The Developing Person
Through the Life Span

Christian Pierre. ***New Friend*** (front cover), ***Road to Opportunity*** (back cover). The luminous colors and figures in *New Friend* and *Road to Opportunity* reflect the hope and discovery apparent in all Pierre's paintings—of adults, animals, plants, landscapes, and children. Pierre has lived in several cultures, under many life circumstances, but she has said that she could never make herself paint anything depressing. Instead, by combining colors, shapes, and composition in ways that simultaneously reflect fantasy and reality, she illustrates life in ways that allow us to recognize truths that we may not have noticed before. Development is about connections—between one age and another, between one group and another, or even between one living creature and another. Joy and affection for every developing person, of whatever age or status, combine as the theme of this text.

SEVENTH EDITION

The Developing Person

Through the Life Span

Kathleen Stassen Berger

Bronx Community College

City University of New York

WORTH PUBLISHERS

Publisher: Catherine Woods

Senior Sponsoring Editor: Jessica Bayne

Developmental Editor: Cecilia Gardner

Marketing Manager: Amy Shefferd

Supplements and Media Editor: Sharon Merritt

Associate Managing Editor: Tracey Kuehn

Project Editor: Vivien Weiss

Art Director, Cover Designer: Barbara Reingold

Interior Designer: Lissi Sigillo

Layout Designer: Paul Lacy

Associate Designer: Lyndall Culbertson

Senior Illustration Coordinator: Bill Page

Illustrations: Todd Buck Illustration and TSI Graphics

Photo Manager: Ted Szczepanski

Photo Researcher: Donna Ranieri

Production Manager: Barbara Anne Seixas

Composition: TSI Graphics

Printing and Binding: R. R. Donnelley & Sons Company

Cover Art: Christian Pierre, *New Friend* (front) and *Road to Opportunity* (back)

Library of Congress Control Number: 2007937431

ISBN-13: 978-0-7167-6072-6

ISBN-10: 0-7167-6072-X

ppbk. ISBN-13: 978-0-7167-6080-1

ppbk. ISBN-10: 0-7167-6080-0

Printed in the United States of America

Third printing

Worth Publishers

41 Madison Avenue

New York, NY 10010

www.worthpublishers.com

Credit is given to the following sources for permission to use the photos indicated:

Part Openers

Corbis, pp. ix, xxxvi

Babystock/Jupiter Images, pp. vi, ix, x, 122, 203

Polka Dot Images/Jupiter Images, pp. vi, xi, 204, 279

Nonstock/Jupiter Images, pp. vi, xi, 280, 359

Brand X Pictures/Jupiter Images, pp. xii, 360, 443

Colin Anderson/Blend Images/Getty Images, pp. vii, xiii, 444, 523

Image Source/Corbis, pp. xiii, 524, 609

Corbis, pp. vii, xiv, 610, 715

Chapter Openers

Tony Savino/The Image Works, pp. ix, 2

Laura Dwight/Corbis, pp. ix, 32

David M. Phillips/Photo Researchers, Inc., p. 60

Rick Gomez/Corbis, pp. x, 90

Marcus Mok/Jupiter Images, pp. x, 124, 203

Jacques Charlas/Stock Boston/PictureQuest, pp. 154, 203

Bruce Yuan-Yue Bi/Lonely Planet, pp. x, 178, 203

Elizabeth Crews, pp. 206, 279

Alloy Photography/Veer, pp. xi, 230, 279

Taxi/Getty Images, pp. xi, 254, 279

Osamu Koyata/Pacific Press Service, pp. 282, 359

Ellen B. Senisi, pp. xi, 306, 359

Sean Sprague/The Image Works, pp. xii, 332, 359

Jupiter Images, pp. 362, 443

Jim Sugar/Corbis, pp. xii, 390, 443

Robert Harding/Getty Images, pp. xii, 414, 443

Mike Watson Images/SuperStock, pp. 446, 523

Marc Charuel/Sygma/Corbis, pp. xiii, 470, 523

Patrick Horton/Lonely Planet, pp. xiii, 498, 523

Lilly Doug/Botanica/Getty Images, pp. 526, 609

Richard I'Anson/Lonely Planet, pp. xiv, 554, 609

Tony Anderson/Taxi/Getty Images, pp. 576, 609

Julie Larsen Maher, pp. xiv, 612, 715

Gloria Wright/Syracuse Newspapers/The Image Works, pp. xiv, 648, 715

Lawrence Manning/Corbis, pp. xv, 678, 715

Christophe Boisvieux/Corbis, pp. xv, Ep-0

ABOUT THE AUTHOR

Kathleen Stassen Berger received her undergraduate education at Stanford University and Radcliffe College, earned an M.A.T. from Harvard University and an M.S. and Ph.D from Yeshiva University. Her broad experience as an educator includes directing a preschool, teaching philosophy and humanities at the United Nations International School, teaching child and adolescent development to graduate students at Fordham University, teaching undergraduates at Montclair State University in New Jersey and at Quinnipiac University in Connecticut, as well as inmates earning paralegal degrees at Sing Sing Prison.

For the past 35 years, Berger has taught at Bronx Community College of the City University of New York. She has taught introduction to psychology, child and adolescent development, adulthood and aging, social psychology, abnormal psychology, and human motivation. Her students—who come from many ethnic, economic, and educational backgrounds and who have a wide range of interests—consistently honor her with the highest teaching evaluations. Her own four children attended New York City public schools, one reason that she was elected as president of Community School Board in District Two.

Berger is also the author of *The Developing Person Through Childhood and Adolescence*. Her developmental texts are currently being used at nearly 700 colleges and universities worldwide and are available in Spanish, French, Italian, and Portuguese as well as English. Her research interests include adolescent identity, sibling relationships, and bullying, and she has contributed articles on developmental topics to the *Wiley Encyclopedia of Psychology*. Berger's interest in college education is manifest in articles published by the American Association for Higher Education and the National Education Association for Higher Education. She continues to teach and learn with every semester and every edition of her books.

BRIEF CONTENTS

CONTENTS

PART III The Play Years 205

PART IV The School Years 281

PART VI

Emerging Adulthood 445

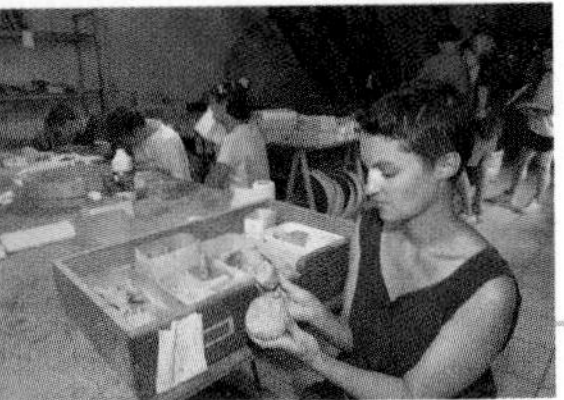

PART VII

Adulthood 525

Preface

Each year, each day, and even each hour is a gift, to be filled with joy and work. At least that is how it seems to me. I write for the tens of thousands of students (in 12 nations and five languages) who will read this book. I hope each of you sees your life as a gift and finds joy and work in this book, as you come to understand and appreciate development.

Change and continuity are the dynamic themes of development. Both are evident in my life and in this book.

I recently sold our house and moved into a new apartment near the Hudson River, beside which I walk almost every day; many gifts there. I watch my children grow, and I realize that their lives and this text are intertwined.

To be specific, my interest in development began in earnest when our first two children (Bethany and Rachel) were infants; as a young professor I often told anecdotes of their early days. Some of those stories appear in this book. A few years later, our third baby (Elissa) cried and needed a walk; that led to an encounter that led to a book contract. Our fourth child (Sarah) was conceived because this text was widely adopted. She is the only one whose photographs we could afford to have taken professionally, and only they made it into this text.

Now all four are adults. Their recent experiences showed me the need for new chapters in this seventh edition, a trio on emerging adulthood. The deaths of my parents and my husband over the past seven years have made me think more deeply about dying; the Epilogue is twice as long as before, with new insights not present in previous editions.

Changes come from the wider community of social scientists as well. Globalization, neuroscience, dynamic systems, and genetic analysis have all provided new insights. This book now has Research Design features, data, and many discussions of the similarities and differences among developing persons worldwide. Further, the integration of mind and body is much better understood, and you will find specifics about the brain and about heredity at every stage of life.

Teaching and writing remain my life's work and passion. I strive to make this text challenging and accessible to every student, remembering that my students were my original reason to write a developmental text. They deserved a text that respected their intellect and experiences, without making development seem dull or obscure. Overall, I believe that a better world is possible because today's students will become tomorrow's wise leaders; this book is my contribution—I hope you see it as a gift—toward that goal.

To learn more about the specifics of this text, including the material that is new to this edition, read on. Or you can turn to the beginning of Chapter 1, and begin your study.

New Material

Every year brings new concepts and research. The best of these are integrated into the text, including hundreds of new references on many topics—among them mirror neurons, the use of prescription medication in young children, autistic spectrum disorders, attachment over the life span, high-stakes testing, brain changes in midlife, and public policy about dying.

Revised Chapters on Adolescence and Emerging Adulthood

I've been sensitive to current research throughout the book, but I've been particularly impressed with the magnitude of the changes that are happening in our understanding of adolescence and the years now referred to as emerging adulthood. As a result, I have spent a lot of time reading and rewriting the six chapters covering the period from age 12 to age 25. Highlights include new discoveries about the adolescent brain (e.g., the prefrontal cortex is not fully mature until the early 20s), the onset of puberty even before the teen years, and the dramatic shift in emerging adulthood—once a time for settling down, but now a time for exploring, learning, and risk taking.

It no longer makes sense to divide adulthood into "early," "middle," and "late," as the previous editions did. Now three chapters (17, 18, and 19) cover emerging adulthood (ages 18 to 25) and the next three chapters (20, 21, and 22) cover adulthood (ages 25 to 65). This reorganization reflects the fact that the major events of those years, including ongoing senescence, expertise, intimate partnership, and parenthood may occur at every age during those 40 years, depending on the specific choices and circumstances of each developing person. The work and love—that is, vocation and family—of adulthood are no longer split between two periods. This new view of adult life is a dramatic example of the way the scientific study of development shifts as new research and theories appear.

TED HOROWITZ / CORBIS

Cognition on Display Shared facials, pedicures, nail painting, eyebrow waxing, and other such beauty rituals are bonding experiences for teenage girls. Parents may blame teen magazines or the superficiality of the culture in general, but their daughters' egocentric thinking may be the true origin of these activities.

Extensive Coverage of Brain Development

Beyond organizational changes, every page of this text reflects new research and theory. Brain development is the most obvious example: Every trio of chapters includes a section on the brain. A sampling of this new material is listed below.

Patterns of developmental growth, pp. 7–8
Mirror neurons, p. 14
Brain development and the epigenetic model of development, pp. 50–51
From one cell to many: Genetic development, pp. 66–67
Genotypes and phenotypes, pp. 73–74
Down syndrome and brain development, pp. 79–80
Fetal brain development, pp. 93–96
Prenatal growth of the brain, p. 97
Teratogens and brain development, pp. 97–99
Brain development during infancy and toddlerhood, pp. 129–136
Sensation, perception, and the brain, pp. 136–139
Brain maturation within the motor cortex, p. 140
Effects of nutrition on the brain, pp. 148–150
Some techniques used by neuroscientists to understand brain function, p. 160
Information processing, p. 161
Measuring infant temperament, pp. 186–188
Synchrony, p. 192
Biosocial development and the brain during early childhood, pp. 207–214
Memory and brain systems, pp. 213–214
Cognitive development and brain maturation during early childhood, pp. 238–239
Emotional regulation during the play years, pp. 258–259
Epigenetic theory, p. 276
The school years: Brain development, pp. 290–303
The school years: Memory formation, p. 311
Hormones in adolescence, pp. 364–365
Brain development in adolescence, pp. 375–380
Drug use in adolescence, pp. 386–387
Cognitive development in adolescence: "Dual-process model" of adolescent thought, p. 398
Information-processing approach: How brain encodes, stores, and retrieves information, p. 473
The aging brain, pp. 530–532
Fluid and crystallized intelligence, pp. 561–562
Brain effects on intelligence, p. 564

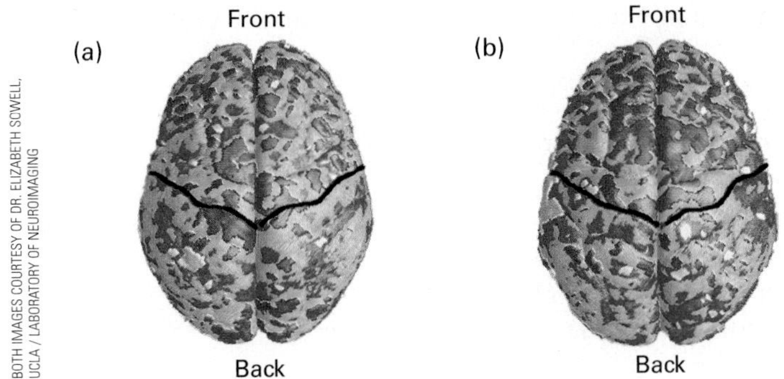

BOTH IMAGES COURTESY OF DR. ELIZABETH SOWELL, UCLA / LABORATORY OF NEUROIMAGING

The Prefrontal Cortex Matures These are composite scans of normal brains of *(a)* children and adolescents and *(b)* adolescents and adults. The red areas indicate both an increase in brain size and a decrease in gray matter (cerebral cortex). The red areas in *(b)* are larger than in *(a)* and are concentrated in the frontal area of the brain, which is associated with complex cognitive processes. The growth of brain areas as their gray matter decreases is believed to reflect an increase in white matter, which consists of myelin—the axon coating that makes the brain more efficient.

The brain in late adulthood, pp. 628–629
Thinking Like a Scientist: Neuroscience and Brain Activity, pp. 656–657
Brain slowdown: Primary and secondary aging, pp. 658–659
Dementia, pp. 662–670
Brain death, p. Ep-3

Research Design

Scientists: Six researchers, sponsored by the RAND Corporation.

Publication: *Pediatrics* (2006). This study was also reported in many news stories.

Participants: Total of 1,461 U.S. teenagers, randomly selected to be representative of all U.S. teens.

Design: Teenagers were interviewed by phone three times over three years and asked which of 16 popular music groups they listened to. Coders rated whether songs contained sexually degrading lyrics. Some participants refused to answer questions about sex, but responses of 938 who were virgins when the study began were analyzed.

Major conclusion: Listening to degrading music about sex, but not other teen music about sex, encourages teenagers to have sexual intercourse.

Comment: This is a correlational study. The longitudinal sequence (music, then intercourse) prompted the conclusions, but others disagree about the relationship between the variables.

New Research Design Feature

A new element appears in this edition, to highlight the science of development. Each chapter includes two or more Research Design boxes. Each is keyed to a study cited in the adjacent text and explains more about the participants and methods of that study. Students are encouraged to read the original studies, which also reveal the many ways—via statistics, hypotheses, and research findings—by which scientists move beyond their original assumptions.

Content Changes to the Seventh Edition

Life-span development, like all sciences, builds on past learning. Many facts and concepts must be restated in every edition of a textbook—stages and ages, norms and variations, dangers and diversities, classic theories and fascinating applications. However, the study of development is continually changed by discoveries and innovations, so no page in this seventh edition is exactly what it was in the sixth edition, much less the first. Highlights of this updating appear below.

Part I: The Beginnings

1. Introduction

- New subsection "Defining Development" discusses the three crucial elements of the science of human development.
- Increased focus on dynamic systems theory.
- Issues and Applications: "My Name Wasn't Mary," about the childhood of poet Maya Angelou.
- New coverage of mirror neurons.
- New discussion of quantitative vs. qualitative research.
- New discussion of protection of research participants.

2. Theories of Development

- Expanded, updated coverage of epigenetic theory.
- Extensively revised discussion of selective adaptation with new examples.
- New subsection on nature–nurture interaction.

3. Heredity and Environment

- Expanded discussion of identical twins.
- New coverage of cloning.
- New coverage of infertility and assisted reproductive technology, including In Person: "I Am Not Happy with Me," about in vitro fertilization.
- New subsection "Visual Acuity," on genetic and cultural factors in nearsightedness.
- New coverage of type 2 diabetes epidemic.

4. Prenatal Development and Birth

- Updated data on preterm births.
- New subsection "Protective Measures," on reducing the risks of teratogens.
- New subsection "Benefits of Prenatal Care," focusing on diagnostic testing.
- Expanded and updated coverage of low birthweight.
- New: A Case to Study: "What Does That Say About Me?"

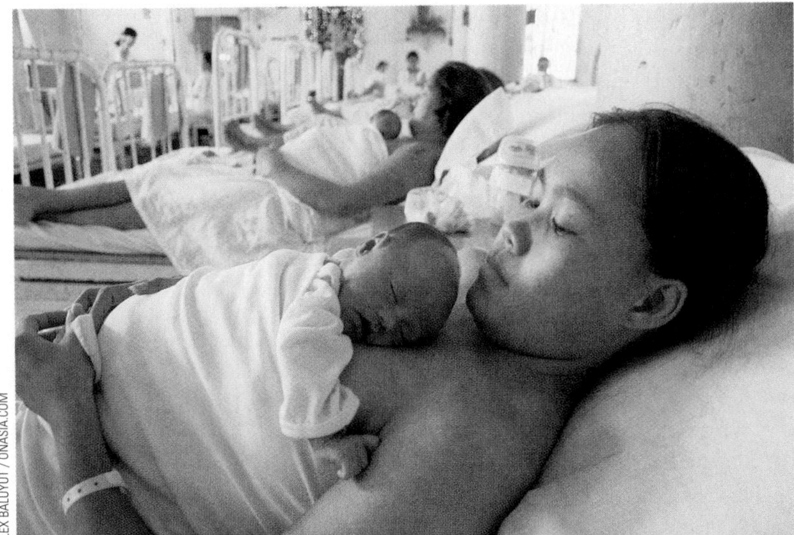
ALEX BALUYUT / ONASIA.COM

A Beneficial Beginning These new mothers in a maternity ward in Manila are providing their babies with kangaroo care.

Part II: The First Two Years

5. The First Two Years: Biosocial Development

- New coverage of co-sleeping
- New subsection "Implications for Caregivers," covering self-righting, plasticity, and sensitive periods in brain development.
- Expanded coverage of infant reflexes, walking, immunization, and breast-feeding.

6. The First Two Years: Cognitive Development

- New subsection on recent research on early affordances.
- New coverage of implicit and explicit memory.
- Updated coverage of the hybrid perspective on language development.

7. The First Two Years: Psychosocial Development

- Updated and expanded coverage of temperament—and what it means for caregivers.
- Expanded coverage of sociocultural theory, with new material on ethnotheories (including A Case to Study: "Let's Go to Grandma's," on the difference between North American and Mayan parents' ethnotheories) and on proximal and distal parenting practices.
- Expanded coverage of synchrony, including Thinking Like a Scientist: The Still-Face Technique, on infants' responses to parental "still face."
- Updated coverage of attachment.
- Updated and expanded coverage of infant day care.

Part III: The Play Years

8. The Play Years: Biosocial Development

- New material on maturation of the prefrontal cortex.
- New section "Emotions and the Brain," on the limbic system and on the effects of stress.
- Updated and reorganized coverage of injuries and abuse, including In Person: "My Baby Swallowed Poison," on strategies for injury prevention.

HAZEL HANKIN

My Youngest at 8 Months When I look at this photo of Sarah, I see evidence of Mrs. Todd's devotion. Sarah's hair is washed and carefully brushed, her jumper and blouse are clean and pressed, and the carpet and stepstool are perfect equipment for standing practice. Sarah's legs—chubby and far apart—indicate that she is not about to walk early; but, given all these signs of Mrs. Todd's attention to caregiving, it is not surprising, in hindsight, that my fourth daughter was my earliest walker.

9. The Play Years: Cognitive Development

- New subsection on theory-theory.
- Expanded and updated coverage of vocabulary development and bilingualism, including new subsection "Constant Change."
- Expanded coverage of preschools, including Montessori, Reggio Emilia, and Head Start.

10. The Play Years: Psychosocial Development

- New subsection "Intrinsic Motivation."
- Expanded discussions of empathy and aggression.
- New box on punishment.
- Expanded, updated coverage of the media and its effects.

Part IV: The School Years

11. The School Years: Biosocial Development

- Revised, expanded, and updated discussion of overweight children.
- New section on physical activity, covering benefits and hazards, neighborhood play, exercise in school, and clubs and leagues.
- Expanded coverage of chronic illness and asthma.
- New subsection on gifted children and mentally retarded children.
- New box on prescribing psychoactive drugs for children.
- New subsection "Autistic Spectrum Disorders."

12. The School Years: Cognitive Development

- Updated, expanded coverage of education, particularly bilingual education, curriculum (internationally and in the United States, including the No Child Left Behind Act), and math instruction in the United States, as well as new subsections on education in Japan and on education and culture.
- New boxes: Issues and Applications: SES and Language Learning; Thinking Like a Scientist: International Achievement Tests; and A Case to Study: Where Did You Learn *Tsunami?*

13. The School Years: Psychosocial Development

- Extensively revised and updated section on the peer group, with new focus on the culture of children, children's moral codes, and social acceptance.

ELLEN B. SENISI / THE IMAGE WORKS

He's Listening With tilted head and pink tutu, this girl exemplifies two of the best characteristics often found in young children: empathy and self-confidence. Responding to her personality and concern, the distressed boy may well decide to rejoin the group.

- New box Thinking Like a Scientist: "I Always Dressed One in Blue Stuff," on parental effects on children's development.
- Expanded, updated material on effects of family income.

Part V: Adolescence

14. Adolescence: Biosocial Development

- New box: A Case to Study: What Were You Thinking? on physical risk taking.
- New section on brain development, focusing on recent brain research, the relationship between brain and behavior, and puberty and biorhythms.
- New box Issues and Applications: Calculus at 8 A.M.?
- Updated discussions of teenage pregnancy and STIs.
- Reorganized, updated discussion of drug use and abuse.

15. Adolescence: Cognitive Development

- New section on the possibilities and problems related to adolescent use of the Internet and other new technologies.
- New major section "Teaching and Learning," with new subsections on middle schools, the transition from middle school to high school, including high-stakes testing, dropouts, school violence, and new approaches.
- New Issues and Applications: Diversity of Nation, Gender, and Income, on an international study of problem-solving abilities of adolescents.

16. Adolescence: Psychosocial Development

- New section "Technology for Everyone," on technology and identity exploration
- New subsections on religious identity and vocational identity.
- Updated and expanded material on sexual/gender identity and political/ethnic identity.
- Updated and expanded material on parent–adolescent relationships.
- New subsection "Cliques and Crowds" (including new In Person: The Berger Daughters Seek Peer Approval).
- New subsection on peer selection and peer facilitation.
- New major section "Sexual Activity."
- Updated material on suicide and parasuicide, including A Case to Study: He Kept His Worries to Himself.
- Updated material on lawbreaking and delinquency, including Thinking Like a Scientist: A Feminist Looks at the Data.

Part VI: Emerging Adulthood

17. Emerging Adulthood: Biosocial Development

- New subsection "Looking Good" on concern with attractiveness.
- Expanded discussions of sexual activity and problems with sex, including new material on STIs and unwanted pregnancies.
- Issues and Applications: Who Gets the Bird Flu Shot? on the question of which age group should be immunized first against bird flu.
- New major section "Health Habits," with subsections on exercise and nutrition.
- New major section "Taking Risks," with new material on social protection, time perspective, and social norms.

18. Emerging Adulthood: Cognitive Development

- New material on cognitive flexibility.
- Revised and updated material on morals and religion.
- Revised and updated material on diversity among college students and on graduates and dropouts.

RUDI VON BRIEL / PHOTO EDIT

Disabled but Vital Therapists find that the most serious consequence of losing a limb is losing the will to live. This young man not only learned to cope with crutches after losing a leg but also regained his spirit: He completed the 26.2-mile New York City marathon.

LOUISE GUBB / CORBIS

Thumbs Up! These graduates in Long Beach, California, are joyful that they have reached a benchmark. Ideally, their diplomas will earn them not only better jobs but also an intellectual perspective that will help them all their lives.

19. Emerging Adulthood: Psychosocial Development

- Updated material on the dimensions of love.
- New section "Family Connections," on continuing family dependence.
- New section "Emotional Development," including sections on well-being, psychopathology (substance abuse, mood disorders, anxiety disorders, schizophrenia), and continuity and discontinuity.

Part VII: Adulthood

20. Adulthood: Biosocial Development

- Updated and revised discussion of the sexual-reproductive system.
- New material on nutrition and obesity.
- New section "Preventive Medicine."
- New material on health and ethnicity.

21. Adulthood: Cognitive Development

- New A Case to Study: "At Very Different Levels," on individual variations over time.
- Revised and updated material on age and culture.
- New material on automatic expert cognition.
- New and updated material on coping with stress, including In Person: An Experienced Parent.

22. Adulthood: Psychosocial Development

- New section "Friends."
- Revised and updated material on marriage. including new material on homogamy and marital equity.
- New section "Caregiving," including new, revised, and updated material on parenthood and on caring for aging parents.
- Extensively revised and updated section on employment.

Part VIII: Late Adulthood

23. Late Adulthood: Biosocial Development

- New Issues and Applications: Getting from Place to Place, on the importance of maintaining mobility.
- Updated and revised section on genetic aging, including discussions of average and maximum life expectancy and selective adaptation.
- New box on theories of aging and attempts to prolong life.

AP PHOTO / RANJIT SINGH

Determined to Vote Older voters tend to have stronger political opinions, more party loyalty, and higher voting rates than younger adults. This Punjabi woman takes an active interest in politics, even though she must depend on her son to carry her to the polling place.

24. Late Adulthood: Cognitive Development

- New A Case to Study: "That Aide Was Very Rude," on sensory declines.
- Revised and updated section on control processes.
- Revised and updated section on secondary aging.
- New A Case to Study: Is It Dementia or Drug Addiction?, on problems of overmedication and drug abuse.
- New section on prevention and treatment of dementia.

25. Late Adulthood: Psychosocial Development

- New Issues and Applications: Thinking Positively.
- New section on recent work and retirement trends and issues.

Epilogue: Death and Dying

- Greatly expanded, revised, and reorganized throughout.
- New main section "Death and Hope," with new material on death throughout the life span, death and religion, acceptance of dying, and choosing death (including new Issues and Applications: Let Terri Schiavo Live/Die/Live/Die).
- New subsection "Seeking Blame and Meaning," including In Person: Blaming Martin, Hitler and Me, on a husband's death.
- Revised and expanded material on diversity of reactions to bereavement.

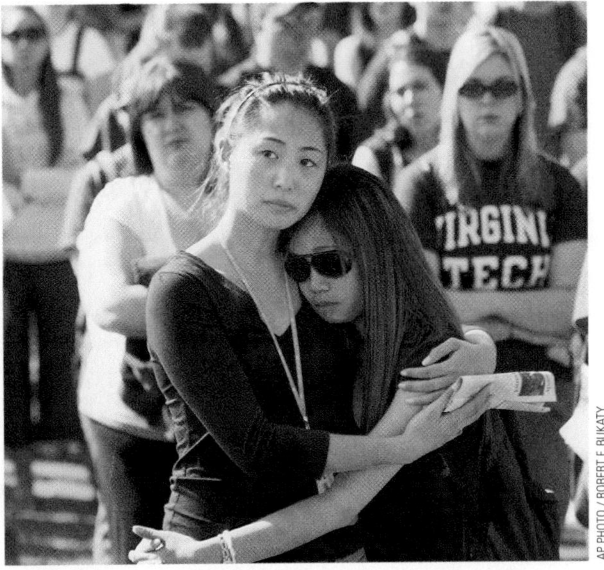

AP PHOTO / ROBERT F. BUKATY

Shared Grief When Seung-Hui Cho, a disturbed student, killed 32 people and wounded 17 on the campus of Virginia Tech in April 2007, many outsiders looked for something or someone to blame—the university's security arrangements and mental health policies, the state's gun laws, even Korean Americans as a group. Students, preferring to seek meaning rather than blame, gathered to pray, sing, and embrace one another.

Ongoing Features

Many characteristics of this book have been acclaimed since the first edition and have been retained in this revision.

Writing That Communicates the Excitement and Challenge of the Field

An overview of the science of human development should be lively, just as real people are. Each sentence conveys tone as well as content. Chapter-opening vignettes bring student readers into the immediacy of development. Examples and explanations abound, helping students make the connections among theory, research, and their own experiences.

Coverage of Diversity

Cross-cultural, international, multiethnic, rich and poor, old and young, male and female, newborn and centenarian—all these words and ideas are vital to appreciating how we all develop. Research uncovers surprising commonalities and notable differences: We are all the same, yet each of us is unique. From the discussion of social contexts in Chapter 1 to the coverage of cultural differences in mourning in the Epilogue, each chapter highlights the possibilities and variations of human life. New research on family structures, immigrants, bilingualism, and ethnic differences in health are among the many topics that illustrate human diversity. Listed here is a smattering of the discussions of culture and diversity in this new edition. Respect for human differences is evident throughout. You will note that examples and research findings from many parts of the world are included, not as add-on highlights, but as integral parts of the description of each age.

PAUL CHESLEY / STONE / GETTY IMAGES

Learning from One Another Every nation creates its own version of early education. In this scene at a nursery school in Kuala Lumpur, Malaysia, note the head coverings, uniforms, bare feet, and absence of boys. None of these elements would be found in most early-childhood education classrooms in North America or Europe.

Observation Quiz (see answer, page 252): What seemingly universal aspects of childhood are visible in this photograph?

Four Generations of Caregiving These four women, from the great-grandmother to her 17-year-old great-granddaughter, all care for one another. Help flows to whoever needs it, not necessarily to the oldest or youngest.

International and domestic diversity in low birthweight, pp. 113–114
International variations in birthing procedures, pp. 110–111
Social support and birth issues: Cultural differences, p. 116
Family sleeping arrangements as an example of cultural traits, p. 128
Association between adoption and IQ of institutionalized Romanian children, pp. 134–135
Ethnic variations in the development of motor skills, pp. 141–142
Ethnicity, infant-care routines by culture, and SIDS, pp. 146–147
Infant nutrition worldwide, pp. 148–150
Cultural variations in language development, pp. 169–171
Influence of culture on emotion, p. 180–181
Applying Erikson's theories across cultures, p. 184
Cross-cultural application of epigenetic theory, p. 185–186
Sociocultural theory, pp. 188–190
Attachment and culture, pp. 193–195
Social referencing, p. 196
Eating habits, p. 208
Cultural adaptation to fine motor skills, p. 217–218
Guided participation (Vygotsky) and social activities, p. 234
Culture and the development of theory of mind, pp. 238–239
International comparison: Children's performance on false-belief tests, p. 239
Language: Word-mapping and culture, p. 241
Bilingualism, cognition, and culture, pp. 244–245
Intrinsic motivation: Emotional regulation and culture, p. 258
Cultural emphasis on prosocial and antisocial behavior, p. 260
How empathy is taught: American vs. Japanese culture, p. 261
Cultural variations in parenting during early childhood, pp. 265–266
Punishment styles by culture, pp. 266–268
Amount of media exposure in various cultures, p. 269
Sociocultural theory and developing gender roles, pp. 275–276
Gender and destiny, p. 277
Size and shape of children, pp. 284–286
Influence of culture on motor skills, p. 287

IQ testing, pp. 293–294
Thinking Like a Scientist: Prescription Drugs, p. 298
Cultural variations in cognition and education in the school years, pp. 309–310
Spectrum disorders and culture, p. 300
Control processes and culture, pp. 312–313
Second-language learning, pp. 315–316
Education around the world, pp. 318–321
International educational assessment, pp. 321–324
Comparison of education in the United States and Japan, pp. 323–324
Culture and education, pp. 328–329
Maintaining tradition in the classroom, p. 330
The culture of children worldwide, pp. 334–337
Friendship and culture, p. 339
Study of bullying in Norwegian schools, p. 341
Diverse household structures, pp. 345–346
Family structure: Culture and ethnic differences, p. 348–350
Cultural variations in parenting and family roles, pp. 349–350
Cultural differences in self-concept/self-esteem, p. 353
Social support and religious faith, pp. 355–356
Impact of environment on the timing of puberty, pp. 366–368
Sexual maturation in various cultures, pp. 373–375
Cultural attitudes toward pregnancy, pp. 380–381
Drug use: Variations by nation, gender, and ethnicity, pp. 384–385
Formal operational thought and culture, p. 395
Identity and religion, ethnicity, and vocation worldwide, pp. 416–419
Teaching and learning, pp. 406–407
International comparisons: Average problem-solving scores among 15-year-olds, p. 408
Adults and teenage conflict: Cultural values, pp. 419–420
United States high school dropout rates by race, p. 410
The peer group for immigrant teens, pp. 425–427
Immigrant youth, p. 425
Adolescent sexuality and culture, pp. 427–429
Sex education: Differences by culture, p. 431
Depression and culture, p. 434–435
Teen suicide rates in various cultures, pp. 435–436
Culture and ages and stages of growth, strength and health, pp. 447–449
Emotional stress and culture, p. 454
Nutrition and culture, p. 457
Eating disorders and culture, p. 459, 461
Cultural variations on violence, p. 466
Kohlberg's postformal thought and culture, pp. 472–473
Stereotype threat, pp. 471, 477–480
Dialectical thought and culture, pp. 480–482
Morals and culture, pp. 483–484
Ethnic identity, pp. 500–502
Anxiety disorders within the cultural context, p. 520
Culture and obesity, p. 542
Diversity and intelligence, pp. 564–565
Culture, cohort, and SES, p. 580
Culture and personality, p. 583
Divorce rates and predictors by culture, p. 595

Diversity and employment, p. 605
Cultural effects of wisdom, p. 27
Centenarians around the world, pp. 643–644
Ethnic discrimination in late adulthood, pp. 687–689
Views of death in major religions, Ep-6–Ep-10
A Case to Study: "Ask My Son and My Husband"; cultural views of communication about dying, pp. Ep-11–Ep-12

Up-to-Date Coverage

I learned from my mentors curiosity, creativity, and skepticism; as a result, I am eager to read and ready to analyze the thousands of journal articles and books on everything from Alzheimer's to zygosity. The recent explosion of research in neuroscience and genetics has challenged me, once again, first to understand and then to explain many complex findings and speculative leaps. My students continue to ask questions and share their experiences, always providing new perspectives and concerns.

Topical Organization within a Chronological Framework

The book's basic organization remains unchanged. Four chapters begin the book with coverage of definitions, theories, genetics, and prenatal development. These chapters function not only as a developmental foundation but also as the structure for explaining the life-span perspective, plasticity, nature and nurture, multicultural awareness, risk analysis, the damage-repair cycle, family bonding, and many other concepts that yield insights for all of human development.

The other seven parts correspond to the major periods of development. Each part contains three chapters, one for each of the three domains: biosocial, cognitive, and psychosocial. The topical organization within a chronological framework is a useful scaffold for students' understanding of the interplay between age and domain. The chapters are color-coded with tabs on the right-hand margins. The pages of the biosocial chapters have green tabs, the cognitive chapters have purple tabs, and the psychsocial chapters have pink tabs.

Four Series of Integrated Features

Four series of deeper discussions appear as integral parts of the text, and only where they are relevant. Readers of earlier editions have particularly liked these series. The categories are "In Person," "A Case to Study," "Thinking Like a Scientist," and "Issues and Applications."

Pedagogical Aids

Each chapter ends with a summary, a list of key terms (with page numbers indicating where the word is introduced and defined), key questions, and three or four application exercises designed to let students apply concepts to everyday life. Key terms appear in boldface type in the text and are defined in the margins and again in a glossary at the back of the book. The outline on the first page of each chapter and the system of major and minor subheads facilitate the survey-question-read-write-review (SQ3R) approach. A "Summing Up" feature at the end of each section provides an opportunity for students to pause and reflect on

DAVID YOUNG-WOLFF / PHOTOEDIT

JOHNER IMAGES / GETTY IMAGES

Same Birthday, Same (or Different?) Genes Twins who are of different sexes or who have obvious differences in personality are dizygotic, sharing only half of their genes. Many same-sex twins with similar temperaments are dizygotic as well. One of these twin pairs is dizygotic; the other is monozygotic.

Observation Quiz (see answer, page 72): Can you tell which pair is monozygotic?

Especially for Teachers You are teaching in a school that you find too lax or too strict, or with parents who are too demanding or too uncaring. Should you look for a different line of work?

➤Response for Teachers (from page 324): Nobody works well in an institution they hate, but, before quitting the profession, remember that schools vary. There is probably another school nearby that is much more to your liking and that would welcome an experienced teacher. Before you make a move, however, assess the likelihood that you could adjust to your current position in ways that would make you happier. No school is perfect; nor is any teacher.

what they've just read. Observation quizzes inspire readers to look more closely at certain photographs, tables, and graphs. The "Especially for . . . " questions in the margins, many of which are new to this edition, apply concepts to real-life careers and social roles.

Photographs, Tables, and Graphs That Are Integral to the Text

Students learn a great deal from this book's illustrations, because Worth Publishers encourages authors to choose the photographs, tables, and graphs and to write captions that extend the content. Appendix A furthers this process by presenting a chart or table for each chapter that contains detailed data for further study.

Supplements

As an instructor myself, I know that supplements can make or break a class. I personally have rejected textbook adoptions because I knew that that publisher historically had provided inaccurate test banks, dull ancillaries, and slow service. That is not the case with Worth Publishers, which has a well-deserved reputation for providing supplements that are extensive and of high quality, for both professors and students. With this edition you will find:

Exploring Human Development: A Media Tool Kit

For this edition, the acclaimed Media Tool Kit takes a technological leap forward. Our materials will now be available online for students and instructors—as well as on CD and (for instructors) VHS and DVD. The tool kit was prepared by a talented team of instructors, including: Victoria Cross, University of California, Davis; Sheridan Dewolf, Grossmont College; Pamela B. Hill, San Antonio College; Lisa Huffman, Ball State University; Thomas Ludwig, Hope College; Cathleen McGreal, Michigan State University; Amy Obegi, Grossmont College;

Michelle L. Pilati, Rio Hondo College; Tanya Renner, Kapiolani Community College; Catherine Robertson, Grossmont College; Stavros Valenti, Hofstra University; and Pauline Zeece, University of Nebraska, Lincoln.

The media activities now offered range from investigations of classic experiments (like the visual cliff and the strange situation) to observations on children's play and adolescent risk taking. More than 50 video clips and animations have been added for this edition—including a stunning new animation of brain development from birth until late life, classic historical footage from Harry Harlow, and spellbinding new footage from a variety of news sources on topics ranging from children in war to the biology of love in middle age. The assessment available on the student tool kit has also been updated and revised—students now can get a better assessment of their learning through randomized, timed quizzes from a large quiz-bank pool.

For instructors, the tool kit includes more than 350 video clips and animations, along with discussion starters and PowerPoint slides available as a set of CD-ROMs, DVDs, VHS tapes, or an online database of more than 350 video clips. The student tool kit includes 49 interactive activities, quizzes, and flashcards. The online student tool kit (available in the spring of 2008) includes more than 70 activities.

PsychPortal

This is the complete online gateway to all the student and instructor resources available with the textbook. PsychPortal brings together all the resources of the media tool kits, integrated with an eBook and powerful assessment tools to complement your course. The ready-to-use course template is fully customizable and includes all the teaching and learning resources that go along with the book, preloaded into a ready-to-use course; sophisticated quizzing, personalized study plans for students and powerful assessment analyses that provide timely and useful feedback on class and individual student performance; and seamless integration of student resources, eBook text, assessment tools, and lecture resources. The quiz bank (featuring more than 80 questions per chapter) that powers the student assessment in both PsychPortal and the Media Tool Kit was written by Pamela Hill, San Antonio College, and Michelle L. Pilati, Rio Hondo College. These questions are not from the test bank!

eBook

The beautiful and interactive eBook fully integrates the complete text and its electronic study tools in a format that instructors and students can easily customize—at a significant savings on the price of the printed text. It offers easy access from any Internet-connected computer; quick, intuitive navigation to any section or subsection, as well as any printed book page number; a powerful notes feature that allows you to customize any page; a full-text search; text highlighting; and a full, searchable glossary.

Companion Web Site

Edited by Catherine Robertson, Grossmont College, the companion Web site (at www.worthpublishers.com/berger) is an online educational setting for students and instructors. It is free, and tools on the site include interactive flashcards in both English and Spanish; a Spanish language glossary; quizzes; annotated Web Links; and Frequently Asked Questions About Development. A password-protected Instructor Site offers a full array of teaching resources, including PowerPoint slides, an online quiz gradebook, and links to additional tools.

"Journey Through the Life Span" Observational Videos

Bringing observational learning to the classroom, this video series allows students to watch and listen to real children as a way of amplifying their reading of the text. "Journey Through the Life Span" offers vivid footage of people of all ages from around the world (North America, Europe, Africa, Asia, and South America), as seen in everyday environments (homes, hospitals, schools, and offices) and at major life transitions (birth, marriage, divorce, being grandparents). Interviews with prominent developmentalists—including Charles Nelson, Barbara Rogoff, Ann Peterson, and Steven Pinker—are integrated throughout to help students link research and theory to the real world. Interviews with a number of social workers, teachers, and nurses who work with children, adults, and the aged give students direct insight into the practical challenges and rewards of their vocations. One hour of unedited footage helps students sharpen their observation skills. Available on VHS and DVD.

"Scientific American Frontiers" Videos for Developmental Psychology

This remarkable resource provides instructors with 17 video segments of approximately 15 minutes each, on topics ranging from language development to nature–nurture issues. The videos can be used to launch classroom lectures or to emphasize and clarify course material. The *Faculty Guide* by Richard O. Straub (University of Michigan) describes and relates each segment to specific topics in the text.

Life-Span Development Telecourse

Transitions Through the Life Span, developed by Coast Learning Systems and Worth Publishers, teaches fundamentals of human development. The course also explores the variety of individual and developmental contexts that influence development, such as socioeconomic status, culture, genetics, family, school, and society. Each video lesson includes specific real-life examples interwoven with commentary by subject matter experts. The course includes 26 half-hour video lessons, a telecourse study guide, and a faculty manual with test bank. The test bank is also available electronically.

eLibrary

The Worth Publishers eLibrary brings together all the existing text and supplementary resources in a single, easy-to-use Web interface. This searchable, Web-based integrator includes materials from the textbook, the Instructor's Resources, and select electronic supplements, including PowerPoint slides and video clips. Through simple browse-and-search tools, instructors can quickly access virtually any piece of content and either download it to a computer or create a Web page to share with students. The eLibrary also features prebuilt, customizable collections for each chapter, allowing adopters to quickly access the "best of" the eLibrary and adapt it for their needs.

Instructor's Resources

This collection of resources written by Richard O. Straub (University of Michigan, Dearborn) has been hailed as the richest collection of instructor's resources in developmental psychology. This manual features chapter-by-chapter previews and lecture guides, learning objectives, springboard topics for discussion and debate, handouts for student projects, and supplementary readings from journal articles. Course planning suggestions, ideas for term projects, and a guide to audiovisual and software materials are also included.

Study Guide

The *Study Guide* by Richard O. Straub helps students evaluate their understanding and retain their learning longer. Each chapter includes a review of key concepts, guided study questions, and section reviews that encourage students' active participation in the learning process. Two practice tests and a challenge test help them assess their mastery of the material.

PowerPoint Slides

A number of different presentation slides prepared by Madeleine L. Tattoon, Riverside Community College, are available on the Web site or on the *Exploring Human Development: Instructor's Media Tool Kit* CD-ROM. There are two prebuilt PowerPoint slide sets for each text chapter—one featuring chapter outlines, the other featuring all chapter art and illustrations. These slides can be used as is or customized to fit individual needs. Video presentation slides provide an easy way to connect chapter content to the selected video clip and follow each clip with discussion questions designed to promote critical thinking. In addition, Madeline Tattoon has produced a set of enhanced lecture slides focusing on key themes from the text and featuring tables, graphs, and figures.

Overhead Transparencies

This set of 50 full-color transparencies consists of key illustrations, charts, graphs, and tables from the textbook.

Test Bank and Computerized Test Bank

The test bank, prepared by Vivian Harper (San Joaquin Delta College) and myself, includes at least 90 multiple-choice and 70 fill-in, true-false, and essay questions for each chapter. Each question is keyed to the textbook by topic, page number, and level of difficulty. The Diploma computerized test bank, available on a dual-platform CD-ROM for Windows and Macintosh, guides instructors step by step through the process of creating a test, and it allows them to quickly add an unlimited number of questions, edit, scramble, or resequence items, format a test, and include pictures, equations, and media links. The accompanying gradebook enables instructors to record students' grades throughout the course and includes the capacity to sort student records, view detailed analyses of test items, curve tests, generate reports, and add weights to grades.

The CD-ROM is also the access point for Diploma Online Testing, which allows instructors to create and administer secure exams over a network or over the Internet. In addition, Diploma has the ability to restrict tests to specific computers or time blocks. Blackboard- and WebCT-formatted versions of each item in the Test Bank are available on the CD-ROM.

Thanks

I'd like to thank the academic reviewers who have read this book in every edition and who have provided suggestions, criticisms, references, and encouragement. They have all made this a better book. I want to mention especially those who have reviewed this edition:

TeneInger Abrom-Johnson, *Prairie View A&M University*
Jackie Adamson, *South Dakota School of Mines & Technology*
Ryan Allen, *The Citadel*
Tracy C. Babcock, *Montana State University*
Don M. Beach, *Tarleton State University*
Kathryn Bojczyk, *Florida State University*
Tanya Boone, *California State University, Bakersfield*
Jennifer L. Boothby, *Indiana State University*
Janine P. Buckner, *Seton Hall University*
Paul Burinskas, *University of Hartford*
Tracie Burt, *Southeast Arkansas College*
Amy Carrigan, *University of Saint Francis*
Julia W. Chang, *Mount St. Mary's College*
Aileen M. Collins, *Chemeketa Community College*
Patricia Ann Crowe, *North Iowa Area Community College*
John Crumlin, *University of Colorado at Colorado Springs*
Linda De Villers, *Chaffey College*
Jacqueline Elder, *Triton College*
Tony Fowler, *Florence-Darlington Technical College*
Don Gasparini, *Manhattan College*
Jessica Gillooly, *Glendale Community College*
Lynn Haller, *Morehead State University*
Myra M. Harville, *Holmes Community College*
Scott L. Horton, *University of Southern Maine, and Mitchell College*
Tasha R. Howe, *Humboldt State University*
Alycia M. Hund, *Illinois State University*
David P. Hurford, *Pittsburg State University*
Russ Isabella, *University of Utah*
D. Lamar Jacks, *Santa Fe Community College*
Jeffrey S. Kaplan, *University of Central Florida*
Michelle L. Kelley, *Old Dominion University*
Kristina T. Klassen, *Northern Idaho College*
Joseph Lao, *Teachers College*
Brian McCoy, *Nichols College*
Joann M. Montepare, *Emerson College*
Melissa Baartman Mork, *Northwestern College*
Ronnie Naramore, *Angelina College*
Alison Paris, *Claremont McKenna College*
Robert Pasnak, *George Mason University*
Michelle L. Pilati, *Rio Hondo College*
Curtis D. Proctor-Artz, *Wichita State University, School of Social Works*
Celinda M. Reese, *Oklahoma State University*
Lilian M. Romero, *San Jacinto College Central Campus*
Rosalind Shorter, *Jefferson Community College*
Peggy Skinner, *South Plains College*
James E. Snowden, *Midwestern State University*
Kevin Sumrall, *Montgomery College*
Margot Sutorius, *Northern Illinois University*
Donna Thompson, *Midland College*
R. Bruce Thompson, *University of Southern Maine*
Dean D. VonDras, *University of Wisconsin—Green Bay*
Robert W. Wildblood, *Indiana University Kokomo*
Wanda A. Willard, *Monroe Community College*
Betsy Wisner, *SUNY Cortland*

In addition, I wish to thank the instructors who participated in our online survey. We've tried very hard to apply the insights gained from their experiences with the sixth edition to make this new edition better.

Jackie Adamson, *South Dakota School of Mines & Technology*
Karin Alaniz, *University of Minnesota, Twin Cities*
Carol Allen, *Miami-Dade Community College, North*
Ariel Anderson, *Western Michigan University*
Don Beach, *Tarleton State University*
Kaye Bedell, *Gavilan College*
Mara Bentley, *Los Angeles Southwest College*
Mark Birchfield, *Warner Southern College*
Margaret Bischoff, *South Texas College*
Kathryn Bojczyk, *Florida State University*
Devorah Bozella, *Mount Aloysius College*
Michael Brislawn, *Bellevue Community College*
Chris Burkett, *Newberry College*
Shawn Christiansen, *Southern Utah University*
Aileen Collins, *Chemeketa Community College*
Melanie Conti, *College of Saint Elizabeth*
Elizabeth DeGiorgio, *Mercer County Community College*
Deborah Dobay, *Chemeketa Community College*
Jill Durby, *Fullerton College*
Pamela Fergus, *Minneapolis Community & Technical College*

Don Gasparini, *Manhattan College*
Michael Gibbons, *Southern Virginia College*
Marian Gibney, *Phoenix College*
Stacey Glaesmann, *San Jacinto College*
Drusilla Glascoe, *Salt Lake Community College*
Arthur Gonchar, *University of La Verne*
Christina Gotowka, *Tunxis Community College*
Amy Guimond, *Arizona State University*
Lisa Hager, *Spring Hill College*
Lynn Haller, *Morehead State University*
Abby Heckman, *Georgia Institute of Technology*
Susan Higgins, *Pennsylvania Valley Community College*
Elaine Hogan, *University of North Carolina at Wilmington*
Scott Horton, *University of Southern Maine*
Abbie Jenks, *Greenfield Community College*
David Johnson, *John Brown University*
Jennifer Jones, *University of New Mexico*
Barbara Kabat, *Sinclair Community College*
Wendy Kallina, *Macon State College*
Janice Kennedy, *Georgia Southern University*
Veena Khandke, *Univ of South Carolina, Spartanburg*
Barbara Lusk, *Collin County Community College*
Brian McCoy, *Nichols College*
Elizabeth Miller, *Northern Illinois University*
Nicholas Murray, *East Carolina University*
Regina O'Shea-Hockett, *Great Basin College-Elko*
Rosamaria Pena, *Laredo Community College*
Donald Ratcliff, *Vanguard University*
Kristina Roberts, *Barstow College*
Edna Ross, *University of Louisville*
Linda Russ, *SUNY University at Buffalo*
Jonathan Schindelheim, *Tufts University*
Eliezer Schnall, *Touro College*
Peggy Skinner, *South Plains College*
Kevin Sumrall, *Montgomery College*
Margo Sutorius, *Northern Illinois University*
Lynda Szymanski, *College of Saint Catherine*
Byron Tharpe, *Jefferson Community College, Southwest*
Kathy Tinsley, *Central Carolina Community College*
Paul Toscano, *College of Southern Maryland*
Connie Veldink, *Everett Community College*
Catherine Wambach, *University of Minnesota, Twin Cities*
Diane Weber, *Gardendale High School*
Larry Weiss, *Suffolk County Community College*
Steve Wisecarver, *Lord Fairfax Community College*

The editorial, production, and marketing people at Worth Publishers are dedicated to meeting the highest standards of excellence. Their devotion of time, effort, and talent to every aspect of publishing is a model for the industry. I particularly would like to thank Stacey Alexander, Jessica Bayne, Anthony Calcara, Cele Gardner, Lorraine Klimowich, Tom Kling, Tracey Kuehn, Paul Lacy, Sharon Merritt, Katherine Nurre, Donna Ranieri, Babs Reingold, Amy Shefferd, Walter Shih, Barbara Seixas, Ted Szczepanski, Vivien Weiss, and Catherine Woods.

Dedication

Billions of people worldwide deserve respect, but humans focus better on one person at a time. Accordingly, I dedicate this book to Jean Montreville, the father of the family in sanctuary at Judson Memorial Church.

Kathleen Stassen Berger

New York, September 2007

The Beginnings

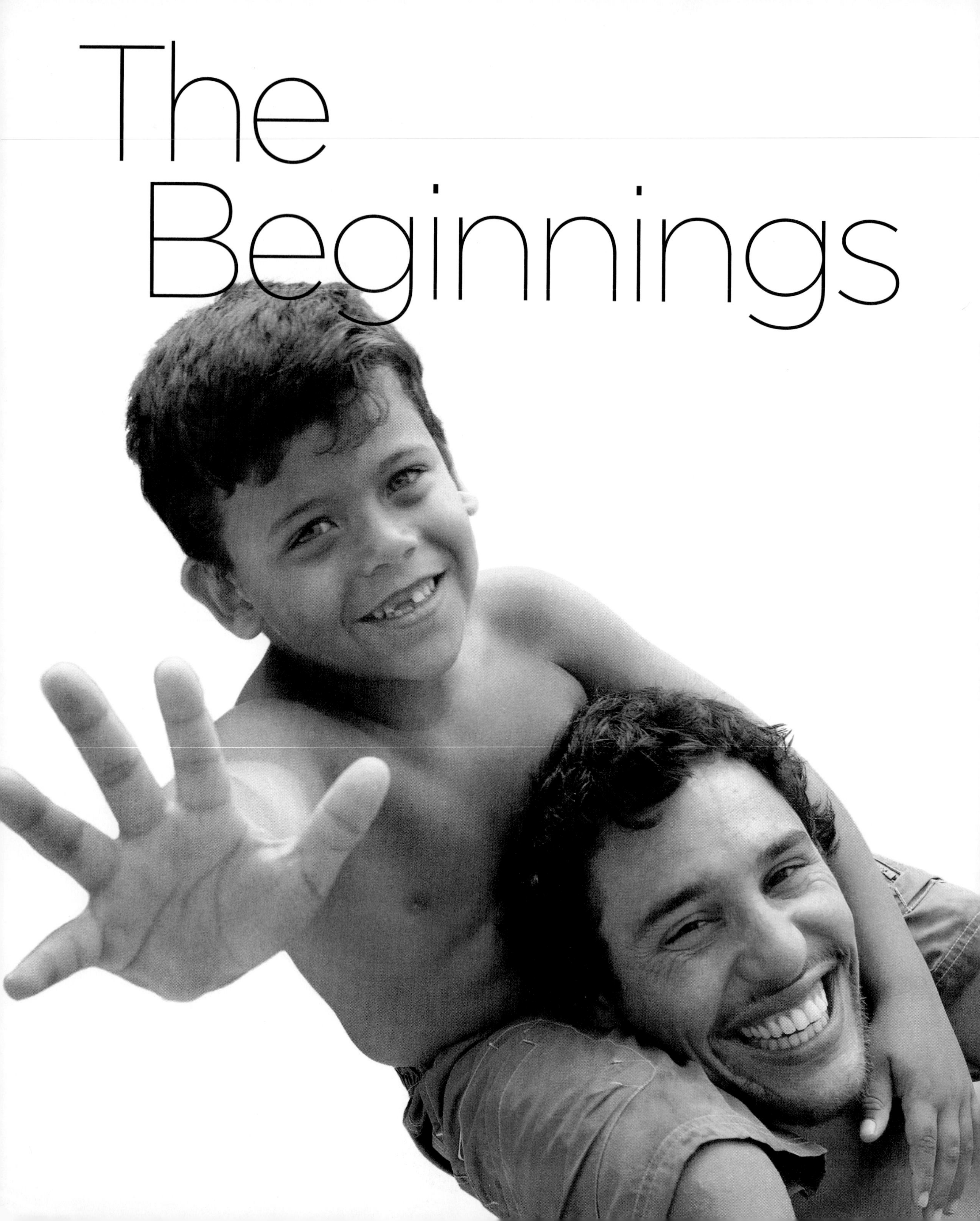

CHAPTER 1
CHAPTER 2
CHAPTER 3
CHAPTER 4

PART I

The science of human development has many beginnings.

Chapter 1 introduces what we study, why, and how. Chapter 2 explains five theories that organize and guide our study. Chapter 3 traces the interaction of heredity and environment, the interplay between the chemical instructions on the genes and the nurturance of the surroundings, from the mother's prenatal diet to the care of the hospice nurse. Chapter 4 details the beginning of human life, from a single dividing cell to a fully formed newborn.

Together these four chapters start our study of human life. A journey around the globe begins with a single step; a life span begins with a millisecond. Turn the page.

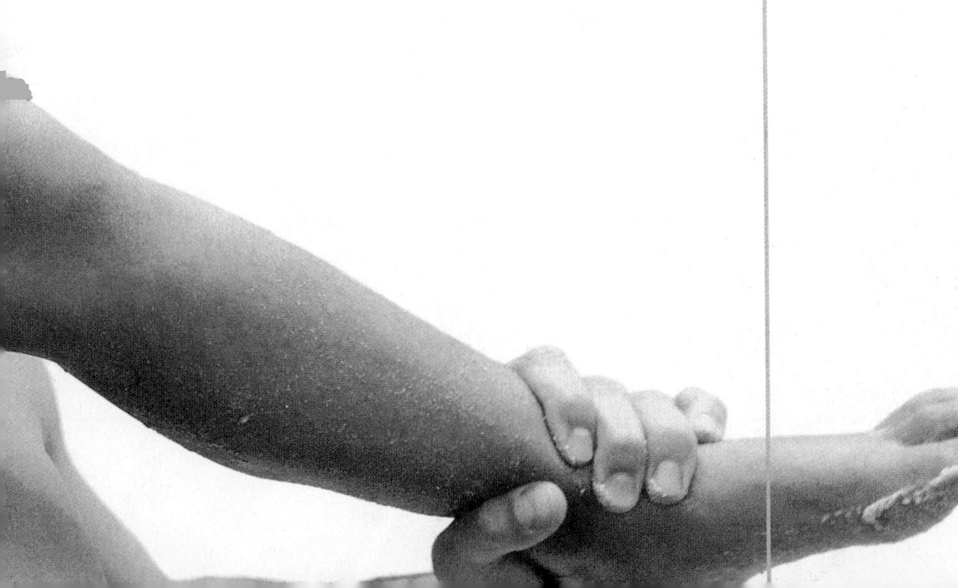

1

CHAPTER OUTLINE

Introduction

What will happen to the baby just born, or to the schoolchild trying to make a friend, or to the emerging adult wondering how to pay for college, or to the elder contemplating retirement? What about you, or your child, or your father—how does anyone become who they are, and what will happen to them tomorrow or 30 years from now? This book is about those people and billions of others, worldwide.

Why should you care? There are dozens of reasons. Some are explained in this chapter and others will become evident as you study. Here is one now: You will look more closely at the people around you, making small moments precious.

This happened to me.

I entered my 8-month-old baby's room to be surprised by a smile and "hahh" as she held on to the slats of her crib, bending her chubby little legs excitedly.

"Hi, Elissa," I grinned back. "You're talking!"

Few people would consider "hahh" talking. But I had learned that language starts with noises and gestures, months before the first identifiable words. I was delighted. You will be joyful, too, in moments you might not have noticed before today.

Defining Development

The **science of human development** *seeks to understand how and why people—all kinds of people, everywhere—change or remain the same over time.* This definition has three crucial elements.

Science

First, and most important, developmental study is a *science*. It depends on theories, data, analysis, critical thinking, and sound methodology, just like every other science does. The goal is to understand "how and why," to discover the processes of development and the reasons for it. As scientists, we ask questions and seek answers.

Science cannot decide the purpose of life; we need philosophy or religion for that. Literature and art can also provide insight beyond the scientific experiment. But "the empirical sciences will show us the way, the means, and the obstacles" involved in making life what we want it to be (Koops, 2003, p. 18).

science of human development The science that seeks to understand how and why people change or remain the same over time. Developmentalists study people of all ages and circumstances.

empirical Based on observation, experience, or experiment; not theoretical.

To say that something is **empirical** means that it is based on data, on many experiences, on demonstrations, on facts. Empirical sciences enable people to live full lives. Without scientific conclusions followed by applications, human life might be "solitary, poor, nasty, brutish, and short," as it was for most people before the scientific revolution (Hobbes, 1651/1997).

Diversity

Second, we study *all kinds of people*—young and old; rich and poor; of every ethnicity, background, sexual orientation, culture, and nationality. The challenge is to identify universalities (beyond birth and death) and differences (beyond everyone's unique genetic code) and then to describe them in ways that simultaneously distinguish and unify all humans.

For example, when you first meet someone, you recognize that person as human (universal) and as your age, or older, or younger (differences within universals; we all have an age). But when you think about yourself or someone you know well, you realize how much more complex each person is. In some ways you are atypical for your age—everyone is. Perhaps you are "wise beyond your years" or you still look at the world with "childlike wonder." Developmental scientists seek to convey both: the generalities and the specifics.

Fiction writers can offer insights in this area, too. In one novel, a vehemently anti-Communist Cuban American asks her teenage daughter to paint a mural of the Statue of Liberty for the opening of a new store. At the public unveiling, the mother sees the mural for the first time: Liberty's torch floats above her grasp and a safety pin is stuck through her nose. The daughter reports:

> The blood has drained from my mother's face and her lips are moving as if she wants to say something but can't find the words. . . . A lumpish man charges Liberty with a pocket knife. . . . Mom swings her new handbag and clubs the guy cold, inches from the painting. . . . And I, I love my mother very much at that moment.
>
> *[Garcia, 2004, pp. 143, 144]*

As for specifics, did this episode actually happen? No, probably not (it appears in a work of fiction). As for generalities, can mother–daughter love overcome generational and political differences? Yes. Researchers have documented the power of family bonds; the dramatic power of this incident arises from that universality.

You might wonder how a novel relates to science, since science, unlike art, depends on objective data, empirical observations, and tested theories. Yet the struggle to understand both the universal and the unique in *all kinds of people* is the goal of both artists and scientists—and, for that matter, of philosophers, preachers, and every other thoughtful person. Using science to study people is an effective means to that end.

Connections Between Change and Time

The third crucial element of the definition is *change or remain the same over time*. The science of human development includes all the transformations and consistencies of human life, from the very beginning to the very end. There is a "reciprocal connection between age-focused developmental specialties [such as infancy, childhood, adolescence, adulthood] and their integration into a life span view" (Baltes et al., 2006, p. 644). That is, each stage is better understood by remembering the whole life, and, conversely, the whole life is understood best by knowing each segment.

Dynamic-Systems Theory

This emphasis on the interaction between people and within each person, such as between parent and child, between prenatal and postnatal life, between ages 2 and 102, is central to the study of the life span. One way to highlight this is via **dynamic-systems theory,** which stresses fluctuations and transitions, "the dynamic synthesis of multiple levels of analysis" (Lerner et al., 2005, p. 38).

dynamic-systems theory A view of human development as always changing. Life is the product of ongoing interaction between the physical and emotional being and between the person and every aspect of his or her environment, including the family and society. Flux is constant, and each change affects all the others.

The word *systems* captures the idea that a change in one part of a person, or family, or society will affect all the other aspects of development, because each part is connected to all the other parts. Dynamic-systems theory may be a new "grand theory of development" (traditional grand theories are explained in Chapter 2) (Spencer et al., 2006, p. 1521). In any case, this perspective is pervasive throughout the human life span, since every moment of life affects all the others.

Applying dynamic-systems theory to human development is a "relatively new" effort (Thelen & Smith, 2006, p. 258), but this perspective has aided natural scientists for over 50 years. They have recognized that systemic change over time is the nature of life:

> Seasons change in ordered measure, clouds assemble and disperse, trees grow to certain shape and size, snowflakes form and melt, minute plants and animals pass through elaborate life cycles that are invisible to us, and social groups come together and disband.
>
> *[Thelen & Smith, 2006, p. 271]*

Bioecological Systems

A leader in understanding levels of development was Urie Bronfenbrenner, who recommended an **ecological-systems approach** to developmental study. He argued that, just as a naturalist studying an organism examines the ecology, or the interrelationship of the organism and its environment, developmentalists need to examine all the systems that surround the development of each person.

ecological-systems approach A vision of how human development should be studied, with the person considered in all the contexts and interactions that constitute a life.

These systems continue to unfold over the natural course of the human life, affecting every thought, action, and emotion (Bronfenbrenner & Morris, 2006). Bronfenbrenner described three nested levels that affect each person (diagrammed in Figure 1.1): *microsystems* (elements of the person's immediate surroundings, such as family and peer group), *exosystems* (such local institutions as school and church), and *macrosystems* (the larger social setting, including cultural values, economic policies, and political processes).

Bronfenbrenner also recognized that conditions change over time, and therefore the *chronosystem* (historical conditions) affects the other three systems. Appreciating the dynamic interaction between the microsystem, the exosystem, and the macrosystem led him to name a fifth system, the *mesosystem,* which involves the connections between systems or between parts of a single system.

One example of a mesosystem is all the connections between home and school, including all the communication processes (letters home, parent–teacher conferences, phone calls, back-to-school nights) between a child's parents and teachers. Another mesosystem is all the connections between work and family, not only direct connections such as family-leave policies and work hours but also connections between such macrosystem factors as unemployment rates, which affect the microsystems of those families in which the head of household cannot find work.

Bronfenbrenner particularly objected to capturing the artificial behavior of a person at one moment, without considering how that behavior has been shaped by overarching systems. Referring in 1974 to research on mother–child attachment (discussed in Chapter 7), he complained, "Much of contemporary developmental

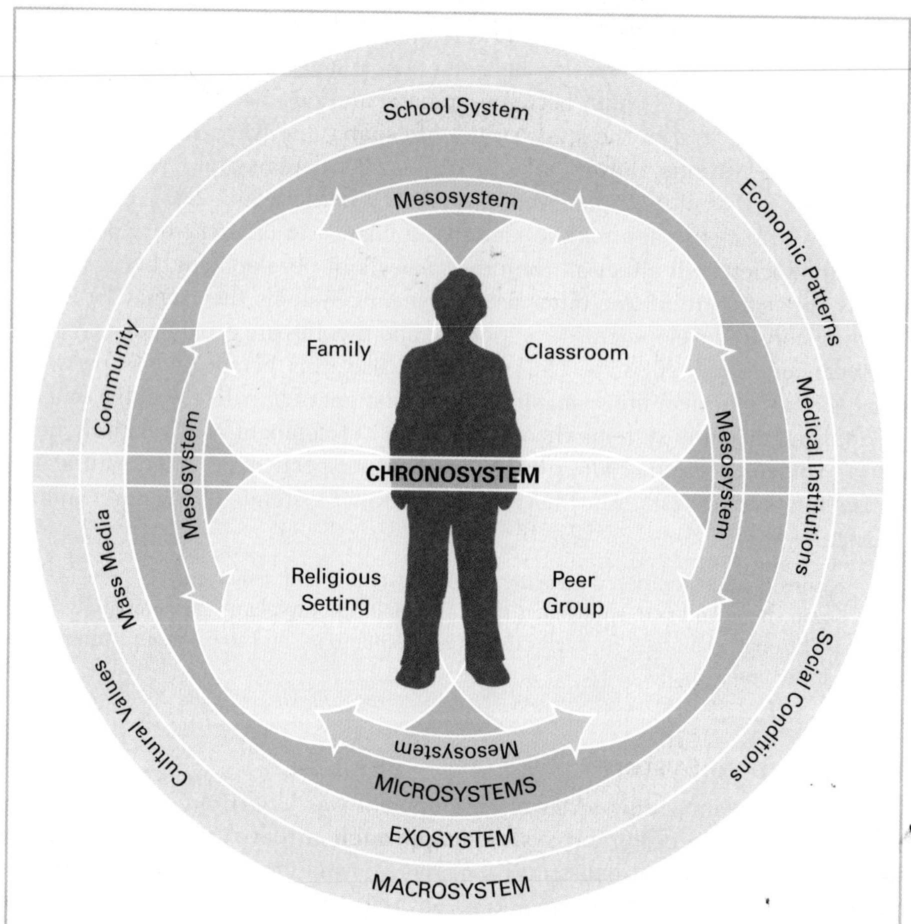

FIGURE 1.1

The Ecological Model According to developmental researcher Urie Bronfenbrenner, each person is significantly affected by interactions among a number of overlapping systems, which provide the context of development. *Microsystems*—family, peer groups, classroom, neighborhood, house of worship—intimately and immediately shape human development. *Mesosystems* refer to interactions among microsystems, as when parents coordinate their efforts with teachers to educate the child. Surrounding and supporting the microsystems are the *exosystems,* which include all the external networks, such as community structures and local educational, medical, employment, and communications systems, that influence the microsystems. Influencing all three of these systems is the *macrosystem,* which includes cultural values, political philosophies, economic patterns, and social conditions. Bronfenbrenner later added a fifth system, the *chronosystem,* to emphasize the importance of historical time.

psychology is the science of the strange behavior of children in strange situations with strange adults for the briefest possible period of time" (p. 1).

Throughout his life, Bronfenbrenner emphasized the importance of studying humans in natural settings, as they actually live their lives. His emphasis on the dynamic biological systems that allow ongoing change inspired him to rename his theory from ecological to *bioecological* (Bronfenbrenner & Morris, 2006). A similar perspective is found in dynamic-systems theory, which holds that "thought is always grounded in perception and action" (Spencer et al., 2006, p. 1529).

This idea that each person develops in various nested contexts, which overlap and interact over time, is central to a dynamic-systems approach to life-span development (Thelen & Smith, 2006) as well as to the bioecological perspective (Bronfenbrenner & Morris, 2006). You will soon see this in all five of the characteristics of life-span study, as well as throughout this book.

SUMMING UP

The science of human development seeks to understand how and why people—all kinds of people, everywhere—change or remain the same over time. As a science, it seeks empirical data to answer crucial questions regarding humans of every age and background. In stressing change, the study of development is dynamic, never static, and focuses on the interaction among people and among the nested levels of influence that external systems have on individual persons.

Five Characteristics of Development

Developmentalists (people from many academic disciplines who study human development) are acutely aware of the reciprocal connection between one moment in life and another. This awareness leads them to five principles that are useful for understanding any age of human life (Baltes et al., 2006; Staudinger & Lindenberger, 2003).

- *Multidirectional.* Change occurs in every direction, not always in a straight line. Gains and losses, predictable growth and unexpected transformations, are evident.
- *Multicontextual.* Human lives are embedded in many contexts, including historical conditions, economic constraints, and family patterns.
- *Multicultural.* Many cultures—not just between nations but also within them—affect how people develop.
- *Multidisciplinary.* Numerous academic fields—especially psychology, biology, education, and sociology, but also neuroscience, economics, religion, anthropology, history, medicine, genetics, and many more—contribute data and insights.
- *Plasticity.* Every individual, and every trait within each individual, can be altered at any point in the life span. Change is ongoing, although neither random nor easy.

Each of these five principles merits further explanation.

Especially for College Students Which pattern of developmental growth best describes the change from high school to college?

Multidirectional

The study of human development is the study of change; development is dynamic, not static. Developmentalists sometimes analyze each fraction of a second, as when a barely perceptible change in a newborn's face reflects a parent's fleeting glance (e.g., Lavelli & Fogel, 2005). More often years, not seconds, are analyzed, revealing unexpected twists and turns.

Gains and Losses

In studying dynamic systems, developmentalists have discovered that each aspect of life (physical health, intellectual growth, social interaction) is multidirectional; any direction—up, down, stable, or erratic—is possible. There is evidence for simple growth, radical transformation, improvement, and decline as well as for continuity—day to day, year to year, and generation to generation (see Figure 1.2). A gain and a loss may occur at the same time, or a loss may lead to a gain or vice versa (Baltes et al., 2006).

When movement occurs, the cause could be something that seems tangential, because the person is systemically affected by a change in any aspect of development. An apparent loss in one dimension is often accompanied by a gain in another. The emphasis on multidirectional change is particularly important in late adulthood, because during old age people tend to focus on the declines, not on the gains. One gain is that many older people become more nurturant toward other family members.

This may be clearer with another example. When newborn babies are held up in a standing position, they move their legs as if walking. It was once thought that this stepping reflex disappeared at about 3 months. At birth, babies have many other reflexes that seem to disappear later. For decades, developmentalists hypothesized that these disappearances reflected losses in brain function, which

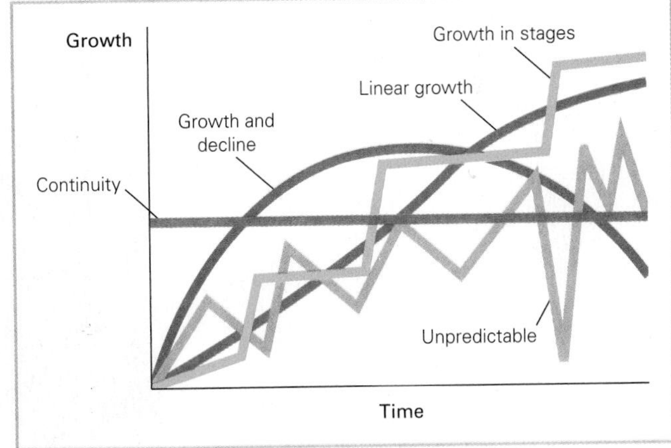

FIGURE 1.2

Patterns of Developmental Growth Many patterns of developmental growth have been discovered by careful research. Although linear (or near-linear) progress seems most common, scientists now find that almost no aspect of human change follows the linear pattern exactly.

they believed were necessary for more advanced brain processes to occur. However, later researchers found that babies still make stepping movements when they are lying on their backs or when their lower bodies are in water. This observation led to the idea that possibly less is lost than is gained. Aha: 3-month-olds have become heavier; their little legs cannot support them, and that's why stepping disappears while standing but not when on their backs or in water (Thelen & Ulrich, 1991).

The Butterfly Effect

One aspect of multidirectional study is that the eventual direction and power of change should not be judged immediately. Small changes may have large effects, because every change affects a dynamic system. The power of a small change is called the **butterfly effect,** after a 1972 speech by weather expert Edward Lorenz, titled "Predictability: Does the Flap of a Butterfly's Wings in Brazil Set Off a Tornado in Texas?"

butterfly effect The idea that a small effect or thing can have a large impact if it happens to tip the balance, causing other changes that create a major event.

The idea of the butterfly effect is that, just as one drop of water might make an overfull glass suddenly spill over, so a small increase in wind velocity caused by a butterfly might be the final force that triggers a storm a thousand miles away. The possibility that small input may result in large output applies to human thoughts and actions as well (Masterpasqua & Perna, 1997). To use a developmental example, one cigarette smoked by a pregnant woman could result in a fetus's death if it is already fragile and underweight for other reasons. Of course, most butterfly wings have no effects, nor do most single cigarettes. The butterfly effect means that a tiny event *could* have an enormous impact, not that it always does.

The opposite can occur: Large changes can affect people in contradictory ways. Lottery jackpot winners become euphoric and then less happy than before (Argyle, 2001; Gilbert, 2006). Christopher Reeve earned fame and fortune as a star in more than 40 films. When he became paralyzed, he first wanted to kill himself but soon welcomed life, explaining that he grew to appreciate other people much more (Reeve, 1999).

➤**Response for College Students** (from page 7): All of them, depending on which aspect of development, in which person, is considered. As the text states, "Any direction is possible."

AP PHOTO / HIDAJET DELIC

Holding On Children from war-torn Kosovo rest at a refugee center near Sarajevo, Bosnia. They are actively coping with their situation as best they can, holding a friend, a little sister, or a loaf of bread in their arms.

Multicontextual

Humans develop in dozens of contexts that profoundly affect their development. Contexts include physical surroundings (climate, noise, population density, etc.) and family patterns. Here we explain only two aspects of the *social context.*

The Historical Context

cohort A group pf people who were born at about the same time and thus move through life together, experiencing the same historical events and cultural shifts.

All persons born within a few years of one another are said to be a **cohort,** a group of people whose shared age means that they travel through life together. Those in a cohort are all affected by the values, events, technologies, and culture of their era. The war in Iraq has a different meaning for U.S. adults whose lives were changed by World War II, the Vietnam War, or the Gulf War.

If you doubt that national trends and events touch individuals, consider your first name—a very personal word chosen especially for you. Look at Table 1.1, which lists the most popular names for boys and girls born into cohorts 20 years apart, beginning in 1925.

The popularity of your name is influenced by the era, and so is your reaction to it. If you are troubled that your name is popular, or rare, or old-fashioned, blame history, not your parents. Cohort affects many other aspects of development. Be grateful you were born after 1900, because severe beatings, deadly childhood diseases, and grueling child labor were common before then, when historical conditions resulted in many unwanted children.

"And this is Charles, our web-master."

Computer Expert in a Baseball Cap Cohort differences become most apparent when new technology appears. Which age group is most likely to download music onto iPods or to send text messages on cellular phones?

The Socioeconomic Context

When social scientists study the socioeconomic context, they often focus on **socioeconomic status,** abbreviated **SES.** Sometimes SES is called "social class" (as in "middle class" or "working class").

socioeconomic status (SES) A person's position in society as determined by income, wealth, occupation, education, place of residence, and other factors.

SES involves more than money, in the form of income or wealth. It is also measured by factors such as occupation, education, and place of residence. The SES of a family consisting of, say, an infant, an unemployed mother, and a father who earns $15,000 a year would be low if the wage earner was an illiterate dishwasher living in an urban slum but would be much higher if that income was earned by a postdoctoral student living on campus and teaching part time.

TABLE 1.1

Which First Names for U.S. Girls and Boys Were Most Popular in 1925, 1945, 1965, 1985, and 2005?

Year	Top Five Girls' Names	Top Five Boys' Names
______	Mary, Dorothy, Betty, Helen, Margaret	Robert, John, William, James, Charles
______	Lisa, Mary, Karen, Kimberly, Susan	Michael, John, David, James, Robert
______	Emily, Emma, Madison, Abigail, Olivia	Jacob, Michael, Joshua, Matthew, Ethan
______	Mary, Linda, Barbara, Patricia, Carol	James, Robert, John, William, Richard
______	Jessica, Ashley, Jennifer, Amanda, Sarah	Michael, Christopher, Matthew, Joshua, Daniel

Guess First If your answers, in order from top to bottom, were 1925, 1965, 2005, 1945, and 1985, you are excellent at detecting cohort influences. If you made a mistake, perhaps that's because the data are compiled from applications for Social Security numbers during each year, so the names of those who did not get a Social Security number are omitted.

ASIM TANVEER / REUTERS / CORBIS

Culturally Acceptable Putting very young children to work is still a widespread custom in many parts of the world. The International Labor Organization estimates that, worldwide, 246 million children aged 5 to 17 are employed—often at very low wages. The children pictured here are working in an embroidery shop in Pakistan.

Observation Quiz (see answer, page 12): Why are they using only their right hands?

As this example illustrates, SES includes advantages and disadvantages, opportunities and limitations, past history and future prospects—all of which affect housing, nutrition, knowledge, and habits. Although low income obviously limits a person, other factors (such as education) can make poverty better or worse.

A question for developmentalists is whether low SES does most damage in infancy, when malnutrition, poor medical care, and low family education could stunt a baby's brain, or in late adulthood, when accumulated stress overwhelms the body's reserves. The answer is not clear; SES is powerful at every age.

Multicultural

Culture affects each human at every moment. Precisely because culture is so pervasive, people rarely notice their culture while they are immersed in it—just as fish do not notice the water they are surrounded by.

Deciding What to Do Each Moment

When social scientists use the term *culture,* they refer to the "patterns of behavior that are passed from one generation to the next . . . [and] that serve as the resources for the current life of a social group" (Cole, 2005, p. 49). The social group may be citizens of a nation, residents of a region within a nation, members of an ethnic group, people living in one neighborhood, or even students in a college class.

Any group may have its own culture—its own values, customs, clothes, dwellings, cuisine, and assumptions. Culture affects every action. For example, some students use highlighters, study in the library, and call professors by their first names; others do not. The reasons are cultural.

Cultures are dynamic, always changing, because children resist some traditional values and adults abandon some aspects of their culture when historical, geographical, or family circumstances change (Smedley & Smedley, 2005). Each

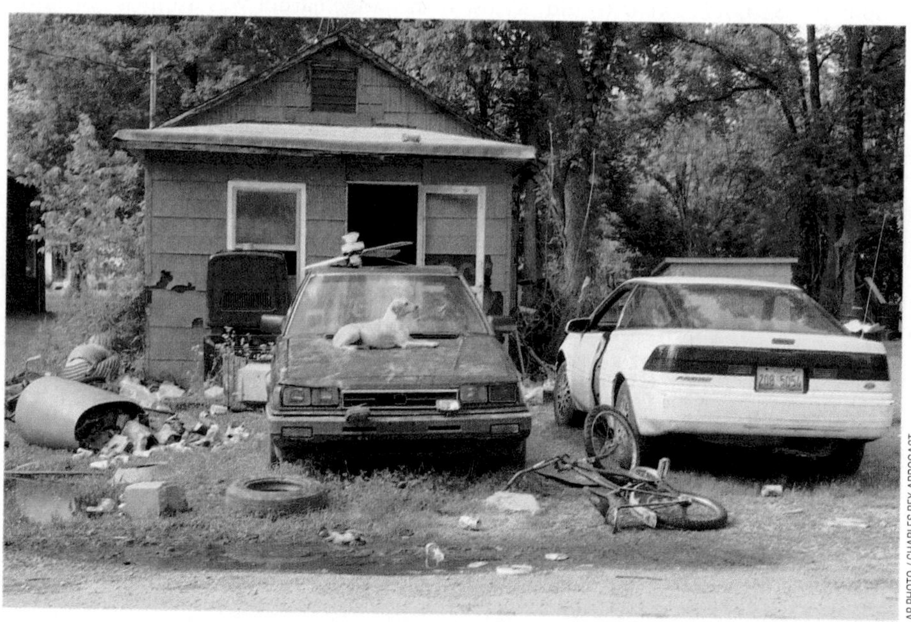

AP PHOTO / CHARLES REX ARBOGAST

The Culture of Poverty In this southern Illinois neighborhood, littered yards are part of a "culture of poverty" that also includes poor nutrition, substandard housing, and an average life expectancy of 52 years.

Observation Quiz (see answer, page 13): A 13-year-old is in this photo, trying to garden. Can you find her?

cohort experiences, and then transmits, a different culture than previous generations did.

People are influenced by more than one culture. In multiethnic nations such as the United States and Canada, many individuals are multicultural, functioning not only within the dominant culture but also within various regional, ethnic, school, and other cultures.

Ethnicity, Race, and Income

Confusion arises whenever people—scientists or nonscientists—refer to ethnic groups, races, cultures, and socioeconomic classes, because these categories overlap. The preceding discussion and the following definitions should clarify the situation.

People of an **ethnic group** share certain attributes, almost always ancestral heritage and often national origin, religion, culture, and language (Whitfield & McClearn, 2005). (*Heritage* refers to customs and traditions passed down to the present; *national origin* refers to one's ancestors' country of birth.) Ethnic categories arise from history, sociology, and psychology, not from biology.

The term **race,** in contrast, has been used to categorize groups of people based on appearance. However, about 95 percent of the genetic differences between one person and another occur *within,* not between, supposed racial groups. Genetic variation is particularly apparent among dark-skinned people whose ancestors were African (Tishkoff & Kidd, 2004). Race is misleading as a biological category.

Instead, although race was long thought to be a valid biological category, it is actually a **social construction,** an idea created by society. That does not render the term meaningless: Perceived racial differences lead to discrimination, and racial identity affects cognition (see the discussion of stereotype threat in Chapter 18). But race "is a socially constructed concept, not a biological one" (Sternberg et al., 2005), and thus racial categories may change over time.

SES overlaps with ethnicity and race. When one careful study found many health differences among Americans of African, Asian, European, and Hispanic heritage living in New England, a close examination found that half of those differences could be traced to SES, not ethnicity (Krieger et al., 2005).

ZHOU GUANGJI / XINHUA PRESS / CORBIS

Heritage Aloft At least ten major ethnic groups make up China's population of more than a billion. This man shows his grandson the multicolored lanterns displayed on Lantern Day in Hangzhou. Other nations, and other parts of China, have no Lantern Day festival, but all have special traditional celebrations of their own.

ethnic group People whose ancestors were born in the same region and who often share a language, culture, and religion.

race A group of people who are regarded (by themselves or by others) as genetically distinct from other groups on the basis of physical appearance.

social construction An idea that is built more on shared perceptions than on objective reality. Many age-related terms, such as childhood, adolescence, yuppies, and senior citizens are social constructions.

REUTERS / JEFF J MITCHELL

No Raisins? For centuries at St. Andrews University in Scotland, new students gave seniors a pound of raisins or else got dunked in a fountain. Wine has replaced raisins, and foam is sprayed instead of water—but on Raisin Monday a social construction lives on.

➤Answer to Observation Quiz (from page 10): They are actually using both hands. The left hand pulls the needle from underneath. Note that they work in rhythm—to keep up the pace as well as to avoid getting in each other's way.

Both national history and SES affect culture and hence development. For example, one cross-cultural study found that learning was stressed for middle-class preschoolers in the United States and Kenya but not for lower-class children in those two nations or for children of any SES in Brazil (Quintana et al., 2006).

The multicultural emphasis in human development requires that researchers be aware of cultural assumptions and values, respecting their power. But culture is dynamic, and people of every ethnic or economic background can accept or reject cultural values. Ethnic, racial, and economic differences do not necessarily determine culture. Consider the childhood experience of poet Maya Angelou, one of many who reshaped U.S. culture during the twentieth century.

issues and applications

"My Name Wasn't Mary"

Maya Angelou was born Marguerite Johnson in 1929 into a community so racially segregated that she thought "white folks couldn't be people because their feet were too small, their skin too white and see-throughy, and they didn't walk on the balls of their feet the way people did—they walked on their heels like horses" (Angelou, 1970, p. 76).

Young Marguerite's best friend was her older brother, Bailey, who gave her the nickname Maya, from "Mya sister," as he called her. At age 10 she began to learn about White people (her "finishing school," she called it) as an apprentice to Miss Glory, who worked as a maid for Mrs. Cullinan. Once, when Marguerite was serving Mrs. Cullinan and her friends:

> One of the women asked, "What's your name, girl?" It was the speckled-face one. Mrs. Cullinan said, "She doesn't talk much. Her name is Margaret." . . .
>
> I smiled at her. Poor thing . . . couldn't even pronounce my name correctly.
>
> "She's a sweet little thing, though."
>
> "Well, that may be, but the name's too long. I'd never bother myself. I'd call her Mary if I were you."
>
> I fumed into the kitchen. That horrible woman would never have the chance to call me Mary because if I was starving I'd never work for her. I decided I wouldn't pee on her if her heart was on fire. . . .
>
> The very next day . . . Miss Glory and I were washing up the lunch dishes when Mrs. Cullinan came to the doorway, "Mary?"
>
> Miss Glory asked, "Who?" . . . "Her name is Margaret, ma'am. Her name's Margaret."
>
> "That's too long. She's Mary from now on. Heat that soup from last night and put it in the china tureen and Mary, I want you to carry it carefully."
>
> Every person I knew had a hellish horror of being "called out of his name." It was a dangerous practice to call a Negro anything that could be loosely construed as insulting because of the centuries of their having been called niggers, jigs, dinges, blackbirds, crows, boots and spooks.
>
> . . . I had to quit the job, but the problem was going to be how to do it. Momma wouldn't allow me to quit for just any reason. . . .
>
> Then Bailey solved my dilemma. He had me describe the contents of the cupboard and the particular plates she liked best. Her favorite piece was a casserole shaped like a fish and the green glass coffee cups. I kept his instructions in mind, so on the next day when Miss Glory was hanging out clothes and I had again been told to serve the old biddies on the porch, I dropped the empty serving tray. When I heard Mrs. Cullinan scream, "Mary!" I picked up the casserole and two of the green glass cups in readiness. As she rounded the kitchen door, I let them fall to the tiled floor.
>
> I could never absolutely describe to Bailey what happened next, because each time I got to the part where she fell on the floor and screwed up her ugly face to cry, we burst out laughing. She actually wobbled around on the floor and picked up shards of cups and cried "Oh, Momma. Oh, dear Gawd. It's Momma's china from Virginia. Oh, Momma, I sorry."
>
> Miss Glory came running in from the yard. . . . "You mean to say she broke our Virginia dishes. What we gone do?"
>
> Mrs. Cullinan cried louder, "That clumsy nigger. Clumsy little black nigger."
>
> Old Speckled Face leaned down and asked, "Who did it, Viola? Was it Mary? Who did it?" . . .

DAN NIERLING, CEDAR FALLS COURIER/THE WATERLOO/AP PHOTO

Today, Everybody Knows Her Name Poet and best-selling author Maya Angelou speaks at the University of Northern Iowa about the healing and saving nature of poetry. She encouraged the members of the audience to become the "composers" of their own lives.

Mrs. Cullinan said "Her name's Margaret, goddam it, her name's Margaret."

And she threw a wedge of broken plate at me. It could have been the hysteria which put her aim off, but the flying crockery caught Miss Glory right over her ear and she started screaming.

I left the front door wide open so all the neighbors could hear.

Mrs. Cullinan was right about one thing. My name wasn't Mary.

[Angelou, 1970, pp. 90–93]

Maya Angelou did not follow the cultural script expected of a poor African American girl. Note, however, that her culture made it unthinkable for her either to ask Mrs. Cullinan to call her "Marguerite" or to tell her mother she wanted to quit.

Why was Maya so unlike Miss Glory, even though they were of the same ethnicity and SES? Cohort and family history are part of the answer. Miss Glory was born 20 years earlier, a descendant of slaves owned by Mrs. Cullinan's family. Mrs. Cullinan and Old Speckled Face were also products of their culture, unaware of the "hellish horror" of renaming.

But this incident demonstrates more than the power of culture to shape perception. It also shows that people sometimes break free of the restrictions imposed by their cohort, culture, or SES.

Multidisciplinary

Powerful forces pull scientists to specialize, to study one phenomenon in one species at one age. This tight focus can provide a deeper understanding of, for instance, the rhythms of vocalization among 3-month-old infants, or the effects of alcohol on adolescent mice, or wives' experiences of husbands' retirement. (Each of these has been studied extensively, and the results inform later sections of this book.)

However, the study of human development requires insight and information from a broad array of disciplines and cross-cutting topics, because each person develops simultaneously in body, mind, and spirit. Although development is often divided into three domains—*biosocial, cognitive,* and *psychosocial*—all three domains interact as part of the dynamic systems that make up a person. (Figure 1.3 provides a full definition of each domain.) For example, although giving birth is primarily biosocial because reproduction is biological, childbirth is also cognitive (it is a decision) and psychosocial (families and cultures vary tremendously in how newborns are treated). Placing a topic within one domain never means that that topic belongs exclusively to that domain, whether biosocial, cognitive, or psychosocial.

➤Answer to Observation Quiz (from page 10): Carolyn Whitaker, in an orange shirt, is at the far left.

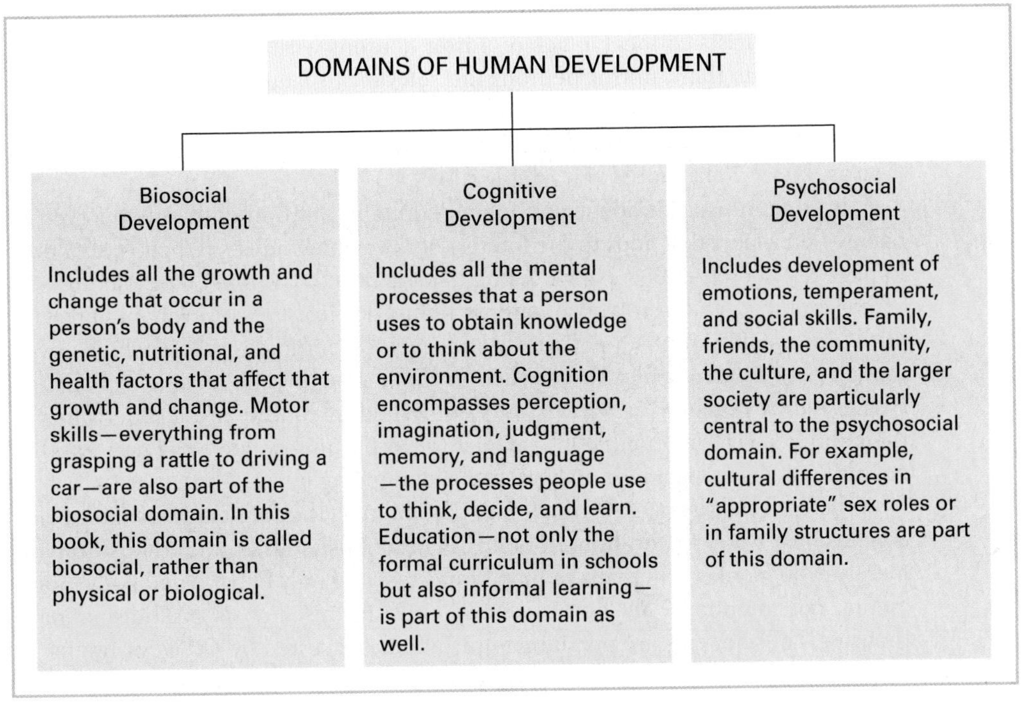

DOMAINS OF HUMAN DEVELOPMENT

Biosocial Development	Cognitive Development	Psychosocial Development
Includes all the growth and change that occur in a person's body and the genetic, nutritional, and health factors that affect that growth and change. Motor skills—everything from grasping a rattle to driving a car—are also part of the biosocial domain. In this book, this domain is called biosocial, rather than physical or biological.	Includes all the mental processes that a person uses to obtain knowledge or to think about the environment. Cognition encompasses perception, imagination, judgment, memory, and language—the processes people use to think, decide, and learn. Education—not only the formal curriculum in schools but also informal learning—is part of this domain as well.	Includes development of emotions, temperament, and social skills. Family, friends, the community, the culture, and the larger society are particularly central to the psychosocial domain. For example, cultural differences in "appropriate" sex roles or in family structures are part of this domain.

FIGURE 1.3

The Three Domains The division of human development into three domains makes it easier to study, but remember that very few factors belong exclusively to one domain or another. Development is not piecemeal but holistic: Each aspect of development is related to all three domains.

Many more disciplines besides biology, psychology, and sociology contribute to our study. As one expert explains: "The study of development is a huge community enterprise that spans generations and many disciplines" (Moore, 2002, p. 74). Multiple disciplines are needed because human beings develop in many domains, in multifaceted contexts, and in diverse cultures.

Although scientists feel a powerful impulse to study just one particular thing, there is also a powerful urge toward interdisciplinary, multifaceted study.

Mirror Neurons

One example of the benefit of the interdisciplinary approach to human development is shown by research on mirror neurons. This began about a decade ago, when neuroscience researchers saw that parts of a monkey's brain responded to observed actions as if the actions were performed by the monkey itself. Thus, when one monkey watched another reach for a piece of fruit, the same brain areas were activated in both monkeys. The researchers located this response in the F5 area of the monkey premotor cortex and called those reflective brain cells **mirror neurons** (Rizzolatti & Craighero, 2004). Hundreds of other experiments have corroborated the existence of mirror neurons.

mirror neurons Brain cells that respond to actions performed by someone else, as if the observer had done that action. For example, the brains of dancers who witness another dancer moving onstage are activated in the same movement areas as would be activated if they themselves did that dance step, because their mirror neurons reflect the activity.

This neuroscientific discovery quickly crossed disciplines and species. Scientists "turned to the human brain and found neural activity that mirrors not only the movement but also the intentions, sensations, and emotions of those around us" (Miller, 2005, p. 945). As "cognitive science meets neurophysiology" (Garbarini & Adenzato, 2004, p. 100), it becomes apparent that mirror neurons affect how people learn, imitate, and think.

Mirror neurons in the human brain reflect gestures, mouth movements, and whole-body actions. When experts in dance or in martial arts watch a performance, their brains are activated as if they themselves were performing (Calvo-Merino et al., 2005).

Implications of Mirror-Neuron Research

Currently, scientists in many disciplines are trying to understand the implications and limitations of this discovery (Wilson & Knoblich, 2005). Anthropologists think it might explain some aspects of cultural transmission or social organization (Adenzato & Garbarini, 2006; Morrison, 2002; Rizzolatti & Craighero, 2004); psychopathologists connect a lack of mirror neurons with autism (Williams et al., 2006); linguists think mirror neurons are relevant to language learning (Buccino et al., 2004); social psychologists wonder whether mirror neurons are one reason people understand other people's intentions and have empathy for those in pain (Harris, 2003; Nakahara & Miyashita, 2005).

Mirror neurons are evident not only in adults but also in children and even in babies—an aspect that adds to the interest of developmentalists (Chen et al., 2004; Lepage & Théoret, 2006). New possibilities are raised that must be explored.

For example, children whose parents fight a lot learn less in school and have difficulty establishing supportive friendships or intimate relationships, even though neither parent has hit or yelled at them directly. The leading explanation (suggested by research) is that parents enmeshed in conflict are less sensitive to their children (Davies et al., 2002). The discovery of mirror neurons raises another possibility: Observing a fight may be like experiencing it.

Although scientists enjoy thinking of possibilities, they are cautious in drawing conclusions. Research on human brains is notoriously difficult. Perhaps humans merely echo monkeys; perhaps human brains respond only to hand and body movements, not intentions. Yet because developmental research is multidisciplinary, thousands of scientists are pursuing implications suggested by monkeys' brains.

Especially for Parents Who Want Their Children to Enjoy Sports While your baby is still too young and uncoordinated to play any sports, what does the research on mirror neurons suggest you might do?

Plasticity

The term *plasticity* denotes two complementary aspects of development: Human traits can be molded (as plastic can be), yet people maintain a certain durability of identity (again, like plastic, which takes decades to disintegrate). Culture and upbringing affect both aspects of plasticity; so do genes and other biological influences.

Plasticity provides both hope and realism—hope because change is possible, and realism because each developing person must build on what has come before. In some ways, plasticity underlies all the other four characteristics of development.

People reexamine earlier values and overcome handicaps throughout their lives, but they cannot erase them. No matter what path a life takes, the journey begins and then proceeds from some particular point, moving up, down, or straight ahead, plastic and multidirectional, connected to context and culture. I have learned all this from David.

Especially for Public Health Professionals
Can immunization protect an embryo?

a case to study

My Nephew David

In the spring of 1967, in rural Kentucky, an epidemic of rubella (German measles) reached two more people: my sister-in-law, who had a sore throat for a couple of days, and her embryo, who was damaged for life. David was born in November. His survival was in doubt. He required immediate surgery for a serious heart ailment, and he was born with thick cataracts on both eyes and malformations of his thumbs, feet, teeth, and spine.

My brother is a professor and his wife is a nurse; their cultural and socioeconomic contexts encouraged them to seek help. Soon a consultant from the Kentucky School for the Blind told them how to help David learn. One instruction was to put him on a large rug to play. If he crawled off the rug, they should say "No" and place him back in the middle. His sense of touch would enable him to explore without bumping into walls.

Progress was slow. At age 3, David could not yet talk, chew solid food, use the toilet, coordinate his fingers, or even walk normally. An IQ test showed him to be severely mentally retarded. Fortunately, although deafness is common in children with rubella syndrome, David could hear. By age 5, one eye had been destroyed, but surgery had removed the cataract on the other eye, allowing some vision.

By then, the social construction that children with severe disabilities are unteachable was changing. David's parents enrolled him in four schools. Two were for children with cerebral palsy; one offered morning classes and the other was open in the afternoon. On Fridays, when both those schools were closed, David attended a school for the mentally retarded. On Sundays he went to church school, his first "mainstreaming"—the social construction that children with special needs should learn with regular children.

At age 7, David entered public school. His motor skills were poor (he had difficulty controlling a pencil); his efforts to read were limited by his faulty vision; and his social skills were impaired (he pinched people and laughed at the wrong times).

By age 10, David had made great strides. He had skipped a year of school and was a fifth-grader. He could read—with a magnifying glass—at the eleventh-grade level. Outside school he began to learn a second language, play the violin, and sing in the choir. He eventually went to college.

David (at right in photo below, with his brothers) now works as a translator of German texts, which he enjoys because "I like

GREG STASSEN

providing a service to scholars, giving them access to something they would otherwise not have" (personal communication with David, 2007). He reported a few years ago that he is

> generally quite happy, but secretly a little happier lately . . . because I have been consistently getting a pretty good vibrato when I am singing, not only by myself but in congregational hymns in church. [I asked what vibrato is; he explained:] When a note bounces up and down within a quarter tone either way of concert pitch, optimally between 5.5 and 8.2 times per second.

Amazing. David is both knowledgeable and happy, and he continues to develop his skills. He also has a wry sense of humor. When I told him that I wasn't progressing as fast as I wanted to in revising this text, even though I was working very hard every day, he replied, "That sounds just like a certain father I know."

The rubella damage will always be with David, limiting his development. But as his aunt, I have watched him defy pessimistic predictions. David is a testament for plasticity: No human is entirely, inevitably restricted by past experiences.

VINCE DE WITT / STOCK, BOSTON

Not the Typical Path This woman's lifelong ambition is to walk the 2,160-mile Appalachian Trail from Maine to Georgia. She is considerably more active than the average member of her cohort.

The five characteristics of human development lead to one conclusion: Nobody is exactly like a typical person of his or her cohort, SES, or culture. Each is influenced in divergent directions by many domains and contexts, whose power varies from person to person. Prediction is never precise. David will always be affected by his early damage, but he was not expected to survive, much less be able to "provide a service" to other people.

SUMMING UP

Each life is characterized by multiple changes that are *multidirectional,* increasing, decreasing, zigzagging, and so on. Development is also *multicontextual,* with every context having an impact. For example, historical and socioeconomic conditions facilitate some paths through life and close off others. A *multicultural* approach to the study of development recognizes that culture is pervasive, affecting every action. Developmental study is also *multidisciplinary,* drawing on biology, psychology, education, sociology, and many other disciplines. *Plasticity* is always evident but never infinite: Humans are neither stuck in their past nor free of it. ■

Developmental Study as a Science

Because the study of development is a science, it is based on *objective* evidence. Because it concerns human life and growth, it is also laden with *subjective* perceptions. This interplay of the objective and the subjective, of the universal and the personal, makes developmental science a challenging, fascinating, and even transformative study.

Adults have heartfelt opinions about how children should be raised; how emerging adults should find work or romance; whether they themselves should marry, or divorce, or have children. Opinions are subjective. Science helps us progress from opinion to truth, from wishes to actual outcomes.

Steps of the Scientific Method

scientific method A way to answer questions that requires empirical research and data-based conclusions.

Scientists ask questions and seek answers. To avoid the distortions of unexamined opinions and to control the biases of personal experience, they use the **scientific method.** This method involves four basic steps and sometimes a fifth:

1. *Ask a question.* On the basis of previous research or a particular theory or personal observation, pose a question. Scientists are curious about almost everything.
2. *Develop a hypothesis.* Reformulate and segment the question into a **hypothesis,** a specific prediction to be tested.
3. *Test the hypothesis.* Design and conduct research to provide empirical evidence (data) about the validity or falsehood of the hypothesis.
4. *Draw conclusions.* Use the evidence to support or refute the hypothesis. Note limitations of the research and alternative explanations.
5. *Make the findings available.* Publish the procedure and results in sufficient detail so that other scientists will be able to evaluate the conclusions or replicate the research.

hypothesis A specific prediction that is stated in such a way that it can be tested and either confirmed or refuted.

Replication is the repetition of a scientific study, using similar procedures with new participants, to verify or dispute the original study's conclusions. Science builds on science: New studies continually refine, refute, replicate, and extend the old.

replication The repetition of a scientific study, using the same procedures on a similar (but not identical) group of participants, in order to verify, refine, or dispute the original study's conclusions.

Between the questions developmental scientists ask (steps 1 and 2) and the answers they find (steps 4 and 5) lies *methodology*—the specific strategies, or methods, used to gather and analyze data and to test hypotheses. A research study's *validity* (does it measure what it purports to measure?), *reliability* (would repeating the measurements produce the same results?), *generalizability* (do the conclusions apply beyond this study?), and *usefulness* (can it solve real-life problems?) affect the power of each study.

Research design can advance or undercut that power. Thus, step 3 is the pivot. Like keystones, without a good design the entire structure will collapse. Some strategies to make research valid, reliable, generalizable, and useful are described in Appendix B. In every chapter, details about the design of some research studies are provided in the margins.

scientific observation A method of testing hypotheses by unobtrusively watching and recording participants' behavior in a systematic and objective manner, either in a laboratory or in a natural setting.

Ways to Test Hypotheses

Now we turn to four methods of testing hypotheses: observations, experiments, surveys, and case studies. Remember, the overall goal is to find evidence that answers questions as accurately as possible.

Observation

Scientific observation requires the researcher to observe and record behavior systematically and objectively. Observations often occur in a naturalistic setting, such as at home, in a school, or in a public park, because such settings encourage people to behave as they usually do. The observer tries to be unobtrusive so that research participants will act naturally. Observation can also occur in a laboratory or in searches of archival data.

Observation has been used to note the worldwide increase in obesity during the past few decades, which has affected children more than any other age group. Obesity rates for U.S. children are charted in Figure 1.4. One important developmental question (step 1 of the scientific method) is, "Why is childhood obesity increasing?" One hypothesis (step 2) is that children today do not get as much exercise as they once did—specifically, most children no longer walk to school. Observation can be used to test this hypothesis (step 3).

Can They See Her? No, and they cannot hear each other. This scientist is observing three deaf boys through a window that is a mirror on the other side. Her observations will help them learn to communicate.

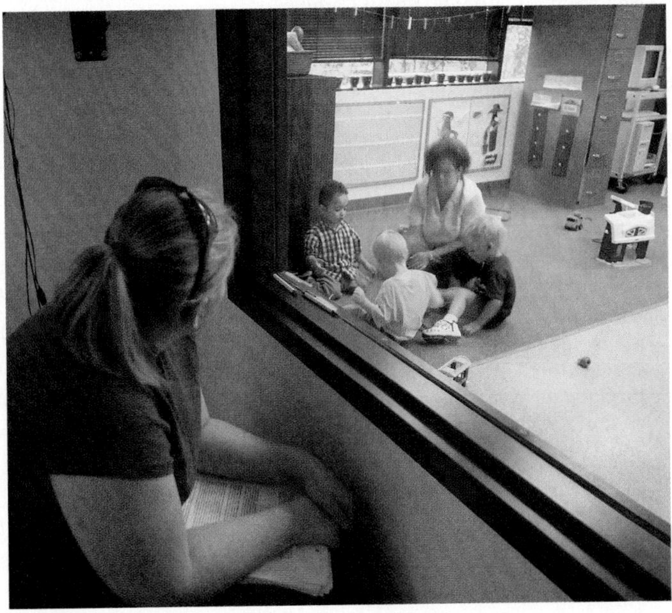

ALAMY

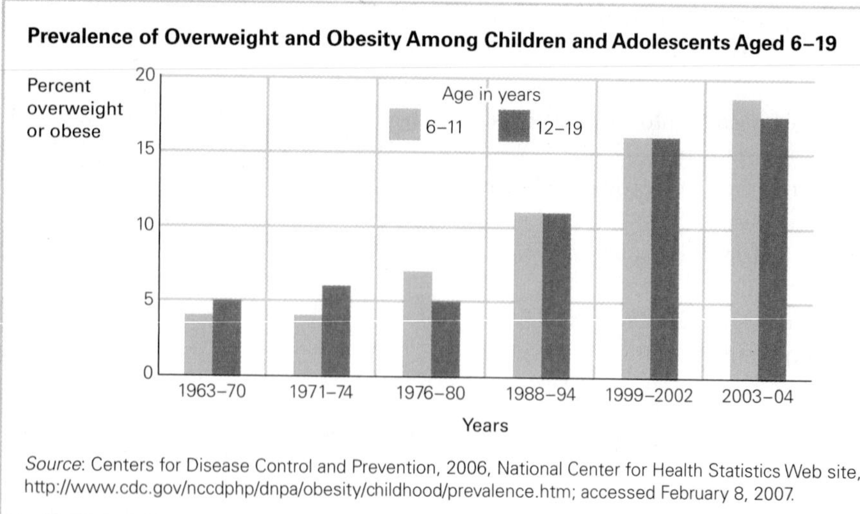

FIGURE 1.4

The Obesity Epidemic The percentage of children and adolescents who are overweight or obese has more than tripled in less than 50 years. The rate of increase has been especially rapid in the past 20 years. Currently, 18 percent of the U.S. population aged 18 or younger have BMI (body mass index) values that are at or above the 95th percentile of the Centers for Disease Control's growth charts, which is the criterion for classification as overweight.

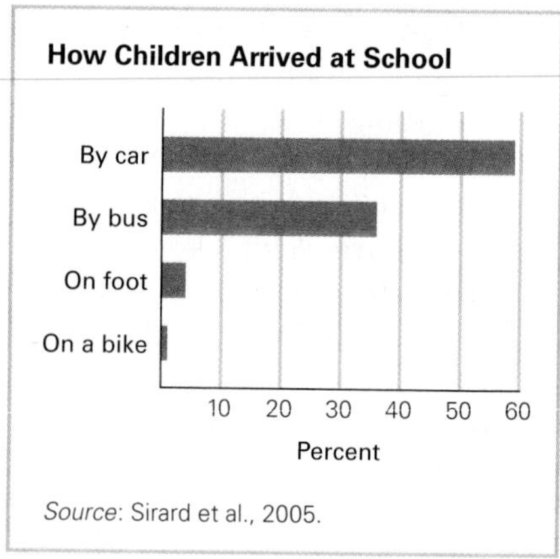

FIGURE 1.5

Why Walk When You Can Ride? An observational study of eight South Carolina elementary schools found that only 5 percent of the children rode their bikes or walked to school. Such a study could not explain *why* so few children got to school under their own steam. For that, an experiment would be needed.

Research Design

Scientists: John Sirard, Barbara E. Ainsworth, Kerri L. McIver, and Russell R. Pate.

Publication: *American Journal of Public Health* (2005).

Participants: Total of 3,911 children attending 8 public elementary schools in and around Columbia, South Carolina. Schools were diverse in SES, ethnicity, and location.

Design: Observational study. Two or three observers at each school, on five consecutive school days, arrived an hour before school started and left two hours later, counting children who arrived via car, bus, bike, or on foot. Similar observations occurred in the afternoon. Weather (e.g., rain) was also noted.

Major conclusion: No matter the SES, ethnic group, urban/suburban neighborhood, or weather, only about 4 percent of the children walked to school and 1 percent rode a bike.

Comment: This is an excellent observational study. However, because the schools were all in one South Carolina community, replication elsewhere is needed.

Several observers went to eight elementary schools (some rural, some urban), noting how the children arrived at school. To make sure they would catch any fluctuations by day of the week, they observed for five consecutive days. As Figure 1.5. shows, 95 percent of the children arrived by car or school bus; only 5 percent got to school under their own power, on foot or on a bicycle (Sirard et al., 2005).

Observation has one major limitation: It does not indicate what *causes* people to do what they do. Do children grow heavier because their parents drive them to school, or do parents drive their children because they are too heavy to walk? Is inactivity the result or the cause of overweight? Observation cannot tell us (see Research Design). An experiment can.

The Experiment

The **experiment** is the research method that scientists use to establish cause. In the social sciences, experimenters typically give people a particular treatment, or expose them to a specific condition, and then note whether their behavior changes.

In technical terms, the experimenters manipulate an **independent variable** (the treatment or special condition, also called the *experimental variable*). They note whether the independent variable affects the specific behavior they are studying, called the **dependent variable** (which, in theory, *depends* on the independent variable). Thus, the independent variable is the new, special treatment; the dependent variable is the result of that treatment.

The purpose of an experiment is to find out whether an independent variable affects the dependent variable. Statistics are often used to analyze the results. Sometimes results are reported by *effect size,* to distinguish slight, moderate, or large effect. Sometimes tests of *significance* are used, to indicate whether the results might have occurred by chance. (A finding that chance would produce the results less than 5 times in 100 is significance at the 0.05 level; 1 time in 100 is 0.01 significance.)

To make sure a change in the dependent variable is caused by the independent variable, experimenters often compare two groups of participants: one that gets the special treatment and the other, similar in every relevant way, that does not. Thus, in a typical experiment (as diagrammed in Figure 1.6), two groups of participants are studied: an **experimental group,** which gets a particular treatment (the independent variable), and a **comparison group** (also called a **control group**), which does not.

To understand the relationship between movement and obesity, investigators (Levine et al., 2005) recruited inactive adults (they described themselves as "couch potatoes") who agreed to wear electronic monitoring equipment to record their bodily movement. The data were automatically recorded 120 times each minute, 24 hours a day. Half the volunteers were lean, and half were overweight. The recordings revealed that the lean adults moved around in "the routines of daily life" more than the overweight adults did (Levine et al., 2005). For instance, they spent an average of nine hours a day on their feet, standing or walking; the obese ones averaged only six hours. So far this is merely observation.

Then came the experiment. Both groups were put on strict diets, the lean group to gain weight and the overweight ones to lose weight, for two months. The overweight participants lost about 20 pounds (8 kg) each, and the lean ones gained about 10 pounds (4 kg) each. (The changes were temporary; most participants returned to their usual weight when they stopped dieting.) Then daily activity was measured again.

The crucial question was whether or not the overweight people moved more than before and the leaner people moved less than before now that their weight had changed. The answer was no. The monitors recorded no significant change. In fact, there was a trend toward *less* movement than before among the heavier people who had lost weight. This shows cause and effect: People do not move less because they are overweight; instead, they are overweight because they move less.

experiment A research method in which the researcher tries to determine the cause-and-effect relationship between two variables by manipulating one variable (called the *independent variable*) and then observing and recording the resulting changes in the other variable (called the *dependent variable*).

independent variable In an experiment, the variable that is introduced to see what effect it has on the dependent variable. (Also called *experimental variable.*)

dependent variable In an experiment, the variable that may change as a result of whatever new condition or situation the experimenter adds. In other words, the dependent variable *depends* on the independent variable.

experimental group A group of participants in a research study who experience some special treatment or condition (the independent variable).

comparison group/control group A group of participants in a research study who are similar to the experimental group in all relevant ways but who do not experience the experimental condition (the independent variable).

Especially for Nurses In the field of medicine, why are experiments conducted to test new drugs and treatments?

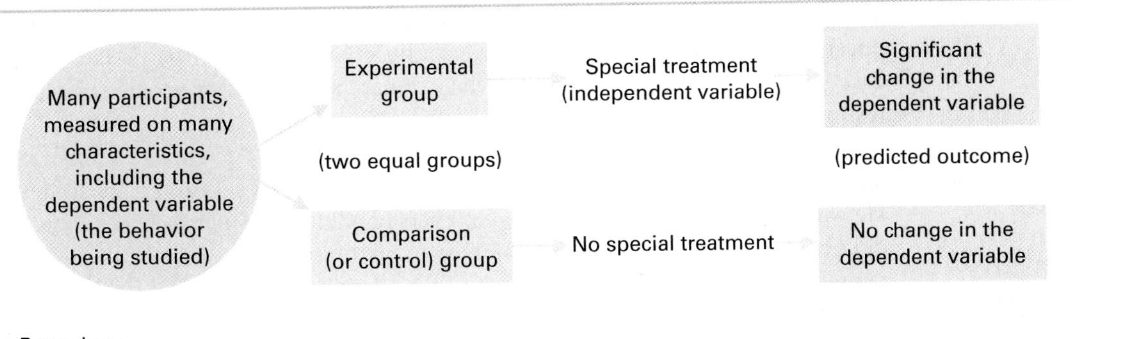

Procedure:

1. Divide participants into two groups that are matched on important characteristics, especially the behavior that is the dependent variable on which this study is focused.
2. Give special treatment, or intervention (the independent variable), to one group (the experimental group).
3. Compare the groups on the dependent variable. If they now differ, the cause of the difference was probably the independent variable.
4. Publish the results.

FIGURE 1.6

How to Conduct an Experiment **Observation Quiz** (see answer, page 23): Does the experimental group always change?

The Survey

survey A research method in which information is collected from a large number of people by interviews, written questionnaires, or some other means.

A third research method is the **survey.** Information is collected from a large number of people by interview, questionnaire, or some other means. This is a quick and direct way to obtain data. However, getting valid survey data is not easy. For example, in every poll designed to predict who will win an election, the surveyed respondents must vote as they say they will, and each of them must reflect the views of the thousands of others in the voting population. Researchers know that these are both uncertainties and therefore adjust for them. The adjustment cannot be precise; many elections are "too close to call."

Further, the wording and the sequence of questions can influence answers, and some respondents present themselves as they would like to be perceived, not as they really are. For example, in a 1998 nationwide telephone survey, 25 percent of parents said their children walked to school. The authors of the observation study described earlier believe that their finding of only 5 percent is "more accurate . . . than survey-based estimates" (Sirard et al., 2005, p. 237).

Especially for Social Scientists What are some of the benefits of cross-cultural research?

Whenever surveys ask husbands and wives, or parents and teachers, or adults and children about the same thing, the two groups' responses differ. For example, "parents portray a much rosier picture of children's well-being than children do of themselves" (Scott, 2000, p. 99).

To illustrate the problems that surveys can pose, note the responses among ninth graders in the United States. More than twice as many boys as girls (12 to 5 percent) say they have experienced sex before age 13 (MMWR, June 9, 2006). That is unlikely, especially since girls reach puberty sooner and their sexual partners are usually older, not younger, boys. Either boys exaggerate or girls underreport their sexual activity. Surveys may not be accurate.

The Case Study

case study A research method in which one individual is studied intensively.

A fourth research method, the **case study,** is an intensive study of one individual. Often the researcher begins by asking the person about past history, current thinking, and future plans. Others (friends, family, teachers) who know the individual are also interviewed. Although some questions are prepared in advance, follow-up questions allow deeper understanding of the nuances of each particular case. A case study can begin less formally, when researchers question people they know, testing ideas in the process.

A case study can provide unanticipated insight. Jeffrey Arnett was a junior professor at the University of Missouri when he interviewed several of his students. He was surprised that the traditional markers of adulthood (marriage and vocation) did not seem important to their happiness or maturation. For example, one student named Angela

> returned to Missouri a year ago after spending two years at Michigan State. . . . She loved being on her own, and she would have liked to finish her bachelor's degree at Michigan State. However, she decided she wanted to change her major from horticulture therapy to "just plain horticulture" and when university officials resisted, she dropped out. . . .
>
> If you look at Angela's life right now, as it is, you might not see much in her favor. She has dropped out of college, and she is working at a job she enjoys but that doesn't pay well and doesn't offer much in the way of long-term prospects. She is living with a boyfriend she doesn't respect and certainly doesn't want to marry. Yet she is reasonably happy with her life, less for what it is now than for what she believes it will be in the future. . . . At age 21, even if she is currently adrift in many ways, all of her hopes are alive and well.
>
> *[Arnett, 2004, pp. 41–44]*

Beginning with such cases, Arnett hypothesized that a new stage of life had developed among 18- to 25-year-olds; he called this stage *emerging adulthood.*

➤**Response for Parents Who Want Their Children to Enjoy Sports** (from page 14): The results of mirror-neuron research imply that people of all ages learn by observing body movements in others. This suggests that parents should make sure their baby gets many chances to watch them (or someone else) throwing balls, running, and playing sports.

➤**Response for Public Health Professionals** (from page 15): No and yes. Embryos cannot be vaccinated, but immunization can prevent the spread of disease and keep a pregnant woman healthy if she already has antibodies.

General statements cannot be proven with case studies, because each person is unique. Beyond that, collecting and interpreting the information reflects individual biases and idiosyncrasies, and case studies are qualitative, not quantitative (a topic discussed later).

No developmental scientist reaches conclusions based only on a case study. At best, a case study raises hypotheses that need more formal exploration. That is exactly what Arnett did, and now many other research designs also find that emerging adulthood is a distinct period in the human life span (Arnett & Tanner, 2006; Settersten et al., 2005). (Emerging adulthood is discussed in Chapters 17–19.)

Studying Change over Time

Developmental scientists use the methods just described—observations, experiments, surveys, and case studies—but they add another dimension. Their research must include time, or aging. Usually they accomplish this by using one of three basic designs: cross-sectional, longitudinal, or cross-sequential (summarized graphically in Figure 1.7).

FIGURE 1.7

Which Approach Is Best? Cross-sequential research is the most time-consuming and most complex approach, but it also yields the best information about development. This is one reason why hundreds of scientists conduct research on the same topics, replicating one another's work—to gain some of the advantages of cross-sequential research without having to wait all those years.

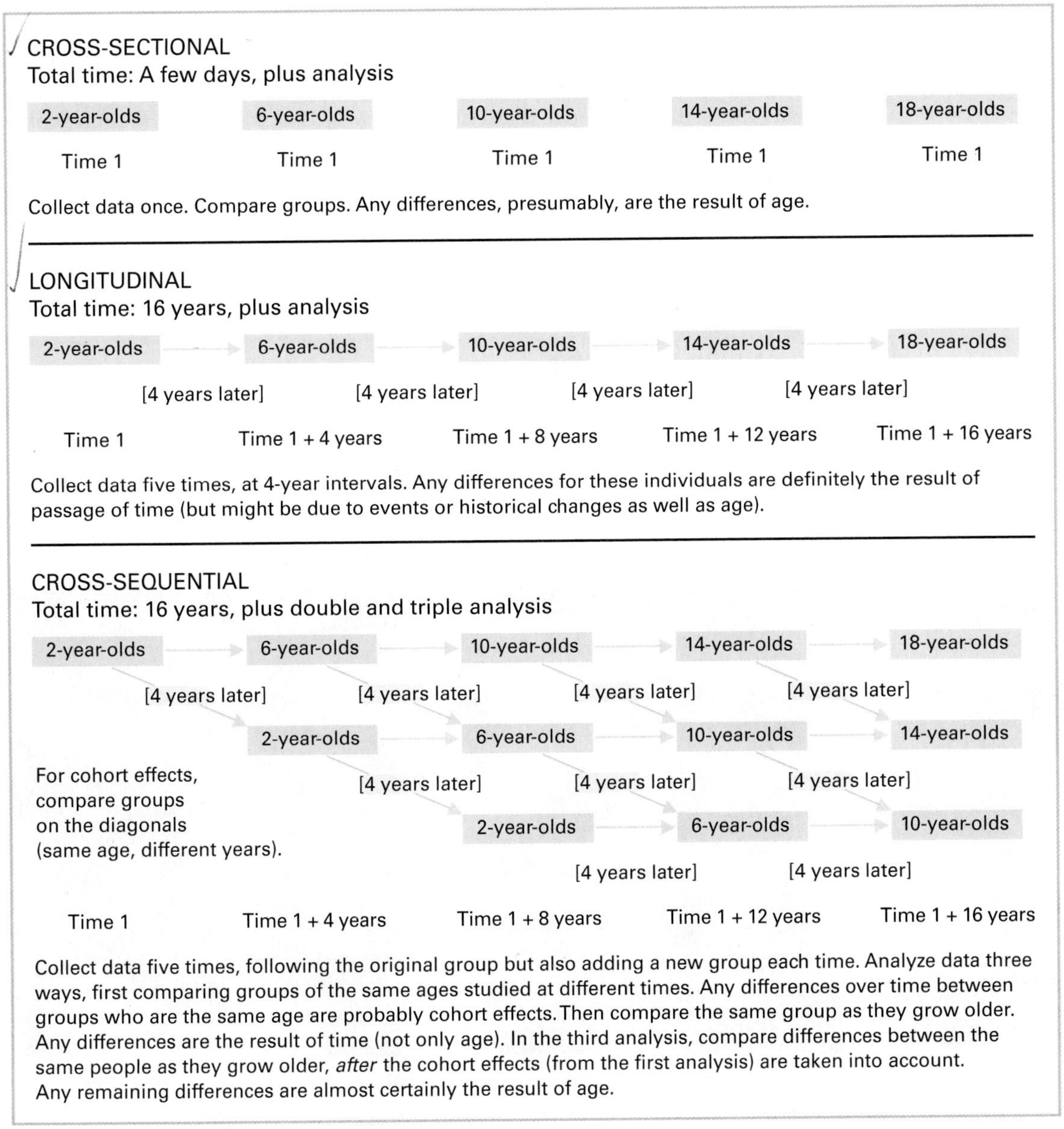

CROSS-SECTIONAL
Total time: A few days, plus analysis

2-year-olds | 6-year-olds | 10-year-olds | 14-year-olds | 18-year-olds
Time 1 | Time 1 | Time 1 | Time 1 | Time 1

Collect data once. Compare groups. Any differences, presumably, are the result of age.

LONGITUDINAL
Total time: 16 years, plus analysis

2-year-olds → 6-year-olds → 10-year-olds → 14-year-olds → 18-year-olds
[4 years later] [4 years later] [4 years later] [4 years later]
Time 1 | Time 1 + 4 years | Time 1 + 8 years | Time 1 + 12 years | Time 1 + 16 years

Collect data five times, at 4-year intervals. Any differences for these individuals are definitely the result of passage of time (but might be due to events or historical changes as well as age).

CROSS-SEQUENTIAL
Total time: 16 years, plus double and triple analysis

2-year-olds → 6-year-olds → 10-year-olds → 14-year-olds → 18-year-olds
[4 years later] [4 years later] [4 years later] [4 years later]
2-year-olds → 6-year-olds → 10-year-olds → 14-year-olds
[4 years later] [4 years later] [4 years later]
2-year-olds → 6-year-olds → 10-year-olds
[4 years later] [4 years later]

For cohort effects, compare groups on the diagonals (same age, different years).

Time 1 | Time 1 + 4 years | Time 1 + 8 years | Time 1 + 12 years | Time 1 + 16 years

Collect data five times, following the original group but also adding a new group each time. Analyze data three ways, first comparing groups of the same ages studied at different times. Any differences over time between groups who are the same age are probably cohort effects. Then compare the same group as they grow older. Any differences are the result of time (not only age). In the third analysis, compare differences between the same people as they grow older, *after* the cohort effects (from the first analysis) are taken into account. Any remaining differences are almost certainly the result of age.

VIC BIDER / INDEX STOCK IMAGERY

SW PRODUCTION / INDEX STOCK IMAGERY

Compare These with Those The apparent similarity of these two groups in gender and ethnic composition makes them candidates for cross-sectional research. Before we could be sure that any difference between the two groups is the result of age, we would have to be sure the groups are alike in other ways, such as socioeconomic status and religious affiliation. Even if two groups seem identical in everything but age, there may be unknown differences.

cross-sectional research A research design that compares groups of people who differ in age but are similar in other important characteristics.

longitudinal research A research design in which the same individuals are followed over time and their development is repeatedly assessed.

Cross-Sectional Research

The most convenient, and thus most common, way to study development is with **cross-sectional research.** Groups of people who differ in age but share other important characteristics (such as education, SES, and ethnicity) are compared. Cross-sectional design seems simple enough, but it is difficult to ensure that the various groups being compared are similar in every important background variable except age.

In addition, historical change might affect one cohort more than another. One example would be the number of people in a cohort. Look at Figure 1.8 on page 24. Do you think that the attitudes, opportunities, or fears of the baby-boom generation are affected by the fact of its huge size? If so, that is a cohort effect that might mistakenly be thought to be an age effect.

Longitudinal Research

To help discover whether age itself, not cohort differences, causes a developmental change, scientists undertake **longitudinal research.** This approach involves collecting data repeatedly on the same individuals as they age. Longitudinal research

(FIRST 5 PICTURES) ©VISCHER FAMILY ARCHIVE / THE IMAGE WORKS

TABLE 1.2

Some Findings from Longitudinal Research

- *Adjustment to parents' divorce.* Negative effects linger, sometimes even into middle age, but not for everyone (Amato & Afifi, 2006; Hetherington & Kelly, 2002).
- *Preventing delinquency.* Patient parenting at age 5, using conversation rather than physical punishment, decreases the likelihood of delinquency 10 years later (Pettit, 2004).
- The *effects of day care.* The quality and extent of child care in infancy and early childhood are less influential than the mother's warmth and responsiveness or coldness and rejection (NICHD, 2005).
- *The stability of personality.* Personality is quite stable over the decades of adulthood. The outgoing, agreeable young adult is likely to become an outgoing, easygoing grandmother (Caspi & Shiner, 2006; McCrae & Costa, 2003).

is particularly useful in studying development over a long age span (Elder & Shanahan, 2006). Some valuable and surprising findings of longitudinal research are given in Table 1.2.

Longitudinal research has several drawbacks. Over time, participants may withdraw, move far away, or die. This can skew the final results if those who disappear are unlike those who stay, and usually they are. In almost every longitudinal study, people of low SES or with serious illnesses are less likely to remain involved. Often researchers cannot find them. Another problem is that participants become increasingly familiar with the questions or the goals of the study and therefore change in ways that a typical person would not.

Probably the biggest problem comes from the changing historical context. Science, popular culture, and politics alter life experiences, and those changes limit the current relevance of data collected on people born decades ago. Meanwhile, waiting for analysis of the effects of longitudinal research harms people living now. For example, dozens of chemicals, drugs, and additives might eventually cause cancer. Yet millions died of lung cancer before longitudinal research proved that 17-year-old smokers risked death at age 67.

➤**Response for Nurses** (from page 19): Experiments are the only way to determine cause-and-effect relationships. If we want to be sure that a new drug or treatment is safe and effective, an experiment must be conducted to establish that the drug or treatment improves health.

➤**Answer to Observation Quiz** (from page 19): No. Note the word *predicted.* The hypothesis is that change will occur for the experimental group and not the control group, but the reason for doing the experiment is to discover whether that prediction does indeed come true.

➤**Response for Social Scientists** (from page 20): Different cultures have different ideas about child rearing. Cross-cultural research provides us with information that may be shared among various cultures and may benefit the children of those cultures.

Six Stages of Life The baby at the far left is Sarah-Maria, born in 1980 in Switzerland. Each of these photos is of a girl at another stage described in this text: infancy (age 1), the play years (age 3), the school years (age 8), adolescence (age 15), emerging adulthood (age 19), and adulthood (age 27).

Observation Quiz (see answer, page 24): Why is there no photo showing the seventh and last stage, late adulthood?

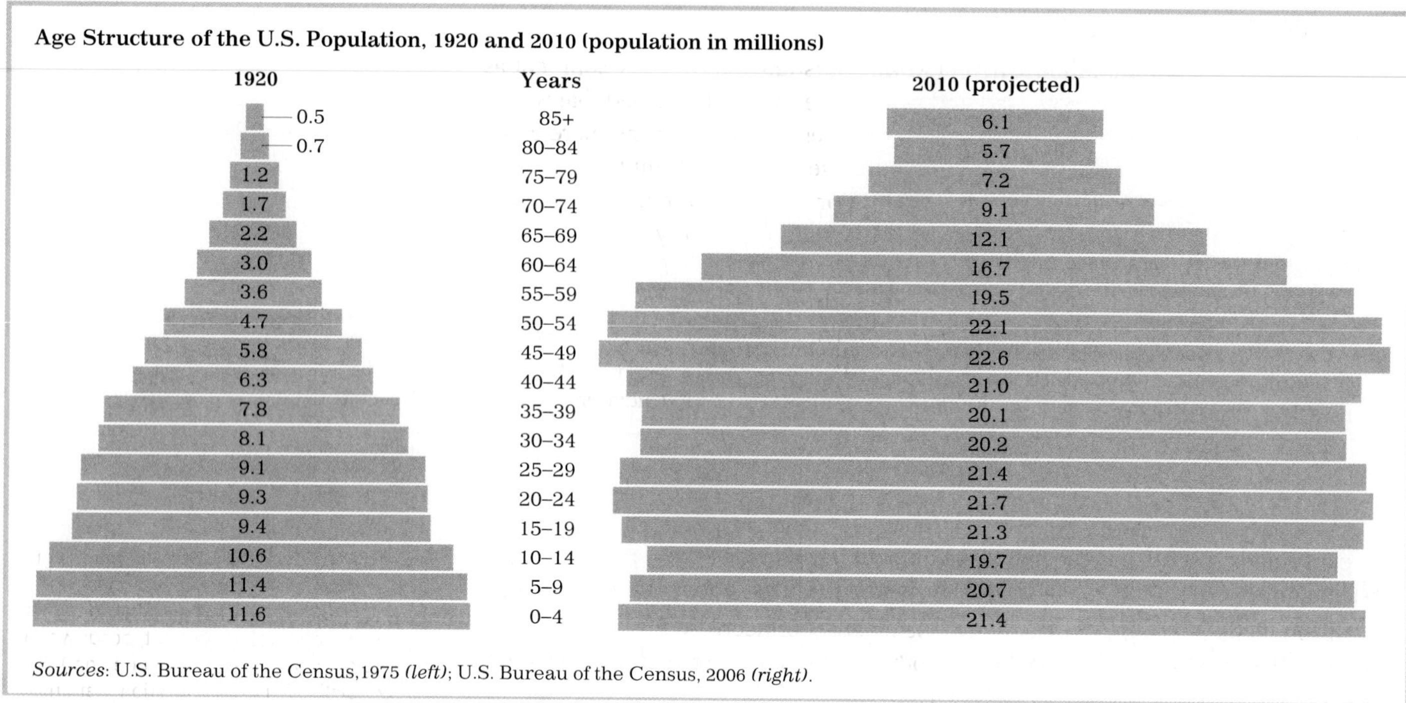

FIGURE 1.8

The Baby-Boom Population Bulge Unlike earlier times, when each generation was slightly smaller than the one that followed, each cohort today has a unique position, determined by the reproductive patterns of the preceding generation and by the medical advances developed during their own lifetime. As a result, the baby boomers, born between 1947 and 1964, represent a huge bulge in the U.S. population. In another three decades, the leading edge of the baby-boom generation, largely intact, will begin moving into the upper age group.

Cross-Sequential Research

Cross-sectional and longitudinal research each have advantages that compensate for the other's disadvantages. Scientists use the two together, often with complex statistical analysis (Hartmann & Pelzel, 2005). The simplest combination is **cross-sequential research** (also referred to as *cohort-sequential research* or *time-sequential research*). With this design, researchers study several groups of people who are of different ages (a cross-sectional approach) and follow all of them over the years (a longitudinal approach).

A cross-sequential design can compare findings for a group of, say, 18-year-olds with findings for the same individuals at age 8, as well as with findings for groups who were 18 a decade or two earlier and groups who are 8 years old at the present (see Figure 1.7). Cross-sequential research thus allows scientists to disentangle differences related to chronological age from those related to historical period.

For example, a cross-sequential study (the Seattle Longitudinal Study) finds that some intellectual abilities (such as vocabulary) increase throughout adulthood and others (such as speed of thinking) decline starting at about age 30 (Schaie, 2005). This study has also discovered that declines in math ability are more closely related to education than to age, a finding that neither cross-sectional nor longitudinal research could have revealed.

cross-sequential research A hybrid research method in which researchers first study several groups of people of different ages (a cross-sectional approach) and then follow those groups over the years (a longitudinal approach). (Also called *cohort-sequential research* or *time-sequential research*.)

SUMMING UP

The scientific method is designed to help researchers answer questions objectively and honestly, with carefully gathered evidence, drawing conclusions based on the data they collect. Methods, findings, and conclusions are reported so that other scientists can build on past work and reexamine results. Researchers observe people unobtrusively, and they conduct experiments under controlled conditions. They may survey hundreds or even thousands of people or study one case in detail. To understand change over time, researchers undertake cross-sectional, longitudinal, and cross-sequential research. Every method has strengths and weaknesses. ■

➤**Answer to Observation Quiz** (from page 23): All of these photos are of the same person, and she will not reach late adulthood until 2045. Longitudinal research shows continuity (that happy smile) and change (her hair).

Especially for Future Researchers What is the best method for collecting data?

Cautions from Science

No doubt the scientific method illuminates and illustrates human development as nothing else does. Facts, hypotheses, and possibilities have all emerged that would not be known without science, and people of all ages are healthier and more capable than they were in previous generations because of it. For example, infectious diseases in children, illiteracy in adults, depression in late adulthood, racism and sexism at every age are much less prevalent today than a century ago. Science is one reason.

Developmental scientists also discover changes that are not beneficial. Television, divorce, shift work, and automobiles are less benign than people first thought.

Although the benefits of science are many, so are the pitfalls. We discuss three of them: misinterpreting data, overdependence on numbers, and unethical practices.

Correlation and Causation

Probably the most common mistake made in the interpretation of research is the confusion of correlation with causation. A **correlation** exists between two variables if one variable is more (or less) likely to occur when the other occurs. A correlation is *positive* if both variables tend to increase together or decrease together, *negative* if one variable tends to increase when the other decreases, and *zero* if no connection is evident. (Try taking the quiz in Table 1.3.)

correlation A number indicating the degree of relationship between two variables, expressed in terms of the likelihood that one variable will (or will not) occur when the other variable does (or does not). A correlation is not an indication that one variable causes the other, only that the two variables are related to the indicated degree.

To illustrate: From birth to age 9, there is a positive correlation between age and height (children grow taller as they grow older), a negative correlation between age and amount of sleep (children sleep less as they grow older), and zero correlation between age and number of toes. None of these correlations is surprising, but many are fascinating, such as the finding that first-born children have higher rates of asthma.

TABLE 1.3

Quiz on Correlation

Two Variables	Positive, Negative, or Zero Correlation?	Why? (Third Variable)
1. Ice cream sales and murder rate	________	________
2. Learning to read and number of baby teeth	________	________
3. Adult gender and number of offspring	________	________

For each of these three pairs of variables, indicate whether the correlation between them is positive, negative, or nonexistent. Then try to think of a third variable that would determine the direction of the correlation. The correct answers are printed upside down below.

Correlations are easy to misinterpret; people assume that one variable causes another. For instance, a longitudinal study found a correlation between teenagers' listening to degrading music (with males depicted as sexually insatiable studs and women as mindless sex objects) and beginning to have sexual intercourse before age 20 (see Table 1.4).

Although the authors of this study say that they cannot be certain of the direction of effects, because correlation is not causation, they write that

> reducing the amount of degrading sexual content in popular music, or reducing young people's exposure to music with this type of content, could delay initiation of intercourse. . . . Intervention possibilities include reaching out to parents of adolescents, to teens, and to the recording industry.
>
> [Martino et al., 2006, p. 338]

Answers:
1. Positive; third variable: heat
2. Negative; third variable: age
3. Zero; each child must have a parent of each sex; no third variable

TABLE 1.4

Correlates of First Sexual Intercourse Before Age 20

Variable	Correlation
Listening to degrading sexual music	0.36*
Having friends who will approve of sex	0.39
Having parents who know where teen is	–0.30
Engaging in heavy petting before age 15	0.47

Source: Martino et al., 2006.
*The correlation between music and first intercourse remained significant and positive after other factors were taken into account.

Research Design

Scientists: Six researchers, sponsored by the RAND Corporation.

Publication: *Pediatrics* (2006). This study was also reported in many news stories.

Participants: Total of 1,461 U.S. teenagers, randomly selected to be representative of all U.S. teens.

Design: Teenagers were interviewed by phone, three times over three years, and asked which of 16 popular music groups they listened to. Coders rated whether songs contained sexually degrading lyrics. Some participants refused to answer questions about sex, but responses of 938 who were virgins when the study began were analyzed.

Major conclusion: Listening to degrading music, but not other teen music about sex, encourages teenagers to have sexual intercourse.

Comment: This is a correlational study. The longitudinal sequence (music, then intercourse) prompted the conclusions, but others disagree about the relationship between the variables.

The researchers assert that lyrics that glorify uncommitted sex encourage teenagers to accept those values. Others who read this study objected. One criminal justice professor at the University of Massachusetts wrote:

> The fact that sexually active kids listen to music with a sexual content should not be surprising. Did we expect they would listen to Mozart's Requiem?
>
> *[Siegel, 2006]*

With correlation, there is always the possibility that the direction is opposite to that hypothesized or that a third variable may be the underlying cause. Did that happen here? (See Research Design.) Alternative explanations from each domain for the connection between sex and music include the following:

- *Biosocial:* Some teenagers have high levels of sexual hormones, which drive them to seek sexual experiences and explicitly sexual music. Sexual intercourse is the result of those hormones (a third variable).
- *Cognitive:* Some teenagers seek sexual experiences, and they find music to reinforce their values (this correlation runs in the opposite direction from the authors' assumption).
- *Psychosocial:* Teenagers idolize some music stars, going to concerts, watching videos, buying posters. They emulate their idol's lifestyle, which may include sexual activities. Listening to music is a by-product of this idolization (a third variable).

Each of these three explanations is possible, as is the original conclusion. Many other hypotheses could be formulated. Correlation indicates connection, not cause.

Quantity and Quality

quantitative research Research that provides data that can be expressed with numbers, such as ranks or scales.

A second caution concerns how much scientists should rely on data produced by **quantitative research** (from the word *quantity*). Quantitative research data can be categorized, ranked, or numbered and thus can be easily translated across cultures. People are asked questions with quantifiable answers—for example, whether they agree or disagree with a statement (only two choices) or whether they do something well, not well, or not at all (three choices). People are also asked to provide factual information, such as what the family income is.

Since quantities can be easily summarized, compared, charted, and replicated, many scientists prefer quantitative research. Statistics, including correlation, significance, and effect size, begin with quantitative data, which has been described as providing "rigorous, empirically testable representations" (Nesselroade & Molenaar, 2003, p. 635).

➤Response for Future Researchers (from page 24): There is no best method for collecting data. The method used depends on many factors, such as the age of participants (infants can't complete questionnaires), the question being researched, and the time frame.

However, by reducing data to categories and numbers, some nuances and individual distinctions are lost. Many developmental researchers use **qualitative research** (from *quality*), asking open-ended questions, reporting answers that are not easily translated into numbers and categories, allowing "a rich description of the phenomena of interest" (Hartmann & Pelzel, 2005, p. 163).

qualitative research Research that considers qualities instead of quantities. Descriptions of particular conditions and participants' expressed ideas are often part of qualitative studies.

Consider this example. A group of kindergarteners began a playground "grass war" triggered by freshly mown grass and a boy who hit Carlotta.

> The grass war now escalates, with girls and boys on both sides becoming involved. In fact, all but a few of the 5-year-old group I am observing are now in the grass war. The war continues for some time until Marina [one of the children] suggests to the children in our group that they make peace. Marina with several children behind her marches up to the boy who hit Carlotta and offers her hand in peace. The boy responds by throwing grass in Marina's face . . . over the objections of another boy who is in his group. Marina stands her ground after being hit with the grass. The second boy pulls his friend aside and suggests that they make peace. The other boy is against the proposal, but eventually agrees and the two then shake hands with Marina. Marina then returns to our group and declares "Peace has been established." The two groups now meet for a round of handshaking.
>
> *[Corsaro & Molinari, 2000, p. 192]*

Notice that this is scientific observation. The researcher did not intervene. At this point, months into his observational study, the children did not expect him to do so. His neutrality allowed him to witness young children, on their own, resolving a conflict.

How would this observation be expressed in numbers? Since the weapon was grass, would this interaction be categorized as a conflict or not? A girl was the peacemaker and a boy started the fight, a gender difference that might be lost in a quantitative study. This particular incident happened in Italy. Does that matter? Without qualitative reports from many other places, we do not know if the Italian location is relevant.

Especially for People Who Have Applied to College or Graduate School Is the admissions process based on quality or quantity?

Qualitative research may seem preferable, in that it reflects cultural and contextual diversity and complexity. But it is also more vulnerable to bias and harder to replicate. Developmentalists pay attention to both kinds of research, sometimes translating qualitative research into quantifiable data, sometimes using qualitative information to suggest hypotheses for quantitative research (Hartmann & Pelzel, 2005).

Ethics in Research

The most important caution for all scientists, especially those studying humans, is to ensure that their research meets the ethical standards of their field. Each academic discipline and professional society involved in the study of human development has a **code of ethics,** or a set of moral principles, and a scientific culture that protect the integrity of research.

code of ethics A set of moral principles that members of a profession or group are expected to follow.

Ethical standards and codes have become increasingly stringent as scientists have become increasingly concerned that "research is not only valid and useful, but also ethical" (Lindsay, 2000, p. 20). Most educational and medical institutions have an *IRB (Institutional Research Board),* a group charged with permitting only ethical research. Although IRBs often slow down scientific study, some research done before they existed was clearly unethical, especially when children, members of minority groups, prisoners, and animals were involved (Blum, 2002; Washington, 2006).

Protection of Research Participants

Researchers must ensure that participation is voluntary, confidential, and harmless. In Western nations, this entails "informed consent" of the participants and, if children are involved, of the parents. In some other nations, this can require consent of the village elders or heads of families, as well as, of course, the research participants themselves (Doumbo, 2005).

The need to protect participants is especially obvious with children, but the same principles apply no matter what the age of the participants (Gilhooly, 2002). These include explaining the purposes and procedures of the study in advance, obtaining written permission to proceed, and allowing the participants to stop at any time.

If researchers discover something that is potentially harmful to any participant, they must stop being dispassionate, objective observers. They must intervene even though their study might be jeopardized. One researcher wanted to learn whether residential care (a form of foster care used in England for children who have special needs or whose parents cannot care for them) is humane. Here is an exchange between the researcher and a boy in residential care:

> **[Researcher:]** Sometimes a person might talk about a situation where they have been harmed by someone. If this happens, I may need to talk to someone else, especially if it is something awful which is still happening to you, or if the person who harmed you may still be hurting someone else. I would want to be able to agree with you what should be done, and who should be told.
>
> **[Resident:]** Well, that's one part of my life I'm not going to be able to talk to you about then, isn't it? I'm not having you deciding who to go and talk to about me.
>
> *[Morris, 1998]*

As you can see, protection of participants sometimes conflicts with the goals of science. The Canadian Psychological Association makes this explicit in its code of ethics, which states that the first principle of ethical research is "respect for the dignity of persons"; the second and the third are "responsible caring" and "integrity in relationships." Fourth is "responsibility to society." All four principles should be observed if possible, but they are ranked in order of importance: Individuals must be safeguarded before the other ethical principles can be followed (Canadian Psychological Association, 2000).

Implications of Research Results

Once a study has been completed, additional ethical issues arise. Scientists are obligated to report research results as accurately and completely as possible, without distorting the results to support any political, economic, or cultural position.

An obvious breach of ethics is to "cook" the data, arranging the numbers so that a particular conclusion seems the only reasonable one. Deliberate falsification is rare; it leads to ostracism from the scientific community, dismissal from a teaching or research position, and, sometimes, criminal prosecution.

A more insidious danger is that research is unintentionally slanted. To prevent this, scientific training, collaboration, and replication are crucial. Numerous precautions are built into methodology, several of which have already been explained. In addition, scientific reports in professional journals include (1) details of the study to allow for replication, (2) a section describing the limitations of the findings, and (3) alternative interpretations of the results.

None of this is to be taken for granted, as one researcher in animal behavior explains: "Desirable modes of scientific conduct require considerable self-awareness as well as a reaffirmation of the old virtues of honesty, skepticism, and integrity" (Bateson, 2005, p. 645). Such virtues need to be stressed for every scholar, writer, and student of child development, including you and me.

There is an additional ethical concern. "In reporting results, . . . the investigator should be mindful of the social, political, and human implications of his research" (Society for Research in Child Development, 1991). What does it mean to be "mindful" of research implications?

In one study, a group of college students who listened to Mozart before taking a cognitive test scored higher than another group who heard no music (Rauscher et al., 1993; Rauscher & Shaw, 1998). The researchers reported this finding, but they did not stress the limitations of the study. They should have been more mindful, because this "Mozart effect" was wildly misinterpreted: The governor of Georgia ordered that all babies born in his state be given a free Mozart CD in order to improve their intelligence, and Florida passed a law requiring every state-funded infant day-care center to play classical music.

In fact, the initial research did not use infants. In a later study that did use children, Mozart did not fare as well as more child-centered music (Schellenberg et al., 2007). The original results could not be replicated (Crncec et al., 2006; McKelvie & Low, 2002).

What Should We Study?

Every reader of this book should consider the most important ethical concern of all: Are scientists answering the questions that are crucial to human development?

- Do we know enough about prenatal nutrition and drugs to protect every fetus?
- Do we know enough about the effects of poverty to enable everyone to be healthy?
- Do we know enough about sexual behavior to eliminate AIDS, unwanted pregnancy, sex abuse, and domestic violence?
- Do we know enough about dying to enable everyone to die with dignity?

The answer to all these questions is a resounding *NO*. The reasons are many, including the fact that each of these questions touches on topics so controversial that some researchers avoid them and few funders support objective studies. Yet ethical standards include more than caring for participants, ensuring confidentiality, and reporting research honestly. Developmentalists have an obligation to study topics that are of major importance for the human family. Many people suffer because questions are unanswered or not even asked.

The next cohort of developmental scientists will build on what is known, mindful of what needs to be explored. That is probably the most important answer to the question posed in the fourth sentence of this chapter: "Why should you care?"

SUMMING UP

Correlations are useful, but they do not prove cause and effect. Quantitative research is more objective and easier to replicate than qualitative research, but it loses the nuances that qualitative research can reveal. Scientists follow codes of ethics to safeguard research participants. Scientists also must be careful to prevent misinterpretations. The most urgent issues are controversial and therefore difficult to study or to report honestly. That is precisely why further scientific research is needed. ■

➤Response for People Who Have Applied to College or Graduate School (from page 27): Most institutions of higher education emphasize quantitative data—the SAT, the GRE, GPA, class rank, and so on. Decide for yourself whether this is fairer than a more qualitative approach.

SUMMARY

Defining Development

1. The study of human development is a science that seeks to understand how people change over time. Sometimes these changes are linear—gradual, steady, and predictable—but more often they are not. Change may be small or large, caused by something seemingly insignificant, like the flap of a butterfly's wings, or something large that affects people in unexpected ways.

2. The dynamic-systems perspective on development is now pervasive in the study of life-span development, evident in the five characteristics of development and in every topic in this text.

3. Development is neither static nor localized; it is the result of interactions among all the systems (microsystems, macrosystems, and exosystems) that impinge on each person. Bronfenbrenner was among many who emphasized the bioecological approach to developmental study.

Five Characteristics of Development

4. Development is multidirectional, multicontextual, multicultural, multidisciplinary, and plastic. It is the product of dynamic systems, so that any change affects an interconnected system, and any person affects all the other people in a family or social group.

5. Each individual develops within unique historical, cultural, and socioeconomic contexts. Life is quite different for a low-income child in a traditional culture, for instance, than for a middle-class child in a modern, multicultural society.

6. One way to subdivide development is by domains, or general aspects of growth and change. This division can be thought of as biosocial, cognitive, and psychosocial, or even body, mind, and social self. All development affects all domains at once as the dynamic-systems perspective makes clear.

7. To understand development, it is necessary to compare many cultures and use research from many disciplines. Nevertheless, because each person has unique genes and experiences, contexts do not determine an individual's development—but they always influence it.

8. *Plasticity* means that change is always possible but is never unrestricted: Childhood becomes the foundation for later growth.

Developmental Study as a Science

9. The five steps of the scientific method lead researchers to question assumptions and to gather data to test conclusions. Although far from infallible, the scientific method helps researchers avoid biases and guides them in asking questions.

10. Commonly used research methods are scientific observation, the experiment, the survey, and the case study. Each method has strengths and weaknesses. The most reliable conclusions can be drawn when various methods all reach similar conclusions and when replications using many subjects in diverse cultures confirm the results.

11. To study change over time, scientists use three research designs: cross-sectional research (comparing people of different ages), longitudinal research (studying the same people over time), and cross-sequential research (combining the other two methods). Each method has advantages.

Cautions from Science

12. A correlation shows that two variables are related but does not prove that one variable causes the other.

13. In qualitative research, information is recorded without being quantified, or translated into numbers. Qualitative research best captures the nuances of individual lives, but quantitative research is easier to replicate and verify.

14. Ethical behavior is crucial in all sciences. Not only must participants be protected, but results must be clearly reported and understood. Scientists must be mindful of the implications of their research.

15. Appropriate application of scientific research depends partly on the training and integrity of the scientists. The most important ethical question is whether the research that is critically needed is being designed, conducted, analyzed, and published.

KEY TERMS

science of human development (p. 3)
empirical (p. 4)
dynamic-systems theory (p. 5)
ecological-systems approach (p. 5)
butterfly effect (p. 8)
cohort (p. 9)
socioeconomic status (SES) (p. 9)
ethnic group (p. 11)
race (p. 11)
social construction (p. 11)
mirror neurons (p. 14)
scientific method (p. 16)
hypothesis (p. 17)
replication (p. 17)
scientific observation (p. 17)
experiment (p. 18)
independent variable (p. 18)
dependent variable (p. 18)
experimental group (p. 19)
comparison group/control group (p. 19)
survey (p. 20)
case study (p. 20)
cross-sectional research (p. 22)
longitudinal research (p. 22)
cross-sequential research (p. 24)
correlation (p. 25)
quantitative research (p. 26)
qualitative research (p. 27)
code of ethics (p. 27)

KEY QUESTIONS

1. What does it mean to say that the study of human development is a science?

2. Give an example of a social construction. Why is it a construction, not a fact?

3. What is the difference between an ethnic group and a culture?

4. What are some cohort differences between you and your parents?

5. Why does the fact that SES and ethnic differences overlap pose a problem?

6. What are the differences between scientific observation and ordinary observation?

7. In what ways can surveys be considered the opposite of case studies?

8. Why would a scientist conduct a cross-sectional study?

9. Why would people refuse to participate or quit before a research study was finished?

10. Cite two probable correlations (positive and negative) regarding how you spend your time.

11. What are the disadvantages and advantages of qualitative research?

12. What is one additional question about development that should be answered?

APPLICATIONS

1. It is said that culture is pervasive but that people are unaware of it. List 30 things you did *today* that you might have done differently in another culture.

2. How would your life be different if your parents were much higher or lower in SES than they are?

3. Design an experiment to answer a question you have about human development. Specify the question and the hypothesis, and then describe the experiment, including the sample size and the variables. (Look first at Appendix B.)

2

CHAPTER OUTLINE

Theories of Development

As we saw in Chapter 1, the science of human development begins with questions. Among the thousands of questions are the following five, each connected to one of the five theories described in this chapter:

1. Do early experiences—of breast-feeding or bonding or abuse—affect adulthood?
2. Does intelligence depend on past instruction, punishment, and examples?
3. Are children and adolescents less logical than adults?
4. Does culture cause variations in adult behavior, such that, say, more people vote in Ontario than in Ohio?
5. If a newborn's parents are alcoholics, should that child never drink?

For every answer, more questions arise: Why or why not? When and how? And the most crucial question of all: So what?

What Theories Do

Each of the five questions listed above is answered yes by one of the five major theories—in order: (1) psychoanalytic theory, (2) behaviorism, (3) cognitive theory, (4) sociocultural theory, and (5) epigenetic theory. Each question is answered less affirmatively by several other theories, perhaps with "not necessarily" or "only sometimes" or even "never."

To find and frame the critical questions regarding development, and then to answer them, we must organize thousands of observations. For that, we need a theory.

A **developmental theory** is a systematic statement of principles and generalizations that provides a coherent framework for understanding how and why people change as they grow older. Developmental theorists "try to make sense out of observations . . . [and] construct a story of the human journey from infancy through childhood or adulthood" (P. H. Miller, 2002, p. 2). Theories connect facts and observations with patterns and explanations, weaving the details of life into a meaningful whole.

As an analogy, imagine building a house. A person could have a heap of lumber, nails, and other materials, but without a blueprint or construction drawings, the heap cannot become a house. Observations of human development are essential raw materials, but theories are needed to put them

developmental theory A group of ideas, assumptions, and generalizations that interpret and illuminate the thousands of observations that have been made about human growth. In this way, developmental theories provide a framework for explaining the patterns and problems of development.

together. As Kurt Lewin (1943) once quipped, "Nothing is as practical as a good theory."

To be more specific:

- Theories lead to pivotal hypotheses, each of which becomes "a direct test of a question" (Salkind, 2004, p. 14).
- Theories generate discoveries.
- Theories offer practical guidance. If a 5-year-old shouts "I hate you!" at his father, the man's reactions (laughing, ignoring, slapping, or asking "Why?") depends on his theory of child development (whether or not he knows it).

grand theories Comprehensive theories of psychology, which have traditionally inspired and directed psychologists' thinking about child development. Psychoanalytic theory, behaviorism, and cognitive theory are all grand theories.

emergent theories Theories that bring together information from many disciplines in addition to psychology and that are becoming comprehensive and systematic in their interpretations of development but are not yet established and detailed enough to be considered grand theories.

Hundreds of theories pertain to developmental science. A few (the psychoanalytic, behaviorist, and cognitive theories) are called **grand theories** because they describe universal processes and development throughout the entire life span. They offer "a powerful framework for interpreting and understanding . . . change and development of all individuals" (Renninger & Amsel, 1997, p. ix). Some (the sociocultural and epigenetic theories) are **emergent theories;** they may become the new systematic and comprehensive theories of the future.

Literally thousands of theories are *minitheories,* about some part of development, perhaps only one age or one domain. For example, one minitheory concerns racial identity (theory of racial socialization), another, friendships in late adulthood (theory of socioemotional selectivity). Minitheories are not presented in this chapter, but remember that, no matter what interests you, theories are a useful way to organize and select your observations.

The distinction between grand and emergent theories is best understood by referring to the multidisciplinary perspective, first noted in Chapter 1. The grand theories of human development originated in the discipline of psychology, while observations and explanations originating in history, biology, sociology, and anthropology led to the emergent theories.

Historical events (notably, increasing globalization and immigration) and genetic discoveries (for example, from the International Hapmap Project, finding alternate versions of genes) highlight the need for the cultural and genetic approaches of the new theories. Two emergent theories (sociocultural and epigenetic) are not yet as coherent as the grand theories, but they are broader than the traditional grand theories that draw only on psychology.

SUMMING UP

Theories are useful—even essential—for scientific study. They provide a framework for organizing the thousands of observations that may be made about any aspect of development. This chapter describes three grand theories—psychoanalytic, behaviorist, and cognitive—and two emergent theories—sociocultural and epigenetic. Throughout the remaining chapters of the book, these five theories will repeatedly be referred to (see the Subject Index entry for each theory). Several minitheories will also be cited. ■

Grand Theories

In the first half of the twentieth century, two opposing theories—psychoanalytic theory and behaviorism (also called *learning theory*)—began as general theories of psychology and later were applied specifically to human development. By midcentury, cognitive theory had emerged, and it gradually became the dominant seedbed of research hypotheses. All three theories are "grand" in that they are comprehensive, enduring, and widely applied (McAdams & Pals, 2006).

Psychoanalytic Theory

Inner drives and motives, many of them irrational, originating in childhood, and unconscious (hidden from awareness), are crucial concepts in **psychoanalytic theory.** These basic underlying forces are thought to influence every aspect of thinking and behavior, from the smallest details of daily life to the crucial choices of a lifetime.

psychoanalytic theory A grand theory of human development that holds that irrational, unconscious drives and motives, often originating in childhood, underlie human behavior.

Freud's Ideas

Psychoanalytic theory originated with Sigmund Freud (1856–1939), an Austrian physician who treated patients suffering from mental illness. He listened to their accounts of dreams and fantasies, thought deeply about Greek drama and "primitive" art, and constructed an elaborate, multifaceted theory.

According to Freud, development in the first six years occurs in three stages, each characterized by sexual pleasure centered on a particular part of the body. In infancy, the erotic body part is the mouth (the *oral stage*); in early childhood, it is the anus (the *anal stage*); in the preschool years, it is the penis (the *phallic stage*), a source of pride and fear among boys and a reason for sadness and envy among girls. Then comes *latency* and, beginning at adolescence and lasting lifelong, the *genital stage* (see Table 2.1).

SUSAN LAPIDES / DESIGN CONCEPTIONS

Childhood Sexuality The girl's interest in the statue's anatomy may just reflect simple curiosity, but Freudian theory would maintain that it is a clear manifestation of the phallic stage of psychosexual development, when girls are said to feel deprived because they lack a penis.

Freud maintained that at each stage, sensual satisfaction (from stimulation of the mouth, anus, or penis) is linked to major developmental needs and challenges. Each stage includes its own potential conflicts. For instance, according to Freud, how people experience and resolve these conflicts—especially those related to weaning, toilet training, and sexual pleasure—determine personality patterns, because "the early stages provide the foundation for adult behavior" (Salkind, 2004, p. 125).

A psychoanalytic interpretation would be that adults may be stuck in unconscious struggles rooted in a childhood stage if they smoke cigarettes (stuck in the oral stage) or keep careful track of money (anal) or are romantically attracted to much older partners (phallic). For all of us, childhood fantasies and memories remain powerful lifelong. If you have ever wondered why lovers call each other "baby" or why many people refer to their spouse as their "old lady" or "sugar

AKG / PHOTO RESEARCHERS, INC.

Freud at Work In addition to being the world's first psychoanalyst, Sigmund Freud was a prolific writer. His many papers and case histories, primarily descriptions of his patients' bizarre symptoms and unconscious sexual urges, helped make the psychoanalytic perspective a dominant force for much of the twentieth century.

daddy," then Freud's theory provides an explanation: The parent–child relationship is the model for all intimacy.

Especially for Adults Who Blame Their Parents Freud believed that every emotional or personality problem adults might have was caused by poor parenting in the first five years of life. Do you think this is true for you?

This idea has been developed by researchers interested in attachment theory, building on the idea that early relationships between parent and child echo throughout life. These researchers have found that "infant attachment history" predicts numerous aspects of intimate relationship functioning (Sroufe et al., 2005, p. 203), including romance (Mikulincer & Goodman, 2006).

Erikson's Ideas

Many of Freud's followers became famous theorists themselves. The most notable in the field of human development was Erik Erikson (1902–1994).

Erikson never knew his biological father. He spent his childhood in Germany, his adolescence wandering through Italy, and his young adulthood in Austria, working with Freud's daughter Anna. He married an American, and he fled to the United States just before World War II. Once in the United States, he continued his interest in various cultures: He studied Harvard students, Boston children at play, and Native Americans.

As you can see, Erikson was interested in cultural diversity, social change, and psychological crises throughout the life span. For example, he wrote a massive case study of Mahatma Gandhi (Erikson, 1969), born in India, educated in

TABLE 2.1

Comparison of Freud's Psychosexual and Erikson's Psychosocial Stages

Approximate Age	Freud (Psychosexual)	Erikson (Psychosocial)
Birth to 1 year	*Oral Stage* The lips, tongue, and gums are the focus of pleasurable sensations in the baby's body, and sucking and feeding are the most stimulating activities.	*Trust vs. Mistrust* Babies either trust that others will care for their basic needs, including nourishment, warmth, cleanliness, and physical contact, or mistrust the care of others.
1–3 years	*Anal Stage* The anus is the focus of pleasurable sensations in the baby's body, and toilet training is the most important activity.	*Autonomy vs. Shame and Doubt* Children either become self-sufficient in many activities, including toileting, feeding, walking, exploring, and talking, or doubt their own abilities.
3–6 years	*Phallic Stage* The phallus, or penis, is the most important body part, and pleasure is derived from genital stimulation. Boys are proud of their penises, and girls wonder why they don't have one.	*Initiative vs. Guilt* Children want to undertake many adultlike activities or fear the limits set by parents and feel guilty.
6–11 years	*Latency* Not really a stage, latency is an interlude during which sexual needs are quiet and children put psychic energy into conventional activities like schoolwork and sports.	*Industry vs. Inferiority* Children busily learn to be competent and productive in mastering new skills or feel inferior and unable to do anything well.
Adolescence	*Genital Stage* The genitals are the focus of pleasurable sensations, and the young person seeks sexual stimulation and sexual satisfaction in heterosexual relationships.	*Identity vs. Role Confusion* Adolescents try to figure out "Who am I?" They establish sexual, political, and vocational identities or are confused about what roles to play.
Adulthood	Freud believed that the genital stage lasts throughout adulthood. He also said that the goal of a healthy life is "to love and to work."	*Intimacy vs. Isolation* Young adults seek companionship and love or become isolated from others because they fear rejection and disappointment. *Generativity vs. Stagnation* Middle-aged adults contribute to the next generation through meaningful work, creative activities, and/or raising a family, or they stagnate. *Integrity vs. Despair* Older adults try to make sense out of their lives, either seeing life as a meaningful whole or despairing at goals never reached.

Britain, a lawyer in South Africa, and leader of the nonviolent revolution that helped India gain independence.

Erikson described eight developmental stages, each characterized by a challenging developmental crisis (summarized in Table 2.1). Although Erikson named two polarities at each stage, he recognized a wide range of outcomes between these opposites. For most people, development at each stage leads to neither extreme but to something in between.

As you can see from Table 2.1, Erikson's first five stages follow the same sequence and include the core concepts of Freud's stages. Erikson, like Freud, believed that the problems of adult life echo the conflicts of childhood. For example, an adult who has difficulty establishing a secure, mutual relationship with a life partner may never have resolved the first crisis of early infancy, trust versus mistrust. However, Erikson's stages differ significantly from Freud's: They emphasize family and culture, not sexual urges, and they continue throughout adulthood.

For Erikson, the resolution of each crisis depends on the interaction between the individual and the social environment as the family and culture construct it. In the stage of initiative versus guilt, for example, children between ages 3 and 6 often want to undertake activities that exceed their abilities or the limits set by their parents. They jump into swimming pools, put their shirts on backwards, make cakes with their own recipes. Such initiatives may lead to pride or failure, with failure perhaps producing guilt.

The outcome of the initiative-versus-guilt crisis depends on how the child seeks independence, how the parents react, and what the society expects. As an example, some families and cultures encourage 5-year-olds to be assertive, seeing them as creative spirits, whereas others call them "rude" or "fresh" if they insist on getting their own way.

Children internalize, or accept, such responses from their parents, peers, and cultures, and those internalized reactions persist throughout life. Even in late adulthood, one person may be bold and outspoken while another fears saying the wrong thing because these two resolved their initiative-versus-guilt stage in opposite ways.

Both Erikson and Freud emphasize the first years of life, and both consider early conflicts when they seek to explain later problems. This is the main criticism of psychoanalytic theory, especially from behaviorists, as you will now see.

CORBIS

What's in a Name?—Erik Erikson As a young man, this neo-Freudian changed his last name to the one we know him by. What do you think his choice means? (See the caption to the next photograph.)

Especially for Teachers Your kindergartners are talkative and always moving. They almost never sit quietly and listen to you. What would Erik Erikson recommend?

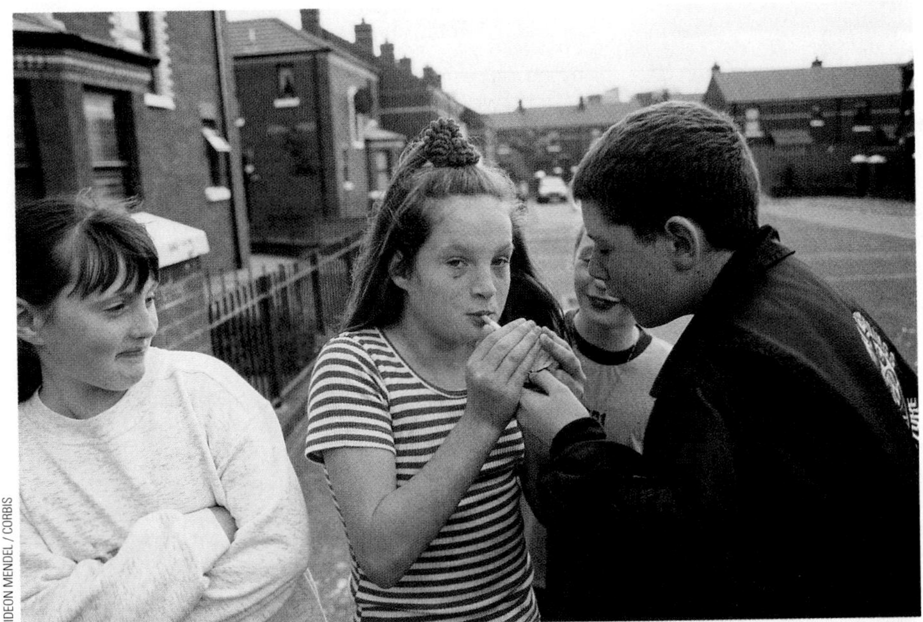

GIDEON MENDEL / CORBIS

Who Are We? The most famous of Erikson's eight crises is the identity crisis, during adolescence, when young people find their own answer to the question "Who am I?" Erikson did this for himself by choosing a last name that, with his first name, implies "son of myself" (Erik, Erik's son). These children in northern Ireland may be smoking because their search for identity is taking place in a sociocultural context that allows an unhealthy path toward adulthood.

Behaviorism

behaviorism A grand theory of human development that studies observable behavior. Behaviorism is also called *learning theory* because it describes the laws and processes by which behavior is learned.

The second grand theory, **behaviorism,** arose in direct opposition to the psychoanalytic emphasis on unconscious, hidden urges (described in Table 2.2). Such urges could not be quantified, and the raw material for Freud's theories came from his patients and Greek drama, which did not seem scientific. Early in the twentieth century, John B. Watson (1878–1958) argued that if psychology was to be a science, psychologists should examine only what they could see and measure: behavior, not thoughts and hidden urges. In Watson's words:

> Let us limit ourselves to things that can be observed, and formulate laws concerned only with those things. . . . We can observe behavior—what the organism does or says.
>
> *[Watson, 1924/1998, p. 6]*

ARCHIVES OF THE HISTORY OF AMERICAN PSYCHOLOGY, THE UNIVERSITY OF AKRON

An Early Behaviorist John Watson was an early proponent of learning theory. His ideas are still influential and controversial today.

According to Watson, if psychologists focus on behavior, they will realize that anything can be learned. He wrote:

> Give me a dozen healthy infants, well-formed, and my own specified world to bring them up in and I'll guarantee to take any one at random and train him to become any type of specialist I might select—doctor, lawyer, artist, merchant chief, and yes, even beggar-man and thief, regardless of his talents, penchants, tendencies, abilities, vocations, and race.
>
> *[Watson, 1924/1998, p. 82]*

Other psychologists, especially in the United States, thought that Watson's emphasis on learning was insightful. They found it difficult to use the scientific method to verify the unconscious motives and drives that Freud described (Cairns & Cairns, 2006). Some developed behaviorism to study actual behavior, objectively and scientifically.

➤Response for Adults Who Blame Their Parents (from page 36): Scientists vehemently disagree about Freud. Some think he was an insightful genius; others believe he was a deluded drug addict. For you, the relevant question might be: If someone else had the same childhood you did, would he or she be just like you?

Laws of Behavior

For every individual at every age, from newborn to centenarian, behaviorists seek the overarching laws that govern how simple actions and environmental responses shape such complex actions as reading a book or making a family dinner. Behaviorists are also called *learning theorists,* because they believe that all behavior is learned step by step. Then they become habits, repeated without much thought, which is true for at least half of what we do (Neal et al., 2006).

TABLE 2.2

Psychoanalytic Theory vs. Behaviorism

Area of Disagreement	Psychoanalytic Theory	Behaviorism
The unconscious	Emphasizes unconscious wishes and urges, unknown to the person but powerful all the same	Holds that the unconscious not only is unknowable but also may be a destructive fiction that keeps people from changing
Observable behavior	Holds that observable behavior is a symptom, not the cause—the tip of an iceberg, with the bulk of the problem submerged	Looks only at observable behavior—what a person does rather than what a person thinks, feels, or imagines
Importance of childhood	Stresses that early childhood, including infancy, is critical; even if a person does not remember what happened, the early legacy lingers throughout life	Holds that current conditioning is crucial; early habits and patterns can be unlearned, even reversed, if appropriate reinforcements and punishments are used
Scientific status	Holds that most aspects of human development are beyond the reach of scientific experiment; uses ancient myths, the words of disturbed adults, dreams, play, and poetry as raw material	Is proud to be a science, dependent on verifiable data and carefully controlled experiments; discards ideas that sound good but are not proven

The specific laws of learning apply to **conditioning,** the processes by which responses become linked to particular stimuli. There are two types of conditioning: classical and operant.

More than a century ago, Russian scientist Ivan Pavlov (1849–1936), after winning the Nobel Prize for his work on animal digestion, noted that his experimental dogs drooled not only when they saw and smelled food but also when they heard the footsteps of the attendants who brought the food. This observation led Pavlov to perform his famous experiments, conditioning dogs to salivate when they heard a bell.

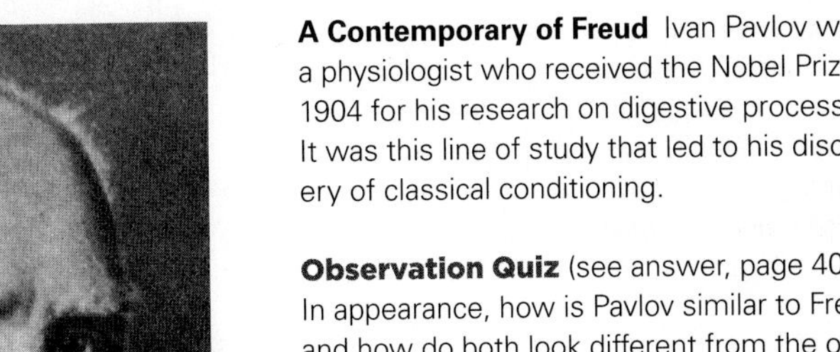

A Contemporary of Freud Ivan Pavlov was a physiologist who received the Nobel Prize in 1904 for his research on digestive processes. It was this line of study that led to his discovery of classical conditioning.

Observation Quiz (see answer, page 40): In appearance, how is Pavlov similar to Freud, and how do both look different from the other theorists pictured?

Pavlov began by ringing the bell just before presenting food. After a number of repetitions of the bell-then-food sequence, dogs began salivating at the bell's sound even when there was no food. This simple experiment demonstrated **classical conditioning** (also called *respondent conditioning*), by which a person or animal is conditioned to associate a neutral stimulus with a meaningful stimulus, gradually responding to the neutral stimulus in the same way as to the meaningful one.

The most influential North American behaviorist was B. F. Skinner (1904–1990). Skinner agreed with Watson that psychology should focus on the scientific study of behavior, and he agreed with Pavlov that classical conditioning explains some behavior. However, Skinner believed that another type of conditioning, **operant conditioning** (also called *instrumental conditioning*), is often crucial, especially in complex learning. In operant conditioning, animals behave in some way and a response occurs. If the response is useful or pleasurable, the animal is likely to repeat the behavior. If the response is painful, the animal is not likely to repeat the behavior.

Pleasant consequences are sometimes called "rewards," and unpleasant consequences are sometimes called "punishments." Behaviorists hesitate to use those words, however, because what people commonly think of as a punishment can actually be a reward, and vice versa. For example, parents punish their children by withholding dessert, by spanking them, by not letting them play, by speaking harshly to them, and so on. But a particular child might, for instance, dislike the dessert, so being deprived of it is actually a reward, not a punishment. Another child might not mind a spanking, especially if he or she craves parental attention. In that family, the intended punishment (spanking) is actually a reward (attention).

Any consequence that follows a behavior and makes the person (or animal) likely to repeat that behavior is called a **reinforcement,** not a reward. Once a behavior has been conditioned, humans and other creatures will do it even if reinforcement occurs only occasionally. Similarly, punishment might make a creature never repeat a certain action. Almost all daily behavior, from socializing with others to earning a paycheck, can be understood as a result of past operant conditioning, according to many behaviorists.

For that reason, early parenting is considered crucial, because it teaches habits that may endure. For instance, if parents want their child to share, when their baby hands them a gummy, half-eaten cracker, they should take the gift with apparent delight and then return it, smiling. Adults should never pull at a toy a child

conditioning According to behaviorism, the processes by which responses become linked to particular stimuli and learning takes place. The word *conditioning* is used to emphasize the importance of repeated practice, as when an athlete gets into physical condition by training for a long time.

classical conditioning The learning process that connects a meaningful stimulus (such as the smell of food to a hungry animal) with a neutral stimulus (such as the sound of a bell) that had no special meaning before conditioning. Also called *respondent conditioning*.

operant conditioning The learning process by which a particular action is followed by something desired (which makes the person or animal more likely to repeat the action) or by something unwanted (which makes the action less likely to be repeated). Also called *instrumental conditioning*.

reinforcement A technique for conditioning behavior in which that behavior is followed by something desired, such as food for a hungry animal or a welcoming smile for a lonely person.

➤Response for Teachers (from page 37): Erikson would note that the behavior of 5-year-olds is affected by their developmental stage and by their culture. Therefore you might design your curriculum to accommodate active, noisy children.

Especially for Teachers Same problem as previously (talkative kindergartners, but what would a behaviorist recommend?

➤Response for Teachers (from page 39): Behaviorists believe that anyone can learn anything. If your goal is quiet, attentive children, begin by reinforcing a moment's quiet or a quiet child, and soon all the children will be trying to remain attentive for several minutes at a time.

➤Answer to Observation Quiz (from page 39): Both are balding, with white beards. Note also that none of the other theorists in this chapter have beards—a cohort difference, not an ideological one.

is holding, encouraging the child to hold tight. Strangers sometimes did that with my children, teaching possessiveness—a lesson I didn't want my children to learn.

The science of human development has benefited from behaviorism. The theory's emphasis on the antecedents and consequences of observed behavior led researchers to realize that many actions that seem to be genetic, or to result from deeply rooted emotional problems, are actually learned. And if something is learned, it can be unlearned. No longer are "the events of infancy and early childhood . . . the foundation for adult personality and psychopathology," as psychoanalysts believed (Cairns & Cairns, 2006, p. 117). People can change, even in old age.

That makes behaviorism a very hopeful theory. It encourages scientists to find ways to eliminate destructive behaviors, among them temper tantrums, phobias, and addictions. Many teachers, counselors, and parents use behaviorist techniques to break undesirable habits and teach new behaviors (Kazdin, 2001). Tantrums cease, phobias disappear, addicts recover, and so on, although not always as easily as the theory predicts.

Like all good theories, both behaviorism and psychoanalytic theory have led to hypotheses and scientific experiments, such as those described in the following feature.

thinking like a scientist

What's a Mother For?

Why do children love their mothers, even if their mothers are mean or unresponsive? Is it because their mothers fed or comforted them when they were infants? To explore such questions, scientists need theories, and then data to disprove or confirm their theories.

Both behaviorism and psychoanalytic theory originally hypothesized that mothers are loved because they satisfy the newborn's hunger and sucking needs. In other words, "the infant's attachment to the mother stemmed from internal drives which triggered activities connected with the libations of the mother's breast. This belief was the only one these two theoretical groups ever had in common" (C. Harlow, 1986). During infancy, mothers were for feeding, and not much else.

Physicians in every hospital were taught that germs caused disease, so they assumed that mothers who kissed and hugged their babies would "spoil" and sicken them. As a consequence, a hundred years ago, orphanages and hospitals kept babies clean and well fed but forbade caregivers to caress them, because "human contact was the ultimate enemy of health" (Blum, 2002, p. 35).

In the 1950s, Harry Harlow (1905–1981), a psychologist who studied learning in monkeys, observed something surprising.

> We had separated more than 60 of these animals from their mothers 6 to 12 hours after birth and suckled them on tiny bottles. . . . During the course of our studies we noticed that the laboratory-raised babies showed strong attachment to the folded gauze diapers which were used to cover the . . . floor of their cages.
>
> [Harlow, 1958, p. 673]

In fact, the infant monkeys seemed more attached to the cloth diapers than to their bottles. This was contrary to the two prevailing theories, since psychoanalytic theory predicted that infants would love whatever satisfied their oral needs and behaviorism predicted that infants would cherish whatever pro-

HARLOW PRIMATE LABORATORY, UNIVERSITY OF WISCONSIN

Clinging to "Mother" Even though it gave no milk, this "mother" was soft and warm enough that infant monkeys spent almost all their time holding on to it. Many infants, some children, and even some adults cling to a familiar stuffed animal when life becomes frightening. According to Harlow, the reasons are the same: All primates are comforted by something soft, warm, and familiar.

vided reinforcing food. Motherless monkeys should love their bottles, not their floorcloths.

Harlow set out to make a "direct experimental analysis" of human love via his monkeys because he believed that "the basic processes relating to affection, including nursing, contact, clinging, and even visual and auditory exploration, exhibit no fundamental differences in the two species" (H. Harlow, 1958). Harlow was troubled that few psychologists recognized the crucial role of physical contact—cuddling, soothing, hugging, and so on—for all social species, including monkeys and humans.

Harlow raised eight infant monkeys, each in a cage with no other animals but with two "surrogate" (artificial) mothers, both mother-monkey size. One surrogate was made of bare wire and the other was covered by soft terrycloth, with a face designed to be ugly—two red bicycle reflectors for eyes and a strip of green for a mouth—but otherwise "soft, warm, and tender, a mother with infinite patience." Four of the baby monkeys were fed by a bottle stuck through the chest of the cloth "mother," the other four by a bottle on the wire "mother" (see Research Design).

Harlow measured how much time each infant monkey spent clinging to each of the two surrogates. The monkeys who had a cloth, milk-providing mother clung to it and ignored the wire mother; this was to be expected, since feeding was connected with mothering. However, even the four babies that fed from the wire mother clung to the cloth mother, going to the wire mother only when hunger compelled them (see Figure 2.1). In short, no attachment to, or love for, the nourishing wire mother could be observed, but the cloth mother had the infants' affection whether or not it provided food. The answer to the question "Does food equal mother love?" was a resounding "No!"

The next question was whether the cloth mothers might reassure infants when frightening events occurred, just as a live mother does. Harlow devised another experiment. He put an unfamiliar mechanical toy into each infant's cage. The monkeys immediately sought comfort from their cloth mother, clinging to the soft belly with one hand and then timidly exploring the new object with the other.

The wire mother provided no such reassurance. Monkeys confronted by the same mechanical toy with access only to their wire mother were terrified—freezing, screaming, shivering, hiding,

Research Design

Scientists: Harry Harlow and many others.

Publication: Reprinted in *Learning to Love: The Selected Papers of H. F. Harlow* (1986), edited by Clara Mears Harlow.

Subjects: Eight infant rhesus monkeys born in Harlow's laboratory.

Design: The monkeys were raised from birth in separate cages, each with two "surrogate mothers": one made of bare wire and the other of wire covered with terrycloth. Half the monkeys were fed by a bottle stuck onto the wire mother, the other half by a bottle stuck onto the cloth mother. Harlow recorded how much time the monkeys spent feeding from and clinging to each mother.

Major conclusion: Monkeys, and presumably all primate infants, need "contact comfort," the warm and soft reassurance of a mother's touch.

Comment: Many design problems are apparent: too few subjects, ethical questions about treatment of animals, and uncertainty about whether data on lab-reared, socially isolated rhesus monkeys applies to humans, or even to other primates in nature. However, the results of this experiment were so dramatic that it has been replicated and revised by dozens of other researchers. Harlow's research revolutionized child care.

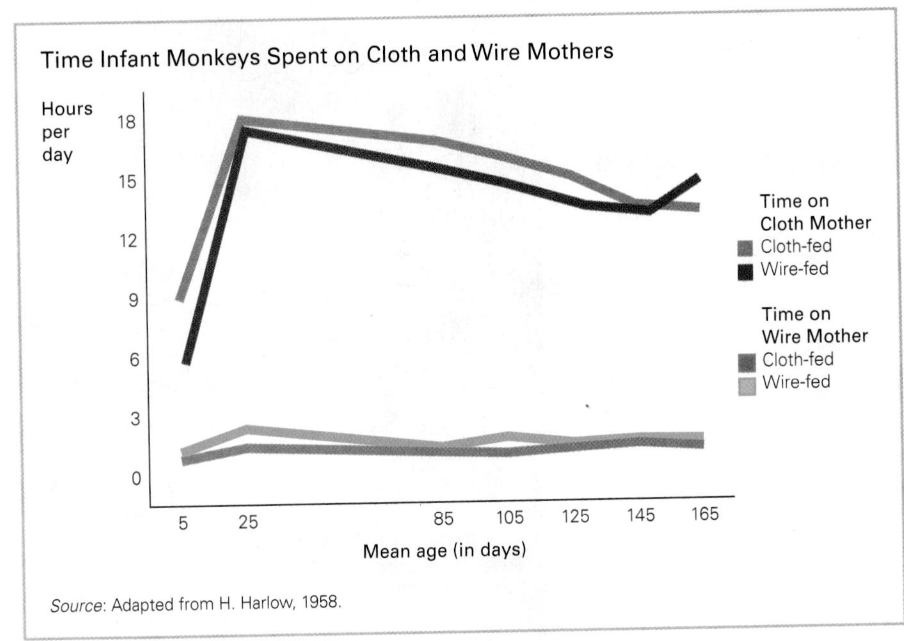

FIGURE 2.1

Softer Is Better During the first three weeks of Harlow's experiment, the infant monkeys developed a strong preference for the cloth-covered "mothers." That preference lasted throughout the experiment, even among the monkeys who were fed by a wire-covered mother.

Observation Quiz (see answer, page 44): At five days, how much time did the wire-fed monkeys (compared with the cloth-fed monkeys) spend on the cloth mothers?

urinating. Harlow concluded that mothering is not primarily about feeding but about what he called "contact comfort" or "love."

Later Harlow's students discovered that mother love involves more than contact. To become psychologically healthy adults, infant monkeys (and humans as well) need interaction with another living, responsive creature (who could be either sex) (Blum, 2002).

Harlow's experiments are a classic example of the use of theories. Although aspects of both behaviorism and psychoanalytic theory were disproved, that is not the most significant point. Remember, theories are meant to be useful, not necessarily true. Because Harlow knew what theories predicted about love and comfort, he was intrigued by the baby monkeys' attraction to the gauze diapers covering the floors of their cages. That led to closer observation, a hypothesis, a clever series of experiments, and some amazing results.

This research revolutionized the treatment of sick or motherless children. Even very tiny, fragile preterm infants now have contact with their parents, typically including very gentle touch—and their chances of survival are better because of it (see Chapter 4).

Today's mothers do much more cuddling and infants do much less crying than their predecessors did a century ago because one creative scientist contrasted theory and observations, performing ingenious experiments to test a hypothesis.

Social Learning

social learning theory An extension of behaviorism that emphasizes the influence that other people have over a person's behavior. Even without specific reinforcement, every individual learns many things via observation and imitation of other people.

Originally, behaviorists believed that all behavior arose from a chain of learned responses, the result of classical and operant conditioning. One refinement of behaviorism came from evidence (from humans as well as monkeys) that all social creatures appreciate another's touch, warmth, reassurance, and example.

This revision is called **social learning theory** (see Figure 2.2). Its central premise is that humans can learn from observing others, without personally experiencing any reinforcement. We learn from other people because we are social beings. We grow up in families, we learn from friends and teachers, we love and hate and admire other people—even when we wish we were more independent.

PHOTOGRAPHER'S CHOICE / GETTY

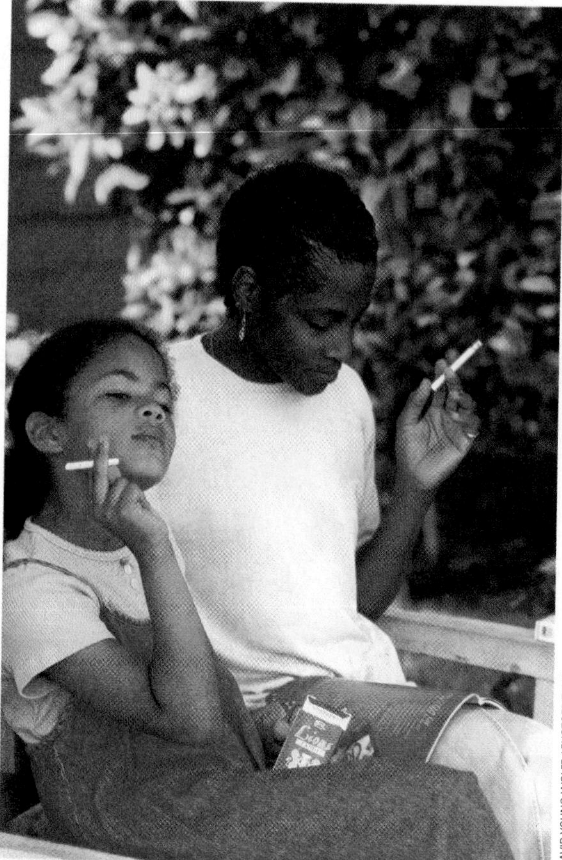

DAVID YOUNG-WOLFF / PHOTOEDIT INC.

Social Learning in Action Social learning validates the old maxim "Actions speak louder than words." If the moments here are typical for each child, the girl on the left is likely to grow up with a ready sense of the importance of this particular chore of infant care. Unfortunately, the girl on the right with a candy "cigarette" may smoke tobacco like her mother—even if her mother warns her not to do so.

Observation Quiz (see answer, page 46): What shows that these children imitate their parents?

An integral part of social learning is **modeling,** in which people observe what someone else does and then copy it. Even hairstyles or dance steps are copied from others—which explains why they change with each generation. Modeling is far more complex than simple imitation, because people model only some actions, of some individuals, in some contexts. For example, you may know people who, as children, were never personally abused but saw their parents hit each other. Some become adults who are violent with their romantic partners, while others are careful to avoid such behavior. These opposite responses support social learning theory; they show the continuing impact of the original example. One child identified with the abuser and the other with the victim, thus, each learned a different lesson. Generally, modeling is likely when the observer is uncertain or inexperienced and when the model is admired, powerful, nurturing, or similar to the observer (Bandura, 1986, 1997).

Learning occurs through:

- **Classical conditioning** Through association, neutral stimulus becomes conditioned stimulus.
- **Operant conditioning** Through reinforcement, weak or rare response becomes strong, frequent response.
- **Social learning** Through modeling, observed behaviors become copied behaviors.

FIGURE 2.2

Three Types of Learning Behaviorism is also called "learning theory" because it emphasizes the learning process, as shown here.

As this example shows, social learning is connected to perceptions and interpretations. It is also related to self-understanding, social reflection, and **self-efficacy,** a feeling of self-confidence that people develop when they have high aspirations and notable achievements (Bandura, 2006).

Self-efficacy explains a paradox found in recent research: Parents who do not believe in their own efficacy and who think their babies are strong-willed are stricter and less responsive than other parents. Why? The explanation from social learning theory is that their own parents probably never let them develop a strong sense of themselves, so they still feel ineffective (Guzell & Vernon-Feagans, 2004). Their parents probably punished them when they tried to assert themselves. Their lack of self-efficacy and their parents' example lead them to be overly controlling with their children.

Current versions of social learning theory incorporate elements of two of the other major theories, cognitive theory and sociocultural theory (Bandura, 2006).

modeling The central process of social learning, by which a person observes the actions of others and then copies them.

self-efficacy In social learning theory, the belief of some people that they are able to change themselves and effectively alter the social context.

cognitive theory A grand theory of human development that focuses on changes in how people think over time. According to this theory, our thoughts shape our attitudes, beliefs, and behaviors.

Cognitive Theory

The third grand theory, **cognitive theory,** emphasizes the structure and development of thought processes. According to this theory, thoughts and expectations profoundly affect attitudes, beliefs, values, assumptions, and actions. Cognitive theory has dominated psychology since about 1980 and has branched into many versions, each adding insights about human development. A major extension of cognitive theory is *information-processing theory,* which focuses on the step-by-step activation of various parts of the brain, as described in Chapter 6 (brain functioning is explained in Chapter 5).

The original cognitive theorist was the Swiss scientist Jean Piaget (1896–1980), who was trained in the natural sciences and studied shellfish. Piaget became interested in the science of human behavior when he got a job in Paris, field-testing questions for a standardized IQ test. Although he was hired to find the age at which children could answer various questions correctly, the *incorrect* answers and the thinking behind them caught his attention. How children think is more revealing, Piaget concluded, than what they know; process, not product, is important.

YVES DEBRAINE / BLACK STAR

Would You Talk to This Man? Children loved talking to Jean Piaget, and he learned by listening carefully—especially to their incorrect explanations, which no one had paid much attention to before. All his life, Piaget was absorbed with studying the way children think. He called himself a "genetic epistemologist"—one who studies how children gain knowledge about the world as they grow up.

Piaget's interest in cognitive development grew as he observed his own three children. He realized that babies are much more curious and thoughtful than other psychologists had imagined. Later he studied hundreds of schoolchildren.

From this work Piaget developed the central thesis of cognitive theory: How people think changes with time and experience, and thought processes always affect behavior. Piaget maintained that cognitive development occurs in four major periods, or stages: *sensorimotor, preoperational, concrete operational,* and *formal operational* (see Table 2.3). These periods are age-related, and, as you will see in

TABLE 2.3

Piaget's Periods of Cognitive Development

Age Range	Name of Period	Characteristics of the Period	Major Gains During the Period
Birth to 2 years	Sensorimotor	Infants use senses and motor abilities to understand the world. Learning is active; there is no conceptual or reflective thought.	Infants learn that an object still exists when it is out of sight (*object permanence*) and begin to think through mental actions.
2–6 years	Preoperational	Children think magically and poetically, using language to understand the world. Thinking is *egocentric,* causing children to perceive the world from their own perspective.	The imagination flourishes, and language becomes a significant means of self-expression and of influence from others.
6–11 years	Concrete operational	Children understand and apply logical operations, or principles, to interpret experiences objectively and rationally. Their thinking is limited to what they can personally see, hear, touch, and experience.	By applying logical abilities, children learn to understand concepts of conservation, number, classification, and many other scientific ideas.
12 years through adulthood	Formal operational	Adolescents and adults think about abstractions and hypothetical concepts and reason analytically, not just emotionally. They can be logical about things they have never experienced.	Ethics, politics, and social and moral issues become fascinating as adolescents and adults take a broader and more theoretical approach to experience.

later chapters, each period fosters particular ways of thinking and acting (Inhelder & Piaget, 1958; Piaget, 1952b).

Intellectual advancement occurs because humans seek **cognitive equilibrium**—that is, a state of mental balance. An easy way (called *assimilation*) to achieve this balance is to interpret new experiences through the lens of preexisting ideas. For example, infants discover that new objects can be grasped in the same way as familiar objects, and adolescents explain the day's headlines as evidence for their existing worldviews. For example, a news story might at first seem surprising, such

cognitive equilibrium In cognitive theory, a state of mental balance in which people are not confused because they can use their existing thought processes to understand current experiences and ideas.

➤Answer to Observation Quiz (from page 41): Six hours, or one-third less time. Note that later on, the wire-fed monkeys (compared with the cloth-fed monkeys) spent equal, or even more, time on the cloth mothers.

© IGAL JUSIDMAN

(a)

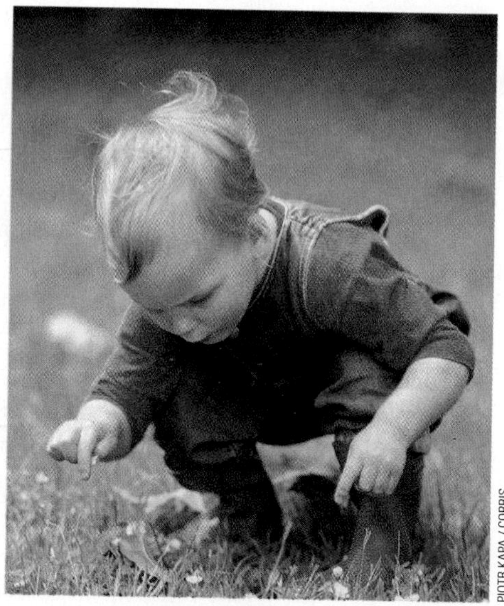

PIOTR KAPA / CORBIS

(b)

How to Think About Flowers A person's stage of cognitive growth influences how he or she thinks about everything, including flowers. *(a)* To 7-month-old Maya, in the sensorimotor stage, flowers are "known" through pulling, smelling, and even biting. *(b)* A slightly older child might be egocentric, wanting to pull up all the flowers within reach, *now.* *(c,d)* At the adult's formal operational stage, flowers can be part of a larger, logical scheme—either to earn money or to cultivate beauty. Thinking is an active process from the beginning of life until the end.

as the report that a suicide bomber had killed 23 people in Afghanistan on February 27, 2007. But, as an analysis of the story noted, most people interpret news headlines using existing concepts, much as Vice President Richard Cheney did when he said that such suicide bombings are proof that terrorism is still a worldwide threat, or as critics of President Bush did when they said that the U.S. government was being distracted by the ongoing conflict in Iraq (Sanger, 2007, p. A-1).

Sometimes a new experience is jarring and incomprehensible. Then the individual experiences cognitive disequilibrium, an imbalance that initially creates confusion. As Figure 2.3 illustrates, disequilibrium leads to cognitive growth because people must adapt their old concepts. Piaget describes two types of adaptation:

- *Assimilation,* in which new experiences are reinterpreted to fit into, or assimilate with, old ideas
- *Accommodation,* in which old ideas are restructured to include, or accommodate, new experiences

Accommodation requires more mental energy than assimilation, but it is sometimes necessary because new ideas and experiences may not fit into existing cognitive structures. Accommodation produces significant intellectual growth, including advancement to the next stage of cognitive development. For example, if your mother says something you never expected her to (such as "I'm going to study ballet"), you will experience cognitive disequilibrium and you will need to adapt. You might *assimilate* your mother's words by deciding she didn't mean what she said. Intellectual growth would occur if, instead, you *accommodate* by expanding and revising your concept of your mother.

Ideally, when people disagree, adaptation is mutual. For example, parents are often startled by their adolescents' strong opinions—perhaps that all drugs should be legalized or that even cigarettes should be outlawed. Parents may grow intellectually if they revise their concepts. As the adolescents become emerging adults, they, too, might revise their notions of their parents. Cognitive growth is active, responsive to clashing ideas and challenging experiences, not primarily dependent on maturation (as postulated in psychoanalytic theory) or repetition (as postulated in behaviorism).

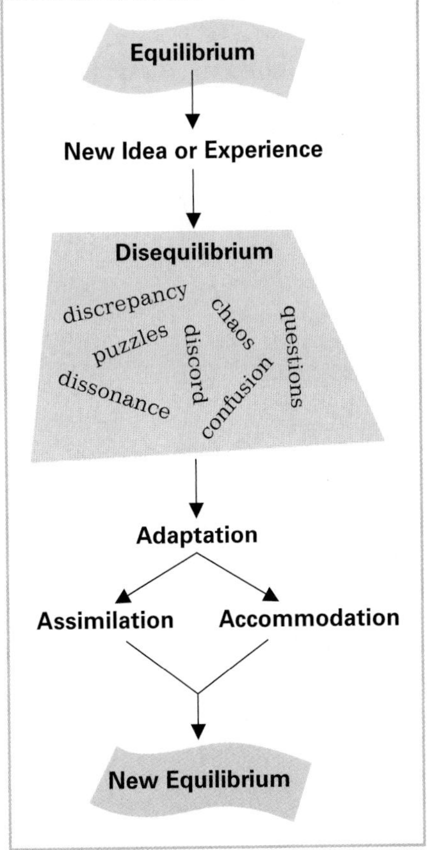

FIGURE 2.3

Challenge Me Most of us, most of the time, prefer the comfort of our conventional conclusions. According to Piaget, however, when new ideas disturb our thinking, we have an opportunity to expand our cognition with a broader and deeper understanding.

RANDY DUCHAINE, BROOKLYN, NY

(c)

PHOTODISC / PUNCHSTOCK

(d)

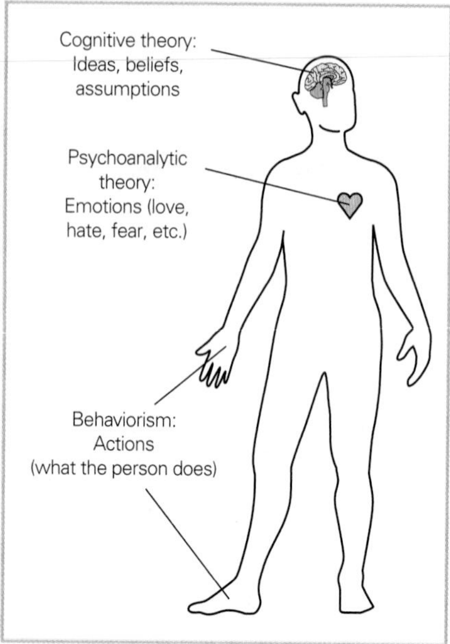

FIGURE 2.4

Major Focuses of the Three Grand Theories

SUMMING UP

The three grand theories originated almost a century ago, each pioneered by men who developed theories so comprehensive and creative that they deserve to be called "grand." Each theory has a different focus: emotions (psychoanalytic theory), actions (behaviorism), or thoughts (cognitive theory) (see Figure 2.4).

Freud and Erikson thought it was important to understand unconscious drives and early experiences in order to understand personality and actions. Behaviorists instead stress experiences in the recent past, especially learning by association, by reinforcement, and by observation. Cognitive theory holds that, to understand people, we need to appreciate how they think. According to Piaget, the way people think changes with age as their brains mature and their experiences challenge their past assumptions.

Emergent Theories

You have surely noticed that the grand theorists were all men born more than a hundred years ago whose biological and academic ancestors were from western Europe and North America. These background variables are limiting. (Of course, female, non-Western, and contemporary theorists are limited by their backgrounds as well.)

Two new theories have emerged that, unlike the grand theories, are multicultural and multidisciplinary, developed not only by men of European ancestry but also by many non-Western, non-White, and female scientists. One, *sociocultural theory*, draws on research in education, anthropology, and history. The other, *epigenetic theory*, arises from biology, genetics, and neuroscience. The wide-ranging multicultural and multidisciplinary approach makes these theories particularly pertinent to our study.

Neither emergent theory has yet developed a comprehensive, coherent explanation of all of human development, of how and why people change. However, both provide significant and useful frameworks leading to better understanding, which is precisely what good theories do.

Sociocultural Theory

Although "sociocultural theory is still emerging" (Rogoff, 1998, p. 687), many developmentalists believe that "individual development must be understood in, and cannot be separated from, its social and cultural-historical context" (Rogoff, 2003, p. 50). The central thesis of **sociocultural theory** is that human development results from the dynamic interaction between developing persons and their surrounding society.

sociocultural theory An emergent theory that holds that development results from the dynamic interaction between each person and the surrounding social and cultural forces.

Cultural Variations

Consider this question: What should you do if your 6-month-old daughter starts to fuss? You could give her a pacifier, turn on a musical mobile, change her diaper, prepare a bottle, rock her, sing a lullaby, offer a breast, shake a rattle, ask for help, or close the door and walk away. Each is the right thing to do in some cultures but not in others. In fact, some parents are warned not to "spoil" their crying babies by picking them up, while others are told that if they let their babies cry, they are abusive and neglectful.

Few adults realize that their responses are shaped by culture, yet this is precisely the case, according to sociocultural theory. Societies provide not only customs but also the tools and theories. For instance, some places have no pacifiers,

➤Answer to Observation Quiz (from page 42): The obvious part of the answer is that one girl is feeding her doll and the other is pretending to smoke a cigarette, but modeling goes far beyond that. Notice that the first girl is holding her spoon at exactly the same angle as her mother is holding hers, and that the positions of the second girl's hand, fingers, and arm mirror her mother's.

bottles, or mobiles—or even diapers or doors. The tools available for baby care profoundly affect parents and infants in ways that echo throughout life. Possessions and privacy are valued much more in some cultures than in others, a value learned in infancy.

The pioneer of the sociocultural perspective was Lev Vygotsky (1896–1934), a psychologist from the former Soviet Union. Vygotsky studied cognitive competency among the ethnically and economically diverse people of his huge nation, as well as among children who were mentally retarded. He studied how Asian farmers used tools, how illiterate people used abstract ideas, and how children learned in school. In his view, each person, schooled or not, is taught by more skilled members of his or her community (Vygotsky, 1934/1986).

Novices must acquire whatever knowledge and capabilities their society requires. This is best accomplished through **guided participation:** Tutors (not only those designated to teach, but also friends and strangers who know more than the novice) engage learners in joint activities, offering not only instruction but also "mutual involvement in several widespread cultural practices with great importance for learning: narratives, routines, and play" (Rogoff, 2003, p. 285).

guided participation In sociocultural theory, a technique in which skilled mentors help novices learn not only by providing instruction but also by allowing direct, shared involvement in the activity. Also called *apprenticeship in thinking.*

Each of us begins life knowing nothing about our culture, which includes such basic knowledge as how and what to eat, when to express emotions, and even how to communicate. Guided participation (also called *apprenticeship in thinking*) is a central concept of sociocultural theory. Learning is informal, social, and pervasive.

Especially for Nurses Using guided participation, how would you teach a young child who has asthma to breathe with a nebulizer?

One of my students recently came to my office with her young son, who eyed my candy dish but held tightly to his mother's hand.

"He can have one if it's all right with you," I whispered.

She nodded and told him, "Dr. Berger will let you have one piece of candy."

He smiled shyly and quickly took one.

"What do you say?" she prompted.

"Thank you," he replied, glancing at me out of the corner of his eye.

"You're welcome," I said.

In that brief moment, all three of us were engaged in guided participation. We were surrounded by cultural traditions and practices, including my role as professor, the fact that I have an office and a candy dish (a custom that I learned from one of my teachers), and the authority of the parent. This mother had taught her son to say thank you, as some families do and others don't. Specifics differ, but all adults teach children skills they may need in their society.

Social interaction is pivotal in sociocultural theory (Wertsch & Tulviste, 2005). This contrasts with learning in the grand theories, which depends, primarily, on either the student or the teacher, not on both simultaneously. In guided participation neither student nor teacher is passive; they learn from each other, through words and activities that they engage in together (Karpov & Haywood, 1998), because "cognitive development occurs in, and emerges from, social situations" (Gauvain, 1998, p. 191).

COURTESY OF DR. MICHAEL COLE, LABORATORY OF COMPARATIVE HUMAN COGNITION, UC, SAN DIEGO

The Founder of Sociocultural Theory Lev Vygotsky, now recognized as a seminal thinker whose ideas are revolutionizing education and the study of development, was a contemporary of Freud, Skinner, Pavlov, and Piaget. Vygotsky did not attain their eminence in his lifetime, partly because his work, conducted in Stalinist Russia, was largely inaccessible to the Western world and partly because he died young, at age 38.

The concept that cultural patterns and beliefs are social constructions (explained in Chapter 1) is easy for sociocultural theorists to grasp. They believe that socially constructed ideas are no less powerful than physical or emotional constraints; indeed, quite the opposite is true. For example, for centuries, women were not allowed to work as firefighters. Reasons centered on their physical limitations (they were too weak to pull hoses), and questions about their judgment (they were too emotional to deal with emergencies). But now it seems that the social reasons (it just wasn't proper) were (and are) more powerful.

Values shape development, even though values are constructed. This point was stressed by Vygotsky, who believed that mentally and physically disabled children should be educated (Vygotsky, 1925/1994). That belief has taken hold in U.S.

culture in the past 30 years, revolutionizing the education of children with special needs (Rogoff, 2003).

The Zone of Proximal Development

According to sociocultural theory, people always learn in the same way, whether they are learning a manual skill, a social custom, or a language. For learning to occur, a teacher (parent, peer, or professional) must locate the learner's **zone of proximal development,** which consists of the skills, knowledge, and concepts that the learner is close to acquiring but cannot yet master without help.

zone of proximal development In sociocultural theory, a metaphorical area, or "zone," surrounding a learner that includes all the skills, knowledge, and concepts that the person is close ("proximal") to acquiring but cannot yet master without help.

Through sensitive assessment of the learner, the teacher engages the student and together, in a "process of joint construction," new knowledge is attained (Valsiner, 2006). The teacher must avoid two opposite dangers: boredom and failure. Some frustration is permitted, but the learner must be actively engaged, never passive or overwhelmed (see Figure 2.5).

To make this seemingly abstract process more concrete, consider an example: a father teaching his daughter to ride a bicycle. He begins by rolling her along, supporting her weight while telling her to keep her hands on the handlebars, to push the right and left pedals in rhythm, and to look straight ahead. As she becomes more comfortable and confident, he begins to roll her along more quickly, praising her for steadily pumping. Within a few lessons, he is jogging beside her, holding only the handlebars. When he senses that she could maintain her balance by herself, he urges her to pedal faster and slowly loosens his grip. Perhaps without even realizing it, she is riding on her own.

Especially for Teachers Following Vygotsky's precepts, how might you teach reading to an entire class of first-graders at various skill levels?

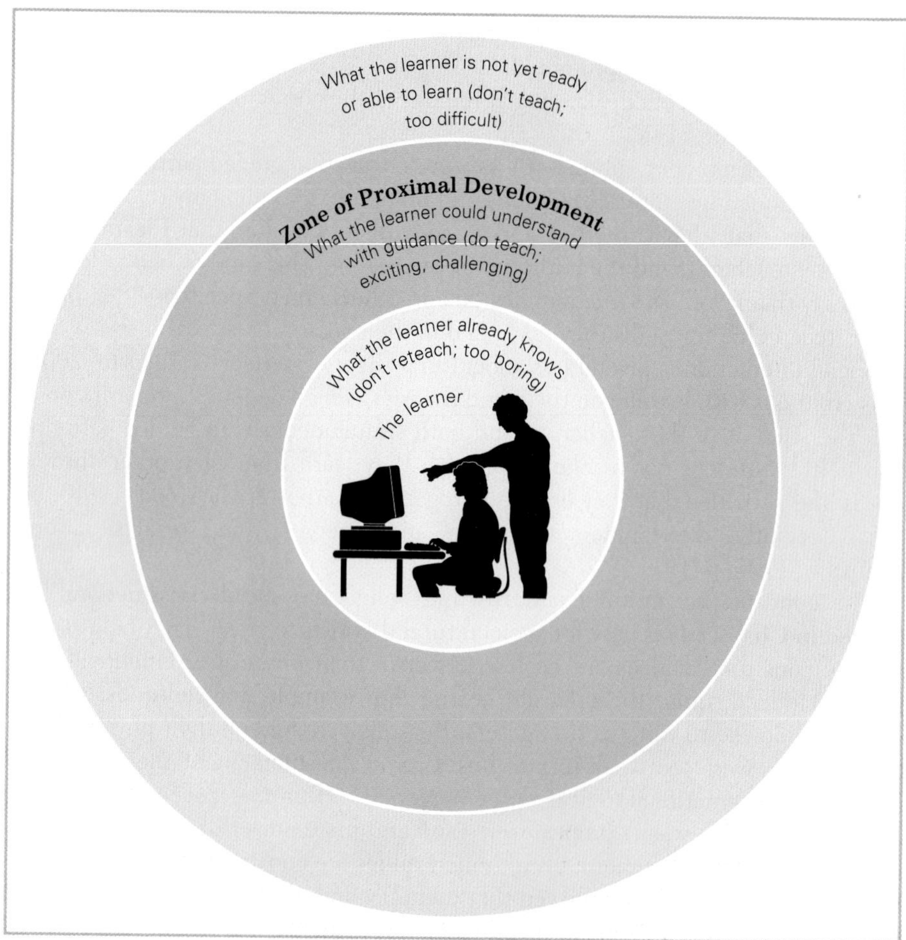

FIGURE 2.5

The Magic Middle Somewhere between the boring and the impossible is the zone of proximal development, where interaction between teacher and learner results in knowledge never before grasped or skills not already mastered. The intellectual excitement of that zone is the origin of the joy that both instruction and study can bring

Note that this is not instruction by preset rules. Sociocultural learning is active: No child learns to ride a bike by reading and memorizing written instructions, and no good teacher merely repeats a prepared lesson.

Because each student has personal traits, experiences, and aspirations, education must be individualized. Learning styles vary: Some children need more assurance than others; some learn best by looking, others by hearing. A mentor needs to sense when support or freedom is needed and how peers can help (they are sometimes the best mentors). Teachers know how the zone of proximal development expands and shifts.

Excursions into and through the zone of proximal development, such as the boy prompted to say "thank you" or the girl learning to balance on a bike, are commonplace for all of us. Our mentors, attuned to ever-shifting abilities and motivation, continually urge a new level of competence; learners ask questions, show interest, and demonstrate progress, thus guiding and inspiring the mentors. When education goes well, both teachers and students are fully engaged and productive. Particular skills and processes vary enormously from culture to culture, but the overall social interaction is the same.

Sociocultural theorists have been criticized for overlooking developmental processes that are not primarily social. Vygotsky's theory, in particular, may neglect the power of genes to guide development, especially if neurological immaturity or disability makes some learning impossible (Wertsch, 1998). Every child can learn, but not every child can learn anything at any moment. Further, while culture is pervasive and informal teachers abound, the prevailing sociocultural values are not necessarily always best.

ARIEL SKELLEY / CORBIS

Learning to Ride Although they are usually not aware of it, children learn most of their skills because adults guide them carefully. What would happen if this father let go?

Epigenetic Theory

The central idea of **epigenetic theory** is that genes interact with the environment to allow development (Gottlieb, 2003). Epigenetic development contrasts sharply with *preformism,* the theory that genes determine every aspect of development.

epigenetic theory An emergent theory of development that considers both the genetic origins of behavior (within each person and within each species) and the direct, systematic influence that environmental forces have, over time, on genes.

Epigenetic theory is the newest developmental theory, but it incorporates several established bodies of research. Many disciplines—including biology (especially the principles of evolution), genetics, and chemistry—provided a foundation. Many psychologists, including Erikson and Piaget, described aspects of their theories as *epigenetic,* recognizing that development builds on genes but is not determined by them.

Many specialties within the social sciences—especially *sociobiology* (the study of how individuals within society seek to pass along their genetic heritage), *evolutionary psychology* (the study of the inherited patterns of behavior that were once adaptive), and *ethology* (the study of animals in their natural environments)—stress the interaction of genes and the environment.

With, On, and Around the Genes

What, then, is new about epigenetic theory? One way to answer that question is to consider the name, derived from the root word *genetic* and the prefix *epi-*. *Genetic* refers to the entire genome, which includes (1) the particular genes that make each person (except monozygotic twins) genetically unique, (2) the genes that distinguish our species as human, and (3) the genes that all living creatures share.

We now know that all psychological as well as all physical traits—from bashfulness to blood type, from moodiness to metabolism, from vocational aptitude to voice tone—are influenced by genes. How religious a person is, or whether someone votes for a liberal candidate, is influenced by genes (Bouchard et al., 2004).

➤**Response for Nurses** (from page 47): You would guide the child in the zone of proximal development, where teacher and child interact. Thus, you might encourage the child to prepare the nebulizer (by putting in the medicine, for instance) and then breathe through it yourself, taking turns with the child.

➤Response for Teachers (from page 48): First of all, you wouldn't teach them "to read"; you would find out each child's skill level and what he or she was capable of learning next, so that instruction would be tailored to each child's zone of proximal development. For some, this might be letter recognition; for others, comprehension of paragraphs they read silently. Second, you wouldn't teach the whole class. You would figure out a way to individualize instruction—maybe by forming pairs, with one child teaching the other; by setting up appropriate computer instruction; or by having parents or other teachers (maybe older children) work with small groups of three or four children.

Even the timing of developmental change is genetic: Humans walk and talk at about 1 year and can have babies in adolescence because genes switch on those abilities (unless something is terribly wrong). Thus, half of epigenetic theory is about the power of genes.

The other half is equally important. The prefix *epi-* means "with," "around," "before," "after," "on," or "near." Thus, *epigenetic* refers to all the surrounding factors that affect the expression of genetic influences. Those factors stop some genes before they have any effect, and they give other genes extensive influence. Some factors cause stress, such as injury, temperature, and crowding; some facilitate, such as nourishing food, loving care, and freedom to play. In "epigenetic programming . . . environmental effects on . . . health or behavior are mediated through altered gene expression" as well as vice versa (Moffitt et al., 2006, pp. 5–6).

Epigenetic theory puts the two halves together in one word to signify this inevitable interaction between genes and the environment. This is illustrated by Figure 2.6, which was first published in 1992 by Gilbert Gottlieb, a leading proponent of epigenetic theory. That simple diagram, with arrows going up and down over time, has been redrawn and reprinted dozens of times to emphasize that dynamic interaction continues in each person's life long after conception (Gottlieb, 1992).

Epigenetic effects are easier to notice in lower animals than in people (Koolhaas et al., 2006). For example, the color of an animal's fur is genetically determined, but environment causes some rabbit species to have white fur in cold climates and brown fur in warm ones.

Even biological sex can be epigenetic. Alligator eggs become males when the nest temperature is 34°C or above during days 7 to 21 of incubation and hatch as females at nest temperatures of 28–31°C (Ferguson & Joanen, 1982). For humans, the age of the parents correlates with the sex of their child, an epigenetic effect. Teenagers conceive more boys.

As development progresses, each person proceeds along the course set by earlier genetic–environmental interactions, which allow a range of possible outcomes called the *reaction range*. Thus, some toddlers cannot be musical masters, because that is above the range of their inherited potential. But they still have a spread of possible reactions to music, depending on their experiences, from being an avid listener to being indifferent to music.

Some aspects of development become less plastic, or changeable, with age (Baltes et al., 2006), which explains why prenatal conditions (e.g., drugs or alcohol) damage the brain and body of a fetus far more than they damage the pregnant woman. However, even in adulthood contexts can change inherited patterns.

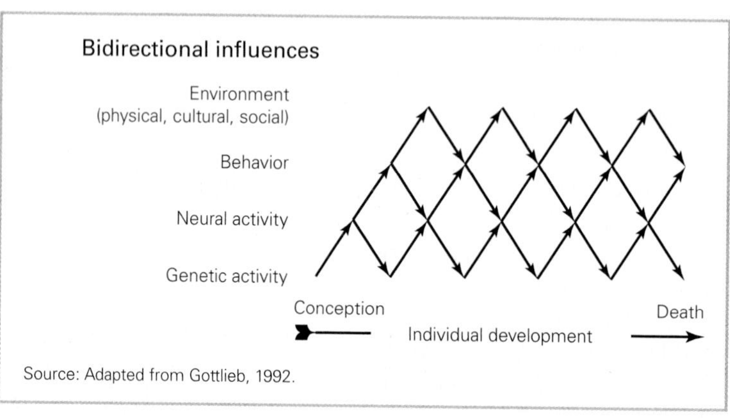

Source: Adapted from Gottlieb, 1992.

FIGURE 2.6

An Epigenetic Model of Development Notice that there are as many arrows going down as going up, at all levels. Although development begins with genes at conception, it requires that all four factors interact.

Observation Quiz (see answer, page 52): According to this diagram, does genetic influence stop at birth?

Dramatic evidence comes from drug addiction. A person's potential to become addicted is genetic. That potential can be realized—a genetically vulnerable person becomes an addict or alcoholic—if the person repeatedly consumes an addictive substance. Thus, addiction is epigenetic, the outcome of the interaction of genes and environment. Even monozygotic twins (who have the same genes) can differ in whether or not they become alcoholics (Moffitt et al., 2006).

Once people are addicts, something in their biochemistry and brain makes them hypersensitive to that drug. For example, one drink makes a nonalcoholic pleasantly tipsy but awakens a powerful craving in the alcoholic. The role of experience in addiction and in creating hypersensitivity to a drug has been demonstrated in countless experiments (Crombag & Robinson, 2004). Nonetheless, as one team of researchers explains:

> Within the epigenetic model, each intermediary phenotype [genetic manifestation] is an outcome as well as a precursor to a subsequent outcome contingent on the quality of person–environment interactions. . . . Sudden shifts . . . can occur. . . . [For example,] 86 percent of regular heroin users among soldiers in Vietnam abruptly terminated consumption upon return to the United States (Robins, Helzer, & Davis, 1975). In effect, a substantial change in the environment produced a major phenotype change.
>
> *[Tarter et al., 1999, p. 672]*

The fact that these addicted soldiers kicked the habit permanently is astonishing to anyone who has watched an addict get "clean" and then relapse time after time. The conventional explanation for the repeated relapses is that, once a person is addicted, the biochemical pull of the drug is too strong to resist. However, the example of the Vietnam veterans suggests that the biochemical (and genetic) aspect of addiction does not work in isolation; the social context (*epi-*) is powerful as well—a point confirmed by more recent research (Baker et al., 2006).

Thus, a crucial aspect of epigenetic theory is that genes never function alone; their potential is not actualized unless certain *epi-* factors occur. For example, many psychological disorders, including schizophrenia, autism, antisocial personality disorder, and some forms of depression, have a genetic component. But none are purely genetic; all are epigenetic, with the severity and even the existence of the psychopathology dependent on environment as well as genes (Krueger & Markon, 2006; Moffitt et al., 2006).

People who inherit a particular variant of one gene (called the short allele of 5-HTT) are more likely to become depressed. However, even people who have this variant do not usually become depressed unless they are maltreated as children or experience stressful events as adults (Caspi et al., 2003). Epigenetic again.

Genetic Adaptation

So far we have described epigenetic factors that affect individuals. Epigenetic factors also affect groups of people and entire species. It is apparent that over billions of years there has been "continual reorganization of epigenetic and genetic determinants." That makes it foolhardy to try to understand species development, even of lower organisms, as solely genetic, transmitted without change over eons (Newman & Müller, 2006, p. 61). **Selective adaptation** of genes and environments is ongoing, which means that the environment favors genes in a population if they increase survival and reproduction. At the same time, selective adaptation makes destructive genes increasingly rare.

Selective adaptation begins when a particular genetic variant benefits the organism that has it, enabling survival and many offspring. About half of those offspring inherit the same gene as their fortunate father or mother. They, too, will

selective adaptation The process by which humans and other organisms gradually adjust to their environment. Specifically, the frequency of a particular genetic trait in a population increases or decreases over generations, depending on whether or not the trait contributes to the survival and reproductive ability of members of that population.

➤**Answer to Observation Quiz** (from page 50): No. Arrows originating with genetic activity extend throughout development until death.

have many children, and thus that beneficial gene will become more common with each succeeding generation. Eventually, almost everyone has that gene and the entire population thrives.

Whether a gene is beneficial, harmful, or neutral depends on the particular environment. For instance, allergy to bee stings is genetic, but inheriting it is no problem if the neighborhood has no bees and the person does not travel. Complex genetic traits depend on the context for their impact. For example, people who inherit fearfulness have an advantage in a hostile place (they may escape attack) but not in a benign environment (they may avoid other people). Similarly, specialized bills (for birds) or teeth (for mammals), which enable creatures to obtain food more easily, perhaps emerged first as a mutation that subsequently spread through the population. Thus, a woodpecker's strong, narrow bill pries insects out of the bark of trees, but a duck's broad, rounded bill strains food from water. So because of genes, a "duck out of water" is a dead duck.

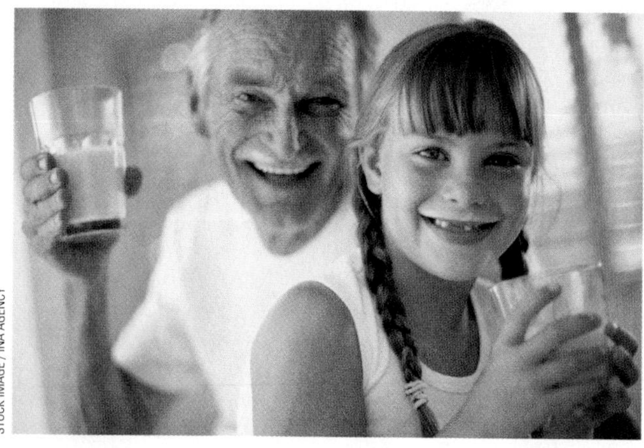

STOCK IMAGE / INA AGENCY

Got Milk! Many people in Sweden (like this pair) and the other Scandinavian countries regularly drink cow's milk and digest it easily. That may be because their ancient occupation of cattle herding coincided with a genetic tendency toward lactose tolerance.

Human differences can also be traced to selective adaptation. All humans may originally have been lactose-intolerant, getting sick if they drank cow's milk; but in regions where dairy farming was introduced thousands of years ago, a few fortunate people had an odd gene that produced an enzyme that let them digest milk. They became healthier than the others, so they had more children. In fact, the genetic variant that allows milk digestion appeared independently in several cattle-herding populations and spread among those people (Gibbons, 2006).

For tribes and clans as well as individuals, the interaction of genes and environment affects survival. Genetic variations are needed when conditions change. If no member of a species inherits some variants of genes needed for adaptation, the entire species can disappear. About 90 percent of all species that ever existed have become extinct, partly *because* none of the animals could adapt to changes in conditions (Buss et al., 1998). Thus far, humans have adapted well, surviving in dramatically diverse climates and ecosystems.

Epigenetic theory suggests that adaptation occurs for all living creatures, no matter where and how they live (Fish, 2002). Consider humans and chimpanzees: Those two species share 99 percent of their genes, yet there are about a million times as many humans alive at this moment than chimpanzees. That 1 percent genetic difference includes several characteristics that have enabled humans to survive and multiply. For instance, as a species, humans are taller than chimpanzees and have longer legs, making it easier for humans to walk long distances. Bipedal (two-legged) locomotion increased mobility, enabling humans (but not chimps) to journey from Africa to distant fertile regions. Humans are the only mammals that have traveled, reproduced, and thrived on every landmass of the world (except Antarctica).

Especially for Students Who are Bored with Reading About Genes How can reading this textbook help you live longer and be happier?

Some aspects of epigenetic theory are widely accepted, including one that helps us understand why human children and parents love each other: It originates with the genes (Hofer, 2006). Children depend for survival on a decade or more of adult care, so for the human species to survive, children and parents must become attached to each other. Consequently, babies instinctively smile at faces, and a newborn's physical appearance and trusting grasp stir almost any adult's protective affection.

Over the millennia, unloved children were likely to die and thus never have children of their own, so parent–child affection became adaptive and widespread among the population. Parental love is strengthened by the same hormones that accompany birth—an example of selective adaptation that I know well.

in person

My Beautiful, Hairless Babies

In the beginning, infants accept help from anyone—a good survival strategy during the centuries when women regularly died in childbirth. By the time they are able to crawl, however, infants are emotionally attached to their specific caregivers and fearful of unfamiliar situations—another good survival tactic.

Both accepting help and forming attachments are evidence of selective adaptation. Infants who stayed near caregivers were unlikely to be lost in a blizzard or eaten by an animal in the jungle—and thus survived to have children of their own. Stressed adults, especially women, are hormonally inclined to "tend and befriend," another survival impulse (Taylor, 2006).

Adults are genetically disposed to nurture babies. Logically, no reasonable person would become a parent. It is irrational to endure sleepless nights, dirty diapers, and years of self-sacrifice. But reason and logic disappear when it comes to mothering, which can be a "minefield" for destructive emotions and actions in mothers, fathers, and children (Hrdy, 2000). Yet millions of adults undergo substantial pain and expense in their quest for the joy of parenthood.

As the mother of four, I have been surprised by the power of genetic programming many times. With my first-born, I asked my pediatrician whether Bethany wasn't one of the most beautiful, perfect babies he had ever seen.

"Yes," he said, with a twinkle in his eyes, "and my patients are better looking than the patients of any other pediatrician in the city."

When my second child was 1 day old, the hospital offered to sell me a photograph of her—hairless, chinless, and with swollen eyelids. I glanced at it and said no, because the photo didn't look at all like her—it made my beautiful Rachel look almost ugly. I was similarly enamored of Elissa and Sarah.

However, I am not only a woman who loves her children; I am also a woman who loves her sleep. On one predawn morning, as I roused myself yet again to feed Sarah, I asked myself why I had chosen for the fourth time to add someone to my life who I knew would deprive me of my precious slumber. The answer, of course, is that some genetic instincts are even stronger than the instinct for comfort.

Open Wide Caregivers and babies elicit responses from each other that ensure survival of the next generation. The caregiver's role in this vital interaction is obvious, but infants do their part. They chirp, meow, whine, bleat, squeal, cry, or otherwise signal hunger—and then open their mouths wide when food arrives. Both the baby birds and the baby human obviously know what to do.

UNEP / SAY BOON FOO / THE IMAGE WORKS

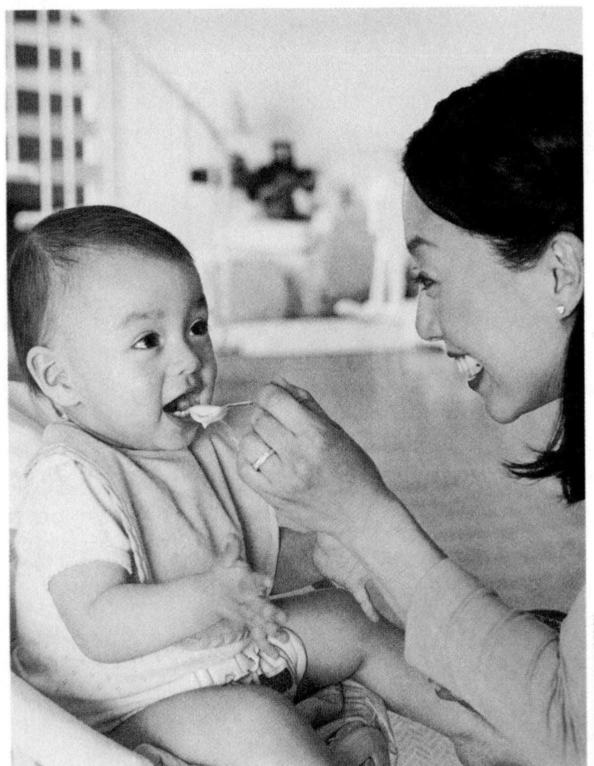

DIGITAL VISION / PUNCHSTOCK

➤Response for Students Who are Bored With Reading About Genes (from page 52): Genetic adaptation of the species has allowed people to learn from one another, thus preventing extinction of the human race. The same process might apply to individuals learning in college.

SUMMING UP

The two emergent theories point in opposite directions. Sociocultural theory looks outward, to the overarching social, historical, and cultural patterns that affect communities, families, and, ultimately, individuals. Sociocultural theory emphasizes that social and cultural groups transmit their values and skills to children through the zone of proximal development, which differs for each learner. By contrast, epigenetic theory begins by looking inward, at thousands of genes, and then moves outward to incorporate the environmental factors that directly affect the expression of those genes. Epigenetic theory includes individual genetic transmission and centuries-old, species-wide adaptation. Both of these emergent theories combine insights, data, and methods from many academic disciplines and take into account current research and techniques. ■

What Theories Contribute

Each major theory discussed in this chapter has contributed a great deal to our understanding of human development (see Table 2.4):

- Psychoanalytic theory has made us aware of the impact of early-childhood experiences, remembered or not, on subsequent development.
- Behaviorism has shown the effect that immediate responses, associations, and examples have on learning.
- Cognitive theory reveals how thoughts, beliefs, and intellectual frameworks affect every aspect of our development.
- Sociocultural theory reminds us that human development is embedded in a rich and multifaceted cultural context, evident in every social interaction.
- Epigenetic theory emphasizes the interaction between genetic instructions and surrounding contexts.

In order, these five theories focus on: early childhood, environment, mind, culture, and genes. No comprehensive view of development can ignore any of these factors.

Each theory has faced severe criticism. Psychoanalytic theory has been faulted for being too subjective; behaviorism, for being too mechanistic; cognitive theory, for undervaluing cultural diversity; sociocultural theory, for neglecting individual initiative; and epigenetic theory, for neglecting the human spirit. Depending on one's perspective, all the major theories can be considered as variations on the universal human experience (McAdams & Pals, 2006). Alternatively, each can be seen as "fundamentally irreconcilable" (Wood & Joseph, 2007, p. 57).

TABLE 2.4

Five Perspectives on Human Development

Theory	Area of Focus	Fundamental Depiction of What People Do	Relative Emphasis on Nature or Nurture?
Psychoanalytic theory	Psychosexual (Freud) or psychosocial (Erikson) stages	Battle unconscious impulses and overcome major crises	More nature (biological, sexual impulses, and parent–child bonds)
Behaviorism	Conditioning through stimulus and response	Respond to stimuli, reinforcement, and models	More nurture (direct environment produces various behaviors)
Cognitive theory	Thinking, remembering, analyzing	Seek to understand experiences while forming concepts and cognitive strategies	More nature (person's own mental activity and motivation are key)
Sociocultural theory	Social context, expressed through people, language, customs	Learn the tools, skills, and values of society through apprenticeships	More nurture (interaction of mentor and learner, within cultural context)
Epigenetic theory	Genes and factors that repress or encourage genetic expression	Develop impulses, interests, and patterns inherited from ancestors	Begins with nature; nurture is also crucial, via nutrients, toxins, and so on

Most developmentalists prefer an **eclectic perspective.** That is, rather than adopt any one of these theories exclusively, they make selective use of all of them, sometimes severely criticizing or ignoring one or another, but always open to surprises from scientific studies that cause rethinking and new theorizing. Research in human development has been characterized as "theoretical pluralism," because no single theory fully explains the behavior of humans through the life span (Dixon & Lerner, 1999).

eclectic perspective The approach taken by most developmentalists, in which they apply aspects of each of the various theories of development rather than adhering exclusively to one theory.

Being eclectic, not tied to any one theory, is beneficial because everyone, scientists as well as laypeople, tends to be biased. It is easy to dismiss alternative points of view, but using all five theories opens our eyes and minds to aspects of development that we might otherwise ignore. Remember the father at the start of this chapter whose 5-year-old said "I hate you"? If the father's first response is a slap, he might recognize that each of these five theories would suggest he reconsider that harsh reaction.

Whatever the limitations of particular theories, developmental theories time and time again illuminate life's myriad experiences and events. Development is dazzling and confusing without some perspective. Ideology and prejudice easily overcome reality without scientific theory and data. One illustration comes from the dispute that has echoed through every decade of developmental study: the nature–nurture controversy.

The Nature–Nurture Controversy

Nature refers to the genes that people inherit. **Nurture** refers to all the environmental influences, beginning with the mother's health and diet during prenatal development and continuing lifelong, including the individual's experiences with family, school, community, society.

nature A general term for the traits, capacities, and limitations that each individual inherits genetically from his or her parents at the moment of conception.

nurture A general term for all the environmental influences that affect development after an individual is conceived.

Nature and Nurture Always Interact

The nature–nurture controversy has many other names, among them *heredity versus environment* and *maturation versus learning*. Under whatever name, the basic question is: How much of any characteristic, behavior, or pattern of development is the result of genes and how much is the result of experiences?

Family responses make a child's genetic tendencies develop. Nature and nurture interact (Moffitt et al., 2006; Reiss et al., 2000). The family responses are elicited by the child's genes, but each parent's genes, status (as biological, adoptive, or stepparent), culture, experience, and so on affect how he or she acts. The combination of child and parent, nature and nurture—not one or the other alone—leads to development.

This interaction is complex—"feedback loops swirling in all directions, all inextricably intertwined" (Lippa, 2002, p. 197)—yet developmentalists seek to understand how nature and nurture interact for each trait. As one expert wrote:

> Both nature and nurture now have seats at the theoretical table, and so the really hard work now begins—to specify, in nitty gritty detail, exactly how the many biological and social environmental factors identified by recent theories weave together.
>
> *[Lippa, 2002, p. 206]*

Theories help with this "really hard work." Imagine a parent and a teacher discussing a child's behavior. Each suggests a possible explanation that makes the other say, "I never thought of that." Having five theories is like having five very perceptive observers. All five are not always on target, but it is certainly better to use alternate theories to expand perception than to stay stuck in one narrow groove. A hand functions best with five fingers, even though some fingers are more useful than others. To get back to nature and nurture, the five theories differ in how and when they see the interaction between the two, and since no simple formula describes the nature–nurture combination, it is helpful to consider many perspectives.

Theoretical Perspectives on Hyperactivity and Homosexuality

Consider two very different human characteristics: hyperactivity and homosexuality. How, and to what extent, are nature and nurture involved in each?

Some children seem always active, running around or restless even when they should be still. They are impulsive, unable to attend to anything for more than a moment. These are symptoms of attention-deficit/hyperactivity disorder, or ADHD (American Psychiatric Association, 2000). The symptoms and treatment are discussed in Chapter 11, but here let us look at how nature and nurture contribute.

Several facts support the idea that this disorder is genetic. Children with ADHD share the following characteristics:

- They are usually boys who have male relatives with the same problem.
- They are overactive in every context, home as well as school.
- They are often calmed by stimulants, such as Ritalin, Adderall, and even coffee.

This last fact convinces many: Since biochemical treatment works, the cause of ADHD must be biochemical—that is, essentially, "nature" (Faraone et al., 2005). Many researchers are looking for better drugs, believing that nature is the cause (e.g., Lopez, 2006).

But wait. There is also evidence that "nurture," or something in the environment, is the cause:

- The rapid increase in ADHD (from 1 to 5 percent of all U.S. children within the past 50 years) cannot be genetic, since selective adaptation takes centuries.
- Many environmental factors correlate with ADHD, including crowded homes, television, lead, food additives, and rigid teaching (e.g., Bateman et al., 2004).

Now consider the influence of nature and nurture on homosexuality. Most social scientists once theorized that homosexuality was the product of nurture. Psychoanalytic theory blamed a weak father and an overbearing mother; behaviorists thought that people learned sexual behavior; cognitive theory suggested that some people's thoughts about family and society led them to rebel by becoming homosexual; sociocultural theorists noted that the frequency of homosexuality in a society depended on whether everyone was expected to be homosexual during adolescence or whether homosexuals were killed, or something in between. Thus nurture, whether within the individual, the family, or the culture, was seen as causing homosexuality.

However, when scientists tried to confirm these theories, they found that children raised by homosexual couples (either adopted or the biological offspring of one of the parents) become heterosexual or homosexual in about the same proportions as children raised by heterosexuals and do not seem particularly rebellious or emotionally disturbed (Patterson, 2006; Wainwright et al., 2004). Researchers following the sociocultural perspective began to make a distinction between **sexual orientation** (erotic inclinations and thoughts) and *sexual expression* (actual behavior); those researchers found that many people have homosexual impulses (nature), which they do not express in hostile cultures but do express in more receptive cultures. Thus nurture affects only expression, not orientation. In fact, depending on definition and context, between 1 percent (self-proclaimed identity of lesbians in the United States) and 21 percent (sexual attraction to other girls among female adolescents in Norway) of people are homosexual (Savin-Williams, 2006). How much of homosexuality is nature and how much is nurture depends partly on definition.

sexual orientation A person's impulses and internal direction regarding sexual interest. A person may be oriented to people of the same sex, of the other sex, or of both sexes. Sexual orientation may differ from sexual expression, appearance, identity, or lifestyle.

No Answers Yet

Both hyperactivity and homosexuality are discussed in greater detail later in this text. This chapter is not the place to decide how much nature or nurture contributes to either of them. Epigenetic theory emphasizes that interaction is key. Choosing nature or nurture is "a dangerous quagmire." According to some psychologists:

> Those who dichotomize sexual orientation into pure biological or social causation fall into a dangerous quagmire. To deny any role for biology affirms an untenable scientific view of human development. Equally harsh and deterministic would be to deny the significance of the environment.
>
> *[Savin-Williams & Diamond, 1997, p. 235]*

Similar complications are evident for ADHD. If one monozygotic twin is hyperactive, the other twin is also likely to be (evidence for nature) but is not always (evidence for nurture) (Lehn et al., 2007).

CREATAS / PUNCHSTOCK

Learning from Dad What is this boy learning from his two fathers? Tennis.

The problem for both homosexuality and hyperactivity is that opinions about them may be harmful. For example, those who emphasize nurture worry that boisterous children are needlessly medicated for ADHD (Breggin, 2001). Many believe that, by not accepting homosexuality as part of nature, societies impair the mental health of people by making them feel ashamed about being who they are (Omoto & Kurtzman, 2006).

Impassioned but opposite opinions about nature and nurture that can lead to developmental harm are evident regarding many other issues in development, including birth defects, school curricula, aggression, marriage, divorce, and retirement. Ideology and ignorance often add to polarization. As one scholar, using the example of aggression, points out: "Individual differences in aggression can be accounted for by genetic or socialization differences, with politically conservative scientists tending to believe the former and more liberal scientists the latter" (M. Lewis, 1997, p. 102). Many questions for developmental scientists become weapons in cultural or political wars.

On nature versus nurture, "opinions shift back and forth between extreme positions" (W. Singer, 2003, p. 438). Because false assumptions lead to contradictory and even harmful policies, it is critical to use scientific inquiry and data as a buffer between opinions and conclusions. How can we avoid extremes, resist the pull of ideology, and overcome bias? Consider theory! Actually, consider more than one theory, and use theory to suggest possibilities and perspectives, which will lead to hypotheses to be explored.

SUMMING UP

As the nature–nurture controversy makes clear, theories are needed to suggest hypotheses, investigation, and, finally, answers, so that objective research can replace personal assumptions. For instance, although it is now known that the parental relationship is not the cause of homosexuality, this conclusion could not be drawn until researchers tested that psychoanalytic hypothesis. Theories are not true or false, but they serve to move the scientific process forward from the first step (ask a question) to the last (draw conclusions). Given the impact of some applications (e.g., the widespread medication of children with ADHD), such progress is sorely needed. ■

SUMMARY

What Theories Do

1. A theory provides a framework of general principles to guide research and to explain observations. Each of the five major developmental theories—psychoanalytic, behaviorist, cognitive, sociocultural, and epigenetic—interprets human development from a distinct perspective, and each provides guidance for understanding how human experiences and behaviors change over time. Good theories are practical: They aid inquiry, interpretation, and daily life.

Grand Theories

2. Psychoanalytic theory emphasizes that human actions and thoughts originate from unconscious impulses and childhood conflicts. Freud theorized that sexual urges arise during three stages of childhood development: oral, anal, and phallic. Parents' reactions to conflicts associated with their children's erotic impulses have a lasting impact on personality, according to Freud.

3. Erikson's version of psychoanalytic theory emphasizes psychosocial development, specifically as societies, cultures, and parents respond to children. Erikson described eight successive stages of psychosocial development, each involving a developmental crisis that occurs as people mature within their context.

4. Behaviorists, or learning theorists, believe that scientists should study observable and measurable behavior. Behaviorism emphasizes conditioning—a learning process. The process of conditioning occurs lifelong, as reinforcement and punishment affect behavior.

5. Social learning theory recognizes that much of human behavior is learned by observing the behavior of others. The basic process is modeling. Children are particularly susceptible to social learning, but all of us learn to be more or less effective because of social influences.

6. Cognitive theorists believe that thought processes are powerful influences on human attitudes, behavior, and development. Piaget proposed that children's thinking develops through four age-related periods, propelled by an active search for cognitive equilibrium.

Emergent Theories

7. Sociocultural theory explains human development in terms of the guidance, support, and structure provided by cultures and societies. For Vygotsky, learning occurs through social interactions, when knowledgeable members of the society guide learners through their zone of proximal development.

8. Epigenetic theory begins with genes, powerful and omnipresent, affecting every aspect of development. Genes are always affected by environmental influences, from prenatal toxins and nutrients to long-term stresses and nurturing families and friends. This interaction can halt, modify, or strengthen the effects of the genes within the person and, via selective adaptation over time, within the species.

What Theories Contribute

9. Psychoanalytic, behavioral, cognitive, sociocultural, and epigenetic theories have each aided our understanding of human development, yet no one theory is broad enough to describe the full complexity and diversity of human experience. Most developmentalists are eclectic, drawing upon many theories.

10. Each theory can shed some light on almost every developmental issue. One example is the nature–nurture controversy. All researchers agree that both genes and the environment influence all aspects of development, but the specific applications that stem from an emphasis on either nature or nurture can affect people in opposite ways. More research is needed, and theories point toward questions that need to be answered.

KEY TERMS

developmental theory (p. 33)
grand theories (p. 34)
emergent theories (p. 34)
psychoanalytic theory (p. 35)
behaviorism (p. 38)
conditioning (p. 39)
classical conditioning (p. 39)
operant conditioning (p. 39)
reinforcement (p. 39)
social learning theory (p. 42)
modeling (p. 43)
self-efficacy (p. 43)
cognitive theory (p. 43)
cognitive equilibrium (p. 44)
sociocultural theory (p. 46)
guided participation (p. 47)
zone of proximal development (p. 48)
epigenetic theory (p. 49)
selective adaptation (p. 51)
eclectic perspective (p. 55)
nature (p. 55)
nurture (p. 55)
sexual orientation (p. 56)

KEY QUESTIONS

1. Why do developmental scientists use theories?

2. How might a psychoanalytic theorist interpret a childhood experience, such as the arrival of a new sibling?

3. How can behaviorism be seen as a reaction to psychoanalytic theory?

4. According to behaviorism, why might some teenagers begin smoking cigarettes?

5. According to Piaget's theory, what happens when a person experiences cognitive disequilibrium?

6. What are the background similarities among Freud, Pavlov, and Piaget?

7. What would a teacher influenced by Vygotsky do?

8. How might sociocultural theory explain how students behave in class?

9. How might epigenetic theory explain the behavior of a pet dog or cat?

10. How might genetic diversity help a species survive?

11. Why are most developmentalists said to be eclectic?

12. Why does it make a difference whether hyperactivity stems primarily from nature or primarily from nurture?

APPLICATIONS

1. Developmentalists sometimes talk about "folk theories," which are theories developed by ordinary people, who may not know that they are theorizing. Choose three sayings commonly used in your culture, such as (from the dominant U.S. culture) "A penny saved is a penny earned" or "As the twig is bent, so grows the tree." Explain the underlying assumptions, or theory, that each saying reflects.

2. Behaviorism has been used to change personal habits. Think of a habit you'd like to change (e.g., stop smoking, exercise more, watch less TV). Count the frequency of that behavior for a week, noting the reinforcers for each instance. Then, and only then, try to develop a substitute behavior by reinforcing yourself for it. Keep careful records; chart the data over several days. What did you learn?

3. The nature–nurture debate can apply to many issues. Ask three people to tell you their theories about what factors create a criminal and how criminals should be punished or rehabilitated. Identify which theory described in this chapter is closest to each explanation you are given.

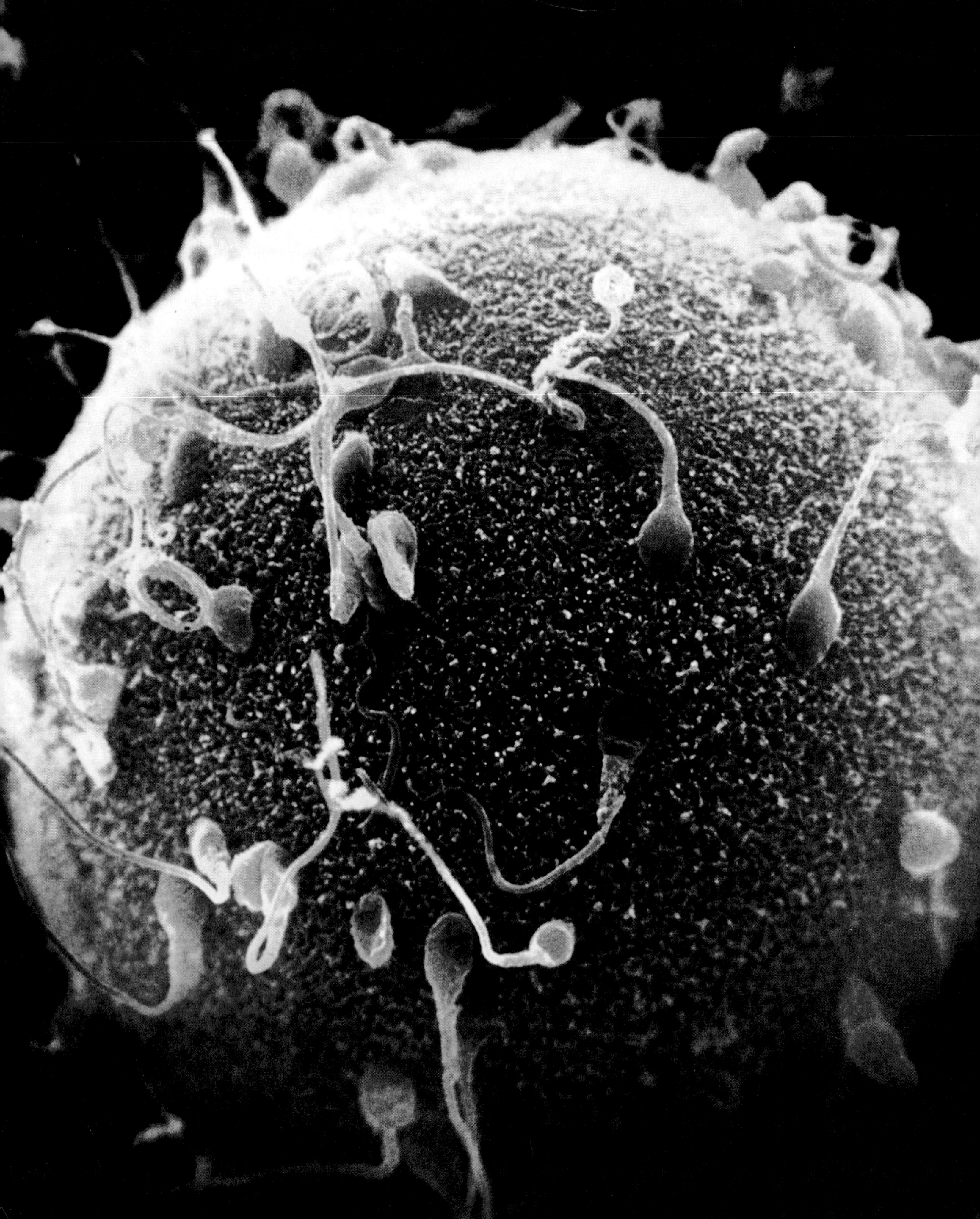

3

CHAPTER OUTLINE

Heredity and Environment

Genes play a leading role in the drama of human development, yet they rarely take center stage. Genes are pervasive and powerful, but they are also hidden and elusive.

One day when I arrived to pick up my daughter Rachel from school, another mother pulled me aside. She whispered that Rachel had fallen on her hand and that her little finger might be broken. My daughter was happily playing, but when I examined her finger, I saw that it was crooked. Trying to avoid both needless panic and medical neglect, I took Rachel home and consulted my husband. He smiled and spread out his hands, revealing the same bent little finger. Aha! An inherited abnormality, not an injury. But why had I never noticed this before?

That bent finger is one small example of millions of genetic surprises in human development. This chapter anticipates and explains some of those mysteries, going behind the scenes to reveal not only what genes are but also how they work. Many ethical issues are raised by genetics, and we will explore those, too. First, the basics.

The Genetic Code

A person is much more than a set of genetic instructions. Although life begins with genes, development is dynamic, ongoing, and interactional. Each person is unlike any other, not only because of unique instructions, locked in DNA, but also because of all the personal, social, and cultural influences that affect each person lifelong.

What Genes Are

To reveal the secrets of the genetic code, we begin by reviewing some biology. All living things are made up of tiny cells. The work of these cells is done by *proteins*. Each cell manufactures certain proteins according to instructions stored at the heart of each cell in molecules of **DNA (deoxyribonucleic acid).** Each molecule of DNA is called a **chromosome,** and these chromosomes contain the instructions to make all the proteins that a living being needs (see Figure 3.1).

Humans have 23 pairs of chromosomes (46 in all). One member of each pair is inherited from each parent. The instructions in these 46 chromosomes are organized into units called genes, with each **gene** (about 25,000

DNA (deoxyribonucleic acid) The molecule that contains the chemical instructions for cells to manufacture various proteins.

chromosome One of the 46 molecules of DNA (in 23 pairs) that each cell of the human body contains and that, together, contain all the genes. Other species have more or fewer chromosomes.

gene A section of a chromosome and the basic unit for the transmission of heredity, consisting of a string of chemicals that code for the manufacture of certain proteins.

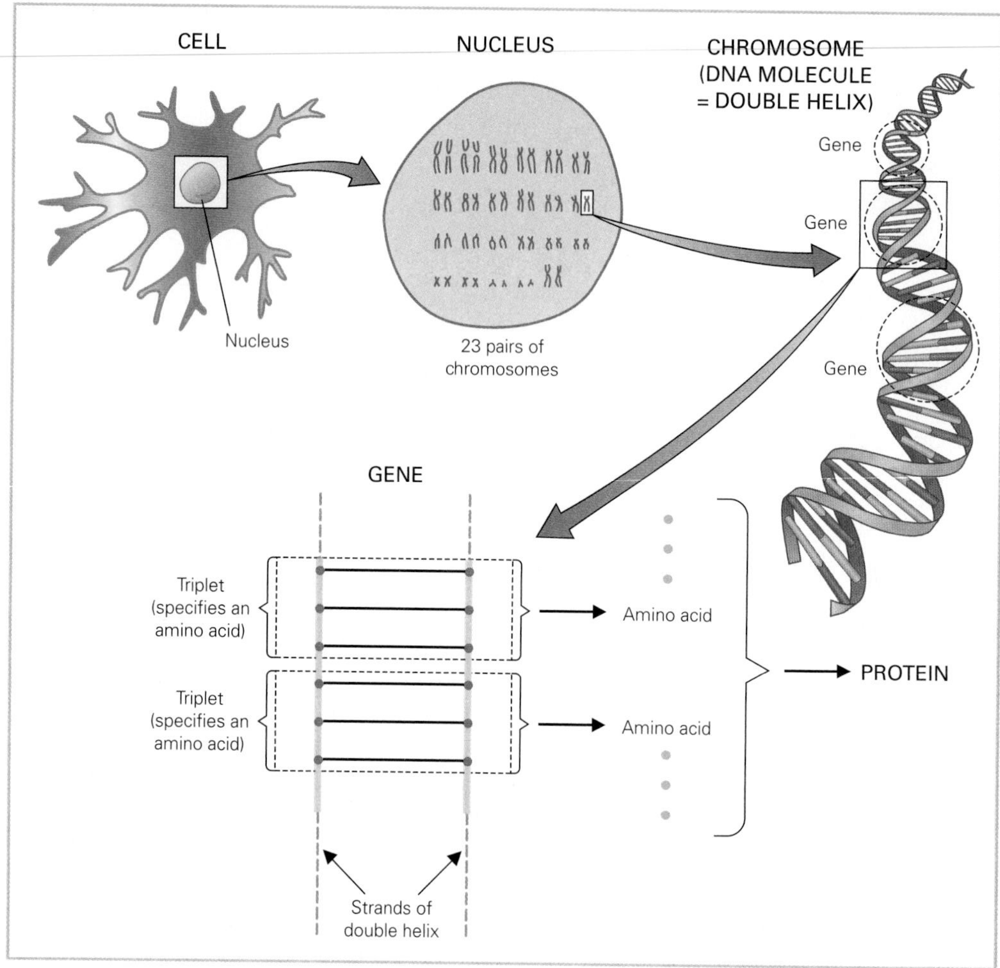

FIGURE 3.1

How Proteins Are Made The genes on the chromosomes in the nucleus of each cell instruct the cell to manufacture the proteins needed to sustain life and development.

in all for a human) located on a particular chromosome. Thus, every gene is a separate section of a chromosome, and each gene contains the instructions for making a specific type of protein.

You are familiar with proteins in the diet. But what exactly is a protein? A protein is composed of a sequence of chemicals, a long string of building blocks called *amino acids.* The recipe that a cell needs to manufacture a protein consists of instructions for stringing together the right amino acids in the right order. These instructions are transmitted to the cell via pairs of only four chemicals called *bases* (*adenine, thiamine, cytosine,* and *guanine,* abbreviated A, T, C, and G), which pair up in only four possible ways (A-T, T-A, C-G, and G-C). There are more than 3 billion pairs in all, and these are arranged in triplets (three pairs) on those 25,000 genes.

Most genes have thousands of precise pairs and triplets, making amino acids (20 types in all). Some instructions are crucial, and any alterations in their code—even a few extra repeats of a triplet—can be fatal. Other unusual codes are normal variations, and still others make no difference that scientists can see (Marcus, 2004).

genome The full set of genes that are the instructions to make an individual member of a certain species.

The entire packet of instructions to make a living organism is called the **genome.** There is a genome for every species of plant and animal. Each person (except monozygotic twins) has a slightly different code, but the human genome is 99.9 percent the same for any two persons. Our similarities far outweigh our differences.

The human genome contains about 25,000 genes (on 46 chromosomes), which instruct the developing body to produce the proteins that make each person unique, yet similar to all other humans. The total is awe-inspiring. As one expert explains:

> If each triplet is considered a word, this sequence of genes is . . . as long as 800 Bibles. If I read the genome out to you at the rate of one word per second for eight hours a day, it would take me a century. . . . This is a gigantic document, an immense book, a recipe of extravagant length, and it all fits inside the microscopic nucleus of a tiny cell that fits easily upon the head of a pin.
>
> *[Ridley, 1999, p. 7]*

There is another amazing part of human genetics: how genes work together to make human beings.

Especially for Number Crunchers A hundred years ago, it was believed that humans had 48 chromosomes, not 46; 10 years ago, it was thought that humans had 100,000 genes, not 25,000. Why?

The Beginnings of Life

Development begins at conception, when a male reproductive cell (*sperm;* plural: *sperm*), penetrates the membrane of a female reproductive cell (*ovum;* plural: *ova*). Each human reproductive cell, or **gamete,** contains 23 chromosomes, half of that person's 46. Thus, although each man has two chromosomes at each site (two at the 10th site, for instance), each of his sperm has only one chromosome at the 10th site. Randomly, about half the time it would be the chromosome 10 he inherited from his mother and half the time the chromosome 10 he inherited from his father.

Since the particular member of each chromosome pair on a given gamete is random, some gametes have one chromosome of the pair, some have the other. Each person can produce 2^{23} different gametes, more than 8 million versions of his or her own 46 chromosomes.

One in 8 million from the father's gamete, which joins with one in 8 million from the mother's gamete, is only the beginning of the vast diversity among humans. People also differ in genes, in triplets and pairs within genes, and in experiences from conception onward.

gamete A reproductive cell; that is, a sperm or ovum that can produce a new individual if it combines with a gamete from the other sex to make a zygote.

zygote The single cell formed from the fusing of two gametes, a sperm and an ovum.

genotype An organism's entire genetic inheritance, or genetic potential.

Matching Genes

When conception occurs in the usual way, some of several million sperm find their way through the vagina, cervix, and uterus and then into a fallopian tube (oviduct), where it might find an ovum. After about an hour, the nucleus of one sperm meets the nucleus of the ovum, and they form a new living cell called a **zygote.** Two reproductive cells have literally become one, and that one new cell is unlike the cells of either parent.

The chromosomes from the father match up with the chromosomes from the mother, so that the zygote contains 23 pairs of chromosomes, arranged in father/mother pairs. The genetic information on those 46 chromosomes constitutes the organism's genetic inheritance, or **genotype,** which endures throughout life, repeated in almost every cell. (Sometimes a zygote has more or fewer than 46 chromosomes, a problem discussed later in this chapter.)

In 22 of the 23 pairs of human chromosomes, both chromosomes are closely matched. Each of these 44 chromosomes is called an *autosome,* which means that it is independent (*auto* means self) of the sex chromosomes (the other 2).

The Moment of Conception This ovum is about to become a zygote. It has been penetrated by a single sperm, whose nucleus now lies next to the nucleus of the ovum. Soon, the two nuclei will fuse, bringing together about 25,000 genes to guide development.

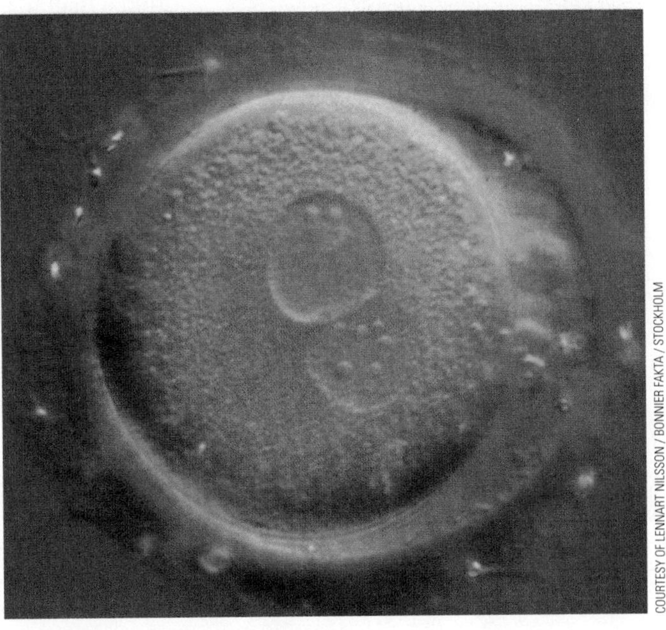

COURTESY OF LENNART NILSSON / BONNIER FAKTA / STOCKHOLM

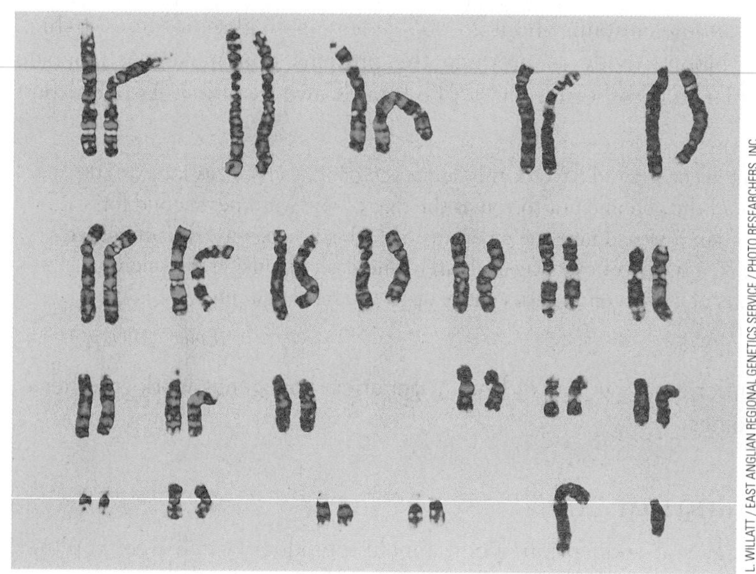

L. WILLATT / EAST ANGLIAN REGIONAL GENETICS SERVICE / PHOTO RESEARCHERS, INC

Mapping the Karyotype A *karyotype* portrays a person's chromosomes. To create a karyotype, a cell is grown in a laboratory, magnified, and then usually photographed. The photo is cut into pieces and rearranged so that the matched pairs of chromosomes are lined up from largest (*at top left*) to smallest (*at bottom right, fourth box from the left*). Shown at the bottom right are the 23rd chromosome pair: XX for a female and XY for a male.

➤**Response for Number Crunchers** (from page 63): There was some scientific evidence for the wrong numbers (e.g., chimpanzees have 48 chromosomes), but the reality is that humans tend to overestimate many things, from the number of genes to their grades on the next test.

Each autosome, from number 1 to number 22, contains hundreds of genes in the same positions and sequence, and each gene on each autosome matches with its counterpart from the other parent at conception. If the gene from one parent is exactly like the gene from the other parent, that gene pair is said to be *homozygous* (literally, "same-zygote"). The match is not always letter perfect, because the codes within a few genes vary slightly. A person with some differences between the code of one gene and that of its counterpart from the other parent is said to be *heterozygous* ("different-zygote") for that trait.

Each version of a gene that has variations is called an **allele.** A person could have the same allele from each parent and be homozygous for that trait or have different alleles and be heterozygous. Usually it does not matter which allele a person has, but some alleles are harmful, especially if the person inherits two of them.

Very rarely, a gene has no counterpart on the other autosome and that gene stands alone. But more than 99.9 percent of the genes on the 22 pairs of chromosomes find a match, usually a homozygotic match but sometimes a heterozygotic one.

allele A slight, normal variation of a particular gene.

Male or Female?

The **23rd pair** is a special case, because these are the sex chromosomes. In females, the 23rd pair is composed of two large X-shaped chromosomes. Accordingly, it is designated **XX.** In males, the 23rd pair has one large X-shaped chromosome and one smaller Y-shaped chromosome. It is called **XY.**

Because a female's 23rd pair is XX, every ovum contains either one X or the other—but always an X. And because a male's 23rd pair is XY, half of his sperm carry an X chromosome and half a Y. The X chromosome is bigger and has more genes, but the Y chromosome has a crucial gene, called SRY, that directs a developing fetus to make male organs. Thus, the sex of a baby depends on which kind of sperm penetrates the ovum—a Y sperm, creating a boy (XY), or an X sperm, creating a girl (XX) (see Figure 3.2).

The natural sex ratio at birth is close to 50/50. (The actual ratio among newborns in the United States is 52 males to 48 females.) This ratio can be affected by serious adversity, such as famine, when male fetuses are more likely to experience **spontaneous abortion** (also called *miscarriage*), or by **induced abortion,** as the following explains.

23rd pair The chromosome pair that, in humans, determines the zygote's (and hence the person's) sex. The other 22 pairs are autosomes, the same whether the 23rd pair is for a male or a female.

XX A 23rd chromosome pair consisting of two X-shaped chromosomes, one each from the mother and the father. XX zygotes become female embryos, female fetuses, and girls.

XY A 23rd chromosome pair consisting of an X-shaped chromosome from the mother and a Y-shaped chromosome from the father. XY zygotes become male embryos, male fetuses, and boys.

spontaneous abortion The naturally occurring termination of a pregnancy before the embryo or fetus is fully developed. (Also called *miscarriage*.)

induced abortion The intentional termination of a pregnancy.

issues and applications

Too Many Boys?

Historically, wars, diseases, and famine sometimes killed many people before they could reproduce. Usually, more girls survived than boys. Because there were far more women than men, and the overall population was dwindling, some cultures encouraged polygamy or single motherhood. Some also allowed men to discard wives who bore no sons (England's King Henry VIII divorced or executed five wives for this reason). Many pregnant women tried to ensure that they would have a boy by resorting to such folk customs as eating "hot" foods. These interventions worked—but only half the time!

Many contemporary cultures still favor boys. For example, in 1979, in an effort to halt starvation by slowing population growth, the government of China began forbidding Chinese couples to have more than one child. (This policy did not apply to members of minority groups or rural residents.) Poverty has been dramatically reduced in China over the two decades since then, but the policy has had one unexpected effect: too many boys. Many Chinese couples want their only child to be a boy because sons are expected to take care of their parents in old age. Millions of female fetuses were aborted, and thousands of newborn girls were made available for adoption. Since 1993, the Chinese government has prohibited prenatal testing solely to determine sex, but "the law has been spottily enforced" (French, 2005, p. 3). In the city of Guiyang, about 75 girls are born for every 100 boys (French, 2005).

Similar data come from other countries. In 1999, in Punjabi, India (where sex-selection laws similar to those in China have been enacted), only 79 females were born for every 100 males (Dugger, 2001). In Nepal, far more women use contraception after the birth of a son than a daughter (Leone et al., 2003), again skewing the sex ratio.

Is this imbalance a private matter or a public concern? Might a society with many males have more learning disabilities, drug abuse, violent crimes, wars, and suicides but fewer nurses, day-care centers, and family caregivers? Chinese doctors worry about the spread of AIDS if young men with no wives turn to risky sex (Cohen, 2004). The Chinese government now allows couples to have two children if both parents are "onlies."

But wait. Gender does not determine behavior directly. Men do not have to abuse drugs or turn to prostitutes. Although women traditionally are caregivers, many single fathers and loving grandfathers provide excellent care of children, and many husbands and sons care for elderly women. In former times, cultures adjusted to having more girls; perhaps today they could adjust to having more boys. Or is there something better about a sex ratio that is close to 50/50?

Unlike China and India, most nations have no laws against sex selection, or about any other attempt to create "designer babies" —children who have the genes the parents prefer. Should they?

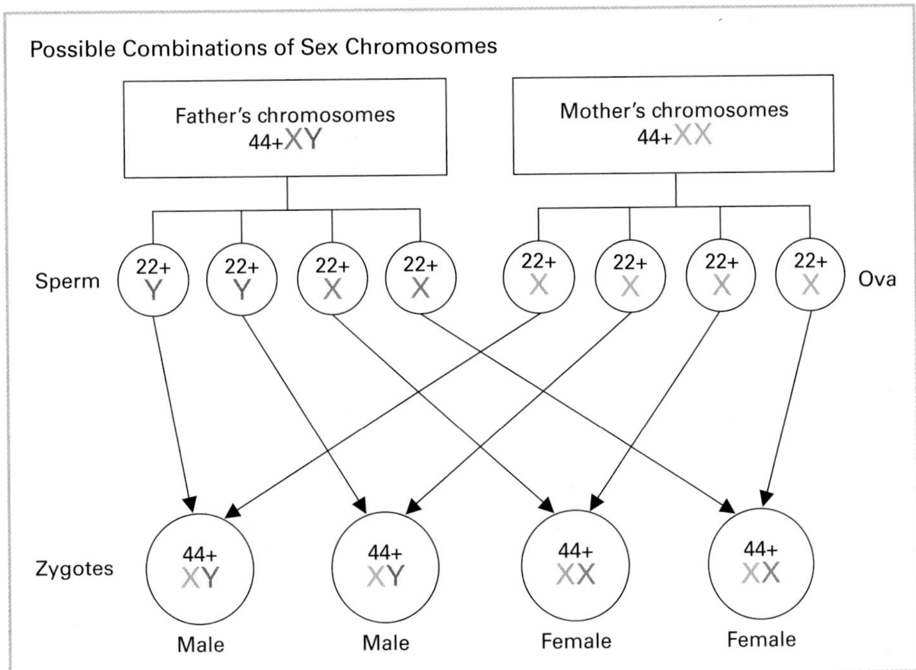

FIGURE 3.2

Determining a Zygote's Sex Any given couple can produce four possible combinations of sex chromosomes; two lead to female children and two, to male. In terms of the future person's sex, it does not matter which of the mother's Xs the zygote inherited. All that matters is whether the father's Y sperm or X sperm fertilized the ovum. However, for X-linked conditions it matters a great deal, because typically one, but not both, of the mother's Xs carries the trait.

Observation Quiz (see answer, page 66): In the chapter-opening photograph (p. 60), can you distinguish the Y sperm from the X sperm?

➤Answer to Observation Quiz (from page 65): Probably not. The Y sperm are slightly smaller, which can be detected via scientific analysis (some cattle breeders raise only steers using such analysis), but visual inspection, even magnified as in the photo, may be inaccurate.

SUMMING UP

The fusion of two gametes (sperm and ovum) creates a zygote, a tiny one-celled creature that has the potential to develop into a human being. One way to describe that process is chemically: DNA is composed of four chemicals that pair up; three of those pairs (a triplet) direct the formation of an amino acid; amino acids in a particular sequence make up proteins; and proteins make a person. Another way to describe it is with numbers: The genetic code for a human being consists of about 3 billion base pairs on 25,000 genes on 46 chromosomes, half from the mother and half from the father. The father's 23rd chromosome pair is XY, which means that half his sperm are X and half are Y; thus, the future baby's sex is determined by which sperm penetrates the ovum and forms a zygote. ■

From One Cell to Many

As already explained, when sperm and ovum combine into a zygote, they establish the *genotype:* all the genes that the developing person has. Creation of an actual person from one cell involves several complex processes of duplication of genetic information, cell division, and differentiation of cells into different types.

phenotype The observable characteristics of a person, including appearance, personality, intelligence, and all other traits.

Some genes on the genotype are ignored and others amplified in the formation of the **phenotype,** which is the actual appearance and manifest behavior of the person. Let's begin by describing the early development of that one original cell.

New Cells, New Functions

Within hours after conception, the zygote begins *duplication* and *division.* First, the 23 pairs of chromosomes duplicate, forming two complete sets of the genome. These two sets move toward opposite sides of the zygote, and the single cell splits neatly down the middle into two cells, each containing the original genetic code. These two cells duplicate and divide, becoming four, which duplicate and divide, becoming eight, and so on.

By the time you (or I, or any other person) were born, your original zygote had become about 10 trillion cells. By adulthood, those cells had become more than 100 trillion. But no matter how large the total number, no matter how much division and duplication occur, almost every cell carries an exact copy of the complete genetic instructions inherited by the one-celled zygote. This explains why DNA testing of any body cell, even one from a drop of blood or a snip of hair, can identify "the real father," "the guilty criminal," or "the long-lost brother."

The fact that every cell in the embryo contains the developing human being's complete genetic code does not mean that any cell could become a person—far from it. At about the eight-cell stage, a third process, *differentiation,* is added to duplication and division. Cells begin to specialize, taking different forms and reproducing at various rates, depending on where they are located. As one expert explains, "We are sitting with parts of our body that could have been used for thinking" (Gottlieb, 2002, p. 172).

As a result of this specialization and differentiation, very early in development cells change from being able to become any part of a creature to being able to become only one part—an eye or a finger, for instance. All cells carry the same genetic information, but cells take on new functions as needed and cannot switch back. An eyelash cannot become a fingernail, although both have the same instructions as the original cell that could have become an eyelash or a fingernail.

Certain genes switch on at particular times, a fact that helps us understand development because it explains why children should not be expected to act like adults. One fascinating aspect of human genetics is that almost half of all human genes affect the brain, not other parts of the body. Genes not only develop neurological functions, they also activate specific aspects of cognitive development, such as the ability to think about abstractions or to plan ahead (Marcus, 2004), neither of which young children can do. Even learning a language begins with genetically triggered maturation of certain brain areas.

Keep in mind that "genes merely produce proteins, not mature traits" (Gottlieb, 2002, p. 164). In other words, the genotype instigates body and brain formation, but the phenotype (the visible traits and behaviors) depends on many genes and on the environment. A zygote might have the genes for becoming, say, a musical genius, but that potential will not be realized without the contributions of many other factors. Epigenesis (see Chapter 2) is pervasive.

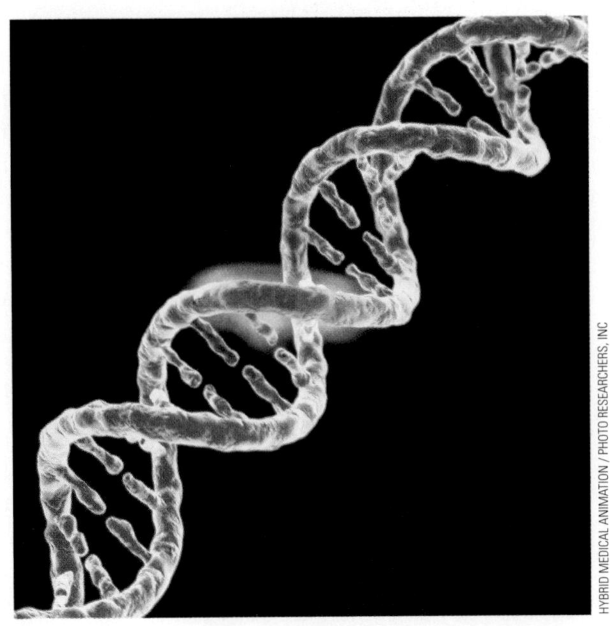

HYBRID MEDICAL ANIMATION / PHOTO RESEARCHERS, INC

Twelve of Three Billion Pairs This is a computer illustration of a small segment of one gene, with several triplets. Even a small difference in one gene, such as a few extra triplets, can cause major changes in the phenotype of a person.

Gene–Gene Interactions

Conception brings together genetic instructions from both parents for every human characteristic. Exactly how do these instructions influence the specific traits that a given offspring inherits? The answer is quite complex, because most traits are **polygenic**—affected by many genes—and **multifactorial**—influenced by many factors.

The **Human Genome Project** is the international effort to map the human genome. Its researchers have found that humans have only about 25,000 genes, 99 percent of which are present in the genomes of other creatures as well. For example, the eyes of flies, mice, and people all originate from the Pax6 gene; another gene produces legs for a butterfly, a cat, a centipede, and a person.

The genetic similarity among living creatures might make you wonder what accounts for the differences. The genomes of humans and chimpanzees are more than 99 percent identical, so why are humans and chimps so different? The answer lies in the activities of 100 or so "regulator" genes, which influence thousands of other genes (Marcus, 2004). Regulator genes make a creature who talks, walks, and thinks as humans do, unlike other animals. Regulator genes regulate genetic interaction, and that makes all the difference.

Human brain size (about 1,400 cubic centimeters) is highly heritable and is quite similar among humans worldwide, especially when compared with the small brains (about 370 cubic centimeters) of our nearest relatives, the chimpanzees (Holden, 2006). Of course, bigger animals (elephants) have bigger brains, but the proportion of brain to body is significantly greater for humans than for other creatures.

Now we'll look at some specifics of gene interaction, in those cases in which the genes exist in several versions (alleles).

polygenic Referring to a trait that is influenced by many genes.

multifactorial Referring to a trait that is affected by many factors, both genetic and environmental.

Human Genome Project An international effort to map the complete human genetic code. This effort was essentially completed in 2001, though analysis is ongoing.

Additive Heredity

Some alleles are **additive genes** because their effects add up to influence the phenotype. When genes interact additively, the trait reflects the contributions of all the genes that are involved. Height, hair curliness, and skin color, for instance, are usually the result of additive genes. Indeed, height is affected by an estimated 100 genes, each contributing a small amount, some to make a person a little taller than average, some a little shorter (Little, 2002).

additive gene A gene that has several alleles, each of which contributes to the final phenotype (such as skin color or height).

In modern nations, most people have ancestors of various heights, hair curliness, skin color, and so on, so their children's phenotype may not reflect the parents' phenotypes, although it always reflects their genotypes. My daughter Rachel (with the crooked little finger) is of average height, shorter than either my husband or I but taller than either of her grandmothers. She apparently inherited some of her grandmothers' genes for relatively short height from us.

Especially for Future Parents Suppose you wanted your daughters to be short and your sons to be tall. Could you achieve that?

How any additive trait turns out depends on all the genes (half from each parent) a child happens to inherit. All additive genes contribute something to the phenotype. To make this more complex, genes interact with each other (called *epistasis*) to produce traits that no ancestor had (Grigorenko, 2003). For instance, the SRY gene on the Y chromosome adds hormones, and one effect of those hormones is to make the boy grow taller. That adds about three inches of height that would not be added if all the autosomes (which carry the height genes) were the same but the 23rd pair was XX instead of XY, so the person was a girl with no SRY.

Dominant–Recessive Heredity

Some alleles are not additive. Of course, the fact that a particular allele is nonadditive doesn't matter with homozygotic pairs, because both genes provide the same instructions. It does matter for heterozygotic pairs. In one nonadditive form, alleles are said to interact in a **dominant–recessive pattern,** which occurs when one allele, the *dominant gene,* is more influential than the other, the *recessive gene.*

dominant–recessive pattern The interaction of a pair of alleles in such a way that the phenotype reveals the influence of one allele (the dominant gene) more than that of the other (the recessive gene).

Sometimes the dominant gene entirely controls the characteristic. In this case, the recessive gene is carried on the genotype but has no obvious effect on the phenotype. For example, blood type B is dominant and blood type O is recessive, which means that a person whose genotype is BO would have B blood type.

An additional factor with blood is Rh-positive or -negative. Rh-negative is recessive, so a person whose blood genotype is Rh-positive *and* Rh-negative would have Rh-positive blood. (Some of the complex relationships of blood genotype and phenotype are shown in Appendix A, p. A-3). For blood transfusion the phenotype, not the genotype, matters.

Blue eyes are determined by a recessive allele and brown eyes by a dominant one. Many recessive traits are not completely hidden. For example, a phenotype of hazel eyes hints at a recessive blue-eye gene.

A special case of the dominant–recessive pattern occurs with genes that are **X-linked,** located on the X chromosome. If an X-linked gene is recessive—as are the genes for most forms of color blindness, many allergies, several diseases, and some learning disabilities—the fact that it is on the X chromosome is critical (see Table 3.1).

X-linked Referring to a gene carried on the X chromosome. If a boy inherits an X-linked recessive trait from his mother, he expresses that trait, since the Y from his father has no counteracting gene. Girls are more likely to be carriers of X-linked traits but are less likely to express them.

Since the Y chromosome is much smaller than the X, an X-linked recessive gene almost always has no dominant counterpart on the Y. For this reason, recessive traits carried on the X chromosome affect the phenotypes of sons much more often than those of daughters (who have another X, which usually has the dominant normal gene). This explains, for instance, why males who have an X-linked disorder, such as color blindness, inherited it from their mothers.

More Complications

As complex as the preceding explanation may seem, it simplifies genetic interaction by making genes appear to be separately functioning entities. But remember that genes merely direct the creation of 20 types of amino acids, which combine to produce thousands of proteins, which then form the body's structures and direct biochemical functions. The proteins of each cell interact with other proteins, nutrients, and toxins.

For any living creature, the outcome of these interactions is difficult to predict. A small alteration in the sequence of base pairs or several extra repetitions in one triplet may be inconsequential or may cascade to create a major problem. The consequences depend on dozens of factors, many of which are not yet understood (Kirkwood, 2003; Plomin & McGuffin, 2003).

TABLE 3.1

The 23rd Pair and X-Linked Color Blindness

X indicates an X chromosome with the X-linked gene for color blindness

23rd Pair	Phenotype	Genotype	Next Generation
1. XX	Normal woman	Not a carrier	No color blindness from mother
2. XY	Normal man	Normal X from mother	No color blindness from father
3. XX	Normal woman	Carrier from father	Half her children will inherit her X. The girls with her X will be carriers; the boys with her X will be color-blind.
4. XX	Normal woman	Carrier from mother	Half her children will inherit her X. The girls with her X will be carriers; the boys with her X will be color-blind.
5. XY	Color-blind man	Inherited from mother	All his daughters will have his X. None of his sons will have his X. All his children will have normal vision, unless their mother also had an X for color blindness.
6. XX	Color-blind woman (rare)	Inherited from both parents	Every child will have one X from her. Therefore, every son will be color-blind. Daughters will be only carriers, unless they also inherit an X from the father, as their mother did.

For example, although females are always XX, one of those X chromosomes is relatively inactive. It seems random whether the dominant X is the one from the mother or the father, and it is not known what the implications are. This is just one example of hundreds of newly discovered complications, especially for human development. To understand these complications, scientists look closely at twins and clones.

Twins

Although every zygote is genetically unique (i.e., has a unique genotype) and most newborns are similarly unique, there is one human exception: monozygotic multiple births.

Rarely—about once in 250 conceptions—on the first day of development, cells not only duplicate but split completely apart, creating two, or four, or even eight identical, separate zygotes. They originate from one (*mono*) zygote. If each implants and grows, they become multiple births, usually **monozygotic (MZ) twins** (also called *identical twins*) but sometimes monozygotic quadruplets or even octuplets.

monozygotic (MZ) twins Twins who originate from one zygote that splits apart very early in development. (Also called *identical twins*.) Other monozygotic multiple births (for example, quadruplets) can occur as well.

Because monozygotic twins originate from the same zygote, their genotype is the same, as are their genetic instructions for physical appearance, psychological traits, vulnerability to diseases, and everything else. One monozygotic twin can donate a kidney for surgical implantation in the other twin with no risk of organ rejection.

Remember that genes start development, affecting every trait, but environment (including chance) is crucial (Kirkwood, 2003). Monozygotic twins differ in birthweight because of where in the mother's uterus each happened to be. Parents treat twins differently, sometimes favoring the larger one, sometimes the smaller (Caspi et al., 2004; Piontelli, 2002).

When monozygotic twins differ in a genetic trait, that helps scientists recognize a nongenetic effect. For example, a pair of 13-year-old monozygotic twins, Brian and Jason, were raised together, which means that their nature (as MZ twins) is

Same Birthday, Same (or Different?) Genes Twins who are of different sexes or who have obvious differences in personality are dizygotic, sharing only half of their genes. Many same-sex twins with similar temperaments are dizygotic as well. One of these twin pairs is dizygotic; the other is monozygotic.

Observation Quiz (see answer, page 72): Can you tell which pair is monozygotic?

identical and much of their environment is shared. Both have Asperger syndrome (explained in Chapter 11). However, Asperger's makes Brian shy and socially awkward, in ways that are quite common for 13-year-olds. He probably would not have been diagnosed were it not for Jason, who displays much more noticeable symptoms of Asperger syndrome—he "fails miserably" in social interaction and his "stilted conversations typically include inappropriate questions and comments" (Bower, 2006, p. 106). Why is one monozygotic twin so much more impaired than the other? Probably because Brian breathed normally at birth, but Jason did not breathe for several seconds until doctors administered oxygen. That loss of oxygen impaired his brain. These boys show that nature matters (both have Asperger's) but that nurture does as well.

dizygotic (DZ) twins Twins who are formed when two separate ova are fertilized by two separate sperm at roughly the same time. (Also called *fraternal twins.*)

Most twins (about two-thirds) are **dizygotic (DZ) twins,** also called *fraternal twins*. They began life as two separate zygotes created by the fertilization of two ova by two sperm at roughly the same time. (Usually, only one ovum is released per month, but sometimes two or more ova become available for fertilization.)

The incidence of dizygotic twins varies by ethnicity and age. For example, DZ twins occur about once in every 11 births among Yoruba women from Nigeria; once in 100 births among British women; and once in 700 births among Japanese women (Gall, 1996; Piontelli, 2002). Women in their late 30s are three times as likely to have DZ twins as are women in their early 20s.

Like all siblings from the same parents, DZ twins have about half of their genes in common. And like any other siblings, they can differ markedly (including in whether they are male or female) or they can look quite similar. Some look so much alike that only genetic tests can determine whether they are monozygotic or dizygotic.

Clones

clone An organism that is produced from another organism through artificial replication of cells and is genetically identical to that organism.

A **clone** is an organism that is produced from another organism through artificial replication of cells and is genetically identical to that organism. Unlike monozygotic twins, which occur naturally, clones are artificially created. Cloning of animals involves removing a cell from a living creature and making it develop into another, genetically identical creature. Since every cell of an organism carries the entire genetic code, cloning is theoretically possible for all living things.

Cloning is routine with plants but is difficult with animals; more than 99 percent of all cloning attempts with animals have failed. The most famous successful animal clone was a sheep named Dolly, created in Scotland in 1997 when a cell from the mammary gland of one ewe was chemically induced to begin duplicating; the embryo was then implanted in the uterus of another ewe. Dolly was the only live birth that resulted from 434 cloning attempts. She aged rapidly and died at age 6, young for a ewe. The scientists who created her have described the hazards of cloning (Wilmut & Highfield, 2006).

Mice are the only mammals that are successfully cloned, time and again. Many other research techniques—including interbreeding, cross-breeding, knocking out genes (disabling a gene to learn its function), and drug dosing—that are unethical with people and that would take years with most animals are used with mice. Mice are helping social scientists learn how to reverse addiction (Crabbe, 2003) and prevent mental illness (Williams, 2003).

For ethical reasons, cloning of humans is illegal, although cloning of cells (not whole organisms) is part of research on many human diseases. Technically, human clones would be possible via **in vitro fertilization (IVF).** Ova are surgically removed from a woman and mixed with sperm. If fertilization occurs, viable zygotes begin to duplicate in vitro, which literally means "in glass" (i.e., a glass laboratory dish). In duplication, sometimes one cell is removed to test for abnormal genes (done only for serious genetic conditions); if the severe condition is not found, the remaining cells are inserted into the woman's uterus to develop into a healthy baby. This is not cloning, and doing so raises no ethical issues.

It is theoretically possible, with IVF, to extract one of those early cells, allow it to duplicate and divide, insert both groups of cells into a woman, and hope that both will implant. This would result in monozygotic twins, a form of cloning that is illegal.

Not at all illegal is the usual in vitro fertilization method. After several zygotes are created and reach the 4- or 8-cell stage, the developing cells are inserted into the uterus. About a third of the time, at least one zygote implants and develops into a baby. Almost half of those times, two or more cell masses implant, and twins or other multiples occur (Society for Assisted Reproductive Technology & American Society for Reproductive Medicine, 2002).

Assisted Reproduction

Depending primarily on age, between 2 and 30 percent of all couples are troubled by **infertility,** defined as the inability to produce a baby after at least a year of trying. The lowest rates of infertility are among emerging adults (age 18–25) who have avoided drugs and sexually transmitted diseases and who live in medically advanced nations; the highest rates worldwide are probably among older couples in South Africa. About one-third of all infertility originates with the woman and one-third with the man; the other one-third is of unknown origin. Counseling, as well as medical intervention, usually includes both partners (Covington & Burns, 2006).

In developed nations, infertile couples often turn to **assisted reproductive technology (ART).** One simple treatment for some female infertility is to use drugs to cause ovulation. For male infertility, sperm from a donor may be inserted into the female partner's uterus, a process called *artificial insemination,* which has been in use for 50 years.

Increasingly common are various techniques that begin with in vitro fertilization, as just described. Although failure is more common than success, a million IVF children (more than half of them twins or triplets) have been born in 40 nations since the first "test-tube" baby was born in England in 1978 (Gerris et al., 2004). The usual reason for IVF is that a woman fails to ovulate or has blocked fallopian tubes. Another reason is low sperm production, which is overcome by injecting a single viable sperm into an ovum (Bentley & Mascie-Taylor, 2000).

Many methods for overcoming infertility result in multiple births. In the United States, triplet births have increased by 500 percent since 1980, according

➤Response for Future Parents (from page 68): Yes, but you wouldn't want to. You would have to choose one mate for your sons and another for your daughters, and you would still have to use sex-selection methods. Even so, it might not work, given all the genes on your genotype. More important, the effort would be unethical, unnatural, and possibly illegal.

in vitro fertilization (IVF) Fertilization that takes place outside a woman's body (as in a glass laboratory dish). Sperm are mixed with ova that have been surgically removed from the woman's ovary. If the combination produces a zygote, it is inserted into the woman's uterus, where it may implant and develop into a baby.

infertility The inability to produce a baby after at least a year of trying to conceive via sexual intercourse.

assisted reproductive technology (ART) A general term for the techniques designed to help infertile couples conceive and then sustain a pregnancy.

to the Center for Health Statistics, and twin births have almost doubled (U.S. Bureau of the Census, 2004). Many couples who thought they could never have any children now have two or three, to the delight of some parents but not of physicians (Newton et al., 2007). (ART is further discussed in Chapter 20.)

in person

"I Am Not Happy with Me"

Successful IVF produces several zygotes. All could be inserted; some could be frozen for later use; some could be used for research; or some could be discarded. Each option is permitted by some nations, clinics, and couples and forbidden by others (Jones & Cohen, 2001). One factor in deciding which option to use is cost: In the United States, each IVF attempt costs about $12,000, with no guarantee of success. Some couples travel to nations with lower costs; others hope to improve their odds by having several zygotes implanted (Newton et al., 2007).

Implantation of more than one zygote creates problems, however. For humans, birthing more than one baby is hazardous for both mother and newborns. Complications of pregnancy, including high blood pressure and toxemia, are common, and multiples are almost always born small and early—twins three weeks early on average, triplets six weeks, and quadruplets nine weeks.

Generally, the more embryos that develop together, the smaller, less mature, and more vulnerable each one is. Throughout life, multiples have higher rates of early death, disease, and disabilities. Triplets, for example, produce more stress in their parents, develop language more slowly, and form weaker social bonds than do equally small single babies or twins (Feldman & Eidelman, 2004).

Since fertility treatments are one cause of multiples, Finland allows only two zygotes to be implanted after in vitro fertilization. The limit is three in Norway and four in several other nations. In Belgium, the government pays only for single-embryo transfers, a policy that has reduced the rate of twins by half (Ombelet, 2007). The United States has no legal limit, but many doctors recommend selective abortion if multiple embryos begin to develop.

ART can separate biological parenthood from child rearing. IVF can be done with donated sperm and ova, with the resulting embryos growing in the uterus of another woman, who can allow yet another couple to adopt the newborn. At birth, that infant already has five "parents." Is that ethical?

Perhaps all ART is unethical, when thousands of children with special needs await loving adoptive parents. When I suggested this to a friend who was infertile, she called me "insensitive, arrogant, and ignorant" because my children had been easily conceived. She said it was no more ethical of me to conceive naturally than for her to use ART. Since then I have read the words of many infertile women. One wrote:

> I just cannot imagine ever feeling good about anything again. I do not even know if my husband will stay with me when he realizes that children are not an option for us. My guess is he will find someone else who will be able to give him a baby. Since I cannot do that, I cannot imagine that he would be happy with me. I am not happy with me.
>
> *[quoted in Deveraux & Hammerman, 1998]*

Complex social issues collide with the personal urge to procreate (Covington & Burns, 2006; Dooley et al., 2003). Compassionate, thoughtful people, including many developmentalists, disagree.

➤Answer to Observation Quiz (from page 70): The Japanese American girls are the monozygotic twins. If you were not sure, look at their teeth, their eyebrows, and the shape of their faces, compared with the ears and chins of the boys.

SUMMING UP

A person's genotype influences almost every characteristic. Genes interact additively, recessively, and in many other ways; almost every trait is polygenic. Human diversity is guaranteed not only by the process of gamete formation and conception but also by life experiences. Each zygote is unlike any other ever conceived; diversity becomes even greater.

Most twins are dizygotic, with no more genes in common than any other siblings. About a third are monozygotic, developing from one zygote and hence having the same genotype. Clones also have the same genotype as the creature they are derived from, but cloning is illegal for humans and problematic for other animals. Some infertile couples turn to assisted reproductive technology (ART) to conceive. ■

From Genotype to Phenotype

The main goal of this chapter is to help every reader grasp the complexity of the interaction between genotype and phenotype. Hundreds of scientists in many nations have studied thousands of twins, both monozygotic and dizygotic, raised together in the same home and raised separately in different homes. When this research began, scientists assumed that monozygotic twins reared together would share both genes and environment and that monozygotic twins raised apart would have the same genes but contrasting environments. This assumption led scientists to hope that twin studies would allow them to distinguish genetic influences from environmental ones (e.g., Segal, 1999).

Members of the next generation of scientists were skeptical. They undertook more research—on stepsiblings, adopted siblings raised together, biological siblings raised apart, and all kinds of twins raised in all kinds of homes (e.g., Reiss et al., 2000; see Research Design). They benefited from molecular analysis, mouse genomes, linkage analysis, and many other methods developed not only to treat physical illness but also used to understand inheritance of psychological traits. They discovered four generalities that virtually all developmentalists accept:

1. Genes affect every aspect of human behavior, including social and cognitive behavior.
2. Most environmental influences on children raised in the same home are *not* shared.
3. Each child's genes elicit other people's responses, and these responses shape development. In other words, a child's environment is partly the result of his or her genes.
4. Children, adolescents, and especially adults choose environments that are compatible with their genes (called *niche-picking*), and thus genetic influences *increase* in adulthood.

[*Ellis & Bjorklund, 2005; Plomin et al., 2003; Posthuma et al., 2003*]

Research Design

Scientists: David Reiss, Jenae M. Neiderhiser, E. Mavis Hetherington, and Robert Plomin.

Publication: *The Relationship Code* (Harvard University Press, 2000), as well as many journals.

Participants: 720 families, each with two children aged 10–18 with varied genetic links: monozygotic twins, dizygotic twins, full siblings, half siblings, and unrelated siblings with biological and stepparents.

Design: Dozens of checklists, interviews, and observations, including longitudinal measures, were used to indicate emotions and cognitive abilities of parents and adolescents, as well as their interactions. Extensive analysis was undertaken to distinguish genetic and environmental effects.

Major conclusion: Genes have a strong impact on every characteristic, but family structure and parental style modify genetic influence.

Comment: By including siblings with so many kinds of relationships to each other and to their parents, with multiple, longitudinal measures, this study untangles some complex nature–nurture interactions.

As you learn more about the interactions among genetic and nongenetic influences, remember to distinguish between a person's *genotype*, or genetic *potential*, and his or her *phenotype*, the actual *expression* of that genetic inheritance in physical appearance, health, intelligence, and actions.

Everyone has many genes in his or her genotype that are not expressed in the phenotype. In genetic terms, each person is a **carrier** of unexpressed genes; that is, a person might "carry" an allele on his sperm or her ova and transmit it to offspring. Only rarely does one gene, or even one pair, cause an identifiable disorder (some instances are described later in this chapter), but combinations of genes might affect the phenotype, additively or in some other way. Schizophrenia, for instance, probably results from many genes, and one reason for the varied types, severity, and developmental patterns of schizophrenia is that each person has a different combination of genes. Each person also has unique experiences, of course, and that difference also affects every mental illness.

carrier A person whose genotype includes a gene that is not expressed in the phenotype. Such an unexpressed gene occurs in half of the carrier's gametes and thus is passed on to half of the carrier's children, who will most likely be carriers, too. Generally, only when the gene is inherited from both parents does the characteristic appear in the phenotype.

About half of all genes affect the brain, not the rest of the body. Thus, personality patterns and cognitive skills are affected by thousands of genetic combinations, with each gene having the potential for small but measurable effects. The specifics depend on other genes, on family, and on culture (Vogler, 2006). A team of eight scientists who are working to decipher the coding variations of 11 million alleles (called the Hapmap Project) put it this way:

> Many different genes distributed throughout the human genome contribute to the total genetic variability of a particular complex trait, with any single gene accounting for no more than a few percent of the overall variability.
>
> [*Hinds et al., 2005, p. 1079*]

COURTESY OF EDNA MORLOK

Too Cute? This portrait of the Genain sisters was taken 20 years before they all developed schizophrenia. However, from their identical hair ribbons to the identical position of their feet, it is apparent that their unusual status as quadruplets set them apart as curiosities. Could their life in the spotlight have nurtured their potential for schizophrenia? There is no way to know for sure.

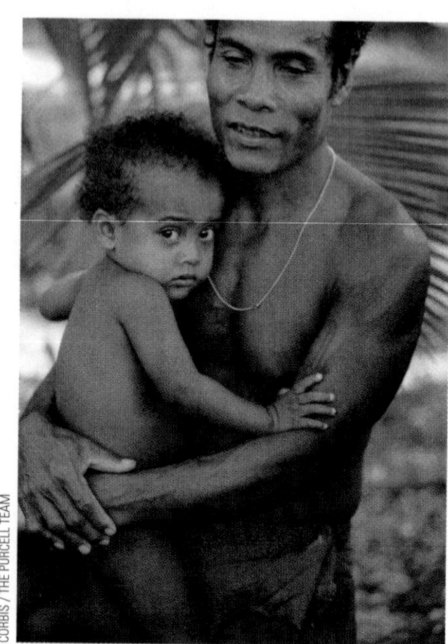

CORBIS / THE PURCELL TEAM

Shyness Is Universal Inhibition is a psychological trait that is influenced by genetics. It is more common at some ages (late infancy and early adolescence) and in some gene pools (natives of northern Europe and East Asia) than others. But every community includes some individuals who are unmistakably shy, such as this toddler in Woleai, more than 3,000 miles west of Hawaii.

Thus, when something is "genetic," that does not mean that its genetic origins are substantial, fixed, or unalterable. It means that it is part of a person's basic foundation, affecting many aspects of life but determining none (T. D. Johnston & L. Edwards, 2002). Rachel's little finger, mentioned in the chapter's opening, was the product of genes, but it might have not been crooked if her prenatal environment had been different.

Every trait, action, and attitude has a genetic component: Without genes, no behavior could exist. But without environment, no gene could be expressed. Now we examine two complex traits: addiction and visual acuity. As you read about two specific expressions (alcoholism and nearsightedness) of those traits, you will see that understanding the progression from genotype to phenotype has many practical uses.

Addiction

At various times, drug addiction, including alcoholism, has been considered a moral weakness and a personality defect. Addicts were locked up in jails or in mental institutions. Some nations tried to stop alcoholism by making alcohol illegal, as the United States did from 1919 to 1933, and most nations have laws forbidding certain drugs and taxes to discourage use of other drugs.

Nonaddicts have long wondered why addicts don't just quit. Now we know that inherited biochemistry makes people vulnerable to various addictions. Anyone can abuse drugs and alcohol, but genes create an addictive pull that can be overpowering, extremely weak, or somewhere in between (Heath et al., 2003).

Alcoholism, particularly, has been studied for decades (Agarwal & Seitz, 2001). The brain patterns of alcoholics' sons who have never consumed alcohol differ from sons of nonalcoholics. The way a person's body digests and metabolizes alcohol allows some people to "hold their liquor" without getting sick and therefore to drink too much; it causes others, notably many East Asians, to sweat and become red-faced after just a few sips. This embarrassing response is one reason many Asians avoid alcohol (Heath et al., 2003).

RAYMOND GEHMAN / CORBIS

Early Death or Long Life? Jerzy Skibo is a Polish farmer pausing to enjoy his lunch of sausage, cheese, and wine. This diet could be unhealthy if he is genetically vulnerable to heart disease or alcoholism. Or he might have protective genes and live to age 100, as some Polish farmers do.

Among people of all ethnicities, reactions to alcohol vary, just as reactions to prescription drugs or many foods vary. Some drinkers become sleepy, others nauseated, others aggressive, and others euphoric. Each of these reactions makes that person more, or less, likely to have another drink.

Especially for People Who Are Easily Bored Is your wish for excitement likely to lead to addiction?

Alcoholism is not simply biochemical. As with all addictions, it is psychological as well. Certain personality traits (a quick temper, a readiness to take risks, and a high level of anxiety) make it more likely that a person will drink and use drugs (Bau et al., 2001; Nielsen et al., 1998). Certain contexts, such as many fraternity parties, make it hard not to drink; other contexts, such as a church in a "dry" county, make it hard to drink.

Gender also mitigates or increases alcoholism, depending on culture. For biological reasons (body size, fat composition, genes for metabolism), women become drunk on less alcohol than men do. In Japan, although women have the same genes as men for metabolizing alcohol, they drink only about a tenth as much. When Japanese women live in the United States, their average alcohol consumption increases about fivefold (Higuchi et al., 1996).

Especially for College Students Who Enjoy a Party You wonder if one of your male friends is an alcoholic because he sometimes drinks too much. He may be OK, though, because he can still talk clearly after drinking twice as much as you do. What should you ask him?

Thus, culture is crucial. If people inherit genes that predispose them to alcoholism but live where alcohol is unavailable (in rural Saudi Arabia, for example), the genotype will never be expressed in the phenotype. Similarly, if alcohol-prone children grow up where alcohol abounds but belong to a religious group that forbids it (such as Seventh-Day Adventists in California), they may escape their genetic destiny. Nature *and* nurture create the alcoholic.

Visual Acuity

Almost every factor that affects overall development also affects vision. Remember that we study change over the life span. People see differently depending on their age:

- Newborns cannot focus more than 2 feet away.
- Children see better each year until about age 8.
- Many adolescents become nearsighted when eyeball shape changes.
- Vision is more likely to improve than to worsen until about age 40.
- In middle age, the elasticity of the lens decreases and the eyeball shape changes again, so that many people become farsighted and need reading glasses.
- Among the old, eye diseases, including cataracts, are common.
- About 10 percent of people over age 90 are blind.

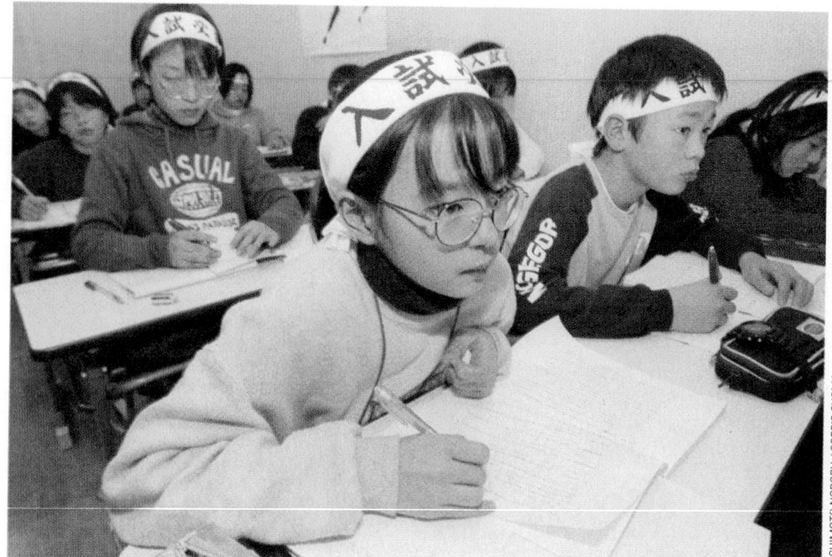
HASHIMOTO NOBORU / CORBIS SYGMA

Young Scholars In Japan and other countries of East Asia, the incidence of nearsightedness is increasing at a rapid rate. One reason may be the amount of time children in those cultures spend indoors studying, which far exceeds the time spent by children in Western societies.

Nearsightedness and Genes

Children usually see quite well, but if they do have a vision problem it is most often nearsightedness (also called *myopia*). Nearsightedness is a symptom in more than 150 genetic syndromes (Morgan, 2003). It may also be caused by physical trauma or illness (such as the rubella virus that caused my nephew David's cataracts; see Chapter 1) or by poor nutrition (such as vitamin A deficiency). Most of these factors cause "high" nearsightedness, so severe that it can lead to blindness.

What about the more common "low" nearsightedness, which makes it hard to read signs that are too far away? A study of British twins found that the Pax6 gene, which governs eye formation, has many alleles that make people somewhat nearsighted (Hammond et al., 2004). This research found heritability of almost 90 percent, which means that if one monozygotic twin is nearsighted, the other twin will almost always be nearsighted, too.

From this and other research, it is evident that genes affect vision. Eye shape is genetic and familial as well as age-related.

➤Response for People Who Are Easily Bored (from page 75): It depends on you. Some people who love risk become addicts; others develop a healthy lifestyle that includes adventure, new people, and exotic places. Any trait can lead in various directions.

Culture and Cohort

If the science of human development arose from the study of only one cohort or culture (such as, in this case, contemporary Britons), scientists might conclude that genes were the major cause of poor vision (Farbrother & Guggenheim, 2001). However, historical and multicultural research finds that environment powerfully influences nearsightedness as well.

The most dramatic example is that if a child's diet is deficient in vitamin A, then he or she will not be able to see well. More than 100,000 African children have partial vision or are blind, for that very reason (West & Sommer, 2001). In their case, genes are irrelevant: The environmental cause and the solution (supplemental vitamin A) are clear.

But what about well-nourished children? Barring trauma or illness, is their visual acuity entirely genetic? Cross-cultural research indicates that it is not.

In Singapore, Taiwan, and Hong Kong, myopia has recently increased so much that the surge has been called an epidemic. The first published research on this phenomenon appeared in 1992, when scholars noticed that, in army-mandated medical exams of all 17-year-old males in Singapore, 43 percent were nearsighted

➤Response for College Students Who Enjoy a Party (from page 75): Your friend's ability to "hold his liquor" is an ominous sign; his body probably metabolizes alcohol differently from the way most other people's do. Alcoholics are often deceptive about their own drinking habits, so you might ask him about the drinking habits of his relatives. If he has either alcoholics or abstainers in his family, you should be concerned, since both patterns are signs of a genetic problem with alcohol. Ask your friend whether he could have only one drink a day for a month. Alcoholics find such restricted drinking virtually impossible.

in 1990 compared with only 26 percent a decade earlier (Tay et al., 1992). Further studies found that nearsightedness increased in Taiwan between ages 6 and 17 from 12 to 84 percent; in Singapore between ages 6 and 9 from 28 to 44 percent; in Hong Kong between ages 7 and 10 from 10 to 60 percent (cited in Grosvenor, 2003). These studies occurred in many circumstances and decades, but the trend was the same.

These increases are partly developmental (remember that nearsightedness increases with puberty), and perhaps some of the young children were already nearsighted but had not yet been diagnosed. Thus, some scholars are not ready to conclude that "myopia is increasing at an 'epidemic' rate, particularly in East Asia" (Park & Congdon, 2004, p. 21).

However, these increases are far higher than they are among children outside East Asia. Further, parents of these same children are much less nearsighted. This suggests an environmental cause (Morgan, 2003; Saw, 2003). What could it be?

One possible culprit is cited again and again: the increasing amount of time children spend studying. In Chapter 12 you will learn that East Asian children are amazingly proficient in math and science, and one reason is that they spend more time doing schoolwork than Western children do. As their developing eyes focus on the pages in front of them, they may lose acuity for objects far away—which is exactly what nearsightedness means. Ophthalmologists suggest that if these children spent more time outside playing, walking, or relaxing in regular daylight, fewer might need glasses (Goss, 2002; Grosvenor, 2003).

As one expert concludes, "The extremely rapid changes in the prevalence of myopia and the dependence of myopia on the level of education indicate that there are very strong environmental impacts" on Asian children's vision (Morgan, 2003, p. 276). Genes are crucial, of course, but it is not surprising that myopia, alcoholism, and almost every other complex human characteristic are highly hereditary *and* highly environmental.

Practical Applications

Some developmental applications of the nature–nurture interaction are obvious. Knowing that genes affect every disorder keeps parents from putting all the blame on their child or their parenting. Knowing that there is a family history of a genetic problem or, better yet, that someone inherited a problem can lead to practical steps. For instance, if alcoholism is in the genes, parents can avoid drinking and their children can be kept away from alcohol. If nearsightedness runs in the family, parents can make sure that children spend time each day playing outdoors.

Of course, nondrinking and outdoor play are recommended for every child, as are dozens of other behaviors, such as flossing the teeth, saying thank you, getting enough sleep, eating vegetables, and writing thank-you notes. However, no child can do everything, and no parent can enforce every proper action. Awareness of genetic vulnerability helps parents set priorities, avoid blame, and take constructive action.

To illustrate, consider one more epidemic. In **type 2 diabetes** (once called *adult-onset diabetes*), the body's production of insulin gradually becomes less efficient. In the United States in 2004, diabetes was the sixth most common cause of death, and it is estimated that 1 in 3 children who were born in 2000 will develop diabetes (Lazar, 2005).

type 2 diabetes A chronic disease in which the body does not produce enough insulin to adequately metabolize carbohydrates (glucose). It was once called *adult-onset diabetes* because it typically developed in people aged 50 to 60; today, however, it often appears in younger people.

Type 2 diabetes is increasing in the United States, partly because obesity leads to expression of the genetic vulnerability (Schwartz & Porte, 2005). Figure 3.3 depicts this, based on data reported in *MMWR* (see Research Design). Some ethnic groups (African Americans, Hispanic Americans, and many Native Americans)

Research Design

Scientists: Hundreds at the U.S. Centers for Disease Control and Prevention.

Publication: *MMWR* (*Morbidity and Mortality Weekly Report*), July 14, 2006.

Participants: Adults living in the United States, contacted by random telephone dialing. The participants had to be over age 18 and willing to answer questions. In 2004, 303,822 (about half those contacted) were interviewed.

Design: This is a repeated, cross-sectional study, interviewing thousands in every state. Standard questions are asked about many health-related behaviors and conditions. Obesity is calculated based on the person's self-reported height and weight.

Major conclusion: Many people have health problems, including almost two-thirds who are overweight many who are diabetic.

Comment: This huge national survey has been repeated over 25 years, with efforts to assure validity. However, people may underreport their weight, diabetics may not be diagnosed, no interviewees are in institutions (e.g., prisons and hospitals), and only people with phones who agree to talk are included. So the rates of obesity and diabetes may be even higher than depicted in Figure 3.3.

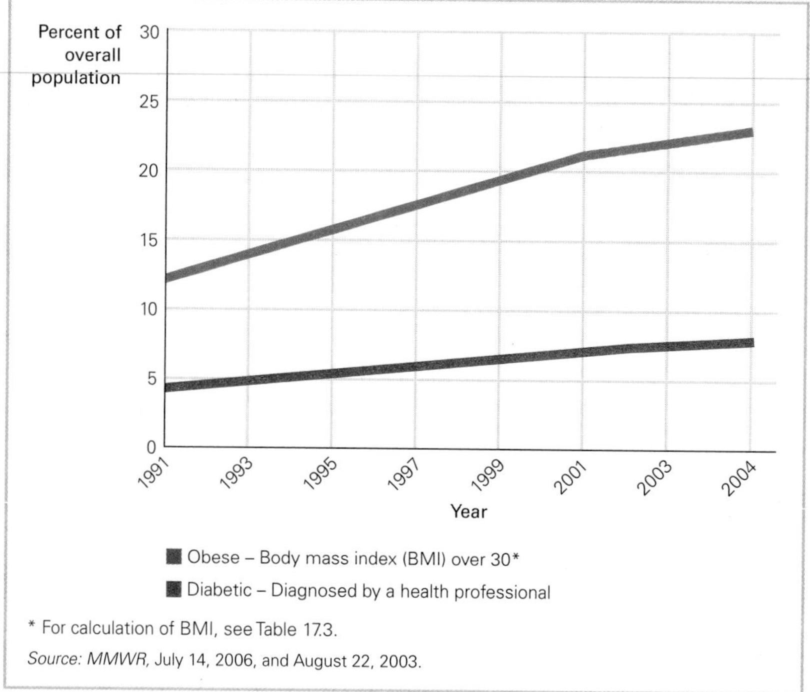

FIGURE 3.3

Getting Worse Obesity is often associated with diabetes, but some people are genetically protected, which means that they can be seriously overweight but disease-free. The graph illustrates that, while obesity and diabetes are both on the rise, the rate of obesity is far higher and is increasing more rapidly than that of diabetes. Detailed data suggest that obesity is often the trigger for the genetic risk of diabetes, but the two conditions do not automatically go hand in hand.

are genetically more vulnerable to diabetes. One reason is that they may have a "thrifty gene" that protected their ancestors in times of famine (Lazar, 2005) but that encourages the accumulation of body fat when food is plentiful (Hildyard & Wolfe, 2002).

Worldwide, the incidence of diabetes is expected to double by 2025, when 300 million people will have the disease (Kiberstis, 2005). The United States now has a childhood obesity epidemic (see Chapter 11), and some adolescents already have type 2 diabetes (Kiberstis, 2005). Knowing this, parents who have diabetic relatives can redouble their efforts to encourage healthy eating and exercise in their children (and themselves). Once again, understanding the interaction between nature and nurture can prevent or moderate genetic problems.

SUMMING UP

Genes affect every trait—whether it be something wonderful, such as a wacky sense of humor; something fearful, such as a violent temper; or something quite ordinary, such as the tendency to be bored. The environment affects every trait as well, in ways that change as maturational, cultural, and historical processes unfold. The expression of genes can sometimes be directed or deflected, depending on the culture and the society and even on the individual and the family. This is apparent in alcoholism, nearsightedness, and type 2 diabetes, all of which have strong genetic roots, distinctive developmental patterns, and environmental triggers. Genes are always part of the story, influential on every page, but they never determine the plot or the final paragraph. ■

Chromosomal and Genetic Abnormalities

We now focus on abnormalities that are caused by an identifiable problem, such as an extra chromosome or a single gene. Such abnormalities are relevant to our study of development for three reasons:

- They provide insight into the complexities of nature and nurture.
- Knowing their origins helps limit their effects.
- Information combats the prejudice that surrounds such problems.

Information is needed as much for the families as for the individuals. Infants born with genetic and chromosomal problems are much more likely to live into adulthood than was the case a few decades ago. This development raises emotional and cognitive issues for their parents and siblings that are not yet well understood (Lewis et al., 2006).

Not Exactly 46 Chromosomes

Gametes with more or fewer than 23 chromosomes are formed for many reasons, both inherited and environmental (such as a parent's exposure to excessive radiation). The variable that most often correlates with chromosomal abnormalities is the age of the mother. Paternal age (if a father is over age 40) is also relevant, but maternal age is more crucial (Crow, 2003), presumably because a woman's ova (which begin to form before she is born) become increasingly fragile by midlife.

Chromosomal abnormalities occur not only in the formation of gametes but also in their early duplication. In those instances, cells of one person may have more or fewer than 46 chromosomes, while other cells of that person have exactly 46. The result is someone who is **mosaic**—that is, who has a mixture of normal and abnormal cells.

Zygotes often have too many or too few chromosomes. One scientist estimates that only half of all conceptions have the usual 46 (Borgaonkar, 1997). Most abnormal zygotes do not duplicate, divide, and differentiate (K. L. Moore & Persaud, 2003). Those that start to grow usually are spontaneously aborted early in pregnancy; other such embryos are aborted by choice when the parents learn about the condition. If a fetus survives to be born, birth is hazardous: About 5 percent of stillborn (dead-at-birth) babies have more than 46 chromosomes (O. J. Miller & Therman, 2001).

Once in about every 200 births, a live infant is born with 45, 47, or, rarely, 48 or 49 chromosomes. Each abnormality leads to a recognizable *syndrome*, a cluster of distinct characteristics that tend to occur together. Usually the cause is three chromosomes (a condition called a *trisomy*) at a particular location instead of the usual two.

GETTY (TAXI)

Is She the Baby's Grandmother? No. Women over age 40 now have a higher birth rate than women that age did just a few decades ago. Later-life pregnancies are more likely to involve complications, but the outcome is sometimes what you see here: a gray-haired mother thrilled with her happy, healthy infant.

Down Syndrome

The most common extra-chromosome condition is **Down syndrome,** also called *trisomy-21* because everyone with Down syndrome has three copies of chromosome 21. The chances that a baby will be born with Down syndrome increase with the mother's age. According to one estimate, a 20-year-old woman has about 1 chance in 800 of carrying a fetus with Down syndrome; a 39-year-old woman, 1 in 67; and a 44-year-old woman, 1 in 16 (see Appendix A, p. A-3). A few decades ago, infants with Down syndrome usually died in early childhood (usually of heart ailments), but now most survive to adulthood.

Some 300 distinct characteristics can result from the presence of that extra chromosome 21. No individual with Down syndrome is quite like another, either

mosaic Having a condition (*mosaicism*) that involves having a mixture of cells, some normal and some with an odd number of chromosomes or a series of missing genes.

Down syndrome A condition in which a person has 47 chromosomes instead of the usual 46, with three rather than two chromosomes at the 21st position. People with Down syndrome typically have distinctive characteristics, including unusual facial features, heart abnormalities, and language difficulties. (Also called *trisomy-21*.)

REUTERS / CLAUDIA DAUT

Universal Happiness All young children delight in painting brightly colored pictures on a big canvas, but this scene is unusual for two reasons: Daniel has trisomy-21, and this photograph was taken at the only school in Chile where normal and special-needs children share classrooms.

in symptoms or in severity, for three reasons: (1) Some are mosaic, having some cells with 46 chromosomes and others with 47; (2) sometimes only part of that third chromosome is present, so the person has, say, 46¼ chromosomes; (3) genes on other chromosomes and environmental experiences differ for each person, so genes on other chromosomes affect that 21st trio.

Despite this variability, most people with trisomy-21 have specific facial characteristics—a thick tongue, round face, slanted eyes—as well as distinctive hands, feet, and fingerprints. Many also have hearing problems, heart abnormalities, muscle weakness, and short stature. They are usually slower to develop intellectually, especially in language (Cohen, 2005). Their eventual intellect varies: Some are severely retarded; others are of average or even above-average intelligence.

Many young children with trisomy-21 are sweet-tempered, less likely to cry or complain than other children. This may become a liability if a child with Down syndrome gets less adult attention and thus less opportunity to learn (Wishart, 1999).

Adults with Down syndrome age faster than other adults, with the ailments of aging usually beginning at about age 30. By middle adulthood, they "almost invariably" develop Alzheimer's disease, which severely impairs their communication skills and makes them much less compliant (Czech et al., 2000). They may develop other problems as well.

This generally pessimistic description, however, does not reflect the actual experience of individuals with Down syndrome. Language does not come easily for them, and many have medical problems. But they may still become happy, proud, and successful young adults. One advised others:

> You may have to work hard, but don't ever give up. Always remember that you are important. You are special in your own unique way. And one of the best ways to feel good about yourself is to share yourself with someone else.
>
> *[Christi Todd, quoted in Hassold & Patterson, 1999]*

AP PHOTO / ALEXANDER ZEMLIANICHENKO

Great Theater A leading man named Sergei Makarov, shown here acting in a Gogol play, is extraordinarily talented. He is a member of Moscow's Theater of Simple Souls, all of whom have Down syndrome. Does "simple souls" evoke pity? No need; a film starring Makarov won the top prize in Russia's national film festival in 2006.

Abnormalities of the 23rd Pair

Every human has at least 44 autosomes and one X chromosome; an embryo cannot develop without an X. However, about 1 in every 500 infants has only one X and no Y (the X stands alone) or has three or more sex chromosomes, not just two (Hamerton & Evans, 2005).

Having an odd number of sex chromosomes impairs cognitive and psychosocial development as well as sexual maturation. The specifics depend on the particular configuration. The only condition in which a person with 45 chromosomes can survive is in the case of a girl with only one X (written as X0, with the 0 standing for no chromosome). This is called *Turner syndrome,* which results in underdeveloped female organs and other anomalies.

Especially for Those Worried About Their Sexuality Might you have an undiagnosed abnormality of your sex chromosome?

If there are three sex chromosomes instead of two, a child may seem normal until puberty, particularly if he is a male with *Klinefelter syndrome,* XXY. Such a boy will be a little slow in elementary school, but not until age 12 or so—when the double X keeps his penis from growing and fat begins to accumulate around his breasts—is it clear that something is wrong. For XXY boys, supplemental hormones can alleviate some physical problems, and special education aids learning—an example of nurture compensating for nature.

Dominant-Gene Disorders

Everyone carries genes or alleles that *could* produce serious diseases or handicaps in the next generation (see Table 3.2). Given that most genes contribute only a small amount to a disorder and that the human genome was just recently mapped, the exact impact of each allele of multifactorial disorders is not yet known (Hinds et al., 2005). However, we do know a great deal about single-gene disorders, since they have been studied for decades.

Most of the 7,000 *known* single-gene disorders are dominant (always expressed). They are easy to notice: Their dominant effects are apparent in the phenotype. With a few exceptions, severe dominant disorders are rare because people who have such disorders rarely have children and thus the gene dies with them.

One exception is *Huntington's disease,* a fatal central nervous system disorder caused by a genetic miscode—this time more than 35 repetitions of a particular triplet. Unlike most dominant traits, the effects of this allele do not begin until middle adulthood. By then a person could have had several children, half of whom would inherit the same dominant gene and therefore would eventually develop Huntington's disease.

Another disorder, which is probably dominant, is *Tourette syndrome.* This condition is common because it is not disabling and because its effects vary (Olson, 2004). About 30 percent of those who inherit the syndrome exhibit recurrent, uncontrollable tics and explosive verbal outbursts, usually beginning at about age 6. The remaining 70 percent have milder symptoms, such as an occasional twitch that is barely noticeable or a postponable impulse to clear their throat. Many children and adults without Tourette's also have such symptoms (Olson, 2004). A person with mild Tourette syndrome might curse and tremor when alone but behave normally in public. Girls who have the Tourette genotype often do not express it, at least not with the obvious tics and verbal explosions of young boys. Tourette syndrome is developmental: It often appears at school age, and sometimes disappears in adolescence.

Fragile X Syndrome

Several genetic disorders are sex-linked, or carried on the X chromosome. Males are thus more likely to be affected by such conditions. One, called **fragile X syndrome,** is caused by a single gene that has more than 200 repetitions of one

fragile X syndrome A genetic disorder in which part of the X chromosome seems to be attached to the rest of it by a very thin string of molecules. The actual cause is too many repetitions of a particular part of a gene's code.

TABLE 3.2

Common Genetic Diseases and Conditions

Name	Description	Prognosis	Probable Inheritance	Incidence*	Carrier Detection?†	Prenatal Detection?
Albinism	No melanin; person is very blond and pale	Normal, but must avoid sun damage	Recessive	Rare overall; 1 in 8 Hopi Indians is a carrier	No	No
Alzheimer's disease	Loss of memory and increasing mental impairment	Eventual death, often after years of dependency	Early onset—dominant; after age 60—multifactorial	Fewer than 1 in 100 middle-aged adults; perhaps 25 percent of all adults over age 85	Yes, for some genes; ApoE4 allele increases incidence	No
Breast cancer	Tumors in breast that can spread	With early treatment, most are cured; without it, death within 3 years	BRCA1 and BRCA2 genes seem dominant; other cases, multifactorial	1 woman in 8 (only 20 percent of breast cancer patients have BRCA1 or BRCA2)	Yes, for BRCA1 and BRCA2	No
Cleft palate, cleft lip	The two sides of the upper lip or palate are not joined	Correctable by surgery	Multifactorial	1 in every 700 births; more common in Asian Americans and American Indians	No	Yes
Club foot	The foot and ankle are twisted	Correctable by surgery	Multifactorial	1 in every 200 births; more common in boys	No	Yes
Cystic fibrosis	Mucous obstructions, especially in lungs and digestive organs	Most live to middle adulthood	Recessive gene; also spontaneous mutations	1 in 3,200; 1 in 25 European Americans is a carrier	Sometimes	Yes, in most cases
Diabetes	Abnormal sugar metabolism because of insufficient insulin	Early onset (type 1) fatal without insulin; for later onset (type 2), variable risks	Multifactorial; for later onset, body weight is significant	Type 1: 1 in 500 births; more common in American Indians and African Americans. Type 2: 1 adult in 6 by age 60	No	No
Deafness (congenital)	Inability to hear from birth on	Deaf children can learn sign language and live normally	Multifactorial; some forms are recessive	1 in 1,000 births; more common in people from Middle East	No	No
Hemophilia	Absence of clotting factor in blood	Death from internal bleeding; blood transfusions prevent damage	X-linked recessive; also spontaneous mutations	1 in 10,000 males; royal families of England, Russia, and Germany had it	Yes	Yes
Hydro-cephalus	Obstruction causes excess fluid in the brain	Brain damage and death; surgery can make normal life possible	Multifactorial	1 in every 100 births	No	Yes
Muscular dystrophy (30 diseases)	Weakening of muscles	Inability to walk, move; wasting away and sometimes death	Recessive or multifactorial	1 in every 3,500 males develops Duchenne's	Yes, for some forms	Yes, for some forms

*Incidence statistics vary from country to country; those given here are for the United States. All these diseases can occur in any ethnic group. Many affected groups limit transmission through genetic counseling; for example, the incidence of Tay-Sachs disease is declining because many Jewish young adults obtain testing and counseling before marriage.

†"Yes" refers to carrier detection. Family history can also reveal genetic risk.

Name	Description	Prognosis	Probable Inheritance	Incidence*	Carrier Detection?†	Prenatal Detection?
Neural-tube defects (open spine)	Anencephaly (parts of the brain missing) or spina bifida (lower spine not closed)	Anencephalic—severe retardation; spina bifida—poor lower body control	Multifactorial; folic acid deficit and genes	Anencephaly—1 in 1,000 births; spina bifida—3 in 1,000; more common in Welsh and Scots	No	Yes
Phenylketonuria (PKU)	Abnormal digestion of protein	Mental retardation, preventable by diet begun by 10 days after birth	Recessive	1 in 100 European Americans is a carrier, especially Norwegians and Irish	Yes	Yes
Pyloric stenosis	Overgrowth of muscle in intestine	Vomiting, loss of weight, eventual death; correctable by surgery	Multifactorial	1 male in 200, 1 female in 1,000; less common in African Americans	No	No
Rett syndrome	Neurological developmental disorder	Boys die at birth. At 6–18 months, girls lose communication and motor abilities	X-linked	1 in 10,000 female births	No	Sometimes
Schizophrenia	Severely distorted thought processes	No cure; drugs, hospitalization, psychotherapy ease symptoms	Multifactorial	1 in 100 people develop it by early adulthood	No	No
Sickle-cell anemia	Abnormal blood cells	Possible painful "crisis"; heart and kidney failure; treatable with drugs	Recessive	1 in 11 African Americans and 1 in 20 Latinos is a carrier	Yes	Yes
Tay-Sachs disease	Enzyme disease	Healthy infant becomes weaker, usually dying by age 5	Recessive	1 in 30 American Jews and 1 in 20 French Canadians and Old Order Amish are carriers	Yes	Yes
Thalassemia	Abnormal blood cells	Paleness and listlessness, low resistance to infections, slow growth	Usually recessive, occasionally dominant	1 in 10 Americans from southern Europe, northern Africa, or south Asia is a carrier	Yes	Yes
Tourette syndrome	Uncontrollable tics, body jerking, verbal outbursts	Appears at about age 5; worsens then improves with age	Dominant, but variable penetrance	1 in 250 children	Sometimes	No

Sources: Briley & Sulser, 2001; Butler & Meaney, 2005; Klug & Cummings, 2000; Mange & Mange, 1999; K. L. Moore & Persaud, 2003; Shahin et al., 2002.

Observation Quiz (see answer, page 84): Is there any ethnic group that does not have a genetic condition that is more common among its members than among the general population?

Response for Those Worried About Their Sexuality (from page 81): That is highly unlikely. Chromosomal abnormalities are evident long before adulthood. It is quite normal for adults to be worried about sexuality for social, not biological, reasons.

triplet (Plomin et al., 2003). (Some repetitions are normal, but not this many.) The repetitions multiply when that X chromosome is passed from one generation to the next.

Although it is an X-linked, single-gene disorder, fragile X syndrome is not strictly recessive or dominant. About two-thirds of females with the fragile X gene are normal; one-third show some mental deficiency. Of males who inherit a fragile X, about 20 percent seem unaffected, about 33 percent are somewhat retarded, and the rest are severely retarded. Many of those have autistic symptoms as well. If a man with a fragile X is normal, half the sons of his daughters (his grandsons) will probably be significantly impaired because of the increased number of repetitions with each generation. But such predictions are approximate as the actual transmission pattern varies.

➤Answer to Observation Quiz (from page 83): No. As you see, all the major groups are mentioned in Table 3.2. In fact, even much smaller groups whose members tend to marry within the group also have higher rates of particular conditions.

The cognitive deficits caused by fragile X syndrome are the most common form of *inherited* mental retardation (many other forms, such as trisomy-21, are not inherited) (Sherman, 2002). In addition to having cognitive problems, children with fragile X syndrome often are shy, with poor social skills (Hagerman & Hagerman, 2002).

Recessive-Gene Disorders

Most recessive disorders are not X-linked. For example, cystic fibrosis, thalassemia, and sickle-cell anemia are all equally common and devastating in males and females (see Table 3.2). About 1 in 12 North Americans is a carrier for one of these three conditions. That high incidence rate results from the fact that although the double recessive pattern is lethal, one recessive gene is protective. For example, carriers of the sickle-cell trait are less likely to die of malaria, which is still a problem in central Africa. Their descendants in North America, including 10 percent of all African Americans, carry a gene that is no longer needed for protection. Cystic fibrosis is most common among people whose ancestors came from northern Europe; carriers may have been protected from cholera.

Especially for History Students Some genetic diseases may have changed the course of history. For instance, the last czar of Russia had four healthy daughters and one son with hemophilia. Once called the royal disease, hemophilia is X-linked. How could this rare condition have affected the monarchies of Russia, England, Austria, Germany, and Spain?

Sometimes a person who carried a lethal gene has many descendants who marry each other. In that case, the genetic disease becomes common in that group. This happened among Jews in one area of eastern Europe, many of whom inherited the recessive Tay-Sachs gene. An infant born with Tay-Sachs disease begins life normally, as a bright, cuddly baby, but then develops slowly and dies before age 5. Many disorders became common because parents of such children tended to have a "replacement" child, who often was a carrier for the same condition. Tay-Sachs also is common among another group with high rates of intermarriage, the French in Louisiana. Probably everyone is a carrier for some recessive disease, but most people do not have children with someone who happens to be a carrier of the same condition.

Genetic Counseling and Testing

Until recently, after the birth of a child with a serious or even fatal disorder, couples blamed fate, not genes or chromosomes. Today, many young adults worry about their genes long before they marry. Almost all adults have a relative with a serious disease that is partly genetic, and they want to know the chances of their children inheriting the same disease.

Who Should Get Counseling, and When?

genetic counseling Consultation and testing by trained experts that enable individuals to learn about their genetic heritage, including harmful conditions that they might pass along to any children they may conceive.

Genetic counseling can relieve some of these worries by providing facts and helping prospective parents discuss issues that are relevant to their decisions.

Counselors must be carefully trained, because many people, especially when considering personal and emotional information, misinterpret words such as "risks" and "probability" (O'Doherty, 2006).

Preconception, prenatal, or even prenuptial genetic testing and counseling are recommended for the following:

- Individuals who have a parent, sibling, or child with a serious genetic condition
- Couples who have a history of spontaneous abortions, stillbirths, or infertility
- Couples from the same ethnic group, particularly if they are relatives
- Women age 35 or older and men age 40 or older

Genetic counselors try to follow two ethical guidelines. First, the results of their clients' tests are kept confidential, beyond the reach of insurance companies and public records. Second, decisions are made by the clients, not by the counselors. These guidelines are not always easy to follow, as the following illustrates.

thinking like a scientist

Who Decides?

One of the most difficult parts of being a scientist is knowing how to use information so it does not harm others. Consider these cases (adapted from Fackelmann, 1994):

1. A pregnant woman and her husband both have achondroplastic dwarfism, a dominant condition that affects appearance (very short stature, large head) but not intellect. They want genetic analysis of the fetus; they plan to abort if the child would be of normal height.
2. A 40-year-old woman is tested and is told that she has the BRCA1 gene. That means she has about an 80 percent chance of developing breast cancer and is at high risk for ovarian and colon cancer. She does not believe these results and wants no one to tell her mother, her four sisters, or her three daughters, some of whom may be in the early stages of cancer.
3. A 30-year-old mother of two daughters (no sons) is a carrier for hemophilia. She requests IVF and pre-implantation analysis so that only male zygotes without the hemophilia-carrying X chromosome will be implanted. Female zygotes, all healthy but half of them carriers, would be destroyed, as would the hemophiliac half of her male zygotes.
4. A couple has a child with cystic fibrosis. They want to know if they both carry the recessive gene, in which case they will have no more children, or if the child's illness was the result of a spontaneous genetic change, as may happen at conception. The test results make it apparent to the counselor that the couple will not have a child with cystic fibrosis, because the husband is not the child's biological father.

Should test results be kept confidential from other family members who are directly affected (as in examples 2 and 4)? Should a client be given information that will lead to a decision that the counselor believes is unethical (as in examples 1 and 3)? Most counselors answer yes, but many students say that they would break confidentiality for examples 2 and 4 and would refuse to test in examples 1 and 3. As a scientist, you might try to explain information so that others reach your conclusions, but your job is research, not opinion. What would you do?

Is Knowledge Always Power?

Genetic counselors, scientists, and the general public usually favor testing, reasoning that having some information is better than having none. However, high-risk individuals (who might hear bad news) do not always want to know, especially if the truth might jeopardize their marriage, their insurance coverage, or their chance of parenthood (Duster, 1999).

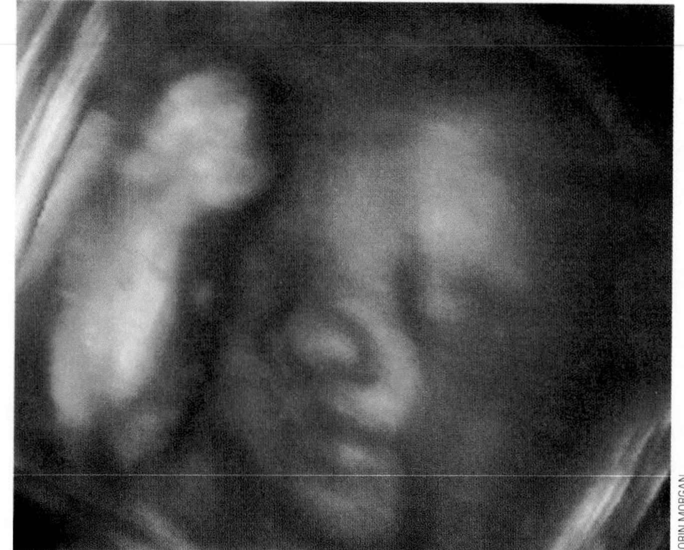

There's Your Baby For many parents, their first glimpse of their future child is an ultrasound image. This is Alice Morgan, 63 days before birth.

For instance, most people who have a 50/50 risk of developing Huntington's disease do not want to know their status unless they are contemplating parenthood. Those who learn that they are *not* carriers often have a more difficult time coping with the news, psychologically, than their siblings who are carriers (Skirton & Patch, 2002).

It is understandable why people might want to know the risk of conceiving a child with a serious disorder or whether a particular fetus has a disorder, especially if the couple already has had a child with that problem. But an entirely different set of issues is raised by testing after birth.

Sometimes testing is helpful, because knowledge can prevent harm. This is the case for **phenylketonuria (PKU),** a recessive condition that is more prevalent among northern Europeans than other population groups (Welsh & Pennington, 2000). Newborns with the double recessive genes for PKU will become severely retarded if they consume phenylalanine, a substance found in many foods. If such a baby is immediately started on a diet free of that amino acid, he or she will develop normally, or close to it (Hillman, 2005).

phenylketonuria (PKU) A genetic disorder in which a child's body is unable to metabolize an amino acid called phenylalanine. Unless phenylalanine is eliminated from the child's diet, the resulting buildup of that substance in body fluids causes brain damage, progressive mental retardation, and other symptoms.

In many nations, including the United States, every newborn is tested for PKU. Dozens of other conditions are often tested for (specifics vary by state and nation), sometimes when no treatment is available. Is that ethical? Might bad news make the parents less affectionate toward their baby, making the problem worse? Counselors disagree (Twomey, 2006).

➤Response for History Students (from page 84): Hemophilia is a painful chronic disease that (before blood transfusions became feasible) killed a boy before adulthood. Though rare, it ran in European royal families, whose members often intermarried, which meant that many queens (including England's Queen Victoria) were carriers of hemophilia and thus were destined to watch half their sons die of it. All families, even rulers of nations, are distracted from their work when they have a child with a mysterious and lethal illness. Some historians believe that hemophilia among European royalty was an underlying cause of the Russian Revolution of 1917 as well as the spread of democracy in the nineteenth and twentieth centuries.

Coping with Uncertainty

Actually, much is uncertain in genetic testing and counseling. Those who learn that they have a harmful dominant gene, or that they and their partner both carry the same dangerous recessive gene, have new information but also new uncertainties. Odds are that half their children will inherit the dominant gene, or that one out of four will have the double recessive, but before actual conception those are merely odds. Some, all, or none of their children *could* have the disease. Each pregnancy is a new risk, another roll of the same dice.

Further, the interaction of genes and the environment makes development over the life span unpredictable, even if the genes are known. For example, some people with sickle-cell anemia suffer terribly and then die young, while others live satisfy-

ROBERT SPENCER / THE NEW YORK TIMES

"The Hardest Decision I Ever Had to Make" That's how this woman described her decision to terminate her third pregnancy when genetic testing revealed that the fetus had Down syndrome. She soon became pregnant again with a male fetus that had the normal 46 chromosomes, as did her two daughters. Many personal factors influence such decisions. Do you think she and her husband would have made the same choice if they had had no other children?

ing lives, with occasional painful crises that can be weathered. Much depends on the family and social context but also on medical treatments yet to be discovered (Gustafson et al., 2006).

People respond to genetic information in different ways. Some couples at high risk refuse to be tested. Others with the exact same genetic risk are tested and then choose sterilization or adoption. Still others take their chances, either accepting the possibility that they may have a seriously ill child or testing the fetus and aborting it if the double recessive is found.

For many problems, including most recessive genetic disorders and chromosomal abnormalities, a definitive diagnosis can be made after conception but not before. Is a couple willing to start a pregnancy and then end it if the embryo would develop into a seriously ill child? One couple that said no and another that said yes are presented in the next chapter, along with a more general discussion of the methods and problems of prenatal testing.

Especially for a Friend A female friend asks you to go with her to the hospital, where she is planning to be surgically sterilized. She says she doesn't want children, especially since her younger brother recently died of sickle-cell anemia, a recessive disease. What, if anything, should you do?

SUMMING UP

Every person is a carrier for some serious genetic conditions. Most of them are rare, which makes it unlikely that the combination of sperm and ovum will produce severe disabilities. Those recessive diseases that are common occur because carriers survived to reproduce as a result of being protected against some conditions that plagued many of our ancestors.

Often a zygote does not have 46 chromosomes. Such zygotes rarely develop, with two primary exceptions: Down syndrome (trisomy-21) and abnormalities of the sex chromosomes. Genetic counseling helps couples clarify their values and understand the risks before they conceive, but every decision raises ethical questions. Counselors try to explain facts and probabilities, but the final decision is made by those directly involved. ■

SUMMARY

The Genetic Code

1. Genes are the foundation for all development, first instructing the living creature to form the body and brain, and then regulating behavior. Human conception occurs when two gametes (an ovum and a sperm, each with 23 chromosomes) combine to form a zygote, 46 chromosomes in a single cell.

2. The sex of an embryo depends on the sperm: A Y sperm creates an XY (male) embryo; an X sperm creates an XX (female) embryo. Every cell of every living creature has the unique genetic code of the zygote that began that life. The human genome contains about 25,000 genes in all.

From One Cell to Many

3. Genes interact in various ways, sometimes additively, with each gene contributing to development, and sometimes in a dominant–recessive pattern. Environmental factors influence the phenotype as well.

4. The environment interacts with the genetic instructions for every trait, even for physical appearance. Every aspect of a person is almost always multifactorial and polygenic.

5. Combinations of chromosomes, interactions among genes, and myriad influences from the environment all assure both similarity and diversity within and between species. This aids health and survival.

6. Twins occur if a zygote splits into two separate beings (monozygotic, or identical, twins) or if two ova are fertilized by two sperm (dizygotic, or fraternal, twins). Monozygotic multiples are genetically the same. Dizygotic multiples have only half of their genes in common, as do all other siblings who have the same parents.

7. Fertility treatments, including drugs and in vitro fertilization, have led not only to the birth of millions of much-wanted babies but also to an increase in multiple births, which have a higher rate of medical problems.

From Genotype to Phenotype

8. Environmental influences are crucial for almost every complex trait. This includes alcoholism and nearsightedness. Some people are genetically susceptible to each of these, but nongenetic factors affect every condition.

9. Knowing the impact of genes and the environment can be helpful. People are less likely to blame someone for a characteristic that is inherited, but realizing that someone is at risk of a serious condition helps with prevention.

Chromosomal and Genetic Abnormalities

10. Often a gamete has fewer or more than 23 chromosomes, creating a zygote with an odd number of chromosomes. Usually such zygotes do not develop. The main exceptions are three chromosomes at the 21st location (Down syndrome, or trisomy-21) or an odd number of sex chromosomes. In such cases, the child has physical and cognitive problems but can live a nearly normal life.

11. Everyone is a carrier for genetic abnormalities, but usually those conditions are recessive (not affecting their phenotype). If dominant, the trait is usually mild, varied, or inconsequential until late adulthood. If being a carrier for a genetic abnormality, such as the sickle-cell trait, is protective, then that gene can become widespread in a population.

12. Genetic testing and counseling can help many couples learn whether their future children are at risk for a chromosomal or genetic abnormality. Genetic testing usually provides information about risks, not actualities. Couples, counselors, and cultures differ in the decisions they make.

KEY TERMS

DNA (deoxyribonucleic acid) (p. 61)
chromosome (p. 61)
gene (p. 61)
genome (p. 62)
gamete (p. 63)
zygote (p. 63)
genotype (p. 63)
allele (p. 64)
23rd pair (p. 64)
XX (p. 64)
XY (p. 64)
spontaneous abortion (p. 64)
induced abortion (p. 64)
phenotype (p. 66)
polygenic (p. 67)
multifactorial (p. 67)
Human Genome Project (p. 67)
additive gene (p. 67)
dominant–recessive pattern (p. 68)
X-linked (p. 68)
monozygotic (MZ) twins (p. 69)
dizygotic (DZ) twins (p. 70)
clone (p. 70)
in vitro fertilization (IVF) (p. 71)
infertility (p. 71)
assisted reproductive technology (ART) (p. 71)
carrier (p. 73)
type 2 diabetes (p. 77)
mosaic (p. 79)
Down syndrome (p. 79)
fragile X syndrome (p. 81)
genetic counseling (p. 84)
phenylketonuria (PKU) (p. 86)

KEY QUESTIONS

1. What are the relationships among proteins, genes, chromosomes, and the genome?

2. How and when is the sex of a zygote determined? Why is the ratio of boy babies to girl babies significant?

3. Which method of identifying a criminal do you think is most accurate: a lineup of suspects, a confession, a fingerprint match, DNA identification? Why?

4. Genetically speaking, how similar are people to one another and to other animals?

5. Sometimes parents have a child who looks like neither of them. How does that happen?

6. What are the differences among monozygotic twins, dizygotic twins, other siblings, and clones?

7. From the prospective parents' perspective, what are the advantages and disadvantages of adoption versus ART?

8. Explain how the course of alcoholism or nearsightedness is affected by nature and by nurture.

9. What are the causes and effects of Down syndrome?

10. Why is genetic counseling a personal decision and usually confidential?

11. Genetic testing for various diseases is much more common than it once was. What are the advantages and disadvantages?

APPLICATIONS

1. Pick one of your traits, and explain the influences that both nature *and* nurture have on it. For example, if you have a short temper, explain its origins in your genetics, your culture, and your childhood experiences.

2. Many adults have a preference for a son or a daughter. Interview adults of several ages and backgrounds about their preferences. If they give the socially preferable answer ("It does not matter"), ask how they think the two sexes differ. Listen and take notes—don't debate. Analyze the implications of the responses you get.

3. Draw a genetic chart of your biological relatives, going back as many generations as you can, listing all serious illnesses and causes of death. Include ancestors who died in infancy. Do you see any genetic susceptibility? If so, how can you overcome it?

4. List a dozen people you know who need glasses (or other corrective lenses) and a dozen who do not. Are there any patterns? Is this correlation or causation?

➤**Response for a Friend** (from page 87): She needs the information you have. She may not be a carrier of the sickle-cell trait (you know she doesn't have the disease, so she has one chance in three of not being a carrier). Even if she is a carrier, she can have a child with the disease only if the father of her child is also a carrier—and then there is only one chance in four. Urge your friend not to do anything irreversible.

4

CHAPTER OUTLINE

Prenatal Development and Birth

Wonder and worry, worry and wonder. Boy or girl? One baby or two? What color hair, eyes, and skin? What shape head, nose, and chin? When, how, and where will birth occur? Will the baby be healthy, well formed, ready for life?

My friend Judy, who taught history at the United Nations School, habitually contrasted the broad sweep of global history and the immediate, local particulars. She did this even when she was pregnant: She rubbed her belly and said, "Statistically, this is probably a Chinese boy."

Judy was right. The majority of newborns are male (about 52 percent), and more of them are Chinese than any other ethnicity (about 25 percent). Given Judy's personal particulars, though, no one was surprised when she gave birth to a European American girl. Judy herself seemed awestruck, repeatedly recounting tiny details, as if no baby like hers had ever appeared before. She was right about that, too.

This anecdote illustrates the dual themes of this chapter. Every topic—prenatal development, possible toxins, birthweight, medical assistance, bonding, and so on—is directly relevant to the 150 million babies born in the world every year. Yet each pregnancy and every birth is unique. This chapter includes both generalities and variations. Learn all you can, and then, if you have a baby, expect to be awed by your personal miracle.

From Zygote to Newborn

The most dramatic and extensive transformation of the entire life span occurs before birth. To make it easier to study, the awesome process of prenatal development is often divided into three main periods. The first two weeks are called the **germinal period;** the weeks from the third through the eighth are the **embryonic period;** the months from the ninth week until birth are the **fetal period.** (Alternative terms are discussed in Table 4.1.)

germinal period The first two weeks of prenatal development after conception, characterized by rapid cell division and the beginning of cell differentiation.

embryonic period The stage of prenatal development from approximately the third through the eighth week after conception, during which the basic forms of all body structures, including internal organs, develop.

fetal period The stage of prenatal development from the ninth week after conception until birth, during which the organs grow in size and mature in functioning.

Germinal: The First 14 Days

You learned in Chapter 3 that the one-celled *zygote* soon begins to duplicate, divide, and differentiate (see Figure 4.1). When the cells take on distinct characteristics and gravitate toward particular positions, the entire cell mass—still very fragile and tiny—is called a **blastocyst.**

blastocyst A cell mass that develops from the zygote in the first few days after conception, during the germinal period, and forms a hollow sphere in preparation for implantation.

TABLE 4.1

Timing and Terminology

Popular and professional books use various phrases to segment pregnancy. The following comments may help to clarify the phrases used.

- *Beginning of pregnancy:* Pregnancy begins at conception, which is also the starting point of *gestational age.* However, the organism does not become an *embryo* until about two weeks later, and pregnancy does not affect the woman (and cannot be confirmed by blood or urine testing) until implantation. Paradoxically, many obstetricians date the onset of pregnancy from the date of the woman's last menstrual period (LMP), about 14 days *before* conception.
- *Length of pregnancy:* Full-term pregnancies last 266 days, or 38 weeks, or 9 months. If the LMP is used as the starting time, pregnancy lasts 40 weeks, sometimes expressed as 10 lunar months. (A lunar month is 28 days long.)
- *Trimesters:* Instead of *germinal period, embryonic period,* and *fetal period,* some writers divide pregnancy into three-month periods called *trimesters.* Months 1, 2, and 3 are called the *first trimester;* months 4, 5, and 6, the *second trimester;* and months 7, 8, and 9, the *third trimester.*
- *Due date:* Although doctors assign a specific due date (based on the woman's LMP), only 5 percent of babies are born on that exact date. Babies born between three weeks before and two weeks after that date are considered "full term" or "on time." Babies born earlier are called *preterm;* babies born later are called *post-term.* The words *preterm* and *post-term* are more accurate than *premature* and *postmature.*

placenta The organ that surrounds the developing embryo and fetus, sustaining life via the umbilical cord. The placenta is attached to the wall of the uterus.

implantation The process, beginning about 10 days after conception, in which the developing organism burrows into the placenta that lines the uterus, where it can be nourished and protected as it continues to develop.

About a week after conception, the blastocyst, now consisting of more than 100 cells, separates into two distinct masses. The outer cells form a shell that will become the **placenta** (the organ that develops within the mother's uterus to protect and nourish the developing creature), and the inner cells form the nucleus of what will next become the embryo.

The first task of the outer cells is to achieve **implantation**—that is, to embed themselves in the nurturing environment of the uterus. Implantation occurs about 10 days after conception and is hazardous (K. L. Moore & Persaud, 2003). At least 60 percent of all natural conceptions and 70 percent of all in vitro conceptions fail to implant (see Table 4.2).

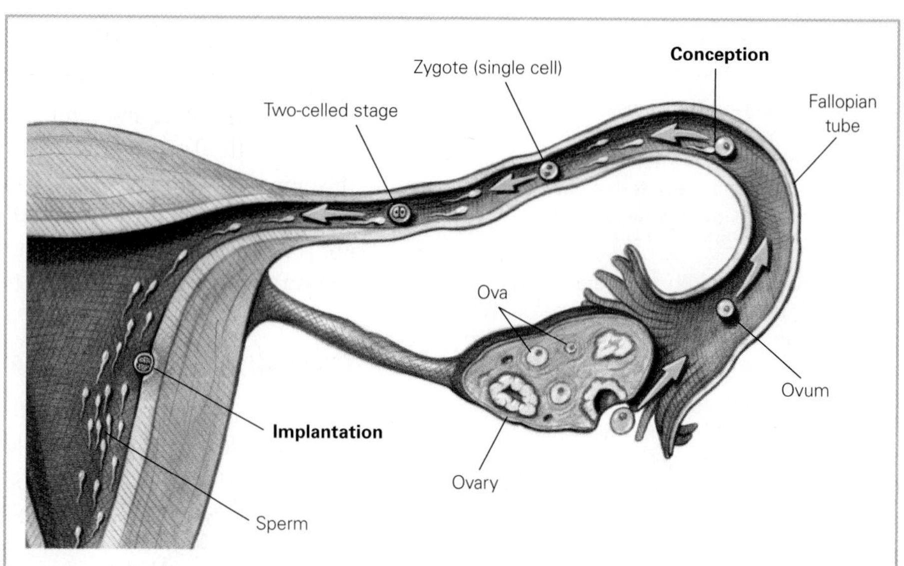

FIGURE 4.1

The Most Dangerous Journey In the first 10 days after conception, the organism does not increase in size because it is not yet nourished by the mother. However, the number of cells increases rapidly as the organism prepares for implantation, which occurs successfully about a third of the time.

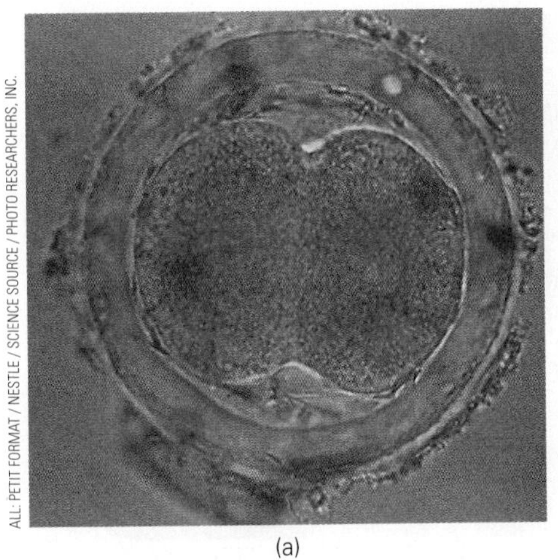
(a)

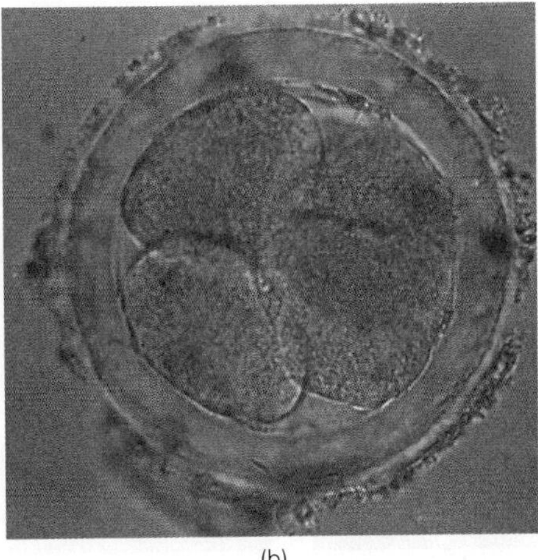
(b)

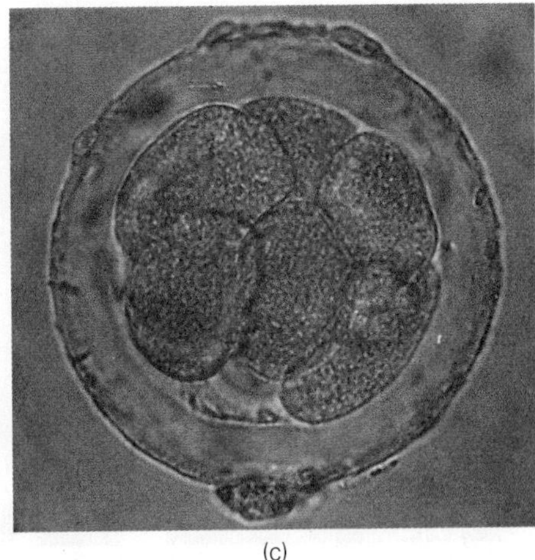
(c)

First Stages of the Germinal Period The original zygote as it divides into *(a)* two cells, *(b)* four cells, and *(c)* eight cells. Occasionally at this early stage, the cells separate completely, forming the beginning of monozygotic twins, quadruplets, or octuplets.

TABLE 4.2

Vulnerability During Prenatal Development

The Germinal Period
At least 60 percent of all developing organisms fail to grow or implant properly and thus do not survive the germinal period. Most of these organisms are grossly abnormal.

The Embryonic Period
About 20 percent of all embryos are aborted spontaneously, most often because of chromosomal abnormalities.

The Fetal Period
About 5 percent of all fetuses are aborted spontaneously before viability at 22 weeks or are stillborn, defined as born dead after 22 weeks.

Birth
About 31 percent of all zygotes grow and survive to become living newborn babies.

Sources: Bentley & Mascie-Taylor, 2000; K. L. Moore & Persaud, 2003.

Embryo: From the Third Through the Eighth Week

The start of the third week initiates the *embryonic period,* when the former blastocyst becomes a distinct being—not yet recognizably human but worthy of a new name, **embryo.** The first sign of a human body structure appears as a thin line (called the *primitive streak*) down the middle of the embryo. This line becomes the *neural tube* 22 days after conception, eventually developing into the *central nervous system*—the brain and spinal cord (K. L. Moore & Persaud, 2003).

embryo The name for a developing organism from about the third through the eighth week after conception.

The head begins to take shape in the fourth week, as eyes, ears, nose, and mouth form. Also in the fourth week, a minuscule blood vessel that will become the heart begins to pulsate, making the cardiovascular system the first to show any activity.

By the fifth week, buds that will become arms and legs appear. The upper arms and then forearms, palms, and webbed fingers form. Legs, feet, and webbed toes, in that order, emerge a few days later, each with the beginning of a skeletal structure. Then—52 and 54 days after conception, respectively—the fingers and toes separate.

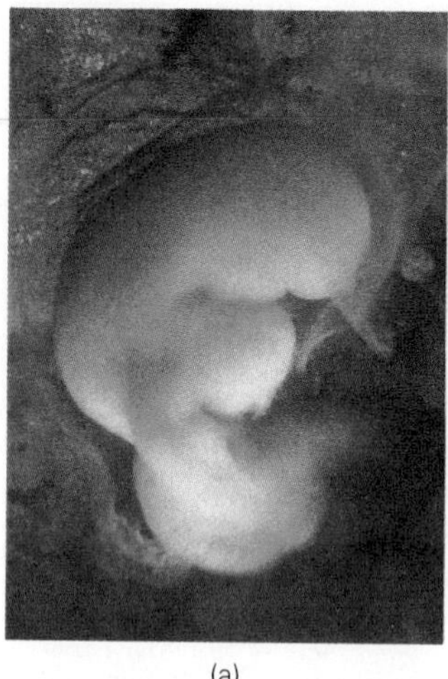
(a)

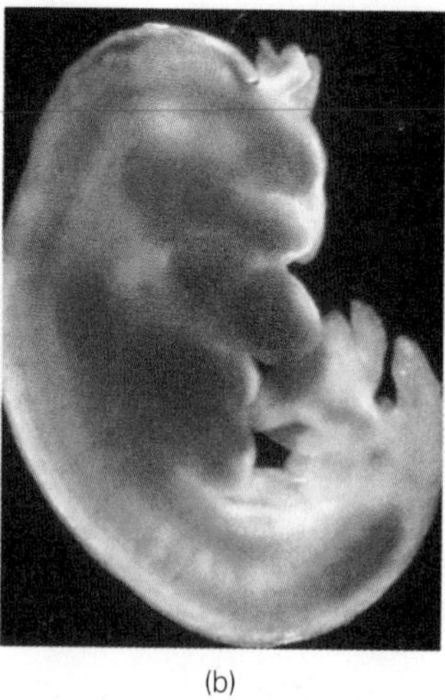
(b)

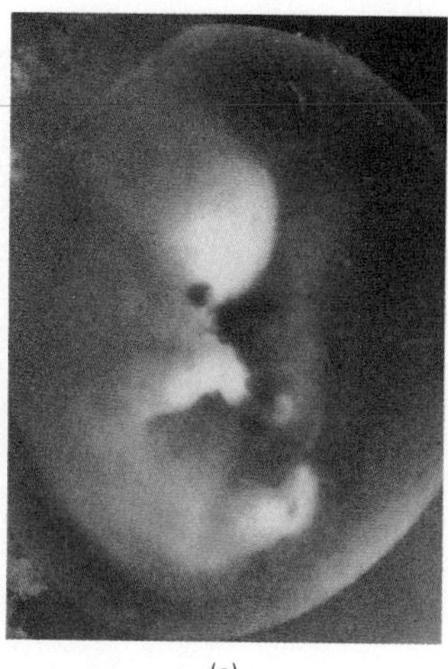
(c)

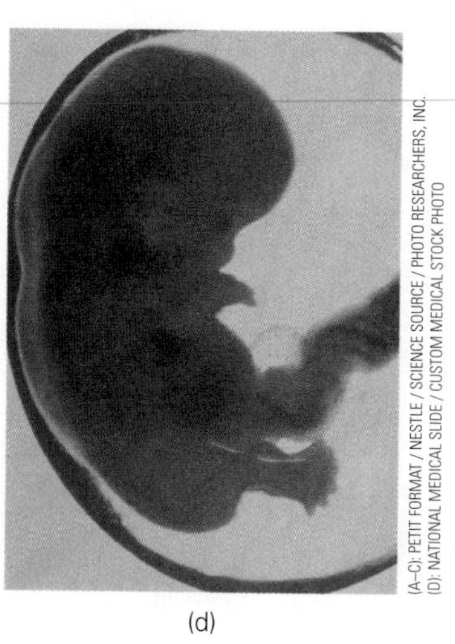
(d)

(A–C): PETIT FORMAT / NESTLE / SCIENCE SOURCE / PHOTO RESEARCHERS, INC. (D): NATIONAL MEDICAL SLIDE / CUSTOM MEDICAL STOCK PHOTO

The Embryonic Period *(a)* At 4 weeks past conception, the embryo is only about ⅛ inch (3 millimeters) long, but already the head *(top right)* has taken shape. *(b)* At 5 weeks past conception, the embryo has grown to twice the size it was at 4 weeks. Its primitive heart, which has been pulsing for a week now, is visible, as is what appears to be a primitive tail, which will soon be enclosed by skin and protective tissue at the tip of the backbone (the coccyx). *(c)* By 7 weeks, the organism is somewhat less than an inch (2½ centimeters) long. Eyes, nose, the digestive system, and even the first stage of toe formation can be seen. *(d)* At 8 weeks, the 1-inch-long organism is clearly recognizable as a human fetus.

At the eighth week after conception (56 days), the embryo weighs just one-thirtieth of an ounce (1 gram) and is about 1 inch (2½ centimeters) long. The head has become rounded, and the features of the face are formed. The embryo has all the basic organs and body parts of a human being, including elbows and knees, nostrils and toes, and a unisex structure called the *indifferent gonad*. It moves frequently, about 150 times an hour (Piontelli, 2002).

Fetus: From the Ninth Week Until Birth

fetus The name for a developing organism from the ninth week after conception until birth.

The developing organism is called a **fetus** from the ninth week after conception until birth. During the fetal period, it develops from a tiny, sexless creature smaller than the last joint of your thumb to a 7½-pound, 20-inch (3,400 grams, 51 centimeters) boy or girl.

The Third Month

Especially for Feminists Many people believe that the differences between the sexes are primarily sociocultural, not biological. Is there any prenatal support for that view?

If an embryo is male (XY), the SRY gene on the Y chromosome commands that male sexual organs develop; with no such command, the indifferent gonad develops into female sex organs. By the 12th week, the genitals are fully formed and are sending hormones to the developing brain. Although most functions of the brain are gender-neutral, hormones cause some sex differences in brain organization by mid-pregnancy (Cameron, 2001).

At the end of the third month, the fetus has all its body parts, weighs approximately 3 ounces (87 grams), and is about 3 inches (7.5 centimeters) long. Early prenatal growth is very rapid, but there is considerable variation from fetus to fetus, especially in body weight (K. L. Moore & Persaud, 2003). The numbers just given —3 months, 3 ounces, 3 inches—are rounded off for easy recollection. (For those on the metric system, "100 days, 100 millimeters, 100 grams" is similarly useful.)

Despite the variations, some aspects of third-month growth are universal. The fetus is too small to survive outside the womb, the organs are not yet functioning, but all the body structures are in place.

The Middle Three Months: Preparing to Survive

In the fourth, fifth, and sixth months, the heartbeat becomes stronger and the cardiovascular system becomes more active. Digestive and excretory systems develop. Fingernails, toenails, and buds for teeth form, and hair grows (including eyelashes).

Amazing as body growth is, the brain is even more impressive, increasing about six times in size and developing many new neurons, or brain cells (in a process called *neurogenesis*), and synapses (*synaptogenesis*), which are connections between neurons. The neurons begin to organize themselves, some dying, some extending long axons to distant neurons (Kolb & Whishaw, 2003). Brain growth and neurological organization continue for years, as you will see in later chapters (in which neurons, synapses, and axons are explained more fully), but the entire central nervous system first emerges during mid-pregnancy.

S. J. ALLEN / INTERNATIONAL STOCK PHOTO

The Fetus At the end of 4 months, the fetus, now 6 inches long, looks fully formed but out of proportion—the distance from the top of the skull to the neck is almost as long as that from the neck to the rump. For many more weeks, the fetus must depend on the translucent membranes of the placenta and umbilical cord (the long white object in the foreground) for survival.

Observation Quiz (see answer, page 96): Can you see eyebrows, fingernails, and genitals?

Advances in fetal brain functioning are critical to attainment of the **age of viability,** the age at which a preterm newborn can survive. That's because the brain regulates basic body functions, such as breathing and sucking. With advanced medical care, the age of viability is about 22 weeks after conception, although most such babies weigh under 500 grams (less than a pound). (For a summary of information about preterm birthweights, see Table 4.7 on page 113.)

age of viability The age (about 22 weeks after conception) at which a fetus might survive outside the mother's uterus if specialized medical care is available.

Babies born before 22 weeks of gestation do not survive. This 22-week barrier has not been reduced by even the most sophisticated respirators and heart regulators, probably because maintaining life requires some brain response (Paul et al., 2006). At 23–26 weeks, the survival rate improves to up to two-thirds (Kelly, 2006; Wilson-Costello et al., 2007).

However, these newborns are vulnerable. A study that compared 8-year-olds who had been born very early with others who had been born "full term" (at 35–40 weeks) found that 20 percent of the preterm children had cerebral palsy, 41 percent had some mental retardation, and only 20 percent had no disabilities (Marlow et al., 2005). Although fewer 22- to 28-week-old newborns were stillborn in the past decade, their mortality and morbidity have not improved, leading one team to suggest that neonatal care has reached its limits (Paul et al., 2006).

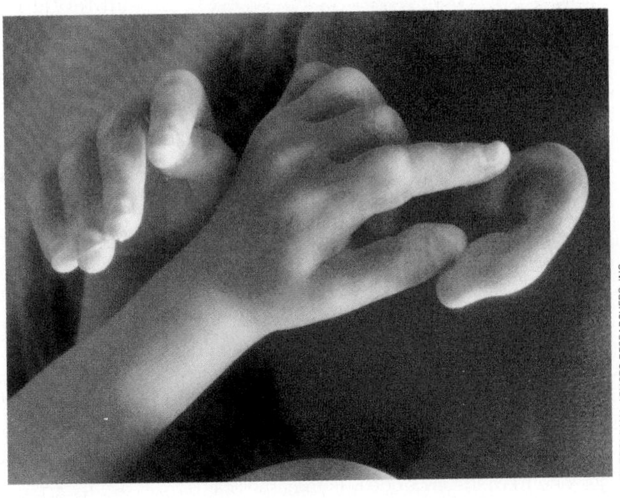

Can He Hear? A fetus, just about at the age of viability, is shown fingering his ear. Such gestures are probably random; but, yes, he can hear.

N. BROMHALL / PHOTO RESEARCHERS, INC.

At about 28 weeks, brain-wave patterns include occasional bursts of activity that resemble the sleep–wake cycles of a newborn (Joseph, 2000), and heart rate and body movement become reactive, not random, decreasing when the fetus needs rest. Because of brain maturation, most babies born at 28 weeks develop normally.

Weight is also significant. By 28 weeks, the typical fetus weighs about 3 pounds (1.3 kilograms), and its chances of survival are 95 percent.

Maturity is more crucial than birthweight. Even very tiny babies sometimes live if they are a few weeks past the age of viability.

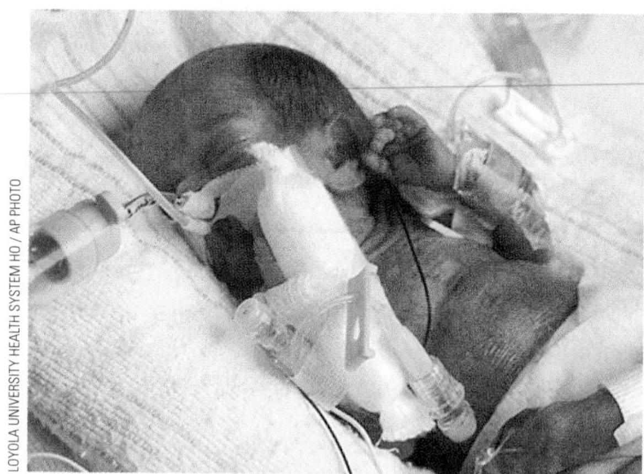
LOYOLA UNIVERSITY HEALTH SYSTEM HO / AP PHOTO

The World's Littlest Baby For reasons discussed in the text, tiny Rumaisa Rahmon has a good chance of living a full, normal life. Rumaisa gained 5 pounds (2,270 grams) in the hospital and then, 6 months after her birth, went home. Her twin sister, Hiba, who weighed 1.3 pounds (600 grams) at birth, had gone home two months earlier. At their one-year birthday, the twins seemed normal, with Rumaisa weighing 15 pounds (6,800 grams) and Hiba 17 (7,711 grams) (CBS News, 2005).

Rumaisa Rahman was born after 25 weeks and 6 days weighing only 8.6 ounces (244 grams). Rumaisa had four advantages besides her gestational maturity: her sex (boys are more likely to die); her birthplace (Chicago's Loyola University Hospital, which specializes in preterm babies); her birth process (cesarean delivery is easier on the fetus); and the reason she was so tiny (she was a twin) (CBS News, 2005).

Another very tiny preterm infant has bucked the odds and survived. Amillia Taylor was born in October 2006 after only 21 weeks and six days in the uterus—a new record. Since she was conceived via IVF, she was actually 22 weeks old at birth, weighing just 10 ounces (284 grams) and measuring a mere 9½ inches. As with Rumaisa, her survival was aided by her sex and place of birth, a specialized neonatal facility within Baptist Children's Hospital of Miami, Florida (Wingert, 2007).

The Final Three Months: From Viability to Full Term

Attaining viability simply means that life outside the womb is *possible*. Each day of the final three months of prenatal growth improves the odds not merely of survival but of a healthy and happy baby.

A viable preterm infant born in the seventh month is a tiny creature requiring intensive hospital care and life-support systems for each gram of nourishment and for every shallow breath. By contrast, after nine months or so, the typical full-term infant is a vigorous person, ready to thrive at home on mother's milk—no expert help, oxygenated air, or special feeding required.

The critical difference between a fragile preterm baby and a robust newborn is maturation of the neurological, respiratory, and cardiovascular systems. In the last three months of prenatal life, brain waves indicate responsiveness; the lungs expand and contract using the amniotic fluid as a substitute for air; and heart valves, arteries, and veins circulate the fetal blood.

Weight gain in the last three months is about 4½ pounds (2,000 grams). This ensures adequate nutrition to the rapidly developing brain and thus avoids severe malnutrition in the second half of pregnancy, which would reduce the baby's ability to learn (Georgieff & Rao, 2001). At full term, human brain growth is so extensive that the *cortex* (the brain's advanced outer layer) forms several folds in order to fit into the skull (see Figure 4.2).

The relationship between mother and child intensifies during the final three months, for fetal size and movements make the pregnant woman very aware of it. In turn, the fetus becomes aware of her sounds (voice and heartbeat), smells (via amniotic fluid), and behavior (Aslin & Hunt, 2001). Regular walking is soothing, and sudden noises cause the fetus to jump. When the mother is highly fearful or anxious, the fetal heart beats faster and body movements increase (DiPietro et al., 2002).

SUMMING UP

In two weeks of rapid cell duplication, differentiation, and finally implantation, the one-celled zygote becomes a blastocyst and then a many-celled embryo. The embryo develops the beginning of the central nervous system (3 weeks), a heart and a face (4 weeks), arms and legs (5 weeks), hands and feet (6 weeks), and fingers and toes (7 weeks), while the inner organs take shape. By 8 weeks, all the body structures, except male and female organs, are in place. Fetal development proceeds rapidly, with weight gain (about 2 pounds, or 900 grams) and brain maturation, which make viability possible by about 22 weeks. Further development of the brain, lungs, and heart make the full-term, 35- to 40-week-old newborn ready for life. ■

➤**Response for Feminists** (from page 94): Only one of the 46 human chromosomes determines sex, and the genitals develop last in the prenatal sequence. Sex differences are apparent before birth, but they are relatively minor.

➤**Answer to Observation Quiz** (from page 95): Yes, yes, and no. Genitals are formed, but they are not visible in this photo. The object growing from the lower belly is the umbilical cord.

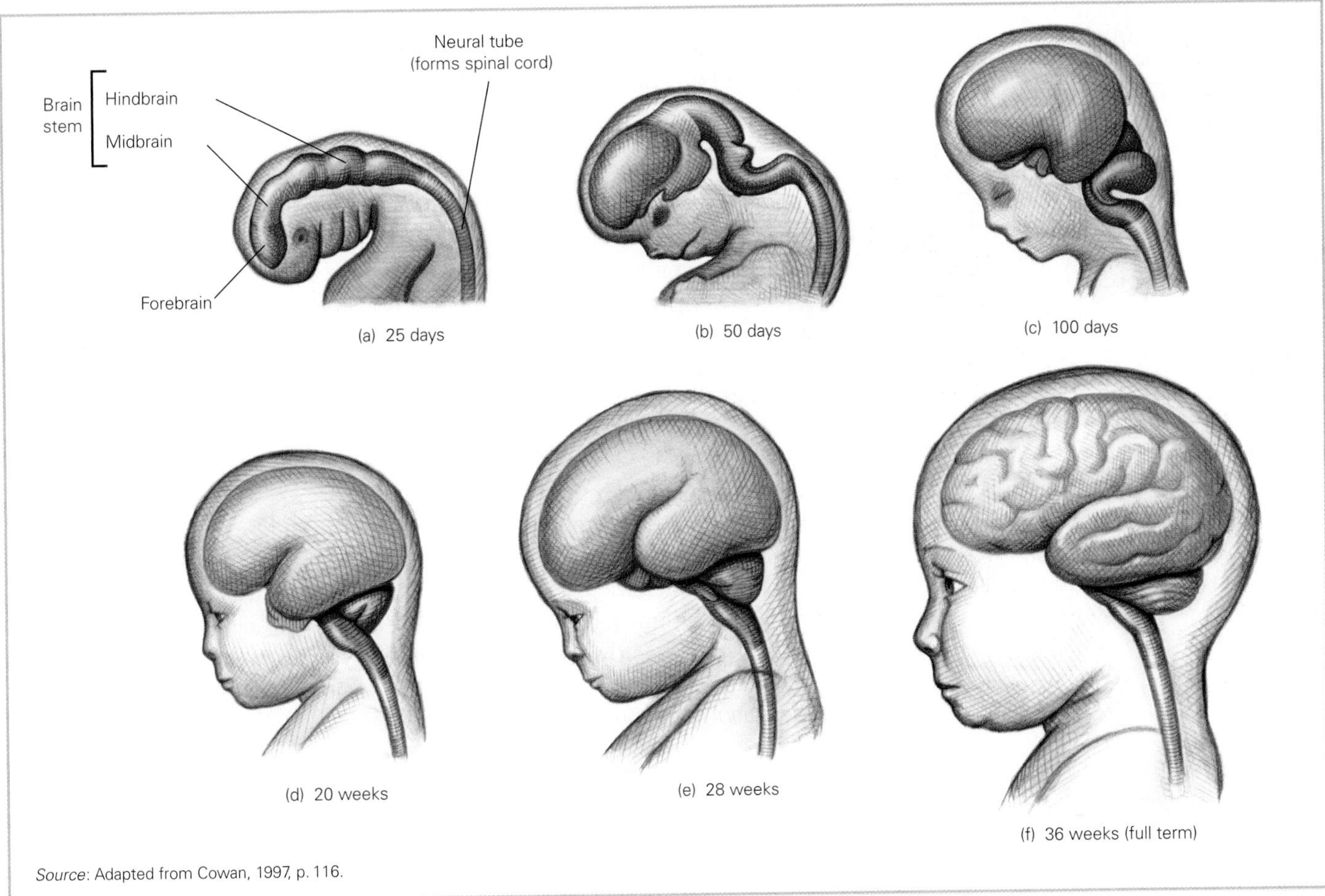

Source: Adapted from Cowan, 1997, p. 116.

FIGURE 4.2

Prenatal Growth of the Brain Just 25 days after conception *(a)*, the central nervous system is already evident. The brain looks distinctly human by day 100 *(c)*. By the 28th week of gestation *(e)*, at the very time brain activity begins, the various sections of the brain are recognizable. When the fetus is full term *(f)*, all the parts of the brain, including the cortex (the outer layer), are formed, folding over one another and becoming more convoluted, or wrinkled, as the number of brain cells increases.

Risk Reduction

Many toxins, illnesses, and experiences can harm a developing person before birth. If this topic alarms you, bear in mind that the large majority of newborns are healthy and capable. Only about 3 percent have major structural anomalies, such as cleft palate, malformed organs, or missing limbs (K. L. Moore & Persaud, 2003), and another 10 percent have minor physical problems that modern medicine can treat, such as an extra digit or an undescended testicle.

Especially for the Friend of a Pregnant Woman Suppose that your friend is frightened of having an abnormal child. She refuses to read about prenatal development because she is afraid to learn about what could go wrong. What could you tell her?

Prenatal development should be thought of not as a dangerous period to be feared but as a natural process to be protected. The goal of *teratology*, the study of birth defects, is to increase the odds that every newborn will have a healthy start. **Teratogens** are substances (such as drugs and pollutants) and conditions (such as severe malnutrition and extreme stress) that increase the risk of prenatal abnormalities.

teratogens Agents and conditions, including viruses, drugs, and chemicals, that can impair prenatal development and result in birth defects or even death.

Teratogens cause not only physical problems but also impaired learning and behavior. Teratogens that harm the brain, making a child hyperactive, antisocial, learning-disabled, and so on, are called **behavioral teratogens.** The origins of

behavioral teratogens Agents and conditions that can harm the prenatal brain, impairing the future child's intellectual and emotional functioning.

➤Response for the Friend of a Pregnant Woman (from page 97): Reassure her that almost all pregnancies turn out fine, partly because most defective fetuses are spontaneously aborted (miscarried) and partly because protective factors are active throughout pregnancy. Equally important, the more she learns about teratogens, the more she will learn about protecting her fetus. Many birth defects and complications can be prevented with good prenatal care.

such problems are difficult to trace, but about 20 percent of all children have behavioral difficulties (usually not noticed until years after birth) that *could* be connected to damage done during the prenatal period.

Determining Risk

It was once believed that the placenta screened out all harmful substances. Then two tragedies occurred. Doctors on an Australian military base traced an increase in blindness among newborns to rubella (German measles) contracted by pregnant women a few months earlier (Gregg, 1941, in Persaud et al., 1985); a sudden increase in European infants born with missing or deformed arms and legs in the late 1950s was traced to a new drug called thalidomide (Schardein, 1976). It became obvious that scientists needed to know how this happened, and teratology began.

risk analysis The science of weighing the potential effects of a particular event, substance, or experience to determine the likelihood of harm. In teratology, risk analysis attempts to evaluate everything that affects the chances that a particular agent or condition will cause damage to an embryo or fetus.

Teratology is a science of **risk analysis,** of weighing the chances that a particular teratogen (substance or condition that could cause harm) will affect the fetus. Understanding risk is crucial for understanding human development; every period of life entails certain risks, and much harm can be avoided.

All teratogens increase *risk,* but none *always* cause damage. Several influential prenatal factors—timing, dosage, and genes—are described here. Other, postnatal influences—such as early care and attachment—are discussed in the three chapters on infancy (5, 6, and 7). Still others—education, friendship, vocation—are discussed later in this text.

Timing of Exposure

One crucial factor is timing—the age of the developing organism when it is exposed to the teratogen. Some teratogens cause damage early in prenatal development, when a particular part of the body is forming. Thalidomide, for example, stopped the formation of arms and legs in weeks 6 or 7 but caused no damage after week 9.

critical period In prenatal development, the time when a particular organ or other body part of the embryo or fetus is most susceptible to damage by teratogens.

The time of greatest susceptibility is called the **critical period.** As you can see in Figure 4.3, each body structure has its own critical period. The entire six weeks of the embryonic stage can be called a critical period for physical structure and form, with the specifics varying somewhat week by week (K. L. Moore & Persaud, 2003).

Because the early days are critical, most obstetricians today recommend that *before* pregnancy, all couples get counseling, stop using recreational drugs (especially alcohol), and update their immunizations (Kuller et al., 2001). In addition, a prospective mother should make sure her body is ready by supplementing a balanced diet with extra folic acid and iron. Not all women follow these recommendations (see Table 4.3).

Since the brain continues to grow throughout prenatal development, there is no safe period for behavioral teratogens. Teratogens that cause preterm birth or low birthweight (notably cigarettes) are particularly harmful in the second half of pregnancy, but, for many reasons, women should stop smoking or ingesting any drugs, and start eating well and taking prenatal vitamins, before conceiving.

Amount of Exposure

threshold effect A situation in which a certain teratogen is relatively harmless in small doses but becomes harmful once exposure reaches a certain level (the threshold).

A second important factor is the dose and/or frequency of exposure. Some teratogens have a **threshold effect;** that is, they are virtually harmless until exposure reaches a certain level, at which point they "cross the threshold" and become damaging (Reece & Hobbins, 2007). Indeed, a few substances are beneficial in small amounts

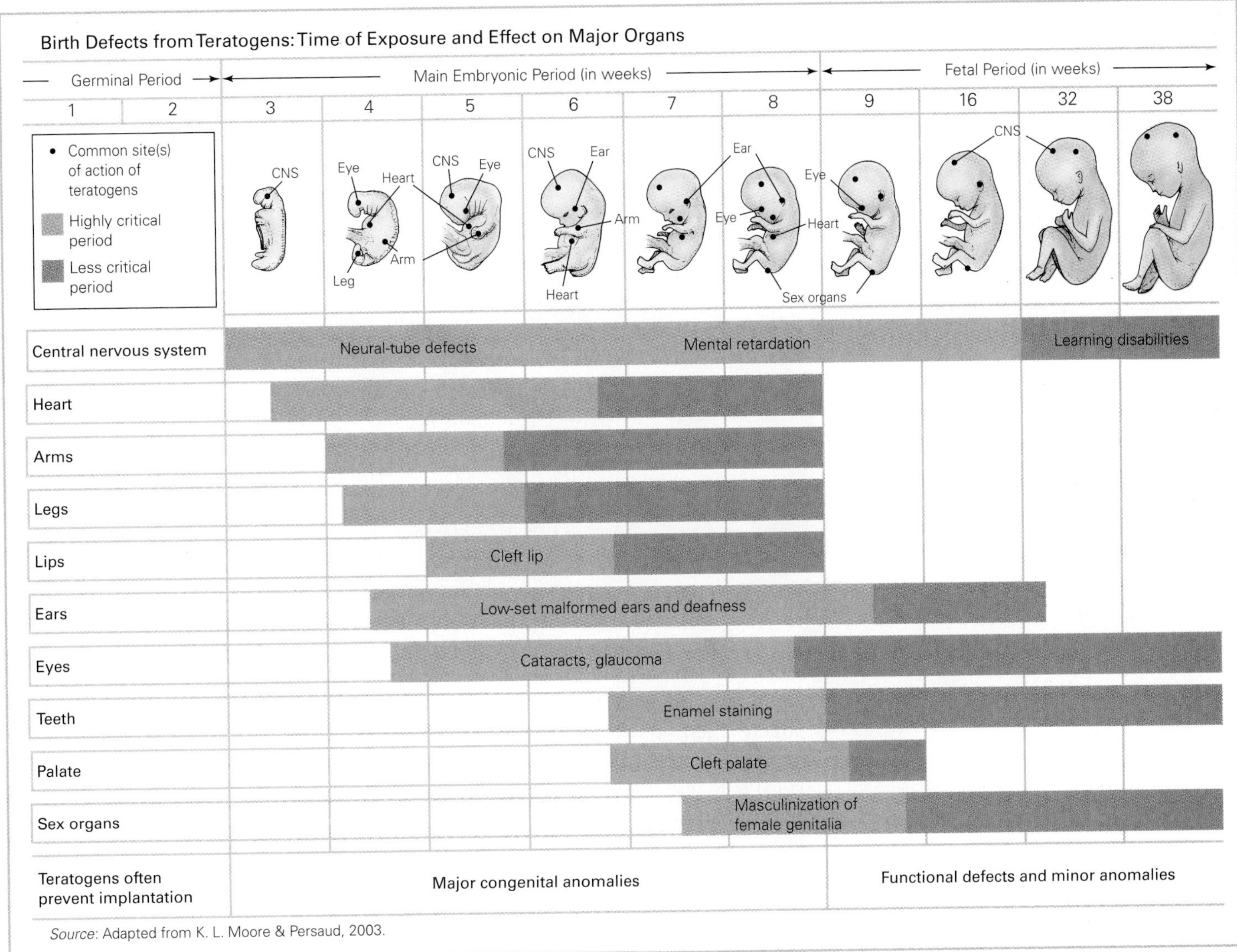

FIGURE 4.3

Critical Periods in Human Development The most serious damage from teratogens *(orange bars)* is likely to occur early in prenatal development. However, significant damage *(purple bars)* to many vital parts of the body, including the brain, eyes, and genitals, can occur during the last months of pregnancy as well.

but fiercely teratogenic in large quantities. For example, vitamin A is an essential part of the prenatal diet, but more than 10,000 units per day may be too much and 50,000 units can cause abnormalities in body structures.

For most teratogens, experts hesitate to specify a safe threshold. One reason is the **interaction effect,** when one teratogen intensifies the impact of another. Alcohol, tobacco, and marijuana interact, doing more harm in combination than any one of them does alone. Ironically, using any one of these three makes a pregnant woman likely to use the others as well.

Especially for Nutritionists Is it beneficial that most breakfast cereals are fortified with vitamins and minerals?

interaction effect The result of a combination of teratogens. Sometimes risk is greatly magnified when an embryo or fetus is exposed to more than one teratogen at the same time.

Genetic Vulnerability

A third factor that determines whether a specific teratogen will be harmful, and to what extent, is the developing organism's genes (Mann & Andrews, 2007). Although

TABLE 4.3

Before You Become Pregnant

What Prospective Mothers Should Do	What Prospective Mothers Really Do (U. S. data)
1. Take a daily multivitamin with folic acid.	1. In 2004, 40 percent of women aged 18 to 45 did so, up from 30 percent in previous years.
2. Avoid binge drinking (defined as 4 or more drinks in a row).	2. One-eighth of all women who might become pregnant (are sexually active, use no contraception) binge-drink (55 percent of binge drinkers are alcoholics).
3. Update immunizations against all teratogenic viruses, especially rubella.	3. Because of laws regarding school admission, most young women in the United States are well immunized.
4. Gain or lose weight, as appropriate.	4. Babies born to underweight women are at risk for low birthweight. Babies born to obese women have three times the usual rate of birth complications.
5. Reassess your use of prescription drugs.	5. Eighty-five percent of pregnant women are taking prescription drugs (not counting vitamins).
6. Know status regarding sexually transmitted diseases.	6. Only a third of sexually active women get tested for the most common STD, chlamydia. Even fewer are screened for other, more dangerous infections, such as syphilis and HIV.

Sources: Andrade et al., 2004; Cedergren, 2004; MMWR, September 17, 2004; MMWR, October 29, 2004; MMWR, December 24, 2004.

precise genetic research has not yet connected fetal genes and teratogens, it is apparent that dizygotic twins, exposed to the same teratogens, experience different effects. Cleft lip, cleft palate, and club foot almost certainly result from a combination of genetic vulnerability, stress, and inadequate nutrition (Botto et al., 2004; Hartl & Jones, 1999).

International comparisons of rates of birth defects also suggest that genes are a factor (World Health Organization, 2003). For example, Japan has relatively low rates of many birth defects, but its rate of newborns with cleft lip is three times that of Canada. The fact that nations, and even regions within nations, have high rates of some defects and low rates of others suggests genetic vulnerabilities and protections.

Genes are known to affect the likelihood of neural-tube defects (see Table 3.2, pp. 82–83). Both spina bifida and microcephaly are more common in some ethnic groups (specifically, among infants of Irish, English, and Egyptian descent) and less common in others (most Asian and African groups), because some groups have more carriers of an allele that decreases the normal utilization of folic acid (Mills et al., 1995). Knowing this led to a solution: If every pregnant woman consumed extra folic acid, the embryos with this allele would still get enough of this B vitamin to develop a normal nervous system.

Since the genes of the fetus are unknown, and the central nervous system begins to form in the third week after conception, women are urged to take vitamins with folic acid *before* becoming pregnant. Only a third of U.S. women take extra folic acid before conception (Suellentrop et al., 2006). However, thanks to a 1996 U.S. law and a 1998 Canadian one, cereal and bread manufactured in those countries are now fortified with folic acid. As a result, folic acid consumption in the United States has increased by 50 percent (Bentley et al., 2006), and neural-tube defects have decreased by 26 percent (MMWR, September 13, 2002). In Europe, where no food fortification has occurred, neural-tube defects have not decreased (Botto et al., 2005).

➤**Response for Nutritionists** (from page 99): Useful, yes; optimal, no. Some essential vitamins are missing (too expensive), and individual needs differ, depending on age, sex, health, genes, and eating habits. The reduction in neural-tube defects is good, but many women do not benefit because they don't eat cereal or take vitamin supplements before becoming pregnant.

In some cases, genetic vulnerability is related to the sex of the developing organism. Generally, males (XY) are at greater risk. That is one explanation for the more frequent spontaneous abortions of male than female fetuses. In addition, boys have more birth defects, learning disabilities, and other problems caused by behavioral teratogens.

Protective Measures

Because of the many variables involved, the results of teratogenic exposure cannot be predicted in individual cases. However, much is known about common and damaging teratogens and about how individuals and society can reduce the risks. Table 4.4, on pages 103–104, lists some teratogens and their effects, as well as preventive measures.

Some pregnant women are exposed to these teratogens with no evident harm, and some defects occur for reasons unknown. Women are advised to avoid all drugs, chemicals in pesticides (including bug spray), construction materials (including solvents), and cosmetics (including hair dye) *before* becoming pregnant.

Such advice is easy to give but not easy to follow. Even doctors should be more careful. A study (see Research Design) of 152,000 births in eight U.S. health maintenance organizations (HMOs) found that doctors wrote an average of three prescriptions per pregnant woman, including many for drugs not declared safe during pregnancy (prescribed for 38 percent) and some for drugs with proven risks to human fetuses (prescribed for 5 percent). Some of those drugs with proven risks (3.4 percent) were in the Food and Drug Administration's category D, meaning that even though they have been proven to be sometimes harmful, they may be worth the risk for the sake of the mother's health. A few (1 percent) were in category X, meaning that they should never be taken because they are proven teratogens and alternatives are available (Andrade et al., 2004).

How could this happen? Perhaps the doctors did not know that their patients were pregnant (the women had already had their first prenatal visit, but they might not have told the prescribing doctor), or perhaps the women did not take the drugs. But women are not always cautious: A nationwide survey has found that some women acknowledge smoking (14 percent) and drinking (5 percent) during the last 3 months of their pregnancies (Suellentrop et al., 2006).

In the past few decades, scientists have identified hundreds of teratogens that *might* harm an embryo or fetus. Almost every common disease, almost every food additive, most prescription and nonprescription drugs (even caffeine and aspirin), trace minerals in the air and water, emotional stress, exhaustion, and even hunger are suspected of impairing prenatal development. Why have scientists not acted on this information, perhaps by calling on the authorities to take away the license of any doctor who prescribed any drug to a pregnant woman or to arrest any woman who smoked or drank?

Remember the scientific method. A hypothesis is tested in many ways, conclusions are tentatively drawn, and researchers note limitations and examine alternative explanations. Most research on teratogens has been done with mice; harm to humans is rarely proven to the satisfaction of every scientist. Definitive proof may take decades, and scientists are taught to be careful.

What would it take for scientists to agree that a substance was a teratogen for humans? A substance would need to be given to hundreds, perhaps thousands, of pregnant women, at various times in the pregnancy (early, late, throughout), with no confounding influences (the women would need to be similar in genes, nutrition, health, medical care). Then their offspring would have to be examined not

Research Design

Scientists: Susan Andrade and others.

Publication: *American Journal of Obstetrics and Gynecology* (2004).

Participants: 152,531 women who gave birth from 1996 to 2000.

Design: Computer search of records from eight HMOs for prescriptions written for these participants between the date of the first prenatal visit and the delivery date.

Major conclusion: Many doctors prescribe drugs for pregnant women that are not known to be safe.

Comment: This method avoids the possibility of women or doctors forgetting or denying drug use during pregnancy. However, some of the women may not have taken the drugs that were prescribed for them, either by their own choice or on advice from a physician. Follow-up research is needed to establish a correlation between birth defects and drugs prescribed.

fetal alcohol syndrome (FAS) A cluster of birth defects, including abnormal facial characteristics, slow physical growth, and retarded mental development, caused by the mother's drinking alcohol while pregnant.

only at birth but for decades afterward, because the damage done by some teratogens becomes evident only in adulthood. For example, many pregnant women took a drug called DES in the 1960s; their adult children have a higher than average risk of problems with their sex organs.

The clash between the urgency of protecting future children and the caution of the scientific method is further illustrated by the story of fetal alcohol syndrome.

thinking like a scientist

On Punishing Pregnant Drinkers

Alcohol in high doses is a proven teratogen. Proof did not come easy; 40 years ago drinking alcohol during pregnancy was believed to be harmless. But some obstetricians noted that a few patients who drank heavily had babies with distorted facial features, including small eyes and a thin upper lip. As those children grew, they turned out to be mentally retarded, impulsive, and hyperactive. This combination was given the name **fetal alcohol syndrome (FAS).**

The diagnosis of FAS was possible because alcohol was widely used. That meant that, once suspicions were raised, the correlation between excessive maternal drinking and fetal harm became "obvious." This hypothesis was tested with thousands of mice and monkeys and with alcoholic women throughout the world, including, recently, in South Africa (May et al., 2005). Replication over the decades has convinced all scientists.

However, not every pregnant woman who drinks heavily has a newborn with FAS. Might the risk of being born with FAS be dose-related or genetic? If FAS is not visibly present, might the infant become hyperactive or a slow learner? Surveys and longitudinal studies have confirmed a correlation between drinking by a pregnant woman and damage to the fetus (Streissguth & Connor, 2001).

© DAVID H. WELLS / CORBIS

Yes, But . . . An adopted boy points out something to his disabled father—a positive interaction between the two. The shapes of the boy's eyes, ears, and upper lip indicate that he was born with fetal alcohol syndrome. Scientists disagree about a correlation between FAS and drinking alcohol during pregnancy.

Not all scientists are convinced. Some infants born to drinking mothers seem unharmed, and many pregnant drinkers have other problems: drug abuse; unstable eating and sleeping patterns; bouts of anxiety, stress, or depression; accidental injuries; domestic violence; sexual infections; malnutrition; illnesses; lack of family support; and inadequate medical care. Any of these can lead to hyperactivity and slower learning in a child, whether the mother drinks or not. Some scientists (especially in Europe) wonder whether occasional, moderate drinking during pregnancy might be acceptable. They note that moderate drinking aids human longevity (Smith & Hart, 2002).

Nevertheless, most doctors in the United States advise pregnant women to abstain completely from alcohol. Moreover, since 1998, four states have authorized "involuntary commitment" (jail or forced residential treatment) for pregnant women who do not stop drinking (National Institute on Alcohol Abuse and Addiction, 2006). Many individual doctors and the American Medical Association fear that the threat of such punishment will cause the women who most need prenatal care to avoid getting it. Developmental scientists ask whether, since every person is powerfully affected by his or her social context, not just pregnant women who drink but also their husbands, mothers, and bartenders should also risk jail.

Of course, that would be madness—millions of people would be jailed. But if that were not done, the law would be selectively enforced, and that is a problem as well. Prejudice might also be involved: The four states that do incarcerate pregnant drinkers (North and South Dakota, Wisconsin, Oklahoma) all have more American Indians than the national average.

Only after a fetus is born does FAS become apparent. To target only one teratogen and to punish women before harm becomes evident is contrary to the scientific method, which seeks proof. But will scientific caution mean that millions of children will suffer because of substances not yet proven to be teratogens? If a pregnant woman you knew ordered a glass of wine, would you try to stop her?

TABLE 4.4

Teratogens: Effects of Exposure and Prevention of Damage

Teratogens	Effects on Child of Exposure	Measures for Preventing Damage
Diseases		
Rubella (German measles)	In embryonic period, causes blindness and deafness; in first and second trimesters, causes brain damage	Get immunized before becoming pregnant
Toxoplasmosis	Brain damage, loss of vision, mental retardation	Avoid eating undercooked meat and handling cat feces, garden dirt
Measles, chicken pox, influenza	May impair brain functioning	Get immunized before getting pregnant; avoid infected people during pregnancy
Syphilis	Baby is born with syphilis, which, untreated, leads to brain and bone damage and eventual death	Early prenatal diagnosis and treatment with antibiotics
AIDS	Baby may catch the virus. If so, illness and death are likely during childhood.	Prenatal drugs and cesarean birth make AIDS transmission very rare.
Other sexually transmitted diseases, including gonorrhea and chlamydia	Not usually harmful during pregnancy but may cause blindness and infections if transmitted during birth	Early diagnosis and treatment; if necessary, cesarean section, treatment of newborn
Infections, including infections of urinary tract, gums, and teeth	May cause premature labor, which increases vulnerability to brain damage	Get infection treated, preferably before becoming pregnant
Pollutants		
Lead, mercury, PCBs (polychlorinated biphenyls), dioxin, and some pesticides, herbicides, and cleaning compounds	May cause spontaneous abortion, preterm labor, and brain damage	Most common substances are harmless in small doses, but pregnant women should still avoid regular and direct exposure, such as drinking well water, eating unwashed fruits or vegetables, using chemical compounds, eating fish from polluted waters
Radiation		
Massive or repeated exposure to radiation, as in medical X-rays	In the embryonic period, may cause abnormally small head (microcephaly) and mental retardation; in the fetal period, suspected but not proven to cause brain damage. Exposure to background radiation, as from power plants, is usually too low to have an effect.	Get sonograms, not X-rays, during pregnancy; pregnant women who work directly with radiation need special protection or temporary assignment to another job
Social and Behavioral Factors		
Very high stress	Early in pregnancy, may cause cleft lip or cleft palate, spontaneous abortion, or preterm labor	Get adequate relaxation, rest, and sleep; reduce hours of employment; get help with housework and child care
Malnutrition	When severe, may interfere with conception, implantation, normal fetal development, and full-term birth	Eat a balanced diet (with adequate vitamins and minerals, including, especially, folic acid, iron, and vitamin A); achieve normal weight before getting pregnant, then gain 25–35 lbs (10–15 kg) during pregnancy
Excessive, exhausting exercise	Can affect fetal development when it interferes with pregnant woman's sleep or digestion	Get regular, moderate exercise
Medicinal Drugs		
Lithium	Can cause heart abnormalities	Avoid all medicines, whether prescription or over-the-counter, during pregnancy unless they are approved by a medical professional who knows about the pregnancy and is aware of the most recent research
Tetracycline	Can harm the teeth	
Retinoic acid	Can cause limb deformities	
Streptomycin	Can cause deafness	
ACE inhibitors	Can harm digestive organs	
Phenobarbital	Can affect brain development	
Thalidomide	Can stop ear and limb formation	

(continued on page 104)

TABLE 4.4 (continued from page 103)

Teratogens: Effects of Exposure and Prevention of Damage

Teratogens	Effects on Child of Exposure	Measures for Preventing Damage
Psychoactive Drugs		
Caffeine	Normal use poses no problem	Avoid excessive use: Drink no more than three cups a day of beverages containing caffeine (coffee, tea, cola drinks, hot chocolate)
Alcohol	May cause fetal alcohol syndrome (FAS) or fetal alcohol effects (FAE) (see Thinking Like a Scientist, p. 102)	Stop or severely limit alcohol consumption during pregnancy; especially dangerous are three or more drinks a day or five or more drinks on one occasion
Tobacco	Increases risk of malformations of limbs and urinary tract, and may affect the baby's lungs	Stop smoking before and during pregnancy
Marijuana	Heavy exposure may affect the central nervous system; when smoked, may hinder fetal growth	Avoid or strictly limit marijuana consumption
Heroin	Slows fetal growth and may cause premature labor; newborns with heroin in their bloodstream require medical treatment to prevent the pain and convulsions of withdrawal	Get treated for heroin addiction before becoming pregnant; if already pregnant, gradual withdrawal on methadone is better than continued use of heroin
Cocaine	May cause slow fetal growth, premature labor, and learning problems in the first years of life	Stop using cocaine before pregnancy; babies of cocaine-using mothers may need special medical and educational attention in their first years of life
Inhaled solvents (glue or aerosol)	May cause abnormally small head, crossed eyes, and other indications of brain damage	Stop sniffing inhalants before becoming pregnant; be aware that serious damage can occur before a woman knows she is pregnant

Note: This table summarizes some relatively common teratogenic effects. As the text makes clear, many individual factors in each pregnancy affect whether a given teratogen will actually cause damage and what that damage might be. This is a general summary of what is known; new evidence is reported almost daily, so some of these generalities will change. Pregnant women or women who want to become pregnant should consult with their physicians.
Sources: Reece & Hobbins, 2007; Mann & Andrews, 2007; O'Rahilly & Müller, 2001; Shepard & Lemire, 2004; L.T. Singer et al., 2002.

Benefits of Prenatal Care

There are many advantages to obtaining early prenatal care (Reece & Hobbins, 2007). Chief among them is protection against teratogens—knowing what medicines to avoid and what foods to eat, for instance. Another advantage is that a *sonogram* (an image of the fetus, taken with sound waves) allows parents and doctors to see if the fetus is developing normally, to anticipate the due date, and to determine if there is more than one fetus. In addition, at least a dozen tests of substances in the mother's blood and urine are routinely done, early and again later in pregnancy, to diagnose problems with the fetus. (Table 4.5 provides information about sonograms and some other prenatal tests.)

Only a few decades ago, most twins came as a surprise to their parents at birth; no more. This information may be life-saving. For instance, in about 15 percent of all twin pregnancies with only one placenta, the bloodstreams of the twins are not separate, and one twin gets too much nourishment from the other. This twin-to-twin transfusion problem often killed both twins, but now it can be detected on a sonogram and treated in mid-pregnancy (Sakata et al., 2006).

Further, since twins are often born too early and too small, a woman carrying twins can try to avoid factors that cause low birthweight, such as poor nutrition, work that includes night shifts and hours of standing, or exhaustion and social stress at home (Croteau et al., 2006). Indeed, every woman who learns that her fetus is growing slowly, or that her blood has insufficient iron, or that her blood pressure is climbing, or that she has gestational diabetes can take measures to moderate all these conditions.

Early prenatal care can also prevent the impact of some deadly teratogens. For example, syphilis and AIDS do not harm the fetus if the woman is diagnosed and treated early in pregnancy. Indeed, only a decade ago, 26 percent of women with HIV would pass the virus on to their baby, who often suffered and died in childhood. Now routine early diagnosis of HIV leads to treatment with antiviral drugs that prevent prenatal transmission of the virus (McDonald et al., 2007; Read, 2005).

Especially for Social Workers When is it most important to convince women to be tested for HIV: a month before pregnancy, a month after conception, or immediately after birth?

TABLE 4.5

Methods of Postconception Testing

Method	Description	Risks, Concerns, and Indications
Pre-implantation testing	After in vitro fertilization, one cell is removed from each zygote at the four- or eight-cell stage and analyzed.	Not entirely accurate. Requires surgery, in vitro fertilization, and rapid assessment. This delays implantation and reduces the likelihood of successful birth. It is used only when couples are at high risk of known, testable genetic disorders.
Tests for pregnancy-associated plasma protein (PAPPA) and human chorionic gonadotropin	Blood tests are usually done at about 11 weeks to indicate levels of these substances.	Indicate normal pregnancy, but false positive or false negative results sometimes occur.
Alpha-fetoprotein assay	The mother's blood is tested for the level of alpha-fetoprotein (AFP), now usually done at mid-pregnancy; often combined with other blood tests and repeat sonogram.	Indicate neural-tube defects, multiple embryos (both cause high AFP), or Down syndrome (low AFP). Normal levels change each week; interpretation requires accurate dating of conception.
Sonogram (ultrasound)	High-frequency sound waves are used to produce a "picture" of the fetus as early as 8 weeks. Sonograms are more accurate later in pregnancy to detect less apparent problems, to confirm earlier suspicions, and to anticipate birth complications.	Reveals problems such as a small head or other body malformations, excess fluid accumulating on the brain, Down syndrome (detected by expert, looking at neck of fetus), and several diseases (for instance, of the kidneys). Estimates fetal age and reveals multiple fetuses, placental position, and fetal growth, all of which are useful in every pregnancy. Sometimes sex is apparent. No known risks, unlike the X-rays that it has replaced.
Chorionic villi sampling (CVS)	A sample of the chorion (part of the placenta) is obtained (via sonogram and syringe) at about 10 weeks and analyzed. Since the cells of the placenta are genetically identical to the cells of the fetus, this can indicate many chromosomal or genetic abnormalities.	Provides the same information as amniocentesis but can be performed earlier. Can cause a spontaneous abortion (1%)
Amniocentesis	About half an ounce of the fluid inside the placenta is withdrawn (via sonogram and syringe) at about 16 weeks. The cells are cultured and analyzed.	Spontaneous abortion caused by the syringe is now very rare (0.05 percent). Detects chromosomal abnormalities and other genetic and prenatal problems. The amniotic fluid also reveals the sex of the fetus. Is done later in pregnancy than other tests, and it takes a week before results are known.

Sources: Eddleman et al., 2006; Malone et al., 2005; K. L. Moore & Persaud, 2003; Newnham et al., 2004; Philip et al., 2004; Wright et al., 2006.

The Legacy of AIDS Orphanages have closed in developed nations because they are no longer needed. In contrast, the need for orphanages is increasing in many parts of the developing world, where AIDS has orphaned 11 million children, according to UNICEF data. These children are in an orphanage in Zimbabwe. Some of them may have inherited the AIDS virus from their parents.

AP PHOTO

➤Response for Social Workers (from page 105): Testing and then treatment are useful at any time, because women who know they are HIV-positive are more likely to get treatment, reduce risk of transmission, and avoid pregnancy. If pregnancy does occur, early diagnosis is best. Getting tested after birth is too late for the baby.

Especially for Women of Childbearing Age If you have decided to become pregnant soon, you cannot change your genes, your age, or your economic status. But you can do three things in the next month or two that can markedly reduce the risk of having a low-birthweight or otherwise impaired baby a year from now. What are they?

Pediatric AIDS has almost disappeared from North America and Europe. It is still on the increase in Africa, where prenatal care is scarce and where, even with care, antiviral drugs are often unavailable or unaffordable. Further, the social stigma of HIV/AIDS is so great that some pregnant women fear that their husbands and families will abandon them if they suspect they are HIV-positive.

One problem with diagnostic tests done early in pregnancy is that about 20 percent of the time, their results suggest that more tests are needed. Many such warnings are "false positives," a test result that is positive for a birth defect, yet the fetus is actually fine. It is also possible to have a "false negative," when the test finds no problem but a defect actually does exist. Usually, the cutoff scores for various prenatal tests are set to produce more false positives than false negatives, but in either case, testing can strain a marriage, as the following illustrates.

a case to study

"What Do People Live to Do?"

John and Martha, graduate students at Harvard, were expecting their second child. Martha was four months pregnant, and her initial prenatal screening revealed an abnormally low level of alpha-fetoprotein (AFP), which could indicate that the fetus had Down syndrome. It was too early for amniocentesis, a more definitive test, so another blood test was scheduled to double-check the AFP level.

John met Martha at a café after a nurse had drawn the second blood sample but before the laboratory reported the test result. Later, Martha wrote about their conversation.

> "Did they tell you anything about the test?" John said. "What exactly is the problem?" . . .
>
> "We've got a one in eight hundred and ninety-five shot at a retarded baby."
>
> John smiled, "I can live with those odds."
>
> I tried to smile back, but I couldn't. . . . I wanted to tell John about the worry in my gut. I wanted to tell him that it was more than worry—that it was a certainty. Then I realized all over again how preposterous that was. "I'm still a little scared."
>
> He reached across the table for my hand. "Sure," he said, "that's understandable. But even if there is a problem, we've caught it in time. . . . The worst case scenario is that you might have to have an abortion, and that's a long shot. Everything's going to be fine."
>
> . . . "I might *have to have* an abortion?" The chill inside me was gone. Instead I could feel my face flushing hot with anger. "Since when do you decide what I *have to* do with my body?"
>
> John looked surprised. "I never said I was going to decide anything," he protested. "It's just that if the tests show something wrong with the baby, of course we'll abort. We've talked about this."
>
> "What we've talked about," I told John in a low, dangerous voice, "is that I am pro-choice. That means I decide whether or not I'd abort a baby with a birth defect. . . . I'm not so sure of this."
>
> "You used to be," said John.

"I know I used to be." I rubbed my eyes. I felt terribly confused. "But now . . . look, John, it's not as though we're deciding whether or not to have a baby. We're deciding what *kind* of baby we're willing to accept. If it's perfect in every way, we keep it. If it doesn't fit the right specifications, whoosh! Out it goes.". . .

John was looking more and more confused. "Martha, why are you on this soapbox? What's your point?"

"My point is," I said, "that I'm trying to get you to tell me what you think constitutes a 'defective' baby. What about . . . oh, I don't know, a hyperactive baby? Or an ugly one?"

"They can't test for those things and—"

"Well, what if they could?" I said. "Medicine can do all kinds of magical tricks these days. Pretty soon we're going to be aborting babies because they have the gene for alcoholism, or homosexuality, or manic depression. . . . Did you know that in China they abort a lot of fetuses just because they're female?" I growled. "Is being a girl 'defective' enough for you?"

"Look," he said, "I know I can't always see things from your perspective. And I'm sorry about that. But the way I see it, if a baby is going to be deformed or something, abortion is a way to keep everyone from suffering—*especially* the baby. It's like shooting a horse that's broken its leg. . . . A lame horse dies slowly, you know? . . . It dies in terrible pain. And it can't run anymore. So it can't enjoy life even if it doesn't die. Horses live to run; that's what they do. If a baby is born not being able to do what other people do, I think it's better not to prolong its suffering."

". . . And what is it," I said softly, more to myself than to John, "what is it that people do? What do we live to do, the way a horse lives to run?"

[Beck, 1999, pp. 132–133, 135]

The second AFP test came back low but in the normal range, "meaning there was no reason to fear that [the fetus] had Down syndrome" (Beck, p. 137).

John thought they had decided to abort a Down syndrome fetus, but his response as they waited for test results had Martha "hot with anger." As Chapter 3 explains, genetic counselors help couples discuss their choices *before* becoming pregnant, but John and Martha had no counseling because they hadn't planned this pregnancy and they were at low risk for any problems, including chromosomal ones.

The opposite of the false positive is the false negative, a mistaken assurance that all is well. The second AFP test was in the reassuring normal range. Martha still had "a worry in my gut." Amniocentesis later revealed that the second AFP was a false negative. The fetus had Down syndrome after all.

Before they conceive, many couples discuss whether or not they would carry a severely abnormal fetus to term. But, as the dialogue between Martha and John reveals, couples tend to be much less certain once pregnancy occurs. We will return to this couple at the end of this chapter. In the meantime, consider another difficult case.

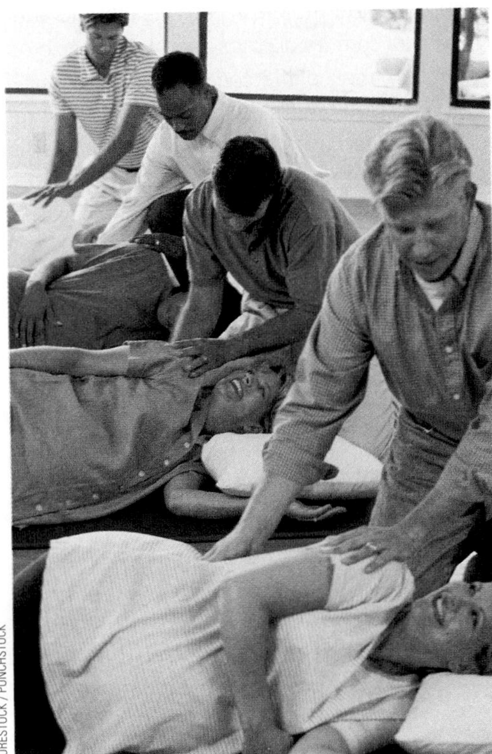

PURESTOCK / PUNCHSTOCK

AP PHOTO / LYNNE SLADKY

The Same Event, A Thousand Miles Apart: Preparing for Birth The husbands of the pregnant American women *(left)* are learning to massage their wives during labor. The pregnant woman in Afghanistan *(above)* and her doctors discuss why labor will soon be induced: One of her twins is not developing normally. Neither is expected to live. Virtually all newborns in developed nations survive; the Afghani woman has already lost two children at birth.

a case to study

"What Did That Say About Me?"

Tom Horan and his wife saw a sonogram that showed that their fetus's legs were bowed and shortened. They were told that the condition could be healed through braces, growth hormones, and surgical procedures in childhood, and they began to think about how they would care for a child who needed so much medical attention.

A closer examination by a specialist revealed other deformities: The left arm was missing below the elbow, and the right hand was undeveloped. Sometimes such deformities signify neurological impairment, the doctors told them, but it was impossible to tell for sure.

> "Our main concern was the quality of life that the child would have, growing up with such extensive limb deformities, even in the absence of cognitive problems," Mr. Horan said.
>
> He and his wife, who have three other children, were reared Roman Catholic and had never considered terminating a pregnancy. Yet even his father, Mr. Horan said, who had long been opposed to abortion, supported their decision to end the pregnancy.
>
> "Confronted with this question and knowing what we knew, it changed his mind," Mr. Horan said. "It's not just a question of right and wrong; it introduces all sorts of other questions that one has to consider, whether it is the survivability of the child, quality of life of parents, quality of life of siblings, social needs. And it becomes much more real when you're confronted with an actual situation."
>
> After the termination, an examination showed . . . an extremely rare condition, Cornelia de Lange syndrome. [The child] would have been severely mentally and physically disabled.
>
> The news was a relief to Mr. Horan, who said he felt sadness and grief, but no regrets. . . . Before the diagnosis, he felt guilt and uncertainty. . . . "I wondered about the ethical implications. . . . What did that say about me?"
>
> *[Harmon, 2004, p. 22]*

The Horans had to reexamine their values, something they did not think necessary before the sonogram. As one review reports, "Most couples say they are both profoundly grateful for the new information and hugely burdened by the choices it forces them to make" (Harmon, 2004, p. 1).

➤Response for Women of Childbearing Age (from page 106): Avoid all drugs (including legal ones, like nicotine and alcohol), check your weight (gain, or lose, some if you are under, or over, the norm), and receive diagnosis and treatment for any infections—not just sexually transmitted ones but those anywhere in the body, including the teeth and gums.

SUMMING UP

Risk analysis is a complex but necessary aspect of prenatal development, especially because the placenta does not protect the fetus from all hazards, such as diseases, drugs, and pollutants. Many factors reduce risk, including the mother's good health and adequate nutrition before pregnancy and early prenatal care (to diagnose and treat problems and to teach the woman how to protect her fetus). Risk is affected by dose, frequency, and timing of exposure to teratogens, as well as by the fetus's genetic vulnerability. Prenatal testing often reassures the prospective parents but may reveal severe problems that require difficult decisions. ■

The Birth Process

For a full-term fetus and a healthy mother, birth can be simple and quick. At some time during the last month of pregnancy, most fetuses change position, turning upside down so that the head is low in the mother's pelvic cavity. They are now in position to be born in the usual way, head first. About 1 in 20 babies does not turn and is positioned to be born "breech," that is, buttocks or, rarely, feet first. Obstetricians sometimes manually turn such fetuses before birth or perform a cesarean section (described below), because breech babies may get insufficient oxygen during labor (Reece & Hobbins, 2007).

Usually about 38 weeks after conception, the fetal brain signals the release of certain hormones that trigger the woman's uterine muscles to contract and relax, starting active labor. Uterine contractions eventually become strong and regular, less than 10 minutes apart.

The baby is born, on average, after 12 hours of active labor for first births and 7 hours for subsequent births (K. L. Moore & Persaud, 2003), although it is not unusual for labor to take twice, or half, as long. Women's birthing positions also vary—sitting, squatting, lying down (Blackburn, 2003), or even immersed in warm water. Figure 4.4 shows the sequence of stages in the birth process.

The Newborn's First Minutes

Do you picture just-delivered babies as being held upside down and spanked so that they will start crying and breathing? Wrong. Gentle handling is best, because newborns usually breathe and cry on their own.

Between spontaneous cries, the first breaths cause the infant's color to change from bluish to pinkish as oxygen begins to circulate. Hands and feet are the last body parts to turn pink. ("Bluish" and "pinkish" refer to the blood color, visible beneath the skin, and apply to newborns of all skin colors.) The eyes open wide; the tiny fingers grab; the tinier toes stretch and retract. The newborn is instantly, zestfully ready for life.

Nevertheless, there is much to be done. Mucus in the baby's throat is removed, especially if the first breaths seem shallow or strained. The umbilical cord is cut to detach the placenta, leaving the "belly button." The placenta is then expelled. If birth is assisted by a trained worker—as are 99 percent of the births in industrialized nations and about half of all births worldwide (Rutstein, 2000)—newborns are weighed, examined to make sure no problems require prompt medical attention, and wrapped to preserve body heat.

FIGURE 4.4

A Normal, Uncomplicated Birth
(a) The baby's position as the birth process begins. *(b)* The first stage of labor: The cervix dilates to allow passage of the baby's head. *(c)* Transition: The baby's head moves into the "birth canal," the vagina. *(d)* The second stage of labor: The baby's head moves through the opening of the vagina ("crowns") and *(e)* emerges completely.

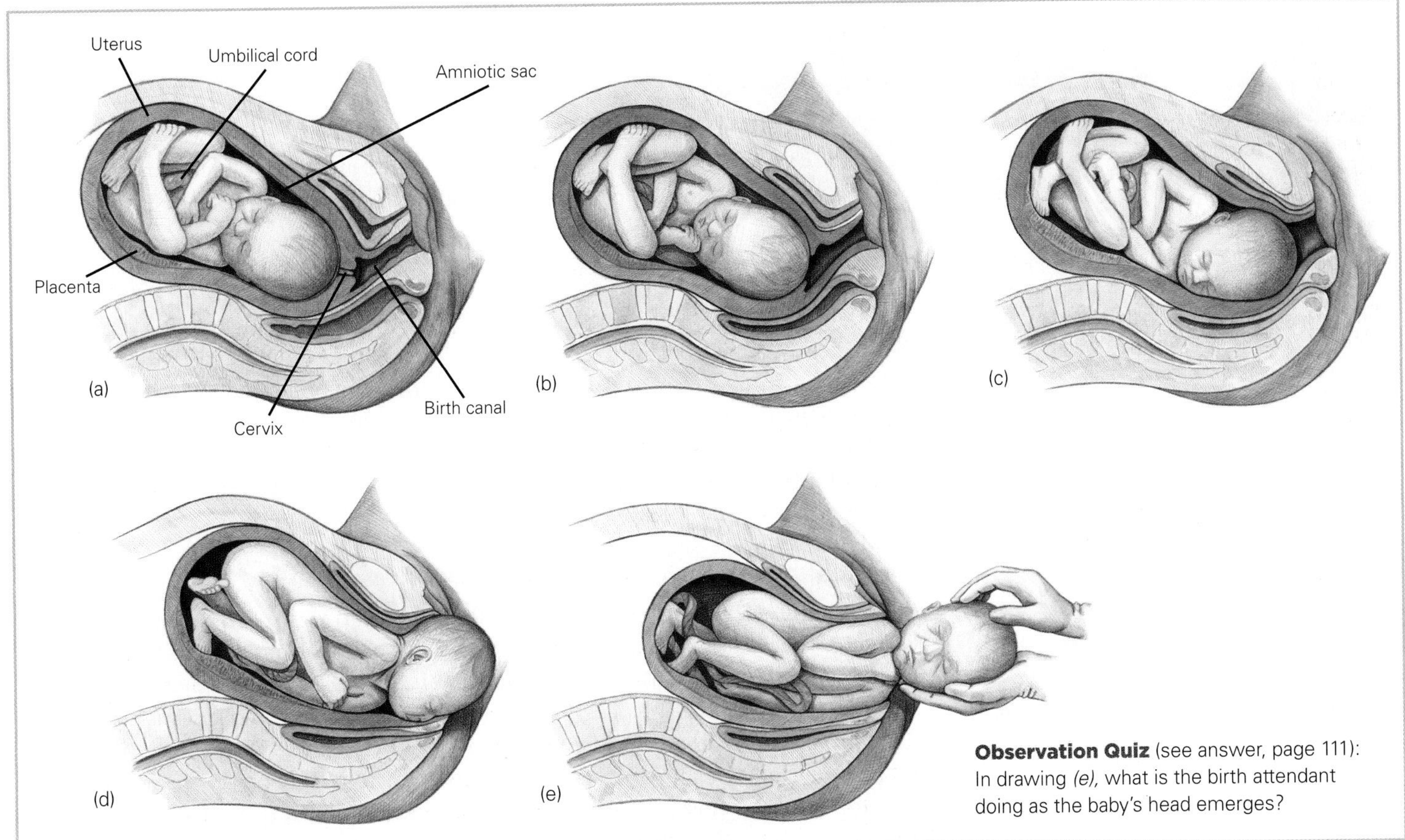

Observation Quiz (see answer, page 111): In drawing *(e)*, what is the birth attendant doing as the baby's head emerges?

TABLE 4.6

Criteria and Scoring of the Apgar Scale

Score	Color	Heartbeat	Reflex Irritability	Muscle Tone	Respiratory Effort
0	Blue, pale	Absent	No response	Flaccid, limp	Absent
1	Body pink, extremities blue	Slow (below 100)	Grimace	Weak, inactive	Irregular, slow
2	Entirely pink	Rapid (over 100)	Coughing, sneezing, crying	Strong, active	Good; baby is crying

Source: Apgar, 1953.

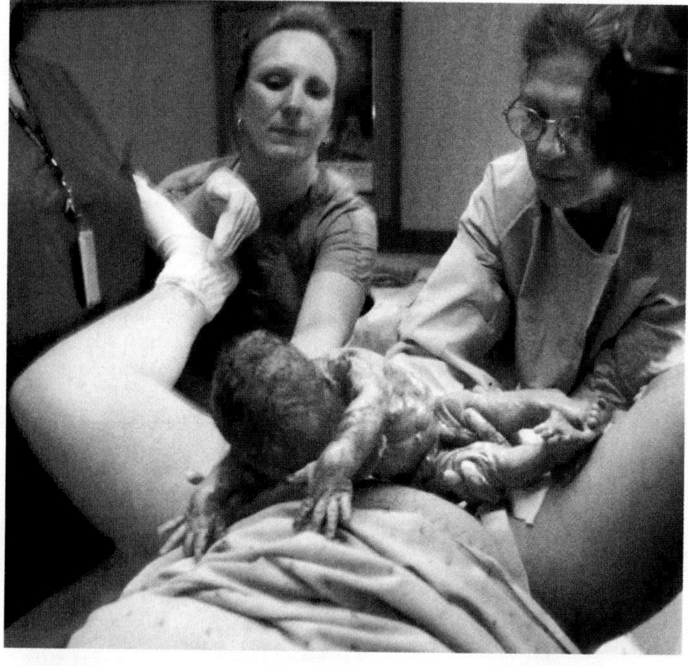

SEAN CAYTON / THE IMAGE WORKS

No Doctor Needed In this Colorado Springs birthing center, most babies are delivered with the help of nurse-midwives. This newborn's bloody appearance and bluish fingers are completely normal; an Apgar test at five minutes revealed that the baby's heart was beating steadily and that the body was "entirely pink."

One widely used assessment is the **Apgar scale** (see Table 4.6). The examiner checks five vital signs—heart rate, breathing, muscle tone, color, and reflexes—at one minute and again at five minutes after birth, assigning each a score of 0, 1, or 2 and totaling all five scores (Moster et al., 2001). The Apgar scale is a quick way for birth attendants to check the baby.

The five-minute Apgar score is the crucial one. An Australian study found that at one minute, many healthy newborns look bluish because they are low on oxygen (saturation rate 63 percent), but the blood level of oxygen quickly rises (to 90 percent or more) (Kamlin et al., 2006). If the five-minute total score is 7 or above, all is well.

If the score is below 7, the infant needs help. If the score is below 4, the newborn is in critical condition, and the attending physician might page "Dr. Apgar," which alerts the neonatalist on duty to rush to the delivery room. Fortunately, most newborns are fine, pink, and alert, which reassures the new parents, who cradle their newborn and congratulate each other.

Variations

How closely any given birth matches the foregoing description depends on the parents' preparation for birth, the physical and emotional support provided by birth attendants, the position and size of the fetus, and the customs of the culture. In developed nations, births usually include drugs to dull pain or speed contractions, sterile procedures, and various hospital protocols to be ready for emergencies and to avoid lawsuits.

Apgar scale A quick assessment of a newborn's body functioning. The baby's color, heart rate, reflexes, muscle tone, and respiratory effort are given a score of 0, 1, or 2 twice—at one minute and five minutes after birth—and the total of all the scores is compared with the ideal score of 10.

cesarean section A surgical birth, in which incisions through the mother's abdomen and uterus allow the fetus to be removed quickly, instead of being delivered through the vagina. (Also called *c-section* or simply *section*.)

Medical Intervention

In about 28 percent of births in the United States, a **cesarean section** is performed. The fetus is removed through incisions in the mother's abdomen and uterus (Hamilton et al., 2004). The rate of surgical birth varies markedly from place to place, with many developed nations having far fewer cesareans than the United States but others having more (see Figure 4.5).

If serious organic abnormalities are evident, microsurgery on tiny hearts, lungs, and digestive systems has been amazingly successful in recent years. If the newborn needs specialized feeding, or warmth, or extra oxygen, that is also available.

Eighty years ago, 5 percent of all newborns in the United States died (De Lee, 1938). Today almost every newborn lives. The death rate in the first days of life is only 1 in 200, with that one almost always in critical condition at birth because of an obvious problem, such as extremely low birthweight or massive birth defects.

In developed nations, newborns are tested for various diseases. If a problem is confirmed by further testing, parents and medical staff can begin protective measures (such as the diet to prevent PKU, explained in Chapter 3) (MMWR, October 15, 2004). Just as during prenatal testing, false positives cause needless worry, and even correct tests may reveal problems that cannot be treated. Nonetheless, most professionals, including those involved with the March of Dimes, advocate testing all newborns for dozens of conditions (Green et al., 2006).

Every year worldwide, obstetricians, midwives, and nurses save millions of lives—of mothers as well as of infants. Indeed, a lack of medical attention during childbirth and illegal abortions are the major reasons why motherhood is still hazardous in the least developed nations; about 1 in 20 women in Africa dies of complications of abortion and birth (Daulaire et al., 2002).

However, intervention is not always best for mother and child. In Pelotas, Brazil, most births are by cesarean (82 percent for private patients in 2004). The rate of low-birthweight infants in that region of Brazil is rising (from 11 to 16 percent in 10 years) because some infants are born before they are ready (Barros et al., 2005). In general, cesareans are easier for the fetus, and quicker for doctor and mother, but increase the rate of birth complications in later pregnancies (Getahun et al. 2006).

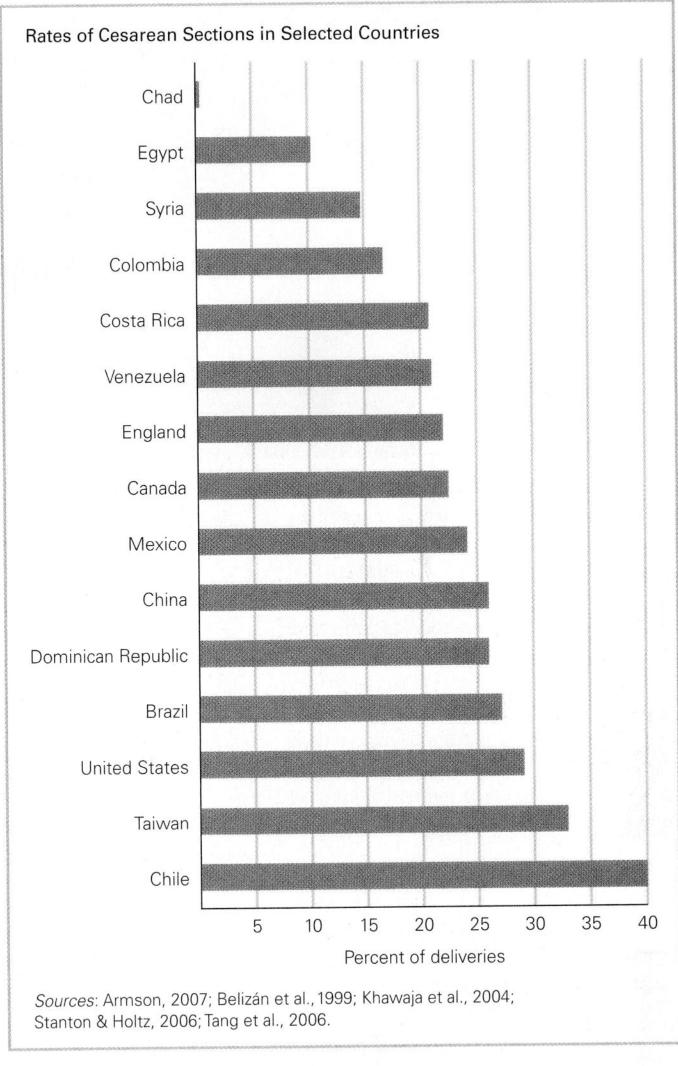

FIGURE 4.5

Too Many Cesareans or Too Few? Rates of cesarean deliveries vary widely from nation to nation. In general, cesarean births are declining in North America and increasing in Africa. Latin America has the highest rates in the world (note that 40 percent of all births in Chile are by cesarean), and sub-Saharan Africa has the lowest. The underlying issue is whether some women who should have cesareans do not get them, while other women have unnecessary cesareans.

Only 1 percent of U.S. births take place at home—about half of these by choice, attended by a doctor or midwife, and half due to unexpectedly rapid birth. Home births are usually quite normal and healthy, but any complications can become more serious while the mother is waiting for emergency medical help (Pang et al., 2002).

In many regions of the world, as modern medicine is introduced, a clash develops between traditional home births attended by a midwife and hospital births attended by an obstetrician: Home births risk complications, and hospital births risk too much intervention. All too often, women must choose one or the other, rather than combining the best features of each. An example of such a combination is reported regarding the Inuit people of northern Canada:

> Until thirty or forty years ago every woman, and most men, learned midwifery skills and knew what to do to help at a birth if they were needed. . . . They helped the woman kneel or squat on caribou skins, and tied the cord with caribou sinews. . . . Since the 1950s, as the medical system took control in the belief that hospital birth was safer, more and more pregnant women were evacuated by air to deliver in large hospitals in Winnipeg and other cities. . . . Around three weeks before her due date a woman is flown south to wait in bed and breakfast accommodation for labor to start, and to have it induced if the baby does not arrive when expected. Anxious about their children left at home, mothers became bored and depressed. . . . Women . . . deliver in a supine position [on their back]

➤**Answer to Observation Quiz** (from page 109): The birth attendant is turning the baby's head after it has emerged; doing this helps the shoulders come out more easily.

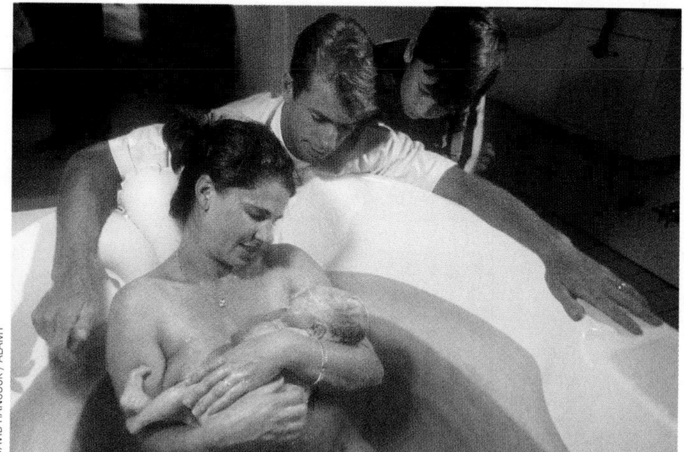

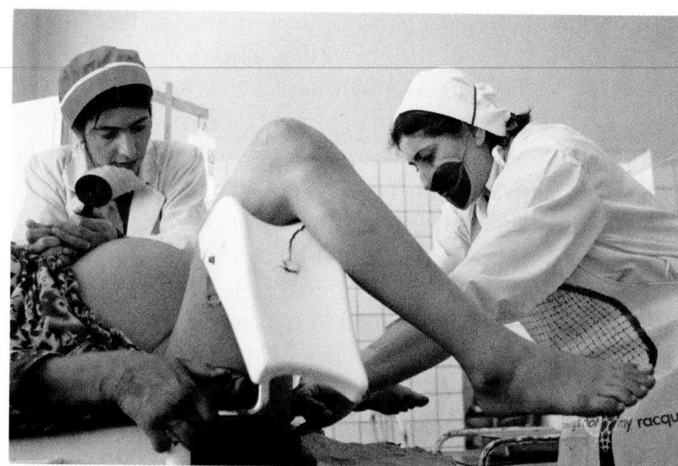

DAVID HANCOCK / ALAMY

NATALIE BEHRING / ONASIA.COM

The Same Event, A Thousand Miles Apart: Back to Basics The physical process of giving birth is the same for all women, but the circumstances vary widely. Many Western women are forgoing the traditional hospital birth in favor of such methods as water birth *(left)*. For women in many developing countries, meanwhile, a sanitary hospital birth would be an improvement—but the hospitals cannot afford even basic supplies. In a delivery room in Afghanistan *(right)*, the doctor is wearing a cooking apron instead of surgical scrubs and an eye mask over her mouth.

> instead of an upright one, which was part of their tradition, and also describe being tied up while giving birth. Many women say that children who have been born in a hospital are different and no longer fit into the Inuit lifestyle. . . . Several new birth centres have now been created [in the Inuit homeland] and nurse-midwives are bringing in traditional midwives as assistants during childbirth, training some Inuit midwives to work alongside them, and at the same time learning some of the old Inuit ways themselves.
>
> *[Kitzinger, 2001, pp. 160–161]*

doula A woman who helps with the birth process. Traditionally in Latin America, a doula was like a midwife, the only professional who attended childbirths. Now doulas are likely to work alongside a hospital's medical staff to help mothers through labor and delivery.

Another example of a traditional custom incorporated into a modern birth is the presence of a **doula.** Long a fixture in many Latin American countries, a doula is a woman who helps other women with labor, delivery, breast-feeding, and newborn care. Increasing numbers of women in North America now hire a professional doula to perform these functions (Douglas, 2002).

From a developmental perspective, such combinations of traditional and modern birthing practices are excellent. Some practices in every culture are helpful and some are harmful to development; a thoughtful combination of traditional and modern is likely to be an improvement over a wholesale rejection of one or the other.

Birth Complications

A *birth complication* includes anything in the newborn, the mother, or the birth process itself that requires special medical attention. When a fetus is already at risk because of a genetic abnormality or exposure to a teratogen, when a mother is unusually young, old, small, or ill, or when labor occurs too soon, birth complications become more likely. Complications usually are part of a sequence of events and conditions that begin long before birth and may continue for years. This means that prevention and treatment must be ongoing. We focus now on one of the most serious complications—lack of oxygen—and one of the most common—low birthweight.

Anoxia

anoxia A lack of oxygen that, if prolonged during birth, can cause brain damage or death to the baby.

Anoxia literally means "no oxygen." Inadequate oxygen during birth can kill the infant if it lasts longer than a few seconds. Some forms of anesthesia once used during the birth process have been discontinued because they slowed down the delivery of oxygen to the fetus or made it more difficult for a newborn to breathe on its own. Lack of oxygen, even for a few seconds, can cause brain damage, especially in a preterm infant.

Cerebral palsy (difficulties with movement and speech resulting from brain damage) was once thought to be caused solely by birth procedures: excessive pain medication, slow breech birth, or delivery by forceps (an instrument used to pull the fetus's head through the birth canal). In fact, however, cerebral palsy often results from genetic vulnerability, worsened by teratogens and a birth that incudes anoxia.

cerebral palsy A disorder that results from damage to the brain's motor centers. People with cerebral palsy have difficulty with muscle control, so their speech and body movements are impaired.

A pair of monozygotic twins were mentioned in Chapter 3, one of whom had a much more severe case of Asperger syndrome than the other. The more severely affected twin also experienced anoxia at birth: He did not begin to breathe on his own; doctors needed to give him oxygen and clear mucus from his throat before he started breathing. That is the likely explanation for his more severe brain damage. Similarly, one reason some people develop schizophrenia is thought to be a bout of anoxia at birth. In both disorders, the underlying problem is genetic, but anoxia can further stress the immature brain.

Anoxia has many causes and is always risky; that's why the fetal heart rate is monitored during labor and why the newborn's color is one of the five criteria on the Apgar scale. How long a fetus can experience anoxia without suffering brain damage depends on genes, weight, neurological maturity, drugs in the bloodstream (either taken by the mother before birth or given by the doctor during birth), and a host of other factors.

Low Birthweight

The World Health Organization defines **low birthweight (LBW)** as a weight of less than 5½ pounds (2,500 grams) at birth. The smallest LBW babies are further grouped into **very low birthweight (VLBW),** a weight of less than 3 pounds, 5 ounces (1,500 grams), and **extremely low birthweight (ELBW),** a weight of less than 2 pounds, 3 ounces (990 grams). Table 4.7 correlates these birthweights with the various stages of prenatal development.

low birthweight (LBW) A body weight at birth of less than 5½ pounds (2,500 grams).

very low birthweight (VLBW) A body weight at birth of less than 3 pounds, 5 ounces (1,500 grams).

extremely low birthweight (ELBW) A body weight at birth of less than 2 pounds, 3 ounces (990 grams).

TABLE 4.7

AT ABOUT THIS TIME: Average Prenatal Weights*

Period of Development	Weeks After Conception	Weight (Nonmetric)	Weight (Metric)	Notes
End of embryonic period	8	1/30 oz.	1 g	
End of first trimester	13	3 oz.	85 g	
At viability (50/50 chance of survival)	22	20 oz.	570 g	A birthweight less than 2 lb., 3 oz. (965 g) is considered extremely low birthweight (ELBW).
End of second trimester	26–28	2–3 lb.	900–1,400 g	Less than 3 lb., 5 oz. (1,500 g) is very low birthweight (VLBW).
End of preterm period	35	5½ lb.	2,500 g	Less than 5½ lb. (2,500 g) is low birthweight (LBW).
Full-term	38	7½ lb.	3,400 g	Between 5½ and 9 lb. (2,500–4,080 g) is considered normal weight.

*To make them easier to remember, the weights are rounded off (which accounts for the inexact correspondence between metric and nonmetric measures). Actual weights vary. For instance, a normal full-term infant can weigh between 5½ and 9 pounds (2,490 and 4,080 grams); a viable infant, especially one of several born at 26 or more weeks, can weigh less than shown here.

The rate of LBW varies widely from nation to nation (see Figure 4.6). The U.S. rate of 8.2 percent in 2005 has been rising steadily over the past two decades and is now higher than it has been in more than 30 years (see Figure 4.7).

Remember that fetal body weight normally doubles in the last trimester of pregnancy, with a typical gain of almost 2 pounds (900 grams) occurring in the final three weeks. Thus, in a **preterm birth,** defined as occurring 3 or more weeks before the standard 38 weeks, the baby usually (though not always) is LBW.

preterm birth A birth that occurs three or more weeks before the full 38 weeks of the typical pregnancy has elapsed—that is, at 35 or fewer weeks after conception.

small for gestational age (SGA) A term for a baby whose birthweight is significantly lower than expected, given the time since conception. For example, a 5-pound (2,265-gram) newborn is considered SGA if born on time but not SGA if born two months early. (Also called *small for dates.*)

Although most preterm babies are LBW because they missed those final weeks of weight gain, some babies are underweight because they gained weight too slowly throughout pregnancy. They are called *small for dates* or **small for gestational age (SGA).** An underweight SGA infant causes more concern than an underweight preterm birth, because SGA signifies impairment during prenatal development.

If a sonogram reveals slow growth, the mother is alerted to see if she can remedy the problem (stop drinking and smoking, eat more, find a less stressful job). But if SGA continues (perhaps because the mother cannot affect it), birth may be induced early or a cesarean performed in order to prevent the neurological consequences of continued slow growth. Newborns who are *both* preterm and SGA make up the most rapidly increasing category of low-birthweight infants (Ananth et al., 2003).

Normally, in the first months outside the womb, a low-birthweight infant gains weight faster than average (called "catch-up growth"). However, a significant number of SGA infants do the opposite and undereat. They are then likely to be diagnosed with "failure to thrive," and be at high risk of becoming mentally slow and physically small (Casey et al., 2006). Problems with the placenta or umbilical cord can cause SGA, as can maternal illness. However, maternal drug use is a far more common cause. Every psychoactive drug slows fetal growth.

Tobacco is the worst and the most prevalent cause of SGA, implicated in 25 percent of all LBW births worldwide. Smoking among pregnant women is declining in the United States but rising in many other nations, especially in Asia. This may increase the rates of LBW shown in Figure 4.6. Prescription drugs can also cause low birthweight. For instance, antidepressants double the incidence of both preterm and SGA infants (Källén, 2004). Some pregnant women need drugs to stave off serious depression, but, as with many measures already mentioned (cesarean sections, genetic testing, anesthesia), the costs and benefits to mother and fetus need to be analyzed case by case (Cohen et al., 2006).

Every psychoactive drug, including prescribed medicines and legal drugs (such as alcohol and nicotine), crosses the placenta and may make a newborn jittery and irritable—signs that the infant is withdrawing from that drug. If the mother is heavily addicted (as with heroin or methadone), the newborn may need to be given some of the drug in order to ease withdrawal.

Another common reason for slow fetal growth is maternal malnutrition. Women who begin pregnancy underweight, who eat poorly during preg-

FIGURE 4.6

Low Birthweight Around the World The LBW rate is often considered a reflection of a country's commitment to its children as well as a reflection of its economic resources.

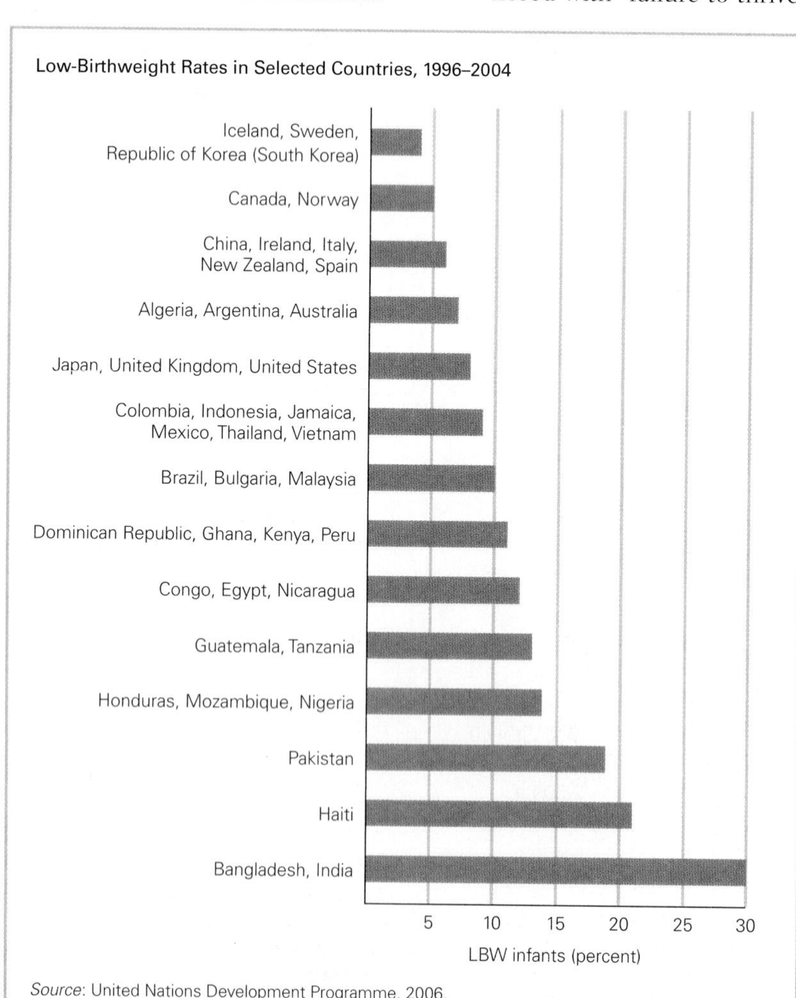

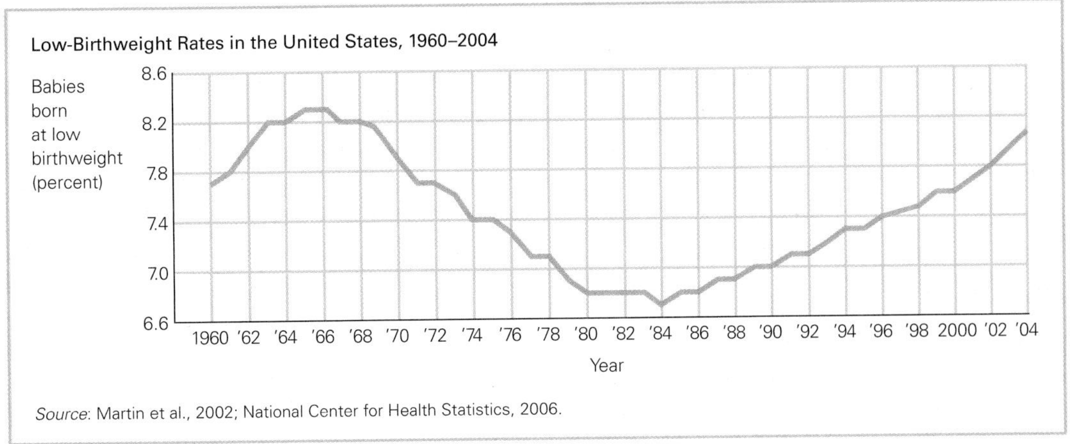

FIGURE 4.7

Not Improving The LBW rate is often taken to be a measure of a nation's overall health. In the United States, the rise and fall of this rate are related to many factors, among them prenatal care, maternal use of drugs, overall nutrition, and number of multiple births.

Observation Quiz (see answer, page 116): In what year was 1 out of every 13 U.S. babies (7.5 percent) born weighing less than 5½ pounds (2,490 grams)?

nancy, or who gain less than 3 pounds (1,360 grams) per month in the last six months are more likely to have an underweight infant. Ironically, obese women (those with BMI over 30) also are at higher risk of having ELBW infants because serious pregnancy complications, such as preeclampsia, require preterm delivery (G. C. S. Smith et al., 2007) (see Table 4.8). The healthiest pregnancies occur in women who are neither too thin nor too heavy. This conclusion came from a study of all the first births in Scotland over a decade, so it is quite reliable (see Research Design).

Malnutrition (not age) is the primary reason teenage girls often have small babies: If they eat haphazardly and poorly, their diet cannot support their own growth, much less the growth of another developing person (Buschman et al., 2001). Unfortunately, many of the risk factors just mentioned—underweight, undereating, underage, and drug use—tend to occur together.

Finally, as you remember from Chapter 3, multiple births are usually LBW. Assisted reproductive technology (ART) has dramatically increased the rate of multiples and thus of LBW (Pinborg et al., 2004). Half of all U.S. in vitro births are multiples.

Research Design

Scientists: Gordon C. S. Smith and four other British researchers.

Publication: *American Journal of Public Health* (2007).

Participants: All 84,701 women in Scotland who had their first child between 1991 and 2001, except those with multiple births, stillbirths, or births after 43 weeks of gestation.

Design: Correlation of mother's weight in early pregnancy with birth outcome.

Major conclusion: Obese women have significantly more elective preterm deliveries (usually because the physician insists), and thus more ELBW infants. The reason is usually preeclampsia (a serious complication during pregnancy), which halts at delivery.

Comment: Although overweight women are less likely to have a spontaneous preterm birth, obese women risk pregnancy complications. Ideally, women should be neither too thin nor too fat when pregnancy begins.

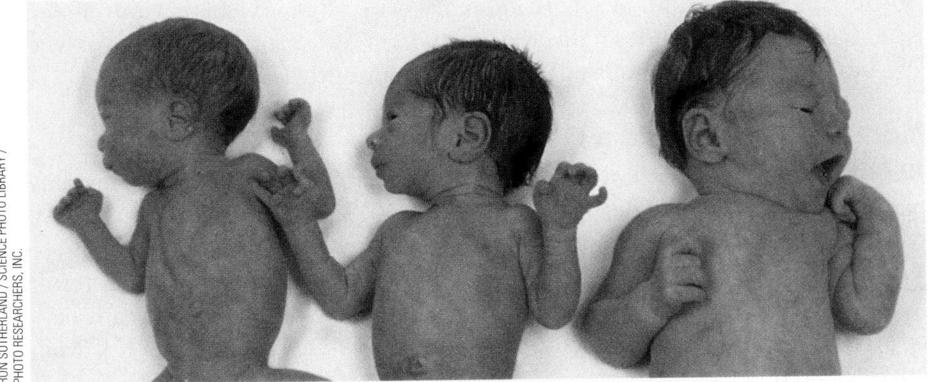

RON SUTHERLAND / SCIENCE PHOTO LIBRARY / PHOTO RESEARCHERS, INC.

Which Baby Is Oldest? The baby at the left is the oldest, at almost 1 month; the baby at the right is the youngest, at just 2 days. Are you surprised? The explanation is that the 1-month-old was born 9 weeks early and now weighs less than 5½ pounds (2,490 grams); the 2-day-old was full-term and weighs almost 8 pounds (3,600 grams). The baby in the middle, born full-term but weighing only 2 pounds (900 grams), is the most worrisome. Her ears and hands are larger than the preterm baby's, but her skull is small; malnutrition may have deprived her brain as well as her body.

TABLE 4.8

Risking Birth Complications: Impact of Mother's BMI

	Incidence of Complication (Percent)			
BMI	Preeclampsia	Spontaneous Preterm Births	Elective Preterm Births	ELBW Newborns
Less than 20 (underweight)	2.2%	5.3%	2.5%	0.4%
20–24.9 (healthy weight)	3.0	3.6	2.3	0.3
25–29.9 (overweight)	4.9	3.3	2.7	0.4
30–34.9 (obese)	7.4	3.1	3.6	0.4
More than 35 (morbidly obese)	10.0	3.0	5.0	1.0

Source: G. C. S. Smith et al., 2007.

Social Support

None of the factors that impede or interrupt prenatal growth are inevitable. Quality of medical care, education, culture, and social support affect every developing person before birth, via their impact on the pregnant woman.

The importance of these factors is made starkly evident in data from Gambia, a poor nation in Africa. Preterm births are highest (17 percent) in July, when many women are working long hours in the fields. SGA births are more common (31 percent) in November, the end of the "hungry season," when most women have been undernourished for three months or more (Rayco-Solon et al., 2005).

Fathers and other relatives, neighbors, cultures, and clinics can reduce risks markedly. For example, the rate of low birthweight among Mexican Americans is lower than the overall U.S. rate, because families are more likely to make sure that their pregnant women do not smoke, drink, or undereat. This is especially true for women who were born in Mexico but give birth in the United States; their babies are remarkably healthy (Aguirre-Molina et al., 2001).

In contrast, there is a high rate of birth complications among women of African American descent, even when they are well nourished, do not use drugs, and obtain good prenatal care. One explanation is that the racism of the larger society adds stress to their lives that they cannot shake off, a factor that takes a toll on African Americans' health overall (Geronimus et al., 2006). Genetic vulnerability is another possibility, but it's unlikely; women from Africa and the Caribbean who give birth in the United States do not have as many birth complications.

Mothers, Fathers, and a Good Start

Birth complications can have a lingering impact on the new family, depending partly on the sensitivity of hospital care (Field, 2001) and the home. In fact, LBW babies are more likely to become adults who are overweight and have health problems, particularly of the heart (Hack et al., 2002). This correlation could result from high levels of stress hormones that the infants experienced in their early days or perhaps because their parents fed them more or raised them differently from other children.

Even when a newborn is small and fragile and must stay in the hospital for weeks after birth, the parents should be encouraged to share in the early caregiving, not only because it benefits the baby but because they, too, are deprived and stressed (Eriksson & Pehrsson, 2005). When the infant's survival and normality are in doubt, many parents feel inadequate, sad, guilty, or angry. Such emotions become more manageable when the parents touch and care for their vulnerable newborn.

➤**Answer to Observation Quiz** (from page 115): In 1998. After having declined, the LBW rate began an upward climb in the mid-1980s.

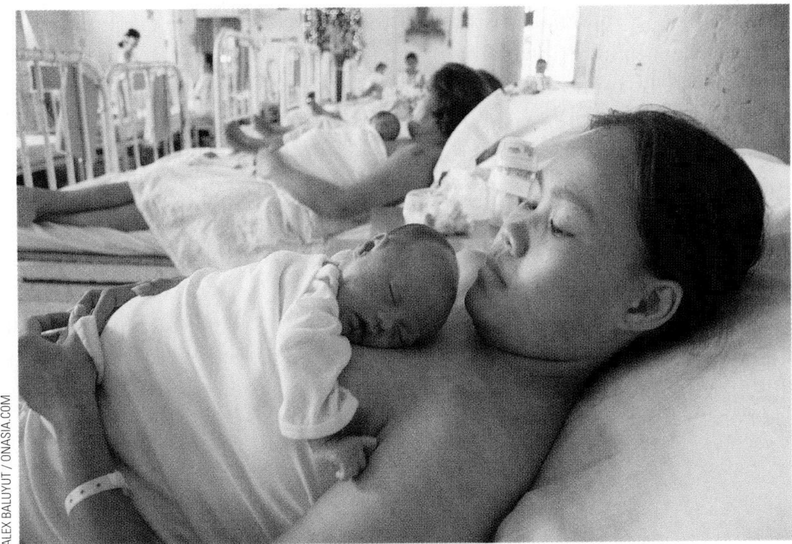
ALEX BALUYUT / ONASIA.COM

A Beneficial Beginning These new mothers in a maternity ward in Manila are providing their babies with kangaroo care.

kangaroo care A form of child care in which the mother of a low-birthweight infant spends at least an hour a day holding the baby between her breasts, like a kangaroo that carries her immature newborn in a pouch on her abdomen. If the infant is capable, he or she can easily breast-feed in this position.

One way to achieve parental involvement is through **kangaroo care,** in which the mother of a low-birthweight infant spends at least an hour a day holding her tiny newborn between her breasts, skin-to-skin, allowing the tiny baby to hear her heart beat and feel her body heat. Fathers also can cradle newborns next to their chests. A comparison study (Feldman et al., 2002) in Israel found that kangaroo-care newborns slept more deeply and spent more time alert than did infants who received standard care. By 6 months of age, infants who had received kangaroo care were more responsive to their mothers. These findings could be the result of either improved infant maturation or increased maternal sensitivity, but either way, this is good news. Other research confirms the benefits of kangaroo care (Ludington-Hoe et al., 2006; Tallandini & Scalembra, 2006).

All humans are social creatures, interacting with their families and their societies. Accordingly, prenatal development and birth involve not only the fetus but also the mother, father, and many others. As you have already read, a woman's chance of avoiding risks during pregnancy depends partly on her family, her ethnic background, and the nation where she lives.

His Baby, Too This new father's evident joy in his baby illustrates a truism that developmental research has only recently reflected: Fathers contribute much more than just half their child's genes.

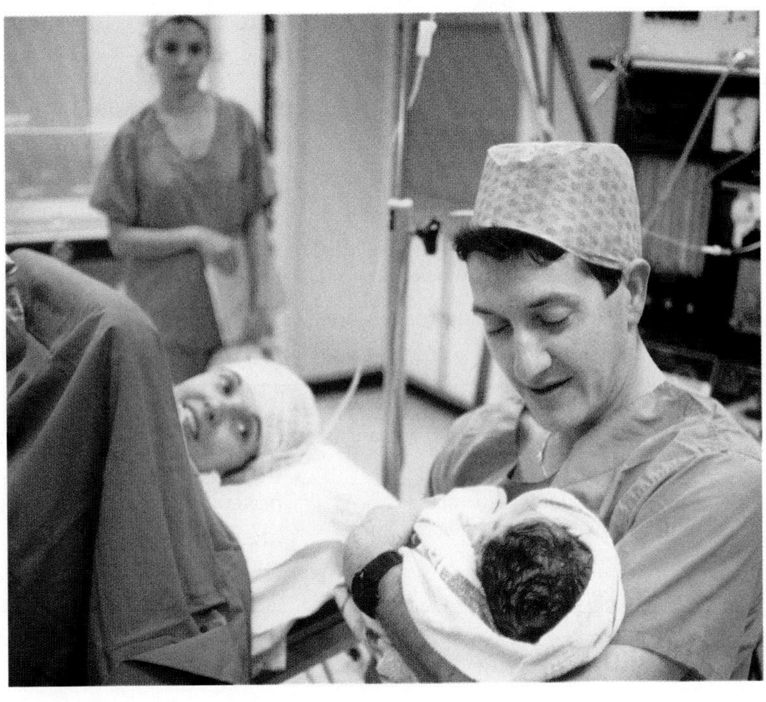
BUBBLES PHOTOLIBRARY / ALAMY

Help from Fathers

Fathers can be crucial. A supportive father-to-be helps a mother-to-be stay healthy, well nourished, and drug-free. Alcohol is not good for a fetus, but neither education nor employment correlates with decreased alcohol consumption during pregnancy. Marriage does (MMWR, April 5, 2002). When it comes to alcohol, at least, husbands seem to help their wives abstain. Overall, a woman's drug consumption and nutrition during pregnancy are powerfully affected by the father's health habits.

An alternate explanation for the correlation between marriage and healthy newborns is that pregnancies within marriage are more often wanted and planned by both parents, and that fact in itself encourages both the pregnant woman and her husband to make sure she takes care of herself. Only about

Especially for Fathers-to-Be When does a man's nongenetic influence on his children begin?

half of all U.S. pregnancies are planned; women who are young and unwed are particularly unlikely to become pregnant intentionally.

Not only by example, but also more directly, fathers and other family members can decrease or increase a mother's stress, which in turn affects her circulation, diet, rest, and digestion and, ultimately, the fetus. One study in northern India found that 18 percent of fathers abused their wives during pregnancy, and the result was a doubling of the rate of fragile newborns and infant death (Ahmed et al., 2006). Another way to see this is that 82 percent of fathers took better care of their wives, to good effect.

The need for social support is mutual. Fathers need reassurance, just as mothers do. Levels of cortisol, a stress hormone, correlate between expectant fathers and mothers: When one parent is stressed, the other often is, too (Berg & Wynne-Edwards, 2002), as the following illustrates.

a case to study

"You'd Throw Him in a Dumpster"

Remember John and Martha, the young couple whose amniocentesis revealed that their fetus had trisomy-21? Martha decided to have the baby, but they had never really discussed the issue. One night at 3:00 A.M., Martha, seven months pregnant, was crying uncontrollably. She told John she was scared.

> "Scared of what?" he said. "Of a little baby who's not as perfect as you think he ought to be?"
>
> "I didn't say I wanted him to be perfect," I said. "I just want him to be normal. That's all I want. Just normal."
>
> "That is total bullshit. . . . You don't want this baby to be normal. You'd throw him in a dumpster if he just turned out to be normal. What you really want is for him to be superhuman."
>
> "For your information," I said in my most acid tone, "I was the one who decided to keep this baby, even though he's got Down's. You were the one who wanted to throw him in a dumpster."
>
> "How would you know?" John's voice was still gaining volume. "You never asked me what I wanted, did you? No. You never even asked me. . . ."
>
> *[Beck, 1999, p. 255]*

This episode ended well, with a long, warm, and honest conversation between the two prospective parents. Both parents learned what their fetus meant to the other, a topic that had been taboo until that night. Adam, their future son, became an important part of their relationship.

This couple's lack of communication up to this point, and the sudden eruption of previously unexpressed emotions, is not unusual during pregnancy or in the days after birth. Honest discussion between expectant or new parents is difficult, especially because birth raises powerful memories from childhood and irrational fears about the future. Some fathers disappear, either literally or by increasing their work hours. Yet open and intimate communication is crucial if a couple is to form a **parental alliance,** a cooperative working relationship between two parents who raise their child together. The need for a parental alliance is evident in an unexpected, yet common, consequence of birth: postpartum depression.

parental alliance Cooperation between a mother and a father based on their mutual commitment to their children. In a parental alliance, the parents agree to support each other in their shared parental roles.

Postpartum Depression

In the days and weeks after birth, between 8 and 15 percent of women experience **postpartum depression,** a sense of inadequacy and sadness (called *baby blues* in the mild version and *postpartum psychosis* in the most severe form) (Perfetti et al., 2004). These rates are for the United States; other nations may be even higher. For example, rates in Pakistan were 36 percent on a standard postpartum scale (Husain et al., 2006). The mother with postpartum depression finds normal baby

postpartum depression A new mother's feelings of inadequacy and sadness in the days and weeks after giving birth.

care (feeding, diapering, bathing) to be very burdensome, and she may have thoughts of neglecting or abusing the infant. Postpartum depression lasting more than a few weeks can have a long-term impact on the child, so it should be diagnosed and treated as soon as possible.

The father's reaction is crucial when a mother experiences postpartum depression. His active caregiving is likely to help the baby thrive and the mother to recover. Some fathers become depressed themselves after birth. Even if the mother is not depressed, the father's depression is likely to affect the baby. One study found that sons of fathers who were depressed after their birth had notable behavior problems as toddlers (Ramchandani et al., 2005).

From a developmental perspective, some causes predate the pregnancy (such as preexisting depression, financial stress, or marital problems); others occur during pregnancy (women are more often depressed two months before birth than two months after); and still others are specific to the infant (health, feeding, or sleeping problems) and to the birth (Ashman & Dawson, 2002; Jones, 2006).

The birth experience itself can affect the woman's well-being. Among those who had babies in the United States between 1993 and 1997, 42 percent had a medical problem (Danel et al., 2003), an added burden for the father as well as the mother. For every woman, birth is stressful, with major hormonal changes, some pain, and a baby who is never exactly what the mother or father anticipated.

Focusing on the parents' emotions raises the question: To what extent are the first hours crucial for the **parent–infant bond,** the strong, loving connection that forms as parents hold, examine, and feed their newborn? It has been claimed that this bond develops in the first hours after birth when a mother touches her naked baby, just as sheep and goats must immediately smell and nuzzle their newborns if they are to nurture them (Klaus & Kennell, 1976). However, research does not find that early skin-to-skin contact is essential for humans (Eyer, 1992; Lamb, 1982). Unlike sheep and goats, most other mammals do not need immediate contact for parents to nurture their offspring. In fact, substantial research on monkeys begins with *cross-fostering,* a strategy in which newborns are removed from their biological mothers in the first days of life and raised by another female or even a male. A strong and beneficial relationship sometimes develops (Suomi, 2002).

Most developmentalists hope that mothers, fathers, and newborns strengthen their relationship in the hours and days after birth. That is a good foundation for the difficult days, nights, and years ahead. But bonding immediately after birth is neither necessary nor sufficient for a strong parental alliance and for parent–child attachment throughout life.

SHEHZAD NOORANI / PETER ARNOLD, INC.

A Teenage Mother This week-old baby, born in a poor village in Myanmar (Burma), has a better chance of survival than he might otherwise have had, because his 18-year-old mother has bonded with him.

parent–infant bond The strong, loving connection that forms as parents hold their newborn.

Especially for Scientists Research with animals can benefit people, but it is sometimes used too quickly to support conclusions about people. When does that happen?

SUMMING UP

Most newborns weigh about 7½ pounds (3,400 grams), score at least 7 out of 10 on the Apgar scale, and thrive without medical assistance. Although modern medicine has made maternal or infant death and serious impairment less common in advanced nations, many critics deplore the tendency to treat birth as a medical crisis instead of a natural event. Developmentalists note that birth complications are rarely the consequence of birth practices alone; prenatal problems are usually involved.

Many factors in the family, fetus, and social conditions lead to low birthweight, a potentially serious and increasingly common problem. Postpartum depression is not rare, but, again, factors before and after birth affect how serious and long-lasting this problem is. Human parents and infants seem to benefit from close physical contact following the birth, but it is not essential for emotional bonding. The family relationship begins before conception, may be strengthened by the birth process, and continues lifelong.

SUMMARY

From Zygote to Newborn

1. The first two weeks of prenatal growth are called the germinal period. During this period, the single-celled zygote develops into a blastocyst with more than 100 cells, travels down the fallopian tube, and implants itself in the lining of the uterus. Most zygotes do not develop.

2. The period from the third through the eighth week after conception is called the embryonic period. The heart begins to beat, and the eyes, ears, nose, and mouth begin to form. By the eighth week, the embryo has the basic organs and features of a human, with the exception of the sex organs.

3. The fetal period extends from the 9th week until birth. By the 12th week, all the organs and body structures have formed. The fetus attains viability at 22 weeks, when the brain is sufficiently mature to regulate basic body functions. Babies born before the 26th week are at high risk of death or disability.

4. The average fetus gains approximately 4½ pounds (2,040 grams) during the last three months of pregnancy and weighs 7½ pounds (3,400 grams) at birth. Maturation of brain, lungs, and heart ensures survival of more than 99 percent of all full-term babies.

Risk Reduction

5. Some teratogens (diseases, drugs, and pollutants) cause physical impairment. Others, called behavioral teratogens, harm the brain and therefore impair cognitive abilities and personality tendencies.

6. Whether a teratogen harms an embryo or fetus depends on timing, amount of exposure, and genetic vulnerability. To protect against prenatal complications, good public and personal health practices are strongly recommended.

7. Many methods of prenatal testing inform pregnant couples how the fetus is developing. Such knowledge can bring anxiety and unexpected responsibility as well as welcome information.

The Birth Process

8. Birth typically begins with contractions that push the fetus, head first, out of the uterus and then through the vagina. The Apgar scale, which rates the neonate's vital signs at one minute and again at five minutes after birth, provides a quick evaluation of the infant's health.

9. Medical intervention can speed contractions, dull pain, and save lives. However, many aspects of the medicalized birth have been faulted. Contemporary birthing practices are aimed at finding a balance, protecting the baby but also allowing more parental involvement and control.

10. Birth complications, such as unusually long and stressful labor that includes anoxia (a lack of oxygen to the fetus), have many causes. Long-term handicaps, such as cerebral palsy, are not inevitable for such children, but careful nurturing from their parents may be needed.

11. Low birthweight (under 5½ pounds, or 2,500 grams) may arise from multiple births, placental problems, maternal illness, malnutrition, smoking, drinking, drug use, and age. Compared with full-term newborns, preterm and underweight babies experience more medical difficulties. Fetuses that grow slowly (SGA) are especially vulnerable.

12. Many women feel unhappy, incompetent, or unwell in the days immediately after giving birth. Postpartum depression may lift with appropriate help; fathers are particularly crucial to the well-being of mother and child, although they also are vulnerable to depression.

13. Kangaroo care is particularly helpful when the newborn is of low birthweight. Mother–newborn interaction should be encouraged, although the parent–infant bond depends on many factors in addition to birth practices.

KEY TERMS

germinal period (p. 91)
embryonic period (p. 91)
fetal period (p. 91)
blastocyst (p. 91)
placenta (p. 92)
implantation (p. 92)
embryo (p. 93)
fetus (p. 94)
age of viability (p. 95)
teratogens (p. 97)
behavioral teratogens (p. 97)
risk analysis (p. 98)
critical period (p. 98)
threshold effect (p. 98)
interaction effect (p. 99)
fetal alcohol syndrome (FAS) (p. 102)
Apgar scale (p. 110)
cesarean section (p. 110)
doula (p. 112)
anoxia (p. 112)
cerebral palsy (p. 113)
low birthweight (LBW) (p. 113)
very low birthweight (VLBW) (p. 113)
extremely low birthweight (ELBW) (p. 113)
preterm birth (p. 114)
small for gestational age (SGA) (p. 114)
kangaroo care (p. 117)
parental alliance (p. 118)
postpartum depression (p. 118)
parent–infant bond (p. 119)

KEY QUESTIONS

1. What are the major differences between an embryo at 2 weeks and at 8 weeks after conception?

2. What are the factors in achieving viability?

3. Since almost all fetuses born at 30 weeks survive, why don't women avoid the last month of pregnancy by having an elective cesarean at that time?

4. Which maternal behavior or characteristic seems most harmful to the fetus: eating a diet low in folic acid, drinking a lot of alcohol, or being HIV-positive? Explain your answer.

5. Reconsider the Horans' decision to abort their fetus. According to this published account, which considerations were crucial for them? If you were in this situation, which considerations would be crucial for you?

6. How much influence do husbands and mothers have on pregnant women? Explain your answer.

7. How have medical procedures helped *and* harmed the birth process?

8. Why do hospitals encourage parents of fragile newborns to provide some care, even if the newborn is in critical condition?

9. What are the differences between a typical pregnancy and birth in Africa and a typical one in North America?

10. What can be done about postpartum depression, for mother, father, and infant?

APPLICATIONS

1. Go to a nearby greeting-card store and analyze the cards regarding pregnancy and birth. Do you see any cultural attitudes (e.g., variations depending on the sex of the newborn or of the parent)? If possible, compare those cards with cards from a store that caters to another economic or cultural group.

2. Interview three mothers of varied backgrounds about their birth experiences. Make your interviews open-ended—let them choose what to tell you, as long as they give at least a 10-minute description. Then compare and contrast the three accounts, noting especially any influences of culture, personality, circumstances, or cohort.

3. People sometimes wonder how any pregnant woman could jeopardize the health of her fetus. Consider your own health-related behavior in the past month—exercise, sleep, nutrition, drug use, medical and dental care, disease avoidance, and so on. Would you change your behavior if you were pregnant? Would it make a difference if your family, your partner, or you yourself did not want a baby?

➤**Response for Fathers-to-Be** (from page 118): It begins before conception and continues throughout prenatal development, through his influence on the mother's attitudes and health.

➤**Response for Scientists** (from page 119): Animal research tends to be used too quickly whenever it supports an assertion that is popular but has not been substantiated by research data, as in the social construction about physical contact being crucial for parent–infant bonding.

The First Two Years

CHAPTER 5

CHAPTER 6

CHAPTER 7

PART II

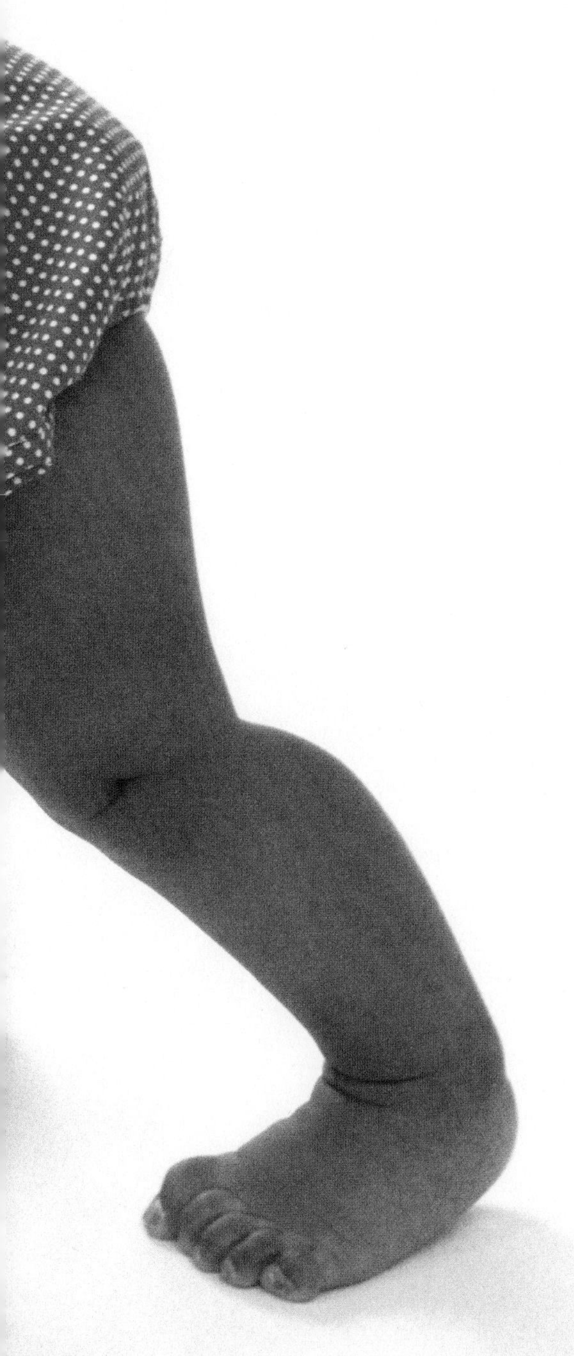

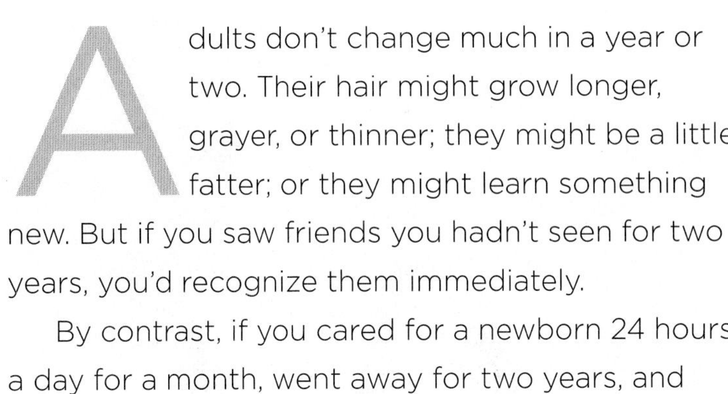

Adults don't change much in a year or two. Their hair might grow longer, grayer, or thinner; they might be a little fatter; or they might learn something new. But if you saw friends you hadn't seen for two years, you'd recognize them immediately.

By contrast, if you cared for a newborn 24 hours a day for a month, went away for two years, and then came back, you might not recognize him or her, because the baby would have quadrupled in weight, grown taller by more than a foot, and sprouted a new head of hair. Behavior would have changed, too. Not much crying, but some laughter and fear—including of you.

A year or two is not much compared with the 75 or so years of the average life span. However, in two years newborns reach half their adult height, talk in sentences, and express almost every emotion—not just joy and fear but also love, jealousy, and shame. The next three chapters describe these radical and awesome changes.

5

CHAPTER OUTLINE

The First Two Years: Biosocial Development

In the first two years, rapid growth is obvious in all three domains—body, mind, and social relationships. Here we chronicle biosocial development: Sit . . . stand . . . walk . . . run! Reach . . . touch . . . grab . . . throw! Listen . . . stare . . . see! Each object, each person, each place becomes something to explore with every sense, limb, and digit.

Invisible developments are even more striking. Infant brains triple in size, with neurons connecting to one another at a dizzying, yet programmed, pace. Tiny stomachs digest more food and more kinds of food, dispatching nourishment to the brain and body to enable phenomenal growth.

Parents and cultures are pivotal to this process, which makes it bio*social*—not merely biological—development. Adults provide the nurture that enables infant growth, with specifics that change daily because infants change daily. As one expert explains, "Parenting an infant is akin to trying to hit a moving target" (Bornstein, 2002, p. 14).

This chapter describes that target as it moves—not only weight, height, and motor skills at key ages but also the brain growth that provides the foundation for all other developments. You will learn in this chapter how to help the infants you know, and some whom you will never meet, make it safely to age 2.

Body Changes

In infancy, growth is so fast, and the consequences of neglect are so severe, that gains need to be closely monitored. Medical checkups, including measurement of height, weight, and head circumference, occur every few weeks at first.

Body Size

Exactly how rapidly does growth typically occur? We saw in Chapter 4 that at birth the average infant weighs 7½ pounds (3,400 grams) and measures about 20 inches (51 centimeters). This means that the typical newborn weighs less than a gallon of milk and is about as long as the distance from a man's elbow to the tips of his fingers.

Infants typically double their birthweight by the fourth month and triple it by their first birthday. Physical growth slows in the second year, but it is still rapid. By 24 months most children weigh almost 30 pounds (13½ kilograms)

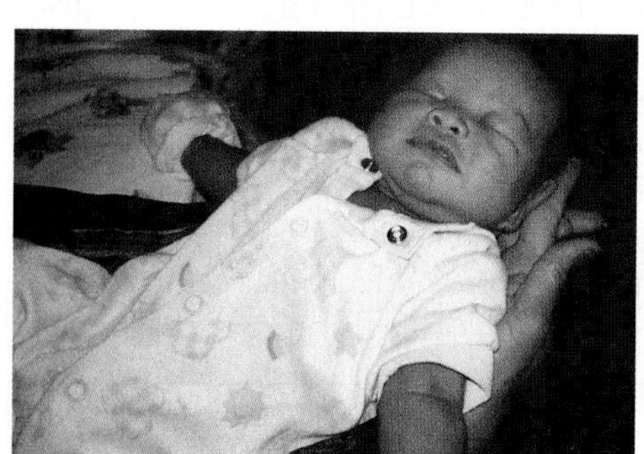

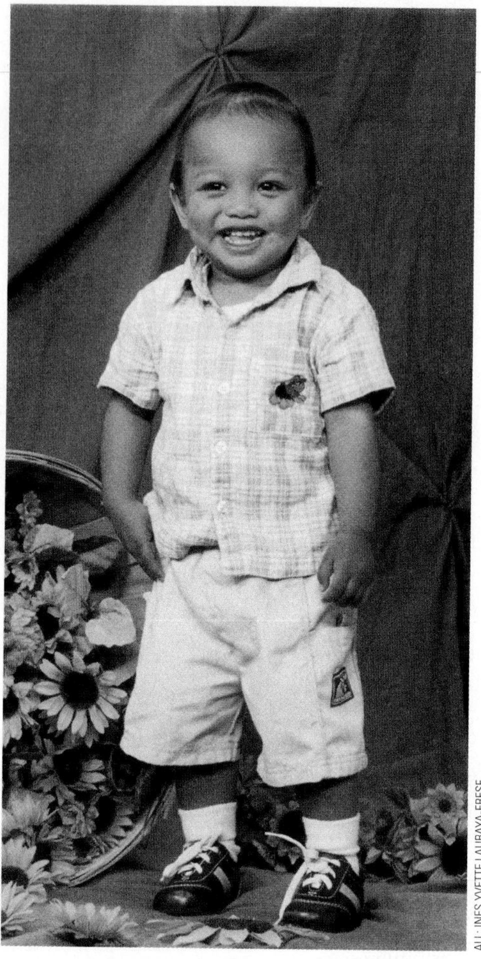

ALL: INES YVETTE LAURAYA-ERESE

Both Amazing and Average Juwan's growth from (*a*) 4 months to (*b*) 12 months to (*c*) 24 months is a surprise and delight to everyone who knows him. At age 2, this Filipino American toddler seems to have become a self-assured, outgoing individual, obviously unique. Yet the norms indicate that he is developing right on schedule—weight, teeth, motor skills, and all.

and are between 32 and 36 inches (81–91 centimeters) tall. This means that typical 2-year-olds are already half their adult height. They are also about 15 to 20 percent of their adult weight, four times as heavy as at birth. (See Appendix A, pp. A-6, A-7.)

norm An average, or standard, measurement, calculated from the measurements of many individuals within a specific group or population.

percentile A point on a ranking scale of 0 to 100. The 50th percentile is the midpoint; half the people in the population rank higher and half rank lower.

Each of the above numbers is a **norm,** an average or standard for a particular population. Norms must be carefully interpreted. The "particular population" for the norms above is a representative sample of North American infants, who may be unlike representative samples of infants from other regions of the world. To understand norms, you also need to understand percentiles. A child who is average is at the 50th **percentile,** a number that is midway between 0 and 100, with half of the children above it and half below it.

Percentiles allow a child's growth to be compared not only with that of other children but also with his or her own prior development. Pediatricians and nurses notice all children whose growth is far from the norms, but they pay closer attention to the ranking: A drop in percentile means that something might be wrong.

Much of the weight increase in the early months is fat, to provide insulation for warmth and a store of nourishment. This stored nutrition keeps the brain growing

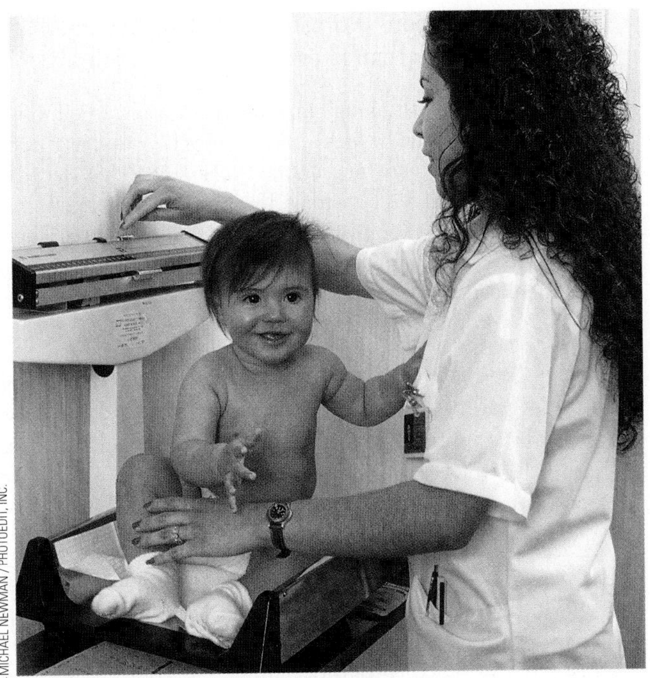

The Weigh-In At her 1-year well-baby checkup, Blair sits up steadily, weighs more than 20 pounds, and would scramble off the table if she could. Both Blair's development and the nurse's protective arm are quite appropriate.

if teething or the sniffles interfere with eating. When nutrition is temporarily inadequate, the body stops growing but not the brain—a phenomenon called **head-sparing** (Georgieff & Rao, 2001). (Chronic malnutrition is discussed later in this chapter.)

head-sparing The biological protection of the brain when malnutrition affects body growth. The brain is the last part of the body to be damaged by malnutrition.

Sleep

New babies spend most of their time sleeping, about 17 hours or more a day. Throughout childhood, regular and ample sleep correlates with normal brain maturation, learning, emotional regulation, and psychological adjustment in school and within the family (Bates et al., 2002; Sadeh et al., 2000). A child who does not sleep well—who wakes up easily or frequently or gets too little sleep—has some kind of health problem, although it is not known if poor sleeping is a cause or a symptom of that problem.

REM sleep Rapid eye movement sleep, a stage of sleep characterized by flickering eyes behind closed lids, dreaming, and rapid brain waves.

Over the first months, the relative amount of time spent in each type or stage of sleep changes. Newborns apparently dream a lot, or at least they have a high proportion of **REM sleep** (rapid eye movement sleep, characterized by flickering eyes, dreaming, and rapid brain waves). Dreaming sleep declines over the early weeks, as does "transitional sleep," the dozing stage when a person is half awake. At 3 or 4 months, quiet sleep (also called slow-wave sleep) increases markedly (Salzarulo & Fagioli, 1999).

At about this time, the various "states" of waking and sleeping become more evident. Thus, although many newborns rarely seem sound asleep or wide awake, by 3 months most babies have periods of alertness, when they are neither hungry nor sleepy, and periods of deep sleep, when noises do not waken them.

Sleep patterns are affected by birth order, newborn diet, and child-rearing practices, as well as by brain maturation. For example, if parents respond to predawn cries with food and play, babies learn to wake up night after night. First-born infants typically

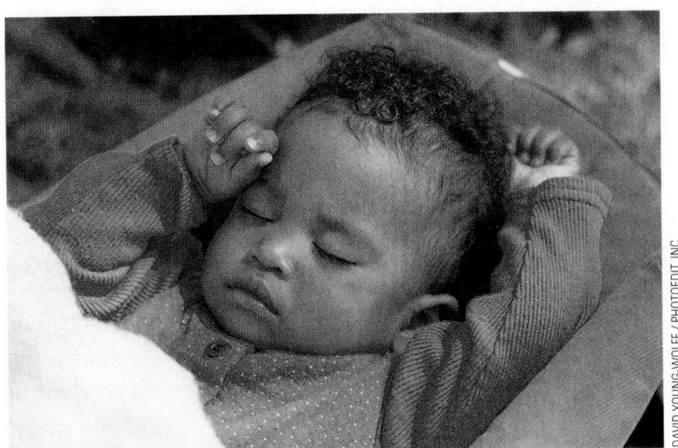

Dreaming, Dozing, or Sound Asleep? Babies spend most of their time sleeping.

Observation Quiz (see answer, page 128): Can you tell which kind of sleep this infant is experiencing?

➤Answer to Observation Quiz (from page 127): The baby's outstretched left arm suggests dreaming, which occupies about six hours of every day's sleep at this age. Direct observation or a video, not a photograph, could demonstrate whether this is REM (dreaming) sleep. Quiet sleep is characterized by shallow breathing, still eyes, and relaxed muscle tone.

"receive more attention" (Bornstein, 2002, p. 28), and that may be why they exhibit more sleep problems than later-borns. Consider this report from one mother:

> I . . . raised my first taking him wherever I went, whenever I went, confident he would adapt. While he was always happy, he was never a good sleeper and his first 4 years were very hard on me (I claim he didn't sleep through the night until he was 4, but I could be wrong, I was so sleep-deprived). . . . [When my third child] came along . . . , I was determined to give her a schedule. . . . She is a GREAT sleeper, happy to go to bed. I am convinced, anecdotally, that schedules are the most important part of this.
>
> *[Freda, personal communication, 1997]*

That is good advice. Developmentalists agree that insisting that an infant conform to the parents' schedule can be frustrating to the parents and, in some cases, harmful to the infant; but letting a child continually interrupt the adults' sleep can be harmful to the parents. Ideally, families interact and adapt until every member's basic needs are met.

One question for many parents is: Where should infants sleep? Traditionally, Western parents put their infants to sleep in a crib in a separate bedroom, unless the family did not have a spare room. Parents in Asia, Africa, and Latin America slept beside their infants, a practice called **co-sleeping** or *bed-sharing*.

co-sleeping A custom in which parents and their children (usually infants) sleep together. (Also called *bed-sharing*.)

Today, many Western parents allow bed-sharing, at least in the first months. In fact, a recent survey of British parents found that half of them slept with their infants some of the time (Blair & Ball, 2004). A study of California families found that about a third practiced co-sleeping from birth; about one-fourth of couples had newborns sleep in another room but allowed their toddlers to sleep with them; and the rest kept babies in a separate room throughout childhood (Keller & Goldberg, 2004).

Co-sleeping does not seem to be harmful unless the adult is drugged or drunk—and thus in danger of "overlying" the baby. According to one report:

> Mothers instinctively take up a protective posture when sharing a bed with their infants, lying in a fetal position with their lower arm above the infant's head and the infant lying within around 20–30 centimeters [about 10 inches] from the mother's chest. The position of the mother's thighs prevents the baby from sliding down the bed.
>
> *[Wailoo et al., 2004, p. 1083]*

Although a videotape analysis found that co-sleeping infants wake up twice as often (six times a night) as solo-sleeping infants (three times), co-sleepers get just as much sleep as solo sleepers because they go back to sleep more quickly (Mao et al., 2004). Sleeping patterns and practices are like other aspects of infant care: Many different paths can lead to normal child development and normal family functioning.

Especially for New Parents You are aware of cultural differences in sleeping practices, and this raises a very practical issue: Should your newborn sleep in bed with you?

SUMMING UP

Birthweight doubles, triples, and quadruples by 4 months, 12 months, and 24 months, respectively. Height increases by about a foot (about 30 centimeters) in the first two years. Such norms are useful as general guidelines, but individual percentile rankings over time indicate whether a particular infant is growing normally. Sleep becomes regular, dreaming less common, and distinct sleep–wake patterns develop, usually including a long night's sleep by age 1. Time spent dreaming decreases to about what it is for an older child. Cultural and caregiving practices influence norms, schedules, and expectations. ■

Brain Development

Recall that the newborn's skull is disproportionately large. That's because it must be big enough to hold the brain, which at birth is already 25 percent of its adult weight. The neonate's body, by comparison, is typically only 5 percent of the adult weight. By age 2, the brain is almost 75 percent of adult brain weight; the child's total body weight is only about 20 percent of its adult weight (see Figure 5.1).

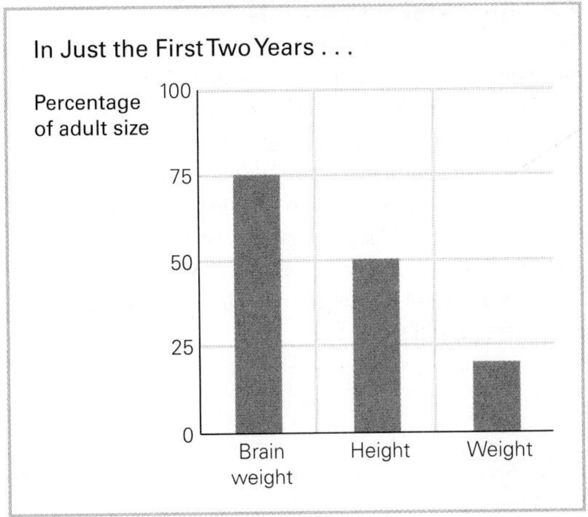
In Just the First Two Years . . .
Percentage of adult size
100
75
50
25
0
Brain weight
Height
Weight

FIGURE 5.1

Growing Up Two-year-olds are barely talking and are totally dependent on adults, but they have already reached half their adult height and three-fourths of their adult brain size. This is dramatic evidence that biosocial growth is the foundation for cognitive and social maturity.

Connections in the Brain

Head circumference provides a rough idea of how the brain is growing, and that is why medical checkups include measurement of the skull. The distance around the head typically increases about 35 percent (from 13 to 18 inches, or from 33 to 46 centimeters) within the first year. Much more significant (although harder to measure) are changes in the brain's communication system. To understand this, we review the basics of neurological development (see Figure 5.2).

Basic Brain Structures

The brain's communication system begins with nerve cells, called **neurons.** Most neurons are created before birth, at a peak production rate of 250,000 new brain cells per minute in mid-pregnancy (Bloom et al., 2001). In infancy, the human brain has billions of neurons. Some neurons are deep inside the brain or in the *brain stem,* a region that controls automatic responses such as heartbeat, breathing, temperature, and arousal. About 70 percent of neurons are in the **cortex,** the brain's six outer layers (sometimes called the *neocortex*) (Kolb & Whishaw, 2003). The cortex is crucial for humans, as is evident in the following three facts:

- About 80 percent of the human brain material is in the cortex.
- In other mammals the cortex is proportionally smaller, and non-mammals have no cortex.
- Most thinking, feeling, and sensing take place in the cortex, although other parts of the brain join in (Kolb & Whishaw, 2003).

neuron One of the billions of nerve cells in the central nervous system, especially the brain.

cortex The outer layers of the brain in humans and other mammals. Most thinking, feeling, and sensing involve the cortex. (Sometimes called the *neocortex.*)

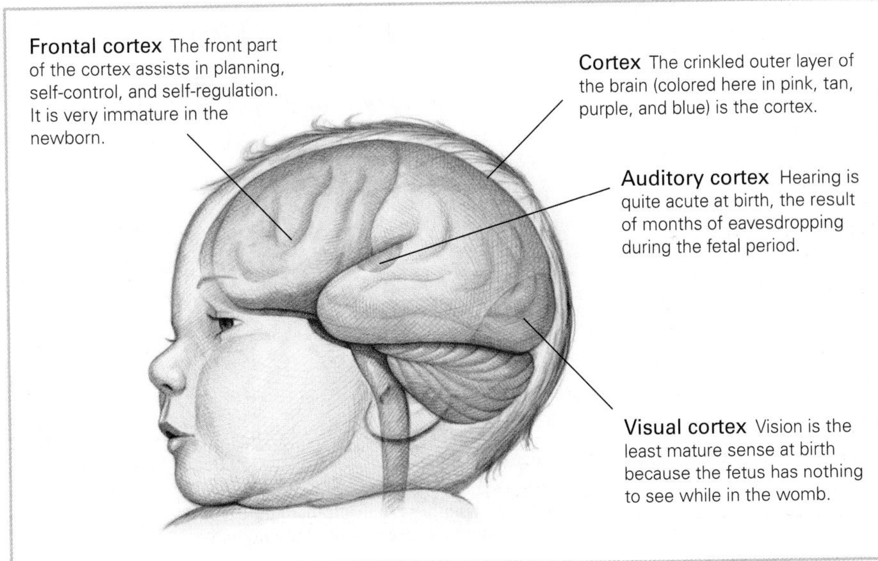
Frontal cortex The front part of the cortex assists in planning, self-control, and self-regulation. It is very immature in the newborn.
Cortex The crinkled outer layer of the brain (colored here in pink, tan, purple, and blue) is the cortex.
Auditory cortex Hearing is quite acute at birth, the result of months of eavesdropping during the fetal period.
Visual cortex Vision is the least mature sense at birth because the fetus has nothing to see while in the womb.

FIGURE 5.2

The Developing Cortex The infant's cortex consists of four to six thin layers of tissue that cover the brain. It contains virtually all the neurons that make conscious thought possible. Some areas of the cortex, such as those devoted to the basic senses, mature relatively early. Others, such as the frontal cortex, mature quite late.

➤**Response for New Parents** (from page 128): From the psychological and cultural perspectives, babies can sleep anywhere as long as the parents can hear them if they cry. The main consideration is safety: Infants should not sleep on a mattress that is too soft, nor should a baby sleep beside an adult who is drunk or drugged or sleeps very soundly (Nakamura et al., 1999). Otherwise, the family should decide for itself where its members would sleep best.

Various areas of the cortex specialize in particular functions. For instance, there is a visual cortex, an auditory cortex, and an area dedicated to the sense of touch for each body part—even for each finger of a person or, in rats, for each whisker (Bloom et al., 2001). Regional specialization within the cortex occurs not only for motor skills and senses but also for particular aspects of cognition.

One of the fascinating aspects of brain specialization is that a particular part of the brain (called the *fusiform face area*) seems dedicated to perception of faces. In newborns, this area is activated not only by real faces but also by visual stimuli (e.g., pictures) that look like faces. The infant's experiences refine perception in this area, so 6-month-olds recognize their mothers and fathers, examine faces of strangers, and no longer pay careful attention to monkey faces (Johnson, 2005).

axon A fiber that extends from a neuron and transmits electrochemical impulses from that neuron to the dendrites of other neurons.

dendrite A fiber that extends from a neuron and receives electrochemical impulses transmitted from other neurons via their axons.

synapse The intersection between the axon of one neuron and the dendrites of other neurons.

Within and between brain areas, neurons are connected to other neurons by intricate networks of nerve fibers called **axons** and **dendrites** (see Figure 5.3). Each neuron has a single axon and numerous dendrites, which spread out like the branches of a tree. The axon of one neuron meets the dendrites of other neurons at intersections called **synapses,** which are critical communication links within the brain. To be more specific, neurons communicate by sending electrochemical impulses through their axons to synapses, to be picked up by the dendrites of other neurons. The dendrites bring the message to the cell bodies of their neurons, which, in turn, convey the message via their axons to still other neurons. Axons and dendrites do not touch at synapses. Instead, the electrical impulses in axons typically cause the release of chemicals called *neurotransmitters,* which carry information

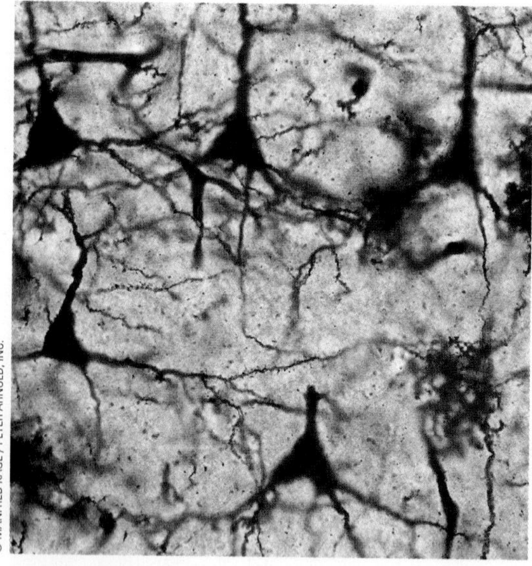

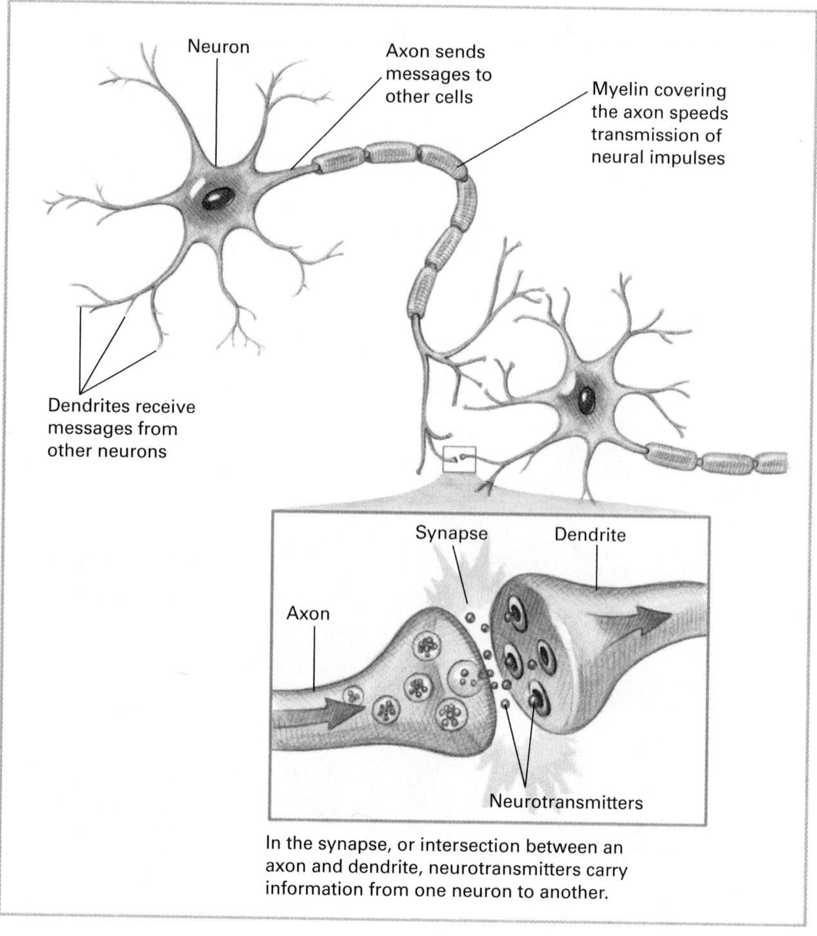

In the synapse, or intersection between an axon and dendrite, neurotransmitters carry information from one neuron to another.

FIGURE 5.3

How Two Neurons Communicate The link between one neuron and another is shown in the simplified diagram at right. The infant brain actually contains billions of neurons, each with one axon and many dendrites. Every electrochemical message to or from the brain causes thousands of neurons to fire simultaneously, each transmitting the message across the synapse to neighboring neurons. The electron micrograph directly above shows several neurons, greatly magnified, with their tangled but highly organized and well-coordinated sets of dendrites and axons.

from the axon of the sending neuron, across the *synaptic gap*, to the dendrites of the receiving neuron, a process speeded up by myelination (described in Chapter 8).

Transient Exuberance and Pruning

At birth, the brain contains more than 100 billion neurons, more than any person will ever use (de Haan & Johnson, 2003). By contrast, the newborn brain has far fewer dendrites and synapses than the person will eventually possess. During the first months and years, rapid growth and refinement in axons, dendrites, and synapses occur, especially in the cortex. Dendrite growth is the major reason that brain weight triples in the first two years (Johnson, 2005).

An estimated fivefold increase in dendrites in the cortex occurs in the 24 months after birth, with about 100 trillion synapses being present at age 2 (Schwartz & Begley, 2002). This early growth is called **transient exuberance,** because the expanded growth of dendrites is followed by *pruning* (see Figure 5.4), in which unused neurons and misconnected dendrites atrophy and die (Barinaga, 2003). (This process is called *pruning* because it resembles the way a gardener might prune a rose bush by cutting away some stems to enable more, or more beautiful, roses to bloom.) Transient exuberance enables neurons to become connected to, and communicate with, a greatly expanding number of other neurons within the brain. Synapses, dendrites, and even neurons continue to form and die throughout life, though more rapidly in infancy than at any other time (Nelson et al., 2006).

Thinking and learning require that such connections between many parts of the brain be made. For example, to understand any word in this text, you need to understand the surrounding words, the ideas they convey, and how they relate to your other thoughts and experiences. Baby brains have the same requirement, although at first they have few experiences to build on, and the various parts of the brain have not yet developed to the adult level or even to the level of a 2-year-old.

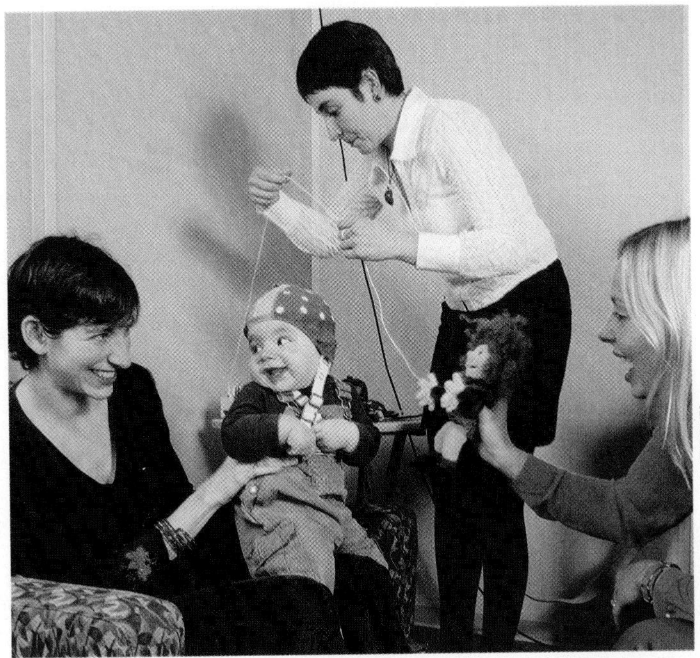

BENJAMIN BENSCHNEIDER / THE SEATTLE TIMES

Electric Excitement Milo's delight at his mother's facial expressions is visible, not just in his eyes and mouth but also in the neurons of the outer layer of his cortex. Electrodes map his brain activation region by region and moment by moment. Every month of life up to age 2 shows increased electrical excitement.

transient exuberance The great increase in the number of dendrites that occurs in an infant's brain during the first two years of life.

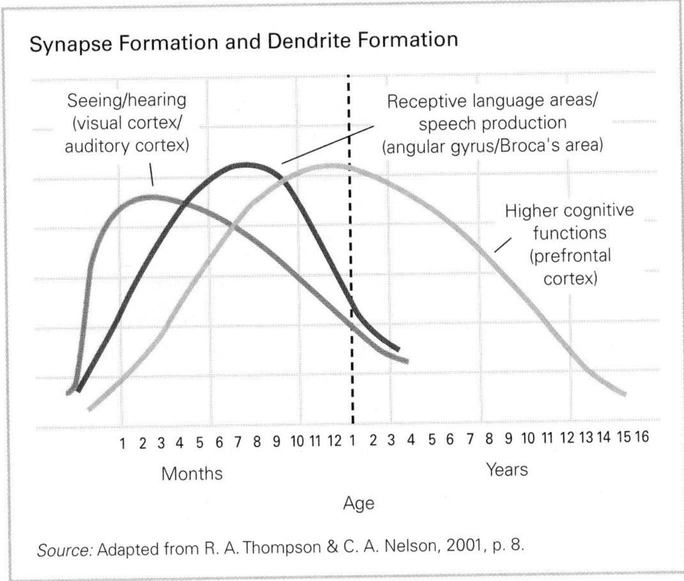

FIGURE 5.4

Brain Growth in Response to Experience These curves show the rapid rate of experience-dependent synapse formation for three functions of the brain (senses, language, and analysis). After the initial increase, the underused neurons are gradually pruned, or inactivated, as no functioning dendrites are formed from them.

Observation Quiz (see answer, page 132): Why do both "12 months" and "1 year" appear on the "Age" line?

➤Answer to Observation Quiz (from page 131): "One year" signifies the entire year, from day 365 to day 729, and that is indicated by its location between "12 months" and "2 years."

Experience Shapes the Brain

The specifics of brain structure and growth depend on genes but also on experience, which produces the "postnatal rise and fall" of synapses (de Haan & Johnson, 2003, p. 5). Soon after exuberant expansion, some dendrites wither away because they are underused—that is, no experiences have caused them to send a message to the axons of other neurons. Strangely enough, this loss increases brain power by promoting a more intricate organization of existing connections; the "increasing cognitive complexity of childhood is related to a loss rather than a gain of synapses" (de Haan & Johnson, 2003, p. 8).

Further evidence of the benefit of cell death comes from neurological research regarding fragile X syndrome (described in Chapter 3), which includes "a persistent failure of normal synapse pruning" (Irwin et al., 2002, p. 194). In children with fragile X syndrome, dendrites are too dense and too long; without pruning, children cannot think normally.

Stress and the Brain

An unfortunate example of the role of experience in brain development begins when the brain produces cortisol and other hormones in response to stress, which happens throughout life (Gunnar & Vasquez, 2001). If the brain produces an overabundance of stress hormones early in life (as when an infant is frequently terrified), then the brain becomes incapable of normal stress responses. Later, that person's brain may either overproduce stress hormones, making the person hypervigilant (always on the alert), or underproduce them, making the person emotionally flat (never happy, sad, or angry).

A kindergarten teacher might notice that one child becomes furious or terrified at a mild provocation and another child seems indifferent to everything. Why? In both cases, the underlying cause could be excessive stress-hormone production in infancy, which changes the way the brain responds to stress. Similarly, if an adult loves or hates too quickly, extremely, and irrationally, the cause could be abnormal brain hormones resulting from early experiences such as abuse (Teicher, 2002).

Necessary and Possible Experiences

A scientist named William Greenough has identified two experience-related aspects of brain development (Greenough et al., 1987):

experience-expectant Refers to brain functions that require certain basic common experiences (which an infant can be expected to have) in order to develop normally.

experience-dependent Refers to brain functions that depend on particular, variable experiences and that therefore may or may not develop in a particular infant.

- The development of **experience-expectant** brain functions requires the individual's exposure to basic common experiences—experiences that almost every infant has and all infants need for normal brain development.
- The development of **experience-dependent** functions depends on the individual's exposure to particular, variable experiences—experiences that some infants in some families and cultures may have but others may not have, and which vary from one infant to another.

The basic, common experiences *must* happen for normal brain maturation to occur, and they almost always do happen: The brain is designed to expect them and use them for growth. Human brain development is dependent on many such *expected* experiences. In deserts and in the Arctic, on isolated farms and in crowded cities, almost all babies do have things to see, objects to manipulate, and people to love them. As a result, their brains develop normally.

In contrast, dependent experiences *might* happen; because of them, one brain differs from another. Particular experiences vary, such as which language babies hear or how their mother reacts to frustration. *Depending* on those particulars, infant brains are structured and connected one way or another, as some dendrites grow and neurons thrive while others die. Consequently, all people are similar, but each person is unique, because of particular early experiences.

This distinction can be made for all mammals. Some of the most persuasive research has been done with songbirds. All male songbirds have a brain region dedicated to listening and reproducing sounds (experience-expectant), but each species in a particular locality learns to produce a slightly different song (experience-dependent) (Knudsen, 1999). Birds develop the neurons that they need: neurons dedicated to learning new songs (canaries) or to finding hidden seeds (chickadees). Both of these functions require experiences that circumstances offer to some birds but not to others (Barinaga, 2003).

EASTCOTT / MOMATINK / THE IMAGE WORKS

Let's Talk Infants evoke facial expressions and baby talk, no matter where they are or which adults they are with. Communication is thus experience-expectant: Young human brains expect it and need it.

Observation Quiz (see answer, page 134): Are these two father and daughter? Where are they?

In unusual situations, knowledge of which developmental events are experience-expectant at what ages is helpful. For example, proliferation and pruning occur at about 4 months in the visual and auditory cortexes. For this reason, treatment of blind or deaf infants (whether with surgery, eyeglasses, or hearing aids) should occur early in life to prevent atrophy of those brain regions that expect sights and sounds (Leonard, 2003). Thus, deaf infants whose deficits are recognized at birth and remediated in their first year become better at understanding and expressing language than do those whose hearing deficits are not noticed until later (Kennedy et al., 2006).

If early visual or auditory neuronal connections are not made, those areas of the brain may become dedicated to other senses, such as touch. Braille, for that reason, is easier for a blind person to read than for a seeing person, because blind people often have more brain cells dedicated to the sense of touch (Pascual-Leone & Torres, 1993).

The language areas of the brain develop most rapidly between the ages of 6 and 24 months, so infants need to hear a lot of speech during that period in order to talk fluently. In fact, speech heard between 6 and 12 months helps infants recognize the characteristics of their local language long before they utter a word (Saffran et al., 2006).

The last part of the brain to mature is the **prefrontal cortex,** the area for anticipation, planning, and impulse control. It is virtually inactive in early infancy but gradually becomes more efficient over the years of childhood and adolescence (Luciana, 2003). Thus, telling an infant to stop crying is pointless, because the infant cannot decide to stop crying. Such decisions require brain functions that are not yet present.

prefrontal cortex The area of cortex at the front of the brain that specializes in anticipation, planning, and impulse control.

Much worse is for an adult to become angry and shake the baby to stop the crying. This can cause **shaken baby syndrome,** a life-threatening condition that occurs when an infant is held by the shoulders and shaken back and forth, sharply and quickly. The shaking stops the crying because of ruptured blood vessels in the brain and broken neural connections. In the United States, brain scans show that more than one in five of all children hospitalized for maltreatment suffer from shaken baby syndrome (Rovi et al., 2004).

shaken baby syndrome A life-threatening condition that occurs when an infant is forcefully shaken back and forth, rupturing blood vessels in the brain and breaking neural connections.

Implications for Caregivers

What does early brain development mean for parents and other caregivers? First, early brain growth is rapid and dependent on experience. This means that caressing a newborn, talking to a preverbal infant, and showing affection toward a toddler

➤Answer to Observation Quiz (from page 133): The man's straight black hair, high cheekbones, and weather-beaten face indicate that he could be an Indian from North or South America. Other clues pinpoint the location more closely. Note his lined, hooded jacket and the low, heat-conserving ceiling of the house—he is an Inuit in northern Canada. A father's attention makes a baby laugh and vocalize, not look away, so this man is not the 6-month-old baby's father. She is being held by a family friend whom she is visiting with her parents.

may be essential to develop the child's full potential. If such experiences are missing from the child's early weeks and months, lifelong damage may result.

Second, each part of the brain has a sequence of growing, connecting, and pruning. Some kinds of stimulation are meaningless before the brain is ready, and some potential learning is irrelevant to a particular person. That means it is advisable to follow the baby's lead to figure out what stimulation is needed. Infants respond most strongly and positively to whatever their brains need; that is why very young babies like to look at and listen to musical mobiles, strangers on the street, and, best of all, their own caregivers.

This preference reflects **self-righting,** the inborn drive to remedy deficits. An infant with limited stimulation will develop the brain by using whatever experiences are available. Babies do not need the latest educational toys—their brains will develop with normal stimulation. Just don't keep them in a dark, quiet place all day long.

self-righting The inborn drive to remedy a developmental deficit.

Human brains are designed to grow and adapt; some plasticity is retained throughout life (Baltes et al., 2006). Brains protect themselves from overstimulation; for example, overstimulated babies sometimes cry or sleep. They also adjust to understimulation, responding to any experience by developing new connections lifelong (Greenough, 1993; Schwartz & Begley, 2002).

Neuroscientists once thought that brains were influenced solely by genes and prenatal influences. By contrast, many social scientists once thought that childhood environment was crucial. Cultures (according to anthropologists) or societies (according to sociologists) or parents (according to psychologists) could be credited or blamed for a child's emotions and actions.

Now most scientists, especially life-span developmentalists, are multidisciplinary, incorporating perspectives from both neuroscience and social science (Nelson et al., 2006). They believe that plasticity is an "inherent property of development" (Johnson, 2005, p. 189), but they do not think plasticity is unlimited. Rather, there are **sensitive periods,** which are times when particular kinds of development are primed to occur (Baltes et al., 2006). The first two years of life are widely considered a sensitive period during which the brain needs some experiences if it is to develop normally.

sensitive period A time when a certain kind of growth or development is most likely to happen or happens most readily.

For an explanation of why social scientists let go of their faith in the brain's ability to recover from deprivation at any age, read the following.

thinking like a scientist

Plasticity and Orphans

How much, and when, can experience affect the brain? Two studies—one involving caged rats and the other involving adopted babies—provide some answers.

In research by Marion Diamond, William Greenough, and their colleagues, some "enriched" rats were raised with other rats in large cages filled with interesting rat toys; other "deprived" rats were isolated in small, barren cages. The rats were randomly assigned, and all came from the same few litters. At autopsy, their brains were examined. The brains of the "enriched" rats were larger and heavier and had more dendrites than the brains of the "deprived" rats (Diamond et al., 1988; Greenough & Volkmar, 1973).

Many other researchers have confirmed this phenomenon: Isolation and sensory deprivation harm the developing brain of a rat, and a complex social environment enhances neurological growth (Curtis & Nelson, 2003). The most recent extensions of this research suggest that rats raised in cognitively stimulating environments are less likely to suffer from brain disease, including Alzheimer's disease, in late adulthood.

Such experiments are unthinkable with humans, but a chilling natural experiment began in Romania in the 1980s, when dictator Nicolae Ceausesçu forbade all birth control and outlawed abortions except for women who had five children or more. Parents were paid for every birth but received no financial support for raising a child. Illegal abortions became the leading cause of death for women age 15–45 (Verona, 2003), and more than 100,000 children were abandoned to crowded, impersonal state-run orphanages (D. E. Johnson, 2000). These children were overstressed and overstimulated because they lacked the buffers of social reassurance and love. They experienced "severe and pervasive restriction of human interactions, play conversation, and experiences" (Rutter & O'Connor, 2004, p. 91).

Ceausesçu was ousted and killed in 1989. During the next two years, thousands of Romanian children were adopted by North American and western European families who believed that "lots of love and good food would change the skinny, floppy waif they found in the orphanage into the child of their dreams" (D. E. Johnson, 2000, p. 154).

All the Romanian adoptees experienced catch-up growth, becoming taller and gaining weight until they reached normal size (Rutter & O'Connor, 2004). However, many showed signs of emotional damage: They were too friendly to strangers, or too angry without reason, or too frightened of normal events (Chisholm, 1998). The children who fared best were adopted before 6 months of age (Rutter, 2006).

For scientists who expected dire consequences, the news was good: "The human infant has built-in 'buffers' against early adversity" (O'Connor et al., 2000). Self-righting was apparent, especially in weight and height. By age 11, children who had been adopted by 6 months were normal in IQ and in other ways.

For those who hoped for the eventual recovery of all these children, however, the news was bad. No further gains occurred after age 6, except for the most severely impaired children, who were still below average. The 11-year-olds who had been adopted after they were 6 months old scored an average of 85 on the WISC IQ test, which is 15 points below normal. Deprivation was also apparent in language and social interaction, abilities controlled by the cortex.

Research on maltreated children in the United States has reached similar conclusions. If maltreatment begins early in life and continues past 1 year, complete social and emotional recovery is much more elusive than catch-up physical growth (Bolger & Patterson, 2003). Plasticity is not infinite; some effects of early deprivation probably persist no matter how nurturant later life is (Rutter, 2006). On the other hand, some plasticity is evident throughout life; some research focuses on a 6-month window, others a year, others two years. Ideally of course, no deprivation occurs at all.

Neither dire nor sunny predictions about maltreated children are accurate. A team of scientists who have devoted their lives to impaired children advise: "Be skeptical about 'miracle' cures of severely affected individuals which appear in the media, or even in scientific journals, while recognizing that partial amelioration can occur in individual cases" (Clarke & Clarke, 2003, p. 131).

Thinking like a scientist means working to stop every government, culture, or family that allows young children to be raised without the experiences they need in order to develop normally. Head-sparing, plasticity, self-righting, and experience-expectant events all compensate for the many imperfections and lapses of human parenting, but they cannot overcome extreme early deprivation that lasts too long.

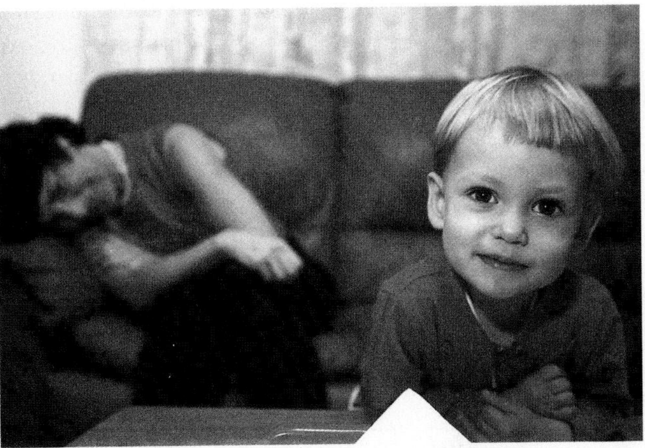

AP / WIDE WORLD PHOTOS

A Fortunate Pair Elaine Himelfarb (shown in the background), of San Diego, California, is shown here in Bucharest to adopt 22-month-old Maria. This adoption was an exception to the Romanian government's ban at the time on international adoptions. Adopted children like Maria, who have been well fed and who are less than 2 years old, are especially likely to develop well.

SUMMING UP

Brain growth is rapid during the first months of life, when dendrites and the synapses within the cortex increase exponentially. By age 2 the brain already weighs three-fourths of its adult weight. Shrinkage of underused and unconnected dendrites begins in the sensory and motor areas and then occurs in other areas. Although some brain development is maturational, experience is also essential—both the universal experiences that almost every infant has (experience-expectant brain development) and the particular experiences whose nature depends on the child's family or culture (experience-dependent brain development). ■

Especially for Social Workers An infertile couple in their late 30s asks for your help in adopting a child from eastern Europe. They particularly want an older child. How do you respond?

Senses and Motor Skills

You learned in Chapter 2 that Piaget called the first period of intelligence the *sensorimotor* stage, emphasizing that cognition develops from the senses and motor skills. The same concept—that infant brain development depends on sensory experiences and early movements—underlies the discussion you have just read.

For that reason, within hours of birth, doctors and nurses make sure the vital organs are functioning, assessing basic senses and motor responses. Many of them use the *Brazelton Neonatal Assessment Scale,* which measures 26 items of newborn behavior (such as cuddling, listening, and self-soothing) as well as several reflexes. Now we describe the sequence in which these abilities—all very immature at birth—develop.

➤**Response for Social Workers** (from page 135): Tell them that such a child would require extra time and commitment, more than a younger adoptee would. Ask whether both are prepared to cut down on their working hours in order to meet with other parents of international adoptees, to obtain professional help (for speech, nutrition, physical development, and/or family therapy), and to help the child with schoolwork, play dates, and so on. You might encourage them instead to adopt a special-needs child from their own area, to become foster parents, or to volunteer at least 10 hours a week at a day-care center. Their response would indicate their willingness to help a real—not imagined—child. If they demonstrate their understanding of what is required, then you might help them adopt the child they want.

Sensation and Perception

All the senses function at birth. Newborns have open eyes, sensitive ears, and responsive noses, tongues, and skin. Throughout their first year, infants use their senses to sort and classify their many experiences. Indeed, "infants spend the better part of their first year merely looking around" (Rovee-Collier, 2001, p. 35).

You may have noticed that very young babies seem to attend to everything, without focusing on anything in particular. Up until about age 1, taste is one of the primary ways humans learn about objects. Babies bring everything to their mouths as soon as they can do so (Adolph & Berger, 2005).

Since all of a newborn's senses function, why don't newborns seem to perceive much? To understand this, you need to understand the distinction between sensation and perception. **Sensation** occurs when a sensory system detects a stimulus, as when the inner ear reverberates with sound or the retina and pupil of the eye intercept light. Thus, sensations begin when an outer organ (eye, ear, skin, tongue, or nose) meets anything in the external world that can be seen, heard, touched, tasted, or smelled.

sensation The response of a sensory system (eyes, ears, skin, tongue, nose) when it detects a stimulus.

perception The mental processing of sensory information, when the brain interprets a sensation.

Perception occurs when the brain notices and processes a sensation. Perception occurs in the cortex, usually as the result of a message from one of the sensing organs—a message that experience suggests might be worth interpreting. Some sensations are beyond comprehension at first: A newborn does not know that the letters on a page might have significance, that Mother's face should be distinguished from Father's face, or that the smells of roses and garlic have different connotations. Perceptions require experience.

Especially for Parents of Grown Children Suppose that you realize that you seldom talked to your children until they talked to you and that you never used a stroller or a walker but put them in cribs and playpens. Did you limit their brain growth and their sensory capacity?

Infant brains are especially attuned to experiences that are repeated, striving to make sense of them (Leonard, 2003). Thus, newborn Emily has no idea that *Emily* is her name, but she has the brain capacity to hear sounds in the usual speech range (not the high sounds that only dogs can hear) and an inborn preference for repeated patterns. At about 4 months, especially when her auditory cortex is rapidly creating and pruning dendrites, the repeated word *Emily* is perceived as well as sensed, and the sound is associated with attention from other people (Saffran et al., 2006).

Before 6 months, Emily may open her eyes and turn her head when her name is called, and she associates the words *Mommy* and *Daddy* with those people. It will take many more months before she tries to say "Emmy" and still longer before she knows that *Emily* is indeed her name or what a mother and father are.

Thus, cognition goes beyond perception. It occurs when people think about and interpret what they have perceived. (Later, cognition no longer requires sensation and perception: People can imagine, fantasize, hypothesize.) There is a sequence of comprehension, from sensation to perception to cognition. A baby's sense organs must function if this sequence is to begin. No wonder the parts of the cortex dedicated to the senses develop rapidly: That is the prerequisite for the other developments.

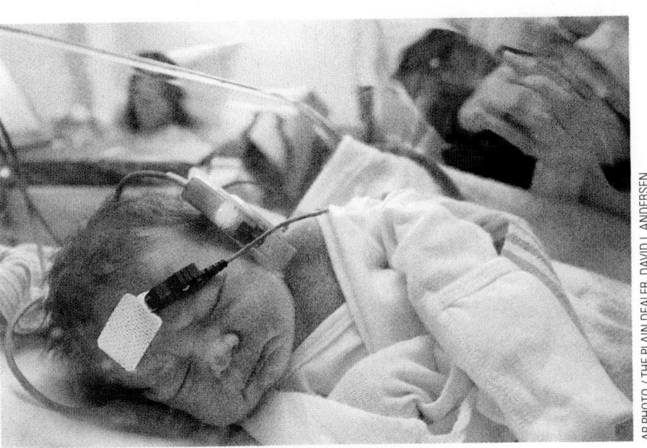

AP PHOTO / THE PLAIN DEALER, DAVID I. ANDERSEN

Before Leaving the Hospital As mandated by a 2004 Ohio law, 1-day-old Henry has his hearing tested via vibrations of the inner ear in response to various tones. The computer interprets the data and signals any need for more tests—as is the case for about 1 baby in 100. Normal newborns hear quite well; Henry's hearing was fine.

Hearing

The sense of hearing is already quite acute at birth. Certain sounds seem to trigger reflexes, even without conscious perception. Sudden noises startle newborns, making them cry; rhythmic sounds, such as a lullaby or a heartbeat, soothe them and put them to sleep. Even in the first days of life, infants turn their heads toward the source of a sound, and they soon begin to adapt that response to connect sight and sound with increasing accuracy (Morrongiello et al., 1998).

Young infants are particularly attentive to the human voice, developing rapid comprehension of the rhythm, segmentation, and cadence of spoken words long before comprehension of their meaning (Saffran et al., 2006). As time goes on, sensitive hearing combines with the developing brain to distinguish patterns of sounds and syllables.

Infants become accustomed to the rules of their language, such as which syllable is usually stressed (various English dialects have different rules), whether changing voice tone is significant (as it is in Chinese), whether certain sound combinations are often or never repeated, and so on. All this is based on very careful listening to human speech, even speech not directed toward them and uttered in a language they do not yet understand.

Seeing

Vision is the least mature sense at birth. Although the eyes open in mid-pregnancy and are sensitive to bright light (if the woman is sunbathing in a bikini, for instance), the fetus has nothing much to see. Newborns are "legally blind"; they see only objects between 4 and 30 inches (10 and 75 centimeters) away (Bornstein et al., 2005).

Soon visual experience combines with maturation of the visual cortex to improve visual ability. By 2 months, infants look more intently at a human face, and, tentatively and fleetingly, smile. Over time, visual scanning becomes more organized and more efficient, centered on important points. Thus, 3-month-olds look more closely at the eyes and mouth, the parts of a face that contain the most information, and they much prefer photos of faces with features over photos of faces with the features blanked out (Johnson & Morton, 1991).

Binocular vision is the ability to coordinate the two eyes to see one image. Because using both eyes together is impossible in the womb, many newborns seem to focus with one eye or the other, or to use their two eyes independently, so that they momentarily look wall-eyed or cross-eyed. At about 14 weeks, binocular vision appears quite suddenly, probably because the underlying brain mechanisms are activated and the infant becomes able to focus both eyes on one thing (Atkinson & Braddick, 2003).

binocular vision The ability to focus the two eyes in a coordinated manner in order to see one image.

Tasting, Smelling, and Touching

As with vision and hearing, the senses of taste, smell, and touch function at birth and rapidly adapt to the social world. For example, one study found that a taste of sugar calmed 2-week-olds but had no effect on 4-week-olds—unless accompanied by a reassuring look from a caregiver (Zeifman et al., 1996). Another study found that sugar is a good pain reliever for newborns (Gradin et al., 2002).

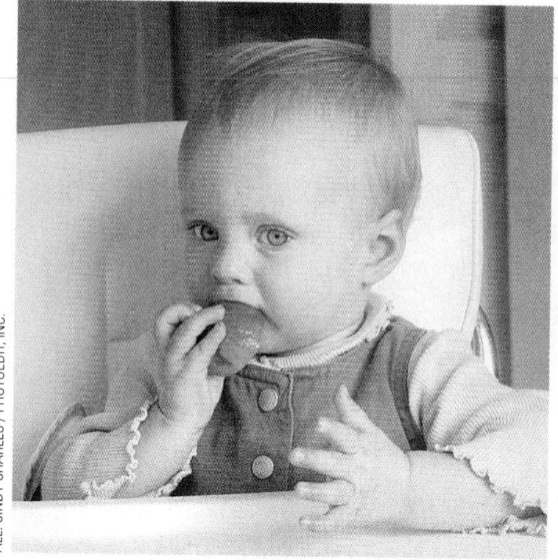

ALL: CINDY CHARLES / PHOTOEDIT, INC.

Learning About a Lime As with every other normal infant, Jacqueline's curiosity leads to taste, then to a slow reaction, from puzzlement to tongue-out disgust. Jacqueline's responses demonstrate that the sense of taste is acute in infancy and that quick brain reactions are still to come.

Similar adaptation occurs for the senses of smell and touch. As babies learn to recognize their caregiver's smell and handling, they relax only when cradled by their familiar caregiver, even when their eyes are closed. The ability to be comforted by touch is one of the important "skills" tested in the Brazelton Neonatal Assessment Scale. Although almost all newborns respond to cuddling, over time they become responsive to whose touch it is and what it communicates. For instance, 12-month-olds respond differently, depending on whether their mother's touch is tense or relaxed (Hertenstein & Campos, 2001).

The entire package of early sensation seems organized for two goals: social interaction (to respond to familiar caregivers) and comfort (to be soothed amid the disturbances of infant life). Even the sense of pain and the sense of motion, which are not among the five basic senses because no body part is dedicated to them, are adapted by infants to aid both socialization and comfort.

The most important experiences are perceived with all the senses at once. Breast milk, for instance, is a mild sedative, so the newborn literally feels happier at the mother's breast, connecting pleasure with taste, touch, smell, and sight.

Because infants respond to motion as well as to sights and sounds, many new parents soothe their baby's distress by rocking, carrying, or even driving (with the baby in a safety seat) while humming a lullaby; here again, infant comfort is connected with social interaction. A variant of this technique is to carry the infant around the house while vacuuming the carpet: Steady noise, movement, and touch combine to soothe distress. In sum, infants' senses are immature, but they function quite well to help babies join the human family.

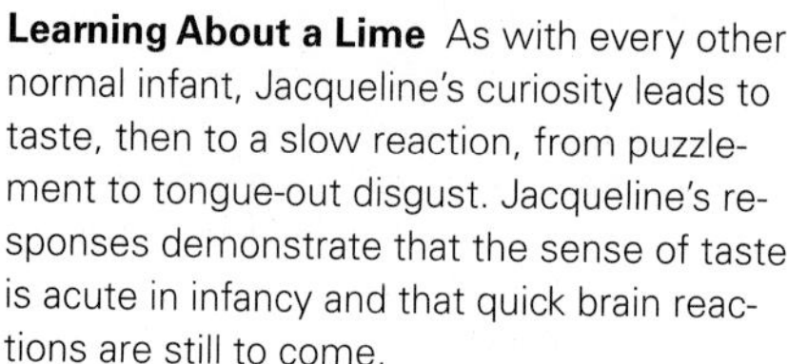

➤Response for Parents of Grown Children (from page 136): Probably not. Experience-expectant brain development is programmed to occur for all infants, requiring only the stimulation that virtually all families provide—warmth, reassuring touch, overheard conversation, facial expressions, movement. Extras such as baby talk, music, exercise, mobiles, and massage may be beneficial but are not essential.

Motor Skills

We now come to the most visible and dramatic advances of infancy, those that ultimately allow the child to "stand tall and walk proud." Thanks to ongoing changes in size and proportion and to increasing brain maturation, infants markedly improve their **motor skills,** which are the abilities needed to move and control the body.

motor skill The learned ability to move some part of the body, from a large leap to a flicker of the eyelid. (The word *motor* here refers to movement of muscles.)

Reflexes

Newborns can move their bodies—curl their toes, grasp with their fingers, screw up their faces—but these movements are not under voluntary control. Strictly speaking, the infant's first motor skills are not really skills but reflexes. A **reflex** is an involuntary response to a particular stimulus. Newborns have dozens of

reflex A responsive movement that seems automatic because it almost always occurs in reaction to a particular stimulus. Newborns have many reflexes, some of which disappear with maturation.

reflexes, 18 of which are mentioned in *italics* below. Three sets of reflexes are critical for survival:

- *Reflexes that maintain oxygen supply.* The *breathing reflex* begins in normal newborns even before the umbilical cord, with its supply of oxygen, is cut. Additional reflexes that maintain oxygen are reflexive *hiccups* and *sneezes,* as well as *thrashing* (moving the arms and legs about) to escape something that covers the face.
- *Reflexes that maintain constant body temperature.* When infants are cold, they *cry, shiver,* and *tuck in their legs* close to their bodies, thereby helping to keep themselves warm. When they are hot, they try to *push away* blankets and then stay still.
- *Reflexes that manage feeding.* The *sucking reflex* causes newborns to suck anything that touches their lips—fingers, toes, blankets, and rattles, as well as natural and artificial nipples of various textures and shapes. The *rooting reflex* causes babies to turn their mouths toward anything that brushes against their cheeks—a reflexive search for a nipple—and start to suck. *Swallowing* is another important reflex that aids feeding, as are *crying* when the stomach is empty and *spitting up* when too much has been swallowed too quickly.

Other reflexes are not necessary for survival but are important signs of normal brain and body functioning. Among them are the following:

- *Babinski reflex.* When infants' feet are stroked, their toes fan upward.
- *Stepping reflex.* When infants are held upright with their feet touching a flat surface, they move their legs as if to walk.
- *Swimming reflex.* When they are laid horizontally on their stomachs, infants stretch out their arms and legs.
- *Palmar grasping reflex.* When something touches infants' palms, they grip it tightly.
- *Moro reflex.* When someone startles them, perhaps by banging on the table they are lying on, infants fling their arms outward and then bring them together on their chests, as if to hold on to something, while crying with wide-open eyes.

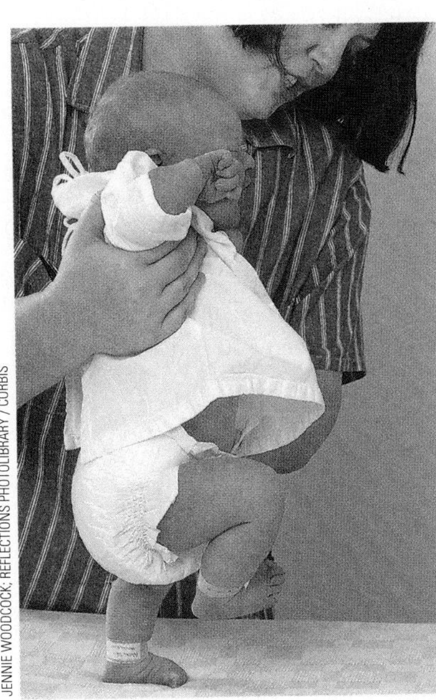
JENNIE WOODCOCK; REFLECTIONS PHOTOLIBRARY / CORBIS

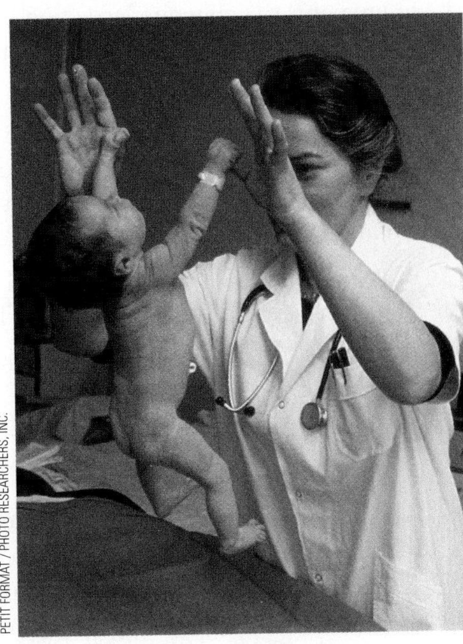
PETIT FORMAT / PHOTO RESEARCHERS, INC.

Never Underestimate the Power of a Reflex For developmentalists, newborn reflexes are mechanisms for survival, indicators of brain maturation, and vestiges of evolutionary history. For parents, they are mostly delightful and sometimes amazing. Both of these viewpoints are demonstrated by three star performers: A 1-day-old girl stepping eagerly forward on legs too tiny to support her body; a newborn grasping so tightly that his legs dangle in space; and a newborn boy sucking peacefully on the doctor's finger.

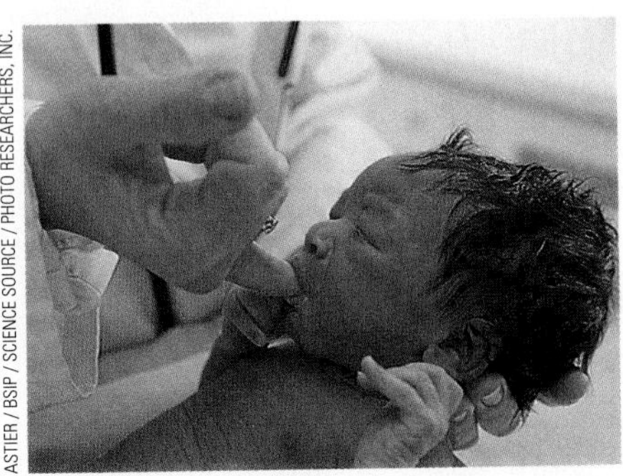
ASTIER / BSIP / SCIENCE SOURCE / PHOTO RESEARCHERS, INC.

Gross Motor Skills

gross motor skills Physical abilities involving large body movements, such as walking and jumping. (The word *gross* here means "big.")

Deliberate actions coordinating many parts of the body, producing large movements, are called **gross motor skills.** These emerge directly from reflexes. Crawling is one example. Newborns placed on their stomachs reflexively move their arms and legs as if they were swimming. As they gain muscle strength, they start to wiggle, attempting to move forward by pushing their arms, shoulders, and upper bodies against the surface they are lying on. Usually by 5 months or so, they become able to use their arms, and then legs, to inch forward on their bellies, a gross motor skill.

Between 8 and 10 months after birth, most infants can lift their midsections and crawl (or *creep,* as the British call it) on "all fours," coordinating the movements of their hands and knees in a smooth, balanced manner (Adolph et al., 1998). Crawling is experience-dependent. Some normal babies never do it, especially if they have always slept on their backs.

It is not true that babies *must* crawl to develop normally. All babies figure out some way to move before they can walk (inching, bear walking, scooting, creeping, or crawling); but many babies who are put to sleep on their backs (as is recommended, to prevent sudden death) resist "tummy time," rolling over and fussing to indicate that they do not want crawling practice (Adolph & Berger, 2005).

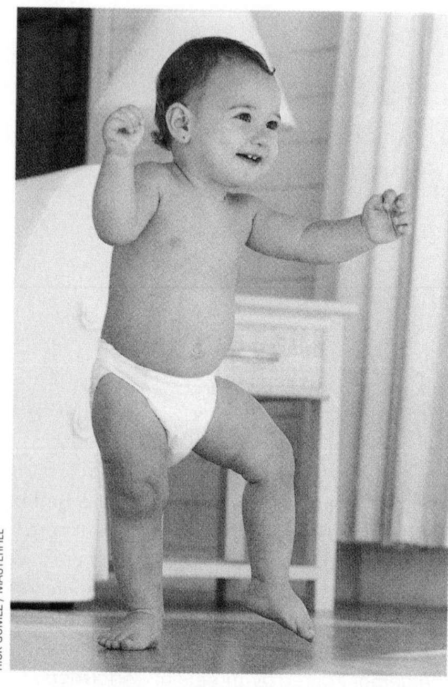

RICK GOMEZ / MASTERFILE

Bossa Nova Baby? This boy in Brazil demonstrates his joy at acquiring the gross motor skill of walking, which quickly becomes dancing whenever music plays.

Sitting also develops gradually, a matter of developing the muscles to steady the heavy top half of the body. By 3 months, babies have enough muscle control to be lap-sitters if the lap's owner provides supportive arms. By 6 months, they can sit unsupported.

Walking progresses from reflexive, hesitant, adult-supported stepping to a smooth, coordinated gait (Bertenthal & Clifton, 1998). Some children can walk while holding on at 9 months, stand alone momentarily at 10 months, and walk well, unassisted, at 12 months. Three factors combine to allow toddlers to walk (Adolph et al., 2003):

- *Muscle strength.* Newborns with skinny legs and infants buoyed by water make stepping movements, but 6-month-olds on dry land do not; their legs are too chubby for their underdeveloped muscles.
- *Brain maturation within the motor cortex.* The first leg movements—kicking (alternating legs at birth and then kicking both legs together or one leg repeatedly at about 3 months)—occur without much thought or aim. As the brain matures, deliberate leg action becomes possible.
- *Practice.* Unbalanced, wide-legged, short strides become a steady, smooth gait after hours of practice.

Once the first two developments have made walking possible, infants become passionate walkers, logging those needed hours of practice. They take steps on many surfaces, with bare feet or wearing socks, slippers, or shoes. They hate to be pushed in their strollers when they can walk.

> Walking infants practice keeping balance in upright stance and locomotion for more than 6 accumulated hours per day. They average between 500 and 1,500 walking steps per hour so that by the end of each day, they have taken 9,000 walking steps and traveled the length of 29 football fields.
>
> *[Adolph et al., 2003, p. 494]*

Fine Motor Skills

fine motor skills Physical abilities involving small body movements, especially of the hands and fingers, such as drawing and picking up a coin. (The word *fine* here means "small.")

Small body movements are called **fine motor skills.** Hand and finger movements are fine motor skills, enabling humans to write, draw, type, tie, and so on. Movements of the tongue, jaw, lips, and toes are fine movements, too. Actually, mouth skills precede finger skills by many months, and skillful grabbing with the feet sometimes precedes grabbing with the hands (Adolph & Berger, 2005). However, hand skills are most praised by adults. Skill at spitting or chewing is not valued as much as skill at copying a letter of the alphabet.

Regarding finger skills, newborns have a strong reflexive grasp but seem to lack hand and finger control. During their first 2 months, babies excitedly stare and wave their arms at an object dangling within reach. By 3 months of age, they can usually touch it; but they cannot yet grab and hold on unless the object is placed in their hands, partly because their eye–hand coordination is too limited.

By 4 months, infants sometimes grab, but their timing is off: They close their hands too early or too late, and their grasp tends to be of short duration. Finally, by 6 months, with a concentrated, deliberate stare, most babies can reach for, grab at, and hold onto almost any object that is of the right size. They can hold a bottle, shake a rattle, and yank a sister's braids.

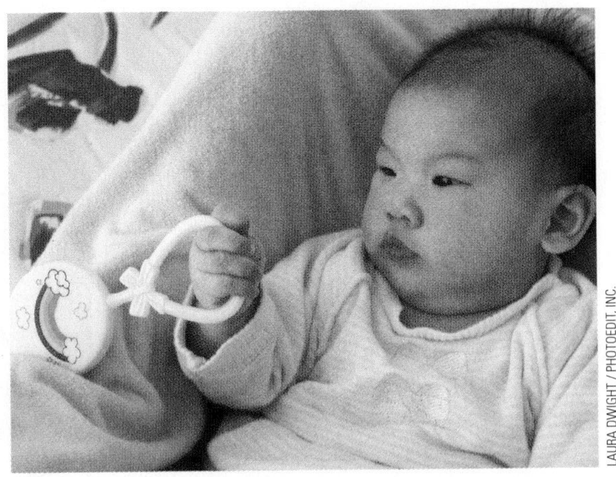

LAURA DWIGHT / PHOTOEDIT, INC.

Mind in the Making Pull, grab, look, and listen. Using every sense at once is a baby's favorite way to experience life, generating brain connections as well as commotion.

Infants need not be able to see their hands to grab; they can grasp a slowly moving object that is lit in an otherwise dark room (Robin et al., 1996). When the lights are on, they use vision to help with accuracy (McCarty & Ashmead, 1999).

Once reaching is possible, babies practice it enthusiastically. In fact, "from 6 to 9 months, reaching appears as a quite compulsive behaviour for small objects presented within arm's reach" (Atkinson & Braddick, 2003, p. 58).

Toward the end of the first year and throughout the second, finger skills improve, as babies master the pincer movement (using thumb and forefinger to pick up tiny objects) and self-feeding (first with hands, then fingers, then utensils). In the second year, grabbing becomes more selective (Atkinson & Braddick, 2003). Toddlers learn when not to pull at sister's braids, Mommy's earrings, and Daddy's glasses, although, as you will learn in the next chapter, curiosity sometimes overwhelms such inhibition.

Ethnic Variations

All healthy infants develop skills in the same sequence, but they vary in the age at which they acquire them. Table 5.1 shows age norms for gross motor skills, based on a large, representative, multiethnic sample of U.S. infants. When infants are grouped by ethnicity, generally African Americans are ahead of Hispanic Americans, who are ahead of European Americans. Internationally, the earliest walkers in the world are in Uganda, where well-nourished and healthy babies walk at 10 months, on average. Some of the latest walkers are in France.

What accounts for this variation? The power of genes is suggested not only by ethnic differences but also by identical twins, who begin to walk on the same day more often than fraternal twins do. Striking individual differences are apparent in infant strategies, effort, and concentration in mastering motor skills, again suggesting something inborn in motor-skill achievements (Thelen & Corbetta, 2002).

But genes are only a small part of most ethnic differences. Cultural patterns of child rearing can affect sensation, perception, and motor skills. For instance, early reflexes are less likely to fade if culture and conditions allow extensive practice. This principle has been demonstrated with legs (the stepping reflex), hands (the grasping reflex), and crawling (the swimming reflex). Senses and motor skills are part of a complex and dynamic system in which practice counts (Thelen & Corbetta, 2002).

TABLE 5.1

At About This Time: Age Norms (in Months) for Gross Motor Skills

Skill	When 50% of All Babies Master the Skill	When 95% of All Babies Master the Skill
Sit, head steady	3 months	4 months
Sit, unsupported	6	7
Pull to stand (holding on)	9	10
Stand alone	12	14
Walk well	13	15
Walk backwards	15	17
Run	18	20
Jump up	26	29

Note: As the text explains, age norms are approximate. Mastering skills a few weeks earlier or later is not an indication of health or intelligence. Mastering them very late, however, is a cause for concern.

Source: Coovadia & Wittenberg, 2004; based primarily on Denver II (Frankenburg et al., 1992).

MIKE GREENLAR / THE IMAGE WORKS

Safe and Secure Like this Algonquin baby in Quebec, many American Indian infants still spend hours each day on a cradle board, to the distress of some non-Native adults until they see that most of the babies are quite happy that way. The discovery in the 1950s that Native American children walked at about the same age as European American children suggested that maturation, not practice, led to motor skills. Later research found that most Native American infants also received special exercise sessions each day, implying that practice plays a larger role than most psychologists once thought.

For example, Jamaican caregivers provide rhythmic stretching exercises for their infants as part of daily care; their infants are among the world's youngest walkers (Adolph & Berger, 2005). Other cultures discourage or even prevent infants from crawling or walking. The people of Bali, Indonesia, never let their infants crawl, for babies are considered divine and crawling is for animals (Diener, 2000). Similar reasoning appeared in colonial America, where "standing stools" were designed for children so they could strengthen their walking muscles without sitting or crawling (Calvert, 2003).

By contrast, the Beng people of the Ivory Coast are proud when their babies start to crawl but do not let them walk until at least 1 year. Although the Beng do not recognize the connection, one reason for this prohibition may be birth control: Beng mothers do not resume sexual relations until their baby begins walking (Gottlieb, 2000).

Although variation in the timing of the development of motor skills is normal, a pattern of slow development suggests that the infant needs careful examination. Slow infants may be retarded, ill, neglected—or perfectly fine, as I know from experience.

in person

The Normal Berger Babies

Cultural beliefs and the demands of daily life affect every parent and baby. When I had our first child, Bethany, I was a graduate student. I had already memorized many norms including "sitting by 6 months, walking by 12." During her first year, Bethany reached all the developmental milestones pretty much on time. However, at 14 months, she was still not walking.

I became anxious. I read about norms with a sharper eye and learned three comforting facts:

- Variation in timing is normal.
- When late walking signifies brain damage, other signs of delayed development are evident. (Thankfully, Bethany was already talking.)
- Norms for motor-skill development vary from nation to nation. (My grandmother came from France, where babies tend to walk late.)

Two months later, Bethany was walking. In my relief, I began marshaling evidence that motor skills are genetic. My students provided additional testimony to the power of genes. Those from

Jamaica, Cuba, and Barbados expected babies to walk earlier than those from Russia, China, and Korea. Many of my African American students proudly cited their sons, daughters, or younger siblings who walked at 10 months, or even 8 months, to the chagrin of their European American classmates.

Believing now in a genetic timetable for walking, I was not surprised when our second child, Rachel, took her first steps at 15 months. Our third child, Elissa, also walked "late"—though on schedule for a Berger child with some French ancestry. By then Bethany had become the fastest runner in her kindergarten.

When our fourth child, Sarah, was born, I was an established professor and author, able to afford a full-time caregiver, Mrs. Todd, from Jamaica. Mrs. Todd thought Sarah was the brightest, most advanced baby she had ever seen—except, perhaps, for her own daughter Gillian. I agreed, but I cautioned Mrs. Todd that Berger children walk late.

"She'll be walking by a year," Mrs. Todd told me. "Maybe sooner. Gillian walked at 10 months."

"We'll see," I replied, confident in my genetic interpretation.

I underestimated Mrs. Todd. She bounced baby Sarah on her lap, day after day. By the time Sarah was 8 months old, Mrs. Todd was already spending a good deal of time bent over, holding Sarah by both hands to practice walking—to Sarah's great delight. Lo and behold, Sarah took her first step at exactly 1 year—late for a Todd baby, but amazingly early for a Berger.

As a scientist, I know that a single case proves nothing. It could be that the genetic influences on Sarah's walking were different from those on her sisters'. Furthermore, she is only one-eighth French, a fraction I had ignored when I sought reassurance regarding Bethany. But in my heart I think it likely that practice, fostered by a caregiver with a cultural tradition unlike mine, made the difference.

HAZEL HANKIN

My Youngest at 8 Months When I look at this photo of Sarah, I see evidence of Mrs. Todd's devotion. Sarah's hair is washed and carefully brushed, her jumper and blouse are clean and pressed, and the carpet and stepstool are perfect equipment for standing practice. Sarah's legs—chubby and far apart—indicate that she is not about to walk early; but, given all these signs of Mrs. Todd's attention to caregiving, it is not surprising, in hindsight, that my fourth daughter was my earliest walker.

SUMMING UP

The five senses (seeing, hearing, tasting, touching, smelling) function quite well at birth, although hearing is far superior to vision, probably because of experience: The fetus has much more to hear than to see. After birth, vision develops rapidly, leading to binocular vision at about the 14th week. Quite sensitive perception from all sense organs is evident by 1 year. The senses work together and are particularly attuned to human interaction.

Motor skills begin with survival reflexes but quickly expand to include various body movements that the infant masters. Infants lift their heads, then sit, then stand, then walk and run. Sensory and motor skills follow a genetic and maturational timetable, but they are also powerfully influenced by experiences, guided by caregivers and culture, and by practice, which infants do as much as their immature and top-heavy bodies allow. ■

Public Health Measures

Although precise worldwide statistics are unavailable, at least 8 billion children were born between 1950 and 2005. About 2 billion of them died before age 5. As high as this figure is, the death toll would have been twice that without advances in child care, especially such aspects of preventive care as childhood immunization, clean water, adequate nutrition, and one particular medical treatment: oral rehydration therapy (giving restorative liquids to children who are sick and have diarrhea). Oral rehydration saves 3 million young children *per year*, almost all in developing nations, but it helps in developed nations as well (Spandorfer et al., 2005).

Most children now live to adulthood (UNICEF, 2006). In the healthiest nations, 99.9 percent who survive the first month (when the sickest and smallest newborns sometimes die) live to age 15. Even in the least healthy nations, where a few decades ago half the children died, now about three-fourths live (see Table 5.2). Public health measures (clean water, adequate food, immunization) are the main reason childhood mortality now is much lower in most nations.

immunization A process that stimulates the body's immune system to defend against attack by a particular contagious disease. A person may acquire immunization either naturally (by having the disease) or through vaccination (by having an injection, wearing a patch, swallowing, or inhaling).

TABLE 5.2

Deaths of Children Under Age 5 in Selected Countries

Country	Number of Deaths per 1,000
Singapore	3*
Iceland	3*
Japan	4†
Italy	4*
Sweden	4
Spain	5†
Australia	5†
United Kingdom	6†
Canada	6
New Zealand	6†
United States	7†
Russia	18†
Vietnam	19*
China	27†
Mexico	27†
Brazil	33†
Philippines	33†
India	74†
Nigeria	194
Afghanistan	257
Sierra Leone	282

* Reduced by at least one-third since 1990.
† Reduced by half since 1990.
Source: UNICEF, 2006.

This table shows the number of deaths per 1,000 children under age 5 for 20 of the 192 members of the United Nations. Most nations have improved markedly on this measure since 1990. Only when war destroys families and interferes with public health measures (as it has in Afghanistan and Sierra Leone) are nations not improving.

Immunization

Measles, whooping cough, pneumonia, and other illnesses were once familiar childhood killers. Although these diseases can still be fatal, especially for malnourished children, they are no longer common in developed nations. Most children are protected because of **immunization,** which primes the body's immune system to defend against a specific contagious disease. This medical development is said to have had "a greater impact on human mortality reduction and population growth than any other public health intervention besides clean water" (J. P. Baker, 2000).

When people catch a contagious disease, their immune system produces antibodies to prevent a recurrence. In a healthy person, a vaccine—a small dose of inactive virus (often via a "shot" in the arm)—stimulates antibodies. Some details about various vaccines are given in Table 5.3. (Immunization schedules, giving the ages at which children and adolescents should be vaccinated, appear in Appendix A, p. A-4.)

Immunization Successes

Stunning successes in immunization include the following:

- Smallpox, the most lethal disease for children in the past, was eradicated worldwide as of 1971. Vaccination against smallpox is no longer needed. Emergency workers are immunized as a precaution against bioterrorism, not a normal outbreak.
- Polio, a crippling and sometimes fatal disease, is very rare. Widespread vaccination, begun in 1955, has led to the elimination of polio in most nations (including the United States). Just 784 cases worldwide were reported in 2003. In 2003, however, rumors about the safety of the polio vaccine halted immunization in northern Nigeria; consequently, polio reappeared in West Africa in 2004, and there were 1,948 cases worldwide in 2005 (Arita et al., 2006).
- Measles (rubeola, not rubella) is disappearing, thanks to a vaccine developed in 1963. Prior to that time, 3 to 4 million cases were reported each year in the United States alone (CDC, 2007). In all of the Americas, fewer than 100 cases of measles occurred in 2003, down from 53,683 in 1997 (MMWR, June 13, 2003). One reason is the introduction of a new method of vaccinating against measles by inhalation rather than injection, now widely used in Mexico.
- A recent success is a newly developed vaccine against rotovirus, which now kills half a million children a year (Glass & Parashar, 2006).

Immunization protects children not only from diseases but also from serious complications, including deafness, blindness, sterility, and meningitis. Each vaccinated child stops the spread of the disease and thus protects others. Newborns may die if they catch a disease; the fetus of a pregnant woman who contracts rubella (German measles) may be born blind, deaf, and brain-damaged; adults who contract mumps or measles become quite ill; and people who have impaired immune systems (who are HIV-positive, very old, or undergoing chemotherapy) can die from "childhood" diseases.

TABLE 5.3

Details About Vaccinations: United States

Vaccine	Year of Introduction*	Peak Annual Disease Total*	2007 Total†	Consequences of Natural Disease*†	Percent of Children Vaccinated (U.S.)†	Known Vaccine Side Effects†
Chicken pox (varicella)	1995	4 million (est.)	34,507	Encephalitis (2 in 10,000 cases), bacterial skin infections, shingles (300,000 per year)	90.0	Fever (1 in 10 doses); mild rash (1 in 20 doses)
DTaP					84.5	Seizures (1 in 14,000), crying, for 3 hours or more (1 in 1,000), fever of 105°F or higher (1 in 16,000)
Diphtheria	1923	206,939	0	Death (5 to 10 in 100 cases), muscle paralysis, heart failure		Adult Td (tetanus and diphtheria) vaccine may cause deep, aching pain and muscle wasting in upper arms
Tetanus	1927	1,560 (est.)	20	Death (1 in 10 cases), fractured bones, pneumonia		
Pertussis	1926 (whole cell) 1991 (acellular)	265,269	8,739	Death (2 in 1,000 cases), pneumonia (10 in 100 cases), seizures (1 to 2 in 100 cases)		Brain disease (0 to 10 in 1 million doses—whole-cell vaccine only)
H influenzae (Type B) (childhood) (all serotypes)	1985	20,000 (est.)	2,231	Death (2 to 3 in 100 cases), meningitis, pneumonia, blood poisoning, inflammation of epiglottis, skin or bone infections	92.6	Redness, warmth, or swelling at injection site (1 in 4); fever of 101°F or higher (1 in 20)
IPV (inactivated) polio vaccine)	1955; improved version used in U.S. since 1987	21,269	0	Death (2 to 5 in 100 cases in children), respiratory failure, paralysis, postpolio syndrome	92.6	Soreness and redness at injection site
MMR					92.3	Seizure caused by fever (1 in 3,000 doses); low platelet count (1 in 30,000 doses)
Measles	1963	894,134	30	Encephalitis (1 in 1,000 cases), pneumonia (6 in 100 cases), death (1 to 2 in 1,000 cases), seizure (6 to 7 in 1,000 cases)		Temporary joint pain and stiffness (1 in 4 teenaged girls and women)
Mumps	1967	152,209	715	Deafness (1 in 20,000 cases), inflamed testicles (20 to 50 in 100 postpubertal males)		
Rubella	1969	56,686	11	Blindness, deafness, heart defects, and/or mental retardation in 85 percent of children born to mothers infected in early pregnancy		
PCV7 (pneumococcal conjugate vaccine)† (childhood)	2000	93,000 (est.)	20,000 (2005 est.)	Death or serious illness caused by meningitis, pneumonia, blood poisoning, ear infections		Fever over 100.4°F (1 in 3); redness, tenderness, or swelling at injection site (1 in 4)

Sources: *Lieu et al., 2000; †Centers for Disease Control and Prevention Web site (www.cdc.gov/vaccines), accessed September 17, 2008.

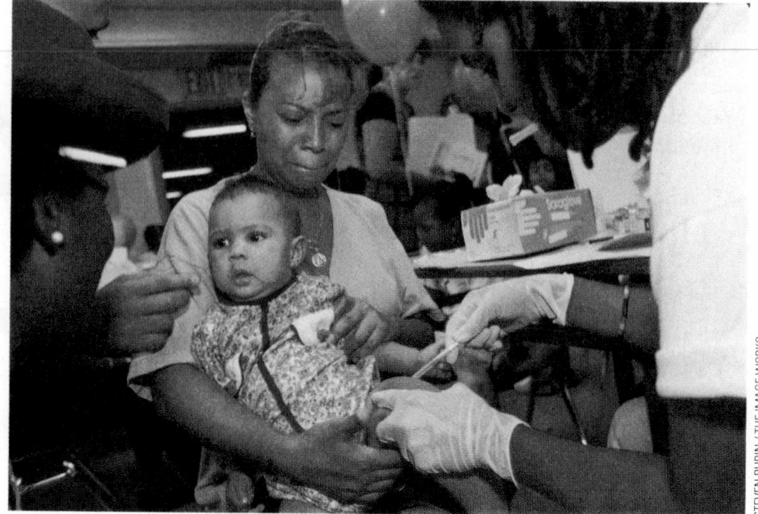

STEVEN RUBIN / THE IMAGE WORKS

Look Away! The benefits of immunization justify the baby's brief discomfort, but many parents still do not appreciate the importance of following the recommended schedule of immunizations.

Problems with Immunization

Parents do not notice if their child does *not* get seriously ill. One doctor, who wants people to attend to disease prevention, laments, "No one notices when things go right" (Bortz, 2005, p. 389). Unfortunately, "minor" diseases can kill. One Kansas father, age 36, caught varicella (chicken pox) from his 9-year-old daughter. He suffered numerous complications and died on March 9, 2002 (MMWR, June 13, 2003). No one in his family had been vaccinated (Kansas did not require varicella immunization for school entry). The 9-year-old was the carrier, but the parents, school, pediatrician, and lawmakers were also part of the problem. Before the vaccine, more than 100 people in the United States died each year from chicken pox and 1 million were itchy and feverish for a week. Fortunately, the death and disease rates have been dramatically reduced (Nguyen et al., 2005).

Especially for Nurses and Pediatricians A mother refuses to have her baby immunized because she wants to prevent side effects. She wants your signature for a religious exemption. What should you do?

Many parents are concerned about potential side effects of vaccinations. However, the risks of the diseases are far greater than the risks from immunization (as Table 5.3 indicates). A review of the published research concludes: "The data demonstrate consistently that the overall benefit of vaccinations ranks among the foremost achievements in modern public health" (Dershewitz, 2002). A hypothesis that the MMR (measles-mumps-rubella) vaccine causes autism has been repeatedly disproved (Shattuck, 2006).

More than 1 million children in developing nations die each year because effective vaccines against AIDS, malaria, cholera, typhoid, and shigellosis are not yet ready for widespread use (Russell, 2002). Another 2 to 3 million die each year from diphtheria, tetanus, and measles because they have not been immunized (Mahmoud, 2004); 100,000 children in India died in 2005 from measles alone (Duggar, 2006). Even in the United States, although most 2-year-olds are fully immunized, only one-third get all their vaccinations on time, with no unneeded extras (Mell et al., 2005).

Sudden Infant Death Syndrome

sudden infant death syndrome (SIDS) A situation in which a seemingly healthy infant, at least 2 months of age, suddenly stops breathing and dies unexpectedly while asleep. The cause is unknown, but it is correlated with sleeping on the stomach and having parents who smoke.

Infant mortality worldwide has plummeted in recent years (see Figure 5.5). Several reasons have already been mentioned: advances in newborn care, better nutrition, access to clean water, and widespread immunization. Another reason is that fewer babies are dying of unknown causes, especially **sudden infant death syndrome (SIDS).**

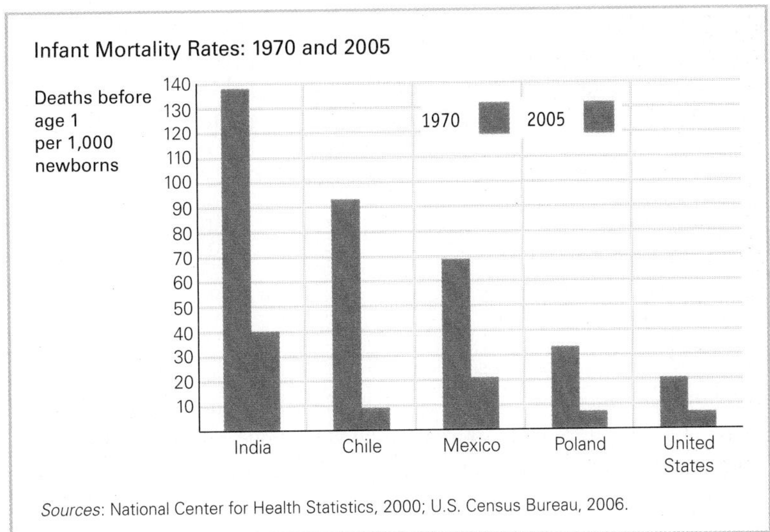

FIGURE 5.5

More Babies Are Surviving Improvements in public health—better nutrition, cleaner water, more widespread immunization—over the past three decades have meant millions of survivors.

Critical Thinking Question (see answer, page 150): The United States seems to be doing very well on reducing infant deaths. Can you suggest another way to present the U.S. data that would lead to another impression?

Still, some young infants who appear healthy—already gaining weight, learning to shake a rattle, starting to roll over, and smiling at their caregivers—die unexpectedly in their sleep. If autopsy and careful investigation find no apparent cause of death, the diagnosis is SIDS (Byard, 2004).

In 1990 in the United States, about 5,000 babies died of SIDS, about 1 infant in 800. Canada, Great Britain, Australia, and virtually every European and South American nation experienced a similar rate. Today, that rate has been cut in half, primarily because fewer infants are put to sleep on their stomachs and because fewer mothers smoke cigarettes. The first of these preventive measures has arisen from an increased awareness of and a greater respect for cultural differences.

Within ethnically diverse nations such as the United States, Canada, Great Britain, Australia, and New Zealand, babies of Asian descent have always been far less likely than babies of European or African descent to succumb to SIDS (Byard, 2004). Although low socioeconomic status (SES) is also a risk factor for SIDS, poverty does not seem to be the primary explanation for this ethnic difference. For example, Bangladeshi infants in England tend to be from low-SES families, yet they are much less vulnerable to SIDS than are traditional British infants from middle-class families. For decades, pediatricians thought that genes were the underlying cause.

Fortunately, awareness of the impact of culture led to examination of infant-care routines. Bangladeshi infants are usually breast-fed, and when they sleep, they are surrounded by family members in a rich sensory environment, hearing noises and feeling the touch of their caregivers. They do not sleep deeply for very long. By contrast, their traditional British age-mates tend to sleep in their own private spaces, and these "long periods of lone sleep may contribute to the higher rates of SIDS among white infants" (Gantley et al., 1993).

Similarly, infants of Chinese heritage rarely die of SIDS (Beal & Porter, 1991). In fact, *before* a worldwide campaign to reduce the risk, only 1 baby in 3,000 in Hong Kong died of SIDS, compared with 1 baby in 200 in New Zealand (Byard, 2004). Why? First, Chinese parents tend to their babies periodically as the infants sleep, caressing a cheek

Sleeping Like a Baby It's best to lay babies on their backs to sleep—even if it's in a hammock in a Cambodian temple.

Especially for Police Officers and Social Workers If an infant died suddenly, what would you look for to distinguish SIDS from homicide?

or repositioning a limb. Second, almost all Chinese infants are breast-fed. This makes them sleep less soundly, and deep sleep is a factor in SIDS. (Cow's milk is harder to digest, so it causes tiredness and thus a deeper sleep.) And third, Chinese parents put their infants to sleep on their backs. This is crucial, as the following explains.

issues and applications

Back to Sleep

When pediatricians, nurses, and anthropologists observed infant care among Asians and Europeans, they noticed a crucial difference: sleeping position. In all the ethnic groups with a low incidence of SIDS, babies were put to sleep on their backs; in all those with high rates, babies slept on their stomachs. The expressed reasons varied. For example, until recently, Benjamin Spock's book of advice for parents (more than 30 million copies sold) recommended stomach sleeping:

> There are two disadvantages to babies sleeping on their back. If they vomit, they're more likely to choke. Also, they tend to keep the head turned toward the same side, usually toward the center of the room. This may flatten that side of the head. It won't hurt the brain, and the head will gradually straighten out, but it may take a couple of years.
>
> *[Spock, 1976, p. 199]*

Contrary advice was provided to Turkish mothers, who were told: "Never put a swaddled baby to sleep on its stomach, for it would not be able to breathe. Instead, put the baby down to sleep on its back" (Delaney, 2000, p. 131).

Both these experts were mistaken: Babies sleeping on their stomachs can breathe, and babies sleeping on their backs do not choke. Neither expert realized the connection between SIDS and sleeping position.

As a new mother, I remember reading these chilling words: "Every once in a while, a baby between the ages of 3 weeks and 7 months is found dead in bed. There is never an adequate explanation, even when a postmortem examination is done" (Spock, 1976, pp. 576–577). I put my babies to sleep on their stomachs, as my mother did with me and as the hospital where they were born did with thousands of newborns every year. My infants survived, but I know parents whose babies did not.

About two decades ago, researchers in Australia advised a group of non-Asian mothers to put their infants to sleep on their backs. Other scientists in other nations tried the same experiment. The results were dramatic: Fewer infants died. For example, one comparison study found that the risk of SIDS was only one-fourth as high when infants slept supine (on their backs) instead of prone (Ponsonby et al., 1993).

It is now accepted that "back to sleep" (as the public-awareness slogan puts it) is safest. Worldwide, SIDS rates have fallen—to 1 in 1,000 in New Zealand, for instance. In the United States, in the four years between 1992 and 1996, the stomach-sleeping rate decreased from 70 to 24 percent, and the SIDS rate dropped from 1.2 to 0.7 per 1,000, a "remarkable success" (Pollack & Frohna, 2001).

Sleeping position does not prevent all SIDS deaths. Low birthweight, overdressed infants, and teenage parenthood are risk factors (Byard, 2004). Maternal smoking is particularly risky (Anderson et al., 2005). Both breast-feeding and pacifier use are protective (Li et al., 2006), perhaps because they strengthen infants' breathing reflexes. Recently, it has been discovered that the existence of too many serotonin receptors in the brain stem, which controls heart rate and breathing, may be a major risk factor for SIDS (Paterson et al., 2006). Infants with this condition do not automatically rouse themselves to breathe when their blood oxygen falls, and death sometimes results. Unfortunately, this abnormality becomes apparent only upon autopsy.

Nutrition

Indirectly, nutrition has been a theme throughout this chapter. You read that pediatricians closely monitor early weight gain, that head-sparing protects the brain from temporary undernourishment, that oral rehydration prevents childhood diarrhea from being fatal. Now, we focus directly on how infants are fed.

Breast Is Best

For most newborns, good nutrition starts with mother's milk. First comes *colostrum,* a thick, high-calorie fluid secreted by the woman's breasts at the birth of her child. After about three days, the breasts begin to produce milk, which is the ideal infant food (see Table 5.4). Mother's milk helps prevent almost every infant illness and allergy (Isolauri et al., 1998). It is always sterile and at body temperature; it contains more iron, vitamins C and A, and many other nourishing substances than cow's or goat's milk.

Babies who are exclusively breast-fed are less likely to get sick. This is true in infancy because breast milk provides antibodies against any disease to which the mother has natural or acquired immunity. Breast-feeding also decreases the risk of diseases that appear in childhood and adulthood, among them asthma, obesity, and heart disease (Oddy, 2004).

The specific fats and sugars in breast milk make it more digestible, and probably better for the infant brain, than any prepared formula (Riordan, 2005). The particular composition of breast milk adjusts to the age of the baby, with breast milk for premature babies distinct from breast milk for older infants.

Quantity increases to meet the demand: Twins and even triplets can grow strong while being exclusively breast-fed for months. In fact, breast milk appears to have so many advantages over formula that critics question the validity of the research: Although studies control for education and income, it is possible that women who choose to breast-feed are better caregivers in some ways not affected by SES. In the United States, a survey finds that parents of breast-fed babies are more likely to be married, college graduates, or immigrants (Gibson-Davis & Brooks-Gunn, 2006; see Research Design).

Bottle-feeding may be better than breast-feeding in unusual circumstances, such as when the mother is HIV-positive or uses toxic or addictive drugs. Even then, however, breast milk may be best. In Africa, HIV-positive women are encouraged to breast-feed because their infants' risk of catching the virus is less than their risk of dying from infections, diarrhea, or malnutrition as a result of improper bottle-feeding. Formula is recommended only if it is "acceptable, feasible, affordable, sustainable, and safe" (WHO, 2000).

Virtually all doctors worldwide recommend exclusive breast-feeding for the first four to six months. Then other foods can be added—especially cereals and bananas,

Research Design

Scientists: Christina Gibson-Davis and Jeanne Brooks-Gunn.

Publication: *American Journal of Public Health* (2006).

Participants: A study called Fragile Families surveyed about 5,000 new mothers from 75 U.S. hospitals.

Design: Mothers and fathers were asked about their social status (e.g., education, marriage, immigration, income, employment) and breast-feeding, with assurance of confidentiality. Questions were asked of both parents soon after birth and again of the mothers a year later.

Major conclusion: A mother's decision to start and continue breast-feeding is affected by many aspects of her social context. U.S.-born mothers are especially less likely to breast-feed.

Comment: This finding is for a population often omitted from other surveys. Confirmation that education and marriage are significant correlates of breast-feeding suggests that husbands and greater exposure to education promote breast-feeding.

➤Response for Nurses and Pediatricians (from page 146): It is very difficult to convince people that their method of child rearing is wrong, although, given what you know, you should try. In this case, listen respectfully and then describe specific instances of serious illness or death from a childhood disease. Suggest that the mother ask her grandparents if they knew anyone who had polio, tuberculosis, or tetanus (they probably did). If you cannot convince this mother, do not despair: Vaccination of 95 percent of toddlers protects the other 5 percent. If the mother has deeply held religious reasons, talk to her clergy adviser, if not to change the mother's mind, at least to understand her perspective.

© JENNIE HART / ALAMY

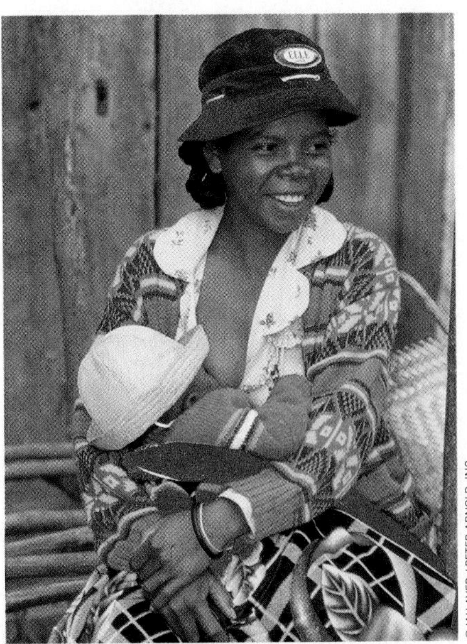

© W.LAYER / PETER ARNOLD, INC.

The Same Event, A Thousand Miles Apart: Breast-Feeding Breast-feeding is universal. None of us would have existed if our foremothers had not successfully breast-fed their babies for millennia. Currently breast-feeding is practiced worldwide, but it is no longer the only way to feed infants, and each culture has particular practices.

Observation Quiz (see answer, page 153): What three differences do you see between these two breast-feeding women—one in the United States and one in Madagascar?

TABLE 5.4

The Benefits of Breast-Feeding
For the Baby
Balance of nutrition (fat, protein, etc.) adjusts to age of baby
Breast milk has micronutrients not found in formula
Less infant illness: including allergies, ear infections, stomach upsets
Less childhood asthma
Better childhood vision
Less adult illness, including diabetes, cancer, heart disease
Protection against measles and all other childhood diseases, since breast milk contains antibodies
Stronger jaws, fewer cavities, advanced breathing reflexes (less SIDS)
Higher IQ, less likely to drop out of school, more likely to attend college
Later puberty, less prone to teenage pregnancy
Less likely to become obese
For the Mother
Easier bonding with baby
Reduced risk of breast cancer and osteoporosis
Natural contraception (with exclusive breast-feeding, for several months)
Pleasure of breast stimulation
Satisfaction of meeting infant's basic need
No formula to prepare; no sterilization needed
Easier to travel with the baby
For the Family
Increased survival of other children (because of spacing of births)
Increased family income (because both formula and medical care are expensive)
Less stress on father, especially at night (he cannot be expected to feed the baby)

Sources: DiGirolamo et al., 2005; Oddy, 2004; Riordan, 2005.

which are easily digested and provide the iron and vitamin C that older infants need. Breast milk should be part of the diet for a year (longer if mother and baby wish). Babies who do not get enough sunlight may need additional vitamin D—whether through supplemental drops or pills or cereal and milk—to prevent rickets (Stokstad, 2003).

In developing nations, breast-feeding dramatically reduces infant death. In the United States and worldwide, more than 90 percent of infants are breast-fed at birth, but only 36 percent are exclusively breast-fed for the first six months. Rates are slightly lower for the least developed nations. By their second birthday, half of the world's infants (especially in poor nations) are still being fed some breast milk, usually at night (UNICEF, 2006).

Whether or not a breast-feeding mother continues to breast-feed for 6 months depends a great deal on her experiences in the first week, when encouragement and practical help are most needed (DiGirolamo et al., 2005). Ideally, nurses visit new mothers at home for several weeks; such visits also increase the likelihood that breast-feeding will continue (Coutinbo et al., 2005).

Malnutrition

Protein-calorie malnutrition occurs when a person does not consume sufficient food of any kind. Roughly 9 percent of the world's children suffer from "wasting," being severely and chronically malnourished because they do not get adequate calories and protein (UNICEF, 2006). These 9 percent are very short for their age and underweight for their height. Many more children are too short *or* too underweight (2 or more standard deviations below the average well-nourished child). According to this criterion, between 25 and 30 percent of the world's children are malnourished (UNICEF, 2006).

protein-calorie malnutrition A condition in which a person does not consume sufficient food of any kind. This deprivation can result in several illnesses, severe weight loss, and sometimes death.

To measure a particular child's nutritional status, compare weight and height with the detailed norms presented in Appendix A, pages A-6 and A-7. A child may simply be genetically short or thin, but a decline in percentile ranking during the first two years is an ominous sign. Birthweight should triple by age 1, and the 1-year-old's legs and cheeks should be chubby with baby fat (which disappears over the next several years).

Chronically malnourished infants and children suffer in three ways:

- Their brains may not develop normally. If malnutrition has continued long enough to affect the baby's height, it may also have affected the brain (Grantham-McGregor & Ani, 2001).
- Malnourished children have no body reserves to protect them against common diseases. About half of all childhood deaths occur because malnutrition makes a childhood disease lethal.
- Some diseases result directly from malnutrition.

➤Answer to Critical Thinking Question (from page 147): The same data could be presented in terms of rate of reduction in infant mortality. Chile's rate in 2005 was only 10 percent of what it had been in 1970—much better than the U.S. rate, which in 2005 was 35 percent of what it had been in 1970. (Other data show that about 25 developed nations have lower infant mortality rates than the United States.)

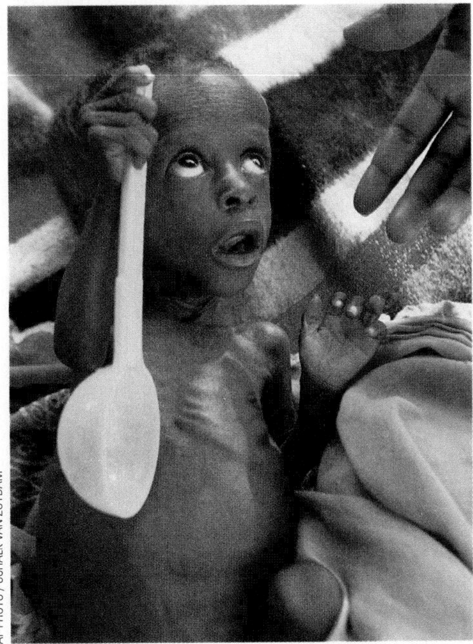
AP PHOTO / SCHALK VAN ZUYDAM

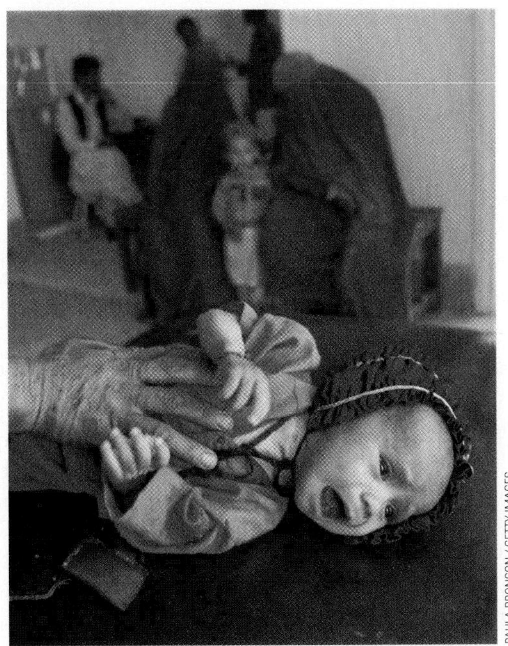
PAULA BRONSON / GETTY IMAGES

The Same Event, A Thousand Miles Apart: Children Still Malnourished Infant malnutrition is common in nations at war (like Afghanistan, *at right*) or with crop failure (like Niger, *at left*). UNICEF relief programs reach only half the children in either nation. The children in these photographs are among the lucky ones.

The worst disease directly caused by malnutrition is **marasmus.** Growth stops, body tissues waste away, and the infant victim eventually dies. Prevention of marasmus begins long before birth, with good nutrition for the pregnant woman. Then breast-feeding on demand (eight or more times a day) and frequent check-ups to monitor the baby's weight can stop marasmus before it begins. Infants who show signs of "failure to thrive" (they do not gain weight) can be hospitalized and treated before brain damage occurs.

Malnutrition after age 1 may cause **kwashiorkor.** Ironically, *kwashiorkor* means "a disease of the older child when a new baby arrives"—signifying cessation of breast-feeding and less maternal attention. In kwashiorkor, the child's growth is retarded; the liver is damaged; the immune system is weakened; the face, legs, and abdomen swell with fluid (edema); the energy level is reduced (malnourished children play less); and the hair becomes thin, brittle, and colorless.

marasmus A disease of severe protein-calorie malnutrition during early infancy, in which growth stops, body tissues waste away, and the infant eventually dies.

kwashiorkor A disease of chronic malnutrition during childhood, in which a protein deficiency makes the child more vulnerable to other diseases, such as measles, diarrhea, and influenza.

SUMMING UP

Many public health practices save millions of infants each year. Immunizing children, putting infants to sleep on their backs, and breast-feeding are simple yet life-saving steps. These are called "public health" measures rather than parental practices because they are affected by culture and national policies.

An underlying theme of this chapter is that healthy biological growth is the result not simply of genes and nutrition but also of a social environment that provides opportunities for growth: lullabies and mobiles for stimulating the infant's senses, encouragement for developing the first motor skills, and protection against disease. Each aspect of development is linked to every other aspect, and each developing person is linked to family, community, and world. ■

➤Response for Police Officers and Social Workers (from page 148): An autopsy, or at least a speedy and careful examination by a medical pathologist, is needed. Suspected foul play must be either substantiated or firmly rejected—so that the parents can be arrested or warned about conditions that caused an accident, or can mourn in peace. Careful notes about the immediate circumstances—such as the infant's body position when discovered, the position of the mattress and blankets, the warmth and humidity of the room, and the baby's health—are crucial. Further, although SIDS victims sometimes turn blue and seem bruised, they rarely display signs of specific injury or neglect, such as a broken limb, a scarred face, an angry rash, or a skinny body.

SUMMARY

Body Changes

1. In the first two years of life, infants grow taller, gain weight, and increase in head circumference—all indicative of development. The norm at birth is 7½ pounds in weight, 20 inches long (about 3,400 grams, 51 centimeters). Birthweight doubles by 4 months, triples by 1 year, and quadruples by 2 years, when toddlers weigh about 30 pounds (13½ kilograms).

2. Sleep gradually decreases over the first two years. As with all areas of development, variations in sleep patterns are normal, caused by both nature and nurture. Co-sleeping is increasingly common for very young infants, and many developmentalists consider it a harmless, or even beneficial, practice.

Brain Development

3. The brain increases dramatically in size, from about 25 to 75 percent of adult weight, in the first two years. Complexity increases as well, with transient exuberance of cell growth, development of dendrites, and formation of synapses. Both growth and pruning aid cognition.

4. Experience is vital for dendrites and synapses to link neurons. In the first year, parts of the cortex dedicated to the senses and motor skills mature. If neurons are unused, they atrophy, and the brain regions are rededicated to other sensations. Normal stimulation, which almost all infants obtain, allows experience-expectant maturation.

5. Most experience-dependent brain growth reflects the varied, culture-specific experiences of the infant. Therefore, one person's brain differs from another's. However, all normal infants are equally capable in the basic ways—emotional, linguistic, and sensory—that humans share.

Senses and Motor Skills

6. At birth, the senses already respond to stimuli. Prenatal experience makes hearing the most mature sense and vision the least mature sense. Vision improves quickly. Infants use their senses to strengthen their early social interactions.

7. Newborns have many reflexes, including the survival reflexes of sucking and breathing. Gross motor skills are soon evident, from rolling over to sitting up (at about 6 months), from standing to walking (at about 1 year), from climbing to running (before age 2).

8. Fine motor skills are difficult for infants, but babies gradually develop the hand and finger control needed to grab, aim, and manipulate almost anything within reach. Experience, time, and motivation allow infants to advance in all their motor skills.

Public Health Measures

9. About 2 billion infant deaths have been prevented in the past half-century because of improved health care. One major innovation is immunization, which has eradicated smallpox and virtually eliminated polio and measles in developed nations.

10. Sudden infant death syndrome (SIDS) once killed about 5,000 infants per year in the United States and thousands more worldwide. This number has been reduced by half since 1990, primarily because researchers discovered that putting infants to sleep on their backs makes SIDS less likely. If mothers stopped smoking, hundreds more infants would survive.

11. Breast-feeding is best for infants, partly because breast milk reduces disease and promotes growth of every kind. Most babies are breast-fed at birth, but less than half are exclusively breast-fed for 6 months, as most doctors worldwide recommend.

12. Severe malnutrition stunts growth and can cause death, directly through marasmus or kwashiorkor and indirectly through vulnerability if a child catches measles, an intestinal disorder, or other illness.

KEY TERMS

norm (p. 126)
percentile (p. 126)
head-sparing (p. 127)
REM sleep (p. 127)
co-sleeping (p. 128)
neuron (p. 129)
cortex (p. 129)
axon (p. 130)
dendrite (p. 130)
synapse (p. 130)
transient exuberance (p. 131)
experience-expectant (p. 132)
experience-dependent (p. 132)
prefrontal cortex (p. 133)
shaken baby syndrome (p. 133)
self-righting (p. 134)
sensitive period (p. 134)
sensation (p. 136)
perception (p. 136)
binocular vision (p. 137)
motor skill (p. 138)
reflex (p. 138)
gross motor skills (p. 140)
fine motor skills (p. 140)
immunization (p. 144)
sudden infant death syndrome (SIDS) (p. 146)
protein-calorie malnutrition (p. 150)
marasmus (p. 151)
kwashiorkor (p. 151)

KEY QUESTIONS

1. In what aspects of development (at any age) would it be best to be at the 10th, 50th, and 90th percentiles? Give an example for each.

2. How might stress hormones affect later development?

3. Why is pruning an essential part of brain development?

4. What is the relationship between the cortex and the dendrites?

5. What are the differences in the visual abilities of a newborn and a 3-month-old?

6. What characteristics of the human brain seem designed for hearing and understanding speech?

7. Why would parents encourage early (before 12 months) or late (after 12 months) walking?

8. In what ways does immunization save lives?

9. What are the signs of malnutrition?

10. Since breast-feeding is best, why do most North American mothers bottle-feed their 6-month-olds?

11. When is it better not to breast-feed an infant?

APPLICATIONS

1. Immunization regulations and practices vary, partly for social and political reasons. Ask at least two faculty or administrative staff members what immunizations students at your college must have and why. If you hear "it's a law," ask why that law is in place.

2. Observe three infants (whom you do not know) in public places such as a store, playground, or bus. Look closely at body size and motor skills, especially how much control each baby has over legs and hands. From that, estimate the age in months, and then ask the caregiver how old the infant is. (Most caregivers know the infant's exact age and are happy to tell you.)

3. *This project can be done alone, but it is more informative if several students pool responses.* Ask 3 to 10 adults whether they were bottle-fed or breast-fed and, if breast-fed, for how long. If anyone does not know, or if anyone expresses embarrassment about how long they were breast-fed, that itself is worth noting. Is there any correlation between adult body size and mode of infant feeding?

➤**Answer to Observation Quiz** (from page 149): The babies' ages, the settings, and the mothers' apparent attitudes. The U.S. mother *(left)* is in a hospital indoors and seems attentive to whether she is feeding her infant the right way. The mother in Madagascar *(right)* seems confident and content as she feeds her older baby in a public place, enjoying the social scene.

6

CHAPTER OUTLINE

The First Two Years: Cognitive Development

This chapter is about infant *cognition,* a word that means "thinking" in a very broad sense, including language, learning, memory, and intelligence in the first two years of life. My aunt's husband, Uncle Henry, boasted that he did nothing with his three children until they were smart enough to talk. He may have found a good excuse to avoid diapering, burping, and bathing, but his beliefs about cognition were wrong. Babies are smart from the first days of life, and they communicate quite well long before they begin talking. Uncle Henry missed his children's most impressive cognitive accomplishments.

Infants strive to organize sensations and perceptions and to understand sequence and direction, the familiar and the strange, objects and people, events and experiences, permanence and transiency, cause and effect. By the end of the first year—often much sooner—babies have succeeded at all these. They have goals and know how to reach them. By the end of the second year, they speak in sentences, think before acting, and pretend to be someone or something (a mother, an airplane) that they know they are not. Smart? Yes.

We begin this chapter by looking at Piaget's framework for observing this amazing intellectual progression, from newborns who know nothing to toddlers who can make a wish, say it out loud, and blow out their birthday candles. We end by asking how cognitive accomplishments, particularly the acquisition of language, occur.

Sensorimotor Intelligence

As you learned in Chapter 2, Jean Piaget was a Swiss scientist, born in 1896. He was "arguably the most influential researcher of all times within the area of cognitive developmental psychology" (Birney et al., 2005, p. 328). Contrary to the popular ideas of his day (including those of my Uncle Henry), Piaget realized that infants are smart and active learners, adapting to experience. And adaptation, according to Piaget, is the essence of intelligence.

Piaget described four distinct periods of cognitive development. The first period begins at birth and ends at about 24 months. Piaget called it **sensorimotor intelligence** because infants learn through their senses and motor skills. This two-year-long period is subdivided into six stages (see Table 6.1).

sensorimotor intelligence Piaget's term for the way infants think—by using their senses and motor skills—during the first period of cognitive development.

TABLE 6.1

The Six Stages of Sensorimotor Intelligence

For an overview of the stages of sensorimotor thought, it helps to group the six stages into pairs. The first two stages involve the infant's responses to its own body.

Primary Circular Reactions	
Stage One (birth to 1 month)	*Reflexes*: sucking, grasping, staring, listening.
Stage Two (1–4 months)	*The first acquired adaptations*: accommodation and coordination of reflexes. Examples: sucking a pacifier differently from a nipple; grabbing a bottle to suck it.
The next two stages involve the infant's responses to objects and people.	
Secondary Circular Reactions	
Stage Three (4–8 months)	*An awareness of things*: responding to people and objects. Example: clapping hands when mother says "patty-cake."
Stage Four (8–12 months)	*New adaptation and anticipation*: becoming more deliberate and purposeful in responding to people and objects. Example: putting mother's hands together in order to make her start playing patty-cake.
The last two stages are the most creative, first with action and then with ideas.	
Tertiary Circular Reactions	
Stage Five (12–18 months)	*New means through active experimentation*: experimentation and creativity in the actions of the "little scientist." Example: putting a teddy bear in the toilet and flushing it.
Stage Six (18–24 months)	*New means through mental combinations*: considering before doing provides the child with new ways of achieving a goal without resorting to trial-and-error experiments. Example: before flushing, remembering that the toilet overflowed the last time, and hesitating.

primary circular reactions The first of three types of feedback loops in sensorimotor intelligence, this one involving the infant's own body. The infant senses motion, sucking, noise, and so on, and tries to understand them.

Stages One and Two: Primary Circular Reactions

In every aspect of sensorimotor intelligence, there is an active (not passive) interaction between the brain and the senses. Sensation, perception, and cognition cycle back and forth (circling round and round) in what Piaget calls a circular reaction. The first two stages of sensorimotor intelligence are examples of **primary circular reactions,** which are reactions that involve the infant's own body.

Stage one, called the *stage of reflexes,* lasts only for a month. It includes senses as well as reflexes, which are the foundation of infant thought. Reflexes become deliberate movements; sensation leads into perception and then cognition. Sensorimotor intelligence begins.

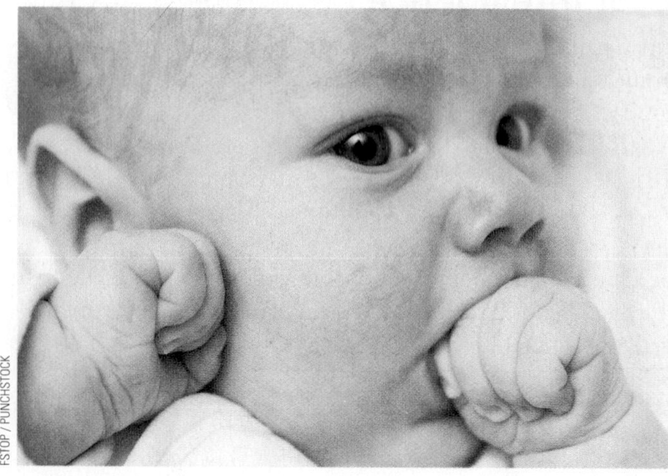

Time for Adaptation Sucking is a reflex at first, but adaptation begins as soon as an infant differentiates a pacifier from her mother's breast or realizes that her hand has grown too big to fit into her mouth. This infant's expression of concentration suggests that she is about to make that adaptation and suck just her thumb from now on.

FSTOP / PUNCHSTOCK

As reflexes adjust, the baby enters stage two, *first acquired adaptations* (also called the stage of first habits). Adaptation is crucial to learning, as it includes both assimilation and accommodation (see p. 45), which the person uses to make sense of experience. This adaptation from reflexes to deliberate action occurs because repeated responses provide information about what the body does and how that action feels.

As an example, newborns suck anything that touches their lips; sucking is one of the strongest reflexes. By about 1 month, infants start to adapt sucking. Some items require not just assimilation but accommodation: Pacifiers need to be sucked without the reflexive tongue-pushing and swallowing that other nipples require. This adaptation is a sign that infants have begun to interpret their perceptions; as they accommodate to pacifiers, they are "thinking."

In other words, adaptation in the early weeks relies primarily on reflexive assimilation: Everything suckable is assimilated as worthy of being sucked until accommodation occurs. After several more months, more adaptation of the sucking reflex is evident. The infant's cognitive responses include: Suck some things to soothe hunger, suck some for comfort, and never suck others (fuzzy blankets, large balls).

Adaptation is apparent when babies are not hungry but want the reassurance of rhythmic sucking. Then they suck a pacifier, or, if their reflexes have not adapted to a pacifier (because one was not offered), they suck thumbs, fingers, or knuckles.

Especially for Parents When should parents decide whether to feed their baby only by breast, only by bottle, or using some combination? When should they decide whether or not to let their baby use a pacifier?

Stages Three and Four: Secondary Circular Reactions

In stages three and four, development switches from primary circular reactions, involving the baby's own body (stages one and two), to **secondary circular reactions,** involving the baby and a toy or another person.

secondary circular reactions The second of three types of feedback loops in sensorimotor intelligence, this one involving people and objects. The infant is responsive to other people and to toys and other objects the infant can touch and move.

During stage three (age 4 to 8 months), infants interact diligently with people and things to produce exciting experiences, *making interesting events last.* Realizing that rattles make noise, for example, they wave their arms and laugh whenever someone puts a rattle in their hand. The sight of something that normally delights an infant—a favorite toy, a smiling parent—can trigger active efforts for interaction.

Stage four (8 months to 1 year) is called *new adaptation and anticipation,* or "the means to the end," because babies now think about a goal and begin to understand how to reach it. Thinking is more innovative in stage four than it was in stage three because adaptation is more complex. For instance, instead of always smiling at Daddy, an infant might assess Daddy's mood first. Stage-three babies merely understand how to continue an experience. Stage-four babies anticipate.

A 10-month-old girl who enjoys playing in the bathtub might see a bar of soap, crawl over to her mother with it as a signal to start her bath, and then remove her clothes to make her wishes crystal clear—finally squealing with delight when the bath water is turned on. Similarly, if a 10-month-old boy sees his mother putting on her coat to leave, he might try to stop her or drag over his own jacket to signal that he wants to go, too.

These examples reveal *goal-directed behavior*—that is, purposeful action. The baby's obvious goal-directedness stems from an enhanced awareness of cause and effect, as well as from better memory for actions already completed and better

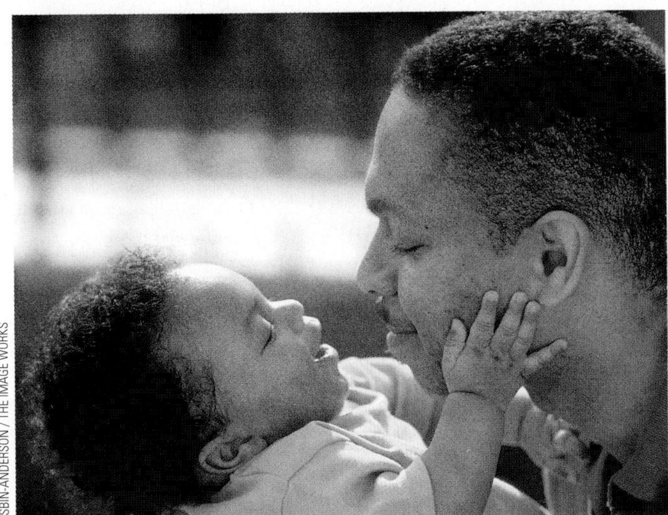

ESBIN-ANDERSON / THE IMAGE WORKS

Talk to Me This 4-month-old is learning how to make interesting sights last: The best way to get Daddy to respond is to vocalize, stare, smile, and pat his cheek.

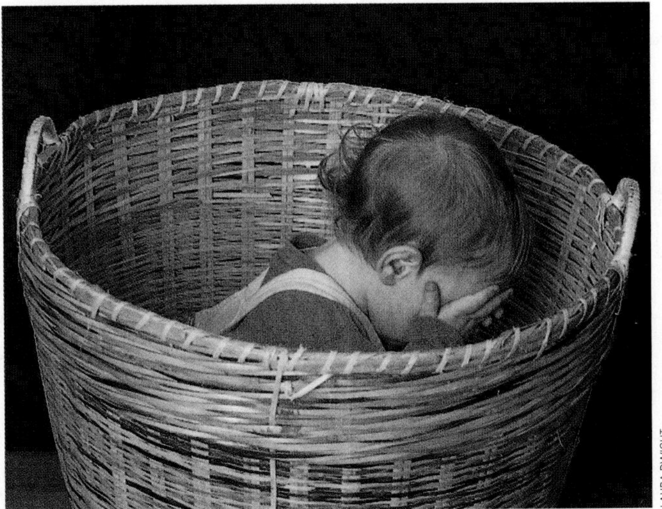

LAURA DWIGHT

Where's Rosa? At 18 months, Rosa knows all about object permanence and hiding. Her only problem here is distinguishing between "self" and "other."

understanding of other people's intentions (Behne et al., 2005; Willatts, 1999). Cognitive awareness coincides with the emergence of the motor skills (e.g., crawling, walking) needed to achieve goals; both developments are the result of neurological maturation (Adolph & Berger, 2006).

object permanence The realization that objects (including people) still exist when they cannot be seen, touched, or heard.

Piaget thought that the concept of **object permanence** emerges at about 8 months. Object permanence refers to the awareness that objects or people continue to exist when they are no longer in sight. Other researchers agreed that a goal-directed search for toys that have fallen from the baby's crib, rolled under a couch, or disappeared under a blanket does not begin to emerge until about 8 months, just as Piaget indicated. However, many current scientists question Piaget's interpretations, as the following explains.

thinking like a scientist

Object Permanence Revisited

Before Piaget, it was assumed that infants understood objects just as adults do. Piaget demonstrated with a simple experiment that that assumption was wrong. An adult shows an infant an interesting toy, covers it with a lightweight cloth, and observes the infant's response. The results:

- Infants younger than 8 months do not search (by removing the cloth).
- At about 8 months, infants search immediately after the object is covered but seem to forget about the object if they have to wait a few seconds.
- By 2 years, children seem to understand object permanence: They search well but not perfectly. Imperfection is evident when playing hide-and-seek: Preschoolers may fear that someone has really disappeared, or they may hide in obvious places (such as behind a coat rack with their feet still visible or as a big lump under a sheet on a bed).

As you learned in Chapter 1, thinking like a scientist means: (1) replication (thousands of scientists in dozens of nations have done this with Piaget's original research design) and (2) questioning the conclusions. Piaget claimed that failure to search for a hidden object meant that infants have no concept of object permanence. Other researchers ask whether other immaturities, such as imperfect motor skills or fragile memory, could mask an infant's understanding that objects still exist when they are no longer visible (Cohen & Cashon, 2006; Ruffman et al., 2005).

Apparently they can. As one researcher points out, "Amid his acute observation and brilliant theorizing, Piaget . . . mistook infants' motor incompetence for conceptual incompetence" (Mandler, 2004, p. 17). A series of clever experiments, in which objects seemed to disappear behind a screen while researchers traced eye movements and brain activity, revealed some inkling of object permanence in infants as young as 4½ months (Baillargeon & DeVos, 1991; Spelke, 1993).

The specific finding that contradicted Piaget is that, long before 8 months, infants showed surprise (by staring longer, for instance) when an object they saw was hidden by a screen and

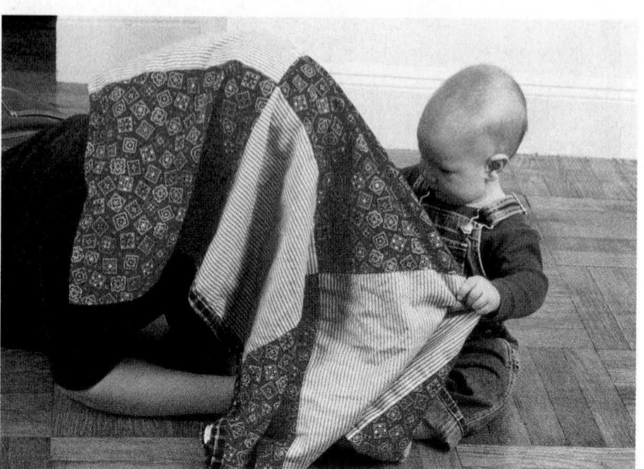

Peek-a-Boo The best hidden object is Mom under an easily moved blanket, as 7-month-old Elias has discovered. Peek-a-boo is fun from about 7 to 12 months. In another month, Elias will search for more conventionally hidden objects. In a year or two, his surprise and delight at finding Mom will fade.

BOTH: LAURA DWIGHT

then vanished, became two objects, or moved in an unexpected way. This reaction suggests object permanence, in that the infants seemed to think the object still existed behind the screen (Baillargeon, 1994).

Further exploration of infant cognition came from a series of experiments in which 2-, 4-, and 6-month-olds watched balls moving behind a screen, sometimes disappearing, sometimes reemerging in a smooth path, sometimes reemerging in the wrong place (Johnson et al., 2003). The 2-month-olds showed no awareness of anything odd, no matter what the balls did; the 4-month-olds showed signs that they knew something was amiss; the 6-month-olds demonstrated (with attentive stares) that they expected the balls to move in the usual way and were surprised when they didn't.

These researchers do not believe that the concept of object permanence (or, at least, perception regarding object trajectories) is inborn. It is the result of maturation and experience, as Piaget thought. The difference between this research and Piaget's is the age at which infants demonstrate the concept. With clever experiments (i.e., relying on visual tracking rather than on the motor skills involved in reaching), researchers have shown that object permanence begins to emerge at 4½ months.

Stages Five and Six: Tertiary Circular Reactions

In their second year, infants start experimenting in deed and in thought, typically acting first and thinking later. **Tertiary circular reactions** begin when 1-year-olds take their first independent and varied actions to discover the properties of other people, animals, and things. Infants no longer simply respond to their own bodies (primary reactions) or to other people or objects (secondary reactions); they also begin new sequences, in a pattern more like a spiral than a closed circle.

The first stage of tertiary circular reactions, Piaget's stage five (age 12 to 18 months), is called *new means through active experimentation.* This builds on the accomplishments of stage four, but goal-directed and purposeful activities become more expansive and creative. Toddlerhood is a time of active exploration, when babies delight in squeezing all the toothpaste out of the tube, taking apart the iPod, uncovering the anthill.

Piaget referred to the stage-five toddler as a **"little scientist"** who "experiments in order to see." Their scientific method is trial and error. Their devotion to discovery is familiar to every adult scientist—and to every parent.

Finally, in the sixth stage (age 18 to 24 months), toddlers begin to anticipate and solve simple problems by using *mental combinations*, an intellectual experimentation that supersedes the active experimentation of stage five. The child is able to put two ideas together, such as that a doll is not a real baby but a doll can be belted into a stroller and taken for a walk. Because they combine ideas, stage-six toddlers think about consequences, hesitating a moment before yanking the cat's tail or dropping a raw egg on the floor. Their strong impulse to discover sometimes overwhelms reflection; they do not always choose wisely. But at least thought precedes action.

Being able to use mental combinations makes it possible for the child to pretend. A toddler might sing to a doll before tucking it into bed. This is in marked contrast to the younger infant, who treats a doll like any other toy, throwing or biting it, or to the stage-five toddler, who tries to pull off the head, arms, and legs to see what is inside.

Piaget describes another stage-six intellectual accomplishment, involving both thought and memory. **Deferred imitation** occurs when infants copy behavior they noticed hours or even days earlier (Piaget, 1962). A classic example is Piaget's daughter, Jacqueline, who observed another child

> who got into a terrible temper. He screamed as he tried to get out of a playpen and pushed it backward, stamping his feet. Jacqueline stood watching him in amazement, never having witnessed such a scene before. The next day, she herself screamed in her playpen and tried to move it, stamping her foot lightly several times in succession.
>
> [Piaget, 1962, p. 63]

tertiary circular reactions The third of three types of feedback loops in sensorimotor intelligence, this one involving active exploration and experimentation. The infant explores a range of new activities, varying his or her responses as a way of learning about the world.

"little scientist" Piaget's term for the stage-five toddler (age 12 to 18 months) who experiments without anticipating the results.

deferred imitation A sequence in which an infant first perceives something that someone else does and then performs the same action a few hours or even days later.

Especially for Parents One parent wants to put all the breakable or dangerous objects away because a toddler is now able to move around independently. The other parent says that the baby should learn not to touch certain things. Who is right?

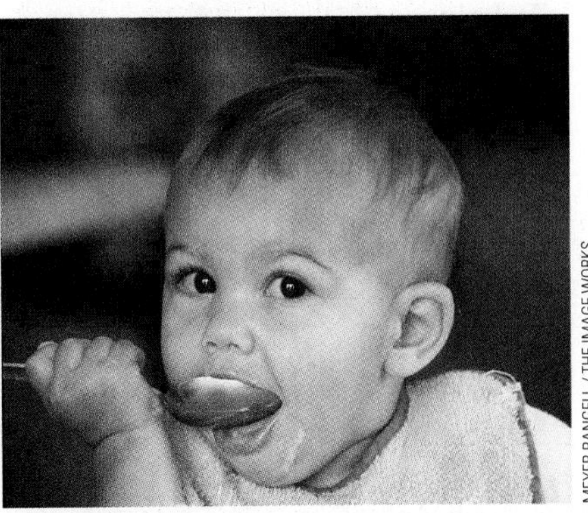
MEYER RANGELL / THE IMAGE WORKS

Bib and Bath Learning to use eating utensils is a cognitively stimulating experience that is largely a matter of trial and—often messy—error.

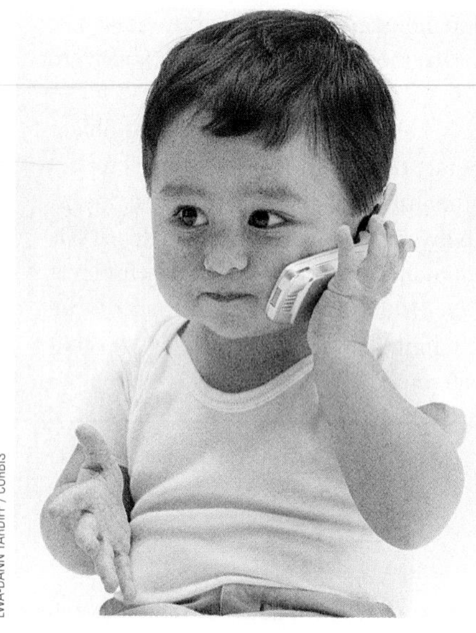

LWA-DANN TARDIFF / CORBIS

I'm Listening This 14-month-old is a master at deferred imitation. He knows how to hold a cell phone and what gestures to use as the "conversation" goes on.

Piaget and Research Methods

Infants reach the various stages of sensorimotor intelligence earlier than Piaget predicted. Not only do 4½-month-olds comprehend object permanence, but many researchers have found that babies pretend and defer imitation as early as 9 months (Bauer, 2006; Meltzoff & Moore, 1999).

One reason Piaget underestimated the speed of infant cognition is that he based his conclusions on what he could see his own three infants do. Direct observation of only three children is a start, but no contemporary researcher would stop there. There are problems with "fidelity and credibility" (Bornstein et al., 2005, p. 287) in collecting data on infants; modern researchers have statistics, design, sample size, and new strategies to overcome these problems (Hartmann & Pelzel, 2005). For example, **habituation** (from the word *habit*) refers to getting used to an experience after repeated exposure to it. Habituation occurs when the school cafeteria serves macaroni day after day or when an infant repeatedly hears the same sound, sees the same picture, plays with the same toy. Evidence of habituation is loss of interest (or, for macaroni, loss of appetite).

habituation The process of getting used to an object or event through repeated exposure to it.

Using habituation as a research strategy involves repeating one stimulus until babies lose interest and then presenting another, slightly different stimulus (a new sound, sight, or other sensation). Babies can indicate in many ways—a longer or more focused gaze; a faster or slower heart rate; more or less muscle tension around the lips; a change in the rate, rhythm, or pressure of suction on a nipple—that they detect a difference between the two stimuli. These often subtle indicators are recorded by technology that was unavailable to Piaget.

By inducing habituation and then presenting a new stimulus, scientists have learned that even 1-month-olds can detect the difference between a *pah* sound and a *bah* sound, between a circle with two dots inside it and a circle without any dots, and much more. Babies younger than 6 months perceive far more than Piaget imagined.

More recent techniques involve measurement of brain activity (see Table 6.2) (Johnson, 2005). In functional magnetic resonance imaging, or **fMRI,** a burst of electrical activity within the brain is recorded, indicating that neurons are firing, which leads researchers to conclude that a particular stimulus has been noticed

fMRI Functional magnetic resonance imaging, a measuring technique in which the brain's electrical excitement indicates activation anywhere in the brain; fMRI helps researchers locate neurological responses to stimuli.

TABLE 6.2

Some Techniques Used by Neuroscientists to Understand Brain Function

Technique	Use	Limitations
EEG (electroencephalogram)	Measures electrical activity in the top layers of the brain, where the cortex is.	Especially in infancy, much brain activity of interest occurs below the cortex.
ERP (event-related potential)	Notes the amplitude and frequency of electrical activity (as shown by brain waves) in specific parts of the cortex in reaction to various stimuli.	Reaction within the cortex signifies perception, but interpretation of the amplitude and timing of brain waves is not straightforward.
fMRI (functional magnetic resonance imaging)	Measures changes in blood flow anywhere in the brain (not just the outer layers).	Signifies brain activity, but infants are notoriously active, which can make fMRIs useless.
PET (positron emission tomography)	Also (like fMRI) reveals activity in various parts of the brain. Locations can be pinpointed with precision, but PET requires injection of radioactive dye to light up the active parts of the brain.	Many parents and researchers hesitate to inject radioactive dye into an infant's brain unless a serious abnormality is suspected.

For both practical and ethical reasons, these techniques have not been used with large, representative samples of normal infants. One of the challenges of neuroscience is to develop methods that are harmless, easy to use, and comprehensive for the study of normal children.

and processed. Using such advanced methods, scientists have been convinced that infants have memories, goals, and even mental combinations in advance of Piaget's stages.

As explained in Chapter 5, many measurements of neurons show that early brain development is wide-ranging: Dendrites proliferate, and pruning is extensive. The first years of life are filled with mental activity and may be prime time for cognitive development (Johnson, 2005). In fact, discoveries have given developmentalists a new worry: People might think that these years are the *only* ones for brain growth. Not so. As 20 leading developmentalists explain, the

> focus on "zero to three" as a critical or particularly sensitive period is highly problematic, not because this isn't an important period for the developing brain, but . . . attention to the period from birth to 3 years begins too late and ends too soon.
>
> [*National Research Council and Institute of Medicine*, 2000, p. 7]

➤Response for Parents (from page 157): Both decisions should be made within the first month, during the stage of reflexes. If parents wait until the infant is 4 months or older, they may discover that they are too late. It is difficult to introduce a bottle to a 4-month-old who has been exclusively breast-fed or a pacifier to a baby who has already adapted the sucking reflex to a thumb.

SUMMING UP

Piaget discovered, described, and then celebrated active infant learning, which he described in six stages of sensorimotor intelligence. Babies use their senses and motor skills to gain an understanding of their world, first with reflexes and then by adapting through assimilation and accommodation. Object permanence, pursuit of goals, and deferred imitation all develop earlier in infancy than Piaget realized. The infant is a little scientist, not only at age 1, as Piaget described so well, but even in the first months of life. Thinking develops before motor skills can execute thoughts. ■

➤Response for Parents (from page 159): It is easier and safer to babyproof the house, because toddlers, being "little scientists," want to explore. However, it is important for both parents to encourage and guide the baby, so it is preferable to leave out a few untouchable items if that will help prevent a major conflict between husband and wife.

Information Processing

Piaget was a "grand" theorist of cognition; he had an appreciation of shifts in the nature of cognition that occur at about ages 2, 6, and 12 years. His sweeping overview, with its notion of distinct stages, contrasts with **information-processing theory,** a perspective modeled on computer functioning, including input, memory, programs, calculation, and output.

information-processing theory A perspective that compares human thinking processes, by analogy, to computer analysis of data, including sensory input, connections, stored memories, and output.

Information-processing theorists believe that a step-by-step description of the mechanisms of thought add insight to our understanding of cognition at every age. Human information processing begins with input picked up by the five senses; proceeds to brain reactions, connections, and stored memories; and concludes with some action, such as a word or gesture. For infants, the output might be moving a hand to uncover a toy (object permanence), saying a word (e.g., *mama*) to signify recognition, or simply staring at a new photo (habituation). For example, instead of crying reflexively at the pain of hunger, an infant might focus on a bottle, remember that it can relieve hunger, reach for it, and then suck on it. Each step of this process requires information processing except the reflexive sucking, and even with that, the older infant is much more effective than the newborn because of better information processing.

Especially for Computer Experts In what way is the human mind not like a computer?

With the aid of the sensitive technology just described, information-processing research has found some impressive intellectual capacities in the infant. For example, concepts and categories seem to develop in the infant brain by about 6 months (Mandler, 2004; Quinn, 2004). This perspective helps tie together various aspects of infant cognition. We review two of these now: affordances and memory. Affordances concern perception or, by analogy, input. Memory concerns brain organization and output—that is, information storage and retrieval.

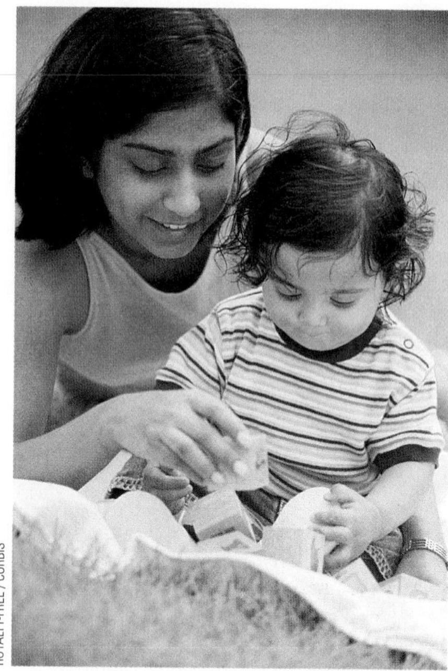

ROYALTY-FREE / CORBIS

Baby in Charge As this mother no doubt realizes, for her toddler, playing with blocks affords touching, stacking, and tossing them, not trying to identify the letters and numbers on them.

Affordances

Perception, remember, is the mental processing of information that arrives at the brain from the sensory organs. It is the first step of information processing the input to the brain. One of the puzzles of development is that two people can have discrepant perceptions of the same situation, not only interpreting it differently but actually observing it differently.

Decades of thought and research led Eleanor and James Gibson to conclude that perception is far from automatic (E. Gibson, 1969; J. Gibson, 1979). Perception—for infants, as for the rest of us—is a cognitive accomplishment that requires selectivity: "Perceiving is active, a process of obtaining information about the world. . . . We don't simply see, we look" (E. Gibson, 1988, p. 5).

The Gibsons contend that the environment (people, places, and objects) *affords*, or offers, many opportunities for perception and for interaction with what is perceived (E. Gibson, 1997). Each of these opportunities is called an **affordance.** Which particular affordance is perceived and acted on depends on four factors: sensory awareness, immediate motivation, current development, and past experience.

affordance An opportunity for perception and interaction that is offered by a person, place, or object in the environment.

As a simple example, a lemon may be perceived as something that affords smelling, tasting, touching, viewing, throwing, squeezing, and biting (among other things). Each of these affordances is further perceived as offering pleasure, pain, or some other emotion. Which of the many affordances a particular person perceives and acts on depends on the four factors just mentioned: sensations, motives, age, and experience. Consequently, a lemon might elicit quite different perceptions from an artist about to paint a still life, a thirsty adult in need of a refreshing drink, and a teething baby wanting something to gnaw on.

Clearly, infants and adults perceive quite different affordances. A toddler's idea of what affords running might be any unobstructed surface—a meadow, a long hallway in an apartment building, or a road. To an adult eye, the degree to which these places afford running may be restricted by such factors as a bull grazing in the meadow, neighbors in the hallway, or traffic on the road. Moreover, young children love to run, so they notice affordances for running; some adults prefer to stay put—so they do not perceive whether running is afforded or not.

➤Response for Computer Experts (from page 161): In dozens of ways, including speed of calculation, ability to network across the world, and vulnerability to viruses. In one crucial way the human mind is better: Computers crash within a few years, while human minds keep working until death.

ROBERT BRENNER / PHOTOEDIT, INC.

Look at Me These 1-year-olds are just learning about the affordances of objects. Thus, a rattle may be pushed against a friend's face to gain the friend's attention. This "little scientist" has not yet discovered that doing so may not be a good idea.

Observation Quiz (see answer, page 164): Are these two toddlers boys or girls?

Research on Early Affordances

As information processing improves over the first year, infants become quicker to recognize affordances. A detailed study traced the responses of infants to eight different displays on a TV screen (Courage et al., 2006; see Research Design). This research measured, among other things, how many times the infants glanced away from the displays, how long their most extensive look lasted, and whether their heart rate slowed down. The older infants were quicker to process the display and decide if it was interesting, a sign of better information processing. For example, the 14-week-olds looked at static dots for 10 seconds at a time, the 20-week-olds for 6 seconds, and babies from 26 to 52 weeks for only 5 seconds.

Developmental trends were apparent, especially for the most interesting display, which was a video from *Sesame Street*. Babies stared at this video for an average of 18 seconds at 14 weeks (usually one long look), 10 seconds at 26 weeks, and then back up to 15 seconds at 52 weeks. According to the researchers, input became quicker with age (hence shorter looks for less interesting things), but cognitive processing advanced (hence more intense looks at *Sesame Street*) (Courage et al., 2006).

Affordances are sought by infants of every age. For instance, one study found that when 9- to 12-month-olds were presented with unknown objects that rattled, rang, squeaked, or were silent, they decided what noise the object afforded on the basis of whether the object's shape was similar to that of another noise-making object. By 12 months, they also used vocabulary: They predicted the noise that an object would make according to whether the object's name was like the name of another object that, they knew, rattled, rang, or squeaked (Graham et al., 2004).

In another experiment, 12- to 24-month-olds watched adults look at or bend a laminated photograph and then followed the example, either looking at or bending it themselves. They did not yet know that photos are primarily for viewing, so they used whichever affordance they had been shown (Callaghan et al., 2004).

Research Design

Scientists: Mary L. Courage, Greg D. Reynolds, and John E. Richards.

Publication: *Child Development* (2006).

Participants: One hundred infants aged 14, 20, 26, 39, and 52 weeks (20 at each age). None had birth complications or known disabilities. Each was tested sitting in the mother's lap.

Design: Babies saw eight displays on a TV monitor, four of them motionless (a face, dots, triangles and lines, a *Sesame Street* scene) and the other four showing the same objects in motion. Duration of looking was measured in seconds by researchers who did not know what the babies saw, and heart rate was measured via an electrocardiogram (EEG).

Major conclusions: Look time and heart rate varied by age and display. Moving displays captured attention more than static ones; human forms were more attractive than geometric designs. The youngest babies often just stared blankly (and showed almost no slowing of heart rate), while the older babies glanced, glanced away, and then looked more closely. Age differences suggested advances in processing; the oldest babies were most "stimulus dependent"—that is, most influenced by the specifics of what they saw.

Comment: This study provides rich data on age and information processing, including one table with 360 data points—72 at each age. This richness complicates analysis, but because the study compares heart rate, look time, age, and display, its conclusions are more reliable.

Sudden Drops

The fact that experience affects which affordances are perceived is quite apparent in studies of depth perception. This research began with an apparatus called the **visual cliff,** designed to provide the illusion of a sudden dropoff between one horizontal surface and another. Mothers were able to urge their 6-month-olds to wiggle toward them over the supposed edge of the cliff, but even with mothers urging, 10-month-olds fearfully refused to budge (E. Gibson & Walk, 1960).

visual cliff An experimental apparatus that gives an illusion of a sudden drop between one horizontal surface and another.

Researchers once thought that inadequate depth perception kept young babies from seeing the drop and that, as the visual cortex became more mature, 8-month-olds could see it. Later research (using advanced technology) found that that interpretation was wrong. Even 3-month-olds notice a drop: Their heart rate slows and their eyes open wide when they are placed over the cliff. But until

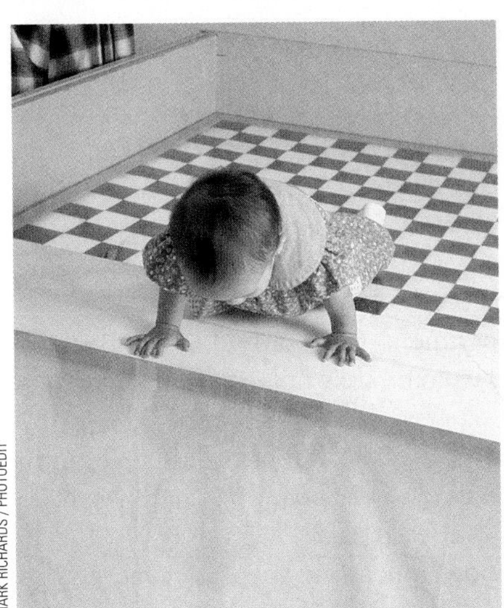

MARK RICHARDS / PHOTOEDIT

Depth Perception This toddler in a laboratory in Berkeley, California, is crawling on the experimental apparatus called a visual cliff. She stops at the edge of what she perceives as a dropoff.

➤Answer to Observation Quiz (from page 162): Surprise! Both babies are girls, named Anne and Sarah. Illustrating the power of stereotyping, many observers would have guessed that they are boys because their blue garments afford masculinity.

they can crawl, they do not realize that crawling over an edge affords falling, perhaps with a frightening and painful result. This depends, of course, on each infant's particular history. The difference is in processing, not input; in affordance, not mere perception. The same process happens with walking: Novice walkers are fearless and reckless; experienced walkers are more cautious and deliberate (Adolph & Berger, 2005).

Movement and People

Despite all the variations from one infant to another in the particular affordances they perceive, two general principles of perception are shared by all infants: dynamic perception and people preference. Both of these principles were demonstrated by the study of the 8 displays mentioned above (Courage et al., 2006).

dynamic perception Perception that is primed to focus on movement and change.

Dynamic perception is primed to focus on movement and change. Infants love motion. As soon as they can, they move their own bodies—grabbing, scooting, crawling, walking. To their delight, these movements change what the world affords them; as a result, perception and body motion advance as quickly as possible (Adolph & Berger, 2005).

Especially for Parents of Infants When should you be particularly worried that your baby will fall off the bed or down the stairs?

Other creatures that move, especially their own caregivers, are among the first and best sources of pleasure, again because of dynamic perception. That is one reason it's almost impossible to teach a baby not to chase and grab a moving dog, a cat, or even a cockroach.

people preference A universal principle of infant perception, consisting of an innate attraction to other humans, which is evident in visual, auditory, tactile, and other preferences.

The other universal principle of infant perception is **people preference.** This characteristic may have evolved over the centuries because humans of all ages survived by learning to attend to, and rely on, one another. As you remember from Chapter 5, all human senses are primed to respond to social stimuli (Bornstein et al., 2005).

Very young babies are interested in the emotional affordances of their caregivers (whether a person is likely to elicit laughter or fear), using their limited perceptual abilities to respond to smiles, shouts, and so on. Infants connect facial expressions with tone of voice long before they understand language. This ability has led to an interesting hypothesis:

> Given that infants are frequently exposed to their caregivers' emotional displays and further presented with opportunities to view the affordances (Gibson, 1959, 1979) of those emotional expressions, we propose that the expressions of familiar persons are meaningful to infants very early in life.
>
> *[Kahana-Kalman & Walker-Andrews, 2001, p. 366]*

Building on earlier research by other scientists on infant perception, these researchers presented infants with two moving images on a video screen. Both images were of a woman, either their mother or a stranger. In one, the woman visibly expresses joy; in the other, sorrow. Each image is accompanied by an audiotape of that woman's happy *or* sad talk. By 7 months, but not before, babies show that they can match emotional words with facial expressions by looking longer at the face expressing the same emotion as in the tone of voice.

One Constant, Multisensual Perception From the angle of her arm and the bend of her hand, it appears that this infant recognizes the constancy of the furry mass, perceiving it as a single entity whether it is standing still, rolling in the sand, or walking along the beach.

ULLI SEER / IMAGE BANK

Some infants in this experiment were only 3½ months old. When they did not know the woman, they failed to match the verbal emotion with the facial expression. In other words, when the face was that of a stranger, these 3½-month-olds did not tend to look more at the happy face when they heard the happy talk or to match sad voice and sad face.

However, when the 3½-month-olds saw their own mother on the video (two images, happy and sad) and heard her happy or her sad voice, they correctly matched visual and vocal emotions. They looked longest at their happy mothers talking in a happy way, but they also looked at their sad mothers when they heard their mother's sad voice—an amazing display of connecting speech tone with facial expressions.

The researchers noticed something else. When infants saw and heard their happy mothers, as opposed to the happy strangers, they smiled twice as quickly, seven times as long, and much more brightly (with cheeks raised as well as lips upturned) (Kahana-Kalman & Walker-Andrews, 2001). Obviously, experience had taught these babies that a smiling mother affords joy. The affordances of a smiling stranger are difficult to judge.

Especially for Parents This research on early affordances suggests a crucial lesson about how many babysitters an infant should have. What is it?

Memory

A certain amount of experience and brain maturation are required in order to process and remember experiences. Infants have great difficulty storing new memories in their first year, and older children are often unable to describe events that occurred when they were younger. But on the basis of a series of experiments, developmentalists now agree that very young infants *can* remember under the following circumstances:

- Experimental conditions are similar to real life.
- Motivation is high.
- Special measures are taken to aid memory retrieval.

The most dramatic evidence for infant memory comes from a series of innovative experiments in which 3-month-olds were taught to make a mobile move by kicking their legs (Rovee-Collier, 1987, 1990). The infants lay on their backs, in their own cribs, connected to a mobile by means of a ribbon tied to one foot (see photograph).

Virtually all the infants began making some occasional kicks (as well as random arm movements and noises) and realized, after a while, that kicking made the mobile move. They then kicked more vigorously and frequently, sometimes laughing at their accomplishment. So far, this is no surprise—self-activated movement is highly reinforcing to infants, part of dynamic perception.

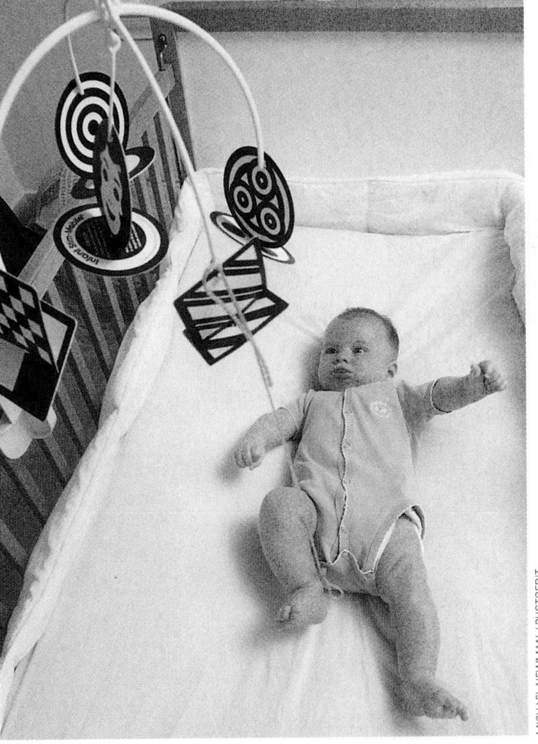

MICHAEL NEWMAN / PHOTOEDIT

He Remembers! In this demonstration of Rovee-Collier's experiment, a young infant immediately remembers how to make the familiar mobile move. (Unfamiliar mobiles do not provoke the same reaction.) He kicks his right leg and flails both arms, just as he learned to do several weeks ago.

Observation Quiz (see answer, page 167): How and why is this mobile unlike those usually sold for babies?

When some infants had the mobile-and-ribbon apparatus reinstalled in their cribs *one week later,* most started to kick immediately; this reaction indicated that they remembered their previous experience. But when other infants were retested *two weeks later,* they began with only random kicks. Apparently they had forgotten what they had learned—evidence that memory is fragile early in life.

Reminders and Repetition

The lead researcher, Carolyn Rovee-Collier, developed another experiment that demonstrated that 3-month-old infants *could* remember after two weeks *if* they had a brief reminder session before being retested (Rovee-Collier & Hayne, 1987). A **reminder session** is any perceptual experience that is intended to help a person recollect an idea, a thing, or an experience.

reminder session A perceptual experience that is intended to help a person recollect an idea, a thing, or an experience, without testing whether the person remembers it at the moment.

In this particular reminder session, two weeks after the initial training, the infants watched the mobile move but were *not* tied to it and were positioned so that they could *not* kick. The next day, when they were again connected to the mobile and positioned so that they *could* move their legs, they kicked as they had learned to do two weeks earlier.

Watching the mobile move on the previous day revived their faded memory. The information about how to make the mobile move was stored in their brains;

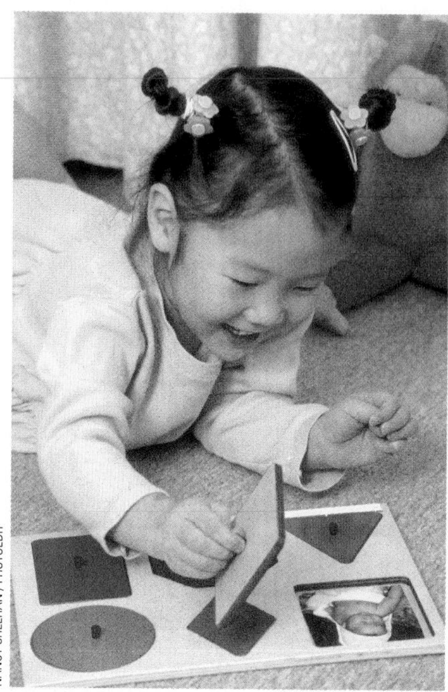

NANCY SHEEHAN / PHOTOEDIT

Memory Aid Personal motivation and action are crucial to early memory, and that is why Noel has no trouble remembering which shape covers the photograph of herself as a baby.

they needed some processing time to retrieve it. The reminder session provided that time. Overall, some early memories can be "highly enduring, and become even more so after repeated encounters with reminders" (Rovee-Collier & Gerhardstein, 1997).

A Little Older, a Little More Memory

After about 6 months, infants can retain information for longer periods of time than younger babies can, with less training or reminding. Toward the end of the first year, many kinds of memory, including that involved in deferred imitation, are apparent (Meltzoff & Moore, 1999). For example, suppose a 9-month-old watches someone playing with a toy he or she has never seen before. The next day, if given the toy, the 9-month-old is likely to play with it in the same way as he or she had observed. (Younger infants do not.)

By the middle of the second year, toddlers can remember and reenact more complex sequences. In one study, 16- and 20-month-olds watched an experimenter perform various activities, such as putting a doll to bed, making a party hat, and cleaning a table (Bauer & Dow, 1994). For each activity, the experimenter used props and gave a brief "instruction" for performing each step. For instance, to clean the table, the experimenter wet it with water from a white spray bottle, saying, "Put on the water"; wiped it with a paper towel, saying, "Wipe it"; and placed the towel in a wooden trash basket, saying, "Toss it."

A week later, most toddlers remembered how to carry out the sequence when they heard "Put on the water. Wipe it. Toss it." They followed what they had seen, not only with the same props but also with different props (for instance, a clear spray bottle, a sponge, and a plastic garbage can). This shows that infants are developing concepts, not imitating behavior (Mandler, 2004). Many other experiments also show that toddlers are thinking conceptually, not just repeating what they have experienced.

Aspects of Memory

Memory is not one thing, "not a unitary or monolithic entity" (Schacter & Badgaiyan, 2001, p. 1). People are inaccurate when they make general statements about their "memory," as in "I have a good memory" or "My memory is failing." Brain-imaging techniques (such as fMRI) reveal many distinct brain regions devoted to particular aspects of memory. There is probably a memory for faces, for sounds, for events, for sights, for phrases, and much more.

One distinction is between *implicit memory*, which is memory for routines and memories that remain hidden until a particular stimulus brings them to mind (like the mobile), and *explicit memory,* which is memory that can be recalled on demand. As you can see in Table 6.3, explicit memory is probably impossible in the first months of life. Some aspects of it are evident after age 1 (see Chapter 9); at about age 5 or 6, when children begin school, explicit memory improves dramatically as those parts of the brain mature (Nelson et al., 2006).

Because there are so many types of memory, it is not surprising that infants remember some things better than others: That's the way human brains are constructed. Thus, early memories may be either fragile or enduring, depending on which type of memory is involved (Nelson & Webb, 2003).

Infants probably store within their brains many emotions and sensations that they cannot readily retrieve, whereas memories of motion (dynamic perception) are remembered once that particular action is cued by the context (as when the infants remembered how to kick to make the mobile move). Once they understand words, a verbal reminder aids retrieval, even after a delay (Bauer, 2006).

➤**Response for Parents of Infants** (from page 164): Constant vigilance is necessary for the first few years of a child's life, but the most dangerous age is from about 4 to 8 months, when infants can move but do not yet have a fear of falling over an edge.

➤**Response for Parents** (from page 165): It is important that infants have time for repeated exposure to each caregiver, because infants adjust their behavior to maximize whatever each particular caregiver affords in the way of play, emotions, and vocalization. Parents should find one steady babysitter rather than several.

TABLE 6.3

The Major Memory Systems and Developmental Tasks

General System	Subsystems	Tasks	Brain Systems Related to Tasks	Infancy Example
Implicit memory (nondeclarative memory)	Procedural learning	Serial reaction time (SRT) task	Striatum, supplementary motor association, motor cortex, frontal cortex	Kick to make mobile move
		Visual expectation paradigm (VExP)	Frontal cortex, motor areas	
	Conditioning	Conditioning	Cerebellum, basal ganglia	Laugh when tickled
	Perceptual representation system	Perceptual priming paradigms	Modality dependent; parietal cortex, occipital cortex, inferior temporal cortex, auditory cortex	Recognize mother's voice
Explicit memory	Pre-explicit memory	Novelty detection in habituation and paired comparison tasks	Hippocampus	Hear difference between sounds
Rare before age 1	Semantic memory (generic knowledge)	Semantic retrieval, word priming, and associative priming	Left prefrontal cortex, anterior cingulate cortex, hippocampal cortex	First spoken words
	Episodic memory (autobiographical)	Episodic encoding	Left prefrontal cortex, left orbitoprefrontal cortex	Remember usual routines of dinner
		Recall and recognition	Right prefrontal cortex, anterior cingulate cortex, parietal cortex, cerebellum, hippocampal cortex	Remember when and how a painful event occurred

Source: Adapted from Nelson & Webb, 2003, p. 103.

SUMMING UP

Infant cognition can be studied using the information-processing perspective, which analyzes each component of how thoughts begin and are organized, remembered, and expressed. Infant perception is powerfully influenced by particular experiences and motivation, so the affordances perceived by one infant differ from those perceived by another. Memory depends on both brain maturation and experience. That is why memory is fragile in the first year (being increased by dynamic perception and reminders) and becomes more evident (although many types of memory remain quite fragile) in the second year. ■

➤**Answer to Observation Quiz** (from page 165): It is black and white, with larger objects—designed to be particularly attractive to infants, not to adult shoppers.

Language: What Develops in the First Two Years?

The acquisition of language, with its thousands of words, idiomatic phrases, grammar rules, and exceptions, is the most impressive intellectual achievement of the young child. In fact, language *is* the most impressive human accomplishment: It differentiates *Homo sapiens* from all other species, and it may be the reason human brains are more complex than those of other animals (Leonard, 2003).

For instance, humans and gorillas are close relatives, with about 99 percent of their genes in common. Gorillas are bigger than people, but an adult gorilla's brain is only one-third as big as a human's and has far fewer dendrites, synapses, and other components. This means that a 2-year-old human has twice as much brainpower as a full-grown gorilla. Many animals communicate, but no species has anything approaching the neurons and networks that support the 6,000 human languages.

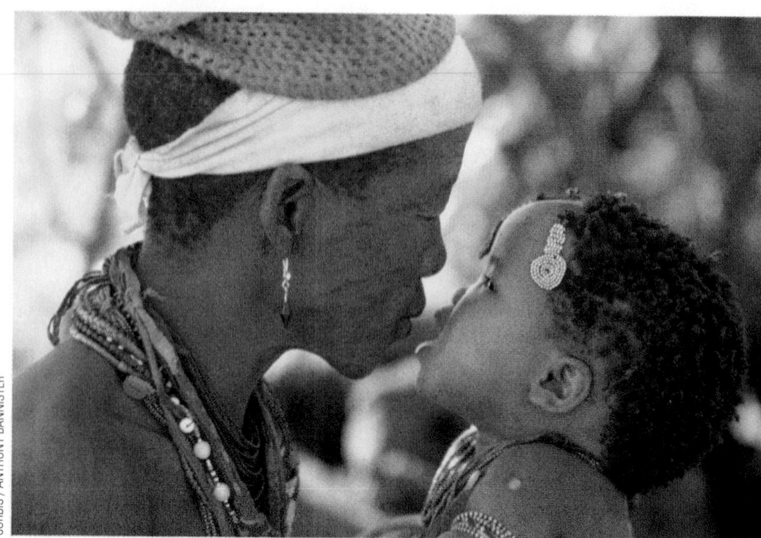

CORBIS / ANTHONY BANNISTER

Too Young for Language? No. The early stages of language are communication through noises, gestures, and facial expressions, very evident here between this !Kung grandmother and granddaughter.

The Universal Sequence

The timing of language acquisition varies; the most advanced 10 percent of 2-year-olds speak more than 550 words, and the least advanced 10 percent speak fewer than 100 words—a fivefold difference (Merriman, 1999). (Some explanations are discussed at the end of this chapter.) But children around the world follow the same sequence of early language development (see Table 6.4).

Listening and Responding

Infants begin learning language before birth, via brain organization and auditory experiences during the final prenatal months. Newborns prefer to hear speech over other sounds; they prefer to listen to high-pitched, simplified, and repetitive adult speech. This form of speech is quite distinct from normal speech. It is sometimes called *baby talk*, since it is talk directed to babies, and sometimes called *motherese*, since mothers all over the world speak it. Both these terms may have misleading implications, so scientists prefer the more formal term **child-directed speech.**

child-directed speech The high-pitched, simplified, and repetitive way adults speak to infants. (Also called *baby talk* or *motherese*.)

Newborns respond to adult noises and expressions (as well as to their own internal pleasures and pain) in many ways, crying, cooing, and making a variety of other sounds even in the first days of life. Their responses gradually become more varied. By 4 months, most babies squeal, growl, gurgle, grunt, croon, and yell, as well as make speechlike sounds (Hsu et al., 2000).

TABLE 6.4

AT ABOUT THIS TIME: The Development of Spoken Language in the First Two Years

Age*	Means of Communication
Newborn	Reflexive communication—cries, movements, facial expressions
2 months	A range of meaningful noises—cooing, fussing, crying, laughing
3–6 months	New sounds, including squeals, growls, croons, trills, vowel sounds
6–10 months	Babbling, including both consonant and vowel sounds repeated in syllables
10–12 months	Comprehension of simple words; speechlike intonations; specific vocalizations that have meaning to those who know the infant well. Deaf babies express their first signs; hearing babies also use specific gestures (e.g., pointing) to communicate.
12 months	First spoken words that are recognizably part of the native language
13–18 months	Slow growth of vocabulary, up to about 50 words
18 months	Vocabulary spurt—three or more words learned per day. Much variation: Some toddlers do not yet speak.
21 months	First two-word sentence
24 months	Multiword sentences. Half the toddler's utterances are two or more words long.

*The ages of accomplishment in this table reflect norms. Many healthy children with normal intelligence attain these steps in language development earlier or later than indicated here.
Source: Bloom, 1993, 1998; Fenson et al., 2000; Lenneberg, 1967.

Babbling

Between 6 and 9 months, babies begin to repeat certain syllables (*ma-ma-ma, da-da-da, ba-ba-ba*), a phenomenon referred to as **babbling** because of the way it sounds. Babbling is experience-expectant; all babies do it, even deaf ones. Responses encourage babbling; deaf babies stop (because they cannot hear responses) and hearing babies continue. All babies make rhythmic gestures, waving their arms as they babble, again in response to the actions of others (Iverson & Fagan, 2004). Toward the end of the first year, babbling begins to sound like the native language; infants imitate what they hear.

babbling The extended repetition of certain syllables, such as *ba-ba-ba,* that begins between 6 and 9 months of age.

Videotapes of deaf children whose parents sign to them show that 10-month-old deaf infants use about a dozen distinct hand gestures—which resemble the signs their parents use—in a repetitive manner similar to babbling. Parents of hearing babies should also use gestures; children understand and express concepts with gestures sooner than with speech (Goldin-Meadow, 2006).

Pointing is an advanced gesture that requires understanding another person's perspective. Most animals cannot interpret pointing; most humans can do so at 10 months. This is one of the intriguing aspects of human development, since pointing indicates a strong preference for social interaction.

STOCK CONNECTION DISTRIBUTION / ALAMY

Lip-Reading Communication begins in early infancy. Infants closely watch speakers' mouth movements and facial expressions. By this baby's age, 5 months, bilingual infants can tell by looking who is speaking French and who is speaking English.

First Words

Finally, at about 1 year of age, the average baby speaks (or signs) a few words. Usually, caregivers understand the first word before strangers do, which makes it hard for researchers to pinpoint exactly what a 12-month-old can say. For example, at 13 months, Kyle knew standard words such as *mama,* but he also knew *da, ba, tam, opma,* and *daes,* which his parents knew to be, respectively, "downstairs," "bottle," "tummy," "oatmeal," and "starfish" (yes, that's what *daes* meant) (Lewis et al., 1999).

In the first months of the second year, spoken vocabulary increases very gradually (perhaps one new word a week). However, 6- to 15-month-olds learn meanings rapidly, and they comprehend about 10 times as many words as they speak (Schafer, 2005; Snow, 2006).

Especially for Caregivers A toddler calls two people "Mama." Is this a sign of confusion?

The Naming Explosion

Once vocabulary reaches about 50 *expressed* words (understood words are more extensive), it builds rapidly, at a rate of 50 to 100 words per month, with 21-month-olds saying twice as many words as 18-month-olds (Adamson & Bakeman, 2006). This language spurt is called the **naming explosion** because many of the early words are nouns, or naming words (Gentner & Boroditsky, 2001).

naming explosion A sudden increase in an infant's vocabulary, especially in the number of nouns, that begins at about 18 months of age.

In almost every language, each significant caregiver (often *dada, mama, nana, papa, baba, tata*), sibling, and sometimes pet is named between 12 and 18 months (Bloom, 1998). (See Appendix A, p. A-4.) Other frequently uttered words refer to the child's favorite foods and to elimination (*pee-pee, wee-wee, poo-poo, ka-ka, doo-doo*).

No doubt you have noticed that all these words have a similar structure: two identical syllables, each a consonant followed by a vowel sound. Many more words follow that pattern—not just *baba* but also *bobo, bebe, bubu, bibi.* Others are slightly more complicated—not just *mama* but also *ma-me, ama,* and so on.

Especially for Nurses and Pediatricians The parents of a 10-month-old have just been told that their child is deaf. They don't believe it, because, as they tell you, the baby doesn't always respond to noises, but he babbles as much as their other children did. What do you tell them?

Cultural Differences

Although all new talkers say names, using similar sounds, and say more nouns than any other part of speech, the ratio of nouns to verbs and adjectives shows cultural

JORGEN SCHYTTE / PETER ARNOLD

Where in the World? Different cultures influence children's language learning in different ways. Children who spend a lot of time with adults receive abundant exposure to the unique speech patterns of their culture.

Observation Quiz (see answer, page 173): What elements in this photograph suggest cultural differences between this family and most European or North American ones?

➤Response for Caregivers (from page 169): Not at all. Toddlers hear several people called "Mama" (their own mother, their grandmothers, their cousins' and friends' mothers) and experience mothering from several people, so it is not surprising if they use "Mama" too broadly. They will eventually narrow the label down to the one correct person.

➤Response for Nurses and Pediatricians (from page 169): Urge the parents to accept the diagnosis and take action. They should begin learning sign language immediately and investigate the possibility of cochlear implants. Babbling has a biological basis and begins at a specified time, in deaf as well as hearing babies. However, deaf babies eventually begin to use gestures more and to vocalize less than hearing babies.

holophrase A single word that is used to express a complete, meaningful thought.

influences (Bornstein et al., 2004). For example, by 18 months, English-speaking infants use relatively more nouns but fewer verbs than Chinese or Korean infants do. Why?

One explanation goes back to the language itself. Chinese and Korean are "verb-friendly," in that verbs are placed at the beginning or end of sentences, which makes them easier to learn. In English, verbs occur in various positions within sentences, and their forms change in illogical ways (think of *go, gone, will go, went*). This irregularity makes English verbs harder than nouns for novice learners (Gentner & Boroditsky, 2001).

An alternative explanation considers the entire social context: Playing with a variety of toys and learning about dozens of objects are crucial in North American culture, whereas East Asian cultures emphasize human interactions—specifically, how one person responds to another. Accordingly, North American infants are expected to name many objects, whereas Asian infants are expected to encode social interactions into language.

Every language has some concepts encoded in adult speech that are easy and some that are hard for infants. English-speaking infants confuse *before* and *after*; Dutch-speaking infants misuse *out* when it refers to taking off clothes; Korean infants need to learn two meanings of *in* (Mandler, 2004).

Learning adjectives is easier in Italian and Spanish than in English or French because of patterns in those languages (Waxman & Lidz, 2006). Specifically, adjectives can stand by themselves without the nouns. If I want a blue cup from a group of multicolored cups, I would ask for "a blue cup" or "a blue one" in English but simply "uno azul" (a blue) in Spanish. Despite such variations, in every language, infants demonstrate impressive speed and efficiency in acquiring both vocabulary and grammar (Bornstein et al., 2004).

Sentences

The first words soon take on nuances of tone, loudness, and cadence that are precursors of the first grammar, because a single word can convey many messages by the way it is spoken. Imagine meaningful sentences encapsulated in "Dada!" "Dada?" and "Dada." Each is a **holophrase,** a single word spoken in such a way that it expresses an entire thought (Tomasello, 2006).

Intonation (variations of tone and pitch) is extensive in babbling and again in holophrases at about 18 months, with a dip in between (at about 12 months). At that one-year point, infants seem to reorganize their vocalization from universal to language-specific (Snow, 2006). They are no longer just singing and talking to themselves (babbling) but communicating with others (uttering holophrases).

Grammar includes all the methods that languages use to communicate meaning. Word order, prefixes, suffixes, intonation, verb forms, pronouns and negations, prepositions and articles—all of these are aspects of grammar. Grammar is obvious when two-word combinations begin, at about 21 months. These sentences follow the word order "Baby cry" or "More juice," rather than the reverse. Soon the child is combining three words, usually in subject–verb–object order in English (for example, "Mommy read book"), rather than any of the five other possible sequences of those words.

grammar All the methods—word order, verb forms, and so on—that languages use to communicate meaning, apart from the words themselves.

A child's grammar correlates with the size of his or her vocabulary (Snow, 2006). The child who says "Baby is crying" is advanced in language development compared with the child who says "Baby crying" or simply the holophrase "Baby" (Dionne et al., 2003). Comprehension advances as well. Their expanding knowledge of both vocabulary and grammar helps toddlers understand what others are saying (Kedar et al., 2006).

If the child's family is bilingual, the acquisition of language is not slowed down, but "development in each language proceeds separately and in a language-specific manner" (Conboy & Thal, 2006, p. 727). Thus an English–French bilingual child who understands the word *on* does not yet necessarily understand *sur.*

Theories of Language Learning

Worldwide, people who are not yet 2 years old already use language well. Bilingual children keep two languages separate, and speak whatever language a given listener understands. Some teenagers compose lyrics or deliver orations that move thousands of their co-linguists. Some adults are fluent in two, three, or even more languages. For many older adults, cognitive abilities decline, but language continues to advance. How do these amazing examples of language learning happen?

Answers come from three schools of thought, each of which is connected to a theory (behaviorism, epigenetic theory, and sociocultural theory, respectively). The first says that infants are directly taught, the second that infants naturally understand language, and the third that social impulses propel infants to communicate.

Each theory of language acquisition has implications for parents and educators, all of whom want children to speak fluently, but none of whom want to teach something that infants cannot learn or that they will learn without instruction. Which theory should guide them?

Cultural Values If his infancy is like that of most babies raised in the relatively taciturn Ottavado culture of Ecuador, this 2-month-old will hear significantly less conversation than infants from most other regions. According to many learning theorists, a lack of reinforcement will result in a child who is insufficiently verbal. In most Western cultures, that might be called maltreatment. However, each culture tends to encourage the qualities it most needs and values, and verbal fluency is not a priority in this community. In fact, people who talk too much are ostracized and those who keep secrets are valued, so encouragement of language may be maltreatment here.

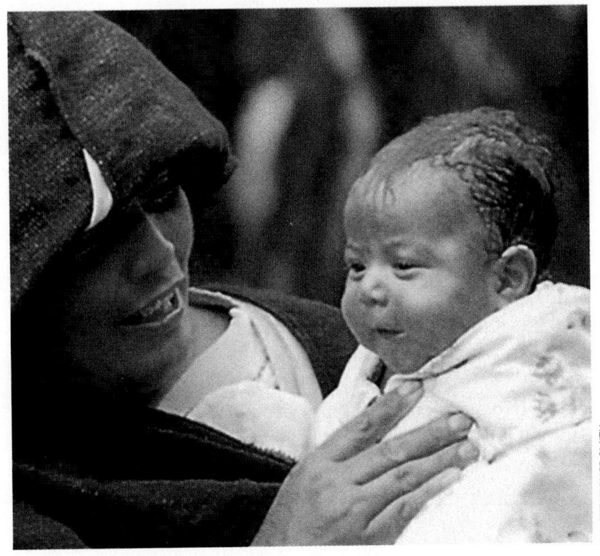

ELLIOTT VARNER SMITH

Theory One: Infants Need to Be Taught

The seeds of the first perspective were planted more than 50 years ago, when the dominant theory in North American psychology was behaviorism, or learning theory. The essential idea was that all learning is acquired, step by step, through association and reinforcement. Just as Pavlov's dogs learned to associate the sound of a bell with the presentation of food (see Chapter 2), behaviorists believe that infants associate objects with words they have heard often, especially if reinforcement occurs.

B. F. Skinner (1957) noticed that spontaneous babbling is usually reinforced. Typically, every time the baby says "ma-ma-ma-ma," a grinning mother appears, repeating the sound as well as showering the

Especially for Nurses and Pediatricians Bob and Joan have been reading about language development in children. They are convinced that language is "hardwired," so they need not talk to their 6-month-old son. How do you respond?

baby with attention, praise, and perhaps food. These affordances of mothers are exactly what the infant wants, and the baby will make those sounds again to get them.

Most parents are excellent instructors. For instance, parents who talk to their young infants typically name each object—"Here is your *bottle,*" "There is your *foot,*" "You want your *juice*?" and so on—often touching and moving the named object at the same time as they speak the target word loudly, clearly, and slowly (Gogate et al., 2000). They also use child-directed speech, capturing the baby's interest with high pitch, short sentences, stressed nouns, and simple grammar—exactly the kind of teaching techniques that behaviorists would recommend.

The core ideas of this theory are the following:

- Parents are expert teachers, although other caregivers help.
- Frequent repetition is instructive, especially when linked to daily life.
- Well-taught infants become well-spoken children.

Behaviorists note that some 3-year-olds converse in elaborate sentences; others just barely put one simple word with another. Such variations correlate with the amount of language teaching the child receives. Parents of the most verbal children teach language throughout infancy—singing, explaining, listening, responding, and reading. For instance, parents of the most verbal children typically read to them every day, even at age 1 (Raikes et al., 2006; see Research Design).

Providing another example, researchers analyzed the language that mothers (all middle-class) used with their preverbal infants, aged 9 to 17 months (Tamis-LeMonda et al., 2001). One mother never imitated her infant's babbling; another mother imitated 21 times in 10 minutes, babbling back as if in conversation. Overall, mothers were most likely to describe things or actions (e.g., "That is a spoon you are holding—spoon"). The range was vast: In 10 minutes, one mother described things only 4 times, while another provided her baby with 33 descriptions.

The frequency of maternal responsiveness at 9 months predicted language acquisition many months later (see Figure 6.1). It was not that noisy infants, whose genes would soon make them start talking, elicited more talk from their mothers. Some quiet infants had noisy mothers, who suggested play activities, described things, and asked questions. Quiet infants with talkative mothers usually became talkative later on.

This research is in keeping with the behaviorist theory that adults teach language and then infants learn it. If adults want language-proficient children who speak, understand, and (later) read well, they must talk to their babies.

Research Design

Scientists: Helen Raikes, Barbara Alexandra Pan, Gayle Luze, Catherine S. Tamis-LeMonda, Jeanne Brooks-Gunn, Jill Constantine, et al.

Publication: *Child Development* (2006).

Participants: From 17 Early Head Start programs, 2,581 mother–infant pairs were interviewed. All were low income; 26 percent were married; 53 percent were high school graduates. About a third each were Americans of European, African, and Hispanic heritage.

Design: When the infants were 14, 24, and 36 months old, their language ability was measured and the mothers were asked how often they read to them and how many books the babies had. The children's language abilities were compared to 15 variables.

Major conclusions: Being read to correlated with language, but early reading (at 14 months) was not as strong a predictor of future language scores as were two other factors, maternal warmth and education. By 36 months, children whose mothers read to them often were quite verbal.

Comment: The size and diversity of this sample add to confidence in the conclusions. Being read to as a baby is one of many factors that foster language. Some of the details of this study could be used to confirm all three theories of language learning discussed here.

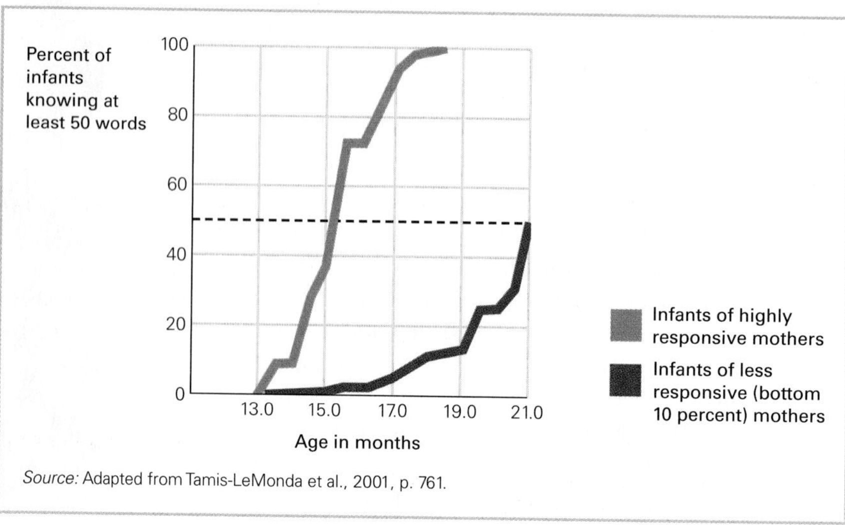

Source: Adapted from Tamis-LeMonda et al., 2001, p. 761.

FIGURE 6.1

Maternal Responsiveness and Infants' Language Acquisition Learning the first 50 words is a milestone in early language acquisition, as it predicts the arrival of the naming explosion and the multiword sentence a few weeks later. Researchers found that half the infants of highly responsive mothers (top 10 percent) reached this milestone as early as 15 months of age and the other half reached it by 17 months. The infants of nonresponsive mothers (bottom 10 percent) lagged significantly behind.

MICHELLE D. BRIDWELL / PHOTOEDIT

Show Me Where Pointing is one of the earliest forms of communication, emerging at about 10 months. As Carlos demonstrates, accurate pointing requires a basic understanding of social interaction, because the pointer needs to take the observer's angle of vision into account.

Theory Two: Infants Teach Themselves

A contrary theory holds that language learning is innate; adults need not teach it. The seeds of this perspective were planted soon after Skinner proposed his theory of verbal learning. Noam Chomsky (1968, 1980) and his followers felt that language is too complex to be mastered merely through step-by-step conditioning. Although behaviorists focus on variations among children in vocabulary size, Chomsky focused on similarities in language acquisition.

Noting that all young children master basic grammar at about the same age, Chomsky cited this *universal grammar* as evidence that humans are born with a mental structure that prepares them to seek some elements of human language—for example, the use of a raised tone at the end of an utterance to indicate a question. Chomsky labeled this hypothesized mental structure the **language acquisition device,** or **LAD.** The LAD enables children to derive the rules of grammar quickly and effectively from the speech they hear every day, regardless of whether their native language is English, Thai, or Urdu.

language acquisition device (LAD) Chomsky's term for a hypothesized mental structure that enables humans to learn language, including the basic aspects of grammar, vocabulary, and intonation.

Other scholars agree with Chomsky that infants are innately ready to use their minds to understand and speak whatever language is offered (Gopnik, 2001). The various languages of the world, as different as they are from one another, are all logical, coherent, and systematic. Infants, who are also logical, are primed to grasp the particular language they are exposed to, making caregiver speech "not a 'trigger' but a 'nutrient'" (Slobin, 2001, p. 438). There is no need for a language trigger, according to theory two, because words are "expected" by the developing brain, which quickly and efficiently connects neurons in the first year to support whichever particular language the infant hears.

➤Answer to Observation Quiz (from page 170): At least four elements are unusual in today's Western families: large size (four children), a child held in the mother's lap to eat (i.e., no high chair for the baby), the father pouring for everyone, and the fact that the whole family, including teenagers, is eating together. This family lives in Mozambique, in southeastern Africa.

Research supports this perspective as well. As you remember, all infants babble *ma-ma* and *da-da* sounds (not yet referring to mother or father) (Goldman, 2001). No reinforcement or teaching is needed; all infants need is for dendrites to grow, mouth muscles to strengthen, neurons to connect, and speech to be heard. Then, in the second year, infants shape their noisemaking quickly to whatever language they hear. Toddlers are naturally endowed to learn vocabulary simply by overhearing it, as many parents discover—occasionally to their dismay (Akhtar et al., 2001).

Theory Three: Social Impulses Foster Infant Language

The third theory is called *social-pragmatic* because it perceives the crucial starting point to be neither vocabulary reinforcement (behaviorism) nor the innate connection (epigenetic), but rather the social reason for language: communication.

BRAND X PICTURES / ALAMY

Not Talking? No words yet, but this infant communicates well with Dad, using eyes, mouth, and hands. What are they telling each other?

According to this perspective, infants communicate in every way they can because humans are social beings, dependent on one another for survival and joy.

Newborns look searchingly at human faces and listen intently to human voices because they seek to respond to emotions, not because they want to know content. Before age 1, infants vocalize, babble, gesture, listen, and point—with an outstretched little index finger that is soon accompanied by a very sophisticated glance to see if the other person is looking at the right spot. These and many other examples show that communication is the servant of social interaction (Bloom, 1998).

Here is an experiment. Suppose an 18-month-old is playing with an unnamed toy and an adult utters a word. Does the child connect that word to the toy? A behaviorist, learning-by-association prediction would be yes, but the answer is no. When toddlers played with a fascinating toy and adults said a word, the toddlers looked up, figured out what the adult was looking at, and assigned the new word to that, not to the fascinating toy (Baldwin, 1993). This supports theory three: The toddlers were socially focused.

According to theory three, then, social impulses, not explicit teaching or brain maturation (as in the first two perspectives), lead infants to learn language, "as part of the package of being a human social animal" (Hollich et al., 2000). They seek to understand what others want and intend, and therefore "children acquire linguistic symbols as a kind of by-product of social action with adults" (Tomasello, 2001).

➤Response for Nurses and Pediatricians (from page 172): While much of language development is indeed hardwired, many experts assert that exposure to language is required. You don't need to convince Bob and Joan of this point, though—just convince them that their baby will be happier if they talk to him.

A Hybrid Theory

Which of these three perspectives is correct? As you can see, each position has been supported by research. Scholars have attempted to integrate all three perspectives, notably in a monograph based on 12 experiments designed by eight researchers (Hollich et al., 2000). The authors developed a hybrid (which literally means "a new creature, formed by combining other living things") of previous theories. They called their model an *emergentist coalition* because it combines valid aspects of several theories about the emergence of language during infancy.

These researchers point out that children learn language to do numerous things—indicate intention, call objects by name, put words together, talk to family members, sing to themselves, express their wishes, remember the past, and much more. Therefore, the scientists hypothesize that some aspects of language are best learned in one way at one age, others in another way at another age.

Especially for Babysitters Should you do anything for your clients' infants besides keeping them safe and clean?

For example, the name of the family dog may be learned by association and repetition, with family members and eventually the dog itself reinforcing the name, a behaviorist process. However, the distinction between *cat* and *dog* may reflect a neurological predilection (epigenetic), which means that the human brain may be genetically wired to differentiate those species.

Which theory do you think explains the fact that the 6-month-old's ability to hear a difference in sounds predicts that child's ability to talk at 13 months, 18 months, and 24 months? This could be the result of listening to many words (behaviorist), of inborn potential (Chomsky), or of social impulses (sociocultural). After intensive study, the scientists who reported that hearing differences lead to spoken proficiency endorsed a hybrid theory, concluding that "multiple attentional, social and linguistic cues" contribute to early language (Tsao et al., 2004, p. 1081).

Another study supporting the hybrid theory began, as did a study previously mentioned (Baldwin, 1993), with infants looking at objects that they had never seen and never heard named. One of each pair was fascinating to babies and the other was boring, specifically "a blue sparkle wand . . . [paired with] a white cabinet latch . . . a red, green, and pink party clacker . . . [paired with] a beige bottle opener" (Pruden et al., 2006, p. 267).

The experimenter said a made-up name (not an actual word), and then the infants were tested to see if they assigned the word to the object that had the experimenter's attention (the dull one) or the one that was interesting to the child. These were 10-month-old infants, not 18-month-old toddlers as in the earlier experiment, and they seemed to assign the word to the fascinating object, not the dull one. This response is what behaviorists, not social-pragmatists, would predict, because the more rewarding object was named.

These researchers interpret their experiment as supporting the emergentist-coalition model, which holds that *how* language is learned depends on the particular circumstances. Behaviorism works for young children, social learning for slightly older ones: "The perceptually driven 10-month-old becomes the socially aware 19-month-old" (Pruden et al., 2006, p. 278).

It makes logical and practical sense for nature to provide several paths toward language learning. Each path may be preferred or more efficient in some stages, cultures, and families, but every child learns to communicate and uses a variety of ways to do so. This hybrid perspective returns the child to center stage: Infants are active learners not only of the concepts described in the first half of this chapter but also of language, and they use many ways to master knowledge. As one expert concludes:

> Word learning theories will have to come to terms with the fact that children . . . are more than perceivers, receivers, or possessors of external supports. Instead, the word learning child is a child with feelings and thoughts about other persons, a child engaged in dynamic real-life events, a child learning to think about a world of changing physical and psychological relationships—in short, a child poised to act, to influence, to gain control . . . to embrace the learning of language for the power of expression it provides.
>
> *[Bloom, 2000, p. 13]*

Especially for Educators An infant day-care center has a new child whose parents speak a language other than the one the teachers speak. Should the teachers learn basic words in the new language, or should they expect the baby to learn the majority language?

SUMMING UP

From the first days of life, babies attend to words and expressions, responding as well as their limited abilities allow—crying, cooing, and soon babbling. Before age 1, they understand simple words and communicate with gestures. At 1 year, most infants speak. Vocabulary accumulates slowly at first, but then more rapidly with the naming explosion and with the emergence of the holophrase and the two-word sentence.

The impressive language learning of the first two years can be explained in many ways. One theory contends that caregivers must teach language, reinforcing the infant's vocal expressions. Another theory relies on the idea of an inborn language acquisition device, a mental structure that facilitates the acquisition of language as soon as maturation makes that possible. A third theory stresses social interaction, implying that infants learn language because they are social beings. A hybrid model combines all three of these theories. Because infants vary in culture, learning style, and social context, the hybrid theory acknowledges that each of the other theories may have some validity at different points in the acquisition of language. ■

SUMMARY

Sensorimotor Intelligence

1. Piaget realized that very young infants are active learners, seeking to understand their complex observations and experiences. Adaptation in infancy is characterized by sensorimotor intelligence, the first of Piaget's four stages of cognitive development. At every time of their lives, people adapt their thoughts to the experiences they have.

2. Sensorimotor intelligence develops in six stages—three pairs of two stages each—beginning with reflexes and ending with the toddler's active exploration and use of mental combinations. In each pair of stages, development occurs in one of three types of circular reactions, or feedback loops, in which the infant takes in experiences and tries to make sense of them.

3. Reflexes provide the foundation for intelligence. The continual process of assimilation and accommodation is evident in the first acquired adaptations, from about 1 to 4 months. The sucking reflex accommodates the particular nipples and other objects that the baby learns to suck. As time goes on, infants become more goal-oriented, creative, and experimental as "little scientists."

4. Infants gradually develop an understanding of objects over the first two years of life. As shown in Piaget's classic experiment, infants understand object permanence and begin to search for hidden objects at about 8 months. Other research finds that Piaget underestimated the cognition of young infants.

Information Processing

5. Another approach to understanding infant cognition is information-processing theory, which looks at each step of the thinking process, from input to output. The perceptions of a young infant are attuned to the particular affordances, or opportunities for action, that are present in the infant's world.

6. Objects that move are particularly interesting to infants, as are other humans. Objects as well as people afford many possibilities for interaction and perception, and therefore these affordances enhance early cognition.

7. Infant memory is fragile but not completely absent. Reminder sessions help trigger memories, and young brains learn motor sequences long before they can remember verbally. Memory is multifaceted; explicit memories are rare in infancy.

Language: What Develops in the First Two Years?

8. Eager attempts to communicate are apparent in the first year. Infants babble at about 6 to 9 months, understand words and gestures by 10 months, and speak their first words at about 1 year.

9. Vocabulary begins to build very slowly until the infant knows approximately 50 words. Then a naming explosion begins. Toward the end of the second year, toddlers begin putting two words together, showing by their word order that they understand the rudiments of grammar.

10. Various theories attempt to explain how infants learn language as quickly as they do. The three main theories emphasize different aspects of early language learning: that infants must be taught, that their brains are genetically attuned to language, and that their social impulses foster language learning.

11. Each of these theories seems partly true. The challenge for developmental scientists has been to formulate a hybrid theory that uses all the insights and research on early language learning. The challenge for caregivers is to respond appropriately to the infant's early attempts to communicate.

KEY TERMS

sensorimotor intelligence (p. 155)
primary circular reactions (p. 156)
secondary circular reactions (p. 157)
object permanence (p. 158)
tertiary circular reactions (p. 159)
"little scientist" (p. 159)
deferred imitation (p. 159)
habituation (p. 160)
fMRI (p. 160)
information-processing theory (p. 161)
affordance (p. 162)
visual cliff (p. 163)
dynamic perception (p. 164)
people preference (p. 164)
reminder session (p. 165)
child-directed speech (p. 168)
babbling (p. 169)
naming explosion (p. 169)
holophrase (p. 170)
grammar (p. 171)
language acquisition device (LAD) (p. 173)

KEY QUESTIONS

1. Why is Piaget's first period of cognitive development called sensorimotor intelligence? Give examples.

2. Give examples of some things adults learn via sensorimotor intelligence.

3. What does the active experimentation of the stage-five toddler suggest for parents?

4. Why are some researchers concerned about too much emphasis being placed on early brain development?

5. How do researchers figure out whether an infant has a concept of something even if the infant cannot talk about it yet?

6. What does research on affordances suggest about cognitive differences between one infant and another?

7. Why would a child remember very little about experiences in infancy?

8. What indicates that toddlers use some grammar?

9. How do deaf and hearing babies compare in early language learning?

10. How would a caregiver who subscribes to the behaviorist theory of language learning respond when an infant babbles?

11. According to the sociocultural theory of language learning, what might explain why an 18-month-old is not yet talking?

12. What does the research on language learning suggest to caregivers?

APPLICATIONS

1. Elicit vocalizations from an infant—babbling if the baby is under age 1, words if older. Write down all the baby says for 10 minutes. Then ask the primary caregiver to elicit vocalizations for 10 minutes, and write these down. What differences are apparent between the baby's two attempts at communication? Compare your findings with the norms described in the chapter.

2. Piaget's definition of intelligence is adaptation. Others consider a good memory or an extensive vocabulary to be a sign of intelligence. How would you define intelligence? Give examples.

3. Many educators recommend that parents read to babies even before the babies begin talking. What theory of language development does this reflect?

4. Test an infant's ability to search for a hidden object. Ideally, the infant should be about 7 or 8 months old, and you should retest over a period of weeks. If the infant can immediately find the object, make the task harder by pausing between the hiding and searching or by secretly moving the object from one hiding place to another.

➤**Response for Babysitters** (from page 174): Yes. Babies need to hear language, so you can assist in their language development by talking and singing to them.

➤**Response for Educators** (from page 175): Probably both. Infants love to communicate, and they seek every possible way to do so. Therefore, the teachers should try to understand the baby, and the baby's parents, but should also start teaching the baby the majority language of the school.

7

CHAPTER OUTLINE

The First Two Years: Psychosocial Development

The dynamic interaction of infants' emotions and their social contexts is the substance of this chapter. You have witnessed this interplay whenever you have seen a tiny baby smile at an engaging face or a toddler flop to the floor, kicking and screaming, after being told "no." I continue to be surprised by mothers and babies.

As I sat on a crowded subway train, a young woman boarded with an infant in one arm and a heavy shopping bag on the other. She tried to steady herself as the train started to move. I asked, "Can I help you?" Wordlessly she handed me . . . the baby. I began softly singing a children's song. The baby was very quiet, keeping her eyes on her mother. That was a psychosocial moment for all three of us.

This chapter opens with a much longer psychosocial episode, the early development of a boy named Jacob. Then we trace infant emotions over the first two years. This discussion is followed by a review of the five theories first described in Chapter 2, with an overview of what each has to say about psychosocial development in infancy. This leads us into an exploration of research on caregiver–infant interaction, particularly *synchrony, attachment,* and *social referencing*—all pivotal to psychosocial development. We then consider the pros and cons of infant day care. The chapter ends with practical suggestions regarding Jacob, whose story appears below.

a case to study

Parents on Autopilot

A father writes about his third child, Jacob:

> [My wife, Rebecca, and I] were convinced that we were set. We had surpassed our quota of 2.6 children and were ready to engage parental autopilot. I had just begun a prestigious job and was working 10–11 hours a day. The children would be fine. We hired a nanny to watch Jacob during the day. As each of Jacob's early milestones passed, we felt that we had taken another step toward our goal of having three normal children. We were on our way to the perfect American family. Yet, somewhere back in our minds we had some doubts. Jacob seemed different than the girls. He had some unusual attributes. There were times when we would be holding him and he would arch his back and scream so loud that it was painful for us.
>
> [*Jacob's father, 1997, p. 59*]

As an infant, Jacob did not relate to his parents (or to anyone else). His parents paid little heed to his psychosocial difficulties, focusing instead on physical development. They noted that Jacob sat up and walked on schedule, and when they "had some doubts," they found excuses, telling themselves that "boys are different" or that Jacob's language delays stemmed from the fact that his nanny spoke little English. As time went on, however, their excuses fell short. His father continues:

> Jacob had become increasingly isolated [by age 2]. I'm not a psychologist, but I believe that he just stopped trying. It was too hard, perhaps too scary. He couldn't figure out what was expected of him. The world had become too confusing, and so he withdrew from it. He would seek out the comfort of quiet, dark places and sit by himself. He would lose himself in the bright, colorful images of cartoons and animated movies.
>
> *[Jacob's father, 1997, p. 62]*

Jacob was finally diagnosed at age 3 with "pervasive developmental disorder." This is a catchall diagnosis that can include autism (discussed in Chapter 11). At the moment, you need to know only that Jacob's psychosocial potential was unappreciated. His despairing parents were advised to consider residential placement because Jacob would always need special care and, with Jacob living elsewhere, they would not be constantly reminded of their "failure." This recommendation did not take into account the commitment that Jacob's parents, like most parents, felt toward their child.

Yet, despite their commitment, they had ignored signs of trouble, overlooking their son's sometimes violent reaction to being held and his failure to talk. The absence of smiling, of social play, and of imitation should have raised an alarm. The father's use of the word *autopilot* shows that he realized this in hindsight. Later in this chapter, you will learn the outcome.

TABLE 7.1

AT ABOUT THIS TIME: Ages When Emotions Emerge

Age	Emotional Expression
Birth	Crying; contentment
6 weeks	Social smile
3 months	Laughter; curiosity
4 months	Full, responsive smiles
4–8 months	Anger
9–14 months	Fear of social events (strangers, separation from caregiver)
12 months	Fear of unexpected sights and sounds
18 months	Self-awareness; pride; shame; embarrassment

Emotional Development

Within the first two years, infants progress from reactive pain and pleasure to complex patterns of social awareness (see Table 7.1). This is the period of life with "high emotional responsiveness" (Izard et al., 2002, p. 767), marked by speedy, uncensored reactions—crying, startling, laughing, raging—and, by toddlerhood, complex responses, from self-satisfied grins to mournful pouts.

Specific Emotions

At first there is pleasure and pain. Newborns look happy and relaxed when fed and drifting off to sleep. They cry when they are hurt or hungry, are tired or frightened (as by a loud noise or a sudden loss of support), or have *colic,* the recurrent bouts of uncontrollable crying and irritability that afflict about a third of all infants in the early months.

Soon, additional emotions become recognizable (Lavelli & Fogel, 2005). Curiosity is increasingly evident as infants distinguish the unusual from the familiar (Kagan, 2002). Happiness is expressed by the **social smile** in response to a human face at about 6 weeks and by laughter at about 3 or 4 months. Parents elicit laughter, and so do adept strangers. Among the Navajo, whoever brings forth that first laugh gives a feast to celebrate that the baby is becoming a person (Rogoff, 2003). Laughter builds as curiosity does, so that a typical 6-month-old not only discovers new things but also laughs loudly, with evident joy.

social smile A smile evoked by a human face, normally evident in infants about 6 weeks after birth.

Anger is evident at 6 months, usually triggered by frustration. It is most apparent when infants are prevented from reaching a graspable object or moving as they wish (Plutchik, 2003). One-year-olds hate to be strapped in, caged in, closed in, or just held tight on someone's lap when they want to explore. Anger in infancy is a healthy response to frustration, unlike sadness, which also appears in the first months. Sadness indicates withdrawal and is accompanied by an increase in the level of *cortisol,* a stress hormone (M. Lewis & D. Ramsay, 2005). Reliable hormone assays are more difficult with infants than with older people, so not all the hormonal changes that accompany infant emotions are known. However, the fact that sadness brings stress suggests that sorrow is not a superficial emotion for infants.

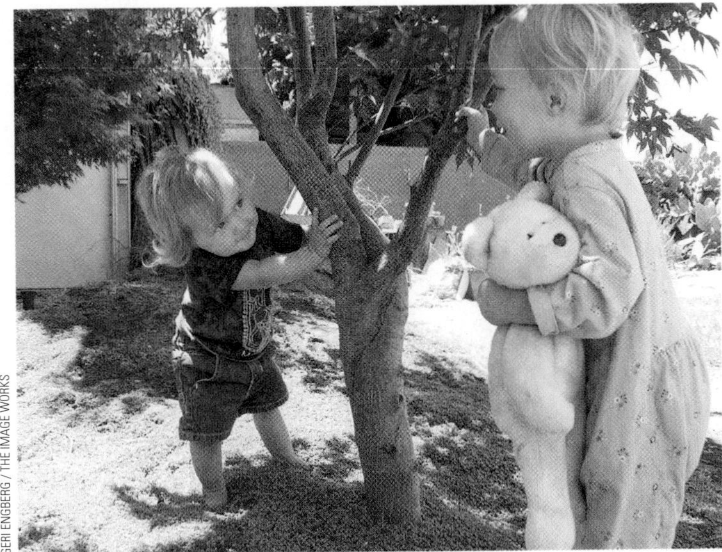
GERI ENGBERG / THE IMAGE WORKS

Friendship Begins Emotions connect friends to each other—these two 1-year-olds as well as friends of any age. The shared smiles indicate a strong social connection. What will they do next?

Fully formed fear in response to some person, thing, or situation (not just distress at a surprise) emerges at about 9 months and then rapidly becomes more frequent as well as more apparent (Kagan, 1998). Two fears are obvious:

- **Stranger wariness,** when an infant no longer smiles at any friendly face, and cries if an unfamiliar person moves too close, too quickly
- **Separation anxiety,** expressed in tears, dismay, or anger when a familiar caregiver leaves

stranger wariness An infant's expression of concern—a quiet stare, clinging to a familiar person, or sadness—when a stranger appears.

separation anxiety An infant's distress when a familiar caregiver leaves; most obvious between 9 and 14 months.

Separation anxiety is normal at age 1, intensifies by age 2, and usually subsides after that. If it remains strong after age 3, it is considered an emotional disorder (Silverman & Dick-Niederhauser, 2004).

Many 1-year-olds fear not just strangers but also anything unexpected, from the flush of a toilet to the pop of a jack-in-the-box, from the sudden closing of elevator doors to the friendly approach of a dog. With repeated experiences and caregiver protection, older infants might themselves enjoy flushing the toilet (again and again) or calling the dog (crying if the dog does *not* come).

Many emotions that emerge in the first months of life take on new strength at about age 1 (Kagan, 2002). Throughout the second year and beyond, anger and fear typically become less frequent but more focused, targeted toward infuriating or terrifying experiences. Similarly, laughing and crying become louder and more discriminating.

New emotions appear toward the end of the second year: pride, shame, embarrassment, and guilt. These emotions require an awareness of other people. They emerge from family interactions, influenced by the culture (Eid & Diener, 2001). For example, pride is encouraged in North American toddlers ("You did it all by yourself"—even when that is

JOURNAL-COURIER / TIFFANY HERMON / THE IMAGE WORKS

Stranger Wariness Becomes Santa Terror For toddlers, even a friendly stranger is cause for alarm, especially if Mom's protective arms are withdrawn. The most frightening strangers are men who are unusually dressed and who act as if they might take the child away. Ironically, therefore, Santa Claus remains terrifying until children are about 3 years old.

Especially for Nurses and Pediatricians Parents come to you concerned that their 1-year-old hides her face and holds onto them tightly whenever a stranger appears. What do you tell them?

untrue), but Asian families discourage pride and cultivate modesty and shame (Rogoff, 2003).

Two-year-olds have many emotional reactions. They are taught which expressions of emotion are acceptable and which are not (Saarni et al., 2006). For example, if a toddler holds on tightly to his mother's skirt and hides his face when a friendly but strange dog approaches, the mother could pick the child up or bend down to pet the dog. The mother's response encourages fear or happiness when a dog next appears.

Self-Awareness

self-awareness A person's realization that he or she is a distinct individual, with body, mind, and actions that are separate from those of other people.

In addition to social interactions, another foundation for emotional growth is **self-awareness,** the infant's realization that his or her body, mind, and actions are separate from those of other people (R. A. Thompson, 2006). At about age 1, an emerging sense of "me" and "mine" leads to a new consciousness of others. As one developmentalist explains:

> With the emergence of consciousness in the second year of life, we see vast changes in both children's emotional life and the nature of their social relationships. . . . The child can feel . . . self-conscious emotions, like pride at a job well done or shame over a failure.
>
> *[M. Lewis, 1997, p. 132]*

Very young infants have no sense of self—at least, of *self* as some people define it. In fact, a prominent psychoanalyst, Margaret Mahler, theorized that for the first 4 months of life infants see themselves as part of their mothers. They "hatch" at about 5 months and spend the next several months developing a sense of themselves as separate from their mothers (Mahler et al., 1975). The period from 15 to 18 months "is noteworthy for the emergence of the *Me-self,* the sense of self as the *object* of one's knowledge" (Harter, 1998, p. 562).

In a classic experiment (M. Lewis & J. Brooks, 1978), babies aged 9–24 months looked into a mirror after a dot of rouge had been surreptitiously put on their noses. If the babies reacted by touching their noses, that meant they knew the mirror showed their own faces. None of the babies less than 12 months old reacted as if they knew the mark was on them (they sometimes smiled and touched the dot on the "other" baby in the mirror). However, those between 15 and 24 months usually showed self-awareness, touching their own noses with curiosity and puzzlement.

LAURA DWIGHT

She Knows Herself This 18-month-old is happy to see herself in her firefighter's helmet. She is adjusting the helmet with her hands on it, and that's evidence that she understands what a mirror is. Note, however, that she is not yet aware that a hat has a front and a back.

Self-recognition usually emerges at about 18 months, at the same time as two other advances: pretending and using first-person pronouns (*I, me, mine, myself, my*). Some developmentalists connect self-recognition with self-understanding (e.g., Gallup et al., 2002), although "the interpretation of this seemingly simple task is plagued by controversy" (Nielsen et al., 2006, p. 166).

Pride and shame seem to be, at this phase, linked to the maturing self-concept, not necessarily to other people's opinions. If someone tells a toddler, "You're very smart," the child may smile but usually already feels smart—and thus is already pleased and proud. Telling toddlers that they are smart, strong, or beautiful may even be unhelpful.

One longitudinal study found that positive comments from mothers to 2-year-olds did *not* lead to more pride or less shame by age 3 (Kelley et al., 2000). However, certain negative comments (such as "You're doing it all wrong") diminished effort and increased shame. Neutral suggestions fostered a willingness to try new challenges. Toddlers' self-esteem seems to result more from accomplishments than from praise.

SUMMING UP

Newborns seem to have only two simple emotions, distress and contentment, which are expressed by crying or looking happy. Very soon curiosity and obvious joy, with social smiles and laughter, appear. By the second half of the first year, anger and fear are increasingly evident, especially in reaction to social experiences, such as encountering a stranger. In the second year, as infants become self-aware, they express emotions connected to themselves, including pride, shame, and embarrassment, and emotions about other people. Universal maturation makes these emotions possible at around 18 months, but context and learning affect their timing, frequency, and intensity. ■

Theories About Infant Psychosocial Development

The five major theories described in Chapter 2 have somewhat different perspectives on the origin and significance of infants' emotions.

Psychoanalytic Theory

Psychoanalytic theory connects biosocial and psychosocial development, emphasizing the need for responsive maternal care. Both major psychoanalytic theorists, Sigmund Freud and Erik Erikson, described two distinct early stages. Freud (1935, 1940/1964) wrote about the *oral stage* and the *anal stage*. Erikson (1963) called his first stages *trust versus mistrust* and *autonomy versus shame and doubt*.

Freud: Oral and Anal Stages

According to Freud (1935), psychological development in the first year of life is in the *oral stage*, so named because the mouth is the young infant's primary source of gratification. In the second year, with the *anal stage*, the infant's main pleasure comes from the anus—particularly from the sensual pleasure of bowel movements and, eventually, the psychological pleasure of controlling them.

Freud believed that both the oral and anal stages are fraught with potential conflicts that have long-term consequences. If a mother frustrates her infant's urge to suck—weaning the infant too early, for example, or preventing the child from sucking on fingers or toes—the child may become distressed and anxious, eventually becoming an adult with an *oral fixation*. Such a person is stuck (fixated) at the oral stage and therefore eats, drinks, chews, bites, or talks excessively, in quest of the mouth-related pleasure denied in infancy.

Similarly, if toilet training is overly strict or if it begins before the infant is mature enough, parent–infant interaction may become locked into a conflict over the toddler's refusal, or inability, to comply. The child becomes fixated and develops an *anal personality*—as an adult, seeking self-control with an unusually strong need for regularity in all aspects of life.

Especially for Nursing Mothers You have heard that if you wean your child too early, he or she will overeat or become an alcoholic. Is it true?

Erikson: Trust and Autonomy

According to Erikson, the first crisis of life is **trust versus mistrust,** when infants learn whether the world can be trusted to satisfy basic needs. Babies feel secure when food and comfort are provided with "consistency, continuity, and sameness of experience" (Erikson, 1963, p. 247). If social interaction inspires trust and security, the child (and later the adult) will confidently explore the social world.

trust versus mistrust Erikson's first psychosocial crisis. Infants learn basic trust if the world is a secure place where their basic needs (for food, comfort, attention, etc.) are met.

JOSE LUIS PELEAZ, INC. / CORBIS

A Mother's Dilemma Infants are wonderfully curious, as this little boy demonstrates. Parents, however, must guide as well as encourage the drive toward autonomy. Notice this mother's expression as she makes sure her son does not crush or eat the flower.

autonomy versus shame and doubt Erikson's second crisis of psychosocial development. Toddlers either succeed or fail in gaining a sense of self-rule over their own actions and bodies.

The next crisis is called **autonomy versus shame and doubt.** Toddlers want autonomy (self-rule) over their own actions and bodies. If they fail to gain it, they feel ashamed of their actions and doubtful about their abilities.

Some cultures encourage independence and autonomy (as in the United States); in others (for example, China) "shame is a normative emotion that develops as parents use explicit shaming techniques" to encourage children's loyalty and harmony within their families (Mascolo et al., 2003, p. 402). Westerners expect toddlers to go through the stubborn and defiant "terrible twos"; parents in many non-Western societies expect the opposite.

Like Freud, Erikson believed that problems arising in early infancy could last a lifetime, creating an adult who is suspicious and pessimistic (mistrusting) or who is easily shamed (insufficient autonomy). These traits could be destructive or not, depending on the norms and expectations of the culture.

Behaviorism

From the perspective of behaviorism, emotions and personality are molded as parents reinforce or punish the child's spontaneous behaviors. For example, if parents smile and pick up their infant at every glimmer of a grin, he or she will become a child—and later an adult—with a sunny disposition. The opposite is also true. Early behaviorists, especially John Watson, expressed this idea in very strong terms:

> Failure to bring up a happy child, a well-adjusted child—assuming bodily health —falls squarely upon the parents' shoulders. [By the time the child is 3] parents have already determined . . . [whether the child] is to grow into a happy person, wholesome and good-natured, whether he is to be a whining, complaining neurotic, an anger-driven, vindictive, over-bearing slave driver, or one whose every move in life is definitely controlled by fear.
>
> [*Watson, 1928, pp. 7, 45*]

social learning Learning by observing others.

Later behaviorists noted that infants also experience **social learning,** which is learning by observing others, as in Albert Bandura's experiment in which young children who had seen an adult punching a rubber Bobo clown treated the doll the same way (Bandura, 1977). Social learning is apparent in many families, when toddlers express emotions—from giggling to cursing—in much the same way their parents or older siblings do. A boy might develop a hot temper, for instance, if his father's outbursts seem to win respect from his mother.

➤Response for Nurses and Pediatricians (from page 182): Stranger wariness is normal up to about 14 months. This baby's behavior actually sounds like secure attachment!

Both psychoanalytic and behaviorist theories emphasize parents. Freud thought that the mother was the young child's first and most enduring "love object," and behaviorists stress the power of a mother over her children. In retrospect, this focus seems too narrow. The other three theories reflect more recent research and the changing historical context.

Cognitive Theory

Cognitive theory holds that thoughts and values determine a person's perspective. Early experiences are important because beliefs, perceptions, and memories make them so, not because they are buried in the unconscious (psychoanalytic theory) or burned into the brain's patterns (behaviorism).

working model In cognitive theory, a set of assumptions that the individual uses to organize perceptions and experiences. For example, a person might assume that other people are trustworthy, and be surprised when this model of human behavior seems in error.

Infants use their early relationships to develop a **working model,** a set of assumptions that become a frame of reference that can be called on later in life (Bretherton & Munholland, 1999; R. A. Thompson & Raikes, 2003). It is called a "model" because these early relationships form a prototype, or blueprint, for later relationships; it is called "working" because, while usable, it is not necessarily fixed or final.

For example, a 1-year-old girl might develop a working model, based on her parents' inconsistent responses to her, that people are unpredictable. All her life she will apply that model whenever she meets a new person. Her childhood relationships will be insecure, and in adulthood she might be on guard against further disappointment. To use Piaget's terminology, she has developed a cognitive *schema* to organize her perceptions. According to cognitive theory, a child's *interpretation* of early experiences is crucial, not necessarily the experiences themselves (Schaffer, 2000).

The hopeful message of cognitive theory is that people can rethink and reorganize their thoughts, developing new working models that are more positive than their original ones. Our mistrustful girl can learn to trust if her later experiences—such as marriage to a faithful and loving husband—provide a new model.

➤Response for Nursing Mothers (from page 183): Freud thought so, but there is no experimental evidence that weaning, even when ill timed, has such dire long-term effects.

Epigenetic Theory

As you remember from Chapter 2, epigenetic theory holds that every human characteristic is strongly influenced by each person's unique genotype. Thus, a child might be happy or anxious not because of early experiences (the three grand theories) but because of inborn predispositions. DNA remains the same from conception on, no matter how emotions are blocked (psychoanalytic theory), reinforced (behaviorism), or interpreted (cognitive theory).

Temperament

Among each person's genetic predispositions are the traits of **temperament,** defined as "constitutionally based individual differences" in emotions, activity, and self-regulation (Rothbart & Bates, 2006, p. 100). "Constitutionally based" means that these traits originate with nature (genes) more than nurture.

temperament Inborn differences between one person and another in emotions, activity, and self-control. Temperament is epigenetic, originating in genes but affected by child-rearing practices.

The concept of temperament is similar to that of personality. Some researchers believe that the line between temperament and personality is unclear (e.g., Caspi & Shiner, 2006). Generally, however, personality traits (e.g., honesty and humility) are considered to be primarily learned, whereas temperamental traits (e.g., shyness and aggression) are considered to be primarily genetic. Although temperamental traits originate with the genes, the way these traits are expressed can be modified by experiences.

CORROON AND COMPANY / MONKMEYER

Twins They were born on the same day and now are experiencing a wading pool for the first time.

Observation Quiz (see answer, page 186): Are these babies monozygotic or dizygotic twins?

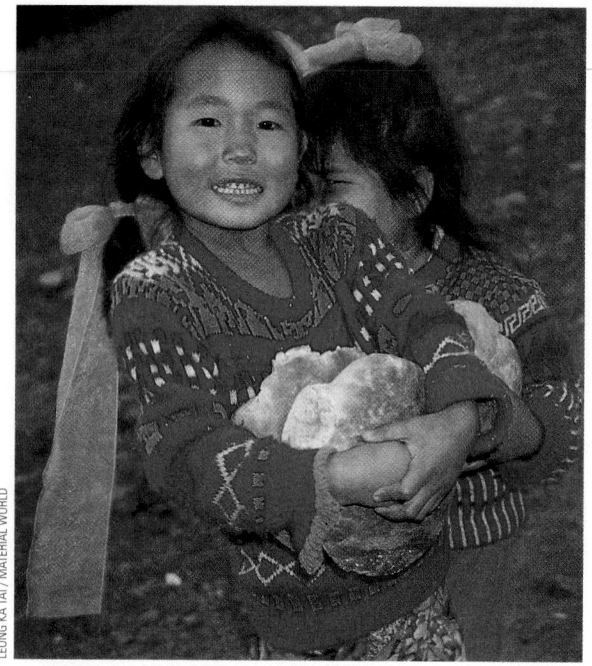

LEONG KA TAI / MATERIAL WORLD

Which Sister Has a Personality Problem? Culture always affects the expression of temperament. In Mongolia and many other Asian countries, females are expected to display shyness as a sign of respect to elders and strangers. Consequently, if the younger of these sisters is truly as shy as she seems, her parents are less likely to be distressed about her withdrawn behavior than the typical North American parent would be. Conversely, they may consider the relative boldness of her older sister to be a serious problem.

In laboratory studies of temperament, some infants have experiences that might be frightening. Four-month-olds might see spinning mobiles or hear unusual sounds. Older babies might confront a noisy, moving robot or a clown who quickly moves close. At such experiences, some children laugh (and are classified as "easy"), some cry ("difficult"), and some are quiet ("slow to warm up") (Fox et al., 2001; Kagan & Snidman, 2004).

The categories of "easy," "difficult," and "slow to warm up" come from a classic study called the *New York Longitudinal Study* (NYLS). Begun in the 1960s, the NYLS was the first among many studies to recognize that each newborn has distinct inborn traits. Although temperament begins in the brain, it is difficult to detect via brain scans, so most of the research uses parents' reports and direct observation. In order to avoid merely reflecting the parents' hopes and biases, researchers ask for specifics. As the NYLS researchers explain:

> If a mother said that her child did not like his first solid food, we . . . were satisfied only when she gave a description such as "When I put the food into his mouth he cried loudly, twisted his head away, and let it drool out."
>
> *[Chess et al., 1965, p. 26]*

According to the NYLS, by 3 months, infants manifest nine temperamental traits that can be clustered into the three categories described above, with a fourth category of "hard to classify" infants:

- Easy (40 percent)
- Difficult (10 percent)
- Slow to warm up (15 percent)
- Hard to classify (35 percent)

Other researchers began by studying adult personality traits and came up with the "Big Five" (whose first letters form the easy-to-remember acronym *OCEAN*):

- Openness: imaginative, curious, welcoming new experiences
- Conscientiousness: organized, deliberate, conforming
- Extroversion: outgoing, assertive, active
- Agreeableness: kind, helpful, easygoing
- Neuroticism: anxious, moody, self-critical

As is further explained in Chapter 22, the Big Five traits are found in many cultures, among people of all ages (McCrae & Costa, 2003). This universality adds to the evidence that some basic temperamental differences are innate, preceding child-rearing practices and cultural values (Rothbart et al., 2000). The Big Five are more complex than the easy/difficult/slow-to-warm-up classifications; but an infant high in agreeableness might be classified as easy, one high in neuroticism would be difficult, and one low in openness would be slow to warm up.

➤Answer to Observation Quiz (from page 185): True tests of zygosity involve analysis of blood type, although physical appearance often provides some clues. Here such clues are minimal: We cannot see differences in sex, coloring, or hand formation—although the shapes of the skulls seem different. The best clue from this photo is personality. Confronting their first experience in a wading pool, these twins are showing such a difference on the approach–withdrawal dimension of temperament that they are probably dizygotic.

The Parents' Role

Studies of temperament find that the traits found in the NYLS or described by the Big Five correspond to clusters of behaviors that appear early in life. Easy babies are happy and outgoing most of the time, adjusting quickly to almost any change. Difficult babies are the opposite: irregular, intense, unhappy, disturbed by every noise, and hard to distract—quite a handful. Slow-to-warm-up babies take their time to adapt to new people and experiences.

One longitudinal study (Fox et al., 2001) identified three distinct groups—positive (exuberant), negative, and inhibited (fearful)—at 4 months. (Many infants fit into none of these groups.) The researchers followed the children in each group, with laboratory measures, mothers' reports, and brain scans at 9, 14, 24, and 48 months. Half were very stable in temperament, reacting the same way and having similar brain-wave patterns when confronted with frightening experiences all four times they were tested.

The other half changed their reaction to frightening experiences on at least one later assessment. Those who had been fearful at 4 months were most likely to change, and the exuberant infants were least likely to change (see Figure 7.1). That speaks to the influence of child rearing, since parents and other adults are likely to coax frightened children to be braver but usually encourage happy children to stay positive.

In response to such adult guidance, infant temperament often changes. In general, however, the interaction between cultural influences and inherited traits tends to shape behavior by early childhood (Rothbart & Bates, 2006). Traits that are present at age 3 often are still evident at age 26 (Caspi et al., 2003).

Whatever their child's temperament, parents need to find a **goodness of fit**—that is, a temperamental adjustment that allows smooth infant–caregiver interaction. With a good fit, parents of difficult children are able to build a close relationship; parents of exuberant, curious children learn to protect them from harm; parents of slow-to-warm-up children give them time to adjust.

In general, stubborn and anxious children (i.e., high in neuroticism) are more affected by their mother's responsiveness than positive children are (Pauli-Pott et al., 2004). Ineffective or harsh parenting *combined with* a negative temperament creates antisocial, destructive children (Caspi et al., 2002). Some children naturally cope easily with life's challenges, whereas "a shy child must control his or her fear and approach a stranger, and an impulsive child must constrain his or her desire and resist a temptation" (Derryberry et al., 2003, p. 1061).

The epigenetic perspective emphasizes that inherited differences in temperament are affected by parental behavior (Kagan & Fox, 2006). Parents must first

Especially for Nurses and Pediatricians Parents come to you with their fussy 3-month-old. They say that they have read that temperament is "fixed" before birth, and they are worried that their child will always be difficult. What do you tell them?

goodness of fit A similarity of temperament and values that produces a smooth interaction between an individual and his or her social context, including family, school, and community.

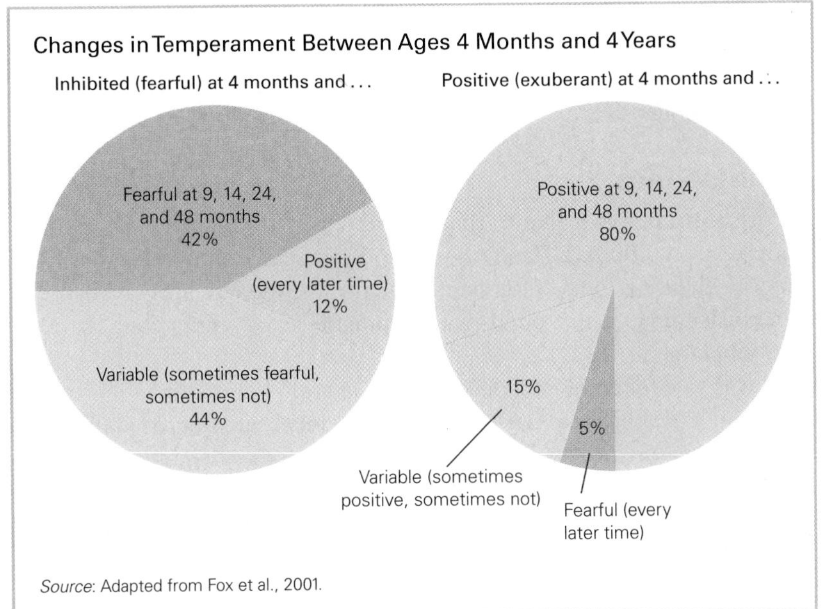

FIGURE 7.1

Do Babies' Temperaments Change? The data suggest that fearful babies are not necessarily fated to remain that way. Adults who are reassuring and do not act frightened themselves can help children overcome an innate fearfulness. Some fearful children do not change, however, and it is not known whether that's because their parents are not sufficiently reassuring (nurture) or because they are temperamentally more fearful (nature).

Observation Quiz (see answer, page 188): Out of 100 4-month-olds who react positively to noises and other experiences, how many are fearful at later times in early childhood?

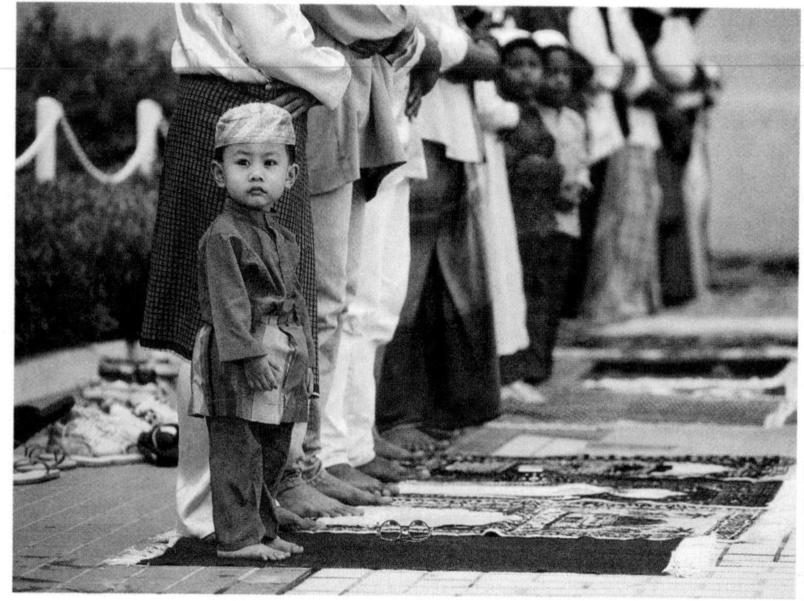

R. IAN LLOYD / MASTERFILE

Learning to Worship This boy in Borneo has learned that Allah is to be shown respect with a covered head and bare feet. He already prays five times a day as part of an ethnotheory that includes concepts of life and death, male and female, good and evil—just like everyone else in the world, although the specifics vary widely.

understand their child's temperamental traits and then teach and guide the child so that those inborn traits are expressed constructively, not destructively.

Many developmentalists caution against too much emphasis on genes, especially in infancy when observations of actual interactions suggest that the mother's parenting style has more influence on the infant's behavior than the infant's temperament does (Roisman & Fraley, 2006). At the same time, it is important to remember that inborn temperament is evident in brain activity as well as in reactions from early infancy, and it influences behavior from childhood through old age (Kagan & Snidman, 2004). (Parenting styles and attitudes are discussed in Chapters 10 and 13.)

➤Response for Nurses and Pediatricians (from page 187): It's too soon to tell. Temperament is not truly "fixed" but variable, especially in the first few months. Many "difficult" infants become happy, successful adolescents and adults.

➤Answer to Observation Quiz (from page 187): Out of 100 4-month-olds, 20 are fearful at least occasionally later in childhood, but only 5 are consistently fearful.

Sociocultural Theory

No one doubts that "human development occurs in a cultural context" (Kagitcibasi, 2003, p. 166). The crucial question is *how much* influence culture has. Sociocultural theorists argue that the influence is substantial, that the entire social and cultural context has a major impact on infant–caregiver relationships and thus on infant development.

Ethnotheories

ethnotheory A theory that underlies the values and practices of a culture and that becomes apparent through analysis and comparison of those practices, although it is not usually apparent to the people within the culture.

An **ethnotheory** is a theory that is embedded in a particular culture or ethnic group (Dasen, 2003). Usually the group members are unaware that their theories underlie their customs. However, as you have already seen with breast-feeding and co-sleeping, many child-rearing practices are connected to ethnotheories (Greenfield et al., 2003).

This is true for emotional development as well. For example, if a culture's ethnotheory includes the idea that ancestors are reincarnated in the younger generation, then "children are not expected to show respect for adults, but adults [are expected to show respect] for their reborn ancestors." Such cultures favor indulgent child-rearing practices, with no harsh punishments. "Western people perceive [these cultures] as extremely lenient" (Dasen, 2003, pp. 149–150).

Especially for Parents of Young Adults U.S. culture includes the term *empty nest,* signifying an ethnotheory about mothers whose children live elsewhere. What cultural values are expressed by that term?

For example, we noted earlier that infants become angry when they are restrained. Nonetheless, many European American parents force their protesting toddlers to sit in strollers, to ride in car seats, to stay in cribs and playpens or behind gates. If toddlers do not lie down quietly to allow diapers to be changed (and few do), some parents simply hold the protesting child still while diapering. Compare this to the approach used by Roberto's parents, below.

a case to study

"Let's Go to Grandma's"

The ethnotheory of Mayan parents includes the belief that children should never be forced to comply with their parents' wishes. When 18-month-old Roberto did not want to wear a diaper, his mother used a false promise, and then a distraction.

> "Let's put on your diaper . . . Let's go to Grandma's . . . We're going to do an errand." This did not work, and the mother invited Roberto to nurse, as she swiftly slipped the diaper on him with the father's assistance. The father announced, "It's over."
>
> *[Rogoff, 2003, p. 204]*

Lack of compliance by toddlers is a problem for many Western parents because their ethnotheory values independence, as Erikson recognized in the name he gave his second stage, autonomy versus shame and doubt. Many Western parents battle with their autonomy-seeking 1-year-olds when the child's self-will manifests itself in stubborn behavior. Yet the parents value independence, so they inadvertently encourage that emotion.

For instance, if a child refuses to get dressed, parents sometimes force compliance by holding the child tight and pulling on clothes as the child cries and kicks. Or, if the room is warm and the child will stay inside, parents might give up and let the child remain half-dressed. Note that, in both cases, one person wins and the other loses, setting the emotional stage for another battle. Roberto's mother chose neither option, even with

> increasing exasperation that the child was wiggling and not standing to facilitate putting on his pants. Her voice softened as Roberto became interested in the ball, and she increased the stakes: "Do you want another toy?" They [father and mother] continued to try to talk Roberto into cooperating, and handed him various objects, which Roberto enjoyed. But still he stubbornly refused to cooperate with dressing. They left him alone for a while. When his father asked if he was ready, Roberto pouted "nono!"
>
> After a bit, the mother told Roberto that she was leaving and waved goodbye. "Are you going with me?" Roberto sat quietly with a worried look. "Then put on your pants, put on your pants to go up the hill." Roberto stared into space, seeming to consider the alternatives. His mother started to walk away, "OK then, I'm going. Goodbye." Roberto started to cry, and his father persuaded, "Put on your pants then!" and his mother asked, "Are you going with me?"
>
> Roberto looked down worriedly, one arm outstretched in half a take-me gesture. "Come on, then," his mother offered the pants and Roberto let his father lift him to a stand and cooperated in putting his legs into the pants and in standing to have them fastened. His mother did not intend to leave; instead she suggested that Roberto dance for the audience. Roberto did a baby version of a traditional dance.
>
> *[Rogoff, 2003, p. 204]*

This is an example of an ethnotheory that "elders protect and guide rather than giving orders or dominating" (Rogoff, 2003, p. 205). A second ethnotheory is apparent as well. Not only did the parents avoid dominating, they also used deception.

If a European American mother threatened to leave and then her child submitted, she probably would take him or her somewhere, because North American ethnotheory holds that false threats lead children to doubt their parents. The bogeyman and Santa Claus are less often invoked by today's educated parents than they were a few generations ago, more because of changed ethnotheory than because of new science.

Proximal and Distal Parenting

Another example of ethnotheory involves how much parents should hold their infants. **Proximal parenting** involves being physically close to a baby, often holding and touching. **Distal parenting** involves keeping one's distance, providing toys, feeding by putting finger food within reach, and talking face to face instead of handling. Those who are convinced that one of these is right are expressing an ethnotheory.

proximal parenting Parenting practices that involve close physical contact with the child's entire body, such as cradling and swinging.

distal parenting Parenting practices that focus on the intellect more than the body, such as talking with the baby and playing with an object.

A longitudinal study comparing child rearing among the Nso people of Cameroon, West Africa, and among Greeks in Athens found marked differences in proximal and distal parenting (H. Keller et al., 2004). The researchers videotaped 78 mothers as they played with their 3-month-old infants. Coders (who did not know the study's hypothesis) rated the play as either proximal (e.g., carrying,

Research Design

Scientists: A team of six from three nations (Germany, Greece, Costa Rica).

Publication: *Child Development* (2004).

Participants: A total of 90 mothers participated when their babies were 3 months old and again when they were 18 months old (32 from Cameroon, 46 from Greece, 12 from Costa Rica). In Greece and Costa Rica, researchers recruited mothers in hospitals. In Cameroon, permission was first sought from the local leader, and then announcements were made among local people.

Design: First, mothers played with their 3-month-olds, and that play was videotaped and coded for particular behaviors. Fifteen months later, the toddlers' self-recognition was assessed with the rouge test, and compliance with preset maternal commands was measured. The mother's frequency of eye contact and body contact with the infant at 3 months was compared with the toddler's self-awareness and compliance at 18 months.

Major conclusion: Toddlers with proximal mothers were more obedient but less self-aware; toddlers with distal mothers tended to show the opposite pattern.

Comment: This is one of the best comparison studies of child-rearing practices in various cultures. Families differed in income and urbanization; these variables need to be explored in other research.

TABLE 7.2

Play Patterns in Rural Cameroon and Urban Greece

Age of Babies	Type of Play	Amount of Time Spent in Play (percent): Nso, Cameroon	Amount of Time Spent in Play (percent): Athens, Greece
3 months	Held by mother	100	31
3 months	Object play	3	40
	Toddler Behavior Measured		
18 months	Self-recognition	3	68
18 months	Compliance (without prompting)	72	2

Source: Adapted from Keller et al., 2004.

swinging, caressing, exercising the child's body) or distal (e.g., face-to-face talking) (see Table 7.2 and Research Design).

The Nso mothers were proximal parents, holding their babies all the time and almost never using objects. The Greek mothers were distal parents, using objects almost half the time and holding their babies less.

The researchers hypothesized that proximal parenting would result in toddlers who were less self-aware but more compliant—traits needed in an interdependent and cooperative society such as rural Cameroon. By contrast, distal parenting might result in toddlers who are self-aware but less obedient—traits needed in modern Athens, where independence, self-reliance, and competition are highly valued.

The predictions were accurate. At 18 months these children were tested on self-awareness (the rouge test) and compliance. The African toddlers didn't recognize themselves in the mirror but obeyed; the opposite was true of the Greek children.

Replicating their own work, these researchers studied a dozen mother–infant pairs in Costa Rica, where play patterns and later toddler behavior were midway between those of the Nso and the Greeks. They then reanalyzed their original longitudinal data, child by child. They found that proximal or distal play at 3 months was highly predictive of toddler behavior, even apart from culture. In other words, Greek mothers who, unlike most of their peers, were proximal parents had more obedient toddlers (H. Keller et al., 2004).

As this study suggested, every aspect of early emotional development interacts with cultural ideas of what is appropriate. For example, other research has found that separation anxiety is more evident in Japan than in Germany, because Japanese infants "have very few experiences with separation from the mother," whereas in Germany "infants are frequently left alone outside of stores or supermarkets" while the mother shops (Saarni et al., 2006, p. 237). From the beginning of life, some emotions are dampened and others are fueled by family responses.

Especially for Parents of Toddlers Your child refuses to stay in the car seat, spits out disliked foods, and almost never does what you say. What can you do?

➤Response for Parents of Young Adults (from page 188): The implication is that human mothers are like sad birds, bereft of their fledglings, who have flown away. Chapter 22 details the accuracy of this ethnotheory.

SUMMING UP

The five major theories differ in their explanations of the origins of early emotions and personality. Psychoanalytic theory stresses the mother's responses to the infant's needs for food and elimination (Freud) or for security and independence (Erikson). Behaviorism also stresses caregiving—especially as parents reinforce the behaviors they want their baby to learn or as they thoughtlessly teach unwanted behaviors.

Learning is also crucial in cognitive theory—not the moment-by-moment learning of behaviorism, but the infant's self-constructed concept, or working model. Epigenetic theory begins with the inherited temperament and then describes how inborn temperament is shaped. Sociocultural theory also sees an interaction between nature and nurture but emphasizes that the diversity of nurture explains much of the diversity of emotions. According to sociocultural theory, child-rearing practices arise from ethnotheories, unexpressed and implicit but very powerful. ■

The Development of Social Bonds

All the theories of development agree that healthy human development depends on social connections, as you have already seen in the abnormal behavior of emotionally deprived Romanian orphans (Chapter 5), in the social exchanges required for language learning (Chapter 6), and in dozens of other examples. All the emotions already described elicit social reactions, and infants are happier and healthier when others (especially their mothers) are nearby (Plutchik, 2003). Now we look closely at infant–caregiver bonds.

Synchrony

Synchrony is a coordinated interaction between caregiver and infant, an exchange in which they respond to each other with split-second timing. Synchrony has been described as the meshing of a finely tuned machine (Snow, 1984), an emotional "attunement" of an improvised musical duet (Stern, 1985), and a smoothly flowing "waltz" (Barnard & Martell, 1995).

synchrony A coordinated, rapid, and smooth exchange of responses between a caregiver and an infant.

Detailed research reveals the mutuality of the interaction: Adults rarely smile at newborns until the infant smiles at them, at which point adults grin broadly and talk animatedly (Lavelli & Fogal, 2005). Since each baby has a unique temperament, parents must be sensitive to their particular infant (Feldman & Eidelman, 2005). Via synchrony, infants learn to read other emotions and to develop the skills of social interaction, such as taking turns and paying attention.

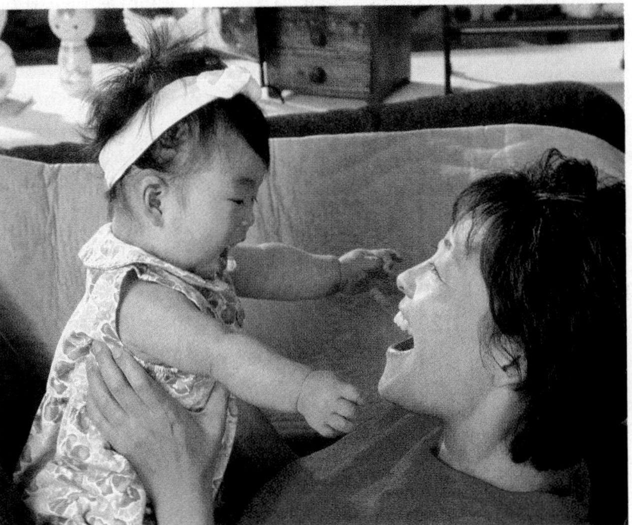

MYRLEEN FERGUSON CATE / PHOTO EDIT

Dance with Me Synchrony in action, with each one's hands, eyes, and open mouth reflecting the other's expression. The close timing of synchrony has been compared to a waltz—and these partners look as if they never miss a beat.

Although infants imitate adults, synchrony usually begins with parents imitating infants (Lavelli & Fogal, 2005). If parents detect an emotion from an infant's expression (easy to do, because infant facial expressions and body motions reflect universally recognizable emotions), and if an infant sees a familiar face expressing that emotion, the infant learns to connect an internal state with an external expression (Rochat, 2001).

For example, suppose an infant is unhappy. An adult who mirrors the distress, and then tries to solve the problem, will teach the infant that although unhappiness is a negative emotion, it is a valid one, and it can be relieved. Obviously, if the adult's reaction to unhappiness is always to feed the infant, that might teach a destructive lesson (food equals comfort regardless of the cause of the distress). But if an adult's reponse is more nuanced (by differentiating hunger, pain, boredom, or fear, for instance, and by responding differently to each), then the infant will learn to perceive the varied reasons for unhappiness and the varied ways of responding to it.

One of the important discoveries regarding synchrony is that adults do not merely echo infant emotions; they try to make them more positive. Thus, when their babies seem angry, mothers tend to react not with anger but with surprise (Malatesta et al., 1989).

➤Response for Parents of Toddlers (from page 190): Remember the origins of the misbehavior—probably a combination of your child's inborn temperament and your own distal parenting. Blended with your ethnotheory, all contribute to the child's being stubborn and independent. Acceptance is more warranted than anger.

Synchrony is experience-expectant, developing connections within the brain (Schore, 2001). For example, parents of triplets spend less time in synchrony with each of them than parents of single infants spend with their child (Feldman et al., 2004); perhaps for that reason, triplet cognition tends to be slightly delayed. Some mothers rarely play with their infants, and that slows down those children's development (Huston & Aronson, 2005). Apparently, infant brains need social interaction to develop to their fullest. Babies usually elicit such interaction (as you have seen when a stranger makes faces to a baby in a public place), but some adults are too overwhelmed to play. In that case, the brain lacks an essential, expected stimulant.

Synchrony becomes more frequent and more elaborate as time goes on; a 6-month-old is a more responsive social partner than a 3-month-old. Parents and infants average about an hour a day in face-to-face play, although variations are apparent from baby to baby, from time period to time period, and from culture to culture (Baildam et al., 2000; Lee, 2000).

thinking like a scientist

The Still-Face Technique

Is synchrony needed for normal development? If no one plays with an infant, how will that infant develop? Experiments using the **still-face technique** have addressed these questions (Tronick, 1989; Tronick et al., 1978). An infant is placed facing an adult, who plays with the baby while a video camera records each partner's reactions. Frame-by-frame comparison of the two videotapes reveals the sequence. Typically, mothers synchronize their responses to the infants' movements, usually with exaggerated tone and expression, and babies reciprocate with smiles and arm waving.

Then, on cue, the adult erases all facial expression and stares with a "still face" for a minute or two. Not usually at 2 months, but clearly at 6 months, babies are very upset by the still face, especially from their parents (less so for strangers). Babies frown, fuss, drool, look away, kick, cry, or suck their fingers.

Interestingly, babies are much more upset when parents show a still face than when parents leave the room for a minute or two (Rochat, 2001). From a psychological perspective, this is healthy: It shows that "by 2 to 3 months of age, infants have begun to expect that people will respond positively to their initiatives" (R. A. Thompson, 2006, p. 29). In one set of experiments, infants became upset if someone had a still face for any reason—to look at a wall, to look at someone else, or merely to look away (Striano, 2004).

In another study, infants experienced not just one but two episodes of a parent's still face. The infants quickly readjusted when their parent became responsive again *if* synchrony characterized the parent–infant relationship. If the parent was typically unresponsive, however, infants stayed upset (with faster heart rate and more fussing) even after the second still-face episode ended (Haley & Stansbury, 2003).

Many research studies lead to the same conclusion: A parent's responsiveness to an infant aids development, measured not only psychosocially but also biologically (with heart rate, weight gain, and brain maturation) (Moore & Calkins, 2004). If a mother is unresponsive to her infant (as usually happens with postpartum depression; see Chapter 4), the father or another caregiver should establish synchrony to help ensure normal development (Tronick & Weinberg, 1997).

still-face technique An experimental practice in which an adult keeps his or her face unmoving and expressionless in face-to-face interaction with an infant.

Attachment

Toward the end of the first year, face-to-face play almost disappears. Once infants can move around and explore, they are no longer content to stay in one spot and follow an adult's facial expressions and vocalizations. Remember that, at about 12 months, most infants can walk and talk, which changes the rhythms of their social interaction (Jaffee et al., 2001). At this time a new type of connection, called *attachment,* replaces synchrony.

attachment According to Ainsworth, "an affectional tie" that an infant forms with the caregiver—a tie that binds them together in space and endures over time.

Attachment is a lasting emotional bond that one person has with another. Attachments form in infancy. According to attachment theory, new close relationships that arise later in life are influenced by these first attachments (R. A.

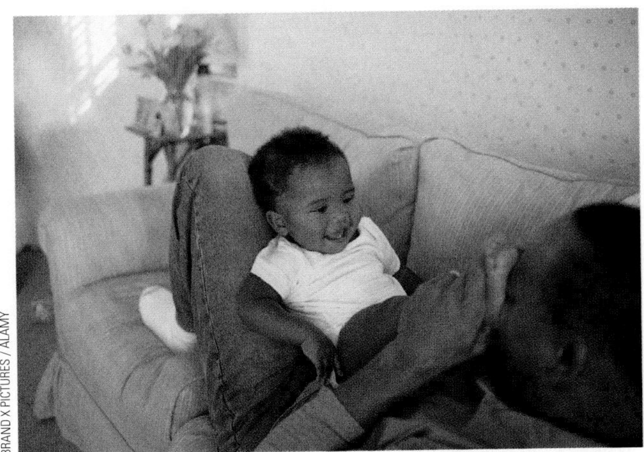
BRAND X PICTURES / ALAMY

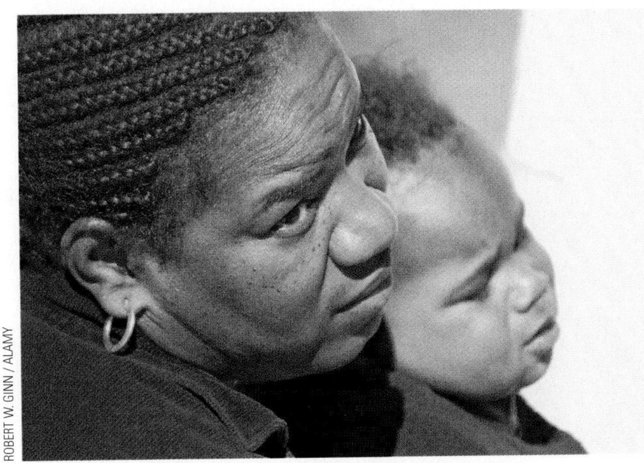
ROBERT W. GINN / ALAMY

Learning Emotions Infants respond to their parents' expressions and actions. If the moments shown here are typical, one young man will be happy and outgoing and the other will be sad and quiet.

Observation Quiz (see answer, page 194): For the pair on the left, where are their feet?

Thompson & Raikes, 2003). In fact, adults' attachment to their own parents, formed decades earlier, affects their relationships with their children. Humans learn in childhood how to relate to people, and those lessons echo lifelong (Grossman et al., 2005; Sroufe et al., 2005).

When two people are attached, they respond to each other in particular ways. Infants show their attachment through *proximity-seeking behaviors,* such as approaching and following their caregivers, and through *contact-maintaining behaviors,* such as touching, snuggling, and holding. A securely attached toddler is curious and eager to explore but maintains contact by looking back at the caregiver.

Caregivers show attachment as well. They keep a watchful eye on their baby and respond sensitively to vocalizations, expressions, and gestures. For example, many mothers or fathers, awakening in the middle of the night, tiptoe to the crib to gaze fondly at their sleeping infant. During the day, many parents instinctively smooth their toddler's hair or caress their child's hand or cheek.

Over humanity's evolutionary history, proximity-seeking and contact-maintaining behaviors contributed to the survival of the species (R. A. Thompson, 2006). Attachment keeps infants near their caregivers and keeps caregivers vigilant.

secure attachment A relationship in which an infant obtains both comfort and confidence from the presence of his or her caregiver.

Secure and Insecure Attachment

The concept of attachment was originally developed by John Bowlby (1969, 1973, 1988), a British developmentalist influenced by both psychoanalytic theory and ethology. Inspired by Bowlby's work, Mary Ainsworth, then a young American graduate student, studied the relationship between parents and infants in Uganda (Ainsworth, 1973).

Ainsworth discovered that virtually all infants develop special attachments to their caregivers. Some infants are more securely attached than others—an observation later confirmed by hundreds of other researchers studying in dozens of nations and cultures (Cassidy & Shaver, 1999; Grossman et al., 2005; Sroufe, 2005; R. A. Thompson, 2006).

Attachment is classified into four types, labeled A–D (see Table 7.3). Infants with **secure attachment** (type B) feel comfortable and confident. The infant derives comfort from being close to the caregiver, and that provides him or her the confidence to explore. The caregiver becomes a base for exploration, giving the child the assurance to venture forth. A toddler might, for example,

Synchrony Father–infant play is often more fun than mother–infant play. This father is teaching his son important lessons about manhood!

MICHAEL NEWMAN / PHOTOEDIT

TABLE 7.3

Patterns of Infant Attachment

Type	Name of Pattern	In Play Room	Mother Leaves	Mother Returns	Toddlers in Category (percent)
A	Insecure-avoidant	Child plays happily	Child continues playing	Child ignores her	10–20
B	Secure	Child plays happily	Child pauses, is not as happy	Child welcomes her, returns to play	50–70
C	Insecure-resistant/ambivalent	Child clings, is preoccupied with mother	Child is unhappy, may stop playing	Child is angry, may cry, hit mother, cling	10–20
D	Disorganized	Child is cautious	Child may stare or yell; looks scared, confused	Child acts oddly—may freeze, scream, hit self, throw things	5–10

scramble down from the caregiver's lap to play with a toy but periodically look back, vocalize a few syllables, and return for a hug.

By contrast, insecure attachment (types A and C) is characterized by fear, anxiety, anger, or indifference. Insecurely attached children have less confidence. Some play without maintaining contact with the caregiver; this is **insecure-avoidant attachment** (type A). An insecurely attached child might instead be unwilling to leave the caregiver's lap; this is **insecure-resistant/ambivalent attachment** (type C).

insecure-avoidant attachment A pattern of attachment in which an infant avoids connection with the caregiver, as when the infant seems not to care about the caregiver's presence, departure, or return.

insecure-resistant/ambivalent attachment A pattern of attachment in which anxiety and uncertainty are evident, as when an infant is very upset at separation from the caregiver and both resists and seeks contact on reunion.

disorganized attachment A type of attachment that is marked by an infant's inconsistent reactions to the caregiver's departure and return.

The fourth category (type D) is called **disorganized attachment;** it may have some elements of any of the other types, but it is clearly different from them. Type D infants may shift from hitting to kissing their mothers, from staring blankly to crying hysterically, from pinching themselves to freezing in place.

About two-thirds of all infants are securely attached (type B). Their mother's presence gives them courage to explore. The father's presence makes some infants even more confident. The caregiver's departure may cause distress; the caregiver's return elicits positive social contact (such as smiling or hugging) and then more playing. A balanced reaction—being concerned about the caregiver's departure but not overwhelmed by it—reflects secure attachment.

Almost a third of all infants are insecure, appearing either indifferent (type A) or unduly anxious (type C). The remaining infants fit into none of these categories and are classified as disorganized (type D).

Measuring Attachment

Strange Situation A laboratory procedure for measuring attachment by evoking infants' reactions to stress.

Ainsworth (1973) developed a now-classic laboratory procedure, called the **Strange Situation,** to measure attachment. In a well-equipped playroom, an infant is closely observed for eight episodes, during which the infant is with the caregiver (usually the mother), with a stranger, with both, or alone.

First, the caregiver and child are together. Then every three minutes the stranger or the caregiver enters or leaves the playroom. Infants' responses to the stress of caregiver departure and stranger presence indicate which type of attachment they have formed to their caregivers. For research purposes, observers are carefully trained and are certified when they are able to accurately differentiate types A, B, C, and D. The key aspects to focus on are the following:

- *Exploration of the toys.* A securely attached toddler plays happily.
- *Reaction to the caregiver's departure.* A secure toddler misses the caregiver.
- *Reaction to the caregiver's return.* A secure toddler welcomes the caregiver.

➤**Answer to Observation Quiz** (from page 193): The father uses his legs and feet to support his son at just the right distance for a great fatherly game of foot-kissing.

(a)

(b)

(c)

ALL: COURTESY OF MARY AINSWORTH

The Attachment Experiment In this episode of the Strange Situation, Brian shows every sign of secure attachment. (*a*) He explores the playroom happily when his mother is present; (*b*) he cries when she leaves; and (*c*) he is readily comforted when she returns.

[It is reactions to the caregiver that indicate attachment; reactions to strangers (whether tears or signs of interest) are a matter of temperament more than of affectional bond.]

Attachment is not always measured via the Strange Situation, which requires that infants be assessed one by one in a laboratory by carefully trained researchers. Sometimes attachment is measured via 90 questions to be sorted by parents about their children or via an extensive interview with parents about their relationships with their own parents. All these measures find a correlation between secure attachment and desirable personality traits and cognitive development. All also find that the type of attachment changes when circumstances (such as the responsiveness of the mother) change. Many aspects of good parenting correlate with secure attachment (see Table 7.4).

TABLE 7.4

Predictors of Attachment Type

Secure attachment (type B) is more likely if:

- The parent is usually sensitive and responsive to the infant's needs.
- The infant–parent relationship is high in synchrony.
- The infant's temperament is "easy."
- The parents are not stressed about income, other children, or their marriage.
- The parents have a working model of secure attachment to their own parents.

Insecure attachment is more likely if:

- The parent mistreats the child. (Neglect increases type A; abuse increases C and D.)
- The mother is mentally ill. (Paranoia increases type D; depression increases type C.)
- The parents are highly stressed about income, other children, or their marriage. (Parental stress increases types A and D.)
- The parents are intrusive and controlling. (Parental domination increases type A.)
- The parents are active alcoholics. (Alcoholic father increases type A; alcoholic mother increases type D.)
- The child's temperament is "difficult." (Difficult children tend to be type C.)
- The child's temperament is "slow to warm up." (This correlates with type A.)

These family and infant characteristics influence a child's attachment status in the ways stated here, but none fully determine it. For example, parental sensitivity predicts only a modest amount of the variation between secure and insecure children. All these correlations have been found in several studies, but none appear in every study, because infant temperaments, contexts, and cultures vary too much.

Insecure Attachment and Social Setting

Early researchers expected secure attachment to "predict all the outcomes reasonably expected from a well-functioning personality" (R. A. Thompson & Raikes, 2003, p. 708). But this turned out not to be the case. Securely attached infants *are* more likely to become secure toddlers, socially competent preschoolers, academically skilled schoolchildren, and better parents (R. A. Thompson, 2006). However, the correlations are not large, and that makes prediction very tentative. Many children shift in attachment status between one age and another (NICHD, 2001; Seifer et al., 2004).

The most troubled children may be those who are classified as type D. If their disorganization makes them unable to develop an effective strategy for dealing with other people (even an avoidant or resistant strategy, type A or C), they may lash out. Sometimes they become hostile and aggressive, difficult for anyone else to relate to (Lyons-Ruth et al., 1999). (An unusually high percentage of the Romanian children who were adopted after age 2 were type D.)

Social Referencing

social referencing Seeking information about how to react to an unfamiliar or ambiguous object or event by observing someone else's expressions and reactions. That other person becomes a social reference.

Infants seek to understand caregivers' emotions. At about age 1, **social referencing** becomes evident when an infant looks to another person for clarification or information, much as someone might consult a dictionary or other "reference" work. A glance of reassurance or words of caution, an expression of alarm, pleasure, or dismay—each becomes a social guide, telling an infant how to react to an unfamiliar situation.

After age 1, when infants reach the stage of active exploration (Piaget) and the crisis of autonomy versus shame and doubt (Erikson), the need to consult caregivers becomes urgent. Toddlers search for cues in gaze and facial expressions, pay close attention to adults' expressed emotions, and watch carefully to detect intentions behind other people's actions (Baldwin, 2000).

Social referencing has many practical applications. Consider mealtime. Caregivers the world over smack their lips, pretend to taste, and say "yum-yum," encouraging toddlers to eat and enjoy their first beets, liver, or spinach. For their part, toddlers become astute at reading expressions, insisting on the foods that the adults *really* like. Through this process, children in some cultures develop a taste for raw fish or curried goat or smelly cheese—foods that children in other cultures refuse.

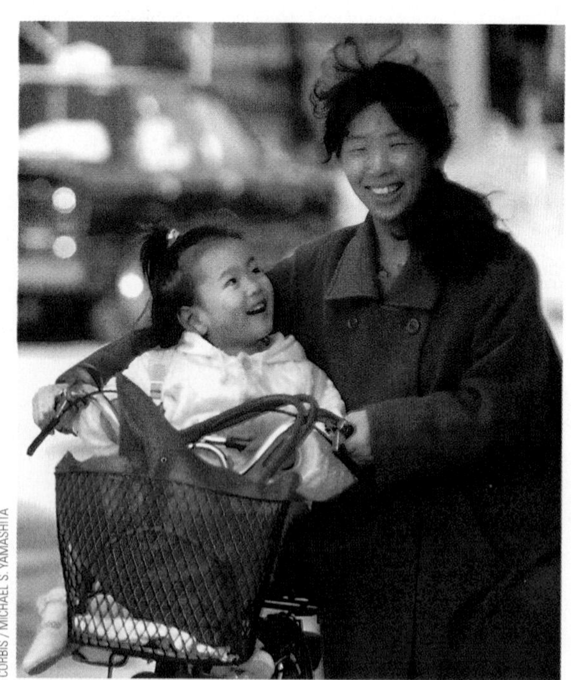

CORBIS / MICHAEL S. YAMASHITA

Social Referencing Should I be happy or scared to ride on a bicycle through the streets of Osaka, Japan? Check with Mom to find out.

Referencing Mothers

Most everyday instances of social referencing occur with mothers. Infants usually heed their mother's wishes, expressed in tone and facial expression. This does not mean that infants are always obedient, especially in cultures where parents and children value independence. Not surprisingly, compliance has been the focus of study in the United States, where it often conflicts with independence.

For example, in one experiment, few toddlers obeyed their mother's request (required by the researchers) to pick up dozens of toys that they had not scattered (Kochanska et al., 2001). Their refusal indicates some emotional maturity: Self-awareness had led to pride and autonomy. The body language and expressions of some of the mothers implied that they did not really expect their children to obey.

These same toddlers were quite obedient when their mothers told them not to touch an attractive toy. The mothers used tone, expression, and words to make this prohibition clear. Because of social referencing, toddlers understood the message. Even when the mothers were out of sight, half of the 14-month-olds and virtually all of the 22-month-olds obeyed. Most (80 percent) of the older toddlers seemed to agree with the mothers' judgment (Kochanska et al., 2001).

Referencing Fathers

In North America, increases in maternal employment have expanded the social references available to infants. Fathers—once thought to be uninvolved with their infants (as was the case with Uncle Henry)—now spend considerable time with their children.

For example, the stereotype is that Latino fathers leave caregiving to their wives. However, a study of more than 1,000 Latino 9-month-olds found "fathers with moderate to high levels of engagement" (Cabrera et al., 2006. p. 1203). Although many possible correlates of father involvement (income, education, age) were analyzed, only one significant predictor of the level of engagement was found: how happy the father was with the infant's mother. Happier husbands tend to be more involved fathers.

The social information that infants get from their fathers tends to be more encouraging than that from mothers, who are more cautious and protective. When toddlers are about to explore, they often seek their father's approval, expecting fun from their fathers and comfort from their mothers (Lamb, 2000; Parke, 1996).

In this, infants show social intelligence, because fathers play imaginative and exciting games. They move their infant's legs and arms in imitation of walking, kicking, or climbing; or play "airplane," zooming the baby through the air; or tap and tickle the baby's stomach. Mothers caress, murmur, read, or sing soothingly; combine play with caretaking; and use standard sequences such as peek-a-boo and patty-cake. In short, fathers are generally more proximal, engaging in play that involves the infant's whole body.

Up, Up, and Away! The vigorous play typical of fathers is likely to help in the infant's mastery of motor skills and the development of muscle control.

Especially for Grandmothers A grandmother of an infant boy is troubled that the baby's father stays with him whenever the mother is away. She says that men don't know how to care for infants, and she notes that he sometimes plays a game in which he tosses his son in the air and then catches him.

Infant Day Care

You have seen that social bonds are crucial for infants. How is this need affected by time spent with paid caregivers? More than half of all 1-year-olds in the United States are in "regularly scheduled" nonmaternal care, sometimes by relatives (usually the father or grandmother) but often not (Loeb et al., 2004). Mothers usually prefer care by a relative because it is the least expensive, often free. However, family care varies in quality and availability. (If a mother is employed, chances are her husband and mother are as well.)

Family day care (children of various ages cared for in someone else's home) is more often used for infants, and older children are more often in **center day care** (several paid caregivers in a place designed for young children). Quality varies in such places, with standards varying markedly from state to state as well as from nation to nation.

In the United States, most parents encounter a "mix of quality, price, type of care, and government subsidies" (Haskins, 2005, p. 168). Some center care is excellent (see Table 7.5), with adequate space, equipment, and trained providers (the ratio of adults to infants should be about 2:5), but it is hard to find. Households with higher incomes are more likely to use center care. In other nations, people of all incomes use center care, funded by the government.

The evidence is overwhelming that good preschool education (reviewed in Chapter 9) is beneficial for young children. Infant day care is more controversial (Waldfogel, 2006), but most developmentalists find that infants are not likely to be harmed by—and, in fact, can benefit from—professional day care (Brooks-Gunn et al., 2002; Lamb, 1998).

family day care Child care that occurs in another caregiver's home. Usually the caregiver is paid at a lower rate than in center care, and usually one person cares for several children of various ages.

center day care Child care in a place especially designed for the purpose, where several paid providers care for many children. Usually the children are grouped by age, the day-care center is licensed, and providers are trained and certified in child development.

Research Design

Scientists: NICHD Early Child Care Research Network, 30 developmentalists cooperating in a study sponsored by the National Institute of Child Health and Human Development (NICHD) .

Publication: Hundreds of research articles in every major child developmental journal and a book, *Child Care and Child Development* (2005), have been published analyzing these data.

Participants: Total of 1,364 mother–infant pairs, from 25 hospitals at 10 sites throughout the United States. Participants were recruited within days after birth. Participating mothers had to be over 18, English-speaking, and healthy.

Design: Ongoing longitudinal study, with many repeated measures from birth to age 10, looking especially at child-care arrangements and at social, emotional, and cognitive development. The data from this study have been used for many purposes; here we focus on correlations between infant care and later development.

Major conclusions: Quality of maternal care is more important than specifics of care. Poor-quality day care, especially in infancy, has some long-term negative effects. Some researchers have found that nonmaternal care for 40 or more hours per week increases the risk of later aggression.

Comment: This study is large, diverse, and ongoing, and it continues to provide fascinating results. One strength is that many regions within the United States were sampled; one weakness is that only one nation was studied. The main drawback is that low-SES and immigrant mothers are not adequately represented.

TABLE 7.5

High-Quality Day Care

High-quality day care during infancy has five essential characteristics:

1. *Adequate attention to each infant.* This means a low caregiver-to-infant ratio and, probably even more important, a small group of infants. The ideal situation might be two reliable caregivers for five infants. Infants need familiar, loving caregivers; continuity of care is very important.
2. *Encouragement of language and sensorimotor development.* Infants should receive extensive language exposure through games, songs, conversations, and positive talk of all kinds, along with easily manipulated toys.
3. *Attention to health and safety.* Cleanliness routines (e.g., handwashing before meals), accident prevention (e.g., no small objects that could be swallowed), and safe areas for exploration (e.g., a clean, padded area for crawling and climbing) are good signs.
4. *Well-trained and professional caregivers.* Ideally, every caregiver should have a degree or certificate in early-childhood education and should have worked with children for several years. Turnover should be low, morale high, and enthusiasm evident. Good caregivers love their children and their work.
5. *Warm and responsive caregivers.* Providers should engage the children in problem solving and discussions, rather than giving instructions. Quiet, obedient children may be an indication of unresponsive care.

For a more detailed evaluation of day care, see the checklist in NICHD, 2005.

A longitudinal study has followed the development of more than 1,300 children from birth to age 11 (NICHD, 2005). The effects of various types of infant care on attachment was a major concern of the researchers, but most analyses of the data found that attachment to the mother is as secure among infants in center care as among infants cared for at home. Like other, smaller studies, this NICHD study confirms that infant day care, even for 40 hours a week before age 1, has much less influence on child development than does the warmth of the mother–infant relationship. Infant and child cognition, especially language learning, advance with center care (NICHD, 2005; see Research Design).

Good infant day care is expensive and scarce, however, because infants need individualized and affectionate attention, which are likely to be in short supply if a caregiver has many infants to care for and limited experience and training (Waldfogel, 2006). Probably for this reason, "disagreements about the wisdom (indeed, the morality) of nonmaternal child care for the very young remain" (NICHD, 2005, p. xiv).

No study finds that children of employed mothers suffer solely because their mothers are working. Many employed mothers make infant care their top priority. For example, time-use research finds that mothers who work full time outside the home spend almost as much time playing with their babies (14½ hours a week) as do mothers without outside jobs (16 hours a week) (Huston & Aronson, 2005). Employed mothers spend half as much time on housework and almost no time on leisure. The study concludes:

> There was no evidence that mothers' time at work interfered with the quality of their relationship with their infants, the quality of the home environment, or children's development. In fact, the results suggest the opposite. Mothers who spent more time at work provided slightly higher quality home environments.
>
> *[Huston & Aronson, 2005, p. 479]*

Other research confirms that much depends on the quality of care, wherever it occurs and whoever provides it. According to the NICHD Early Child Care Research Network, early day care seems detrimental *only* when the mother is in-

➤Response for Grandmothers (from page 197): Fathers can be great caregivers, and most mothers prefer that the father provide care. It's good for the baby and the marriage. Being tossed in the air is great fun (as long as the father is careful and a good catcher!). A generation or two ago, mothers seldom let fathers care for infants. Fortunately, today's mothers are less likely to act as gatekeepers, shutting the fathers out.

Especially for Day-Care Providers A mother who brings her child to you for day care says that she knows she is harming her baby but must work out of economic necessity. What do you say?

sensitive *and* the infant spends more than 20 hours a week in a poor-quality program in which there are too few caregivers, with too little training) (NICHD, 2005).

Although the mother's sensitivity is the best predictor of a child's social skills, day care can have a significant effect, too. Some children, especially boys, who receive extensive nonmaternal care are more quarrelsome and have more conflicts with their teachers than does the average student (NICHD, 2003).

The negative effects of poor care have also been found in a study in Israel of 758 infants. Those cared for at home by an attentive father or grandmother seemed to do very well, as did those in a high-quality day-care center. However, those cared for in a center with untrained caregivers and only one adult for five infants fared poorly (Sagi et al., 2002). Other studies also find that a 5:1 ratio of infants to adults is too high; 5:2 not only allows caregivers to provide better instruction and support but also makes children more cooperative (de Schipper et al., 2006).

ANN HEISENFELT / AP PHOTO

Secure Attachment Kirstie and her 10-month-old daughter Mia enjoy a moment of synchrony in an infant day-care center sponsored by a family-friendly employer, General Mills. High-quality day care and high-quality home care are equally likely to foster secure attachment between mother and infant.

Regarding home care, children whose primary caregiver is depressed fare worse than they would in center care (Loeb et al., 2004). Many studies find that out-of-home day care is better than in-home care if an infant's family does not provide adequate stimulation and attention (Ramey et al., 2002; Votruba-Drzal et al., 2004).

Among the benefits of day care is the opportunity to learn to express emotions. When a toddler is temperamentally very shy or aggressive, he or she is less likely to remain so if caregivers and other children are available as social references (Fox et al., 2001; Zigler & Styfco, 2001). But no expert would say that *all* infants are better off either in day care or at home.

Especially for Potential Day-Care Providers What are some of the benefits and costs of opening and running a day-care center?

SUMMING UP

Infants seek social bonds, which they develop with one or several people. Synchrony begins in the early months: Infants and caregivers interact face to face, making split-second adjustments in their emotional responses to each other. Synchrony evolves into attachment, an emotional bond with adult caregivers. Secure attachment allows learning to progress; insecure infants are less confident and may develop emotional impairments. As infants become more curious and as they encounter new toys, people, and events, they use social referencing to learn whether such new things are fearsome or fun.

The emotional connections evident in synchrony, attachment, and social referencing may occur with mothers, fathers, other relatives, and day-care providers. Instead of harming infants, as was once feared, nonmaternal care sometimes enhances infants' psychosocial development. The quality and continuity of child care matter more than who provides it. ■

Conclusions in Theory and Practice

You have seen in this chapter that the first two years are filled with psychosocial interactions, all of which result from genes, maturation, culture, and caregivers. Each of the five major theories seems plausible. No single theory stands out as the best.

All theorists agree that the first two years are crucial, with early emotional and social development influenced by the parents' behavior, the quality of day care, cultural patterns, and inborn traits. It has not been proven whether one influence, such as a good day-care center, compensates for another, such as a depressed mother (although parental influence is always significant). Multicultural research

TABLE 7.6

AT ABOUT THIS TIME: Infancy

Approximate Age	Characteristic or Achievement
3 months	Rolls over Stays half-upright in stroller Uses two eyes together Grabs for object; if rattle in hand, can shake it Makes cooing noises Joyous recognition of familiar people
6 months	Sits up, without adult support (but sometimes using arms) Grabs and can grasp objects with whole hand Smiles and laughs Babbles, listens, and responds with facial expression Tries to crawl (on belly, not yet on all fours) Stands and bounces with support (on someone's lap, in a bouncer) Begins to shows signs of anger, fear, attachment
12 months	Stands without holding on Crawls well Takes a few unsteady steps Uses fingers, including pincer grasp (thumb and forefingers) Can feed self with fingers Speaks a few words (*mama, dada, baba*) Strong attachment to familiar caregivers Apparent fear of strangers, of unexpected noises and events
18 months	Walks well Runs, but also falls Tries to climb on furniture Speaks 50–100 words; most are nouns Begins toilet training Likes to drop things, throw things, take things apart Recognizes self in mirror
24 months	Runs well Climbs up (down is harder) Uses simple tools (spoon, large marker) Combines words (usually noun/verb, sometimes noun/verb/noun) Can use fingers to unscrew tops, open doors Very interested in new experiences and new children

An Eventful Time This table lists aspects of development that have been discussed in Chapters 5, 6, and 7. Throughout infancy, temperament and experience affect when and how babies display the characteristics and achievements listed here. The list is meant as a rough guideline, not as a yardstick for indicating a child's progress in intelligence or any other trait.

has identified a wide variety of practices in different societies. These discoveries imply that no one event (such as toilet training, in Freud's theory) determines emotional health.

On the basis of what you have learned, you could safely advise parents to play with their infants; respond to their physical and emotional needs; let them explore; maintain a relationship; pay attention to them; and expect every toddler to be sometimes angry, sometimes proud, sometimes fearful. Parental actions and attitudes may or may not have a powerful impact on later development, but they certainly can make infants happier or sadder. Parental attentiveness leads to synchrony, attachment, and social referencing, which are crucial to infant and toddler development.

Such generalities are not good enough for Jacob, or for all the other infants who show signs of malnutrition, delayed language, poor social skills, abnormal emotional development, insecure or disorganized attachment, or other deficits. In dealing with individual children who have problems, we need to be more specific.

Jacob was 3 years old but not talking. Even in his first year, his psychosocial development was impaired. Looking at Table 7.6 on infant development, you can see that even at 3 months he was unusual in his reaction to familiar people. All infants need one or two people who are emotionally invested in them from the first days of life, and it is not clear that Jacob had anyone, including his nanny, who did not speak English, or his parents. There is no indication of synchrony or attachment.

Something had to be done, as the parents eventually realized. They took Jacob for evaluation at a major teaching hospital. He was seen by at least 10 experts, none of whom said anything encouraging. The diagnosis was "pervasive developmental disorder," which suggests serious brain abnormality.

Fortunately, Jacob's parents then consulted a psychiatrist who specialized in children with psychosocial problems (Greenspan & Wieder, 2003). He showed them how to relate to Jacob, saying, "I am going to teach you how to play with your son." They learned about "floor time," four hours a day set aside to get on their son's level and interact: Imitate him, act as if they are part of the game, put their faces and bodies in front of his, create synchrony even though Jacob did not initiate it.

The father reports:

> We rebuilt Jacob's connection to us and to the world—but on his terms. We were drilled to always follow his lead, to always build on his initiative. In a sense, we could only ask Jacob to join our world if we were willing to enter his. . . . He would drop rocks and we would catch them. He would want to put pennies in a bank and we would block the slot. He would want to run in a circle and we would get in his way.
>
> I remember a cold fall day when I was putting lime on our lawn. He dipped his hand in the powder and let it slip through his fingers. He loved the way it

> felt. I took the lawn spreader and ran to the other part of our yard. He ran after me. I let him have one dip and ran across the yard again. He dipped, I ran, he dipped, I ran. We did this until I could no longer move my arms.
>
> *[Jacob's father, 1997, p. 62]*

Jacob's case is obviously extreme, but many infants and parents have difficulty establishing synchrony. From the perspective of early psychosocial development, nothing could be more important than a connection like the one Jacob and his parents established.

> In Jacob's case it worked. He said his first word at age 3, and by age 5 . . . he speaks for days at a time. He talks from the moment he wakes up to the moment he falls asleep, as if he is making up for lost time. He wants to know everything. "How does a live chicken become an eating chicken? Why are microbes so small? Why do policemen wear badges? Why are dinosaurs extinct? What is French? [A question I often ask myself.] Why do ghosts glow in the dark?" He is not satisfied with answers that do not ring true or that do not satisfy his standards of clarity. He will keep on asking until he gets it. Rebecca and I have become expert definition providers. Just last week, we were faced with the ultimate challenge: "Dad," he asked: "Is God real or not?" And then, just to make it a bit more challenging, he added: "How do miracles happen?"
>
> *[Jacob's father, 1997, p. 63]*

Miracles do not always happen. Children with pervasive developmental disorder usually require special care throughout childhood; Jacob may continue to need extra attention. Nevertheless, almost all infants, almost all the time, develop strong relationships with their close family members. The power of early psychosocial development is obvious to every developmentalist and, it is hoped, to every reader of this text.

➤Response for Day-Care Providers (from page 198): Reassure the mother that you will keep her baby safe and will help to develop the baby's mind and social skills by fostering synchrony and attachment. Also tell her that the quality of mother–infant interaction at home is more important than anything else for psychosocial development; mothers who are employed full time usually have wonderful, secure relationships with their infants. If the mother wishes, you can discuss ways she can be a more responsive mother.

➤Response for Potential Day-Care Providers (from page 199): A high-quality day-care center needs trained and responsive adults and a clean, safe space—all of which can be expensive and may mean that you will have to charge higher fees than many families can afford to pay. The main benefit for you is knowing that you can make a major contribution to the well-being of infants and their families.

SUMMARY

Emotional Development

1. Two emotions, contentment and distress, appear as soon as an infant is born. Anger emerges with restriction and frustration, between 4 and 8 months of age, and becomes stronger by age 1.

2. Reflexive fear is apparent in very young infants. However, fear of something specific, including fear of strangers and fear of separation, does not appear until toward the end of the first year.

3. In the second year, social awareness produces more selective fear, anger, and joy. As infants become increasingly self-aware at about 18 months, emotions—specifically, pride, shame, and affection—emerge that encourage an interface between the self and others.

Theories About Infant Psychosocial Development

4. According to all five major theories, caregiver behavior is especially influential in the first two years. Freud stressed the mother's impact on oral and anal pleasure; Erikson emphasized trust and autonomy.

5. Behaviorists focus on learning; parents teach their babies many things, including when to be fearful or joyful. Cognitive theory holds that infants develop working models based on their experiences.

6. Epigenetic theory emphasizes temperament, a set of genetic traits whose expression is influenced by the environment. Parental practices inhibit and guide a child's temperament, but they do not create it. Ideally, a good fit develops between the parents' actions and the child's personality.

7. The sociocultural approach notes the impact of social and cultural factors on the parent–infant relationship. Ethnotheories shape infant emotions and traits so that they fit well within the culture. Some cultures encourage proximal parenting (more physical touch); others promote distal parenting (more talk and object play).

The Development of Social Bonds

8. By 3 months, infants become more responsive and social, and synchrony begins. Synchrony involves moment-by-moment interaction. Caregivers need to be responsive and sensitive. Infants are disturbed by a still face because they expect and need social interaction.

9. Attachment, measured by the baby's reaction to the caregiver's presence, departure, and return in the Strange Situation, is crucial. Some infants seem indifferent (type A—insecure-avoidant) or overly dependent (type C—insecure-resistant/ambivalent), instead of secure (type B). Disorganized attachment (type D) is the most worrisome form.

10. Secure attachment provides encouragement for infant exploration. As they play, toddlers engage in social referencing, looking to other people's facial expressions to detect what is fearsome and what is enjoyable.

11. Fathers are wonderful playmates for infants, who frequently consult them, as well as their mothers, as social references.

12. Day care for infants seems, on the whole, to be a positive experience, especially for cognitive development. Psychosocial characteristics, including secure attachment, are influenced more by the mother's warmth than by the number of hours spent in nonmaternal care. Quality of care is crucial, no matter who provides that care.

Conclusions in Theory and Practice

13. Experts debate exactly how critical early psychosocial development may be: Is it the essential foundation for all later growth or just one of many steps along the way? However, all infants need caregivers who are committed to them and are dedicated to encouraging each aspect of early development.

KEY TERMS

social smile (p. 180)
stranger wariness (p. 181)
separation anxiety (p. 181)
self-awareness (p. 182)
trust versus mistrust (p. 183)
autonomy versus shame and doubt (p. 184)
social learning (p. 184)
working model (p. 184)
temperament (p. 185)
goodness of fit (p. 187)
ethnotheory (p. 188)
proximal parenting (p. 189)
distal parenting (p. 189)
synchrony (p. 191)
still-face technique (p. 192)
attachment (p. 192)
secure attachment (p. 193)
insecure-avoidant attachment (p. 194)
insecure-resistant/ambivalent attachment (p. 194)
disorganized attachment (p. 194)
Strange Situation (p. 194)
social referencing (p. 196)
family day care (p. 197)
center day care (p. 197)

KEY QUESTIONS

1. How would a sensitive parent respond to an infant's distress?

2. How do emotions in the second year of life differ from emotions in the first year?

3. What are similarities and differences in the two psychoanalytic theories of infancy?

4. How might synchrony affect the development of emotions in the first year?

5. What is an example of an ethnotheory of your culture that differs from those of other cultures?

6. What are the similarities between epigenetic and sociocultural theories of infant emotions?

7. Why would a mother and father choose not to care for their infant themselves, 24/7?

8. What are the advantages and disadvantages of three kinds of nonmaternal infant care: relatives, family day care, and center day care?

9. Attachments are said to be lifelong. Describe an adult who is insecurely attached.

10. How would psychosocial development be affected if an infant spent every day in a crowded day-care center—for example, a center with eight infants for every caregiver?

11. In terms of infant development, what are the differences between employed and unemployed mothers?

APPLICATIONS

1. One cultural factor influencing infant development is how infants are carried from place to place. Ask four mothers whose infants were born in each of the past four decades how they transported them—front or back carriers, facing out or in, strollers or carriages, car seats or on mother's laps, and so on. Why did they choose the mode(s) they chose? What are their opinions and yours on how that cultural practice might affect infants' development?

2. Observe synchrony for three minutes. Ideally, ask the parent of an infant under 8 months of age to play with the infant. If no infant is available, observe a pair of lovers as they converse. Note the sequence and timing of every facial expression, sound, and gesture of both partners.

3. Telephone several day-care centers to try to assess the quality of care they provide. Ask about such factors as adult–child ratio, group size, and training for caregivers of children of various ages. Is there a minimum age? If so, why was that age chosen? Analyze the answers, using Table 7.5 as a guide.

PART II The Developing Person So Far: The First Two Years

BIOSOCIAL

Body Changes Over the first two years, the body quadruples in weight and the brain triples in weight. Connections between brain cells grow increasingly dense, with complex neural networks of dendrites and axons. Neurons become coated with an insulating layer of myelin, sending messages faster and more efficiently, and the various states—sleeping, waking, exploring—become more distinct. Experiences that are universal (experience-expectant) and culture-bound (experience-dependent) both aid brain growth, partly by allowing pruning of unused connections between neurons.

Senses and Motor Skills Brain maturation underlies the development of all the senses. Seeing, hearing, and mobility progress from reflexes to coordinated voluntary actions, including focusing, grasping, and walking. Culture is evident in sensory and motor development, as brain networks respond to the particulars of each infant's life.

Public Health Infant health depends on immunization, parental practices (including "back to sleep"), and nutrition (ideally, breast milk). Survival rates are much higher today than they were even a few decades ago, yet in some regions of the world infant growth is still stunted because of malnutrition.

COGNITIVE

Sensorimotor Intelligence and Information Processing As Piaget describes it, during the first two years (sensorimotor intelligence) infants progress from knowing their world through immediate sensory experiences to being able to "experiment" on that world through actions and mental images. Information-processing theory stresses the links between input (sensory experiences) and output (perception). Infants develop affordances, their own ideas regarding the possibilities offered by the objects and events of the world. Recent research finds traces of memory at 3 months, object permanence at 4 months, and deferred imitation at 9 months—all much younger ages than Piaget described.

Language Interaction with responsive adults exposes infants to the structure of communication and thus language. By age 1, infants can usually speak a word or two; by age 2, language has exploded, as toddlers talk in short sentences and add vocabulary words each day. Language develops through reinforcement, neurological maturation, and social motivation.

PSYCHOSOCIAL

Emotions and Theories Emotions develop from basic newborn reactions to complex, self-conscious responses. Infants' increasing self-awareness and independence are shaped by parents, in a transition explained by Freud's oral and anal stages, by Erikson's crises of trust versus mistrust and autonomy versus shame and doubt, by behaviorism in the focus on parental responses, and by cognitive theory's working models. Much of basic temperament—and therefore personality—is inborn and apparent throughout life, as epigenetic theory explains. Sociocultural theory stresses cultural norms, evident in parents' ethnotheories that guide them in raising their infants.

The Development of Social Bonds Early on, parents and infants respond to each other by synchronizing their behavior in social play. Toward the end of the first year, secure attachment between child and parent sets the stage for the child's increasingly independent exploration of the world. Insecure attachment—avoidant, resistant, or disorganized—signifies a parent–child relationship that hinders infant learning. Infants become active participants in social interactions. Fathers and day-care providers, as well as mothers, encourage infants' social confidence.

The Play Years

CHAPTER 8
CHAPTER 9
CHAPTER 10

PART III

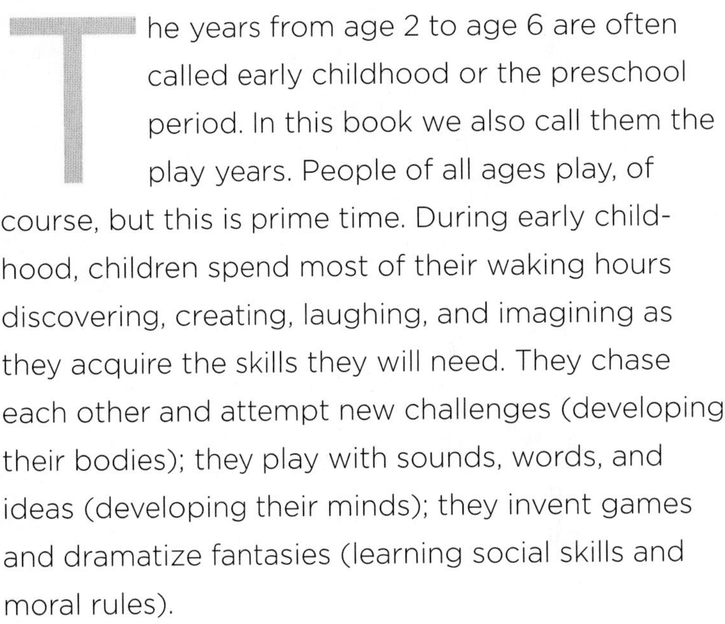

The years from age 2 to age 6 are often called early childhood or the preschool period. In this book we also call them the play years. People of all ages play, of course, but this is prime time. During early childhood, children spend most of their waking hours discovering, creating, laughing, and imagining as they acquire the skills they will need. They chase each other and attempt new challenges (developing their bodies); they play with sounds, words, and ideas (developing their minds); they invent games and dramatize fantasies (learning social skills and moral rules).

Playfulness makes young children exasperating as well as delightful. To them, growing up is a game, and their enthusiasm for it seems unlimited—whether they are quietly tracking a beetle through the grass or riotously turning their bedroom into a shambles. Their minds seem playful, too, when they explain that "a bald man has a barefoot head" or that "the sun shines so children can go outside to play."

If you expect young children to sit quietly or think logically, you'll be disappointed. But if you enjoy play, then these children will bring you joy.

8

CHAPTER OUTLINE

The Play Years: Biosocial Development

When you were 3 years old, I hope you wanted to fly like a bird, a plane, or Superman, and I hope someone kept you safe. Protection is needed, as well as appreciation of this period of development. Do you remember learning to skip or to write your name? Three-year-olds try all these, but they shuffle instead of skip, and they forget letters of the alphabet. By age 6, they can skip, write, and much more, as long as they have had enough practice.

Thus, not only do children grow bigger and stronger, they also become more skilled at hundreds of tasks. These advances and the need to protect children against serious problems that sometimes occur, are themes of this chapter.

Body Changes

Compared with cute and chubby 1-year-olds, 6-year-olds are grown up. As in infancy, the body and brain develop according to powerful epigenetic forces, biologically driven as well as socially guided, experience-expectant and experience-dependent (as explained in Chapter 5).

Growth Patterns

Just comparing a toddling 1-year-old and a cartwheeling 6-year-old makes some differences obvious. During the play years, children become slimmer as the lower body lengthens and baby fat turns to muscle. In fact, the body mass index (or BMI, the ratio of weight to height) is lower at age 5 than at any other age in the entire life span (Guillaume & Lissau, 2002). Gone are the protruding belly, round face, short limbs, and large head that characterize the toddler. The center of gravity moves from the breastbone to the belly button, enabling cartwheels and many other motor skills.

Increases in height and weight accompany these changes in proportions. Each year from age 2 through 6, well-nourished children add almost 3 inches (about 7 centimeters) and gain about 4½ pounds (2 kilograms). By age 6, the average child in a developed nation weighs about 46 pounds (21 kilograms) and is 46 inches (117 centimeters) tall. (As my nephew David said at that point, "In numbers I am square now.")

A typical 6-year-old:

- Is at least 3½ feet tall (more than 100 centimeters)
- Weighs between 40 and 50 pounds (between 18 and 22 kilograms)
- Looks lean, not chubby (ages 5–6 are lowest in body fat)
- Has adult-like body proportions (legs constitute about half the total height)

When many ethnic groups live together in the same developed nation, children of African descent tend to be tallest, followed by those of European descent, then Asians, and then Latinos. However, height differences *within* groups are greater than the average differences between groups. Body size is especially variable among children of African descent, because Africans are more genetically diverse than people from other continents (Goel et al., 2004).

Over the centuries, low-income families encouraged their children to eat, so that they would have a reserve of fat to protect them in times of famine. Now the same pattern has become destructive. In Brazil, for example, undernutrition caused two-thirds of all nutrition problems in 1975. By 1997, overnutrition was the most common problem (Monteiro et al., 2004).

A detailed study of 2- to 4-year-olds in low-income families in New York City found many overweight children, with the proportion increasing as income fell (Nelson et al., 2004). Further, more 4-year-olds than 2-year-olds were overweight (27 percent compared with 14 percent), which suggests that eating habits, not genes, were the cause. Overweight children were more likely to be of Hispanic (27 percent) or Asian (22 percent) descent than of African (14 percent) or European background (11 percent).

Such problems are not limited to New York City. Worldwide, an epidemic of adult heart disease and diabetes is spreading, and the major cause is the overfeeding of children (Gluckman & Hanson, 2006). It has been predicted that by 2020 more than 228 million adults worldwide will have diabetes (more in India than in any other nation) as a result of unhealthy eating habits acquired in childhood.

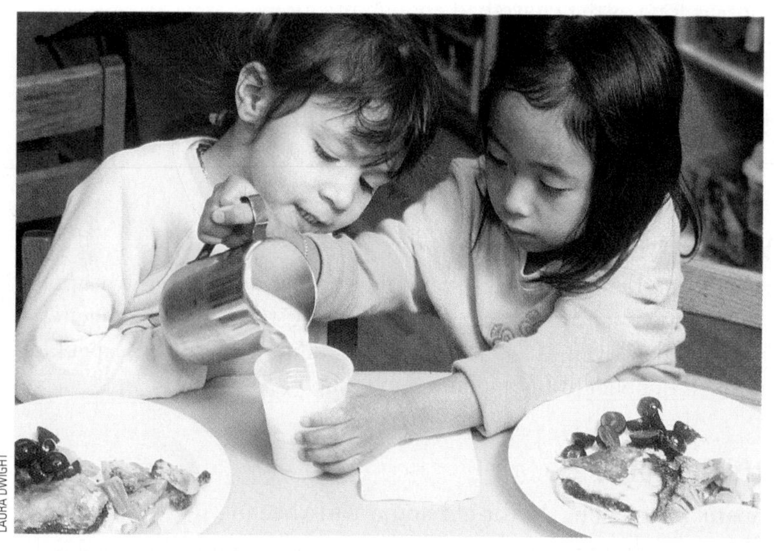

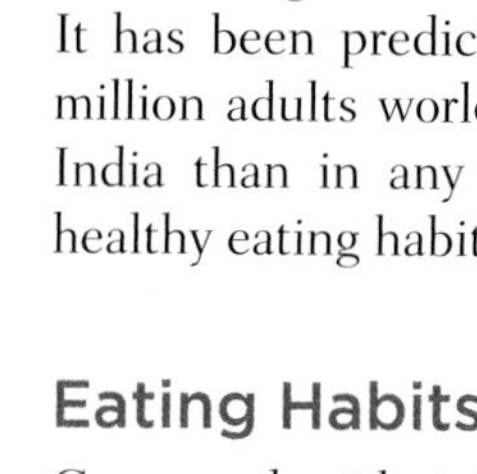

LAURA DWIGHT

No Spilled Milk This girl is demonstrating her mastery of the motor skills involved in pouring milk, to the evident admiration of her friend. The next skill will be drinking it—not a foregone conclusion, given the lactose intolerance of some children and the small appetites and notorious pickiness of children this age.

Observation Quiz (see answer, page 211): What three things can you see that indicate that this attempt at pouring will probably be successful?

Eating Habits

Compared with infants, young children—especially modern children, who play outdoors less than their parents or grandparents did—need far fewer calories per pound of body weight. Consequently, appetite decreases between ages 2 and 6. Instead of appreciating this natural development, many parents fret, threaten, and cajole their children into eating more than they should ("Eat all your dinner, and you can have ice cream").

Nutritional Deficiencies

Although most children in developed nations consume enough calories, they do not always obtain adequate iron, zinc, and calcium. For example, consumption of calcium is lower than it was 20 years ago because children today drink less milk and more soda (Jahns et al., 2001). Another problem is sugar. Many cultures encourage children to eat sweets, in birthday cake, holiday candy, desserts, and other treats. Yet sugar causes tooth decay, the most common disease of young children in developed nations (Lewit & Kerrebrock, 1998).

Sweetened cereals and drinks that are advertised as containing 100 percent of a day's vitamin requirements are a poor substitute for a balanced diet for many reasons besides their high sugar content. One is that some essential nutrients have probably not yet been identified, much less listed on food labels. Another is that fresh fruits and vegetables provide more than vitamins; they also provide other diet essentials, such as fiber and fat.

Just Right

Many young children are quite compulsive about daily routines, including meals. They insist on eating only certain foods, prepared and placed in a particular way. This rigidity, known as the "just right" or "just so" phenomenon, would be pathological in adults but is normal and widespread among young children. For example:

> Whereas parents may insist that the child eat his vegetables at dinner, the child may insist that the potatoes be placed only in a certain part of the plate and must not touch any other food; should the potatoes land outside of this area, the child may seem to experience a sense of near-contamination, setting off a tirade of fussiness for which many 2- and 3-year-olds are notorious.
>
> *[Evans et al., 1997]*

Most young children's food preferences and rituals are far from ideal. (One 3-year-old I know wanted to eat only cream cheese sandwiches on white bread; one 4-year-old, only fast-food chicken nuggets.) When 1,500 parents were surveyed about their 1- to 6-year-olds (Evans et al., 1997), over 75 percent reported that their children's just-right phase peaked at about age 3, when the children:

- Preferred to have things done in a particular order or in a certain way
- Had a strong preference to wear (or not wear) certain clothes
- Prepared for bedtime by engaging in a special activity, routine, or ritual
- Had strong preferences for certain foods

By age 6, this rigidity fades somewhat (see Figure 8.1). Another team of experts puts it this way: "Most, if not all, children exhibit normal age-dependent obsessive compulsive behaviors [which are] usually gone by middle childhood" (March et al., 2004, p. 216).

The best advice for parents is probably to be patient until the just-right obsession fades away. Insistence on a particular routine, a preferred pair of shoes, or a favorite cup can usually be accommodated until the child gets a little older.

Overeating is another story. Almost no young child anywhere in the world, except in times of famine or war, is underfed during these years. Ideally, children would have only healthy foods to eat, a strategy that would protect their health lifelong (Gluckman & Hanson, 2006). Instead, at least in the United States, most children have several unhealthy snacks each day (Jahns et al., 2001).

Especially for Parents of Fussy Eaters
You prepare a variety of vegetables and fruits, but your 4-year-old wants only French fries and cake. What should you do?

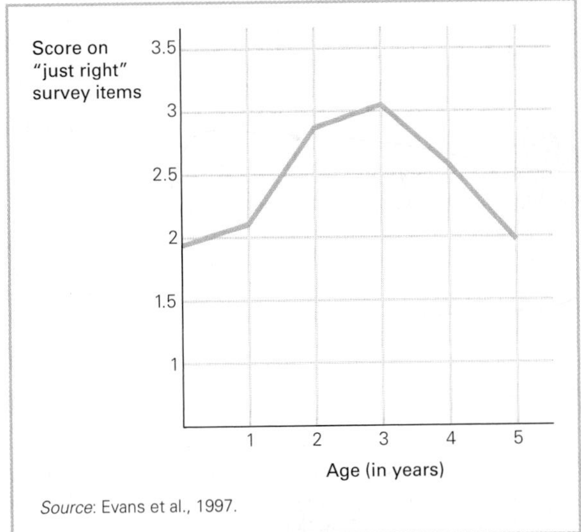

FIGURE 8.1

Young Children's Insistence on Routine
This chart shows the average scores of children (who are rated by their parents) on a survey indicating the child's desire to have certain things—including food selection and preparation—done "just right." Such strong preferences for rigid routines tend to fade by age 6.

SUMMING UP

During the play years, children grow steadily taller and proportionately thinner, with variations depending on genes, gender, nutrition, income, and other factors. Overweight is more common than underweight. One reason is that adults encourage overeating. Another is that young children usually have small appetites and picky habits but are rewarded with foods that are high in calories yet low in nutrition. ■

➤Response for Parents of Fussy Eaters (from page 209): The nutritionally wise answer would be to offer *only* fruits, vegetables, and other nourishing, low-fat foods, counting on the child's eventual hunger to drive him or her to eat them. However, centuries of cultural custom make it almost impossible for parents to be wise in such cases. Perhaps the best you can do is to discuss the dilemma with a nutritionist or pediatrician, who can advise you about what to do for your particular child.

Brain Development

Brains grow rapidly even before birth. By age 2, not only have brains increased in size but also a great deal of pruning of dendrites has already occurred. The 2-year-old brain weighs 75 percent of what it will weigh in adulthood. (The major structures of the brain are diagrammed in Appendix A, p. A-30.)

Since most of the brain is already present and functioning, what remains to develop after age 2? The most important parts! Those functions of the brain that make us most human are the ones that develop after infancy, enabling quicker, more coordinated, and more reflective thought (Kagan & Herschkowitz, 2005). Brain growth after infancy is a crucial difference between humans and other animals.

Speed of Thought

myelination The process by which axons become coated with myelin, a fatty substance that speeds the transmission of nerve impulses from neuron to neuron.

After infancy, continued proliferation of the communication pathways (dendrites and axons) results in some brain growth. However, most of the increase in brain weight (to 90 percent of adult weight by age 5) occurs because of **myelination** (Sampaio & Truwit, 2001). *Myelin* is a fatty coating on the axons that speeds signals between neurons, like insulation wrapped around electric wires to aid conduction.

The effects of myelination are most noticeable in early childhood (Nelson et al., 2006). Greater speed becomes pivotal when several thoughts must occur in rapid succession. By age 6 most children can listen and then answer, catch a ball and then throw it, write the alphabet in sequence, and so on.

Especially for Early-Childhood Teachers You know you should be patient, but you feel your frustration rising when your young charges dawdle on the walk to the playground a block away. What should you do?

Parents must still be patient when listening to young children talk, when helping them get dressed, or when watching them try to write their names. All these tasks are completed more slowly by 6-year-olds than by 16-year-olds. However, thanks to myelination, preschoolers are at least quicker than toddlers, who may take so long that they forget what they were doing before they finish.

Connecting the Brain's Hemispheres

corpus callosum A long band of nerve fibers that connect the left and right hemispheres of the brain.

One part of the brain that grows and myelinates rapidly during the play years is the **corpus callosum,** a band of nerve fibers that connect the left and right sides of the brain (see Figure 8.2). Growth of the corpus callosum makes communication between the two brain hemispheres more efficient, allowing children to coordinate the two sides of the brain or body. Failure of the corpus callosum to develop normally may result in serious disorders, including autism (Diwadkar & Keshavan, 2006).

lateralization Literally, sidedness. The specialization in certain functions by each side of the brain, with one side dominant for each activity. The left side of the brain controls the right side of the body, and vice versa.

To understand the significance of coordination of the two brain hemispheres, you need to realize that the two sides of the body and brain are not identical. Each side specializes, so each is dominant for certain functions—a process called **lateralization.** Lateralization, or "sidedness," is apparent not only in right- or left-handedness but also in the feet, eyes, ears, and the brain itself. Such specialization is epigenetic, prompted by genes, prenatal hormones, and early experiences.

The Left-Handed Child

Infants and toddlers usually prefer one hand over the other for grabbing a spoon, a rattle, and so on. For centuries, parents who saw a preference for the left hand forced their children to be right-handed. Indeed, since most people are right-handed, the common assumption was that right-handedness was best. This bias is still evident in language. In English, a "left-handed compliment" is insincere, and no one wants to be "left back" or "out in left field." In Latin, *dexter* (as in *dexterity*) means "right" and *sinister* means "left" (and also "evil"). *Gauche,* which in English means "socially awkward," is the French word for "left."

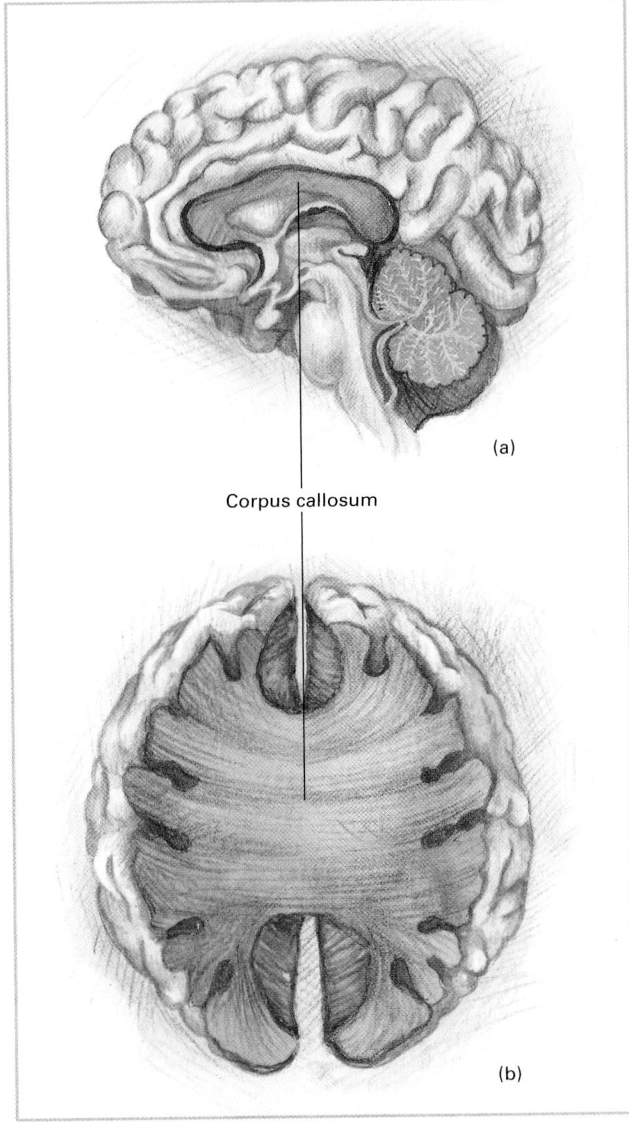

FIGURE 8.2

Connections Two views of the corpus callosum, a band of nerve fibers (axons) that convey information between the two hemispheres of the brain. When developed, this "connector" allows the person to coordinate functions that are performed mainly by one hemisphere or the other. *(a)* A view from between the hemispheres, looking toward the right side of the brain. *(b)* A view from above, with the gray matter removed in order to expose the corpus callosum.

Customs, including taboos, also favor right-handed people. For example, in many Asian and African nations, only the left hand is used for wiping after defecation; it is a major insult to give someone anything with that "dirty" hand.

Developmentalists advise against trying to switch a child's handedness, not only because this causes needless parent–child conflict but also because it might interfere with the natural and necessary process of lateralization. Left-handed adults tend to have thicker corpus callosa than others, which may enable better coordination of both sides of the body (Cherbuin & Brinkman, 2006). A disproportionate number of artists, musicians, and sports stars are left-handed.

Especially for Left-Handed Adults If you have a left-handed child (as you very well might, since handedness is partly genetic), at what age would you try to switch him or her?

The Whole Brain

Through studies of people with brain damage as well as through brain imaging, neurologists have determined how the brain's hemispheres specialize: The left half controls the right side of the body and contains the areas dedicated to logical reasoning, detailed analysis, and the basics of language; the right half controls the left side of the body and contains the areas dedicated to generalized emotional and creative impulses, including appreciation of most music, art, and poetry. Thus, the

➤Answer to Observation Quiz (from page 208): The cup, the pitcher, and the person. The cup has an unusually wide opening; the pitcher is small and has a sturdy handle; and the girl is using both hands and giving her full concentration to the task.

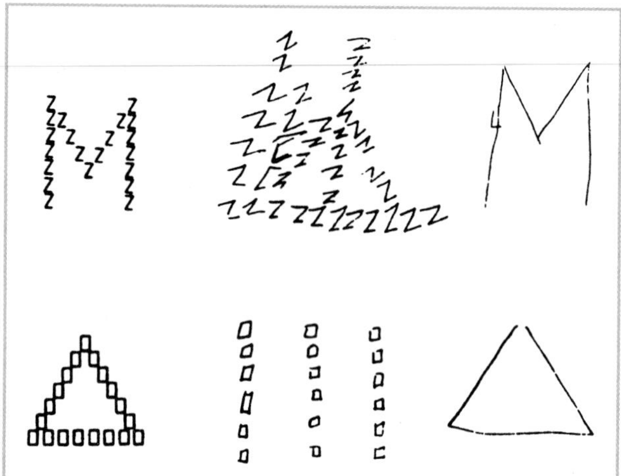

FIGURE 8.3

Copy What You See Brain-damaged adults were asked to copy the figure at the left in each row. One person drew the middle set, another the set at the right.

Observation Quiz (see answer, page 214): Which set was drawn by someone with left-side damage and which set by someone with right-side damage?

left side notices details and the right side grasps the big picture—a distinction that should provide a clue in interpreting Figure 8.3.

No one (except severely brain-damaged people) is exclusively left-brained or right-brained. Every cognitive skill requires both sides of the brain, just as gross motor skills require both sides of the body (Hugdahl & Davidson, 2002). Because older children have more myelinated fibers in the corpus callosum to speed signals between the two hemispheres, better thinking and less clumsy actions are possible for them.

Planning and Analyzing

You learned in Chapter 5 that the *prefrontal cortex* (sometimes called the *frontal cortex* or *frontal lobe*) is an area in the very front part of the brain's outer layer (the cortex), under the forehead. It "underlies higher-order cognition, including planning and complex forms of goal-directed behavior" (Luciana, 2003, p. 163). The prefrontal cortex is crucial for humans; it is said to be the *executive* of the brain because all the other areas of the cortex are ruled by prefrontal decisions. For example, a person might feel anxious on meeting someone new, whose friendship may be valuable in the future. The prefrontal cortex can calculate and plan, not letting the anxious feelings prevent the acquaintance.

Maturation of the Prefrontal Cortex

The frontal lobe "shows the most prolonged period of postnatal development of any region of the human brain" (Johnson, 2005, p. 210), with dendrite density and myelination increasing throughout childhood and adolescence (Nelson et al., 2006). Several notable benefits of maturation of the prefrontal cortex occur from ages 2 to 6:

- Sleep becomes more regular.
- Emotions become more nuanced and responsive to specific stimuli.
- Temper tantrums subside.
- Uncontrollable laughter or tears become less common.

In one series of experiments, 3-year-olds consistently made a stunning mistake (Zelazo et al., 2003). The children were given a set of cards with clear outlines of trucks or flowers, some red and some blue. They were asked to "play the shape game," putting trucks in one pile and flowers in another. Three-year-olds can do this correctly, as can some 2-year-olds and almost all older children.

No Writer's Block The context is designed to help this South African second-grader concentrate on her schoolwork. Large, one-person desks, uniforms, notebooks, and sharp pencils are manageable for the brains and skills of elementary school children, but not yet for preschoolers.

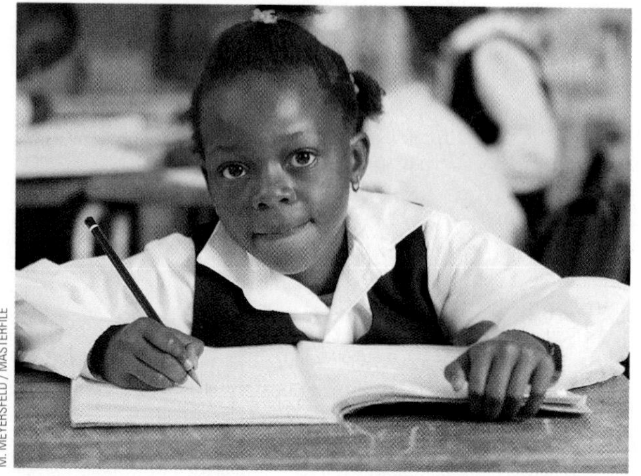

M. MEYERSFELD / MASTERFILE

Then the children were asked to "play the color game," sorting the cards by color. Most of them failed at this task, sorting by shape instead. This study has been replicated in many nations, and 3-year-olds usually get stuck on their initial sorting pattern (Diamond & Kirkham, 2005). Most older children, even 4-year-olds, make the switch.

When this result was first obtained, experimenters wondered whether the children didn't know their colors, so the scientists switched the order, first playing "the color game." Most 3-year-olds did that correctly. Then, when they were asked to play "the shape game," they still sorted by color. Even with a new set of cards, such as yellow or green rabbits or boats, they still tend to sort by the criterion (either color or shape) that was used in their first trial.

Researchers are looking into many possible explanations for this surprising result (Müller et al., 2006; Yerys & Munakata, 2006). All agree, however, that something in the executive function of the brain must mature before children are able to switch from one way of sorting objects to another.

An everyday example is the game Simon Says, in which children are supposed to follow the leader *only* when his or her orders are preceded by the words "Simon says." Thus when leaders touch their noses and say, "Simon says touch your nose," children are supposed to touch their noses; but when leaders touch their noses and merely say, "Touch your nose," no one is supposed to follow the example. Young children quickly lose at this game because they impulsively do what they see and are told to do. Older children are better at it because they can think before acting.

Maturation of the prefrontal cortex is also discussed in Chapters 5, 11, and 14.

➤Response for Early-Childhood Teachers (from page 210): One solution is to remind yourself that the children's brains are not yet myelinated enough to enable them to quickly walk, talk, or even button their jackets. Maturation has a major effect, as you will observe if you can schedule excursions in September and again in November. Progress, while still slow, will be a few seconds faster in November than it was in September.

Attention

A major function of the prefrontal cortex is to focus attention and thus to curb impulsiveness. A 3-year-old jumps from task to task and cannot be still, even in church or any other place that requires quiet. Similarly, younger children may want to play with a toy that another child has but lose interest by the time that toy becomes available.

The opposite of the impatient child is the child who plays with one toy for hours. **Perseveration** is the name for the tendency to persevere in, or stick to, one thought or action. Perseveration is evident in the card-sorting study and in young children's tendency to repeat one phrase or question again and again or to throw a tantrum when their favorite TV show is interrupted. That tantrum itself may perseverate: The child's crying may become uncontrollable and unstoppable, as if the child is stuck in that emotion.

perseveration The tendency to persevere in, or stick to, one thought or action for a long time.

Impulsiveness and perseveration are opposite behaviors with the same underlying cause: immaturity of the prefrontal cortex. Over the play years, brain maturation (innate) and emotional regulation (learned) decrease both impulsiveness and perseveration. Children gradually become able to pay attention when necessary (de Haan & Johnson, 2003).

➤Response for Left-handed Adults (from page 211): Preferably never! Most left-handed adults are quite proud of their distinctiveness. Developmentalists now recommend that natural dominance prevail. However, if you still want your child to switch, early childhood is too late, as brain lateralization has begun. In the first weeks of life, you might encourage right-handedness—but don't insist.

Emotions and the Brain

Now that we have looked at the brain structures involved in planning and analyzing, we turn to the *limbic system*, an area of the brain that is crucial in the expression and regulation of emotions. Both expression and regulation advance during the play years (more about that in Chapter 10). Three major parts of the limbic system are the amygdala, the hippocampus, and the hypothalamus.

The **amygdala,** a tiny structure deep in the brain (named after an almond, because it is about that shape and size), registers emotions, both positive and negative, especially fear (Nelson et al., 2006). Increased activity of the amygdala is one reason some young children have terrifying nightmares or sudden terrors.

amygdala A tiny brain structure that registers emotions, particularly fear and anxiety.

Fear can overwhelm the prefrontal cortex and disrupt a child's ability to reason. If a child is scared of, say, a lion in the closet, an adult should open the closet door and tell the lion to go home, not laugh or insist that the fear is nonsense.

Especially for Brain Experts Why do most neurologists think the limbic system is an oversimplification?

The amygdala responds to facial expressions (Vasa & Pine, 2004). This is part of social referencing, explained in Chapter 7. If a child sees a parent look terrified when a strange dog approaches, the child may also feel extreme fear, and if this recurs often enough, the child's amygdala may become hypersensitive. If instead the parent conveys pleasure or curiosity about the dog, the child will probably overcome initial feelings of fear because of another structure in the brain's limbic system, the hippocampus.

The **hippocampus** is located right next to the amygdala. It is a central processor of memory, especially memory of locations. The hippocampus responds to the

hippocampus A brain structure that is a central processor of memory, especially the memory of locations.

➤Answer to Observation Quiz (from page 212): The middle set, with its careful details, reflects damage to the right half of the brain, where overall impressions are formed. The person with left-brain damage produced the drawings that were just an M or a Δ, without the details of the tiny z's and rectangles. With a whole functioning brain, people can see both "the forest and the trees."

➤Response for Brain Experts (from page 213): The more we discover about the brain, the more complex we realize it is. Each part has specific functions *and* is connected to every other part.

hypothalamus A brain area that responds to the amygdala and the hippocampus to produce hormones that activate other parts of the brain and body.

anxieties of the amygdala with memory; it makes the child remember, for instance, that Mother petted a dog at a neighbor's house.

Memories of location are fragile in early childhood because the hippocampus is still developing. Indeed, every type of memory has its own timetable (Nelson & Webb, 2003); for example, memory for context is less advanced than memory for content, and *source memory* (of when, where, and how a certain fact was learned) is hazy (Cycowicz et al., 2003). A preschool child might claim "No one told me that. I always knew it" or might remember that something happened but misremember who was involved.

The amygdala and the hippocampus are sometimes helpful, sometimes not, depending on how useful fear and memory are. Some children, because their amygdala and hippocampus are not well developed, might be fearless when they should remember past events and be cautious. When the amygdala is surgically removed from animals, they are fearless in situations that should scare them; cats will stroll nonchalantly along when monkeys are nearby, for instance—something no normal cat would do (Kolb & Whishaw, 2003).

A third part of the limbic system, the **hypothalamus,** responds to signals from the amygdala (arousing) and the hippocampus (usually dampening) to produce hormones that activate other parts of the brain and body (see Figure 8.4). Ideally, this occurs in moderation. If excessive stress hormones flood the brain, part of the hippocampus may be destroyed. Permanent deficits in learning and memory may result (Davis et al., 2003).

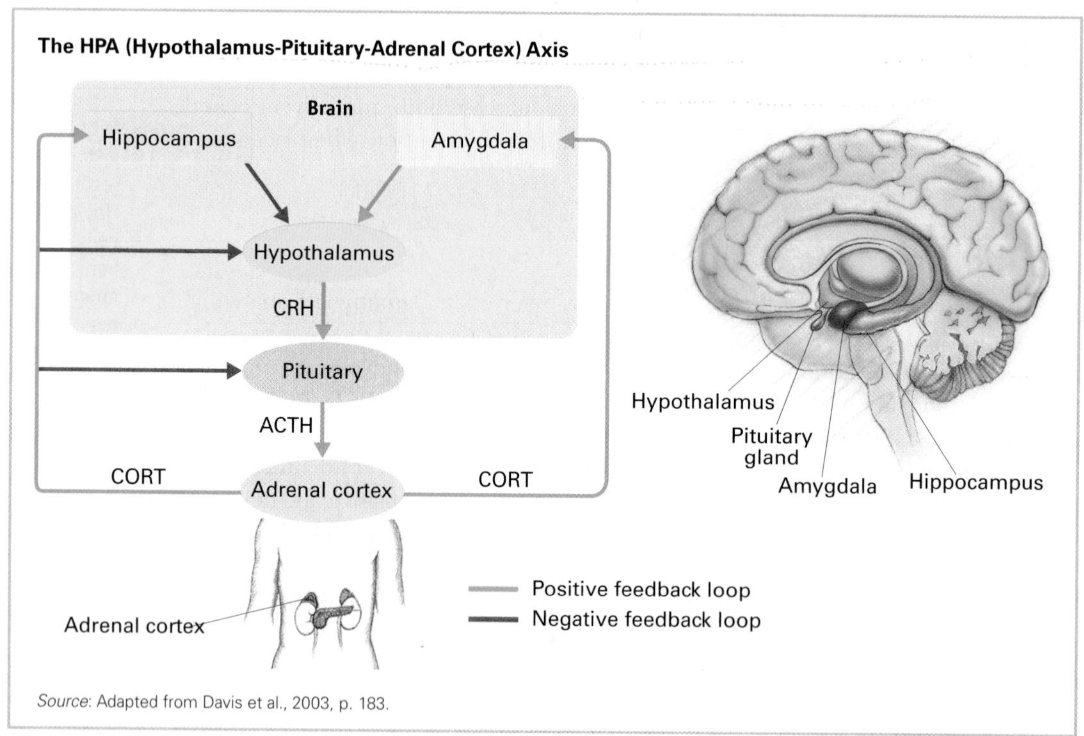

FIGURE 8.4

A Hormonal Feedback Loop This diagram simplifies a hormonal linkage, the HPA axis, involving the limbic system. Both the hippocampus and the amygdala stimulate the hypothalamus to produce CRH (corticotropin-releasing hormone), which in turn signals the pituitary gland to produce ACTH (adrenocorticotropic hormone). ACTH then triggers the production of CORT (glucocorticoids) by the adrenal cortex (the outer layers of the adrenal glands, atop the kidneys). The initial reaction to something frightening may either build or disappear, depending on other factors, including memories, and on how the various parts of the brain interpret that first alert from the amygdala. (Some other components of this mechanism have been omitted for the sake of clarity.)

Stressful experiences—meeting new friends, entering school, visiting a strange place—probably foster growth if the child has someone or something to moderate the stress. In an experiment, brain scans and tests of hormone levels measured stress in 4- to 6-year-olds after a fire alarm. Two weeks later, they were questioned about the event. Compared with less reactive children, those with higher stress reactions to the alarm remembered more with a friendly interviewer but less with a stern interviewer (Quas et al., 2004).

Other research also finds that preschoolers remember traumatic experiences better if the interviewer is a warm and attentive listener (Bruck et al., 2006). But stress should not be relentless, without long recovery, because developing brains are fragile; "prolonged physiological responses to stress and challenge put children at risk for a variety of problems in childhood, including physical and mental disorders, poor emotional regulation, and cognitive impairments" (Quas et al., 2004, p. 379).

Prolonged stress, with emotional and cognitive impairment, seemed to occur for the thousands of Romanian children in orphanages (see Chapter 5). When they saw pictures of happy, sad, frightened, and angry faces, their limbic systems were less reactive than were those of Romanian children living with their parents. The brains of the orphans were less lateralized, suggesting less specialized, less efficient thinking (Parker & Nelson, 2005).

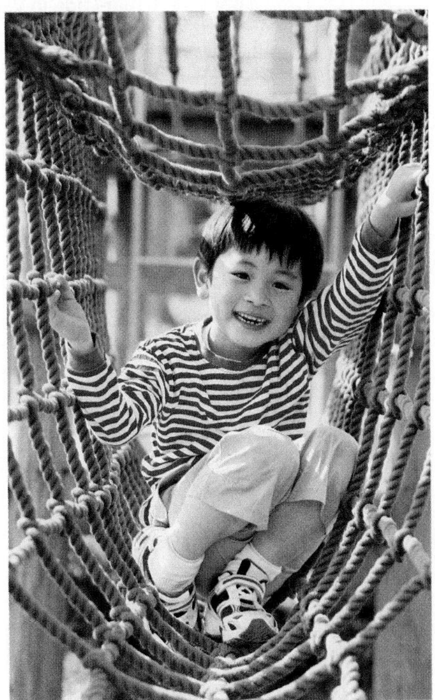

DIGITAL VISION / PUNCHSTOCK

The Joy of Climbing Would you delight in climbing on an unsteady rope swing, like this 6-year-old in Japan (and almost all his contemporaries worldwide)? Each age has special sources of pleasure.

Motor Skills

Maturation of the prefrontal cortex improves impulse control, while myelination of the corpus callosum and lateralization of the brain permits better coordination. No wonder children move with greater speed and grace as they age from 2 to 6, becoming better able to direct and refine their actions. (Table 8.1 lists approximate ages for the acquisition of various motor skills.)

TABLE 8.1

AT ABOUT THIS TIME: **Motor Skills at Ages 2–6***

Approx. Age	Skill or Achievement
2 years	Run for pleasure, without falling (but bumping into things) Climb chairs, tables, beds, out of cribs Walk up stairs Feed self with spoon Draw lines, spirals
3 years	Kick and throw a ball Jump with both feet off the floor Pedal a tricycle Copy simple shapes (e.g., circle, rectangle) Walk downstairs Climb ladders
4 years	Catch a ball (not too small or thrown too fast) Use scissors to cut Hop on either foot Feed self with fork Dress self (no tiny buttons, no ties) Copy most letters Pour juice without spilling Brush teeth
5 years	Skip and gallop in rhythm Clap, bang, sing in rhythm Copy difficult shapes and letters (e.g., diamond shape, letter *S*) Climb trees, jump over things Use knife to cut Tie a bow Throw a ball Wash face, comb hair
6 years	Draw and write with one hand Write simple words Scan a page of print, moving the eyes systematically in the appropriate direction Ride a bicycle Do a cartwheel Tie shoes Catch a ball

*Context is crucial. (Many 6-year-olds cannot tie shoelaces because they have no shoes with laces.)

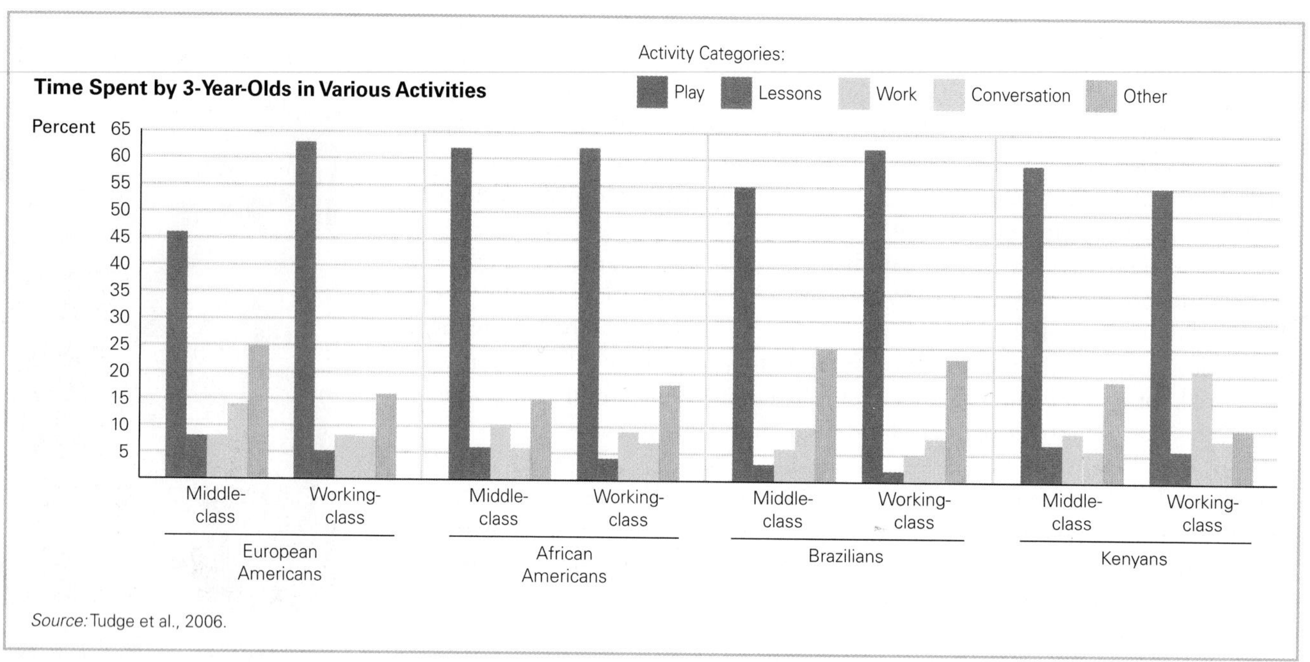

FIGURE 8.5

Mostly Playing When researchers studied 3-year-olds in the United States, Brazil, and Kenya, they found that, on average, the children spent more than half their time playing. Note the low percentages of both middle- and working-class Brazilian children in the Lessons category, which included all intentional efforts to teach children something. There is a cultural explanation: Unlike parents in Kenya and the United States, most Brazilian parents believe that children this age should not be in organized day care.

Research Design

Scientists: Jonathan Tudge and others (e.g., researchers in Brazil and Kenya).

Publication: *Child Development* (2006).

Participants: About 20 3-year-olds from each of four ethnic groups: European American and African American in Greensboro, North Carolina; Luo in Kisumu, Kenya; and European descent in Porto Alegre, Brazil. On the basis of parents' education and occupation, half the children in each group were from middle-class families and half were from working-class families.

Design: Children were observed for 20 hours each in their usual daytime activities. The child wore a wireless microphone; every 6 minutes, the observer recorded what the child was doing. Later the time was allocated among five categories: Lessons (deliberate attempts to impart information), Work (household tasks), Play (activities for enjoyment), Conversation (sustained talk with adults about things not the current focus of activity), and Other (eating, bathing, sleeping).

Major conclusion: All eight groups spent much more time playing than doing anything else. Much larger differences were found in time spent in lessons, work, and conversation.

Comment: Many features of good research are evident in this study.

According to a study of middle-class and working-class children in Brazil, Kenya, and the United States (Tudge et al., 2006; see Research Design), young children spend the majority of their waking time in play, more than they spend in three other important activities (doing chores, learning lessons, or having conversations with adults) combined (see Figure 8.5). Mastery of gross and fine motor skills is one result of the extensive active play of young children.

Gross Motor Skills

Gross motor skills—which, as defined in Chapter 5, involve large body movements—improve dramatically. When you watch children play, you can see clumsy 2-year-olds who fall down and sometimes bump into each other, but you can also see 5-year-olds who are both skilled and graceful.

Most North American 5-year-olds can ride a tricycle; climb a ladder; pump a swing; and throw, catch, and kick a ball. Some can skate, ski, dive, and ride a bicycle—activities that demand balance as well as coordination. In some nations, 5-year-olds swim in oceans or climb cliffs. A combination of brain maturation, motivation, and guided practice makes each of these skills possible.

Adults need to make sure children have safe space, time, and playmates; skills will follow. According to sociocultural theory, children learn best from peers who demonstrate whatever skills—from catching a ball to climbing a tree—the child is ready to try.

Fine Motor Skills

Fine motor skills, which involve small body movements (especially those of the hands and fingers), are harder to master. Pouring juice into a glass, cutting food with a knife and fork, and achieving anything more artful than a scribble with a pencil require muscular control, patience, and judgment that are beyond most 2-year-olds.

Many fine motor skills involve two hands and thus both sides of the brain: The fork stabs the meat while the knife cuts it; one hand steadies the paper while the other writes; tying shoes, buttoning shirts, pulling on socks, and zipping zippers require both hands. An immature corpus callosum and prefrontal cortex may be the underlying reason that shoelaces get knotted, paper gets ripped, and zippers get stuck. Short, stubby fingers and confusion about handedness add to the problem.

Especially for Immigrant Parents You and your family eat with chopsticks at home, but you want your children to feel comfortable in Western culture. Should you change your family's eating customs?

BANANA STOCK / PICTUREQUEST

Snip, Snip Cutting paper with scissors is a hard, slow task for a 3-year-old, who is just beginning to develop fine motor control. Imagine wielding blunt "safety" scissors and hoping that the paper will be sliced exactly where you want it to be.

Artistic Expression

During the play years, children are imaginative, creative, and not yet self-critical. They love to express themselves, especially if their parents applaud, display their artwork, and otherwise communicate approval. It may be that the relative immaturity of the prefrontal cortex allows imagination free rein, without the social anxiety of older children, who might say "I can't draw" or "I am horrible at dancing."

All forms of artistic expression blossom during early childhood. Children love to dance around the room, build an elaborate tower of blocks, make music by pounding in rhythm, and put bright marks on shiny paper.

Children's artwork reflects their unique perception and cognition. For example, researchers asked young children to draw a balloon and, later, a lollipop. To adults, the drawings were indistinguishable, but the children who made the drawings were quite insistent as to which was which (Bloom, 2000) (see Figure 8.6).

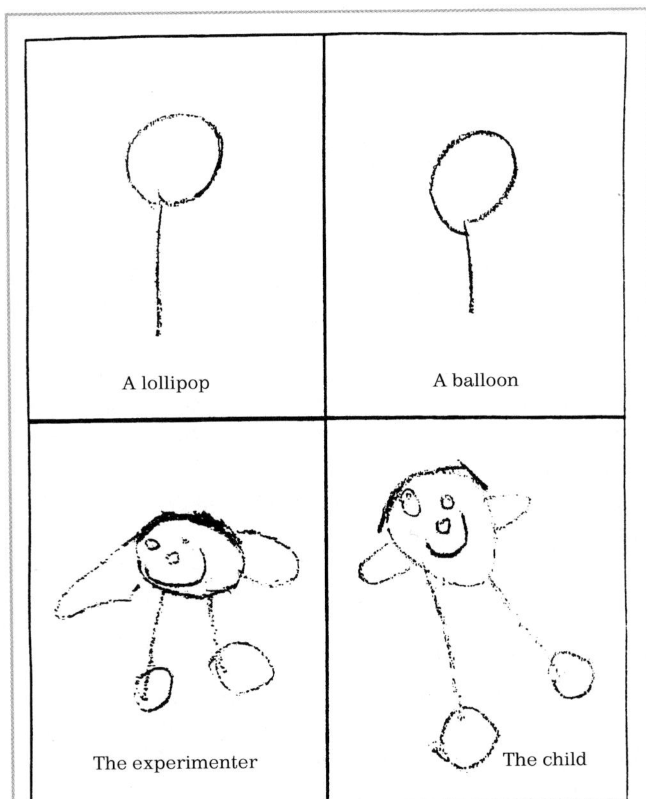

FIGURE 8.6

Which Is Which? The child who made these drawings insisted that the one at top left was a lollipop and the one at top right was a balloon (not vice versa) and that the drawing at bottom left was the experimenter and the one at bottom right was the child (not vice versa).

(a)

(b)

(c)

(A) NICOLE VILLAMORA (B) LAURA DWIGHT (C) BLEND IMAGES / ALAMY

No Ears? *(a)* Jalen was careful to include all seven of her family members who were present when she drew her picture. She tried to be realistic—by, for example, portraying her cousin, who was slumped on the couch, in a horizontal position. *(b)* Elizabeth takes pride in a more difficult task, drawing her family from memory. All have belly buttons and big smiles that reach their foreheads, but they have no arms or hair. *(c)* By age 6, this Virginia girl draws just one family member in detail—nostrils and mustache included.

In every artistic domain, from dance to sculpture, maturation of brain and body is gradual and comes with practice. For example, when drawing the human figure, 2- to 3-year-olds usually draw a "tadpole"—a circle for a head with eyes and sometimes a smiling mouth, and then a line or two beneath to indicate the rest of the body. Gradually, children's drawings of people evolve from tadpoles into more human forms.

Tadpoles are "strikingly characteristic" of children's art (Cox, 1993); they are drawn universally, in all cultures. Similarly, children worldwide seek places to climb—on rocky hillsides, playground structures, and the dining room table—imagining as they play. They like challenges that they can meet.

SUMMING UP

The brain continues to mature during early childhood, with myelination in several crucial areas. One is the corpus callosum, which connects the left and right sides of the brain and therefore the right and left sides of the body. Increased myelination speeds up actions and reactions. The prefrontal cortex enables impulse control, allowing children to think before they act as well as to stop one action in order to begin another. As impulsiveness and perseveration decrease, children become better able to learn. Several key areas of the brain—including the amygdala, the hypothalamus, and the hippocampus—make up the limbic system, which also matures from ages 2 to 6. The limbic system aids emotional expression and control. Maturation of the brain leads to better control of the body and hence to development of motor skills. ■

Injuries and Abuse

Throughout this text, we have assumed that parents want to foster their children's development and protect them from danger. That is true in the vast majority of families. Yet more children die of violence—either accidental or deliberate—than from any other cause.

In the United States, where accurate death records are kept, out of every 100,000 1- to 4-year-olds, 10.9 died accidentally, 2.5 died of cancer (the leading fatal disease at this age), and 2.4 were murdered in 2003 (U.S. Bureau of the Census, 2006).

Young children are more vulnerable to injuries and abuse than are slightly older ones, partly because they are impulsive yet dependent on others, as we have just seen. Much of the harm to children can be prevented, and that is our primary reason for discussing this topic in detail.

➤Response for Immigrant Parents (from page 217): Children develop the motor skills that they see and practice. They will soon learn to use forks, spoons, and knives. Do not abandon chopsticks completely, because young children can learn several ways of doing things, and the ability to eat with chopsticks is a social asset.

Avoidable Injury

Worldwide, injuries cause millions of premature deaths among young adults as well as children: Not until age 40 does any disease overtake accidents as a cause of mortality. Among children, the 1- to 4-year-olds are most vulnerable to accidental death and injury (MMWR, September 3, 2004).

Age-related trends are apparent in the particular kinds of injuries. Teenagers and young adults are most often killed as passengers or drivers in motor-vehicle accidents. Falls are more often fatal for the very young (under 24 months) and very old (over 80 years) than for preschoolers. For preschoolers, fatal accidents are more likely to involve poison, fire, choking, or drowning.

Why do small children have so many accidents? Immaturity of the prefrontal cortex makes young children impulsive, so they plunge into dangerous places and activities (Zeedyk et al., 2002). Unlike infants, their motor skills allow them to run, leap, scramble, and grab in a flash. Their curiosity is boundless; their impulses are uninhibited.

Injury Control

As one team of experts notes, "Injuries are not unpredictable, unavoidable events. To a large extent, society chooses the injury rates it has" (Christoffel & Gallagher, 1999, p. 10). How could a society *choose* unnecessarily high rates of injury, pain, and lifelong damage? Injury prevention is no accident; it is a choice made by parents, by legislators, and by society as a whole.

To understand this, consider the implications of the terminology. The word *accident* implies that an injury is a random, unpredictable event. If anyone is at fault, a careless parent or an accident-prone child might be blamed. This is called the "accident paradigm"; it implies that "injuries will occur despite our best efforts," and it allows the general public to feel blameless (Benjamin, 2004, p. 521).

In response, experts now prefer the term **injury control** (or **harm reduction**) instead of accident prevention. Injury control implies that harm can be minimized if appropriate controls are in place. Minor mishaps are bound to occur, but the damage is reduced if a child falls on a safety surface instead of concrete, if a car seat protects the body in a crash, if a bicycle helmet cracks instead of a skull, if the swallowed pills come from a tiny bottle.

injury control/harm reduction Practices that are aimed at anticipating, controlling, and preventing dangerous activities; these practices reflect the beliefs that accidents are not random and that injuries can be made less harmful if proper controls are in place.

Only half as many 1- to 5-year-olds in the United States were fatally injured in 2005 as in 1985, thanks to laws that govern poisons, fires, and cars. But now the leading cause of unintentional death for children aged 1 to 5 is drowning in a swimming pool (Brenner et al., 2001). To prevent most such deaths, government officials need only require that any body of water near a home have a high fence around it.

A pool-fencing ordinance in southern California allowed one side of the enclosure to be the wall of a house, with a door that could be locked. This seemed reasonable to homeowners but not to pediatricians. The law protected trespassing children but not the family's own children, who knew how to open those doors. After the law was passed, California child drownings did not decline (Morgenstern et al., 2000).

(a)

MANOR PHOTOGRAPHY / ALAMY

(b)

INMAGINE

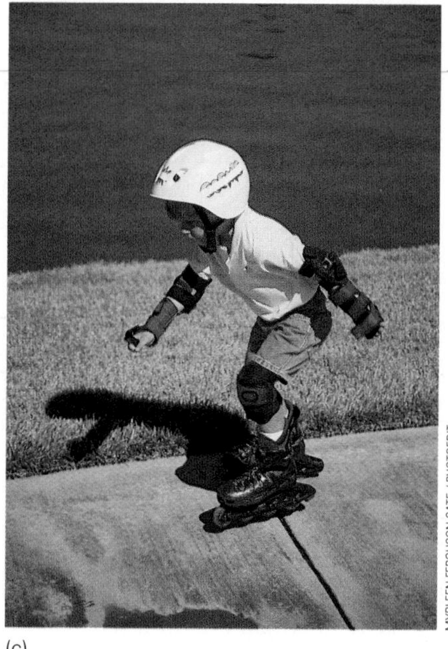
(c)

MYRLEEN FERGUSON CATE / PHOTOEDIT

And If He Falls . . . None of these children is injured, so no tertiary prevention is needed. Photos *(b)* and *(c)* both illustrate secondary prevention. In photo *(a)*, the metal climbing equipment with large gaps and peeling paint is hazardous. Primary prevention suggests that this "attractive nuisance" be dismantled.

Three Levels of Prevention

Injury prevention should begin long before any particular child, parent, or politician does something foolish or careless. Of the three levels of prevention described below, the one that is least noticed by individuals but most effective overall is the first level (Cohen et al., 2007).

- In **primary prevention,** the overall situation is structured to make injuries less likely. Primary prevention fosters conditions that reduce everyone's chance of injury, no matter what their circumstances.
- **Secondary prevention** is more specific, averting harm to individuals in high-risk situations.
- **Tertiary prevention** begins after an injury, limiting the damage it causes. Tertiary prevention saves lives and reduces the number and severity of permanent disabilities.

primary prevention Actions that change overall background conditions to prevent some unwanted event or circumstance, such as injury, disease, or abuse.

secondary prevention Actions that avert harm in a high-risk situation, such as stopping a car before it hits a pedestrian.

tertiary prevention Actions, such as immediate and effective medical treatment, that are taken after an adverse event such as illness or injury occurs, and are aimed at reducing the harm or preventing disability.

To illustrate, the rate of pedestrian deaths in motor-vehicle accidents has steadily decreased in the past 20 years because of all three levels of prevention. How does each level contribute to this welcome decline?

Primary prevention includes sidewalks, speed bumps, pedestrian overpasses, brighter streetlights, and single-lane traffic circles (Retting et al., 2003; Tester et al., 2004). Cars have been redesigned (e.g., better headlights and brakes) and drivers' skills improved (e.g., as a result of more frequent vision tests and stronger drunk-driving penalties).

Especially for Urban Planners Describe a neighborhood park that would benefit 2- to 5-year-olds.

Secondary prevention reduces the dangers in high-risk situations. For children this means requiring flashing lights on stopped school buses, employing school-crossing guards, refusing alcohol to teenagers, and insisting that young children walk with adults, who are more careful crossing streets. For the aged, this means longer red lights and well-marked crosswalks.

The distinction between primary prevention and secondary prevention is not clear-cut. In general, secondary prevention is more targeted, focusing on specific risk groups (e.g., young children) and proven dangers (e.g., walking to school) rather than on the overall culture, politics, or environment.

Finally, *tertiary prevention* reduces damage after accidents. Laws against hit-and-run driving, improved emergency-room procedures (e.g., faster action to re-

RICHARD RANSIER / CORBIS

A Safe Leap What makes this jump safe as well as fun are the high fences on all sides of the pool, the adequate depth of the water, and the presence of at least one adult (taking the picture).

duce brain swelling), and more effective rehabilitation are examples of tertiary prevention. Speedy and well-trained ambulance teams may be the most important: If an injured person arrives at a hospital within the "golden hour" after an accident, the chances of recovery are much better (Christoffel & Gallagher, 1999). In many European countries, tertiary prevention has involved redesigning the fronts of cars so that they are less destructive to pedestrians when accidents do occur (Retting et al., 2003).

Many measures at all three levels have been instituted, to good effect. In the United States, pedestrian deaths decreased from 8,842 in 1990 to 4,600 in 2004 (U.S. Bureau of the Census, 2006). Similar trends are found in almost every nation, for almost every fatal injury.

Especially for Socially Aware Students In the "In Person" feature below, how did Kathleen Berger's SES protect Bethany from serious harm?

in person

"My Baby Swallowed Poison"

The first strategy that most people think of for preventing injury to young children is parental education. However, public health research finds that laws that apply to everyone are more effective than education, especially if parents are not ready to learn and change or are overwhelmed by the daily demands of child care.

For example, the best time to convince parents to use an infant seat in their car (which has saved thousands of young lives) is before they bring their newborn home from the hospital. Voluntary use of car seats is much less common than mandated use.

As one expert explains: "Too often, we design our physical environment for smart people who are highly motivated" (Baker, 2000). In real life, everyone has moments of foolish indifference. At those moments, automatic safety measures save lives.

I know this firsthand. My daughter Bethany, at age 2, climbed onto the kitchen counter to find, open, and swallow most of a bottle of baby aspirin. Where was I? A few feet away, nursing our second child and watching television. I did not notice what Bethany was doing until I checked on her during a commercial.

What prevented serious injury? Laws limiting the number of baby aspirin per container (primary prevention), my pediatrician telling me on my first well-baby checkup to buy syrup of ipecac (secondary prevention), and my phone call to Poison Control (tertiary prevention). I told the stranger who answered the phone, "My baby swallowed poison." He calmly asked me questions and then told me to make Bethany swallow ipecac so that she'd throw up the aspirin. I did and she did. I still blame myself, but I am grateful for all three levels of prevention that protected my child.

MISHAWAKA POLICE DEPARTMENT / GETTY IMAGES

Nobody Watching? Madelyn Gorman Toogood looks around to make sure no one is watching before she slaps and shakes her 4-year-old daughter, Martha, who is in a car seat inside the vehicle. A security camera recorded this incident in an Indiana department store parking lot. A week later, after the videotape was repeatedly broadcast nationwide, Toogood was recognized and arrested. The haunting question is: How much child abuse takes place that is not witnessed?

Child Maltreatment

The next time you read news headlines about some horribly neglected or abused child, think of these words from a leading researcher in child maltreatment:

> Make no mistake—those who abuse children are fully responsible for their actions. However, creating an information system that perpetuates the message that offenders are the only ones to blame may be misleading. . . . We all contribute to the conditions that allow perpetrators to succeed.
>
> *[Daro, 2002, p. 1133]*

We all contribute in the sense that the causes of child maltreatment are multifaceted, involving not only the parents but also the maltreated children, the community, and the culture. For example, infants are most at risk of being maltreated if they themselves are difficult (fragile, needing frequent feeding, crying often) *and* if their mothers are depressed and do not feel in control of their lives or their infants *and* if the family is under stress because of poverty (Bugental & Happaney, 2004).

Maltreatment Noticed and Defined

Noticing is the first step. Until about 1960, people thought child maltreatment was rare and usually consisted of a sudden attack by a disturbed stranger. Today, thanks to a pioneering study based on careful observation in one Boston hospital (Kempe & Kempe, 1978), we know better: Maltreatment is neither rare nor sudden and the perpetrators are often the child's own parents. That makes it much worse: Ongoing maltreatment, with no safe haven, is much more damaging to children than a single brief incident, however abusive (Manly et al., 2001).

child maltreatment Intentional harm to or avoidable endangerment of anyone under 18 years of age.

child abuse Deliberate action that is harmful to a child's physical, emotional, or sexual well-being.

child neglect Failure to meet a child's basic physical, educational, or emotional needs.

With this recognition came a broader definition: **Child maltreatment** now refers to all intentional harm to, or avoidable endangerment of, anyone under 18 years of age. Thus, child maltreatment includes both **child abuse,** which is deliberate action that is harmful to a child's physical, emotional, or sexual well-being, and **child neglect,** which is failure to appropriately meet a child's basic physical or emotional needs.

The more that researchers study child maltreatment, the more apparent the harmful effects of neglect become (Hildyard & Wolfe, 2002). As one team wrote, "Severe neglect occurring in the early childhood years has been found to be particularly detrimental to successful adaptation" (Valentino et al., 2006, p. 483). How frequently does maltreatment occur? It is impossible to say. Not all cases of maltreatment are noticed, not all that are noticed are reported, and not all that are reported are substantiated.

reported maltreatment Harm or endangerment about which someone has notified the authorities.

substantiated maltreatment Harm or endangerment that has been reported, investigated, and verified.

Reported maltreatment occurs when the authorities have been informed about the situation. Since 1993, the number of *reported* cases of maltreatment in the United States has ranged from 2.7 million to 3 million a year (U.S. Department of Health and Human Services, 2006). Cases of **substantiated maltreatment** are those that have been investigated and verified (see Figure 8.7). The number of *substantiated* cases in 2004 was 872,000 (one-fourth of which victimized 2- to 5-year-olds), or about 1 maltreated child in every 70 aged 2 to 5 (U.S. Department of Health and Human Services, 2006). This 3-to-1 ratio of reported to substantiated cases can be attributed to three factors:

- Each child is counted once, even if repeated maltreatment is reported.
- Substantiation requires proof in the form of unmistakable injuries, serious malnutrition, or a witness willing to testify. Such evidence is not always available.
- A report may be false or deliberately misleading (less than 1 percent).

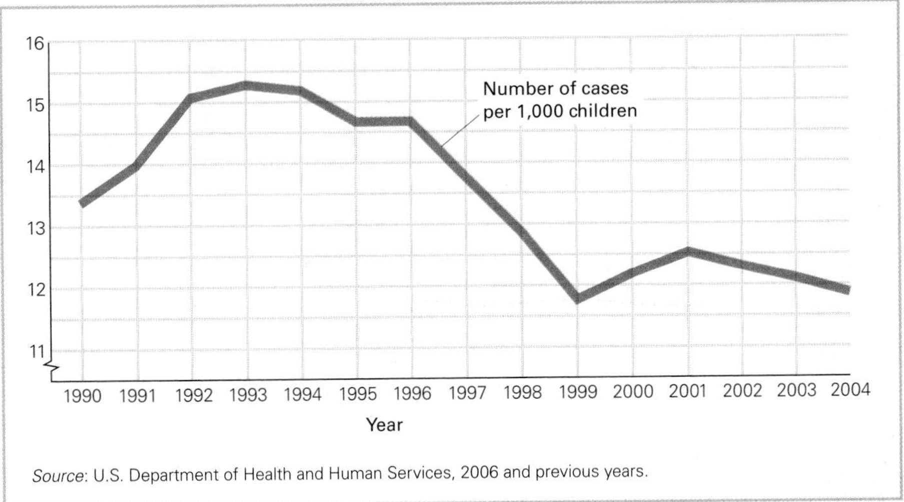

FIGURE 8.7

Rates of Substantiated Child Maltreatment, United States, 1990–2004 The number of reported and substantiated cases of maltreatment of children under age 18 in the United States is too high, but there is some good news: The rate has declined significantly from the peak in 1993.

Observation Quiz (see answer, page 225): The dot for 1999 is close to the bottom of the graph. Does that mean it is close to zero?

Research Design

Scientists: Jon Hussey and others at the University of North Carolina.

Publication: *Pediatrics* (2006).

Participants: Total of 15,197 young adults, interviewed at age 18–26 as part of the third wave of a large longitudinal study called Add Health, which began in 1995 with a representative sample of over 20,000 U.S. adolescents.

Design: Participants were asked to report, confidentially (via headphones and a computer, a method that yields more accurate answers than face-to-face or written questions do), whether their caregivers had ever maltreated them. Questions were specific (e.g., "slapped, hit, or kicked"), and participants indicated how often the behavior occurred (once, twice, or more).

Major conclusions: Maltreatment was common: One in four had been physically abused. Each type of maltreatment was associated with multiple health risks.

Comment: Although one would hope that these rates are overestimates, actual rates may be even higher, for three reasons: (1) Young adults tend to idealize their childhood; (2) the original participants were all in high school and had their parents' permission to respond to the survey; and (3) the participants in this third wave of interviews were, on average, more advantaged than those who dropped out or could not be found.

How often does maltreatment go unreported? According to a national, confidential survey of young adults in the United States, 1 in 4 had been physically abused ("slapped, hit, or kicked" by a parent or other adult caregiver) before sixth grade and 1 in 22 had been sexually abused ("touched or forced to touch someone else in a sexual way") (Hussey et al., 2006; see Research Design).

One reason for these high rates may be that young adults were asked if they had *ever* been mistreated by someone who was caring for them, while most other sources report *annual* rates. The authors of this study think the rates they found are *underestimates*!

Warning Signs of Maltreatment

Often the first sign of maltreatment is delayed development, such as slow growth, immature communication, lack of curiosity, or unusual social interactions. All these difficulties may be evident even at age 1 (Valentino et al., 2006).

During the play years, a maltreated child may seem fearful, startled by noise, defensive and quick to attack, and confused between fantasy and reality. These may be symptoms of **post-traumatic stress disorder (PTSD),** a disorder first identified in combat veterans, then in adults who had experienced some emotional injury or shock (in reaction to a serious accident or violent crime, for example). It now seems evident in some maltreated children (De Bellis, 2001; Yehuda, 2006).

post-traumatic stress disorder (PTSD) A delayed reaction to a trauma or shock, which may include hyperactivity and hypervigilance, displaced anger, sleeplessness, sudden terror or anxiety, and confusion between fantasy and reality.

By school age, neglected children tend to be withdrawn and self-critical; abused children tend to be aggressive; neither is resilient to stress. At every age, maltreated children are less likely to have friends (Manly et al., 2001).

Table 8.2 lists signs of maltreatment, both neglect and abuse. None of these signs are proof, but whenever any of them occurs, it signifies trouble. Many nations, including the United States, now require professionals who deal with children (teachers, nurses, social workers, doctors, police officers) to report any suspected maltreatment. Not all professionals know when to be suspicious, however. For

➤**Response for Urban Planners** (from page 220): The adult idea of a park— a large, grassy open place—is not best for young children. For them, you would design an enclosed area, small enough and with adequate seating to allow caregivers to socialize while watching their children. The playground surface would have to be protective (since young children are clumsy), with equipment that encouraged both gross motor skills (such as climbing) and fine motor skills (such as sandbox play). Swings are not beneficial, since they do not develop many motor skills. Teenagers and dogs should have their own designated areas, far from the youngest children.

TABLE 8.2

Signs of Maltreatment in Children Aged 2 to 10
Injuries that do not fit an "accidental" explanation: bruises on both sides of the face or body; burns with a clear line between burned and unburned skin; "falls" that result in cuts, not scrapes
Repeated injuries, especially broken bones not properly tended
Fantasy play, with dominant themes of violence or sexual knowledge
Slow physical growth, especially with unusual appetite or lack of appetite
Ongoing physical complaints, such as stomachaches, headaches, genital pain, sleepiness
Reluctance to talk, to play, or to move, especially if development is slow
No close friendships; hostility toward others; bullying of smaller children
Hypervigilance, with quick, impulsive reactions, such as cringing, startling, or hitting
Frequent absences from school, changes of address, or new caregivers
Expressions of fear rather than joy on seeing the caregiver

Source: Adapted from Scannapieco & Connell-Carrick, 2005.

Especially for Nurses While weighing a 4-year-old, you notice several bruises on the child's legs. When you ask about them, the child says nothing and the parent says the child bumps into things. What should you do?

instance, child patients are reported for maltreatment three times more often in teaching hospitals (where ongoing education is part of the hospital's mission) than in regular hospitals, where "child abuse and neglect are underidentified, underdiagnosed, and undercoded" (Rovi et al., 2004, p. 589). Would better reporting make a difference? It might have for a child known as B.V.

a case to study

A Series of Suspicious Events

Three million reported cases of maltreatment per year in the United States seems like a huge number, yet most cases of neglect are not reported. Consider one team's report on a child in a low-income family:

> B.V., a 2-year-old male, was found lying face down in the bathtub by an 8-year-old sent to check on him. He had been placed in the bathtub by his mother, who then went to the kitchen and was absent for approximately 10 minutes. B.V. was transported by ambulance to a local hospital. He was unresponsive and had a rectal temperature of 90 degrees Fahrenheit. After medical treatment, the child's breathing resumed, and he was transported to a tertiary care hospital. B.V. remained in the pediatric intensive care unit for 9 days with minimal brain function and no response to any stimuli. He was then transferred to a standard hospital room where he died 2 days later. The mother refused to have an autopsy performed. Subsequently, the death certificate was signed by an attending physician, and cause of death was pneumonia with anoxic brain injury as a result of near-drowning.
>
> The CPS [Child Protective Services] worker advised B.V.'s mother that 10 minutes was too long to leave a 2-year-old in the bathtub unsupervised. B.V.'s mother replied that she had done it many times before and that nothing had happened. Further examination of the medical chart revealed that prior to B.V.'s death, he had a sibling who had experienced an apparent life-threatening event (previously termed a "near miss" sudden infant death syndrome). The sibling was placed on cardiac and apnea (breathing) monitors for 7 to 8 months. In addition, B.V. had been to the children's hospital approximately 2 weeks prior for a major injury to his big toe. B.V.'s toe had been severed and required numerous stitches. The mother stated that this incident was a result of the 4-year-old brother slamming the door on B.V.'s foot. Furthermore, B.V. had been seen in a different local hospital for a finger fracture the month before his death. None of the available reports indicate the mother's history of how the finger fracture occurred.
>
> *[Bonner et al., 1999, pp. 165–166]*

No charges were filed in this death. The team notes:

> This case illustrates chronic supervisory neglect. . . . The series of suspicious events that preceded the death did not result in protective or preventive services for the family.
>
> *[Bonner et al., 1999, p. 166]*

This case is indeed a chilling example of "chronic supervisory neglect." Professionals who dealt with the family ignored many medical signs that something was wrong—the sibling's "near-miss" SIDS, the fractured finger, and the severed toe. No mention is made of language, emotions, or social skills, which probably would have raised alarm as well.

Even after death, the neglect of neglect continued. No help was provided for the 8-year-old who found his dying brother or for the 4-year-old who reportedly severed the toddler's toe. These children were also at high risk of maltreatment. Indeed, they had already been maltreated: Children are damaged by chronic feelings of helplessness and danger (De Bellis, 2001).

Physical abuse and neglect are most likely to be experienced by children who:

- Are under age 6
- Have two or more siblings
- Have an unemployed or absent father
- Have a mother who did not complete high school
- Live in a poor, high-crime neighborhood

All these risk factors were present for B.V. If he had not been poor, he might have had a private pediatrician, who might have noticed the danger he was in. If his mother had had fewer children and a supportive husband, she might have watched him in the tub. A higher level of education might have helped her understand how to cope. Neighbors and relatives might have helped. Instead, B.V. died.

Consequences of Maltreatment

The impact of any child-rearing practice is affected by the cultural context. Certain customs (such as circumcision, pierced ears, and spanking) are considered abuse in some cultures but not in others, and their actual effects on children vary accordingly. Children suffer if their parents seem not to love them according to their community's standards for parental love.

Maltreatment compromises basic health in every way (Hussey et al., 2006). Abused and neglected children are more often injured, sick, and hospitalized for reasons not directly related to their maltreatment (Kendall-Tackett, 2002).

Many neglectful parents do not enroll their children in day-care centers or schools that would teach them well. Visits to a park, to a zoo, to the grandparents' home, or to a neighbor child's house are infrequent, since social isolation is a result as well as a cause of child maltreatment. Maltreated children learn less and suffer more.

REUTERS / SANJIB MUKHERJEE

Abuse or Athletics? Four-year-old Budhia Singh ran 40 miles in 7 hours with adult marathoners. He says he likes to run, but his mother (a widow who allowed his trainer to "adopt" him because she could not feed him) has charged the trainer with physical abuse. The government of India has declared that Singh cannot race again until he is fully grown. If child, parent, and community approve of some activity, can it still be maltreatment?

Although biological and academic handicaps are substantial, deficits are even more apparent in the child's social skills. Maltreated children often regard other people as hostile and exploitative; hence, they are less friendly, more aggressive, and more isolated than other children. The longer their abuse continues and the earlier it started, the worse their peer relationships are (Manly et al., 2001; Scannapieco & Connell-Carrick, 2005).

A life-span perspective reveals that all these deficits can continue lifelong. Maltreated children and adolescents are often bullies or victims or both. Adults who were severely maltreated in childhood (physically, sexually, or emotionally) often use drugs or alcohol to numb their emotions; they often enter unsupportive relationships, become victims or aggressors, sabotage their own careers, eat too much or too little, and generally engage in self-destructive behavior (M. G. Smith & Fong, 2004). From a developmental perspective, the worst consequences result from chronic neglect, which is least likely to be reported.

Three Levels of Prevention, Again

Just as with injury control, there are three levels of prevention of maltreatment. The ultimate goal is to stop it before it begins. This is *primary prevention;* it focuses on the mesosystem and exosystem (see Chapter 1). Examples of primary-prevention conditions include stable neighborhoods; family cohesion; income equality; and measures that decrease financial instability, family isolation, and teenage parenthood.

Secondary prevention involves spotting the warning signs and intervening to keep a problematic situation from getting worse. For example, insecure attachment,

➤Response for Socially Aware Students (from page 221): Preschoolers from families at all income levels can have accidents, but Kathleen Berger's SES allowed her to have a private pediatrician as well as the income to buy ipecac "just in case." She also had a working phone and the education to know about Poison Control.

➤Answer to Observation Quiz (from page 223): No. The number is actually 11.8 per 1,000. Note the little squiggle on the graph's vertical axis below the number 11. This means that numbers between zero and 11 are not shown.

MIKE BOOTH / ALAMY

Where's Mom? Inside the shop, buying something for her baby. In many European towns, as here in Largs, Scotland, parents consider it beneficial to let the baby wait outside and breathe fresh air rather than join them inside. In the United States, parents have been jailed for doing this. Can both cultures be right?

Especially for the General Public You are asked to give a donation to support a billboard campaign against child abuse and neglect. You plan to make charitable contributions totaling $100 this year. How much of this amount should you contribute to the billboard campaign?

especially of the disorganized type (described in Chapter 7), is a sign of a disrupted parent–child relationship. Someone needs to repair that interaction. Secondary prevention includes measures such as home visits by nurses or social workers, high-quality day care, and preventive medical treatment—all designed to help high-risk families.

Tertiary prevention includes everything intended to reduce the harm when maltreatment has already occurred. Reporting and substantiating abuse are only the first steps. Action is needed. Someone must help the family or remove the child. If hospitalization is required, intervention should have begun much earlier. At that point, care is more expensive and hospitalization is longer than for other conditions (Rovi et al., 2004); in addition, lengthy hospitalization further damages the fragile parent–child bond.

Children fare better when they are secure in their environment, whether they live with their biological parents who have learned to provide good care, with a

The Same Event, A Thousand Miles Apart: Fun with Grandpa Grandfathers, like those shown here in Japan and India, often delight their grandchildren. Sometimes, however, they protect them—either in kinship care, when parents are designated as neglectful, or as secondary prevention before harm is evident.

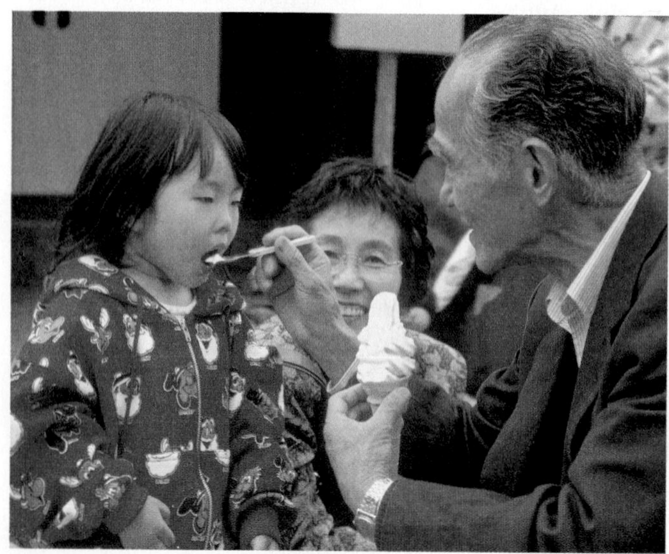

PHOTO JAPAN / ALAMY

STEVE MCCURRY / MAGNUM

STEPHANIE MAZE / CORBIS

Tertiary Prevention Adoption has been these children's salvation, particularly for 9-year-old Leah, clinging to her mother. The mother, Joan, has five adopted children. Adoption is generally better than foster care for maltreated children, because it is a permanent, stable arrangement.

foster family, or with an adoptive family. **Permanency planning** involves efforts by authorities to find a home that will nurture the child until adulthood (Waddell et al., 2004).

In **foster care,** children are officially removed from their parents' custody and entrusted to another adult who is paid to nurture them. In 2004 more than half a million children in the United States were in foster care. About half of them were in a special version of foster care called **kinship care,** in which a relative of the maltreated child becomes the foster caregiver (U.S. Department of Health and Human Services, 2004). This estimate is for official kinship care; three times as many children are informally cared for primarily by relatives who are not their parents.

In the United States, most foster children are from low-income families; half are African American or Latino; and many have multiple physical, intellectual, and emotional problems (Pew Commission on Foster Care, 2004). Despite these problems, children develop better in foster care (including kinship care) than with their original abusive families if a supervising agency screens foster families and provides ongoing financial and emotional support (Berrick, 1998).

However, many agencies are inadequate. One obvious failing is that many move children from one home to another for reasons that are unrelated to the child's behavior or wishes. Foster children average three placements before finding a permanent home (Pew Commission on Foster Care, 2004).

Adoption is the preferred permanent option, but judges and biological parents are reluctant to release children for adoption, and some agencies reject all but "perfect" families—those headed by a heterosexual married couple who are middle class, and of the same ethnicity as the child, and in which the wife is not employed. Since a healthy permanency, not perfection, is the goal, most experts want adoption restrictions loosened, courts to act more quickly in the interests of the children, and permanent guardianship allowed if adoption is impossible.

permanency planning An effort by authorities to find a long-term living situation that will provide stability and support for a maltreated child. A goal is to avoid repeated changes of caregiver or school, which can be particularly harmful for the child.

foster care A legal, publicly supported plan in which a maltreated child is removed from the parents' custody and entrusted to another adult, who is paid to be the child's caregiver.

kinship care A form of foster care in which a relative of a maltreated child becomes the approved caregiver.

➤**Response for Nurses** (from page 224): Any suspicion of child maltreatment must be reported, and these bruises are suspicious. Someone in authority must find out what is happening so that the parent as well as the child can be helped.

SUMMING UP

As they move with more speed and agility, young children encounter new dangers, becoming seriously injured more often than older children. Three levels of prevention are needed. Laws and practices should be put in place to protect everyone (primary

➤**Response for the General Public** (from page 226): Maybe none of it. Educational campaigns seldom change people's habits and thoughts, unless they have never thought about an issue at all. If you want to help prevent child abuse and neglect, you might offer free babysitting to parents you know who seem overwhelmed, or you might volunteer for a community group that helps troubled families.

prevention); supervision, forethought, and protective measures should prevent mishaps (secondary prevention); and when injury occurs, treatment should be quick and effective and changes should be made to avoid repetition (tertiary prevention).

Each year, abuse or neglect is substantiated for almost a million children in the United States. About 2 million other cases are reported but not substantiated, and millions more are not reported. Preventing maltreatment of all kinds is urgent but complex, because the source is often the family system and the cultural context, not a deranged stranger. Primary prevention includes changing the social context to ensure that parents protect and love their children. Secondary prevention focuses on families at high risk—the poor, the young, the drug-addicted. In tertiary prevention, the abused child is rescued before further damage occurs. ■

SUMMARY

Body Changes

1. Children continue to gain weight and height during early childhood. Many become quite picky eaters.

2. Culture, income, and family customs all affect children's growth. Worldwide, an increasing number of children have unbalanced diets, eating more fat and sugar and less iron and calcium than they need. Childhood obesity is increasingly common, because children exercise less and snack more than children once did, laying the foundation for chronic adult illness.

Brain Development

3. Myelination is substantial during early childhood, speeding messages from one part of the brain to another. The corpus callosum becomes thicker and functions much better. The prefrontal cortex, known as the executive of the brain, is strengthened as well.

4. Brain changes enable more reflective, coordinated thought and memory; better planning; and quicker responses. Many brain functions are localized in one hemisphere of the brain. Left/right specialization is apparent in the brain as well as in the body.

5. The expression and regulation of emotions are fostered by several brain areas, including the amygdala, the hippocampus, and the hypothalamus. Abuse in childhood may cause an overactive amygdala and hippocampus, creating a flood of stress hormones that interfere with learning.

6. Gross motor skills continue to develop, so that clumsy 2-year-olds become 6-year-olds able to move their bodies in whatever ways their culture values and they themselves have practiced, as long as height and judgment are not required.

7. Muscle control, practice, and brain maturation are also involved in the development of fine motor skills. Young children enjoy expressing themselves artistically, developing their motor skills as well as their self-expression.

Injuries and Abuse

8. Accidents are by far the leading cause of death for children, with 1- to 4-year-olds more likely to suffer a serious injury or premature death than older children. Biology, culture, and community conditions combine to make some children more vulnerable.

9. Injury control occurs on many levels, including long before and immediately after each harmful incident, with primary, secondary, and tertiary prevention. Laws seem more effective than educational campaigns. Close supervision is required to protect young children from their own eager, impulsive curiosity.

10. Child maltreatment typically results from ongoing abuse and neglect by a child's own parents. Each year almost 3 million cases of child maltreatment are reported in the United States, almost 1 million of which are substantiated.

11. Health, learning, and social skills are all impeded by ongoing child abuse and neglect. Physical abuse is the most obvious form of maltreatment, but neglect is common and probably more harmful.

12. Foster care, including kinship care, is sometimes necessary. Permanency planning is needed because frequent changes are harmful to children. Primary and secondary prevention helps parents care for their children and reduces the need for tertiary prevention.

KEY TERMS

myelination (p. 210)
corpus callosum (p. 210)
lateralization (p. 210)
perseveration (p. 213)
amygdala (p. 213)
hippocampus (p. 213)
hypothalamus (p. 214)
injury control/harm reduction (p. 219)
primary prevention (p. 220)
secondary prevention (p. 220)
tertiary prevention (p. 220)
child maltreatment (p. 222)
child abuse (p. 222)
child neglect (p. 222)
reported maltreatment (p. 222)
substantiated maltreatment (p. 222)
post-traumatic stress disorder (PTSD) (p. 223)
permanency planning (p. 227)
foster care (p. 227)
kinship care (p. 227)

KEY QUESTIONS

1. How are growth rates, body proportions, and motor skills related during early childhood?

2. Does low family income tend to make young children eat more or less? Explain your answer.

3. What are the crucial aspects of brain growth that occur after age 2?

4. How do emotions, and their expression, originate in the brain?

5. Why do public health workers prefer to speak of "injury control" or "harm reduction" instead of accidents?

6. What conditions are best for children to develop their motor skills?

7. What are the differences among the three kinds of prevention?

8. What are the arguments for and against laws to protect children from injury?

9. Why might neglect be worse than abuse?

10. What are the advantages and disadvantages of foster care?

11. What are the advantages and disadvantages of kinship care?

APPLICATIONS

1. Keep a food diary for 24 hours, writing down what you eat, how much, when, how, and why. Then think about nutrition and eating habits in early childhood. Do you see any evidence in yourself of imbalance (e.g., not enough fruits and vegetables, too much sugar or fat, not eating when you are hungry)? Did your food habits originate in early childhood, in adolescence, or at some other time?

2. Go to a playground or other place where young children play. Note the motor skills that the children demonstrate, including abilities and inabilities, and keep track of age and sex. What differences do you see among the children?

3. Ask several parents to describe each accidental injury of each of their children, particularly how it happened and what the consequences were. What primary, secondary, or tertiary prevention measures would have made a difference?

4. Think back on your childhood and the friends you had at that time. Was there any maltreatment? Considering what you have learned in this chapter, why or why not?

9

CHAPTER OUTLINE

The Play Years: Cognitive Development

I was among dozens of adults on a subway who were captivated by a little girl, perhaps 3 years old, with sparkling eyes and many braids. She sat beside a large stranger, looking at her mother, who stood about 6 feet to her left, holding onto a pole. The little girl repeatedly ducked her head behind the stranger and said, "You can't see me, Mama," unaware not only that her stockinged legs and shiny shoes stuck out in front of her but also that her whole body was constantly visible to her mother.

Like that little girl, every young child has much to learn. They are sometimes *egocentric,* understanding only their own perspective. Among their developing ideas is a *theory of mind,* an understanding of how minds work (as in knowing that your mother can sometimes see you when you cannot see her).

Since children learn so much from age 2 to 6, developmentalists have gained a new respect for early education. No longer merely "day care," or "home care," early learning is now considered vital, whether it occurs at home or in a center.

The halting, simple sentences of the typical 2-year-old become the nonstop, complex outpourings of a talkative 6-year-old, who can explain almost anything. How does that happen? This chapter describes thinking and learning from age 2 to 6, including remarkable advances in language as well as thought.

Piaget and Vygotsky

Jean Piaget and Lev Vygotsky (introduced in Chapter 2) are justly famous for their descriptions of cognition. Their theories, especially in what they have to say about the eager learning of young children, are "compatible in many ways" (Rogoff, 1998, p. 681).

Piaget: Preoperational Thinking

For Piaget, early childhood is the second of four stages of cognition. He termed cognitive development between the ages of about 2 and 6 **preoperational intelligence,** which goes beyond senses and motor skills (sensorimotor intelligence) to include language and imagination. Preoperational thinking is magical and self-centered; *pre-*operational means that the child is not yet ready for logical operations (or reasoning processes) (Inhelder & Piaget, 1964).

preoperational intelligence Piaget's term for cognitive development between the ages of about 2 and 6; it includes language and imagination (in addition to the senses and motor skills of infancy), but logical, operational thinking is not yet possible.

Obstacles to Logical Operations

Piaget described four characteristics of thinking in early childhood, all of which make logic difficult: centration, focus on appearance, static reasoning, and irreversibility.

centration A characteristic of preoperational thought in which a young child focuses (centers) on one idea, excluding all others.

egocentrism Piaget's term for children's tendency to think about the world entirely from their own personal perspective.

Centration is the tendency to focus on one aspect of a situation to the exclusion of all others. Young children may, for example, insist that lions and tigers seen at the zoo or in picture books cannot be cats, because the children "center" on the house-pet aspect of the cats they know. Or they may insist that Daddy is a father, not a brother, because they center on the role that each family member fills for them. The latter example illustrates a particular type of centration, *ego-centration,* which Piaget called **egocentrism,** literally self-centeredness. Egocentric children contemplate the world exclusively from their personal perspective.

Piaget did not equate egocentrism with selfishness. Consider, for example, a 3-year-old who chose to buy a model car as a birthday present for his mother, stubbornly convinced that she would be delighted. In fact, his "behavior was not selfish or greedy; he carefully wrapped the present and gave it to his mother with an expression that clearly showed that he expected her to love it" (Crain, 2005, p. 108).

focus on appearance A characteristic of preoperational thought in which a young child ignores all attributes that are not apparent.

static reasoning Thinking that nothing changes: Whatever is now has always been and always will be.

irreversibility The idea that nothing can be undone; the inability to recognize that something can sometimes be restored to the way it was before a change occurred.

A second characteristic of preoperational thought is a **focus on appearance** to the exclusion of other attributes. A girl given a short haircut might worry that she has turned into a boy. In preoperational thought, a thing is whatever it appears to be.

Third, preoperational children use **static reasoning,** assuming that the world is unchanging, always in the state in which they currently encounter it. A young boy might want the television turned off while he goes to the bathroom, assuming that when he returns, he can pick up the program exactly where he left off.

The fourth characteristic of preoperational thought is **irreversibility.** Preoperational thinkers fail to recognize that reversing a process sometimes restores whatever existed before. A 3-year-old might cry because his mother put lettuce on his hamburger. Overwhelmed by his desire to have things "just right" (as explained in Chapter 8), he might reject the hamburger even after the lettuce is removed because he believes that what is done cannot be undone.

Especially for Parents Who Want Their Children to Eat Better How can Piaget's theory help you encourage your child to eat?

Conservation and Logic

Piaget devised many experiments demonstrating the constraints on thinking that result from preoperational reasoning. A famous set of experiments involved **conservation,** the fact that the amount of something remains the same (is conserved) despite changes in its appearance.

conservation The idea that the amount of a substance remains the same (i.e., is conserved) when its appearance changes.

Suppose two identical glasses contain the same amount of liquid, and the liquid from one glass is poured into a tall, narrow glass. If young children are asked whether one glass contains more liquid or they both contain the same, they will insist that the narrower glass, in which the liquid level is higher, has more.

All four characteristics of preoperational thought are evident in this mistake. Young children fail to understand conservation of liquids because they focus (*center*) on what they see (*appearance*), noticing only the immediate (*static*) condition. It does not occur to them that they could reverse the process and re-create the liquid level of a moment earlier (*irreversibility*). (See Figure 9.1 for other examples.)

Limitations of Piaget's Research

Notice that Piaget's test of conservation required the child's words, not actions. Other research has found that even 3-year-olds can distinguish appearance from reality if the test is nonverbal or playful (Sapp et al., 2000). Many children indicate that they know something via their gestures before they say it in words (Goldin-Meadow, 2006).

COURTESY OF KATHLEEN BERGER

Demonstration of Conservation My youngest daughter, Sarah, here at age 5¾, demonstrates Piaget's conservation-of-volume experiment. First, she examines both short glasses to be sure they contain the same amount of milk. Then, after the contents of one are poured into the tall glass and she is asked which has more, she points to the tall glass, just as Piaget would have expected. Later she added, "It looks like it has more because it's taller," indicating that some direct instruction might change her mind.

Tests of Various Types of Conservation

Type of Conservation	Initial Presentation	Transformation	Question	Preoperational Child's Answer
Volume	Two equal glasses of liquid.	Pour one into a taller, narrower glass.	Which glass contains more?	The taller one.
Number	Two equal lines of checkers.	Increase spacing of checkers in one line.	Which line has more checkers?	The longer one.
Matter	Two equal balls of clay.	Squeeze one ball into a long, thin shape.	Which piece has more clay?	The long one.
Length	Two sticks of equal length.	Move one stick.	Which stick is longer?	The one that is farther to the right.

FIGURE 9.1

Conservation, Please According to Piaget, until children grasp the concept of conservation at (he believed) about age 6 or 7, they cannot understand that the transformations shown here do not change the total amount of liquid, checkers, clay, and wood.

➤Response for Parents Who Want Their Children to Eat Better (from page 232): It may help if you take each of the four characteristics of preoperational thought into account. Because of egocentrism, having a special place and plate might assure the child that this food is exclusively his or hers. Since appearance is important, food should look tasty. Since static thinking dominates, if something healthy is added (e.g., grate carrots into the cake, add milk to the soup), the addition should be done before the food is given to the child. In the reversibility example in the text, the lettuce should be removed out of the child's sight and the "new" hamburger presented.

Researchers now believe that Piaget underestimated the conceptual ability of young children, just as he underestimated it in infants (Halford & Andrews, 2006). He designed his experiments to reveal what young children seemed *not* to understand, rather than to identify what they could understand, and he relied on the children's words in an experimental setting rather than their nonverbal signs in a play context.

Vygotsky: Social Learning

It is undeniable that young children's thinking is often magical and self-centered. For many years, this aspect of cognition dominated descriptions of early childhood by developmentalists, especially Piaget.

Vygotsky was the first leading developmentalist to emphasize a second aspect of early cognition: Young children are not always egocentric; they can be very sensitive to the wishes and emotions of others. This second aspect emphasizes the social side of preschool thought, which contrasts with Piaget's emphasis on the individual.

Especially for Aunts and Uncles It is a special family occasion, and you want to take presents to your nieces and nephews. What should you take?

Children as Apprentices

Vygotsky believed that every aspect of children's cognitive development is embedded in a social context (Vygotsky, 1935/1987). Children are curious and observant. They ask questions—about how machines work, why weather changes, where the sky ends—assuming that others know the answers.

apprentice in thinking Vygotsky's term for a person whose cognition is stimulated and directed by older and more skilled members of society.

guided participation The process by which people learn from others who guide their experiences and explorations.

In many ways, a child is what Vygotsky called an **apprentice in thinking,** someone whose intellectual growth is stimulated and directed by older and more skilled members of society. The parents and older siblings are usually the child's teachers (Maynard, 2002; Rogoff, 2003). If the child attends a day-care program, learning from "more capable peers" is central (C. Thompson, 2002).

According to Vygotsky, children learn because their elders do the following:

- Present challenges
- Offer assistance (not taking over)
- Provide instruction
- Encourage motivation

With the help of their mentors, children learn to think by means of their **guided participation** in social experiences and in explorations of their universe, with both the mentor and the child talking as well as acting. For example, children learning to draw or write or dance are quite willing to copy from one another. A child who is copied is not resentful but rather appreciates the recognition.

The reality that children are curious about everything, learning and remembering whatever they experience, is evidence of cognition. The ability to learn (not the measure of what is known) indicates intelligence. Vygotsky (1935/1978) said: "What children can do with the assistance of others might be in some sense even more indicative of their mental development than what they can do alone" (p. 5).

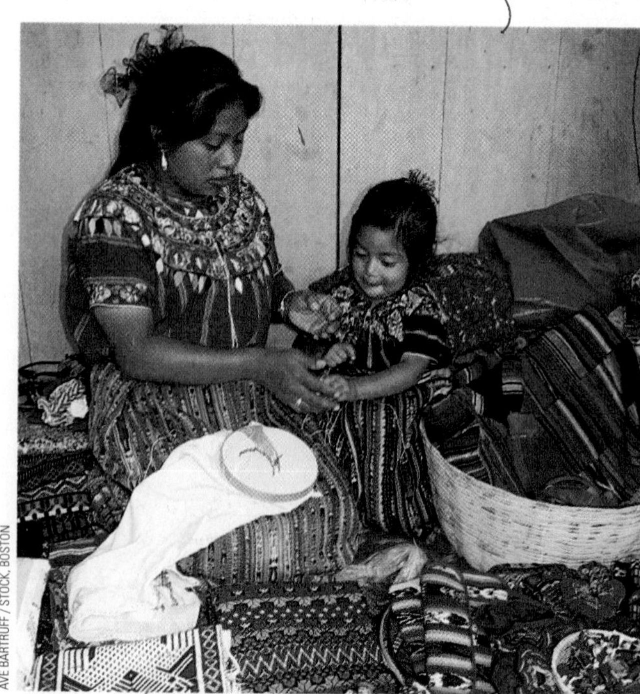

AVE BARTRUFF / STOCK, BOSTON

Guided Participation Through shared social activity, adults in every culture guide the development of their children's cognition, values, and skills. Typically, the child's curiosity and interests, rather than the adult's planning for some sort of future need, motivate the process. That seems to be the case as this Guatemalan girl eagerly tries to learn her mother's sewing skills.

Scaffolding

As you saw in Chapter 2, Vygotsky believed that for each developing individual, there is a **zone of proximal development (ZPD),** which includes all the skills that the person can perform with assistance but cannot quite perform independently. How and when children master their potential skills depends, in part, on the willingness of others to provide **scaffolding,** or temporary sensitive support, to help them traverse that zone.

zone of proximal development (ZPD) Vygotsky's term for the skills that a person can exercise only with assistance, not yet independently. ZPD applies to the ideas or cognitive skills a person is close to mastering as well as to more apparent skills.

scaffolding Temporary support that is tailored to a learner's needs and abilities and aimed at helping the learner master the next task in a given learning process.

Good caregivers scaffold often, teaching children to look both ways before crossing a street (while holding the child's hand) or letting them stir the batter for a cake (perhaps stirring a few times themselves to make sure the ingredients are well mixed).

Scaffolding is particularly important for experiences that are directly cognitive—that is, ones that will produce better understanding of words and ideas. For example, adults reading to 3-year-olds usually provide excellent scaffolding—explaining, pointing, listening—toward the child's ZPD in response to the child's needs at the moment (Danis et al., 2000). The sensitive reader would never tell the child to be quiet and listen but might instead prolong the session by asking the child questions.

Siblings can also provide scaffolding. In one study in Chiapas, Mexico, 8-year-old Tonik taught his 2-year-old sister, Katal, how to wash a doll. After several minutes of demonstrating and describing, Tonik continues:

> **Tonik:** Pour it like this. (Demonstrates)
> **Tonik:** Sister, pour it. (Hands glass)
> **Tonik:** Look! Pour it.
> **Katal:** (Pours, with some difficulty)
> **Tonik:** Like that. (Approval)
> **Katal:** (Looks away)
> **Tonik:** It's finished now.
>
> *[quoted in Maynard, 2002, p. 977]*

Note that when Katal looked away, Tonik wisely declared the session finished. Such a response, not criticism, encourages the learner to participate in later apprenticeships. Motivation is crucial in early education—one reason why sensitive social interaction is so powerful.

Especially for Someone Teaching a Friend to Drive You want to teach a friend to drive using your car, but you fear a temper explosion or a crash. How would Vygotsky advise you to proceed?

Language as a Tool

Vygotsky believed that words are used to build scaffolds, developing cognition. Just as a builder could not construct a house without tools, the mind needs language. Talking, listening, reading, and writing are tools to advance thought.

Language advances thinking in two ways. First, internal dialogue, or **private speech,** occurs when people talk to themselves, developing new ideas (Vygotsky, 1934/1987). Young children use private speech often, typically talking out loud to review, decide, and explain events to themselves (and, incidentally, to anyone else within earshot). Older preschoolers use private speech more selectively and effectively, sometimes in a whisper or even without any audible sound (Winsler et al., 2000). Adults use private speech quietly, and write down their ideas to help them think.

private speech The internal dialogue that occurs when people talk to themselves (either silently or out loud).

The second way in which language advances thinking, according to Vygotsky, is by mediating the social interaction that is vital to learning. This **social mediation** function of speech occurs during both formal instruction (when teachers explain things) and casual conversation.

social mediation A function of speech by which a person's cognitive skills are refined and extended through both formal instruction and casual conversation.

Language used in social mediation is evident as children, guided by their mentors, learn numbers, recall memories, and follow routines. Among the differences between 2-year-olds and 6-year-olds is that the latter can count objects, assigning one number per item (called one-to-one correspondence), can remember accurately (although false memories can confuse anyone), and can verbalize scripts (such as the usual scenario for a birthday party or a restaurant meal).

Adult instruction and verbal encouragement are crucial for all these cognitive accomplishments (e.g., Hubbs-Tait et al., 2002; Mix et al., 2002). Thus, by age 3 or 4, children's brains are mature enough to comprehend numbers, store memories, and know routines, but whether or not a child actually demonstrates this understanding depends on family, school, and culture. Language is a key mediator between brain potential and what children actually understand and remember because other people teach via the words children use to think (Haden et al., 2001; Schneider & Pressley, 1997).

➤Response for Aunts and Uncles (from page 234): Remember that preschool children focus on appearances and are egocentric. Whatever you give a 2- to 5-year-old must be seen as equal to any present you give another child. Thus, you would choose identical gifts (perhaps markers, toys, or articles of clothing), so that no child can compare presents and decide that you love another child more.

SUMMING UP

Cognition develops rapidly from age 2 to 6. Children's active search for understanding was first recognized by Piaget, who realized that children of this age are generally not capable of performing logical operations (which is why he called this period *preoperational*). Their egocentrism limits their understanding and they center on only one thing at a time, focusing on appearance. Their thinking is static, not dynamic. They do not understand reversibility.

Vygotsky emphasized the social and cultural aspects of children's cognition. He believed that children must be properly guided as apprentices, within their zones of proximal development. Language is a tool that mediates between the child's curiosity and the mentor's knowledge. ■

➤Response for Someone Teaching a Friend to Drive (from page 235): Use guided participation, and scaffold the instruction so it does not all come at once. Both you and your student might hold the steering wheel at first, and practice in a large, empty parking lot. Be sure to provide lots of praise and days of practice.

Children's Theories

Both Piaget and Vygotsky realized that children actively work to understand their world. Recently, many other developmentalists have attempted to show exactly how children's knowledge develops. Children seek to explain what they experience, especially why and how people behave as they do. If no one provides satisfying explanations, they develop their own answers.

Theory-Theory

One theory of cognitive development begins with the human drive to develop theories, a drive that is especially apparent in early childhood. The term **theory-theory** refers to the idea that children construct theories to explain everything they see and hear:

theory-theory The idea that children attempt to explain everything they see and hear by constructing theories.

> More than any animal, we search for causal regularities in the world around us. We are perpetually driven to look for deeper explanations of our experience, and broader and more reliable predictions about it. . . . Children seem, quite literally, to be born with . . . the desire to understand the world and the desire to discover how to behave in it.
>
> *[Gopnik, 2001, p. 66]*

Thus, according to theory-theory, the best conceptualization of, and explanation for, mental processes in young children is that humans always seek reasons, causes, and underlying principles. Figure 9.2, with its narrative-style "recipe" for cooking a turkey, captures the essential idea of theory-theory: that children don't want logical definitions but rather explanations of various things, especially things that involve them.

Especially for Adults Answering a 3-Year-Old's Questions A characteristic of young children is that they ask questions, often frustrating adults by asking "Why?" getting an answer, and immediately asking "Why?" again. Now that you know that such questions are almost always about purpose, not science, how would you answer the question "Why is my brother bad?" or "Why is there night?"

Exactly how are explanations sought in early childhood? In one study, Mexican American mothers kept detailed diaries of every question their 3- to 5-year-olds

A whole turkey

1 big bag full of a whole turkey (Get the kind with no feathers on, not the kind the Pilgrims ate.)
A giant lump of stuffin'
1 squash pie
1 mint pie
1 little fancy dish of sour berries
1 big fancy dish of a vegetable mix
20 dishes of all different candies; chocolate balls, cherry balls, good'n plenties and peanuts

Get up when the alarm says to and get busy fast. Unfold the turkey and open up the holes. Push in the stuffin' for a couple of hours. I think you get stuffin' from that Farm that makes it.

I know you have to pin the stuffin' to the turkey or I suppose it would get out. And get special pins or use big long nails.

Get the kitchen real hot, and from there on you just cook turkey. Sometimes you can call it a bird, but it's not.

Then you put the vegetables in the cooker—and first put one on top, and next put one on the bottom, and then one in the middle. That makes a vegetable mix. Put 2 red things of salt all in it and 2 red things of water also. Cook them to just ½ of warm.

Put candies all around the place and Linda will bring over the pies.

When the company comes put on your red apron.

FIGURE 9.2

Unfold the Turkey This recipe (from *Smashed Potatoes*, edited by Jane Martel) shows many characteristics of preschool thought, among them literal interpretation of words ("Sometimes you can call it a bird, but it's not") and an uncertain idea of time ("Push in the stuffin' for a couple hours") and quantity ("A giant lump of stuffin' ").

asked and how the mothers responded (Kelemen et al., 2005; see Research Design). Generally, younger children asked more questions than older children, and more educated mothers heard (or recorded) more questions. This study focused particularly on children's curiosity and how adults respond.

Most of the questions were about human behavior and characteristics (see Figure 9.3). For example, children asked, "Why do you give my mother a kiss?" "Why is my brother bad?" "Why do women have breasts?" and "Why are there Black kids?" Fewer questions were about nonliving things ("Why does it rain?") or objects ("Why is my daddy's car white?").

Many questions concerned the underlying purpose of various natural phenomena, although parents usually responded as if children were asking about science instead. For example, when children asked why women have breasts, parents would tell them about hormones and maturation, not that breasts are for feeding babies.

Research Design

Scientists: Deborah Kelemen and others.

Publication: *Developmental Psychology* (2005).

Participants: A total of 48 Mexican American mothers and their 3- to 5-year-olds. Most of the women were born in Mexico and all lived in central California at the time of the study.

Design: After an initial interview, the researchers phoned the mothers every two days for two weeks to hear what "Why?" or "How?" questions the children asked and what answers the children were given.

Major conclusion: Children ask many questions about the purpose of things and about human behavior; they seem less curious about inanimate objects.

Comment: These families were often bilingual, immigrant, and religious. These characteristics may not have affected the results, but replication is needed to find out for sure. Ideally, children's actual questions would be tape-recorded, not simply reported by the mothers (whose reports might be distorted by unconscious biases).

FIGURE 9.3

Questions, Questions Parents found that most of their children's questions were about human behavior—especially the parents' behavior toward the child. Children seek to develop a theory to explain things, so the question "Why can't I have some candy?" is not satisfactorily answered by "It's almost dinnertime."

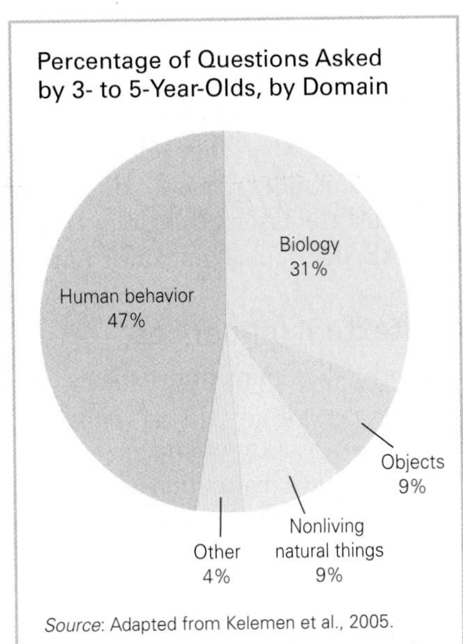

Theory of Mind

Human mental processes—thoughts, emotions, beliefs, motives, and intentions—are among the most complicated and puzzling phenomena that we encounter every day. Adults seek to understand why people fall in love, or vote as they do, or make foolish choices. Children are puzzled about a playmate's unexpected anger, a sibling's generosity, or an aunt's too-wet kiss.

To know what goes on in another's mind, people develop a "folk psychology," an understanding of others' thinking called **theory of mind.** Theory of mind typically appears rather suddenly (Wellman et al., 2001), in "an important intellectual change at about 4 years" (Perner, 2000, p. 396).

theory of mind A person's theory of what other people might be thinking. In order to have a theory of mind, children must realize that other people are not necessarily thinking the same thoughts that they themselves are. That realization is seldom possible before age 4.

Belief and Reality: Understanding the Difference

Actually, theory of mind includes many concepts, some of which are difficult for much older children. However, a sudden leap in understanding does seem to occur at about age 4. What is it that children suddenly understand? Between the ages of 3 and 6, children come to realize that thoughts may not reflect reality. This idea leads to the theory-of-mind concept that people can be deliberately deceived or fooled—an idea that is beyond the understanding of most younger children, even when they have themselves been deceived.

➤Response for Adults Answering a 3-Year-Old's Questions (from page 236): Do not talk about the toy the brother broke or explain the earth's rotation! Instead, connect the answer to the child. You might say, "Your brother probably wishes he had your toy" or "There's night so you know when it is time to go to sleep."

Consider an experiment. An adult shows a 3-year-old a candy box and asks, "What is inside?" The child says, naturally, "Candy." But the child has been tricked:

> **Adult:** Let's open it and look inside.
> **Child:** Oh . . . holy moly . . . pencils!
> **Adult:** Now I'm going to put them back and close it up again. (*Does so*) Now . . . when you first saw the box, before we opened it, what did you think was inside it?
> **Child:** Pencils.
> **Adult:** Nicky [friend of the child] hasn't seen inside this box. When Nicky comes in and sees it . . . what will he think is inside it?
> **Child:** Pencils.
>
> [*adapted from Astington & Gopnik, 1988, p. 195*]

Especially for Social Scientists Can you think of any connection between Piaget's theory of preoperational thought and 3-year-olds' errors in this theory-of-mind task?

This experiment has become a classic, performed with thousands of children from many cultures. Three-year-olds almost always confuse what they know now with what they once thought and what someone else might think. Another way of describing this is to say that they are "cursed" by their own knowledge (Birch & Bloom, 2003), too egocentric to grasp other perspectives.

As a result, young children are notoriously bad at deception. They play hide-and-seek by hiding in the same place time after time, or their facial expression betrays them when they tell a fib. Closely related is their inability to change their minds (remember perseveration from Chapter 8), even when they recognize that they must think something new. With static reasoning (characteristic of preoperational thought), changing one's mind is difficult.

Contextual Influences

Recently, developmentalists have asked what, precisely, strengthens theory of mind at about age 4. Is this change more a matter of nature or of nurture, of brain maturation or of experience?

Neurological maturation is a plausible explanation. In one study, 68 children aged 2½ to 5½ were presented with four standard theory-of-mind situations, including a Band-Aid box that really contained pencils (similar to the candy-box experiment just described) (Jenkins & Astington, 1996). More than one-third of the children succeeded at all four tasks, and more than one-third failed at three or four. Age was the main factor: The 5-year-olds were most likely to succeed on all tasks, the 4-year-olds had middling success, and the 3-year-olds were most likely to fail every time.

This age-related advance suggests that context is less crucial than maturation of the brain's prefrontal cortex (Perner et al., 2002). Further evidence that brain maturation is a prerequisite for theory of mind is the fact that impaired brain functioning is the most likely cause of autism (see Chapter 11), and many autistic children are advanced in numerical understanding but slow to develop theory of mind (Baron-Cohen, 1995).

Two other influences that are affected by context are key: language and siblings. Children with greater verbal fluency (at any age) are more likely to have a theory of mind. This is partly the result of experience, especially mother–child conversations that involve thoughts and wishes (Ruffman et al., 2002). Deaf children are delayed in developing a theory of mind, probably because their language development is delayed (Lundy, 2002).

When the effects of both age and language ability are accounted for, a third important factor emerges: having at least one older brother or sister (Jenkins & Astington, 1996). One researcher estimates that, in theory-of-mind development, "two older siblings are worth about a year of chronological age" (Perner, 2000, p. 383). The arguing, agreeing, competing, and cooperating that siblings normally do apparently lead children to understand that their own thinking is not shared by everyone.

A study comparing theory of mind among young children in preschools in Canada, India, Peru, Samoa, and Thailand found that the Canadian children were slightly ahead and the Samoan children were slightly behind, but across cultures most of the children in the study sample passed the false-belief tests (such as a culture-fair version of the one involving pencils in the candy box) by age 5 (see Figure 9.4). The researchers concluded that brain maturation was the primary factor in the acquisition of theory of mind but that language development and social interaction were also influential (Callaghan et al., 2005).

The child's own logic and maturation are important (Piaget), but language and social interaction are mediators (Vygotsky) once the necessary brain structures are in place. In most cultures, "a certain amount of experience hearing and participating in conversation" occurs by age 3, allowing theory of mind to develop (Callaghan et al., 2005, p. 382).

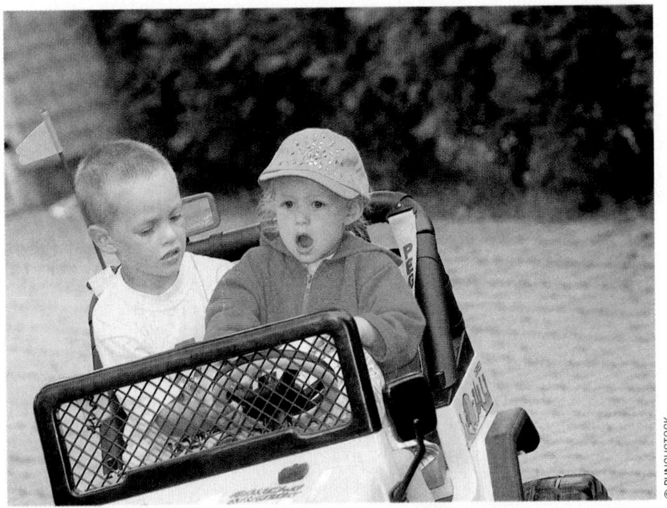

Road Rage? From their expressions, it looks as if this brother and sister may crash their toy jeep and cry, each blaming the other for the mishap. But a benefit of such sibling interactions is that they can advance theory of mind by helping children realize that people do not always think the same way.

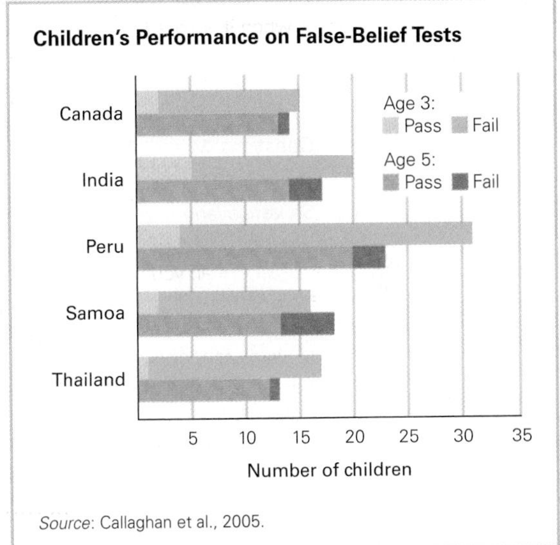

FIGURE 9.4

Few at Age 3, Most by Age 5 The advantage of cross-cultural research is that it can reveal universal patterns. Although the number of children in each group is small (from 31 3-year-olds in Peru to 13 5-year-olds in Thailand), the pattern is obvious. Something changes at about age 4.

SUMMING UP

Scholars have recently noted that children develop theories to explain whatever they observe, and those theories do not necessarily spring from explanations given to them by adults. Children seem to be much more interested in the underlying purpose of events within the grand scheme of life; adults are more focused on immediate scientific causes. Many researchers have explored the development of theory of mind, the understanding that other people can have thoughts and ideas that are unlike one's own. Neurological maturation, linguistic competence, family context, and culture all affect the attainment of theory of mind at about age 4. ■

Language

Language is pivotal to cognition in early childhood, as we have seen in the examples of Vygotsky's social mediation and the development of theory of mind. Language is also the leading cognitive accomplishment during these years: 24-month-old children begin this period with short sentences and limited vocabulary, and 6-year-olds end it with the ability to understand and discuss almost anything (see Table 9.1).

critical period A time when a certain development *must* happen if it is ever to happen. For example, the embryonic period is critical for the development of arms and legs. It was once thought that early childhood was the critical period for language learning, but today it is considered a *sensitive period*.

sensitive period A time when a certain type of development is most likely to happen and happens most easily. For example, early childhood is considered a sensitive period for language learning.

Maturation and myelination added to extensive social interaction make age 2 to 6 the usual time for learning language. Indeed, scientists once thought that these years were a **critical period,** the *only* time when a first language could be mastered and the best time for learning a second or third language. This hypothesis has been disproven. Millions of older children and adults learn to be fluent in second languages (Bialystok, 2001; Hakuta et al., 2003).

Nonetheless, early childhood is a **sensitive period** for language learning—for rapidly and easily mastering vocabulary, grammar, and pronunciation. Young children are sometimes called "language sponges" because they soak up every drop of language they encounter.

TABLE 9.1

AT ABOUT THIS TIME: **Language in Early Childhood**

Approximate Age	Characteristic or Achievement
2 years	*Vocabulary:* 100–2,000 words *Sentence length:* 2–6 words *Grammar:* Plurals, pronouns, many nouns, verbs, adjectives *Questions:* Many "What's that?" questions
3 years	*Vocabulary:* 1,000–5,000 words *Sentence length:* 3–8 words *Grammar:* Conjunctions, adverbs, articles *Questions:* Many "Why?" questions
4 years	*Vocabulary:* 3,000–10,000 words *Sentence length:* 5–20 words *Grammar:* Dependent clauses, tags at ends of sentences ("... didn't I?" "... won't you?") *Questions:* Peak of "Why?" questions; also many "How?" and "When?" questions
5 years	*Vocabulary:* 5,000–20,000 words *Sentence length:* Some seem unending (". . . and . . . who . . . and . . . that . . . and . . .") *Grammar:* Complex, sometimes using passive voice ("Man bitten by dog"); subjunctive ("If I were . . .") *Questions:* Include some about differences (male/female, old/young, rich/poor)

They also talk a lot—to adults, to each other, to themselves, to their toys—unfazed by mispronunciation, misuse, stuttering, or other impediments to fluency. Note a crucial developmental asset as well: Language comes easily because, compared with most older children and adults, young children are not as self-conscious about what they say.

Vocabulary

In childhood, new words are added rapidly. The average child knows about 500 words at age 2 and more than 10,000 at age 6. One scholar says that 2- to 6-year-olds learn 10 words a day (Clark, 1995); another estimates one word for every two waking hours from about age 2 to age 20 (Pinker, 1994). The *naming explosion* (explained in Chapter 6) becomes a more general explosion, with new verbs, adjectives, adverbs, and conjunctions as well as many more nouns mastered during early childhood.

Precise estimates of vocabulary vary because contexts are diverse; the estimates given here may be high. However, all researchers agree that vocabulary builds quickly and that most children could learn far more language than they do. Every child could probably become fluently bilingual if their context encouraged that.

Fast-Mapping

fast-mapping The speedy and sometimes imprecise way in which children learn new words by mentally charting them into categories according to their meaning.

How does the vocabulary explosion occur? After painstakingly learning one word at a time at age 1, children develop an interconnected set of categories for words, a kind of grid or mental map, which makes speedy vocabulary acquisition possible. The process is called **fast-mapping** (Woodward & Markman, 1998) because, rather than figuring out an exact definition after hearing a word used in several contexts, children hear a word once and tentatively stick it into one of the categories on their mental language map.

Like more conventional mental mapping, language mapping is not always precise. Thus, when asked where Nepal is, most people can locate it approximately ("in Asia"), but few can name each bordering country. Similarly, children quickly learn new animal names, for instance, because they are mapped in the brain close to already-known animal names. Thus, *tiger* is easy to map if you know *lion*. A trip to the zoo facilitates fast-mapping of dozens of animal words, especially since zoos scaffold such learning by placing similar animals together.

The benefit of knowing at least one word of a category is evident in a classic experiment. A preschool teacher taught a new word by saying, "Give me the chromium tray, not the red one" (Carey, 1985). Those children who already knew *red* quickly grasped the new word, *chromium,* and remembered it more than a week later. Those children who knew no color words did not remember the new word (a week later, they could not select a chromium object) because they were unable to map it (Mandler, 2004).

Another set of experiments began in cultures whose languages had only a few counting words: the equivalents of *one, two,* and *many*. People in such cultures were much worse at estimating quantity because they did not have the words to guide them (Gordon, 2004). Mapping and understanding a new number word, such as *nineteen,* is easier if one already knows a related word, such as *nine*.

Generally, the more linguistic clues children already have, the better their fast-mapping is (Mintz, 2005). To increase vocabulary, parents should talk to them often, adding new vocabulary (Hoff & Naigles, 2002). Alas, preschoolers also map words their parents would rather they didn't, as I learned.

MICHAEL WICKES / THE IMAGE WORKS

What's That? By far the best way for a parent to teach a young child new vocabulary is by reading aloud. Ideally, the interaction should be a very social one, with much pointing and talking, as this Idaho pair demonstrate. If such experiences are part of her daily routine, this little girl not only will develop language but also will be among the first of her classmates to learn how to read.

in person

"Mommy the Brat"

Fast-mapping has an obvious benefit: It fosters quick acquisition of vocabulary. However, it also means that children *seem* to know words merely because they use them when, in actuality, their understanding of the words' meaning is quite limited.

Realizing that children often do not fully comprehend the meanings of words they use makes it easier to understand—and forgive—their mistakes. I still vividly recall an incident when my youngest daughter, then 4, was furious at me.

Sarah had apparently fast-mapped several insulting words into her vocabulary. However, her fast-mapping did not provide precise definitions or reflect nuances. In her anger, she called me first a "mean witch" and then a "brat." I smiled at her innocent imprecision, knowing the first was fast-mapped from fairy tales and the second from comments she got from her older sisters. Neither label bothered me, as I don't believe in witches and my brother is the only person who can appropriately call me a brat.

But then Sarah let loose an X-rated epithet that sent me reeling. Struggling to contain my anger, I tried to convince myself that fast-mapping had left her with no real idea of what she had just said. "That word is never to be used in this family!" I sputtered. My appreciation of the speed of fast-mapping was deepened by her response: "Then how come Rachel [her older sister] called me that this morning?"

Words and the Limits of Logic

Closely related to fast-mapping is logical extension: After learning a word, children use it to describe other objects in the same category. One child told her father she had seen some Dalmatian cows on a school trip to a farm. He understood her because he remembered that she had petted a Dalmatian dog the weekend before.

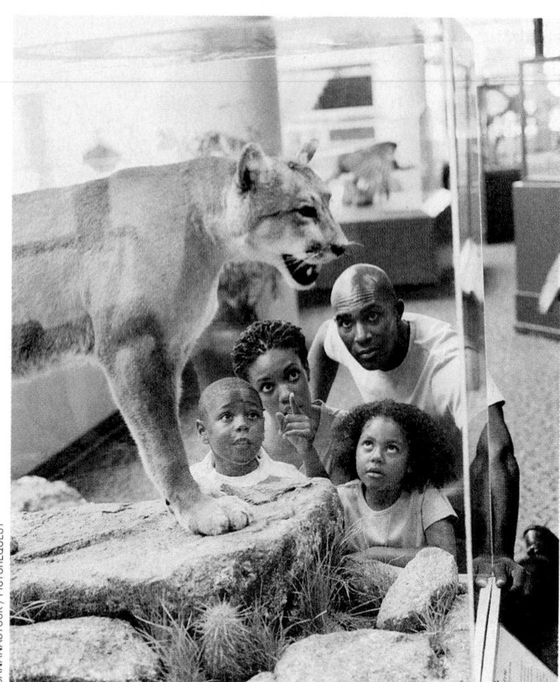

BANANASTOCK / PICTUREQUEST

Fangs for the Memories Museums, zoos, parks, farms, factories—all provide abundant opportunities for vocabulary building and concept formation. These parents may be teaching their children not only *mountain lion* but also *habitat*, *carnivore*, and *incisors*.

Children use their available vocabulary to cover all the territory they want to talk about (Behrend et al., 2001). They use logic to figure out what words mean—for instance, deciding that butter comes from butterflies and birds grow from bird seed.

One child, jumping on a bed, knew that *live with* means reside in the same home.

Mother: Stop. You'll hurt yourself.
Child: No I won't. (*Still jumping*)
Mother: You'll break the bed.
Child: No I won't. (*Still jumping*)
Mother: OK. You'll just have to live with the consequences.
Child: (*Stops jumping*) I'm not going to live with the consequences. I don't even know them.

[adapted from Nemy, 1998]

An experiment in teaching the names of parts of objects (e.g., the spigot of a faucet) found that children learned much better if the adults named the object that had the part, and then spoke of the part in the possessive (e.g., "See this butterfly? Look, this is its thorax") (Saylor & Sabbagh, 2004). This finding shows that how a new word is presented affects the likelihood that a child will learn that word.

Young children have difficulty with words that express comparisons (such as *tall* and *short*, *near* and *far*, *high* and *low*, *deep* and *shallow*) because they do not understand that the meaning of these words depends on the context (Ryalls, 2000). Young children who know that one end of the swimming pool is the deep end might obey parental instructions to stay out of deep puddles by splashing through every puddle they see, insisting that none of them are deep.

Words expressing relationships of place and time—such as *here*, *there*, *yesterday*, and *tomorrow*—are difficult as well. More than one pajama-clad child has awakened on Christmas morning and asked, "Is it tomorrow yet?" A child told to "stay there" or "come here" may not follow instructions, partly because the terms are confusing.

One example of childlike understanding comes from Italian preschoolers who were discussing a war nearby. They seemed to understand the issues, advocating peace. But their words revealed their egocentrism. Giorgia, age 4, said, "The daddies, mommies, and children get their feelings hurt by war" (Abbott & Nutbrown, 2001, p. 123).

Grammar

Chapter 6 noted that the *grammar* of language includes the structures, techniques, and rules that are used to communicate meaning. Word order and word repetition, prefixes and suffixes, intonation and emphasis—all are part of grammar.

By age 3, English-speaking children understand many aspects of grammar. They know word order (subject/verb/object), saying "I eat the apple," not any of the 23 other possible sequences of those four words. They also use plurals, tenses (past, present, and future), and nominative, objective, and possessive pronouns (*I/me/mine* or *my*). They use articles (*the, a, an*) correctly, even though the use of articles in English has many complexities.

Parents' input and encouragement, as well as their use of grammar, lead directly to faster and more correct language use by children (Barrett, 1999; Hoff & Naigles, 2002). In a study of twins (who are often delayed in grammar because they experience less individualized conversation), researchers found that the speed and scope of language learning depended on how much the parents spoke

➤**Response for Social Scientists** (from page 238): According to Piaget, preschool children focus on appearance and on static conditions (so they cannot mentally reverse a process). Further, they are egocentric, believing that everyone shares their point of view. No wonder they believe that they had always known that the candy box held pencils and that their friend would know that, too.

to each twin (Rutter et al., 2003). Some parents speak more to one twin than the other, and that difference affects language development.

Each specific aspect of language develops differently, because many genetic and environmental influences have an impact, and no two children have the same influences. Genes may be more influential for expressive than for receptive language, since the latter is more dependent on experience (Kovas et al., 2005). Grammar is strongly influenced by experience.

Young children learn grammar so well that they tend to apply rules when they should not. This tendency, called **overregularization,** creates trouble when a language includes many exceptions, as English does. An example involves one of the first grammatical rules that English-speaking children apply: the addition of a final *-s* to form the plural of a noun. Many young children overregularize, talking about *foots, tooths, sheeps,* and *mouses.*

overregularization The application of rules of grammar even when exceptions occur, so that the language is made to seem more "regular" than it actually is.

A fascinating aspect of the increasing intelligence of young children is that many of them first say words correctly and then, when they understand the rule, start making overregularizing mistakes. Although even the first sentences show some understanding of grammar, it takes many years before children use all the grammar structures of their native language correctly (Tomasello, 2006).

Learning Two Languages

In today's world, bilingualism is an asset, even a necessity. Yet as they grow up, language-minority children (those who speak a language that is not the dominant language of their nation) are at a disadvantage in almost every measure. They are more likely to do poorly in school, to feel ashamed, to become unemployed as adults, and so on (see Chapter 12). Learning the majority language is crucial for them, but how should this learning happen?

What Is the Goal?

The first question that must be answered is, What is the goal of having a second language? Parents, teachers, and the public often disagree. Should young children become bilingual, learning two distinct languages? Some say no, arguing that young children need to become proficient in one, and only one, language and that trying to teach them two languages might confuse them. Others say yes, arguing that everyone should learn at least two languages and that the language-sensitive years of early childhood are the best time for it.

The second argument has more research support. Remarkably, soon after the vocabulary explosion, young children are able to master two languages' distinct sets of words and grammar, with each language's characteristic pauses, pronunciations, intonations, and gestures (Bates et al., 2001; Mayberry & Nicoladis, 2000). Adults who are bilingual can use one language and temporarily inhibit the other, experiencing no confusion, thanks to a specific area of the brain that stores language and uses the appropriate words (Crinion et al., 2006).

Young children have difficulty with pronunciation in every language, but this does not slow down their learning of a second language, as it does for adults. When expressing themselves, many of them transpose sounds (*magazine* becomes *mazagine*), drop consonants (*truck* becomes *ruck*), convert difficult sounds

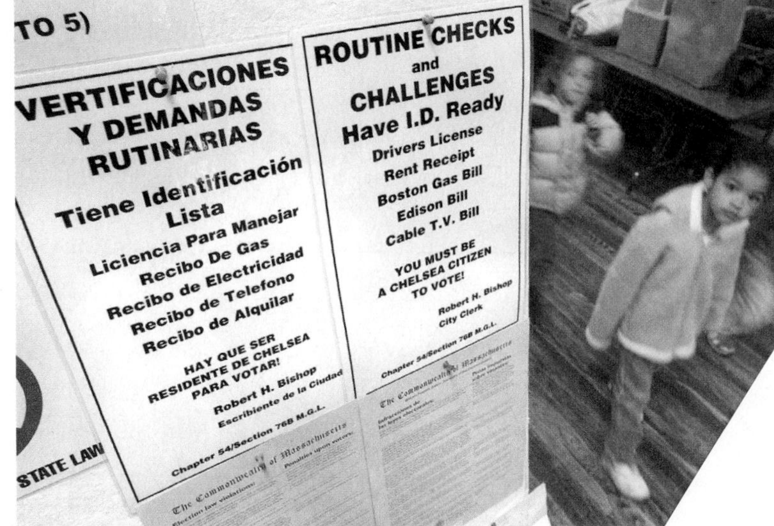

Tiene Identificación Lista Are you pleased or angered by this bilingual sign at a school in Chelsea, Massachusetts, that serves as a polling place on election day? In this election, voters were deciding whether or not to eliminate government funding for bilingual education. Those who favored immersion argued that signs like this one would soon become unnecessary if children were taught only in English. Those who favored bilingual education held that without it, children from minority-language families would be likely to drop out of school before mastering *any* language.

(*father* becomes *fadder*), and make other errors. But they can hear better than they can talk (receptive more than expressive). For example, my daughter Rachel at age 4 asked for a "yeyo yayipop." Her father said, "You want a yeyo yayipop?" She replied, "Daddy, sometimes you talk funny."

Bilingualism, Cognition, and Culture

Since language is integral to culture, bilingualism is embedded in emotions of ethnic pride and fear. This reality hampers developmental research. One group of researchers explains:

> A question of concern to many is whether early schooling [in the play years] in English for language minority children harms the development and/or maintenance of their mother tongue and possibly children's language competence in general. . . . [The] debate quickly and unfortunately becomes . . . hampered by extreme and emotional political positions.
>
> *[Winsler et al., 1999, p. 350]*

Especially for Immigrant Parents You want your children to be fluent in the language of your family's new country, even though you do not speak that language well. Should you speak to your children in your native tongue or in the new language?

Research finds that bilingualism has both advantages and disadvantages. Supporters point out, correctly, that children who speak two languages by age 5 are less egocentric in their understanding of language and more advanced in their theory of mind. Opponents point out, also correctly, that bilingual children often are less fluent in one or both languages, slowing down reading as well as other linguistic skills (Bialystok, 2001).

This last fact makes many who speak the dominant language strive to have every child learn that language. This issue is of particular importance in California, where more than half of all public school children have parents who are immigrants. Many such parents find that their children make a *language shift,* becoming more fluent in their new language than in their home language (Min, 2000; S.-L. C. Wong & M. G. Lopez, 2000).

It is not unusual for 5-year-olds to understand their parents' language but refuse to speak it, especially if their parents understand the dominant language. Nor is it unusual for adults to depend on a child as interpreter when they deal with monolingual bureaucrats. This dependency, which amounts to a role reversal, makes practical sense, but it widens the gap between child and parent. (Even native-born monolingual families have a generational and cohort parent–child gap.)

One Family's Multiculturalism One of the first cultural preferences to travel successfully is food, and Italian cuisine is one of the world's most popular. This family lives in New York, the parents were born in Taiwan, their children are learning to speak both Chinese and English—and they all love pepperoni pizza.

SUSAN KUKLIN / PHOTO RESEARCHERS, INC.

Language shift and role reversal are unfortunate, not only for the child and the parents but also for the society. Having many bilingual citizens is a national strength, and respect for family traditions is a bulwark against adolescent rebellion. Yet young children are preoperational: They center on the immediate status of their parents and their language, on appearances more than past history or future benefits. No wonder many shift toward the dominant language.

Again, what is the goal of second-language learning? Parents are reluctant to deprive children of their roots, heritage, and identity, and yet they know that speaking, reading, and writing the dominant language are necessary for success (Suarez-Orozco & Suarez-Orozco, 2001). Many adults who are proud of their home language criticize members of their ethnic group who have "lost" their heritage language. But they also know that their children will face discrimination if they speak with a "foreign" accent and are less than fluent in the dominant language.

The best solution seems to be for every child to become a **balanced bilingual,** fluent in two languages, speaking both so well that no audible hint suggests the other language. Is balanced bilingualism possible? Yes. In many nations, during these sensitive play years, children become fluent in two or more languages.

balanced bilingual A person who is fluent in two languages, not favoring one or the other.

Constant Change

The basics of language learning—explosion, fast-mapping, overregularization, extensive practice—apply to bilingual learning. Parents who want a child to learn two languages need to intensify the child's exposure to both languages.

Fortunately, children have a powerful urge to communicate and a readiness to learn as much as they can. This was dramatically illustrated by children in Nicaragua at a boarding school for the deaf (Siegal, 2004). Their teachers tried to teach spoken Spanish and used no sign language. (This strategy is no longer common, since it is now clear that deaf children learn best if they are taught sign language from infancy. However, war delayed the teachers' awareness of this finding.)

The children in Nicaragua invented their own sign language, using it among themselves and teaching it to the new arrivals. Their created language flourished, with each new generation of children refining it. Younger children were more fluent than older ones because they built on what had already been invented, adding new gestures.

Similarly, established languages continually change. In English in the past few decades, the word *Negro* gave way to *Black,* which was soon replaced by *African American*. New terms include *hip-hop*, *e-mail*, *DVD*, *spam*, *blog*, *cell* (phone), *rap* (music), *buff* (in shape), and hundreds more. Words from other languages have become basic English vocabulary, such as *salsa, loco, amour, kowtow,* and *mensch*. Some key terms in this book, *doula* and *kwashiorkor* among them, originated in other languages. Young people learn such changes before adults do.

SUMMING UP

Children aged 2 to 6 have impressive linguistic talents. They explode into speech, from about a hundred words to many thousands, from halting baby talk to fluency. Fast-mapping and grammar are among the sophisticated devices they use, strategies that can backfire. No other time in the entire life span is as sensitive to language learning, especially to mastering pronunciation. Children can readily learn two languages during these years. Extensive exposure to both languages is necessary to become a balanced bilingual. ■

Early-Childhood Education

A hundred years ago children had no formal education until first grade, which is why it was called "first" and why younger children were called "preschoolers." Today most 3- to 5-year-olds in developed nations are in school (see Figure 9.5 for U.S. trends), partly because research "documents the rapid development and great learning potential of the early years" (Hyson et al., 2006, p. 6).

Names of early educational institutions differ (such as preschool, nursery school, day care, pre-primary), but names do not indicate the nature of a program. We will consider three clusters: child-centered, teacher-directed, and intervention programs.

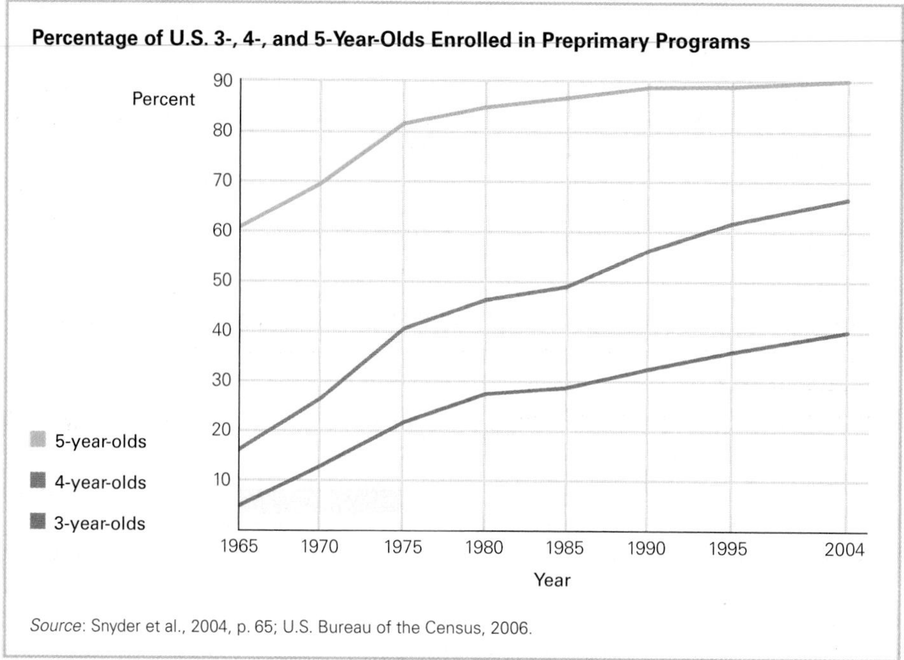

FIGURE 9.5

Changing Times As research increasingly finds that preschool education provides a foundation for later learning, more and more young children are in educational programs.

Child-Centered Programs

Many programs are developmental, or child-centered, stressing children's development and growth. This approach stresses children's need to play and explore rather than to follow adult directions (Weikart, 1999). Many child-centered programs use a Piaget-inspired model that allows children to discover ideas at their own pace. The physical space and the materials—dress-up clothing, art supplies, puzzles, blocks of many sizes, and other toys—are organized to encourage self-paced exploration.

Many child-centered programs encourage artistic expression. Some educators argue that young children "are all poets" in that they are gifted in seeing the world more imaginatively than older people do. According to advocates of child-centered programs, this peak of creative vision should be encouraged; children should be given lots of opportunities to tell stories, draw pictures, dance, and make music for their own delight (Egan & Ling, 2002).

Child-centered programs also show the influence of Vygotsky, who thought that children learn from other children, with adult guidance. For example, in order to learn number skills, classrooms have games that include math (counting objects, keeping score), routines that use measurements (daily calendars, schedules), and number guidelines (only three children in the blocks corner, two volunteers to get the juice).

"We teach them that the world can be an unpredictable, dangerous, and sometimes frightening place, while being careful not to spoil their lovely innocence. It's tricky."

Montessori Schools

One type of preschool that is child-centered began a hundred years ago, when Maria Montessori opened nursery schools for poor children in Rome. She believed that children needed structured, individualized projects to give them a sense of accomplishment, such as completing particular puzzles, using a sponge and water to clean a table, and drawing shapes.

Like Piaget (her contemporary), Montessori (1936/1966) realized that children have different thoughts and needs from adults. They learn from activities that adults might call play, and teachers should provide tasks that dovetail with the cognitive eagerness of the child. For example, because they have a need for order, for language learning, and for using all their senses, children will learn from exercises that allow them to develop these skills.

Today's Montessori schools still emphasize individual pride and accomplishment, presenting many literacy-related tasks (such as outlining letters and looking at books) to the children at age 4 or so (Lillard, 2005). Many tasks differ from those Montessori developed, but the underlying philosophy is the same. Children collaborate with each other and do not sit quietly while a teacher instructs them. That is what makes this child-centered, although some things children enjoy (pretend play, for example) are not Montessori.

The goal is for the children to feel proud of themselves and engaged in learning. Many aspects of Montessori's philosophy are in accord with current developmental research, and that is one reason this kind of school remains popular in many nations. A study of 5-year-olds in inner-city Milwaukee who were chosen by lottery to attend Montessori programs found that they were better at pre-reading and early math tasks, as well as at theory of mind, than a group of their peers who had not been selected (Lillard & Else-Quest, 2006).

The Reggio Emilia Approach

Another form of early-childhood education is called the *Reggio Emilia approach* because it was inspired by a program pioneered in the Italian town of that name, where today 13 infant–toddler centers and 21 preschools are funded by the city. Almost all local parents want their children to participate; there is a waiting list, and more centers are planned.

In Reggio Emilia, every preschooler is encouraged to master skills not usually seen in American schools until age 7 or so, such as writing and using tools, but no child is *required* to engage in such learning (Edwards et al., 1998). There is no large-group instruction, with formal lessons in, say, forming letters or cutting paper. Children are seen as "rich and powerful learners" and as "competent, creative individuals" (Abbott & Nutbrown, 2001, pp. 24, 47), each with his or her own learning needs and artistic drive.

Appreciation of the arts is evident not only in the children's activities but also in the physical design of the schools. Every Reggio Emilia school has a large central room where children gather, with floor-to-ceiling windows open to a spacious, plant-filled playground. Big mirrors are part of every school's décor (again fostering individuality), and children's art is displayed on white walls and hung from high ceilings. Among the characteristics of Reggio Emilia programs (now evident in every developed nation) are a low teacher/child ratio, ample space, and abundant materials.

One of the distinctive features of the curriculum is that a small group of children become engaged in long-term projects of their choosing. Such projects foster the children's pride in their accomplishments (which are displayed for all to admire) while teaching them to plan and work together.

➤**Response for Immigrant Parents** (from page 244): Children learn by listening, so it is important for you to speak with them often, and it is probably best to do so in both languages. Depending on how comfortable you are with the new language, you might prefer to read to your children, sing to them, and converse with them primarily in your native language and find a good preschool where they will learn the new language. The worst thing you could do would be to restrict speech in either tongue.

Another Place for Children High ceilings, uncrowded play space, varied options for art and music, a glass wall revealing trees and flowers—all these features reflect the Reggio Emilia approach to individualized, creative learning for young children. Such places are rare in nations other than Italy.

Observation Quiz (see answer, page 250): How many children appear in this photograph and how many are engaged in creative expression?

Teachers have 6 hours of work time each week without the children, which they spend planning activities, having group discussions, and talking to parents. Parental involvement is expected: They teach in special subject areas, meet with one another, and receive frequent reports, often with photographs, written observations, and their child's artwork. The entire town is proud of their children and schools.

Teacher-Directed Programs

Unlike Reggio Emilia, some programs stress academics taught by the teacher to the entire class. The curriculum teaches children letters, numbers, shapes, and colors, as well as how to listen to the teacher and sit quietly. Praise and other reinforcements are given for good behavior, and time-outs (brief separation from activities) are punishments.

In teacher-directed programs, there is a clear distinction between the serious work of schooling and the cozy play of home. As one German boy explained:

> So home is home and kindergarten is kindergarten. Here is my work and at home is off-time, understand? My mum says work is me learning something. Learning is when you drive your head, and off-time is when the head slows down.
>
> *[quoted in Griebel & Niesel, 2002, p. 67]*

The teachers' goal is to make all children "ready to learn" when they enter elementary school. Some of these programs explicitly teach basic skills, including reading, writing, and arithmetic, sometimes with the teacher asking questions that all the children answer together. Children are given practice in forming letters, sounding out words, counting objects, and writing their names. If a 4-year-old learns to read, that is success. (In a developmental program, it might arouse suspicion that the child was not being allowed enough time to play.) Many teacher-directed programs were inspired by behaviorism, which emphasizes step-by-step learning and repetition.

The contrast between child-centered and teacher-directed philosophies is evident in many areas, not only in lessons but also in social interactions. For instance, if one child bothers another child, should the second child tell the teacher, or should the two children work it out by themselves? If one child bites another, should the biter be isolated, reprimanded, or—as sometimes happens—should the victim be allowed to bite back? Each preschool has rules for such situations, which vary because of contrasting philosophies.

Intervention Programs

Developmental scientists, linking research findings and practical applications, have discovered that early childhood is a prime learning period. It is also evident that some children learn much more than others. Five-year-olds differ dramatically in their ability to learn, talk, and even listen. The main reason is thought to be exposure to language and other learning opportunities that some parents provide and others do not (Hart & Risley, 1995).

Many nations try to narrow the gap by offering high-quality early education. Some nations (e.g., China, France, Italy, and Sweden) make programs available to all children; others vary (for example, in the United States, Oklahoma, and some other states provide full-day kindergarten and preschool education for all children, while other states provide only a few hours a day for those who are particularly needy).

Especially for Parents In trying to find a preschool program, what should a parent look for?

Head Start

In the United States, the most widespread early-childhood-education program is Project Head Start, which began in 1965 and continues to this day. This federal program was designed for low-income or minority children who were thought to need a "head start" on their education. The quality and results of Head Start programs vary from place to place. Some long-term effects are unknown, because scientific evaluation was not included in the original planning (Phillips & White, 2004).

Nevertheless, Head Start has provided half-day education for millions of 3- to 5-year-olds, boosting their social and learning skills at least temporarily, and has probably provided long-term benefits as well (Zigler et al., 1996). Some programs are now 6 hours long rather than 3, because researchers realize that learning correlates with the length of school time.

There are many problems in evaluating Head Start. Over the decades, its goals have been diffuse and varied, from lifting families out of poverty to promoting literacy, from providing dental care and immunizations to teaching standard English. Some teachers practice child-centered education and others prefer a teacher-directed approach; some consider parents part of the problem and others regard parents as allies. In any case, intervening with parents has proven difficult (Powell, 2006).

Many of the early Head Start programs had no specific curriculum or goals, which made valid evaluation impossible (Whitehurst & Massetti, 2004). An added problem has been the political turmoil that surrounds the topics of poverty, government programs, and the education of young children in the United States. The federal government has continued to fund Head Start year after year, partly because early education is proven to be beneficial in dozens of ways, but the program's priorities and direction have changed continually as the political winds have shifted (Zigler & Styfco, 2004).

Learning Is Fun The original purpose of the Head Start program was to boost disadvantaged children's academic skills. The most enduring benefits, however, turned out to be improved self-esteem and social skills, as is evident in these happy Head Start participants, all crowded together.

Observation Quiz (see answer, page 251): How many of these children are in close physical contact without discomfort or disagreement?

LAURA DWIGHT

➤Answer to Observation Quiz (from page 248): Eight children, and all of them are engaged in creative projects—if the boy standing at right is making music, not just noise, with that cymbal.

Experimental Programs

The same social imperatives that led to Head Start also led to several intensive programs (involving many hours and years, with cognitive emphasis) that have been well evaluated through longitudinal research. Three projects in particular have excellent follow-up data: one in Michigan, called Perry or High/Scope (Schweinhart & Weikart, 1997; Schweinhart et al., 2005); one in North Carolina, called Abecedarian (Campbell et al., 2001); and one in Chicago, called Child–Parent Centers (Reynolds, 2000; Reynolds et al., 2004).

All three programs enrolled children from low-income families for several years before kindergarten, all compared experimental groups of children with matched control groups, and all reached the same conclusion: Early education can have substantial long-term benefits, which become apparent when the children are in the third grade or later.

Children in these three programs scored higher on math and reading achievement tests by age 10 than did other children from the same backgrounds, schools, and neighborhoods. They were significantly less likely to be placed in special classes for slow or disruptive children or to repeat a year of school. In adolescence, they had higher aspirations and a greater sense of achievement and were less likely to be mistreated. As young adults, they were more likely to attend college and less likely to go to jail.

All three research projects found that direct cognitive training (not simply letting children play), with specific instruction in various school-readiness skills, was useful as long as each child's needs and talents were considered. The curriculum was neither child-centered nor teacher-directed, but a combination. Parents were engaged with the child's learning.

Although these programs were expensive (perhaps as much as $15,000 annually per child in 2007 dollars), many believe that the decreased need for special education and other social services eventually makes such programs a wise investment. Indeed, one economist calculates that governments eventually spend at

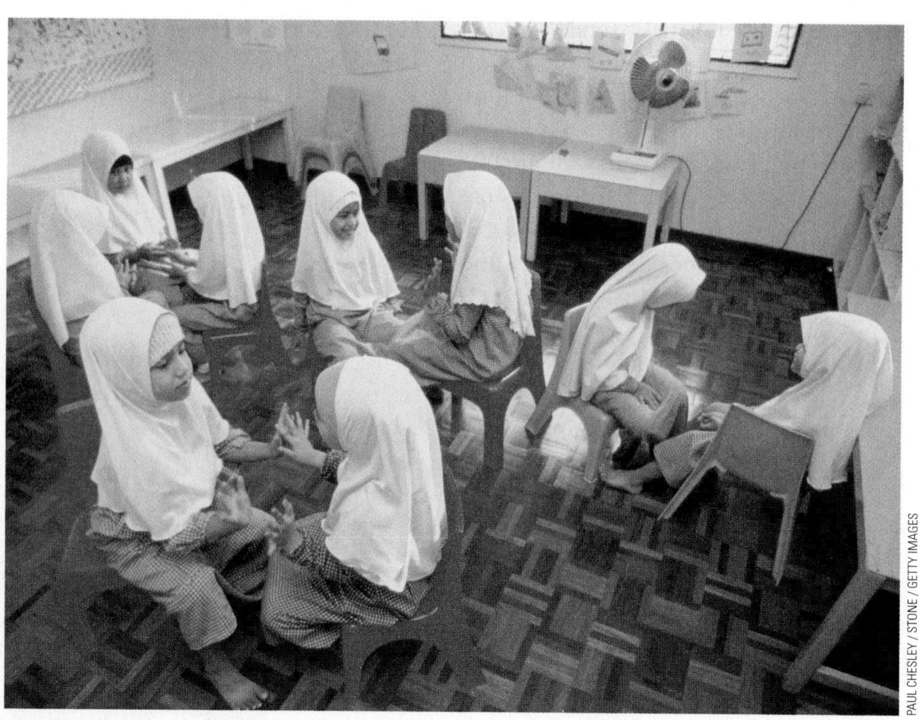

PAUL CHESLEY / STONE / GETTY IMAGES

Learning from One Another Every nation creates its own version of early education. In this scene at a nursery school in Kuala Lumpur, Malaysia, note the head coverings, uniforms, bare feet, and absence of boys. None of these elements would be found in most early-childhood education classrooms in North America or Europe.

Observation Quiz (see answer, page 252): What seemingly universal aspects of childhood are visible in this photograph?

least five times more per person when children do not have the benefit of an intensive preschool program (Lynch, 2004). Children from low-income families who did not attend preschool have higher rates of many costly conditions later in life: special education (four times more expensive per student per year); unemployment (no taxes); and even imprisonment ($150,000 per inmate per year).

Costs and Benefits

The financial aspect may be especially significant. For many early-childhood educators, Reggio Emilia is the gold standard because the teacher/child ratio is low and the physical space is luxurious, but the cost per child for such a program is about twice that of most other types of preschool care.

Since parents pay the bulk of the cost of preschool education in the United States (except for some intervention programs), Reggio Emilia is beyond the means of most families. Child-centered programs open to all children may be feasible only in places with community support and a low birth rate (like Italy, where most families have only one child).

A key finding from all the research is that the quality of early-childhood education counts. The most recent reauthorization of Head Start emphasizes educational quality and evaluative research (Lombardi & Cubbage, 2004). Comparisons of programs find that the specific curricula and philosophy matter less than teachers who know how to respond to the needs of young children. Generally, an educational, center-based program is better than family day care or home care, but high-quality home care is better than a low-quality day-care center (Clarke-Stewart & Allhusen, 2005).

Some characteristics of quality care have been described in Chapter 7: safety, adequate space and equipment, a low adult/child ratio, positive social interactions among children and adults, and trained staff (and educated parents) who are likely to stay in the program. Continuity helps, for the child as well as for the adults. One of the best questions that parents comparing options can ask is, "How long has each staff member worked at this center?"

Curriculum is also important, especially by age 4 or 5. Best may be programs with an emphasis on learning, reflected in a curriculum that includes extensive practice in language, fine and gross motor skills, and basic number skills. Such programs may be found in child-centered or teacher-directed schools. As this chapter emphasizes, young children love to learn and can master many skills and ideas, as long as adults do not expect them to think and behave like older children.

Beyond that, history teaches that new research will find additional cognitive potential among 2- to 6-year-olds and additional strategies to develop that potential. Valid evaluation (longitudinal comparisons with experimental and control groups) are still rare. Some readers of this book will undertake the research and staff the schools that will update our view of cognition in childhood.

SUMMING UP

Research, particularly on preschool programs for children in low-income families, has proved that high-quality early education benefits children, who improve in language, in social skills, and in prospects for the future (Clarke-Stewart & Allhusen, 2005). A variety of programs, including child-centered (Montessori and Reggio Emilia) and teacher-directed are available—although sometimes very expensive. Nations, states, and parents differ in what they seek from early education for their children, and programs vary in teacher preparation, curriculum, physical space, and adult/child ratios. ■

➤Answer to Observation Quiz (from page 249): All five—not four (look again at the right-hand side of the photograph)!

➤Response for Parents (from page 249): There is much variation. None fit every parent's values. However, children should be engaged in learning, not allowed to sit passively or to squabble with one another. Before deciding, parents should look at several programs, staying long enough to see the children in action and the teachers showing warmth and respect for the children.

SUMMARY

Piaget and Vygotsky

1. Piaget stressed the egocentric and illogical aspects of thought during the play years. He called this stage preoperational thought because young children often cannot yet use logical operations to think about their observations and experiences.

2. Young children, according to Piaget, sometimes focus on only one thing (centration) and see things only from their own viewpoint (egocentrism), remaining stuck on appearances and on current reality. They cannot understand that things change, actions can be reversed, and other people have other perspectives.

3. Vygotsky stressed the social aspects of childhood cognition, noting that children learn by participating in various experiences, guided by more knowledgeable adults or peers. That guidance assists learning within the zone of proximal development, which encompasses the knowledge and skills that the child has the potential to learn.

4. According to Vygotsky, the best teachers use various hints, guidelines, and other tools to provide the child with a scaffold for new learning. Language is a bridge of social mediation between the knowledge that the child already has and the learning that the society hopes to impart. For Vygotsky, words are a tool for learning that both mentor and child use.

Children's Theories

5. Children develop theories, especially to explain the purpose of life and their role in it. Among these theories is theory of mind—an understanding of what others may be thinking. Notable advances in theory of mind occur at around age 4. Theory of mind is partly the result of brain maturation, but a child's language and experiences (in the family and community) also have an impact.

Language

6. Language develops rapidly during early childhood, which is a sensitive period but not a critical one for language learning. Vocabulary increases dramatically, with thousands of words added between ages 2 and 6. In addition, basic grammar is mastered.

7. Many children learn to speak more than one language. Ideally, children become balanced bilinguals, equally proficient in two languages, by age 6.

Early-Childhood Education

8. Organized educational programs during early childhood advance cognitive and social skills, although specifics vary a great deal. Montessori and Reggio Emilia are two child-centered programs that began in Italy and now are offered in many nations. Behaviorist principles led to many specific practices of teacher-directed programs.

9. Head Start is a government program that generally helps low-income children. Longitudinal research on three other programs for low-income children has demonstrated that early-childhood education reduces the likelihood of later problems. Graduates of these programs are less likely to need special education and more likely to become law-abiding, gainfully employed adults.

10. Although many preschool programs are successful, the quality of early education matters. Children learn best if there is a clear curriculum and if the adult–child ratio is low. The training and continuity of early-childhood teachers are also important.

KEY TERMS

preoperational intelligence (p. 231)
centration (p. 232)
egocentrism (p. 232)
focus on appearance (p. 232)
static reasoning (p. 232)
irreversibility (p. 232)
conservation (p. 232)
apprentice in thinking (p. 234)
guided participation (p. 234)
zone of proximal development (ZPD) (p. 235)
scaffolding (p. 235)
private speech (p. 235)
social mediation (p. 235)
theory-theory (p. 236)
theory of mind (p. 238)
critical period (p. 240)
sensitive period (p. 240)
fast-mapping (p. 240)
overregularization (p. 243)
balanced bilingual (p. 245)

➤**Answer to Observation Quiz** (from page 250): Three aspects are readily apparent: These girls enjoy their friendships; they are playing a hand-clapping game, some version of which is found in every culture; and, most important, they have begun the formal education that their families want for them.

KEY QUESTIONS

1. Piaget is often criticized for his description of early cognition. Why is this, and is the criticism fair? (Discuss with particular reference to preoperational thought.)

2. Give an example of the process of cognition in early childhood as Vygotsky would describe it, highlighting at least three of his specific concepts.

3. What are the main similarities between Vygotsky and Piaget?

4. How would parents act differently toward their child according to whether they agreed with Piaget or with Vygotsky?

5. How does Piaget's idea of egocentrism relate to the research on theory of mind?

6. How does fast-mapping apply to children's learning of curse words?

7. How do children learn grammar without formal instruction?

8. What are the differences between child-centered and teacher-directed instruction?

9. Why is there disagreement about the extent to which Head Start benefits children?

10. Why do some cities and nations provide much better preschool education than others?

APPLICATIONS

The best way to understand thinking in early childhood is to listen to a child, as applications 1 and 2 require. If some students have no access to children, they should do application 3 or 4.

1. Replicate one of Piaget's conservation experiments. The easiest one is conservation of liquids (pictured in Figure 9.1). Find a child under age 5, and make sure the child tells you that two identically shaped glasses contain the same amount of liquid. Then carefully pour one glass of liquid into a narrower, taller glass. Ask the child which glass now contains more or if the glasses contain the same amount.

2. To demonstrate how rapidly language is learned, show a preschool child several objects and label one with a nonsense word the child has never heard. (*Toma* is often used; so is *wug*.) Or choose a word the child does not know, such as *wrench, spatula,* or a coin from another nation. Test the child's fast-mapping.

3. Theory of mind emerges at about age 4, but many adults still have trouble understanding other people's thoughts and motives. Ask several people why someone in the news did whatever they did (e.g., a scandal, a crime, a heroic act). Then ask your informants how sure they are of their explanation. Compare and analyze the reasons as well as the degrees of certainty. (One person may be sure of an explanation that someone else thinks is impossible.)

4. Think about an experience in which you learned something that was initially difficult. To what extent do Vygotsky's concepts (guidance, language mediation, apprenticeship, zone of proximal development) explain the experience? Write a detailed, step-by-step description of your learning process as Vygotsky would describe it.

10

CHAPTER OUTLINE

- **Emotional Development**
  - Initiative Versus Guilt
  - Psychopathology
  - Empathy and Antipathy
- **Parents**
  - Parenting Style
  - ISSUES AND APPLICATIONS: Planning Punishment
  - The Challenge of Media
- **Becoming Boys and Girls**
  - Theories of Gender Differences
  - IN PERSON: Berger and Freud
  - Gender and Destiny

The Play Years: Psychosocial Development

Imagine that you have two children, a typical 2-year-old and a 6-year-old. What a contrast! If you take your 2-year-old to the playground, don't become absorbed in conversation. Before you realize it, your child may be crying atop a high slide, tasting a sandbox cake, grabbing a toy, or, worse, nowhere to be seen. Meanwhile, as long as adults are nearby, your 6-year-old is probably safe, sliding and sharing, not swallowing sand or disappearing without permission.

This chapter describes that 2-to-6 transformation. Maturation and motivation are crucial; so are emotions and experiences. Psychosocial development is multifaceted, involving genes, gender, parents, peers, and culture, all readily apparent in this chapter.

Emotional Development

Learning when and how to express emotions (made possible as the emotional hotspots of the brain become linked to the executive functions) is the preeminent psychosocial accomplishment between ages 2 and 6 (N. Eisenberg et al., 2004). Children who master this task, called **emotional regulation,** become more capable in every aspect of their lives (Denham et al., 2003; Matsumoto, 2004).

emotional regulation The ability to control when and how emotions are expressed. This is the most important psychosocial development to occur between the ages of 2 and 6, though it continues throughout life.

Emotions are regulated and controlled by 6-year-olds in ways unknown to exuberant, expressive, and often overwhelmed toddlers. Children learn to be friendly to new acquaintances but not too friendly, angry but not explosive, frightened by a clown but not terrified, able to distract themselves and limit their impulses if need be. (All these abilities emerge during the preschool period and continue to develop throughout life.) Now we explain some specific aspects of emotional regulation.

Initiative Versus Guilt

Initiative is saying something new, extending a skill, beginning a project. Depending on the outcome (including the parents' response), some initiatives make children feel guilty—a consequence that can make children afraid to try new activities again. Children internalize past experiences of pride or shame, thus affecting their self-esteem or feelings of guilt.

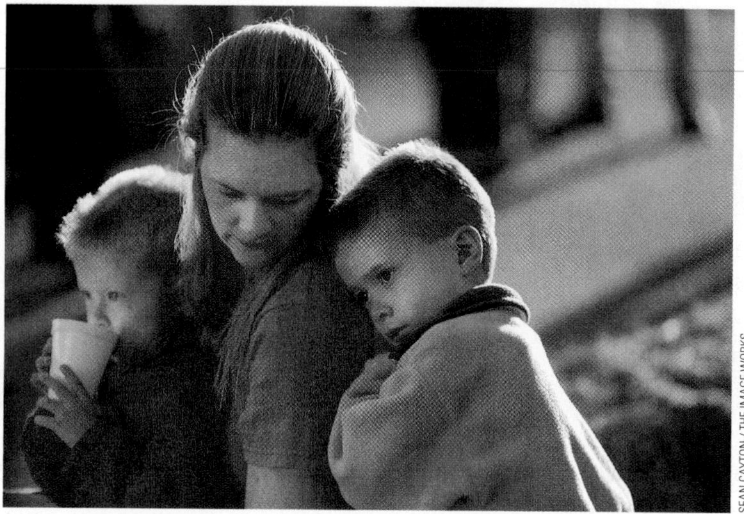
SEAN CAYTON / THE IMAGE WORKS

Close Connection Unfamiliar events often bring developmental tendencies to the surface, as with the curious boy and his worried brother, who are attending Colorado's Pikes Peak or Bust Rodeo breakfast. Their attentive mother keeps the livelier boy calm and reassures the shy one.

Observation Quiz (see answer, page 259): Mother is obviously a secure base for both boys, who share the same family and half the same genes but are different ages: One is 2 and the other is 4. Can you tell which boy is younger?

initiative versus guilt Erikson's third psychosocial crisis. Children begin new activities and feel guilty when they fail.

self-esteem How a person evaluates his or her own worth, either in specifics (e.g., intelligence, attractiveness) or overall.

self-concept A person's understanding of who he or she is. Self-concept includes appearance, personality, and various traits.

More generally, positive enthusiasm, effort, and self-evaluation characterize ages 3 to 6, according to Erik Erikson's psychosocial theory. During what he called his third developmental stage, **initiative versus guilt,** Erikson described self-esteem as emerging from the acquisition of skills and competencies described in the previous two chapters.

Self-esteem is the belief in one's own ability, a personal estimate of success and worthiness. As self-esteem builds, children become more confident and independent. The autonomy of 2-year-olds, often expressed as stubborn reactions, becomes the initiative of 5-year-olds, often seen in their self-motivated activities. In the process, children form a **self-concept,** or understanding of themselves, which includes not only self-esteem but also facts such as gender and size.

Balancing one's own wishes with the expectations embedded in the social context is not easy, especially if one's only playmate has been a mother who never thwarted the child's initiative. For example, one child (about age 3) was new to peers and to preschool:

> She commanded another child, "Fall down. Go on, do what I say." When the other child stayed stalwartly on his feet, she pushed him over and was clearly amazed when he jumped up and said, "No pushing!" and the teacher came over and reproved her.
>
> *[Leach, 1997, p. 474]*

In this example, the more experienced child has a strong self-concept that he was ready to defend. The inexperienced girl was "reproved," not punished. The teacher hoped she would internalize the rule so that she would feel guilt (not shame) if she broke it again. Most older children and adults, but fewer 4- or 5-year-olds, experience guilt when their initiative clashes with the rules and regulations they have learned (Lagattuta, 2005).

Pride

Erikson recognized that typical 3- to 5-year-olds have immodest and quite positive self-concepts, holding themselves in high self-esteem. They believe that they are strong, smart, and good-looking—and thus that any goal is quite achievable. Whatever they are (self-concept) is also thought to be good (for instance, little boys are proud of being male).

In the play years, children are confident that their good qualities will endure but that any bad qualities (even biological traits such as poor eyesight) will disappear with time (Lockhart et al., 2002). As one group of researchers explained:

> Young children seem to be irrepressibly optimistic about themselves. . . . Consider, for example, the shortest, most uncoordinated boy in a kindergarten class who proclaims that he will be the next Michael Jordan.
>
> *[Lockhart et al., 2002, pp. 1408–1409]*

The new initiative that Erikson describes is aided by a longer attention span (made possible by neurological maturity); now children have a purpose for what they do. Concentrated attention is believed to be crucial for later competence of all kinds, but concentration is not an automatic result of brain growth.

Self-esteem and concentration are connected to motivation, cognition, and experience, all of which correlate with maturation but are not caused by it. For example, 6-year-olds who have been chronically mistreated feel inadequate and incompetent, with abnormally low self-esteem (Kim & Cicchetti, 2006).

Feeling proud of oneself is the foundation for practice and then mastery, as children learn to pour juice or climb a tree. For most children, self-criticism does not arise until later. Preschoolers predict that they can solve impossible puzzles, remember long lists of words, change every undesirable trait, and control the dreams that come when they are asleep (Stipek et al., 1995; Woolley & Boerger, 2002). Such naive predictions, sometimes called "protective optimism," help them learn (Lockhart et al., 2002) because they are not afraid to try new things.

ARIEL SKELLEY / CORBIS

Happy and Colorful No wonder this 5-year-old is proud—her picture is worth framing. High self-esteem is one of the strengths of being her age. Can you imagine a 9-year-old holding an equally colorful picture so proudly?

Guilt and Shame

Notice that Erikson called the negative consequence of this crisis "guilt," not shame. Erikson believed that because children develop self-awareness, they feel guilty when they realize their own mistakes. Generally, guilt means that people blame themselves because they have done something wrong, while shame means that people feel that others are blaming them.

Shame can be based on what is, such as one's ethnic background. In this case, the shame is rooted in the belief that others devalue those of certain ethnicities or minorities. To counter such feelings of shame, many parents of minority children (Mexican, African, or Indian American, among others) wisely make sure their children feel proud of their identity (Parke & Buriel, 2006).

Guilt and shame often occur together, though they do not necessarily go hand in hand. For example, children who misbehave may shame the parents, but the parents do not usually feel guilty. Or a person could feel guilty (of driving too fast, for instance) but not ashamed.

Many thoughtful people believe that guilt is a more mature emotion than shame because guilt is internalized (Bybee, 1998; Tangney, 2001; Zahn-Waxler, 2000). Guilt originates within; it may bother a person even if no one else knows about the misdeed. Shame depends on other people; it comes from knowing that someone else might see and criticize what a person has done. Thus, Erikson's expectation of shame at age 2 and guilt by age 5 signifies emotional maturation during these years.

Especially for College Students Is extrinsic or intrinsic motivation more influential in your study efforts?

Intrinsic Motivation

The idea that guilt comes from within highlights the distinction between **intrinsic motivation** and **extrinsic motivation.** Intrinsic motivation is evident when a person does something for the joy of doing it—such as a musician who plays simply for the delight of making music, even if no one else is around to hear it. Extrinsic motivation comes from outside (*ex-*), when the reason to do something is to gain praise or some other reward from someone else.

intrinsic motivation Goals or drives that come from inside a person, such as the need to feel smart or competent.

extrinsic motivation The need for rewards from outside, such as material possessions or someone else's esteem.

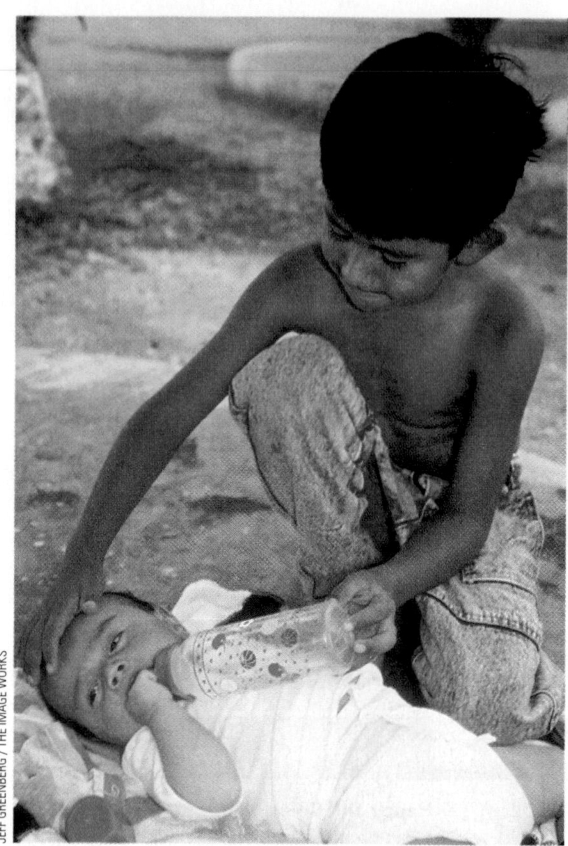
JEFF GREENBERG / THE IMAGE WORKS

Emotional Regulation Older brothers are not famous for being loving caregivers. However, in the Mayan culture, older children learn to regulate their jealousy and provide major care for younger siblings while their parents work.

Observation Quiz (see answer, page 260): What do you see that suggests that this boy is paying careful attention to his brother?

For the most part, preschool children are intrinsically motivated. They enjoy learning, playing, and practicing for their own joy, not because someone else sets a goal for them. For instance, when they play games, young children might not keep score; the fun is in playing more than in winning.

In a classic experiment, preschool children were given Magic Markers with which to draw and then placed into one of three groups with different conditions: (1) no award, (2) expected award (told *before* they had drawn anything that they would get a certificate), and (3) unexpected award (they heard "You were a big help" and received a certificate *after* they had drawn something) (Lepper et al., 1973). When the children returned to their classrooms, observers noted how often they chose to draw. Those who got the expected award drew less than those with the unexpected award. This was interpreted to mean that the extrinsic award undercut intrinsic motivation.

This research triggered a flood of studies. Researchers tried to uncover whether, when, and how rewards should be given. The consensus is that praising or paying a person after work has been done encourages that behavior, as long as the reinforcement is based on actual accomplishment. However, if substantial rewards are promised in advance for something that the person already enjoys doing, the extrinsic consequences may backfire by diminishing intrinsic motivation (Cameron & Pierce, 2002; Deci et al., 1999).

Cross-cultural research makes this more complex. Cultures differ regarding which emotions need regulation and which internal and external motivations work best. For example, children are especially encouraged to overcome their fears in the United States, to modify their anger in Puerto Rico, to temper their pride in China, and to control their aggression in Japan (Harwood et al., 1995; Hong et al., 2000; J. G. Miller, 2004). Emotional regulation is valuable everywhere, but cultures differ in the specifics (Matsumoto, 2004).

Psychopathology

At every age, developmentalists are concerned with preventing or treating *psychopathology,* which is an illness or disorder (*-pathology*) that involves the mind (*psycho-*). The first signs of psychopathology in children usually involve emotions that seem to overwhelm the child. Emotional regulation begins with impulse control. Often the impulse that most needs control is anger, because "dysregulated anger may trigger aggressive, oppositional behavior" (Gilliom et al., 2002, p. 222). Before such regulation, a frustrated 2-year-old might flail at another person or lie down screaming and kicking. A 5-year-old usually has more self-control, perhaps pouting and cursing, but not hitting and screaming.

Emotional Balance

Without adequate control, emotions overpower children. This occurs in two, seemingly opposite, ways. Some children have **externalizing problems:** They lash out in impulsive anger, attacking other people or things. They are sometimes called "undercontrolled."

externalizing problems Difficulty with emotional regulation that involves outwardly expressing emotions in uncontrolled ways, such as by lashing out in impulsive anger or attacking other people or things.

internalizing problems Difficulty with emotional regulation that involves turning one's emotional distress inward, as by feeling excessively guilty, ashamed, or worthless.

Other children have **internalizing problems:** They are fearful and withdrawn, turning emotional distress inward. They are sometimes called "overcontrolled." Both externalizing and internalizing children are unable to regulate their emotions properly or, more precisely, unable to regulate the *expression* of their emotions. They do not exercise enough control or they control themselves too much (Caspi & Shiner, 2006; Hart et al., 2003).

Emotional regulation is in part neurological, a matter of brain functioning. Because a child's ability to regulate emotions requires thinking before acting, deciding whether and how to display joy, anger, or fear, emotional regulation is the province of the prefrontal cortex, the executive area of the brain. As you remember from Chapter 8, the prefrontal cortex reacts to the limbic system (by acting or inhibiting action), including those parts of the brain (including the amygdala) where powerful emotions, especially fear and anxiety, form.

Normally, neurological advances in the prefrontal cortex occur at about age 4 or 5, when children become less likely to throw a temper tantrum, provoke a physical attack, or burst into giggles (Kagan & Hershkowitz, 2005). Throughout the period from age 2 to 6, violent outbursts, uncontrollable crying, and terrifying phobias diminish, and the capacity for self-control—such as not opening a wrapped gift immediately if asked to wait—becomes more evident (Carlson, 2003; Grolnick et al., 2006).

Emotional differences between younger and older children begin within the brain, perhaps going beyond simple maturation to differences more closely linked to the XX or XY chromosomes (Colder et al., 2002). Although girls are better at regulating their externalizing emotions, they are less successful with internalizing ones. By adolescence, undercontrolled boys may be delinquents; overcontrolled girls may be anxious or depressed (Pennington, 2002).

➤Answer to Observation Quiz (from page 256): Size is not much help, since children grow slowly during these years and the heads of these two boys appear about the same size. However, emotional development is apparent. Most 2-year-olds, like the one at the right, still cling to their mothers; most 4-year-olds are sufficiently mature, secure, and curious to watch the excitement as they drink their juice.

➤Response for College Students (from page 257): Both are important. Extrinsic motivation includes parental pressure and the need to get a good job after graduation. Intrinsic motivation includes the joy of learning, especially if you can express that learning in ways others recognize. Have you ever taken a course that was not required and was said to be difficult? That was intrinsic motivation—a sign that you will benefit from your college studies.

Differences in Early Care

Neurological damage can occur during early development, either prenatally (if a pregnant woman is stressed, ill, or a heavy drug user) or in infancy (if an infant is chronically malnourished, injured, or frightened). Extensive stress can kill some neurons and stop others from developing properly (Sanchez et al., 2001). This may affect the child's ability to regulate his or her emotions—the temper tantrum of a particular 5-year-old may not be as readily controllable as for most kindergarten children.

Early care prevents or worsens innate problems with emotional control. Highly stressed infant rats develop abnormal brain structures. However, if stressed rat pups are raised by nurturing mothers, their brains are protected by hormones elicited by their mothers, who lick, nuzzle, groom, and feed them often (J. Kaufman & Charney, 2001). Similarly in humans, nurturing caregivers guide reactive children toward emotional regulation, helping them become more competent than many other children (Hane & Fox, 2006; Quas et al., 2004).

FRANK SIMONETTI / STOCK CONNECTION / PICTUREQUEST

Who's Chicken? Genes and good parenting have made this boy neither too fearful nor too bold. Appropriate caution is probably the best approach to meeting a chicken.

The harm of poor caregiving is evident in maltreated 4- to 6-year-olds. Most such children (80 percent in one study) are "emotionally disregulated," either indifferent or extremely angry when strangers criticize their mothers (Maughan & Cicchetti, 2002). If neglect or abuse occurs in the first few years, it is more likely to cause internalizing or externalizing problems than mistreatment that begins when the child is older, probably because it harms the developing brain (Lopez et al., 2004; Manly et al., 2001).

Always remember that many influences affect each child. Nurture and nature interact, influencing the brain as well as behavior, through "multiple converging pathways," many originating in the brain but also activated by experiences (Cicchetti & Walker, 2001, p. 414).

Empathy and Antipathy

With increasing social awareness and decreasing egocentrism (as reviewed in Chapter 9), two other emotions develop: **empathy,** an understanding of the feelings and concerns of others, and **antipathy,** a dislike or even hatred of other people.

empathy The ability to understand the emotions of another person, especially when those emotions differ from one's own.

antipathy Feelings of anger, distrust, dislike, or even hatred toward another person.

➤Answer to Observation Quiz (from page 258): Look at his hands, legs, and face. He is holding the bottle and touching the baby's forehead with delicacy and care; he is positioning his legs in a way that is uncomfortable but suited to the task; and his eyes and mouth suggest he is giving the baby his full concentration.

Empathy is not the same as sympathy, which is feeling sorry *for* someone. It is feeling sorry *with* someone, feeling their pain as if it were one's own. Research with mirror neurons (see Chapter 1) suggests that observing someone else may activate the same areas of the brain as in the person directly involved. This is how empathy works. Antipathy likewise is a personal and emotional reaction, much stronger than merely disagreeing with someone.

Preschoolers develop empathy, but as you may remember from the Chapter 9 discussion of egocentrism and theory of mind, they do not always read others' emotions accurately (Saarni et al., 2006). For instance, when a person says in a very sad voice, "I came in first place in a race," virtually every 6-year-old judges the person to be unhappy, but almost no child younger than 6 recognizes the importance of tone (Morton et al., 2003). In other words, it takes maturity to correctly read tone, expression, and body language when they contradict what the child would feel in that situation.

Especially for Adults Who Are Unhappy What would prompt a young child to cheer someone up?

Young children (ages 3 and 4) also confuse another person's intentions and desires, a mistake that older children and adults rarely make (Leslie et al., 2006; Schult, 2002). Finally, young children can experience too much empathy, becoming so distressed by someone else's problem that they are not able to help (Saarni et al., 2006). An overly empathetic 3-year-old whose friend bumped his head may be overwhelmed with sadness and unable to find ice, tell an adult, or even express words of comfort.

Leading to Behavior

prosocial behavior Feeling and acting in ways that are helpful and kind, without obvious benefit to oneself.

antisocial behavior Feeling and acting in ways that are deliberately hurtful or destructive to another person.

Ideally, empathy leads to **prosocial behavior,** being helpful and kind without gaining any obvious benefit. Expressing concern, offering to share food or a toy, and including a shy child in a game or conversation are examples of prosocial behavior.

Antipathy can lead to **antisocial behavior,** deliberately injuring someone or destroying something that belongs to another (Caprara et al., 2001). Antisocial actions include verbal insults, social exclusion, and physical assaults. An antisocial 4-year-old might look another child in the eye, scowl, and then kick him hard without provocation.

By age 4 or 5—as a result of brain maturation, theory of mind, emotional regulation, and interactions with caregivers—most children can be deliberately prosocial or antisocial, with prosocial behavior generally increasing from age 3 to 6 and beyond (N. Eisenberg et al., 2006). Imagine that a boy hits his mother. If he is a toddler, the mother usually realizes that he is experimenting, a tertiary circular reaction, and she should stop him with a stern expression but not feel personally attacked.

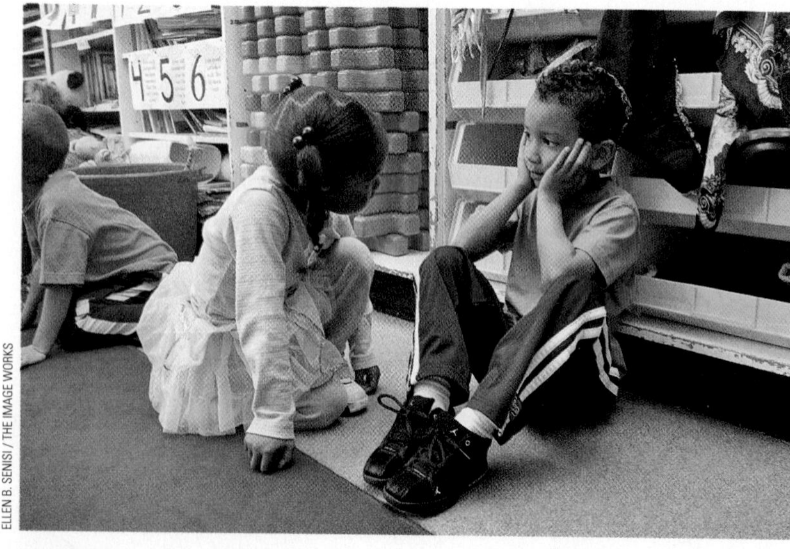

ELLEN B. SENISI / THE IMAGE WORKS

He's Listening With tilted head and pink tutu, this girl exemplifies two of the best characteristics often found in young children: empathy and self-confidence. Responding to her personality and concern, the distressed boy may well decide to rejoin the group.

However, if her son is 5, something is seriously wrong. In fact, according to a study in Montreal, when 5-year-olds are mean to their mothers (physically or verbally), that signifies a disturbed relationship, and the child is headed for externalizing problems with others at school, with friends, and probably later in life (Moss et al., 2004).

Cultures vary in how much they allow, punish, or encourage both prosocial and antisocial behavior, as well as in what particular behaviors are considered good and bad. In one specific example (see Figure 10.1), when Japanese and U.S. mothers were helping their 4-year-olds with a puzzle, the Japanese mothers were likely to emphasize mutuality (e.g., "This puzzle is hard for us"), while the

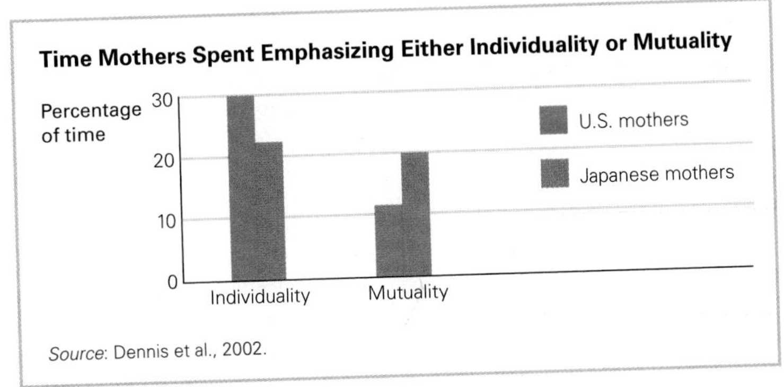

FIGURE 10.1

How Empathy Is Taught During free play with their 4-year-olds, Japanese mothers were more likely than U.S. mothers to emphasize mutuality, or interdependence. U.S. mothers tended to stress individuality, or self-reliance. This study demonstrates the role of culture in children's development of empathy.

Research Design

Scientists: Tracy A. Dennis, Pamela Cole, Carolyn Zahn-Waxler, and Ixchiro Mizuta.

Publication: *Child Development* (2002).

Participants: Sixty 4-year-olds in two groups of 30, one in Japan and one in the United States.

Design: Mothers played with their children while their interaction was videotaped. Later, coders who were blind to the hypothesis coded the mother's and the child's actions and speech in more than 20 categories. One was individuality and one was autonomy. Validity and reliability checks on the coding helped ensure standardization.

Major conclusion: Many similarities and a few differences (some opposite to the stereotypes) were found. Japanese mothers emphasized mutuality much more, and U.S. mothers emphasized individuality.

Comment: The two groups were closely matched on many factors, including child's age, parents' age, and education. This suggests that the differences were primarily cultural. Replication, with 4-year-olds in these and other nations, is needed.

U.S. mothers tended to emphasize individuality (e.g., "You are having a hard time with this puzzle") (Dennis et al., 2002; see Research Design). If this is typical, then Japanese children might learn to empathize more than U.S. children would.

Preschool children are capable of feeling empathy for others of their own group (national, ethnic, religious, or familial) without feeling antipathy toward people of other groups, never realizing that their values and goals are not universally shared (Verkuyten, 2004). In fact, their innocence can be astonishing, as researchers found in Northern Ireland: Most 6-year-olds said they did not know of any problems between the Catholics and Protestants (Sani & Bennett, 2004). Meanwhile, many adults in their communities felt such antipathy that even killing was possible.

Most young children are not prejudiced against other children because of background characteristics such as gender or ethnicity. A 5-year-old girl might say "I hate boys" because her older sister says that, but she may consider a boy her best friend. Typically, best friends are of the same sex and background, but that is because of personal interests more than categories (Rubin et al., 2006). When children are prejudiced (and some are), that usually begins when they are older, influenced by family and culture (Nesdale, 2004; Ruble et al., 2004). More often, young children feel empathy toward any child who is hurt, hungry, or otherwise in trouble.

Aggression

The gradual regulation of emotions and emergence of antipathy is nowhere more apparent than in the most antisocial behavior of all, *active aggression,* which occurs when a child's dislike erupts into action. Learning when and how to be aggressive is a major goal of the play of young children. This is evident on close observation of rough-and-tumble play; or in the fantasies of domination and submission that shine through sociodramatic play; or in the sharing of art supplies, construction materials, and wheeled vehicles (J. D. Peterson & Flanders, 2005). Children learn to inhibit their angry impulses in emotional regulation.

Researchers recognize many types of aggression, described in Table 10.1. **Instrumental aggression** is very common among young children, who often want something they do not have and will try, without thinking, to get it. **Reactive aggression** is impulsive as well, and this type, particularly, becomes better controlled with emotional regulation. Finally, **bullying aggression** is the most ominous, when a child seems to deliberately hurt another.

Especially for Young Adults When you were younger, you might have had an imaginary friend with whom you played, slept, and talked. Does this mean you were emotionally disturbed?

instrumental aggression Hurtful behavior that is intended to get or keep something that another person has.

reactive aggression An impulsive retaliation for another person's intentional or accidental actions, verbal or physical.

bullying aggression Unprovoked, repeated physical or verbal attack, especially on victims who are unlikely to defend themselves.

TABLE 10.1

The Four Forms of Aggression

Type of Aggression	Definition	Comments
Instrumental aggression	Hurtful behavior that is aimed at gaining something (such as a toy, a place in line, or a turn on the swing) that someone else has	Often increases from age 2 to 6; involves objects more than people; quite normal; more egocentric than antisocial.
Reactive aggression	An impulsive retaliation for a hurt (intentional or accidental) that can be verbal or physical	Indicates a lack of emotional regulation, characteristic of 2-year-olds. A 5-year-old should be able to stop and think before reacting.
Relational aggression	Nonphysical acts, such as insults or social rejection, aimed at harming the social connections between the victim and others	Involves a personal attack and thus is directly antisocial; can be very hurtful; more common as children become socially aware.
Bullying aggression	Unprovoked, repeated physical or verbal attack, especially on victims who are unlikely to defend themselves	In both bullies and victims, a sign of poor emotional regulation; adults should intervene before the school years. (Bullying is discussed in Chapter 13.)

➤**Response for Adults Who Are Unhappy** (from page 260): Young children are not good at guessing emotions from voice tone, facial expression, or sarcasm. They are naturally sympathetic if an adult sheds a few tears while describing a sad event, thereby expressing feelings clearly and directly.

➤**Response for Young Adults** (from page 261): No. In fact, imaginary friends are quite common, especially among creative children.

Bullying is not always physical; it can be verbal or relational when the goal is to disrupt a child's friendships. Physical aggression declines over the preschool and school-age years, but verbal attacks may increase (Dodge et al. 2006). So might *relational aggression* (described in Chapter 13).

Bullying is apparent among some young children, with boys particularly likely to use physical attacks. Preschool bullies must be stopped, and victims must learn to defend themselves, lest the bully/victim patterns continue throughout middle childhood and adolescence. The various forms of bullying and the consequences are described in detail in Chapter 13, on school-age children.

Aggression follows a developmental pattern, becoming less common, but more hurtful, with time. Infants are very aggressive; they naturally pinch, slap, and even bite others. In Richard Tremblay's dramatic words, "The only reason babies do not kill each other is that we do not give them knives or guns" (quoted in Holden,

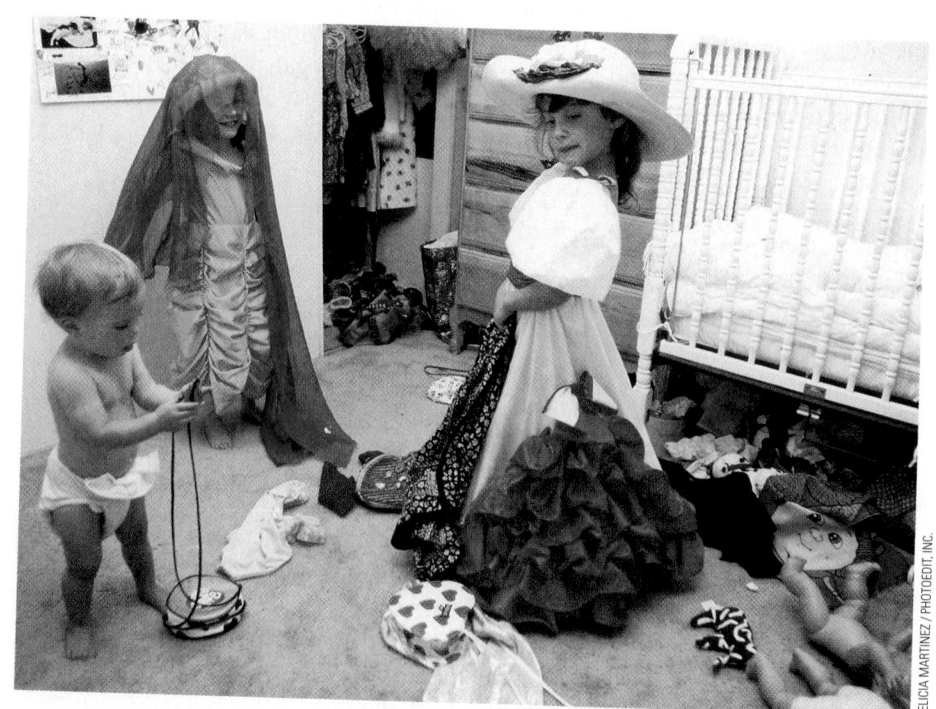

FELICIA MARTINEZ / PHOTOEDIT, INC.

Ladies and Babies A developmental difference is visible here between the 14-month-old's evident curiosity and the 4-year-old friends' pleasure in sociodramatic play. The mother's reaction—joy at the children's mastery play or irritation at the mess they've made—is less predictable.

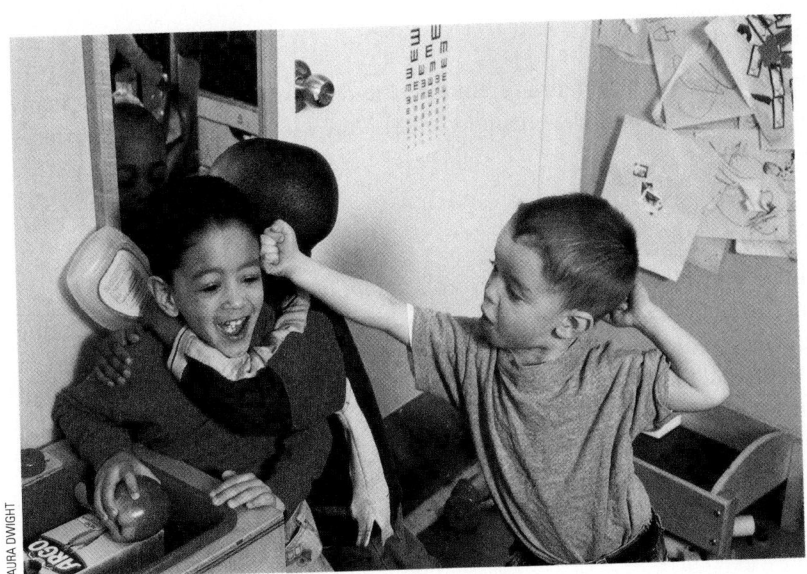
LAURA DWIGHT

Male Bonding Sometimes the only way to distinguish aggression from rough-and-tumble play is to look at the faces. The hitter is not scowling, the hittee is laughing, and the hugger is just joining in the fun. Another clue that this is rough-and-tumble play comes from gender and context. These boys are in a Head Start program, where they are learning social skills, such as how to avoid fighting.

2000, p. 580). Fortunately, babies are not strong and they have no weapons, giving parents time to teach them some self-control before any serious harm occurs.

Almost all 2-year-olds are still somewhat aggressive, but the incidence of such behavior diminishes over the next two years. If a child has not begun to modify his or her antisocial behavior by age 3 or 4, that child may be violent throughout childhood, adolescence, and early adulthood (Loeber et al, 2005; Tremblay & Nagin, 2005). However, if parents have a good relationship with their child and they help him or her decrease aggression, then the child will probably do well, academically and socially, displaying only average aggression by middle childhood (NICHD Early Child Care Research Network, 2004).

Remember that emotions need regulation, not repression. Since overcontrol, not just undercontrol, can lead to psychological problems, some assertive and self-protective behaviors are probably beneficial (Hawley, 1999). An internalizing 4-year-old who cries and retreats from every threat may become a victim, overwhelmed by anxiety or depression later on. Thus, some aggression in early childhood is quite normal (NICHD Early Child Care Network, 2004).

As self-esteem and the self-concept build, children become more likely to defend their interests. As emotional regulation increases, they do not attack without reason. Normal 4-year-olds have *learned* to choose issues and targets as well as to control the type and intensity of aggression (Tremblay & Nagin, 2005).

RICHARD HUTCHINGS / PHOTOEDIT INC.

A Real Fight? Could be. We cannot see the boys' faces, and we do not know what led up to this moment.

Observation Quiz (see answer, page 264): Are any signs of a serious fight visible?

SUMMING UP

As Erikson describes, pride, purpose, and initiative are integral components in the self-concept of young children. Preschoolers typically have high self-esteem. Children who have difficulty with emotional regulation often develop internalizing or externalizing problems. Many researchers believe that emotional regulation is the foundation for later social skills and cognitive growth, as children become more prosocial and less antisocial, expressing empathy more than anger. Some aggression is normal in young children, who gradually learn to regulate their anger. ■

➤Answer to Observation Quiz (from page 263): No. Boys acting out of antipathy kick and pummel, grab and pull, bite and pound. None of that is shown here.

Parents

We have seen that young children's emotions and actions are affected by many factors, including brain maturation and culture. Now we focus on another primary influence: parents.

Parenting Style

Parents differ a great deal in what they believe about children and how they act with them. Although thousands of researchers have traced the effects of parenting on child development, the work of one person, 40 years ago, continues to be most influential. Diana Baumrind (1967, 1971) studied 100 preschool children, all from California, almost all middle-class European Americans. (The cohort and cultural limitations of this sample were not obvious at the time.)

Baumrind found that parents differed on four important dimensions:

- *Expressions of warmth.* Some parents are very affectionate, others cold and critical.
- *Strategies for discipline.* Parents vary in whether and how they explain, criticize, persuade, ignore, and punish.
- *Communication.* Some parents listen patiently; others demand silence.
- *Expectations for maturity.* Parents vary in standards for responsibility and self-control.

Baumrind's Three Patterns of Parenting

On the basis of these dimensions, Baumrind identified three parenting styles (see Table 10.2).

authoritarian parenting Child rearing with high behavioral standards, punishment of misconduct, and low communication.

permissive parenting Child rearing with high nurturance and communication but rare punishment, guidance, or control.

authoritative parenting Child rearing in which the parents set limits but listen to the child and are flexible.

- **Authoritarian parenting.** The parents' word is law, not to be questioned. Misconduct brings strict punishment, usually physical (but not so harsh as to be considered abusive). Authoritarian parents set down clear rules and hold high standards. They do not expect children to give their opinions; discussion about emotions is especially rare. (One adult from such a family said that the question "How do you feel?" had only two possible answers: "Fine" and "Tired.") Authoritarian parents love their children, but they seem aloof, rarely showing affection.
- **Permissive parenting.** Permissive parents make few demands, hiding any impatience they feel. Discipline is lax partly because permissive parents have low expectations for maturity. Instead, permissive parents are nurturing and accepting, listening to whatever their offspring say. They want to be helpful, but they do not feel responsible for shaping their children.
- **Authoritative parenting.** Authoritative parents set limits and enforce rules, but they also listen to their children. The parents demand maturity, but they are usually forgiving (not punishing) if the child falls short. They consider themselves guides, not authorities (as authoritarian parents do) or friends (as permissive parents do).

As explained in Chapter 8, no researcher has ever found that abusive or neglectful parenting helps children. This means that authoritarian parents must take care not to punish too often or too harshly and that permissive parents must be concerned about, not indifferent to, their children's well-being.

Many other researchers continue to study parenting styles. The three-part description above, although still influential, is too simple (e.g., Bornstein, 2006; Galambos et al., 2003; Lamb & Lewis, 2005; Parke & Buriel, 2006). Baumrind's original sample was limited (very little economic, ethnic, or cultural diversity):

TABLE 10.2

Characteristics of Parenting Styles Identified by Baumrind

	Characteristics				
				Communication	
Style	Warmth	Discipline	Expectations of Maturity	Parent to Child	Child to Parent
Authoritarian	Low	Strict, often physical	High	High	Low
Permissive	High	Rare	Low	Low	High
Authoritative	High	Moderate, with much discussion	Moderate	High	High

She focused on style more than daily processes; she did not take into account the child's substantial contribution to parent–child relationships; and she did not realize that some authoritarian parents are very loving and that some permissive parents guide their children with words, if not with rules.

Children growing up with these three styles have been followed longitudinally, and the following correlations have been reported (Baumrind, 1991; Steinberg et al., 1994):

- *Authoritarian* parents raise children who are likely to be conscientious, obedient, and quiet but not especially happy. The children tend to feel guilty or depressed, internalizing their frustrations and blaming themselves when things don't go well. As adolescents, they sometimes rebel, leaving home before age 20.
- *Permissive* parents raise unhappy children who lack self-control, especially in the give-and-take of peer relationships. Inadequate emotional regulation makes them immature and impedes friendships, which is the main reason for their unhappiness. They tend to live at home, still dependent, in early adulthood.
- *Authoritative* parents raise children who are successful, articulate, happy with themselves, and generous with others. These children are usually liked by teachers and peers, especially in cultures where individual initiative is valued.

An especially important factor regarding parenting style during the preschool years is a child's temperament. Fearful children and impulsive children need different parental responses (Kochanska et al., 2001; Van Leeuwen et al., 2004). This means that any simple formula of the best parenting is likely to be wrong in some cases; a child's personality and the social context are always significant.

Cultural Variations

Effective Chinese American, Caribbean American, and African American parents are often stricter than effective parents of northern or western European backgrounds (Chao, 2001; Wachs, 1999). It is important to acknowledge that multicultural and international research has found that specific discipline methods and family rules are less important than parental warmth, support, and concern (McLoyd & Smith, 2002; Parke & Buriel, 2006). Children from every ethnic group and every country benefit if they believe that their parents appreciate them; children everywhere suffer if they feel rejected and unwanted (Khaleque & Rohner, 2002; Maccoby, 2000).

An example of the role of culture in discipline comes from the contrast between mothers in Japan and in the United States. Japanese mothers tend to use reasoning, empathy, and expressions of disappointment to control their children more than North American mothers do. These techniques work well, partly because the

Especially for Political Activists Many observers contend that children learn their political attitudes at home, from the way their parents treat them. Is this true?

LAURA DWIGHT

Parenting Style This woman is disciplining her son, who does not look happy about it.

Observation Quiz (see answer, page 270): Which parenting style is shown here?

Japanese mother–child relationship is strongly affectionate (it is called *amae,* a close interpersonal bond) (Rothbaum et al., 2000).

Would North American parents successfully raise their children if they expressed more sympathy and less anger with their misbehaving 4-year-olds? There is no simple answer. But cross-cultural differences in disciplining young children are apparent (e.g., physical punishment is illegal in some Scandinavian nations, common in some Latin American ones).

Dozens of other differences in values, climate, economy, history, and so on are evident between nations (and among groups within nations). Each of these factors could affect child-rearing practices. It is impossible to draw simple conclusions about discipline and adult personality, because definitive research linking cross-cultural variables has not been done (Matsumoto & Yoo, 2006).

Given this appreciation that cultural differences reflect a group's adaptation to its specific setting, developmentalists hesitate to recommend any one particular style of parenting as best for everyone (Dishion & Bullock, 2002; J. G. Miller, 2004). That does not mean that they believe all parents function equally well—far from it. Signs of serious trouble are obvious in a child's behavior, including several mentioned in this chapter: overcontrol, undercontrol, bullying, and antisocial play. Ineffective parenting is not the only explanation for such problems, but it is one common cause. Solutions, however, vary.

Discipline and Punishment

A particular issue for many developmentalists and parents is discipline, which varies a great deal from family to family, culture to culture. Given what researchers have learned about cognition (that children do not understand complex causes), ideally parents anticipate misbehavior and guide their children toward patterns that will help them lifelong. But parents cannot always anticipate and prevent problems; punishment is sometimes necessary.

No disciplinary technique works quickly and automatically to teach any and all children desired behavior. It is easy to stop a child for a moment, with a threat or a slap, but it is hard to shape behavior so that the child gradually internalizes the parents' standards. Yet this is the goal and sometimes the result. Between ages 2 and 6, children learn to reflect on consequences, to control their emotions, and to bring their actions closer to what their parents expect. The child becomes self-regulating, not just obedient.

In every nation and family, the first step is clarity about what is expected. What is "rude" or "nasty" or "undisciplined" behavior in one community is often accepted, even encouraged, in another. Each family needs to decide its goals and make them explicit for the child. Parents have a wide range of expectations and thoughts regarding child rearing, although they are often unaware of them (Bornstein, 2006; Bugental & Grusec, 2006). This diversity is all the more reason both parents need to discuss their expectations—to form a strong *parental alliance.*

The second step is to remember what the child is able to do. Many parents forget how immature children's control over their bodies and minds is. For instance, some parents punish children for wetting

Pay Attention Children develop best with lots of love and attention. They shouldn't have to ask for it!

"He's just doing that to get attention."

TABLE 10.3

Relating Discipline to Developmental Characteristics During Early Childhood

1. *Remember theory of mind.* Young children gradually come to understand things from other viewpoints. Encouraging empathy ("How would you feel if someone did that to you?") increases prosocial and decreases antisocial behavior.
2. *Remember emerging self-concept.* Young children are developing a sense of who they are and what they want. Adults should protect that emerging self, neither forcing 3-year-olds to share their favorite toys nor saying, "Words do not hurt." Instead, children need to know when and how to protect their favorite possessions and their emerging sense of self. For instance, a child can learn not to bring a toy to school unless he or she is willing to share it with everyone.
3. *Remember the language explosion and fast-mapping.* Young children are eager to talk and think, but they say more than they really understand. Children who "just don't listen" should not always be punished, because they may not have understood a command. Discussion before and after they misbehave helps children learn.
4. *Remember that young children are not yet logical.* The connection between misdeed and punishment needs to be immediate and transparent, but usually it is not. If you were spanked as a child, do you remember why? Did you ever do the same misdeed again?

➤**Response for Political Activists** (from page 265): There are many parenting styles, and it is difficult to determine each one's impact on children's personalities. At this point, attempts to connect early child rearing with later political outlook are speculative at best.

Especially for Parents Suppose you agree that spanking is destructive, but you sometimes get so angry at your child's behavior that you hit him or her. Is your reaction appropriate?

the bed, but no child deliberately wets the bed. Three-year-olds are clumsy and irrational; they inevitably break things and tell "lies."

Punishment should be rare, reserved for misdeeds that the child understands and could reasonably control. Other developmental characteristics to remember are listed in Table 10.3, and different methods of punishment are discussed in the following.

psychological control A disciplinary technique that involves threatening to withdraw love and support and that relies on a child's feelings of guilt and gratitude to the parents.

issues and applications

Planning Punishment

Physical punishment (slapping, spanking, or beating) is used more on children between the ages of 2 and 6 than on children of any other age group. Many parents believe that spanking is acceptable, legitimate, and sometimes necessary, and they often remember being spanked themselves.

However, the life-span perspective reminds us of long-term consequences. Physical punishment works at the moment it is administered—spanking stops a child's misbehavior—but longitudinal research finds that children who are physically punished are likely to become bullies, delinquents, and then abusive adults. Domestic violence of every type—spousal abuse, threats, and insults—correlates with antisocial behavior in childhood and then adulthood (Jaffee et al., 2004; Straus, 1994). Of course, many children who are spanked do not become violent adults. Spanking increases the risk, but other factors (poverty and temperament, among others) are stronger influences. Nonetheless, developmentalists wonder why parents would increase any risk. Since physical punishment increases the possibility of aggression and only temporarily increases obedience, it is not recommended (Amato & Fowler, 2002; Gershoff, 2002).

In truth, every form of punishment may have unintended consequences. Another method, **psychological control,** uses guilt and the child's gratitude toward the parent and may damage a child's initiative and achievement (Barber, 2002).

Consider the results of a study of an entire cohort (the best way to obtain an unbiased sample) of children born in Finland (Aunola & Nurmi, 2004). Their parents were asked 20 questions about their approach to child rearing. The following four items, which the parents rated from 1 ("Not at all like me") to 5 ("Very much like me"), measured psychological control:

1. *My child should be aware of how much I have done for him/her.*
2. *I let my child see how disappointed and shamed I am if he/she misbehaves.*
3. *My child should be aware of how much I sacrifice for him/her.*
4. *I expect my child to be grateful and appreciate all the advantages he/she has.*

The higher the parents scored on psychological control, the lower the children's math scores. The connection grew stronger as the children advanced in school. Math achievement suffered most if parents were high in both psychological control and affection (e.g., they frequently hugged their children) (Aunola & Nurmi, 2004). Other research also finds that psychological control can depress children's achievement and social acceptance, although affection does not always make things worse (Barber, 2002).

One disciplinary technique often used in North America is the **time-out,** in which an adult requires the child to sit quietly apart from other people for a few minutes. For young children, a time-out can be quickly effective; one minute of time-out per year of age is suggested. Another common practice is *withdrawal of love,* when the parent expresses disappointment or looks sternly at the child, as if the child were no longer lovable.

A third method is *induction,* in which the parents talk with the child, getting the child to understand why the behavior was wrong. Conversation helps children internalize standards, but listening takes time and patience from the child as well as from the adult. Since 3-year-olds do not understand causes and consequences, they cannot answer an angry "Why did you do that?"

Each method varies in consequences and effectiveness, depending on the child's temperament, the culture, the parents' personalities, and the parent–child relationship. For example, a time-out is effective *if* the child prefers to be with other people. One version of time-out for older children is suspension from school, which works if the child wants to be in the classroom. However, if a child dislikes school, time-out becomes a reinforcement for the child (and the teacher), making future disobedience more likely.

There is no simple answer partly because children's personalities and parental pressures vary. As a mother, I know that patient guidance is necessary and that prevention is better than punishment, but emotions can be overwhelming. Rachel, at age 3, took a glass orange juice bottle from the refrigerator, dropping it on the kitchen floor. It shattered. I wanted to slap her. "Time-out!" I yelled, putting her on the couch (20 feet away) until I cleaned it up. I needed that time-out more than she did.

Parents have powerful emotions, memories, and stresses. That's why punishment is not a simple issue. One young child who was disciplined for fighting protested, "Sometimes the fight just crawls out of me." Ideally, punishment won't just crawl out of the parent.

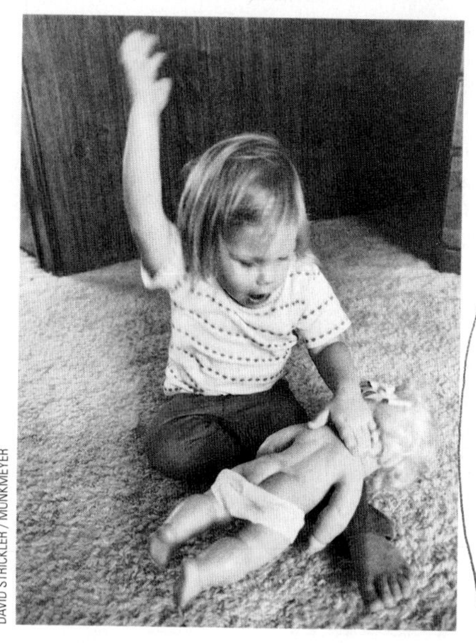

Angela at Play Research suggests that being spanked is a salient and memorable experience for young children, not because of the pain but because of the emotions. Children seek to do what they have learned; they know not only how to place their hands but also that an angry person does the hitting. The only part of the lesson they usually forget is what particular misdeed precipitated the punishment. Asked why she is spanking her doll, Angela will likely explain, "She was bad."

time-out A disciplinary technique in which a child is separated from other people for a specified time.

The Challenge of Media

Some people (not parents) imagine that parenting is straightforward and that good parents always have good children. Not so. Children are emotionally immature, sometimes angry or fearful or defiant. Preschoolers, in particular, talk when they should be quiet, run when they should walk, show off when they should be modest.

Further, each cohort of parents is faced with challenges that their parents never confronted. Currently, those challenges include new junk food; far more single-parent families than in the past (about 40 percent, discussed in the following chapters); earlier sexual awareness; and an explosion of media, including the Internet (Comstock & Scharrer, 2006).

Parents allow their young children to watch television or use the computer not only because the children demand it but also because video keeps children engaged. Parents easily ignore the possible impact on the emotionally immature child, who is dazzled by fast-moving images and entranced by cartoon figures that have no empathy. Almost no preschooler understands "the motivated purpose of a commercial as a self-interested vehicle intended to benefit the advertiser" (Comstock & Scharrer, 2006, p. 833).

KEEP OUT

B. Smaller

"Why don't you get off the computer and watch some TV?"

Experts advise parents to minimize media exposure, including no television before age 2. Six major organizations devoted to the health of children (the American Psychological Association, the American Academy of Pediatrics, the American Medical Association, the American Academy of Child and Adolescent Psychiatry, the American Academy of Family Physicians, and the American Psychiatric Association) implore parents to stop exposing their children to video violence—whether in cartoons, in situation comedies, in video games, or on the evening news. This leaves almost nothing to watch (C. A. Anderson & Bushman, 2002).

Did you notice that all six organizations have *American* in their titles? That requires a cross-cultural advisement: Most of the research reported here studied U.S. children watching U.S. media (C. A. Anderson & Bushman, 2002; Roberts & Foehr, 2004). Readers need to ask themselves whether this limits the conclusions reported here or whether American media are so pervasive that the same problems exist worldwide.

TABLE 10.4

Average Daily Exposure to Electronic Media

Age 2 to 4 Years	Hours per Day
White	3:18
Black	4:30
Hispanic	3:37
Age 5 to 7 Years	**Hours per Day**
White	3:17
Black	4:16
Hispanic	3:38

Source: Adapted from Roberts & Foehr, 2004.

The Importance of Content

Most young children of every ethnic and economic group in the United States spend more than three hours each day using some sort of media (see Table 10.4). Among young children, television is the most popular medium. Almost every home has at least two televisions, and children usually watch apart from their parents, often in their own rooms. By age 3, more than one-fourth of all children already have a television in their bedrooms, and this percentage rises as children grow older (Roberts & Foehr, 2004).

What do children see? The "good guys," whether in cartoons or police dramas, do as much hitting, shooting, and kicking as the "bad guys," yet the consequences of their violence are sanitized, justified, or made comic. Almost all the good guys are male and White. Women are usually portrayed as victims or adoring girlfriends, not as leaders—except in a very few girl-oriented programs that boys rarely watch.

Attempts to restrict children's watching have limited success. For instance, many TV programs and movies are now labeled regarding their appropriateness for children, but this is voluntary and many producers refuse to do it. Parents can install a V-chip in their television to limit what children can see, but few families have done so successfully. For many reasons, such voluntary measures have little effect on children's exposure to violence and sex, especially for children who are most vulnerable.

Evidence from every perspective and method confirms that violence is pervasive and that children of all ages who watch violence on television become more violent themselves (C. A. Anderson et al., 2003; Huesmann et al., 2003; J. G. Johnson et al., 2002; Singer & Singer, 2005). For example, they are more likely to get into fights with each other and even to break things and hurt people when they grow up. For obvious reasons, extensive longitudinal research has not been published for the newer media, but virtually all developmentalists expect that sexual messages and aggression on all media (DVDs, MP3 players, the Internet) undermine optimal development of young children (Comstock & Scharrer, 2006).

Past research gives parents good reason to limit their children's media involvement. Consider the results of a longitudinal study that began with children at about age 5 and queried those same children again as adolescents (D. R. Anderson et al., 2001; see Research Design).

Preschoolers who watched a lot of violence on television and copied the actions of cartoon characters were more violent and less creative. They had lower grades in school when they were older. This was true for both sexes and evident in every subject, but some correlations were particularly strong. For instance, 5-year-old

Research Design

Scientists: Daniel Anderson, Aletha C. Huston, Kelly L. Schmitt, Deborah L. Linebarger, and John C. Wright.

Publication: *Monographs of the Society for Research in Child Development* (2001).

Participants: A total of 570 adolescents from Massachusetts and Kansas, whose television watching and other characteristics were studied in depth (viewing diaries recorded exactly what they watched).

Design: These participants and their television viewing were first studied at age 5. As adolescents, they were asked questions about their current lives, and their high school transcripts were obtained. Researchers controlled for many factors (e.g., SES, gender, region), seeking correlations between viewing habits at age 5 and behavior at age 16 or so. Efforts were made to understand causation, not just correlation.

Major conclusion: Sixty-five correlations were found between television viewing at preschool and adolescent behavior and characteristics. Most but not all effects were negative, leading to the conclusion that content matters: "Marshall McLuhan appears to have been wrong. The *medium* is not the message. The *message* is the message" (p. 134).

Comment: These researchers wisely followed up on hundreds of preschoolers who had been carefully surveyed many years earlier. The result confirms the conclusions of many cross-sectional and shorter longitudinal studies: Television in the early years affects behavior in school. The other interesting result was not predicted by those most critical of TV: The content of some programs facilitates learning.

Dangerous Toy? Would this 4-year-old at the computer be safer playing outside with a ball?

girls generally watched less violence than boys did, but when they did, the effects were greater.

There were also some positive effects of early television watching, depending on the programs watched. Young children who watched only educational programs (mostly *Sesame Street* and *Mr. Rogers' Neighborhood*) became teenagers who earned higher grades and read more than other high school students did, especially if they were boys. This study also examined what the children watched as adolescents and again found an impact, almost always negative.

From a developmental perspective, early childhood is the best time to raise this issue because that is when household media habits are established. Young children are strongly influenced by their parents and older siblings, who often watch TV during meals or spend hours with television, computer, and hand-held video games. Already in 1999, one-fourth of all 6-year-olds had played a computer or video game within the past 24 hours (Roberts & Foehr, 2004). And the numbers are rising each year.

Early childhood is a vulnerable period for media effects for other reasons as well. First, young children spend more time in front of TV and computer screens than do people of any other age group. Second, young children are not very knowledgeable about society, culture, and people; they are novices at interpreting and regulating emotions. For example, when a cartoon animal or even a person explodes on the screen, they are more likely to cheer than to cry.

➤Answer to Observation Quiz (from page 266): The authoritative style. Note the firm hold this woman has on her defiant son; he must listen (evidence that she is not permissive). Also note that she is talking to him, not hitting or yelling, and that her expression is warm (evidence that she is not authoritarian).

The Effects on Family life

Probably the worst effect of the media is how it interferes with family life. Children benefit when their parents are involved in their lives, as already apparent in the discussion of parenting patterns. As you have seen, language development (the crucial cognitive achievement of early childhood) depends on hours of one-on-one conversations every day. Likewise, emotional regulation (the crucial psychosocial accomplishment of early childhood) depends on parental responsiveness.

Unfortunately, all the research reports that the more media a family uses, the less time they spend together. Parents and children talk only briefly when they watch together, and they rarely watch together. In most families, parents and children have their own TVs, often in separate rooms. Further interfering with family time, the television often stays on during meals and even when no one is watching.

"Have some respect for my learning style."

Video Style Children who spend a lot of time watching television and playing video games are likely to develop a visual learning style. They get used to receiving information in the form of vivid images and brief scenes, making it harder for them to concentrate on and comprehend anything that is longer and presented in verbal form.

All told, the result is "parental abdication of oversight on children's media behavior" (Roberts & Foehr, 2004, p. 202). Not only do the media cut into the time children spend with their parents, they also reduce the amount of time children spend in imaginative and social play—and thus on learning.

Although many adults hope that more time spent with one type of media would mean less time spent with another, this is not the case. The only exception is with print: Children who read many books tend to watch less TV (Roberts & Foehr, 2004). It is not surprising that grades suffer and impulsive violence increases as children watch more TV.

No wonder those six organizations recommend limited television. But few parents can enforce a total prohibition. (When you read about fast-mapping in Chapter 9, did you wonder why Sarah called me angry names? It was because I had momentarily unplugged the TV.) Parents can, however, limit their own and their children's media exposure and play, read, and talk with their children more. Few children know a proven fact: An animated parent can be more entertaining than Mickey Mouse.

SUMMING UP

Over the past 40 years, Diana Baumrind and most other developmentalists have found that authoritative parenting (warm, with guidance) is more effective than either authoritarian (very strict) or permissive (very lenient) parenting. In any culture, children thrive when their parents appreciate them and care about their accomplishments. The children of parents who are uninvolved, uncaring, or abusive are seldom happy, well-adjusted, and high-achieving.

Good parenting is not achieved by following any one simple rule; children's temperaments vary, and so do cultural patterns. The media pose a particular challenge worldwide because children are attracted to colorful, fast-paced images, yet violent TV programs, in particular, lead to more aggressive behavior. Parental monitoring of the quality and quantity of the media—the underlying messages as well as the overt themes—to which children are exposed is recommended by every expert. ■

➤Response for Parents (from page 267): The worst time to spank a child is when you are angry, because you might seriously hurt the child and because the child will associate anger with violence and may follow your example. You would do better to learn to control your anger and develop other strategies for discipline and for prevention of misbehavior.

Becoming Boys and Girls

Identity as a male or female is an important feature of a child's self-concept, a major source of self-esteem (with each gender believing that it is best) (Powlishta, 2004). The first question asked about a newborn is "Boy or girl?" and parents select gender-distinct clothes, blankets, diapers, and even pacifiers. Toddlers already know their own sex, and children become more aware of gender with every passing year of childhood (Maccoby, 1998).

Social scientists attempt to distinguish between **sex differences,** which are the biological differences between males and females, and **gender differences,** which are culturally imposed masculine or feminine roles and behaviors. In theory, this may seem like a straightforward separation, but, as with every nature–nurture distinction, the interaction between sex and gender makes it hard to separate the two (Hines, 2004).

sex differences Biological differences between males and females, in organs, hormones, and body type.

gender differences Differences in the roles and behavior of males and females that originate in the culture.

Even 2-year-olds can apply gender labels (*Mrs., Mr., lady, man*) consistently. That simple cognitive awareness becomes, by age 3, a rudimentary understanding that sex distinctions are lifelong (although some pretend, hope, or imagine otherwise). By age 4, children are convinced that certain toys (such as dolls or trucks) and certain roles (such as nurse or soldier) are appropriate for one gender but not the other (Bauer et al., 1998; Ruble et al., 2006).

Throughout the play years, children confuse gender and sex. Awareness that a person's sex is a biological characteristic, not determined by words, opinions, or clothing, develops gradually, becoming firm at age 8 or so (Szkrybalo & Ruble, 1999). This uncertainty about the biological determination of sex was demonstrated by a 3-year-old who went with his father to see a neighbor's newborn kittens. Returning home, the child told his mother that there were three girl kittens and two boy kittens. "How do you know?" she asked. "Daddy picked them up and read what was written on their tummies," he replied.

Theories of Gender Differences

Experts as well as parents disagree about what proportion of observed gender differences is biological (perhaps hormones, brain structure, body shape) and what proportion is environmental (perhaps embedded in the culture or in the family)

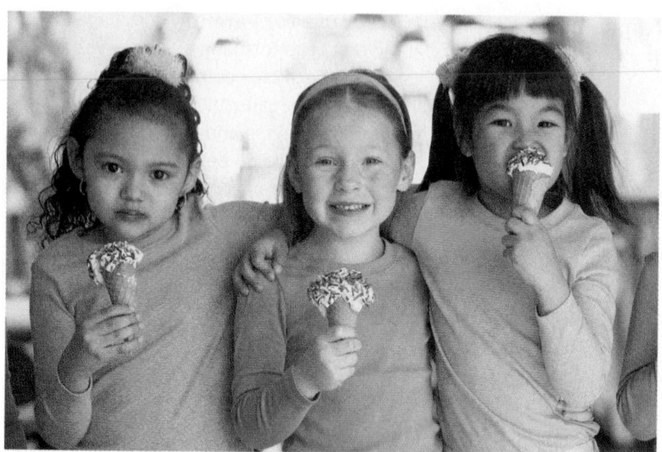

Biology or Culture? Could the trio on the left dress as pirates and the three on the right all eat ice cream cones with multicolored sprinkles? If they did, and if new photographs were taken, would their expressions, clothes, closeness, and hair switch as well? Probably not: By age 5, dozens of differences between boys and girls are evident.

(Leaper, 2002; Ruble et al., 2006). For example, you read earlier that girls are often ahead of boys in emotional regulation. Is that connected to the twenty-third pair of chromosomes that affects brain development, or is it that parents treat their sons and daughters differently? Evidence supports both.

Neuroscientists tend to look for male–female brain differences, and they find many; sociologists tend to look for male–female family and culture patterns, and they also find many. Similar but varied predilections apply to historians, anthropologists, political scientists, and psychologists of every perspective. Consider the explanations for sex/gender differences during early childhood from each of our five theories.

Psychoanalytic Theory

phallic stage Freud's third stage of development, when the penis becomes the focus of concern and pleasure.

Freud (1938) called the period from about age 3 to 6 the **phallic stage** because he believed its central focus is the *phallus,* or penis. At about 3 or 4 years of age, said Freud, the process of maturation makes a boy aware of his male sexual organ. He begins to masturbate, to fear castration, and to develop sexual feelings toward his mother.

Oedipus complex The unconscious desire of young boys to replace their father and win their mother's exclusive love.

These feelings make every young boy jealous of his father—so jealous, according to Freud, that every son secretly wants to replace his dad. Freud called this the **Oedipus complex,** after Oedipus, son of a king in Greek mythology. Abandoned as an infant and raised in a distant kingdom, Oedipus later returned to his birthplace and, not realizing who they were, killed his own father and married his mother. When he discovered what he had done, he blinded himself in a spasm of guilt.

Freud believed that this ancient drama has been replayed for two millennia because it dramatizes emotions all boys feel about their parents—both love and hate. Every male feels guilty because of the incestuous and murderous impulses that are buried in his unconscious. Boys fear that their fathers will inflict terrible punishment if their secret impulses are discovered.

superego In psychoanalytic theory, the judgmental part of the personality that internalizes moral standards of the parents.

In self-defense, boys develop a powerful conscience called the **superego,** which is quick to judge and punish "the bad guys." According to Freud's theory, a young boy's fascination with superheroes, guns, kung fu, and the like arises from his unconscious urges to kill his father. An adult man's homosexuality, homophobia, or obsession with punishment might be explained by an imperfectly resolved phallic stage.

Freud offered several descriptions of the phallic stage in girls. One centers on the **Electra complex** (also named after a figure in classical mythology). the Electra complex is similar to the Oedipus complex in that the little girl wants to eliminate the same-sex parent, her mother, and become intimate with the opposite-sex parent, her father.

Electra complex The unconscious desire of girls to replace their mother and win their father's exclusive love.

Children of both sexes cope with their guilt and fear through **identification,** that is, by allying themsleves with another person—the same-sex parent—by symbolically taking on that person's behavior and attitudes. Because they cannot replace their parents, young boys copy their fathers' mannerisms, opinions, actions, and so on, and girls copy their mothers'. Both sexes exaggerate the appropriate male or female role.

identification An attempt to defend one's self-concept by taking on the behaviors and attitudes of someone else.

Since the middle of the twentieth century, social scientists generally have agreed that Freud's explanation of sexual and moral development "flies in the face of sociological and historical evidence" (David et al., 2004, p. 139). More recently, however, some of Freud's ideas have become more acceptable to psychologists. I myself have softened my criticism of Freud, as the following explains.

in person

Berger and Freud

My family's first "Electra episode" occurred in a conversation with my eldest daughter, Bethany, when she was about 4 years old:

Bethany: When I grow up, I'm going to marry Daddy.
Mother: But Daddy's married to me.
Bethany: That's all right. When I grow up, you'll probably be dead.
Mother: *(determined to stick up for myself)* Daddy's older than me, so when I'm dead, he'll probably be dead, too.
Bethany: That's OK. I'll marry him when he gets born again.

At this point, I couldn't think of a good reply, especially since I had no idea where she had gotten the concept of reincarnation. Bethany saw my face fall, and she took pity on me:

Bethany: Don't worry, Mommy. After you get born again, you can be our baby.

The second episode was a conversation I had with my daughter Rachel when she was about 5:

Rachel: When I get married, I'm going to marry Daddy.
Mother: Daddy's already married to me.
Rachel: *(with the joy of having discovered a wonderful solution)* Then we can have a double wedding!

The third episode was considerably more graphic. It took the form of a "valentine" left on my husband's pillow by my daughter Elissa, who was about 8 years old at the time. It is reproduced at right.

Finally, when my youngest daughter, Sarah, turned 5, she also expressed the desire to marry my husband. When I told her she couldn't, because he was married to me, her response revealed one more hazard of watching TV: "Oh, yes, a man can have two wives. I saw it on television."

I am not the only feminist developmentalist to be taken aback by her own children's words. Nancy Datan (1986) wrote about the Oedipal conflict: "I have a son who was once five years old. From that day to this, I have never thought Freud mistaken." Obviously, these bits of "evidence" do not prove that Freud was correct. I still think he was wrong on many counts. But I now find Freud's description of the phallic stage less bizarre than I once did.

Pillow Talk Elissa placed this artwork on my husband's pillow. My pillow, beside it, had a less colorful, less elaborate note—an afterthought. It read "Dear Mom, I love you too."

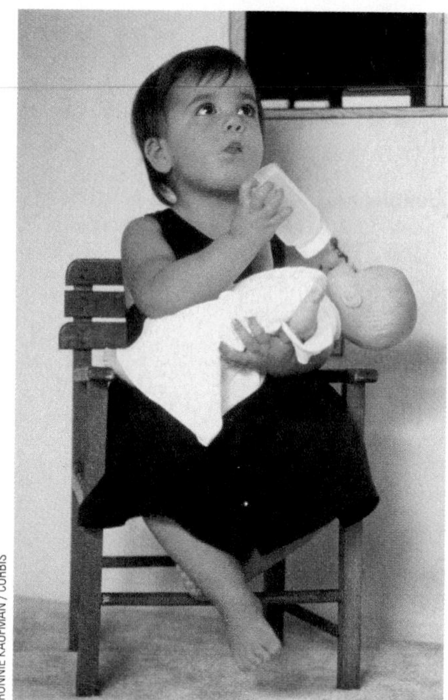
RONNIE KAUFMAN / CORBIS

Rehearsal for Future Motherhood This preschooler is demonstrating three behaviors that are considered appropriate for girls and are almost never seen in boys: She is wearing a dress, tucking one crossed leg behind the other, and cradling and "feeding" a doll.

Behaviorism

In contrast with psychoanalytic theorists, behaviorists believe that virtually all roles are learned and therefore result from nurture, not nature. To behaviorists, gender distinctions are the product of ongoing reinforcement and punishment.

Some evidence supports this aspect of learning theory. Parents, peers, and teachers all reward behavior that is "gender appropriate" more than behavior that is "gender inappropriate." For example, "adults complement a girl when she wears a dress but not when she wears pants" (Ruble et al., 2006, p. 897). According to social learning theory, children themselves notice the ways men and women behave and then internalize the standards they observe, becoming proud of themselves when they act like "little men" and "little ladies" (Bandura & Bussey, 2004; Bussey & Bandura, 1999).

The male–female distinction seems to be more significant to males than to females (Banerjee & Lintern, 2000; David et al., 2004). Boys are more often criticized for being "sissies" than girls are criticized for being "tomboys." Fathers, more than mothers, expect their daughters to be feminine and their sons to be tough.

Behaviorists believe children learn about proper behavior not only directly (such as receiving a gender-appropriate toy or a father's praise) but also indirectly, through social learning. Children model their behavior particularly after that of people they perceive to be nurturing, powerful, and yet similar to themselves. For young children, those people are usually their parents. And parental attitudes about gender differences become increasingly influential as children become more aware of the thoughts and attitudes other people might hold (Tenenbaum & Leaper, 2002).

This theory explains why gender prejudice is particularly strong during the play years. If a college man wants to teach young children, his classmates will probably respect him and may know another man who made the same choice. If a 4-year-old boy wants the same thing, his peers will laugh because their experience has been quite gender-segregated. As one professor reports:

> My son came home after 2 days of preschool to announce that he could not grow up to teach seminars (previously his lifelong ambition, because he knew from personal observation that everyone at seminars got to eat cookies) because only women could be teachers.
>
> *[Fagot, 1995, p. 173]*

Cognitive Theory

Cognitive theory offers an alternative explanation for the strong gender identity that becomes apparent during the play years. Cognitive theorists focus on children's understanding—on the way a child intellectually grasps a specific issue or value. Children develop concepts about their experiences, developing many schemas or general beliefs. In this case, a **gender schema** is the child's understanding of sex differences (Kohlberg et al., 1983; Martin et al., 2002).

gender schema A cognitive concept or general belief based on one's experiences—in this case, a child's understanding of sex differences.

Young children, they point out, have many gender-related experiences but not much cognitive depth. They tend to see the world in simple terms. For this reason, they categorize male and female as opposites, even when some evidence contradicts such a sexist assumption. Nuances, complexities, exceptions, and gradations about gender (as well as about everything else) are beyond the intellect of the preoperational child.

The self-esteem and self-concept that young children develop lead to a cognitive drive to categorize themselves as male or female and then to behave in a way that fits the category. For that reason, cognitive theorists see "Jill's claim that she is a girl because she is wearing her new frilly socks as a genuine expression of her gender identity" (David et al., 2004, p. 147).

An example comes from a 3½-year-old boy whose aunt called him *cute*. He insisted he should be called *handsome* instead (Powlishta, 2004). Obviously he had developed gender-based categories, and he wanted others to see him as the young man his own cognition had decided he was.

According to cognitive theory, children develop a mental set, or a cognitive schema, which biases their views of whatever experiences they have. For 2- to 6-year-olds, that cognitive schema is, of necessity, quite simple, which is why their sex stereotyping peaks at about age 6.

Cognitive theory differs from social learning theory in that "while both theories explain how the social reality of sex differences is internalized, social learning theory proposes that society socializes children, while cognitive developmental theory proposes that children actively socialize themselves" (David et al., 2004, pp. 139–140).

Sociocultural Theory

Proponents of the sociocultural perspective point out that many traditional cultures enforce gender distinctions with dramatic stories, taboos, and terminology. In societies where adult activities and dress are strictly separated by gender, girls and boys attend sex-segregated schools and virtually never play together. Regardless of how strictly gender distinctions are enforced in different cultures, however, children all over the world adopt whatever patterns of talking, behaving, and even thinking that are prescribed for their sex (Leaper & Smith, 2004).

ARIEL SKELLEY / CORBIS

Trick or Treat? Any doubt about which of these children are girls and which are boys? No. Any question about whether such strict gender distinctions are appropriate at age 4? Maybe.

Every society has powerful values and attitudes regarding preferred behavior for men and women, and every culture teaches these values to its young, even though the particular tasks assigned to males and to females vary. To sociocultural theorists, this proves that society, not biology, segregates the sexes and transmits its version of proper male or female behavior (Kimmel, 2004).

This is blatantly apparent during adolescence, when sexual urges might drive young people to seek out the other sex. Instead, in most nations, young people work beside adults of the same sex as themselves and socialize in sex-segregated but cross-age groups, "from the pottery making sessions of the Hopi to the gathering parties of the !Kung Bushmen to the groups of Sicilian women neighbors, sitting together as they embroider" (Schlegel, 2003, pp. 243–244).

To break through the restrictiveness of culture and to encourage individuals to define themselves primarily as humans, rather than as males or females, some parents and teachers have embraced the idea of androgyny. As psychologists use the term, **androgyny** means a balance, within a person, of traditionally masculine and feminine characteristics. To achieve androgyny, boys would be encouraged to be nurturant and girls to be assertive so that they can develop less restrictive, gender-free self-concepts (Bem, 1993). However, androgyny does not necessarily lead to a healthier self-concept (Ruble et al., 2006).

androgyny A balance, within a person, of traditionally male and female psychological characteristics.

Sociocultural theory stresses that androgyny (or any other gender concept) cannot be taught simply through parental reinforcement, as behaviorism might propose. Children will not be androgynous unless their culture promotes such ideas and practices—something no culture has done. Why not? The reasons may lie buried far deeper in human nature than in political forces or social values. That is what epigenetic theory suggests.

Especially for Gender Idealists Suppose you want to raise an androgynous child. What do you think would happen if you told no one your newborn's sex, dressed it in yellow and white rather than pink or blue, and gave it a gender-neutral name, such as Chris or Lee?

Epigenetic Theory

We saw in Chapter 2 that epigenetic theory contends that our traits and behaviors are the result of interaction between genes and early experience—not just for each of us as individuals but for the human race as a whole. The idea that gender differences are based in genetics is supported by recent research in neurobiology, which has found dozens of biological differences between male and female brains (Hines, 2004). Sex hormones, circulating before birth, affect the brain throughout life, as male and female brains differ not only in overall size (male brains are larger) but also in connections between parts (female brains often have more connections) and in many other ways.

In nonhuman creatures, sex differences in brain shape and function are legion. For example, male and female voices differ partly because of vocal control systems within the brains of all jawed vertebrates. In an experiment, male and female hormones quickly changed the brain impulses, altering the pattern of vocalization in a fish species. The authors believe this may apply to all "vocal vertebrates," including people (Remage-Healey & Bass, 2004).

Although epigenetic theory stresses the biological and genetic origins of behavior, it also recognizes that the environment can shape, enhance, or halt those genetic impulses. Here is one example: Girls seem to be genetically inclined to talk earlier than boys, perhaps because in prehistoric times, when women stayed behind to care for the children while the men hunted, women had to become more adept at social interaction. Consequently, female brains evolved to favor language (Gleason & Ely, 2002).

Today, women still specialize in caregiving, using language to show support and agreement, while men are still more assertive, favoring speech that is more directive, with shorter, louder sentences. Even when these patterns are shown to be stereotypes that no longer apply to a specific person, genetic adaptation of the species may have led to sex differences that began several millennia ago and would take centuries to change.

Researchers repeatedly find that girls tend to be more responsive to language than boys and that mothers and daughters typically talk more than fathers and sons (Leaper, 2002; Leaper & Smith, 2004; Maccoby, 1998). The female advantage in language is more apparent from ages 2 to 5 than at any other age (Leaper & Smith, 2004). Those are the sensitive years when the brain is most likely to respond to language and thus when epigenetic effects are most likely to appear.

In the same way, all sex and gender differences may have genetic, hormonal roots, for reasons that originated millions of years ago and helped our ancestors form families and thus survive. Modern society has quite different needs and can create different conditions that may enhance or redirect those inherited tendencies.

Such redirection is uncommon. Accordingly, male–female distinctions are among the first that children recognize, and by age 5 children show a strong same-sex favoritism as well as strong impulses to avoid playing with toys they believe belong to the other gender. Preschool boys avoid dolls, a preference that seems as evident in the twenty-first century as in historic times (Ruble et al., 2006).

Gender and Destiny

The first and last of our five major theories—psychoanalytic theory and epigenetic theory—emphasize the power of biology. A reader might seize on those theories to decide that, since gender-based behavior and sexual stereotypes originate in the body and brain, they are difficult to change. But the other three theories—behaviorism, cognitive theory, and sociocultural theory—all present persuasive evidence for the influence of family and culture.

Thus, our five major theories lead in two opposite directions:

- Gender differences are rooted in biology.
- Biology is not destiny: Children are shaped by their experiences.

Given nature and nurture, both these conclusions are valid. That creates a dilemma. Since human behavior is plastic, what gender patterns *should* children learn, ideally? Answers vary among developmentalists as well as among mothers, fathers, and cultures.

If children responded only to their own inclinations, some might choose behaviors, express emotions, and develop talents that are taboo—even punished—in certain cultures. In Western societies, little boys might put on makeup, little girls might play with guns, and both sexes might play naked outside in hot weather. Whether these behaviors should be permitted is a question for adults, not children.

My daughter Bethany, at about age 5, challenged one of my young male students to a fight.

"Girls don't fight," he said, laughing.

"Nobody fights," I sternly corrected him.

To this day I wonder if my response, although cast in unisex words, was nonetheless quite female. Should I have just left it alone, allowing my student to teach Bethany gender norms? Or should I have championed androgyny, telling Bethany that girls can fight and urging my student to engage in the same rough-and-tumble play fighting that might have occurred if she were a boy? I remember this incident now, years later, because I am still not sure of the answer.

➤Response for Gender Idealists (from page 275): Since babies are raised by a society and community as well as by their parents, and since some gender differences are biological, this attempt at androgyny would not succeed. First, other interested parties would decide for themselves that the child was male or female. Second, the child would sooner or later develop gender-specific play patterns, guided by other boys or girls.

SUMMING UP

Young boys and girls are seen as quite different, not only by parents and other adults but especially by the children themselves. Gender stereotypes are held most forcefully at about age 6. Each of the five major theories has an explanation for this phenomenon: Freud describes unconscious incestuous urges; behaviorists note social reinforcement; cognitive theorists describe immature categorization; sociocultural explanations focus on patterns throughout the culture; and epigenetic theory begins with the hereditary aspects of brain and body development. Although each theory offers an explanation, theories don't answer questions about moral and social values. Perhaps that is why cultures and individuals draw contradictory conclusions about everyday practices regarding sex and gender. ■

SUMMARY

Emotional Development

1. Regulation of emotions is crucial during the play years, when children learn emotional control. Emotional regulation is made possible by maturation of the brain, particularly of the prefrontal cortex, as well as by experiences with parents and peers.

2. In Erikson's psychosocial theory, the crisis of initiative versus guilt occurs during the play years. Children normally feel pride and self-esteem, sometimes mixed with feelings of guilt.

3. Both externalizing and internalizing problems indicate impaired self-control. Many severe emotional problems that are evidence of psychopathology are first evident during these years.

4. Empathy, which leads to prosocial behavior, and antipathy, which leads to antisocial behavior, develop during early childhood. These emotions come from within the child, but family experiences either enhance or undercut the process.

5. As children become more aware of themselves and their peers, they regulate their aggression. Instrumental aggression occurs when children fight over toys and privileges, and reactive aggression occurs when children react to being hurt. More worrisome is bullying aggression, damaging to both aggressor and victim.

Parents

6. Three classic styles of parenting have been identified: authoritarian, permissive, and authoritative. Generally, children are more successful and happy when their parents express warmth and set guidelines. Parenting that is rejecting and uninvolved is harmful.

Punishment should fit not only the age and temperament of the child but also the culture.

7. Children are prime consumers of many kinds of media, usually for several hours a day, often without their parents' involvement. Content is crucial. The themes and characters of many television programs and video games can lead to increased aggression, as shown in longitudinal research.

Becoming Boys and Girls

8. Even 2-year-olds correctly use sex-specific labels, and young children become aware of gender differences in clothes, toys, future careers, and playmates. Gender stereotypes, favoritism, and segregation peak at about age 6.

9. Nature and nurture are both involved with sex and gender; disentangling them is very difficult. Every type of scientist and each major theory has a perspective on sex and gender distinctions.

10. Freud emphasized that children are attracted to the opposite-sex parent and eventually seek to identify, or align themselves, with the same-sex parent. Behaviorists hold that gender-related behaviors are learned through reinforcement and punishment (especially for males) and social modeling.

11. Cognitive theorists note that simplistic preoperational thinking leads to gender schema and therefore stereotypes. Sociocultural theorists point to the many male–female distinctions apparent in every society.

12. An epigenetic explanation notes that some sex differences result from hormones affecting brain formation. Experiences enhance or halt those neurological patterns.

13. Thus each theory has an explanation for the sex and gender differences that are apparent everywhere. Parents need to decide which differences are useful to encourage and which are destructive.

KEY TERMS

emotional regulation (p. 255)
initiative versus guilt (p. 256)
self-esteem (p. 256)
self-concept (p. 256)
intrinsic motivation (p. 257)
extrinsic motivation (p. 257)
externalizing problems (p. 258)
internalizing problems (p. 258)
empathy (p. 259)
antipathy (p. 259)
prosocial behavior (p. 260)
antisocial behavior (p. 260)
instrumental aggression (p. 261)
reactive aggression (p. 261)
bullying aggression (p. 261)
authoritarian parenting (p. 264)
permissive parenting (p. 264)
authoritative parenting (p. 264)
psychological control (p. 267)
time-out (p. 268)
sex differences (p. 271)
gender differences (p. 271)
phallic stage (p. 272)
Oedipus complex (p. 272)
superego (p. 272)
Electra complex (p. 273)
identification (p. 273)
gender schema (p. 275)
androgyny (p. 275)

KEY QUESTIONS

1. How can adults help children develop self-esteem?

2. What are the differences between shame and guilt?

3. What is the connection between temperament and emotional regulation?

4. How do early caregiving and culture affect emotional control?

5. How do parenting styles relate to cultural differences?

6. What are the advantages and disadvantages of physical punishment?

7. What are the consequences of using time-out and of psychological control?

8. How do children change from age 2 to 6 in their male and female roles and behaviors?

9. Describe the differences among three of the five theories of sex differences.

10. List the similarities between two of the five theories of sex differences.

APPLICATIONS

1. Observe the interactions of two or more young children. Sort your observations into four categories: emotion, reasons, results, and emotional regulation. Note every observable emotion (laughter, tears, etc.), the reason for it, the consequences, and whether or not emotional regulation was likely. For example: "Anger: friend grabbed toy; child suggested sharing; emotional regulation probable."

2. Ask three parents about punishment, including their preferred type, at what age, for what misdeeds, and by whom. Ask your three informants how they were punished and how that affected them. If your sources agree, find a parent (or a classmate) who has a different view.

3. Gender indicators often go unnoticed. Go to a public place (park, restaurant, busy street) and spend at least 10 minutes recording examples of gender differentiation, such as articles of clothing, mannerisms, interaction patterns, and activities. Quantify what you see, such as baseball hats on eight males and two females or (better but more difficult) four male–female conversations, with gender difference in length and frequency of talking, interruptions, vocabulary, and so on.

PART III The Developing Person So Far: The Play Years

BIOSOCIAL

Body Changes Children continue to grow from ages 2 to 6, but their rate of growth slows down. Normally the BMI (body mass index) is lower at about age 5 than at any other time of life. Children often become more discriminating eaters, eating too much unhealthy food and refusing to eat certain other foods altogether.

Brain Development Both the proliferation of neural pathways and myelination continue. Specific parts of the brain (including the corpus callosum, prefrontal cortex, amygdala, hippocampus, and hypothalamus) begin to connect, allowing lateralization and coordination of left and right as well as less impulsivity and perseveration. Gross motor skills, such as drawing, develop more slowly.

Injuries and Maltreatment Injury control is particularly necessary in these years, since far more children worldwide die of avoidable accidents than of diseases. Child abuse and neglect are likely in homes with many young children and few personal or community resources. Prevention requires that abused children be protected from further harm (tertiary prevention), that risk factors be reduced (secondary prevention), and—most difficult but crucial—that social changes make maltreatment less likely (primary prevention).

COGNITIVE

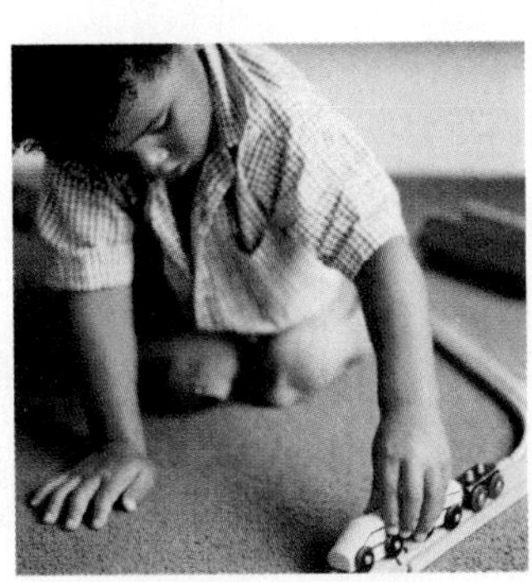

Piaget and Vygotsky Piaget stressed the young child's egocentric, illogical perspective, which prevents the child from grasping concepts such as conservation. Vygotsky stressed the cultural context, noting that children learn extensively from others. Many children develop their own theories, including a theory of mind as they realize that not everyone thinks as they do.

Language Language abilities develop rapidly. By age 6, the average child knows 10,000 words and demonstrates extensive grammatical knowledge. Young children are quite capable of becoming balanced bilinguals if their social context is encouraging.

Early Childhood Education Young children are avid learners as they play. Child-centered, teacher-directed, and intervention programs can all nurture learning; the actual outcome depends on the skill and number of teachers.

PSYCHOSOCIAL

Emotional Development Self-esteem is usually high during the play years. In Erikson's stage of initiative versus guilt, self-concept emerges, as does the ability to regulate emotions. Externalizing problems may be the result of too little emotional regulation; internalizing problems may result from too much control. Empathy produces prosocial behavior; antipathy leads to antisocial actions. Aggression takes many forms: Instrumental aggression is quite normal; bullying aggression is ominous.

Parents Parenting styles that are warm and responsive, with much communication, are most effective in encouraging the child's self-esteem, autonomy, and self-control. This parenting style is called authoritative. The authoritarian and permissive styles are less beneficial, especially if spanking or psychological control is used as discipline. Extensive use of television and other media by children can disrupt family life.

Becoming Boys and Girls Children develop stereotypic concepts of sex differences (biological) and gender differences (cultural). Theories give contradictory explanations of nature and nurture, but all agree that sex and gender identities become increasingly salient to young children.

The School Years

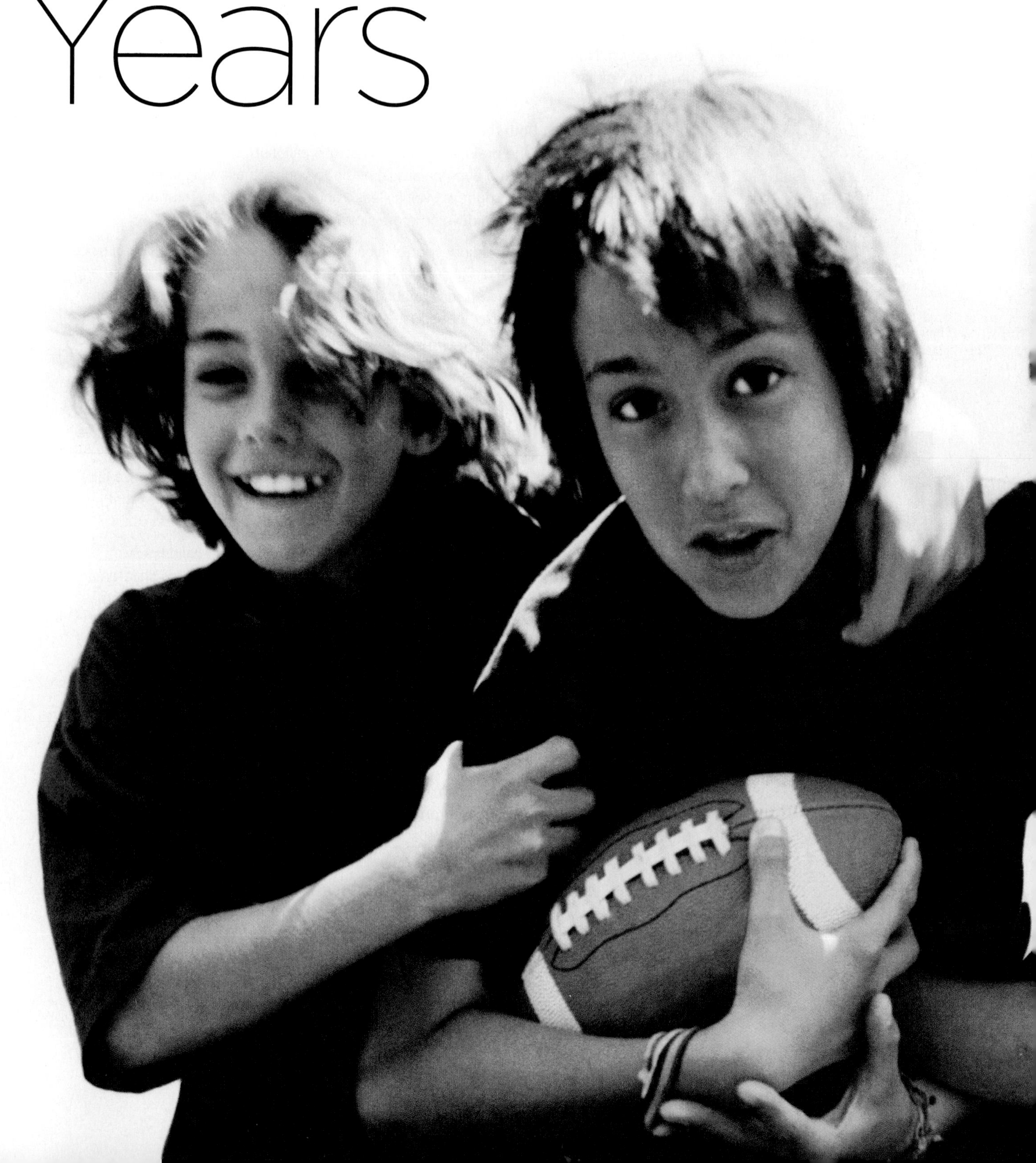

PART IV

Families and cultures have always stressed education for children who are past early childhood but not yet adolescents. In some cultures and centuries, girls and poor children were not sent to school; they learned how to perform the tasks required of adults in their cultures. Today, most children worldwide—including girls and less advantaged boys—begin their education before early childhood and continue after adolescence, preparing for school or building on what they have learned. But the period from age 7 to 11 is still prime time for learning—hence these are "the school years." Although sometimes called middle childhood, we have chosen to emphasize what is special about these years—and schooling is it.

If asked to pick the best years of the entire life span, you might choose ages 7 to 11 and defend your choice persuasively. For many children, these healthy and productive years allow measured (not dramatic) growth; mastery of new athletic skills; and acquisition of concepts, vocabulary, and intellectual abilities. In psychosocial development, children typically appreciate their parents, make new friends, and are proud of their nationality, gender, and ethnicity.

All this is true for many, but not all. Some school-age children struggle with special educational needs; some live in dysfunctional families; some cope with poverty or homelessness; some contend with obesity, chronic health problems, learning disabilities, or bullying. The next three chapters celebrate the joys and acknowledge the difficulties of these school years.

全脂牛乳
全脂牛乳

11

CHAPTER OUTLINE

The School Years: Biosocial Development

Context changes, so everything changes. No longer do children depend entirely on their families to dress, feed, and wash them, or to send them to a preschool where they encounter a limited number of similar children. By age 6 or 7, self-care (dressing, eating, bathing) is routine and attendance at school is mandated—usually a school with a formal curriculum and, often, hundreds of fellow learners from many backgrounds.

This chapter describes similarities among all school-age children, but also differences that suddenly become significant—in size, in health, in learning ability, and in almost everything else. Children make comparisons, and almost every child sometimes feels inadequate. I moved a thousand miles in the second grade, entering a new school. I was self-conscious and lonely. Cynthia talked to me; she seemed willing to be my friend.

"We cannot be friends," she told me, "because I am a Democrat."

"So am I," I answered. (I knew my family believed in democracy.)

"No you're not. You are a Republican," she said.

I was stunned. We never became friends.

Neither Cynthia nor I realized that each child is unusual in some way (perhaps from another culture, family type, or, in this case, political background) and yet capable of friendship with children who are different. I wish that some adult had noticed my loneliness and helped me. Cynthia would have made a good friend.

A Healthy Time

Genetic and environmental factors safeguard childhood. Most fatal childhood diseases and accidents occur before age 7, and by the school years a measure of caution and several doses of vaccine are protective. Even during times of high infant mortality and before immunization, school-age children have always been quite hardy, protected until they reach their reproductive years and can produce the next generation.

The same factors operate today. **Middle childhood,** the period after early childhood and before adolescence, approximately from age 7 to 11, is the healthiest period of the entire life span (see Figure 11.1). Fatal illness is very rare and mortal injuries are unusual during this time.

middle childhood The period between early childhood and early adolescence, approximately from age 7 to 11.

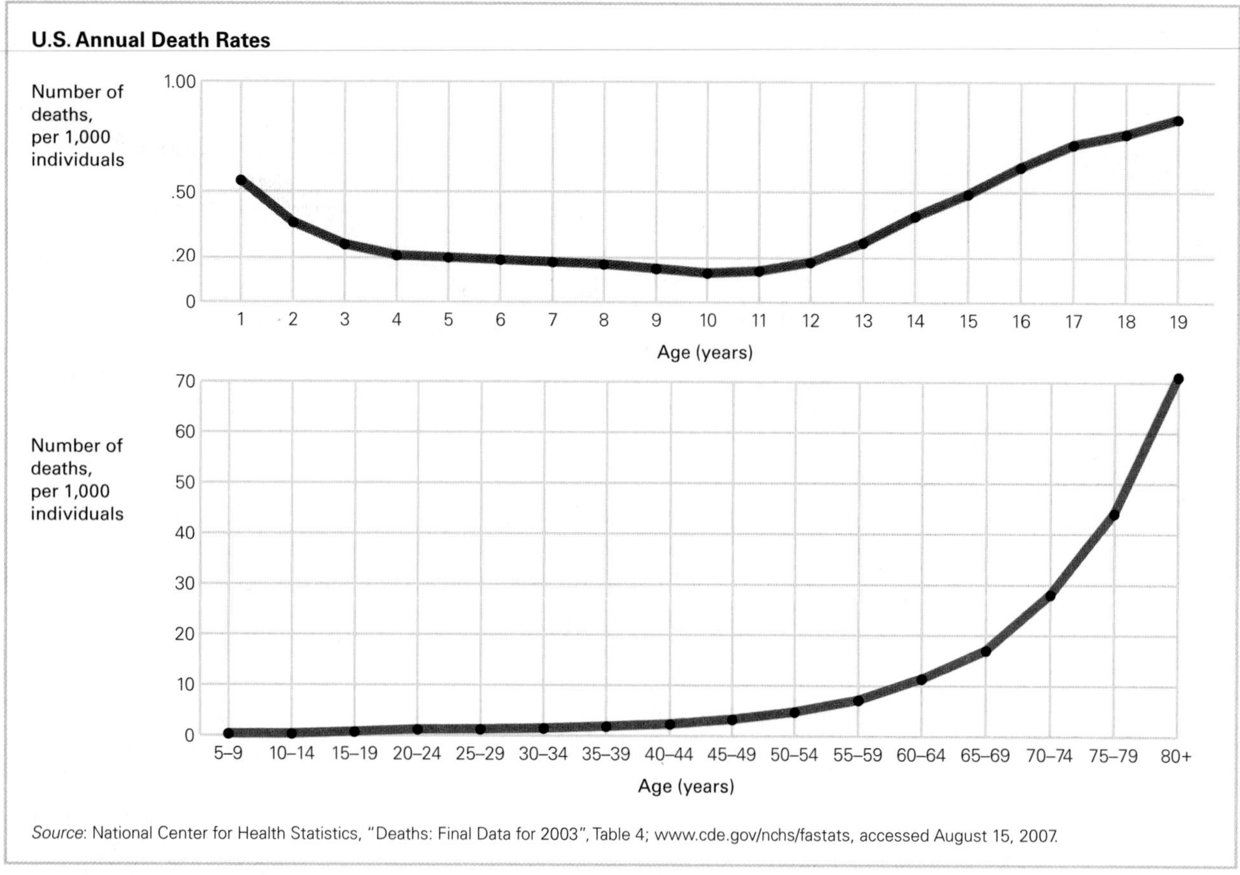

Source: National Center for Health Statistics, "Deaths: Final Data for 2003", Table 4; www.cde.gov/nchs/fastats, accessed August 15, 2007.

FIGURE 11.1

Death at an Early Age? Almost Never! Schoolchildren are remarkably hardy, as measured in many ways. These charts show that death rates for 7- to 11-year-olds are lower than those for children under 7 or over 11 and about a hundred times lower than for adults.

Observation Quiz (see answer, page 286): From the bottom graph, it looks as if ages 9 and 19 are equally healthy, but they are dramatically different in the top graph. What is the explanation?

overweight In an adult, having a BMI (body mass index) of 25 to 29. In a child, being above the 85th percentile, based on the U.S. Centers for Disease Control's 1980 standards for his or her age and sex.

obesity In an adult, having a BMI (body mass index) of 30 or more. In a child, being above the 95th percentile, based on the U.S. Centers for Disease Control's 1980 standards for his or her age and sex.

Size and Shape

The rate of growth slows down, allowing school-age children to undertake their basic self-care, from brushing their teeth to buttoning their jackets, from making their own lunch to walking to school. Muscles become stronger: The average 10-year-old can throw a ball twice as far as a 6-year-old. Lung capacity expands: With each passing year, children run faster and exercise longer without breathing more heavily (Malina et al., 2004).

In fact, partly because of slower growth and stronger muscles, during these years children can master almost any motor skill that doesn't require adult size. For instance, 9-year-olds can race their elders on bicycles, but they can't compete in adult basketball.

Culture, motivation, and practice are crucial for any motor skill. This is illustrated by the use of chopsticks, a fine motor skill that is attained in chopstick-using cultures by half of the 4-year-olds and virtually all the 6-year-olds (Wong et al., 2002), but by almost no 7- to 11-year-olds elsewhere.

Typically, school-age children in developed nations eat enough, as their bodies grow taller. Healthy 6-year-olds tend to have the lowest body mass index (BMI, a number expressing the relationship of height to weight) of any age group (Guillaume & Lissau, 2002) and, until puberty, children typically stay slim.

As you know, however, not every school-age child is slim. The most common nutritional problem at this age is **overweight,** defined as having a BMI above the 85th percentile of the growth charts as compiled (according to age and sex) by the U.S. Centers for Disease Control. **Obesity** is defined as having a BMI above the 95th percentile. (The definitions for adults are different: a BMI between 25 and 29 for overweight and 30 or above for obesity).

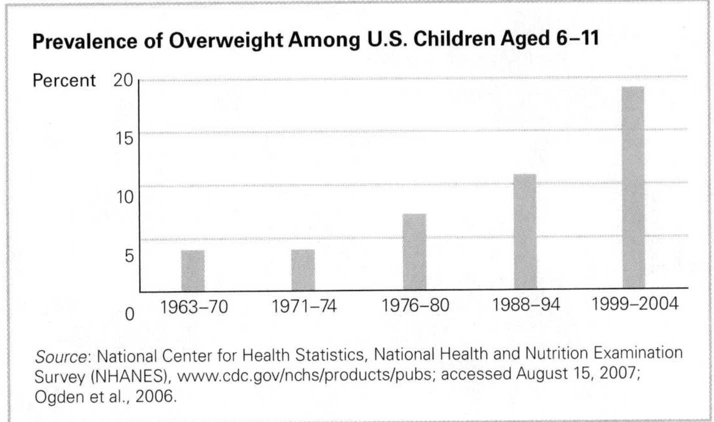

FIGURE 11.2

No Improvement in Sight The prevalence of overweight among 6- to 11-year-olds increased by 8 percentage points between 1988 and 1994 and between 1999 and 2004. The picture is not much brighter among adolescents: Overweight among 12- to 19-year-olds increased by 6 percentage points, from 11 percent to 17 percent, during the same period.

The average child of every age, family income, nationality, and cultural group is heavier today than in 1980 (see Figure 11.2). Older and poorer children show the most worrisome gains (Ogden et al., 2006). Quality of food (e.g., high-calorie, low-nutrition "junk foods"), not quantity, is the problem. Even in China, where more than a billion people are poor, obesity is becoming a medical problem (Gu et al., 2005). Poverty no longer means starvation, except in nations beset by famine or war, where crop failures and forced migration make food very scarce.

Excess weight hinders development in every domain. Overweight children exercise less and have higher blood pressure, risking health problems in adulthood, including type 2 diabetes (which is increasing among older children), heart disease, and stroke. School achievement often decreases, self-esteem falls, and loneliness rises with excessive increases in weight (Friedlander et al., 2003; Guillaume & Lissau, 2002; Mustillo et al., 2003).

Especially for Teachers A child in your class is overweight, but you are hesitant to say anything to the parents, who are also overweight, because you do not want to insult them. What should you do?

What makes one child more vulnerable to being overweight than another of the same age? Genes are part of the explanation; they affect activity level, food preferences, body type, and metabolic rate. People who inherit from both parents a particular allele of a gene called FTO (as about 16 percent of all children of European ancestry do) are much more likely to be obese than are other children (Frayling et al, 2007). It is not known how often this genetic combination is found in children of other backgrounds.

But genes do not act alone: "Fat runs in families but so do frying pans, which makes it hard to know whether DNA or dripping is more to blame for today's plague of obesity" (Jones, 2006, p. 1879).

Vulnerable children become obese because of the influence of an estimated 250 genes and because of many influences in the environment, including their parents' and grandparents' diets (Gluckman & Hanson, 2006). Studies suggest dozens of other environmental culprits. For instance, children who daily watch more than two hours of television and drink more than two servings of soda ("pop") are more often overweight than are those who do neither (Institute of Medicine, 2005).

Adults may not realize that their children are overweight and thus may not think that they have any reason to limit their consumption of junk food, their time spent playing video games and watching TV, and their lack of physical activity. For instance, in one study of obese African American children, only 30 percent of the parents acknowledged that their children were overweight (Young-Hyman et al., 2003).

All The Same These boys are all friends in the third grade, clowning in response to the camera—as school-age boys like to do. Outsiders might notice the varied growth rates and genetic differences, but the boys themselves are more aware of what they have in common.

LAURA DWIGHT

MICHAEL NEWMAN / PHOTO EDIT

Will She Drink Her Milk? The first word many American children read is *McDonald's,* and they all recognize the golden arches. Fast food is part of almost every family's diet—one reason the rate of obesity has doubled in every age group in the United States since 1980. Even if the young girl stops playing with her straw and drinks the milk, she is learning that soda and French fries are desirable food choices.

Especially for Parents Suppose that you always serve dinner with the television on, tuned to a news broadcast. Your hope is that your children will learn about the world as they eat. Can this practice be harmful?

If parents do recognize the problem, their attempt to put the child on a diet may boomerang. One study of 7- to 12-year-olds found that "restricting access to certain foods increases rather than decreases preference. Forcing a child to eat a food will decrease liking for that food" (Benton, 2004, p. 858). A better strategy is for adults to keep their own weight down and to exercise with the child (Patrick et al., 2004).

Physical Activity

Active play benefits children in every way, not only with weight and motor skills. Children often play joyfully, "fully and totally immersed" (Loland, 2002, p. 139). Much more than for younger children, the maturation of body and brain enables school-age children to join in active games. For them, the benefits of sports can last a lifetime:

- Better overall health
- Less obesity
- Appreciation of cooperation and fair play
- Improved problem-solving abilities
- Respect for teammates and opponents of many ethnicities and nationalities

Answer to Observation Quiz (from page 284): Look at the vertical axis. From age 1 to 20, the annual death rate is less than 1 in 1,000.

There are hazards as well:

- Loss of self-esteem as a result of criticism from teammates or coaches
- Injuries (the infamous "Little League elbow" is one example)
- Reinforcement of prejudices (especially against the other sex)
- Increases in stress (evidenced by altered hormone levels, insomnia)
- Time and effort taken away from learning academic skills

Where can children potentially reap the benefits and avoid the hazards? Three possibilities are neighborhoods, schools, and sports leagues.

➤Response for Teachers (from page 285): Speak to the parents, not accusingly (because you know that genes and culture have a major influence on body weight), but helpfully. Alert them to the potential social and health problem that their child's weight poses. Most parents are very concerned about their child's well-being and will work with you to improve the child's snacks and exercise level.

Neighborhood Games

Neighborhood play is flexible; children improvise to meet their needs. Rules, boundaries of where play can occur, and times are adapted to children's availability (usually any school-age children whose parents let them). Stickball, touch football, tag, hide-and-seek, jump rope, and dozens of other games that involve running and catching, or kicking and jumping, can go on forever, or at least until dark. The play is active and interactive, ideal for children.

Modern life has made informal neighborhood games increasingly scarce. Exploding urbanization means fewer open areas that are both fun and safe. For example, Mexico City had an estimated 3 million residents in 1970 and 20 million in 2005; an inevitable result is overcrowding, with less space for children to play.

Further, many parents keep their children inside because of "stranger danger"—although "there is a much greater chance that your child is going to be dangerously overweight from staying inside than that he is going to be abducted" (Layden, 2004, p. 96). Homework, television, and video games all compete with outdoor play.

Keep It Rolling This boy in Orissa, India, is using an old bicycle tire as a hoop. Although they use different objects, children everywhere have the impulse to play, and many of their games are the same.

Observation Quiz (see answer, page 289): Is this boy malnourished?

Exercise in School

When opportunities for neighborhood play are scarce, physical education in school is an alternative. Good gym teachers know developmentally appropriate, cooperative games and exercises for children (Belka, 2004). However, children may enjoy sports but hate physical education. One author cites an example of two children who participate enthusiastically in sports every weekend but have a different attitude in school:

> Their current softball unit in physical education hardly provokes any excitement. There are 18 students on each side, sides that are formed in an ad hoc manner each lesson. . . . Few students get turns to pitch, and many are satisfied playing the deepest of outfield positions in order to have minimal involvement in the game.
>
> *[Hastie, 2004, p. 63]*

As schools are pressured to increase reading and math knowledge (see Chapter 12), time for physical education and recess has declined to a few hours a week. Typically, many children share a confined space, spending more time waiting than moving.

Athletic Clubs and Leagues

Private or nonprofit clubs and organizations offer opportunities for children to play. Culture and family influence this type of play: Some children learn golf, others tennis, others boxing. Cricket and rugby are common in England and in former British colonies, such as Australia and Jamaica; baseball is common in Japan, the United States, Cuba, Panama, and the Dominican Republic; soccer is central in many European, African, and Latin American nations.

The best-known organized recreation program for children is Little League, with 2.7 million children playing baseball and softball on 180,000 teams in 75 countries. When it began in 1939, Little League had only three teams of boys aged 9–12. Now it includes girls, younger and older children, and 22,000 children with disabilities, an expansion that indicates the desire of children and their parents to play sports—increasingly less available at school or on a neighborhood vacant lot.

Despite possible problems, most children enjoy organized sports. One adult confesses:

> I was a lousy Little League player. Uncoordinated, small, and clueless are the accurate adjectives I'd use if someone asked politely. . . . What I did possess, though, was enthusiasm. Wearing the uniform—cheesy mesh cap, scratchy polyester shirt, old-school beltless pants, uncomfortable cleats and stirrups that never stayed up—gave me a sort of pride. It felt special and made me think that I was part of something important.
>
> *[Ryan, 2005]*

"Just remember son, it doesn't matter whether you win or lose—unless you want Daddy's love."

Especially for Phys. Ed. Teachers A group of parents of fourth- and fifth-graders has asked for your help in persuading the school administration to sponsor a competitive sports team. How should you advise the group to proceed?

Belonging is important to every child, but that point raises one final problem with organized children's sports: Many children are left out (Collins, 2003). Parents must pay their children's fees, transport them to practices and games, and support their children's teams. Children who are from poor families, who are not well coordinated, or who have chronic illnesses are less likely to belong to sports teams. Those are the very children who could benefit most from the exercise.

Chronic Illness

We noted that middle childhood is generally a healthy time, more so now in every nation of the world than just 30 years ago. Immunization has reduced deaths dramatically, and serious accidents, fatal illnesses, and even minor diseases are less common.

In the United States, the improved health of school-age children is evidenced in fewer chronic illnesses, less exposure to environmental toxins, and fewer surgeries performed in childhood. Hearing impairments and anemia are half as frequent as they were two decades ago, and only 1 percent of 5- to 10-year-olds had elevated blood levels of lead in 2001, compared with almost 30 percent in 1978 (MMWR, May 27, 2005; see Research Design). Elevated blood lead correlates with many disabilities, especially affecting the brain (mental retardation, hyperactivity).

Research Design

Scientists: Nine scientists working for three U.S. government agencies: Environmental Protection, Housing and Urban Development, and Centers for Disease Control and Prevention.

Publication: *Mortality and Morbidity Weekly Report* (MMWR) of May 27, 2005, published by the Massachusetts Medical Society.

Participants: A large, representative U.S. sample is examined every few years as part of NHANES (the National Health and Nutrition Examination Survey). The study cited was the 1999–2002 survey, and these data were from blood tests of 6,283 people aged 6–19.

Design: Blood levels of lead were analyzed by spectrophotometry in a CDC laboratory. The cutoff for an "elevated" level was 10 μg per deciliter, a standard recognized by many public health authorities.

Major conclusion: Compared with previous NHANES data, a marked decrease in blood levels of lead was found among all groups. The decrease was attributed to "coordinated, intensive efforts" that included removing lead from gasoline, paint, and the metal used to make food cans.

Comment: This study confirmed that a public health campaign to reduce exposure to lead was succeeding. The data also reveal some problems: Children under 6 years are about 10 times more likely to have elevated lead levels than are adolescents, and rates are still relatively high among African and Latino Americans.

Health-related problems still occur, of course. About 13 percent of all children have special health needs, some of which get worse during the school years, including Tourette syndrome, stuttering, and allergies. Such conditions often have social side effects, impairing children's learning as well as peer acceptance. Relatively minor problems, such as walking with a limp, wearing glasses, repeatedly having to blow one's nose, or even having a visible birthmark, may make children self-conscious.

Basic practices, such as eating a balanced diet, getting enough exercise and sleep, and breathing clean air, continue to be important for health and learning during these years; some evidence suggests that they become more important. Just 50 years ago, most poor children lived in rural areas; they exercised more and breathed cleaner air than city children. Now most poor children live in cities. The children who are at risk of illness for economic or social reasons are also the most vulnerable if basic health needs are not met—which is all too often the case (Buckhalt et al., 2007; Dilworth-Bart & Moore, 2006).

Any chronic condition that limits active play, impedes focused attention, or prevents regular school attendance correlates with emotional and social problems of every kind. For illustration, we examine the condition that is the most common reason for children to miss school: asthma.

Asthma

Asthma is a chronic inflammatory disorder of the airways that makes breathing difficult. Although asthma affects people of every age, rates are highest among school-age children and are increasing worldwide (Bousquet et al., 2007). In the United States, asthma affects 9 percent of all children under age 18, with higher rates for Puerto Rican (19 percent) and African American (13 percent) children. These rates are about twice as high as they were in 1980 (Akinbami, 2006).

asthma A chronic disease of the respiratory system in which inflammation narrows the airways from the lungs to the nose and mouth, causing difficulty in breathing. Signs and symptoms include wheezing, shortness of breath, chest tightness, and coughing.

Many researchers are studying the possible causes of asthma, including genetic factors. Suspect alleles have been identified, but asthma has varied genetic roots (Bossé & Hudson, 2007).

In any case, as you saw with obesity, genes increase the risk of asthma, but environment is crucial. Some experts suggest a "hygiene hypothesis," the idea that contemporary children are so overprotected from viruses and bacteria that they do not get the infections and childhood diseases that would strengthen their immune systems (Busse & Lemanske, 2005; Tedeschi & Airaghi, 2006).

Several aspects of modern life—carpets, pets inside the home, airtight windows, less outdoor play—are known to contribute to the increased rates of asthma (Tamay et al., 2007). Many allergens that trigger asthma attacks (pet dander, cigarette smoke, dust mites, cockroaches, and mold) are more concentrated in today's well-insulated homes than in the houses of a century ago. Air pollution is also a problem. A study in Mongolia, where many people still live in sparsely populated and poor rural areas, confirmed that asthma increases with modern, city life, even though Mongolian urban dwellers are still quite poor (Viinanen et al., 2007).

Especially for School Nurses For the past month, a 10-year-old fifth-grade girl has been eating very little at lunch and has visibly lost weight. She has also lost interest in daily school activities. What should you do?

Prevention of Asthma

The three levels of prevention discussed in Chapter 8 apply to every chronic health problem, including asthma. *Primary prevention* is the most difficult. Better ventilation of schools and homes, decreased pollution, eradication of cockroaches, and construction of many more outdoor play areas would make asthma less common by helping all children.

The benefit of primary prevention was revealed during the 1996 Summer Olympics in Atlanta, Georgia. Various measures aimed at reducing traffic congestion (e.g., free mass transit) also reduced air pollution and, unexpectedly, cut the number of asthma attacks almost in half (Friedman et al., 2001). Similar conclusions, using an entirely different methodology, were found regarding air pollution and asthma in Beijing (Pan et al., 2007).

KATHY MCLAUGHLIN / THE IMAGE WORKS

Pride and Prejudice In some city schools, asthma is so common that using an inhaler is a sign of prestige, as suggested by the facial expressions of these two boys. The prejudice is more apparent beyond the walls of this school nurse's room, in a society that allows high rates of childhood asthma to occur.

Secondary prevention reduces the occurrence of asthma among high-risk children. When asthma runs in the family, then breast-feeding and ridding the house of dust, pets, smoke, and other allergens cut the rate of allergies and asthma in half (Elliott et al., 2007; Gdalevich et al., 2001). For asthma (as well as all other health problems), regular checkups aid secondary prevention.

Finally, *tertiary prevention* (reducing the damage caused by asthma once it develops) includes the prompt use of injections and inhalers, which markedly reduce acute wheezing and overnight hospitalizations (Glauber et al., 2001). The use of hypoallergenic materials (e.g., for mattress covers) can also reduce the rate of asthma attacks—but not by much, probably because tertiary prevention at home occurs too late (MMWR, January 14, 2005).

Adequate tertiary prevention is provided for less than half the children with asthma in the United States. Why? One reason is economic. One-third of school-age children, including more than half of African American and Hispanic children, have no health insurance (U.S. Department of Health and Human Services, 2004). Another reason is mistrust of doctors (mostly White, high-income older men) by parents of young children (often non-White, low-income young women).

Language and cultural barriers add to the problem. Among one group of immigrant mothers of asthmatic children, 88 percent thought drugs were overused in the United States, and 72 percent did not give their children the medication their doctors prescribed (Bearison et al., 2002). In a large multiethnic study, half the parents who bought drugs for childhood asthma did not acknowledge that their child was asthmatic (Roberts, 2003). It may be that the prescribing doctor did not explain, or that the parents did not understand, or that they refused to acknowledge a chronic illness.

Children reflect their parents' attitudes. Only half of a group of 8- to 16-year-olds with asthma followed their doctor's advice about medication; those children

➤Response for Parents (from page 286): Habitual TV watching correlates with obesity, so you may be damaging your children's health rather than improving their intellect. Your children would probably profit more if you were to make dinner a time for family conversation.

➤Answer to Observation Quiz (from page 287): Although malnutrition is common in India, school-age children worldwide are more often too fat than too thin. This boy has healthy hair; his ribs do not show; and, most important, he seems to have adequate energy and coordination for active play. Although a definitive answer depends on percentiles, he is probably just fine.

➤**Response for Phys. Ed. Teachers** (from page 288): Discuss with the parents their reasons for wanting the team. Children need physical activity, but some aspects of competitive sports are better suited to adults than to children. Recommend that the parents think of ways to foster their children's health and cooperative spirit without the element of competition.

who were older, minority, and low-income were least likely to comply (McQuaid et al., 2003). This lack of compliance among older children is also a major problem in the treatment of diabetes, PKU, sickle-cell anemia, and almost every other chronic childhood condition.

Asthma and many other adult health problems can be prevented during the school years if two things occur. First, parents must be diligent in providing regular preventive care for dental health (early treatment prevents later tooth loss and gum disease), eye health (specific exercises can postpone the need for glasses), spine curvature (a back brace may encourage normal growth), and so on. Second, children must develop the habit of taking care of their health so that their adolescent rebellion erupts in some way (such as green hair) that does not make them sick.

SUMMING UP

School-age children are usually healthy, strong, and capable. Immunizations during the play years protect them against childhood diseases, and developmental advances give them sufficient strength and coordination to take care of their own basic needs (eating, dressing, bathing). However, their growing awareness of themselves and of each other makes every physical condition a potential problem that might interfere with peer acceptance and school attendance. Obesity and asthma are two notable examples. Both have genetic and early-childhood origins, but both become more problematic during middle childhood. Primary prevention is crucial, but many children do not get the safe, active play or the ongoing care that they need. ■

Brain Development

Recall that, in early childhood, emotional regulation, theory of mind, and left–right coordination emerge. The maturing corpus callosum connects the two hemispheres of the brain. The prefrontal cortex—the executive part of the brain—plans, monitors, and evaluates. These developments continue in middle childhood. We look now at advances in reaction time, attention, and automatization, and at ways to measure brain activity, particularly tests of ability that indicate whether a child is developing as expected.

Advances in Brain Functioning

reaction time The time it takes to respond to a stimulus, either physically (with a reflexive movement such as an eye blink) or cognitively (with a thought).

Increasing myelination results "by 7 or 8 years of age, in a massively interconnected brain" (Kagan & Herschkowitz, 2005, p. 220). One consequence is a reduction in **reaction time,** the length of time it takes to respond to a stimulus. Over the decades of adulthood, reaction time slowly lengthens again. Consequently, for instance, grandparents might lose to a teenage grandchild at rapid-response video games but be fairly matched with an 8-year-old one.

Advances in the "mental control processes that enable self-control" (Verté et al., 2005, p. 415) allow planning for the future, which is beyond the ability of the impatient younger child. Now children can analyze possible consequences before they lash out in anger or dissolve in tears and can figure out when a curse word seems advisable (on the playground to a bully, perhaps) and when it does not (in the classroom or at home).

selective attention The ability to concentrate on some stimuli while ignoring others.

Neurological advances allow children to process different types of information in many areas of the brain at once and to pay special heed to the most important elements. **Selective attention,** the ability to concentrate on some stimuli while ignoring others, is crucial for early school competence (NICHD Early Child Care Research Network, 2003). Selective attention requires ongoing myelination and the increased production of neurotransmitters (chemical messengers) and improves noticeably at about age 7. School-age children not only notice various stimuli (which is one form of attention) but can also judge the appropriate response when several possibilities conflict (Rueda et al., 2007).

Attention deficits may underlie many of the problems seen in 6-year-olds, including poor motor skills that gradually improve with age (Wassenberg et al., 2005). Motor and cognitive impairments are not entirely the result of inattention, but inattention is part of the problem.

In the classroom, selective attention allows children to listen, take concise notes, and ignore distractions (all very difficult at age 6, better by age 10). In the din of the cafeteria, children can understand one another's gestures and expressions and respond quickly. Playing ball, batters ignore the other team's attempts to distract them, while alert fielders start moving into position as soon as a ball is hit their way. Selective attention underlies all of these abilities.

➤Response for School Nurses (from page 289): Something is wrong, and you (or the school psychologist, or both) should talk to the girl's parents. Ask whether they, too, have noticed any changes. Recommend that the child see her pediatrician for a thorough physical examination. If the girl's self-image turns out to be part of the problem, stress the importance of social support.

Another major advance in brain function in middle childhood is **automatization,** the repetition of a sequence of thoughts and actions until it becomes automatic, or routine. At first, almost all behaviors under conscious control require careful and slow thought. After many repetitions, as neurons fire in sequence, actions become automatic and patterned. Less thinking is needed because firing one neuron sets off a chain reaction.

automatization A process in which repetition of a sequence of thoughts and actions makes the sequence routine, so that it no longer requires conscious thought.

Increased myelination and hours of practice lead to the "automatic pilot" of cognition (Berninger & Richards, 2002). Consider a child learning to read. At first, eyes (sometimes aided by a finger) concentrate, painstakingly making out letters and sounding out each one. This sequence of actions leads to perception of syllables and then words. Eventually the process becomes so automatic that a glance at a billboard results in reading without any intentional effort.

Automatization is apparent in the acquisition of every skill. Speaking a second language, reciting the multiplication tables, and writing one's name are haltingly, even painfully, difficult at first but then gradually become automatic. A transformation to a more efficient form of neural processing, freeing the brain for more advanced reading, speaking, computation, and writing, is the reason for this advance (Berninger & Richards, 2002). Practice makes perfect (almost).

DIGITAL VISION / GETTY IMAGES

Neurons at Work Brain development is evident in this duet, since playing the piano requires selective attention, practice, and automatization, as does singing in harmony. These girls are about 9 years old; compare their proficiency with the piano banging and off-key singing of the typical preschooler.

Measuring the Mind

Measuring developmental changes in brain functioning can be done via repeated brain scans, such as the fMRI. One laboratory reported that the cortex (the top layers of the brain) is relatively thin at the beginning of childhood and then grows thicker during the school years, reaching a peak at about age 8. The brains of children who are very intelligent follow the same pattern, but it is more pronounced (notably thinner and then thicker) and the thickening develops more slowly, particularly in the prefrontal cortex (Miller, 2006).

Intriguing research like this is arduous and expensive; it has not yet been replicated or even fully understood. More often, mental processes are measured via written questions on a standardized test. Each child's answers are compared with those of other children the same age (to assess aptitude) or the same school grade (to measure achievement).

FIGURE 11.3

In Theory, Most People Are Average Almost 70 percent of IQ scores fall within the normal range. Note, however, that this is a norm-referenced test. In fact, actual IQ scores have risen in many nations; 100 is no longer exactly the midpoint. Further, in practice, scores below 50 are slightly more frequent than indicated by the normal curve shown here, because severe retardation is the result not of the normal distribution but of genetic and prenatal factors.

Observation Quiz (see answer, page 295): If a person's IQ is 110, what category is he or she in?

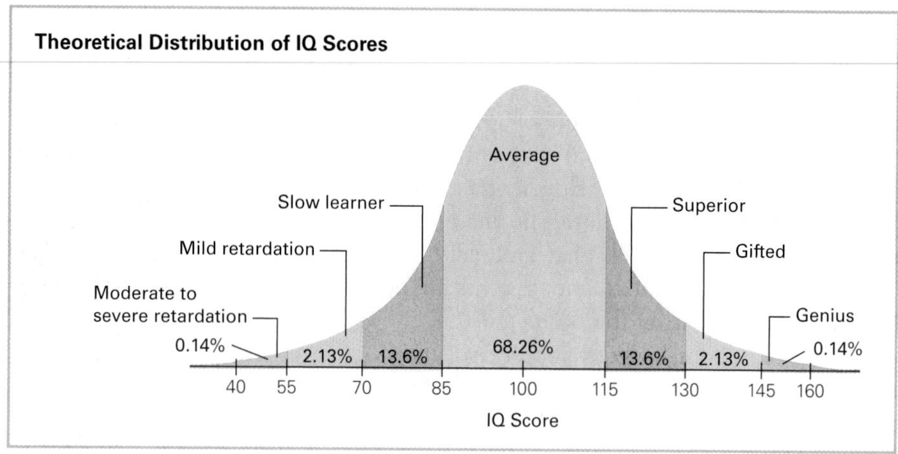

aptitude The potential to master a particular skill or to learn a particular body of knowledge.

IQ tests Tests designed to measure intellectual aptitude, or ability to learn in school. Originally, intelligence was defined as mental age divided by chronological age, times 100—hence the term *intelligence quotient,* or *IQ.*

achievement tests Measures of mastery or proficiency in reading, math, writing, science, or any other subject.

Aptitude and Achievement

In theory, **aptitude** is the potential to master a particular skill or to learn a particular body of knowledge. The most important aptitude for school-age children is intellectual aptitude, or the ability to learn in school. Intellectual aptitude is measured by **IQ tests** (see Figure 11.3).

In theory, achievement is distinct from aptitude. Achievement is not what a person *might* learn but what a person *has* learned. **Achievement tests** are taken routinely by students (as mandated in the United States by the No Child Left Behind Act, discussed in Chapter 12), measuring learning in reading, math, writing, science, and other subjects.

The words *in theory* precede those definitions because aptitude and achievement tests are designed to measure different traits; but the scores on them are highly correlated, not just for individuals but also for nations, according to a study of 46 countries (Lynn & Mikk, 2007). Both aptitude and achievement also correlate with wealth, individually and nationally (Lynn & Vanhanen, 2002). It is not surprising, then, that a child's IQ score predicts later education and then adult success. To be specific, children with high IQs usually earn good grades in school and graduate from college. As adults, they typically hold professional or managerial jobs, marry, and own homes (Sternberg et al., 2001).

Flynn Effect The rise in average IQ scores that has occurred over the decades in many nations.

The average IQs of entire nations have risen substantially—a phenomenon called the **Flynn Effect,** after the researcher who first described it (Flynn, 1999). At first, the Flynn Effect was doubted because IQ was thought to be totally genetic and genes don't change. But developmentalists now agree that the Flynn Effect is real (Rodgers & Wänström, 2007) and believe that the reasons are environmental, including better health, smaller families, and more schooling.

Especially for People Who Know Their IQ Score How would you interpret scores of 125, 100, and 75?

IQ is an abbreviation for "intelligence quotient." Originally, an IQ score was based on an actual quotient: mental age (as indicated on the test) divided by chronological age, and the result was then multiplied by 100. Children whose test performance equals the average performance of all children the same age have a mental age equal to their chronological age. In that case, mental age divided by chronological age equals 1, and 1 times 100 gives an IQ of 100. Thus, an IQ of 100 is exactly average.

The current method of calculating IQ is more complicated, but it is still assumed that a person's aptitude for learning increases through adolescence, so dividing the score by years of age equals the IQ. An IQ of 100 is held to be average at any age. In adulthood, aptitude is assumed *not* to change year by year (see Chapter 21). About two-thirds of people of all ages have an IQ between 85 and 115. Almost all (96 percent) are between 70 and 130.

Highly regarded and widely used IQ tests include the *Stanford-Binet* test, now in its fifth edition (Roid, 2003), and the *Wechsler* tests. There are Wechsler tests for preschoolers (the WPPSI, or Wechsler Preschool and Primary Scale of Intelligence), for adults (the WAIS, or Wechsler Adult Intelligence Scale), and for school-age children—the **WISC, or Wechsler Intelligence Scale for Children,** now in its fourth edition (Wechsler, 2003).

The WISC has 10 subtests, including tests of vocabulary, general knowledge, memory, and visual awareness, each of which provides a score. The Wechsler tests allow calculation of two IQ scores, one "verbal" (measured by tests of vocabulary, word problems, etc.) and the other "performance" (solving puzzles, copying shapes, etc.).

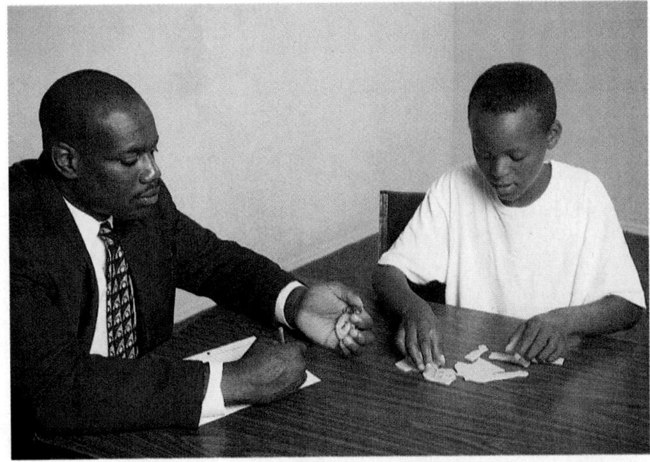

LEW MERRIM / MONKMEYER

Performance IQ This puzzle, part of a performance subtest on the Wechsler IQ test, seems simple until you try it. The limbs are difficult to align correctly, and time is of the essence. This boy has at least one advantage over most African American boys who are tested. Especially during middle childhood, boys tend to do better when their examiner is of the same sex and ethnicity.

Gifted or Retarded

A child with a very high IQ (usually above 130) may be considered gifted and placed in "gifted and talented" classes. In the United States, school policies and programs for gifted children vary from state to state. In 2000, 14 percent of children in Oklahoma were in gifted classes; in Vermont, only 1 percent were (Digest of Educational Statistics, 2005). Very high IQs are just as common among children in Vermont as in Oklahoma, but adults—voters, legislators, educators—in these two states have decided to educate these children in different ways.

Thirty years ago the definition of **mental retardation** was straightforward: All children or adults with an IQ below 70 were classified as mentally retarded, with further subdivisions for progressively lower scores: mild retardation, 55–70; moderate retardation, 40–54; severe retardation, 25–39; profound, below 25. Each of these categories signified different expectations, from "educable" (mildly retarded, able to learn to read and write) to "custodial" (profoundly retarded, unable to learn any skills). However, the mere label *mentally retarded* sometimes led parents and teachers to expect less of a child than the child was actually capable of, which reduced learning.

Further, in the population as a whole, where the average IQ is 100, only about 2 percent of children score below 70; but children in many immigrant, low-income, and minority groups have an average IQ well below 100. The reason is probably cultural bias embedded in the IQ tests, not those children's lack of intellectual aptitude. The result is that disproportionate numbers of those children (significantly more than 2 percent) are designated mentally retarded (Edwards, 2006; Pennington, 2002). That seems unfair.

Accordingly, the current definition stipulates that, in addition to having an IQ below 70, children who are designated as mentally retarded must be unusually far behind their peers in adaptation to life. Thus, a 6-year-old who, without help, gets dressed, fixes breakfast, walks to school, and knows the names of her classmates would not be considered mentally retarded, even if she had an IQ of 65. Adaptation is often measured with the Vineland Test of Adaptive Intelligence or some other assessment tool (Venn, 2004).

Wechsler Intelligence Scale for Children (WISC) An IQ test designed for school-age children. The test assesses potential in many areas, including vocabulary, general knowledge, memory, and spatial comprehension.

mental retardation Literally, slow, or late, thinking. In practice, people are considered mentally retarded if they score below 70 on an IQ test and if they are markedly behind their peers in adaptation to daily life.

Criticisms of IQ Testing

Many developmentalists criticize IQ tests. They argue that no test can measure potential without also measuring achievement and that every test score reflects the culture of the people who wrote, administer, and take it (Armour-Thomas & Gopaul-McNicol, 1998; Cianciolo & Sternberg, 2004). Even tests designated as culture-free, because they ask children to perform universally familiar tasks like drawing a person or naming their classmates, depend on cultural experiences.

Developmentalists also know that intellectual potential does in fact change over the life span. A child who needs special education in an early grade might later be classified as above average, or even gifted, like my nephew David (see Chapter 1). Like any other psychological test, an IQ test is a snapshot, providing a static, framed view of a dynamic, ever-developing brain at work.

Many measures are thus used to indicate learning potential. If an 8-year-old cannot read, for instance, vision and hearing assessments are done; then tests of comprehension, word recognition, and phonetic skills are given to supplement the IQ test. If brain damage is suspected, tests of balance and coordination ("Hop on one foot," "Touch your nose") or of brain–eye–hand connection ("Copy this drawing of a diamond") are useful.

Even with a battery of tests, assessment may be inaccurate, especially when tests that have been standardized in the United States are used in cultures where academic intelligence is not prized (Sternberg & Grigorenko, 2004).

> Like many other Western technological inventions (such as the printing press, the sewing machine, the bicycle, and the tractor), the intelligence test (popularly known as the IQ test) has been widely exported around the world. Like tractors, intelligence tests bring with them both ostensible utility and hidden implications.
>
> [*Serpell & Haynes, 2004, p. 166*]

© OWEN FRANKEN / STOCK, BOSTON

Demonstration of High IQ? If North American intelligence tests truly reflected all aspects of the mind, children would be considered mentally slow if they could not replicate the proper hand, arm, torso, and facial positions of a traditional dance, as this young Indonesian girl does brilliantly. She is obviously adept in kinesthetic and interpersonal intelligence. Given her culture, it would not be surprising if she were deficient in the logical-mathematical intelligence required to use the Internet effectively or to surpass an American peer in playing a video game.

A more fundamental criticism concerns the very concept that there is one general thing called intelligence (often referred to as *g*, for general intelligence). Humans may have *multiple intelligences.* If they do, then the use of a test to find one IQ score is based on a false premise. Robert Sternberg (1996) describes three distinct types of intelligence:

- *Academic,* measured by IQ and achievement tests
- *Creative,* evidenced by imaginative endeavors
- *Practical,* seen in everyday problem solving

Other psychologists stress a kind of intelligence called *emotional intelligence,* including the ability to regulate one's emotions and perceptive understanding of other people's feelings. Emotional intelligence is thought to be more important than intellectual ability in determining success in adulthood (Goleman, 1995; Salovey & Grewal, 2005).

The most influential of all multiple-intelligence theories is Howard Gardner's, which describes eight intelligences: linguistic, logical-mathematical, musical, spatial, bodily-kinesthetic (movement), interpersonal (social understanding), intrapersonal (self-understanding), and naturalistic (understanding of nature, as in biology, zoology, or farming) (Gardner, 1983, 1999; Gardner & Moran, 2006).

A person might be gifted spatially but not linguistically (a visual artist who cannot describe her work), or someone might have interpersonal but not naturalistic intelligence (a gifted clinical psychologist whose houseplants wither). Gardner's theory has been influential in education, especially with young children (e.g., Rettig, 2005); it has also been widely criticized (Kincheloe, 2004; Visser et al., 2006; Waterhouse, 2006).

According to those who hold that humans have multiple intelligences, standard IQ tests measure only part of brain potential. If intelligence is the multifaceted jewel that Gardner believes it to be, tests and schools need to expand their curricula so that every child can shine.

Especially for Teachers What are the advantages and disadvantages of using Gardner's eight intelligences to guide your classroom curriculum?

SUMMING UP

During middle childhood, neurological maturation allows faster, more automatic reactions. Selective attention enables focused concentration in school and in play. Aptitude tests, including IQ tests, compare mental age to chronological age. Actual learning is measured by achievement tests. The concept that an IQ score measures underlying aptitude (*g*) is challenged by Robert Sternberg, Howard Gardner, and others, who believe that the brain contains not just one aptitude but many. Determining who is gifted and who is retarded may be useful for educators, but there is much more change in IQ scores than originally imagined. Adaptation to circumstances is crucial. ■

➤Answer to Observation Quiz (from page 292): He or she is average. Anyone with a score between 85 and 115 is of average IQ.

➤Response for People Who Know Their IQ Score (from page 292): Above average, average, and below average compared with others the same age. For example, if three children are 12 years old, one might have a mental age (as determined by the test) of 15, another 12, and the third, 8. Then their IQ scores would be: $15/12 = 1.25 \times 100 = 125$ (above average); $12/12 = 1 \times 100 = 100$ (average); $8/12 = 0.75 \times 100 = 75$ (below average).

Children with Special Needs

Parents watch with pride as their offspring become smarter, taller, and more skilled. These feelings may mingle with worry when their children are not like other children. Often slowness, impulsiveness, or clumsiness is the first problem to be noticed; other problems become apparent once formal education begins.

Such **children with special needs** require extra help in order to learn because of differences in their physical or mental characteristics. Many of them seem fine until they encounter the demands of primary school. One example is Billy.

children with special needs Children who, because of a physical or mental disability, require extra help in order to learn.

a case to study

Billy: Dynamo or Dynamite?

Billy was born full term after an uncomplicated pregnancy; he sat up, walked, and talked at the expected ages. His parents were proud of his energy and curiosity: "Little Dynamo," they called him affectionately. He began to read on schedule, and he looked quite normal. But when Billy was in third grade, his teacher, Mrs. Pease, referred him to a psychiatrist because his behavior in class was "intolerably disruptive" (Gorenstein & Comer, 2002, p. 250), as the following episode illustrates:

> Mrs. Pease had called the class to attention to begin an oral exercise: reciting a multiplication table on the blackboard. The first child had just begun her recitation when, suddenly, Billy exclaimed, "Look!" The class turned to see Billy running to the window.
>
> "Look," he exclaimed again, "an airplane!"
>
> A couple of children ran to the window with Billy to see the airplane, but Mrs. Pease called them back, and they returned to their seats. Billy, however, remained at the window, pointing at the sky. Mrs. Pease called him back, too.
>
> "Billy, please return to your desk," Mrs. Pease said firmly. But Billy acted as though he didn't even hear her.
>
> "Look, Mrs. Pease," he exclaimed, "the airplane is blowing smoke!" A couple of other children started from their desks.
>
> "Billy," Mrs. Pease tried once more, "if you don't return to your desk this instant, I'm going to send you to Miss Warren's office." [Billy did sit down, but before Mrs. Pease could call on anyone, Billy blurted out the correct answer to the first question she asked.]
>
> Mrs. Pease tried again. "Who knows 3 times 7?" This time Billy raised his hand, but he still couldn't resist creating a disruption.
>
> "I know, I know," Billy pleaded, jumping up and down in his seat with his hand raised high.
>
> "That will do, Billy," Mrs. Pease admonished him. She deliberately called on another child. The child responded with the correct answer.
>
> "*I* knew that!" Billy exclaimed.
>
> "Billy," Mrs. Pease told him, "I don't want you to say one more word this class period."
>
> Billy looked down at his desk sulkily, ignoring the rest of the lesson. He began to fiddle with a couple of rubber bands, trying to see how far they would stretch before they broke. He looped the rubber bands around his index fingers and pulled his hands farther and farther apart. This kept him quiet for a while; by this point, Mrs. Pease didn't care what he did, as long as he was quiet. She continued conducting the multiplication lesson while Billy stretched the rubber bands until finally they snapped, flying off and hitting two children, on each side of him. Billy let out a yelp of surprise, and the class turned to him.
>
> "That's it, Billy," Mrs. Pease told him, "You're going to sit outside the classroom until the period is over."
>
> "No!" Billy protested. "I'm not going. I didn't do anything!"
>
> "You shot those rubber bands at Bonnie and Julian," Mrs. Pease said.
>
> "But it was an accident."
>
> "I don't care. Out you go!"
>
> Billy stalked out of the classroom to sit on a chair in the hall. Before exiting, however, he turned to Mrs. Pease. "I'll sue you for this," he yelled, not really knowing what it meant.
>
> *[Gorenstein & Comer, 2002, pp. 250–251]*

➤**Response for Teachers** (from page 294): The advantages are that all the children learn more aspects of human knowledge and that many children can develop their talents. Art, music, and sports should be an integral part of education, not just a break from academics. The disadvantage is that they take time and attention away from reading and math, which might lead to less proficiency in those subjects on standard tests and thus to criticism from parents and supervisors.

You will read more about Billy later in this chapter.

Dozens of specific diagnoses lead to classification as a child with special needs, including anxiety disorder, Asperger syndrome, attachment disorder, attention-deficit disorder, autism, bipolar disorder, conduct disorder, clinical depression, developmental delay, and Down syndrome. In the United States, two-thirds of school-age children with special needs are said to have a learning or language disability—neither of which may have been evident in earlier years or may still be evident in later years.

Every special need probably begins with a biological anomaly, perhaps the extra chromosome of Down syndrome or simply an unusual allele that affects some neurological connections. Biology is only the beginning; the social context affects how disabling the condition becomes.

Using Language Carefully: People First

Labels can stereotype and restrict rather than describe and enable. *People-first* designations are preferred when speaking or writing about people with special needs. The idea is to begin with the general human term (e.g., *child, boy, person*) and add "with [the type of special need]." Thus, we write about *children with autism,* not autistic children, *people with AIDS,* not AIDS patients.

Further, the names of syndromes are no longer expressed in the possessive. For example, people with three chromosomes at the 21st pair (trisomy-21) do not have "Down's syndrome," although a Dr. Down first described the condition in 1866. They are now referred to as people with *Down syndrome* (no *'s*) so as not to imply that their condition belongs to someone else.

In addition, some people choose to refer to themselves as *challenged,* not *handicapped,* because challenges can more readily be overcome. *Disability* is preferred over *handicap.*

Developmental Psychopathology

developmental psychopathology The field that uses insights into typical development to study and treat developmental disorders, and vice versa.

One part of the science of development is called **developmental psychopathology,** which links the study of typical development to that of various disorders, and vice versa. The goal is "to understand the nature, origins, and sequelae [consequences] of individual patterns of adaptation and maladaptation over time" (Davies & Cicchetti, 2004, p. 477).

Four lessons from developmental psychopathology apply to everyone:

1. *Abnormality is normal.* Most people sometimes act oddly, and those with serious disabilities are, in many respects, like everyone else.
2. *Disability changes year by year.* Someone who is severely disabled at one stage may become quite capable, or vice versa.
3. *Adulthood may be better or worse.* Prognosis is difficult. Many infants and children with serious disabilities that affect them psychologically (e.g., blindness) become happy and productive adults. Conversely, some conditions become more disabling at maturity, when interpersonal skills become more important.
4. *Diagnosis depends on the social context.* According to the widely used ***Diagnostic and Statistical Manual of Mental Disorders* (DSM-IV-TR),** "nuances of an individual's cultural frame of reference" must be considered before a diagnosis can be made (American Psychiatric Association, 2000, p. xxxiv). Perhaps psychopathology resides "not in the individual but in the adaptiveness of the relationship between individual and context" (Sameroff & MacKenzie, 2003, p. 613).

***Diagnostic and Statistical Manual of Mental Disorders* (DSM-IV-TR)** The American Psychiatric Association's official guide to the diagnosis (not treatment) of mental disorders. (*IV-TR* means "fourth edition, Test Revision.")

We now focus on only three of the many categories of disorders that developmental psychopathologists study: attention deficits, learning disabilities, and autistic spectrum disorders. Understanding these three can lead to a better understanding of all children.

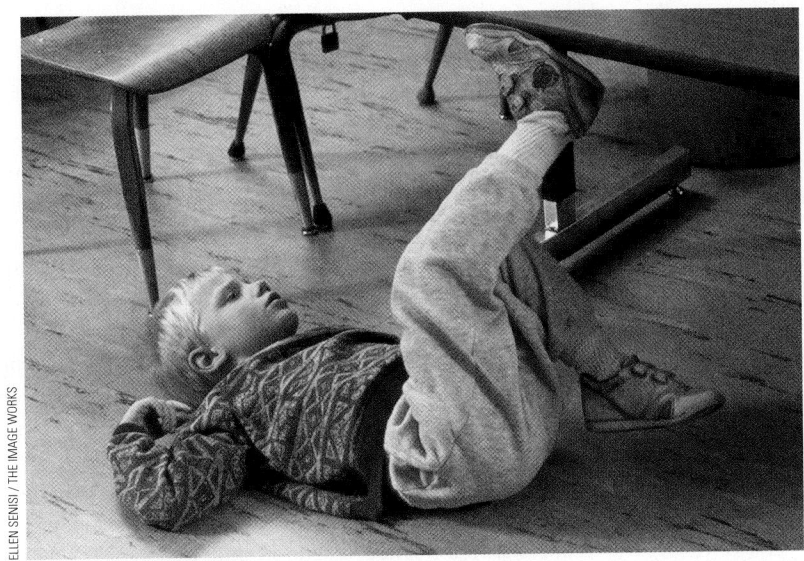

ELLEN SENISI / THE IMAGE WORKS

Not a Cure-All Ritalin has been found to calm many children with ADHD—but it does not necessarily make them models of good behavior. Like this 5-year-old boy with multiple handicaps, including ADHD (for which he is given Ritalin), they are still capable of having a tantrum when frustrated.

Attention-Deficit Disorders

A major problem for about 10 percent of all young children is that they have difficulty paying attention. They have an attention-deficit disorder (ADD), which is sometimes accompanied by an impulse to be continually active, leading to one of the most exasperating developmental disruptions, **attention-deficit/hyperactivity disorder (ADHD).** Children with ADHD have three problems: They are inattentive, impulsive, and overactive, with individual variations in which of these three is most evident (Barkley, 2006).

attention-deficit/hyperactivity disorder (ADHD) A condition in which a person not only has great difficulty concentrating for more than a few moments but also is inattentive, impulsive, and overactive.

After sitting down to do homework, a child with ADHD might look up, ask questions, think about playing, get a drink, fidget, squirm, tap the table, jiggle his or her legs, and go to the bathroom—and then start the whole sequence again. The child's difficulty may be caused by a slow-developing prefrontal cortex, an overactive limbic system, or an imbalance of neurotransmitters (Wolraich & Doffing, 2005). No matter what the cause, their brains make it hard to pay attention, and this often becomes a lifelong problem (Barkley, 2006).

Especially for Health Workers Parents ask that some medication be prescribed for their kindergarten child, who they say is much too active for them to handle. How do you respond?

About 5 percent of U.S. children are diagnosed with ADHD (more boys than girls, more European Americans than Latinos). One such child was Billy, the 8-year-old already described, who ran to the window when he was supposed to stay seated and who blurted out the answers without waiting to be called on. Children with ADHD often think they are being punished unfairly. Remember that Billy complained: "*I* knew that!", "I didn't do anything!", and finally "I'll sue you."

Often, other disorders are comorbid with ADHD (Barkley, 2006). (**Comorbidity** means the presence of two or more unrelated disease conditions at the same time in the same person.) Some comorbid conditions, such as delinquency, may be consequences of untreated ADHD, but many predate it and may have the same underlying cause. Among these conditions are "conduct disorder, depression, anxiety, Tourette syndrome, dyslexia, and bipolar disorder, . . . autism and schizophrenia" (Pennington, 2002, p. 163).

comorbidity The presence of two or more unrelated disease conditions at the same time in the same person.

The most effective treatment for ADHD is usually medication plus psychotherapy, with training for parents and teachers (Abikoff & Hechtman, 2005). Curiously, many drugs that are stimulants for adults, including amphetamines (e.g., Adderall) and methylphenidate (Ritalin), calm down children with ADHD. Prescribing drugs for children is controversial, with some fearing overdosing while others argue that refusing to prescribe drugs for ADD is akin to withholding insulin from a diabetic. The following feature details the ongoing debate.

thinking like a scientist

Overdosing and Underdosing

In the United States, more than 2 million children and adolescents under age 18 take prescription drugs to regulate their emotions and behavior. This rate doubled between 1987 and 1996 (Brown, 2003; Zito et al., 2003). It has leveled off in recent years but remains high, with 1 in 20 children aged 6 to 12 taking stimulants (usually for ADHD) (Zuvekas et al., 2006).

The most commonly prescribed drug is Ritalin, but at least 20 other psychoactive drugs, including Prozac, Zoloft, and Paxil, are being used to treat children as young as 2 for depression, anxiety, and many other conditions (Gorski, 2002). Few of these substances have been studied with children, who might respond better with higher or lower doses than those given to adults (Brown, 2003).

Many people fear that drugs are prescribed too early and too often. One writer contends:

> Squirming in a seat and talking out of turn are not "symptoms" and do not reflect a syndrome. [Such behaviors may be] caused by anything from normal childhood energy to boring classrooms or overstressed parents and teachers. We should not suppress these behaviors with drugs.
>
> *[Breggin & Baughman, 2001, p. 595]*

Almost all child psychologists agree that drugs are both underused and overused in treating children with ADHD (Angold et al., 2000; Brown, 2003). Some children who would benefit are never given medication; other children are given more medication than they need. Dosage is a particular concern, because children's weight and metabolism change continuously, so that a dose that is right at age 5 might be too low at age 10. Further, overdosage could be especially problematic when brains and bodies are still developing.

We all have opinions about drugs: Some of us are suspicious of anything that is not natural; others believe that medication can cure almost anything. Thinking like a scientist requires looking at evidence, not being swayed by preconceived ideas. Of course, it is impossible to be entirely objective, but many researchers, doctors, and parents try to consider the particular needs of each child rather than acting on general principles.

One group of researchers, seeking to find out whether drugs helped children with ADHD, began with small doses that were gradually increased until behavior improved as much as possible without side effects. After several weeks at that optimal dose, the children were given a placebo for a week. The children, parents, and teachers knew that this might occur but did not know when. Without the medication, the children's ability to function deteriorated rapidly, according to all observers. That convinced the scientists that the medication was effective (Hechtman et al., 2005).

Might childhood drug treatment for psychological problems (whether or not the origin is in the brain) have long-term consequences? This is a common fear. A particular concern is that such children will become drug dependent and will abuse chemical substances as adolescents. However, longitudinal research comparing nonmedicated and medicated children with ADHD finds the opposite: Childhood medication reduces the risk of adolescent drug abuse (Faraone & Wilens, 2003).

Far fewer children are diagnosed with ADHD in Europe than in North America. In the United States, rates of medication are highest among boys from low-income, non-Hispanic, southern households (see Table 11.1) (Martin & Leslie, 2003; Rowland et al., 2002; Witt et al., 2003; Zito et al., 2003). To a scientist, these differences suggest that culture and setting, not just biochemistry, influence diagnosis and treatment. Might girls in Kansas or London be underdiagnosed or English-speaking boys in Mississippi be overdiagnosed? Is prejudice at work here?

A British writer suggests that the diagnosis of ADHD is a way for low-income families to get more public money, part of the "madhouse of modern Britain, where families of badly behaved children are rewarded by the state" (McKinstry, 2005). Such an opinion obviously reflects bias more than science, but it indicates the need for public understanding.

Thinking like a scientist means asking questions. For each child, exactly what genetic or environmental conditions foster ADHD and what intervention is best (not just drugs, but which drug at what dose; not just family, but which child-rearing practices and family structures; not just school, but which teacher and placement)? Literally thousands of scientists in dozens of nations are seeking answers.

Ritalin was prescribed for Billy, and his parents and teacher were taught how to help him. He "improved considerably," becoming able not only to stay in his seat and complete his schoolwork but also to make friends (Gorenstein & Comer, 2002).

TABLE 11.1

Rates of Diagnosis and Medication for ADHD

	Percent Diagnosed with ADHD	Percent of Those Diagnosed Taking Medication for ADHD
Girls	4.7	63
Boys	14.8	73
1st and 2nd grades	7.4	70
3rd, 4th, and 5th grades	12.2	72
Non-Hispanic White	10.8	76
Non-Hispanic Black	9.1	56
Hispanic	4.0	53

Source: Rowland et al., 2002.

Learning Disabilities

Many people have some specific **learning disability** that leads to difficulty mastering a particular skill that most other people acquire easily. If Gardner's theory of multiple intelligences is correct, almost everyone has a learning disability. Perhaps one person is clumsy (low on kinesthetic intelligence), while another sings off key (low in musical intelligence).

A learning disability becomes problematic when the child falls markedly behind in some aspect of school curriculum, despite the best efforts of the child and the teacher. The child may have an average or above-average IQ but "scattered" scores on subtests, with some high and others low. The child may seem less capable in some areas than in others.

Learning disabilities do *not* usually result in lifelong impediments. Children typically find ways to compensate; they learn effective strategies to work around their deficiency. As an adult, such a child may function well. This seems to have been true of Winston Churchill, Albert Einstein, and Hans Christian Andersen, all of whom probably had learning disabilities as children. Or an adult may feel inferior, afraid to do many things, because of childhood disability.

LAURA DWIGHT

learning disability A marked delay in a particular area of learning that is not caused by an apparent physical disability, by mental retardation, or by an unusually stressful home environment.

Is She Dyslexic? No. Some young readers have difficulty "tracking" a line of print with their eyes alone. Using a finger to stay on track can be a useful temporary aid.

One common learning disability is **dyslexia,** which refers to unusual difficulty with reading. No single test accurately diagnoses dyslexia (or any other learning disability), because every academic achievement includes many skills (Sofie & Riccio, 2002). A child with a reading disability might have trouble sounding out words but excel in other reading skills, such as comprehension and memory of printed text. Thus, various forms of dyslexia have been identified.

Poor listening skills are often at the root of dyslexia. Early theories of dyslexia hypothesized that visual difficulties—e.g., reversals of letters (reading *was* instead of *saw*) and mirror writing (*b* instead of *d*)—were the origin, but in fact dyslexia originates with speech and hearing problems (Pennington, 2002). An early warning occurs if a 3-year-old does not talk clearly and does not experience a language explosion. Early speech therapy might not only improve talking but also reduce or prevent later reading problems.

dyslexia Unusual difficulty with reading; thought to be the result of some neurological underdevelopment.

➤Response for Health Workers (from page 297): Medication helps some hyperactive children, but not all. It might be useful for this child, but other forms of intervention should be tried first. Compliment the parents on their concern about their child, but refer them to an expert in early childhood for an evaluation and recommendations. Behavior-management techniques geared to the particular situation, not medication, will be the first strategy.

Autistic Spectrum Disorders

Autism is a disorder characterized by woefully inadequate social skills. Two decades ago, it was considered a single, rare disorder affecting fewer than one in a thousand children, who experienced "an extreme aloneness that, whenever possible, disregards, ignores, shuts out anything . . . from the outside" (Kanner, 1943). Children who developed slowly but were not so withdrawn were diagnosed as being mentally retarded or as having a "pervasive developmental disorder." Now such children are usually said to have an **autistic spectrum disorder,** which characterizes about 1 in every 150 8-year-olds (three times as many boys as girls) in the United States (MMWR, February 9, 2007).

There are three signs of an autistic spectrum disorder: delayed language, impaired social responses, and unusual play. Underlying all three is a kind of emotional blindness (Scambler et al., 2007). Children with any form of autism

autism A developmental disorder marked by an inability to relate to other people normally, extreme self-absorption, and an inability to acquire normal speech.

autistic spectrum disorder Any of several disorders characterized by inadequate social skills, impaired communication, and abnormal play.

find it difficult to understand the emotions of others. Consequently, they do not want to talk, play, or otherwise interact with anyone. The problem may be a deficit in the brain's mirror neurons (see Chapter 1; Oberman & Ramachandran, 2007) that makes them feel alien, like an "anthropologist on Mars," as one adult with autism expressed it (Sacks, 1995).

Because autistic disorders cover a wide spectrum, or range, their degree of severity varies. Some children never talk, rarely smile, and play for hours with one object (such as a spinning top or a toy train). Others, including those with **Asperger syndrome,** are called "high-functioning," which means that they are unusually intelligent in their specialized area and that their speech is close to normal. However, their social interaction is impaired. Still others are slow in all three areas (language, social interaction, play) but are not as severely impaired as are children with classic autism.

Asperger syndrome A specific type of autistic spectrum disorder characterized by extreme attention to details and deficient social understanding.

Some children with autistic characteristics show signs in early infancy (no social smile, for example) and continue to resist social contact. Others improve by age 3 (Chawarska et al., 2007). Still others (about a fourth) start out developing normally and then deteriorate (MMWR, February 9, 2007). The most dramatic example of the latter pattern occurs in girls with Rhett syndrome. They seem normal at first, but their brains develop very slowly and are much smaller than those of other children the same age (Bienvenu, 2005).

In other children with autism, the problem may be too much neurological activity, not too little. Their heads are large, and parts of the brain (especially the limbic system) are unusually sensitive to noise, light, and other sensations (Schumann et al., 2004). The effect was described by Temple Grandin, a woman with autism:

> Every time you take the kid into Wal-Mart, he's screaming. Well, the reason for that is that the fluorescent lights are flickering and driving him crazy, the noise in there hurts his ears, the smells overpower his nose. Wal-Mart is like being inside the speaker at a rock and roll concert.
>
> *[Medscape Psychiatry and Mental Health, 2005]*

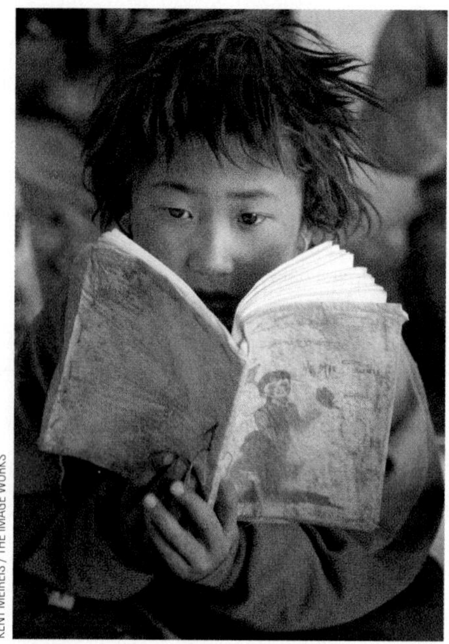

KENT MEIREIS / THE IMAGE WORKS

Culture Clash This Tibetan boy attends a Chinese school. Chinese is very difficult to learn to read, especially if it is not one's native language. He may indeed have learned to decode the printed symbols—or he may have learned to fake it.

ALAN CAREY / THE IMAGE WORKS

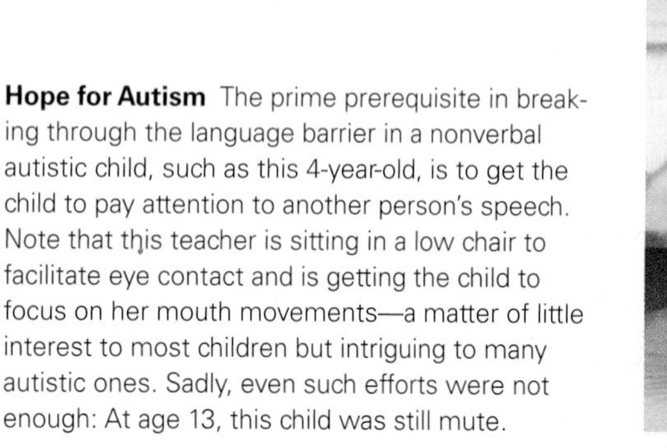

Hope for Autism The prime prerequisite in breaking through the language barrier in a nonverbal autistic child, such as this 4-year-old, is to get the child to pay attention to another person's speech. Note that this teacher is sitting in a low chair to facilitate eye contact and is getting the child to focus on her mouth movements—a matter of little interest to most children but intriguing to many autistic ones. Sadly, even such efforts were not enough: At age 13, this child was still mute.

The incidence of autistic spectrum disorders may have tripled during the 1990s, as reported in California, Minnesota, and other areas. Certainly the number of children receiving special educational services because of autistic disorders has increased dramatically (Newschaffer et al., 2005).

This increase may reflect an expanded definition of the condition, earlier diagnosis, and availability of special education (before 1980, children diagnosed as autistic were not provided special education in the United States) (Gurney et al., 2003; Parsell, 2004). This hypothesis received support from a detailed study in Texas, showing that, over a six-year period, the number of children with autism tripled in the wealthiest school districts but did not change in the poorest districts (with fewer specialists) (Palmer et al., 2005; see Research Design).

Another possibility is that some new teratogen is harming many embryonic or infant brains. One suspect was thimerosal, an antiseptic containing mercury that is used in childhood immunizations. Many parents of autistic children first noticed their infants' impairments after their MMR (measles-mumps-rubella) vaccinations (Dales et al., 2001).

This immunization hypothesis has been disproven. Of all 500,000 children born in Denmark from 1991 to 1998, about a fifth never received MMR vaccinations. They were just as likely to be diagnosed with autistic spectrum disorders as those who were vaccinated (Madsen et al., 2002). Further, thimerosal was removed from vaccines a decade ago, but the rates of autism are still rising.

Many other substances (pesticides, cleaning chemicals, some of the ingredients in nail polish) remain to be tested. Problems with risk analysis (explained in Chapter 4) are evident in this research, as in all research in developmental psychopathology. Scientists are not sure exactly why some children have autistic spectrum disorders, nor why symptoms vary.

It is known, however, that the original cause of autistic spectrum disorders is biological (genes, stress, perhaps chemicals). But treatment that relieves symptoms of autism involves early education. Each core symptom (problems with language, social connections, and play) has been a focus of treatment.

In programs that emphasize language, one-on-one training with teachers and parents helps children learn to communicate. Usually, this training involves applied behavior analysis, with data collection and intervention that reinforces each step in the right direction, a method developed from behavioral theory (Wolery et al., 2005). Other programs emphasize play (Greenspan & Wieder, 2006), as with Jacob in Chapter 7. Remember that when Jacob's parents learned to play with him, his language abilities improved dramatically.

Still other programs stress attachment (Beppu, 2005). Achieving even stronger parent–child bonds of attachment is a goal favored in Japan, where "successful diagnosis of high-functioning autism and Asperger syndrome has resulted in high detection rates" (p. 204). In one program, a 6-year-old boy with autism noticed his older brother pouring water and tried to take a turn. "When his mother praised him, [the boy] looked back at his mother with a smile and poured his water even more eagerly" (p. 211). According to this therapist, the boy's smile and pride were signs that he was aware of social praise and formed an attachment by connecting with his mother.

Research Design

Scientists: Raymond Palmer, Stephen Blanchard, and David Mandall designed the study, and C. R. Jean provided critical interpretation.

Publication: *American Journal of Public Health,* (2005).

Participants: All 1,040 school districts in Texas over six school years, 1994 to 2001.

Design: The school districts were sorted into tenths according to their resources: income, salaries, community wealth, proportion of disadvantaged students and so on. Within each tenth, the number of students designated as autistic was tallied each year.

Major conclusion: Increases in rate of students with autistic spectrum disorders correlated with wealth, from an increase of 300 percent in districts in the top two-tenths to no change in the bottom tenth. For every 10,000 children, 21 in the top districts and 3 in the bottom districts were designated as having autism.

Comment: These findings, covering an entire state, suggest that increases in the incidence of autism are caused by better diagnosis, greater availability of special education, and perhaps parental insistence on diagnosis and treatment.

Educating Children with Special Needs

For all children with special needs, individualized instruction before age 6 can help them develop better learning strategies (Berninger & Richards, 2002; Silver & Hagin, 2002). Even children with severe symptoms of autism can be helped, although few ever learn to function normally (Ben-Itzchak & Zachor, 2007). For

TABLE 11.2

Laws Regarding Special Education in the United States*

PL (Public Law) 91-230: Children with Specific Learning Disabilities Act, 1969

Recognized learning disabilities as a category within special education. Before 1969, learning-disabled children received no special education or services.

PL 94-142: Education of All Handicapped Children Act, 1975

Mandated education of all school-age children, no matter what disability they might have, in the *least restrictive environment (LRE)*—which meant with other children in a regular classroom, if possible. Fewer children were placed in special, self-contained classes, and even fewer in special schools. This law required an *individual education plan (IEP)* for each child with special needs, specifying educational goals and periodic reassessment.

PL 105-17: Individuals with Disabilities Education Act [IDEA], 1990; updated 1997 and 2004

Refers to "individuals," not children (to include education of infants, toddlers, adults), and to "disabilities," not handicaps. Emphasizes parents' rights in placement and IEP.

*Other nations have quite different laws and practices, and states and school districts within the United States vary in interpretation and practice. Consult local support groups, authorities, and legal experts, if necessary.

all disorders, psychologists advocate "preventive intervention rather than waiting to intervene when language and learning problems begin to cast a long and wide shadow" (Plomin, 2002, p. 59).

Although the underlying physiological roots of childhood disorders are probably the same everywhere, the education of children with special needs during the school years varies dramatically. Most children with special needs are first spotted by a teacher (not a parent or pediatrician), who makes a *referral,* a request for evaluation. Then other professionals observe and test the child. If they agree that the child has special needs, they discuss an **individual education plan (IEP)** with the parent (see Table 11.2). Some parents want such specialized help; others dread the social consequences of special education for their child.

individual education plan (IEP) A document that specifies educational goals and plans for a child with special needs.

Before 1960, most children with special needs simply left school—they either dropped out or were forced out. Some were never even accepted to any school at all. That changed in the United States with a 1969 law that required that all children be educated. At first, children with special needs were placed together, but neither their social skills nor their academic achievement advanced.

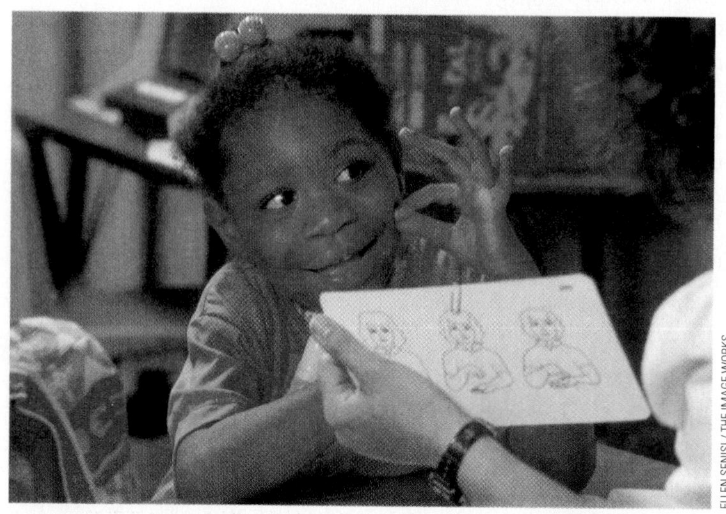

ELLEN SENISI / THE IMAGE WORKS

She Knows the Answer Physical disabilities often mushroom into additional emotional and cognitive problems. However, a disability can be reduced to a minor complication if it is recognized and if appropriate compensation or remediation is made a part of the child's education. As she signs her answer, this deaf girl shows by her expression that she is ready to learn.

LAURA DWIGHT

Every Child Is Special One reason for a school policy of inclusion is to teach children to accept and appreciate children who have special needs. The girl with Down syndrome (in yellow) benefits from learning alongside her classmates, as they learn from her. An effective teacher treats every child as a special individual.

In response, a 1975 U.S. law called the *Education of All Handicapped Children Act* mandated that children with special needs must learn in the **least restrictive environment (LRE).** Often that meant educating them with children in the regular class, a policy called *mainstreaming*.

least restrictive environment (LRE) A legal requirement that children with special needs be assigned to the most general educational context in which they can be expected to learn.

Some schools set aside a **resource room,** where mainstreamed children with special needs spent time with a teacher who worked individually with them. However, pulling children out of the regular classroom so that they could spend time in the resource room sometimes undermined their friendships and learning.

resource room A room in which trained teachers help children with special needs, using specialized curricula and equipment.

Another approach, **inclusion,** seemed wiser. Children with special needs were "included" in the general classroom, with "appropriate aids and services" (special help from a trained teacher who worked with the regular teacher).

inclusion An approach to educating children with special needs in which they are included in regular classrooms, with "appropriate aids and services," as required by law.

In theory, parents decide what education their children receive. This is not always the case, however, partly because experts, teachers, and parents often disagree about the goals and practices of special education (Connor & Ferri, 2007; Rogers, 2007). Currently, children with special needs typically have fewer friends and learn less than other children, no matter what placement they are given (Wiener & Schneider, 2002).

Compared with the United States, most other nations recognize fewer children with special needs and have fewer laws and specialized teachers for helping those children. It is not clear whether singling them out for special education is better or worse for children with special needs.

SUMMING UP

Many children have special learning needs that originate in their brain development. Developmental psychopathologists emphasize that no one is typical in every way; the passage of time sometimes brings improvement and sometimes not. People with attention-deficit disorders, learning disabilities, and autistic spectrum disorders may function adequately or may have lifelong problems, depending on severity, family, school, and culture as well as on comorbid conditions. Specifics of diagnosis, prognosis, medication, and education are debatable; no child learns or behaves exactly like another. ■

SUMMARY

A Healthy Time

1. Middle childhood is a time of steady growth and few serious illnesses. Increasing independence and self-care allow most school-age children to be relatively happy and competent.

2. Childhood obesity is becoming a worldwide epidemic. Although genetics plays a role in body weight, less exercise and the greater availability of unhealthy food are also culprits. Many adults, including parents, have not fully recognized this problem, which allows contempory children to be heavier than children a generation ago.

3. Physical activity not only retards obesity, it aids health and joy in many ways. Current environmental conditions make child play increasingly scarce.

4. Most other health problems are less common than they were 30 years ago, but the incidence of asthma is increasing. Although the origins of asthma are genetic and the triggers are specific allergens, effective primary prevention involves extending the breast-feeding period, making sure children get more outdoor play, and reducing air pollution.

Brain Development

5. Brain development continues during middle childhood, enhancing every aspect of development. Myelination increases, speeding communication between neurons. The prefrontal cortex and the corpus callosum continue to mature, allowing not only analysis and planning but also selective attention and automatization.

6. IQ tests are designed to quantify intellectual aptitude. Most such tests emphasize language and logical ability and predict school achievement. IQ tests also reflect the culture in which they were created.

7. Achievement tests measure what a person has actually accomplished. Most standard achievement tests measure academic learning. Sometimes measuring adaptation to daily life is crucial, especially in diagnosing mental retardation.

8. Critics contend that intelligence is actually manifested in multiple ways, which conventional IQ tests are too limited to measure. The concept of multiple intelligences recognizes creative and practical abilities, some of which are difficult to test.

Children with Special Needs

9. Developmental psychopathology uses an understanding of normal development to inform the study of unusual development. Four general lessons have emerged: Abnormality is normal; disability changes over time; adolescence and adulthood may make a condition better or worse; and diagnosis depends on context. Every disability has a physical and psychic component.

10. Children with attention-deficit/hyperactivity disorder (ADHD) have potential problems in three areas: inattention, impulsiveness, and overactivity. The treatment for attention deficits is a combination of medication, home management, and education. Stimulant medication often helps children with ADHD to learn, but the dosage must be carefully monitored.

11. Some young children with obvious educational or psychological disabilities are recognized, referred, evaluated, diagnosed, and treated in early childhood. For the most part, however, behavioral or learning problems are not spotted until children enter elementary school and are compared with other children in a setting that demands maturity and learning.

12. Children with autistic spectrum disorders typically show odd and delayed language ability, impaired interpersonal skills, and unusual play. Several specific disorders, including Asperger syndrome and Rhett syndrome, fall under this category. Autism may improve with intensive early education but never disappears.

13. People with learning disabilities have unusual difficulty in mastering a specific skill that other people learn easily. The most common learning disability that manifests itself during the school years is dyslexia, unusual difficulty with reading. Children with learning disabilities can be helped if the problem is spotted early and if the assistance is individualized to suit the particular child.

14. About 10 percent of all school-age children in the United States receive special education services. These services begin with an IEP (individual education plan) and assignment to the least restrictive environment.

15. Inclusion of children with special needs into regular education may aid the social skills of all children. However, inclusion does not meet every child's needs.

KEY TERMS

middle childhood (p. 283)
overweight (p. 284)
obesity (p. 284)
asthma (p. 288)
reaction time (p. 290)
selective attention (p. 290)
automatization (p. 291)
aptitude (p. 292)
IQ tests (p. 292)
achievement tests (p. 292)
Flynn Effect (p. 292)
Wechsler Intelligence Scale for Children (WISC) (p. 293)
mental retardation (p. 293)
children with special needs (p. 295)
developmental psychopathology (p. 296)
Diagnostic and Statistical Manual of Mental Disorders (DSM-IV-R) (p. 296)
attention-deficit/hyperactivity disorder (ADHD) (p. 297)
comorbidity (p. 297)
learning disability (p. 299)
dyslexia (p. 299)
autism (p. 299)
autistic spectrum disorder (p. 299)
Asperger syndrome (p. 300)
individual education plan (IEP) (p. 302)
least restrictive environment (LRE) (p. 303)
resource room (p. 303)
inclusion (p. 303)

KEY QUESTIONS

1. How does the growth of the school-age child compare with the growth of the younger child?

2. What are the main reasons for the recent increase in childhood obesity?

3. What measures to reduce asthma would also benefit all other children?

4. How does reaction time affect a child's ability to learn and behave?

5. What are some good uses of intelligence tests?

6. What are some misuses of intelligence tests?

7. Why was the field of developmental psychopathology created?

8. Why might parents decide to ask a doctor to prescribe Ritalin for their child?

9. What are the signs of autistic spectrum disorders?

10. How could it happen that an adult might have a learning disability that was never spotted?

APPLICATIONS

1. Compare play spaces for children in different neighborhoods—ideally, urban, suburban, and rural areas. Note size, safety, and use. How might children's weight and motor skills be affected?

2. Developmental psychologists believe that every teacher should be skilled at teaching children with a wide variety of needs. Does the teacher-training curriculum at your college or university reflect this goal? Should all teachers take the same courses, or should some teachers be specialized? Give reasons for your opinions.

3. Internet sources vary in quality, no matter what the topic, but this may be particularly true of Web sites designed for parents of children with special needs. Pick one childhood disability or disease and find several information sources on the Internet devoted to that condition. How might parents evaluate the information provided?

4. Special education teachers are in great demand. In your local public schools, what is the ratio of regular to special education teachers? How many are in self-contained classrooms, resource rooms, and inclusion classrooms? What does your data reveal about the education of children with special needs in your community?

12

CHAPTER OUTLINE

The School Years: Cognitive Development

School-age children are learners. As long as it's not too abstract, they can learn almost anything: how to divide fractions, when to surf the Web, what to feed an orphaned kitten, and much more. Each day advances knowledge a tiny bit.

Time matters, but the depth and content of learning reflect motivation more than maturation—motivation guided by cultural priorities and channeled by brain networks. Thus, nurture and nature interact to allow each child's mind to develop. Every school-age child is primed to learn, and adults everywhere are eager to teach.

In the United States, concerns that children were not learning enough led to a federal law called *No Child Left Behind,* which was passed in 2001 and is scheduled for revision and renewal in 2007. Meanwhile, the people of Japan worried that their children felt too much academic pressure, so their government in 2002 began *yutori kyoiku,* which means "more relaxed education." Both these policies, and many other ideas about education, are described later in this chapter.

First, however, we describe theories and research on cognitive development during the school years. By the time you finish this chapter, you will understand what school-age children might learn and why adults argue about it.

Building on Theory

Every theory, as Chapter 2 stressed, is practical. The dominant theories of cognition in school-age children, as expressed by Jean Piaget, Lev Vygotsky, and information-processing theorists, have been used to structure education.

Piaget and School-Age Children

In Piaget's view, the most important cognitive structure attained in middle childhood is called **concrete operational thought,** characterized by a collection of concepts that enable children to reason.

Piaget thought that many logical concepts are almost impossible for younger children to comprehend but that children begin to understand them sometime between ages 5 and 7 (Inhelder & Piaget, 1964). Soon they apply logic in *concrete* situations—that is, situations that deal with visible, tangible, real things. Children thereby become more systematic, objective, scientific—and educable—thinkers.

concrete operational thought Piaget's term for the ability to reason logically about direct experiences and perceptions.

An Example: Classification

classification The logical principle that things can be organized into groups (or categories or classes) according to some characteristic they have in common.

One crucial logical concept is **classification,** the organization of things into groups (or *categories* or *classes*) according to some property that they have in common. For example, a child's parents and siblings are classified as belonging to a group called family. Other common classes are people, animals, food, and toys. Each class includes some elements and excludes others, and each is part of a hierarchy. Food, for instance, contains the subclasses of meat, grains, fruits, and so on.

Most subclasses can be further divided: Meat includes poultry, beef, and pork, which again can be further subdivided. It is apparent to adults who have mastered classification, but not always to children, that items at the bottom of the hierarchy belong to every higher category (bacon is always pork, meat, and food) but that the process does not work in reverse (most foods are not bacon).

Piaget developed many experiments to reveal children's understanding of classification. For example, an examiner shows a child a bunch of nine flowers—seven yellow daisies and two white roses (revised and published in Piaget et al., 2001). The examiner makes sure the child understands "flowers," "daisies," and "roses." Then comes the crucial question: "Are there more daisies or more flowers?" Until about age 7, most children say, "More daisies." Pushed to justify their answer, the youngest children usually have no explanation, but some 6- or 7-year-olds say that there are more yellow ones than white ones or that, because the daisies are daisies, they aren't flowers (Piaget et al., 2001). By age 8, most children have a solid understanding of the classification of objects they can see (concrete objects, not yet hypothetical ones) and they confidently answer, "More flowers than daisies."

VEER

After "Gee Whiz!" After he sees the magnified image that his classmate expects will amaze him, will he analyze his observations? Ideally, concrete operational thought enables children to use their new logic to interpret their experiences.

The Significance of Logic

What do Piaget's classification experiments mean? Despite Piaget's interpretation, they do *not* prove a dramatic logical shift between preoperational and concrete operational thought. Other research finds that classification appears before middle childhood (Halford & Andrews, 2006). Even infants seem to have brain networks ready to categorize what they see (Quinn, 2004), and 4-year-olds can judge whether a certain food is breakfast food, junk food, both, or neither (S. P. Nguyen & Murphy, 2003).

Nonetheless, Piaget's experimentation revealed something important. What develops during middle childhood is the ability to use mental categories and subcategories flexibly, inductively, and simultaneously. This is apparent with flowers and daisies or (a greater challenge) with cars, which can be transportation, toys, lethal weapons, imports, consumer products, Toyotas, SUVs, and so on. Although preschool children can categorize, older children are more precise and flexible in classification, so that they are able to separate the essential from the irrelevant (Hayes & Younger, 2004).

identity The logical principle that certain characteristics of an object remain the same even if other characteristics change.

reversibility The logical principle that a thing that has been changed can sometimes be returned to its original state by reversing the process by which it was changed.

The same flexibility is evident for other logical concepts. Remember from Chapter 9 that younger children do not understand conservation because they are swayed by appearance. School-age children grasp the concept of **identity,** the principle that objects remain the same even if some characteristics appear to shift. A ball is still a ball when it rolls into a hole; a child is the same person awake and asleep.

They also understand **reversibility,** the principle that things can return to their original state. By middle childhood, a child might prove conservation by using identity ("It's still the same milk") or by reversing the process (pouring the liquid back into the first container).

Piaget realized that school-age children gradually become more logical, less egocentric, and quite concrete in their understanding. This is evident not only in Piaget's experiments but also in research regarding math, physics, sickness, and so on (Astuti et al., 2004; C. Howe, 1998; Keil & Lockhart, 1999).

This movement away from egocentrism toward a more flexible logic was illustrated by 5- to 9-year-olds who were asked about two hypothetical boys—David, who thought chocolate ice cream was yucky, and Daniel, who found chocolate ice cream yummy. Most 5-year-olds (63 percent) thought David was wrong, and many felt he was bad or stupid as well. By contrast, virtually all (94 percent) of the 9-year-olds thought both boys could be right, and few were critical of David (Wainryb et al., 2004).

Vygotsky and School-Age Children

Vygotsky (1934/1994) also felt that educators should consider the thought processes of the child. This approach was a marked improvement over the dull "meaningless acquisition" approach of many educators, which rendered the child "helpless in the face of any sensible attempt to apply any of this acquired knowledge" (pp. 356–357), which was apparent not only in Vygotsky's home nation (Russia), but in schools worldwide.

The Role of Instruction

Unlike Piaget, who stressed the child's own discovery of important concepts, Vygotsky regarded instruction by others as crucial, with peers and teachers providing the bridge between the child's developmental potential and the necessary skills and knowledge. In each child's zone of proximal development, or almost-understood ideas, other people are crucial.

Confirmation of the role of social interaction comes from children who, because of their school's entry-date requirement, are relatively old kindergarteners or young first-graders. Learning among 5-year-old first-graders (those who were born in December, for instance) far exceeds that of 5-year-olds who are only slightly younger but who (because they were born in January) are in kindergarten.

Additional confirmation comes from the effect on children of high-quality teaching. There is a direct correlation between the percentage of qualified teachers in a school and learning, even when other factors (SES, prior achievement, neighborhood) are considered (Wayne & Youngs, 2003).

Remember that, for Vygotsky, formal education is only one of many contexts for learning. Children are apprentices as they play with each other, watch television, eat dinner with their families, and engage in other daily interactions.

In short, Vygotsky's emphasis on the sociocultural context contrasts with Piaget's more maturational approach. Vygotsky believed that cultures (tools, customs, and people) teach people. The social setting guides children in their zone of proximal development. For example, a child who is surrounded by adults who read for pleasure, by well-stocked bookcases, and by street signs is likely to read sooner than a child with little or no exposure to any of these things—even if both are in the same classroom—because the former is enticed into the zone of reading.

Especially for Teachers How might Piaget's and Vygotsky's ideas help in teaching geography to a class of third-graders?

Cultural Variations

Most research on children's cognition has been done in North America and western Europe, but the same patterns are apparent worldwide. In Zimbabwe, for example, children's understanding of classification is influenced not only by their

VICTOR RUIZ CABALLERO / AP / WIDE WORLD PHOTOS

Street Smarts Javier Garcias sells candy and cigarettes on the streets of San Salvador, the capital of El Salvador, from 5:00 A.M. until 1:00 P.M. and from 5:00 P.M. to 8:00 P.M. In between, he goes to school. That combination of work experience and formal education may add up to excellent math skills—if Javier is awake enough to learn.

age (Piaget) but also by factors related to social interactions (Vygotsky), such as the particulars of their schooling, and by their family's SES (Mpofu & van de Vijver, 2000).

The most detailed international example comes from Brazil, specifically from the street children who sell fruit, candy, and other products to earn their living. Many have never attended school and consequently score poorly on standard math achievement tests. This is no surprise to developmentalists, who have seen many examples of slower academic proficiency in children who are unschooled (Rogoff et al., 2005).

However, most young Brazilian peddlers are adept at pricing their wares, making change, and giving discounts for large quantities—a set of operations that must be recalibrated almost every day because of inflation, wholesale prices, and customer demand. These children calculate "complex markup computations and adjust for inflation in these computations by using procedures that were widespread in their practice but not known to children in school" (Saxe, 1999, p. 255).

Thus, the knowledge of advanced math that is reflected in these street children's cognitive performance comes from three sources:

- Demands of the situation
- Learning from other sellers
- Daily experience

None of this would surprise Vygotsky, who would expect that street culture would teach children what they needed to know. The researchers found that school was not completely irrelevant. The best math skills were demonstrated by children who had some schooling as well as street experience (Saxe, 1991).

Today's educators and psychologists regard both Piaget and Vygotsky as insightful theorists. Developmentalists' understanding of how children learn depends largely on "a framework that was laid down by Piaget and embellished by Vygotsky" (C. Howe, 1998, p. 207). In other words, Piaget's appreciation that children are eager learners, trying to understand the world in ways limited by their maturation, has been developed by Vygotsky. Vygotsky realized how much children learn from each other and from their teachers—as long as those mentors know what motivation and understanding the children already possess.

Information Processing

information-processing theory The view of cognition as comparable to the functioning of a computer and as best understood by analyzing each aspect of that functioning—sensory data input, connections, stored memories, and output.

An alternative approach to understanding cognition arises from **information-processing theory.** As you learned in Chapter 6, this approach takes its name from computer functioning. Computers receive and store vast quantities of information (numbers, letters, pixels, or other coded symbols) and then use software programs to process that information.

People, too, take in large amounts of information. They use mental processes to perform three functions: search for specific units of information when needed (as a search engine does); analyze (as software programs do); and express the analysis in a format that another person (or a networked computer) can interpret. By tracing the paths and links of each of these functions, scientists can better understand the mechanisms of learning. Information processing focuses on the specifics of a child learning a particular thing, not on theories but on details. It's thinking that progresses from models and hypotheses to practical demonstrations (Munakata, 2006).

Learning is particularly rapid in childhood, even without explicit adult instruction. As they search, analyze, and express information, many 7- to 11-year-olds not only soak up knowledge in school but also outscore their elders in video games, memorize the lyrics of popular songs, and recognize out-of-towners by the clothes they wear. Some children, by age 11, beat their elders at chess, play music so well that adults pay to hear them, or write poems that are published. Other children live by their wits on the street or become soldiers in civil wars, learning lessons that no child should know (Grigorenko & O'Keefe, 2004). All this is evidence of rapid acquisition of knowledge.

As with a computer, greater efficiency in learning requires more than just the storage of information within the brain. Greater efficiency requires retrieval strategies and analysis, which make 11-year-olds better thinkers than 7-year-olds, who are better thinkers than 3-year-olds. Nonetheless, as with computers, memory is crucial.

➤Response for Teachers (from page 309): Here are two of the most obvious ways. (1) Use logic. Once children can grasp classification and class inclusion, they can understand cities within states, states within nations, and nations within continents. Organize your instruction to make logical categorization easier. (2) Make use of children's need for concrete and personal involvement. You might have the children learn first about their own location, then about the places where relatives and friends live, and finally about places beyond their personal experience (via books, photographs, videos, and guest speakers).

Memory

Sensory memory (also called the *sensory register*) is the first component of the human information-processing system. It stores incoming stimuli for a split second after they are received, to allow them to be processed. To use terms first explained in Chapter 5, *sensations* are retained for a moment so that some of them can become *perceptions*. This first step of sensory awareness is already quite good in early childhood, improves slightly until about age 10, and remains adequate until late adulthood.

sensory memory The component of the information-processing system in which incoming stimulus information is stored for a split second to allow it to be processed. (Also called the *sensory register*.)

Once some sensations become perceptions, the brain selects meaningful perceptions to transfer to working memory for further analysis. It is in **working memory** (previously called *short-term memory*) that current, conscious mental activity occurs. Working memory improves steadily and significantly every year from age 4 to age 15 (Gathercole et al., 2004). For example, capacity increases, and sounds are remembered. These improvements are possible in part because of changes in the brain: increased myelination and dendrite formation in the prefrontal cortex—the massive interconnection described in Chapter 11.

working memory The component of the information-processing system in which current conscious mental activity occurs. (Also called *short-term memory*.)

Finally, some information is transferred to **long-term memory,** which stores it for minutes, hours, days, months, or years. The capacity of long-term memory—how much information can be crammed into one brain—is virtually limitless by the end of middle childhood. Together with sensory memory and working memory, long-term memory assists in organizing ideas and reactions. Crucial to the process of measuring and using long-term memory is not merely *storage* (how much material has been deposited) but also *retrieval* (how readily the material can be brought into working memory to be used). Retrieval is easier for some memories—especially memories of vivid, highly emotional experiences—than for others.

long-term memory The component of the information-processing system in which virtually limitless amounts of information can be stored indefinitely.

Especially for Teachers How might your understanding of memory help you teach a 2,000-word vocabulary list to a class of fourth-graders?

Speed and Knowledge

Having looked at the components of the information-processing system, let's look more closely at two keys to cognitive development in school-age children: greater speed and greater knowledge.

Speed of thinking continues to increase throughout the first two decades of life. Neurological maturation, including ongoing myelination, helps to account for these changes (Benes, 2001). So does experience.

Repetition (pronouncing the same word, rehearsing the same dance step, adding the same numbers) makes neurons fire in a coordinated and seemingly instantaneous sequence (Merzenich, 2001). As children repeatedly use their intellectual skills, processes that once required hard mental labor become automatic.

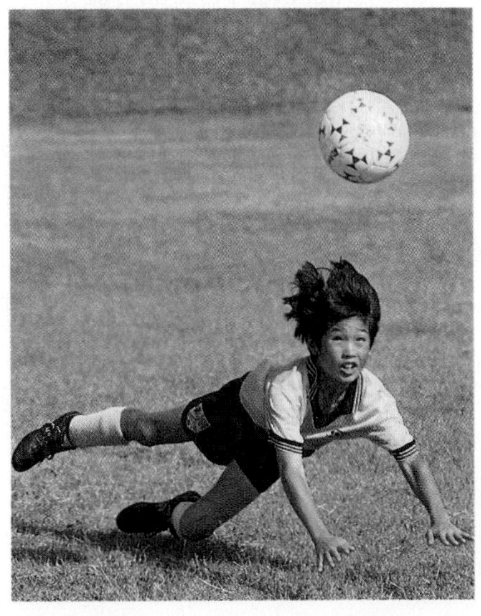

Eye on the Ball This boy's concentration while heading the ball and simultaneously preparing to fall is a sign that he has practiced this maneuver enough times that he can perform it automatically. Not having to think about what to do on the way down, he can think about what to do when he gets up, such as pursuing the ball or getting back to cover his position.

➤Response for Teachers (from page 311): Children this age can be taught strategies for remembering by making links between working memory and long-term memory. You might break down the vocabulary list into word clusters, grouped according to root words, connections to the children's existing knowledge, applications, or (as a last resort) first letters or rhymes. Active, social learning is useful; perhaps in groups the students could write a story each day that incorporates 15 new words. Each group could read its story aloud to the class.

This *automatization* (described in Chapter 11) increases processing speed, frees up memory capacity, allows more information to be remembered, and advances thinking in every way (Demetriou et al., 2002).

Progress from initial effort to automatization often takes years, making repetition and practice essential. Many children lose cognitive skills over the summer because the lack of daily schooling for a few months erases earlier academic learning (Alexander et al., 2007). Even adults who leave college for a decade feel "rusty" when they first return. The most problematic aspect of children's television watching may be that it crowds out time for reading and thus reduces achievement (Roberts & Foehr, 2004). Not until something is overlearned does it become automatic.

knowledge base A body of knowledge in a particular area that makes it easier to master new information in that area.

The more people know, the more they can learn and remember. That is, having an extensive **knowledge base,** a broad body of knowledge in a particular subject area, makes it easier to master new information in that area. Ongoing development of knowledge depends on past experience, current opportunity, and personal motivation. This is evident from millions of school-age children: Their knowledge base is far greater in some domains, and far smaller in others, than their parents or teachers would like.

A British study provides an example (Balmford et al., 2002; see Research Design). Schoolchildren were asked to identify 10 out of a random sample of 100 Pokémon creatures and 10 out of 100 types of wildlife common in the United Kingdom. As you can see in Figure 12.1, the 4- to 6-year-olds knew only about a third of the 20 items but could identify more living things than imaginary ones. In contrast, 8- to 11-year-olds recognized more Pokémon creatures than living things. A peak in Pokémon knowledge occurred at about age 9, more for boys than girls (gender breakdowns are not shown in the graph). It is easy to understand why: Third-grade boys were often intensely engaged in collecting Pokémon cards.

Research Design

Scientists: Andrew Balmford, Lizzie Clegg, Tim Coulson, and Jennie Taylor.

Publication: *Science* (2002) (a weekly journal published by the American Association for the Advancement of Science).

Participants: A total of 109 British schoolchildren, aged 4–11.

Design: Each child was asked to name 20 pictures, 10 of British wildlife (plants, mammals, invertebrates, and birds) and 10 of Pokémon characters, randomly chosen from two packs of 100. To be considered correct, the children did not have to name the genus of insect or plant (saying "beetle" was enough), but they had to do so for mammals (e.g., "badger"). Pokémon creatures had to be identified by their correct names.

Major conclusion: Children are great learners, but they do not learn much about nature. Identification increased markedly from age 4 to 8, from 32 percent to 53 percent for natural creatures, and from 7 to 78 percent for Pokémon characters.

Comment: This straightforward study is presented as a wake-up call for conservationists. The authors quote Robert Pyle: "What is the loss of a condor to a child who has never seen a wren?"

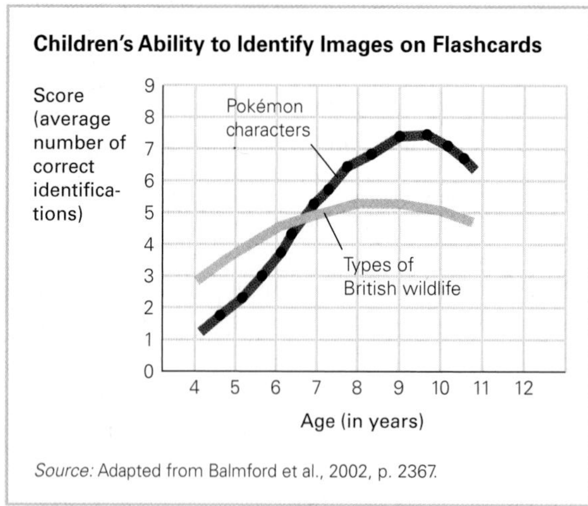

FIGURE 12.1

Knowledge of the Real and the Imaginary Every child's knowledge base expands with age, but the areas of special interest tend to shift as the child grows older. At about 8 years of age, British schoolchildren's ability to identify Pokémon characters on flashcards began to surpass their ability to identify real-life animals and plants.

Observation Quiz (see answer, page 314): What does this graph suggest about the state of wildlife conservation in the United Kingdom in the year 2020?

Control Processes

control processes Mechanisms (including selective attention, metacognition, and emotional regulation) that combine memory, processing speed, and knowledge to regulate the analysis and flow of information within the information-processing system.

The mechanisms that put memory, processing speed, and the knowledge base together are called **control processes;** they regulate the analysis and flow of information within the system. Control processes include selective attention, metacognition, and emotional regulation. They assume an executive role in the information-processing system. When someone concentrates on only the crucial part of the material bombarding the sensory memory, or summons a rule of thumb from long-term memory to working memory, or uses the knowledge base to connect new information, control processes are active. They organize, decide, and direct, as the chief executive officer of a large corporation is supposed to do.

Control processes develop spontaneously with age, but they are also taught. Sometimes this teaching is explicit. For instance, classroom instruction often includes spelling rules such as "*i* before *e* except after *c*" and helpful sentences for remembering things such as the order of the planets from the sun ("My Very Eager Mother Just Sent Us Nine Pizzas"—Mercury, Venus, Earth, Mars, Jupiter, Saturn, Uranus, Neptune, Pluto). Once children know these, they can use the same techniques to make up their own mnemonic devices (memory aids). In fact, now that Pluto is no longer considered a planet, they have an opportunity to do so.

Sometimes it is more implicit. Cultures teach children general strategies, such as whether they should learn by attending to one thing at a time, as is the expectation in North American schools, or should learn while doing other things, as some cultures (for example, in Latin America) encourage. This latter approach is not necessarily inefficient because "simultaneous attention may be important when learning relies on observation of ongoing events" (Correa-Chavez et al., 2005, p. 665).

BACHMANN / PHOTO RESEARCHERS, INC.

They've Read the Book Acting in a play based on *The Lion, the Witch, and the Wardrobe* suggests that these children have metacognitive abilities beyond those of almost any preschooler. Indeed, the book itself requires a grasp of the boundary between reality (the wardrobe) and fantasy (the witch). "Thinking about thinking" is needed in order to appreciate the allegory.

Observation Quiz (see answer, page 314): Beyond understanding the book, what are three examples of metacognition implied here? Specifically, how does the ability to memorize lines, play a part, and focus on the play illustrate metacognition?

During the school years, children develop a more comprehensive form of thinking called **metacognition,** sometimes called *thinking about thinking*. Metacognition is the ability to evaluate a cognitive task to determine how best to accomplish it and then to monitor and adjust one's performance on that task.

metacognition "Thinking about thinking," or the ability to evaluate a cognitive task to determine how best to accomplish it, and then to monitor and adjust one's performance on that task.

Marked advances in metacognition occur when children become better aware of what they know and what they need to learn. School-age children with such an awareness might, for example, test themselves to judge whether they have learned their spelling words, rather than insisting (as younger children might) that they know it all (Harter, 1999).

With the advances in metacognition come strikingly evident improvements in children's ability to store information so that retrieval is possible. The relationship is clear, for example, from an experiment in which 7- and 9-year-olds memorized two lists of 10 items each (M. L. Howe, 2004). Some children had separate lists of toys and vehicles; others had two mixed lists, with toys and vehicles combined in both. A day later, they were asked to remember one of the lists. Having had separate lists of toys and vehicles helped the 7-year-olds somewhat, compared to the 7-year-olds with mixed lists, but having organized lists was particularly beneficial for the 9-year-olds. They remembered notably more items than did other 9-year-olds whose lists had mixed toys and vehicles.

Some of these children had been explicitly told about the categories of the lists and some had not. That did not make much difference, because the 9-year-olds spontaneously noted the categories, and that helped them remember (M. L. Howe, 2004). In other words, the 9-year-olds used metacognitive skills without prompting.

The relative benefits of spontaneous use of metacognition versus instruction in memory techniques have been the focus of decades of research (Pressley & Hilden, 2006). Such research has thus looked at both discovery (inspired by Piaget) and explicit scaffolding (inspired by Vygotsky) from an information-processing perspective.

It is apparent that during the school years, children benefit from learning specific cognitive strategies in every academic subject (math, reading, writing, science),

➤Answer to Observation Quiz (from page 312): As the authors of this study observe, "People care about what they know." As their knowledge about their country's animal and plant life declines with age, these British children's concern for wildlife conservation is likely to decline, too.

especially if they are given practice over weeks and months. To use the language of computers, once a program is installed, if the operator uses it frequently and understands its application, output is faster and more accurate. That works for children, too.

SUMMING UP

Piaget and Vygotsky both recognized that school-age children are avid learners who actively build on the knowledge they already have. Piaget emphasized the child's own logical thinking, as the principles of classification, identity, and reversibility are understood during concrete operational thought. Research inspired by Vygotsky and the sociocultural perspective fills in Piaget's outline with details of the actual learning situation. Cultural differences can be powerful; specific instruction and practical experience make a difference.

An information-processing analysis highlights many components of thinking that advance during middle childhood. Although sensory memory and long-term memory do not change much during these years, the speed and efficiency of working memory improve dramatically, which makes school-age children better thinkers than they previously were. Another advantage of older children is that past learning results in a greater knowledge base.

In addition, control processes, such as selective attention and metacognition, enable children to become more strategic thinkers, able to direct their minds toward whatever they are motivated to learn and adults are motivated to teach. ■

➤Answer to Observation Quiz (from page 313): (1) Memorizing extensive passages requires an understanding of advanced memory strategies that combine meaning with form. (2) Understanding how to play a part so that other actors and the audience respond well requires a sophisticated theory of mind. (3) Staying focused on the moment in the play despite distractions from the audience requires selective attention.

Language

As you remember, many aspects of language advance rapidly before middle childhood. By age 6, children have mastered most of the basic vocabulary and grammar of their first language, and many even speak a second language. However, as we will now see, because school-age children have the abilities described in the chapter to this point (noted by Piaget, Vygotsky, and information-processing theorists), they advance in language.

Some school-age children learn as many as 20 new words a day and apply grammar rules they did not use before. These new words and applications are unlike the language explosion. Increases in logic, flexibility, memory, speed of thinking, metacognition, and connections between facts enhance the learning of a first and second language (Kagan & Herschkowitz, 2005).

Vocabulary and Pragmatics

Young children know the names of thousands of objects, and they understand many other parts of speech as well. But school-age children are more flexible and logical in their knowledge and use of vocabulary, understanding metaphors, prefixes and suffixes, and compound words.

For example, 2-year-olds know *egg,* but 10-year-olds also know *egg salad, egg-drop soup, eggless, eggplant, egghead,* and *walking on eggshells, egg on my face,* and *last one in is a rotten egg.* They understand that each of these expressions is logically connected to *egg* (benefits of the knowledge base) but is also distinct from the dozen uncooked eggs in the refrigerator. They use each expression in the appropriate contexts.

Especially for Parents You've had an exhausting day but are setting out to buy groceries. Your 7-year-old son wants to go with you. Should you explain that you are so tired that you want to make a quick solo trip to the supermarket this time?

One aspect of language that advances markedly in middle childhood is pragmatics, the practical use of language, including communication with varied audiences in different contexts. This ability is obvious to linguists when they listen to children talk informally with their friends and formally with their teachers or parents, never calling the latter a rotten egg—regardless of whether they are the last one to sit down to dinner or not.

Children are thus able to switch back and forth, depending on the audience, between different manners of speaking, or "codes." Each code includes many aspects of language—tone, pronunciation, gestures, sentence length, idioms, vocabulary, and grammar. Sometimes the switch is between formal code (used in academic contexts) and informal code (used with friends); sometimes it is between dialect or vernacular (used on the street) and standard or proper speech. Many children use a new code in text messaging, with numbers (411), abbreviations (LOL), and emoticons (☺).

During middle childhood, many children excel at pragmatics, using the appropriate code in each context. They not only adjust to their audience but can use logic to do so, applying grammatical rules when they need to. Children need help from teachers to become fluent in the formal code so that they will be able to communicate with educated adults from many places. The peer group teaches the informal code, and each local community teaches dialect and pronunciation.

RACHEL EPSTEIN / THE IMAGE WORKS

Connections Basic vocabulary is learned by age 4 or so, but the school years are best for acquiring expanded, derivative, and specialized vocabulary, especially if the child is actively connecting one word with another. With his father's encouragement, this boy in San Jose, California, will remember *Jupiter, Mars,* and the names of the other planets and maybe even *orbit, light-years,* and *solar system.*

Second-Language Learning

The most obvious need for school-age children to use various codes pragmatically occurs when children speak one language at home and another at school. Almost every nation's population includes many children who speak a minority language, and most of the world's 6,000 languages are never used in school. Consequently, about a billion children are educated in a language other than their mother tongue (John-Steiner et al., 1994). Many will lose fluency in their first language. It is estimated that at least 5,000 languages will die by 2050 (May, 2005).

In the United States, 4 million students (10 percent of the school population) are **English-language learners (ELLs)** (formerly called LEP, limited English proficiency) and thus do not yet speak English well. Many live with their co-linguists in California, Texas, New York, New Jersey, and Florida, while others are surrounded by people who cannot converse with them. Many public school classes (43 percent) have at least one ELL student (Zehler et al., 2003).

English-language learner (ELL) A child who is learning English as a second language.

Middle childhood is a good time for learning a second language. As explained earlier, children aged 7 to 11 are eager to communicate, are logical, and have an ear (and brain) for nuances of code and pronunciation. Experience in Canada, in Israel, and in many other nations proves that most children can become fluent in two languages before puberty (DeKeyser & Larson-Hall, 2005).

In the United States, as in many other countries, some students learning the majority language in school have a first language that is relatively close to it, while others have a quite different first language. Those who already read and write Spanish, French, or another Romance language have a foundation for learning English, since the letters, many sounds, and some words are similar. If their teachers show them how to sound out letters and recognize words that are cognates, they grasp English more quickly (Carlo et al., 2004). Children whose first language uses different symbols and has a markedly different sound system, as is the case, for example, with Arabic and Asian languages, have a harder time (Snow & Kang, 2006).

Many American children, most notably from Asian American backgrounds, make a *language shift,* replacing their original language with English rather than becoming fluent in both languages (Tse, 2001). Partly to avoid this, many Asian communities provide "heritage" language classes after school or on Saturdays. In the 1990s in the Los Angeles area, there were 80 Chinese heritage schools with

➤Response for Parents (from page 314): Your son would understand your explanation, but you should take him along if you can do so without losing patience with him. Any excursion can be a learning opportunity. You wouldn't ignore his need for food or medicine; don't ignore his need for learning. While shopping, you can teach vocabulary (does he know *pimientos, pepperoni, polenta?*), categories ("root vegetables," "freshwater fish"), and math (which size box of cereal is cheaper?). Explain in advance that you need him to help you find items and carry them and that he can choose only one item that you wouldn't normally buy. Seven-year-olds can understand rules, and they enjoy being helpful.

15,000 pupils. Despite such classes, many Asian American children lose their original language (Liu, 2006). This is unfortunate, not only because fluently bilingual adults are needed but also because language is intimately connected to values and emotions, and parents and others fear language loss may represent a loss of culture. Immigrant parents want their children to maintain their culture even as they want their children to succeed.

Bilingual speakers are aware of the connection between language and emotion, and they choose how to say what to whom (Myers-Scotton & Bolonyai, 2001). Things learned in English are more readily remembered in English, and things learned in the original language are remembered better in that language (Marian & Fausey, 2006).

Many educators fear that immigrant children may suffer if they are expected to relinquish their first language.

> Challenges of adaptation to a new language and culture for child migrants are reflected in data about their academic achievement. Language minority children are at demonstrably greater risk than native speakers of experiencing academic difficulty . . . in the United States, . . . in the Netherlands, . . . in Great Britain, . . . and in Japan.
>
> *[Snow & Kang, 2006, p. 76]*

Experts agree that all children should learn to speak and write in the majority language while not losing their native tongue, and that those children who already speak the majority language should learn a second language, ideally before puberty. Experts do not agree on the best way to reach these goals. Political controversies have made objective research difficult; no single approach has been proven to be best for all children in all contexts (Bialystok, 2001; Hinkel, 2005; Snow & Kang, 2006).

total immersion A strategy in which instruction in all school subjects occurs in the second (majority) language that a child is learning.

bilingual education A strategy in which school subjects are taught in both the learner's original language and the second (majority) language.

ESL (English as a second language) An approach to teaching English in which all children who do not speak English are placed together and given an intensive course in basic English so that they can be educated in the same classroom as native English speakers.

Approaches range from **total immersion,** in which instruction in all school subjects occurs entirely in the second (majority) language, to the opposite approach, in which children learn in their first language until the second language can be taught as a "foreign" tongue. Variations between these extremes include **bilingual education,** with instruction in two languages, and, in North America, **ESL (English as a second language),** programs in which ELL children are taught intensively and exclusively in English to prepare them for regular classes.

The success of any of these methods seems to depend on the literacy of the home (the specific language used at home matters less than the frequency of reading, writing, and listening), the warmth and skill of the teacher, and the overall cultural context. Any method tends to fail if children feel shy, stupid, or lonely because of their language.

Second-language learning remains controversial in the United States, even among immigrants who do not speak English. Cognitive research leaves no doubt that school-age children *can* learn a second language if it is taught logically, step by step, and they *can* maintain their original language. The best strategies included a language-rich environment (at home and school), with ample reading, writing, and speaking instruction.

The likelihood of parents, school, and culture encouraging bilingualism in children is affected by the socioeconomic status of the family and of the minority group. This is one explanation for the experience of Korean immigrant children, who usually have more success at learning English in the United States than the typical immigrant child but do much worse in Japan (where they often are at the bottom of the economic ladder). An overview finds that "language teaching has always been susceptible to political and social influences" (Byram & Feng, 2005, p. 926). Let's take a closer look at the role of SES in language learning.

issues and applications

SES and Language Learning

Decades of research throughout the world have found a powerful connection between language development and socioeconomic status (Plank & MacIver, 2003). Compared with their peers, children from low-SES families tend to fall behind in talking, then in reading, and then in other subjects. Not only do children from low-income families have smaller vocabularies, but their grammar is simpler (fewer compound sentences, dependent clauses, and conditional verbs) and their sentences are shorter (Hart & Risley, 1995; Hoff, 2003).

The information-processing perspective forces us to look at specifics of daily input that might affect the child's brain and thus the child's ability to learn language. Possibilities abound—lead in house paint, inadequate prenatal care, lack of a nourishing breakfast, overcrowded household, too few books at home, teenage parenthood, authoritarian child rearing . . . the list could go on and on. All of these correlate with low SES, but no one of them has been proven to be in itself a major cause of poor language learning.

There are two factors, however, that *do* appear to play an important role in the connection between low SES and poor language learning. One is extent of early exposure to language. Unlike parents with higher education, many less educated parents tend not to speak extensively or elaborately with their children. The reasons correlate with low income (financial stress, not enough time for each child, neighborhood noise) but are not caused by it. In one study, researchers observed young children at home for three years, recording an average of 30 hours of talk per family. Children in high-SES families heard about 2,000 words an hour, while children in low-SES families heard only about 600 words per hour (Hart & Risley, 1995). Many studies have found a "powerful linkage" between adult linguistic input and later child output (Weizman & Snow, 2001, p. 276). Remember that dendrites in the brain grow to accommodate the child's experiences, including experience with language.

A second factor is expectation. Many people believe that teachers' and parents' expectations are the reason some children master language quickly while others do not, and SES may affect expectations. Expectations can, of course, make a positive difference. For example, E. P. Jones, who won the 2004 Pulitzer Prize for his novel *The Known World* (E. P. Jones, 2003), grew up in a very poor family, headed by a single mother who was illiterate. Jones writes:

> For as many Sundays as I can remember, perhaps even Sundays when I was in the womb, my mother has pointed across "I" street to Seaton [school] as we come and go to Mt. Carmel [church].
> "You gonna go there and learn about the whole world."
>
> *[E. P. Jones, 1992/2003, p. 29]*

He did.

SUMMING UP

Children continue to learn language rapidly during the school years. They become more flexible, logical, and knowledgeable, figuring out the meaning of new words. Many converse with friends using informal speech and master a more formal code in school. Millions become proficient in a second language, a process facilitated by teachers who help them see connections between the new language and their original one, and by peers who do not make them feel ashamed. Speaking and listening to each child, in school and at home, continues to help with language learning. ■

Teaching and Learning

School-age children are great learners. They develop strategies, accumulate knowledge, apply logic, and think quickly. Magical and egocentric thinking no longer dominate, yet 7- to 11-year-olds are not yet as resistant to authority as adolescents sometimes are.

Children universally are given responsibility and instruction at about age 7, because that is when their bodies and brains are ready. Traditionally, this occurred within the family, but now 95 percent of the world's 7-year-olds are in school. Communities and cultures choose what happens at school, including what children learn.

Schools are pivotal. In the United States, this is particularly true for young children whose families are immigrants, have low SES, and/or do not speak the majority language. Two such children, both educated in southern California, describe their experiences.

> *Yolanda:*
> When I got here [from Mexico at age 7], I didn't want to stay here, 'cause I didn't like the school. And after a little while, in third grade, I started getting the hint of it and everything and I tried real hard in it. I really got along with the teachers. . . . They would start talking to me, or they kinda like pulled me up some grades, or moved me to other classes, or took me somewhere. And they were always congratulating me.
>
> *Paul:*
> I grew up . . . ditching school, just getting in trouble, trying to make a dollar, that's it, you know? Just go to school, steal from the store, and go sell candies at school. And that's what I was doing in the third or fourth grade. . . . I was always getting in the principal's office, suspended, kicked out, everything, starting from the third grade.
>
> My fifth grade teacher, Ms. Nelson . . . she put me in a play and that like tripped me out. Like, why do you want me in a play? Me, I'm just a mess-up. Still, you know, she put me in a play. And in the fifth grade, I think that was the best year out of the whole six years. I learned a lot about the Revolutionary War. . . . Had good friends. . . . We had a project we were involved in. Ms. Nelson . . . just involved everyone. We made books, this and that. And I used to write, and wrote two, three books. Was in a book fair. . . . She got real deep into you. Just, you know, "Come on now, you can do it." That was a good year for me, fifth grade.
>
> [*quoted in Nieto, 2000, pp. 220, 249*]

Note that initially Yolanda didn't like the United States because of school, but her teachers "kind of pulled me up." By third grade she was beginning to get "the hint of it." For Paul, school was where he sold stolen candy and where his teachers sent him to the principal, who suspended him. Ms. Nelson's fifth grade, though it was "a good year" for him, was too late; Paul was sent to a special school and probably (suggested, not confirmed in the text) had been in jail by age 18.

FIGURE 12.2

What Money Can't Buy The United States spends more on elementary school education, but U.S. students do not learn more than students in other developed nations. Depending on your personal and political perspective, you can blame the children, the teachers, the curriculum, or government policies.

Observation Quiz (see answer, page 320): Four other nations have relatively high per capita spending on education. Do you know anything else noteworthy about them?

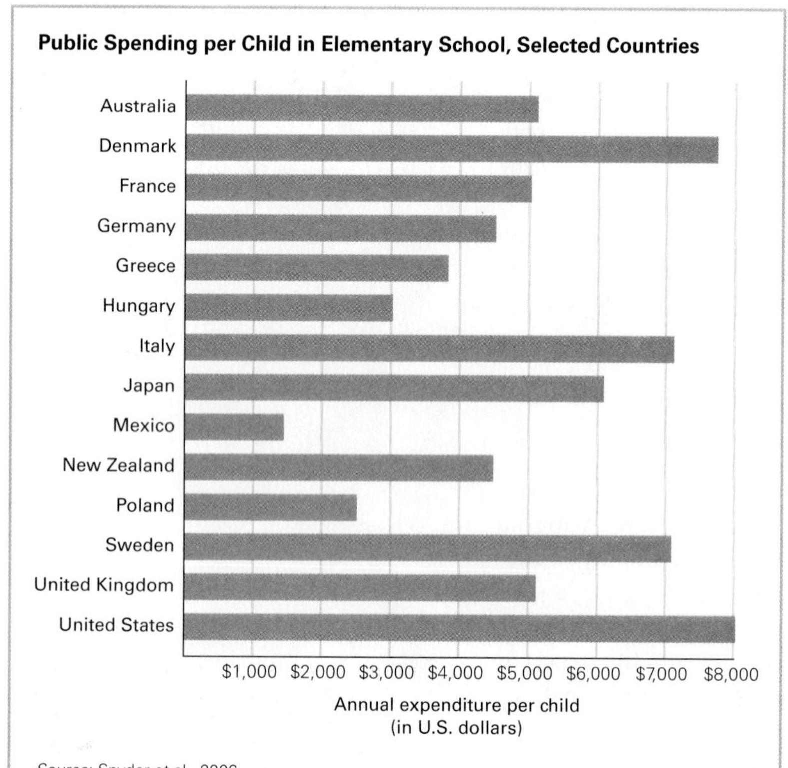

Curriculum

Everywhere children are taught to read, write, and do arithmetic, although beyond basic skills, nations vary in how and what they teach their children and how much they spend to do it (see Figure 12.2). For example, reasoned speaking and logical argument are taught in Russia and France but not in India or the United States (Alexander, 2000); memorization is important in India but is less so in England. In some places, physical education and the arts are essential; in France, for example, every week physical education takes three hours and arts education more than two hours (Marlow-Ferguson, 2002). Even nations that are geographically and culturally close to each other differ in specifics. For example, every elementary school student in Australia spends at least two hours per week studying science, but this is true for only 23 percent in nearby New Zealand (Snyder et al., 2004).

When, how, to whom, and whether second-language instruction should occur also varies markedly from nation to nation. Within some nations, including the United States, second-language instruction varies from district to district, as already explained. Even in the same district and under the same policy, teacher quality is crucial, as the quotations from Yolanda and Paul illustrate and as research has confirmed (Hinkel, 2005). In other nations, including most European countries, every elementary school child learns at least one language in addition to his or her native tongue.

Religious instruction is another major variable. In some nations, every public school teaches religion. For instance, Finnish schools require religious education —but provide parents only three choices: Lutheran, Christian Orthodox, or nonsectarian (Marlow-Ferguson, 2002). In other nations, religious instruction is forbidden in state-sponsored schools. This is true in the United States, where 88 percent of children attend public schools; the other 12 percent are home-schooled (2 percent) or attend a private school (10 percent), often with a religious bent (U.S. Department of Education, 2006). Almost every nation has some private schools that are sponsored by religious groups. Again, international variation is large. Sixteen percent of French children attend church-related schools; only 1 percent of Japanese children do (Marlow-Ferguson, 2002).

Especially for Parents Suppose you and your school-age children move to a new community that is 50 miles from the nearest location that offers instruction in your faith or value system. Your neighbor says, "Don't worry, they don't have to make any moral decisions until they are teenagers." Is your neighbor correct?

Another major difference is whether the parents, the local community, the state, or the nation decides curriculum. The following is from a minister of education in Australia:

> Education is a national priority and it is too important to be left at the mercy of state parochialism . . . with an increasingly mobile workforce, why should students and teachers be disadvantaged when they move interstate from one educational system to another?
>
> *[Bishop, quoted in Manzo, 2007, p. 40]*

In Australia local control of curriculum clashes with a push for national standards. The same clash is at the heart of the controversy in the United States over the **No Child Left Behind Act** of 2001, a federal law that mandates annual standardized achievement tests for public school children beginning in the third grade. If schools do not meet the achievement standards (which keep rising) for several years, parents can transfer their children out, and low-scoring schools will lose funding and may have to close.

No Child Left Behind Act A U.S. law passed by Congress in 2001 that was intended to increase accountability in education by requiring standardized tests to measure school achievement. Many critics, especially teachers, say the law undercuts learning and fails to take local needs into consideration.

Some states (e.g., Utah) have opted out of No Child Left Behind. Other states have achievement tests that allow most schools to progress (and thus get funding). The **National Assessment of Educational Progress (NAEP),** a federal Department of Education project that measures achievement in reading, mathematics, and other subjects over time, finds fewer children proficient in various skills than state tests show (see Figures 12.3 and 12.4). Yet

National Assessment of Educational Progress (NAEP) An ongoing and nationally representative measure of children's achievement in reading, mathematics, and other subjects over time; nicknamed "the Nation's Report Card."

> local control of public schools is a hallowed tradition in American education and there has long been antipathy to the idea of a national test. . . . Some state educators say comparisons are unfair because NAEP is too rigorous and was designed to chart long-term trends, not to measure what states feel students should know.
>
> *[Vu, 2007]*

One problem with national standards, as is evident with NAEP, is that states disagree about what children should know and how they should learn it. Many schools (71 percent in one study) cut back on parts of the curriculum (especially art or music) in order to offer more instruction in reading and math (Rentner et al., 2006). One reason for this shift in emphasis is that No Child Left Behind implemented **Reading First,** reflecting the notion that the primary item of curriculum (and the primary goal of national standards and topic of achievement tests) should be reading. In addition, nationally approved materials for teaching

Reading First A federal program that was established by the No Child Left Behind Act and that provides states with funding for early reading instruction in public schools, aimed at ensuring that all children learn to read well by the end of the third grade.

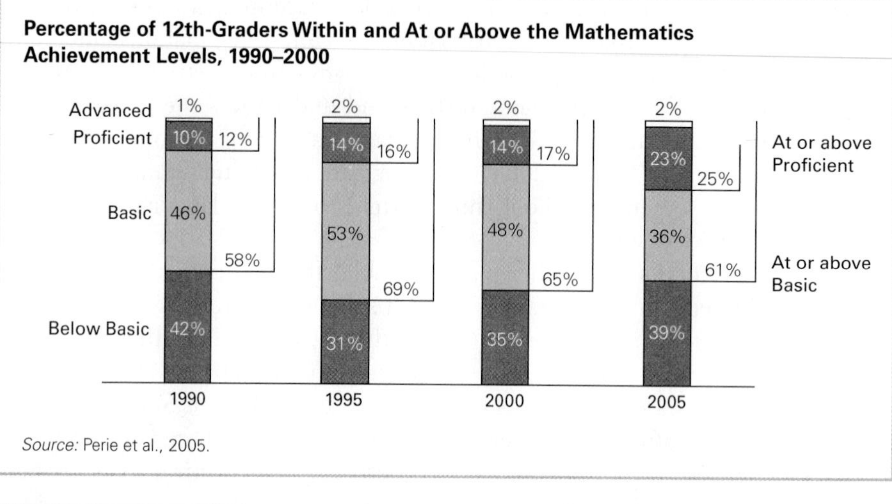

Source: Perie et al., 2005.

FIGURE 12.3

Better or Worse? Should a country's education policy emphasize helping more students become "Proficient" or better in mathematics or trying to make sure that fewer students score "Below Basic"? The United States seems to be choosing the former, with more resources allocated to the schools where students score high in math achievement.

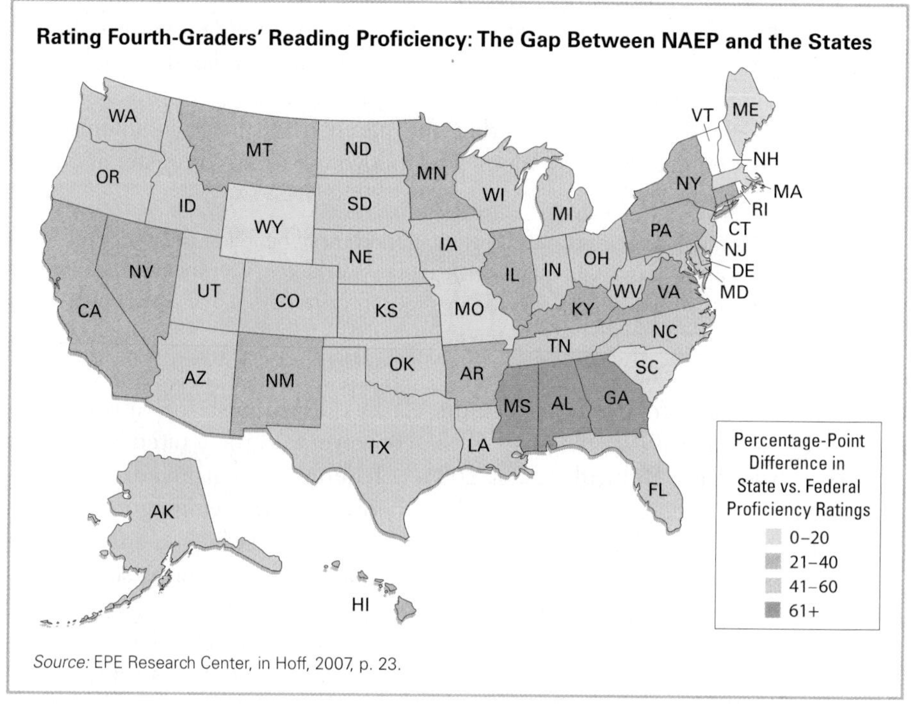

Source: EPE Research Center, in Hoff, 2007, p. 23.

FIGURE 12.4

Local Standards Each state sets its own level of proficiency, which helps low-scoring states obtain more federal money for education, but it may undercut high standards for student learning.

reading favor the phonics side of the reading wars (discussed below) (Manzo, 2006). For all these reasons, reauthorization of No Child Left Behind, scheduled for 2007, required major revision.

In addition to formal mandates, there is a **hidden curriculum,** which consists of the unrecognized lessons that children absorb in school. The hidden curriculum typically involves such matters as tracking, teacher characteristics, discipline, teaching methods, sports competition, student government, and extracurricular activities. For example, if most of the teachers are different from most of the children in terms of gender, ethnicity, or economic background, the hidden message may be that some children are not expected to succeed in school.

hidden curriculum The unofficial, unstated, or implicit rules and priorities that influence the academic curriculum and every other aspect of learning in school.

One obvious manifestation of the hidden curriculum is the physical setting. Some schools have spacious classrooms; wide hallways; personal computers; and large, grassy playgrounds. Others have small, poorly equipped rooms and cement play yards or "play streets," closed to traffic for a few hours a day. A former New York State Commissioner of Education explained:

➤**Answer to Observation Quiz** (from page 318): Denmark, Italy, Japan, and Sweden have very low birth rates and thus have relatively few schoolchildren.

> If you ask the children to attend school in conditions where plaster is crumbling, the roof is leaking and classes are being held in unlikely places because of overcrowded conditions, that says something to the child. . . . If, on the other hand, you send a child to a school in well-appointed or [adequate facilities], that sends the opposite message. That says this counts. You count. Do well.
>
> [*Sobol, quoted in* Campaign for Fiscal Equity v. State of New York, *2001*]

In some countries, school is held outdoors. Students sit quietly on the ground. The school day must end whenever it rains. What messages does this kind of school setting convey?

In all these variations in curriculum, those who advocate one "best" practice risk becoming tangled in ideology, politics, and culture, disconnected from the findings of educational research (Rayner et al., 2001). On their part, children do not necessarily learn what policy makers intend, or even what their own teachers teach. Intended, implemented, and attained curricula are three different things (Robitaille & Beaton, 2002).

➤Response for Parents (from page 319): No. In fact, these are prime years for moral education. You might travel those 50 miles once or twice a week or recruit other parents to organize a local program. Whatever you do, don't skip moral instruction. Discuss and demonstrate your moral and religious values, and help your children meet other children who share those values.

The Outcome

Most parents, teachers, and political leaders believe that their children are learning what they need. Parents give higher ratings to their children's schools than nonparents in their community do, although nonparents do rate their own community's schools higher than schools nationwide (Snyder et al., 2004). Similarly, many parents of home-schooled and private school children believe that public schools are worse than research finds them to be (Green & Hoover-Dempsey, 2007; Lubienski & Lubienski, 2005).

This does not necessarily mean that parents are fooling themselves, only that people disagree about what children should learn and how to best measure that learning (Elmore et al., 2004; R. S. Johnson, 2002). Objective, international tests do not put an end to these disagreements, as the following explains.

TIMSS (Trends in Math and Science Study) An international assessment of the math and science skills of fourth- and eighth-graders. Although the TIMSS is very useful, scores are not always comparable, because sample selection, test administration, and content validity are hard to keep uniform.

thinking like a scientist

International Achievement Tests

Objective assessment of educational achievement might be done by comparing results from international, culture-neutral tests. Ideally, each nation would give the same tests, under the same conditions, to a representative group of children of a particular age and year of schooling. Such even-handed comparisons are impossible, however, because educational practices vary too widely in different countries. For example, Scottish children, who begin school at age 4, have a three-year advantage over Russian children, who usually begin school at age 7 (Mullis et al., 2004).

Despite such problems, international tests are useful. One such assessment, administered periodically to fourth- and eighth-graders worldwide, is called the **TIMSS (Trends in Math and Science Study).** The average 10-year-old in Singapore is ahead of the top 5 percent of U.S. students in math, according to the TIMSS. Fourth-graders in Hong Kong, Japan, and Chinese Taipei (Taiwan) also did better than their counterparts

"Big deal, an A in math. That would be a D in any other country."

in western nations. This trend of East Asian superiority continues through high school (see Table 12.1).

Canada, England, and the United States are above average on the TIMSS, but not by much. The lowest-ranking nations—Tunisia, Morocco, and the Philippines (not shown in the table)—do not have a long history of universal fourth-grade education. No very poor nations participated in the testing, finding it too expensive, too discouraging, or too difficult.

Is the TIMSS fair? Here is a sample math question for fourth-graders:

> Jasmine made a stack of cubes the same size. The stack had 5 layers, and each layer had 10 cubes. What is the volume of the stack?
> a. 10 cubes
> b. 15 cubes
> c. 30 cubes
> d. 50 cubes

Is this item equally difficult for children in every nation, or are East Asians favored?

TABLE 12.1

TIMSS Rankings of Average Math Achievement Scores of Eighth-Graders, Selected Countries*

Country	Year 2003	1999	1995
Singapore	1	1	1
Korea	2	2	2
Hong Kong	3	3	4
Japan	4	4	3
Netherlands	5	6	6
Canada**	6	5	7
Hungary	7	8	8
Czech Republic	8	7	5
Russian Federation	9	9	9
Australia	10	10	10
United States	11	11	12
New Zealand	12	12	11
Cyprus	13	13	13
Iran	14	14	14

*Not all of the countries that participated in TIMSS (25 in 2003) are reported because most of them did not give this test in all three years. Eighth-grade rankings are given here; the fourth-grade rankings are similar, but not as much comparative data are available.

**Results for Canada are for the provinces of Ontario and Quebec only and thus are not strictly comparable with other countries' average scores.

Source: International Association for the Evaluation of Educational Achievement, 2003; http://timss.bc.edu, accessed April 25, 2007.

Progress in International Reading Literacy Study (PIRLS) Inaugurated in 2001, a planned five-year cycle of international trend studies in the reading ability of fourth-graders.

Western nations score better on international reading assessments, such as the **Progress in International Reading Literacy Study (PIRLS).** In the first round of testing, in 2001, only 3 of the 35 participating nations (Sweden, England, and Bulgaria) surpassed the United States in the percentage of fourth-graders who read in the top 10 percent.

For all international tests, data can be interpreted in various ways. For instance, critics of U.S. education focus more on math and science (assessed by the TIMSS) than on reading (assessed by the PIRLS). Those who are concerned about educational disparities notice the spread between the children in the top fourth (above the 75th percentile) and the bottom fourth (below the 26th percentile). On the PIRLS, 24 nations had a wider spread than the United States, and ten had less disparity (Sweden, England, Bulgaria, Canada, the Netherlands, Lithuania, Latvia, the Czech Republic, France, Hong Kong) (Mullis et al., 2003).

Gender differences in performance are both confirmed and refuted by the data. Internationally, girls are ahead in verbal skills (by 4 percentage points, on average) and boys in math, but nations differ from one another much more than boys do from girls, and the gender spread varies. To pick two extremes, Scottish fourth-grade boys averaged 11 points higher in math than girls, but Filipino girls averaged 9 points above the boys. National scores ranged from 339 (Tunisia) to 594 (Singapore), a much greater difference than the gender differences. Such results led one team to propose a *gender similarities hypothesis* that males and females are similar on most measures, with very few exceptions (Hyde & Linn, 2006).

International testing is too costly to be done every year. Current TIMSS analysis is of tests conducted in 2003. Students worldwide are taking a TIMSS test in 2007, and the results will be reported and analyzed by 2009. Beyond the slow

SHEHZAD NOORANI / PETER ARNOLD, INC.

Catching Up with the West These Iranian girls are acting out a poem that they have memorized from their third-grade textbook. They attend school in a UNICEF-supported Global Education pilot project. Their child-centered classes encourage maximum participation.

reporting of results, another problem is that both participation and emphasis vary from nation to nation. For cultural and cost reasons, some nations participate in TIMSS but not PIRLS (e.g., Japan and South Korea), or in PIRLS but not TIMSS (e.g., Iran and Greece), or in neither (most developing nations). The United States has participated in both, as well as in PISA (Programme for International Assessment), a third international test designed to assess 15-year-olds' ability to apply knowledge (reviewed in Chapter 15). The United States scores well in reading and poorly in applications, but its middling TIMSS scores are most widely publicized.

Especially for Future Research Scientists What should you watch for in news reports about the TIMSS data?

Education Wars and Assumptions

Adults differ in their beliefs about what children should learn—and how. Virtually every aspect of education is not merely debatable; it has caused bitter dispute. Almost everyone has opinions about Japanese education, about teaching reading, about learning math, and many other issues, and those opinions often do not square with the research findings, as you will now see.

Japanese Education

How good is Japanese education? Your answer is probably affected by whether you were educated in Japan or elsewhere. The Japanese are much more critical of their schools than people in the United States are of them.

Ever since Harold Stevenson first compared schoolchildren in North America and Japan (H.W. Stevenson, Lee, et al., 1990; H.W. Stevenson, Chen, et al., 1993), many Americans have envied Japanese education. Japanese children spend more time in school, with longer days, weeks (including Saturday mornings), and years (only one month of summer vacation). Children study at school (and so have less free time) and at home (and so have fewer household chores). Three-fourths of them attend *juko*, private classes that supplement public school.

Japanese teachers are respected by students and parents, and they learn from one another; time is specifically scheduled for collaboration (Stigler & Hiebert, 1999). Further, the Japanese government funds and guides education. That involvement by national government fosters equity and allows children who move mid-year from one region to another to lose no time in catching up with their new classmates. Absenteeism is low, and less than 2 percent of high school students leave school before graduation.

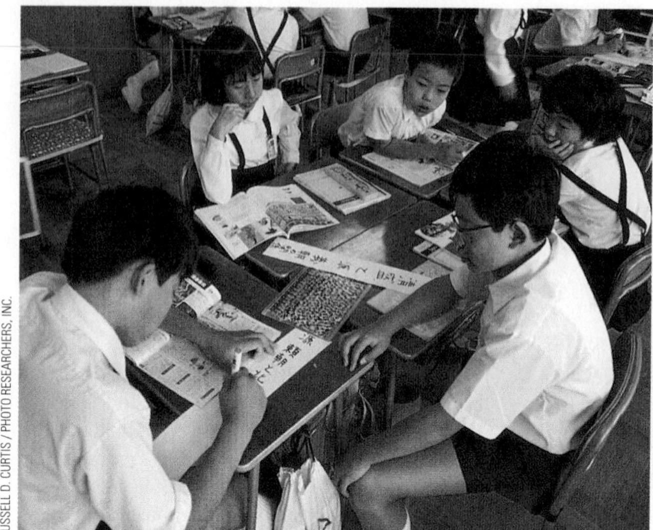

RUSSELL D. CURTIS / PHOTO RESEARCHERS, INC.

Collaborative Learning Japanese children are learning mathematics in a more structured and socially interactive way than are their North American counterparts.

All these factors and others are cited to explain why Japanese children score far above their U.S. peers in math and science. The contrast was among the reasons almost all U.S. Congress members voted for No Child Left Behind in 2001: The program anticipated that every child in the United States would eventually learn as well and as much as Japanese children do.

Meanwhile, in Japan, many parents and government officials express disappointment with the outcomes of public education (Hosaka, 2005; Sugie et al., 2006). Some Japanese children need help developing metacognitive skills that are not taught in school, partly because large class sizes and detailed curriculum requirements make individualized attention difficult (Ichikawa, 2005). In addition, the system may sacrifice creativity and independent thought, at least according to Western critics (Kohn, 2006).

In 2002 the Japanese eased educational and testing requirements by instituting *yutori kyoiku,* which means "more relaxed education." The required curriculum was reduced by 30 percent to allow more emphasis on learning to think rather than memorizing facts to get high test scores (Magara, 2005). The long-term results, like the results of No Child Left Behind, are not yet known.

Especially for Teachers You are teaching in a school that you find too lax or too strict, or with parents who are too demanding or too uncaring. Should you look for a different line of work?

The Reading Wars

Reading is complex. The ability to read with speedy, automatic comprehension is the cumulative result of many earlier steps—from looking closely at pictures (at age 2 or earlier) to learning to figure out unknown technical words (at age 10 and beyond). There are two distinct methods of teaching children to read: phonics and whole language (Rayner et al., 2001). Clashes over the two approaches have led to "serious, sometimes acrimonious debate, fueling the well-named 'reading wars'" (Keogh, 2004, p. 93).

phonics approach Teaching reading by first teaching the sounds of each letter and of various letter combinations.

Historically, schools used the **phonics approach** (from the root word for "sound"), in which children learn to read by learning letter–sound correspon-

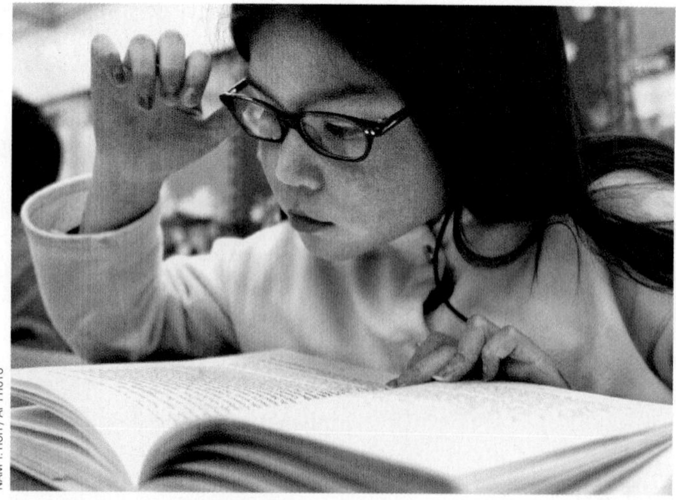

NAM Y. HUH / AP PHOTO

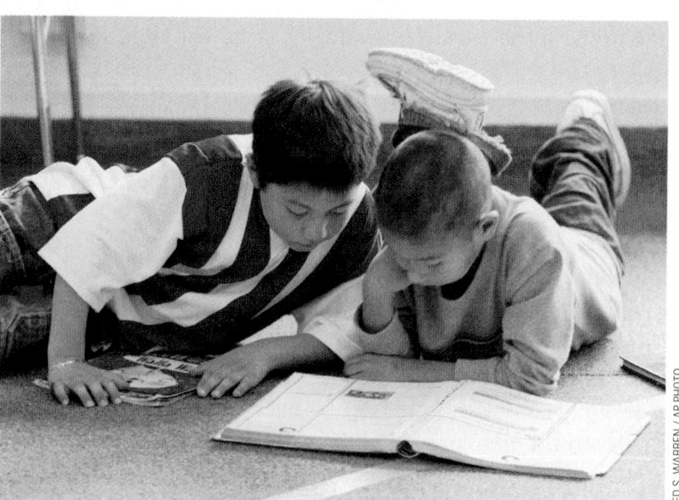

TED S. WARREN / AP PHOTO

Reading with Comprehension *(left)* Reading and math scores in third-grader Monica's Illinois elementary school showed improvement under the standards set by the No Child Left Behind Act. The principal noted a cost for this success in less time spent on social studies and other subjects. *(right)* Some experts believe that children should have their own books and be able to read them wherever and however they want. This strategy seems to be working with Josue and Cristo, two 8-year-olds who were given books through their after-school program in Rochester, Washington.

dences in order to decipher simple words. This approach seemed to be supported by behaviorism (see Chapter 2) and, more recently, by information-processing theory in that step-by-step instructions, with frequent repetition, was favored.

Piaget's theory—that children learn on their own as soon as their minds are ready—provided the rationale for another method, called the **whole-language approach.** For concrete operational thinkers, Piaget's followers explained, abstract, decontextualized memorization (as in traditional phonics) is difficult. Literacy is the outcome of natural motivation in talking and listening, reading and writing. When teachers instruct using the whole-language approach, young children (in addition to reading) draw, talk, and write. They also invent their own spelling, because many languages, including English, are too variable to be spelled phonetically (see Figure 12.5).

whole-language approach Teaching reading by encouraging early use of all language skills—talking and listening, reading and writing.

However, unlike talking, which is experience-expectant, reading and writing are experience-dependent. Children need instruction, as Vygotsky might argue. Beginning readers may need to be taught to translate spoken words into printed ones, and vice versa. Some children may never "discover" how to read on their own.

Research arising from every contemporary developmental theory has noted the uniqueness of each child as a beginning reader, including individual patterns of language proficiency, learning style, and maturation. In practical terms, this means that phonics may be essential for those children who need help learning how to sound out new words. Targeted early instruction in letter–sound combinations may be crucial (Torgesen, 2004). Score one for phonics.

Yet for comprehension and memory, children need to make connections between concepts, not just between letters. Thus, children need to read books that are challenging and interesting and must write about their own experiences and interests. Score one for whole language.

The answer to this tie is also a truce in the reading wars. A focus on phonics need not undercut instruction that motivates children to read, write, and discuss with their classmates and their parents. For reading comprehension and fluency, phonemic awareness is a beginning, but other aspects of literacy are important as well (Muter et al., 2004). As the editors of a leading publication for teachers explain:

> In any debate on reading instruction that counterposes a focus on skills with a focus on enjoyment—or that pits phonological skills against the knowledge necessary to comprehend grade-level material—there is only one good answer: Kids need both.
>
> [The Editors, *American Educator*, 2004, p. 5]

Fortunately, experts on the two sides in the reading wars have stopped their bitter feud. Most developmentalists and many reading specialists now believe that teachers should use a variety of methods and strategies, for there are "alternate pathways in learning to read" (Berninger et al., 2002, p. 295). Research leaves little doubt that in the early grades systematic phonics instruction "is important" (Camilli et al., 2003, p. 34) but that it should not come at the expense of meaning and pleasure.

Researchers are less sure of "the best approaches and methods of reading and writing instruction for students older than age 9 and interventions for those who are struggling readers in grades 4–12" (McCardle & Chhabra, 2004, pp. 472–473). It is, however, known that, for older children, reading instruction can and should be connected to literature, history, science, and other areas of study. An expanding knowledge base aids comprehension and helps avoid the "fourth-grade slump." One teacher who knew that and taught accordingly may have saved some people's lives.

From karla to My mom
its No fare
that You mad
me Lat my Lade
bug Go Wat
If I was your
mom and I mad
You tack your
Lade bug Tam
Shr You Wad
be sad like me
that lade bug
mat of ban a orfan
so You sod ov lat me
hav it ane wae

FIGURE 12.5

"You Wud Be Sad Like Me" Although Karla uses invented spelling, her arguments show that she is reasoning quite logically; her school-age mind is working quite well. (If you have trouble deciphering Karla's note, turn the book upside down for a translation.)

➤Response for Future Research Scientists (from page 323): The next set of published results of the TIMSS is expected in 2009. As someone who knows how to think like a scientist, see if the headlines accurately reflect the data.

"From Karla to my mom. It's no fair that you made me let my lady bug go. What if I was your mom and I made you take your lady bug. I am sure you would be sad like me. That lady bug might have been an orphan. So you should have let me have it anyway."

a case to study

Where Did You Learn *Tsunami*?

Before December 26, 2004, perhaps 1 percent of the world's population knew the word *tsunami*. I was in the other 99. Over Christmas that year, when my nephew Bill said we should pray for the victims of the tsunami, I marveled that he could pronounce a word that I had not known until I read that day's headlines.

Even among the 1 percent who knew the word, few understood it. Some British 10-year-olds were the exceptions. In early December 2004 their teacher, Andrew Kearny, had shown them a video clip of survivors of a tsunami that struck Hawaii in the 1950s and had drawn a diagram on the board that his students copied into their exercise books. Tilly Smith was his student.

> Two weeks later, Tilly was on Maikhao Beach in Phuket, Thailand, with her parents and her 7-year-old sister. Suddenly, the tide went out, leaving a wide stretch of sand where the ocean had been. Most tourists stood gawking at the disappearing ocean, but Tilly grabbed her mother's hand: "Mummy, we must get off the beach now. I think there's going to be a tsunami."
>
> Tilly's parents alerted other holiday makers nearby, then raced to tell their hotel staff in Phuket. The hotel swiftly evacuated Maikhao Beach, and minutes later a huge wave crashed onto the sand, sweeping all before it. Incredibly, the beach was one of the few in Phuket where no one was killed.
>
> *[Larcombe, 2005]*

Tilly and her family survived for many reasons: Tilly remembered what she had learned; her parents heeded her warning; higher ground was nearby. But some credit goes to her teacher, who did more than list *tsunami* as a vocabulary word. He used examples and activities to give the concept meaning. Ten-year-olds are ready to learn and remember as long as knowledge is concrete (Piaget) and instruction includes examples and active participation (Vygotsky). This is not just good fortune, but also good education.

The Math Wars

Mathematics instruction in the United States has become even more problematic than instruction in reading, for a number of reasons. First, economic development depends on science and technology, and math is vital in both those fields. Second, many children hate math, as suggested by a 2007 Google search that found 36,100 sites for "math phobia" and just 171 for "reading phobia," a 210-to-1 ratio. Third, U.S. students are weaker in math than students from other nations, especially East Asian nations, at least as measured by TIMSS. This last reason makes math education vulnerable to quick solutions suggested by angry adults—not the best way to develop curriculum.

One reason the United States does not rank higher may be just that: The battle over how to teach math is not always to the benefit of children (Boaler, 2002). According to one report, "U.S. mathematics instruction has been scorched in the pedagogical blaze known as the 'math wars'—a divide between those who see a need for a greater emphasis on basic skills in math and others who say students lack a broader, conceptual understanding of the subject" (Cavenaugh, 2005, p. 1).

Historically, math was taught by rote; children memorized number facts, such as the multiplication tables, and filled page after page of workbooks. In reaction against this approach, many educators, inspired especially by Piaget and Vygotsky, sought to make math instruction more active and engaging, less a matter of memorization than of discovery (Ginsburg et al., 1998).

This newer approach is controversial. Many parents and educators believe that children need to memorize number facts. Educators as well as mathematicians stress that math involves a particular set of rules, symbols, and processes that must be taught, with limits to the role discovery can play (Mervis, 2006).

As with reading, researchers have attempted to understand what teachers can do to help children learn, and enjoy, math. TIMSS experts videotaped 231 math classes in three nations—Japan, Germany, and the United States—to analyze national differences (Stigler & Hiebert, 1999). The U.S. teachers presented math

➤Response for Teachers (from page 324): Nobody works well in an institution they hate, but, before quitting the profession, remember that schools vary. There is probably another school nearby that is much more to your liking and that would welcome an experienced teacher. Before you make a move, however, assess the likelihood that you could adjust to your current position in ways that would make you happier. No school is perfect; nor is any teacher.

at a lower level than did their German and Japanese counterparts, with more definitions but less coherence and connection to what the students had learned in other math classes. The "teachers seem to believe that learning terms and practicing skills is not very exciting" (p. 89).

In contrast, the Japanese teachers were excited about math instruction, working collaboratively and structuring lessons so that the children developed proofs and alternative solutions, alone and in groups. Teachers used social interaction (among groups of children and groups of teachers) and sequential curricula (lessons for each day, week, and year built on previous math knowledge), often presenting the students with problems to solve in groups.

Some have suggested that teachers should dispel math anxiety by convincing students that they are good at math. This seems unlikely to be helpful. In the United States, 51 percent of eighth-graders are highly confident of their math ability, even though their scores on international math achievement tests are unimpressive. Among 46 nations, only Israel has a higher level of math confidence (59 percent) (Snyder et al., 2006). Unfortunately, achievement seems to fall as confidence rises. The highest math achievement scores are from China (Taipei), which has the lowest proportion of students who are highly confident of their math ability (26 percent).

One idea that follows from information-processing theory is to make each grade of elementary school math build on the previous year's instruction. This idea is now endorsed by the National Council of Teachers of Mathematics (NCTM), an influential group in the United States. For example, second-graders will learn addition, subtraction, and place value; multiplication, fractions, and decimals will be saved for the fourth grade (Mervis, 2006). Whether this plan will be implemented and attained remains to be seen; children and parents like to believe that they are advanced in math, and learning multiplication and fractions in second grade confirms their belief, even though it will eventually slow down their basic understanding.

Other Assumptions

The educational landscape is filled with other controversies and assumptions that are commonly held but debatable. For example, in the past 20 years adults have become convinced that children learn from homework, and even kindergarten children often bring work home. Yet one researcher finds that homework undermines learning instead of advancing it (Kohn, 2006).

Similarly, although many parents choose to send their children to schools with smaller class sizes, the evidence about their effect is mixed (Blatchford, 2003; Hanushek, 1999). Wide international variation is apparent, from a teacher–pupil ratio of 10 to 1 in Denmark to 30 to 1 in Turkey. Smaller is not necessarily better, as evidenced by Asian nations with high ratios that tended to have high math and science scores (Snyder et al., 2006).

Data on class size thus "do not lend themselves to straightforward implications for policy" (NICHD Early Child Care Research Network, 2004, p. 66; see Research Design). Even a famous study in Tennessee, which found that smaller classes in kindergarten benefited children for several years, is open to various interpretations (Finn & Achilles, 1999).

Other reforms, in addition to reducing class size, that have been strongly advocated—and strongly opposed—include raising teacher salaries; improving professional education; extending school hours; expanding the school year; creating charter schools; allowing school vouchers; and increasing sports, music, or silent reading. These might, or might not, help children learn. Valid, replicated, unbiased research is thus far lacking. One review of the impact of class size concludes:

Research Design

Scientists: NICHD Early Child Care Research Network, consisting of 29 leading child-care researchers.

Publication: *Developmental Psychology*, (2004).

Participants: A total of 890 children in their second year of school in 651 elementary school classrooms. These children were part of a cohort of 1,634 children followed since birth, from 10 research sites, in various locations in the United States.

Design: Children's achievement and social outcomes were measured, as were teacher behaviors, via a structured three-hour observation in each classroom. Measures were first adjusted to reflect the children's academic and social backgrounds (e.g., SES, gender) and the teachers' backgrounds (e.g., education, ethnicity). Many factors were controlled to learn the effects of class size (which ranged from 10 to 39 students per teacher).

Major conclusions: Class size was irrelevant for many measures. Smaller classes (less than 20) were better in some ways but not all. For example, first-graders in smaller classes tended to develop better word attack skills but were more disruptive. Their teachers were less structured but showed more warmth.

Comment: This study (cited in earlier chapters) features a large, geographically varied, longitudinal sample that allows controls for preexisting factors. However, the sample had few high-risk children (a newborn was excluded if the mother was under 19, did not speak English, or lived in an unsafe neighborhood).

> Reductions in class size are but one of the policy options that can be pursued to improve student learning. Careful evaluations of the impacts of other options, preferably through the use of more true experiments, along with an analysis of the costs of each option, need to be undertaken. However, to date there are relatively few studies that even compute the true costs of large class-size reduction programs, let alone ask whether the benefits . . . merit incurring the costs.
>
> *[Ehrenberg et al., 2001]*

Especially for School Administrators
Children who wear uniforms in school tend to score higher on reading tests. Why?

Similar conclusions apply for most other education reforms. Another review, this one about home schooling, charter schools, and vouchers, complains of "the difficulty of interpreting the research literature on this topic, most of which is biased and far from approaching balanced social science" (Boyd, 2007, p. 7). The call for "evidence-based" reforms is appreciated by developmentalists, as by all other scientists. Unfortunately, as experience with Reading First has illustrated, bias can creep in when it is left to political leaders to decide which evidence is valid (Manzo, 2006).

Culture and Education

As you can see, many controversies regarding cognitive development as it relates to education are political more than developmental. Piaget, Vygotsky, information-processing theory, and, in earlier decades, progressive education and behavior modification have all been used to support particular practices, sometimes for good reasons, sometimes not. To conclude this chapter, we highlight again the sometimes hidden role of culture.

Here are excerpts from two letters to a local newspaper in British Columbia, Canada (quoted in K. Mitchell, 2001, pp. 64–65). One mother wrote:

> Our children's performances are much lower both in academic and moral areas. I noticed the children have learned very little academically. They learned to have self-confidence instead of being self-disciplined; learned to speak up instead of being humbled; learned to be creative instead of self-motivated; and learned to simplify things instead of organizing. All of these characteristics were not balanced, and will be the source of disadvantage and difficulties in children in this competitive society.

Another parent responded:

> She wants her children to be self-disciplined, humble, self-motivated and organized, instead of being self-confident, assertive, creative and analytic. . . . These repressive, authoritarian, "traditional" parents who hanker for the days of yore, when fresh-faced school kids arrived all neatly decked out in drab-grey uniforms and shiny lace-up leather shoes, are a menace to society.

In this district, many families were immigrants from Asia (including the author of the first letter), while others and almost all the school administrators and teachers were from families that had been in Canada for generations. Similar conflicts erupt in every community that has diverse groups of families or a difference in background between the teachers and the children.

Recognizing this problem is only a beginning. For example, in another Canadian community, Inuit children were taught in Inuit by Inuits for their first two years of school and were then taught in French or English, the majority languages, by non-Inuits. The Inuit teachers prepared the children for the transition by teaching French and English as a second language, and later teachers worked to increase their students' language proficiency. Both groups of teachers realized that they were failing. Relatively few Inuit children became fluent in a second language, and most dropped out before high school graduation. Other research has found that many aboriginal adolescents (as members of Canada's First Nations are called) become alienated from their native culture and then become depressed or even suicidal as adolescents (Chandler et al., 2003). The problem may seem to be a failure of bilingual education—perhaps total immersion coming too soon or too late. But culture, not language, may be the pivotal factor.

A scientist using naturalistic observation found much more than a language shift between grades 2 and 3 (Eriks-Brophy & Crago, 2003). The Inuit teachers encouraged group learning and cooperation, almost never explicitly judging an individual student's response. By contrast, the non-Inuit teachers often criticized behaviors that the earlier teachers encouraged, such as group cooperation (which the non-Inuit teachers called "talking out of turn"), helping each other ("cheating"), and attempts to answer ("stupid mistakes").

A specific example illustrates this pattern. A common routine in North American schools is called initiation/response/evaluation: The teacher asks a question, a child responds, and the teacher states whether the response is correct or not. An analysis of 14 teachers in this Inuit school found that the initiation/response/evaluation routine dominated the instruction of the non-Inuit teachers (60 percent) but not that of the Inuit teachers (18 percent) (Eriks-Brophy & Crago, 2003). For example, an Inuit teacher showed a picture and asked:

Teacher: This one. What is it?
Student: Tutuva (*an insect*).
Teacher: What is it?
Student: Tutuva.
Teacher: All of us, look carefully.
Student: Kituquianluti (*another insect, this time correct. The teacher nodded and breathed in.*)

In contrast, a non-Inuit third-grade teacher asked:

Teacher: Richard, what is this?
Richard: It is an ear.
Teacher: Good.
Teacher: Rhoda, what is this?
Rhoda: Hair.
Teacher: No. What is this?
Rhoda: Face.
Teacher: It is a face.
Rhoda: It is a face.
Teacher: Very good, Rhoda.

[quoted in Eriks-Brophy & Crago, 2003]

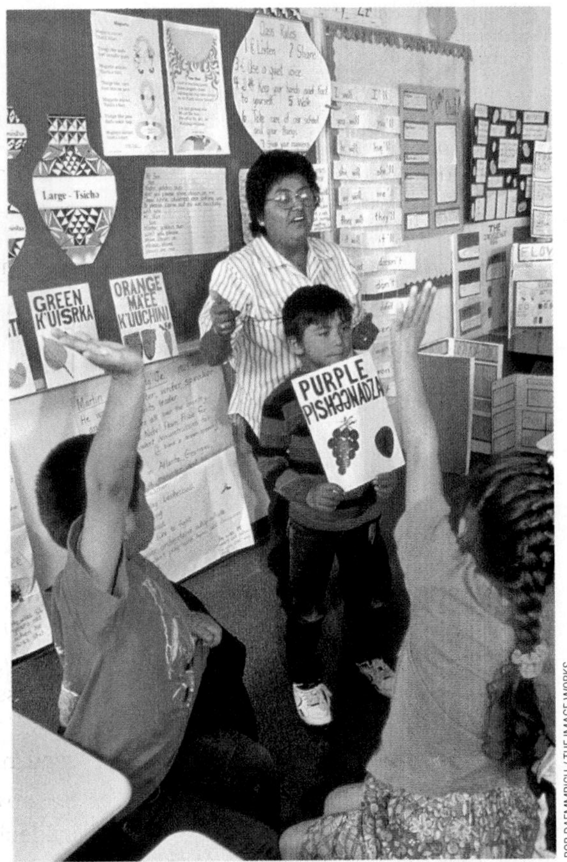

BOB DAEMMRICH / THE IMAGE WORKS

Hidden Curriculum This informal, bilingual first-grade class in Acoma Pueblo, New Mexico, is a contrast to the U.S. government's nineteenth-century policy of sending all Native American children to English-only boarding schools.

Observation Quiz (see answer, page 330): What three social constructions about proper education for Pueblo children do you see?

Note that the first teacher never verbally evaluated the child (merely nodding and breathing to signal correctness), but the second teacher did so at least three times ("good," "no," "very good"). No wonder the children were confused and discouraged. They were unprepared to make a cultural shift as well as a language one.

Such problems can emerge anywhere. Teaching methods are the outcome of cultural beliefs, a "social system that evolves over time" (Eriks-Brophy & Crago, 2003, p. 397), often hidden from the teachers themselves. Underlying the issues that parents seize on—discipline, phonics, and math scores—are deeper issues involving culture and values.

Every child wants to learn, every teacher wants to teach, and every family wants the best for its children. This makes differences in curricula and methods much

Maintaining Tradition Some would say that these Vietnamese children in Texas are fortunate. They are instructed in two languages by a teacher who knows their culture, including the use of red pens for self-correction as well as teacher correction. Others would say that these children would be better off in an English-only classroom.

OB DAEMMRICH / THE IMAGE WORKS

harder to reconcile than more obvious cultural manifestations. No one cares if a particular child eats goat, chitlings, or whale for dinner, but people everywhere care about what their own—and their neighbors'—children learn.

➤Response for School Administrators (from page 328): The relationship reflects correlation, not causation. Wearing uniforms is more common when the culture of the school emphasizes achievement and study, with strict discipline in class and a policy of expelling disruptive students.

➤Answer to Observation Quiz (see answer, page 330): The ideas that (1) learning colors is important, (2) children should raise their hands to be called on individually, and (3) words should be written. (Note that the Pueblo words for colors are much longer than the English equivalents—harder for first-grade readers.) Indeed, the very idea of bilingual education is a social construction, approved by most Americans but not necessarily by research.

SUMMING UP

Societies throughout the world recognize that school-age children are avid learners and that educated citizens are essential to economic development. However, schools differ in what and how children are taught. The nature and content of education raise ideological and political concerns. Examples are found in the reading wars, the math wars, class size, and bilingual education. Research finds that direct instruction (in phonics; in mathematical symbols and procedures; in the vocabulary, grammar, and syntax of second languages) is useful, even essential, if children are to master all the skills that adults want them to learn. Also crucial are motivation, pride, and social interaction. School-age children are great learners, but they cannot learn everything. Adults decide the specifics, and cultural values are apparent in every classroom. ■

SUMMARY

Building on Theory

1. According to Piaget, children begin concrete operational thought at about age 6 or 7. Egocentrism diminishes and logic begins. School-age children can understand classification, conservation, identity, and reversibility.

2. Vygotsky stressed the social context of learning, including the specific lessons of school and the overall influence of culture. International research finds that maturation is one factor in the cognitive development of school-age children (as Piaget predicted) and that cultural and economic forces are also influential (as Vygotsky predicted).

3. An information-processing approach examines each step of the thinking process, from input to output, using the computer as a model. Humans are more creative than computers, but this approach is useful for understanding memory, perception, and expression.

4. Memory begins with information that reaches the brain from the sense organs. Then selection processes allow some information to reach working memory. Finally, long-term memory stores some images and ideas indefinitely, retrieving some parts when needed.

5. Selective attention, a broader knowledge base, logical strategies for retrieval, and faster processing advance every aspect of cognition. Repeated practice makes thought patterns and skill sets almost automatic, requiring little time or conscious effort.

6. Children become better at controlling and directing their thinking as the prefrontal cortex matures. Consequently, metacognition advances.

Language

7. Language learning improves in many practical ways, including expanded vocabulary, as words are logically linked together. Many children learn a second language, succeeding if they are well taught. Children of low SES are usually lower in linguistic skills, primarily because they hear less language and adult expectations for their learning are low.

Teaching and Learning

8. Nations and experts agree that education is critical during middle childhood, and 95 percent of the world's children now attend primary school. Schools differ in what and how they teach, especially in the hidden curriculum.

9. International assessments are useful as comparisons, partly because few objective measures of learning are available. In the United States, the No Child Left Behind law and the National Assessment of Educational Progress attempt to raise the standard of education, with mixed success.

10. The "reading wars" pit advocates of phonics against advocates of the whole-language approach. These wars have quieted somewhat, as research finds that phonological understanding is essential for every child who is just learning to read but that motivation and vocabulary are important as well.

11. Math learned by rote and math learned via social interaction are the two sides of the "math wars." Math and science achievement are higher in East Asian nations than elsewhere, perhaps because in those countries math lessons are sequential and interactive.

12. Cultural differences in assumptions about education are frequent, but scientific research on the best way for children to learn is scarce. For example, many people believe that children learn better in small classes, but the research is inconclusive.

KEY TERMS

concrete operational thought (p. 307)
classification (p. 308)
identity (p. 308)
reversibility (p. 308)
information-processing theory (p. 310)
sensory memory (p. 311)
working memory (p. 311)
long-term memory (p. 311)
knowledge base (p. 312)
control processes (p. 312)
metacognition (p. 313)
English-language learner (ELL) (p. 315)
total immersion (p. 316)
bilingual education (p. 316)
ESL (English as a second language) (p. 316)
No Child Left Behind Act (p. 319)
National Assessment of Educational Progress (NAEP) (p. 319)
Reading First (p. 319)
hidden curriculum (p. 320)
TIMSS (Trends in Math and Science Study) (p. 321)
Progress in International Reading Literacy Skills (PIRLS) (p. 322)
phonics approach (p. 324)
whole-language approach (p. 325)

KEY QUESTIONS

1. How do logical ideas help children understand classification?

2. According to Vygotsky, if children never went to school, how would cognitive development occur?

3. What are differences among the three kinds of memory?

4. What are the differences between language learning in early and middle childhood?

5. What are the advantages and disadvantages in teaching children who do not speak English in English-only classes?

6. How does metacognition affect the ability to learn something new?

7. What are some of the differences in education in various parts of the world?

8. Why are international tests of learning given, and what are some of the problems with such tests?

9. How might a hidden curriculum affect what a child might learn?

10. Why are disagreements about curriculum and method sometimes called "wars," not merely differences of opinion?

APPLICATIONS

1. Visit a local elementary school and look for the hidden curriculum. For example, do the children line up? Why or why not, when and how? Does gender, age, ability, or talent affect the grouping of children or the selection of staff? What is on the walls? Are parents involved? If so, how? For everything you observe, speculate about the underlying assumptions.

2. Interview a 7- to 11-year-old child to find out what he or she knows *and understands* about mathematics. Relate both correct and incorrect responses to the logic of concrete operational thought.

3. What do you remember about how you learned to read? Compare your memories with those of two other people, one at least 10 years older and the other at least 5 years younger than you. Can you draw any conclusions about effective reading instruction? If so, what are they? If not, why not?

4. Talk to two parents of primary school children. What do they think are the best and worst parts of their children's education? Ask specific questions and analyze the results.

13

CHAPTER OUTLINE

The School Years: Psychosocial Development

In middle childhood, children break free from the closely supervised and limited arena of younger years. They venture forth in the neighborhood, community, and school, experiencing friendships, rivalries, and other social complexities.

From Cinderella to Harry Potter, school-age children's favorite stories use the extraordinary—either magical or coincidental—as a scaffold for deeper themes: friendship, mistrust of adults, sharp wits, and the heroic battle of good against evil. These are standard themes that children love.

This chapter examines the interplay between expanding freedom and guiding forces, between brave adventures and adult society, between valuing peers and needing parents. We look first at friends and families, then at the children themselves, especially at their coping strategies and inner strengths.

The Peer Group

Getting along with peers is especially crucial during middle childhood, "central to living a full life and feeling good" (Borland, 1998, p. 28). Difficulties with peers can cause serious problems, and being well-liked is protective, especially for children from conflicted, punitive, or otherwise stressful homes (Criss et al., 2002; Rubin et al., 2006).

There is an important developmental progression in peer relationships. Younger children have friends and learn from them, but their egocentrism makes them less affected by another's acceptance or rejection. School-age children, in contrast, are well aware of their classmates' opinions, judgments, and accomplishments.

One way to characterize this is to distinguish between "two distinct but intimately intertwined aspects of self" (Harter, 2006, p. 508): the "I-self" and the "me-self." The I-self is the self as subject—a person who thinks, acts, and feels independently; the me-self is the self as object—a person reflected, validated, and critiqued by others (Harter, 2006).

In middle childhood, the me-self is crucial, because of the new strength of **social comparison,** comparing oneself with other people even when no one else explicitly makes the comparison. School-age children become much more socially aware, judging themselves as worse or better than other people in hundreds of ways. Ideally, social comparison helps children value

social comparison The tendency to assess one's abilities, achievements, social status, and other attributes by measuring them against those of other people, especially one's peers.

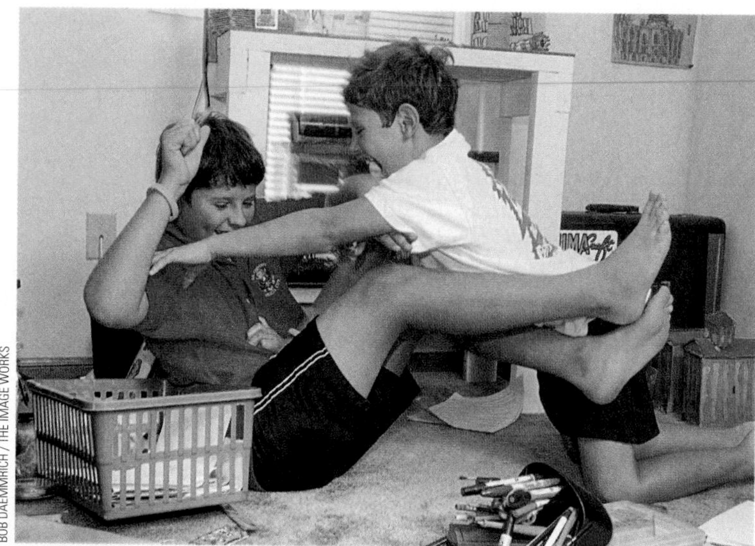

BOB DAEMMRICH / THE IMAGE WORKS

How to Play Boys teach each other the rituals and rules of engagement. The bigger boy shown here could hurt the smaller one, but he won't; their culture forbids it in such situations.

the abilities they have and abandon the imaginary, rosy self-evaluation of preschoolers (Grolnick et al., 1997; Jacobs et al., 2002).

The Culture of Children

Peer relationships, unlike adult–child relationships, involve partners who negotiate, compromise, share, and defend themselves as equals. Children learn social lessons from each other that grown-ups cannot teach, not only because adults are from a different generation but also because they are not peers. Adults sometimes command obedience, sometimes allow dominance, but always are much older and bigger.

The **culture of children** includes the particular rules and rituals that are passed down from slightly older children without adult approval. "Ring around the rosy, ashes, ashes, all fall down," for instance, originated with children coping with death (Kastenbaum, 2006). (*Rosy* is short for *rosary*.)

Throughout the world, the culture of children encourages independence from adult society. By age 10, if not before, peers pity those (especially boys) whose parents kiss them in public ("momma's boy"), tease children who please the teachers ("teacher's pet," "suck up"), and despise those who betray other children to adults ("tattletale," "grasser," "snitch," "rat"). Keeping secrets from adults is part of the culture of children.

culture of children The particular habits, styles, and values that reflect the set of rules and rituals that characterize children as distinct from adult society.

Clothes often signify independence and peer-group membership. Many 9-year-olds refuse to wear clothes their parents buy because they are too loose, too tight, too long, too short, or wrong in color, style, brand, or in some other way invisible to adults.

Since children adopt the manners and values of their peers, parents may encourage their children to form certain friendships (Dishion & Bullock, 2002). This succeeds with young children, but not with older ones, some of whom prefer friends who talk "dirty" or defy authority. The culture of children may include **deviancy training,** when children show each other how to avoid adult restrictions (Snyder et al., 2005). Some consequences of this are harmless (passing a note during class), others are not (shoplifting, spray-painting graffiti, cigarette smoking).

deviancy training The process whereby children are taught by their peers to avoid restrictions imposed by adults.

JEFF GREENBERG / THE IMAGE WORKS

Yu-Gi-Oh The specifics vary tremendously—stamps, stickers, liquor ads, matchbooks, baseball cards, and many more—but the impulse to collect, organize, and trade certain items is characteristic of school-age children. For a few years, in south Florida and elsewhere, the coveted collector's item was Yu-Gi-Oh cards.

One aspect of the culture of children that bothers many adults in developed nations is sexism. Gender stereotypes become more elaborate during the school years, when children much prefer to play with other children of their own sex (Ruble et al., 2006). While gender segregation is strongly maintained (especially among the boys), racial and ethnic prejudice is usually not (Nesdale, 2004). Indeed, schoolchildren's sense of justice and fairness helps them recognize and reject prejudice, first when it affects someone else and then themselves (C. S. Brown & Bigler, 2005; Killen, 2007).

As already apparent in deviancy training, the culture of children is not always benign. For example, because communication with peers is a priority, children may quickly master a second language but also spout curses, accents, and slang if that signifies being in synch (or "up," or "down") with their peers' culture.

KYUYA KAMAZAWA / HAGA / THE IMAGE WORKS

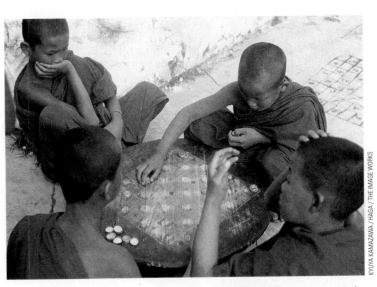

The Rules of the Game These young monks in Myanmar (formerly Burma) are playing a board game that adults also play, but the children have some of their own refinements of the general rules. Children's peer groups often modify the norms of dominant culture, as is evident in everything from superstitions to stickball.

Attitudes are affected by friends as well. Remember Yolanda and Paul (from Chapter 12)?

> *Yolanda:*
> There's one friend . . . she's always been with me, in bad or good things . . . She's always telling me, "Keep on going and your dreams are gonna come true."
>
> *Paul:*
> I think right now about going Christian, right? Just going Christian, trying to do good, you know? Stay away from drugs, everything. And every time it seems like I think about that, I think about the homeboys. And it's a trip because a lot of the homeboys are my family, too, you know?
>
> [*quoted in Nieto, 2000, pp. 220, 149*]

Children's Moral Codes

Ages 7 to 11 are:

> years of eager, lively searching on the part of children . . . as they try to understand things, to figure them out, but also to weigh the rights and wrongs . . . This is the time for growth of the moral imagination, fueled constantly by the willingness, the eagerness of children to put themselves in the shoes of others.
>
> [*Coles, 1997*]

The validity of that statement is suggested by a meta-analysis of dozens of studies: Generally, school-age children are more likely to behave prosocially than are younger children (Eisenberg & Fabes, 1998).

A similar idea arises from the theory of *social efficacy*—that people come to believe that they can affect their circumstances; this belief then leads to action that changes the social context. As Bandura writes, "the human mind is generative, reflective, proactive and creative, not merely reactive" (2006, p. 167). Those are exactly the cognitive traits that come to the fore in middle childhood, and they result in moral engagement, a drive to understand and weigh in on moral arguments. Empirical studies show that, throughout middle childhood, children readily suggest moral arguments to distinguish right from wrong (Killen, 2007).

Emotion, particularly empathy (stronger now because children are more aware of each other), is one force that drives this interest in right and wrong. Peer culture and personal experience is another. For example, children in multiethnic schools are better able to argue against prejudice (Killen et al., 2006). Intellectual maturation is a fourth, as we will now see.

TABLE 13.1

Kohlberg's Three Levels and Six Stages of Moral Reasoning

Level I: Preconventional Moral Reasoning
The goal is to get rewards and avoid punishments; this is a self-centered level.

- *Stage One: Might makes right* (a punishment and obedience orientation). The most important value is to maintain the appearance of obedience to authority, avoiding punishment while still advancing self-interest. Don't get caught!
- *Stage Two: Look out for number one* (an instrumental and relativist orientation). Each person tries to take care of his or her own needs. The reason to be nice to other people is so that they will be nice to you.

Level II: Conventional Moral Reasoning
Emphasis is placed on social rules; this is a community-centered level.

- *Stage Three: "Good girl" and "nice boy."* Proper behavior is behavior that pleases other people. Social approval is more important than any specific reward.
- *Stage Four: "Law and order."* Proper behavior means being a dutiful citizen and obeying the laws set down by society, even when no police are nearby.

Level III: Postconventional Moral Reasoning
Emphasis is placed on moral principles; this level is centered on ideals.

- *Stage Five: Social contract.* Obey social rules because they benefit everyone and are established by mutual agreement. If the rules become destructive or if one party doesn't live up to the agreement, the contract is no longer binding. Under some circumstances, disobeying the law is moral.
- *Stage Six: Universal ethical principles.* General, universally valid principles, not individual situations (level I) or community practices (level II), determine right and wrong. Ethical values (such as "life is sacred") are established by individual reflection and may contradict egocentric (level I) or social and community (level II) values.

Stages of Moral Reasoning

Much of the developmental research on children's morality began with Piaget's descriptions of the rules used by children as they play (Piaget, 1932/1997). This led to Lawrence Kohlberg's explanation of the cognitive stages of morality (Kohlberg, 1963). Kohlberg's research involved asking children and adolescents (and eventually adults) about various moral dilemmas. The story of a poor man named Heinz, whose wife was dying, serves as an example. A local druggist had the only cure for the wife's illness, an expensive drug that sold for 10 times what it cost to make.

> Heinz went to everyone he knew to borrow the money, but he could only get together about half of what it cost. He told the druggist that his wife was dying and asked him to sell it cheaper or let him pay later. But the druggist said "no." The husband got desperate and broke into the man's store to steal the drug for his wife. Should the husband have done that? Why?
>
> [*Kohlberg, 1963*]

The crucial factor in Kohlberg's scheme is not the final answer, but the *reasons* for it. For instance, a person might say the husband should steal the drug because he needs his wife to care for him, or because people will blame him if he lets his wife die, or because trying to save her life is more important than obeying the law. Each reason indicates a different level of moral reasoning.

Kohlberg described three levels of moral reasoning, with two stages at each level (see Table 13.1) and with clear parallels to Piaget's stages of cognition. **Preconventional moral reasoning** is similar to preoperational thought in that it is egocentric. **Conventional moral reasoning** parallels concrete operational thought in that it relates to current, observable practices. **Postconventional moral reasoning** is similar to formal operational thought because it uses logic and abstractions, going beyond what is concretely observed in a particular society.

According to Kohlberg, intellectual maturation, as well as experience, advances moral thinking. During middle childhood, children's answers shift from being primarily preconventional to conventional: Concrete thought and peer experiences help children move past the first two stages to the next two.

Kohlberg has been criticized for not taking cultural or gender differences into account. For example, caring for family members is much more important to many people than Kohlberg seemed to recognize. In terms of children's psychosocial development, Kohlberg did not seem to recognize the shift from adult to peer values. School-age children are quite capable of questioning or ignoring adult rules that seem unfair (Turiel, 2006).

preconventional moral reasoning Kohlberg's first level of moral reasoning, emphasizing rewards and punishments.

conventional moral reasoning Kohlberg's second level of moral reasoning, emphasizing social rules.

postconventional moral reasoning Kohlberg's third level of moral reasoning, emphasizing moral principles.

What Children Value

Sociocultural contexts are always influential at any stage. Moral specifics vary between and within nations, even within one ethnic group in one region. Yolanda and Paul, both Hispanic Americans from southern California, had quite different opinions about the value of education.

> *Yolanda:*
> I feel proud of myself when I see a [good] grade. And like [if] I see a C, I'm going to have to pull this grade up. . . . I like learning. I like really getting my mind working. . . . [Education] is good for you.

> *Paul:*
> I try not to get influenced too much, pulled into what I don't want to be into. But mostly, it's hard. You don't want people to be saying you're stupid. "Why do you want to go to school and get a job? . . . Drop out."
>
> *[quoted in Nieto, 2000, pp. 220, 221, 252]*

In developed nations, almost all parents value education and expect children to respect their teachers and other elders, but children do not necessarily do so (Cohen et al., 2006). They seek respect from each other. In other cultures, adults may not value school or friendship as much as children do.

> In rural Kenyan villages, the most competent children are often those viewed as having . . . accurate knowledge regarding natural herbal medicines that are used to treat parasites and other illnesses. . . . In many rural Alaska Yup'ik villages, the most competent children are often those viewed as having . . . superior hunting and gathering skills.
>
> *[Sternberg & Grigorenko, 2004, p. ix]*

As in this example, people disagree about which traits are most important in children. To cite an example familiar in developed nations, some parents want creative, lively offspring and others prefer obedient, quiet ones. But as Kenya, Alaska, and every other nation strives to modernize, political leaders, teachers, and many of the children themselves value school success.

Similarly, children's moral precepts are not necessarily the ones that adults endorse. Parents who want a lively child may watch with dismay as their school-age child starts acting lackadaisical and bored (which in the culture of children may be "cool"); parents who want an obedient child may have a defiant one. Three common values among 6- to11-year-olds are: Protect your friends, don't tell adults what is happening, and don't be too different from your peers (which explains both apparent boredom and overt defiance.)

Social Acceptance

Some children are well-liked, others not; but the children in each group change over time (Kupersmidt et al., 2004; Ladd, 2005). In a study conducted over six years, researchers asked 299 children which classmates they wanted, or did not want, as playmates. Overall, about a third of the children were popular (often chosen), about half were average (sometimes chosen), and about a sixth were unpopular (often rejected), with some change in the size of each cluster from year to year. Almost every child (89 percent) changed from one cluster to another over the six years. Only 2 percent were unpopular every year, and only 6 percent were consistently popular (Brendgen et al., 2001).

Culture and cohort affect the reasons why children are liked. For example, in North American culture, shy children are consistently not popular; in contrast, a study conducted in 1990 in Shanghai found that shy children were respected and often popular (Chen et al., 1992). Over the next 12 years, however, Chinese culture changed; assertiveness became more valued. This was shown in a new survey from the same Shanghai schools, which found that shy children were less popular than their shy predecessors had been (Chen et al., 2005). This cultural change also meant that fewer children identified themselves as shy.

Among young children in the United States, the most popular children are "kind, trustworthy, cooperative." Particularly as children grow older (around the time of fifth grade), a new group appears—children who are "athletic, cool, dominant, arrogant, and . . . aggressive." They are feared and respected, high in social status, but not necessarily liked (Cillessen & Mayeux, 2004a, p. 147).

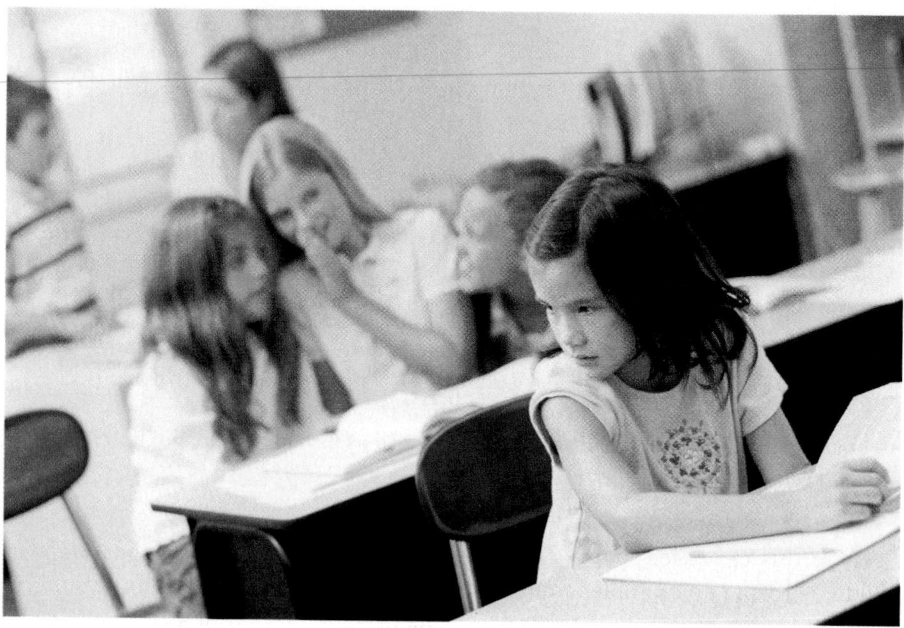

ALAMY

Loneliness Are the girls in the background whispering about the girl in the foreground loudly enough for her (but not the teacher) to hear? Perhaps this social situation is not what it appears to be, but almost every classroom has one or two rejected children, the targets of gossip, rumors, and social isolation.

Another development is the emergence of three distinct types of unpopular children. Some are *neglected,* not really rejected; they are ignored but not shunned. This may not be damaging to the child, especially if he or she has a supportive family or outstanding talent (in music or the arts, say) (Sandstrom & Zakriski, 2004).

The other two types of unpopular children suffer active rejection. Some are **aggressive-rejected**—disliked because they are antagonistic and confrontational. Others are **withdrawn-rejected**—disliked because they are timid, withdrawn, and anxious. Children of these two types have much in common: They tend to misinterpret social situations and to lack emotional regulation, and they are often mistreated at home (Pollak et al., 2000).

aggressive-rejected Rejected by peers because of antagonistic, confrontational behavior.

withdrawn-rejected Rejected by peers because of timid, withdrawn, and anxious behavior.

Social Awareness

Interpretation of social situations (akin to emotional intelligence, discussed in Chapter 11) may be crucial for peer acceptance. **Social cognition** is the ability to understand human interactions, an ability that begins developing in infancy (with social referencing) and continues in early childhood (as children develop a theory of mind). In most cases, social cognition is well-established in middle childhood. Children with impaired social cognition are likely to be rejected (Gifford-Smith & Rabiner, 2004; Ladd, 2005).

social cognition The ability to understand social interactions, including the causes and consequences of human behavior.

One extensive two-year study of social awareness began with 4½- to 8-year-olds. The researchers found that school-age children improve not only in social cognition but also in a related ability called **effortful control,** which entails modifying impulses and emotions. As a result of these improvements, the older children in this study had fewer emotional problems than did the younger ones, based on parents' reports (N. Eisenberg et al., 2004).

effortful control The ability to regulate one's emotions and actions through effort, not simply through natural inclination.

Well-liked children generally assume that social slights, from a push to an unkind remark, are accidental. Therefore, in contrast with rejected children, a social slight does not provoke fear, self-doubt, or anger. Given a direct conflict between themselves and another child, well-liked children think of the future of that relationship, seeking a compromise to maintain the friendship (Rose & Asher, 1999). These prosocial impulses and attitudes are a sign of social maturity, rare in rejected children (Gifford-Smith & Rabiner, 2004).

Friendship

Although school-age children value acceptance by the entire peer group, personal friendship is even more important to them (Erwin, 1998; Ladd, 1999; Sandstrom & Zakriski, 2004). Indeed, if they had to choose between being popular but friendless and having close friends but being unpopular, most children would take the friends. That is a healthy choice. Friendship leads to psychosocial growth and buffers against psychopathology.

A longitudinal study of peer acceptance (popularity) and close friendship (mutual loyalty) among fifth-graders found that both affected social interactions and emotional health 12 years later but that close friends were more important (Bagwell et al., 2001).

Another study found that children had about the same number of acquaintances no matter what their home backgrounds, but those from violent homes had fewer close friends and were lonelier. The authors explained, "Skill at recruiting surface acquaintances or playmates is different . . . from the skill required to sustain close relationships," and the latter is needed if the child is to avoid loneliness, isolation, and rejection (McCloskey & Stuewig, 2001, p. 93).

CAROL BECKWITH & ANGELA FISHER / HAGA / THE IMAGE WORKS

Friends and Culture Like children everywhere, these children—two 7-year-olds and one 10-year-old, of the Surma people in southern Ethiopia—model their appearance after that of slightly older children, in this case adolescents who apply elaborate body paint for courtship and stick-fighting rituals.

Observation Quiz (see answer, page 340): Are they boys or girls?

Friendships become more intense and intimate as children grow older, an expected development with improvement in social cognition and effortful control. Compared to age 6, by age 10, children demand more of their friends, change friends less often, become upset when a friendship breaks up, and find it harder to make new friends. Gender differences persist in activities (girls talk more while boys play games), but both boys and girls want best friends (Erwin, 1998; Underwood, 2004).

By age 10, most children know how to be a good friend. For example, when fifth-graders were asked how they would react if other children teased their friend, they almost all said they would ask their friend to do something fun with them, reassuring them that "things like that happen to everyone" (Rose & Asher, 2004).

Older children tend to choose best friends whose interests, values, and backgrounds are similar to their own. In fact, by the end of middle childhood, close friendships are almost always between children of the same sex, age, ethnicity, and socioeconomic status. This occurs not because children become more prejudiced over the course of middle childhood (they do not) but because they seek friends who understand and agree with them (Aboud & Amato, 2001; Aboud & Mendelson, 1996; Powlishta, 2004).

Bullies and Victims

Almost every adult remembers isolated attacks, occasional insults, and unexpected social slights in childhood. Many adults also remember good friends who kept them from being bullied.

Defining Terms

bullying Repeated, systematic efforts to inflict harm through physical, verbal, or social attack on a weaker person.

Bullying is defined as repeated, systematic attacks intended to harm those who are unable or unlikely to defend themselves and who have no protective social network. Bullying occurs in every nation, in every community, and in every kind of school (religious or secular, public or private, progressive or traditional, large or small), although some schools have much less bullying than others of the same

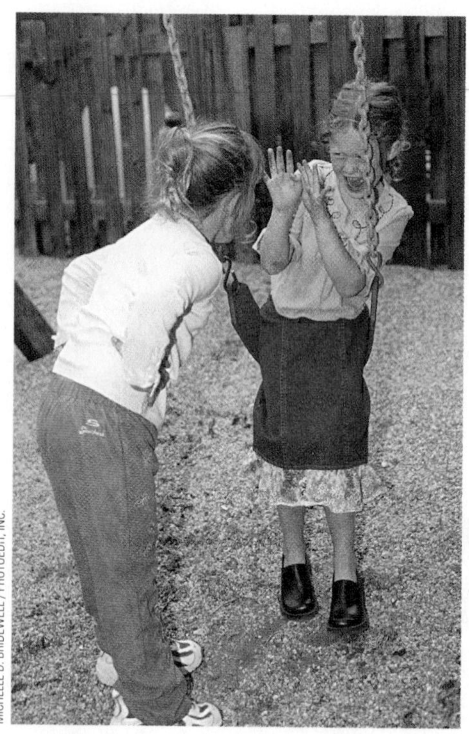

MICHELLE D. BRIDEWELL / PHOTOEDIT, INC.

JONATHAN NOUROK / PHOTOEDIT, INC.

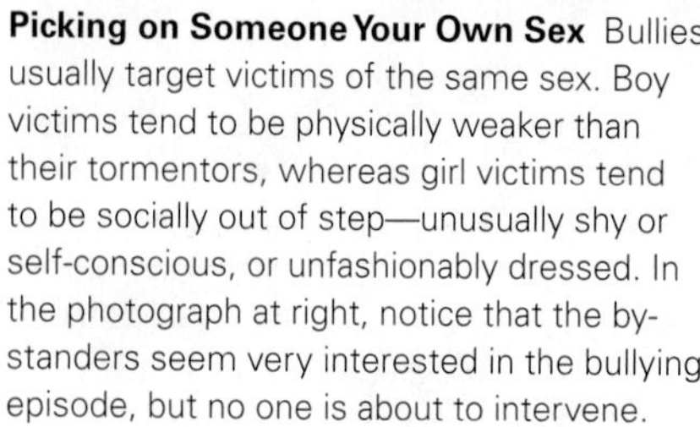

Picking on Someone Your Own Sex Bullies usually target victims of the same sex. Boy victims tend to be physically weaker than their tormentors, whereas girl victims tend to be socially out of step—unusually shy or self-conscious, or unfashionably dressed. In the photograph at right, notice that the bystanders seem very interested in the bullying episode, but no one is about to intervene.

type. Bullying may be *physical* (hitting, pinching, or kicking), *verbal* (teasing, taunting, or name-calling), or *relational* (designed to halt peer acceptance).

A key word in this definition is *repeated.* Victims of bullying typically endure shameful experiences again and again—being forced to hand over lunch money, laugh at insults, drink milk mixed with detergent, and so on, with others watching and no one defending them.

Victims of bullying tend to be "cautious, sensitive, quiet . . . lonely and abandoned at school. As a rule, they do not have a single good friend in their class" (Olweus et al., 1999, p. 15). Most victims are withdrawn-rejected, but some are aggressive-rejected, called **bully-victims** (or *provocative victims*) (Unnever, 2005). Bully-victims are "the most strongly disliked members of the peer group," with neither friends nor sympathizers (Sandstrom & Zakriski, 2004, p. 110).

bully-victim Someone who attacks others, and who is attacked as well. (Also called *provocative victims* because they do things that elicit bullying, such as taking a bully's pencil.)

Most bullies are *not* rejected. They have a few admiring friends (henchmen). Unless they are bully-victims, they are socially perceptive—but without the empathy of prosocial children. Especially over the years of middle childhood, they become skilled at avoiding adult awareness, attacking victims who can be counted on not to resist.

Boy bullies are often big; they target smaller, weaker boys. Girl bullies are often sharp-tongued; they harass shyer, more soft-spoken girls. Boys tend to use force (physical aggression), while girls tend to mock, ridicule, or spread rumors (relational aggression). This is a generality; many bullies of both sexes use multiple tactics.

Bullying may originate with a genetic predisposition or a brain abnormality, but parents, teachers, and peers usually succeed in teaching children to restrain their aggressive impulses before middle childhood (part of effortful control). However, families that create insecure attachment, provide a stressful home life, or include hostile siblings tend to intensify children's aggression (Cairns & Cairns, 2001; Ladd, 2005).

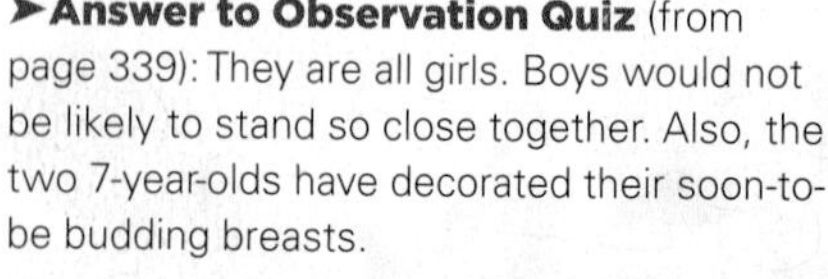

➤Answer to Observation Quiz (from page 339): They are all girls. Boys would not be likely to stand so close together. Also, the two 7-year-olds have decorated their soon-to-be budding breasts.

The consequences of bullying can echo for years. Many victims develop low self-esteem, and some explode violently at times; many bullies become increasingly cruel (Berger, 2007). Over time, both bullies and victims incur social costs, including impaired social understanding and relationship difficulties (Pepler et al., 2004). Even bystanders suffer (Nishina & Juvonen, 2005), liking school less. Perhaps mirror neurons make them feel pain when observing victimization (Berger, 2007).

Can Bullying Be Stopped?

Most children who are attacked find ways to halt ongoing victimization, by ignoring, retaliating, defusing, or avoiding. A study of older children who were bullied one year but not the next indicated that finding new friends was crucial (P. K. Smith, et al., 2004). Friendship helps current victims, but bullies may find new targets. More successful efforts change conditions in the whole school, including the behaviors of teachers and bystanders.

Especially for Former Victims of Bullying Almost everyone was bullied at some point in childhood. When you remember such moments, how can you avoid feeling sad and depressed?

This "whole-school" strategy is advocated by Dan Olweus, a pioneer in antibullying efforts. In 1982, after three victims of bullying in Norway killed themselves, the government asked Olweus to survey Norway's 90,000 school-age children. He reported much more bullying than adults realized: 14 percent of the children in grades 2–5 said that they were victims "now and then" and 10 percent admitted that they deliberately hurt other children (Olweus, 1993).

To stop bullying, Olweus used an ecological-systems approach, involving every segment of the school. He sent pamphlets to parents, showed videos to students, trained school staff, and increased supervision during recess. In each classroom, students discussed how to stop bullying and befriend lonely children. Bullies and their parents were counseled. Twenty months later, Olweus surveyed the children again. Bullying had been reduced by half (Olweus, 1992).

Similar efforts have been tried in dozens of nations, after surveys found high rates of bullying. For example, a Canadian study reported that about a third of the boys and a fourth of the girls had bullied another child in the previous two months (Pepler et al., 2004). However, interventions have usually been less successful than Olweus's original effort.

Especially for Parents of an Accused Bully Another parent has told you that your child is a bully. Your child denies it and explains that the other child doesn't mind being teased.

In the United States, one recent intervention produced a decrease in observed bullying but not in reported bullying (Frey et al., 2005; see Research Design). After another much-acclaimed effort in Texas, reported bullying actually increased (Rosenbluth et al., 2004). Several studies have discovered that putting troubled students together in a therapy group or a classroom tends to increase aggression in all of them (Kupersmidt et al., 2004). Older children are particularly stuck in their patterns; some high school efforts have backfired.

FRANK FOURNIER / WOODFIN CAMP & ASSOCIATES

FRANK FOURNIER / WOODFIN CAMP & ASSOCIATES

Shake Hands or Yell "Uncle" Many schools, such as this one in Alaska, have trained peer mediators who intervene in disputes, hear both sides, take notes, and seek a resolution. Without such efforts, antagonists usually fight until one gives up, giving bullies free rein. Despite Alaska's higher rate of adolescent alcohol abuse, the state's adolescent homicide rate is lower than the national average.

Research Design

Scientists: Karin S. Frey, Miriam K. Hirschstein, Jennie L. Snell, Leihua V. S. Edstron, Elizabeth MacKenzie, and Carole J. Broderick (all from The Committee on Children).

Publication: *Developmental Psychology* (2005).

Participants: All third- to sixth-graders in six schools.

Design: Confidential surveys and playground observations were conducted at six schools (three experimental and three control), both before and after interventions at the experimental schools. In the experimental schools, administrative changes (such as better supervision at recess) were coupled with a special 12-week curriculum taught by all the third- to sixth-grade teachers.

Major conclusion: Bullying is hard to stop. Playground observations found that bullying at the three control schools increased more over the school year than in the experimental schools (60 percent compared with 11 percent). However, children's attitudes and self-reported victimization did not improve.

Comment: This is good science, with experimental and control groups, before-and-after measures, observations, and questionnaires. It shows, unfortunately, that the culture of children and schools resists change.

Even in elementary school, well-intentioned measures, such as letting children solve problems on their own or assigning guards to the school, may make the situation worse. Teaching social cognition to victims may seem like a good idea, but the problem arises from the school culture more than from the victims. Many anti-bullying projects report discouraging results (J. D. Smith, et al., 2004; P. K. Smith & Ananiadou, 2003).

A review of all research on successful ways to halt bullying (Berger, 2007) finds the following to be true:

- The whole school must change, not just the identified bullies.
- Intervention is more effective in the younger grades.
- Evaluation is critical. Programs that appear to be good might actually be harmful.

This final point merits special emphasis. Some programs make a difference; some do not; only objective follow-up can tell. The best recent success was reported from a multifaceted effort that involved every school in one town over eight years. Victimization was reduced from 9 to 3 percent (Koivisto, 2004). Sustained and comprehensive effort may be what is needed.

SUMMING UP

School-age children develop their own culture, with customs and morals that encourage them to be loyal to each other. Moral development is affected by cognitive maturation and cultural values, with school-age children being more influenced by the ethics of their peer groups than by adults. All 6- to 11-year-olds need social acceptance and close, mutual friendships, to protect against loneliness and depression.

Most children experience some peer rejection as well as acceptance. However, some are repeatedly rejected and friendless, becoming victims of bullying. Bullying occurs everywhere, but the frequency and type depend on the school climate, on the culture, and on the child's age and gender. Efforts to reduce bullying have rarely been successful; a whole-school approach seems best. ■

Families and Children

No one doubts that genes affect temperament as well as ability, that peers are vital, and that schools and cultures influence what, and how much, children learn. Many people are also convinced that parental practices make a decided difference in how children develop. On this last point, some developmental researchers have expressed doubts, suggesting that genes, peers, and communities are so powerful that there may be little room left for parents (Ladd & Pettit, 2002; McLeod et al., 2007; O'Connor, 2002).

As already detailed (see Chapter 3), a substantial part of a person's behavior can be traced to heredity. This statement is based on research and statistical analysis of many traits found in monozygotic twins (genetically identical) separated at birth and raised in different homes (environment is not identical) (Canli, 2006; Lykken, 2006; Plomin et al., 2002; Wright, 1999).

Some human traits (such as height and hearing) are largely genetic; others (especially complex traits, including moral values) are far less so.

Nothing is entirely genetic or entirely environmental: Genes always interact with the environment, which amplifies the power of some genes and mutes the expression of others (see Chapter 1). Also, as the dynamic-systems approach reminds us, the relationship between genes and the environment for any particular

➤**Response for Former Victims of Bullying** (from page 341): Although children who are victims of bullying often feel inferior and alone, you now know that adults should have stopped the bully. Now you can become angry at the adults who should have protected you. You can also be proud of yourself for having eventually gotten through or escaped the situation. Your anger and pride may replace your lingering sadness and depression.

trait changes over time. Here we focus on the environmental component of child development between ages 6 and 10.

Shared and Nonshared Environment

Environment is subdivided into *shared environment* (e.g., household influences that are the same for two people, such as children reared together) and *nonshared* (e.g., when siblings have different friends and different teachers). Surprisingly, careful research has repeatedly found that nonshared environmental factors are more influential on siblings than are shared ones. This fact has led some to conclude that parents have little influence on how school-age children develop (e.g., Harris, 1998, 2002).

The latest findings, however, reassert the power of parents. The analysis of shared and nonshared influences was correct, but the assumption was wrong. Children raised in the same household do *not* necessarily share the same home environment. If the family moves, parents divorce, or one or both lose a job, each child is affected differently; thus, these environmental influences are nonshared. Further, parents' attitudes toward each of their children vary, as the following makes clear.

➤**Response for Parents of an Accused Bully** (from page 341): The future is ominous if the charges are true. Your child's denial is a sign that there is a problem. (An innocent child would be worried about the misperception instead of categorically denying that any problem exists.) You might ask the teacher what the school is doing about bullying. Family counseling might help. Because bullies often have friends who egg them on, you may need to monitor your child's friendships and perhaps befriend the victim. Talk matters over with your child. Ignoring the situation might lead to heartache later on.

thinking like a scientist

"I Always Dressed One in Blue Stuff . . ."

One way to measure family influence is to compare children of varying genetic similarity (twins, full siblings, stepsiblings, adopted children) raised in the same household (Reiss et al., 2000). The extent to which children share alleles (100 percent for monozygotic twins, 50 percent for full siblings, 25 percent for half-siblings, much less for unrelated individuals such as stepsiblings and adopted children) can be used to calculate how much of the variation in a trait is inherited. The remaining variation presumably arises from the environment.

This seems simple enough. However, every research design aimed at studying the links between parental behavior and child behavior is vulnerable to criticism (see Figure 13.1). Consequently, an expert team of scientists, noting the flaws in earlier research, set out to compare 1,000 sets of monozygotic twins reared by their biological parents (Caspi et al., 2004).

The team assessed each child's temperament by asking the mothers and teachers to fill out a detailed, standardized checklist. They also assessed every mother's attitudes toward each child. These ranged from very positive ("my ray of sunshine") to very negative ("I wish I never had her. . . . She's a cow, I hate her") (quoted in Caspi et al., 2004, p. 153).

Many mothers described personality differences between their twins and assumed these were innate. The mothers did not realize that they themselves may have created many of these differences. For example, one mother spoke of her identical daughters:

> Susan can be very sweet. She loves babies . . . she can be insecure . . . she flutters and dances around. . . . There's not much between her ears. . . . She's exceptionally vain, more so than Ann. Ann loves any game involving a ball, very sporty, climbs trees, very much a tomboy. One is a serious tomboy and one's a serious girlie girl. Even when they were babies I always dressed one in blue stuff and one in pink stuff.
>
> *[quoted in Caspi et al., 2004, p. 156]*

Some mothers were much more cold and rejecting toward one twin than toward the other:

> He was in the hospital and everyone was all "poor Jeff, poor Jeff" and I started thinking, "Well, what about me? I'm the one's just had twins. I'm the one's going though this, he's a seven-week-old baby and doesn't know a thing about it." . . . I sort of detached and plowed my emotions into Mike.
>
> *[quoted in Caspi et al., 2004, p. 156]*

After she was divorced, this mother blamed Jeff for favoring his father: "Jeff would do anything for Don but he wouldn't for me, and no matter what I did for either of them it wouldn't be right" (p. 157). She said Mike was much more lovable.

The researchers controlled for genes, gender, age, and personality differences in kindergarten (by measuring, among other things, antisocial behavior as assessed by the children's kindergarten teachers). They found that twins whose mothers were more negative toward them tended to *become* more antisocial than their co-twin. The rejected twins were more likely to fight, steal, and hurt others at age 7 than at age 5 after all background factors were taken into account. Mothers' attitudes were obviously influential.

Many other nonshared factors—peers, teachers, and so on—are important. But this change in identical twins confirms the popular belief: Parents matter. The assumption that parents and a home provide a completely shared environment for all their children is false. As everyone with siblings can attest, each child's family experiences are unique.

FIGURE 13.1

Improvements in Research Design Before designing a study, researchers identify the weaknesses of earlier studies so that they can consider ways of avoiding them. This chart shows the preliminary analysis made by the team that found that parents' attitudes have a direct effect on children's behavior. As they realized, "continuing refinements" in research design are always possible.

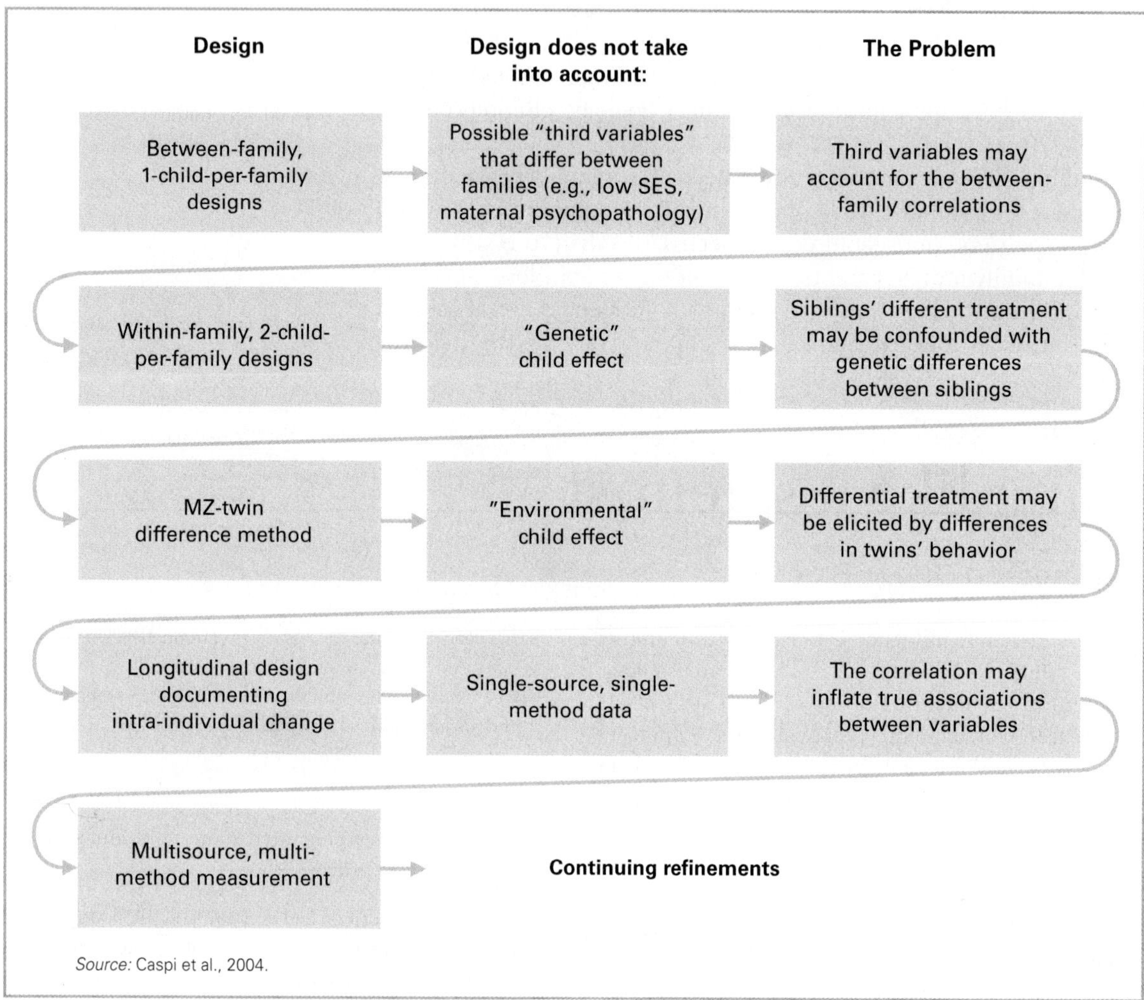
Design
Design does not take into account:
The Problem
Between-family, 1-child-per-family designs
Possible "third variables" that differ between families (e.g., low SES, maternal psychopathology)
Third variables may account for the between-family correlations
Within-family, 2-child-per-family designs
"Genetic" child effect
Siblings' different treatment may be confounded with genetic differences between siblings
MZ-twin difference method
"Environmental" child effect
Differential treatment may be elicited by differences in twins' behavior
Longitudinal design documenting intra-individual change
Single-source, single-method data
The correlation may inflate true associations between variables
Multisource, multi-method measurement
Continuing refinements
Source: Caspi et al., 2004.

Family Function and Dysfunction

family structure The legal and genetic relationships (e.g., nuclear, extended, step) among relatives in the same home.

family function The way a family works to meet the needs of its members. Children need families to provide basic material necessities, encourage learning, develop self-respect, nurture friendships, and foster harmony and stability.

Exactly what do school-age children require from their families, and what factors in family structure make it likely (or unlikely) that they will get it? **Family structure** refers to the legal and genetic connections among related people living in the same household. **Family function** refers to the way a family works to care for its members.

The most important family function for people of all ages is to afford a safe haven of love and encouragement. Beyond that, people of various ages need different things from their families: Infants need frequent caregiving and social interaction; teenagers need both freedom and guidance; young adults need peace and privacy; the aged need respect and appreciation.

KATHY MCLAUGHLIN / THE IMAGE WORKS

Meeting Her Need for Fit and Fashion A 10-year-old's rapidly growing feet frequently need new shoes, and peer pressure favors certain styles of footwear. Here, Rebekah's sisters wait and watch as their mother tries to find a boot that fits her and is fashionable.

School-age children thrive if their families function for them in five ways:

1. *Provide basic necessities:* Children aged 6 to 11 can eat, dress, wash, and sleep without help, but someone must provide food, clothing, and shelter.
2. *Encourage learning.* School-age children must master academic and social skills. Families can support and guide their education.
3. *Develop self-respect.* As they become cognitively mature, school-age children become self-critical and socially aware. Families can help their children feel competent and capable.
4. *Nurture peer relationships.* School-age children need friends, and families can provide the time and opportunity to develop those friendships.
5. *Ensure harmony and stability.* School-age children need protective and predictable family routines, since they are particularly troubled by conflict and change. Families can provide this kind of stability and security.

Thus, families provide resources, both material and cognitive, as well as emotional and social support. No family always functions perfectly, but some malfunctions are worse than others at various points of the life span. Family structures do not determine function, but they affect it, as do other family characteristics, particularly income.

Diverse Structures

The effects of family structure on family function are many, but before explaining them we need to distinguish *household* from structure. A household as defined by the United States Census is all the people who live together in the same home. Many households, worldwide, are not made up of members of a single family—that is, they are not "family households" (Georgas et al., 2006). Often, a household consists of one person living alone (26 percent of all households in the United States in 2005) or of nonrelatives living together (6 percent in the United States). Among family households, most do not include children under age 18, usually because they consist of a married couple living alone.

Here we focus on family households that include a school-age child (about one-fourth of all households). Table 13.2 briefly describes common family structures within these households in the United States. More than half of all school-age children live in two-parent homes as part of a **nuclear family** (a married couple and their biological offspring); worldwide as well, this is the most common family structure (Georgas et al., 2006). Nuclear families include families in which parents live together but are not legally married; they *cohabit*. Depending partly on local customs, they are sometimes considered married.

nuclear family A family that consists of a father, a mother, and their biological children under age 18.

In the United States, more than a fourth of all school-age children currently live in a **single-parent family,** with only one parent. This is the dominant form among African Americans. Most European American children will spend some time in a single-parent family before age 18.

single-parent family A family that consists of only one parent and his or her biological children under age 18.

The nuclear and single-parent family structures are sometimes contrasted with the **extended family,** in which children live not only with one or both of their parents but also with other relatives (usually grandparents, but often aunts, uncles, and cousins as well). Extended families are common among low-income families and in poor nations, partly because household expenses and responsibilities can be shared.

extended family A family of three or more generations living in one household.

TABLE 13.2

Common Family Structures (with percentages of U.S. children aged 6–11 in each family type)

Two-Parent Families (67%)

Most human families have two parents. These families are of several kinds.

1. **Nuclear family** (56%) Named after the nucleus (the tightly connected core particles of an atom), the nuclear family consists of a husband and wife and their biological offspring. About half of all families with children are nuclear. This category includes extended families in which both parents live with the parents of one of the spouses or when a grandparent couple acts as mother and father.
2. **Stepparent family** (8%) Divorced fathers (Stewart et al., 2003) are particularly likely to remarry. Usually his children from a previous marriage do not live with him, but if they do, they are in a stepparent family. Mothers are less likely to remarry, but when they do, the children often live with her and their stepfather. Many children spend some time in a stepparent family, but relatively few spend their entire childhood in such families.
   Blended family A stepparent family that includes children born to several families, such as the biological children from the spouses' previous marriages and the biological children of the new couple. This type of family is a particularly difficult structure for school-age children.
3. **Adoptive family** (3%) Although as many as one-third of infertile married couples adopt children, fewer adoptable children are available than in earlier decades, which means that most adoptive families have only one or two children. A single parent is sometimes an adoptive parent, but this is unusual.
4. **Polygamous family** (0%) In some nations, it is common for one man to have several wives, each bearing his children.

One-Parent Families (28%)

One-parent families are increasingly common, but they tend to have fewer children than two-parent families.

1. **Single mother, never married** (11%) Many babies (about a third of all U.S. newborns) are born to unmarried mothers, but most of these mothers intend to marry someday (Musick, 2002). Many of them do get married, either to their baby's father or to someone else. By school age, their children are often in two-parent families.
2. **Single mother—divorced, separated, or widowed** (12%) Although many marriages end in divorce (almost half in the United States, less in other nations), many divorcing couples have no children and many others remarry. Thus, many divorced women do not have school-age children living with them.
3. **Single father, divorced or never married** (5%) About one in five divorced or unmarried fathers has physical custody of the children. This structure is uncommon, but it is the most rapidly increasing form.

Other Family Types (5%)

Some children live in special versions of one- or two-parent families, described here.

1. **Extended family** Many children live with their grandparents as well as with one or both of their parents.
2. **Grandparents alone** For some school-age children, their one or two "parents" are their grandparents, because the biological parents are dead or otherwise unable to live with them. This family type is increasing, especially in Africa, where an epidemic of AIDS is killing many parents.
3. **Homosexual family** Some school-age children live in a homosexual family, usually when a custodial parent has a homosexual partner. Less often, a homosexual couple adopts children or a lesbian has a child. Varying laws and norms determine whether these are one- or two-parent families.
4. **Foster family** This family type is usually considered temporary, and the children are categorized by their original family structure. Otherwise, they are in one- or two-parent families depending on the structure of their foster family.

Source: Percentages are estimated from U.S. Bureau of the Census, 2007.

The distinctions among family types are not clear-cut, especially regarding extended families. Most nuclear and single-parent families have close connections with other relatives who often live nearby, share meals, provide emotional and financial support, and otherwise function as an extended family. Further, especially in developing nations, extended families who technically are in one household nonetheless have private living areas within the home for each couple and their children, as occurs in nuclear families (Georgas et al., 2006).

Especially for Readers Whose Parents Are Middle-Aged Your mother tells you that she misses taking care of young children and wants to become a foster parent. How do you advise her?

Connecting Structure and Function

Family structure and family function are intertwined. The crucial question for children is whether the family living arrangements make it more, or less, likely that several adults are devoted to their well-being.

From this perspective, single-mother families may be problematic, because such households are likely to be low-income and unstable in that they are most likely to change structure as well as location (Raley & Wildsmith, 2004). Furthermore, there is only one adult who often has many roles to fill besides being a parent. Children in single-mother families "are at greatest risk," faring worse in school and in adult life (Carlson & Corcoran, 2001, p. 789).

A **blended family,** the structure in which a married couple combine offspring from earlier partnerships, also risks instability. Blended families tend to be wealthier than single-parent families, but older children leave, new babies arrive, and marriages dissolve more often than do first marriages. The likelihood that children will thrive in blended families depends on the adults' economic and emotional security; blended families are not necessarily better for children than single-parent families.

blended family A family that consists of two adults and the children of the prior relationships of one or both parents and/or the new partnership.

Nuclear families tend to function best for children, partly because people who marry and stay married tend to have personal and financial strengths that also make them better parents. Correlational statistics show that, compared with adults who never marry, married adults tend to be wealthier, better educated, healthier, more flexible, and less hostile—even before they marry.

Especially for Single Parents You have heard that children raised in one-parent families will have difficulty in establishing intimate relationships as adolescents and adults. What can you do about this possibility?

On average, biological and adoptive parents are more dedicated to their children than are step or foster parents. For these reasons, children growing up in nuclear families are more likely to have someone to teach them to brush their teeth, to read to them at bedtime, to check their homework, and so on, as well as to plan for their future, saving for college and inculcating health habits.

BILL ARON / PHOTOEDIT, INC.

A Comfortable Combination The blended family—husband, wife, and children from both spouses' previous marriages—often breeds resentment, depression, and rebellion in the children. That is apparently not the case for the family shown here, which provides cheerful evidence that any family structure is capable of functioning well.

➤Response for Readers Whose Parents Are Middle-Aged (from page 347): Foster parenthood is probably the most difficult type of parenthood, yet it can be very rewarding if all needed support is available and a long-term arrangement is likely. Advise your mother to make sure that medical, educational, and psychological help is available if needed and that the placement agency truly cares about children's well-being.

Every family type is affected by culture (Heuveline & Timberlake, 2004). For example, many French parents are not married, but they share household and child-rearing tasks and are less likely to separate than are married adults in the United States. Thus, the cohabiting structure functions well for French children. However, in the United States, cohabiting parents split up more than married parents. This makes that structure, on average, less functional for children (S. L. Brown, 2004).

More generally, the effect of marriage and divorce on parenthood varies not only by nation but also by ethnic group. Compared with other American ethnic groups, divorced and single-parent families are not as common among Hispanic Americans and Asian Americans, and marriage usually entails devotion to child rearing by both parents. Children benefit.

However, if divorce does occur, it is more life-changing. Divorced Hispanic American fathers are *less* likely to stay involved with their children than are divorced fathers of other ethnic groups (King et al., 2004). (Data are not available for Asian American divorced fathers.)

Every study finds exceptions to these patterns. In any family type, some children develop well and others are harmed. It is "not enough to know that an individual lives in a particular family structure without also knowing what takes place within that structure" (Lansford et al., 2001, p. 850). Function, not structure, is key.

Family Trouble

We now look at two factors that interfere with family function in every nation: low income and high conflict (Georgas et al., 2006). Financial stress and family fighting often co-occur because they feed on each other. Imagine this scene.

Suppose a 3-year-old spills his milk, as every 3-year-old sometimes does. In a well-functioning, financially stable family, the parents then teach the child how to mop up a spill. They pour more milk, perhaps with a comment that encourages family harmony, such as, "Everyone makes mistakes sometimes."

What if the parents are already overwhelmed by unemployment, overdue rent, an older child who wants money for a school trip? What if the last of the food stamps bought that milk? Conflict erupts, with shouting, crying, and accusations (a sibling claiming, "He did it on purpose"; the 3-year-old saying, "You pushed me"; an uncle adding, "You should teach him to be careful"). Poverty can make anger spill over when the milk does.

Family Income

As in this example, family income correlates with both function and structure. Directly or indirectly, all five functions benefit from adequate income (Conger & Donellan, 2007; Gershoff et al., 2007; Yeung et al., 2002), especially at ages 6 to 9 (Gennetian & Miller, 2002).

To understand exactly how income affects child development, consider the *family-stress model,* which holds that the crucial question to ask about any risk factor (such as low income, divorce, unemployment) is whether or not it increases the stress on a family. In developed nations, poverty may not directly prevent children from having adequate food, clothing, and other necessities, since adults are usually able to secure at least the minimum needed. In that case, low income may not add to stress.

However, for many families, economic hardship increases stress, which results in the worry and tension that make adults more likely to be harsh and hostile with their partners and children (Conger et al., 2002; Parke et al., 2004). Thus, the adults' stressed and stressful *reaction* to poverty is crucial. Many intervention

➤Response for Single Parents (from page 347): Do not get married mainly to provide a second parent for your child. If you were to do so, things would probably get worse rather than better. Do make an effort to have friends of both sexes with whom your child can interact.

programs aim to educate poor parents so that their reactions to their children become more encouraging and patient than hostile (McLoyd et al., 2006).

Reaction to wealth may be a problem, too. Children in high-income families have a disproportionate share of emotional problems, which sometimes lead to drug abuse and delinquency. One reason, again, is thought to be the stress from parents who pressure their children to be superstars (Luthar, 2003).

In low-income families, however, an emphasis on parental reaction (not on income) may be misplaced. Poverty itself—inadequate child care, poor health care, possible homelessness, and so on—may cause stress. Perhaps raising household income, thereby reducing stress, would be better for children than focusing on problematic parenting styles and dysfunctional reactions.

That conclusion might be drawn from an eight-year natural experiment (Costello et al., 2003). This study began by assessing psychopathology among 1,420 school-age children, many of whom were Native American. For children of every ethnicity, those from poor homes averaged four symptoms of mental disturbance, compared with only one symptom among the nonpoor.

VALICA BOUDRY / AP PHOTO

The One-Parent Family Single parents are of two types: never married and formerly married. This divorcée is a pediatrician, so she and her daughter have a higher income than many other one-parent families. To combat the other hazards faced by single parents—including loneliness, low self-esteem, and ongoing disputes with the former spouse—she has established a divorce resource center in her hometown in Michigan.

Midway through the study, about 200 children suddenly were no longer in poor families, primarily because a new casino began paying each Native American adult about $6,000 per year. Among those children, the incidence of externalizing symptoms fell, reaching the same low levels as among the children who were not poor when the study began (Costello et al., 2003). For these children, at least, no parent education was needed to change reactions and relieve the family stress.

Other research also suggests that reducing family financial stress directly benefits the children. In extended families that include several well-educated wage earners, the children are likely to become well educated and happy. Children in single-mother households do much better if their father pays child support (J. W. Graham & Beller, 2002) or if the nation subsidizes single parents (as Austria and Iceland do) (Pong et al., 2003).

Especially for Readers Who Are Not Parents Should children call their parents by their first names and wear whatever they choose? Or should children be deferential toward adults and be pushed to excel in school?

In general, economic hardship (either chronic poverty or sudden loss of income) leads to anger and depression among the adults, which makes them hostile toward their partners and their children—and thus not the loving, firm, caring parents they could be (Conger et al., 2002; Parke et al., 2004). This is affected by ethnicity and culture, but the trends are universal. Economic distress impairs family functioning.

Harmony and Stability

The second crucial factor for school-age children is harmony and stability, each of which can be considered separately but which both work together (Buehler & Gerard, 2002; Khaleque & Rohner, 2002). Ideally, parents form a parental alliance, learning to cooperate and thus protecting the children. The need for harmony explains why blended families can be problematic (Hetherington & Kelly, 2002). Jealousy, stress, and conflict tend to arise when children have to share a home with other children and must adjust to the authority of another adult. In such situations, smooth parental alliances can take years to form.

In any family structure, children's well-being declines if family members fight, especially if parents physically or verbally abuse each other. In contrast, children may learn valuable lessons from parental disagreements that result in compromise and reconciliation (Cummings et al., 2003). But if a fight escalates, or one parent walks out and the other sobs, that may harm a child.

➤Response for Readers Who Are Not Parents (from page 349): This is a trick question. The crucial factor in child rearing is parents' genuine warmth toward the child. While neither approach mentioned in the question reflects the ideal, authoritative style, both can produce happy, successful children.

Especially for Parents Who Want to Divorce and Remarry A couple want to divorce each other and marry other people. At what age is this least harmful to children?

FIGURE 13.2

When Parents Fight and Children Blame Themselves Husbands and wives who almost never disagree are below the first standard deviation (–1 SD) in verbal marital conflict. Couples who frequently have loud, screaming, cursing arguments are in the highest 15 percent (+1 SD). In such high-conflict households, children are not much affected—*if* they do not blame themselves for the situation. However, if children do blame themselves, they are likely to have internalizing problems, such as nightmares, stomachaches, panic attacks, and feelings of loneliness.

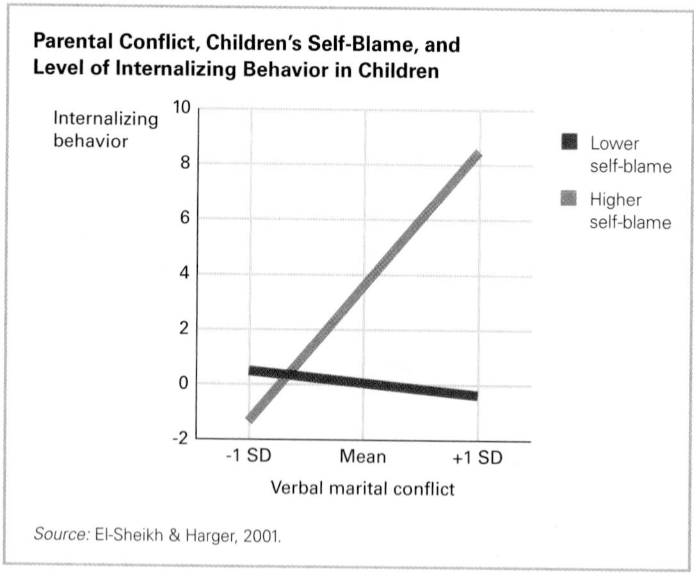

Every family transition affects the children. They are more likely to quit school, leave home, use drugs, become delinquent, and have early love affairs if their families change more frequently or drastically than average (McLanahan et al., 2005). Some family structures typically undergo multiple transitions as children grow. For instance, most unmarried mothers change jobs, residences, and romantic partners several times before their children are fully grown (Bumpass & Lu, 2000).

Changing homes is particularly hard for school-age children (who have a special need for continuity), yet each year about 16 percent of all U.S. children move from one home to another, a rate three times that of adults over age 50 (U.S. Bureau of the Census, 2007). Even a move that parents consider an improvement may upset school-age children who lose their friends. A move to another culture is obviously especially hard.

The problems associated with moving were shown by a study in Japan, where junior employees are often transferred for several years to strengthen company cohesiveness. If the employee is a father, about half the time his family moves with him. Researchers compared the children who moved to those who did not, expecting to find the benefits of daily contact with fathers. However, the school-age children did better if they stayed put, even with absent fathers (Tanaka & Nakazawa, 2005). (Their mothers, however, were more stressed, illustrating that each change affects family members differently.)

Worldwide, children are more likely to move as family income falls. Hardest hit are school-age children who are homeless or refugees. In the United States, homeless children move, on average, two to three times *a year* before moving into a shelter (Buckner et al., 1999), a major threat to their well-being.

Household harmony and continuity can be fostered by communities, as seems to be the case with some immigrant and African American communities. Children benefit when single mothers are not isolated, when men who aren't part of the household become "social fathers" to them, and when nearby grandmothers and other adults provide free and nurturing child care.

By contrast, sometimes a child's peace of mind is jeopardized by conflict in the family or neighborhood. Parents disturb a child's development if they push their children to take sides in a marital dispute or if they give one child authority over another. Grandparents and parents fighting over child-rearing practices can also be harmful.

An intriguing study of 8- to 11-year-olds assessed three factors: conflict between parents, stress reactions in children, and each child's feelings. By far the most important correlate with children's problems was not the marital discord but the children's feelings of self-blame or vulnerability. When children "do not perceive that marital conflict is threatening to them and do not blame themselves" (El-Sheikh & Harger, 2001, p. 883), they are much less troubled (see Figure 13.2).

SUMMING UP

Parents influence child development, with some families functioning better than others. For school-age children, families serve five crucial functions: to provide basic necessities, to encourage learning, to develop self-respect, to nurture friendships, and to provide harmony and stability. Low income, conflict, and transitions interfere with these functions, no matter what the family structure.

The nuclear, two-parent family is the most common, but a sizable minority of families are headed by a single parent (including one-fourth of all families of school-age children in the United States). Two-parent families tend to provide more income, stability, and adult attention. Extended families, grandparent families, one-parent families, blended families, and adoptive families can raise successful, happy children, although each of these has its own vulnerabilities. No structure inevitably either harms children or guarantees good family function.

TABLE 13.3

AT ABOUT THIS TIME: Signs of Psychosocial Maturation Between Ages 6 and 11

Children are more likely to have specific chores to perform at home.
Children are more likely to have a weekly allowance.
Children are expected to tell time, and they have set times for various activities.
Children have more homework assignments, some over several days.
Children are less often punished physically, more often with disapproval or withdrawal of privileges.
Children try to conform to peer standards in such matters as clothing and language.
Children influence decisions about their after-school care, lessons, and activities.
Children use media (TV, computers, video games) without adult supervision.
Children are given new responsibility for younger children, pets, or, in some cultures, employment.

The Nature of the Child

We have now discussed peers and parents, the two most important social influences on school-age children. However, each child is an individual, not simply a social being reacting to others. Table 13.3 shows some of the practical ways that children become much more responsible and mature over these years.

To delve more deeply into the nature of the school-age child, we turn first to psychoanalytic theory, which puts forth a very specific description. Then we look at current developmental research, which provides a different perspective.

Psychoanalytic Theory

Psychoanalytic theory stresses that school-age children are eager to learn about their expanding social universe. Sigmund Freud described this period as **latency,** when emotional drives are quiet and unconscious sexual conflicts are submerged. Latency is a "time for acquiring cognitive skills and assimilating cultural values as children expand their world to include teachers, neighbors, peers, club leaders, and coaches. Sexual energy continues to flow, but it is channeled into social concerns" (P. H. Miller, 2002, p. 131).

Erik Erikson agreed that middle childhood is an emotionally quiet period. The child "must forget past hopes and wishes, while his exuberant imagination is tamed and harnessed to the laws of impersonal things," becoming "ready to apply himself to given skills and tasks" (Erikson, 1963, pp. 258, 259). During Erikson's crisis of **industry versus inferiority,** children busily try to master whatever abilities their culture values.

latency Freud's term for middle childhood, during which children's emotional drives and psychosocial needs are quiet (latent). Freud thought that sexual conflicts from earlier stages are only temporarily submerged, to burst forth again at puberty.

industry versus inferiority The fourth of Erikson's eight psychosocial development crises, during which children attempt to master many skills, developing a sense of themselves as either industrious or inferior, competent or incompetent.

LINDSAY HEBBERD / WOODFIN CAMP & ASSOCIATES

Celebrating Spring No matter where they live, 7- to 11-year-olds seek to understand and develop whatever skills are valued by their culture. They do so in active, industrious ways, as described in behaviorism as well as cognitive, sociocultural, psychoanalytic, and epigenetic theories. This universal truth is illustrated here, as four friends in Assam, northeastern India, usher in spring with a Bihu celebration. Soon they will be given sweets and tea, which is the sociocultural validation of their energy, independence, and skill.

➤Response for Parents Who Want to Divorce and Remarry (from page 350): Children usually prefer that their parents stay together, unless one parent is abusive. There is no best age for children when it comes to parents' getting divorced. However, it is probably worst if such major family transitions occur just when children are undergoing major transitions of their own, such as starting school or beginning puberty.

Children judge themselves as either *industrious* or *inferior*—that is, competent or incompetent, productive or failing, winners or losers. Being productive not only is intrinsically joyous but also fosters the self-control that is a crucial defense against emotional problems (Bradley & Corwyn, 2005).

Concerns about inferiority are evident in the schoolchild's ditty: "Nobody likes me. Everybody hates me. I think I'll go out and eat some worms." This lament has endured for generations because it captures, with humor that children can appreciate, the self-doubt that many school-age children feel.

Self-Concept

The following self-description could have been written by many 10-year-olds:

> I'm in the fourth grade this year, and I'm pretty popular, at least with the girls. That's because I'm nice to people and can keep secrets. Mostly I am nice to my friends, although if I get in a bad mood I sometimes say something that can be a little mean. I try to control my temper, but when I don't, I'm ashamed of myself. I'm usually happy when I'm with my friends, but I get sad if there is no one to do things with. At school, I'm feeling pretty smart in certain subjects like Language Arts and Social Studies. I got As in these subjects on my last report card and was really proud of myself. But I'm feeling pretty dumb in Math and Science, especially when I see how well a lot of the other kids are doing. Even though I'm not doing well in those subjects, I still like myself as a person, because Math and Science just aren't that important to me. How I look and how popular I am are more important. I also like myself because I know my parents like me and so do other kids. That helps you like yourself.
>
> *[quoted in Harter, 1999, p. 48]*

This excerpt (from a book written by a scholar who has studied the development of children's self-concept for decades) captures the nature of school-age children. As already explained, social comparison ("especially when I see how well a lot of the other kids are doing"), effortful control ("I try to control my temper"), loyalty ("can keep secrets"), and appreciation of peers and parents ("I know my parents like me and so do other kids") are typical.

Note that the child's self-concept no longer mirrors the parents' perspective. Every theory and every perceptive observer notes that school-age children recognize themselves as individuals, distinct from what their parents and teachers think of them.

One study that confirmed this began by asking, "Who knows best what you are thinking? . . . how tired you are? . . . your favorite foods?" and so on (Burton & Mitchell, 2003). Unlike 3-year-olds who might answer, "Mommy," and rely on a parent to tell them, "Oh, you are tired, it's time for your nap," school-age children become increasingly sure of their own minds. In this study, few (13 percent) of the 5-year-olds but most (73 percent) of the 10-year-olds thought that they knew themselves better than their parents or teachers did (Burton & Mitchell, 2003).

Increases in self-understanding and social awareness come at a price. Self-criticism and self-consciousness tend to rise from age 6 to 12, as self-esteem dips (Merrell & Gimpel, 1998), especially for children who live with unusual stresses (e.g., an abusive or alcoholic parent) (Luthar & Zelazo, 2003).

If children are already quite anxious and stressed, reduced self-esteem tends to lead to lower academic achievement (Pomerantz & Rudolph, 2003). This is particularly true of children who are rejected by classmates (Flook et al., 2005). A loss of self-pride in middle childhood may foreshadow emotional uncertainty and psychic stress in adolescence—not the usual path, but the one often followed by children who feel inferior (Graber, 2004).

As you can see, self-esteem is tricky. If it is unrealistically high, it may produce less effortful control and thus lower achievement (Baumeister et al., 2003), but the same consequences may occur if it is unrealistically low. Children who appreciate themselves and appreciate other children (i.e., when self and peers both fare well in social comparison) tend to have more friends and to be prosocial, able to defend a friend if the occasion arises. In contrast, children who like themselves but not their peers are more likely to be aggressive bullies (Salmivalli et al., 2005).

Cultural differences make self-esteem more complex. Many cultures expect children to be modest. For example, Australians say that "tall poppies" are cut down, and the Japanese discourage social comparison to make oneself feel superior (Toyama, 2001). Although Chinese children often excel at mathematics, only 1 percent said that they were "very satisfied" with their performance in that subject (Snyder et al., 2004). Does their dissatisfaction increase their achievement? Would this scarcity of self-esteem occur in other nations?

It is apparent that the combination of high self-esteem and low opinion of others is destructive; such children tend to have few friends, show more aggression, and be more lonely (Salmivalli et al., 2005). Academic and social competence are aided by realistic evaluation of objectively measured achievement, not by unrealistically high self-esteem (Baumeister et al., 2003). Achieving the proper balance is not easy, although each year of middle childhood tends to bring children closer to this goal.

Coping and Overcoming

As you have seen in these three chapters on middle childhood, the school-age child's expanding social world and developing cognition can bring disturbing problems. Some serious health impairments (e.g., obesity and asthma) affect psychosocial development, and children with special needs become painfully aware of their differences. Speaking a minority language may hinder academic learning and impair self-esteem. Some children are socially inept, rejected, or even victimized, and many have hostile or stressed parents and are in poor or unstable families.

Resilience and Stress

Surprisingly, some children seem unscathed by their problematic, stressful environments. They have been called "resilient" or even "invincible." Those who are familiar with recent research, however, use these terms cautiously, if at all (see Table 13.4). As dynamic-systems theory reminds us, although some children cope better than others, none are impervious to their social context (Jenson & Fraser, 2006; Luthar et al., 2003).

Resilience has been defined as "a dynamic process encompassing positive adaptation within the context of significant adversity" (Luthar et al., 2000, p. 543). Note the three parts of this definition:

resilience The capacity to adapt well to significant adversity and to overcome serious stress.

- Resilience is *dynamic,* not a stable trait. That means a given person may be resilient at some periods but not others.
- Resilience is a *positive adaptation* to stress. For example, if rejection by a parent leads a child to establish closer relationships with others, perhaps a grandparent or the parent of a neighbor child, that is resilience.
- Adversity must be *significant*. Some adversities are comparatively minor (large class size, poor vision), and some are major (victimization, neglect).

One important discovery is that many small stresses that might be called "daily hassles" can accumulate to become major if they are ongoing. Each stress can make other stresses more likely to be harmful (Fergusson & Horwood, 2003; Hammen, 2003).

TABLE 13.4

Dominant Ideas About Challenges and Coping in Children, 1965–Present

1965	All children have the same needs for healthy development.
1970	Some conditions or circumstances—such as "absent father," "teenage mother," "working mom," and "day care"—are harmful for every child.
1975	All children are *not* the same. Some children are resilient, coping easily with stressors that cause harm in other children.
1980	Nothing inevitably causes harm. Indeed, both maternal employment and preschool education, once thought to be risk factors, usually benefit children.
1985	Factors beyond the family, both in the child (low birthweight, prenatal alcohol exposure, aggressive temperament) and in the community (poverty, violence), can be very risky for the child.
1990	Risk–benefit analysis finds that some children seem to be "invulnerable" to, or even to benefit from, circumstances that destroy others. (Some do well in school despite extreme poverty, for example.)
1995	No child is invincibly resilient. Risks are always harmful—if not in education, then in emotions.
2000	Risk–benefit analysis involves the interplay among all three domains (biosocial, cognitive, and psychosocial), including factors within the child (genes, intelligence, temperament), the family (function as well as structure), and the community (including neighborhood, school, church, and culture). Over the long term, most people overcome problems, but the problems are real.
Today	The focus is on strengths, not risks. Assets in the child (intelligence, personality), the family (secure attachment, warmth), the community (good schools, after-school programs), and the nation (income support, health care) must be nurtured.

Sources: Luthar, 2003; Luthar et al., 2000; Maton et al., 2004; Walsh, 2002; Werner & Smith, 2001; Jenson & Fraser, 2006.

Resilience Is Real This table simplifies the progression of ideas about resilience; some older ideas are still valid, and some newer ideas were first expressed decades ago. Nonetheless, the emphasis has shifted over the past 40 years, as research evidence and thoughtful critiques have deepened understanding of resilience in children.

One example is the noise of airplanes overhead. If a child lives near an airport, that stress happens several times a day, but for just a minute at a time. A study of 2,844 children living near three major airports found that the noise impaired the reading ability of some (not all) (Stansfeld et al., 2005). A more chilling example comes from research on the children who survived Hurricane Katrina. Many experienced several stresses (see Figure 13.3) and have a much higher rate of psychological problems than they did before the hurricane hit (see Viadero, 2007).

Daily routines may build up stress. For example, a depressed mother may have little effect on her child if an emotionally stable and available father buffers her influence or if the mother herself functions well when she is with the child. However, her depression may become a significant stress if the child must, day after day, prepare for school, supervise and discipline younger siblings, and keep friends at a distance because the mother wants quiet.

A key aspect of resilience is the ability of children to develop their own friends, activities, and skills. After-school activities are one arena for this; participation in extracurricular programs correlates with better emotional and academic functioning (NICHD Early Child Care Research Network, 2004).

To encourage resilience, community, religious, and government programs can develop extracurricular activities for all children, from 4-H to midnight basketball, from choir to Little League. Children who can choose their own activities from many possibilities are likely to find an area of competence and develop a view of themselves as industrious, not inferior.

This was apparent in a 40-year study in Hawaii that began with children born into poverty, often to parents who were alcoholic or mentally ill. Amazingly, about a third of these children coped well. By middle childhood, they were already finding ways to avoid family stresses, choosing instead to achieve in school, to make good friends, and to find nonparental mentors. By adolescence, these children had distanced themselves from their parents. As adults, they left family problems behind (many moved far away) and established their own healthy relationships (Werner & Smith, 1992, 2001).

As was true for many of these children, school can often be an escape. An easygoing temperament and a high IQ help (Curtis & Cicchetti, 2003), but they are not essential. In the Hawaii study, "a realistic goal orientation, persistence, and 'learned creativity' enabled . . . a remarkable degree of personal, social, and occupational success," even for children with evident learning disabilities (Werner & Smith, 2001, p. 140).

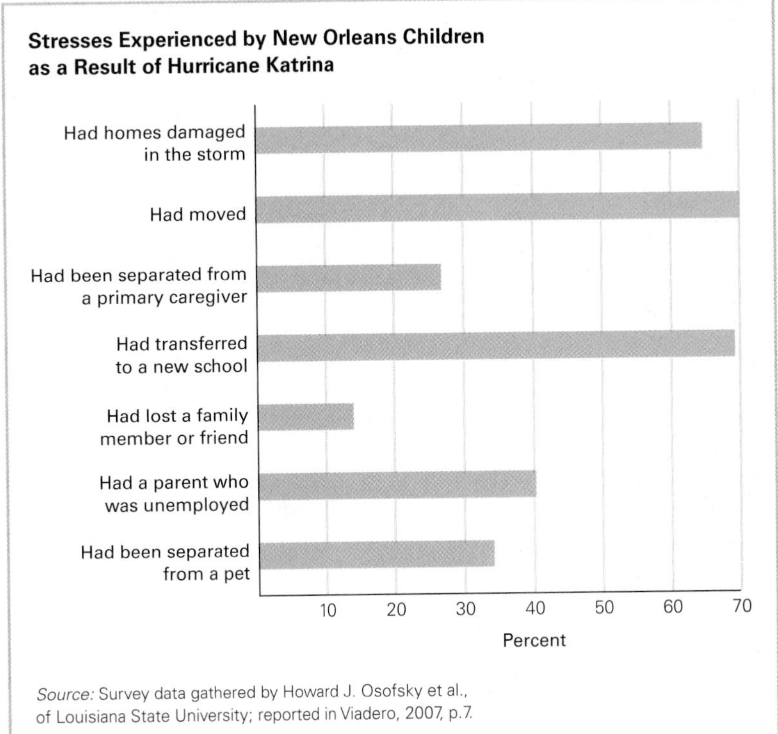

FIGURE 13.3

Enough Stress for a Lifetime Many children experienced more than one kind of severe stress during Hurricane Katrina and its aftermath. That disaster inflicted more stress on the children of New Orleans than most adults ever experience in their lifetime, and its long-term impact will likely be dramatic.

Social Support and Religious Faith

A major factor that helps children deal with problems—one we have already touched on—is the social support they receive. A strong bond with a loving and firm parent can see a child through many difficulties. Even in war-torn or deeply impoverished neighborhoods, secure attachment to a parent who has been consistently present since infancy tends to foster resilience (Masten & Coatsworth, 1998; Yates et al., 2003).

Many immigrant children do well in their new culture, academically and emotionally, despite all their stresses, if their families and schools are supportive (Fuligni, 2001). Other research also finds that parenting practices can buffer stress even for impoverished children living in very adverse conditions (Wyman et al., 1999).

Compared with the small, homebound lives of younger children, the expanding social world of school-age children allows new possibilities for social support. A network of supportive relatives is a better buffer than having only one close parent (Y. Jackson & Warren, 2000). Friends help, too, as already shown with bullying. Grandparents, unrelated adults, peers, and even pets can help children cope with stress (Borland, 1998).

Especially for Religiously Observant Adults A child you know seems much more religious than his or her parents are, and the parents are upset because the child believes things that they do not. What should be done?

B CHILD / AP PHOTO

Grandmother Knows Best About 20,000 grandmothers in Connecticut are caregivers for their grandchildren. This 15-year-old boy and his 17-year-old sister came to live with their grandmother in New Haven after their mother died several years ago. This type of family works best when the grandmother is relatively young and has her own house, as is the case here.

Children naturally try to deal with problems, a self-righting characteristic that seems evident in all humans, from the toddler who stands up after a tumble (Chapter 5) to the very old person who faces death with equanimity (Chapter 25). However, to right themselves, even well-equipped, well-intentioned school-age children must connect to at least one other person. One study concludes:

> When children attempt to seek out experiences that will help them overcome adversity, it is critical that resources, in the form of supportive adults or learning opportunities, be made available to them so that their own self-righting potential can be fulfilled.
>
> *[Kim-Cohen et al., 2004, p. 664]*

An example of such self-righting potential is children's use of religion, which often provides social support via an adult from the same community. As the authors of one study explain, "The influences of religious importance and participation . . . are mediated through trusting interaction with adults, friends and parents who share similar views" (King & Furrow, 2004, p. 709).

The religious convictions of children are very diverse (Levesque, 2002), but faith itself can be psychologically protective, in part because it helps children reinterpret their experiences. Parents can provide religious guidance, but by middle childhood, some children pray and attend religious services more often than their parents do. Research shows that church involvement particularly helps African American children in communities where social stresses and racial prejudice abound (Akiba & García-Coll, 2004).

Adults may not realize that many children (by age 8 but not at age 4) believe that prayer is communication, and they expect that prayer will make them feel better, especially when they are sad or angry (see Research Design and Figure 13.4) (Bamford & Lagattuta, 2007). Thus, religious beliefs become increasingly useful as school-age children cope with their problems.

In accord with their self-righting impulses, children try to develop competencies. They find social supports, if not in their families then among their friends or

Research Design

Scientists: Christi Bamford and Kristin H. Lagattuta.

Publication: Not quite published! This was a poster at the Society for Research in Child Development conference, held in Boston in April 2007. All the other studies cited in this text are published, but this one is included partly to inspire young researchers.

Participants: A total of 100—20 each at ages 4, 6, and 8, and 40 college students at the University of California. Family backgrounds were equally divided between those who considered themselves very religious, somewhat religious, and not religious.

Design: Participants were shown faces depicting various emotions and picture stories of children in various situations who decided to pray. They were asked when and why people might pray as well as how they would feel afterward.

Major conclusions: Compared with younger children, 8-year-olds were more likely to believe that prayer is used for gratitude and for making something better. They also thought people would feel better after they prayed.

Comment: Exploring the religious beliefs of children is an important topic, but it is not often done in psychological research. This study is a good beginning, but culture (even for nonreligious families) affects beliefs. Replication in another nation is needed.

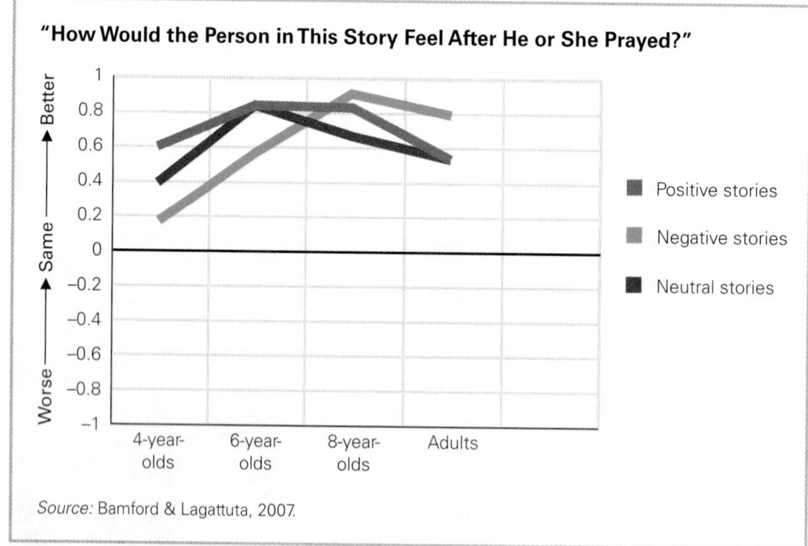

FIGURE 13.4

Help Me, God The numbers on this graph are the averages when people were asked how characters in various scenarios would feel after praying. There were only three choices: better (= 1), same (= 0) or worse (= −1). As you can see, virtually all the 8-year-olds thought prayer would make a person feel better.

unrelated adults. School success, religious faith, after-school achievements—any or all of these can help a child overcome problems. As two experts explain:

> Successful children remind us that children grow up in multiple contexts—in families, schools, peer groups, baseball teams, religious organizations, and many other groups—and each context is a potential source of protective factors as well as risks. These children demonstrate that children are protected not only by the self-righting nature of development, but also by the actions of adults, by their own actions, by the nurturing of their assets, by opportunities to succeed, and by the experience of success. The behavior of adults often plays a critical role in children's risks, resources, opportunities, and resilience.
>
> *[Masten & Coatsworth, 1998, p. 216]*

BILL ARON / PHOTOEDIT, INC.

Become Like a Child Although the particulars vary a great deal, school-age children's impulses toward industriousness, stability, and dedication place them among the most devout members of every religious faith.

SUMMING UP

Children gain in maturity and responsibility during the school years. According to psychoanalytic theory, the relative quiet of the latency period makes it easier for children to master new skills and to absorb their culture's values. To Erikson, the crisis of industry versus inferiority generates self-doubt in many school-age children.

Researchers have found that school-age children develop a more realistic self-concept. They cope by becoming more independent, using school achievement, after-school activities, supportive adults, and religious beliefs to help them overcome whatever problems they face.

A strength-based understanding of children moves our focus from problems (e.g., divorce, bullies) to assets (e.g., family harmony, social understanding). If low-income parents are not overwhelmed, children will not be, either. Similarly, social skills can prevent children from becoming bullies or victims. At every age, the characteristics of the person interact with past developmental history and current conditions to produce either a well-functioning, benevolent person or the opposite.

Adolescence, the subject of the next three chapters, is a continuation of middle childhood as well as a radical departure from it. Stresses and strains continue to accumulate. Risk factors, including drug availability and sexual urges, become more prevalent. Fortunately, for many young people, protective resources and constructive coping also increase (Masten, 2001). Personal competencies, family support, and close friends get most people through childhood (as we saw in this chapter), adolescence, and, eventually, adulthood. ■

➤Response for Religiously Observant Adults (from page 355): Because religious beliefs are often helpful to children, because respect for family is emphasized by virtually all religions, and because maturation usually makes people more tolerant, it may be best to let the child develop his or her own beliefs without interference. Of course, parents should set a good example and protect children from harm, no matter what the source.

SUMMARY

The Peer Group

1. Peers are crucial in the social development of the school-age child. Each group of children has a culture of childhood, passed down from slightly older children.

2. School-age children are very interested in differentiating right from wrong. The culture of children is one source of school-age morality, and so is cognitive maturity. Kohlberg described three levels of moral reasoning, with children gradually gaining in moral wisdom.

3. Popular children may be cooperative and easy to get along with or may be competitive and aggressive. Much depends on the age and culture of the children.

4. Rejected children may be neglected, aggressive, or withdrawn. All three types have difficulty interpreting the normal give-and-take of childhood. Close friendships become increasingly important as children grow.

5. Bullying is common among school-age children and has long-term consequences for bullies and victims. Bullying is hard to stop without a multifaceted, long-term, whole-school approach.

Families and Children

6. Families influence children in many ways, as do genes and peers. The five functions of a supportive family are: to satisfy children's physical needs; to encourage them to learn; to help them develop friends; to protect their self-respect; and to provide them with a safe, stable, and harmonious home.

7. The most common family structure, worldwide, is the nuclear family, with other relatives nearby and supportive. Other structures include single-parent, stepparent, blended, adoptive, and grandparent. Generally, it seems better for children to have two parents rather than one because a parental alliance can support their development. Structure matters less than function.

8. Income affects family functioning. Poor children are at greater risk for emotional and behavioral problems because the stress of poverty often hinders effective parenting. Conflict is also harmful, even when the child is not directly involved.

9. No particular family structure guarantees good—or bad—child development. Any change in family residence or structure, including divorce and remarriage, is likely to hinder school achievement and friendship formation.

The Nature of the Child

10. All theories of development acknowledge that school-age children become more independent and capable in many ways. In psychoanalytic theory, Freud described latency, when psychosexual needs are quiet; Erikson emphasized industry, when children are busy mastering various tasks.

11. All children are affected by any major family or peer problems they encounter. Resilience is more likely to be found in children with social support, independent activities, personal assets, and religious faith.

12. Children develop their self-concept during these years, based on a more realistic assessment of their competence than at earlier years.

KEY TERMS

social comparison (p. 333)
culture of children (p. 334)
deviancy training (p. 334)
preconventional moral reasoning (p. 336)
conventional moral reasoning (p. 336)
postconventional moral reasoning (p. 336)
aggressive-rejected (p. 338)
withdrawn-rejected (p. 338)
social cognition (p. 338)
effortful control (p. 338)
bullying (p. 339)
bully-victim (p. 340)
family structure (p. 344)
family function (p. 344)
nuclear family (p. 346)
single-parent family (p. 346)
extended family (p. 346)
blended family (p. 347)
latency (p. 351)
industry versus inferiority (p. 351)
resilience (p. 353)

KEY QUESTIONS

1. How does a school-age child develop a sense of self?

2. The culture of children strongly disapproves of tattletales. How does this affect child development?

3. Why is social rejection particularly devastating during middle childhood?

4. Describe the personal characteristics of a bully and a victim.

5. How do schools, families, and cultures contribute to the incidence of bullying?

6. What is the difference between family function and family structure?

7. What are the advantages and disadvantages of a stepparent family?

8. Why is a safe, harmonious home particularly important during middle childhood?

9. What is the psychoanalytic view of middle childhood?

10. What makes it more likely that a child will cope successfully with major stress?

APPLICATIONS

1. Go someplace where school-age children congregate, such as a schoolyard, a park, or a community center, and use naturalistic observation for at least half an hour. Describe what popular, average, withdrawn, and rejected children do. Note at least one potential conflict (bullying, rough-and-tumble, turf, etc.). Describe the sequence and the outcome.

2. Focusing on verbal bullying, describe at least two times when someone said a hurtful thing to you and two times when you said something that might have been hurtful to someone else. What are the differences between the two types of situations?

3. How would your childhood have been different if your family structure had been different, such as if you had (or had not) lived with your grandparents, if your parents had (or had not) gotten divorced, if you had (or had not) lived in a foster family?

4. The chapter suggests that school-age children develop their own theology, distinct from the one their parents teach them. Interview a child, aged 6 to 12, asking what he or she thinks about God, sin, heaven, death, and any other religious topics you think relevant. Compare the child's responses with the formal doctrines of the faith of his or her parents.

PART IV The Developing Person So Far: The School Years

BIOSOCIAL

A Healthy Time During middle childhood, children grow more slowly than they did earlier or than they will during adolescence. Exercise habits are crucial for health and happiness. Prevalent physical problems, including obesity and asthma, have genetic roots and psychosocial consequences.

Brain Development Brain maturation continues, leading to faster reactions and better self-control. Practice aids automatization and selective attention, which allow smoother and quicker action. Which specific skills are mastered depends largely on culture, gender, and inherited ability, all of which are reflected in intelligence tests. Children have many abilities not reflected in standard IQ tests.

Special Needs Many children have special learning needs. Early recognition, targeted education, and psychological support can help them, including those with autism spectrum disorders, specific learning disabilities, and attention deficit disorders.

COGNITIVE

Building on Theory Beginning at about age 7, Piaget noted, children attain concrete operational thought, including the ability to understand the logical principles of classification, identity, and reversibility. Vygotsky emphasized that children become more open to learning from mentors, both teachers and peers. Information-processing abilities increase, including greater memory, knowledge, control, and metacognition.

Language Children's increasing ability to understand the structures and possibilities of language enables them to extend the range of their cognitive powers and to become more analytical in vocabulary. Children have the cognitive capacity to become bilingual.

Education Formal schooling begins worldwide, although the specifics depend on culture. International comparisons reveal marked variations in overt and hidden curriculum, as well as in learning, between one nation and another. The United States, with the No Child Left Behind Act, is moving toward more testing and increased emphasis on basic skills. Other nations—notably Japan—are moving in other directions. The reading and math wars pit traditional education against a more holistic approach to learning.

PSYCHOSOCIAL

Peers The peer group becomes increasingly important as children become less dependent on their parents and more dependent on friends for help, loyalty, and sharing of mutual interests. Moral development, influenced by peers, is notable during these years. Rejection and bullying become serious problems.

Families Parents continue to influence children, especially as they exacerbate or buffer problems in school and the community. During these years, families need to meet basic needs, encourage learning, foster self-respect, nurture friendship, and—most important—provide harmony and stability. Most one-parent, foster, or grandparent families are better than a nuclear family with two biological parents in open conflict, but family structure does not guarantee optimal functioning. Household income and family stability benefit children of all ages, particularly in middle childhood.

The Nature of the Child Theorists agree that many school-age children develop competencies and attitudes to defend against stress. Some children are resilient, coping well with problems and finding support in friends, family, school, religion, and community.

Adolescence

CHAPTER 14

CHAPTER 15

CHAPTER 16

PART V

Would you ride with an unskilled driver? When my daughter Bethany had her learner's permit, I tried to convey confidence. Not until a terrified "Mom! Help!" did I grab the wheel to avoid hitting a subway kiosk. I should have helped sooner, but it is hard to know when children become adults, able to manage without their mothers.

As an adolescent, Bethany was neither child nor adult. A century ago, puberty began later: Soon after puberty, many teenage girls married and boys found work. Depending on customs and family income, some married or entered the labor force even before adolescence and some much later. Even today, in some developing nations, by age 10 some boys are working and some girls are betrothed.

It has been said that *adolescence begins with biology and ends with society.* Today, adolescence tends to begin earlier biologically and end later sociologically than it once did. Growth is uneven in both domains; some aspects of the brain mature at puberty (emotional excitement) and some much later (reflection). This led one observer to liken adolescence to "starting turbo-charged engines with an unskilled driver" (Dahl, 2004, p. 17).

In the next three chapters (covering ages 11–18), we begin with biology (the growth increases of puberty) and move toward society (the roles that teenagers take on). Understanding adolescence is more than an intellectual challenge: Those turbo-charged engines need skilled guidance. Get ready to grab the wheel.

14

CHAPTER OUTLINE

Adolescence: Biosocial Development

The body changes of early adolescence rival those of infancy in speed and drama but differ in one crucial way: Adolescents are aware. Even tiny changes (a blemish, a fingernail) matter when a person watches his or her own body transforming.

I once overheard a conversation among three teenagers, including my daughter Rachel. All three were past the awkward years, now becoming beautiful. They were discussing the imperfections of their bodies. One spoke of her fat stomach (what stomach? I could not see it), another of her long neck (hidden by her silky, shoulder-length hair), and my Rachel complained not only about a bent finger but also about her feet!

The reality that children grow into men and women is no shock to any adult. But for teenagers, heightened self-awareness often triggers surprise and even horror, joy, or despair. This chapter describes normal biosocial changes, including growing bodies, emerging sexuality, and maturing brains, and then two possible problems.

That's What Friends Are For Jennifer's preparations for her prom include pedicure and hairstyle, courtesy of her good friends Khushbu and Meredith. In every generation and society the world over, teenagers help their same-sex friends prepare for the display rituals involved in coming of age, but the specifics vary by cohort and culture.

MIKE KING / AP PHOTO

Puberty Begins

puberty The time between the first onrush of hormones and full adult physical development. Puberty usually lasts three to five years. Many more years are required to achieve psychosocial maturity.

menarche A girl's first menstrual period, signaling that she has begun ovulation. Pregnancy is biologically possible, but ovulation and menstruation are often irregular for years after menarche.

spermarche A boy's first ejaculation of sperm. Erections can occur as early as infancy, but ejaculation signals sperm production. Spermache occurs during sleep (in a "wet dream") or via direct stimulation.

Puberty refers to the years of rapid physical growth and sexual maturation that end childhood, eventually producing a person of adult size, shape, and sexual potential. The forces of puberty are unleashed by a cascade of hormones that produce external signs as well as the heightened emotions and sexual desires that many adolescents experience. The process normally starts between ages 8 and 14. The biological changes follow a common sequence (see Table 14.1).

For girls, puberty begins with growth of the nipples and initial pubic hair, then a peak growth spurt, widening of the hips, the first menstrual period (**menarche**), final pubic-hair pattern, and full breast development. The current average age of menarche among well-nourished girls is about 12 years, 8 months (Malina et al., 2004), although, as you will soon see, variation in timing is quite normal.

For boys, the usual sequence is growth of the testes, initial pubic hair, growth of the penis, first ejaculation of seminal fluid (**spermarche**), facial hair, peak growth spurt, voice deepening, and final pubic-hair growth (Biro et al., 2001; Herman-Giddens et al., 2001). The modal age of spermarche is just under 13 years, the same as for menarche.

Typically, physical growth and maturation are complete four years after the first signs appear, although some individuals (usually late developers) add height, and most (especially early developers) gain more fat and muscle in their late teens or early 20s.

Hormones

hormone An organic chemical substance that is produced by one body tissue and conveyed via the bloodstream to another to affect some physiological function. Various hormones influence thoughts, urges, emotions, and behavior.

Just described are the visible changes of puberty. An invisible event begins the entire process, namely a marked increase in certain **hormones,** which are natural

TABLE 14.1

AT ABOUT THIS TIME: The Sequence of Puberty

Girls	Approximate Average Age*	Boys
Ovaries increase production of estrogen and progesterone†	9	
Uterus and vagina begin to grow larger	9½	Testes increase production of testosterone†
Breast "bud" stage	10	Testes and scrotum grow larger
Pubic hair begins to appear; weight spurt begins	11	
Peak height spurt	11½	Pubic hair begins to appear
Peak muscle and organ growth (also, hips become noticeably wider)	12	Penis growth begins
Menarche (first menstrual period)	12½	Spermarche (first ejaculation); weight spurt begins
First ovulation	13	Peak height spurt
Voice lowers	14	Peak muscle and organ growth (also, shoulders become noticeably broader)
Final pubic-hair pattern	15	Voice lowers; visible facial hair
Full breast growth	16	
	18	Final pubic-hair pattern

*Average ages are rough approximations, with many perfectly normal, healthy adolescents as much as three years ahead of or behind these ages.

†Estrogens and testosterone influence sexual characteristics, including reproduction. Charted here are the increases produced by the gonads (sex glands). The ovaries produce estrogens and the testes produce androgens, especially testosterone. Adrenal glands produce some of both kinds of hormones (not shown).

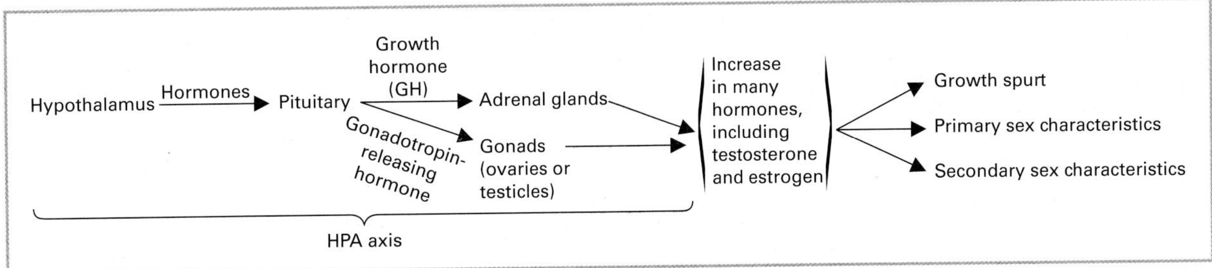

FIGURE 14.1

Biological Sequence of Puberty Puberty begins with a hormonal signal from the hypothalamus to the pituitary gland. The pituitary, in turn, signals the adrenal glands and the ovaries or testes to produce more of their hormones.

chemicals in the bloodstream that affect every body cell. Hormones regulate hunger, sleep, moods, stress, sexual desire, and much more.

At least 23 hormones affect human growth and maturation, several of which increase markedly in the months before the first signs of puberty. Technically, those first straggly pubic hairs are "a late event" in the process (Cameron, 2004, p. 116).

You learned in Chapter 8 that the production of many hormones is regulated deep within the brain, where biochemical signals from the hypothalamus signal another brain structure, the **pituitary.** The pituitary produces hormones that stimulate the **adrenal glands,** small glands located above the kidneys at either side of the lower back. The adrenal glands produce more hormones. This **HPA axis** (hypothalamus-pituitary-adrenal) is the route followed by hormones that regulate stress, growth, sleep, appetite, and sexual excitement as well as puberty (see Figure 14.1).

pituitary A gland in the brain that responds to a signal from the hypothalamus by producing many hormones, including those that regulate growth and control other glands, among them the adrenal and sex glands.

adrenal glands Two glands, located above the kidneys, that produce hormones (including the "stress hormones" epinephrine [adrenaline] and norepinephrine).

HPA axis The hypothalamus-pituitary-adrenal axis, a route followed by many kinds of hormones to trigger the changes of puberty and to regulate stress, growth, sleep, appetite, sexual excitement, and various other bodily changes.

Sex Hormones

At adolescence, the pituitary also activates the **gonads,** or sex glands (ovaries in females; testes, or testicles, in males). One hormone in particular, GnRH (gonadotropin-releasing hormone), causes the gonads to enlarge and dramatically increase their production of sex hormones, chiefly **estradiol** in girls and **testosterone** in boys. These hormones affect the entire body shape and function.

Estrogens (including estradiol) are considered female hormones, and androgens (including testosterone) are considered male hormones, but the adrenal glands produce both in everyone. Unlike those produced by the adrenal glands, the hormones produced by the gonads are sex-specific. After a decrease during childhood, testosterone skyrockets in boys—up to 20 times the pre-pubescent level (Roche & Sun, 2003). For girls, estradiol increases to about 8 times the childhood level (Malina et al., 2004).

The activated gonads eventually produce gametes (sperm and ova), whose maturation and release are heralded by spermarche or menarche, signifying that the young person has the biological potential to become a parent. (Peak fertility comes years later, but ovulation and ejaculation signify the possibility of pregnancy.)

gonads The paired sex glands (ovaries in females, testicles in males). The gonads produce hormones and gametes.

estradiol A sex hormone, considered the chief estrogen. Females produce more estradiol than males do.

testosterone A sex hormone, the best known of the androgens (male hormones); secreted in far greater amounts by males than by females.

Sudden Emotions

Remember that the HPA axis leads from brain to body to behavior. The behaviors that adolescents are best known for are emotional and sexual—moodiness and lust that overtake the formerly predictable, seemingly asexual, child. Hormones influence this. To be specific:

- Testosterone at high or accelerating levels stimulates rapid arousal of emotions, especially anger.
- Hormonal bursts lead to quick emotional extremes (despair, ecstasy).
- For many boys, the increase in androgens causes sexual thoughts and a desire to masturbate.
- For many girls, the fluctuating estrogens increase happiness in the middle of the menstrual cycle (at ovulation) and sadness or anger at the end.

Especially for Parents of Teenagers Why would parents blame adolescent moods on hormones?

Although adults experience these same hormonal effects, during puberty hormones are more erratic and powerful, less familiar and controllable, and they come in bursts, not a steady flow (Cameron, 2004; Susman & Rogol, 2004). Further, when adults experience hormonal changes (especially during pregnancy and birth), cognitive maturation helps control the effects.

Hormones sometimes make adolescents seek sexual activity and sometimes arouse excitement, pleasure, and frustration. But human thoughts and emotions not only result from physiological and neurological processes—they also *cause* them (Damasio, 2003). An adolescent's reactions to how other people respond to breasts, beards, and body shapes evoke emotions that, in turn, affect hormones—just as hormones affect emotions—with the particular emotional reaction not directly tied to specific hormones (Alsaker & Flammer, 2006).

This is clearer with an example. Suppose a 13-year-old girl hears a lewd remark, provoked by her developing breasts in a too-tight shirt. She might feel a surge of anger, fear, or embarrassment, but it is the remark, not her hormones, that arouses her. Her emotions might cause a rise in stress hormones and sexual ones as well.

Evidence for a complex link between hormones and emotions came from a study of 56 adolescents who were late to begin puberty (Schwab et al., 2001). Doctors prescribed treatment every 3 months: injections of hormones (low, medium, or high doses of testosterone or an estrogen) alternating with injections of a placebo (which had no hormones). Gradually, the outward signs of puberty appeared.

Every three months, other measures were taken: the level of sex hormones (measured via blood tests) and the emotions felt by the adolescents (via a questionnaire). An emotional shift occurred, indirectly caused by the hormones. Over the two years, moods became more positive, not directly because of hormones in the body but presumably because the teenagers were happy with their physical development.

Surprisingly, happiness and sadness did not correlate with shifting hormonal levels. The teenagers did not seem emotionally aroused by the level of hormones in their systems—with one exception. Both boys and girls reported more anger when they had had *moderate* amounts of hormones, not the highest levels of testosterone (for the boys) or estrogens (for the girls) (Susman & Rogol, 2004).

Both 12 The ancestors of these two Minnesota 12-year-olds came from northern Europe and West Africa. Their genes have dictated some differences between them, including the timing of puberty, but these differences are irrelevant to their friendship.

SKJOLD PHOTOGRAPHS / THE IMAGE WORKS

When Will Puberty Start?

Hormones cascading into the bloodstream always trigger the changes of puberty. However, age of onset varies. Age 11 or 12 is most likely, but a rise in hormones is still considered normal in those as young as age 8 or as old as age 14. This variation is not random but is affected by genes, body fat, and stress (Ellis, 2004).

Genes

The genes on the sex chromosomes markedly affect the onset of puberty. Among well-nourished children, at least one girl (XX) in a fifth-grade class has already developed breasts and begun to grow to adult height. Not until age 18 or so has her last male classmate (XY) sprouted facial hair and grown to man-size.

On average, girls are about two years ahead of boys in height. However, hormonally and sexually girls are ahead by only a few months, not by years (Malina et al., 2004), because the height spurt occurs about midway in female pubescence (before menarche) but is a late event (after spermarche) for boys.

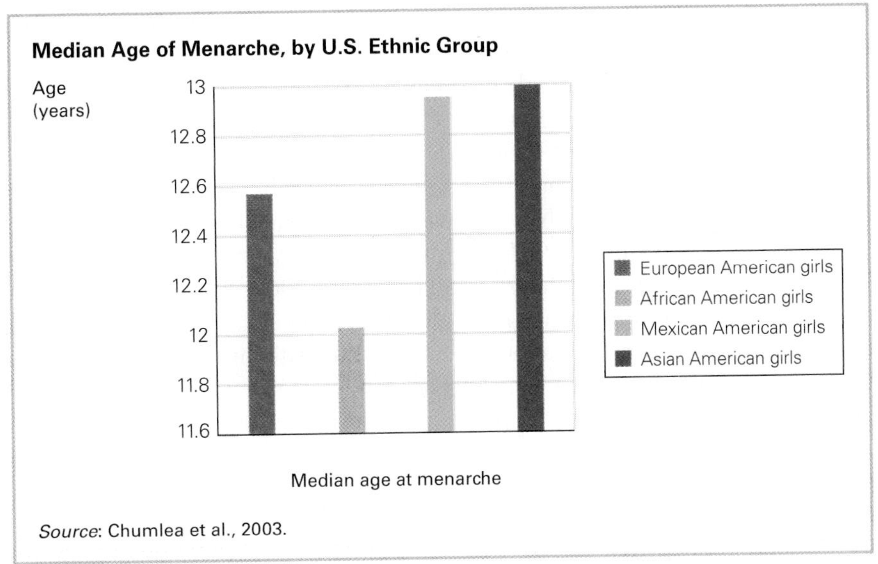

FIGURE 14.2

Usually by Age 13 The median age of menarche (when half the girls have begun to menstruate) differs somewhat among ethnic groups in the United States.

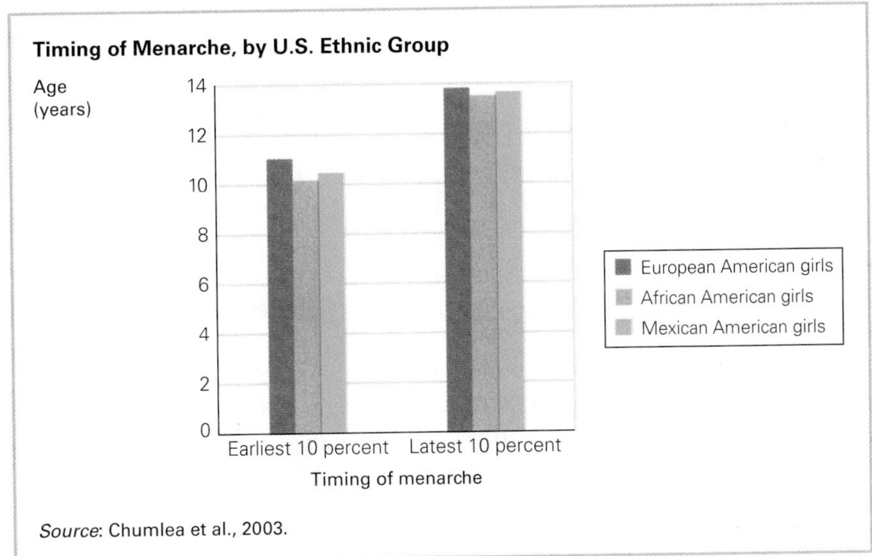

FIGURE 14.3

Almost Always by Age 14 This graph shows the age of menarche for the earliest and latest 10 percent of girls in three U.S. ethnic groups. Note that, especially for the slow developers (those in the 90th percentile), ethnic differences are very small.

Observation Quiz (see answer, page 368): At first glance, ethnic differences seem dramatic in Figure 14.2 but minimal in Figure 14.3. Why is this first glance deceptive?

Genes influence the timing of puberty in other ways as well. Monozygotic twins are more alike than same-sex dizygotic twins (Roche & Sun, 2003). Ethnic variations in pubertal timing are partly genetic (see Figure 14.2). In the United States, African Americans tend to reach puberty earlier than do European Americans or Hispanic Americans (see Figure 14.3). Asian Americans average several months later (Herman-Giddens et al., 2001; Malina et al., 2004).

Ages in Europe also vary, probably for genetic reasons. Northern European girls are said to reach menarche at 13 years, 4 months, on average, and southern European girls do so at an average age of 12 years, 5 months (Alsaker & Flammer, 2006).

Body Fat

The genetic differences noted above are apparent only when every child is well fed. Puberty starts earlier in the cities of India and China than in the remote villages, probably because rural children are often hungry. In Poland and Greece, urban–rural differences are shown in that puberty occurs a year earlier in Warsaw

➤Response for Parents of Teenagers (from page 366): If something causes adolescents to shout "I hate you," to slam doors, or to cry inconsolably, parents may decide that hormones are the problem. This makes it easy to disclaim personal responsibility for the teenager's anger. However, research on stress and hormones suggests that this comforting attribution is too simplistic.

than in Polish villages and 3 months earlier in Athens than in the rest of Greece (Malina et. al, 2004).

Worldwide, stocky individuals begin puberty before those with thinner builds. Some believe that hormones in the food supply cause earlier puberty, and others believe that hormones cause weight gain rather than vice versa (Ellison, 2002). Neither of these theories has been proven. Nonetheless, it is apparent that menarche occurs later in girls who have little body fat (because they are undernourished or overexercised) and that most girls weigh at least 100 pounds (45 kilograms) before their first period (Berkey et al., 2000).

In both sexes, chronic malnutrition delays puberty. This probably explains why puberty did not occur until about age 17 in the sixteenth century. In the early twentieth century, menarche occurred on average at age 15 in Norway, Sweden, and Finland (Tanner, 1990), compared with age 12 or 13 today.

secular trend A term that refers to the earlier and greater growth of children due to improved nutrition and medical care over the last two centuries.

These are examples of the **secular trend,** a term that refers to earlier and greater growth of children over the last two centuries as nutrition and medical care have improved. Over the twentieth century, each generation experienced puberty a few months earlier than did the preceding one (Alsaker & Flammer, 2006).

The secular trend seems to have stopped in developed nations (Roche & Sun, 2003). This has a specific application. Probably, after considering the gender differential (men are on average about 5 inches taller than women), today's young adults will be about as tall as their parents unless chronic illness or undernourishment as a child is a factor.

➤Answer to Observation Quiz (from page 367): The major reason is the vertical axis, which covers a total of 1½ years in Figure 14.2 and 14 years in Figure 14.3. In addition, the outliers (top and bottom 10 percent) in Figure 14.2 show less variation than the median in Figure 14.3

Stress

The production of many hormones is directly connected to stressful experiences via the HPA axis (Sanchez et al., 2001). Because stress affects reproductive hormones, many young women experience irregular menstruation when they leave home for college or take trips abroad, and many couples find it easier to become pregnant on vacation than when they are working.

Stress affects pubertal hormones as well, paradoxically by *increasing* (not decreasing) them. Puberty tends to arrive earlier if a child's parents are sick, addicted, or divorced, or when the neighborhood is violent and impoverished (Herman-Giddens et al., 2001; Hulanicka, 1999; Moffitt et al., 1992).

Before concluding that stress *causes* early puberty, however, you need to know that not every scientist agrees that this is the case (Ellis, 2004). Since puberty is partly genetic, it could be that adults who reached puberty early are likely to marry and become parents young, which might make them more likely to be undereducated, depressed, angry, and divorced. Consequently, their children would live with conflicted, divorce-prone parents and thus experience early puberty not because of the conflict but because of their genes.

However, at least one careful longitudinal study of 87 girls did find a direct link between stress and puberty (Ellis & Garber, 2000). Those girls who fought with their mothers and who lived with an unrelated man (stepfather or mother's boyfriend) also had earlier puberty, even when genes and weight were taken into account. The longer a girl lived with a man who was not her father, the earlier she reached menarche.

Animal research also implicates stress. Mice, rats, and opossums under stress become pregnant at younger ages than do other members of their species (Warshofsky, 1999). Further, female mice reach puberty earlier if, as infants, they were raised with unrelated adult male mice (Caretta et al., 1995).

The evidence for the stress hypothesis is sufficiently strong to wonder why stress would trigger puberty. Logically, conflicted or stepfather families would benefit if the opposite happened—if teenagers looked and acted like children and could not reproduce. But that does not happen. One explanation comes from evolutionary theory:

> Over the course of our natural selective history, ancestral females growing up in adverse family environments may have reliably increased their reproductive success by accelerating physical maturation and beginning sexual activity and reproduction at a relatively early age.
>
> *[Ellis & Garber, 2000, p. 486]*

In other words, in past stressful times, adolescent parents could replace themselves before they died, passing on family genes. Natural selection favored genes that adapted to wars, famine, and sickness by initiating early puberty. Currently, early sexuality and reproduction lead to social disruption, not social survival, but the human genome has been shaped over millennia. Although many explanations are possible for the link between stress and early puberty, the evidence continues to find the correlation (Romans et al., 2003).

Especially for Parents Worried About Early Puberty Suppose your cousin's 9-year-old daughter has just had her first period, and your cousin blames hormones in the food supply for this "precocious" puberty. Should you change your young daughter's diet?

Too Early, Too Late

For most adolescents, only one aspect of timing is important: their friends' schedules. No one wants to be early or late, with early particularly hard for girls, late for boys. Why?

Think about the early-maturing girl. If she has visible breasts in the fifth grade, the boys tease her; they are awed by the sexual creature in their midst. She must fit her womanly body into a school chair designed for younger children, and she may hide her breasts in large T-shirts and bulky sweaters and refuse to undress for gym. Early-maturing girls tend to have lower self-esteem, more depression, and poorer body image than later-maturing girls (Compian et al, 2004; Mendle et al., 2007).

Some early-maturing girls have boyfriends several years older, which adds status but more complications, including drug and alcohol use (Weichold et al., 2003). They are "isolated from their on-time-maturing peers [and] tend to associate with older adolescents. This increases their emotional distress" (Ge et al., 2003, p. 437).

Cohort is crucial for boys. Early-maturing boys who were born around 1930 often became leaders in high school and beyond (M. C. Jones, 1965). Early-maturing boys also tend to be more successful as adults (Taga et al., 2006). However, if early-maturing boys live in stressful urban neighborhoods (with poverty, drugs, and violence) and if their parents are unusually strict, they are likely to befriend law-breaking, somewhat older boys (Ge et al., 2002). For both sexes, early puberty currently correlates with early romance, sex, and parenthood, which lead to later depression and other psychosocial problems (B. Brown, 2004; Siebenbruner et al., 2007).

Late puberty may also be difficult, especially for boys. Ethnic differences in age of puberty can add to ethnic tensions in high school. Remember that Asian American youth tend to experience later puberty. In one multiethnic high school, the "quiet Asian boys" were teased because they were shorter and thinner than their classmates, much to their dismay (Lei, 2003). This is a likely explanation for the greater peer discrimination experienced by the Chinese youth in another school (Greene et al., 2006; see Research Design). In a third multiethnic high school, Samoan students were small numerically but advanced in puberty. As a result, they were respected by their classmates of all backgrounds, able to moderate tensions between African and Mexican Americans (Staiger, 2006). Interactions among students in all three of these schools illustrate the importance of physical appearance for many adolescents. Puberty can enhance or diminish a person's status with peers, depending partly on when it occurs.

Research Design

Scientists: Melissa L. Greene, Niobe Way, and Kerstin Pahl.

Publication: *Developmental Psychology* (2006).

Participants: A total of 136 high school students at a multiethnic high school in New York City.

Design: Six times over the four years of high school, students answered questionnaires about discrimination, ethnic identity, depression, and self-esteem.

Major conclusion: For all four ethnic groups (Black, Asian American, Puerto Rican, and other Latino), perceived peer discrimination had a greater impact on self-esteem than did perceived adult discrimination. The Asian Americans averaged higher levels of perceived discrimination than any other group; the Black Americans were second.

Comment: This study is a welcome step toward multifaceted, multiethnic, longitudinal research on adolescents. More is needed to provide, as the researchers write, "a thorough examination of the impact of experiences of discrimination on well-being."

➤**Response for Parents Worried About Early Puberty** (from page 369): Probably not. If she is overweight, her diet should change, but the hormone hypothesis is speculative. Genes are the main factor; she shares only 1/8 of her genes with her cousin.

Nutrition

All the changes of puberty depend on nutrition, yet many adolescents are deficient in necessary vitamins or minerals. A five-year longitudinal study found that eating habits get worse throughout the teen years (N. I. Larson et al., 2006).

Diet Deficiencies

Fewer than half of all teenagers consume the recommended daily dose of 15 milligrams of iron, found in green vegetables, eggs, and meat—all spurned in favor of chips, sweets, and fast food. Because menstruation depletes the body of iron, more adolescent girls are anemic than those in any other age or gender group (Belamarich & Ayoob, 2001). Adolescent boys also suffer from anemia, especially if they engage in physical labor or competitive sports, because muscles need iron (Blum & Nelson-Mmari, 2004).

Calcium is another example. About half of adult bone mass is acquired from ages 10 to 20, yet few adolescents consume enough calcium to prevent osteoporosis, which causes disability, injury, and death among older adults. Milk drinking has declined; most North American children once drank at least a quart a day. In 2005 among ninth-graders, only 14 percent of U.S. girls and 24 percent of boys drank even 24 ounces (¾ liter) of milk a day. By twelfth grade, the rates were 10 and 18 percent (MMWR, June 9, 2006).

Nutritional deficiencies result from the choices young adolescents are allowed, even enticed, to make. There is a direct link between deficient diets and the availability of vending machines in schools (Cullen & Zakeri, 2004). Fast-food establishments cluster around high schools, if zoning permits, and many such places are hangouts for teenagers.

One reason is price. At least experimentally, 10- to 14-year-olds choose healthy foods if they are cheaper than unhealthy ones (Epstein et al., 2006), but milk and fruit juice are more expensive than fruit punch or soda, and McDonald's charges more for a salad than a hamburger. Only 20 percent of high school students in 2005 ate five or more servings of fruits or vegetables a day (MMWR, June 9, 2006), worse than a decade ago (29 percent) (MMWR, August 14, 1998).

Body Image

body image A person's idea of how his or her body looks.

Another reason for poor nutrition is anxiety about **body image**—that is, a person's idea of how his or her body looks. Since puberty alters the entire body, it is almost impossible for teenagers to welcome every change. Unfortunately, their perceptions are distorted; they tend to focus on and exaggerate the problems.

Girls diet because they want to be thinner, and they notice that boys tend to date thinner girls (Halpern et al., 2005). Many boys want to look taller and stronger, a concern that increases from ages 12 to 17 (D. Jones & Crawford, 2005). Children of ethnic minorities are bombarded with faces and bodies in films and advertisements that have features and shapes quite different from those their genes will produce.

Many stressed teenagers eat erratically or ingest drugs (especially diet pills or steroids), hoping to lose weight (the girls) or to gain muscles (the boys). Their obsession can backfire. Some adolescents give up, becoming flabby and fat instead of strong and thin. About 12 percent of all U.S. teenagers are overweight according to international standards, more than in any other nation that has been studied (Lissau et al., 2004). As bad as that is, almost two-thirds (62 percent) of all U.S. adolescent girls and almost a third of the boys are trying to lose weight, according to a nationwide U.S. survey of 14,000 high school students (MMWR, June 9, 2006).

Some social scientists believe that the epidemic of obesity (discussed in detail in Chapters 11 and 20) can be a direct result of the wish to be thinner (e.g., P. F. Campos, 2004). Adolescent obesity increases the risk of premature death, at least for women, partly because overweight women are more likely to be suicidal (van Dam et al., 2006). Girls are more likely than boys to be obsessed with weight, an obsession that can lead to extreme dieting. Eating disorders typically begin in early adolescence and grow worse by young adulthood. (Anorexia and bulimia nervosa are discussed in detail in Chapter 17.)

LAURA DWIGHT

Does He Like What He Sees? During adolescence, all the facial features do not develop at the same rate, and the hair often becomes less manageable. If B. T. here is typical, he is not pleased with the appearance of his nose, lips, ears, or hair.

SUMMING UP

Puberty usually begins between ages 8 and 14 (typically at about 11) in response to hormones deep within the brain, from the hypothalamus to the pituitary to the adrenal and sex glands. Hormones affect the emotions as well as the physique, with adolescent outbursts caused by the combination of hormones and sociocultural reactions to visible body changes. Many factors, including genes, body fat, and probably stress, affect when puberty begins. Generally, puberty begins earlier than in past centuries, although this aspect of the secular trend is stopping. Early puberty (especially for girls) or late puberty (especially for boys) is problematic. All adolescents are vulnerable to poor nutrition and body image worries. ■

The Transformations of Puberty

Every body part changes during puberty. For simplicity, the transformation from a child into an adult is traditionally divided into two parts: growth and sexuality. We will use that division here and add a third aspect, the transformation of the brain. In actuality, however, every aspect of pubescent growth involves all three.

For example, suppose a young adolescent suddenly notices darker and thicker hair growing on his or her legs, which everyone experiences as part of puberty. If the child is a girl, she will probably shave her legs, feeling quite womanly when she nicks herself before developing a light touch or buying a depilatory. If the child is a boy, he may search for new hair on his upper lip, his chin, and his chest, to mark his manhood. Thus a sexless sign of maturity (hair on the legs) is seen as sexual, and thoughts and memories stored in the brain affect the adolescent's proud reaction.

Growing Bigger and Stronger

The first set of changes during puberty is the **growth spurt**—a sudden, uneven jump in the size of almost every part of the body, turning children into adults. Growth proceeds from the extremities to the core (the opposite of the proximal-distal growth of the prenatal and infant periods). Thus, fingers and toes lengthen before hands and feet; hands and feet before arms and legs; arms and legs before the torso.

growth spurt The relatively sudden and rapid physical growth that occurs during puberty. Each body part increases in size on a schedule: Weight usually precedes height, and the limbs precede the torso.

Because the torso is the last body part to grow, many pubescent children are temporarily big-footed, long-legged, and short-waisted, appearing to be "all legs and arms" (Hofmann, 1997, p. 12). If young teenagers complain that their jeans don't fit, they are probably correct, even if those same jeans fit their shorter-waisted, thinner body when their parents paid for them a month before. (Parents had advance warning when they had to buy shoes for their children in adult shoe sizes.)

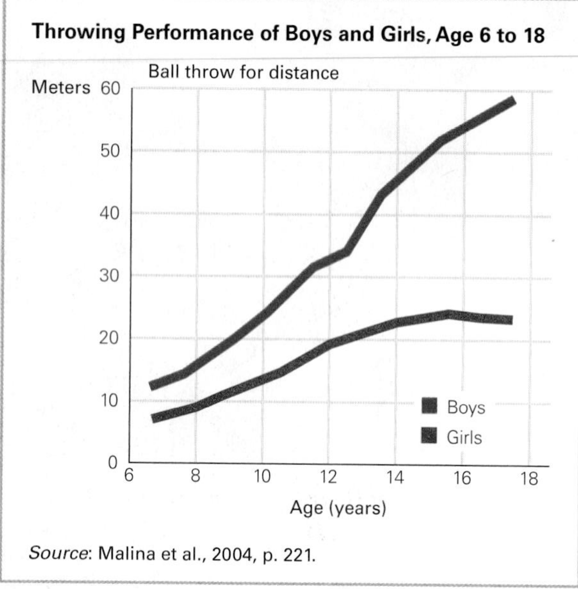

FIGURE 14.4

Big Difference All children experience an increase in muscles during puberty, but gender differences are much more apparent in some gross motor skills than others. For instance, upper-arm strength increases dramatically only in boys.

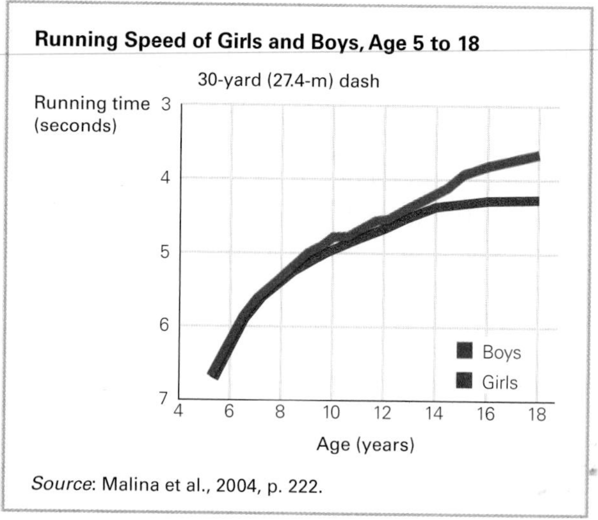

FIGURE 14.5

Little Difference Both sexes develop longer and stronger legs during puberty.

Observation Quiz (see answer, page 374): At what age does the rate of increase in the average boy's muscle accelerate?

Sequence: Weight, Height, Muscles

As the bones lengthen and harden (visible on an X-ray) and the growth spurt begins, children eat more and gain weight. Exactly when, where, and how much weight is gained depends on heredity, diet, exercise, and gender, with girls gaining much more fat than boys. By age 17, the average girl has twice as much fat as her male classmate, whose increased weight is mostly muscle (Roche & Sun, 2003).

A height spurt follows the weight spurt, burning up some fat and redistributing the rest. A year or two after the height spurt, the muscle spurt occurs. Thus, the pudginess and clumsiness of early puberty is usually gone by late adolescence. On average, a boy's arm muscles are twice as strong at age 18 than at age 8, enabling him to throw a ball four times as far (Malina et al., 2004). Arm muscles show the most sex difference (see Figure 14.4); other muscles are more gender-neutral. For instance, running speed increases over adolescence in both sexes, with boys not much faster than girls (see Figure 14.5).

Other Body Changes

For both sexes, organs grow and become more efficient. Lungs triple in weight, and adolescents breathe more deeply and slowly. The heart doubles in size and beats more slowly (which decreases the pulse), while blood pressure and volume both increase (Malina et al., 2004). These changes increase physical endurance, enabling many teenagers to run for miles or dance for hours.

Note that both weight and height increase *before* the growth of muscles and internal organs, which means that athletic training and weight lifting should be tailored to an adolescent's size the previous year, to spare their immature muscles and organs. Sports injuries are the most common school accidents, increasing at puberty. One reason is that, because height precedes increases of bone mass, young adolescents are more vulnerable to fractures than are adults until old age (Roche & Sun, 2003).

Only one organ system, the lymphoid system (which includes the tonsils and adenoids), *decreases in size,* thus making teenagers less susceptible to respiratory ailments. Mild asthma, for example, often switches off at puberty (Busse & Lemanske, 2005), and teenagers have fewer colds than younger children do.

Another organ system, the skin, changes in marked ways, making bodies oilier, sweatier, and more prone to acne. Hair also changes. During puberty, hair on the head and limbs becomes coarser and darker, and new hair grows under arms, on faces, and above sex organs (pubic hair, from which puberty was named). Visible facial and chest hair is sometimes considered a sign of manliness, although hairiness in either sex depends on genes as well as hormones.

CLEVE BRYANT / PHOTOEDIT

Male Pride Teenage boys typically feel serious pride when they first need to shave. Although facial hair is taken as a sign of masculinity, a person's hairiness is actually genetic as well as hormonal. Further evidence that the Western world's traditional racial categories have no genetic basis comes from East Asia: Many Chinese men cannot grow beards or mustaches, but most Japanese men can.

Sexual Maturation

The second set of changes turns boys into men and girls into women. Sexual characteristics signify this transformation, as do many impulses and behaviors.

Sexual Body Changes

Primary sex characteristics are defined as those parts of the body that are directly involved in conception and pregnancy. During puberty, every primary sex organ (the ovaries, the uterus, the penis, and the testes) increases in size and matures in function. By the end of the process, reproduction is possible.

At the same time as maturation of the primary sex characteristics, **secondary sex characteristics** develop. Secondary sex characteristics are bodily features that do not directly affect fertility (hence they are secondary) but that signify masculinity or femininity. One obvious secondary sexual characteristic is body shape, virtually unisex in childhood. At puberty, males grow taller than females (by 5 inches, on average) and become wider at the shoulders, while girls develop breasts and a wider pelvis.

Breasts and hips are often considered signs of womanhood; but neither is required for conception, and thus both are secondary, not primary, sex characteristics. Secondary sex characteristics may be important psychologically, if not biologically. For example, many girls buy "minimizer," "maximizer," "training," or "shaping" bras. Many boys are horrified to notice a swelling around their nipples—a normal and temporary result of the erratic hormones of early puberty.

A welcome secondary sex characteristic is a lower voice as the lungs and larynx grow, a change most noticeable in boys. Girls also develop lower voices, which is why throaty female voices are considered sexy.

The pattern of growth at the scalp line differs for the two sexes, but few people notice that. Instead, they notice gender markers in hair length and style, which can attain the status of a secondary sex characteristic. Adolescents spend considerable time, money, and thought on their visible hair—growing, shaving, curling, straightening, brushing, combing, styling, dyeing, wetting, drying . . .

primary sex characteristics The parts of the body that are directly involved in reproduction, including the vagina, uterus, ovaries, testicles, and penis.

secondary sex characteristics Physical traits that are not directly involved in reproduction but that indicate sexual maturity, such as a man's beard and a woman's breasts.

Sexual Activity

The primary and secondary sex characteristics just described are not the only manifestations of the sexual hormones. Fantasizing, flirting, hand-holding, staring, displaying, and touching are all done in particular ways to reflect gender, availability, and culture. As already explained, hormones trigger thoughts and emotions, but the social context shapes thoughts into enjoyable fantasies, shameful preoccupations, frightening impulses, or actual contact.

Some experts believe that boys are more influenced by hormones and girls by culture (Baumeister et al., 2007). Perhaps. When a relationship includes sexual intimacy, girls seem more concerned about the depth of the romance than boys do

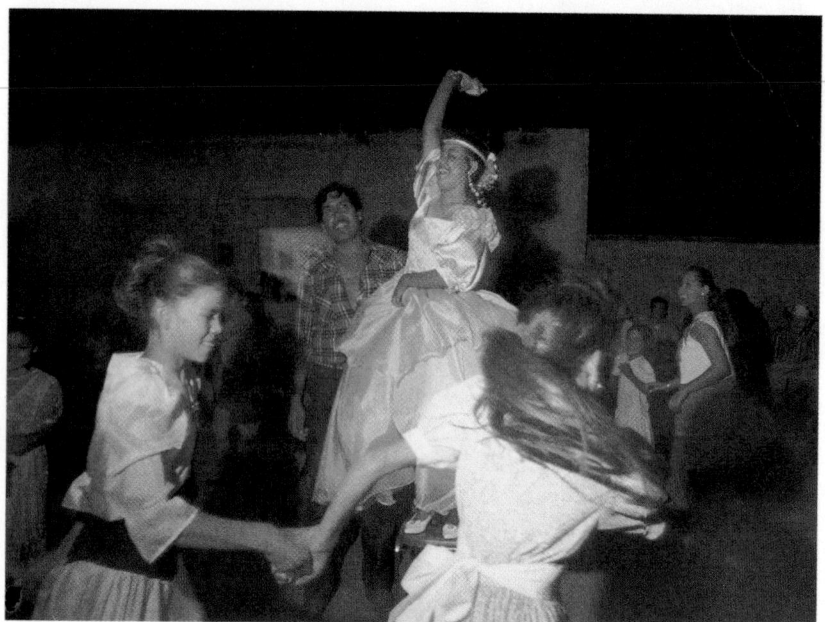

A Woman at 15 Dulce Giovanna Mendez dances at her *quinceañera,* the traditional fifteenth-birthday celebration of a Hispanic girl's sexual maturity. Dulce lives in Ures, Mexico, where many older teenagers marry and have children. This was the expected outcome of puberty in earlier decades in the United States as well.

(Zani & Cicognani, 2006). However, both sexes are influenced by hormones and society. All have sexual interests they did not previously have (biology), which produce behaviors that teenagers in other nations would not necessarily engage in (culture) (Moore & Rosenthal, 2006).

Cultural norms affect who is likely to be a person's first sexual partner. Individuals might think that this is a very private and personal choice, but evidence suggests not.

For example, North American adolescents of both sexes tend to express sexual impulses with partners about the same age, which is also true in many European nations (Zani & Cicognani, 2006). However, in Finland and Norway, girls tend to become sexually experienced later than boys. In Greece and Portugal, the opposite is true (Teitler, 2002). Men in Nigeria are expected to seek inexperienced younger teens for sexual partners and to give them gifts. By contrast, emerging adult males in Thailand are expected to seek older, experienced women (World Health Organization, 2005).

These generalities do not apply to everyone within those nations. Subgroups as well as cohorts always differ, again for cultural reasons. One specific was found in a survey of 704 adolescents in Ghana: More 16-year-old girls than boys were sexually experienced, but those experienced girls usually had only one partner whereas the boys had several. Muslim youth were less often experienced than Christians, who were less experienced than those of neither faith (Glover et al., 2003).

As in Ghana, religious teachings affect sexual behavior for many teenagers worldwide; this was apparent in a study of adolescents in Israel and the United States, with many youth being influenced by their faith. For Muslim teenagers, romances seldom included sexual intimacy, even in thought (Magen, 1998). For example, one Arab Israeli boy reported on "the most wonderful and happiest day of my life":

> A girl passed our house. And she looked at me. She looked at me as though I were an angel in paradise. I looked at her, and stopped still, and wondered and marveled. . . . [Later] she passed near us, stopped, and called my friend, and asked my name and who I am. I trembled all over and could hardly stand on my feet. I used my brain, since otherwise I would have fallen to the floor. I couldn't stand it any longer and went home.
>
> *[quoted in Magen, 1998, pp. 97–98]*

Cohort as well as culture have notable effects on sexual activity. For most of the twentieth century, surveys in North America have reported increasing proportions of adolescents becoming sexually active. This trend reversed in 1990. For example, according to the CDC's Youth Risk Behavior Survey (MMWR, 2006), 62 percent of eleventh-graders in the United States had had intercourse in 1991, but only 51 percent had in 2005. The double standard (with boys expected to be more sexually active than girls) also declined, as male rates came closer to female ones (see Figure 14.6). Ethnic differences among high school students were also apparent. Rates of sexual experience for African Americans were down 13 percentage points (from 81 to 68 percent), for European Americans down 7 percentage points (from 50 to 43 percent), and for Latinos down 2 percentage points (from 53 to 51 percent).

➤Answer to Observation Quiz (from page 372): About age 13. This is most obvious in ball throwing (see Figure 14.4), but it is also apparent in the 30-yard dash.

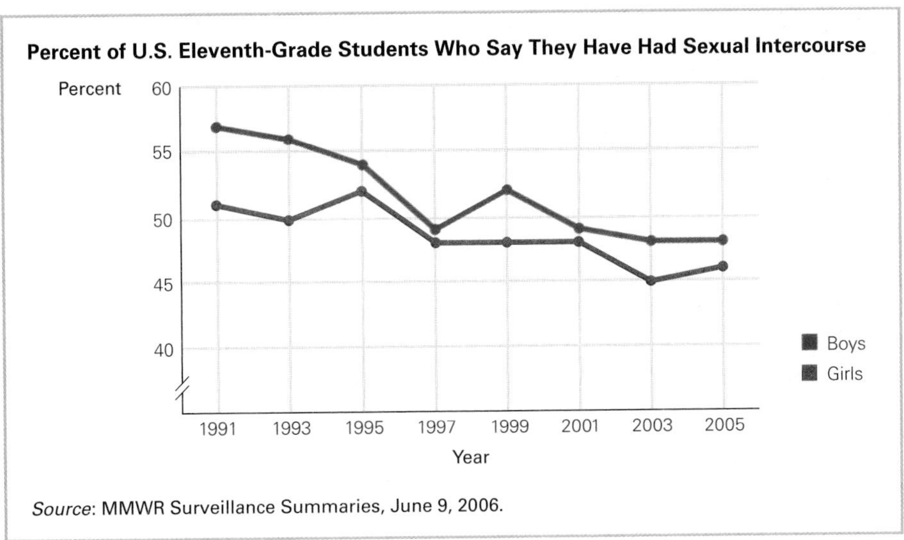

FIGURE 14.6

Surprise! Two trends are apparent from this graph. First, fewer adolescents are sexually experienced than was the case 15 years ago. Second, the gap between the sexes is shrinking. This is confirmed by other data, including the number of eleventh-graders who say they have had four or more partners, which showed a 10 percent male–female gap in 1991 and a 5 percent gap in 2005. Both trends (decline and sexual convergence) are found in other nations, and neither was predicted by researchers a few decades ago.

All these examples demonstrate that a universal experience (specifically, rising hormones) that produces another universal experience (specifically, growth of primary and secondary sex characteristics) takes many forms, depending on cohort and culture.

Brain Development

As with all the other changes of puberty, adolescent brain growth is the consequence of hormones, maturation, and experience, which together cause uneven yet rapid growth. The limbic system (fear, emotional impulses) matures before the prefrontal cortex (planning ahead, emotional regulation). Neuroscientists and developmentalists are working to understand exactly how emotions and logic connect, as the following explains.

a case to study

What Were You Thinking?

Laurence Steinberg is a noted expert on adolescent thinking. He is also a father.

> When my son, Benjamin, was 14, he and three of his friends decided to sneak out of the house where they were spending the night and visit one of their girlfriends at around two in the morning. When they arrived at the girl's house, they positioned themselves under her bedroom window, threw pebbles against her windowpanes, and tried to scale the side of the house. Modern technology, unfortunately, has made it harder to play Romeo these days. The boys set off the house's burglar alarm, which activated a siren and simultaneously sent a direct notification to the local police station, which dispatched a patrol car. When the siren went off, the boys ran down the street and right smack into the police car, which was heading to the girl's home. Instead of stopping and explaining their activity, Ben and his friends scattered and ran off in different directions through the neighborhood. One of the boys was caught by the police and taken back to his home, where his parents were awakened and the boy questioned.
>
> I found out about this affair the following morning, when the girl's mother called our home to tell us what Ben had done. . . . After his near brush with the local police, Ben had returned to the house out of which he had snuck, where he slept soundly until I awakened him with an angry telephone call, telling him to gather his clothes and wait for me in front of his friend's house. On our drive home, after delivering a long lecture about what he had done and about the dangers of running from armed police in the dark when they believe they may have interrupted a burglary, I paused.
>
> "What were you thinking?" I asked.
>
> "That's the problem, Dad," Ben replied, "I wasn't."
>
> *[Steinberg, 2004, pp. 51, 52]*

Steinberg finds his son insightful. "The problem is not that Ben's decision-making was deficient. The problem is that it was nonexistent" (Steinberg, 2004, p. 52). In his analysis, Steinberg points out a characteristic of adolescent thought: When emotions are intense, especially with peers, the logical part of the brain shuts down.

This is not reflected in questionnaires that require teenagers to respond to paper-and-pencil questions regarding hypothetical dilemmas. On those tests, teenagers think carefully and answer correctly. They know the risks of sex and drugs. However,

> the prospect of visiting a hypothetical girl from class cannot possibly carry the excitement about the possibility of surprising someone you have a crush on with a visit in the middle of the night. It is easier to put on a hypothetical condom during an act of hypothetical sex than it is to put on a real one when one is in the throes of passion. It is easier to just say no to a hypothetical beer than it is to a cold frosty one on a summer night.
>
> *[Steinberg, 2004, p. 43]*

Steinberg believes that, to understand how the brain actually works, abstract questionnaires are inadequate. Adolescent thinking is more variable than earlier researchers believed (Kuhn, 2006). Now that scientists realize the limitations of prior research, and neuroscientists have data from fMRI and other brain scans, new discoveries about adolescent brain functioning are on the horizon.

Ben reached adulthood safely. Some other teenagers, with less cautious police or less diligent parents, do not. Ideally, research on adolescent brains will help protect adolescents from their own dangerous ones (Monastersky, 2007).

Especially for Parents Worried About Their Teenager's Risk Taking You remember the risky things you did at the same age, and you are alarmed by the possibility that your child will follow in your footsteps. What should you do?

Caution Versus Thrills

Much more interdisciplinary research is needed to integrate neurology and psychology. Caution is needed, lest "incomplete brain development [becomes] an explanation for just about everything about teens that adults have found perplexing, from sleep patterns to risk taking and mood swings" (Kuhn, 2006, p. 59). The fMRI, the PET, and other measures are expensive and complex, and longitudinal, reliable, multifactorial research on the brains of typical 10- to 17-year-olds is not yet extensive. As one expert explains:

> We stand at the edge of very exciting new research developments as new neuroimaging technologies come online, but at present we are groping in the dark in many respects. . . . The work on adolescent development is particularly recent.
>
> *[Keating, 2004, p. 69]*

With excitement tempered by caution, scientists trace many hallmarks of adolescent thinking and behavior to the brain. It is thrilling to learn that the frontal lobes are the last part of the brain to mature, with ongoing myelination from ages 10 to 25. In the words of a leading neuroscientist:

> The frontal lobes are essential for . . . response inhibition, emotional regulation, planning, and organization, which may not be fully developed in adolescents . . . [which suggests that brain immaturity underlies much] troublesome adolescent behavior.
>
> *[Sowell et al., 2007, p. 59]*

Uneven Growth

You learned in Chapter 11 that the brain functions well in middle childhood, as dendrites, myelination, and the corpus callosum allow "a massively interconnected brain" (Kagan & Herschkowitz, 2005, p. 220). Yet you just read that the immature prefrontal cortex may allow "troublesome adolescent behavior." Is this a contradiction? Regression? Eight-year-olds would probably not sneak out at 2 A.M. to throw pebbles at a girl's window. If the idea occurred to them, they would probably think twice and stay in bed.

Actually, there is no contradiction. Adolescents are quite capable of rational thinking. However, they don't necessarily *use* that capacity to "think twice" before acting. As in the rest of the teenager's body, brain growth is uneven. Myelination and maturation proceed from inside to the cortex and from back to front (Sowell et al., 2007).

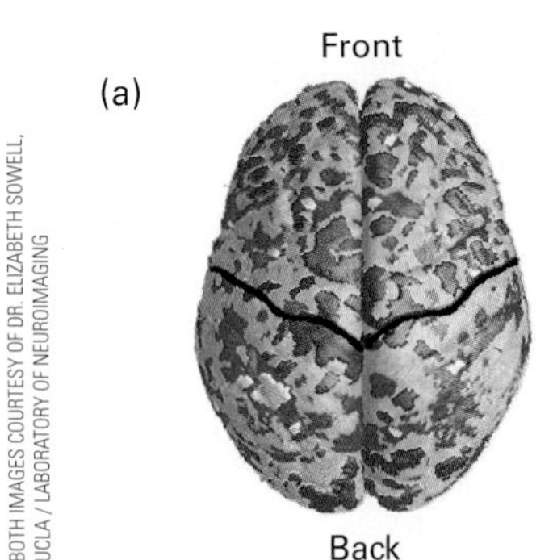

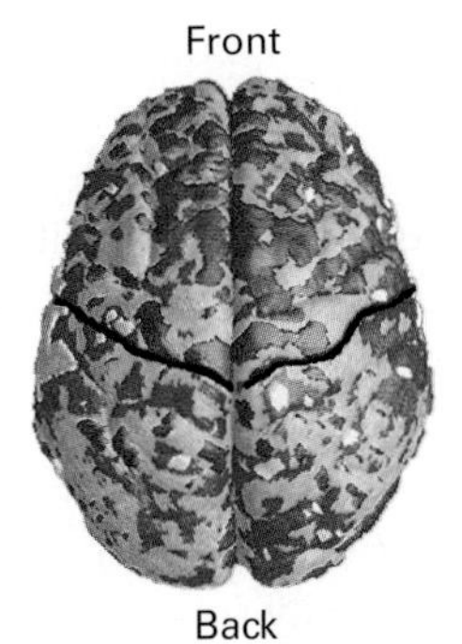

BOTH IMAGES COURTESY OF DR. ELIZABETH SOWELL, UCLA / LABORATORY OF NEUROIMAGING

The Prefrontal Cortex Matures These are composite scans of normal brains of *(a)* children and adolescents and *(b)* adolescents and adults. The red areas indicate both an increase in brain size and a decrease in gray matter (cerebral cortex). The red areas in *(b)* are larger than in *(a)* and are concentrated in the frontal area of the brain, which is associated with complex cognitive processes. The growth of brain areas as their gray matter decreases is believed to reflect an increase in white matter, which consists of myelin—the axon coating that makes the brain more efficient.

Further, the hormones of puberty seem to affect the amygdala more directly than they affect the cortex, which is more influenced by age and experience. The combination of the sequence of brain maturation and the effects of early puberty mean that the limbic system (deep inside) matures years before the prefrontal cortex.

Since the amygdala specializes in quick emotional reactions—sudden anger, joy, fear, despair—and the prefrontal cortex (called the executive) coordinates, inhibits, and strategizes, this uneven maturation puts adolescents

> at increased risk for emotional problems and disorders because the brain systems that activate emotions . . . are developed before the capacity for volitional effortful control of these emotions is fully in place.
>
> *[Compas, 2004, p. 283]*

The maturing limbic system is particularly attracted to strong, immediate sensations, unchecked by the slowly maturing prefrontal cortex. For this reason,

> Adolescents *like* intensity, excitement, and arousal. They are drawn to music videos that shock and bombard the senses. Teenagers flock to horror and slasher movies. They dominate queues waiting to ride the high-adrenaline rides at amusement parks. Adolescence is a time when sex, drugs, *very* loud music, and other high-stimulation experiences take on great appeal. It is a developmental period when an appetite for adventure, a predilection for risks, and a desire for novelty and thrills seem to reach naturally high levels.
>
> *[Dahl, 2004, pp. 7, 8]*

Such intense experiences are sought because they short-circuit the emotional regulation of the prefrontal cortex.

When stress, arousal, passion, sensory bombardment, drug intoxication, or deprivation are extreme, the brain is overtaken by impulses that might shame adults. Teenagers brag about being so drunk they were "wasted," "bombed," "smashed," describing a state most adults would try to avoid. Some teenagers choose to spend a night without sleep, a day without eating, or to exercise in pain.

The consequences may be especially severe in the twenty-first century, because puberty precedes adult employment and family life by a decade or more and because guns, drugs, and sex can turn a momentary lapse of judgment into a lethal mistake. It seems that the hormones that trigger the body changes of puberty do not also trigger the brain changes, which are more affected by birth date than body size.

Twisted Memorial This wreck was once a Volvo, driven by a Colorado teenager who ignored an oncoming train's whistle at a rural crossing. The car was hurled 167 feet and burst into flames. The impact instantly killed the driver and five teenage passengers. They are among the statistics indicating that accidents, many of which result from unwise risk taking, kill 10 times more adolescents than diseases do.

DOMINIC CHAVEZ / THE DENVER POST / AP PHOTO

Neurological Advances

With increased myelination, reactions become lightning fast. The white matter, which includes the axons and dendrites that link one neuron to another, increases throughout adolescence, again from

➤Response for Parents Worried About Their Teenager's Risk Taking (from page 376): You are right to be concerned, but you cannot keep your child locked up for the next decade or so. Since you know that some rebellion and irrationality are likely, try to minimize them by not boasting about your own youthful exploits, by reacting sternly to minor infractions to nip worse behavior in the bud, and by making allies of your child's teachers.

back to front (Sowell et al., 2007). Additional pruning occurs, and the dopamine system (neurotransmitters that bring pleasure) is very active.

Before these advances are complete (about age 25), new connections between one synapse and another ease acquisition of new ideas, words, memories, personality patterns, or dance steps (Keating, 2004). As you might imagine, values acquired during adolescence are more likely to endure than those learned later, after brain links are more firmly established.

Adolescent brain immaturity can be used positively or negatively. The fact that "the prefrontal cortex is still developing . . . confers benefits as well as risks. It helps explain the creativity of adolescence and early adulthood, before the brain becomes set in its ways. But it also makes adolescents more prone to addiction" (Monastersky, 2007, p. A17).

One expert bemoans "the deleterious consequences of drug use [which] appear to be more pronounced in adolescents than in adults, a difference that has been linked to brain maturation" (Moffit et al., 2006, p. 12). Another scholar celebrates adolescent passion that "intertwines with the highest levels of human endeavor: passion for ideas and ideals, passion for beauty, passion to create music and art" (Dahl, 2004, p. 21).

Thus, adolescent experiences can teach compassion or mistrust, political participation or isolation. Those who care about the next generation need attend to the life lessons that adolescents are learning, providing "scaffolding and monitoring" until brains and skills can function well on their own (Dahl, quoted in Monastersky, 2007, p. A18).

Body Rhythms

Brain rhythms affects body rhythms (Buzsáki, 2006). The hypothalamus and pituitary regulate hormones that affect stress, appetite, sleep, and so on. As you know, the brain of every living creature responds to natural changes.

Seasons affect reproduction (more births occur in spring), weight (gains in winter), and, in some species, migration and hibernation. Diurnal (daily) rhythms affect tiredness, hunger, alertness, elimination, body temperature, nutrient balance, blood composition, moods, and so on. (Some people wake up cheery and others cranky, switching moods by nightfall.)

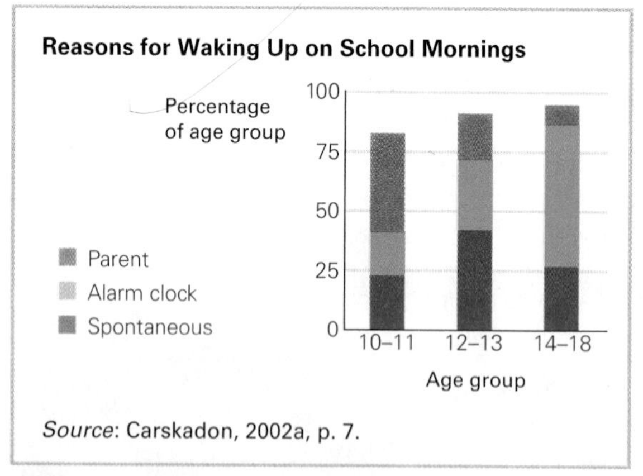

FIGURE 14.7

Sleep Deprivation Humans naturally wake up once they've had enough sleep. Few high school students wake up spontaneously, and many sleep later on weekends than on school days. These facts suggest that most teenagers need more sleep. Depression and irritability correlate with insufficient sleep.

All creatures have a day–night cycle. That's why jet lag affects people who fly east–west across the globe, changing time zones, but not those who fly the same distance north–south. Because of diurnal rhythms, people cannot get their recommended 60 hours of sleep per week by staying awake 24 hours for four days and then sleeping 20 hours on each of the other three. The diurnal rise and fall of body chemicals, melatonin among them, make sleep elusive sometimes and impossible to postpone at other times.

Puberty alters biorhythms. Hormones from the pituitary often cause a "phase delay" in sleep–wake patterns: Many teens are wide awake at midnight but half-asleep all morning. Because adult brains are naturally alert in the morning and sleepy at night, social patterns set by adults do not necessarily accommodate adolescent rhythms.

One consequence is sleep deprivation for many teenagers, who naturally stay up late but who nonetheless are forced to wake up early. Evidence for this is that teenagers seldom waken spontaneously on weekdays (see Figure 14.7) and often "sleep in" on weekends (Andrade & Menna-Barreto, 2002).

Uneven sleep schedules (more sleep on weekends, with later bedtimes and daytime sleeping) are common among teenagers, yet this unevenness decreases well-being just as overall sleep deprivation does (Fuligni & Hardway, 2006). Girls are particularly likely to be sleep-deprived, which decreases their grades and happiness (Fredriksen et al., 2004).

issues and applications

Calculus at 8 A.M.?

Biology designs teenage bodies to be alert at midnight and tired all morning, perhaps falling asleep in school (see Figure 14.8). School schedules reflect culture, not biorhythms.

Some parents fight biology. They command their wide-awake teen to "go to sleep," they hang up on classmates who phone after 10 P.M., they set early curfews, and they drag their offspring out of bed for school. (An opposite developmental clash occurs when parents tell their toddlers to stay in their cribs after dawn.)

Data on the phase delay of adolescence led social scientists at the University of Minnesota to ask 17 school districts to consider a later starting time for high school. Most adults opposed the idea.

Teachers generally thought that early morning was the best time to learn. Many (42 percent) parents of adolescents thought school should begin before 8 A.M. In fact, some (20 percent) wanted their teenagers out of the house by 7:15 A.M., as did only 1 percent of those with younger children. Bus drivers hated rush hour; cafeteria workers wanted to leave by mid-afternoon; police said teenagers should be off the streets by 4 P.M.; coaches needed sports events to end before dark; employers hired teens to staff the afternoon shift; community program directors wanted to schedule the gym for nonschool events (Wahlstrom, 2002).

Despite the naysayers, one school district experimented. In Edina, Minnesota, high school began at 8:30 A.M. (previously 7:25 A.M.) and ended at 3:10 P.M., not 2:05 P.M. After one year, most (93 percent) parents and virtually all students approved. One student said, "I have only fallen asleep in school once this whole year, and last year I fell asleep about three times a week" (quoted in Wahlstrom, 2002, p. 190). The data showed fewer absent, late, disruptive, or sick students (the school nurse became an advocate) and higher grades.

Other school districts reconsidered. Minneapolis, which had started high school at 7:15 A.M., changed the starting time to 8:40 A.M. Again, attendance improved, as did graduation rate. School boards in South Burlington (Vermont), West Des Moines (Iowa), Tulsa (Oklahoma), Arlington (Virginia), and Milwaukee (Wisconsin) voted in favor of later starting times, switching on average from 7:45 A.M. to 8:30 A.M. (Tonn, 2006). Unexpected advantages appeared: financial savings (more efficient energy use) and, at least in Tulsa, unprecedented athletic championships.

But change is hard. Researchers believe that "without a strategic approach, the forces to maintain the status quo in the schools will prevail" (Wahlstrom, 2002, p. 195). Few college students choose 8 A.M. classes. Why?

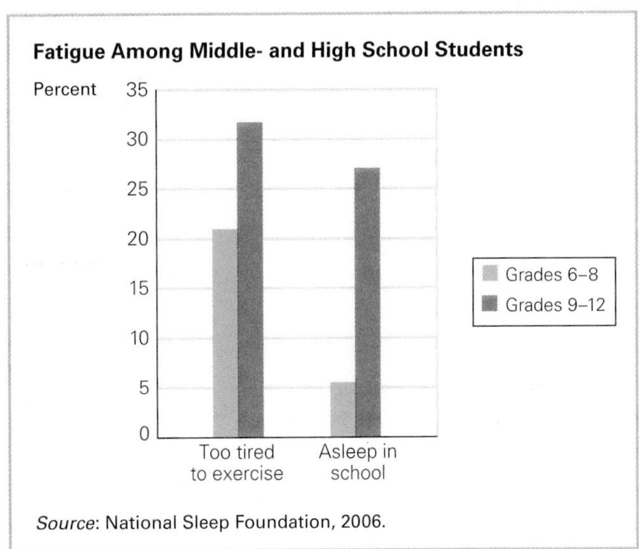

FIGURE 14.8

Dreaming and Learning? This graph shows the percent of U.S. students who, once a week or more, fall asleep in class or are too tired to exercise. Not shown are those who are too tired overall (59 percent for high school students) or who doze in class "almost every day" (8 percent).

Sleep deprivation and irregular sleep schedules are associated with many other difficulties, such as falling asleep while driving, insomnia in the middle of the night, distressing dreams, and mood disorders (depression, conduct disorder, anxiety) (Carskadon, 2002b; Fredriksen et al., 2004; Fuligni & Hardway, 2006).

Especially for Those Who Appreciate Folk Wisdom What is meant by "The early bird catches the worm" and "Early to bed and early to rise, makes a man healthy, wealthy, and wise"?

SUMMING UP

The growth spurt, sexual differentiation, and brain maturation are notable during the years after the first signs of puberty. Physical growth proceeds from the extremities to the center, so the limbs grow before the internal organs. Weight precedes height, which precedes muscles and growth of the internal organs. Both boys and girls increase in sexual interest as their bodies develop and their hormone levels rise, with sexual behavior and thoughts powerfully affected by culture.

The hormones of puberty probably cause the brain's emotional hot spots to further myelinate as well as grow. Adult functioning of the prefrontal cortex depends less on specific hormones and more on age and experience; thus it matures later. Uneven neurological advancement may be one reason adolescents take irrational risks and enjoy intense sensory experiences. Reactions quicken and emotional memories endure. The brain affects body rhythms, notably in the phase delay that makes adolescents stay up late at night. As a result of school schedules, many adolescents are sleep-deprived. ■

Possible Problems

Growth and sexual awakening, emotional intensity and hormonal rushes—all of this can be quite wonderful. However, as you will read in each of the chapters on adolescence and emerging adulthood, maturation can bring problems. Typically, if a young person has one problem, he or she also has several others—true for about 20 percent of all young people. That means that 80 percent are not bedeviled by problems; for them, adolescence is more joyful than troubled. Remember that as we look at sex and drugs, serious problems for a minority.

Sex Too Soon

Adolescent sexuality in the twenty-first century can be problematic for three reasons:

- Puberty occurs at young ages. Early sexual experiences correlate with depression and drug use.
- Raising a child has become more complex, which means that teenage pregnancy is no longer welcomed or expected.
- Sexually transmitted infections are more common and dangerous.

The first item on this list, sexual relationships, is discussed in Chapter 16, where the main discussion of teen romance and friendship occurs. The other two items, pregnancy and infections, each have specific health impacts, so they are discussed below.

Teenage Pregnancy

There is good news about pregnancy under age 18: It is about half as common as it was 20 years ago in the United States and in many other nations (MMWR, February 4, 2005). Not only are teen births less frequent, the abortion rate has also decreased. Contraception use is higher and teen intercourse is lower.

Nonetheless, if a girl under age 15 becomes pregnant, as about 25,000 U.S. girls did in 2002 (a rate higher than in any other developed nation), she is at greater risk of almost every complication—including spontaneous and induced abortion, high blood pressure, stillbirth, cesarean section, a low-birthweight baby, and even death—than she would have been if she had waited five years or more (Menacker et al., 2004).

In some nations (notably sub-Saharan Africa), inadequate medical care makes pregnancy the leading cause of death for teenage girls (Reynolds et al., 2006). In regions where almost everyone is malnourished, the youngest mothers die of birth complications three times more often than do older women (Blum & Nelson-Mmari, 2004).

If a pregnant teenager has an abortion (as two-thirds of all pregnant U.S. girls under age 15 do), she avoids the problems of a sustained pregnancy and birth, but she encounters other complications, partly because the younger a woman is, the later in pregnancy she is likely to abort (MMWR, November 24, 2006).

Throughout puberty, bodies add bone, redistribute weight, and gain height, while the inner organs (including the uterus) mature. Pregnancy interferes with this, because another set of hormones directs the body to sustain new life. Nature protects the fetus, which may take essential nutrients (especially calcium and iron) from the mother. If normal pubescent growth is deflected, that causes the girl to become a shorter and sicker woman than she otherwise would have been.

If a young woman lives in a developed nation and obtains good medical care, the serious biological consequences of adolescent pregnancy are rare. Unfortunately, the youngest teenagers are likely to postpone seeing a doctor, which increases the risk of complications. Even in Sweden, with good nutrition and free prenatal care, an early teen birth impairs health and achievements lifelong (Olausson et al., 2001).

If a baby of a teen mother is born healthy, he or she is still likely to experience numerous complications later on, including poor health; inadequate education; low intelligence; and anger at his or her family, community, and society (Borkowski et al., 2007). That takes a greater toll on the mother as she cares for her child.

Many college students reading this book know teenage mothers. Such young women may obtain good medical care, stay in school, and get help from her family and the child's father. In such a case, adolescent mothers are likely to be resilient, becoming competent young women by age 30 or so (Borkowski et al., 2007). As with the other problems of life, no single burden is insurmountable, although it would be easier on the body to postpone pregnancy until all growth is complete.

Sexual Infections

A **sexually transmitted infection (STI)** (formerly known as a sexually transmitted disease [STD] or venereal disease [VD]) is any infection transmitted through sexual contact (oral or genital). Worldwide, sexually active teenagers have higher rates of the most common STIs (*gonorrhea, genital herpes,* and *chlamydia*) than any other age group (World Health Organization, 2005).

sexually transmitted infection (STI) A disease spread by sexual contact, including syphilis, gonorrhea, genital herpes, chlamydia, and HIV.

The most lethal STIs, specifically AIDS and syphilis, are more commonly caught by people in their 20s, but teenagers are vulnerable to them as well, especially if they already have an STI or if they have sex with an older person. One statistic makes the point: In the United States, young persons aged 15–24 constitute only one-fourth of the sexually active population but account for half of all sexually transmitted infections (MMWR, October 20, 2006).

One reason is purely biological. Fully developed women have some natural biological defenses against STIs, but this is less true for pubescent girls, who are more likely to catch every STI, including AIDS, from an infected partner (World Health Organization, 2005). It is not known whether adolescent boys are also more vulnerable to infection.

It is known that, for many reasons, sexually active boys and girls under age 16 are particularly likely to contract an STI (Kaestle et al., 2005) but are unlikely to seek immediate treatment and alert their sexual partners. Not only are they ashamed and afraid, but many do not recognize symptoms, nor do they believe that medical treatment will be confidential.

An added complication occurs for partners of the same sex. Especially for youths in the United States, such relationships are usually kept secret; thus it is even more difficult for them to seek treatment than it is for heterosexual teenagers.

Many STIs have no symptoms but severe consequences (MMWR, August 4, 2006). For example, chlamydia, the most frequently reported disease (more often than any other sexual or nonsexual disease), can cause lifelong infertility. Another

➤Response for Those Who Appreciate Folk Wisdom (from page 379): Folk wisdom is a good way to understand popular culture. In this case, adults enshrined their natural rhythms with aphorisms approving adult sleep–wake patterns.

common STI is human papillomavirus (HPV), which increases the chances of fatal uterine cancer. Human immunodeficiency virus (HIV) can have no symptoms for years, and then cause AIDS and death. There are literally hundreds more STIs (James, 2007).

Especially for Health Practitioners How might you encourage adolescents to seek treatment for STIs?

Unless a teenager has regular checkups with lab testing (which few do), he or she may not realize that an STI is at work. Many STIs can be prevented with immunization and confidential counseling. Although most of the research has been done on girls, the problem may be even worse for boys, who are particularly unlikely to see a doctor unless they are seriously injured.

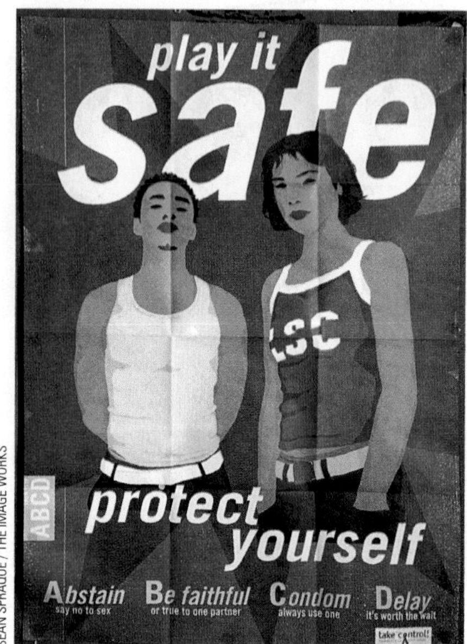

SEAN SPRAGUE / THE IMAGE WORKS

No Safer? Educational posters and even intense educational programs have little proven effect on the incidence of AIDS among adolescents. This poster was displayed outside an HIV testing center in Windhoek, Namibia, a country that has one of the highest HIV infection rates in the world.

Protection

Preventing and treating STIs is only one of many reasons teenagers should have regular medical care. Basic information is no longer the usual problem. Almost every teenager knows that pregnancy and STIs can be prevented by abstinence or regular and proper use of condoms, but whether that information is translated into practice depends on peers, partners, and adults. Confidence in a familiar medical provider can be crucial.

National differences are striking. In France, 91 percent of adolescents use contraception (usually a condom) at first intercourse (Michaud et al., 2006), partly because every French high school is required to provide free, confidential medical care. However, far fewer Italian, German, and U.S. teenagers use condoms. For instance, in the United States, only 46 percent of sexually active high school senior girls used a condom during their most recent sexual encounter (MMWR, June 9, 2006).

Sex education is discussed in Chapter 16. Before leaving this topic, however, we need to note one mistake especially common in early adolescence, already apparent in our discussion of body image. Teenagers tend to confuse appearance and reality, not realizing that a polite, well-dressed partner could have an STI. For example, one girl in Malawi (where AIDS is epidemic) thought she was safe because her partner was known to her and "my mother knows his mother" (quoted in World Health Organization, 2005, p. 11).

Sexual Abuse

We should not leave the topic of sexuality without noting that **child sexual abuse,** which includes any sexual activity between a juvenile and an older person, is most common just after puberty. Every study finds that virtually every adolescent problem (including drug abuse, eating disorders, suicide, and pregnancy) is more common in adolescents who are sexually abused. Some eventually become abusers as well (Barbaree & Marshall, 2006).

child sexual abuse Any erotic activity that arouses an adult and excites, shames, or confuses a child, whether or not the victim protests and whether or not genital contact is involved.

Young people who are sexually exploited have difficulty establishing sexual relationships. This is true during the abuse, because the abuser often isolates the victim from his or her peers, and later on, because past memories interfere with normal sexuality.

Sex abuse is more common between the ages of 10 and 15 than at any other time, and it is a major problem in every nation. The United Nations reports that millions of young adolescents are forced into marriage, genital surgery, and prostitution (often across national borders) each year (Pinheiro, 2006). Exact numbers are elusive. Almost every nation has laws against sexual abuse, but these laws are rarely enforced, and adults often let disgust and sensationalism crowd out efforts to prevent, monitor, and eliminate the problem (Davidson, 2005).

Data on substantiated childhood sexual abuse in the United States confirm that, as elsewhere, the rate is higher among 12- to 15-year-olds than among younger children (U.S. Department of Health and Human Services Administration on

TABLE 14.2

Age and Sex Abuse: United States, 2005

Age	Number of Substantiated Victims	Percent of Maltreatment That Is Sex Abuse
0–3	5,407	2.1
4–7	18,547	8.2
8–11	19,136	11.2
12–15	29,768	17.3
16–18	8,676	16.8

Source: U.S. Department of Health and Human Services Administration on Children, Youth, and Families, 2006

Children, Youth, and Families, 2006). Girls are particularly vulnerable, although boys are also at risk. But overall rates are declining, perhaps because adolescents are becoming better informed about sexual activity (Finkelhor & Jones, 2004). Nonetheless, almost thirty thousand 12- to 15-year-olds were substantiated victims of sexual abuse in the United States in 2005 (see Table 14.2), a statistic that underscores that teenagers need protection, not just information (U.S. Department of Health and Human Services Administration on Children, Youth, and Families, 2006).

Drug Use and Abuse

Innocence is also reflected in drug use, as few adolescents imagine that they could become addicted. Most experiment and observe no immediate harm, enjoying the thrill of doing something that adults think they are too young to do. Worldwide, most young people use at least one drug before age 18.

An annual nationwide survey of U.S. high school seniors called Monitoring the Future began in 1975 and continues to this day (see Research Design). In 2006, many seniors drank alcohol (73 percent), puffed a cigarette (47 percent), and smoked marijuana (42 percent) (Johnston et al., 2007) (see Figure 14.9). Drug use is down in the United States over the life of the survey, but the number of available drugs has increased, as have prescription-type drugs (e.g., barbiturates and tranquilizers).

Research Design

Scientists: Lloyd D. Johnston, Patrick M. O'Malley, Jerald G. Bachman, and John E. Schulenberg.

Publication: Monitoring the Future is online. Print copies are available from the National Institute on Drug Abuse in Bethesda, Maryland.

Participants: In 2006, 48,500 students in 410 high schools, throughout the United States.

Design: Beginning in 1975, scientists from the University of Michigan surveyed adolescents each year, asking about drug use, drug availability, and personal attitudes. The basic questions have remained the same, with new drugs added (e.g., Vicodin, OxyContin). Data are reported by age, sex, ethnicity, and region.

Major conclusion: Over the 32 years of the survey, drug use declined, rose, and recently declined again. New drugs continue to appear, and sometimes old drugs become more popular again. Use is more affected by attitudes than by availability.

Comment: This study tracks many cohort changes within the United States. Interested readers should access the latest reports online. Note that other nations often show different patterns and that Monitoring the Future does not usually include high school dropouts.

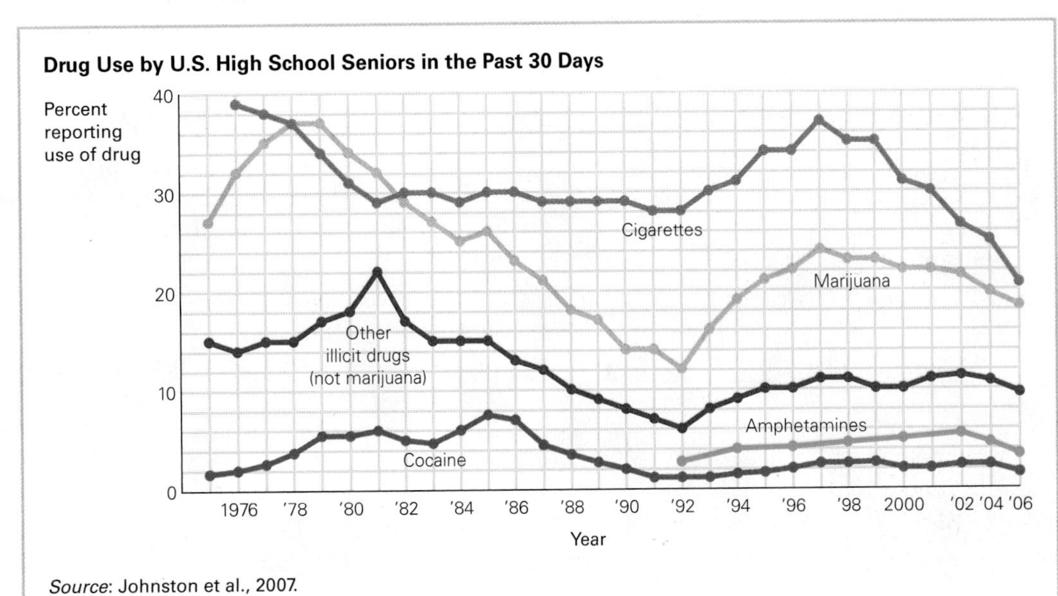

FIGURE 14.9

Rise and Fall By asking the same questions year after year, the Monitoring the Future study shows notable historical effects. It is encouraging that something in society, not in the adolescent, makes drug use increase and decrease and that the most recent data show a decline. However, as Chapter 1 emphasized, survey research cannot prove what causes change.

Variations by Nation, Gender, and Ethnicity

One of the fascinating aspects of adolescent drug use is how variable it is, which indicates that much more than biology is involved. In some nations, young adolescents drink alcohol more often than they use any other drug; in others, smoking is more common than drinking. In many places (especially eastern Europe), teenagers use both alcohol and tobacco more than in the United States; in still other places, teenagers rarely use any drugs at all (Buelga et al., 2006; Eisner, 2002).

Laws and family practices are part of the reason for these variations, but not the only reasons. For example, in many Arab nations, alcohol is strictly forbidden; in many European nations, children drink wine with dinner; in many Asian nations, anyone may smoke anywhere; in the United States, smoking is forbidden in many public places.

Even nations with common boundaries differ radically (Buelga et al., 2006). For example, among 15-year-olds, 9.4 percent of those in Switzerland were heavy users of marijuana compared with only 3.3 percent in Italy. More Canadian youth smoke marijuana, but fewer smoke cigarettes, than in the United States. Laws are only part of the explanation: Although marijuana is legal and widely available in the Netherlands, Dutch 15-year-olds are among the lowest heavy users (2.8 percent) of any developed nation (Buelga et al., 2006).

Gender differences are apparent for most drugs in most nations, with boys having higher rates of use than girls. In the United States, cigarette smoking is unisex, but an international survey (131 nations) of 13- to 15-year-olds found that more boys than girls are smokers (except in some European nations), including three times as many boys as girls in Southeast Asia (Warren et al., 2006). According to another international survey, this one of 31 nations, boys are also almost twice as likely as girls to have tried marijuana (26 versus 15 percent) (ter Bogt et al., 2006).

For North Americans, the good news is that adolescents begin drug use later than in many other nations. A significant minority (about 20 percent) never use any drugs, usually because of religious values (C. Smith, 2005). However, the United States leads the world in the number of available drugs, including synthetic narcotics, unknown in most nations. During 2006, 10 percent of U.S. high school seniors used Vicodin and 4 percent used OxyContin (Johnston et al., 2007).

A particular problem is using drugs before age 13, because doing so is more likely to interfere with brain and body growth as well as to lead to serious problems

➤Response for Health Practitioners (from page 382): Many adolescents are intensely concerned about privacy and fearful of adult interference. This means your first task is to convince the teenagers that you are nonjudgmental and that everything is confidential.

Especially for Older Brothers and Sisters A friend said she saw your 13-year-old sister smoking. Should you tell your parents?

MARK PETERS / CORBIS

STUART FRANKLIN / MAGNUM PHOTOS

The Same Event, A Thousand Miles Apart: Teen Approaches to Drinking Adolescents everywhere drink alcohol, including these girls at a high school prom in New York City *(left)* and at a sidewalk café in Prague *(right)*. Cultural differences affect the specifics but not the general trend toward teenage experimentation with drugs and alcohol.

Observation Quiz (see answer, page 386): Can you spot three cultural differences between these two groups?

later on. One large U.S. survey revealed that, among ninth-graders, 34 percent said that they had begun drinking before age 13, 19 percent that they had smoked a cigarette, and 11 percent that they had tried marijuana (MMWR, June 9, 2006). Monitoring the Future found that 16 percent of eighth-graders reported past use of inhalants (which can be unexpectedly and rapidly fatal), again beginning before the teen years (Johnston et al., 2007).

Rates also vary among U.S. ethnic groups (see Figure 14.10). European American teens use the most drugs and African and Asian Americans the least. Hispanic adolescent drug use may be increasing, especially marijuana smoking by younger teens who speak English well (Delva et al., 2005).

Why would any teenager, in any nation, use drugs, especially if forbidden by law and against parental wishes? One reason is that, for many adolescents, peers are more important than parents. "In young adolescence, use of substances . . . provides a form of commerce with the social world" (Dishion & Owen, 2002, p. 489). In other words, socially awkward pubescent children (especially boys) use drugs to establish friendships and be part of a peer group.

Another reason is that the neurological drive for intense sensations without the caution of a fully mature prefrontal cortex makes adolescents seek a quick and intense rush, as explained by a Spanish expert:

> Teenagers and young adults use licit and illicit drugs to look for states of excitement that make their relationships with others more intense and satisfying and that make their spare time activities more stimulating.
>
> *[Buelga et al., 2006, p. 351]*

LAUREN GREENFIELD

Looking Cool The tight clothing, heavy makeup, multiple rings, and cigarettes are meant to convey to the world that Sheena, 15, and Jessica, 16, are mature, sophisticated women.

Observation Quiz (see answer, page 386): Did these girls buy their own cigarettes?

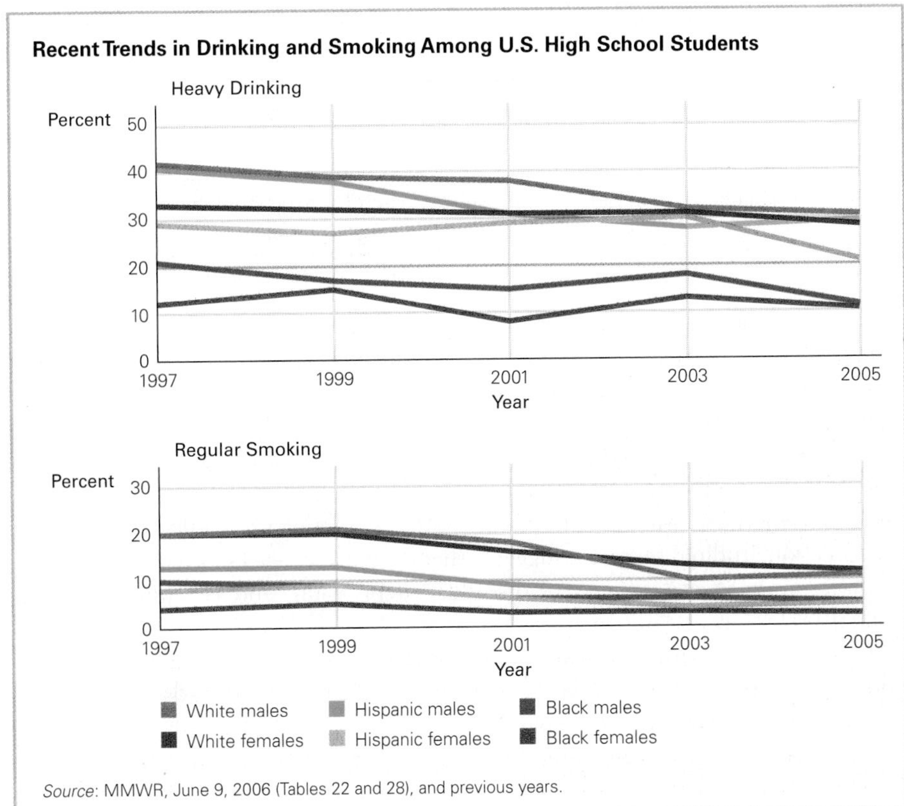

FIGURE 14.10

Less Drinking, Still Too Much Smoking The overall downward trend in both binge drinking and regular smoking by adolescents is good news, but changing many high school students' minds about getting drunk or smoking daily remains difficult.

Observation Quiz (see answer, page 387): Which of these categories of people is least likely to drink alcohol during adolescence? Which category seems most affected by cohort changes in regular smoking?

➤**Response for Older Brothers and Sisters** (from page 384): Smoking is very addictive; urge your sister to stop now, before the habit becomes ingrained. Most adolescents care more about immediate concerns than about the distant possibility of cancer or heart disease, so tell your sister about a smoker you know whose teeth are yellow, whose clothing and hair reek of smoke, and who is shorter than the rest of his or her family. Then tell your parents; they are your best allies in helping your sister have a healthy adolescence.

➤**Answer to Observation Quiz** (from page 384): The most important difference is that, because moderate alcohol use during adolescence is accepted in most European countries, the girls in the Czech Republic are casual about drinking in public. In addition, the American girl is drinking straight from the bottle, and she is drinking hard liquor—both generally frowned upon in Europe.

Especially for College Roommates You and your roommate respect each other's privacy, but your roommate is jeopardizing his or her health by getting drunk every weekend and practicing unsafe sex. What should you do?

➤**Answer to Observation Quiz** (from page 385): No; they bummed them off a stranger at this San Jose, California, shopping mall. If you answered no, you probably had in mind the fact that most states, including California, are strictly enforcing their laws against selling cigarettes to minors. You may also have noticed the awkward way the girls are holding their cigarettes and realized that they have not yet been smoking long enough to have become addicted to nicotine.

Harm from Drugs

Since drugs are widely used and bring peer bonding and excitement, many adolescents think adults exaggerate the harm of teen drug use. That may be, but developmentalists see many immediate and long-term consequences. It would be far better if adolescents and their communities could postpone experimentation and never get to steady use. Here are some of the reasons.

During puberty, the body and the brain are destined to grow. Drugs interfere with healthy eating and digestion, particularly important during puberty. All psychoactive drugs impair the appetite, but tobacco is worst of all. Smoking or chewing tobacco decreases food consumption and interferes with the absorption of nutrients. This is one reason adolescent smokers become shorter and heavier adults.

In fact, all kinds of tobacco (bidis, cigars, pipes, chewing tobacco) decrease growth, a particularly serious problem in India, where undernutrition is chronic and tobacco use (typically not via cigarettes) is widespread (Warren et al., 2006). Since internal organs mature after the height spurt, drug-using teenagers who appear full-grown may still damage their hearts, lungs, brains, and reproductive systems.

For North Americans, alcohol is the most commonly abused drug, which is particularly harmful for the brain. Steady drinking impairs memory and self-control (not just temporarily) by damaging the hippocampus and the prefrontal cortex (S. A. Brown et al., 2000; De Bellis et al., 2005; White & Swartzwelder, 2004).

When nonhuman animals are forced to drink alcohol, addiction occurs and brain abnormalities result, with animals choosing the drug rather than nourishment. Among rats, adolescents likely drank more than adults in the same condition, and they were slower to solve problems (De Bellis et al., 2005; Sircar & Sircar, 2005).

Many adolescents know the damage of alcohol and cigarettes from observing adults, but they remain oblivious to the dangers of marijuana. Johanna explained:

> I started off using about every other weekend, and pretty soon it increased to three to four times a week. . . . I started skipping classes to get high. I quit soccer because my coach was a jerk. My grades dropped, but I blamed that on my not being into school. . . . Finally some of my friends cornered me and told me how much I had changed, and they said it started when I started smoking marijuana. They came with me to see the substance-abuse counselor at school.
>
> *[quoted in Bell, 1998, p. 199]*

Adolescents who regularly smoke marijuana are likely to drop out of school, become teenage parents, and be unemployed (Chassin et al., 2004). Marijuana affects memory, language proficiency, and motivation (Lane et al., 2005)—all especially crucial during adolescence.

For decades, researchers have noted that many drug-using adolescents distrust their parents, injure themselves, hate their schools, and get in trouble with the law. One hypothesis was that the psychic strains of adolescence led to drug use. However, longitudinal research suggests that drug use causes more problems than it solves, often *preceding* anxiety disorders, depression, and rebellion (Chassin et al., 2004).

Perhaps because drugs appear to make problems better but actually make them worse, more drugs are sought for those worse problems, which leads to abuse and addiction. Like Johanna above, many adolescents do not notice when they move past use (experimenting) to *abuse* (causing harm) and then *addiction* (needing the drug to feel normal). Addiction may take years, but Monitoring the Future reports that, in 2006, 25 percent of high school seniors were binge drinkers (5 or more

TABLE 14.3

Adolescent Drug Use Predicts Adult Drug Use

As High School Senior	Odds Ratio at Age 35
Binge drinking	3.7 for heavy drinking
Marijuana use	8.7 for marijuana use
Other illicit drugs	5.3 for cocaine use
	3.4 for abuse of prescription drugs
Cigarette smoking, tried	3.3 for regular smoking
Cigarette smoking, in past month	12.7 for regular smoking
Cigarette smoking, regular	42.5 for regular smoking

Source: Merline et al., 2004.

Still Smoking? Binge drinkers in high school are 3.7 times more likely to become heavy drinkers at midlife compared with those who were not binge drinkers. Adults generally stick to the same drugs they used in high school (very seldom crossing over from smoking cigarettes to using cocaine, for instance), except that illicit drug users often switch to abusing prescription drugs.

alcoholic drinks in a row in the past two weeks), 12 percent were daily cigarette smokers, and 5 percent were daily marijuana users (Johnston et al., 2007). All these suggest addiction.

Indeed, all psychoactive drugs are addictive, physically or psychologically, with addiction more likely the younger a person is at first use (see Table 14.3). Compared with nonusing high school students, users think they are using drugs as a *temporary* respite, but early users often use the same drug at age 35, when most people who first try drugs in college have quit (Merline et al., 2004). For example, adolescent binge drinkers are almost four times more likely to drink heavily at midlife than those who did not binge in high school (even if they drank heavily at age 20).

Learning from Experience

As you just read, any drug that affects the brain is more harmful and yet more attractive during adolescence than later. Herein lies another example of the "unskilled driver," referenced in the beginning of these chapters. Wisdom about use and abuse, about moderation versus addiction, about tolerance and impairment, and about particular risks comes with experience. A common phenomenon is **generational forgetting,** the idea that each new generation forgets what the previous generation learned about harmful drugs (Chassin et al., 2004; Johnston et al., 2007).

generational forgetting The idea that each new generation forgets what the previous generation learned about harmful drugs.

Why does generational forgetting occur? One reason is that teenagers tend to distrust adults, who experienced a different drug scene. For example, the most widely used drug prevention program in U.S. high schools, project DARE, features adults (usually police officers) telling high school students about the dangers of drugs. DARE has no impact on later drug use, according to several reliable studies (West & O'Neal, 2004).

Similarly, some antidrug advertisements and scare tactics ("your brain on drugs") have the opposite effect from that intended, probably because they make the drug seem exciting (Block et al., 2002; Fishbein et al., 2002).

This does not mean that trying to halt early drug use is hopeless. Massive ad campaigns in Florida and California have cut adolescent smoking in half, in part by having teenagers help design the publicity. Throughout the United States, higher prices and better law enforcement have led to a marked decline in smoking among younger adolescents. In 2006, only 9 percent of eighth-graders had smoked cigarettes in the past month, compared with 21 percent 10 years earlier (Johnston et al., 2007).

➤**Answer to Observation Quiz** (from page 385): Black females are least likely to drink alcohol, with Black males the next-lowest group. The White males' and females' rate of smoking dropped from 21 percent to 10 percent in just the four years from 1999 to 2003.

➤Response for College Roommates (from page 386): Think about how you would feel if your roommate died because you kept quiet. Discuss your concerns with your roommate, presenting facts as well as feelings. You cannot make anyone change, but you must raise the issue. You might also consult the college health service.

Similarly, the declining U.S. rates of adolescent sex, birth, and abortion, as well as all the variations in drug use just described, suggest that adolescent biology is far from destiny, that the emotions and sexual impulses of puberty need not be harmful.

As you will see in the next two chapters, experiences of peers, guidance from elders, and application of research together have helped most young people avoid the hazards of this age period. The energy and sexuality of the teen years are fondly remembered by many adults. So it should be for everyone.

SUMMING UP

Although many adolescents are not yet sexually active or users of drugs, others are, with a substantial minority involved in such activities before age 15. Early pregnancy takes a physiological as well as psychological toll; early sexually transmitted infections are particularly likely to spread; early use of alcohol, nicotine, or marijuana is particularly likely to slow down development of the brain and body. Because of generational forgetting, adolescents learn best from other members of the same generation, which makes it more difficult to warn them about the hazards of sex and drugs. ■

SUMMARY

Puberty Begins

1. Puberty refers to the various changes that transform a child's body into an adult one. Even before the teenage years begin, biochemical signals from the hypothalamus to the pituitary gland to the adrenal glands (the HPA axis) increase testosterone, estrogen, and various other hormones. These hormones cause the body to grow and change.

2. Puberty is accompanied by many emotions. Some, such as quick mood shifts and thoughts about sex, are directly caused by hormones, but most are only indirectly hormonal. Instead, they are caused by reactions (from others and from the young persons themselves) to the body changes of adolescence.

3. The visible changes of puberty normally occur anytime from about age 8 to 14; puberty most often begins between ages 10 and 13. The young person's sex, genetic background, body fat, and level of family stress all contribute to this variation.

4. Girls generally begin and end the process before boys do. Adolescents who do not reach puberty at about the same age as their friends experience additional stresses. Generally (depending on culture, community, and cohort), early-maturing girls have the most difficult time of all.

5. To sustain body growth, most adolescents consume large quantities of food, although they do not always make healthy choices. One reason for poor nutrition is anxiety about body image.

The Transformations of Puberty

6. The growth spurt is an acceleration of growth in every part of the body. Peak weight increase usually precedes peak height, which is then followed by peak muscle growth. The lungs and the heart also increase in size and capacity, and body rhythms (especially sleep) change.

7. Sexual characteristics emerge at puberty. The maturation of primary sex characteristics means that by age 13 or so, menarche and spermarche have occurred, and the young person is soon capable of reproducing. In many ways, the two sexes experience the same sexual characteristics, although they emerge in different ways.

8. Secondary sex characteristics are not directly involved in reproduction but do signify that the person is a man or a woman. Body shape, breasts, voice, body hair, and numerous other features differentiate males from females. Sexual activity is influenced more by culture than by physiology.

9. Various parts of the brain mature during puberty, each at its own rate. The neurological areas dedicated to emotional arousal (including the amygdala) mature ahead of the areas that regulate and rationalize emotional expression (the prefrontal cortex). Consequently, many adolescents seek intense emotional experiences, untempered by rational thought.

10. The prefrontal cortex matures by early adulthood, allowing better planning and analysis. Throughout this period, ongoing myelination and experience allow faster and deeper thinking.

Possible Problems

11. Among the problems that adolescents face is sex before their bodies and minds are ready. Pregnancy before age 16 takes a physical toll on a growing girl, and STIs at any age can lead to infertility and even death.

12. Most adolescents use drugs, especially alcohol and tobacco, although such substances impair growth of the body and of the brain. Prevention and moderation are possible, but programs need to be carefully designed to avoid generational forgetting.

KEY TERMS

puberty (p. 364)
menarche (p. 364)
spermarche (p. 364)
hormone (p. 364)
pituitary gland (p. 365)
adrenal glands (p. 365)
HPA axis (p. 365)
gonads (p. 365)
estradiol (p. 365)
testosterone (p. 365)
secular trend (p. 368)
body image (p. 370)
growth spurt (p. 371)
primary sex characteristics (p. 373)
secondary sex characteristics (p. 373)
sexually transmitted infection (STI) (p. 381)
child sexual abuse (p. 382)
generational forgetting (p. 387)

KEY QUESTIONS

1. What aspects of puberty are under direct hormonal control?

2. What psychological responses result from the physical changes of puberty?

3. How do nature and nurture combine to enable young people to become parents?

4. Why is experiencing puberty "off time" especially difficult?

5. What are the similarities of puberty for males and females?

6. What are the differences of puberty for males and females?

7. Name three reasons many adolescents have nutritional deficiencies.

8. Why is body image particularly likely to be distorted in adolescence?

9. Almost all neuroscientists agree about certain aspects of brain maturation. What are these aspects?

10. Why are sexually active adolescents more likely to contract STIs than are sexually active adults?

11. What can help prevent teenage drug abuse?

APPLICATIONS

1. Visit a fifth-, sixth-, or seventh-grade class. Note variations in the size and maturity of the students. Do you see any patterns related to gender, ethnicity, body fat, or self-confidence?

2. Interview two to four of your friends who are in their late teens or early 20s about their memories of menarche or spermarche, including their memories of others' reactions. Do their comments indicate that these events are emotionally troubling for young people?

3. Talk with someone who became a parent before the age of 20. Were there any problems with the pregnancy, the birth, or the first years of parenthood? Would the person recommend young parenthood? What would have been different had the baby been born three years earlier or three years later?

4. Adults disagree about the dangers of drugs. Find two people with very different opinions (e.g., a parent who would be horrified if his or her child used any drug and a parent who believes that young people should be allowed to drink or smoke at home). Ask them to explain their reasons, and write these down without criticism or disagreement. Later, present each with the arguments from the other person. What is the response? How open, flexible, and rational does it seem to be? Why are beliefs about drugs so deeply held?

WE LOVE
KOBE

15

CHAPTER OUTLINE

Adolescence: Cognitive Development

I drove four strangers to the distant birthday party of a mutual friend. One young man spoke forcefully for hours, explaining why people should bear arms, citizens should support third-party candidates, parents should be honest with their children, everyone should love each other despite differences in sexual orientation. And more.

My other three passengers were older. They bristled at his attitude and his assertions. One said "Yes, but . . ." Another, "No, because . . . " I also tried. He did not budge. Then he said he was 16 (he looked older). Argument stopped. Knowing his age explained his thinking and quieted us.

Like this young man, adolescents combine ego, logic, and emotion. Sometimes ego overwhelms logic; sometimes emotion overrides both. This chapter will describe the egocentrism of early adolescence and then teenagers' intellectual advances in analysis and intuition (called dual-processing). Schools do not always accommodate such cognitive characteristics, as we will also explore.

Adolescent Thinking

Brain maturation, intense conversations, additional years of schooling, moral challenges, and increased independence all occur between ages 11 and 18. The combination furthers cognition. Scientists disagree as to how much each of those five characteristics contributes to advances in adolescent thought. They agree, however, that there is "enormous variability in cognitive functioning among normal adolescents, with some performing no better than third graders on many reasoning tasks and others performing as well as or better than most adults" (Kuhn & Franklin, 2006, p. 955).

To understand any single adolescent of any age, keep variability in mind: Although egocentrism is typically evident at the beginning of adolescence, intuition in the middle, and logic at the end, any one of these forms of cognition may appear in any adolescent at any time.

Egocentrism

During puberty, people center many of their thoughts on themselves. They wonder how others perceive them; they try to make sense of conflicting feelings about their own parents, school, and classmates; they think deeply (but not always realistically) about their future; they ruminate with close friends, analyzing every nuance of what they did and might have done.

TED HOROWITZ / CORBIS

Cognition on Display Shared facials, pedicures, nail painting, eyebrow waxing, and other such beauty rituals are bonding experiences for teenage girls. Parents may blame teen magazines or the superficiality of the culture in general, but their daughters' egocentric thinking may be the true origin of these activities.

Young adolescents not only think intensely about themselves, they also imagine what others think about them. This is called **adolescent egocentrism,** first described by David Elkind (1967). Remember from Chapter 9 that *egocentric* means "self at the center."

The difference between egocentrism during adolescence and the same trait during preoperational thought (p. 231) is that adolescents, unlike younger children, have a well-developed theory of mind. They know that other people have their own thoughts. Their egocentrism does not ignore others. Instead, it distorts their understanding of what others might be thinking, especially about them.

In egocentrism, adolescents regard themselves as uniquely special and much more socially significant (noticed by everyone) than they actually are. Accurately imagining someone else's perspective is especially difficult when egocentrism rules (Lapsley, 1993). For example, Ben (see Chapter 14, p. 375) did not think how police officers might perceive a gang of young men fleeing from a patrol car at 2 A.M.

Egocentrism leads people to interpret another's behavior as related to themselves. A stranger's frown or a teacher's critique could make a teenager conclude that "no one likes me," and then deduce that "I am unlovable" or even "I dare not appear in public." More positive casual reactions—a smile from a sales clerk or an extra-big hug from a younger brother—could lead to the thought "I am great" or "Everyone loves me," with similarly distorted self-perception.

adolescent egocentrism A characteristic of adolescent thinking that leads young people (ages 10 to 13) to focus on themselves to the exclusion of others. A young person might believe, for example, that his or her thoughts, feelings, and experiences are unique, more wonderful or awful than anyone else's.

As part of egocentrism, acute self-consciousness about appearance is probably higher between ages 10 and 14 than earlier or later (Rankin et al., 2004). Young adolescents would rather not stand out from their peers, hoping instead to blend in racially, religiously, and economically. They believe that other people are as egocentric as they are. As one girl said:

> I am a real worrier when it comes to other people's opinions. I care deeply about what they say, think and do. If people are very complimentary, it can give you a big confidence boost, but if people are always putting you down you feel less confident and people can tell. A lot of advice that is given is "do what you want and don't listen to anyone else," but I don't know one person who can do that.
>
> *[quoted in J. H. Bell & Bromnick, 2003, p. 213]*

The Invincibility Fable

Elkind gave several aspects of adolescent egocentrism special names. One is the **invincibility fable,** the idea that one is invincible, never defeated, protected from harm. Some young people seem convinced that, unlike other mortals, they will not be hurt by fast driving, unprotected sex, addictive drugs, or self-starvation. When they do any of these things and survive without injury, they feel special and proud, not lucky and thankful.

invincibility fable An adolescent's egocentric conviction that he or she cannot be overcome or even harmed by anything that might defeat a normal mortal, such as unprotected sex, drug abuse, or high-speed driving.

For instance, one survey found that only 1 in 20 teenage cigarette smokers thought they would be smoking in five years, even though two-thirds had already tried to stop and failed, and most teenage smokers become addicted to nicotine and are still smoking years later (Siqueira et al., 2001). Evidence about other people may be ignored if an adolescent believes that he or she is independent and exceptional, impervious to human vulnerability.

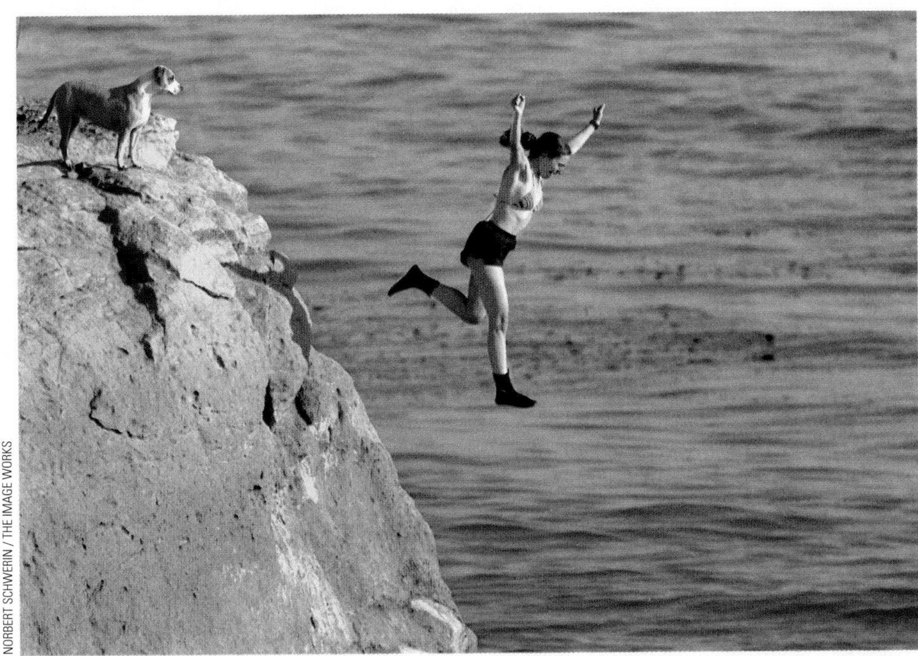

NORBERT SCHWERIN / THE IMAGE WORKS

Not Me! A young woman jumps into the Pacific Ocean near Santa Cruz, California, while at a friend's birthday party. The jump is illegal, yet since 1975, 52 people have died taking that leap off these cliffs. Hundreds of young people each year decide that the thrill is worth the risk, aided by the invincibility fable and by what they think are sensible precautions. (Note that she is wearing shoes. Also note that the dog has apparently decided against risking a jump.)

In every nation, those who volunteer for military service—hoping to be sent into combat—are more likely to be under age 20 than over it. Young recruits take risks, in the military as well as in civilian life, more often than older, more experienced soldiers (Killgore et al., 2006).

Imaginary Audience

Egocentrism also creates an **imaginary audience.** Many adolescents seem to believe that they are at center stage, with all eyes on them, that others are as intensely interested in them as they themselves are. As a result, they are continually imagining how others react to their appearance and behavior.

imaginary audience The other people who, in an adolescent's egocentric belief, are watching, and taking note of, his or her appearance, ideas, and behavior. This belief makes many teenagers very self-conscious.

The imaginary audience can cause teenagers to enter a crowded room as if they are the most attractive human beings alive. They might put studs in their lips or blast music for all to hear, calling attention to themselves. The reverse is also possible: They might avoid scrutiny lest someone notice a blemish on their chin or a stain on their sleeve. Many a 12-year-old balks at going to school with a bad haircut or the wrong shoes.

Especially for Parents of Adopted Children Should adolescents be told if they were adopted?

This explains many adolescents' concern about the audience of their peers, who presumably judge every visible oddity of their appearance and behavior. No wonder, then, that one adolescent remarked, "I would like to be able to fly if everyone else did; otherwise it would be rather conspicuous" (quoted in A. Steinberg, 1993). Another, age 12, explained:

> I dress different now that I'm in middle school. I used to not care about my clothes—I'd wear whatever my mom bought for me. But now I really care [and] take time to think about it. So it bugs me when my mom yells at me for wearing jeans with holes or big shirts. It's a big deal to her if my clothes aren't clean. She thinks my teachers will think she's a bad mother or something.
>
> *[Daniel, quoted in R. Bell, 1998, p. 59]*

Note that this young adolescent imagines that his mother is troubled by her own audience, who are the teachers in his school. It is typical to begin with imagined reactions of other people and end by judging the foolishness of one's parents, as two teens named Bethany and Jim illustrate.

in person

Bethany and Jim

It was a humid midsummer afternoon. Bethany prevailed on me to go with her to the Metropolitan Museum of Art. When we climbed up to street level from the subway station, we encountered a sudden downpour. Bethany stopped and became angry—at me!

> **She:** You didn't bring an umbrella? You should have known.
> **Me:** It's OK—we'll walk quickly. It's a warm rain.
> **She:** But we'll get all wet.
> **Me:** No problem. We'll dry.
> **She:** But people will see us with our hair all wet.
> **Me:** Honey, no one cares how we look. And we won't see anyone we know.
> **She:** That's OK for you to say. You're already married.

I asked, incredulously, "Do you think you are going to meet your future husband here?"

She looked at me as if I were unbelievably stupid. "No, of course not. But people will look at me and think, 'She'll never find a husband looking like that!'"

Another example is reported by a father, himself a psychotherapist:

> The best way I can describe what happens [during adolescence] is to relate how I first noticed the change in my son. He was about 13 years of age. . . . I was driving 65 miles an hour in a 55-mile-an-hour zone.
>
> He suddenly turned toward me and shouted, "Dad!"
>
> I was startled and responded by saying, "What is it, Jim!"
>
> Then there was this pause as he folded his arms and turned slowly in my direction and said, "Dad, do you realize how fast you are driving this car?" . . .
>
> "Oh, I'm doing 65 miles per hour!" (as if I didn't know it).
>
> He then came right back at me and said, "Dad! Do you know what the speed limit is on this highway?"
>
> "Yes, Jim, it's 55 miles an hour."
>
> He then said, "Dad! Do you realize that you are traveling 10 miles over the speed limit! . . . Don't you care about my life at all! Do you have any idea of how many thousands of people lose their lives every year on our nation's highways who exceed the speed limit!"
>
> Now I was beginning to get angry and I responded by saying, "Look, Jim, I have no idea how many people are killed every year, you were right I shouldn't have been speeding; I promise I won't ever do it again, so let us just forget it!"
>
> Not being satisfied, he continued, "Dad! Any idea what would happen if the front wheel of this car came off doing 65 miles per hour, how many lives you might jeopardize!"
>
> He kept on with this for another 10 minutes until I finally got him quiet for about 20 seconds! Then he came back at me and said, "Dad! I've been thinking about this."
>
> Once he said that, I knew I was in deep trouble! You see, my son was so easy to deal with before he started to think!
>
> *[Garvin, 1994, pp. 39–41]*

Bethany and Jim ("Don't you care about my life at all!") were egocentric, with an imaginary audience ("People will look at me and think"), but socially aware ("You're already married," "thousands of people"). That's adolescent egocentrism.

Egocentrism Reassessed

After Elkind first described adolescent egocentrism, some psychologists blamed it for every teenage problem, from drug use to pregnancy, from rebellion to apathy (Eckstein et al., 1999). A more recent wave of research has found that many adolescents do not feel invincible. Moreover, egocentrism "may signal growth toward cognitive maturity" (Vartanian, 2001, p. 378) and is not necessarily irrational; other adolescents their age *are* judging them (J. H. Bell & Bromnick, 2003).

For example, one 13-year-old moved to Los Angeles from a small town:

> When I got to school the first day, everyone looked at me like I was from outer space or something. It was like, "Who's that? Look at her hair. Look at what she's wearing." That's all anybody cares about around here; what you look like and what you wear. I felt like a total outcast. As soon as I got home, I locked myself in my room and cried for about an hour. I was so lonely.
>
> *[Tina, quoted in R. Bell, 1998, p. 78]*

The phrase "all anybody cares about around here" does not apply only to Los Angeles. The same words could have been written by a young adolescent who moved from Los Angeles to a small town or by almost any middle school student who was new to a school anywhere. Part of this girl's reaction may have been egocentric, if she imagined more scrutiny than actually occurred, but it does seem that young adolescents sometimes reject their peers who dress or act in abnormal ways.

➤Response for Parents of Adopted Children (from page 393): Probably not now. Most counselors believe that adopted children should be told very early. Adolescents may react irrationally to learning new information about themselves.

Formal Operational Thought

In sorting through their life experiences, adolescents develop logic. Jean Piaget was the first to notice and describe this advance. He realized that cognitive processes, not just cognitive contents, can shift after childhood to a level called **formal operational thought.** Adolescent thinking is no longer limited by personal experiences (as in concrete operations): Adolescents can consider abstractions (Inhelder & Piaget, 1958).

One way to distinguish formal and concrete thinking is to remember the school curriculum. Younger children multiply real numbers (4×8); adolescents can multiply unreal numbers, such as $(2x)(3y)$ or even $(-5xy^2)(3zy^3)$. Younger children study other cultures by learning about daily life—drinking goat's milk or building an igloo, for instance, whereas adolescents grasp concepts like "gross national product" and "fertility rate" and can figure out how these phenomena affect politics. Younger students plant carrots and feed rabbits; adolescents examine cells and bacteria.

WILL MCINTYRE / PHOTO RESEARCHERS, INC.

Abstraction Way Beyond Counting on Fingers and Toes This high school student explains an algebra problem, a behavior that requires a level of hypothetical and abstract thought beyond that of any concrete operational child—and of many adults. At the beginning of concrete operational thought, children need blocks, coins, and other tangible objects to help them understand math. By later adolescence, in the full flower of formal operational thought, such practical and concrete illustrations are irrelevant.

formal operational thought In Piaget's theory, the fourth and final stage of cognitive development, characterized by more systematic logic and the ability to think about abstract ideas.

Piaget's Experiments

Piaget and his colleagues devised a number of tasks that demonstrate formal operational thought (Inhelder & Piaget, 1958). They show that, "in contrast to concrete operational children, formal operational adolescents imagine all possible determinants . . . [and] systematically vary the factors one by one, observe the results correctly, keep track of the results, and draw the appropriate conclusions" (P. H. Miller, 2002).

In one experiment (diagrammed in Figure 15.1), children balance a scale by hooking weights onto the scale's arms. To master this task, a person must realize that the heaviness of the weights and their distance from the center interact reciprocally to affect balance. Therefore, a heavier weight close to the center can be counterbalanced with a lighter weight far from the center. For example, a 12-gram weight placed 2 centimeters to the left of the center might balance a 6-gram weight placed 4 centimeters to the right.

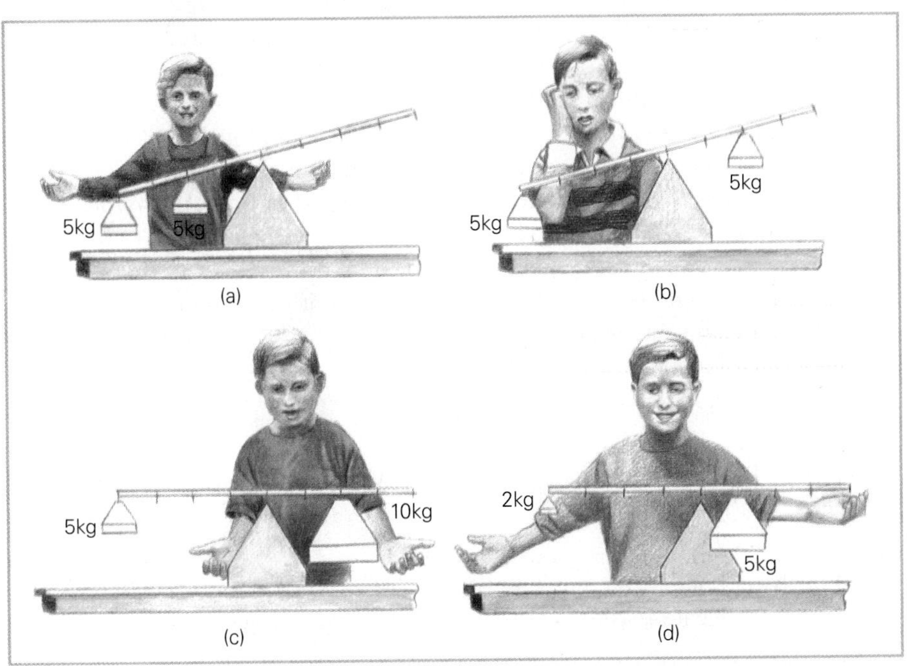

FIGURE 15.1

How to Balance a Scale Piaget's balance-scale test of formal reasoning, as it is attempted by *(a)* a 4-year-old, *(b)* a 7-year-old, *(c)* a 10-year-old, and *(d)* a 14-year-old. The key to balancing the scale is to make weight times distance from the center equal on both sides of the center; the realization of that principle requires formal operational thought.

This concept was completely beyond the ability or interest of 3- to 5-year-olds. In Piaget's experiments, they randomly hung different weights on different hooks. By age 7, children realized that the scale could be balanced by putting the same amount of weight on each arm, but they didn't know or care that the distance from the center was important.

By age 10, at the end of their concrete operational stage, children thought about location, but they used trial and error, not logic. They succeeded with equal weights at equal distances and were pleased when they balanced different weights, but they did not figure out the formula.

Finally, by about age 13 or 14, some children hypothesized the reciprocal relationship between weight and distance, tested this hypothesis, and formulated the mathematical formula, solving the balance problem accurately and efficiently. Piaget attributed each of these advances to attainment of the next cognitive stage.

Hypothetical-Deductive Thought

One hallmark of formal operational thought is the capacity to think of possibility, not just reality. Adolescents "start with possible solutions and progress to determine which is the real solution" (Lutz & Sternberg, 1999, p. 283). "Here and now" is only one of many alternatives including "there and then," "long, long ago," "nowhere," "not yet," and "never." As Piaget said:

> *Possibility* no longer appears merely as an extension of an empirical situation or of action actually performed. Instead, it is *reality* that is now secondary to *possibility*.
>
> *[Inhelder & Piaget, 1958, p. 251; emphasis in original]*

hypothetical thought Reasoning that includes propositions and possibilities that may not reflect reality.

Adolescents are therefore primed to engage in **hypothetical thought,** reasoning about *what-if* propositions that may or may not reflect reality. For example, consider:

> If dogs are bigger than elephants, and
>
> If mice are bigger than dogs,
>
> Are elephants smaller than mice?

Younger children, presented with such counterfactual questions, answer no. They have seen elephants and mice, so the logic escapes them. Some adolescents answer yes. They understand what *if* means (adapted from Moshman, 2005).

Hypothetical thought transforms a person's perceptions, though not necessarily for the better. Reflection about serious issues becomes complicated because many possibilities are considered, sometimes sidetracking logical conclusions about the immediate issues (Moshman, 2005).

For example, a survey of U.S. teenagers' religious ideas found that most 13- to 17-year-olds considered themselves religious and thought that practicing their particular faith would help them avoid hell. However, they hesitated to follow that conviction to the next logical step by trying to convince their friends to believe as they did. As one explained, "I can't speak for everybody, it's up to them. I know what's best for me, and I can't, I don't, preach" (C. Smith & Denton, 2005, p. 147).

Similarly, a high school student who wanted to keep a friend from committing suicide hesitated to judge her friend's intentions because

> to . . . judge [someone] means that whatever you are saying is right and you know what's right. You know it's right for them and you know it's right in every situation. [But] you can't know if you are right. Maybe you are right. But then, right in what way?
>
> *[quoted in Gilligan et al., 1990]*

Although adolescents are not sure what is "right in what way," they see what is wrong. At every age it is easier to criticize something than to create it, but criticism itself shows an advance in reasoning. (Recall Jim, who lectured his father about speed limits because he "started thinking.") Unlike younger children, adolescents do not necessarily accept current conditions. They criticize everything from the way their mother cooks spaghetti to how the world calendar counts the year. They criticize what is, precisely because of their hypothetical thinking.

Abstract Thinking

In developing the capacity to think hypothetically, by age 14 or so, adolescents become capable of **deductive reasoning,** which begins with an abstract idea or premise and then uses logic to draw specific conclusions (Galotti, 2002; Keating, 2004). By contrast, as you remember from Chapter 12, **inductive reasoning** predominates during the school years, as children accumulate facts and personal experiences to aid their thought.

In essence, a child's reasoning goes like this: "This creature waddles and quacks. Ducks waddle and quack. Therefore, this must be a duck." This reasoning is inductive: It progresses from particulars ("waddles like" and "quacks like") to a general conclusion ("it's a duck"). By contrast, deduction progresses from the general to the specific: "If it's a duck, it will waddle and quack" (see Figure 15.2).

deductive reasoning Reasoning from a general statement, premise, or principle, through logical steps, to figure out (deduce) specifics. (Sometimes called *top-down thinking.*)

inductive reasoning Reasoning from one or more specific experiences or facts to a general conclusion; may be less cognitively advanced than deduction. (Sometimes called *bottom-up reasoning.*)

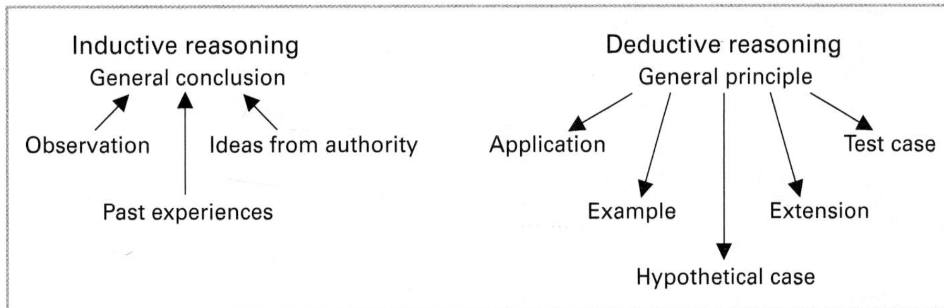

FIGURE 15.2

Bottom Up or Top Down? Children, as concrete operational thinkers, are likely to draw conclusions on the basis of their own experiences and what they have been told. This is called inductive, or bottom-up, reasoning. Adolescents can think deductively, from the top down.

Most developmentalists agree with Piaget that adolescent thought can be qualitatively different from children's thought (Fischer & Bidell, 1998; Flavell et al., 2002; Keating, 2004; Moshman, 2005). They disagree about whether this change is quite sudden (Piaget) or gradual (information-processing theory); about whether change results from context (sociocultural theory) or biological changes (epigenetic theory); about whether changes occur universally in every domain (Piaget) or more selectively (all the other theories). Some adolescents and adults still reason like concrete operational children, and "no contemporary scholarly reviewer of research evidence endorses the emergence of a discrete new cognitive structure at adolescence that closely resembles . . . formal operations" (Kuhn & Franklin, 2006, p. 954). In other words, logical thinking becomes more possible at adolescence, but it is probably not a "discrete new structure," sudden or universal, as Piaget seemed to believe.

These criticisms of Piaget are familiar from previous chapters. There is much more cognitive variability at every age than Piaget seemed to recognize. Piaget "launched the systematic study of adolescent cognitive development" (Keating, 2004, p. 45), but his description is not the final word.

Testing Juice How much vitamin C does orange juice contain? You could ask the producer, but adolescents would prefer to find out for themselves, as these chemistry students are doing.

Intuitive, Emotional Thought

As many developmentalists over the past three decades have shown, the fact that adolescents *can* use hypothetical-deductive reasoning does not necessarily mean that they *do* use it (Kuhn & Franklin, 2006). Adolescents find it much easier and quicker to forget about logic and follow their impulses.

Two Modes of Thinking

dual-process model The notion that two networks exist within the human brain, one for emotional and one for analytical processing of stimuli.

Advanced logical thought is counterbalanced by the increasing power of intuitive thinking, leading to recognition of a **dual-process model** of adolescent cognition (Keating, 2004).

Researchers are increasingly convinced that the brain has at least two distinct pathways, called dual-processing networks. The two processing networks have been designated by various names: intuitive/analytic, implicit/explicit, contextualized/decontextualized, creative/factual, unconscious/conscious, gist/quantitative, emotional/intellectual, experiential/rational.

You may remember another pair discussed at length in Chapter 14—the limbic system and the prefrontal cortex. Each of these pairs refers to the same two modes, although every pair of terms describes a slightly different dichotomy. Both modes advance during the second decade of life. The first half of each pair is the more commonly used. It is preferred unless circumstances compel activation of the second, more taxing, mode.

intuitive thought Thought that arises from an emotion or a hunch, beyond rational explanation. Past experiences, cultural assumptions, and sudden impulses are the precursors of intuitive thought. (Also called *contextualized* or *experiential thought.*)

analytic thought Thought that results from analysis, such as a systematic ranking of pros and cons, risks and consequences, possibilities and facts. Analytic thought depends on logic and rationality.

- The first mode begins with a prior belief, past experience, or common assumption, rather than with a logical premise. This is called **intuitive** (or *contextualized* or *experiential*) **thought.** Thoughts spring forth from memories and feelings. Intuitive cognition is quick and powerful; it feels "right."
- The second mode is the formal, logical, hypothetical-deductive thinking described by Piaget. This is called **analytic thought,** because it involves rational analysis of many factors whose interactions must be calculated, as in the scale-balancing problem. Analytic thinking requires a certain level of intellectual maturity, brain capacity, motivation, and practice.

BOB DAEMMRICH / THE IMAGE WORKS

Reality and Fantasy Because teenagers can think analytically and hypothetically, they can use computers not only to obtain factual information and to e-mail friends but also to imagine and explore future possibilities. This opportunity may be particularly important for adolescents like 17-year-old Julisa *(right)*. She is a student in a high school in Brownsville, Texas, that offers computer labs and other programs to children of migrant laborers.

In the words of one researcher, there are "two systems but one reasoner" (De Neys, 2006, p. 428), which means that when people use emotional reasoning they are less able to use analytic reasoning. Another scholar writes about "two brain networks" that interact, explaining that the intuitive one dominates during adolescence (L. Steinberg, 2007, p. 56). Neither mode is always best; ideally, a person learns to coordinate both modes as "one reasoner."

Thoughts in each mode either coexist or conflict, and *both* advance during adolescence (Galotti, 2002; Klaczynski, 2005; Moshman, 2005; Reyna, 2004). As detailed in Chapter 14, the foundation for these cognitive advances is the brain, which allows "stronger, more effective neuronal connections" (Kuhn & Franklin, 2006. p. 957).

Comparing Intuition and Analysis

Paul Klaczynski has conducted many studies comparing the thinking of children, young adolescents, and older adolescents (usually 9-, 12-, and 15-year-olds). In one, Klaczynski (2001) presented 19 logical problems. For example:

> Timothy is very good-looking, strong, and does not smoke. He likes hanging around with his male friends, watching sports on TV, and driving his Ford Mustang convertible. He's very concerned with how he looks and with being in good shape. He is a high school senior now and is trying to get a college scholarship.
>
> *Based on this [description], rank each statement in terms of how likely it is to be true. . . . The most likely statement should get a 1. The least likely statement should get a 6.*

_____ Timothy has a girlfriend.

_____ Timothy is an athlete.

_____ Timothy is popular and an athlete.

_____ Timothy is a teacher's pet and has a girlfriend.

_____ Timothy is a teacher's pet.

_____ Timothy is popular.

In ranking these statements, most (73 percent) of the students made at least one analytic error. Their mistake was to rank a double statement (e.g., athlete *and* popular) as more likely than a single statement included in it (athlete *or* popular). A double statement cannot be more likely than either of its parts; therefore, those 73 percent were illogical and wrong. This error is an example of intuitive thought: The adolescents jumped to the more inclusive statement, taking a quick, experiential leap rather than sticking to the logical task at hand.

In this study, almost all adolescents were analytical and logical on some of the 19 problems but not on others. Logic improved with age and education, although not with IQ. Klaczynski (2001) concluded that, even though teenagers *can* use logic, "most adolescents do not demonstrate a level of performance commensurate with their abilities" (p. 854).

What would motivate high school students to use—or fail to use—their newly acquired analytic mode of thinking? These students had learned the scientific method in school, and they knew that scientists use empirical evidence and deductive reasoning. But they did not always think like scientists. Why not?

Dozens of experiments and extensive theorizing have found some answers (Diamond & Kirkham, 2005; Klaczynski, 2005; Kuhn & Franklin, 2006). Essentially, logic is more difficult; it does not always feel right. Once people (of any age) reach an emotional conclusion (sometimes called a "gut feeling"), they resist changing their mind, avoiding logic that might reveal their poor judgment.

PETER HVIZDAK / THE IMAGE WORKS

Her Whole Brain Chess players like this girl, who is competing in a Connecticut championship match, must be analytic, thinking several moves ahead. But sometimes an unexpected intuitive move unnerves the opposition and leads to victory.

Egocentrism makes rational analysis even more difficult, as one psychologist discovered when her teenage son called to be picked up late one night from a party that had "gotten out of hand." The boy heard

> his frustrated father lament "drinking and trouble—haven't you figured out the connection?" Despite the late hour and his shaky state, the teenager advanced a lengthy argument to the effect that his father had the causality all wrong and the trouble should be attributed to other covariates, among them bad luck.
>
> *[Kuhn & Franklin, 2006, p. 966]*

Research confirming the difficulty of thinking scientifically comes from experiments on the **sunk cost fallacy,** which is the mistaken assumption that, because a person has already spent money, time, or effort (a cost already "sunk"), the person should spend more of the same. People of all ages make this error, investing money to repair a lemon of a car, staying in a class they are failing, and so on. An example used in the research asked people whether they would watch more of a movie they disliked if they had paid for it (e.g., on pay-per-view TV) than they would if it were free. People of all ages said yes (Klaczynski & Cottrell, 2004).

sunk cost fallacy The belief that if time or money has already been invested in something, then more time or money should be invested. Because of this fallacy, people spend money trying to fix a "lemon" of a car or sending more troops to fight for a losing cause.

Adolescents are better than younger children at recognizing the sunk cost fallacy, realizing that "just because you made a mistake in paying to see a stupid movie, you don't need to torture yourself by watching the whole thing." In this, as in all research, variability is evident: Logic is not universal at adolescence.

Better Thinking

Sometimes adults define "better thinking" as a more cautious approach (as in the connection between "trouble" and alcohol above). Adults are particularly critical of the egocentrism that leads a teenager to risk future addiction by experimenting with drugs or to risk pregnancy and AIDS in order to avoid the awkwardness of using a condom.

But adults may be egocentric in this judgment, assuming that adolescents share their values. Parents want healthy, long-living children, and they conclude that adolescents miscalculate or use faulty reasoning when they make decisions that risk their lives. Adolescents, however, value social warmth and friendship. A 15-year-old who is offered a cigarette might make a rational decision to choose social acceptance over the distant risk of cancer (Engels et al., 2006).

Adolescent thinking (including egocentrism) can be positive, not necessarily more selfish or irrational than adult thinking (Reyna & Farley, 2006). As one expert explains, "Zeal in adolescents can fuel positive humanistic efforts to feed the poor and care for the sick, yet it can also lead to dogmatic attitudes, intolerance . . . passions captured by a negatively charismatic figure like Adolf Hitler or Osama bin Laden" (Dahl, 2004, p. 21). Adolescents are said to "ride the waves of historical events" (B. Brown & Larson, 2002, p. 12), being noble or naive depending on the immediate context.

At every age, sometimes the best thinking is "fast and frugal" (Gigerenzer et al., 1999). The systematic, analytic thought that Piaget described may be slow and costly—wasting precious time when a young person would rather act than think.

Generally, adolescents use their minds with more economy than children do and may be as logical as adults are. As the knowledge base increases, thinking processes accelerate; analysis and intuition become more forceful. With age, thinking gains efficiency and is less likely to go off on a tangent. It is efficient to use formal, analytic thinking in science class and to use emotional, experiential thinking (which is quicker and more satisfying) for personal issues, and this tends to happen (Kuhn & Franklin, 2006).

Which mode of thinking is best when the topic is religious beliefs? Most adolescents use intuitive, not analytic, thinking for religion, as the following explains.

Research Design

Scientist: Christian Smith (with more than 100 colleagues and graduate students).

Publication: *Soul Searching,* Oxford University Press (2005).

Participants: Between 2001 and 2003, in the National Study of Youth and Religion, 3,360 13- to 18-year-olds and one of their parents were interviewed by phone. A subsample of 287 were interviewed privately in person. To secure a representative sample, a random-digit-dial telephone survey of families throughout the United States was conducted to find families with at least one member between the ages of 13 and 17 who would be willing to talk.

Design: Each participant was asked questions regarding religion, school, family, sex, and drugs. Data were analyzed and reported by religious allegiance, family background, and various beliefs.

Major conclusion: Religion *is* important to most adolescents, who are much less critical or disaffected than has been portrayed.

Comment: Research on religious beliefs and development has been avoided by many scientists, partly because any conclusions are likely to be rejected by some adherents and partly because it is not easy to distinguish religious from cultural beliefs. This study is part of a new wave of research; much more needs to be published in order to understand the role of religion in development.

thinking like a scientist

Teenage Religion

As you remember from Chapter 1, scientists build on previous research or theories, replicating, extending, or disputing the work of others. Scientists question assumptions, seeking empirical evidence to verify or refute cultural myths. This is a formal operational approach.

Some impressionistic descriptions of teenagers and religion (e.g., Flory & Miller, 2000) emphasize cults and sects. Young congregants gather, "dressed as they are, piercings and all, and express their commitment by means of hip-hop and rap music, multimedia presentations, body modification, and anything else that can be infused with religious meaning" (Ream & Savin-Williams, 2003, p. 51). This evokes emotions: Many adults consider piercings and rap music to be the antithesis of true faith. Impressions, however, neither verify nor refute—only science does.

A team of researchers began by "reading many published overview reports on adolescence . . . with the distinct impression that American youth simply do not have religious or spiritual lives" (C. Smith & Denton, 2005, p. 4). But, thinking like scientists, they sought evidence (see Research Design).

The researchers found that most adolescents (71 percent) felt close to God and believed in heaven, hell, and angels. Most identified with the same tradition as their parents (78 percent Christian, 3 percent Jewish or Muslim). Some were agnostic

(2 percent), and 16 percent said they were not religious, although many of those attended church and prayed. Less than 1 percent were decidedly unconventional (e.g., Wiccan).

Beliefs seemed egocentric, with faith seen as a personal tool to be used in times of difficulty (e.g., taking an exam). Most adolescents (60 percent) said they believed "many religions might be true." One said, "I think every religion is important in its own respect. You know, if you're Muslim, then Islam is the way for you. If you are Jewish, well, that's great too. If you're Christian, well, good for you. It's just whatever makes you feel good about you" (quoted in C. Smith & Denton, 2005, p. 163).

Many respondents (82 percent) claimed that their beliefs were important to their daily life. One boy explained that religion kept him from doing "bad things, like murder or something," and one girl said:

> [Religion] influences me a lot with the people I choose not to be around. I would not hang with people that are, you know, devil worshipers because that's just not my thing, I could not deal with that negativity.
>
> *[C. Smith & Denton, 2005, p. 139]*

The author doubts that "socializing with Satanists is a real issue in this girl's life" or that this boy "struggles with murderous tendencies" (C. Smith & Denton, 2005, p. 139). Although daily life in modern America presents many ethical issues, few adolescents used theology to guide them. Less than 1 percent connected religion with repentance, seeking justice, or loving one's neighbor. For most, religious beliefs were intuitive, not analytic. Religion seemed to assure the invididuals that they were OK (those who were most devout were less depressed) and, occasionally, to bolster their criticisms of their parents.

Especially for Religious Leaders Suppose you believe very strongly in some tenet of your faith, but the youth group includes teenagers who act contrary to your belief. What should you do?

SUMMING UP

Thinking reaches heightened self-consciousness at puberty, when adolescent egocentrism may be apparent. Some young adolescents have unrealistic notions about their place in the social world, imagining themselves as invincible, unique, and the center of attention. This self-awareness is often criticized by adults, but it shows a cognitive advance and may be shaped by the social context.

Piaget thought the fourth and final stage of intelligence, called formal operational thought, began in adolescence. He found that adolescents improve in deductive logic and hypothetical thinking. Other researchers confirm that logic often improves in the second decade of life but also recognize another mode of thinking. The second form is experiential thinking, quicker and more intense than formal operational thought. Because every form of thought advances during adolescence, teenagers know more, think faster, and use systematic analysis and abstract logic beyond the capability of younger children. Emotional passions, with fast and frugal thinking, may be preferred over logical, methodical thought. ■

Teaching and Learning

Given the nature of the adolescent mind, what and how should teenagers be taught? Many educators, developmentalists, political leaders, and parents want to know exactly what curriculum and school structures are best for 11- to 18-year-olds. We cannot present any one answer here, because no single answer is supported by the research. Various scientists, nations, and schools are trying opposite strategies, some of which are based on opposite, but logical, hypotheses. We can, however, provide some definitions, facts, and possibilities.

Secondary education—traditionally grades 7 through 12—is the term used to describe the school years after elementary or grade school (known as *primary education*) and before college or university (known as *tertiary education*). The importance of secondary education is widely recognized, as adults in every nation are healthier and wealthier if they have graduated from high school. Worldwide, "secondary education has [the] transformational ability to change lives for the better. . . . For young people all over the world, primary education is no longer enough" (World Bank, 2005, xi–xii).

secondary education Literally the period after primary education and before tertiary education. It usually occurs from about age 12 to 18, although there is some variation by school and by nation.

➤Response for Religious Leaders (from page 401): This is not the time for dogma; teenagers intuitively rebel against authority. Nor is it the time to keep quiet about your beliefs, because teenagers need some structure to help them think. Instead of going to either extreme, begin a dialogue. Listen respectfully to their expressions of concern and emotion, and encourage them to think more deeply about the implications of their actions.

Even such a seemingly irrelevant condition as heart disease (the leading killer worldwide) is about 50 percent more common among those who never graduated from high school compared with those who graduated but never went to college (MMWR, February 16, 2007). This statistic comes from the United States, but data from every nation and every ethnic group indicate that high school graduation is a surprising boon.

Partly for this reason, the number of students in secondary schools is increasing faster than in primary or tertiary schools. In 2004, 78 percent of the world's children received some secondary education, including virtually all the 10- to 14-year-olds in the Americas, East Asia, and Europe, but just 64 percent of them in South Asia and 36 percent in sub-Saharan Africa (UNESCO, 2006).

Although almost everyone agrees that adolescents should be educated, and although no one doubts that secondary education correlates with health and wealth for individuals as well as for nations, many disagree about what and how students should be taught.

Middle School: Less Learning

In the United States and many other nations, separate schools have been created for children who have outgrown (literally) primary school. These were all once called high schools, with younger students put in separate schools called junior high schools. Now, with puberty occurring earlier than in years past (often at age 11), many intermediate **middle schools** have been established to educate sixth- (and sometimes fifth-) graders alongside seventh- and eighth-graders (who had previously been in junior high schools). Ninth-graders are often reassigned into high schools.

middle school A school for the grades between elementary and high school. Middle school can begin with grade 5 or 6 and usually ends with grade 8.

During the middle school years, academic achievement often slows down and behavioral problems become more commonplace. The first year of middle school is called the "low ebb" of learning (Covington & Dray, 2002), when many teachers feel ineffective (Eccles, 2004). This affects later education: "Long term academic trajectories—the choice to stay in school or to drop out and the selection in high school of academic college-prep courses versus basic level courses—are strongly influenced by experience in grades 6–8" (Snow et al., 2007, p. 72).

Especially for Middle School Teachers You think your lectures are interesting and you know you care about your students, yet many of them cut class, come late, or seem to sleep through it. What do you do?

Many developmentalists think that one crucial problem is that students lose connection to teachers, partly because middle school scheduling means each teacher has dozens, sometimes hundreds, of students. Throughout secondary education, bonding between students and teachers is key to learning as well as to avoiding risks (Crosnoe et al., 2004).

Students' relationships with one another also deteriorate, partly because students suddenly find themselves with hundreds of strangers, many older and bigger than they are. Because new middle school students have many classmates they have never seen before, first impressions become especially significant. Unfortunately, this coincides with the physiological changes described in Chapter 14 that make each developing person acutely aware of every detail of appearance.

At this age, friendships and peer groups are crucial for providing validation. Several studies find that, unlike in elementary school, in middle schools aggressive and drug-using students tend to be admired over those who are conscientious and studious (Allen et al., 2005; Mayeux & Cillessen, 2007). To stay or become popular, many middle school students stop associating with unpopular peers (Rose et al., 2004). This may deprive them of the opportunity to learn from those among the ranks of the unpopular who are studious—the so-called geeks and nerds. But many students at this age would rather sacrifice their academic standing than risk social exclusion.

One longitudinal study that followed children from preschool through high school provides an example of the changes that can occur in the middle school years. Of all the children in the study, James was one of the most promising. In his early school years, he was an excellent reader whose mother took great pride in him—her only child. Once James entered middle school, however, the situation changed:

> Although still performing well academically, James began acting out. At first his actions could be described as merely mischievous, but later he engaged in much more serious acts, such as drinking and fighting, which resulted in his being suspended from school. He said, "The kids were definitely afraid of me but that didn't stop them" from being his friends.
>
> *[Snow et al., 2007, p. 59]*

In middle school James felt disconnected from his teachers and counselors and said he had "a complete lack of motivation." While at the end of primary school James said he planned to go to college, by the time he reached the tenth grade, he had dropped out of school.

Often family conflicts increase at around the time middle school begins (Shanahan et al., 2007). For instance, James and his abusive father blamed each other for every problem. His mother escaped blame, but she mistakenly thought that James was as self-sufficient as his physical growth made him appear. She "talked about how independent James was for being able to be left alone to fend for himself, [while] he described himself as isolated and closed off" (Snow et al., 2007, p. 59).

Although James is only one student, his experiences were not atypical in this longitudinal study. The problems of young adolescents are "widespread and almost certainly multiply determined" (Snow et al., 2007, p. 63), that is, pervasive, with many causes. Middle schools can push some vulnerable children over the edge. Many developmentalists agree that, instead of being supportive of developing egos, middle schools are "developmentally regressive" (Eccles, 2004, p. 141)—taking a step backward. To pinpoint the developmental mismatch, note that just when egocentrism leads young people to feelings of shame or fantasies of stardom (performing for an imaginary audience), they are scheduled to change rooms, teachers, and classmates every 40 minutes or so. That makes public acclaim, personal recognition, or even private comfort difficult. When extracurricular activities become competitive, fragile egos shun the possible glare of coaches, advisers, or other students. Grades often fall in middle school, because teachers grade more harshly and students are less conscientious.

One way that young adolescents cope with stress is to blame their troubles on others—classmates, teachers, parents, nations. This may help explain the results of a study in Los Angeles: Those in more ethnically diverse schools felt safer and less lonely (Juvonen et al., 2006; see Research Design). The scientists suggest that students who feel victimized "can attribute their plight to the prejudice of other people" rather than blame themselves (Juvonen et al., 2006, p. 398).

How can middle schools encourage rather than discourage adolescent learning? Many middle school reforms are under way, with varying success (Roney et al., 2004).

Remember that answers are not clear, but that adolescent egocentrism is particularly strong in early adolescence and that intuitive thought generally overwhelms logic. Developmental research finds that egocentrism, intuitive thought, and logic coexist in every classroom. Middle school teachers need to consider the particular ideas and styles of each individual. The emotional and personal excitement of role-playing, debating, and group interaction may keep students engaged.

Research Design

Scientists: Jaana Juvonen, Adrienne Nishina, and Sandra Graham.

Publication: *Psychological Science* (2006).

Participants: A total of 2,000 middle school students from 99 classrooms in 11 Los Angeles middle schools, all low income, with ethnic diversity.

Design: Students answered questionnaires about safety, loneliness, victimization, and self-worth. Diversity was calculated by the likelihood that any two random students in a class or a school would be of the same race. Particular focus was placed on the two groups with the greatest number of students—Latino and African American.

Major conclusion: Diversity in the classrooms as well as in the schools led to less loneliness and a greater feeling of safety.

Comment: As the authors point out, "the possibility that there is safety in diversity—as opposed to safety in numbers—is an optimistic one" (p. 399). The focus on low-income Mexican and African Americans is commendable. This research needs to be extended to include, for example, Asian minority students who, according to other research, experience more bullying.

BOB DAEMMRICH / THE IMAGE WORKS

Isolated No More This huge lunchroom in a Texas high school could make any student sad, anxious, and lonely. Technology can help, though. This ninth-grade girl has her cell phone and MP3 player, so a potentially lonely lunch break is a happy, sociable time instead.

Bullying and social exclusion need to be stopped. Some research has found that "differential learning," treating "students as individual learners" within each class, advances learning in middle schools (May & Supovitz, 2006, p. 252).

Technology and Cognition

Adults have divergent perspectives regarding technology and teenage cognition. Some hope that computers will be a boon to learning, creating a new generation of better-informed, technologically savvy youth. Others fear that technology will undercut respect for adults and schools, that egocentrism will go wild when adolescents realize what their parents don't know (Hern & Chaulk, 1997; Roschelle et al., 2000).

The rise of new technology, however, is far outpacing any attempts by adults to stop, or even slow, its impact. A mere two decades ago, no one knew about the World Wide Web, instant messaging, chat rooms, blogs, iPods, Blackberries, and digital cameras. Yet today, teenagers are intimately acquainted with all of these technologies, even going as far as creating whole new texting "languages" to communicate with one another. In 1995, only half of all U.S. public schools had Internet capacity; now all do (see Figure 15.3) (U.S. Bureau of the Census, 2007).

The "digital divide," bemoaned in the 1990s because it separated boys from girls and rich from poor (Dijk, 2005; Norris, 2001) has been bridged. In the United States, the greatest divider between Internet users and nonusers is now age. To be specific, in 2005 (the year of the latest reliable statistics) the proportion of adolescents who used the Internet (78 percent) was by far the largest of any age group. The proportion of elderly Internet users was lowest (20 percent) (Snyder et al., 2006). Income and ethnicity gaps are shrinking every year, and the gender gap has all but disappeared, but age differences remain.

Technology is no longer limited only to developed nations. Teenagers worldwide use the Internet for, among other things, information about sex that their schools and parents do not provide (Borzekowski & Rickert, 2001; Gray et al., 2005; Suzuki & Calzo, 2005). An international political project involving 3,000 adolescents from 129 nations linked all of them via e-mail, some from home and others through nearby schools, libraries, or Internet cafés (see Figure 15.4). (Cassell et al., 2006).

Computers are now often seen as essential tools for education. This is exaggerated (those with and without computer access do equally well on various tests), but it is thought that Internet use

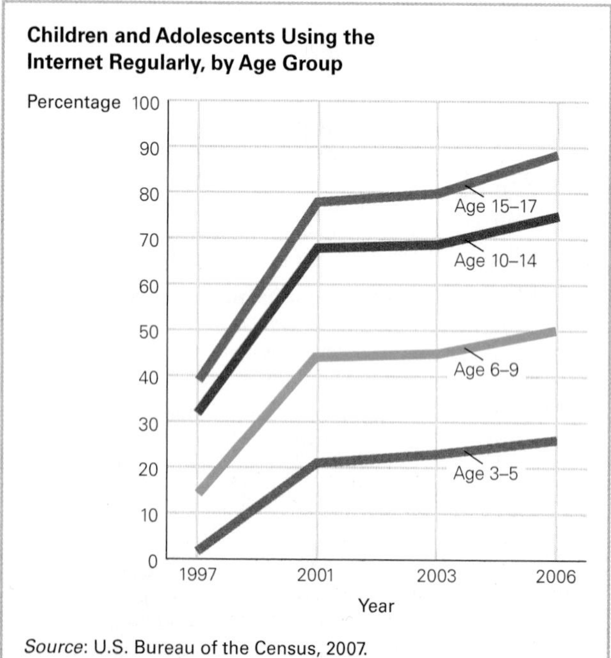

FIGURE 15.3

Logging On This graph shows the explosive increase in Internet use by children of all ages, especially teenagers, that has occurred since the mid-1990s. By age 18, almost every U.S. teenager is using the Internet at home, at school, or both, to check news, connect with friends, or find information. (*Note:* The data for 1997–2003 used identical questions and reliable survey methods from the annual Current Population Reports, published by the U.S. Bureau of the Census. Because CPR data for 2006 were not yet available as of this writing, the percentages given for that year are estimates and are not directly comparable with the data for other years.)

Hello . . . . I believe that Katia has spoken for most of us when she tells us how discouraged she is. I have heard it from many other people and have heard of stagnation in other discussion groups. I am very frustrated right now. The groups I am in aren't doing much. . . . It's awfully discouraging! But think of it from the perspective that we are all part of an incredible process, a process which has never before happened in the history of humanity. We are all children, essentially "dumped" into virtual rooms with a broad topic in mind, and the rest is ultimately up to us. It's difficult! The process, like any (life, school, work, a hike, everything) has its ups and downs. That sounds kind of trite—but it's true. And it's inevitable. And it is very valuable for us as human beings. Perhaps even more so than changing the world, we are learning and growing personally, which IS indirectly shaping the future. . . . Practically speaking, I have a suggestion as to how we all can move forward from this point, and get out of the "rut."

1. Every group, think clearly and put something together in writing asking the question, "What is our ultimate goal?" I think that putting a finger on all of the objectives both practical and philosophical will be a good starting point.

2. Then, start by making a timeline to carry out those objectives—dividing them, starting small and then building it up. For example, "In the first two weeks we need to figure out a general organizational flow for our project. The week following that, we need to go into finer details and figure out what sub-groups will exist. The 4th week, we need to figure out how people will be elected and how people will carry out the tasks in each group. Blah, blah, blah."

. . . And, through time and through perseverance, it will take off! I hope that we can all move forward and get back into the fun and excitement of our work and play. I am so privileged to know all of you. I feel happy and look forward to all the years we will have together. What are all your thoughts?

Source: Quoted in Cassell et al., 2006.

FIGURE 15.4

Discouraged, But . . . You might think that the logical analysis shown in this e-mail must come from a wise adult; but, no, the writer is 14 years old. He is in India, writing to adolescents he had not met in nations he had not seen. This project joined adolescents worldwide in a junior political summit.

may improve reading and spatial skills. In an experiment conducted with 10- to 18-year-olds (mostly African American from low-income families) who were given free Internet access at home, both reading scores and school grades were found to rise (Jackson et al., 2006).

Traditional research conducted before the technology explosion found that, with time, education, and experience, adolescents are more likely to move past egocentric thought and think logically and deductively. Perhaps the information overload of the World Wide Web will push adolescents toward deductive reasoning faster. Conversely, e-mail may allow adolescents to express egocentric thoughts and intuitive impulses that are better kept private. Cyberbullying is an example (Li, 2007).

Similar mixed consequences are apparent in many aspects of technology. Many advances (e.g., cell phones, e-mail, texting) require social interaction, which adolescents need for cognitive growth (Subrahmanyam et al., 2006). Online communication makes friends closer (Valkenburg & Peter, 2007). Even shy teens create screen names and engage in discussion at a distance, perhaps furthering thought and communication without the danger and intimacy of more direct contact. This may be especially important for teenagers who feel socially isolated.

On the other hand, intuitive thought, especially when propelled by emotions without analysis by the prefrontal cortex, can be dangerous. Teenagers may use technology to distance themselves from adults. Adolescents are pushed toward risk rather than caution when they are with peers (L. Steinberg, 2007).

To get a better understanding of the uses and misuses of the Internet, consider the following example. Currently, more than 400 Web sites are dedicated to "cutting," the self-injury done primarily to relieve depression and guilt (Whitlock et al., 2006). Cutting is addictive, particularly for adolescent girls (Yates, 2004). Analysis of a representative sample of 3,219 posts on cutting sites found that most were helpful, allowing self-injuring adolescents to "establish interpersonal intimacy . . . ,

➤Response for Middle School Teachers (from page 402): Students need both challenge and involvement; avoid lessons that are too easy or too passive. Create small groups; assign oral reports, debates, and role-plays; and so on. Remember that adolescents like to hear one another's thoughts and their own voices.

[which is] especially difficult for young people struggling with intense shame, isolation, and distress" (Whitlock et al., 2006, p. 415). The most common theme of the messages was informal support (28 percent), with many other posts describing formal treatment (7 percent, usually positively) and emotional triggers (20 percent) (Whitlock et al., 2006). This makes it seem as if technology was helpful for young women who once were isolated in their pain. Some sites, however, provided suggestions for concealment (9 percent) or information on techniques and paraphernalia (6 percent). Here is one chilling exchange:

> Poster 1: Does anyone know how to cut deep without having it sting and bleed too much?
>
> Poster 2: I use box cutter blades. You have to pull the skin really tight and press the blade down really hard. You can also use a tourniquet to make it bleed more.
>
> Poster 3: I've found that if you press your blade against the skin at the depth you want the cut to be and draw the blade really fast it doesn't hurt and there is blood galore. Be careful, though, 'cause you can go very deep without meaning to.
>
> *[quoted in Whitlock et al., 2006, p. 413]*

RAJESH KUMAR SINGH / AP PHOTO

Middle School Slump? These students in rural India are the same age as middle school students in developed nations, but their enthusiasm for school has not waned. One reason is that they do not take education for granted; only a select few are able to stay in school beyond age 11. Another reason may be seen here: The government is trying to upgrade the curriculum by providing traveling, Internet-connected computers.

Web sites directed at young people who are vulnerable to self-starvation, homophobia, violent sex, racism, and so on may encourage them, making these problems worse.

Overall, it is easy to see egocentrism and intuitive thought in adolescent use of technology; it is also easy to see the educational possibilities. However, it is not obvious how adults can guide teenagers through the current maze of technology. The next generation of researchers, some of them adolescents themselves a decade ago, may provide some answers.

Transitions and Translations

Developmentalists are able to make one definitive contribution to the issue of how adolescents learn best. Many studies have found that changes, even positive ones, are disruptive. As a result, transitions from one school to another are difficult, usually decreasing a person's ability to function and learn. Changing schools just when the growth spurt and sexual characteristics develop is bound to create stress.

Remember from Chapter 12 that ongoing minor stresses can become overwhelming if they accumulate. This may lead to psychic problems, as one expert explains:

> A number of disorders and symptoms of psychopathology, including depression, self-injury behavior, substance abuse, eating disorders, bipolar disorder, and schizophrenia have striking developmental patterns corresponding to transitions in early and late adolescence.
>
> *[Masten, 2004, p. 310]*

Of course, the transition to middle school or high school cannot be blamed for every disorder, since hormones, body shape, sexual impulses, family, and culture also contribute. Genes for psychopathology and sensation seeking might activate at puberty, causing havoc for those with no emotional control (E. F. Walker, 2002). However, since the first year of a new school often correlates with increased bullying and decreased achievement *and* the onset of depression and eating disorders (as does the first year of high school or college), schools need to pay special attention to the psychic needs of new students. There are a number of different measures that can be taken to ease the stress these students might feel, including teaching all such students in a separate area; avoiding transitions by extending elementary school to include grade 8; restructuring secondary schools to comprise grades 7 through 12 (as Japan recently did); and allowing families more choice, information, and involvement in each adolescent's education.

One particular problem occurs when the adults and many of the students in a new school are notably different from those in the old school, to whose culture the students are accustomed. Contrary to the study that found that diversity within classrooms was protective in middle school, other research has found that students entering high schools where they are suddenly in the minority may feel alienated and worried about their academic success (Benner & Graham, 2007). Advance involvement of students and families might ease the transition.

As mentioned in Chapter 12, researchers distinguish *intended, implemented,* and *attained* curricula (Robitaille & Beaton, 2002). *Intended* curriculum refers to the content that educational leaders prescribe, *implemented* curriculum means what the teachers and school administrators offer, and *attained* curriculum refers to what the students learn.

Strong intentions can lead to blame if the intentions are not realized. Teachers can be faulted for not implementing curricula, and students can be blamed for not learning what is taught. The result is reduced esteem and motivation among both teachers and students. From a developmental perspective, this direction is the opposite of what it should be. The attained learning is crucial, and intentions and implementation should be readjusted if students are not learning as they should—which is often the case with students who are new to a school.

Teaching and Learning in High School

As we have seen, adolescents can think abstractly, analytically, hypothetically, and logically—as well as personally, emotionally, intuitively, and experientially. By high school, the curriculum and teaching style are often quite analytic and abstract. In theory and sometimes in practice, high schools advance analytic ability in adolescents, so they can use logic to override the "biases that not only preserve existing beliefs but also perpetuate stereotypes and inhibit development" (Klaczynski, 2005, p. 71). That is good, but is it overdone?

Most academic subjects emphasize logic, often with laboratory experiments or historical documents that require the students to make systematic deductions. This is exactly what formal operational thinking enables adolescents to do and what the best assessments try to measure.

issues and applications

Diversity of Nation, Gender, and Income

Problem solving is a centerpiece of formal operational thinking. To assess this ability in 15-year-olds, an exam was prepared and administered under the auspices of PISA (Programme for International Student Assessment). This exam asked 250,000 students in 41 nations to answer questions intended to determine skill level in decision making, system analysis, and troubleshooting. The following is an example of one of the problems appearing on the exam.

The Zedish Community Service is organizing a five-day Children's Camp. Forty-six children (26 girls and 20 boys) have signed up for the camp, and 8 adults (4 men and 4 women) have volunteered to attend and organize the camp.

Adults
Mrs. Madison
Mrs. Carroll
Ms. Grace
Ms. Kelly
Mr. Stevens
Mr. Neill
Mr. Williams
Mr. Peters

Dormitories	
Name	**Number of beds**
Red	12
Blue	8
Green	8
Purple	8
Orange	8
Yellow	6
White	6

Dormitory rules:

1. Boys and girls must sleep in separate dormitories.
2. At least one adult must sleep in each dormitory.
3. The adult(s) in a dormitory must be of the same gender as the children.

Children's Camp—Question 1

Dormitory Allocation

Fill in the table to allocate the 46 children and 8 adults to dormitories, keeping to the rules.

Name	Number of Boys	Number of Girls	Name(s) of Adult(s)
Red			
Blue			
Green			
Purple			
Orange			
Yellow			
White			

Response Coding Guide for Children's Camp Question 1

Full Credit

Code 2: 6 conditions to be satisfied

- Total girls = 26
- Total boys = 20
- Total adults = four female and four male

About one in five 15-year-olds were "reflective, communicative problem solvers," as those who answered most questions correctly were called. Most earned partial credit. About one in six were "below basic" (skipping questions or making many mistakes). East Asian students generally did well (almost none at the lowest level), as did students from Finland, Australia, New Zealand, and Canada. Among developed nations, Italian and U.S. students had the lowest scores (with about one in four below basic), although Mexican, Brazilian, and Indonesian students scored much lower (see Table 15.1).

Table 15.2 suggests that the biological advent of puberty (which is experienced by age 15 in every nation) and biological sex differences (notable by age 15) do not affect intellectual achievement as much as cultural and schooling differences do. As the text makes clear, scientists do not yet agree as to which elements of culture and school are crucial. Students who took the exam went astray in many ways. Some ignored essential elements (as in the camp problem, not realizing that the adults needed beds), some confused numbers (e.g., switching boys and girls), while others skipped certain problems entirely. Unlike on multiple-choice tests, an intuitive thinker could not use quick guessing; analysis and written responses were required.

Beyond national variation, the scientists were interested in economic, gender, and family structure disparities. On gender, differences were few and insignificant, even though problem-solving ability correlates with math ability and boys usually do better at math. Boys had a wider range of scores than girls, with a higher proportion at the highest and lowest levels.

A particular concern was whether family and background factors affected learning. National policies can reduce socioeconomic differences among adults, and educational practices can compensate for children whose families do not teach them higher-order skills. But when the data were separated by family and background, the results varied markedly by nation. For example, in the United States it made little difference whether a child was native-born or not, but in Germany it made a big dif-

TABLE 15.1

Average Problem-Solving Scores Among 15-year-olds

(Note: The highest possible score was 700, the lowest 200; the international average was 500.)

Country	Average Score	Country	Average Score
Korea	550	Spain	481
Hong Kong	548	Italy	469
Japan	547	United States	477
Canada	529	Portugal	470
New Zealand	533	Turkey	408
Australia	530	Mexico	384
France	519	Brazil	371
Sweden	509	Indonesia	361
Ireland	498		

Source: Organisation for Economic Co-operation and Development, 2004.

School or Culture? Notable differences are apparent between nations, but the reasons are not obvious. Is the culture of some nations less conducive to problem solving, or are the schools of some nations less adept at teaching formal operational thought?

TABLE 15.2

Factor	Average Difference	Little or No Impact	Large Impact
Parental occupation	76 points	Korea, China-Macao	Belgium, Germany
Immigrant child	36 points	Canada, United States	Germany, Switzerland
Single-parent family	23 points	Austria, Brazil	United States, Belgium
Parental education	20 points	Sweden, Portugal	Hungary, Uruguay
Gender	4 points (F)	Canada, United States	Iceland (F); China-Macao (M)

ference. In 16 nations it made no significant difference whether a child lived with one parent or two, but in the United States this correlated with 44 points of difference. Overall, although parental occupation (which usually signifies income) had an effect in every nation, with children at each socioeconomic level scoring lower than children in the next-higher tier, no background factor was as significant as the national differences, which varied by nearly 200 points.

Focus on the Brightest

From a developmental perspective, the fact that high schools emphasize formal thinking makes sense, since by the later years of adolescence, many students are capable of attaining that level. Few do, however, unless adults teach them to do it, and it may be that the lack of logic among many adults is due to their lack of education in such thinking (Kuhn & Franklin, 2006).

Some nations are trying to raise their standards of education, partly so that more students will achieve the highest levels of thought. In the United States, an increasing number of high school students are enrolled in classes that are designed to be more rigorous, with externally scored exams, either the IB (International Baccalaureate) or the AP (Advanced Placement).

In 2006, about 3 million U.S. students earned a high school diploma and more than 1 million took at least one Advanced Placement class. The hope is that taking such classes will lead to better thinking, or at least higher achievement, though it is yet to be proven (McNeil, 2007; Viadero, 2006).

Another manifestation of the same trend is the greater number of requirements for receiving an academic diploma that all students must attain; no one is allowed to earn a vocational or general diploma unless the parents specifically request it (Olson, 2005). Many schools require two years of math beyond algebra, a year of laboratory science, and two years of history.

Finally, an increasing number of U.S. states require passing a **high-stakes test** in order to graduate. (Any exam for which the consequences of failing are severe is called a high-stakes test. Traditionally, such tests were used when adults sought professional licenses—e.g., for lawyers, doctors, and clinical psychologists.) Some see this as raising standards; others see it as destroying learning, in that teachers who "teach to the test" stress neither logic nor intuition (Nichols & Berliner, 2007).

high-stakes test An evaluation that is critical in determining success or failure. If a single test determines whether a student will graduate or be promoted, that is a high-stakes test.

Ironically, just when more U.S. schools are instituting high-stakes tests, many East Asian nations are moving in the opposite direction (Fujita, 2000). The trend in Japan is toward fewer academic requirements for high school students, school five days a week instead of six, and less "examination hell," as the high-stakes tests have been called. The science adviser to the prime minister of Japan is seeking more flexibility in education in order to promote more innovation in Japanese society. He wants "high school students [to] study whatever they are interested in" rather than to narrow their study to attain high scores on one final test (quoted in Normile, 2007).

Especially for High School Teachers You are much more interested in the nuances and controversies than in the basic facts of your subject, but you know that your students will take high-stakes tests on the basics and that their scores will have a major impact on their futures. What should you do?

High-stakes tests are often the subject of fierce debate. Unfortunately, it is the students who find themselves caught in the middle. In California in 2006, for example, 41,700 students (many of them from low-income Mexican American families) completed the credits for graduation but failed the state's high-stakes exam. Days before graduation, a judge ruled that the tests were discriminatory and that these students had earned their diplomas (McKinley, 2006). The state won an appeal. Those 41,700 students were not granted diplomas (Jacobson, 2006); some went to summer school to try again and some quit.

➤Response for High School Teachers (from page 409): It would be nice to follow your instincts, but the appropriate response depends partly on pressures within the school and on the expectations of the parents and administration. A comforting fact is that adolescents can think about and learn almost anything if they feel a personal connection to it. Look for ways to teach the facts your students need for the tests as the foundation for the exciting and innovative topics you want to teach. Everyone will learn more, and the tests will be less intimidating for your students.

Focus on the Dropouts

Not every student who begins secondary school stays to finish it. Rates of those aged 11 to 18 who are enrolled in school vary from less than 20 percent in the poorest nations (Niger, Cambodia) to 100 percent in the richest (Japan, Sweden) (World Bank, 2005).

Developed nations typically require students to be in school until they reach a certain age, usually between 14 and 18, with age 16 being the average (Education Week, 2007). In the United States and Canada, 90 percent of all teenagers are either students or high school graduates. Most of the dropouts leave toward the end of their secondary school career, at age 17 or so.

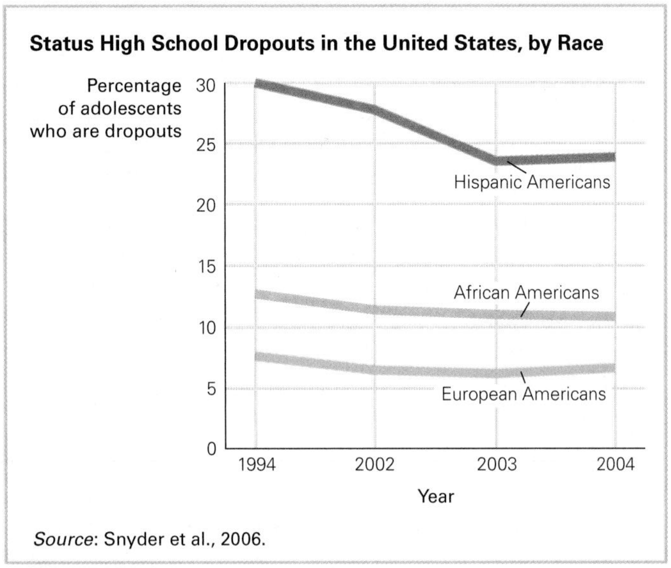

Status High School Dropouts in the United States, by Race

Percentage of adolescents who are dropouts
30
25
20
15
10
5
0
1994
2002
2003
2004
Year
Hispanic Americans
African Americans
European Americans

Source: Snyder et al., 2006.

FIGURE 15.5

No diploma This graph shows a recent increase in the percentage of 16- to 24-year-old status dropouts who are not in high school and who do not have a high school diploma.

Whenever high-stakes tests are a requisite for graduation, there is a "potential unintended consequence" of more high school dropouts (Christenson & Thurlow, 2004, p. 36). Twenty-three U.S. states now require exit exams to graduate; in those states, fewer students graduate (Robelen, 2006). Between 2003 and 2004 in the United States, the dropout rate increased (Hoff, 2005). As with all statistics, many interpretations of the increasing dropout rate are possible, although everyone seems to agree that a high school education is beneficial for later life (Orfield, 2004).

Interpretation is even more complicated in this case because dropout statistics are presented in many ways. "Status dropouts" are 18- to 24-year-olds who are not in school and who have no diploma (see Figure 15.5). Not counted are 19-year-olds who are still in high school or young adults who left school but earned a GED (General Education Diploma, granted on passing a series of exams). Another way to count is to note how many entering ninth-graders have not graduated four years later. By this measure, the dropout rate is more than 50 percent in some schools.

If a school, or a school district, wants to reduce the dropout rate, one alternative is to make graduation easier. On the other hand, if more and more requirements are added, the dropout rate will increase. Is this a sign of a successful school or a failing one? Those most likely to drop out are those of low income and minority ethnicity. Is that acceptable?

Taking a long view, the percentage of status dropouts has gradually decreased in the United States over the past 30 years, from about 14 to 10 percent. However, the percentage of those who left in their senior year (not earlier) increased, from 26 percent of all the dropouts to 40 percent. Again, many interpretations are possible.

Especially for Students Who Recently Left High School Which would be better: leaving without a diploma during one's senior year of high school or leaving in the ninth grade, before all those additional years?

Student Engagement

Surprisingly, students who are capable of passing their classes are as likely to drop out as those with learning disabilities. Persistence, diligence, and motivation seem to play a more crucial role than intellectual ability when it comes to earning a high school diploma (Fredricks et al., 2004). Many adolescents express boredom and unhappiness with school ("Algebra sucks," "*The Odyssey* is boring"), especially when they are complaining to their friends (Larson, 2000; Lyons, 2004). Adolescents seek to be admired by their peers, which may mean appearing to be detached from education. Attachment to school and assessment of self-competence typically falls in each consecutive year of high school, particularly for boys (Fredricks & Eccles, 2002; Porche et al., 2004; Wigfield et al., 1997).

Teachers, researchers, and developmentalists describe adolescents—honor students as well as delinquents—as having "high rates of boredom, alienation, and disconnection from meaningful challenge" (Larson, 2000). That conclusion comes from an American study, but similar conclusions have been found from as far away as Australia, where teachers were asked what problems they had with their students (Little, 2005). As you can see in Figure 15.6, middle school students can be disruptive, but high school students are often disengaged.

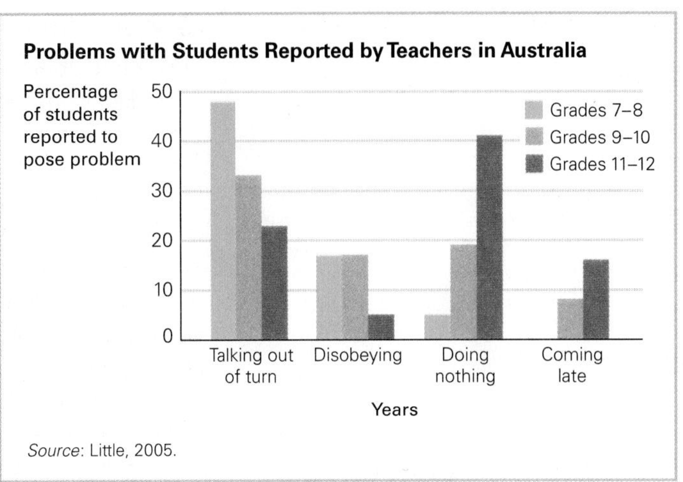

FIGURE 15.6

Teacher's Complaints Teachers around the globe concur that each adolescent age group poses its own particular set of behavioral problems in school. This chart is based on data as reported by teachers in Australia. Which is worse: a student who is actively disruptive or one who has stopped caring?

One reason may be that only formal operational thought is promoted, while egocentric and intuitive thought, which are more relational and social, are excluded. Schedules limit social interaction by allowing only a few minutes between classes and not allowing students to gather informally on school grounds before or after classes. Budget cutting often targets extracurricular activities first, which undercuts attachment to school (Fredricks & Eccles, 2006).

Teachers are hired for their expertise in one or more academic fields, not for their ability to relate to adolescents. They are able to answer complex questions about the intricacies of theoretical physics, advanced calculus, and iambic pentameter, but they are often ill equipped to deal effectively with troubled students. Instead, these students are usually sent to meet with a guidance counselor, who more often than not is responsible for hundreds of students. The result is that egocentric and intuitive thought may be devalued to the point that some adolescents feel that they themselves are devalued.

Especially for High School Guidance Counselors Given what you know about adolescent thinking, should you spend more time helping students with college applications, with summer jobs, with family problems, or with course selection?

So what can be done to encourage adolescents to be more engaged with school? While there is no single, definitive answer to this question, there are many possible avenues to explore.

One possible improvement may be to keep high schools small. Extensive research suggests that 200 to 400 is the ideal number of students to have in a high school, partly because there is more opportunity for almost every student to be involved in some sort of team or club. Nevertheless, two-thirds of high school students in the United States attend schools with enrollments of over 1,000 (Snyder et al., 2006). Big schools are more economical, but they do not necessarily increase learning and motivation (Eccles et al., 2003).

Another option is to encourage extracurricular activities, because there are "developmental benefits of participation in extracurricular activities for many high school adolescents" (Fredricks & Eccles, 2006, p. 712). Athletic teams elicit emotions and school bonding, which explains why students on such teams (even those who are not star athletes) are less prone to use drugs or alcohol, have a low incidence of depression, and earn higher grades. Overall, adolescents who are active in school clubs and athletic teams are more likely to graduate and go to college (Mahoney et al., 2005).

Again, these are only suggestions. A review of adolescent education throughout the world finds that "no culture or nation has worked out a surefire educational psychology to guarantee that every one of the youth is motivated in school" (Larson & Wilson, 2004, p. 318). Other ideas, some from other nations, may be better. Further experimentation and research are needed to determine more effective methods, given that current structures and curricula seem to leave many students disengaged (Fredricks et al., 2004).

School Violence

The same practices that foster motivation and education can also prevent violence. The data from the United States over the past decade suggest that fewer fights are breaking out in school but that students are more afraid of school than they have been in the past.

Students are unlikely to be destructive or afraid if they are engaged in learning, bonding with their teachers and fellow students, and involved in school activities. Such students create a protective shield throughout the school, for "students are well aware of the problem children in their own classrooms . . . [but] for such information to flow from students to administrators requires an atmosphere where sharing in good faith is respected and honored" (Mulvey & Cauffman, 2001).

According to a survey of all the principals in Texas middle and high schools, several measures seem to be effective in reducing school crime, including setting clear rules for student behavior, rewarding students for attendance, and organizing more sporting events within (and not just between) schools (Cheurprakobkit & Bartsch, 2005).

This study also showed that measures that increase fear, such as installing metal detectors and handing out strict punishments, are more likely to increase violence than decrease it. Primary prevention to improve the school climate is needed because measures that (1) increase peer friendships, (2) strengthen teacher–student relationships, and (3) promote student involvement tend to reduce violence. Programs that teach conflict resolution have also had some success, perhaps because they make a point of accomplishing the three goals just mentioned (e.g., Breunlin et al., 2002). Unfortunately, however, some efforts boomerang. Some programs designed to reduce bullying, halt drug use, and prevent delinquency have in fact had the opposite effect. Evaluation is crucial.

➤Response for Students Who Recently Left High School (from page 410): In terms of adolescent cognition, the diploma is merely a piece of paper, and the education gained in all those years is the true reward. On the other hand, the diploma is used as a credential for college admission and job applications. The answer to this question depends on whether you think learning in high school has intrinsic value or is aimed toward an extrinsic reward.

SUMMING UP

Secondary education is an integral aspect of cognitive development. However, researchers and nations disagree about how best to teach adolescents. Middle schools tend to be less personal, less flexible, and more tightly regulated than elementary schools, all of which may contribute to declining student achievement. Transitions are difficult for children, especially when the demands of puberty and the self-centeredness of egocentrism are at work. Students and educators alike turn to technology—for different reasons. It is not clear that the benefits of Internet use outweigh possible problems, but it is clear that most adolescents use various forms of technology every day.

High school education can advance thinking of all kinds, including analytic and intuitive thinking, in every domain. But it is often only formal operational thinking that is taught and tested. High-stakes testing reflects an effort to equalize achievement and increase accountability, but it may result in a less creative curriculum and increase the number of students who drop out before earning a diploma. Essential to safe and successful secondary education are activities that encourage students to engage intellectually with ideas, each other, and teachers. ■

➤Response for High School Guidance Counselors (from page 411): It depends on what your particular students need; schools vary a great deal. However, all students need to talk and think about their choices and options so that they will not act impulsively. Therefore, providing information and a listening ear might be the most important thing you can spend time doing. You will also want to keep all students in challenging and interesting classes until they graduate. Encouraging teachers and administrators to improve educational structures and to increase student motivation is a worthwhile endeavor.

SUMMARY

Adolescent Thinking

1. Cognition in early adolescence may be egocentric, a kind of self-centered thinking. Adolescent egocentrism gives rise to the invincibility fable and the imaginary audience.

2. *Formal operational thought* is Piaget's term for the last of his four periods of cognitive development. He tested and demonstrated formal operational thought with various problems that might be encountered by students in a high school science or math class, such as figuring out how to adjust weights on a balance scale.

3. Adolescents are no longer earthbound and concrete in their thinking; they prefer to imagine the possible, the probable, and even the impossible, instead of focusing on what is real. They develop hypotheses and explore, using deductive reasoning.

4. Intuitive thinking, also known as contextualized or experiential thinking, becomes more forceful during adolescence. Few teenagers always use logic, although they are capable of doing so. Emotional, intuitive thinking is quicker and more satisfying, and sometimes better.

Teaching and Learning

5. Secondary education—after primary and before tertiary (college)—is the fastest growing area of education in the world, partly because it correlates with the health and weath of individuals and nations. Most of the world's children now receive some secondary schooling.

6. Middle school students tend to be bored by school, difficult to teach, and hurtful to one another. One reason may be that middle schools are not structured to accommodate egocentrism or intuitive thinking.

7. Many forms of psychopathology increase at the transition to middle school, to high school, and to college. Although transitions are always stressful, this may be particularly true in adolescence.

8. Adolescents use technology, particularly the Internet, more than people of any other age. They reap many educational benefits from doing so, but there may be hazards as well.

9. Education in high school seems to emphasize formal operational intelligence. In the United States, the demand for more accountability has led to more AP classes and high-stakes testing. This may have unintended consequences, including a higher dropout rate.

10. Low motivation is often a problem among secondary school students. Especially in very large schools, few are actively involved in sports or other school activities, which promote school bonding and thus engagement. If students feel disconnected from the teachers and the school, they are more likely to be violent.

KEY TERMS

adolescent egocentrism (p. 392)
invincibility fable (p. 392)
imaginary audience (p. 393)
formal operational thought (p. 395)
hypothetical thought (p. 396)
deductive reasoning (p. 397)
inductive reasoning (p. 397)
dual-process model (p. 398)
intuitive thought (p. 398)
analytic thought (p. 398)
sunk cost fallacy (p. 399)
secondary education (p. 401)
middle school (p. 402)
high-stakes test (p. 409)

KEY QUESTIONS

1. What are some of the behavioral consequences of adolescent egocentrism?

2. Why are adolescents particularly concerned about the imaginary audience?

3. What characteristics of the balance-scale question make it a measure of cognition?

4. What are the advantages of intuitive thought?

5. How might intuition and analysis lead to opposite conclusions?

6. Why are middle schools called developmentally regressive?

7. Why are transitions a particular concern for educators?

8. What are the advantages and disadvantages of high-stakes testing?

9. What are the most motivating features of a good secondary school?

10. What factors increase and decrease the likelihood of school violence?

APPLICATIONS

1. Describe a time when you overestimated how much other people were thinking about you. How was your mistake similar to and different from adolescent egocentrism?

2. Talk to a teenager about politics, families, school, religion, or any other topic that might reveal the way that young person thinks. Do you hear any adolescent egocentrism? Intuitive thinking? Systematic thought? Flexibility? Cite examples.

3. Think of a life-changing decision you have made. How was the decision based on logic and how on emotion? What would have changed if you had given it more thought—or less?

4. Visit a local high school or middle school. Describe the hidden curriculum (class assignments, rules, nonacademic activities, etc.). How does it encourage adolescent learning?

हैं राही प्यार के
लाल कुआं

16

CHAPTER OUTLINE

Adolescence: Psychosocial Development

A 17-year-old writes:

> I am interested in everything. I like new technology, computers, videos. I have a guitar that I play at home. I usually go to play basketball with my friends . . . Briefly, I feel good. I am friendly and I have a sense of humor . . . Love, friendship, honesty and self-assurance are the most important values in a person's life.
>
> *[quoted in van Hoorn et al., 2000, p. 22]*

This adolescent could be male or female and could be living almost anywhere—Tokyo, Topeka, Toronto, or your hometown. In fact, he lives in Pécs, Hungary. While he was growing up, his nation changed its political and economic system, and as a teenager he often heard gunfire from neighboring Yugoslavia, which was undergoing a bloody civil war that led to the birth of three new countries. Yet he says, without irony, "There were no essential, important events in my life, only that I was born" (quoted in van Hoorn et al., 2000, p. 22).

This boy is similar to adolescents everywhere, influenced more by microsystems of families and friends than by changes in exosystems (such as political upheaval). Culture is influential, mediated through the family, but many teenagers seem oblivious to its effects.

Almost always, adolescents seek a unique identity that is "honest and self-assured"; they value "love and friendship" from their parents and peers. This chapter begins with a description of the identity quest and then discusses relationship needs and patterns. At the end of this chapter, two obstacles to growth are described: depression and delinquency.

Identity

Psychosocial development during adolescence is often understood as a search for **identity,** for a consistent understanding of oneself. Each young person wants to know "Who am I?"

As Erik Erikson described it, life's fifth psychosocial crisis is **identity versus diffusion.** The search for identity is the primary crisis of adolescence—a crisis in which young people struggle to reconcile their understanding of themselves as unique but with a connection to their heritage and to the larger society (Erikson, 1968).

identity A consistent definition of one's self as a unique individual, in terms of roles, attitudes, beliefs, and aspirations.

identity versus diffusion Erikson's term for the fifth stage of development, in which the person tries to figure out "Who am I?" but is confused as to which of many possible roles to adopt.

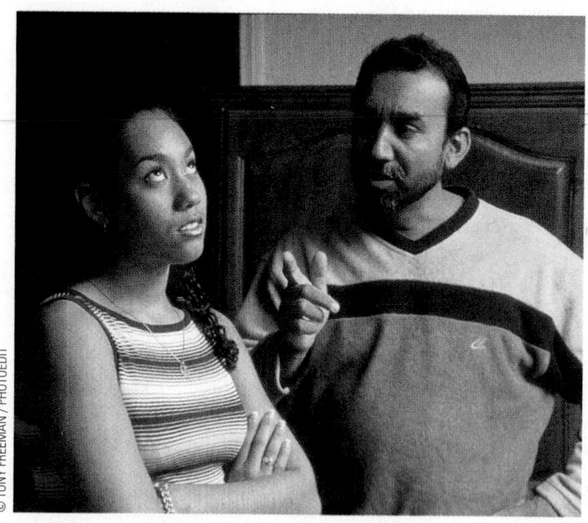

I'm a Big Girl Now Young teenagers are likely to use their musical taste, their clothing and hairstyles, and sometimes their facial expression to make it very obvious to parents that they are no longer the obedient, predictable children they once were.

identity achievement Erikson's term for the attainment of identity, or the point at which a person understands who he or she is as a unique individual, in accord with past experiences and future plans.

identity diffusion A situation in which an adolescent does not seem to know or care what his or her identity is.

foreclosure Erikson's term for premature identity formation, which occurs when an adolescent adopts parents' or society's roles and values wholesale, without questioning and analysis.

moratorium A way for adolescents to postpone making identity achievement choices by finding an accepted way to avoid identity achievement. Going to college is the most common example.

Identity achievement is the ultimate psychosocial goal, according to Erikson. Adolescents seek to establish their own identities by reconsidering all the goals and values set by their parents and culture, accepting some and rejecting others. Adolescents maintain continuity with their past in order to move toward their future (Chandler et al., 2003).

Erikson first labeled this crisis "identity versus diffusion" in the middle of the twentieth century, an era unlike today in politics, social context, developmental research, and adolescent self-concept. Over the past half-century, major psychosocial shifts have made the search for identity longer and given it new dimensions (Côté, 2006; Nurmi, 2004). In addition to achievement, at least three other identity statuses have been described: diffusion, foreclosure, and moratorium (Marcia, 1966).

Not Yet Achieved

The opposite of identity achievement is **identity diffusion,** a lack of commitment to any goals or values, with apathy concerning every role. Even the usual social demands, such as putting away clothes, making friends, completing school assignments, and thinking about college or employment, are beyond the diffused adolescent. Instead, too much sleep, long hours of mind-numbing television, and a turn from one romance to another with neither passion nor distress are typical. The response to school failure, parental criticism, missed deadlines, lost papers is, "Whatever."

Identity **foreclosure** occurs when young people short-circuit their search by not questioning traditional values (Marcia, 1966; Marcia et al., 1993). They might simply accept roles and customs from their parents or culture, never exploring alternatives. An example of foreclosure might be a boy who has always anticipated following in his father's footsteps. If his father is a doctor, he might take advanced chemistry and biology in high school; if his father is a day laborer, he might drop out of school at age 16. For many young people, foreclosure is a comfortable shelter, a way to avoid the stress of forging a new path.

Another shelter, considered more mature, is **moratorium,** a kind of time-out. Societies provide many moratoria, chosen by adolescents just as they are graduating from high school. Identity achievement would mean selecting a mate and a career, as people once did at about age 16 to 18. Moratorium is a way to postpone such choices.

The most obvious moratorium in North America is going to college, because colleges encourage studying many disciplines (general education) and provide a rejoinder to any older relative who urges settling down to marriage and career. Other institutions that allow postponement of identity are the military; religious mission work; and various internships in government, academe, and industry.

Unlike identity diffusion, adolescents in moratorium try to do what is required (as student, soldier, missionary, or whatever), but they consider it temporary, not their final identity. The U.S. Army once advertised, "Be all you can be," but it also promised that, once you had become whatever you could be, you could reenter civilian life with more maturity and education than when you enlisted. Then you might be ready to achieve identity.

Four Arenas of Identity Achievement

Erikson (1968) highlighted four aspects of identity: religion, sex, politics, and vocation. Terminology and emphasis have changed, yet these four domains remain important.

Religious Identity

The distinctions among diffusion, foreclosure, moratorium, and achievement are evident in religious identity, which few teenagers achieve. Diffusion is evident in those who drift along with whatever faith their parents or their friends favor. One teenager said, "At the moment religion's not that important. I guess when I get older it might become more so, but right now being with my friends and having fun and being a teenager is more important to me" (quoted in C. Smith, 2005, p. 159).

Most religions expect young people to struggle with theological questions, with a moratorium on commitment. For example, those who want to be Roman Catholic priests or nuns must undergo years of testing and training before they are allowed to assume that role. Mormons expect everyone to complete a year or two of missionary work before marriage. A sizable minority of Amish adolescents take part in a tradition known as *rumspringa* ("running around"), where they "venture out into the world" (Stevick, 2001, p. 166). As young adults, many return to the fold, choosing to be baptized in the Amish faith after their exploration of the world beyond their community.

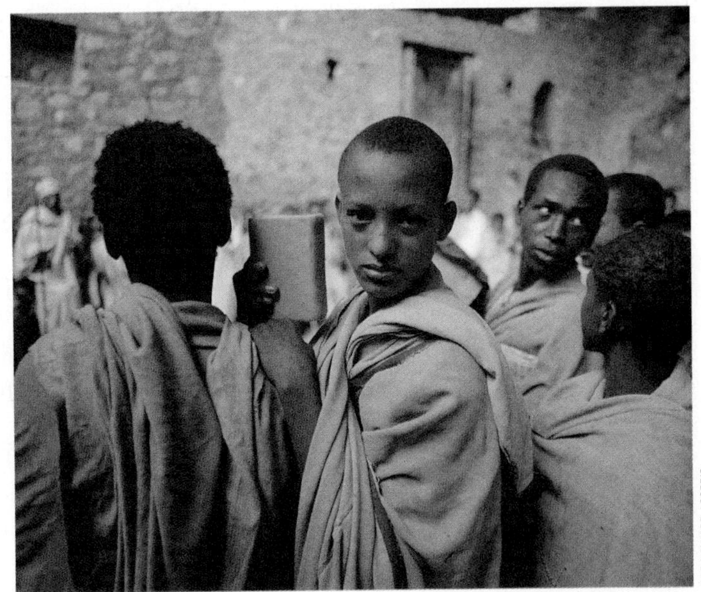

ROB HOWARD / CORBIS

A Religious Life These young adolescents in Ethiopia are studying to be monks. Their monastery is a haven in the midst of civil strife. Will the rituals and beliefs also provide them with a way to achieve identity?

Foreclosure would involve accepting a faith without questioning. The survey of religion highlighted in the previous chapter (pp. 400–401) found that 8 percent of the participating teenagers considered themselves to be devout (C. Smith, 2005). They often prayed, read scripture, and attended services. It is impossible to know whether those devout teenagers had foreclosed or had achieved their religious identity sooner than most. Time will tell. Those who foreclosed might "lose" their faith, but those who achieved will likely deepen their commitment.

Sexual/Gender Identity

Erikson's term *sexual identity* has, over the past 50 years, been replaced by *gender identity*. As you remember from Chapter 10, for social scientists *sex* and *sexual* refer to biological male/female characteristics and *gender* refers to cultural and social characteristics.

A half-century ago, Erikson and other psychoanalytic theorists thought of males and females as opposites (P. Y. Miller & Simon, 1980). They assumed that, although many adolescents were temporarily confused about their sexual identity, they would soon identify as men or women and adopt sex-appropriate roles (Erikson, 1968; Freud, 1958/2000).

Later, cross-cultural research and a changing cultural environment, prodded by the multicultural perspective and by historical change, revealed the limitations of that assumption (Lippa, 2002). Sexual identity

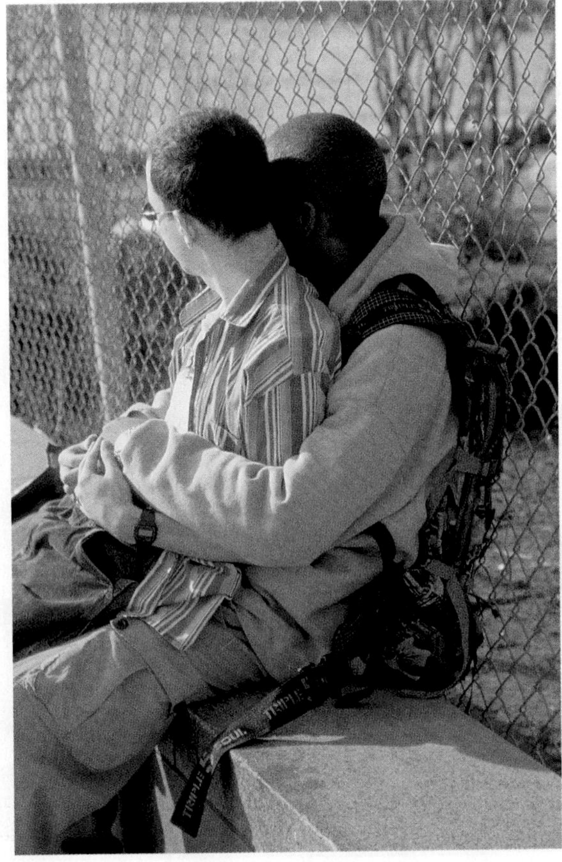

LEE SNIDER / THE IMAGE WORKS

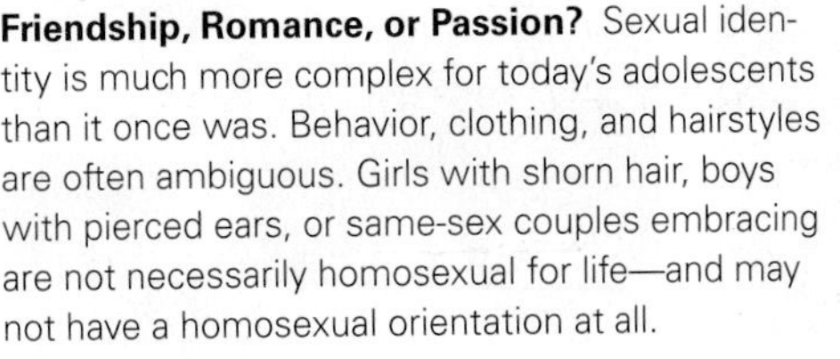

Friendship, Romance, or Passion? Sexual identity is much more complex for today's adolescents than it once was. Behavior, clothing, and hairstyles are often ambiguous. Girls with shorn hair, boys with pierced ears, or same-sex couples embracing are not necessarily homosexual for life—and may not have a homosexual orientation at all.

gender identity A person's acceptance of the roles and behaviors that society associates with the biological categories of male and female.

sexual orientation A term that refers to whether a person is sexually and romantically attracted to others of the same sex, the opposite sex, or both sexes.

became known as **gender identity** (Denny & Pittman, 2007), which now refers primarily to a person's self-definition as male or female. Gender identity usually leads to gender role and sexual orientation, but not always (Galombos, 2004).

A related term, **sexual orientation,** refers to a person's erotic desires. The word *orient* can be interpreted to mean "turns toward," and thus sexual orientation refers to whether a person is romantically attracted to people of the other sex, the same sex, or both sexes. Sexual orientation can be relatively strong or weak, and it can be acted upon, unexpressed, or even unconscious.

Adolescents feel strong sexual drives, but many are not sure how and with whom to express them. That is why gender identity, gender role, and sexual orientation all become issues during adolescence (Baumeister & Blackhart, 2007). This topic is discussed in more detail later in this chapter.

Political/Ethnic Identity

In Erikson's day, achieving political identity meant identifying with a particular political party. Today, as with the young man quoted at the opening of this chapter, many adolescents seem oblivious to national and international politics (Kinder, 2006; Torney-Purta et al., 2001). Once they are old enough to vote—if they vote at all—they usually say they choose the person, not the party.

Since Erikson's time, political values and attitudes have been increasingly influenced by ethnic loyalty rather than political party; hence the term *identity politics.* For many adolescents, ethnic identity becomes an important aspect of their overall identity (Phinney, 2006).

Within the United States, ethnic identity is central to many adolescents of African, Asian, and Hispanic descent, who contend with their group's history, their parents' perspectives, and their own experiences, often blending these various components of their backgrounds into personal values and actions. As with all adolescents, they struggle to find their own identities while remaining connected to their roots.

The need to establish ethnic identity arises in early adolescence and peaks at about age 15 (French et al., 2006; Pahl & Way, 2006). Ethnic identity continues to evolve for years, partly because social and historical circumstances change. As one developmentalist contends, for ethnic minorities, "the need to explore the implications of their group membership may extend the identity exploration period throughout the 20s and often beyond" (Phinney, 2006, p. 118).

The Same Event, A Thousand Miles Apart: Learning in School For these two groups of Muslim girls, the distance between their schools in Dearborn, Michigan *(left),* and Jammu, Kashmir *(right),* is more than geographical. The schools' hidden curricula teach different lessons about the roles of women.

Observation Quiz (see answer, page 421): What three differences are evident?

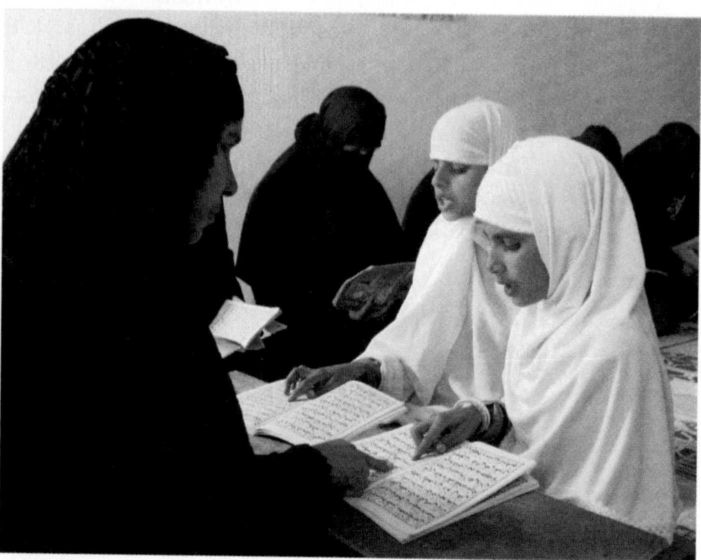

Ethnicity also becomes salient for many European Americans, especially those whose families connect ethnicity with religion (as happens for millions of adolescents in other nations as well). Each political or ethnic identity affects language, manners, dating patterns, clothing, values, and so on (Trimble et al., 2003).

Vocational Identity

Vocational identity in the twenty-first century is usually postponed until age 25 or later, for a variety of reasons. One is that few teenagers can find meaningful work (Csikszentmihalyi & Schneider, 2000). Another is that most available jobs are quite different from what they were a generation ago, making foreclosure difficult. A third is that the required skills for many vocations take years to attain, which makes selecting a vocation at age 16 premature.

To the surprise of many adults, not only is it premature for adolescents to decide on a vocation, but adolescent employment itself may be harmful. Several studies in the United States have found that a job during high school requiring 20 or more hours per week can impede identity formation, family relationships, academic achievement, and career success (Greenberger & Steinberg, 1986; Staff et al., 2004). Money earned is often spent on drugs, clothes, cars, and entertainment.

Overall, many aspects of the identity search have become more arduous than they seemed to be when Erikson first described them (Zimmer-Gembeck & Collins, 2003). Fifty years ago, the drive to become an independent and autonomous person was thought to be the "key normative psychosocial task of adolescence" (p. 177). Today researchers are aware that identity achievement before age 18 is elusive.

SUMMING UP

Erikson's fifth psychosocial crisis, which was first described more than 50 years ago and depicts adolescence as a time to search for a personal identity, still resonates with those who study contemporary teenagers. Patterns of diffusion, foreclosure, and moratorium are still apparent. One thing that has changed, however, is the length of the process, with few young people developing a firm sense of who they are and what path they will follow. The specific aspects of identity—religious, political, sexual, and vocational—have taken new forms and schedules as well. Ethnic identity is pivotal for many contemporary teenagers, who need to incorporate their group history into current reality. ■

Relationships

The changing seas of development are never sailed alone. At every turn, a voyager's family, friends, and community provide sustenance, directions, ballast for stability, and a safe harbor when it is time to rest. Social forces also provide a reason to move ahead or change direction. In adolescence, when the winds of change blow particularly strong, adults and contemporaries are valuable shipmates.

Adults and Teenagers

Adolescence is often characterized as a time of waning adult influence, a period when young people distance themselves from the values and behaviors of their elders. There is some validity to this observation, but it need not be true, nor is such a disconnect necessarily a good sign. In fact, when young people feel valued by their communities, trusted by teachers, and connected to adults, they are far

Not in My Kitchen Both parents and teenagers are invested in their relationship, but each generation has its own perspective on their interactions.

Observation Quiz (see answer, page 422): What do you see in the body positions of these two that suggests a generational conflict?

bickering Petty, peevish arguing, usually repeated and ongoing.

less likely to abuse drugs, leave school, take unnecessary risks, and so on (Benson, 2003; Stanton & Burns, 2003).

Parents are crucial for support and guidance (Collins & Laursen, 2004), but other adults can also contribute substantially to the development of adolescents. "Supportive relationships with non-parent adults are considered to be among the key developmental assets predicting positive youth outcomes" (Rhodes & Roffman, 2003, p. 195). These nonparent adults can be other relatives, teachers, church leaders, or even the parents of friends; all can contribute to a rich social network that sustains healthy development (Parke & Buriel, 2006).

Conflicts at Home

Parent–adolescent relationships are pivotal, but not always peaceful. Disputes arise when a child's drive for independence clashes with the parents' customary control. The specifics depend on many factors, including age, gender, and culture.

Parent–adolescent conflict typically peaks in early adolescence, especially between mothers and daughters (Arnett, 1999; Granic et al., 2003; Laursen et al., 1998). Usually it manifests as **bickering**—repeated, petty arguments (more nagging than fighting) about routine, day-to-day concerns, such as cleanliness, clothes, chores, and schedules. Some bickering may indicate a healthy family, since close relationships almost always include some conflict (Smetana et al., 2004).

Few parents can resist commenting about dirty socks thrown on the floor or a ring through a newly pierced eyebrow, and few adolescents can calmly listen to "expressions of concern" without feeling unfairly judged. Parents want their children to be present at family dinners and to go along for visits to relatives, while teenagers just want to be with their friends. Parents notice resistance and fear the worst—addiction, jail, disappearance.

After a period during which bickering occurs regularly, most parents typically adjust by granting more autonomy, and "friendship and positive affect typically rebound to preadolescent levels" (Collins & Laursen, 2004, p. 337). Normally, teenagers adjust as well; by age 18, increased emotional maturity and reduced egocentrism bring some appreciation of their parents.

In some families, however, downright neglect on the part of the parents can result in a decidedly different outcome. Sixteen-year-old Joy's stepfather said, "Teens all around here [are] doing booze and doing drugs. . . . But my Joy here ain't into that stuff" (C. Smith, 2005, p. 10). In fact, Joy was smoking pot, drinking alcohol, and having sex with her boyfriend. She once overdosed on her mother's medicine and lay unconscious for two days before anyone even noticed. Obviously, she was in far worse trouble than most "teens all around here."

Regarding parent–adolescent relationships, it is also important to note cultural differences in expectations and patterns. Some cultures value family harmony above all else, and in these cultures both generations usually avoid conflict. This peaceableness may be either repressive or healthy, depending on the cultural perspective. It could be that adolescent rebellion is a social construction, assumed to be necessary by middle-class Westerners but not necessarily by those of other cultures or socioeconomic status (Larson & Wilson, 2004).

"So I blame you for everything—whose fault is that?"

That is speculation. It is known, however, that the topics and the processes of conflict vary from place to place. For example, Japanese youth expect autonomy in their choice of music but parental guidance in their romantic choices, which might make a U.S. adolescent bristle (Hasebe et al., 2004). In the United States, conflict is normal, but "expressed hostility" is not, and it is likely to lead to disobedient, cheating, lying adolescents, even when the influence of deviant friends is taken into account (Buehler, 2006).

In every nation, it is not only cultural norms but also family customs that affect the topics, timing, and severity of parent–child disagreement. Role models are quite influential, those provided not only by parents (especially if the parents fight with each other) but also by siblings. For instance, if older siblings are aggressive, sexually active, or drug users, younger siblings are more likely to follow their example than to learn from their mistakes (Bank et al., 2004; Brody, 2004; East & Kiernan, 2001). Conflict with parents peaks earlier for younger than elder siblings, which indicates again the power of a family role model (Shanahan et al., 2007; see Research Design).

Especially for Mothers Why would young adolescent daughters and their mothers be most likely to bicker?

Research Design

Scientists: Lilly Shanahan, Susan M. McHale, D. Wayne Osgood, and Ann C. Crouter.

Publication: *Developmental Psychology* (2007).

Participants: Families consisting of two siblings living with their married parents, 201 in total. The elder children were 10 to 14 years old at the start of the study, and their siblings were one to four years younger.

Design: At four intervals over five years, participants were asked about the frequency of fights with each parent in 11 domains (e.g., chores, appearance, health, relationships).

Major conclusions: Conflict peaked at about age 13 for first-born children and at about age 9 for second-born. Younger siblings had fewer conflicts overall than first-borns.

Comment: This study considers several family interaction patterns over time. Not only do younger siblings tend to follow their elder siblings (called spill-over) but parents also tend to learn from experience, finding ways to avoid conflicts by the time the second child reaches puberty. Research on other types of families might show whether this pattern holds for them as well.

Closeness with the Family

As we have just seen, conflict is only one dimension of the parent–child relationship, easy to notice though not necessarily the most important. Another key factor that may have an even greater impact on the parent–child relationship is overall closeness, which has four specific aspects:

- Communication (Do parents and teens talk openly with one another?)
- Support (Do they rely on one another?)
- Connectedness (How emotionally close are they?)
- Control (Do parents encourage or limit adolescent autonomy?)

No developmentalist doubts that the first two, communication and support, are helpful, if not essential. Patterns set in place during childhood continue. If these patterns are positive, they can buffer some of the turbulence of adolescence (Cleveland et al., 2005; Collins & Laursen, 2004).

Regarding connectedness and control, consequences vary and observers differ. Consider this example, written by one of my students:

> I got pregnant when I was sixteen years old, and if it weren't for the support of my parents, I would probably not have my son. And if they hadn't taken care of him, I wouldn't have been able to finish high school or attend college. My parents also helped me overcome the shame that I felt when . . . my aunts, uncles, and especially my grandparents found out that I was pregnant.
>
> *[personal communication with "I.," 2004]*

My student is grateful to her parents, but others might wonder whether her early motherhood allowed her parents too much control and necessitated a dependent connection at a time when she should have been finding her own identity. A study of pregnant adolescents in the United States found that young mothers and their children fared best if the parents were supportive but did not take over the care of the child completely (Borkowski et al., 2007). An added complexity is that my student's parents had emigrated from South America: Cultural differences in family expectations may have been a factor in her pregnancy and in her family's response.

➤Answer to Observation Quiz (from page 418): Facial expressions, degree of adult supervision, and head covering. (Did you notice that the Kashmiri girls wear a tight-fitting cap under their one-piece white robes?)

An important correlate of family closeness in the United States is **parental monitoring**—that is, parental knowledge about the child's whereabouts, activities, and companions. When monitoring is part of a warm, supportive relationship, the child is likely to become a confident, well-educated adult, avoiding drug use and risky sex (Barnes et al., 2006; Fletcher et al., 2004).

parental monitoring Parents' ongoing awareness of what their children are doing, where, and with whom.

➤Answer to Observation Quiz (from page 420): The mother's folded arms show her determination to keep her son in line. The young man sits on the kitchen counter, with cap but without shoes, to stress his independence.

However, if parents are too restrictive and controlling, that correlates with depression and other disorders, possibly resulting in adolescents who habitually deceive their parents. Worst of all may be *psychological control* (a threat to withdraw love and support; see Chapter 10) (Barber, 2002). Apparently, adolescents need freedom in order to feel competent and loved. Parental monitoring itself may be harmful when, instead of indicating a warm connection with the adolescent, it derives from harsh suspicion (Stattin & Kerr, 2000).

Ongoing Influence

Finding the right balance is difficult. Each family adjusts to personalities and cultures. The worst thing to do is to give up. Even if teenagers seem oblivious or defiant, parents can still be influential; this is true for all families, not only for intact, middle-class ones (B. Brown, 2005; Richardson, 2004).

One detailed study measured the self-esteem of low-income minority students in a large New York City high school. They found that the school climate had little impact on self-esteem but that "parents are a primary presence in their children's emotional lives throughout adolescence," whether they are African American, Latino, or Asian American (Greene & Way, 2005, p. 171).

Of course, genes, maturation, and friendships also affect a child's personality and activities. But parents have a decided impact through guidance, modeling, and past decisions that affect the child (e.g., neighborhood and school choices). Children tend to follow their parents' examples in many activities, including religious involvement, drug use, and sports preferences (Rose, 2007).

Overall, effective parenting before the teen years is protective during adolescence; ineffective parenting during childhood may produce angry, uncontrollable youth (Cleveland et al., 2005; Li et al., 2002). This pattern continues. A longitudinal study found a correlation between parenting style used when children were in seventh grade and any problems (delinquency, risky sex, drug use, etc.) they had by the time they were in eleventh grade. These researchers wrote:

> When parents permit too much freedom, they may put their young adolescents at risk for a negative peer context, but they can also put their young adolescents at risk if they are perceived as being too intrusive.
>
> *[Goldstein et al., 2005, p. 409]*

➤Response for Mothers (from page 421): Conflicts typically occur about habits of dress and cleanliness. Mothers are most directly involved with daily enforcement, and daughters are traditionally more docile—so their rebellion produces surprise and resistance in their mothers.

Peer Support

Parental influence is most direct in childhood and at the beginning of adolescence. Then peer influence becomes more apparent. From hanging out with a crowd to whispering with a confidant, peers make life a joy rather than a burden. As one high school boy said, "A lot of times I wake up in the morning and I don't want to go to school, and then I'm like, you know, I have got this class and these friends are in it, and I am going to have fun. That is a big part of my day—my friends" (quoted in Hamm & Faircloth, 2005, p. 72).

Cliques and Crowds

Adolescents group themselves into cliques and crowds (Collins & Steinberg, 2006; Eckert, 1989), which help "bridge the gap between childhood and adulthood" (Bagwell et al., 2001, p. 26). A cluster of close friends is called a **clique,** who are loyal to one another and who exclude outsiders. A **crowd** is a larger group of adolescents who share common interests, though they may not necessarily be friends. Crowds may be based predominantly on race or ethnicity, or on some personal characteristic or activity, such as the "brains," "jocks," "skaters," or

clique A group of adolescents made up of close friends who are loyal to one another while excluding outsiders.

crowd A larger group of adolescents who have something in common but who are not necessarily friends.

"burnouts." Crowds guide students' decisions about clothes, music, drugs, classes, and so on, although allegiance to a crowd is much looser than to a clique. For example, a student could dress like others in a crowd (with preppy shirts, trench coats, or baggy pants) but not endorse the same values as other members of that crowd. A crowd may use small signs of identity (a certain brand of backpack, a particular greeting) that adults do not notice but members of other crowds do (Strouse, 1999).

Cliques and crowds provide both social control and social support. They promote group norms, not necessarily directly but through criticism and exclusion of people who do not conform (B. Brown & Klute, 2003). Compared with primary school children, many adolescents consider appearance and style (often in opposition to adult norms) important for peer acceptance, as I learned within my own family.

Especially for Parents of a Teenager Your 13-year-old comes home after a sleepover at a friend's house with a new, weird hairstyle—perhaps cut or colored in a bizarre manner. What do you say and do?

in person

The Berger Daughters Seek Peer Approval

Our oldest daughter wore the same pair of jeans to tenth grade, day after day. She washed them each night by hand, and, at her request, I put them in the dryer very early each morning. My bewildered husband watched us both ("Is this some weird female ritual?"). He encouraged her to wear other clothes, to no avail. Years later she explained that she wanted her classmates to think she didn't care how she looked. If she varied her clothing, they would think she did care, and then they might criticize her.

Our second daughter was 16 when she told me she had pierced her ears again. She wanted to wear more earrings at once than anyone in my generation did. My response: "Does this mean you are going to take drugs?" She laughed at my naiveté, happy at my disapproval.

At age 15, our third daughter was diagnosed with Hodgkin's disease, a form of cancer. My husband and I weighed divergent opinions from four physicians, all explaining why their treatment would minimize the risk of death. She had her own priorities: "I don't care what you choose, as long as I keep my hair." (Her hair fell out temporarily, but now her health is good.)

Our youngest, in her first year of middle school, refused to wear her jacket even on the coldest days, much to her teachers' and parents' dismay. In high school, she offered an explanation: She wanted her peers to think she was tough.

What strikes me now is how oblivious I was to my children's need for peer respect. At the time, it did not occur to me that it would explain their seemingly bizarre actions. I reacted as a mother, not as a wise developmentalist. As my husband said, "I knew they would become adolescents, but I did not realize we would become parents of adolescents."

Choosing Friends

Peers are constructive as often as they are destructive (B. Brown, 2004). The adult fear of **peer pressure,** which usually means social pressure to conform to negative peer activities, ignores the other possibility—that "friends generally encourage socially desirable behaviors" (Berndt & Murphy, 2002, p. 281). Members of a clique or crowd support each other in joining sports teams, studying for exams, avoiding smoking, and applying to college.

Young people *can* lead one another into trouble, however. Collectively, peers sometimes provide **deviancy training,** when one person shows another how to rebel against social norms (Dishion et al., 2001). Especially if adolescents believe that their most popular, most admired peers are having sex, or doing drugs, or ignoring homework, then "social contagion" spreads destructive behavior (Rodgers, 2003).

To understand the true impact of peers, two concepts are helpful: *selection* and *facilitation.* In **peer selection,** teenagers select friends whose values and interests they share, abandoning friends who follow other paths. Acquaintances test

peer pressure Encouragement to conform with one's friends or contemporaries in behavior, dress, and attitude; usually considered a negative force, as when adolescent peers encourage one another to defy adult authority.

deviancy training Destructive peer support in which one person shows another how to rebel against authority or social norms.

peer selection An ongoing, active process whereby adolescents select friends on the basis of shared interests and values.

each other with secrets, with money, and in other ways before becoming friends. Friendships dissipate if a person feels betrayed. Peer selection during adolescence is an ongoing, active process (Way & Hamm, 2005).

peer facilitation The encouragement adolescent peers give one another to partake in activities or behaviors they would not otherwise do alone, whether constructive or destructive.

As for **peer facilitation,** peers encourage one another to do things that few would dare alone. They give each other specific suggestions (Let's all skip school on Friday!) and support (Congratulations on that A!). Peer facilitation is evident for both constructive and destructive behaviors—everything from using drugs on one end of the spectrum to studying on the other.

In fact, both selection and facilitation can work in any direction (Lacourse et al., 2003). One teenager joins a clique whose members smoke cigarettes and drink beer, and the group takes the next step, perhaps sharing a joint at a party. Another teenager might choose friends who enjoy math, and all of them might decide to enroll in AP calculus. This was true for Lindsay, who says:

> [Companionship] makes me excited about calculus. That is a hard class, but when you need help with calculus, you go to your friends. You may think no one could be excited about calculus, but I am. Having friends in class with you definitely makes school more enjoyable.
>
> *[quoted in Hamm & Faircloth, 2005, p. 72]*

An interesting experiment compared adolescents (ages 13 to 16), emerging adults (ages 18 to 22), and adults (over age 24) (Gardner & Steinberg, 2005). They played 15 rounds of a video driving game, "Chicken." Periodically, the screen would flash a yellow light, indicating that soon (from one to several seconds later) a wall would appear. The participants had to decide when to brake. The goal was to keep driving as long as possible and avoid crashing into the wall. Points were gained for travel time, but a crash erased all the points from that trial.

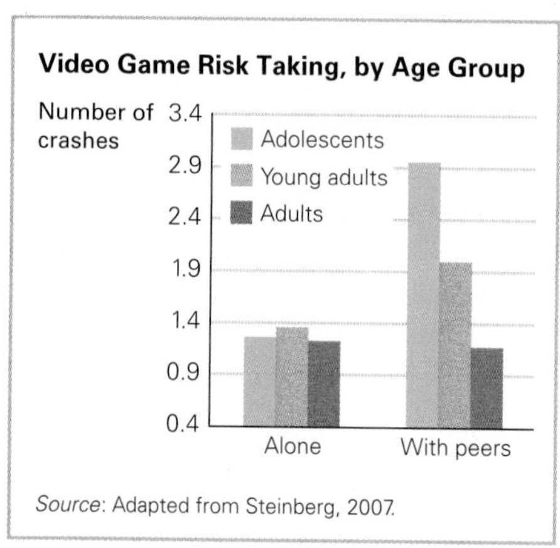

FIGURE 16.1

Admire Me Everyone wants to accumulate points in a game, earn high grades, and save money—*unless* one is a teenager and other teens are watching. Then a desire to obtain peer admiration by taking risks may overtake caution. At least in this game, teenage participants chose to lose points and increase crashes when other teens were present.

The participants were randomly assigned to one of two conditions: playing alone or with two peers (same sex and age group, but not necessarily same ethnic group). When they played alone, adolescents, emerging adults, and adults all averaged one crash per session; one crash was enough to make them wary. Adults were as cautious when playing with peers as they were when playing alone. But for adolescents, playing with peers facilitated their willingness to take a chance: They crashed three times, on average (see Figure 16.1) (Gardner & Steinberg, 2005; Steinberg, 2007).

That was the outcome for all the ethnic groups combined, but an interesting result was found when those who were non-White (about half the sample) were analyzed separately. The adolescents were far more likely to crash when they were with their peers than when they were alone, but the non-White adults were more cautious when with peers than when alone. Boys were more affected by peers than girls were.

Facilitation is usually mutual, not a matter of a rebel leading an innocent astray (B. Brown & Klute, 2003). In the video-driving experiment, each of the triad took 15 trials while the other two watched and waited for their turn. Witnessing a crash did not diminish the willingness to risk (Gardner & Steinberg, 2005).

A teenager from another study explained:

> The idea of peer pressure is a lot of bunk. What I heard about peer pressure all the way through school is that someone is going to walk up to me and say, "Here, drink this and you'll be cool." It wasn't like that at all. You'd go somewhere and everyone else would be doing it and you'd think, "Hey, everyone else is doing it and they seem to be having a good time—now why wouldn't I do this?" In that sense, the preparation of the powers that be, the lessons that they tried to drill into me, they were completely off. They had no idea what we are up against.
>
> *[quoted in Lightfoot, 1997]*

Thus, adolescents both choose and are chosen by their peers. High-functioning adolescents have close friends who themselves are high-achieving, with no major emotional problems. The opposite also holds: Those who are drug users, sexually active, and alienated from school choose compatible friends and provide mutual support to continue on that path (Crosnoe & Needham, 2004).

One other aspect should be mentioned, because it shows why parents tend to blame their child's misbehavior on his or her peers. When adolescents say that they must wear something or go somewhere because "everyone else is doing it," they lighten their responsibility (Ungar, 2000). Peers deflect, and defend against, adult criticism.

➤Response for Parents of a Teenager (from page 423): Remember: Communicate, do not control. Let your child talk about the meaning of the hairstyle. Remind yourself that a hairstyle in itself is harmless. Don't say "What will people think?" or "Are you on drugs?" or anything that might give your child reason to stop communicating.

Friends of Both Sexes

Romance and sexual activity are important to adolescents and will be discussed shortly. But more important than lovers are friends. Adults sometimes worry about boy–girl contact, assuming that teenage children will have sex if adults are not nearby. They also worry about close boy–boy buddies, fearing homosexuality. However, it is not uncommon for teenagers to have close, even passionate, friendships with peers of both the same sex and the opposite sex, with no romantic undertones.

Close relationships help adolescents establish their identity and deal with cliques and crowds. Disruption of friendships can cause jealousy or depression, but this does not suggest anything sexual: Adolescents rely on friends more than on sexual partners. Friendships are likely to last for years, whereas teenage romances are often short-lived (B. L. Barber, 2006; Collins & van Dulmen, 2006; Feiring, 1999; Way & Hamm, 2005).

Immigrant Youth

Friends play a special role for the millions of immigrant adolescents (either those born abroad or those whose parents were born in another nation). This includes one-third of all adolescents in Frankfurt, one-half in Amsterdam, and two-thirds in Los Angeles and New York. Many immigrant children become model youth, earning higher grades and seeming to be better adjusted than those of the same ethnicity whose families are not immigrants (Fuligni, 1998; Rumbaut & Portes, 2001).

Especially for Teachers of Immigrants Your immigrant students' parents never come to open-school nights or answer the written notes you send home. What should you do?

The immigrants' parents and younger siblings depend on them. They help out at home and mediate between the old and new cultures (see Figure 16.2) (Tseng, 2004). Adolescents benefit from this arrangement, in that they gain respect within their families and experience community support, encouragement, and ethnic pride—all of which help them in a hostile environment (Fuligni et al., 2005). Conflict can arise if the parents seek to maintain traditional practices that differ markedly from those of teenage culture (Suarez-Orozco & Suarez-Orozco, 2001).

Adolescents want to respect their parents and fit in with their peers—a sometimes impossible combination. One example is that Western adolescents expect their parents to listen to them, while many immigrant adults expect their children to silently heed their advice (Collins & Steinberg, 2006). Immigrant friends with the same stresses help adolescents negotiate conflicting cultures, traditions, and desires, preventing foreclosure or open rebellion.

For example, Layla's parents were raised in Yemen, but the family now lives near Detroit. At age 15, Layla was sent back to Yemen to marry her father's nephew. She later returned to her Michigan public high school and tried to keep her marriage secret (she wore no ring).

For Layla, her school was "both liberating and a sociocultural threat" (Sarroub, 2001, p. 390). In the United States, the cultural assumption is that adolescents

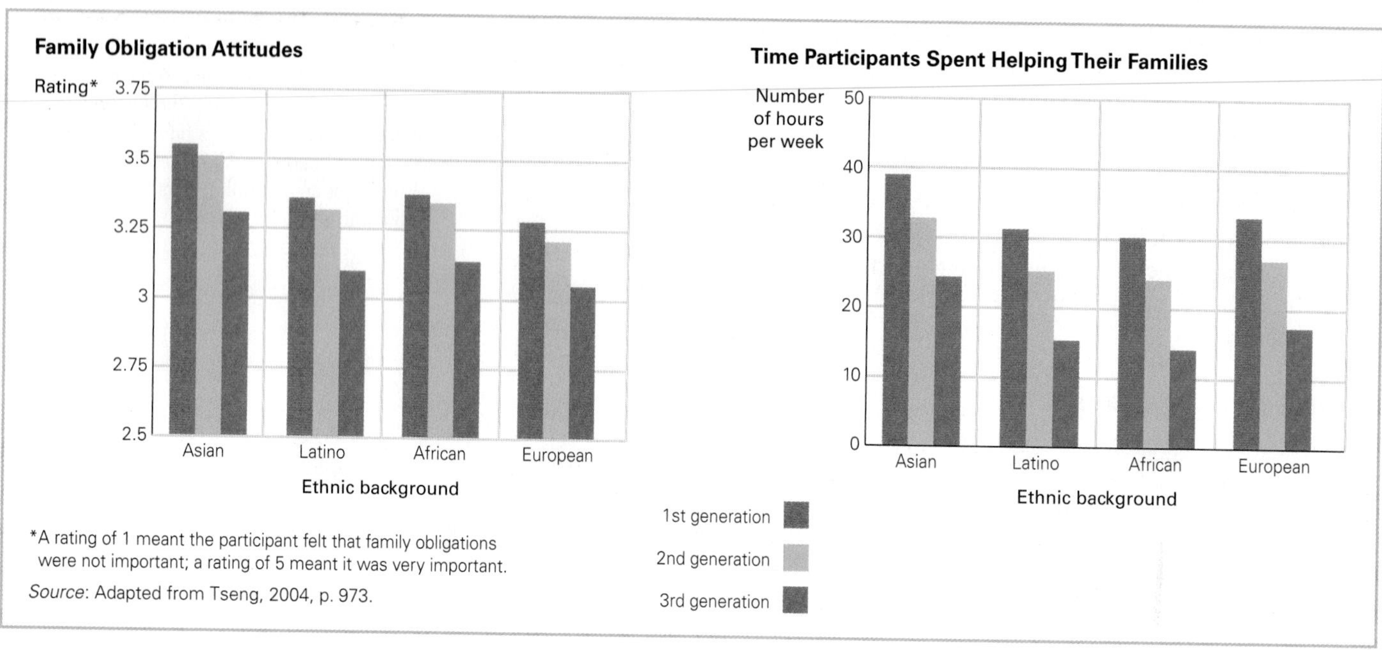

FIGURE 16.2

A Sense of Duty Nearly 1,000 U.S. college students from four ethnic groups were asked how important they thought family obligations were and how much time they spent each week helping their families (by, for example, doing household chores, translating for their parents, taking care of siblings, or working in the family business).

Observation Quiz (see answer, page 428): How many hours a week does the average immigrant college student spend helping out at home?

should speak their minds, dress as they choose, and question adult authority. Gender difficulties made it worse: Equal education for both sexes is built into U.S. law, but "the gender gap in education in Yemen is among the highest in the world, with more than half of the women illiterate" (UNICEF, 2005).

Layla respected her parents and adhered to Islam, but she resisted many aspects of her heritage. For example, she was troubled that her father chewed qaat (a narcotic that is legal in Yemen but illegal in the United States), that he wanted her to wear a long Arab dress (she wore jeans instead), and that he did not agree with her plan to get a divorce and go to college. Layla especially resented Yemeni tradition, which allowed boys more freedom than girls.

> At times Layla was confused and unhappy at home. She . . . preferred going to school where she could be with her Yemeni friends who understood her problems and with whom she could talk. "They make me feel, like, really happy. I have friends that have to deal with the same issues." . . . Layla was often angry that girls in Yemen were taken out of school. . . . She thought that the boys had been given too much freedom, much more than the girls.
>
> *[Sarroub, 2001, pp. 408–409]*

Friends may be particularly important when it comes to protecting the self-esteem of immigrant youth from Asian backgrounds, who seem to suffer from lower self-esteem than their European American or African American counterparts as well as to experience more discrimination from other adolescents (Greene & Way, 2005; Greene et al., 2006). They are also more involved with their families, as Figure 16.2 shows.

For many teenagers, immigrants and nonimmigrants alike, peers become "like family," "brothers and sisters" (Way et al., 2005). In violent neighborhoods, friends not only defend against attacks but also help each other avoid physical fights. One 16-year-old boy said about his friend:

> Well, with him when I'm in an argument with somebody that disrespected me and he just comes out and backs me up and says "Yo, Chris, don't deal with that. Yo, let's just go on," you know, 'cause I could snap.
>
> *[quoted in Way et al., 2005, p. 48]*

To "snap" is a potential danger for all adolescents, given their quick reactions of intuitive thought. Having friends who say, "Don't deal with that" can help calm them and protect them from self-destruction.

SUMMING UP

Relationships with peers of both sexes as well as adults are crucial during adolescence. Parents and adolescents often bicker over small things, but parental monitoring and ongoing communication are helpful to adolescent psychosocial health. Parental neglect or excessive parental control can foster adolescent rebellion.

Peers aid adolescents in their search for self-esteem and maturity. Some peer groups encourage self-destructive, antisocial behavior, but most help teenagers to cope with the biological, social, and emotional stresses of this period. Friends, cliques, and crowds are chosen by adolescents and vice versa: Selection and facilitation explain how adolescents influence each other. For all teenagers, friends of both sexes are important. Immigrant adolescents are particularly influenced by their friends, as they try to make a place for themselves and succeed in cultures unlike those that guided their parents. ■

➤Response for Teachers of Immigrants (from page 425): Perhaps the parents cannot read English, or work or family obligations may prevent them from coming to school in the evening. You might ask your student to set up a home visit for you at a suitable time for the parents. Then go to praise their child more than criticize.

Sexuality

No arena highlights the overlapping influences of parents, peers, and the wider community more clearly than sexuality. Human nature endows adolescents with strong sexual impulses. Adults then direct those impulses toward frightening dreams, pleasurable fantasies, stolen glances, sexual arousal, or early pregnancy.

Before Committed Partnership

Decades ago, Dexter Dunphy (1963) described the sequence of male–female relationships during childhood and adolescence:

1. Groups of friends, exclusively one sex or the other
2. A loose association of girls and boys, with public interactions within a crowd
3. Small mixed-sex groups of the advanced members of the crowd
4. Formation of couples, with private intimacies

Culture affects timing and manifestations, but subsequent research in many nations still finds the same sequence. Youth in many lands, and even of many species, exclude the other sex in childhood and are attracted to them by adulthood, which suggests that biology is at work more so than culture (B. Brown, 2004; Connolly et al., 2000; Weisfeld, 1999).

In modern developed nations, where puberty begins at about age 10 and marriage does not usually occur until much later, each of these four stages typically lasts several years. Same-sex groups dominate in elementary school and often continue through middle and high school in cliques or sports teams, when groups of same-sex friends talk about the other sex but spend little time in one-on-one private interaction. Early, exclusive romances are often a sign of social trouble, not maturity (B. Brown, 2004).

Romances

The first romances appear in high school, rarely lasting more than a year, with girls more likely to say they have a steady boyfriend than vice versa. Committed couples form later. While romantic partners can often provide emotional support,

© DONNA RANIERI / BLINKSTOCK

©RICHARD LORD / THE IMAGE WORKS

The Same Event, A Thousand Miles Apart: Teenagers in Love No matter where in the world they are, teenage couples broadcast their love in universally recognized facial expressions and body positions. Samantha and Ryan *(top)*, visiting New York City from suburban Philadelphia, are similar in many ways to the teen couple *(bottom)* in Chicute, Mozambique, even though their social contexts are dramatically different.

teenage romances are more about companionship than physical intimacy (Furman et al., 2007).

Breakups are common; so are unreciprocated crushes. Both can be emotionally devastating, in part because often entire high school crowds ("the smallest of small towns") are witnesses (Schwartz, 2006). It is not unusual for a teenager in love to find it difficult to sleep, study, or even eat. Adolescents are then devastated by rejection, often contemplating revenge or suicide (Fisher, 2006). At this point, peer support can be a lifesaver.

Overall, healthy romances are one manifestation of a life replete with good relationships with parents and peers (Laursen & Mooney, 2007). That triple support network means that a fight with a parent, a slight from a peer, or the breakup of a romance can be taken in stride because the other two arenas of social support provide comfort and reassurance.

Homosexual Youth

For homosexual adolescents, complications slow down the formation of friendship and romantic bonds. To begin with, many do not acknowledge their sexual orientation, sometimes not even to themselves. It may be that having a defined orientation, either homosexual or heterosexual, is less important among today's youth than it was when Erikson wrote about sexual identity half a century ago (Savin-Williams, 2005).

In one confidential study of more than 3,000 ninth- to twelfth-grade teenagers, only 0.5 percent identified themselves as gay or lesbian (Garofalo et al., 1999), far fewer than the 1 to 7 percent (varying by culture and gender) of adults who so identify (Savin-Williams, 2006). Retrospectively, many homosexual men report that they became aware of their sexual interests at about age 11 but told no one until age 17 (Maguen et al., 2002). Past cohorts of gay youth had higher rates of clinical depression, drug abuse, and even suicide than their heterosexual peers; it is not known if the current cohort has avoided these problems (Savin-Williams & Diamond, 2004).

Most girls who later identify as lesbian are oblivious to, or in denial of, their sexual urges in adolescence, partly because sexual self-knowledge may be more difficult for girls (Baumeister & Blackhart, 2007). Unlike gay men, many lesbians first recognize their sexuality in emerging adulthood via a close friendship that becomes romantic (Savin-Williams & Diamond, 2004).

Cultural expectations add to the complications. For example, in many Latino cultures, "adolescents who pursue same-sex sexuality are viewed by their communities as having fundamentally failed as men or women" (Diamond & Savin-Williams, 2003, p. 399). Many gay youth of every ethnicity date members of the other sex to hide their true orientation (Brown, 2006).

About 10 percent of heterosexual adults report that they had same-sex encounters or desires as adolescents (Laumann et al., 1994). It is not known whether such inclinations are part of normal sexual awakening for most adolescents (only a fraction of whom report it) or whether many bisexual teenagers become exclusively heterosexual later on.

In the Add Health study, of those few who reported *exclusive* same-sex attraction at the first data collection, only 11 percent reported exclusive same-sex attraction a year later. Most had changed to exclusively other-sex attraction, and one-third reported no sexual attraction at all (Udry & Chantala, 2005).

Eleanor Maccoby (1998), an expert on gender, finds that "a substantial number of people experiment with same-sex sexuality at some point in their lives, and a small minority settle into a life-long pattern of homosexuality" (p. 191). Sexual

➤Answer to Observation Quiz (from page 426): The average for all three groups of Asians is about 33 hours.

experimentation is common in adolescence, but no one knows how many constitute that "substantial number" who "experiment with same-sex sexuality."

Much remains to be discovered about friendship, romance, and sexuality during adolescence (Brown, 2006). Research ethics require parental permission before questions are asked of anyone younger than 18, and many parents refuse to let strangers ask their children about sex.

Learning About Sex

Historically, intense romantic attachments in adolescence were often considered a threat to normal development because they disrupted traditional bonding (Coontz, 2006). Arranged childhood marriages (often to uncles or cousins), monasteries, no-fault divorces, chastity belts, shotgun weddings, polygamy—each of these has been considered normal in some cultures and barbaric in others.

Today, parents and societies continue to be concerned about adolescent sexual relationships, with education (accurate or not, via schools or the media) being the most commonly used method to control adolescent sexuality. As is probably apparent to every reader, current messages about teenage sexuality are contradictory. Consistent and reliable guidance is scarce.

One example is oral sex, which parents and teachers rarely discuss. The lack of information leads many adolescents to conclude that it is "safe," a dangerously egocentric notion (Kalmuss et al., 2003). Another example is AIDS. Worldwide, less than half of teenagers understand how AIDS is transmitted. In South Africa, 5.5 million adults (19 percent of the population, mostly young adults) are HIV-positive—the highest number in the world (UNAIDS, 2006). One reason is that, until 2003, the government spread misinformation about AIDS.

The opposite may be true in the United States, where young adolescents overestimate the risk of AIDS because adults use fear of AIDS to keep adolescents from engaging in sex (Reyna & Farley, 2006). Fortunately, throughout the world AIDS is much better understood than it was a decade ago. Every continent has at least one nation where transmission rates are down (UNAIDS, 2006).

Peers

Adolescent sexual behavior is strongly influenced by the example of other adolescents. Many teens discuss details of romance and sex with other members of their clique, expecting their sexual behavior to gain them approval from their friends (Laursen & Mooney, 2007). Often, the boys brag and the girls worry about gaining a "reputation." Specifics depend on the peers: All members of a clique may be virgins, or all may be sexually active.

Among contemporary U.S. teens, some church-based crowds take a "virginity pledge," vowing to postpone sexual intercourse. If the group considers itself a select minority and virginity is one of its distinguishing features, then that becomes significant for all group members (Bearman & Brückner, 2001). When crowds disperse at high school graduation, members who had taken the pledge are more likely to marry and less likely to use contraception than are other adolescents. As a result, many become parents at a relatively early age but fewer become single parents (Johnson & Rector, 2004).

Sexual interaction is also strongly influenced by whether or not an adolescent is in an ongoing romantic relationship. Probably for this reason, adolescents who are early to experience puberty and who are physically attractive are also likely to be sexually experienced.

Parents

Parents play a pivotal role in teenagers' sexual decisions, via monitoring, modeling, and conversation. Children who discuss sex with their parents take fewer risks, avoid pressure to have sex, and think that their parents provide good information (Blake et al., 2001; Jaccard et al., 2002; B. C. Miller et al., 2001).

Especially for Young Adults Suppose your parents never talked to you about sex or puberty. Was that a mistake?

However, honest discussions are uncommon. In one study, mothers were asked whether their teens had had sex (Jaccard et al., 1998). Then the teens were asked the same question, in confidence. The difference between the two sets of replies was astounding (see Figure 16.3). For instance, more than one-third of the 14-year-olds were sexually active, but only about one-third (13 percent of 35 percent) of the mothers of those sexually active teens knew it.

Most mothers (72 percent) reported that they had talked with their teens about sex, but only 45 percent of the teens agreed (Jaccard et al., 1998). Thus, 27 percent of mother–child pairs did not agree about whether the topic had ever been discussed—a gap that remained when this study was replicated (Jaccard et al., 2000).

Parents also overestimate how much their children believe their advice. One study concludes that "parent perceptions of how much credibility, trust, and accessibility they think they have established with their adolescents bear only a weak relationship to adolescent characterizations of parent credibility, trust, and accessibility" (Guilamo-Ramos et al., 2006, p. 1242).

Religious parents are more hesitant to talk about sex (except to warn their teens against it) (Regnerus, 2005), but religion is *not* the most significant correlate of whether parent–child conversations occur; gender and age are. Parents are more likely to talk to daughters than to sons and to older adolescents (over 15) than younger ones. This is not good news, since young adolescent boys are most likely to heed, and need, advice about safe sex (Kirby, 2001).

One problem is that parents underestimate adolescents' capacity to engage in responsible sex. For example, another study found that only 23 percent of mothers and 33 percent of fathers thought that most teenagers were capable of using

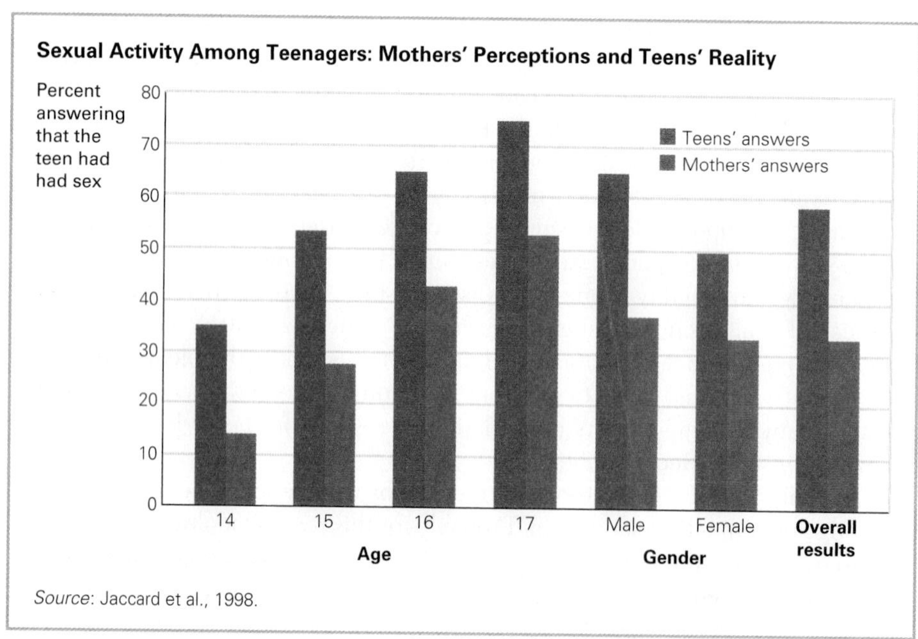

FIGURE 16.3

Mother Doesn't Always Know This graph shows the discrepancy between the answers mothers gave to the question "Is your child sexually active?" and the answers teenagers gave when asked for the truth. Notice which age group and gender had the largest gaps—younger teens and boys!

a condom correctly (M. E. Eisenberg et al., 2004). Parental example may be as important as conversations: Adolescents who live with both biological parents are less than half as likely to begin a sexual relationship as are those who don't (Blum et al., 2000; Ellis et al., 2003).

Sex Education in School

Almost all parents want other adults to provide up-to-date sex education (including information on safe sex and contraception) for adolescents (Landry et al., 2003; Yarber et al., 2005), partly because parents realize that methods and diseases have changed since they were teenagers. Developmentalists agree that sex education belongs in the schools, as well as in parent–child conversations, since adolescents need to learn from trusted and experienced adults before they misinform each other.

The United States began a massive experiment in 1998, spending about a billion dollars over 10 years to promote *abstinence-only* sex education. The goal was to teach adolescents to wait until marriage before becoming sexually active. These programs emphasized the need for younger teens to feel confident in themselves, able to say no to sex. No information about nonabstinent ways to prevent STIs or pregnancy was provided because it was feared that such information might encourage sexual activity.

Fortunately, funding included longitudinal evaluation (four to six years after the start of the curriculum) using sound scientific methodology. Unfortunately, however, the special curriculum had little effect. About half of students in both the experimental and control groups had sex by age 16. The number of partners and use of contraceptives was the same with or without the special curriculum (Trenholm et al., 2007; see Research Design). The comparison groups knew slightly more about preventing disease or pregnancy, but this did not affect behavior.

Although adults often disagree about what children should be taught, no curriculum to date has dramatically affected age of sexual activity. The best programs start before high school, include assignments that require parent–child communication, focus on behavior and not just information, and last for years (Kirby, 2002; Weaver et al., 2006). Even so, whether or not an adolescent follows the urge to become sexually active depends more on family, peers, and culture than on classes. Sex education can, however, affect some of the specifics of that activity. For example, in a Texas program, half of the ninth-graders—the experimental group—received a two-year curriculum stressing safe sex as well as abstinence (Coyle et al., 2001). Teachers involved parents and provided medical referrals for students who asked for them (both highly recommended practices).

Three years later, a survey found that students in both groups began intercourse at the same age (Coyle et al., 2001). The one benefit was that those in the experimental group had sex less often and used condoms more often than those in the comparison group. The researchers wonder if the program started too late: One-fourth of the ninth-graders had already had sex.

Most European schools teach about sexual responsibility, masturbation, and oral and anal sex—subjects that are rarely covered in U.S. sex-education programs. Rates of teenage pregnancy in most European nations are less than half those in the United States. School curriculum is only one of many possible reasons.

Worldwide, both genders need sex education, as is widely recognized in North America and Europe but not in many developing nations. Some parents still use a double standard, warning their daughters of sexual dangers while encouraging experimentation by their sons (UNAIDS, 2006). This is no longer usual in the United States, as demonstrated by one ninth-grade boy who said:

Research Design

Scientists: Christopher Trenholm, Barbara Devaney, Ken Fortson, Lisa Quay, Justin Wheeler, and Melissa Clark.

Publication: Report to the U.S. Department of Health and Human Services by the Mathematica Policy Research (2007).

Participants: Students in Powhatan, Virginia; Milwaukee, Wisconsin; Miami, Florida; and Clarksdale, Mississippi, were randomly assigned to be enrolled in the abstinence-only classes or not. Both groups were large enough to allow valid comparisons (1,209 in the experimental groups, 848 in the control groups).

Design: All four cities' programs were intense (more than 50 contact hours) and all began early (between ages 10 and 12). Significant differences among the four regions allowed the scientists to discover whether one version of abstinence-only education was more effective than the other and whether one population (for example, two were rural and two were urban) responded better than another. Four to six years after the programs began, students (then age 16, on average) were asked about their knowledge and behavior.

Major conclusion: No matter what the programs were, the abstinence-only curriculum had no impact on sexual experience (51 percent of both groups had had intercourse, on average at age 14) and virtually no impact on other aspects of behavior. For example, some adults thought that abstinence-only students would not use condoms, but condom use was equal in both groups (only 9 percent of those who were sexually active never used a condom).

Comment: Neither the best hopes nor the worst fears about abstinence-only programs were confirmed. This report encourages researchers to evaluate efforts to change adolescent behavior, and its findings were one reason Congress stopped funding abstinence-only programs in 2007.

> I do look forward to it, if it's with a good girl, a good person. I'm going to make sure to wear protection, make sure she doesn't have a disease, make sure we know what to do if the protection doesn't work. Make sure we know the consequences of it, make sure she would know the consequences of what would happen if not everything went right.
>
> *[quoted in Michels et al., 2005, p. 594]*

His five "make sures" illustrate the benefits of education and analytic thinking. Will he still think the same way a few years from now?

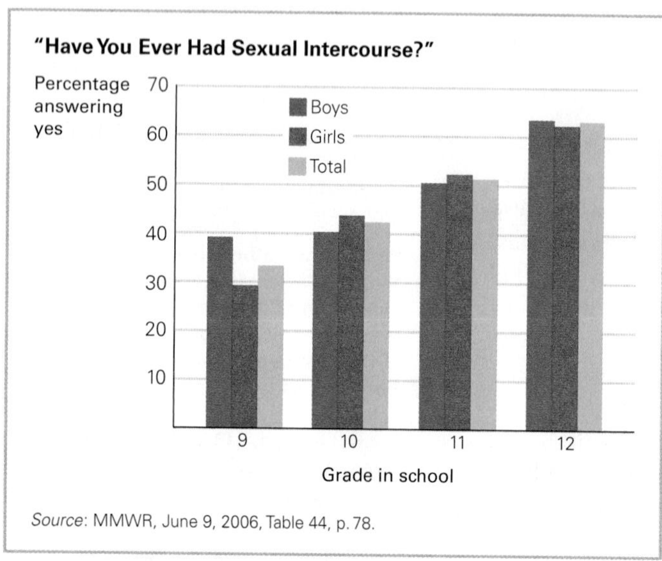

FIGURE 16.4

Is Everybody Doing It? No. About one-third of high school seniors and 53 percent of all students in grades 9 through 12, both boys and girls, are still virgins. The data for this graph are from the Youth Risk Behavior Survey, a national survey that asks the same questions of thousands of U.S. students in the ninth through twelfth grades each year. In 2005, 14,000 students in 159 public and private schools in 44 states were surveyed. Some other U.S. surveys find higher rates (these percentages do not include high school dropouts, who are more often sexually active than adolescents who stay in school), but the scope and annual repetition of this survey make trends apparent.

Observation Quiz (see answer, page 436): How do boys' and girls' rates of sexual activity compare?

Especially for an Adult Friend of a Teenager If your 14-year-old friend asks you where to get "the pill," what do you say?

Sexual Behavior

Not all teenagers are having sex. Rates vary from nation to nation; almost no teenagers are sexually active in some places, almost all in others. In the United States in 2005, about half of all teenagers had sexual intercourse by age 16 (or the eleventh grade), which is a little bit later than a decade earlier (see Figure 16.4).

Norms vary markedly within each nation. In the U.S. Youth Risk Behavior Survey of high school students, three-fourths of the boys in Baltimore said they had had intercourse, but less than one-third of San Francisco girls said they had (MMWR, June 9, 2006).

Teenage sex troubles many adults who married before having sex because they wanted to avoid unwed pregnancy, which often led to abortion, adoption, or unplanned weddings. In 1960, only 13 percent of all teenage mothers in the United States were unmarried, compared with 81 percent in 2003 (U.S. Bureau of the Census, 1972, 2006). Note, however, that these data refer to *unwed* motherhood. Other statistics are encouraging:

- *Teen births overall have decreased dramatically in every nation.* For example, between 1960 and 2005, the adolescent birth rate in China was cut in half (reducing the world's population by about a billion by 2007) and the U.S. teen birth rate was reduced by a third. This decline is continuing in every ethnic group and nation. For instance, in 1990, 5.7 percent of all Asian American births were to teenagers; in 2004 only 3.4 percent were—a 40 percent reduction.
- *The use of "protection" has increased.* Contraception, particularly condom use among adolescent boys, has doubled in most nations since 1990. The U.S. Youth Risk Behavior survey found that 77 percent of sexually active ninth-grade boys used a condom during their most recent intercourse (MMWR, June 9, 2006). About 20 percent of U.S. teenage couples now use the pill *and* condoms, preventing both pregnancy and infection (Manlove et al., 2003).
- *The teen abortion rate is also down.* In the United States, only half as many teenagers had abortions in 2003 as in 1973 (MMWR, November 24, 2006). The teen abortion rate continues to decline, even though the adult rate has been rising since 2000.

These facts lead to one hopeful conclusion: Although bodies and hormones have changed little in recent decades, teenage responses to biological drives have changed dramatically. Public policy and social norms affect decisions that seem to be personal and private (Teitler, 2002).

For developmentalists in the United States, there remains one troubling set of statistics. Proportionately speaking, teenage girls in the United States have far more births than do their peers in any other developed nation (eight times the rate in Japan, twice the rate in Canada and Great Britain). The reason is not because they are having more sex but because they use less contraception.

SUMMING UP

Adolescents have always been interested in sex, and societies have always attempted to control sexual expression. Given the earlier onset of puberty and later marriages, adolescents are especially needful of accurate information and guidance. Parents, peers, and schools sometimes provide this information, not always teaching adolescents what they need to know. Parents are influential role models. However, many are slow to talk with their children about sex. Schools can teach adolescents, but sex education needs to begin before students become sexually active. About half of all U.S. adolescents have experienced intercourse by age 16, a rate that has not increased over the past decade. The data show a shift in adolescent sexual behavior, including fewer births and more contraception. ■

➤Response for Young Adults (from page 430): Yes, but maybe you should forgive them. Ideally, parents should talk to their children about sex, presenting honest information and listening to the child's concerns. However, many parents find it very difficult to do this because they feel embarrassed and ignorant. Try bringing up the subject now; your parents may feel more comfortable discussing it with a young adult than with a child or adolescent.

Sadness and Anger

Adolescence is usually a wonderful time, perhaps better for current generations than ever before. As you have read, identity achievement is less rushed; parents and friends are usually helpful; pregnancy and marriage are less common than before. More teenagers are in school, fewer are malnourished, almost none die of disease. The editor of the leading academic journal on adolescence considers this period more joyful than problematic (Brown, 2005).

Nonetheless, for a troubled few, serious problems plague development. Most problems are **comorbid,** which means that two or more disorders ("morbidities," in medical jargon) coexist in the same person. An angry adolescent who is, say, unusually aggressive is also at higher risk of dropping out of school, being arrested, and dying accidentally. A sad teenager who uses illegal drugs before age 15 is also more vulnerable to depression, unwanted pregnancy, and suicide.

comorbidity A situation in which two or more unrelated illnesses or disorders occur at the same time.

Distinguishing between normal moodiness and pathological problems is complex. Some emotional reactions are quite normal: Many adolescents are less happy and angrier than they were as children. For a few, however, emotions become extreme, pathological, even deadly, if they are not noticed and ameliorated.

Depression

The general emotional trend from late childhood through adolescence is toward less confidence. A dip at puberty is found in every study, although many studies find that African Americans tend to be higher overall self-esteem and Asian Americans lower. Some studies find a rise in self-esteem over the years of secondary school and college, while others do not (Fredricks & Eccles, 2002; Greene & Way, 2005; Harter, 1999). Data from one cross-sequential study, shown in Figure 16.5, indicated that boys start out more confident than girls but decline faster as they grow older. It is a myth that only girls, not boys, lose confidence at puberty (Barnett & Rivers, 2004).

There are sex differences in morbidity, however, with girls much more likely to be seriously depressed than boys. For some adolescents, the sobering self-awareness that is typical in adolescence leads to **clinical depression,** an overwhelming feeling of sadness and hopelessness that disrupts all normal, regular activities.

clinical depression Feelings of hopelessness, lethargy, and worthlessness that last two weeks or more.

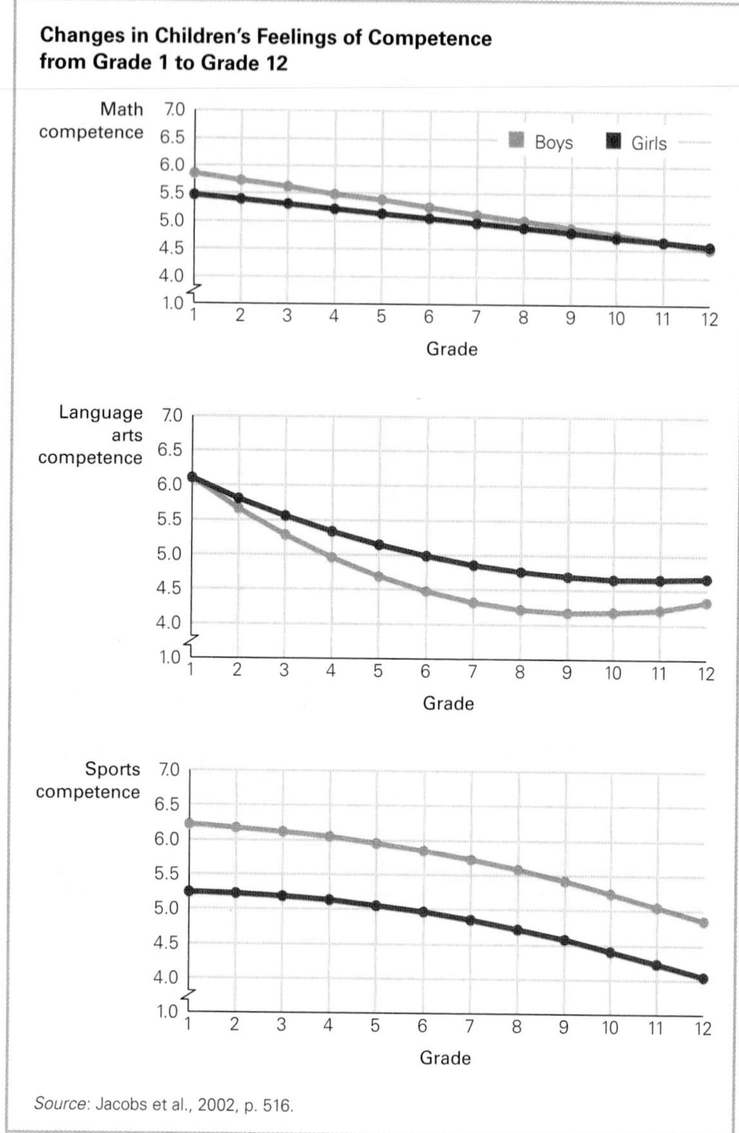

FIGURE 16.5

All the Children Are Above Average U.S. children, both boys and girls, feel less and less competent in math, language arts, and sports as they move through grades 1–12. Their scores on tests of feelings of competence could range from 1 to 7, and the fact that the twelfth-grade average was between 4 and 5 indicates that, overall, teenagers still consider themselves above average.

The causes of depression include genetic vulnerability and a depressed mother who was the adolescent's primary caregiver in infancy (Cicchietti & Toth, 1998; Murray et al., 2006). These conditions predate adolescence, but something happens at puberty to push many vulnerable children into despair. The rate of clinical depression more than doubles during this time, to an estimated 15 percent, affecting about 1 in 5 teenage girls and 1 in 10 teenage boys (Graber, 2004).

It is not known whether the reasons for the gender differences are primarily biological, psychological, or social (Alloy & Abramson, 2007; Ge et al., 2001; Graber, 2004; Hankin & Abramson, 2001). Obviously, girls experience different hormones, but they are also subject to gender-specific pressures from families, peers, and cultures. Recently, a cognitive explanation has been suggested for girls' higher rates of depression. **Rumination**—talking about, remembering, and mentally replaying past experiences—is more common among females than males. When the incident replayed is unpleasant, rumination can lead to depression (Alloy et al., 2003). Rumination may make girls sadder, but it also may protect them from lonely, impulsive actions, as we will now see.

Suicide

Teenagers are just beginning to explore life. When trouble comes (failing a class, ending a romance, fighting with a parent), they don't always know that better days lie ahead. As you have just read, this kind of stress can lead to depression and, in more extreme cases, thoughts of suicide. **Suicidal ideation**—that is, "serious, distressing thoughts about killing oneself"—peaks at about age 15 (Rueter & Kwon, 2005).

Suicidal ideation is so common that it could be considered a normal part of adolescence. One study revealed that, for two weeks or more in the past 12 months, more than one-third (37 percent) of U.S. high school girls felt so hopeless that they stopped doing some of their usual activities and more than one-fifth (22 percent) seriously thought about suicide. The corresponding rates for boys are 20 percent and 12 percent (MMWR, June 9, 2006).

Suicidal ideation is common; completed suicides are not. Adolescents are actually *less* likely to kill themselves than adults are. Many people mistakenly think suicide is more frequent in adolescence for four reasons:

- The rate, low as it is, is much higher than it once was (see Figure 16.6).
- Statistics on "youth" often include emerging adults, whose suicide rates are higher.
- Adolescent suicides are more likely to capture media attention than adult suicides are.
- Suicide *attempts* (parasuicide) are probably more common between the ages of 15 and 20.

Instead of *attempted suicide* or *failed suicide,* experts prefer the term **parasuicide,** defined as any potentially lethal action against the self that does not result

rumination Repeatedly thinking and talking about past experiences; can contribute to depression.

suicidal ideation Thinking about suicide, usually with some serious emotional and intellectual or cognitive overtones.

parasuicide Any potentially lethal action against the self that does not result in death.

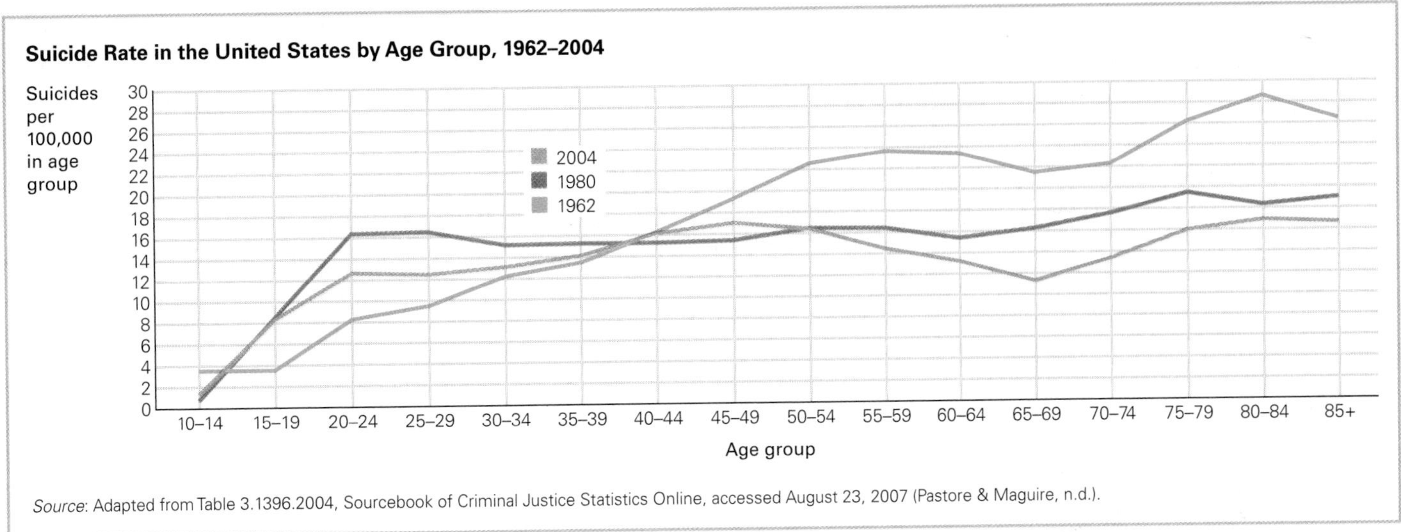

Source: Adapted from Table 3.1396.2004, Sourcebook of Criminal Justice Statistics Online, accessed August 23, 2007 (Pastore & Maguire, n.d.).

FIGURE 16.6

Much Depends on Age A historical look at U.S. suicide statistics reveals two trends, both of which were still apparent in 2004. First, older teenagers today are two times more likely to take their own lives than in 1960, but less likely than in 1980. Second, suicide rates overall are down, but they continue to be highest among elderly people age 75 and older.

Observation Quiz (see answer, page 437): In a typical cross-section of 1,000 U.S. 15- to 19-year-olds, how many committed suicide in 2004?

in death. Adolescent emotions and confusion typically disguise intent, even to the individuals themselves, which makes a distinction between attempted and completed suicide inaccurate. *Parasuicide* is thus a more accurate term. After a potentially lethal episode, many adolescents feel relieved that they survived.

International rates of teenage parasuicide fall between 6 and 20 percent, a range reflecting cultural differences in frequency and in data collection. Here is a specific one: Among eleventh-graders in U.S. high schools during the year 2005, 11 percent of the girls and 4.5 percent of the boys said they had tried to kill themselves (see Table 16.1). The rate of completed suicide for ages 15 to 19 in the United States that year was only 4 per 100,000, which is 0.004 percent (see Table 16.2). Where ideation leads depends on four factors (Berman et al., 2006; Goldsmith et al., 2002):

- Availability of guns
- Parental supervision
- Availability of alcohol and other drugs
- Culture

TABLE 16.1

Suicidal Ideation and Parasuicide Among U.S. High School Students, 2005

		Seriously Considered Attempting Suicide	Parasuicide (Attempted Suicide)	Parasuicide Requiring Medical Attention	Actual Suicide (ages 15–19)
Overall		**16.9%**	**8.5%**	**2.3%**	Less than 0.01% (about 7 per 100,000)
Girls:	9th grade	23.9	14.1	4.0	
	10th grade	23.0	10.8	2.4	Girls: About 2 per 100,000
	11th grade	21.6	11.0	2.9	
	12th grade	18.0	6.5	2.2	
Boys:	9th grade	12.2	6.8	2.1	
	10th grade	11.9	7.6	2.2	Boys: About 11 per 100,000
	11th grade	11.9	4.5	1.4	
	12th grade	11.6	4.3	1.0	

Source: MMWR, Youth Risk Behavior Survey, June 9, 2006.

TABLE 16.2

U.S. Suicide Rates of 15- to 19-Year-Olds by Ethnic Group, 2004

	Males (rate per 100,000)	Females (rate per 100,000)	Females as Percent of Total
American Indian and Alaskan Native	22.7	9.1	25%
European American	13.4	2.6	16%
Hispanic American	9.1	2.0	20%
African American	6.9	2.3	13%
Asian American	5.7	3.3	29%

Source: Anderson & Smith, 2005.

The first three factors suggest why youth suicide in North America and Europe has doubled since 1960: Adolescents have more access to guns, alcohol, and drugs and have less adult supervision than they once did. Culture also has an effect: Rates are higher in eastern Europe than in western Europe, in the southwestern than the southeastern United States, on the continent of Africa than the continent of South America. For all these differences, culture is a plausible explanation.

Suicide rates show definite ethnic and gender differences as well, perhaps for cultural reasons (Berman et al., 2006; Tatz, 2001). Here are some examples.

Gender is the most dramatic and universal factor influencing suicide. Although depression and parasuicide are more common among females, completed suicide is more common among males (except in China). One reason is that men tend to shoot themselves (usually an instantly lethal method) rather than overdose (which allows time for intervention) (Gould, 2003). Boys tend to have greater access to guns. For example, in California seven times as many boys aged 12 to 17 own guns than girls (Sorenson & Vittes, 2004).

cluster suicides Several suicides committed by members of a group within a brief period of time.

Adolescents are particularly influenced by media reports and therefore are susceptible to **cluster suicides,** which are several suicides within a group over a few months. If a student's "tragic end" is sentimentalized, it may elicit suicidal ideation, parasuicides, and completed suicides among that student's schoolmates (Joiner, 1999). Adolescent cluster suicides seem particularly prevalent among students who identify with a subgroup, such as members of an Indian tribe (Beauvais, 2000). Overall, if one teenager commits suicide, special care must be taken to prevent his or her acquaintances from following that example.

Socioeconomic groups also share subcultures. Wealth and education decrease the risk of many adolescent disorders, but not suicide—quite the opposite, in fact. The reason may be related to cluster suicides and news reports, which typically highlight the potential of the deceased young person in headlines (e.g., "Honor Student Kills Self"). Such media coverage may lead other honor students to think about suicide.

➤**Answer to Observation Quiz** (from page 432): Girls tend to become sexually active a little later than boys, but by the eleventh grade, almost equal percentages of the two sexes have had sexual intercourse.

Since 1990, rates of adolescent suicide have fallen, perhaps because of more effective use of antidepressants (Gould, 2003). A British study suggested that such drugs increase suicidal ideation (not suicide), but recent analysis of 27 controlled clinical trials (similar to experiments, only with participants who have a particular illness or disorder) found that antidepressants far more often help young people who are depressed or anxious than increase suicidal ideation (Bridge et al., 2007). In one study of 439 depressed 12- to 17-year-olds, the best outcome was for those who received *both* cognitive-behavioral therapy and medication (March et al., 2004).

➤**Response for an Adult Friend of a Teenager** (from page 432): Practical advice is important: Steer your friend to a reputable medical center that provides counseling for adolescents about various methods of avoiding pregnancy (including abstinence). You don't want your friend using ineffective or harmful contraception or becoming sexually active before he or she is ready. Try to respond to the emotions behind the question, perhaps addressing the ethics and values involved in sexual activity. Remember that adolescents do not always do the things they talk about, nor are they always logical; but they can analyze alternatives and assess consequences if adults lead them in that direction.

When adolescent suicides are reported by age, gender, and ethnicity, statistics from the past two decades find one group that does not follow the general trend of fewer deaths. African American males aged 15 to 19 are more likely to kill themselves now than they were 20 years ago, although their rates remain below those of American boys of European descent. Many cultural hypotheses have been offered, including fewer employment opportunities, more guns, and a reluctance to ask for help, especially if it means treatment for mental illness (Joe, 2003).

For all groups, the data show that intervention and treatment reduce the occurrence of suicide if the warning signs are heeded (Aseltine & DeMartino, 2004). Consider the following case.

a case to study

He Kept His Worries to Himself

Bill is 17, a senior in high school. A good student, hard working, some would say "driven," Bill has achieved well and is hoping to go to either Harvard or Stanford next year. He is also hopeful that his college career will lead him to medical school and a career as a surgeon like his father. Bill is a tall, handsome boy, attractive to girls but surprisingly shy among them. When he socializes, he prefers to hang out in groups rather than date; in these groups, he is likely to be seen deep in introspective discussion with one girl or another. Introspection has no place on the school football team, where this past season Bill led all receivers in pass catches. Nor does he appear at all the quiet type in his new sports car, a gift from his parents on his 17th birthday. The elder of two sons, Bill has always been close to his parents, and a "good son." Perhaps for these reasons, he has been increasingly preoccupied as verbalized threats of separation and divorce become common in his parents' increasingly frequent conflicts. These worries he has kept largely to himself.

[Berman et al., 2006, pp. 43–44]

If you were Bill's friend, would you find help for him? Unfortunately, Bill had no close friends. Even his parents did not realize he was troubled until "Bill's body was brought to the local medical examiner's office; he put his father's .22-caliber handgun to his head and ended his life in an instant" (Berman et al., 2006, p. 44).

In retrospect, there had been warning signs—no friends, male or female; his parents' conflicts; his foreclosure on his father's profession; his drive for perfection (Harvard or Stanford, football star); no older siblings to help him. Does the gift of a sports car signify that his parents had ignored his emotional needs? Might he have been worried about his sexuality, fearing rejection? Why was his father's gun loaded and accessible? The report does not mention any postmortem testing for alcohol or other drugs, a notable omission. Denial may still be a problem, even after death.

More Destructiveness

Like low self-esteem and suicidal ideation, bouts of anger are common in adolescence. Many adolescents slam doors, defy parents, and tell friends exactly how badly other teenagers (or siblings or teachers) have behaved. Some teenagers "act out," becoming destructive, particularly if they are boys. They steal, damage property, or injure others.

Is such behavior normal? Most developmentalists who agree with psychoanalytic theory (see Chapter 2) answer yes. A leading advocate of this view was Anna Freud (Sigmund's daughter, herself a prominent psychoanalyst), who wrote that adolescent resistance to parental authority was "welcome . . . beneficial . . . inevitable." She explained:

> We all know individual children who, as late as the ages of fourteen, fifteen or sixteen, show no such outer evidence of inner unrest. They remain, as they have been during the latency period, "good" children, wrapped up in their family relationships, considerate sons of their mothers, submissive to their fathers, in accord with the atmosphere, idea and ideal of their childhood background. Convenient as this may be, it signifies a delay of their normal development and is, as such, a sign to be taken seriously.
>
> *[A. Freud, 1958/2000, p. 263]*

Contrary to Freud, many psychologists, most teachers, and almost all parents are quite happy with well-behaved, considerate teenagers. For them, a "good" child is not a serious sign at all. Which view is valid? Both. Adolescents vary, and understanding that variation is crucial to helping them cope with emotional stresses.

Some teenagers never become destructive. Their good behavior does not predict a later explosion or breakdown. In fact, according to a 30-year longitudinal study from Dunedin, New Zealand, by age 26 men who had never been delinquent usually had college degrees, "held high-status jobs, and expressed optimism about their own futures" (Moffitt, 2003, p. 61).

➤**Answer to Observation Quiz** (from page 435): Statistically speaking, none. The rates are given per 100,000 in each age group. This means that fewer than 1 in 10,000 teens commit suicide in a year.

©MICHAEL NEWMAN / PHOTO EDIT

ALAMY

The Same Event, A Thousand Miles Apart: Following Tradition Adolescents worldwide flout adult conventions. Here, for instance, note the necklace on one of these boys in a Los Angeles high school *(left)* and the dyed red hair (or is it a wig?) on one of the girls in a Tokyo park *(right)*. As distinctive as each of these eight rebels is, all are following a tradition for their age group—just as their parents probably did when they were adolescents.

Of the many longitudinal studies that have now been completed, most conclude that increased anger at puberty is normal but that most young people express that anger in acceptable ways (yelling at their peers, complaining about adult behavior). Worse is explosive anger (breaking something, hurting someone), but that may not necessarily signal later problems. A minority, about 7 percent (and more boys than girls), are steadily aggressive throughout childhood and early adolescence (Broidy et al., 2003).

Breaking the Law

A word about terminology: *Juvenile delinquents* are lawbreakers under age 18. Some laws apply only to juveniles (for drinking, buying cigarettes, and breaking curfews) and some to everyone (for stealing, raping, and killing). Our main concern here is the more serious offenses, although restricting minor offenses may prevent some of the most destructive consequences of anger.

Aggression and serious crime are more frequent during adolescence than at any other period of life. Worldwide, arrests rise rapidly at about age 12, peak at about age 16, and then decline slowly with every passing decade of adulthood (Rutter, 1998). The particulars vary by nation and cohort, but, almost always, the arrest rate for violent crimes is twice as high for an older teenager as for an average adult.

incidence How often a particular behavior or circumstance occurs.

prevalence How widespread within a population a particular behavior or circumstance is.

Most crime data focus on **incidence,** obtained by determining the ages of all people who are arrested. This does not indicate **prevalence**—that is, how widespread lawbreaking is. To explain this distinction, suppose that only a few repeat offenders commit almost all the crimes. In that case, the prevalence would be low, even though the incidence was high. *If* this were true, and *if* adolescents on the path to a criminal career could be spotted early and then imprisoned, the *incidence* of adolescent crime would plummet because those few offenders could no longer commit their many crimes.

Developmentalists over the past few decades have concluded that imprisoning juvenile criminals as adults is a failing strategy that may even increase crime rather than reducing it. Juveniles are experimenters; they have not yet settled on any career, let alone a criminal one (Farrington, 2004). Most have no more than one serious brush with the law, and even chronic offenders are usually convicted of a mix of offenses—some minor, some serious.

Prevalence is high: Many adolescent offenders commit one or a few crimes each, rather than a few offenders committing hundreds each (Snyder, 1998). For example, one study of urban seventh-graders found that 79 percent of the sample of 1,559 (both sexes, all races, from parochial as well as public schools) had committed at least one crime (stolen something, damaged property, or hurt someone physically) but less than one-third had committed five or more such acts (Nichols et al., 2006).

Police records are imperfect measures because only about one-fourth of young lawbreakers are arrested, or even caught and then warned and released (Dodge et al., 2006). For example, another confidential study of an entire birth cohort (Fergusson & Horwood, 2002) found that the average boy admitted to more than three serious offenses between the ages of 10 and 20 and the average girl to one—although very few had ever been arrested. Self-reports generally find the same patterns but a much higher incidence and prevalence than official statistics: The peak is at age 16, with almost no one reporting a *first* serious offense before age 10 or after age 20 (Dodge et al., 2006).

Adolescent males are arrested at least three times as often as females. In the United States, African Americans are arrested at least three times as often as European Americans, who are themselves arrested at least three times as often as Asian Americans (Pastore & Maguire, 2005). Self-reports find much smaller gender and ethnic differences (Dodge et al., 2006), another reason why incidence statistics are suspect. The self-report data on girls is unsettling, at least to me (see the following).

Especially for Police Officers You see some 15-year-olds drinking beer in a local park when they belong in school. What do you do?

thinking like a scientist

A Feminist Looks at the Data

"Sugar and spice, and everything nice, that's what little girls are made of" was a rhyme I showed my mother soon after I learned to read, announcing, "That proves it." It confirmed that I was better than my older brother, who, like all little boys, was made of "snakes and snails and puppy dog tails." As my mother tells it, I have always been proud to be female, a feminist, a girl, and then a woman. However, as an adult scientist, I look at data.

A quick look at statistics shows that adolescent girls *are* nicer than boys. For example, among U.S. high school seniors who graduated in 2003, 11 percent of the boys, but only 4 percent of the girls, had been arrested one or more times in the previous year (Pastore & Maguire, 2005). Among high school seniors who, five or more times in the past year, have hurt someone badly enough to need bandages or a doctor, the male–female ratio is 10 to 1 (3 percent to 0.3 percent) (Pastore & Maguire, 2005).

I also reflect on expert opinion. "Boys are far more antisocial than girls," concludes a review of antisocial behavior written by three men, all developmental researchers I respect (Dodge et al., 2006, p. 73).

But I know the difference between wishful thinking and data, between official incidence and self-reported prevalence, between direct and indirect aggression. Several female scholars have suggested that girls prefer relational aggression, manifested in gossip, social exclusion, and the spreading of rumors. That would mean that girls' antisocial impulses would be less noticeable than those of boys, who are more likely to hit and kick (Crick et al., 2001; Underwood et al., 2003).

The research finds that girls are not always nice (Moffitt et al., 2001). The study of high school seniors cited above found that 47 percent of the girls, but only 38 percent of the boys, had gotten into five or more arguments or fights with their parents that year (Pastore & Maguire, 2005). A study of seventh-graders found that more girls than boys reported getting angry and losing self-control (Nichols et al., 2006).

Women are not always nice either. Among heterosexual couples, women are more likely to curse, hit, and even injure their partners than men are (Archer, 2000; Moffitt et al., 2001). Mothers mistreat their children at least twice as often as fathers do (U.S. Department of Health and Human Services Administration on Children, Youth, and Families, 2006).

Females seem to be less likely to express anger in public, physical ways. They are more likely to talk their way out of an arrest when they are teenagers. However, neither sex is exclusively "everything nice." My brother is usually kind, and there are some "snakes and snails" in me.

AP PHOTO / DAYTONA BEACH NEWS-JOURNAL, DAVID TUCKER

Do You Know This Boy? Warren Messner fights back tears as he is sentenced in a Daytona Beach, Florida, courtroom for the 2005 beating murder of a homeless man. Messner is 16; he was sentenced to be imprisoned until he is 39. Like most teenage criminals, he was unhappy at school and broke the law with friends, three other boys who also pleaded guilty.

Causes of Delinquency

Two clusters of factors, one from childhood and one from adolescence, predict antisocial behavior and serious crime (Lahey et al., 2003).

The first cluster relates to brain functioning. Short attention span, severe child abuse, hyperactivity, inadequate emotional regulation, maternal cigarette smoking, slow language development, low intelligence, early and severe malnutrition, autistic tendencies—none of these factors necessarily leads to delinquency, but all correlate with it (Brennan et al., 2003).

These factors are more common among boys from low-income families. However, no matter what a child's gender or socioeconomic status, neurological impairment increases the risk that a child will become a **life-course-persistent offender** (Moffitt et al., 2001), a term for someone who breaks the law before and after adolescence as well as during it.

The second cluster of causes appears in adolescence, and these risk factors are primarily psychosocial, not biological. They include deviant friends; few connections to school; being biologically mature but being treated like a child (a "maturity gap"); living in a crowded, violent neighborhood; unemployment; drug use; and close relatives (especially older siblings) in jail. This cluster is also more prevalent among low-income, urban adolescent boys, but almost all adolescents experience some of them. Any teen with these problems is at risk of becoming an **adolescence-limited offender,** whose criminal activity stops by age 21 (Moffitt, 1997, 2003). Adolescence-limited offenders were not perfect as children, but unlike their life-course-persistent peers, they were not the worst behaved in their class or the first to use drugs, have sex, or be arrested.

life-course-persistent offender A person whose criminal activity typically begins in early adolescence and continues throughout life; a career criminal.

adolescence-limited offender A person whose criminal activity stops by age 21.

Adolescence-limited offenders tend to break the law with their friends, facilitated by their chosen antisocial clique or crowd. There are more boys than girls in this group, but the gender gap in lawbreaking is narrower than it is in earlier adolescence (Moffitt et al., 2001). By mid-adolescence, rap sheets of adolescence-limited offenders resemble those of their life-course-persistent peers, but their childhood provides hope. If they can be protected from various snares that could handicap them for life (such as quitting school, time in prison, drug addiction, early parenthood), they may grow out of their criminal behavior (Moffitt, 2003). This is especially likely if they are female, live in a harmonious two-parent family, avoid alcohol and other drugs, do well in school, are religious, and have parents who monitor activity. None of these six factors is a guarantee, but they all help.

Make no mistake: Adolescent lawbreaking is neither inevitable nor insignificant; quite the contrary. Antisocial behavior tends to escalate in individuals and communities during adolescence. Such behavior needs to be halted early on, before it becomes truly dangerous to the young delinquent and any potential victims, who are usually other adolescents. Fighting, drug use, and vandalism are unacceptable. Adult prison terms for adolescents may lead to more crimes later in life, but ignoring adolescent rebellion is not helpful either.

When it comes to halting delinquency, relationships are crucial. Such is the finding from studies of *therapeutic foster care,* a course of treatment that provides intensive caregiving for young adolescents who are already troubled and antisocial delinquents (Chamberlain et al., 2002). In this program, foster parents are given extra help, training, and payment to establish a relationship with a foster child as well as with his or her teachers. Delinquents in therapeutic foster care are arrested only half as often as those in traditional care.

Overall, close relationships with supportive adults and avoidance of deviant peers helps rebellious youth (adolescence-limited or not) stay within bounds (Barnes et al., 2006; Kumpfer & Alvarado, 2003). Some adolescents never become depressed or delinquent, and those who do usually improve by age 20 (Broidy et al., 2003; Crockett et al., 2006; Wiesner et al., 2005). As is evident throughout this chapter, family and friends usually help teenagers find their identity and navigate through whatever difficulties they face. This process continues in emerging adulthood, as explained in the next trio of chapters.

➤Response for Police Officers (from page 439): Avoid both extremes: Don't let them think this situation is either harmless or serious. You might take them to the police station and call their parents in. However, these adolescents are not life-course-persistent offenders; jailing them or grouping them with other lawbreakers might encourage more serious acts of rebellion.

SUMMING UP

Compared with people of other ages, many adolescents experience sudden and extreme emotions that lead to powerful sadness and anger. These feelings are usually expressed within supportive families, friendships, neighborhoods, and cultures that contain and channel them. For some teenagers, however, emotions are unchecked or intensified by their social contexts. This situation can lead to suicide attempts (especially for girls), to minor lawbreaking (for both sexes), and, more rarely, to completed suicide and arrests (especially for boys). Intervention works best when it reduces the contextual risks (such as access to guns and drugs) and develops healthy relationships between the adolescent and constructive peers and adults. ■

SUMMARY

Identity

1. Adolescence is a time for self-discovery. According to Erikson, adolescents seek their own identity, sorting through the traditions of their families and cultures.

2. Many young adolescents either foreclose on their options without exploring possibilities or experience diffusion before reaching moratorium or identity achievement. In general, identity achievement takes much longer for contemporary adolescents than it did half a century ago, when Erikson first described it.

3. Identity achievement can occur in many domains, including religious identity, sexual identity (now often called gender identity), political identity (often replaced by ethnic identity), and vocational identity.

Relationships

4. Parents continue to influence their growing children, despite bickering over minor issues. Ideally, from age 10 to 18, communication and warmth remain high within the family, while parental control decreases and adolescents develop autonomy.

5. Cultural differences in timing of conflicts and particulars of monitoring are evident. Too much parental control, with psychological intrusiveness, is harmful.

6. Peers can be beneficial or harmful, depending on particular friends, cliques, and crowds. Friends can lead each other astray, providing training in deviance, or can encourage each other constructively.

7. Peers are particularly crucial for immigrant adolescents, who often have a strong commitment to family values but who also try to adjust to new norms and customs. Most immigrant adolescents do well in school and help their families.

8. Friendships with both sexes are important for self-concept and maturation. Romance need not be part of such close friendships.

Sexuality

9. Misinformation about sex can be very harmful and is common throughout the world. Parents and peers provide some sex education to adolescents but do not necessarily do it well.

10. In the United States, most adults want schools to teach adolescents about sex, but the specifics of the curriculum are controversial. No program (including abstinence-only) has made much difference in the age at which adolescents become sexually active, although some effectively encourage protection against pregnancy and disease.

11. Many European nations have more extensive sex education, begun earlier, than does the United States. The teenage birth rate has fallen and use of contraception has increased in every nation, although the U.S. rates of adolescent pregnancy are much higher than in other developed nations.

Sadness and Anger

12. Almost all adolescents lose some of the confidence they had when they were children. A few individuals become chronically sad and depressed, intensifying problems they had in childhood.

13. Many adolescents think about suicide. Parasuicides are not rare, especially among adolescent girls. Few adolescents actually kill themselves; most who do so are boys. Drugs, alcohol, guns, alienation from parents and peers, and lifelong depression increase the risk of suicide.

14. Almost all adolescents become more independent and angry as part of growing up. According to psychoanalytic theory, emotional turbulence is normal during these years. Often, rebelliousness manifests itself in delinquency, especially among adolescent boys.

15. Treatment and punishment of delinquents must take into account differences in origin. Adolescence-limited delinquents should be prevented from hurting themselves or others. Life-course-persistent offenders have problems that start in early childhood and extend into adulthood. Therapeutic foster care is one treatment that seems effective.

KEY TERMS

identity (p. 415)
identity versus diffusion (p. 415)
identity achievement (p. 416)
identity diffusion (p. 416)
foreclosure (p. 416)
moratorium (p. 416)
gender identity (p. 418)
sexual orientation (p. 418)
bickering (p. 420)
parental monitoring (p. 421)
clique (p. 422)
crowd (p. 422)
peer pressure (p. 423)
deviancy training (p. 423)
peer selection (p. 423)
peer facilitation (p. 424)
comorbidity (p. 433)
clinical depression (p. 433)
rumination (p. 434)
suicidal ideation (p. 434)
parasuicide (p. 434)
cluster suicides (p. 436)
incidence (p. 438)
prevalence (p. 438)
life-course-persistent offender (p. 440)
adolescence-limited offender (p. 440)

KEY QUESTIONS

1. What is the difference between identity achievement and identity diffusion?

2. What factors might make it particularly easy, or particularly difficult, for someone to establish his or her ethnic identity?

3. Give several examples of decisions a person must make in establishing gender identity.

4. Why and how do parents remain influential during their children's teen years?

5. How and when can peer pressure be helpful, and how can it be harmful?

6. What is the usual developmental pattern of relationships between boys and girls?

7. What are the common mistakes parents make in regard to their adolescent children's sexuality?

8. What facts are encouraging and discouraging about sexual experiences among adolescents in the United States?

9. In what ways can adolescent suicide be considered common and in what ways uncommon?

10. How do personal and cultural factors increase the risk of adolescent suicide?

11. How are adolescence-limited and life-course-persistent offenders similar, and how are they different?

APPLICATIONS

1. Teenage cliques and crowds may be more important in large U.S. high schools than elsewhere. Interview two people who spent their teenage years in small schools, or in another nation, about the peer relationships in their high schools. Describe and discuss any differences you find.

2. Locate a news article about a teenager who committed suicide. Were there warning signs that were ignored? Does the report inadvertently encourage cluster suicides?

3. Research suggests that most adolescents have broken the law but that few have been arrested or incarcerated. Is this true for people you know? Ask 10 of your fellow students whether they broke the law when they were under 18 and, if so, how often and in what ways. Assure them of confidentiality and ask specific questions about minor lawbreaking (e.g., drinking, skipping school) as well as things that would be considered crimes for adults (e.g., stealing, injuring someone else). What hypothesis arises about lawbreaking in your cohort?

4. As a follow-up to Application 3, ask your fellow students about the circumstances. Was their lawbreaking done with peers or alone? What was the effect of the responses of police, parents, judges, and peers? Explain how the circumstances and responses relate to adolescent psychosocial development.

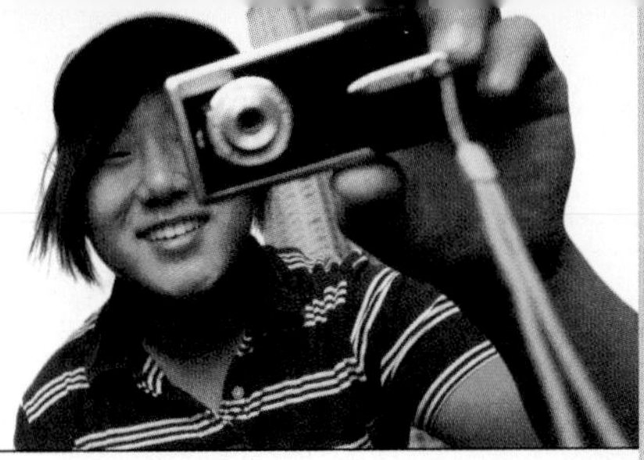

PART V The Developing Person So Far: Adolescence

BIOSOCIAL

Puberty Puberty begins adolescence, as the child's body becomes much bigger (the growth spurt) and more sexual. Both sexes experience increased hormones, reproductive potential, and primary as well as secondary sexual characteristics. Brain growth, hormones, and social contexts combine to make every adolescent more interested in sexual activities, with possible hazards of early pregnancy and sexual abuse.

Drugs Another hazard is drug use and abuse, which slows growth and increases risks. Adolescents are attracted to psychoactive drugs, but there is diversity in what drugs they try, if any. In most nations, boys use more drugs than girls do; in North America; the gender difference is small. Also in North America, alcohol is most commonly used, with much lower rates of cigarette smoking than in most European and Asian nations.

COGNITIVE

Adolescent Thinking Adolescents think differently than younger children do. Piaget stressed their new ability to use abstract logic, which is part of formal operational thought. Many adolescents can think hypothetically and deductively, as they are taught to do in science classes. Elkind recognized adolescent egocentrism, as many younger teens think they are invincible or that everyone else notices what they do and wear. Many more recent scholars find that intuitive thought increases during adolescence, with emotional and experiential (or dual-process) thinking overcoming logic at times.

Teaching and Learning Secondary education promotes individual and national health and success. Nations vary in how many of their adolescents graduate from high school, for reasons of culture and economics. Particularly in the United States, middle schools have been considered the "low ebb" of education, when grades and achievement fall, bullying increases, and many teachers and students become disenchanted with learning. International tests find some marked differences in achievement. In the United States, high-stakes tests required before high school graduation are the latest effort to improve standards of learning for adolescents.

PSYCHOSOCIAL

Identity Adolescent psychosocial development includes a search for identity, as Erik Erikson described. Adolescents seek to forge their own identity, combining childhood experiences, cultural values, and their unique aspirations. The four contexts of identity are religion, sex, vocation, and politics/ethnicity. Few adolescents achieve identity in these four arenas; identity diffusion and foreclosure are more likely.

Relationships Families continue to be influential, despite rebellion and bickering. Adolescents seek autonomy but also rely on parental support. Friends and peers of both sexes are increasingly important. For heterosexual as well as homosexual youth, friends may be crucial in helping teenagers achieve sexual identity. Romances often begin in adolescence. About half of all teens in the United States become sexually active. Among developed nations, the United States has higher rates of teen pregnancy and less comprehensive sex education.

Sadness and Anger Depression and rebellion become serious problems for a minority of adolescents. This troubled group is at some risk of suicide (rates are lower than for adults) and violent criminality (rates are higher than for adults). Most adolescents break the law, but their delinquency is adolescence-limited; they eventually become law-abiding adults. Some, however, are life-course-persistent delinquents.

Emerging Adulthood

CHAPTER 17

CHAPTER 18

CHAPTER 19

PART VI

Social scientists traditionally cite three roles as signifying adulthood: employee, spouse, and parent. Those roles were expected, even coveted, once puberty was over. Children looked forward to being "all grown up," anticipating privileges (like driving and drinking) that were denied them.

By contrast, many contemporary young adults avoid those three classic roles. Especially in developed nations, the ages 18 to 25 are characterized by more education, later marriage, fewer births, and postponed career choices. It is a time for exploration, not settling down. People in their early 20s try out various jobs, lifestyles, partners, ideas, and values.

Of course, not all young adults stretch the time between adolescence and adulthood. Particularly in developing nations, many begin work, marriage, and parenthood before age 20, just as their parents and grandparents did. But globalization has accelerated a trend first apparent among wealthier youth. Now adolescents and young adults everywhere put off adult roles as long as they can, seeking more education and independence than older generations in their community ever had. Emerging adulthood has become a new life stage and, here, a new trio of chapters.

17

CHAPTER OUTLINE

Emerging Adulthood: Biosocial Development

"How does it feel to be your age?" Elissa asked me at my recent birthday dinner.

"I don't feel old, but the number makes me think that I am."

"Twenty-five is old, too," Sarah said. (She had celebrated her birthday two weeks earlier.)

We laughed, but understood. Although at one time age 18 or 21 was considered the beginning of adulthood, age 25 has become the new turning point. People of all ages now believe that, in their mid-20s, young adults should devise "a good plan for what they are going to do with the rest of their life" (Pew Research Center, 2007, p. 11).

Over the past few decades, a sociocultural shift has pushed forward the age at which people are expected to commit to career and family, or at least to have "a good plan." The years between adolescence and adulthood have become distinct, containing a generation called the Millennials (Goldsmith et al., 2003) or Gen Y (American Demographics, 2002) (a decade ago, this age group was called Generation X) and constituting a life period called the "frontier of adulthood" (Settersten et al., 2005) or "emerging adulthood" (Arnett, 2004; Crouter & Booth, 2006), the label used here.

As this chapter explains, emerging adults have distinct biosocial characteristics, some of which have always been part of the human experience and some of which are new. At least in developing nations, many emerging adults are healthier than earlier generations yet are more vulnerable to eating disorders, violent death, and drug abuse. We begin with the good parts.

Growth, Strength, and Health

Today, as they have been for centuries, the years from 18 to 25 are prime time for hard physical work, athletic achievement, and reproduction. Before learning the details, consider the imperfect connection between biosocial development and age.

Ages and Stages

For children, physical maturation correlates with chronological age and developmental stage. Infancy begins at birth; adolescence begins at puberty. The play years and the school years also have biological markers, less dramatic but still apparent in the brain.

In childhood, age signifies cognitive norms and abilities. No one would mistake a 3-month-old for a 3-year-old or a 7-year-old for a 17-year-old or expect them to learn in the same way. A controversial topic in education is "redshirting," starting a child in kindergarten a year later than the law allows. The reason for redshirting is that one year adds physical, cognitive, and social maturity, allowing a young child to be an advanced kindergartner. Obviously, birthdays matter for children (Weil, 2007).

This is not true for adults. Chronological age is an imperfect guide to development. A 40-year-old, for instance, could have a body that functions like that of a typical person a decade older or younger. In college, adults of all ages attend class together. No professor prejudges students' intellect based on age.

Social roles vary as well. Unlike in childhood, when virtually all 6- to 10-year-olds live with their parents and go to school, in adulthood a group of 40-year-olds, for example, might include some never married, some divorced several times, some expecting their first child, some grandparents. Age is not definitive even within one community, much less when comparing cohorts or cultures.

Nonetheless, developmentalists cluster adults into chronological groups and report differences between one age group and another. For example, cited throughout this chapter is a survey conducted by the Pew Research Center (2007) that compares generations (see Research Design). The authors acknowledge that "boundaries that separate generations are indistinct" but proceed to distinguish the following: ages 18 to 25 (Generation Next, born 1981–1988), ages 25 to 40 (Generation X, born 1966–1980), ages 40 to 60 (Baby Boomers, born 1946–1964), and age 60 and older (Seniors, born before 1946).

Why do surveys (and books such as this one) continue to compare adult age groups, even though chronological age is an imperfect guide? Although age variations need to be considered, developmentalists nonetheless believe that cohort and age affect behavior.

For example, although you are not precisely like the average person your age, over the next 10 years maturation and experience will affect you. Developmental research can alert you to some of the pressures and possibilities of your next decade, to help you accomplish what you want. Taking this one step further, people in your cohort share some biological and sociological characteristics with others their age, especially when compared with those 20 or 40 years older.

The goal of our study remains to predict "changes over time" (Chapter 1) to allow optimal growth at each life period. People follow patterns, which vary by age, culture, and cohort. For instance, the average age of marriage in the United States is about 25 for women and 27 for men (see Table 17.1), significantly later than in the mid-twentieth century (21 and 24) (U.S. Bureau of the Census, 1952, 2006) Knowing that is useful if you are not yet married.

Many such age differences result more from social factors than biological ones and thus differ by culture, even in the same community. This is apparent among the current cohort in the largest state in Germany: Age of marriage for those of Turkish descent averages 21 for women and 24 for men, while for those of tradi-

Research Design

Scientists: Andrew Kohut, director of the Pew Research Center for the People and the Press, and hundreds of others.

Publication: *A Portrait of "Generation Next"* (2007).

Participants: A total of 1,501 adults from throughout the United States, with an "oversample" of emerging adults.

Design: Answers to telephoned questions about habits, values, and opinions were compared by age group, with special care and methods to ensure validity.

Major conclusion: Emerging adults differ markedly from older generations in many ways (such as use of technology and attitudes about homosexuality) but not in others (such as views on abortion).

Comments: Although the Pew scientists designed their research to obtain valid results (e.g., contacting young adults via cell phone), surveys are always vulnerable to bias. The report notes two possible problems: wording and inadvertent selection bias (e.g., those who have no phones might have given different answers). A third possible problem is the human tendency to say one thing and do another. Confirmation from direct behavioral research is needed.

TABLE 17.1

At About This Time . . . Following Certain Patterns, By Age (U.S., 2006)

Age 18—Graduate from high school

Age 18–19—Enroll in college (65 percent of high school graduates go to college)

Age 22—Leave college (of those who entered college)

Age 25*—Steady employment

Age 25†—Women: Average age of first marriage

Age 26—Women's first birth (of those who have children; about 20 percent do not)

Age 27†—Men: Average age of first marriage

*At age 20–24, many have jobs but half this group has been with the current employer less than a year.

†This is the age at which half the cohort has married. It is the median but not the mean, because no one knows when, or if, the other half will marry.

These are estimates, based primarily on data from the United States Bureau of the Census. Ages vary by source and nation, but all report older ages for the current cohort compared with prior generations.

Sources: Dye, 2005; U.S. Bureau of the Census, 2006.

tional German ancestry, the ages are 29 and 32 (Caldwell, 2007). You may have been told that you are too young to marry even though you are older than your grandparents were when they were wed.

Variations add complexity, but also understanding. Soon you will read about possible problems arising from current emerging adults' later age of marriage. Knowing about adult development allows better anticipation and prevention of these potential problems.

Overall, then, adult developmental trends are well worth description. Labels and boundaries are fluid, variation is vast, yet patterns characterize people at each age. Lockstep stages or chronological demarcations—no. Clusters and modes—yes. Insight—we hope so.

Strong and Attractive Bodies

Maximum height is usually reached by age 16 for girls and 18 for boys, except for a few late-maturing boys who gain another inch or two by age 21. During emerging adulthood, muscles grow and shape changes in ways that differ by sex, with males gaining more arm muscle and females more hip fat. By age 22 women have attained adult breast and hip size and men have reached full shoulder width and upper-arm strength. Although standards of beauty vary by culture, worldwide male–female differences in waist/hip ratio and arm muscles add to sexual allure (Singh, 2004), as emphasized by the clothes they wear.

Especially for a Competitive Young Man Given the variations in aging muscle, how might a 20-year-old respond if he loses an arm-wrestling contest against his father?

Physical strength for both sexes increases in the 20s. Emerging adults are more capable than people of any other age group of running up a flight of stairs, lifting a heavy load, or gripping an object with maximum force. Strength gradually decreases over the years, with some muscles weakening more quickly than others: Back and leg muscles shrink faster than the arm muscles, for instance (Masoro, 1999). This is apparent in older baseball players who are still capable of hitting home runs long after they've ceased being able to steal bases.

Every body system, including the digestive, respiratory, circulatory, and sexual-reproductive systems, functions optimally at the beginning of adulthood (Aspinall, 2003). Serious diseases are not yet apparent, and some childhood ailments are outgrown. For instance, childhood asthma disappears as often as it continues, according to a careful longitudinal study in New Zealand (Sears et al., 2003). Even the common cold is less frequent.

In a mammoth survey, 96.4 percent of young adults in the United States rated their health as good, very good, or excellent, and only 3.6 percent rated it as fair or poor (National Center for Health Statistics, 2006). Similarly, 96 percent of 18- to 24-year-olds report no activity limitations due to chronic health conditions, a rate better than that of any other age group (see Figure 17.1). The Pew study found that only 2 percent of emerging adults consider health their most important problem, compared with 15 percent of those over age 25 (Pew Research Center, 2007).

Lifelong, preventive health care protects health. If this were the only way to stay healthy, then a great many emerging adults would be sick, because most avoid doctors unless they are injured or pregnant. Each year in the United States, the average young adult sees a health professional once, compared with about 10 annual medical visits for the typical adult age 75 or older (National Center for Health Statistics, 2006).

FIGURE 17.1

Strong and Independent Looking at this graph, do you wonder why twice as many 5- to 17-year-olds as 18- to 24-year-olds are said to be limited in daily activities? The answer relates to who reports the limitations. Parents answer for children; adults answer for themselves. Parents tend to be more protective, reporting that chronic conditions (mostly ADD and asthma) limit what their children can do.

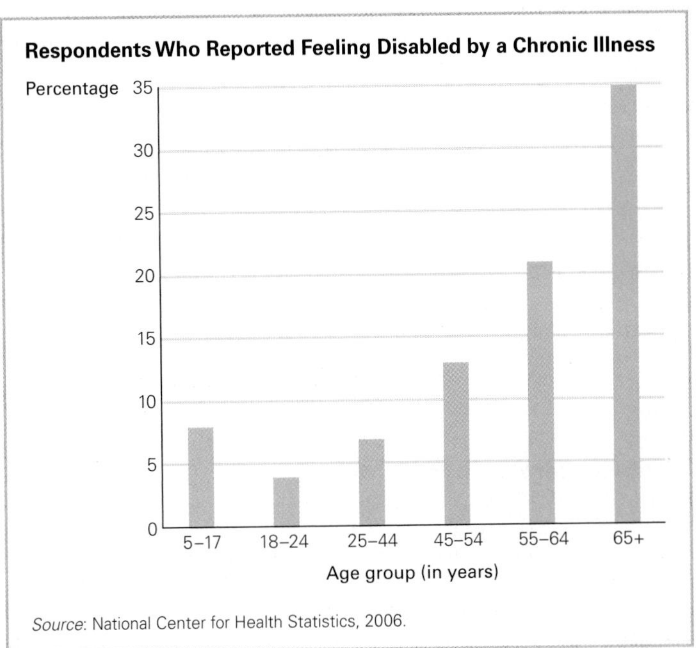

Source: National Center for Health Statistics, 2006.

TABLE 17.2

U.S. Deaths from the Top Four Diseases, by Age

Age Group	Annual Rate per 100,000
15–24	8
25–34	18
35–44	71
45–54	235
55–64	656
65–74	1,632
75–84	3,706
85+	8,981

Source: National Center for Health Statistics, 2006.

Young and Healthy Young adults rarely die of diseases, including the top four: heart disease, cancer, stroke, and obstructive pulmonary disease. These are annual rates, which means that for each person, the chance of death in that decade is 10 times the yearly rate. Thus, a 15-year-old has less than 1 chance in 10,000 of dying of disease before age 25; a 75-year-old has more than 1 chance in 3 of dying of disease before age 85. (As reported later in this chapter, non-disease deaths show a different pattern.)

Fortunately, bodies are naturally healthy during these years. The immune system is strong, fighting off everything from the sniffles to cancer (Henson & Aspinall, 2003). Usually, blood pressure is normal, teeth have no new cavities, heart rate is steady, the brain functions well, and lung capacity is sufficient. Many diagnostic tests, such as PSA (for prostate cancer), mammograms (for breast cancer), and colonoscopy (for colon cancer), are not recommended until age 40, unless family history or warning signs suggest otherwise. Death from disease is rare worldwide (Heuveline, 2002), as Table 17.2 details for the United States.

Bodies Designed for Health

This rosy picture does not mean that emerging adults are unaffected by the passing years. The process of aging, called **senescence** (discussed in detail in Chapter 20), begins as soon as full growth is reached. Habits established in early adulthood affect health later on. However, few emerging adults are aware of senescence because of two biological processes we now describe: homeostasis and organ reserve.

Bodies in Balance

Many body functions are designed for **homeostasis,** a state of equilibrium maintained by interactions of all the body's physiological systems. Many homeostatic responses are regulated in the brain by the pituitary, sometimes called "the master gland," which defends the body via various hormonal shifts (the *HPA axis*, described on p. 215) to maintain homeostasis (Timiras, 2003). Homeostasis works most quickly and efficiently during emerging adulthood, which is one reason emerging adults are less likely to get sick, fatigued, or obese than older adults.

Examples of homeostasis are all around us. When people exercise, their greater use of oxygen automatically leads to more rapid breathing and heart rate to deliver more oxygen to their cells. If the air temperature rises, people sweat, move slowly, and thirst for cold drinks—all to cool off. When it gets chilly, people shiver to increase body heat. If they are really cold, their teeth chatter, a kind of shivering.

Each person's internal thermometer is slightly different. Bodies adjust to past experiences, and younger people are generally warmer than older ones. This explains why people who grew up in different climates react differently to weather and why your mother tells *you* to put on a sweater because *she* is cold. For everyone, however, homeostasis helps maintain equilibrium.

The other major reason young adults rarely experience serious illness is **organ reserve,** an extra capacity of each organ that allows the body to cope with stress or physiological extremes. Aging of the body reduces the capacity of each organ and body system, but the reduction rarely affects daily life (Aspinall, 2003). For instance, hearing is most acute at about age 12, but unless a teenager and an adult are both listening for footsteps outside, for example, tiny hearing losses are imperceptible. (The teenager would usually hear those footsteps first.)

Not only in emerging adulthood, but at least until middle age, declines in homeostasis and organ reserve are usually unnoticed. A 40-year-old pregnant woman might notice that her kidneys, blood pressure, and lung capacity are less resilient than when she was pregnant at age 20, but she is unaware of any slowdown when she is not expecting a baby.

Bodies have a muscle reserve as well, and this reserve is directly related to physical strength. Maximum strength *potential* typically begins to decline by age 30. However, few adults develop all of their possible strength, and even if they did, 50-year-olds retain 90 percent of the muscle reserve they had at age 20 (Rice & Cunningham, 2002). Indeed, if a 50-year-old begins lifting weights, he or she may become stronger than ever.

senescence The process of aging, whereby the body becomes less strong and efficient.

homeostasis The adjustment of all the body's systems to keep physiological functions in a state of equilibrium. As the body ages, it takes longer for these homeostatic adjustments to occur, so it becomes harder for older bodies to adapt to stress.

organ reserve The capacity of organs to allow the body to cope with stress, via extra, unused functioning ability.

➤Response for a Competitive Young Man (from page 449): He might propose a stair-climbing race and win, since leg strength declines faster than arm strength. Of course, intergenerational competition has psychic ramifications; perhaps the son should simply say "congratulations" and leave it at that.

The most important muscle of all, the heart, shows a similar pattern (Cameron & Bulpitt, 2003). The heart is amazingly strong during emerging adulthood: Only 1 in 50,000 North American young adults dies of heart disease each year. The average *maximum* heart rate—the number of times the heart can beat per minute under extreme stress—declines as the reserve is reduced, beginning at about age 25. But the *resting* heart rate remains very stable. Once again, peak potential performance declines, but normal functioning is not affected by aging until late adulthood.

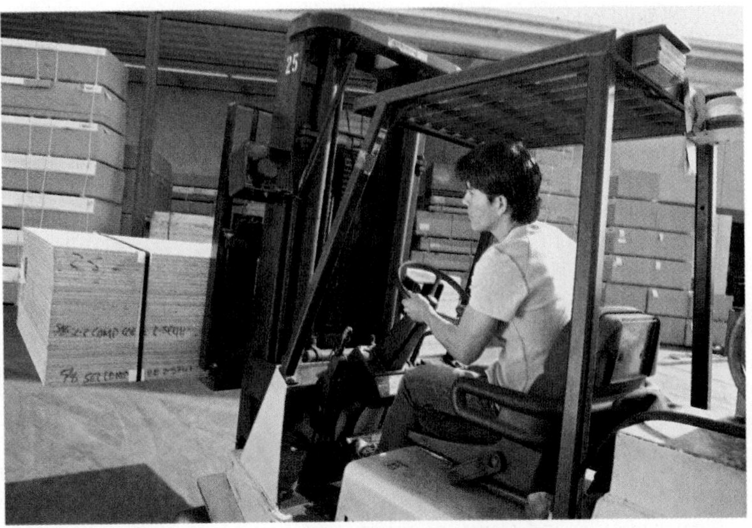

MIKE WATSON IMAGES LTD / PUNCHSTOCK

The Best Employee At his age, this worker's body is in ideal condition for safely operating a forklift: His vision is sharp, his hand is steady, and his reactions are quick.

Even in the smaller changes of aging, such as the wearing down of the teeth or loss of cartilage in the knees, serious reductions are not normally evident until old age. As one expert explains, "A remarkable feature of aging is that various organs and structures have evolved to 'last a lifetime'" (Holliday, 1995). Whether that lifetime is closer to 100 years or to a mere 65 depends largely on health habits established in early adulthood, as we will soon describe. First, consider the implications of the overall excellent health of young adults if an epidemic of avian influenza—"bird flu"—were to occur.

issues and applications

Who Should Get the Bird Flu Shot?

Health officials must make choices regarding immunizing the population against H5N1, the virus that causes avian influenza. Their priorities should reflect ethics and social science research, yet discussion of these issues has barely begun (Emanuel & Wertheimer, 2006; Silverstein et al., 2006).

Currently, the only humans who have contracted this disease are those (butchers, for example) who have had close contact with infected birds. As of summer 2007, no known transmission from human to human had occurred. Social scientists fear that scare tactics might backfire, yet efforts to prepare do not sufficiently take into account the ethical and practical aspects of halting the virus (Basili & Franzini, 2006; Nerlich & Halliday, 2007).

Epidemiologists predict that the H5N1 virus, like the 1918 bird flu that killed millions, will eventually mutate and spread among humans. It is impossible to know which mutation will allow such transmission, which means that no precise vaccine can be developed in advance.

Once human-to-human infection occurs, the virus can be isolated and analyzed. Then it could take as much as a year for 75 million doses of effective vaccine to be developed, far fewer than needed for the earth's 6 to 8 billion people (Poland, 2006). Scientists are working feverishly to find faster and more effective ways to produce vaccine (one report puts the time lag at four months, not a year), but even with scientific breakthroughs, months will elapse between the first human-to-human transmission and the availability of enough vaccine for everyone (Morse et al., 2006). Meanwhile, thousands, millions, or maybe billions of people will catch the bird flu. Many of them will die.

Finding novel ways to produce sufficient vaccine quickly is only half the battle. The other half is to decide the best way to allocate vaccine, to implement quarantine, and to slow transmission so that millions of lives are spared.

Very little is known about this half. A simple suggestion—keeping sick people at home in a room with a closed door—may or may not be effective (Morse et al., 2006). Another possibility—halting all air travel—was first thought to be useful but was later discounted (Enserink, 2006). International cooperation is erratic; data on acceptance of vaccines are contradictory (Fedson, 2005; Slonim et al., 2006; D. Smith, 2006). We know that with smallpox, for example, sometimes people rioted to be first in line to be vaccinated; other times, they refused the vaccine. What does that say about H5N1?

Given limited supply, someone must decide priorities. Health workers are usually at the top of the list; they are most likely to be exposed and most needed to fight the disease. The people in the nation where bird flu first appears need the vaccine first, an argument forcefully made by Indonesia, which is likely to be that nation (Enserink, 2007). However, other nations may not donate scarce vaccine, an ethical issue.

Should one age group be prioritized? Emerging adults' immune systems are more responsive to immunization than the systems of older adults, which means that any vaccine is more effective in young adults. However, homeostasis, organ reserve, and advanced hospital care mean that sick 18- to 25-year-olds are less likely to die than are infants or those who are elderly or frail. (That's why the oldest and most feeble receive conventional flu shots first.)

But to slow down transmission, the targets should be *disease vectors*—that is, people and conditions that increase the spread of illness. Children and schools are potent disease vectors. For this reason, should the bird flu arrive, the current U.S. plan is to shut down all schools.

Emerging adults are also prime disease vectors, but their interactions are more difficult to halt. They come in close contact with many others—as employees without private offices, as passengers on buses and trains, as international travelers staying in communal hostels, as social beings who mingle in crowded dance clubs and bars. In the 1918 flu outbreak, emerging adults had the highest death rates, not because flu was a more potent killer for them (it was not) but because more of them caught the disease (Barry, 2005).

Considering emerging adults as disease vectors is not theoretical. An outbreak of almost 100,000 cases of mumps occurred recently in England and Wales. It spread rapidly among emerging adults (see Figure 17.2), partly because they were in contact with other young adults but also because of a lapse in required immunization. One young Briton flew to the United States as a summer camp counselor. He became sick a week after he arrived, and he passed mumps to 12 campers (all from the United States) and 19 counselors (almost all from abroad). Quarantine required 513 people to stay isolated at the camp for most of the summer until no one else became sick (MMWR, February 24, 2006).

Currently in the United States, adults are at the bottom of the vaccine priority list, lower than embalmers (who might be more exposed) (Emanuel & Wertheimer, 2006). Yet to prevent a pandemic, emerging adults as disease vectors may need to be first. In 1918, many officials lied, and more deaths resulted. More U.S. people died of the flu than died in World War I (Barry, 2005). Past experience with SARS and TB suggests that emerging adults are unlikely to insist on vaccination; political leaders are unlikely to have young adults immunized first and thus allow frail people to die, even if doing so would save more lives in the long term. Should they?

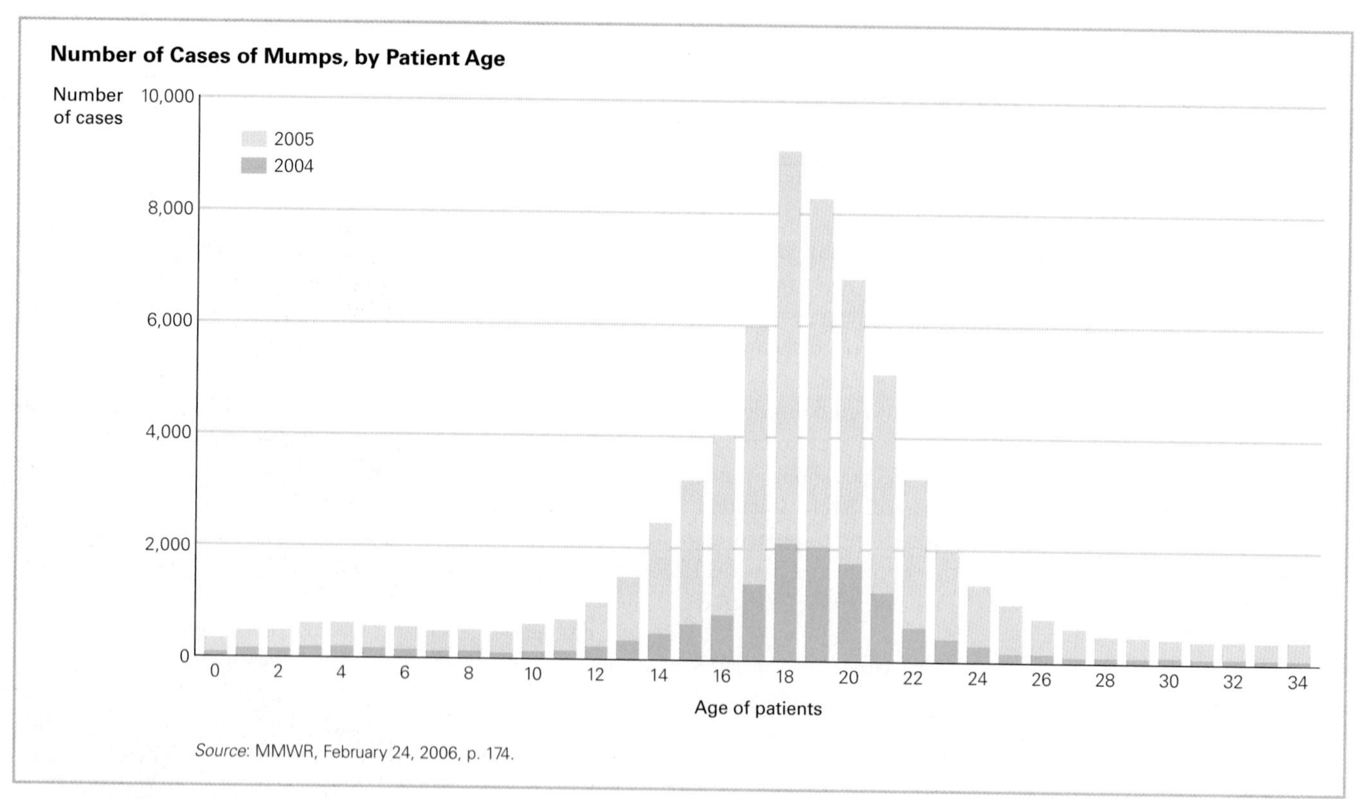

FIGURE 17.2

Not a Childhood Disease In this British outbreak, young adults were major disease vectors for mumps, which is inaccurately considered a childhood disease. The places with the highest rates of transmission were college campuses.

Appearance

Partly because of their overall health, strength, and activity, most emerging adults look vital and attractive. The oily hair, pimpled faces, and awkward limbs of adolescence are gone, and the wrinkles and hair loss of adulthood have not yet appeared. Muscles are stronger and obesity is less common during emerging adulthood than earlier or later in life. Newly prominent fashion models, popular singers, and film stars tend to be in their early 20s, looking fresh and glamorous.

Vanity about personal appearance is generally frowned upon, so it is not surprising that a cross-cultural study of 19- to 26-year-olds in the United States, New Zealand, India, and China found few who admitted that they are intensely concerned about their appearance (Durvasula et al., 2001). Yet emerging adults spend more money on their own clothes and shoes than adults of any other age (American Demographics, 2002). When they exercise, their main reason is fitness and weight control, unlike older adults, whose main motivation is health (Biddle & Mutrie, 2001).

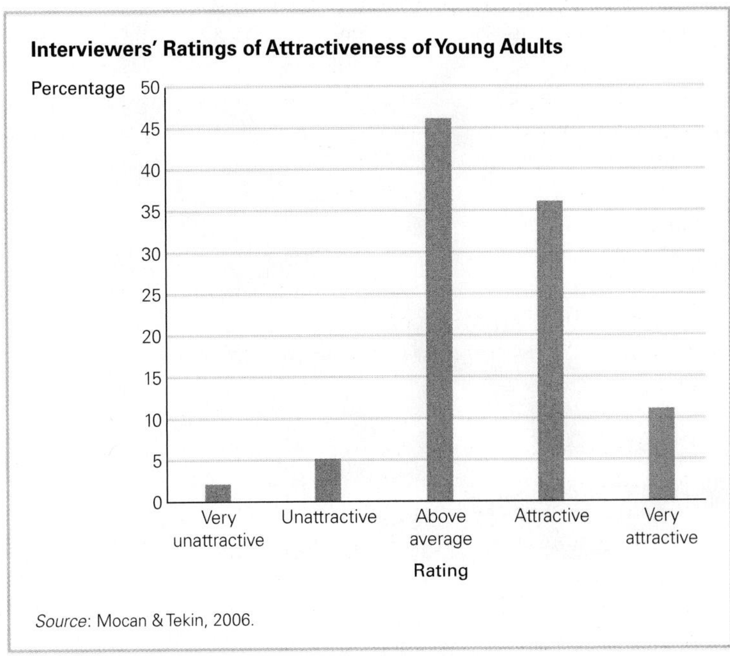

FIGURE 17.3

Hey, Good-Looking When thousands of the Add Health study's adolescent participants were reinterviewed as emerging adults, many had become more attractive, as rated by the interviewers.

Some of this concern about appearance is connected to sexual drives, since appearance attracts sexual interest. Young adults care about how they look because, quite naturally, they want attention from each other. Further, these are the years when many people seek employment. Attractiveness (in clothing as well as body and face) correlates with better jobs and higher pay (Hamermesh et al., 2002).

No wonder young adults try to look their best. Usually, they succeed. In the Add Health Longitudinal study of a large representative sample of U.S. teenagers (Blum et al., 2000), the participants were interviewed for a third time when they were young adults, and the interviewers noted how attractive each respondent was. Only 7 percent were rated unattractive or very unattractive (see Figure 17.3), a much smaller proportion of the very same people as they were rated at earlier ages. Other data also find that adults of all ages rate this age group better looking than any other (Mocan & Tekin, 2006).

Sexual Activity

As already mentioned, the sexual-reproductive system is at its strongest during emerging adulthood. Young adults have a strong sex drive; fertility is greater and miscarriage is less common; orgasm is more frequent; and testosterone, the hormone associated with sexual desire, is significantly higher for both men and women at age 20 than at age 40 (Anis, 2007; Huang, 2007).

Most people who have ever lived were born to women younger than 25 years old, when mothers were most likely to survive pregnancy and childbirth. Some women kept bearing children until menopause, but peak fertility as well as peak newborn survival has always been between the maternal ages of 18 and 25. With unprotected intercourse, pregnancy occurs during emerging adulthood within 3 months, on average. Both sexes become less fertile with age (Hassan & Killick, 2003). (Infertility is discussed in Chapter 20.)

However, for today's emerging adults, these physiological assets can become liabilities. The sex drive leads to many joyous interactions, but whereas it once led to marriage and parenthood, many young adults today want sex but do not want spouses or children (Lefkowitz & Gillen, 2006). In earlier times, if a woman did

Together Again Although biologists and psychologists describe the differences between the sexes, the reality is that young adult men and women are similar in many ways. Both seek one special other person and are thrilled to be together.

JUPITERIMAGES / BRAND X / ALAMY

Love Without Pregnancy Not only government policy but also modern contraception has changed the nature of loving relationships for young Chinese couples. This Shanghai couple may marry, they may have sex, and they may be together for fifty years or more, but they will probably have only one child.

not want to become pregnant, she had few options other than abstinence. Several completely unscientific "methods" were tried (such as walking in seven circles right after sex), but they resulted in many unwanted babies being born. Today there is "a plethora of methods" (Bayer, 2007, p. 231) that actually work.

The reality that sex need not entail pregnancy is one reason that people are marrying later. Attitudes have changed along with practice. A national poll finds that most 18- to 24-year-olds think premarital sex is "not wrong at all," while only 18 percent of those over age 65 agree (T. W. Smith, 2005). The Pew survey (Pew Research Center, 2007) found that 75 percent of emerging adults think their generation has more "casual sex" than the previous generations.

Most emerging adults still believe that marriage is a serious and desirable commitment that they expect to make in the future. Although they condone premarital sex, most emerging adults (80 percent) believe that extramarital sex is "always wrong" (T. W. Smith, 2005). Obviously, premarital sex postpones marriage without sexual deprivation; no wonder most emerging adults value it. However, this new pattern makes two complications more likely: distress and disease.

Emotional Stress

Confidential surveys find that contemporary emerging adults have more partners and more sexual intercourse than adults who are somewhat older. Their physical relationships usually involve emotional connections because, at least in the United States, most sexually active adults have one steady partner at a time, a pattern called *serial monogamy* (Laumann & Michael, 2001).

Emerging adults in France (reputedly a highly erotic culture) also follow this pattern of serial monogamy (Gagnon et al., 2001). Indeed, although research among emerging adults in traditional cultures is unavailable, sex and commitment may be intertwined by nature. Human physiological responses affect neurological patterns as well as vice versa. As one scientist explains, those who engage in casual sex can trigger the brain system for attachment (as well as for romantic love), leading to "complex, unanticipated emotional entanglement with psychologically and socially unsuitable mating partners" (H. E. Fisher, 2006, p. 12).

Such "unanticipated emotional entanglement" is likely to produce emotional stress. Most sexual interactions include unspoken assumptions. Generally speaking, attitudes about the purpose of sex fall into one of three categories (Laumann & Michael, 2001):

1. *Reproduction.* About one-fourth of all people in the United States (more women than men; more older adults than younger ones) believe that the primary purpose of sex is reproduction. They promote abstinence until marriage, and for them the only acceptable contraception is abstinence when the woman is fertile. Emerging adults with this perspective are likely to marry relatively young, pressured not only by their parents but also by their values and sexual desires.
2. *Relationship.* Most people in the United States (more women than men) believe that the main purpose of sex is to strengthen pair bonding. This is the dominant belief among emerging adults. For this group the preferred sequence is dating, falling in love, deciding to be faithful, having sex, perhaps living together, and finally (if both are "ready" for commitment) marriage and parenthood. Emotional complexities arise if one partner is further along in this sequence, but at least both are on the same path.

3. *Recreation.* About one-fourth of all people in the United States (more men than women, especially young men) believe that sex is "a fundamental human drive and a highly pleasurable physical and mental experience" (Cockerham, 2006, p. 25), sought primarily for enjoyment. Ideally, both partners achieve orgasm, without commitment. As already explained, this attitude may be difficult to sustain.

These labels and generalities come from the United States (Laumann & Michael, 2001), but these same three are evident elsewhere (although not in the same proportions). For example, a study of Canadian college students found that about 30 percent were celibate, waiting for their lifelong partner; about 60 percent were sexually active and faithful in their relationships; and about 10 percent were experimenters. The latter used fewer condoms and were more accepting of sex with acquaintances (like the recreation group above) (Netting & Burnett, 2004).

©ELLEN SINISI / THE IMAGE WORKS

Do They Talk? This couple in Schenectady, New York, are in a "long-term relationship," probably years from marriage. We hope they agree about what they would do if she got pregnant, or if he found someone else, or if either was offered a great job or university scholarship in another state. Few emerging adult couples discuss such matters until they happen.

Assumptions about the purpose of sex are usually mutual when romance involves people who were raised within the same religion and culture. In that case, attitudes about fidelity, pregnancy, love, and abortion are understood by both partners, even when not discussed. Currently, however, many emerging adults leave their childhood community and "have a number of love partners in their late teens and early twenties before settling on someone to marry" (Arnett, 2004, p. 73). They may feel misused and misled because "choices about sex are not the disassociated, disembodied, hedonistic and sensuous affairs of the fantasy world; they are linked, and rather tightly linked by their social embeddedness, to other domains of our lives" (Laumann & Michael, 2001, p. 22). Without realizing it, each partner may be embedded in a worldview that the other does not share—or even imagine.

An added complication is gender identity (discussed in Chapter 16). Whereas former generations identified as either male or female, either heterosexual or homosexual, some emerging adults refuse to categorize themselves, saying they are in all, or none, of these categories (Savin-Williams, 2005).

If two love partners hold differing assumptions about the purpose of sex or the nature of gender, emotional pain and frustration are likely to follow. One might accuse the other of betrayal, an accusation the other considers patently unfair. Romantic breakups are often the result of such disagreements, and they sometimes lead to depression and suicide, both of which are more frequent in emerging adulthood than they once were. But it is not known how often misunderstandings are at the root of such depression.

One thing that is known, however, is that the second set of possible problems —an increase in sexually transmitted infections—is the direct result of the new sexual patterns among today's young adults.

Sexually Transmitted Infections

Sexually transmitted infections (STIs) have been part of life since the beginning of time. However, the incidence is much higher today than ever before. Half of all emerging adults in the United States have had at least one STI (Lefkowitz & Gillen, 2006). Some STIs are relatively minor and easily treatable, but others can lead to potentially serious health problems. Even when STIs have no symptoms (about half the time), infertility and even death can be the eventual outcome (James, 2007).

Public health experts recommend that in order to prevent the spread of infection people see a doctor and get tested six months after the end of a sexual relationship before having sex with a new partner. Few people, especially few emerging adults, take this advice. Most begin new relationships almost immediately, sometimes starting a new sexual liaison before the old one is even over (Foxman et al., 2006). Monogamy is the pattern while the relationship is ongoing, but a very quick transition occurs at the end. Rapid transmission of STIs is one result.

Worldwide, sex workers have added to the current epidemic of STIs. It used to be that prostitution, often referred to as "the world's oldest profession," was local in scope, with regard to both prostitutes and their clients. Today, with international flight being relatively easy and readily available, diseases caught from infected prostitutes are quickly spread from nation to nation by clients who travel the globe (James, 2007).

This is particularly tragic with HIV/AIDS, first confined primarily to gay men in major U.S. cities and then to injection drug users who shared needles. Within 20 years, primarily because of the sexual activities of young adults, HIV became a worldwide epidemic. In many nations, more victims are heterosexual and female than homosexual and male, and less than half receive the lifesaving drugs they need.

Some nations, notably Thailand, Zimbabwe, and Uganda, have reduced the incidence of AIDS by persuading sex workers and their clients to use condoms as well as by encouraging young women to delay marriage (Hayes & Weiss, 2006). At least in theory, if brides are old enough to choose their future husbands, they are more likely to marry younger men who are HIV-negative. Postponing marriage and educating sex workers are probable explanations for decreases in HIV in southern India among 15- to 24-year-olds (not among older adults) (Kumar et al., 2006). Overall, however, young adults are the main STI vectors as well as the main victims (Cockerham, 2006).

SUMMING UP

Emerging adulthood is a distinct period of life, from roughly ages 18 to 25. Not every young adult is typical of this stage, and age boundaries throughout adulthood change with each culture and cohort. Nonetheless, emerging adults tend to share many characteristics. They are strong, healthy, and attractive as well as endowed with well-functioning organ systems. Homeostasis and organ reserve protect them. Typically, they satisfy their strong sexual appetites with a series of romantic relationships that last for months or years—although they avoid the commitment of marriage and parenthood. Two hazards from this new pattern, not always anticipated, are emotional distress and sexually transmitted infections. STIs are epidemic and serious. Young adults, as well as societies, need to change their sexual behavior patterns to prevent harm. ■

Habits and Risks

Emerging adults experiment and select from many options. Some begin good habits and sustain them lifelong; others make destructive choices. We focus first on two vital choices, exercise and nutrition, and then describe the ways in which taking certain risks can either help or harm development.

Exercise

Exercise at every stage of life protects against serious illness, even if a person has other bad habits, such as smoking and overeating (Carnethon et al., 2003; Manson et al., 1999). Exercise reduces blood pressure, strengthens the heart and lungs, and makes depression, osteoporosis, heart disease, arthritis, and even some cancers less likely. Health benefits from exercise are substantial for men and women, old and young, former sports stars and those who never joined an athletic team.

By contrast, sitting for long hours correlates with almost every unhealthy condition, especially heart disease and diabetes, both of which bring additional health hazards (Hu et al., 2003). Even a little movement—gardening, light housework, walking up the stairs or to the bus—helps. Walking briskly for 30 minutes a day, five days a week, is better; more intense exercise (swimming, jogging, bicycling, and the like) is ideal.

Among the goals for adults listed in *Healthy People 2010* (a nationwide health agenda launched by the U.S. Department of Health and Human Services) are that 25 percent of trips outside the house be walking (not driving) and that 30 percent of the population exercise 30 minutes a day at least five days a week (McElroy, 2002). Being active during early adulthood is crucial, although few inactive young adults realize it.

A study called CARDIA (Coronary Artery Risk Development in Adulthood) began with 18- to 30-year-olds who were followed into middle age. Those who were the least fit were four times more likely to have diabetes and high blood pressure 15 years later. The probable reason is that circulatory problems began, unnoticed, in early adulthood (Carnethon et al., 2003).

Fortunately, it is natural for emerging adults to keep moving—to climb stairs, run to the store, join intramural college and company athletic teams, play neighborhood games, jog, sail, or bicycle (Biddle & Mutrie, 2001). Especially in developing nations, they take jobs that require movement and strength. In the United States, emerging adults walk more and drive less than older adults, and about two-thirds of them reach the standard of exercising 30 minutes a day, five days a week (National Center for Health Statistics, 2006).

Maybe this generation will maintain good exercise habits, but research suggests otherwise. Past generations quit exercising when marriage, parenthood, and career became more demanding. Young adults, aware of this tendency, can choose friends and communities that support, rather than preclude, staying active. To be specific:

1. *Friendship.* People exercise more if their friends do so, too. Because social networks typically shrink with age, adults need to maintain, or begin, friendships that include movement, such as meeting a friend for a jog instead of a beer or playing tennis instead of going to a movie.
2. *Communities.* In some places, exercise is facilitated with easy access to walking and biking paths, ample fields and parks, and subsidized pools and gyms. Most colleges provide these amenities, but most neighborhoods and nations do not. Exceptions include Germany and the Netherlands, which have tripled their bike paths and banished cars from many streets, extending the average life span of their citizens by two years (Pucher & Dijkstra, 2003). Health experts cite extensive research showing that community design can have a positive effect on the levels of obesity, hypertension, and depression (Jackson, 2003; McElroy, 2002).

Especially for Emerging Adults Seeking a New Place to Live People move more often between the ages of 18 and 25 than at any later time. Currently, real estate agents describe sunlight, parking, and privacy as top priorities for their young clients. What else might emerging adults ask when selecting a new home?

Eating Well

Nutrition is another lifelong habit embedded in culture. "You are what you eat" is an oversimplification, but at every stage of life, diet affects development. Fortunately, in most cultures, long before the invention of vitamin pills and bathroom scales, young adults ate enough but not too much.

set point A particular body weight that an individual's homeostatic processes strive to maintain.

body mass index (BMI) The ratio of a person's weight in kilograms divided by his or her height in meters squared.

For body weight there is a homeostatic **set point,** or settling point, which makes people eat when they are hungry and stop eating when they are full. The set point is affected by age, genes, diet, hormones, and exercise. Overfeeding or starvation disrupts homeostasis (people who are malnourished in their first months of life are especially vulnerable to obesity), but, barring unusual circumstances, nature works to keep every bodily system in balance.

This is particularly true for young adults. Weight is often measured via the **body mass index (BMI),** which is the ratio between weight and height (see Table 17.3). A normal weight is between 20 and 25 BMI. Above 25 is considered overweight; BMI of 30 or more is considered obese. Emerging adulthood is the time when the greatest proportion of people are within the normal range.

Emerging adults can change childhood patterns of all kinds. For this reason, they consume more bottled water, organic foods, and non-meat diets than older adults, and many become more fit. A large British study found that about half those who were obese as children become normal-weight young adults, with healthier eating and social patterns (Viner & Cole, 2005).

Readiness to change old patterns can have the opposite effect as well. A U.S. study found that young adults eat more fast food (store-bought pizza, burgers, and so on) than those of other ages. Indeed, they eat four times as many such meals as adults over age 55 do (Bowman & Vinyard, 2003).

Although some emerging adults lose excess weight, others gain too much. According to the British study cited above, 12 percent of normal-weight teenagers

TABLE 17.3

Body Mass Index (BMI)

To find your BMI, locate your height in the first column, then look across that row. Your BMI appears at the top of the column that contains your weight.

BMI	19	20	21	22	23	24	25	26	27	28	29	30	35	40
Height (in feet and inches)	**Weight** (in pounds)													
4'10"	91	96	100	105	110	115	119	124	129	134	138	143	167	191
4'11"	94	99	104	109	114	119	124	128	133	138	143	148	173	198
5'0"	97	102	107	112	118	123	128	133	138	143	148	153	179	204
5'1"	100	106	111	116	122	127	132	137	143	148	153	158	185	211
5'2"	104	109	115	120	126	131	136	142	147	153	158	164	191	218
5'3"	107	113	118	124	130	135	141	146	152	158	163	169	197	225
5'4"	110	116	122	128	134	140	145	151	157	163	169	174	204	232
5'5"	114	120	126	132	138	144	150	156	162	168	174	180	210	240
5'6"	118	124	130	136	142	148	155	161	167	173	179	186	216	247
5'7"	121	127	134	140	146	153	159	166	172	178	185	191	223	255
5'8"	125	131	138	144	151	158	164	171	177	184	190	197	230	262
5'9"	128	135	142	149	155	162	169	176	182	189	196	203	236	270
5'10"	132	139	146	153	160	167	174	181	188	195	202	207	243	278
5'11"	136	143	150	157	165	172	179	186	193	200	208	215	250	286
6'0"	140	147	154	162	169	177	184	191	199	206	213	221	258	294
6'1"	144	151	159	166	174	182	189	197	204	212	219	227	265	302
6'2"	148	155	163	171	179	186	194	202	210	218	225	233	272	311
6'3"	152	160	168	176	184	192	200	208	216	224	232	240	279	319
6'4"	156	164	172	180	189	197	205	213	221	230	238	246	287	328
	Normal						Overweight					Obese		

Source: National Heart, Lung, and Blood Institute, n.d.

Calculating Adult BMI One objective assessment of appropriate weight is the amount of body fat as represented by the body mass index (BMI). A person's BMI is calculated by dividing his or her weight (in kilograms) by height (in meters) squared. Since most U.S. readers do not know their weight and height on the metric system, this table calculates BMI for them. A healthy BMI is between 19 and 25. A very muscular person may be healthy at a BMI of 26 or even 27, because muscle and bone weigh more than fat.

become obese by age 30 (Viner & Cole, 2005). Particular nutritional hazards await immigrant young adults who decide to "eat American." They might avoid curry, hot peppers, or wasabi—each of which has been discovered to have health benefits—and eat too much American fast food, which tends to be high in fat, sugar, and salt.

➤Response for Emerging Adults Seeking a New Place to Live (from page 457): Since neighborhoods have a powerful impact on health, a person could ask to see the nearest park, to meet a neighbor who walks to work, or to contact a neighborhood sports league.

Eating Disorders

Obesity is considered an eating disorder. It is discussed in Chapter 20 because it is more common in middle adulthood than in early adulthood. Most other eating disorders are especially prevalent in emerging adulthood (Shannon, 2007), when the average woman wants to be 8 pounds lighter and the average man 5 pounds heavier, even though both are usually of normal weight (Mintz & Kashubeck, 1999). Throughout adulthood women wish to be thinner, as confirmed by an Australian study of women aged 20 to 84. However, obsession about weight loss was greatest in the youngest women; the middle-aged women weighed more but worried less (Tiggemann & Lynch, 2001).

anorexia nervosa A serious eating disorder in which a person restricts eating to the point of emaciation and possible starvation. Most victims are high-achieving females in early puberty or early adulthood.

bulimia nervosa An eating disorder in which the person, usually female, engages repeatedly in episodes of binge eating followed by purging through induced vomiting or use of laxatives.

Dieting sometimes leads to **anorexia nervosa,** a disorder of self-starvation. Individuals voluntarily undereat and overexercise, depriving their vital organs of nourishment. Between 5 and 20 percent of victims die (Mitchell & McCarthy, 2000). The direct cause of death is usually organ failure, although many young women with anorexia are severely depressed and at increased risk of suicide.

According to DSM-IV-TR (American Psychiatric Association, 2000), anorexia nervosa is diagnosed when four symptoms are evident:

- Refusal to maintain a body weight that is at least 85 percent of normal for age and height
- Intense fear of weight gain
- Disturbed body perception and denial of the problem
- In adolescent and adult females, lack of menstruation

If someone's BMI is 18 or lower, or if she (or, less often, he) loses more than 10 percent of body weight within a month or two, anorexia is suspected.

Although anorexia may have existed in earlier centuries (think of the saints who refused all food), the disease was undiagnosed before about 1950, when some high-achieving, upper-class young women in the United States grew so thin that they died. Soon anorexia became evident in other developed nations, and now it is evident worldwide, especially in urban areas (Walcott et al., 2003).

Asian, African, and Latin American emerging adults once seemed immune, probably because their cultures are less plagued with the obsession to be skinny. However, they are no longer exempt. One team of experts, writing for clinicians, stated, "It is critical that the possibility of eating and body image concerns are considered for all individuals, regardless of ethnic background" (Dounchis et al., 2001, p. 82). Genes make anorexia more likely: If a young woman has a close relative, especially a monozygotic twin, with this disorder or with severe depression, she is at added risk.

About three times as common as anorexia is the other major dieting disorder of our time, **bulimia nervosa.** The person (again, usually female) with bulimia repeatedly overeats compulsively, consuming thousands of calories within an hour or two, and then purging through either induced vomiting or excessive use of laxatives. Bingeing and purging is common among women during emerging adulthood; some studies find that half of all college women have done so at least once (Fairburn & Brownell, 2002). Bulimia is present worldwide, in virtually every major city (Walcott et al., 2003).

AP PHOTO / EUGENIO SAVIO

Only a Few Months Left to Live Brazilian supermodel Ana Carolina Reston is shown walking the runway about a year before she died in 2006, weighing just 88 pounds. Anorexia has become a worldwide illness.

Most people with bulimia are close to normal in weight and therefore unlikely to starve to death. However, they can experience serious health problems, including severe damage to the gastrointestinal system and cardiac arrest from the strain of electrolyte imbalance (Shannon, 2007). Bingeing without purging is another eating disorder. Some binge eaters become extremely overweight because of a genetic defect, but this is not usual (Branson et al., 2003).

To warrant a clinical diagnosis of bulimia, bingeing and purging must occur at least once a week for three months, with uncontrollable urges to overeat and a distorted self-concept of body size. Between 1 and 3 percent of women in the United States are clinically bulimic during early adulthood (American Psychiatric Association, 2000). Some experts argue that the DSM-IV-TR definition of anorexia and bulimia is too restrictive and that many more young women than 3 percent have severe eating disorders (Henig, 2004).

Theories of Eating Disorders

In all eating disorders, consumption is disconnected from the internal cues of hunger, serving some psychological or social need rather than homeostasis (Shannon, 2007). A developmental perspective finds that eating disorders may originate early in life, not only with genes but also with early hunger (which alters the set point) and family food habits. According to one explanation:

> Parental control in child feeding may have unintended effects on the development of eating patterns; [especially with] emphasis on "external" cues in eating and decreased opportunities for the child to experience *self*-control. . . . Parental pressure to eat may result in food dislike and refusal, and restriction may enhance children's liking and consumption of restricted foods.
>
> *[J. O. Fisher & Birch, 2001, p. 35]*

It is not surprising that eating disorders are rooted in childhood, since that is true for most serious problems. But why are females 10 times as likely as males to engage in such destructive self-sabotage? Is nature or nurture the reason? Each of the five theories described in Chapter 2 offers an explanation:

- A *psychoanalytic* hypothesis is that women develop eating disorders to separate psychically from their overbearing mothers, who provided their early feeding. Refusing food becomes a disturbed way to achieve independence.
- *Behaviorism* notes that for some people with low self-esteem (more often women than men), fasting, bingeing, and purging are powerful, immediate reinforcers in that they relieve emotional distress, setting up a destructive stimulus–response chain.
- One *cognitive* explanation is that when young adult women compete with men in jobs and careers, they seek to project a strong, self-controlled, masculine image antithetical to the buxom, fleshy body of the ideal woman of the past.
- *Sociocultural* explanations include the cultural pressure to be "slim and trim" and model-like—a pressure felt strongly by today's emerging adult women, who seek autonomy from their parents and admiration from their peers but not marriage or motherhood.
- The *epigenetic* perspective emphasizes genes and the evolutionary mandate to reproduce. If a girl fears sex and motherhood, then a bony appearance, lack of menstruation, and food obsession quiet her sexual impulses and preclude pregnancy. Anorexia may be "an adaptive postponement" or "a maladaptive suppression of fertility" (Mealey, 2003, pp. 11–12).

Each of these theories may provide insight. Which is most relevant to the following case?

a case to study

"Too Thin, As If That's Possible"

Julia was the elder of two daughters in a suburban two-parent family. She was a model high school student, partly because her mother checked her homework and because both parents monitored her closely. She decided to join the track and cross-country teams for two reasons—to strengthen her college applications and to control her weight. She had no boyfriends; her parents disapproved of high school romances. Julia writes about her first semester of college:

> I have never before felt so much pressure. Because my scholarship depends both on my running and on my maintaining a 3.6 grade point average, I've been stressed out much of the time. Academic work was never a problem for me in the past, but there's just so much more expected of you in college.
>
> It was pressure from my coach, my teammates, and myself that first led me to dieting. . . . I know that my coach was really disappointed in me. He called me aside about a month into the season. He wanted to know what I was eating, and he told me the weight I had gained was undoubtedly hurting my performance. He said that I should cut out snacks and sweets of any kind, and stick to things like salad to help me lose the extra pounds, and get back into shape. He also recommended some additional workouts. I was all for a diet—I hated that my clothes were getting snug. . . . At that point, I was 5 feet, 6 inches and weighed 145 pounds. When I started college I had weighed 130 pounds. . . .
>
> Once I started dieting, the incentives to continue were everywhere. My race time improved, so my coach was pleased. I felt more a part of the team and less like an outsider. My clothes were no longer snug, and when they saw me at my meets my parents said I looked great. I even received an invitation to a party given by a fraternity that only invited the most attractive . . . women. After about a month, I was back to my normal weight of 130 pounds.
>
> . . . I set a new weight goal of 115 pounds. I figured if I hit the gym more often and skipped breakfast altogether, it wouldn't be hard to reach that weight in another month or so. Of course, this made me even hungrier by lunchtime, but I didn't want to increase my lunch size. I found it easier to pace myself with something like crackers. I would break them into several pieces and only allow myself to eat one piece every 15 minutes. The few times I did this with friends in the dining hall I got weird looks and comments. I finally started eating lunch alone in my room. . . . I couldn't believe it when the scale said I was down to 115 pounds. I still felt that I had excess weight to lose. Some of my friends were beginning to mention that I was actually looking too thin, as if that's possible.
>
> . . . All of which brings me to the present time. Even though I'm running great and I'm finally able to stick to a diet, everyone thinks I'm not taking good enough care of myself. . . . I'm doing my best to keep in control of my life, and I wish that I could be trusted to take care of myself.

Julia's roommate writes:

> There were no more parties or hanging out at meals for her. . . . We were all worried, but none of us knew what to do. . . . I looked in the back of Julia's closet. A few months ago I had asked to borrow a tampon. She opened a new box and gave me one. The same box was still there with only that one missing. For the first time, I realized how serious Julia's condition could be.
>
> A few days later, Julia approached me. Apparently she just met with one of the deans, who told her that she'd need to undergo an evaluation at the health center before she could continue practicing with the team. She asked me point blank if I had been talking about her to anyone. I told her how her mother had asked me if I had noticed any changes in her over the past several months, and how I honestly told her yes. She stormed out of the room and I haven't seen her since. I know how important the team is to Julia, so I am assuming that she'll be going to the health center soon. I hope that they'll be able to convince her that she's taken things too far, and that they can help her to get better.
>
> *[quoted in Gorenstein & Comer, 2002, pp. 275–280]*

Julia is a classic case of anorexia nervosa, with rapid weight loss, denial, and lack of menstruation. She believes she is "finally able to stick to a diet" and is "in control," when in fact she is addicted to exercise and weight loss. Serious depression is linked to anorexia; suicide is a danger.

It is not surprising that Julia's coach, parents, and friends did not notice her eating disorder sooner. This time lag is common: "By the time the anorexic reaches the point at which the disorder is clinically identified, she has already become entrapped in a complex web of psychological attitudes" (R. A. Gordon, 2000). Before that point, many people encourage rapid weight loss instead of welcoming the normal weight gain of a healthy developing woman.

Actually, when her coach suggested she diet, Julia's weight after a month of college—145 pounds (65.7 kilograms) for an athlete who is five feet, six inches (1.6 meters) tall—was within the normal range. With a BMI of 25.6, she was only slightly overweight (and, since muscle is heavier than fat, many experts would not consider her overweight at all). Certainly, she was far from obese. Yet everyone was pleased when she lost 15 pounds in a month. Although Julia was in danger, her parents and the fraternity boys encouraged her to continue dieting.

Considering all five theories, each seems plausible. Julia may have been overly dependent on her mother (psychoanalytic), reinforced for weight loss (behaviorism), suffering from distorted thinking (cognitive), surrounded by a culture that encouraged thinness (sociocultural), and avoidant of parties and romance (epigenetic). The theories lead to a concern for her younger sister: Vulnerability to eating disorders is genetic, familial, and cultural. Julia not only needs to get well; she also needs to protect her sister.

Taking Risks

Now we look closely at something that brings both ecstasy and despair. Emerging adults bravely, or foolishly, take risks. Risk taking is not only age-related; it is also genetic and hormonal. Some people—more often males than females—are naturally more daring than others. Thus those who are genetically impulsive, *and* male, *and* emerging adults are most likely to be brave or foolish.

Societies as well as individuals benefit because each generation of emerging adults takes chances. Enrolling in college, moving to a new state or nation, getting married, having a baby—all these endeavors are risky. So is starting a business, filming a documentary, entering an athletic contest, enlisting in the military, and joining the Peace Corps. Emerging adults take these risks, and the rest of society is grateful.

Destructive risks are apparent as well, including having sex without a condom, driving without a seat belt, carrying a loaded gun, and abusing drugs. Accidents, homicides, and suicides are the three leading causes of death among people aged 15 to 25, killing more of them than all diseases combined. This is true even in nations where infectious diseases and malnutrition are rampant. The only national exception is South Africa, where death from AIDS is more frequent than suicide, though it is obviously connected to risk taking as well (Hayes & Weiss, 2006).

edgework Occupations or recreational activities that involve a degree of risk or danger. The prospect of "living on the edge" makes edgework compelling to some individuals.

extreme sports Forms of recreation that include apparent risk of injury or death and that are attractive and thrilling as a result. Motocross is one example.

Edgework

Before lamenting risk taking, we need to recognize the attraction of **edgework**—that is, living on the edge by skillfully managing stress and fear to attain some goal (Lyng, 2005). The joy is in the intense concentration and mastery; edgework is more compelling if failure risks disaster.

Many occupations include edgework, from firefighting to bond trading. One edgework occupation, bicycle messengering, has moments of timeless pleasure. As one social scientist explains, "Their entire lives are wrapped inside a distinct messenger lifestyle that cherishes thrills and threats of dodging cars as they speed through the city" (Kidder, 2006, p. 32; see Research Design).

Most companies pay messengers per delivery, which gives them incentive to run red lights and ride against traffic, but a few companies pay an hourly wage and provide health insurance. One skilled messenger took a job with one of the latter kind of companies because he was getting married and needed better pay and benefits; he complained bitterly that the joy was gone (Kidder, 2006).

Many young adults cannot find a job that satisfies their need for danger. Instead they seek the edge in recreation—climbing mountains, skydiving, and so on. Each of these activities has social guidelines that celebrate risk but not stupidity; novices are shunned until they are recognized as "members of the same tribe" (Laurendeau & van Brunschot, 2006; Lyng, 2005, p. 4).

Other manifestations of the risk-taking impulse are competitive **extreme sports,** which were nonexistent before emerging adults were classified as a distinct age group. For example, freestyle motocross was "practically invented" in the mid-1990s by Brian Deegan and Mike Metzger when they were about 20 years old (Higgins, 2006a). Motocross involves riding motorcycles over barriers and off ramps, including a 50-foot-high leap into "big air." As rider and cycle fall, points are gained by doing tricks, such as backward somersaults. Today,

Research Design

Scientist: Jeffrey Kidder.

Publication: *Sociological Forum* (2006).

Participants: Kidder was a participant-observer: He worked as a bicycle messenger, socialized with other messengers, competed in illegal riding contests, and attended conferences.

Design: By writing field notes, listening carefully, and reading extensively, Kidder connected sociological theories of labor and edgework with his experiences.

Major conclusions: Bicycle messengering has thrills and challenges beyond the monetary rewards (which are quite low). Emerging adults who lack degrees first take the job because they need work. Some stay on because, as one said, "It is the job that I love."

Comment: As a participant-observer, Kidder provides insight and detail regarding dangerous, dirty, and law-breaking work that few scientists understand. As always with qualitative work, the scientist is a filter. Another participant-observer, or another type of study, might report discrepant results.

> As a result of their longevity, Deegan and Metzger [now in their early thirties] are considered legends, graybeard veterans in a much younger man's game. . . . One has lost a kidney and broken a leg and both wrists; the other has broken arms and legs and lost a testicle. Watching them perform, many observers wonder whether they have lost their minds.
>
> *[Higgins, 2006a]*

Observers who wonder about the sanity of these two young men are long past their own daredevil days, but many emerging adults are attracted to extreme sports. One, Travis Pastrana, won the 2006 X Games motocross competition at age 22 with a double backflip because, as he explained, "The two main things are that I've been healthy and able to train at my fullest, and a lot of guys have had major crashes this year" (quoted in Higgins, 2006b). Major crashes are part of every sport Pastrana enjoys.

Drug Abuse

The same impulse that is admired in edgework can also lead to behaviors that are clearly destructive, not only for individuals but for the community as well. The most studied of these destructive behaviors are drug abuse and addiction, both examples of edgework (Reith, 2005) and both more common during contemporary emerging adulthood than at any other age or era.

Drug abuse and addiction can involve a range of drugs, from the perfectly legal to the highly illegal. In fact, two of the most harmful and addictive substances—nicotine and alcohol—are legal in the United States. From a health perspective, legality is irrelevant. What matters is the direct effects of abuse and addiction.

drug abuse The ingestion of a drug to the extent that it impairs the user's biological or psychological well-being.

drug addiction A condition of drug dependence in which the absence of the given drug in the individual's system produces a drive—physiological, psychological, or both—to ingest more of the drug.

Drug abuse occurs whenever a person uses a drug that is harmful to physical, cognitive, or psychosocial well-being. Technically, even one-time use of a legal drug can be abuse. Abuse *usually* entails frequent use (e.g., smoking marijuana regularly) or high doses (e.g., four or more alcoholic drinks on a single occasion).

Drug abuse can eventually lead to **drug addiction,** a condition of dependence in which the absence of a drug causes intense cravings for it in order to satisfy a need. The need may be either physical (to stop the shakes, settle one's stomach, or sleep) or psychological (to quiet fear or lift depression). Withdrawal symptoms are the telltale signs of addiction.

Some adolescents and older adults abuse drugs, but emerging adults have the highest rates of heavy drinking, pill-popping, and illicit drug use. Being with peers, especially in college, seems to encourage drug abuse. In fact, the category of emerging adults least likely to abuse drugs is women who do not go to college, perhaps because many live with their families.

Rates of addiction and abuse fall over the years of adulthood, a decline attributed to both maturity and marriage (Eisner, 2002). One U.S. survey found that 69 percent of the marijuana smokers and 67 percent of the cocaine users had quit by age 30, as had 11 percent of the drinkers (Chen & Kandel, 1995). Other data show a less dramatic decline: Patterns are affected by historical trends as well as age. Each drug in each region has a particular trajectory, influenced partly by use when the adults were adolescents. However, the overall trend is curvilinear, rising during emerging adulthood and then falling with maturity (Johnston et al., 2006). (See Figure 17.4.)

ANDREW LICHTENSTEIN / THE IMAGE WORKS

"Eggs and Kegs" Alcohol serves as a social lubricant for many young adults. In this regular ritual, college students ("eggheads") in the Albany, New York, area gather to drink beer until the last keg runs out, toward dawn. By then, most of them have made new friends and are tired but happy. Others, however, are sick, angry, and tearful.

Tobacco use is an exception to this developmental pattern, probably because nicotine is so highly addictive with little immediate impairment. Not until about age 60 (when health effects become obvious) do smoking rates fall dramatically (U.S. Bureau of the Census, 2006).

Drugs illustrate a problem with numerous kinds of risks. At first, thrills and benefits outweigh hazards, partly because generational forgetting (pp. 387) leads

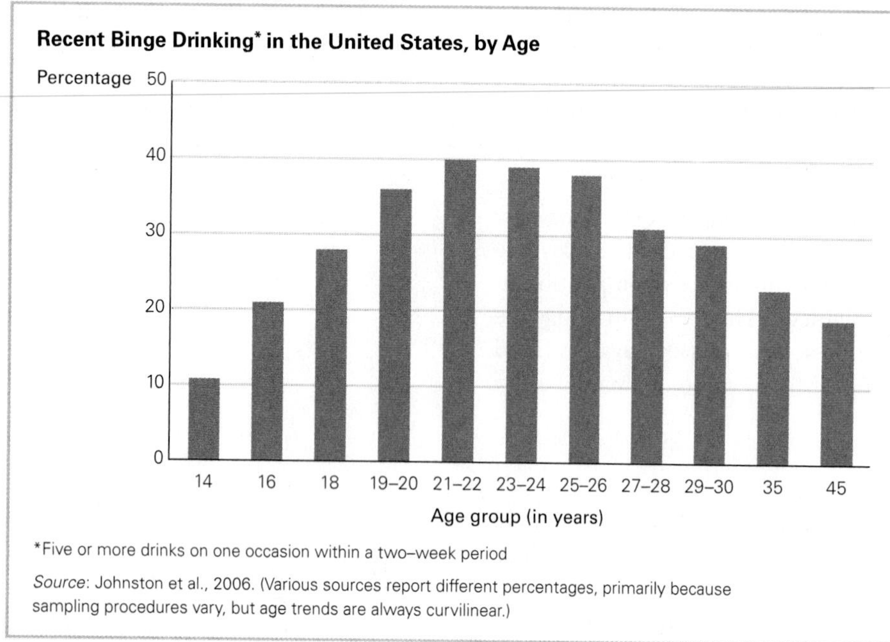

*Five or more drinks on one occasion within a two-week period

Source: Johnston et al., 2006. (Various sources report different percentages, primarily because sampling procedures vary, but age trends are always curvilinear.)

FIGURE 17.4

Laws and Choices Abusive drinking is common throughout adulthood. Laws seem to have some effect on those under the age of 21, and then experience and social setting affect adults as they mature.

each generation to ignore the advice of older adults. Alcohol, for instance, reduces social anxiety, a problem for those who enter college, start a new job, speak to strangers, or embark on a romance. Crossing the line between use and abuse does not ring alarms for young adults, who justify drug use because of the momentary relief it affords and who have not yet seen peers impaired and addicted. Lack of personal witnessing makes generational forgetting possible. Disapproval of drug use is lower during emerging adulthood than at any other age (Johnston et al., 2006).

Long-term data show that drug abuse impairs later life. Those who use drugs heavily in high school are less likely to go to college (Johnston et al., 2006). Those who use drugs heavily in emerging adulthood are less likely to earn a degree, find a good job, or sustain a romance (Eisner, 2002). They are also more likely to get sick and die. For instance, a 21-year study in Scotland found that young adult men who drank heavily doubled their risk of dying by middle age (Hart et al., 1999).

delay discounting The tendency to undervalue, or downright ignore, future consequences and rewards in favor of more immediate gratification.

The fact that young adults ignore later consequences is an example of a logical error called **delay discounting,** the tendency to undervalue, or discount, events in the future. If offered a choice between, say, $100 now and $110 later, delay discounting leads people to undervalue (discount) the delayed reward and choose the immediate one. Delay discounting occurs at every age (for example, lottery winners usually choose to take half immediately rather than all in installments). Emerging adults are particularly likely to underestimate delayed consequences.

This tendency explains a paradox. As a result of school classes and media messages, almost all emerging adults know the life-threatening risks of drug abuse and unprotected sex. Nonetheless, they consume addictive drugs and have sex with partners whose history they do not know. Why? Delay discounting.

Emerging adults who are addicted to drugs are also likely to think they can stop on their own. This belief may help explain another discrepancy noted by researchers: "Perhaps the greatest treatment-related paradox is that although early young adulthood is the time of highest pathological alcohol involvement, treatment for AUDs [alcohol use disorders] appears to peak in later adulthood" (Sher & Gotham, 1999).

issues and applications

What's Wrong with the Men?

It is dangerous to be a young man in the twenty-first century. In the United States, almost 1 male in every 100 dies from suicide, homicide, or an accident between the ages of 15 and 25 (U.S. Bureau of the Census, 2007). (These rates do not include deaths of soldiers.)

Young men drive recklessly, have unprotected sex, enjoy extreme sports, abuse alcohol, take illegal drugs, gamble, volunteer for combat, carry guns, and more. Women and older men do these things, too, but far less often. As a result, emerging adult men die violently four times as often as women of the same age and more often than males of any other age—with the exception of those over age 75, who are more prone to accidents.

Violent death rates among young men in Canada, Mexico, and Australia are almost as high as those in the United States (see Figure 17.5), with differences in specifics (cause of death) but not the sex ratio. For example, Canada has three times as many suicides as homicides, whereas in the United States more young men are killed by someone else than by themselves. Similarly, however, in both nations more men than women die young, and accidents are the leading cause.

Worldwide, four times more young men than women commit suicide or die in motor-vehicle accidents, and six times as many are murdered, almost always by another young man who—in turn, may be killed in retribution. When the data are reported by nation or by ethnic group, the male-to-female ratio for violent death ranges from 3:1 to 10:1 (Heuveline, 2002).

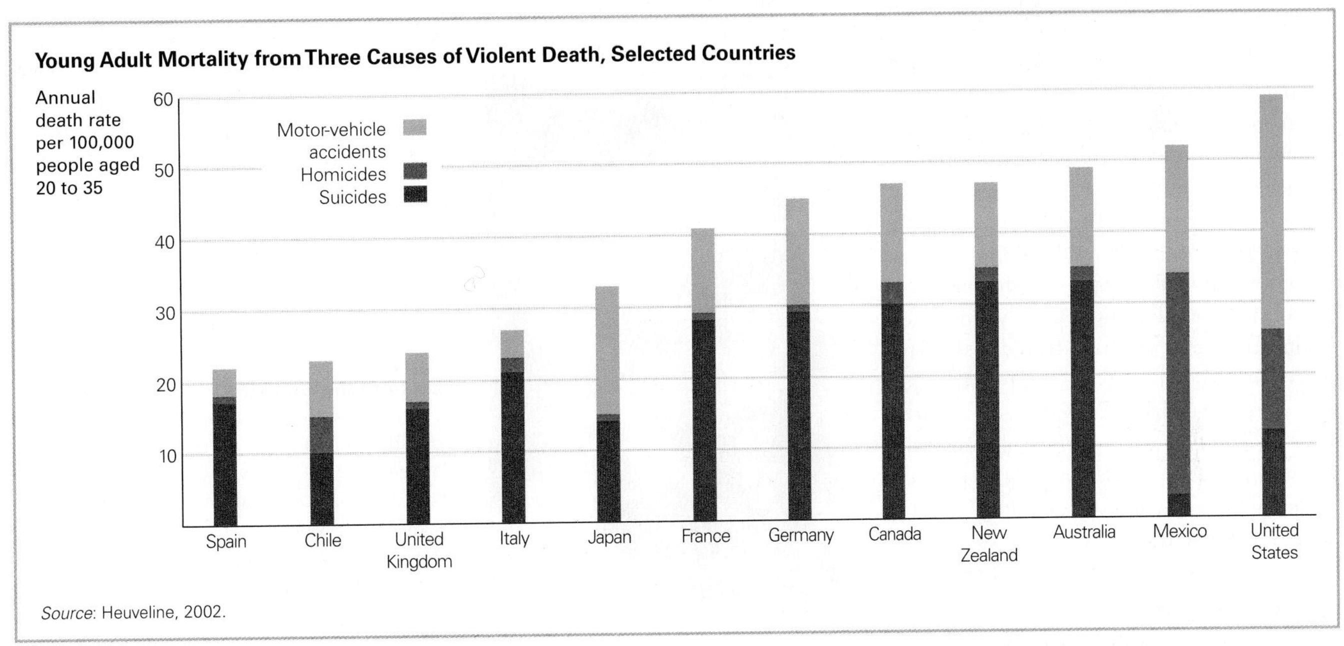

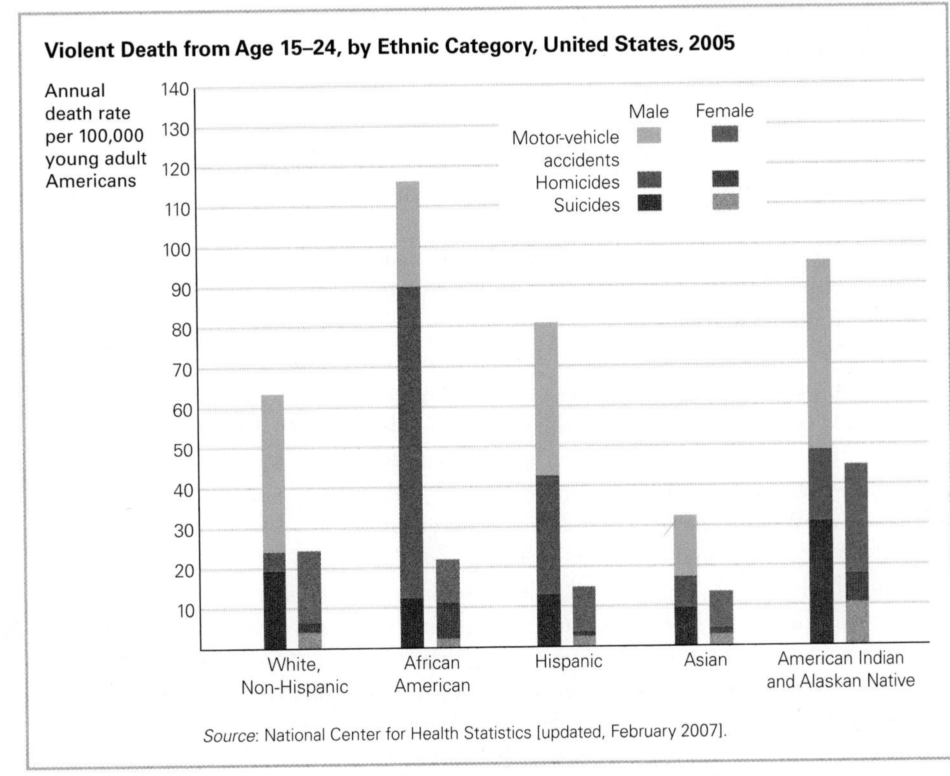

FIGURE 17.5

A Dangerous Time of Life These graphs show the rates of violent death among young adults in selected countries worldwide *(top)* and by U.S. ethnic category *(bottom)*. Worldwide data take years to gather; most of these nations have reduced violent deaths over the last decade. The U.S. data are more recent and are for ages 15–24. Ethnic differences have narrowed over the past decade, but they are still readily apparent. Emerging adulthood is the peak period for all forms of violent death except suicide, which has higher rates among older white males and older Asian females than among young adults.

Observation Quiz (see answer, page 467): In the United States, which group has the smallest gender disparity? Which has the largest?

Why are young men so vulnerable? Biology is a prime hypothesis. The hormone testosterone increases dramatically from boyhood to manhood, and its level often correlates with impulsive, uncontrolled, and angry reactions. This correlation is far from perfect, however: Many studies of humans and other animals find that testosterone is not always a trigger for risk taking and violence (Van Goozen, 2005).

According to another theory from biology, men want to be chosen as sex partners, so they try to prove to potential mates that they are strong and brave, capable of producing superior offspring (Archer, 2004). Thus, although young women may not take risks themselves, they may admire men who do.

A more psychosocial theory is that men respect other men who do dangerous things. Edgework is much more a male endeavor than a female one, with other males acting as companions, rivals, and admirers (Lyng, 2005). A study of young men who had been seriously wounded by other young men found that most of them feared loss of respect and therefore were more concerned about revenge than survival (Rich & Grey, 2005). Another researcher, explaining why men choose more lethal means of parasuicide (guns more often than drugs), notes that men feel that surviving a suicide attempt is feminine, but completed suicide is masculine (Canetto, 1997).

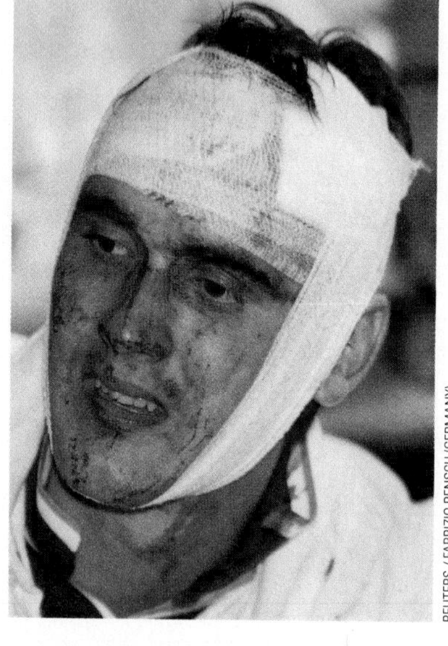

REUTERS / FABRIZIO BENSCH (GERMANY)

Far from the Wild West Europeans and Asians consider the United States a violent nation, the only developed country that imposes the death penalty and the one with the highest homicide rate. But they could look closer to home for examples of violence. This young man is one of hundreds injured in rioting after a soccer match in southern Germany between England and Sweden.

These explanations seem partially valid, but cultural variations require additional analysis. The male/female ratio for violent deaths varies between nations and within them, as well as for each group and type of death. For instance, in the United States, among Latino and African American young adults, the male-to-female sex ratio for firearm deaths is 12:1, compared with 4:1 for Asian Americans of the same age group (National Center for Health Statistics, 2006). Culture, not biology, must be the reason.

Obviously, biological sex is not the only influence on risk taking. Family upbringing and social norms can override male–female biology or roles to influence people (Holder, 2006). If we understood the reasons for such differences, perhaps thousands more emerging adult men would survive unscathed, at least until age 30.

Social Norms

social norms The standards of behavior within a given society or culture, based more on how people should behave than on how they actually behave.

As you have probably realized, one discovery from the study of human development might reduce risk taking and improve health habits among emerging adults—the power of **social norms.** Social norms are standards for typical behaviors within a particular society. They are particularly strong for emerging adults. Now more than in earlier generations, young adults are independent of their parents and do not yet have life partners or children. They seek the approval of others of their generation; social norms matter.

Not only are contemporary emerging adults immersed in social settings (colleges, parties, concerts, sports events) where risk takers are widely admired, they notice these people, such as the classmate who brags that he waited until the last minute and wrote a term paper in one night or the star athlete who did something dangerous and unexpected. Noticing such individuals leads many emerging adults to overestimate the prevalence of risk takers and thus to be influenced by them.

In one experiment, several small groups of college students were offered as much alcohol as they wanted as they socialized with each other. In some groups, one student was secretly recruited in advance to drink heavily; in others, one student was assigned to drink very little; in a third condition, there was no student confederate. In those groups with a heavy drinker, the average student drank more than those in groups with a light drinker or no designated drinker. In these latter two conditions, consumption was the same. Thus, they followed the norm set by the risk takers, not by the cautious ones (reported in Miller & Carroll, 2006).

The U.S. military has provided a natural experiment regarding social norms, with a similar conclusion. In 1990, more military men than civilians abused drugs (including alcohol), with a few loud abusers influencing the rest. Then expectations changed and prohibitions were enforced. Although only a few of the worst offenders were actually charged with drug use, by 1997, only half as many soldiers as civilians were using drugs (Ammerman et al., 1999). Social expectations and perceived norms changed; behavior followed.

The power of social norms is evident in the popularity of extreme sports. For instance, a small group of British men formed the Dangerous Sports Club when they were young adults. They thought of trying bungee jumping on April Fools' Day in 1979. On that day, at first they all backed off, telling the press it was a foolish joke. But later in the afternoon, after drinking, one was filmed bungee jumping. Thousands of other young men saw the video, and before long, bungee jumping became a fad.

A similar story holds for other extreme sports—hang gliding, ice climbing, pond swooping, base jumping—never imagined until one daredevil young adult inspired thousands of others (Cockerham, 2006). Other risky sports, once attractive to hundred of thousands, have become safer, less edgy, and therefore less popular. Boxing, for example, was much more popular 50 years ago than today, now that rules make severe injury less likely.

This research has led to the **social norms approach,** an attempt to reduce risk taking by conducting surveys of emerging adults and using the results to make them aware of the prevalence of various behaviors. About half the colleges in the United States have surveyed alcohol use on their campuses and reported the results (Berkowitz, 2005; Wechsler et al., 2003). In general, when college students realize that most of their classmates study hard, avoid binge drinking, refuse drugs, and are sexually abstinent, faithful, or protected, they are more likely to follow these social norms. Of course, if social norms surveys suggest to lonely, temperate, conscientious students that they are odd, then the opposite of the desired effect may result, with those students engaging in more rather than less risky behavior (Schultz et al., 2007).

Implications

Consider again the developmental problems raised by emerging adults' impulse to experiment and explore. We would all suffer if young adults were timid, traditional, and afraid of innovation. They need to befriend strangers, try new foods, explore ideas, travel abroad, and sometimes risk their lives. The tasks that await—graduating from college, finding a challenging job, getting married, becoming a parent—are all impossible for people who are overly cautious and unwilling to take chances.

But risks should be taken carefully. If the independence of emerging adults leads them to throw caution to the wind, if edgework includes injury, if delay discounting means consequences are ignored, then life itself may be cut short. A college education correlates with better health—including more exercise, healthier eating, less drug use, and longer life (Adler & Snibbe, 2003). This is all the more reason to guard against the foolish risks that seem to accelerate during college.

One of my older students, John, told the class about his experience as an emerging adult. His attitude was amused pride at first. But by the end of his narrative, he was troubled by his actions, partly because John was now the father of a little boy he adored, and he realized that his son might become an equally reckless young man. John told us that, during a vacation break in his first year of college, he and two of his male friends were sitting, bored, on a beach. One friend proposed swimming to an island, barely visible on the horizon. They immediately set

➤**Answer to Observation Quiz** (from page 465): The smallest gender differences are among American Indian and Alaskan Natives; the largest difference is between Hispanic males and females.

social norms approach A method of reducing risky behavior that uses emerging adults' desire to follow social norms by making them aware, through the use of surveys, of the prevalence of various behaviors within their peer group.

out. After swimming for a long time, John realized that he was only about a third of the way there, that he was tired, that the island was merely an empty spit of sand, and that he would have to swim back. He turned around and swam to shore. The friend who made the proposal eventually reached the island. The third boy became exhausted and almost drowned (a passing boat rescued him).

What does this episode signify about the biosocial development of emerging adults? It is easy to understand why John started swimming. The influence of delay discounting, male ego, and social context is evident, as is that of the three friends' joy in their strong arms, lungs, and abilities. Young men like to be active, feeling their physical strength.

Like John, many adults remember fondly the risks they took when they were younger. They forget the friends who caught STIs, who had abortions, who became addicts or alcoholics, or who died young, and they ignore the reality that their younger brothers and sons might do the same. Emerging adulthood is a strong and healthy age, but it is not without serious risks. Why attempt to swim to a distant island? More thinking (Chapter 18) or social rescuing (Chapter 19) may be needed.

SUMMING UP

Emerging adulthood is generally a time of excellent health, but bad choices regarding habits and risks can have harmful effects on development. Good exercise habits established in young adulthood contribute greatly to overall health in middle age and beyond, while sedentary individuals are more likely to develop diabetes and high blood pressure. Good eating habits are also key to preventing these diseases, as well as obesity. While emerging adults are less likely to become obese than are older adults, they are more likely to develop potentially deadly eating disorders such as anorexia and bulimia.

Risk taking is common during young adulthood, and risks can range from the worthwhile (going to college) to the destructive (unprotected sex). In general, males tend to engage in risky behavior more than females do. Some choose edgework occupations—firefighting, for instance—that involve a degree of danger. Emerging adults are particularly vulnerable to drug and alcohol abuse and addiction. Problems arise in part because they seek excitement and in part because they seek the approval of others of their generation. In addition, emerging adults tend to discount or even ignore the potential consequences of risky behavior in favor of a more immediate, though less logical, payoff. Violent death, especially of young men, is too common. ■

SUMMARY

Growth, Strength, and Health

1. Emerging adulthood is a new period of development, characterized by later marriage and more education. Age variations are apparent throughout development; nonetheless, ages 18 to 25 can be described as a distinct period.

2. Most young adults are strong and healthy. All the body systems function optimally during these years; death from disease is rare.

3. Homeostasis and organ reserve help ensure that emerging adults feel strong and recover quickly from infections and injuries. The gradual slowdowns of senescence begin as soon as puberty is complete but are not yet noticed.

4. Emerging adults are usually physically and sexually attractive. This is also the peak time for sexual desire.

5. Reproduction is most successful during emerging adulthood because both male and female bodies are at peak fertility. However, most people this age do not yet want to become parents. Contraception now makes sex without parenthood possible.

6. Sexual relationships before marriage are accepted by most young adults, although they may not realize that being sexually active makes other problems more likely. Disagreement about the purpose of sex—reproduction, relationship, or recreation—can cause emotional stress between partners.

7. Another problem is sexually transmitted infections, which are much more common now than in earlier generations because many young adults have several sexual relationships before marriage. Infertility and even death can result from untreated STIs.

Habits and Risks

8. Many emerging adults engage in adequate exercise, protecting their long-term health by so doing. Ideally, they choose friends and neighborhoods that will keep them active.

9. Good nourishment is important lifelong. Women are especially vulnerable to unhealthy dieting, which can lead to serious eating disorders such as anorexia and bulimia nervosa.

10. Risk taking increases during emerging adulthood, with the thrills of edgework being particularly attractive to young men. Many risks can have life-threatening consequences, including drug abuse and addiction, unprotected sex, and extreme sports. During emerging adulthood, men in particular are at high risk of violent death.

11. Cultural as well as gender variations are evident in risk taking and violent death. Social norms are particularly powerful during these years. These two facts can reduce the hazards of risk taking, as seems to have occurred among college students who drink heavily.

KEY TERMS

senescence (p. 450)
homeostasis (p. 450)
organ reserve (p. 450)
set point (p. 458)
body mass index (BMI) (p. 458)
anorexia nervosa (p. 459)
bulimia nervosa (p. 459)
edgework (p. 462)
extreme sports (p. 462)
drug abuse (p. 463)
drug addiction (p. 463)
delay discounting (p. 464)
social norms (p. 466)
social norms approach (p. 467)

KEY QUESTIONS

1. What age range does emerging adulthood encompass, and what social conventions tend to characterize this period?

2. How and why is physical attractiveness of greater concern to emerging adults than to other age groups?

3. In what ways are the concepts of organ reserve and homeostasis comforting to young adults?

4. How are differing attitudes about the purpose of sex likely to lead to emotional stress?

5. What role can friendships and communities play in maintaining good exercise habits?

6. How can concern about being fat become a health hazard?

7. Why are young adults particularly susceptible to drug use and abuse?

8. What are some ways in which risk taking among emerging adults is influenced by delay discounting?

9. What are the sex differences in the rate of violent deaths, and to what degree are they the result of nature or nurture?

10. How do social norms affect the incidence of health problems in early adulthood?

11. What are the advantages to society of risk taking among young men?

APPLICATIONS

1. What would your priorities be in deciding which groups should receive flu vaccine? Rank professions, ages, nationalities, and other factors, with at least 20 categories overall. Then compare your list with a classmate's, discussing the reasons for similarities and differences.

2. Describe an incident during your emerging adulthood when taking a risk could have led to disaster. What were your feelings at the time? What would you do if you knew that a child of yours was about to do the same thing?

3. Describe the daily patterns of someone you know who has unhealthy habits related to eating, exercise, drug abuse, risk taking, or some other aspect of lifestyle. What would it take for that person to change his or her habits? Consider the impact of time, experience, medical advice, and fear.

4. Use the library or Internet to investigate changes over the past 50 years in the lives of young adults in a particular nation or ethnic group. What caused those changes? Are they similar to the changes reported in the United States?

18

CHAPTER OUTLINE

Emerging Adulthood: Cognitive Development

What did you learn today? When I asked my young children, I sometimes heard about things of no interest to me (like how a bunny eats a carrot); when I asked my adolescents, I sometimes got silence. A child might answer by reciting cold facts, and some adolescents might cynically reply, "Nothing." Adults might say something that connects people and ideas, something thoughtful. But not always; adults do not always think like adults. Nonetheless, beginning in early adulthood, cognition sometimes changes in quality, quantity, speed, topics, efficiency, depth, values, and skills. When and how this happens are topics in this book's three chapters on adulthood cognition.

Cognitive development can be described using many approaches:

- The *stage approach* evaluates whether a new stage or level is reached, such as a postformal stage of thinking and reasoning in adulthood.
- The *psychometric approach* analyzes intelligence by means of IQ tests and other measures.
- The *information-processing approach* studies how the brain encodes, stores, and retrieves information.

All three approaches provide valuable insights into the complex patterns of cognition throughout the life span. Yet, much more than in childhood, as already emphasized in Chapter 17, chronological age is an imperfect marker in adulthood: Adults of various ages think at various levels.

To avoid repetition and confusion, each of the book's remaining chapters on cognitive development (this one and Chapters 21 and 24) emphasize only one approach: a stage theory that focuses on postformal thought here, psychometrics in Chapter 21, and information processing in Chapter 24.

Each chapter also includes age-related topics. (For example, the effects of college education on cognition are described in this chapter.) College has major impact among emerging adults, as you will learn—and as I learned from my children when they sometimes dismissed my innovative political opinions as "first wave" (which meant "old-fashioned"). Each chapter on adult cognition also includes research on various adult ages, since mere age does not determine how adults think. Discussions of morality, religion, and creativity appear and reappear since they are relevant at every age.

Postformal Thought

Thinking in adulthood differs from earlier thinking in three major ways: It is more practical, more flexible, and more dialectical. Each of these aspects will be discussed in turn. Taken together, they are sometimes thought of as constituting a postformal stage of cognitive development, combining a new "ordering of formal operations" with a "necessary subjectivity" (Sinnott, 1998, p. 24). This occurs gradually, not at any particular year or decade.

The Practical and the Personal: A Fifth Stage?

postformal thought A proposed adult stage of cognitive development, following Piaget's four stages, that goes beyond adolescent thinking by being more practical, more flexible, and more dialectical (that is, more capable of combining contradictory elements into a comprehensive whole).

Postformal thought is so called because it follows Piaget's fourth stage, formal operational thought (Arlin, 1984, 1989). This proposed fifth stage is considered the practical one, characterized by "problem finding," not just "problem solving." Adults do not wait for someone else to present a problem to solve. Instead, they take a more flexible and comprehensive approach as they consider various aspects of a situation beforehand, noting difficulties and anticipating problems, dealing with them rather than denying, avoiding, or procrastinating because planning realistically is so difficult.

Compare that with the thinking of adolescents, who may try to use their formal analysis to distill universal truths, develop arguments, and resolve the world's problems. Or they may think spontaneously, using emotions that might lead them astray. The combination of emotion and analysis, applied to practical problems, eludes them. For example, they may impulsively join a protest against child labor in Pakistan but may be unable to figure out when and how they should prepare for a chemistry test. Both activities are important for different reasons, but the teenager has difficulty balancing goals and priorities. Teenagers prefer to use quick, intuitive thought and then act; they can rationally analyze issues, but they rarely think through the specific and practical consequences of their actions.

In adulthood, intellectual skills are harnessed to real educational, occupational, and interpersonal concerns. Conclusions and consequences matter much more. As an example familiar to most college students, professors, in contrast to high school teachers, typically announce assignments and due dates for the entire semester and expect students "to decide for themselves when to do [the work, invoking] that dreaded phrase *time management*" (Howard, 2006, p. 15). Teachers realize that emerging adults only gradually master that skill, so they tailor their expectations to their students' abilities.

Adults accept and adapt to the contradictions and inconsistencies of everyday experience, becoming less playful and more practical. They consider most of life's answers to be provisional, not necessarily permanent; they take irrational and emotional factors into account. For example, planning when to begin writing a term paper that is due in a month may take into account personal emotions (e.g., anxiety, perfectionism), other obligations (at home and at work), and practical considerations (fact checking, library reserves, computer availability, proper formatting). Ignoring all this until the last day is something teenagers might do; emerging adults in college are expected to know better.

Really a Stage?

Some scholars doubt that childhood cognition develops in stages. When the issue is whether stages of adult cognition exist, almost everyone is dubious. Piaget and many other stage theorists, who describe stages of childhood, never imagined a "postformal" stage. If reaching a "stage" means attaining a new set of cognitive skills (as from sensorimotor to preoperational), then adulthood has no stages.

Piaget considered formal operations to be the final cognitive stage, and brain researchers report that the prefrontal cortex finally is developed by age 20 or so.

However, despite evidence that the brain and mind are fully grown by emerging adulthood (although brain changes are continual, with new dendrites connecting and unused neurons dying), certain ways of thinking are evident in adulthood that are rarely found earlier. Context and culture are crucial: A 30-year-old in one place and time may think quite differently from someone the same age in another place and at a different time (Blanchard-Fields et al., 1999). Non-Western cultures also describe adult thought as qualitatively different from adolescent thought, although not everyone sees this as a distinct stage. In Hinduism, for instance, a stage of social embeddedness (similar to problem finding) lasts through middle age, and then a new stage appears at which people are expected to be less engaged in immediate social concerns (Saraswathi, 2005).

In general, although stages that are neurologically based do not appear in adulthood, many scholars find a "qualitative and quantitative change in cognitive functioning through the adult life span" (Schaie & Willis, 2000, pp. 175–178). The term *fifth stage* may be a misnomer, but a new cognitive level is reached if adult life circumstances allow it (Labouvie-Vief, 2006).

A recent study explored the concept that adults think differently than adolescents do. Researchers who did not know the participants' ages categorized participants' descriptions of themselves as *self-protective* (high in self-involvement, low in self-doubt), *dysregulated* (fragmented, overwhelmed by emotions or problems), *complex* (valuing openness and independence above all), or *integrated* (able to regulate emotions and logic). As life experiences accumulated, adults expressed themselves differently. No one under age 20 was at the advanced "integrated" stage, but some adults of every age were (see Figure 18.1). The largest shift occurred between adolescence and emerging adulthood, although not until age 30 were a third at the complex level (Labouvie-Vief, 2006).

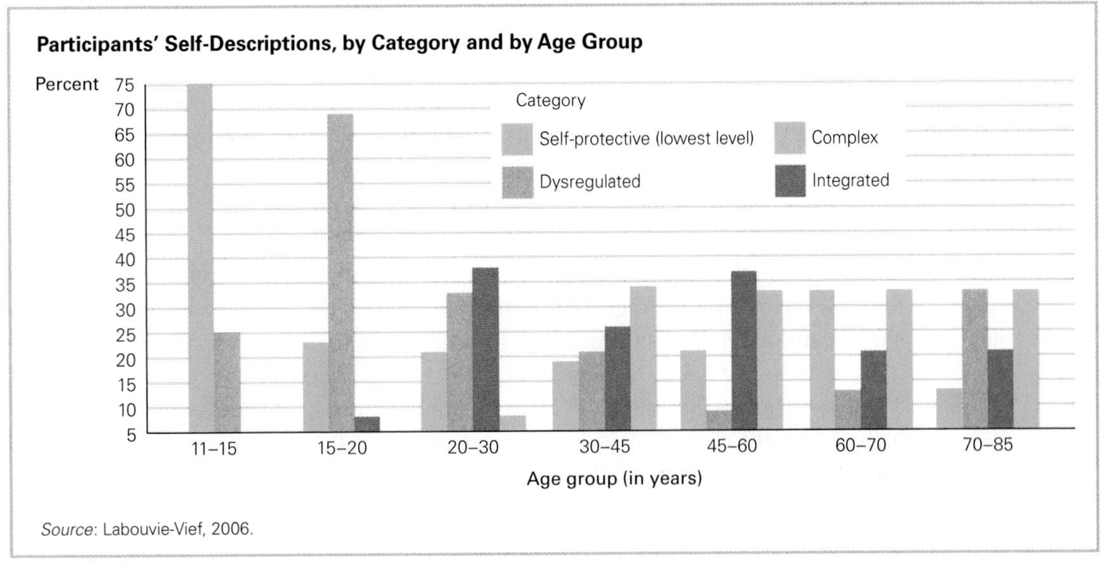

FIGURE 18.1

Talk About Yourself People gradually became less self-centered and less confused as they described themselves over the years of adulthood. Many adults, but no children or adolescents, achieved a level of self-acceptance at which emotions and reason were integrated.

Combining Subjective and Objective Thought

subjective thought Thinking that is strongly influenced by personal qualities of the individual thinker, such as past experiences, cultural assumptions, and goals for the future.

objective thought Thinking that is not influenced by the thinker's personal qualities, but involves facts and numbers that are universally considered true and valid.

One of the practical skills of postformal thinking is combining subjective and objective thought. **Subjective thought** arises from the personal experiences and perceptions of an individual; **objective thought** follows abstract, impersonal logic. Traditional models of formal operational thought devalue subjective feelings, personal faith, and emotional experience while overvaluing objective, logical thinking. Piaget's description of the advanced adolescent is one such model (Klaczynski, 2005), although you remember that intuitive thought is also evident.

Purely objective, logical thinking may be maladaptive when we are dealing with the complexities and commitments of daily life. Subjective feelings and individual experiences must be taken into account because objective reasoning alone is too limited, rigid, and impractical (Sinnott, 1998). Yet subjective thinking is also limited. Truly mature thought involves the interaction between abstract, objective forms of processing and expressive, subjective forms. Adult thought does not abandon objectivity; instead, "postformal logic combines subjectivity and objectivity" (Sinnott, 1998, p. 55) to become personal and practical.

Consolidating Emotions and Logic

Solving the complex problem of combining affect (emotion) and cognition (logic) is the crucial intellectual accomplishment of adulthood. During most of adulthood, "increasing consolidation of more complex cognitive-affective structures continues. . . . Emerging adulthood truly does emerge as a somewhat crucial period of the life span" because "complex, critical, and relativizing thinking emerges only in the 20s" (Labouvie-Vief, 2006, p. 78). Without this consolidation of intellect and emotion (that is, "cognitive-affective structures"), behavioral extremes (such as binge eating, anorexia, obesity, addiction, and violence) or cognitive extremes (such as believing that one is the greatest or the lowest person on earth) are common. By contrast, adults are better able to balance personal experience with knowledge.

As an example of such balance, a student of mine named Laura wrote:

> Unfortunately, alcoholism runs in my family. . . . I have seen it tear apart not only my uncle but my family also. . . . I have gotten sick from drinking, and it was the most horrifying night of my life. I know that I didn't have alcohol poisoning or anything, but I drank too quickly and was getting sick. All of these images flooded my head about how I didn't want to ever end up the way my uncle was. From that point on, whenever I have touched alcohol, it has been with extreme caution. . . . When I am old and gray, the last thing I want to be thinking about is where my next beer will come from or how I'll need a liver transplant.

Especially for Someone Who Has to Make an Important Decision Which is better: to go with your gut feelings or to consider pros and cons as objectively as you can?

Laura's thinking about alcohol is postformal in that it combines knowledge (e.g., of alcohol poisoning) with emotions (images flooded her head). Note that she is cautious, not abstinent: She does not need to go to the extreme of becoming alcoholic (as some college students do) and then to the other extreme of avoiding even one sip (as recovering alcoholics must). This development of postformal thought regarding alcohol is seen in most U.S. adults over time: Those in their early 20s are most likely to abuse alcohol (Bingham et al., 2005), but with a few years of experience and cognitive maturity, most are more mature with their drinking by age 25 or 30, drinking occasionally and moderately from then on (Schulenberg et al., 2005).

Looking at all the research makes it apparent that combining emotions and logic is a challenge when the issue at stake is deeply personal. In Chapter 15, you read that adolescents' cognition suffers when their own religion is under attack or when intuitive thinking overwhelms formal operational thought. The same problem happens to many adults, but some adults are better able than others to put emotions into perspective. In general, teenagers use either objective *or* subjective reasoning, but adults can combine the two (Blanchard-Fields et al., 1999).

Cognitive Flexibility

The ability to be practical—to predict, to plan, and to combine objective and subjective mental processes—is valuable; it is fortunate that adults can reach that postformal level. However, plans can go awry. For example, corporate restructuring might require looking for another job, a failure of birth control might mean dealing with an unwanted pregnancy, a parent's illness might require changing one's plans for higher education. Almost every adult experiences such events. Those with cognitive flexibility avoid retreating into either emotions or intellect. Instead they reflect on their options, combining emotions and reason, taking time to select the best course of action (Lutz & Sternberg, 1999; Wethington, 2000).

Thus, a hallmark of postformal cognition is intellectual flexibility. This comes from the realization that each person's perspective is only one of many; that each problem has many potential solutions; and that knowledge is dynamic, not static (Sinnott, 1998). Emerging adults begin to realize that "there are multiple views of the same phenomenon" (Baltes et al., 1998, p. 1093). Listening to other people, considering their opinions without immediately agreeing or disagreeing, is a sign of flexibility.

Working Together

Consider flexibility in trying to solve this problem:

> Every card in a pack has a letter on one side and a number on the other. Imagine that you are presented with the following four cards, each of which has something on the back. Turn over only those cards that will confirm or disconfirm this proposition: *If a card has a vowel on one side, then it always has an even number on the other side.*
>
> E 7 K 4
>
> Which cards must be turned over?

The difficulty of this puzzle is "notorious" (Moshman, 2005, p. 36). Almost everyone wants to turn over the E and the 4; almost everyone is mistaken. In one experiment with college students working on their own, 91 percent got it wrong. However, when groups of college students who had guessed wrong on their own discussed the problem, 75 percent got it right, avoiding the 4 card (even if it has a consonant on the other side, the statement could still be true) and selecting the E and the 7 cards (if the 7 has a vowel on the other side, the proposition is proved false). They were able to think things through, changing their minds after listening to others (Moshman & Geil, 1998). This is cognitive flexibility.

Daily life for young adults shows many signs of such flexibility. The very fact that emerging adults marry and become parents later than previous generations did (as reviewed in Chapter 17) suggests that, couple by couple, thinking processes are not tied to childhood experiences or traditional norms. Similarly, college plans (courses to be taken, majors declared, careers sought, degrees earned) typically change several times between students' first and last semesters, as advice from other students and professors, as well as personal experience, provides new information (T. Miller et al., 2005).

Such data on behavioral change could be attributed to many factors other than cognitive flexibility. However, research specifically examining adult cognition finds

➤Response for Someone Who Has to Make an Important Decision (from page 474): Both are necessary. Mature thinking requires a combination of emotions and logic. To make sure you use both, take your time (don't just act on your first impulse) and talk with people you trust. Ultimately, you will have to live with your decision, so do not ignore either intuitive or logical thought.

that adults are more likely than children to imagine several solutions for every problem and then to take care in selecting the best one.

For example, in one study, adults of various ages were asked to suggest solutions to 15 life problems (Artistico et al., 2003). Most participants found several possible solutions for each dilemma, as postformal thinkers (but not concrete or formal thinkers) usually do. The more familiar the problem, the more possibilities were suggested. For example, losing motivation to finish a college degree evoked an average of four solutions from younger adults but only one or two from older adults. By contrast, a concern of late adulthood, the desire to have relatives visit more frequently, evoked an average of four solutions from older adults but only two from younger adults.

Research on problem-solving abilities of adults of various ages concludes that emerging adults are better problem solvers than both adolescents and the oldest adults. The reason is cognitive: Young adults are better able to set aside their stereotypes and are not limited by familiar ideas (Klaczynski & Robinson, 2000; Thornton & Dumke, 2005).

The ability to find multiple solutions to any practical problem is one hallmark of postformal thought (Sinnott, 1998). Of course, individuals differ in their cognitive flexibility, and experience helps. Evidence comes from another study, in which older adults were asked what a man should do if his lawn needs mowing but his doctor has told him to take it easy (Marsiske & Willis, 1995, 1998). Think of as many solutions as you can. Now look at Table 18.1 (on page 478). If you see solutions that did not occur to you, remember that this problem is more familiar to older than younger adults. After adolescence, when people encounter complex problems, maturity and experience help them become more strategic as well as more flexible: They seek advice and control their initial impulses (Byrnes, 2005).

Countering Stereotypes

Cognitive flexibility, particularly the ability to change one's childhood assumptions, is needed to counter stereotypes. Look at the U.S. survey findings diagrammed in Figure 18.2.

Not only do younger adults hold less gender-stereotyped views than older ones, but a close look at age trends (comparing cohort changes over a 24-year period) reveals that many adults changed their minds about men's political superiority. Half of the 18- to 24-year-olds who thought in 1972–1974 that men were better at politics no longer held that idea 24 years later. That this is a genuine cognitive shift is suggested by other data from the same survey showing that opinions did not shift much on non-stereotype issues and that, over these years, the attitudes of younger and older generations converged (T. W. Smith, 2005; see Research Design). Since childhood experiences and historical circumstances differ for each cohort, this convergence indicates that adults can reflect on current experiences and can override childhood stereotypes.

Less prejudice regarding women in politics is apparent not only in opinions but also in behavior: In 1973 the U.S. Senate was exclusively male, but in 2006 there were 14 female senators. The same political trend is apparent worldwide: Dozens of female heads of state

FIGURE 18.2

Older and Wiser? As evidence for adult postformal thought, half of the young adults in 1973 who thought men were better at politics than women changed their minds by middle age. Other data from the same survey indicate that adults have become less prejudiced about gender, race, and sexuality but have not changed their minds about other matters. This shows that opinions during adulthood change because of experiences and reflection, not simply because of maturation.

Observation Quiz (see answer, page 478): How much change over 25 years is found in the opinions of the cohort who were emerging adults in 1973?

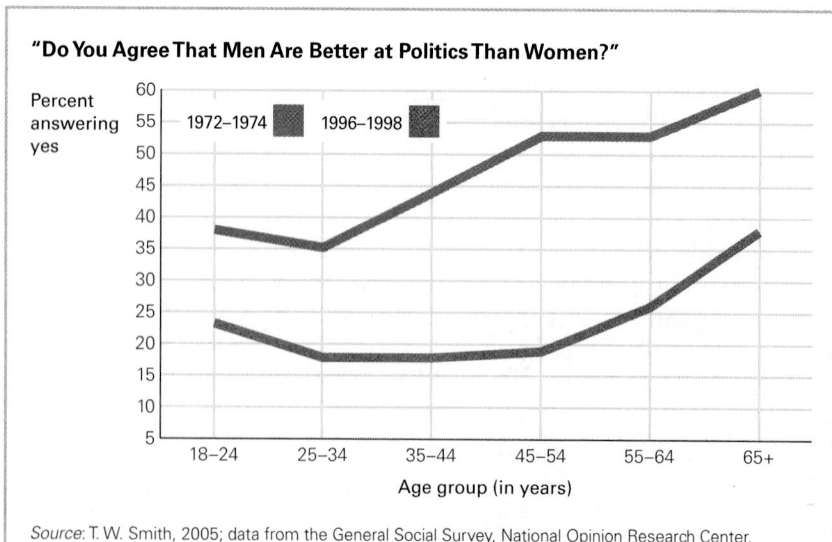

Source: T. W. Smith, 2005; data from the General Social Survey, National Opinion Research Center.

have been elected over the past few decades; both Chile and Liberia elected their first woman president in 2006.

Research on changes in racial prejudice in adulthood merits closer study. Many European American children and adults harbor some implicit bias against African Americans; this bias is detectable in their slower reaction time when mentally processing photos of African Americans as compared with photos of European Americans (Baron & Banaji, 2006). By adulthood, however, most people in the United States today believe that they are not racially prejudiced, and their behavior reveals no bias (at least in explicit tests in a research laboratory). Thus, many adults have both unconscious prejudice and rational nonprejudice, a combination that illustrates dual processing (explained on p. 398). Cognitive flexibility allows adults to recognize their emotional biases and to change their behaviors—both difficult without openness and flexibility.

People are often unaware of their stereotypes, even when those false beliefs harm themselves. One of the most pernicious self-prejudices is called **stereotype threat,** the worry that other people assume that you, yourself, are stupid, lazy, oversexed, or worse because of your race, sex, age, or weight (Steele, 1997). The mere *possibility* of being negatively stereotyped arouses emotions that can disrupt cognition as well as emotional regulation (Inzlicht et al., 2006).

Not everyone experiences stereotype threat, and not every context evokes it. The feeling is particularly strong as ethnic and gender identities are being developed (Good et al., 2003), a process that begins in adolescence and is usually completed in emerging adulthood (as explained in Chapters 16 and 19).

Stereotype threat is particularly likely when circumstances remind the person of a possible threat "in the air," not an overt threat (Steele, 1997). For example, in one study, young adults first answered a questionnaire that assessed how strongly they identified with their gender and then tried to solve 20 difficult math problems (Schmader, 2002). Half of the participants simply took the test, but the other half were told that the purpose of the exam was to discover sex differences, which reminded them of the stereotype that women are deficient in math. Men and women scored equally well, except for one group that had lower average scores: women who heard that sex differences would be assessed *and* who identified strongly with their sex. Apparently, the possible threat triggered anxiety, which interfered with their performance.

Another possible example is that African American men have lower grades in high school and earn far fewer college degrees than their peers, including their

Research Design

Scientist: T. W. Smith.

Publication: General Social Survey (GSS), National Opinion Research Center (2005).

Participants: Between 700 and 3,000 adults in U.S. households every year or two since 1972.

Design: Questions were answered regarding demographic characteristics (age, ethnicity, SES) and social issues. Participants' opinions were then categorized by age and chronological year. The Smith study combines several years.

Major conclusion: Opinions did not shift much on nonstereotype issues. Over the years, the attitudes of younger and older generations converged.

Comment: This convergence indicates that with improved cognitive flexibility, adults can reflect on current experiences to potentially override preconceived notions or stereotypes established in childhood.

stereotype threat The possibility that one's appearance or behavior will be misread to confirm another person's oversimplified, prejudiced attitudes.

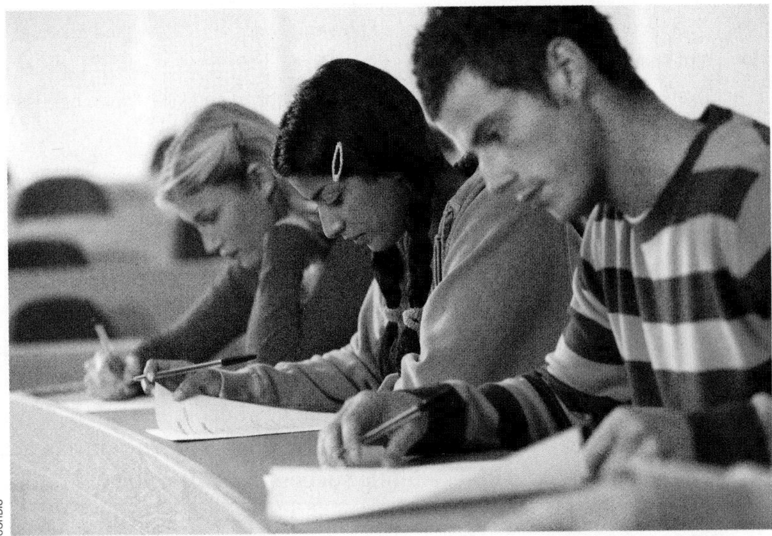

CORBIS

The Threat of Bias If students fear that others expect them to do poorly in school because of their ethnicity or gender, they may not identify with academic achievement and do worse on exams than they otherwise would have.

Observation Quiz (see answer, page 478): Which of these three college students taking an exam is least vulnerable to stereotype threat?

TABLE 18.1

Four Adults' Solutions to an Everyday Problem: Examples of Practical Creativity

Problem: Let's say that a 67-year-old man's doctor has told him to take it easy because of a heart condition. It's summertime and the man's yard needs to be mowed, but the man cannot afford to pay someone to mow the lawn. What should he do?

Subject A

- Do not mow the yard.
- Pray that someone will do it for me . . . Let my church know I have a need . . . Tell any help agency.
- If I have children . . . let them know of my need.

Subject B

- If the man has a yard, he must be living in a house. The best thing he could do would be to sell the house and move into an apartment with no yard or upkeep.
- He could trade services with a younger neighbor. The neighbor would mow his lawn in return for the man walking the neighbor's dog, watching his children, etc.
- He could call his city or county human services department . . . and ask if there are volunteers.
- He could ask a grandson to mow it without pay.

Subject C

- Immediately start planning to live in a situation that is suitable to his condition. Plan ahead.
- In the meanwhile, he should see if relative or friend could help him until he changes abode.
- Possibly he could exchange the mowing for some service he can do, like babysitting or tutoring.
- Be sure to get a second medical opinion.
- Talk to his church or organization people. Trade services.
- Check civic organizations.
- Possibly [borrowing] a riding mower might be suitable—until he changes abode.
- Get a part-time job, and earn enough to pay for help.

Subject D

- Move to quarters not having a yard to maintain.
- Cover lawn with black plastic sheeting . . . remove plastic in fall and sow rye grass.
- Rent a room to a man who will care for yard as part payment of room.
- Marry a young physical training teacher who loves yard work.
- Tether sheep in yard.
- Buy a reconditioned remote-controlled power mower, shrubbery, and flowers.
- Plant shade trees.
- Cover yard with river rock and/or concrete and apply weed killer when necessary.
- Plant a vegetable garden in yard.
- Plant a grain seed and sell harvest.

Sources: Marsiske & Willis, 1995, 1998, in Adams-Price, 1998, pp. 100–101.
The problem comes from Denney and Pearce, 1989.

➤Answer to Observation Quiz (from page 476): About half of those who thought men were better at politics changed their minds (from 38 percent agreement to 19 percent).

➤Answer to Observation Quiz (from page 477): It depends on what is being tested and on the students' backgrounds. White males are generally least vulnerable, but if the test is about literature and if the male student believes that men are not as good as women at writing about poetry and fiction, his performance on the exam may be affected by that stereotype.

genetic peers, African American women. Although social and economic inequality is part of the reason, a cognitive interpretation is also possible (Cokley, 2003; Sackett et al., 2004). If African American males become aware of a stereotype that they are good athletes but poor scholars, it might make them anxious and then make them disidentify with academic success. That would lead to disengagement from studying, and then to lower grades and test scores (Ogbu, 2003).

Stereotype threat may affect people from many groups. In addition to those already cited, members of "caste-like minorities in industrial and nonindustrial nations throughout the world (e.g., the Maoris of New Zealand, the Baraku of Japan, the Harijans of India, the Oriental Jews of Israel, and the West Indians of Great Britain)" all show evidence of stereotype threat (Steele, 1997, p. 623).

How do unconscious prejudices relate to postformal thought? Since everyone has some childhood stereotypes hidden in their brain, adults need flexible cognition to overcome them, abandoning prejudices learned earlier. Is this possible? Yes, as the following explains.

thinking like a scientist

Reducing Stereotype Threat

Stereotype threat can make women and minorities doubt their intellectual ability. That doubt reduces learning if they become anxious in academic contexts, performing below their potential.

Many programs attempt to raise the academic achievement of individuals whose potential seems unrealized. Surprisingly successful are colleges whose students are predominantly women or African American (Astin & Osequera, 2002; Freeman & Thomas, 2002). Perhaps context is crucial: If everyone in a group has the same background, stereotype threat is diminished.

But what can reduce stereotype threat when students are a minority at their college? In theory, people will be less threatened by any stereotype if they believe that achievement depends more on their effort than on inborn, genetic traits (Steele, 1997). In other words, if adults accept that IQ can be improved through hard work, they can overcome handicaps caused by stereotype threat.

This idea led to a hypothesis: Intellectual performance increases if people *internalize* (believe wholeheartedly, not just intellectually) the idea that intelligence is plastic and can be changed. One group of scientists tested this hypothesis, building on two findings from prior research: (1) Stereotype threat regarding intellectual ability is powerful among African Americans, and (2) people are more likely to accept and internalize ideas when they express those ideas, a phenomenon called "saying is believing."

In an experiment, researchers recruited African American and European American students at Stanford University, where African Americans are a small minority (Aronson et al., 2002; see Research Design). The students were randomly divided into three equal groups. For Group I, attitudes regarding college were measured before and after the experimental period, but no intervention occurred.

Students in Groups II and III experienced almost identical interventions, in three sessions. First, they read a letter supposedly written by a struggling junior high student, and they were asked to write an encouraging response that included current research on intelligence. In the second session, the experimenter praised their letters and gave them a thank-you note ostensibly from the younger student. They were then to encourage other young students by preparing a speech, which was videotaped as a first draft and later, at the third session, was taped again in a "final" version. All three sessions were designed to help them internalize a message about intelligence.

The only difference between Groups II and III was in the particular research they learned about (via a video as well as written text) and were asked to incorporate into their letters and speeches. Group II was told to emphasize that there are multiple intelligences (see Chapter 11). Group III was asked to explain that intelligence expands with effort and that new neurons may grow (e.g., Segalowitz & Schmidt, 2003). This later research undercuts the notion that racial differences in IQ are genetic, thus reducing stereotype threat.

The intervention in Group III succeeded. Compared with participants in Groups I and II, participants in Group III changed their ideas about the plasticity of intelligence, and African Americans in particular improved their attitudes about

Research Design

Scientists: Joshua Aronson, Carrie Fried, and Catherine Good.

Publication: *Journal of Experimental Social Psychology* (2002).

Participants: A total of 79 Stanford undergraduates of both sexes, 42 African American and 37 European American.

Design: Students with the same measures were divided into three groups—Group I had no intervention, Group II learned about multiple intelligences, and Group III learned that intelligence depends on effort, not innate ability. They answered questionnaires about attitudes toward college, IQ, and GPA before and after the intervention (if any). Results were adjusted so that scores on the SAT (a standardized test of ability) were equalized, which means that individuals were compared with others of the same tested potential.

Major conclusion: Compared with participants in Groups I and II, those in Group III changed their ideas about the plasticity of intelligence, so the intervention in Group III succeeded in reducing stereotype threat.

Comments: This experiment and other research suggest that although stereotype threat is powerful, emotions about cognition can change.

academic achievement, reported more joy in learning, and increased their average grades (see Table 18.2).

This experiment and other research suggest that stereotype threat is powerful and that emotions about cognition can change. Emerging adults who have suffered from racial prejudice and whose social context elicits stereotype threat can show cognitive flexibility, reducing anxiety, increasing learning, and raising their grades.

TABLE 18.2

Attitudes and Grades in Academic Term Following Stereotype-Threat Experiment

	Group I (no intervention)		Group II (IQ is multiple)		Group III (IQ is malleable)	
	Blacks	Whites	Blacks	Whites	Blacks	Whites
Value placed on academics, from 1 (lowest) to 7 (highest)	3.5	5.7	3.9	5.7	4.8	5.6
Average grade	B	B+	B	B+	B+	A–

Source: Aronson et al., 2002.

Dialectical Thought

dialectical thought The most advanced cognitive process, characterized by the ability to consider a thesis and its antithesis simultaneously and thus to arrive at a synthesis. Dialectical thought makes possible an ongoing awareness of pros and cons, advantages and disadvantages, possibilities and limitations.

thesis A proposition or statement of belief; the first stage of the process of dialectical thinking.

antithesis A proposition or statement of belief that opposes the thesis; the second stage of the process of dialectical thinking.

synthesis A new idea that integrates the thesis and its antithesis, thus representing a new and more comprehensive level of truth; the third stage of the process of dialectical thinking.

With all aspects of postformal thinking, advanced thinking at any point of adulthood is a "promise, not reality" (Labouvie-Vief, 2006). Postformal thought, at its best, becomes **dialectical thought,** said to be the most advanced cognitive process (Basseches, 1984, 1989; Riegel, 1975). The word *dialectic* refers to a philosophical concept (developed by the German philosopher Georg Hegel in the early nineteenth century) that every idea or truth bears within itself the opposite idea or truth. Other philosophers and cultures over the centuries also recognized dialectical thought (Wong, 2006).

To use the words of philosophers, each idea, or **thesis,** implies an opposing idea, or **antithesis.** Dialectical thought involves considering both these poles of an idea simultaneously and then forging them into a **synthesis**—that is, a new idea that integrates both the original and its opposite. Note that the synthesis is not a compromise; it is a new idea that incorporates both original ideas. For example, many young children idolize their parents (thesis), many adolescents are highly critical of their parents (antithesis), and many emerging adults appreciate their parents but realize they are influenced by their background and age (synthesis).

Because ideas always initiate their opposites, change is continuous. Each new synthesis deepens and refines the thesis and antithesis that initiated it: Dialectical change results in developmental growth (Sinnott, 1998).

Dialectical thinking involves the constant integration of beliefs and experiences with all the contradictions and inconsistencies of daily life. Educators who agree with Russian theorist Lev Vygotsky that learning is a social interaction within the zone of proximal development (with learners and mentors continually adjusting to each other) are taking a dialectical approach to education (Vianna & Stetsenko, 2006). Dialectical processes are readily observable by life-span researchers, who believe that "the occurrence and effective mastery of crises and conflicts represent not only risks, but also opportunities for new development" (Baltes et al., 1998, p. 1041). As Chapter 1 emphasized, life-span change is multidirectional, ongoing, and often surprising—a dynamic, dialectical process.

A "Broken" Love Affair

Let's look at an example of dialectical thought familiar to many: the end of a love affair (Basseches, 1984). A nondialectical thinker is likely to believe that each person has stable, independent traits. Faced with a troubled romance, then, the nondialectical thinker concludes that one partner (or the other) is at fault, or perhaps the relationship was a mistake from the beginning because the two were a "bad match."

By contrast, dialectical thinkers see people and relationships as constantly evolving; partners are changed by time as well as by their interaction. Adjustment is necessary and inevitable for every couple. Therefore, a romance does not become troubled because the partners are fundamentally incompatible or because one or the other is at fault but because both have changed without adapting. Marriages do not "break" or "fail"; they either continue to develop over time (dialectically) or stagnate. Ideally, both members of a relationship develop dialectical processes, with each partner recognizing the needs of the other and moving forward with a new synthesis (McCarthy & McCarthy, 2004).

Does this happen in practice as well as in theory? Perhaps. Certainly teenage marriages are more likely to end in divorce than adult marriages are. People of all ages are upset when a romance ends, but, perhaps because of neurological immaturity, the younger a person is, the more likely he or she is to be overcome by jealousy or despair, unable to find the synthesis (Fisher, 2006). Older couples may be less likely to divorce because both partners think more dialectically and therefore move from thesis ("I love you because you are perfect") past antithesis ("I hate you because you can't do anything right") to synthesis ("Neither of us is perfect, but together we can grow").

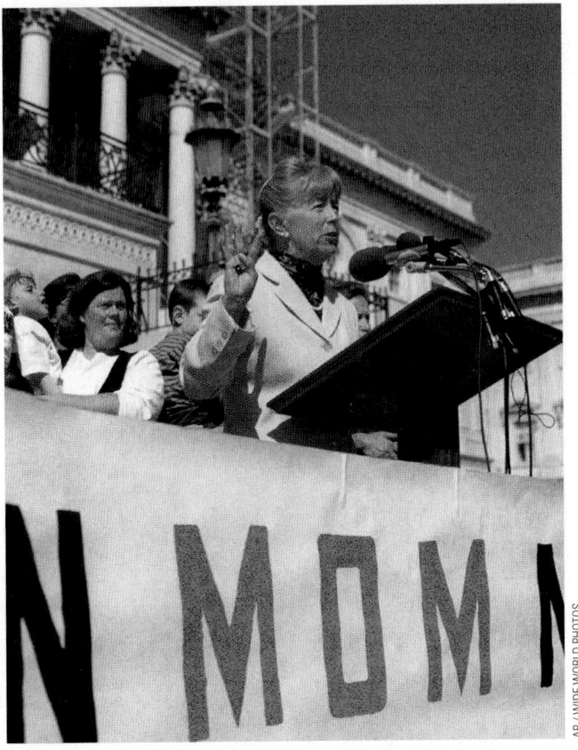

AP / WIDE WORLD PHOTOS

One Woman's Dialectical Journey In dialectical thinking, individuals develop new thoughts that seem opposed to their original thinking. Eventually, a new cognitive pattern incorporates both the original idea and the opposing one. In 1994, Carolyn McCarthy thought of herself primarily as a wife, mother, nurse (thesis)—until her husband was senselessly murdered, and her son seriously wounded, by a gunman on a shooting rampage on a commuter train. She began to question many basic assumptions in her life and in the social order (antithesis). In particular, she opposed her Republican congressman—whom she had previously supported—because he was against gun control. This led to a synthesis in which she herself ran for Congress, as a Democrat, winning the seat to become a public advocate for a much wider community.

Observation Quiz (see answer, page 483): What event is Representative McCarthy promoting?

A similar dialectical process occurs among other people in close relationships (Montgomery & Baxter, 1998). This was very evident in a study of grandmothers, mothers, and daughters, whose relationships were rife with contradictions between "unified opposites" (Miller-Day, 2004, p. 77).

New demands, roles, responsibilities, and even conflicts become opportunities for growth (Wethington, 2002). Dialectically, a student might enroll in a course in a subject area that is unfamiliar, an employee might seek an unexpected promotion, a young adult might leave his parents' household and move to another town. In such situations, when comfort collides with the desire for growth, dialectical thinkers find a new synthesis, gaining insight (Newirth, 2003).

Dialectical thinking is more often found in middle-aged people than in emerging adults, and it is rare in adolescents (Vukman, 2005). Regression is possible. Degradation of complex thinking can be caused by any emotionally charged event, such as the death of a friend; the start of a new romance; or, according to developmentalist Gisela Labouvie-Vief (2006), a national tragedy such as the terrorist attacks of September 11, 2001, to which most adults reacted with an emotional surge of patriotism, heroism, fear, and prejudice.

Culture and Dialectics

Does cultural background affect cognitive processes? Probably. Several researchers believe that ancient Greek philosophy led Europeans to use analytic, absolutist logic—to take sides in a battle between right and wrong, good and evil—whereas Confucianism and Taoism led the Chinese and other Asians to seek compromise, the "Middle Way." Asians tend to think holistically, about the whole rather than the parts, seeking the synthesis because "in place of logic, the Chinese developed a dialectic" (Nisbett et al., 2001, p. 305). (Of course, such cultural distinctions exaggerate the variability in both places.)

In one series of experiments, Asian and European American students were asked to respond to various situations like this one:

> Mary, Phoebe, and Julie all have daughters. Each mother has held a set of values that has guided her efforts to raise her daughter. Now the daughters have grown up, and each of them is rejecting many of her mother's values. How did it happen and what should they do?
>
> *[Peng & Nisbett, 1999]*

As part of this research, judges who did not know the ethnic backgrounds of the respondents scored the answers as to whether they sought some middle ground (a dialectical response) or took sides. For example, a response like "Both mothers and daughters have failed to understand each other" is a dialectical statement, whereas "Mothers have to recognize that daughters have a right to their own values" is not (Peng & Nisbett, 1999). Asians were more often dialectical, searching for a compromise that satisfied both generations.

Another series of studies compared three groups of students: one group consisting of Koreans in Seoul, Korea; one of Korean Americans who had lived most of their lives in the United States; and one of U.S.-born European Americans. Participants were told:

> Suppose you are the police officer in charge of a case involving a graduate student who murdered a professor. . . . As a police officer, you must establish motive.
>
> *[Choi et al., 2003]*

Participants were given a list of 97 items of information and were asked to identify the ones they would want to know about as they looked for the killer's motive. Some of the 97 items were clearly relevant (e.g., whether the professor had publicly ridiculed the graduate student), and virtually every student in all three groups wanted to know about them. Some were clearly irrelevant (e.g., the graduate student's favorite color), and almost everyone left them out. Other items were questionable (e.g., what the professor was doing that fateful night; how the professor was dressed). Compared with both groups of Americans, the students in Korea asked for 15 more items, on average. The researchers believe that students in Seoul had been taught by their culture to include the entire context in order to find a holistic, balanced synthesis (Choi et al., 2003).

Describe This Scene According to some research, Asians tend to take in the whole scene, whereas European are likely to focus on the central image.

Observation Quiz (see answer, page 484): What peripheral details are more likely to be noticed by an Asian than by a European?

AP PHOTO / KEITH SRAKOCIC

Dialectical thought affects priorities and values. Extensive cross-cultural research on well-being finds that Western adults are happiest when they achieve a personal triumph, but Chinese adults are happiest when they find a synthesis of several social roles (Lu, 2005). Other research finds a positive correlation between the frequency of experiencing joy and distress among Asian Americans as well as among Japanese in Japan. No such correlation was found among European and Hispanic Americans (Scollon et al., 2005). One interpretation is that dialectical thinkers seek a balance of happy and unhappy moments, reminding themselves of certain joys when they are sad and vice versa.

Researchers agree that notable differences between Eastern and Western thought are the result of nurture, not nature—that "cognitive differences have ecological, historical and sociological origins" (Choi et al., 2003, p. 47), not genetic ones. None insist that one way of thinking is always better than the other. In fact, the notion that there is one "best way" is not dialectical, although most developmentalists think that a flexible process of reflection and change is more advanced than simply sticking to one thesis.

SUMMING UP

Adult thinking both advances and declines over many decades, not following a strict chronological timetable or proceeding to a universally recognized stage. Some believe that a fifth stage of cognition follows Piaget's fourth stage of formal operational thought, although most researchers prefer to think of adult thinking as potentially reaching new levels, not a new stage. Postformal thinking is characterized by more practical, flexible, and dialectical thought.

The real-life responsibilities that are typical in adulthood advance cognition, in part because neither logical analyses nor emotional reactions are adequate in isolation. Adults are better able to abandon their stereotypes and adapt their long-term relationships because of their cognitive advances. Some adults think dialectically, with thesis leading to antithesis and then synthesis. This ever-changing, dynamic cognition is characteristic of intellectually advanced adults and is more evident in some contexts and cultures than others. ■

➤Answer to Observation Quiz (from page 481): Reading the letters on the sign helps if you are not only good at guessing the missing words but also politically astute about gun control. She is promoting the Million Mom March that was held in May 2000 to demand stronger gun-control laws.

Morals and Religion

According to many researchers, adult responsibilities, experiences, and education affect moral reasoning and religious beliefs. This maturation of values appears first in emerging adulthood and continues through middle age (Pratt & Norris, 1999). As one expert said:

> Dramatic and extensive changes occur in young adulthood (the 20s and 30s) in the basic problem-solving strategies used to deal with ethical issues. . . . These changes are linked to fundamental reconceptualizations in how the person understands society and his or her stake in it.
>
> *[Rest, 1993, p. 201]*

According to research by this expert, one stimulus for young adult shifts in moral reasoning is college education, especially if coursework includes extensive discussion of moral issues or if the student's future profession (such as law or medicine) requires subtle ethical decisions.

It is known that many emerging adults enter college expecting to deepen their values. In a U.S. survey of new college students, about 40 percent said they thought it was important to develop a meaningful philosophy of life, and the same percentage hoped to integrate spirituality into their lives. About 65 percent planned to help other people who were in difficulty (*Chronicle of Higher Education*, 2006). In general, when students finish college, they report having experienced a "small, steady gain throughout college on developing their own values and ethical standards" (Komives & Nuss, 2005, p. 163).

Which Era? What Place?

Before going further, we need to clarify the relationship between morals and culture. Moral values are powerfully affected by circumstances, including national background, culture, and era. Think about historical and national differences in body covering (topless? head coverings? burka?), diet (pork? beef? vegan?), and much more. These practices are rooted in moral principles, such as the value and purpose of nonhuman animals. Indeed, culture determines whether a particular

➤**Answer to Observation Quiz** (from page 482): Asians are more likely to notice the telephone poles and wires, the long shadows on the street, the trees in the foreground and at top right, the varied designs of the building roofs, the street lights, the white church spire in the distance. If you are a native-born U.S. resident, you may have missed most of these details but come close to identifying the place and time: an American city (specifically, Pittsburgh) in the late 1990s (specifically, 1997).

practice is a moral issue at all. For example, in the United States, abortion is considered a moral issue, but it is less so in Japan, where specifics (e.g., did the pregnancy result from rape?) are more important than decontextualized principles (Sahar & Karasawa, 2005).

The power of culture makes it difficult to assess whether adult morality changes with age. Further, age-related differences in opinions can be judged as improvements or declines, depending on one's own standards. For example, U.S. data show that, as people age from 20 to 50, they tend to become less supportive of homosexual rights, of divorce, and of the right to publish pornography but more supportive of public spending on mass transit and health (T. W. Smith, 2005).

However, it does seem that the process (not necessarily the outcome) of moral thinking improves with age. One important aspect is that adults become less dogmatic. As one scholar explains it, "The evolved human brain has provided humans with cognitive capacity that is so flexible and creative that every conceivable moral principle generates opposition and counter principles" (Kendler, 2002, p. 503).

Evidence for moral growth abounds in biographical and autobiographical literature. Most readers of this book probably know someone (or may be that someone) who had a narrow, shallow outlook on the world at age 18 and then developed a broader, deeper perspective in adulthood. However, few scientific studies of moral development have been published. At least one longitudinal study found more understanding and empathy for other people among young adults than among the same people when they were adolescents (Eisenberg et al., 2005).

Dilemmas for Emerging Adults

It is fortunate that adolescent egocentrism ebbs, because emerging adults often experience moral dilemmas. They are no longer bound by their parents' rules or by their childhood culture (which they questioned during their identity crisis), but they are not yet connected to a family of their own. As a result, they must decide for themselves what to do about sex, drugs, education, vocation, and many other matters.

One set of dilemmas concerns sexuality, reproduction, and relationships—topics that can be discussed at length but are only mentioned as examples here. Carol Gilligan believes that decisions about contraception and abortion advance moral thinking, especially for women (Gilligan, 1981; Gilligan et al., 1990). According to Gilligan, the two sexes approach these decisions differently. Women are raised to develop a **morality of care.** They give human needs and relationships the highest priority. In contrast, men are taught to develop a **morality of justice;** their emphasis is on distinguishing right from wrong.

morality of care In Gilligan's view, moral principles that reflect the tendency of females to be reluctant to judge right and wrong in absolute terms because they are socialized to be nurturant, compassionate, and nonjudgmental.

morality of justice In Gilligan's view, moral principles that reflect the tendency of males to emphasize justice over compassion, judging right and wrong in absolute terms.

Other research does not support Gilligan's description of gender differences in morality. Factors such as education, specific dilemmas (some situations evoke care and some justice), and culture correlate more strongly than gender with whether a person's morality emphasizes relationships or absolutes (Juujärvi, 2005; Vikan et al., 2005; Walker, 1984). For example, those with less education (no longer characteristic of women) are more swayed by immediate relationships.

Emerging adulthood is "a crucial time for the development of a world view" (Arnett, 2004, p. 166), not only about sex and relationships but also about career and lifestyle. Finding a job and new friends, meeting coworkers and neighbors, all within a global economy and with advanced communication (Internet, satellite videos, international music), means that contemporary emerging adults learn about ethical principles that differ radically from their own. Because these experiences cluster in early adulthood, as postformal thinking advances, young adults think deeply about moral issues.

Freedom of choice may become problematic. Some emerging adults cherish their independence from family restraints and childhood prejudices. However, others develop "an acute sense of alienation and impermanence as they grow up with a lack of cultural certainty and a lack of clear guidelines for how life is to be lived" (Arnett, 2001, p. 776). Researchers are discovering that people are happiest with some choice (adults stuck in their childhood home are less happy) but not too much (Schwartz, 2004).

issues and applications

Clear Guidelines for Cheaters

Cheating is wrong; cheaters should be punished. That is part of my moral code. Yet I have read that moral values are influenced by culture and that flexible, dialectical thinking is mature. My reading made me halt my immediate, emotional reaction when I discovered three identical answers on the essay portion of one of my tests. I wondered if my students knew that there were cheaters among them. I handed out an anonymous questionnaire. The results:

- Thirty-five percent were certain cheating was going on in the class.
- Fifty-two percent strongly suspected it.
- Thirteen percent thought there was no cheating.

I was shocked. Why had no one told me? What should I do? In the next class, I divided the students into groups, told each group to figure out what my response should be, and left the room.

When I returned, I learned that my students did not share my dismay. Some noncheaters felt superior (cheaters are "only hurting themselves"). Some expressed ethnic prejudice (foreign students "whisper things in their language"). Some thought cheating was my fault ("Your tests are too hard") or a good thing (we should "help our friends"). Obviously, my culture clashed with theirs.

These numbers echo a nationwide poll of high school students, titled "A Whole Lot of Cheating Going On," in which only a third of the students said that "not very much" cheating occurred in their schools (Keifer, 2004). My horror is shared by many other professors. One review called cheating "endemic" to all colleges (Whitley & Keith-Spiegel, 2002), and a summary found that all professors abhor plagiarism, although they differ widely in their definitions and punishments (Robinson-Zañartu et al., 2005). And my students are similar to others; almost all college students know of cheating but almost no student reports it, and faculty are much less aware than students are (Hard et al., 2006).

Obviously, professors and students view cheating differently. This was confirmed by a professor of anthropology, who spent a year enrolled as a student at her university. She writes: "I wish students could more readily see . . . that finding a student cheating is not a triumphant moment, as one student suggested to me, but an upsetting one" (Nathan, 2006, p. 11). To me, cheating means that I have failed.

But wait. Using dialectical thinking, I realized that my culture (in this case, the academic system) considers cheating a dishonest attack on education, but student culture may see it as cooperation and mutual support. Students cheat more if they are closely connected to colleges—that is, if they attend full-time, live on campus (see Table 18.3), and belong to fraternities or sororities (Storch & Storch, 2002). My thesis is that cheating is evil; their antithesis is that cheating may help someone get a diploma.

A political scientist reports that students who cheat are making a rational choice in that they weigh the benefit of a higher grade against the unlikely cost of being caught and failing the class (Woessner, 2006). In this way, using someone else's work can be seen as a solution to a social problem. Note that this is a

TABLE 18.3

"Some Forms of Cheating Are Necessary to Get the Grades I Want": College Students Who Agree

Student Characteristics	Percentage Agreeing
All students	8%
Type of institution	
Two-year colleges	5
Four-year institutions	9
Universities	11
Attendance	
Full-time	9
Part-time	3
Gender	
Men	10
Women	5
Resident status	
Residence hall or fraternity	11
Commuter	6
Age	
25 or younger	10
Over 25	3

Source: Data cited in McCabe & Trevino, 1996.

solution used by politicians with speechwriters, celebrities with ghost writers, authors of some best-sellers, and members of collectivist cultures where people are expected to help their family and friends. For none of them is this considered cheating.

That is not my perspective. But postformal thinking requires me to combine my emotions with logic. My synthesis is not to change my moral code but to make it explicit, part of the culture of my classroom. I no longer assume that my students share my values. I ask students to sit far apart during tests; I use alternate versions of exams; and I require creative, current homework. If cheating occurs, I talk privately to all the offenders, trying to combine consequences with cognitive growth.

Measuring Moral Growth

How can we assess whether a person uses postformal thinking regarding moral choices? In Lawrence Kohlberg's scheme, people discuss standard moral dilemmas, responding however they choose to various probes. Over decades of longitudinal research, Kohlberg (Chapter 13) noted that some respondents in his sample seemed to regress at young adulthood, from postconventional to conventional thought. On further analysis of the responses, this shift was seen as an advance because the young adults incorporated human social concerns (Labouvie-Vief, 2006). They were dialectical, reaching a new level.

Defining Issues Test (DIT) A series of questions developed by James Rest and designed to assess respondents' level of moral development by having them rank possible solutions to moral dilemmas.

The **Defining Issues Test (DIT)** is another way to measure moral thinking; it does not require thoughtful analysis of the level of reasoning. The DIT has a series of questions with specific choices. For example, in one of the DIT dilemmas, a news reporter must decide whether to publish some old personal information that will damage a political candidate. Respondents rank their priorities, from personal benefits ("credit for investigative reporting") to higher goals ("serving society"). This ranking of items leads to a number score, which makes it easier to correlate moral development with other aspects of adult cognition, experience, and life satisfaction (Schiller, 1998). In general, DIT scores rise with age and education because adults gradually become less doctrinaire and self-serving and more flexible and altruistic (Rest et al., 1999).

This observation was recently confirmed by a study of adolescents and young adults in the Netherlands (Raaijmakers, 2005; see Research Design). The relationship between the DIT and delinquency was intriguing because thought shifted from justification for past behavior to guidance for future behavior. In adolescence, DIT scores rose among those who rarely broke the law. However, in early adulthood, a rise in DIT scores *preceded* a drop in delinquency. For adults, then, moral thinking produced moral behavior, not just vice versa.

Research Design

Scientist: Quinten A. W. Raaijmakers.

Publication: *International Journal of Behavioral Development* (2005).

Participants: A total of 846 Dutch youth, both male and female, ages 15–23 at outset, 21–29 at conclusion.

Design: Anonymous questionnaires about self-reported delinquency and scores on the Defining Issues Test. Results were compared by age (cross-sectionally) and over several years (longitudinally).

Major conclusions: In adolescence, DIT scores rose among those who rarely broke the law. In early adulthood, a rise in DIT scores *preceded* a drop in delinquency.

Comment: The results indicate that for adults, moral thinking produces moral behavior, not vice versa. A question that arises with all research is whether people in another nation would respond the same way.

Stages of Faith

A similar process may occur for the development of faith. James Fowler (1981, 1986) developed a sequence of six stages of faith, building on the work of Piaget and Kohlberg:

- *Stage 1: Intuitive-projective faith.* Faith is magical, illogical, imaginative, and filled with fantasy, especially about the power of God and the mysteries of birth and death. It is typical of children ages 3 to 7.
- *Stage 2: Mythic-literal faith.* Individuals take the myths and stories of religion literally, believing simplistically in the power of symbols. God is seen as rewarding those who follow His laws and punishing others. Stage 2 is typical from ages 7 to 11, but it also characterizes some adults. Fowler cites a woman who says extra prayers at every opportunity, to put them "in the bank."
- *Stage 3: Synthetic-conventional faith.* This is a conformist stage. Faith is conventional, reflecting concern about other people and favoring "what feels

AP PHOTO / GENE J. PUSKAR

LUDOVIC CAREME / CORBIS

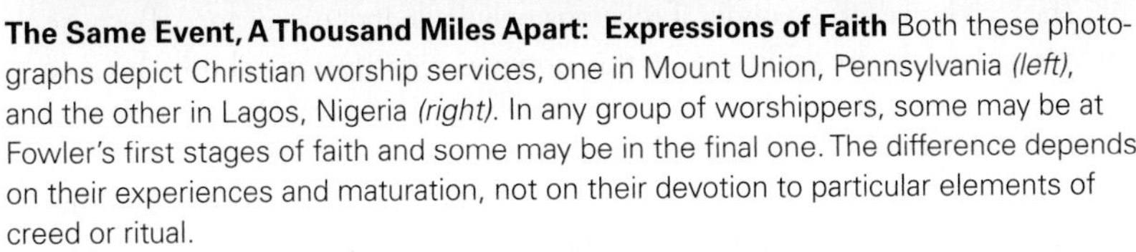

The Same Event, A Thousand Miles Apart: Expressions of Faith Both these photographs depict Christian worship services, one in Mount Union, Pennsylvania *(left)*, and the other in Lagos, Nigeria *(right)*. In any group of worshippers, some may be at Fowler's first stages of faith and some may be in the final one. The difference depends on their experiences and maturation, not on their devotion to particular elements of creed or ritual.

right" over what makes intellectual sense. Fowler quotes a man whose personal rules include "being truthful with my family. Not trying to cheat them out of anything. . . . I'm not saying that God or anybody else set my rules. I really don't know. It's what I feel is right."

- *Stage 4: Individual-reflective faith.* Faith is characterized by intellectual detachment from the values of the culture and from the approval of other people. College may be a springboard to stage 4, as the young person learns to question the authority of parents, teachers, and other powerful figures and to rely instead on his or her own understanding of the world. Faith becomes an active commitment.
- *Stage 5: Conjunctive faith.* Faith incorporates both powerful unconscious ideas (such as the power of prayer and the love of God) and rational, conscious values (such as the worth of life compared with that of property). People are willing to accept contradictions, obviously a postformal manner of thinking. Fowler says that this cosmic perspective is seldom achieved before middle age.
- *Stage 6: Universalizing faith.* People at this stage have a powerful vision of universal compassion, justice, and love that compels them to live their lives in a way that many other people think either saintly or foolish. A transforming experience is often the gateway to stage 6, as happened to Moses, Muhammad, the Buddha, and St. Paul and, more recently, Mohandas Gandhi, Martin Luther King, Jr., and Mother Teresa. Stage 6 is rarely achieved.

If Fowler is correct, faith, like other aspects of cognition, progresses from a simple, self-centered, one-sided perspective to a more complex, altruistic (unselfish), and many-sided view. Although not everyone agrees with Fowler's particular stages, the role of religion in human development is now widely accepted, especially when people are confronted with "unsettling life situations" (Day & Naedts, 1999; Miller & Thoresen, 2003). Faith, apparently, is one way people combat stress, overcome adversity, and analyze challenges. Other evidence suggests that this process continues over the years of adulthood, with young adults least likely to attend religious services and to pray (Wilhelm et al., 2007). Changes over the decades of adulthood may or may not signify a higher religious stage.

In any case, like almost all forms of thinking and analyzing, faith changes as life does. Cognition in adulthood is not stagnant. It is difficult, however, to imagine that one's own thinking, or morality, or faith is less than it will be in another decade or two. My own experience is one example.

in person

Faith and Tolerance

When I was in college, I once spoke with a young woman whose religious beliefs seemed naive. She hadn't given her faith much thought. Wanting to deepen her thinking without being harsh, I asked, "How can you be so sure of what you believe?"

Instead of recognizing the immaturity of her thought, she startled me by replying, "I hope that someday you reach the certainty that I have."

In the years since that conversation, I have encountered many other people whose religious beliefs seem too pat, too unquestioning, too immature; yet I realize that they might think that my faith is less advanced than theirs. When someone tells me that he or she is praying for me and my family, I respond graciously and gratefully and do not judge their beliefs. Does this mean that my cognition has become more flexible, more dialectical? Has my own faith moved up the hierarchy that Fowler described?

Hunter Lewis (2000) observed that "people need to consider their own values, consider them seriously, consider them for themselves" (p. 248). I agree, and I think Fowler's description of six stages of faith can aid such consideration. There is a problem, however: I wonder if religious beliefs do indeed advance. Because so few people are at the upper stages (just as almost no one reaches Kohlberg's stage 6, and few adults always use postformal thought), the implication is that most of us are immature.

Judging someone else's faith, as Fowler seems to do, strikes me as arrogant and self-satisfied—traits antithetical to my beliefs. Yet I judge cognitive growth as I teach. Is this one of the contradictions of life that adults learn to live with, or am I justifying an irrational set of values? It troubles me to describe stages of faith that are beyond most adults. I like to think I am at stage 6, or at least 5. But now, at least, I recognize the possibility that my own faith may not be as advanced as I imagine.

SUMMING UP

Moral issues challenge cognitive processes, as adults move beyond the acceptance of authority in childhood and beyond the rebellion of adolescence. Cultural values always affect beliefs, so it is particularly difficult to judge one's own moral position held in adulthood as advanced compared with another person's position. According to Gilligan, gender shapes a person's moral priorities, but other researchers disagree. Some people become more open and reflective in their moral judgments and in their religious faith as they mature and as personal experiences and education deepen their ethical understanding. However, as globalism advances, young adults encounter conflicting value systems and divergent religious faiths; this exposure presents potential challenges and practical difficulties. It is not obvious that some people are more advanced in morals and faith than others, although postformal thinking should advance moral judgment as well as other forms of thinking. ■

Cognitive Growth and Higher Education

Many readers of this textbook have a personal interest in the final topic of this chapter, the relationship between college education and cognition. All the evidence is positive: College graduates seem to be not only healthier and wealthier than other adults but also deeper and more flexible thinkers. These conclusions are so powerful that scientists view them with suspicion: Might selection effects or historical trends, rather than college education itself, lead to such encouraging correlations? Let us look at the data.

The Effects of College

Contemporary students attend college primarily to secure better jobs and to learn specific skills (especially in knowledge and service industries, such as information technology, global business, and health care). Their secondary goal is general education (Komives & Nuss, 2005). This is true not only in the United States (see Figure 18.3) but also in many other nations (Jongbloed et al., 1999).

One of the students in a course I taught at Quinnipiac University in 2004 acknowledged both goals:

> A higher education provides me with the ability to make adequate money so I can provide for my future. An education also provides me with the ability to be a mature thinker and to attain a better understanding of myself. . . . An education provides the means for a better job after college, which will support me and allow me to have a stable, comfortable retirement.
>
> *[E., age 18]*

LOUISE GUBB / CORBIS

Thumbs Up! These graduates in Long Beach, California, are joyful that they have reached a benchmark. Ideally, their diplomas will earn them not only better jobs but also an intellectual perspective that will help them all their lives.

Such worries about future costs and retirement income may seem premature in an 18-year-old, but this is not unusual. About half of all U.S. students take out loans to pay for college, and many are concerned about the impact the debt will have on their economic future.

Statistics confirm the economic value of college. For example, in the year 2003 in the United States, the average annual income of full-time workers with a BA degree was $68,000, compared with $33,000 for people with only a high school diploma (U.S. Bureau of the Census, 2007).

College also correlates with better health: College graduates everywhere smoke less, eat better, exercise more, and live longer. They are also more likely to be spouses, homeowners, and parents of healthy children. Does something gained in college—perhaps knowledge, self-control, less of a tendency toward depression, or better job prospects—affect health in positive ways? All these seem likely, although researchers are not certain how much each element contributes (Adler & Snibbe, 2003).

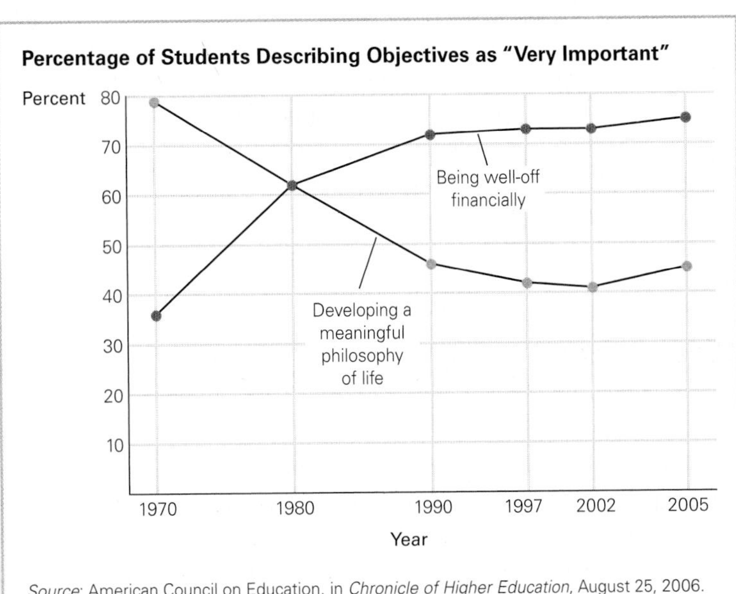

Source: American Council on Education, in *Chronicle of Higher Education*, August 25, 2006.

FIGURE 18.3

Primary Reason for Going to College: Wealth Versus Wisdom The American Council on Education surveys college freshmen every year. Cohort shifts are particularly significant regarding income.

Observation Quiz (see answer, page 490) Does a generation gap exist between current professors and their students?

➤Answer to Observation Quiz (from page 489): Maybe. If their professors are in their 60s and have not changed their values since their college days, a large gap is apparent. Other evidence presented in this chapter, however, suggests that neither of these conditions necessarily holds.

Looking specifically at cognitive development, does college make people more likely to combine the subjective and objective in a flexible, dialectical way? Probably. College seems to improve verbal and quantitative abilities, knowledge of specific subject areas, skills in various professions, reasoning, and reflection. According to one comprehensive review:

> Compared to freshmen, seniors have better oral and written communication skills, are better abstract reasoners or critical thinkers, are more skilled at using reason and evidence to address ill-structured problems for which there are no verifiably correct answers, have greater intellectual flexibility in that they are better able to understand more than one side of a complex issue, and can develop more sophisticated abstract frameworks to deal with complexity.
>
> *[Pascarella & Terenzini, 1991, p. 155]*

Note that many of these abilities characterize postformal thinking.

Some research finds that thinking becomes more reflective and expansive with *each year* of college (Clinchy, 1993; King & Kitchener, 1994; Perry, 1981). First-year students believe that clear and perfect truths exist; they are distressed if their professors do not explain these truths. Freshmen tend to gather knowledge as if facts were nuggets of gold, each one separate from other bits of knowledge and each one pure and true. One first-year student said he was like a squirrel, "gleaning little acorns of knowledge and burying them for later use" (quoted in Bozik, 2002, p. 145).

This initial phase is followed by a wholesale questioning of personal and social values, including doubts about the idea of truth itself. If a professor makes an assertion without extensive analysis and evidence, upper-level students are skeptical. No fact is taken at face value, much less stored intact for future use.

Finally, as graduation approaches, after considering many ideas, students become committed to certain values, even as they realize their opinions might change (Pascarella & Terenzini, 1991; Rest et al., 1999). Facts have become neither gold nor dross, but rather useful steps toward a greater understanding.

According to one classic study (Perry, 1981, 1999), thinking progresses through nine levels of complexity over the four years that lead to a bachelor's degree, moving from a simplistic either/or dualism (right or wrong, success or failure) to a relativism that recognizes a multiplicity of perspectives (see Table 18.4). Perry found that the college experience itself causes this progression: Peers, professors, books, and class discussion all stimulate new questions and thoughts. In general, the more years of higher education and of life experience a person has, the deeper and more dialectical that person's reasoning becomes (Pascarella & Terenzini, 1991).

Especially for Those Considering Studying Abroad Given the effects of college, would it be better for a student to study abroad in the first year or last year of a college education?

Which aspect of college is the primary catalyst for such growth? Is it the challenging academic work, professors' lectures, peer discussions, the new setting, living away from home? All are possible. Every scientist finds that social interaction and intellectual challenge advance thinking. College students themselves expect classes and conversations to further their thinking—which is exactly what occurs (Kuh et al., 2005). This is not surprising, since development is "a dialectical process" between individuals and social structures (Giele, 2000, p. 78). College is a social structure dedicated to fostering cognitive growth.

Changes in the College Context

You probably noticed that Perry's study was first published in 1981. The undergraduates he studied were at Harvard. Conclusions based on elite college students 30 years ago may no longer apply, especially because both sides of the dialectic—students and social structures—have changed. The fact just cited that college and

TABLE 18.4

Perry's Scheme of Cognitive and Ethical Development During College

Freshmen	Position 1	Authorities know, and if we work hard, read every word, and learn Right Answers, all will be well.
Dualism modified	Transition	But what about those Others I hear about? And different opinions? And Uncertainties? Some of our own Authorities disagree with each other or don't seem to know, and some give us problems instead of Answers.
	Position 2	True Authorities must be Right, the others are frauds. We remain Right. Others must be different and Wrong. Good Authorities give us problems so we can learn to find the Right Answer by our own independent thought.
	Transition	But even Good Authorities admit they don't know all the answers *yet!*
	Position 3	Then some uncertainties and different opinions are real and legitimate *temporarily,* even for Authorities. They're working on them to get to the Truth.
	Transition	But there are *so many* things they don't know the Answers to! And they won't for a long time.
Relativism discovered	*Position 4a*	Where Authorities don't know the Right Answers, everyone has a right to his own opinion; no one is wrong!
	Transition	Then what right have They to grade us? About what?
	Position 4b	In certain courses Authorities are not asking for the Right Answer. They want us to *think* about things in a certain way, *supporting* opinion with data. That's what they grade us on.
	Position 5	Then *all* thinking must be like this, even for Them. Everything is relative but not equally valid. You have to understand how each context works. Theories are not Truth but metaphors to interpret data with. You have to think about your thinking.
	Transition	But if everything is relative, am I relative too? How can I know I'm making the Right Choice?
	Position 6	I see I'm going to have to make my own decisions in an uncertain world with no one to tell me I'm Right.
	Transition	I'm lost if I don't. When I decide on my career (or marriage or values), everything will straighten out.
Commitments in relativism developed	Position 7	Well, I've made my first Commitment!
	Transition	Why didn't that settle everything?
	Position 8	I've made several commitments. I've got to balance them—how many, how deep? How certain, how tentative?
	Transition	Things are getting contradictory. I can't make logical sense out of life's dilemmas.
Seniors	Position 9	This is how life will be. I must be wholehearted while tentative, fight for my values yet respect others, believe my deepest values right yet be ready to learn. I see that I shall be retracing this whole journey over and over—but, I hope, more wisely.

Source: Perry, 1981, 1999.

universities are designed to foster cognitive growth does not necessarily mean that they succeed, especially because student expectations shape learning and student goals differ from institutional values (Ferrari et al., 2005; Howard, 2005). Administrators and faculty still hope for ongoing intellectual growth, but let's look more closely at how the college context has changed.

Changes in the Students

College is no longer for the elite few. Far more emerging adults are in college today than ever before. For instance, in the first half of the twentieth century, in western Europe, Japan, and North America, fewer than one in every twenty young adults earned a college degree. In 2000 almost one in three did (Rhodes, 2001). Although the percentages are far lower in Latin America, Africa, and Asia, the rates of college attendance in every nation have increased several times over (see Table 18.5).

Worldwide, three times as many students are in colleges or universities today than in 1975. The greatest expansion has occurred in nations that were British colonies. For example, when India became independent in 1948, only 100,000

TABLE 18.5

Number of Students Enrolled in College in Selected Countries, 1980 and 2002

About nine times more in 2002 than in 1980		
Iran	184,000	1,714,000
China	1,663,000	15,186,000
About six times more in 2002 than in 1980		
Nigeria	150,000	948,000
Three to four times more in 2002 than in 1980		
Egypt	716,000	2,154,000
Bangladesh	240,000	879,000
Argentina	491,000	2,207,000
Colombia	272,000	990,000
India	3,545,000	11,215,000
United Kingdom	827,000	2,241,000
Australia	324,000	1,012,000
About two times more in 2002 than in 1980		
Philippines	1,276,000	2,427,000
Italy	360,000	507,000
Mexico	930,000	2,237,000
World	**51,037,000**	**119,332,000**

Source: Snyder et al., 2006.

First Generation in College College has become increasingly popular among emerging adults. As is apparent from the sizable increases in enrollment since 1980, most of the parents of current students never attended college. They provide motivation and encouragement, but they can offer little practical advice.

students were in college. By the early twenty-first century, India had 11 million college students (Digest of Education Statistics, 2006).

Further, "everyone knows that college students in the early twenty-first century are more diverse in every possible way" (Moneta & Kuh, 2005, p. 68). The most obvious change is gender: In 1970, most college students were male; now in every developed nation except Germany, a majority of students are female. In addition, students' ethnic, economic, religious, and cultural backgrounds are more varied. More students are parents, are older than age 25, attend part-time, and live and work off-campus—all true worldwide.

Student experiences, history, skills, and goals are changing as well. Most are technologically savvy, having spent more hours using computers than watching television or reading. Personal blogs, chat rooms, and pages on Facebook.com and MySpace.com have exploded, often unbeknownst to college staff. College majors are changing. Fewer students concentrate in the liberal arts and more specialize in business and the professions (e.g., law and medicine). Students have different priorities today: Fewer seek general education and more seek financial security (see Figure 18.4).

Such changes are not always welcome. For instance, many developing nations still make college less accessible to women, and men generally still prefer to marry women who have less education than they do. A 2006 law in India designed to increase the numbers of postsecondary students from lower castes led to a nationwide student strike. Some U.S. affirmative action policies, put in place in the 1970s to increase minority admissions to college, were declared unconstitutional in the 1990s.

Many administrators and faculty wish that more current students studied the liberal arts. Among them is the past president of Cornell University, who deplores "narrow job training." He believes that

> questions of our common humanity, once confronted by the liberal arts, are now hushed or ignored, even though we have never needed them more. A young man or woman will become a more humane physician after some exposure to Shakespeare and Dostoyevsky. . . . We need specialist professionals with generalist views.
>
> *[Rhodes, 2001, p. 35]*

Changes in the Institutions

As students are changing, so are colleges. Worldwide there are thousands of new colleges. Some nations, including China and Saudi Arabia, have recently built huge new universities. The United States has twice as many institutions of higher learning in 2005 as it had in 1970, with increases particularly in the number of two-year colleges. In 1955 in the United States, only 275 junior colleges existed; 50 years later there were more than 1,000 such colleges, now called community colleges. For-profit colleges were scarce until about 1980; now there are about 850 of them in the United States (*Chronicle of Higher Education*, 2006).

Compared with earlier decades, current colleges offer more career programs and hire more part-time faculty; in the United States in 2003, 44 percent of college faculty members were part-time, compared with 22 percent in 1970. Newer faculty are more likely to be women and/or minorities. The proportion of tenured full professors who are European American males has decreased, although they still predominate; in 2005 in the United States, two-thirds of all faculty at the top rank were men. Specifics vary in each nation, but the trends toward more minority and part-time faculty are worldwide.

➤Response for Those Considering Studying Abroad (from page 490): Since one result of college is that students become more open to other perspectives while developing their commitment to their own values, foreign study might be most beneficial after several years of college. If they study abroad too early, some students might be either too narrowly patriotic (they are not yet open) or too quick to reject everything about their national heritage (they have not yet developed their own commitments).

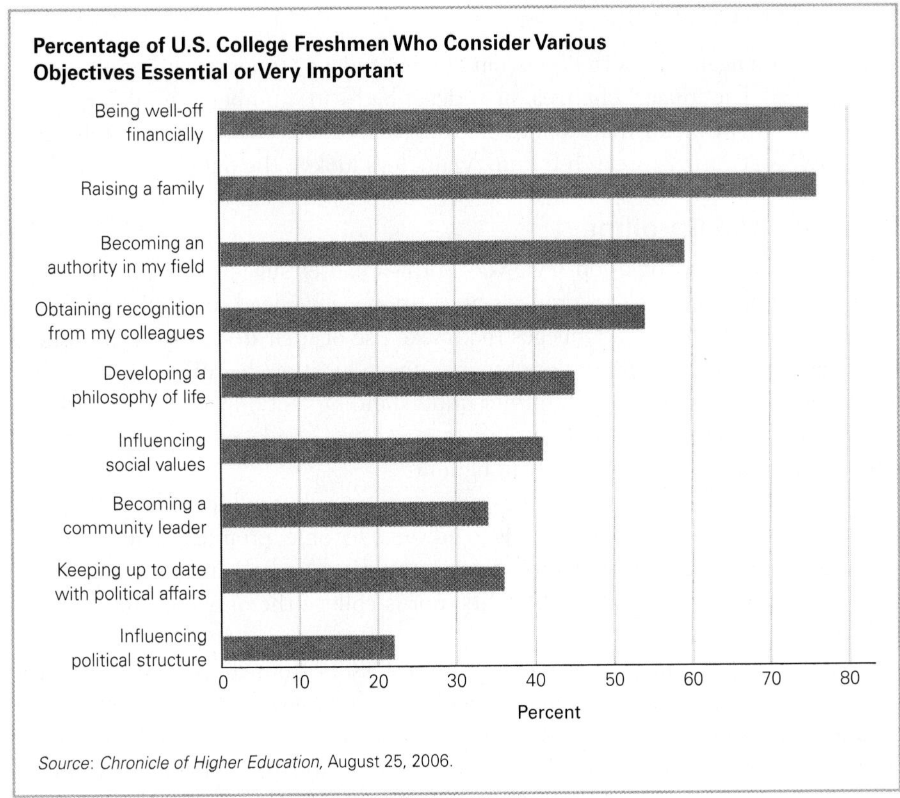

FIGURE 18.4

Personal Aspirations The American Council on Education began surveying college freshmen in 1966. Over the decades, students have gradually become more interested in their personal success and less concerned about larger issues of developing a philosophy and acting on it. For example, keeping up to date on politics was important to 58 percent in 1966 but to less than half as many (27 percent) in 1998. It rose to 36 percent in 2005.

Enrollment in public colleges has expanded, with more than 25,000 undergraduates at each of 100 public universities in the United States. Private colleges still outnumber public ones by about 3:2, but more than 75 percent (about 13 million) of all U.S. college students attend publicly sponsored institutions. They are less expensive than private colleges, but no college is free (although some students, with financial aid, pay no tuition).

Family income, not individual ability, continues to be the most significant influence on whether a particular emerging adult will attend college and, once enrolled, will graduate (J. King, 2005). Only 48 percent of low-income students earn a degree or certificate within 6 years of beginning college. The dropout rate is particularly high among community college students. When they enroll, 80 percent say they are likely to earn a bachelor's degree, but less than 20 percent of them do (Brint, 2003).

The chance of leaving college without a degree becomes greater as income falls, as the size of the college increases, and as other life obligations (such as parenthood) accumulate. Living off campus and working full time make dropping out more likely (J. King, 2004).

Verified dropout statistics overall are elusive, because some students who leave college return several years later, and almost half transfer from one school to another. California statistics may be most accurate, since students are tracked within that state's extensive system of more than 400 public institutions of higher education. The president of California State at Monterey Bay writes:

> We know, statistically, that in America, out of 100 ninth graders, 18 will have a baccalaureate or an associate's degree 10 years later . . . 32 out of 100 don't graduate from high school in four years (many more than we admitted), and . . . of the 68 who graduate, 60 percent go to college, and . . . 50–60 percent graduate within six years.
>
> *[P. Smith, 2004, p. 139]*

Evaluating the Changes

This situation again raises the question of what today's students get out of attending college. The major changes just described—in numbers, in diversity, in dropouts—might mean that college no longer produces the "greater intellectual flexibility" that earlier research found. Again, let's look at the data.

Diversity and Enrollment

diversity Variety or heterogeneity within a certain category, such as plants or animals. For developmentalists, diversity involves differences among groups of people based on such characteristics as race, gender, culture, age, family income, and sexuality.

All the evidence on cognition reviewed in this chapter suggests that interactions with people of different backgrounds and various views lead to intellectual challenges and deeper thought. Colleges that make use of their **diversity**—via curriculum, class assignments, discussions, cooperative education, learning communities, and so on—help students stretch their understanding, not only of differences and similarities among people but also of themselves (Nagda et al., 2005). Young adults of all backgrounds are likely to benefit.

Of course, college education does not automatically produce a leap ahead in cognitive development. College tends to advance income, promote health, deepen thinking, and increase tolerance of differing political, social, and religious views, but not everyone receives these benefits; nor is college the only path to cognitive growth.

Nonetheless, listening to students and professors from diverse backgrounds, thinking new thoughts, and reading books never known before almost always broaden a person's perspective. College classes that are career-based, as well as courses in the liberal arts, raise ethical questions and promote moral thinking (Rest et al., 1999). Higher education still seems to be "a transforming element in human development" (Benjamin, 2003, p. 11).

A special benefit may come from students who are parents, are employed, attend school part-time, and are older than 30. They enliven conversations and discussions with their fellow students. These students themselves make some crucial choices: Full-time study and part-time work are much more likely to foster learning than is the opposite combination (Pascarella, 2005), which means that students of all backgrounds learn more if they involve themselves more in the campus community.

Graduates and Dropouts

If postformal thinking—the ability to cope with the complexities of personal emotions and logical decision making—is the result of higher education, does a high dropout rate mean that many college students leave before reaching that level of cognition? Many do not have family or friends who have graduated before them. Do frustrating curricula, time-management complications, social challenges, and financial requirements prevent them from reaping the benefits of college? According to one research team, many young students lack the cultural knowledge or cognitive maturity to acquire the "social know-how" needed to navigate through college. Some "adapt to complexities better as they proceed through college," but that depends on their staying long enough to attain "basic skills or increased maturity" (Deil-Amen & Rosenbaum, 2003, p. 141).

A specific concern here is the expansion of public institutions. Does that make it harder for students to acquire the skills they need to succeed in college? Probably private colleges offer some advantages to young adults of all incomes and backgrounds, including less risk of dropping out. The reasons for the lower dropout rate are many, some having more to do with the student than the institution. However, "the extent of learning and cognitive growth that happens during the first

United States? Canada? Guess Again! These students attend the University of Capetown in South Africa, where previous cohorts of Blacks and Whites would never have been allowed to socialize so freely. Such interactions foster learning, as long as stereotype threat does not interfere.

year of college does not appear to be highly dependent on the characteristics of the institution one attends" (Pascarella, 2005, p. 130). Much more important are the student's openness to learning; engagement with education; learning style; and the particular classmates, professors, and curriculum—all of which can be found in some colleges of every type.

Intellectually inclined and financially secure high school graduates are more likely to attend and then graduate from college than their poorer, less studious contemporaries. That means that some benefits universally linked to college (health, income) are actually the result of precollege factors. However, when selection effects are taken into account, college still aids cognitive development. Some college is better than none, because the first semesters are especially important. One expert explains: "The growth in some content areas (e.g., English, mathematics, social sciences) and in critical thinking that occurs during the first year of college represents a substantial part of the total growth in those areas attributable to the undergraduate experience" (Pascarella, 2005, p. 130).

A valid comparison can be made with young adults who never attend college. When 18-year-old high school graduates of similar backgrounds and abilities are compared, those who begin jobs rather than college achieve less and feel more dissatisfied than those who earn a college degree (Schulenberg et al., 2005). Between 1980 and 2006, about 25 million immigrants, almost all poor and non-White, arrived in the United States. Many of their children are now of college age. Those who attend college do much better, economically and intellectually, than other children of immigrants from the same countries of origin who do not. Even those who attend a community college and then drop out fare better than those without any college experience at all (Trillo, 2004). Similar findings come from comparing native-born Americans: By age 24, those who attended college and postponed parenthood are more thoughtful, more secure, and seem to be better positioned for a successful adulthood (Osgood et al., 2005).

For many readers, none of this comes as a surprise. Tertiary education stimulates thought, no matter how old the student is. From first-year orientation to graduation, emerging adults do more than learn facts and skills pertaining to their majors; they think deeply and reflectively, as postformal thinkers do.

SUMMING UP

Many life experiences advance thinking processes. College is one of them, as years of classroom discussion, guided reading, and conversations with fellow students from diverse backgrounds can lead students to consider more ideas as well as to engage in more dynamic and dialectical reasoning. College enrollments have increased in many nations, particularly at publicly supported colleges and universities. A major problem is that many students drop out before learning what they need to know, but even a little higher education seems to produce cognitive advancement. It seems likely that although the context differs from that of a few decades ago, college education still promotes cognitive development. ■

SUMMARY

Postformal Thought

1. Adult cognition can be studied in any of several ways: using a postformal approach, a psychometric approach, or an information-processing approach. This chapter focuses on postformal thinking.

2. Many researchers believe that, in adulthood, the complex and conflicting demands of daily life sometimes produce a new cognitive perspective, which can be called postformal thought. This is not a true stage because it is not tied to maturation, but adults can think at a level that few adolescents reach.

3. Postformal thought is practical, flexible, and dialectical. Adults use their minds to solve the problems that they encounter, anticipating and deflecting difficulties.

4. One hallmark of adult thought is the ability to combine emotions and rational analysis. This ability is particularly useful in responding to emotionally arousing situations, as when childhood prejudices or stereotype threats appear.

5. Dialectical thinking synthesizes complexities and contradictions. Instead of seeking absolute, immutable truths, dialectical thought recognizes that people and situations are dynamic, ever-changing.

Morals and Religion

6. Thinking about questions of morality, faith, and ethics may also progress in adulthood. Specific moral opinions are strongly influenced by culture and context, but adults generally become less self-centered as they mature.

7. As people mature, life confronts them with ethical decisions, including many related to human relationships and the diversity of humankind. According to Fowler, religious faith also moves toward universal principles, past culture-bound concepts.

Cognitive Growth and Higher Education

8. Research over the past several decades indicates not only that college graduates are wealthier and healthier than other adults but also that they think at a more advanced level. Over the years of college, students gradually become less inclined to seek absolute truths from authorities and more inclined to make their own decisions.

9. Today's college students are unlike those of a few decades ago. In every nation, the sheer number of students has multiplied, and students' backgrounds are more diverse in every way.

10. Colleges as institutions have also changed, becoming larger and more career oriented; in addition, enrollment in publicly funded institutions has increased. Faculty are more often part-time, and more diverse as well.

11. Although both students and institutions have changed, even an incomplete college education still seems to advance young adults, intellectually and financially. Indeed, some of the changes, particularly the increased diversity, are likely to foster deeper thinking.

KEY TERMS

postformal thought (p. 472)
subjective thought (p. 474)
objective thought (p. 474)
stereotype threat (p. 477)
dialectical thought (p. 480)
thesis (p. 480)
antithesis (p. 480)
synthesis (p. 480)
morality of care (p. 484)
morality of justice (p. 484)
Defining Issues Test (DIT) (p. 486)
diversity (p. 494)

KEY QUESTIONS

1. What are three approaches to the study of adult cognition?

2. What are the main characteristics of postformal thinking?

3. How does the emotional intensity of a problem affect the reasoning ability of individuals of different ages?

4. Show how an example from the text (cheating in college or the end of a love affair) illustrates thesis, antithesis, and synthesis.

5. Describe your own example of dialectical reasoning, other than cheating in college and the end of a love affair.

6. Is postformal thinking a stage in the Piagetian sense of the term? Why or why not?

7. How does the moral thinking of adults differ from that of children and adolescents? Why?

8. How does culture affect morality? Pick one specific moral issue, and show that ideas about the "right" answer are affected by cultural differences.

9. According to research, how does college education affect the way people think?

10. What are the main differences between college students today and 30 years ago?

APPLICATIONS

1. Read a biography or autobiography that includes information about the person's thinking from age 18 to 30, paying particular attention to practical, flexible, and dialectical thought. How did personal experiences, education, and intellectual ideas affect the person's thinking?

2. Some ethical principles are thought to be universal, respected by people of every culture. Think of one such idea, and analyze whether it is accepted by the world's major religions.

3. Statistics on changes in students and in colleges are fascinating, but only a few are reported here. Find other data, perhaps from another nation (a reference librarian can help you find many data sources). Report the data and discuss causes and implications.

4. One way to study cognitive development during college is to study yourself and your classmates. Compare thoughts and decisions at the beginning of college and at graduation. Remembering that case studies are provocative but not definitive, identify some hypotheses about college and intellectual growth from your personal experiences that you would like to examine, and explain how you might do so.

19

CHAPTER OUTLINE

Emerging Adulthood: Psychosocial Development

In psychosocial development, even more than in physical or cognitive development, the hallmark of contemporary adult life is diversity: Adults vary widely in maturity, family, work, and lifestyle. For emerging adults who are less restricted by family or culture, the choices for education, work, friends, and partners are mind-boggling. For other young adults, especially in poorer nations or earlier times, adulthood options are (or were) quite limited. The patterns described soon in friendship, love, and psychological health are relevant to all, but diversity is particularly dramatic for the current generation.

Looking back, I now see many signs of this new diversity. For instance, when I was 20, Phoebe and Peggy were my two closest friends. As expected by our parents and culture, we anticipated becoming happy brides, wives, and mothers, even describing our wedding dresses and naming our children.

Anticipations clashed with social change. Over the years of our adulthood, we had three husbands and five children—average for our culture and cohort. But Phoebe never married or had children. She started her own business, becoming a millionaire who owns a house near the Pacific Ocean. Peggy married, divorced, remarried, and had one child at age 40. She earned a PhD and, after many academic jobs, finally found the work she loves, as a massage therapist.

None of us did what we expected or what was average, but in our diversity came fulfillment. When I last saw Phoebe, I complained that my young-adult daughters are single. She smiled, put her hand on mine, and said, "Please notice. I never married or had children. I am happy." So is Peggy. So am I. So are most adults, in all their diversity, as this chapter begins to explain.

Identity Achieved

When Erik Erikson first described his eight stages, most developmentalists believed that identity was usually achieved before adulthood. No more. Additional years between leaving high school and shouldering adult responsibilities have extended the identity crisis.

As was true 50 years ago, the search for identity (see Chapter 16) begins at puberty, but it continues much longer; most emerging adults are still seeking to establish precisely who they are (Côté, 2006; R. O. Kroger, 2006). Erikson believed that, at each stage, the outcome of earlier crises provides the foundation of each new era, as is evident in emerging adulthood (see Table 19.1).

TABLE 19.1

Erikson's Eight Stages of Development

Stage	Virtue/Pathology	Possible in Emerging Adulthood If Not Successfully Resolved
Trust vs. mistrust	Hope/withdrawal	Suspicious of others, making close relationships difficult
Autonomy vs. shame and doubt	Will/compulsion	Obsessively driven, single-minded, not socially responsive
Initiative vs. guilt	Purpose/inhibition	Fearful, regretful (e.g., very homesick in college)
Industry vs. inferiority	Competence/inertia	Self-critical of any endeavor, procrastinating, perfectionistic
Identity vs. role diffusion	Fidelity/repudiation	Uncertain and negative about values, lifestyle, friendships
Intimacy vs. isolation	Love/exclusivity	Anxious about close relationships, jealous, lonely
Generativity vs. stagnation	Care/ rejectivity	[In the future] Fear of failure
Integrity vs. despair	Wisdom/disdain	[In the future] No "mindfulness," no life plan

Source: Erikson, 1982.

Past as Prologue In elaborating his eight stages of development, Erikson associated each stage with a particular virtue and a type of psychopathology, as shown here. He also thought that earlier crises could reemerge, taking a specific form at each stage. Here are some possible problems (not directly from Erikson) that could occur in emerging adulthood if earlier crises were not resolved.

Worldwide, emerging adults ponder religious commitments, gender roles, political loyalties, and career options, trying to reconcile hopes for the future with beliefs acquired in the past. Although none of these four identities are necessarily set by age 18, two of them, ethnic and vocational identity, now seem almost impossible to achieve during adolescence. Therefore, we discuss them further here.

Ethnic Identity

In the United States and Canada, about half of the 18- to 25-year-olds are either children of immigrants or native-born adults of African, Asian, Indian (Aboriginal in Canada), or Latino descent. For them, ethnicity is a significant aspect of identity (Phinney, 2006). Most such individuals identify with very specific ethnic groups. For example, unlike adolescents, as emerging adults they identify as Vietnamese, Pakistani, or Korean Americans, not simply as Asian (Dion, 2006).

Similarly, those who are descendants of American slaves no longer call themselves colored or Negro, but African American. This is true for almost everyone of that ethnicity, but the first age groups to self-identify as African American were older adolescents and younger adults. Ethnicity is particularly important to many emerging adults.

More than any other age group, emerging adults meet many people of other backgrounds. They become aware of national and international history, customs, and prejudices. Their experiences shape the specifics of their ethnic identity because "without a context, identity formation and self-development cannot occur" (Trimble et al., 2003, p. 267).

Many European Americans, realizing the importance of ethnicity for their friends at college or at work, become more conscious of their own background and religion. Like the Vietnamese or Koreans mentioned above, they might go beyond identifying as Catholic or Jewish, for instance, and call themselves Ukrainian Catholic or Russian Jewish.

Although everyone struggles to forge an identity, this is particularly difficult for immigrants because combining past and future means reconciling their parents'

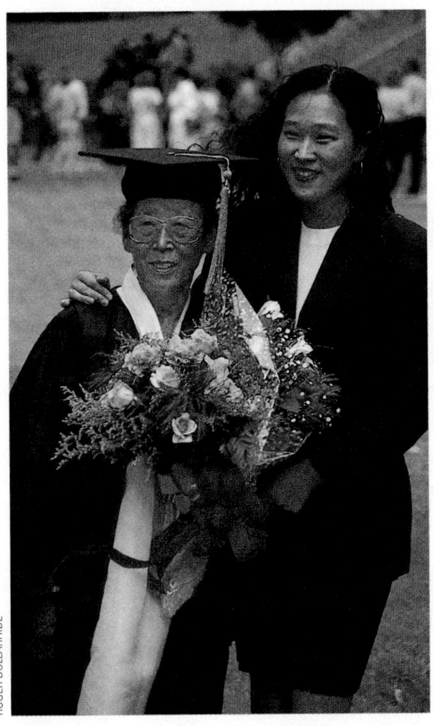

ROGER DOLLARHIDE

SALLY CASSIDY

The Same Event, A Thousand Miles Apart: Family Generations In developed countries, the social clock now permits grandmothers to be college graduates *(left)* and discourages teenagers from becoming mothers. This is in marked contrast to developing nations such as Indonesia, where grandmothers never go to college and many young teenagers, like this Javanese girl *(right)*, become mothers.

Observation Quiz (see answer, page 503): Although these pairs are separated by 6,000 miles and at least 30 years, they display two similiarities that are universal to close relationships of every kind. What are they?

background with their new social context. Conflicts often arise, not only regarding choice of vocation or partner (as can happen with any emerging adult) but in something more basic, "the assumption that these choices should be made independently by the young adult daughter or son" (Dion, 2006, p. 303). Young immigrants are often expected to be proud of their ethnic roots, and many are, but they are also expected by their peers to make independent choices about their future. Many clash with their parents as they do so.

A study of adolescent immigrants in 13 nations found that ethnic pride generally correlated with self-esteem but not necessarily with social adjustment. These participants were not yet adults, which may be one reason they had not yet found an appropriate balance between ethnic roots and national loyalty. Many aspects of ethnic identity were yet to be resolved (Berry et al., 2006; see Research Design).

The choice of an ethnic identity affects language, manners, romance, employment, neighborhood, religion, clothing, and values. Some aspects of identification are easier than others (Trimble et al., 2003), but ethnic identity is always complex:

- It is reciprocal, both a personal choice and a response to others.
- It depends on context and therefore changes with time and circumstances.
- It is multifaceted: Emerging adults choose some attributes and reject others.

The changing contexts of life require ethnic identity to be reestablished at each phase, perhaps with one identity in adolescence, another in emerging adulthood, and still another as a parent. Those whose parents are from different ethnic groups must deal with added complexity. By emerging adulthood, many self-identify with whichever group experiences more prejudice (Herman, 2004).

Consider Kevin Johnson, son of a European American and Mexican American. As a high school student, he thought of himself as Anglo, but as an emerging adult he chose to identify as Mexican, criticizing his parents for not teaching him Spanish. As an adult, he married a Mexican American, gave his children Spanish names, and sent them to bilingual schools (Johnson, 1999).

Research Design

Scientists: John W. Berry, Jean S. Phinney, David L. Sam, and Paul Vedder.

Publication: *Immigrant Youth in Cultural Transition,* Erlbaum (2006).

Participants: From 13 "settler" nations, 7,997 13- to 18-year-olds, about one-third of them native-born and the other two-thirds from 26 immigrant groups. In addition, 3,165 of their parents participated.

Design: Participants completed questionnaires about ethnic identity, school problems, personal issues, and relations with parents. The results were compared by nation, age, and ethnic group.

Major conclusions: Similarities among all of the adolescents (including native-borns) were more apparent than differences. The immigrant adolescents' responses to their new nations were called integration, national identity, ethnic identity, and diffusion, which could be compared to Erikson's identity achievement, two forms of foreclosure, and diffusion. Another finding is the "immigration paradox"—recently arrived youth had fewer behavior problems than their native-born peers.

Comment: Much more research is needed on the development of immigrant youth; this study is a welcome step in that direction. Additional research needs observations, not just

AP / WIDE WORLD PHOTOS

A Woman Now Two young girls participate in the traditional coming-of-age ceremony in Japan. Their kimonos and hairstyles are elaborate and traditional, as is the sake (rice wine) they drink. This is part of the ceremony signifying passage from girlhood to womanhood.

Observation Quiz (see answer, page 504): At what age do you think this event occurs in Japan—15, 16, 18, or 20?

As with Kevin Johnson, who went to Harvard and decided to live in California (not Mexico), each adult chooses which facets of his or her ethnic identity to adopt and how to express them. In adolescence, many second-generation immigrants criticize their parents for speaking their original language and for restricting their teenagers' dating choices (Ghuman, 2003; Portes & Rumbaut, 2001). In emerging adulthood or adulthood, however, some of those same individuals adopt traditional values and practices.

For this reason, college classes in ethnic studies include many emerging adults who want to learn about their culture. Because ethnicity is multifaceted and changing, no young adult conforms to his or her ethnic past precisely. Meanwhile, every culture of the world keeps developing. Some former immigrants visit their "home" country and find that they are strangers (Long & Oxfeld, 2004).

Thus, in the globalization of the twenty-first century, when people seek to form an ethnic identity, combining past and future is a complex but crucial task. Background cannot be ignored, but it must not become a retreat. This was powerfully expressed by one young adult:

> Questioning their identity, as inevitable as that experience is, is not enough. To have passed through the ambiguities, contradictions, and frustration of cultural schizophrenia is to have passed only the first test in the process. . . . We need to embody our own history. *El pueblo que pierde su memoria pierde su destino:* The people who forgets its past, forfeits its future.
>
> *[Gaspar de Alba, 2003, pp. 211–212]*

Vocational Identity

Establishing a vocational identity is considered part of growing up not only by developmental psychologists influenced by Erikson but also by emerging adults themselves (Arnett, 2004). For many, that is one reason they go to college, which not only provides a moratorium but also is considered an important step toward a career (see Table 19.2).

A correlation between college education and income has always been evident, and it is even stronger in the twenty-first century because fewer unskilled jobs are available and more knowledge-based jobs have been created. The correlation is not perfect (1 percent of those in the top one-fifth income bracket are not high school graduates), but it is very high (77 percent in that top bracket have at least a bachelor's degree) (Swanson, 2007).

TABLE 19.2

Top Six "Very Important" Reasons for Deciding to Attend College*

Reason	Percent
To learn more about things that matter to me	78 percent
To be able to get a better job	72 percent
To be able to make more money	71 percent
To get training for a specific career	69 percent
To gain a general education and appreciation of ideas	65 percent
To prepare myself for graduate or professional school	58 percent

*Based on a national survey of students entering four-year colleges in the United States in Fall 2005.
Source: Chronicle of Higher Education, August 25, 2006.

Among today's youth, higher education is necessary for both sexes. In the United States, of those earning advanced degrees—master's, doctoral, or professional—57 percent are women (*Chronicle of Higher Education,* 2006).

Most (75 percent) emerging adults work while they are in college (*Chronicle of Higher Education,* 2006). Whether in college or not, most young adults move from job to job, not considering any of them their vocational identity. Between ages 18 and 27, the average U.S. worker has eight jobs (U.S. Bureau of the Census, 2006).

This job history does not foster higher vocational status or income. Overall, however, tertiary education is increasingly needed for careers that allow promotions and, eventually, high salaries (Olson, 2007).

Charles, a 27-year old Princeton graduate, is typical. He has worked for the same advertising agency for a year but still thinks of himself as a "temp," able to leave the company at any moment to pursue a career in music. He explains: "I'm single. I don't have a car or a house or a mortgage or a significant other that's pulling me in another direction, or kids or anything. I'm highly portable, and I can basically do what I want as long as I can support myself" (quoted in Arnett, 2004, p. 37).

Many developmentalists wonder if vocational identity is an illusion in the current employment market (Moen & Roehling, 2004). Perhaps adults of all ages should see work the way Charles and many young adults do, as a way to earn money while they satisfy their creative, self-expressive impulses elsewhere. Although most societies are structured as if all workers were steady, dedicated, and full-time, this may be irrational in the current economy (Vaupel & Loichinger, 2006).

> Some young adults assume that they will find a vocational niche that is perfect for their aspirations and talents. They have high expectations for work. They expect to find a job that will be an expression of their identity. . . . However, there is a dark side to the work prospects of emerging adults. With such high expectations for what work will provide to them, with the expectation that their jobs will serve not only as a source of income but as a source of self-fulfillment and self-expression, some of them are likely to find that the actual job they end up in for the long term falls considerably short of this ideal.
>
> *[Arnett, 2004, pp. 143, 163]*

AP PHOTO / TED S. WARREN

For the Time Being Every company would like to hold on to its skilled employees. That is one reason the title of this young woman's job, at one of Starbucks' nearly 15,000 stores worldwide, is "barista," not "waitress." Nevertheless, most emerging adults consider their current jobs only temporary stops on the way toward lifelong careers.

SUMMING UP

The identity crisis continues in emerging adulthood, as young people seek to establish their own unique path toward adulthood. Ethnic identity is especially important, but difficult, for those who realize they are a minority within their nation. Often, the specifics of ethnic identity change with maturation as well as with historical change. Vocational identity is also an ongoing search. Although most emerging adults are employed at many jobs between the ages of 18 and 25, few are sure of their career identity. College education improves job prospects and eventual income. Nonetheless, vocational identity may remain elusive. ■

➤Answer to Observation Quiz (from page 501): Physical touching (note their hands) and physical synchrony (note their bodies leaning toward each other).

Intimacy

In Erikson's theory, after achieving identity, people experience **intimacy versus isolation.** This crisis arises from the powerful desire to share one's personal life with someone else. Without intimacy, adults suffer from loneliness and isolation. Erikson explains:

> The young adult, emerging from the search for and the insistence on identity, is eager and willing to fuse his identity with others. He is ready for intimacy, that is, the capacity to commit himself to concrete affiliations and partnerships and to develop the ethical strength to abide by such commitments, even though they call for significant sacrifices and compromises.
>
> *[Erikson, 1963, p. 263]*

intimacy versus isolation The sixth of Erikson's eight stages of development. Adults seek someone with whom to share their lives in an enduring and self-sacrificing commitment. Without such commitment, they risk profound aloneness and isolation.

➤Answer to Observation Quiz (from page 502): The most obvious clue—that the girls look like teenagers—is misleading. Remembering that the social clock is somewhat slower in developed nations and that Asian adolescents mature relatively late, you might accurately guess age 20, five years after Quinceañera, the similar Latina occasion, and four years after the European American "Sweet Sixteen."

As will be explained in Chapter 22, other theorists have different words for the same human need: *affiliation, affection, interdependence, communion, belonging, love*. All agree that adults seek to become friends, lovers, companions, and partners. The urge for social connection is a powerful human impulse, at least as powerful as the sexual drive, discussed in Chapter 17.

All intimate relationships have much in common—not only in the psychic needs they satisfy but also in the behaviors they require (Reis & Collins, 2004). Intimacy progresses from attraction to close connection to ongoing commitment. Each relationship demands some personal sacrifice, including vulnerability that brings deeper self-understanding and shatters the isolation caused by too much self-protection. As Erikson explains, to establish intimacy, the young adult must

> face the fear of ego loss in situations which call for self-abandon: in the solidarity of close affiliations [and] sexual unions, in close friendship and in physical combat, in experiences of inspiration by teachers and of intuition from the recesses of the self. The avoidance of such experiences . . . may lead to a deep sense of isolation and consequent self-absorption.
>
> *[Erikson, 1963, pp. 163–164]*

According to a more recent theory, an important aspect of close human connections is "self-expansion," the idea that each of us enlarges our understanding, our experiences, and our resources through our intimate friends, lovers, and relatives (Aron et al., 2004–2005). Intimacy and self-expansion are desirable parts of the human experience, which each person may seek somewhat differently.

Friendship

Throughout life, friends defend against stress and provide joy (Bukowski et al., 1996; Krause, 2006). They are chosen for the very qualities (e.g., understanding, tolerance, loyalty, affection, humor) that make them good companions, trustworthy confidants, and reliable sources of support. Unlike family members, friends are earned; they choose us. No wonder having close friends is positively correlated with happiness and self-esteem lifelong.

Choosing Friends

Friends, new and old, are particularly crucial during emerging adulthood, especially for those who do not have a steady romantic partner (Kalmijn, 2003). At this stage of life, family obligations are minimal, since few emerging adults have a spouse, dependent children, or elderly parents. Instead, they have friends.

In college, work, and community, as well as in various chosen activities (from aerobics classes to zoological society memberships), young adults have many acquaintances who provide advice, companionship, information, and sympathy (Radmacher & Azmitia, 2006). Emerging adulthood is when close friendships form; people tend to make more friends during these years than at any later period.

gateways to attraction The various qualities, such as appearance and proximity, that are prerequisites for the formation of close friendships and intimate relationships.

How do acquaintances become friends? Four factors are **gateways to attraction** (Fehr, 1996):

1. Physical attractiveness (even in platonic same-sex relationships)
2. Apparent availability (willingness to talk, to do things together)
3. Frequent exposure
4. Absence of exclusion criteria (no unacceptable characteristics)

The first two factors on this list are straightforward. Humans throughout the centuries have been attracted to others who are good-looking and seem interested in them. People want friends and partners who appear healthy and strong and who are willing to spend the time and effort needed to establish a friendship.

The third factor, exposure, is surprisingly powerful (Bornstein, 1989). Lifelong friends from college are more often those who chanced to live on the same dorm floor rather than one floor above. Work acquaintances might become friends if they ride the same bus home.

The need for exposure helps explain a developmental process. Childhood friendships may fade over time because friends no longer see each other when, as emerging adults, they go to college, especially if one family moves away. E-mail, phone calls, and letters can fill some of this gap, but unless adult friends are in frequent contact, sometimes face to face, they "lose touch" and the friendship withers.

Exposure does not always lead to friendship, of course. College roommates become close friends if they share personal confidences, but they sometimes discover exclusion criteria and keep their distance (Gore et al., 2006). It takes time and effort to maintain an adult friendship, as close friends know, including scheduling time together. Equity of effort in maintaining the friendship adds to both friends' satisfaction (Oswald et al., 2004).

The fourth factor, **exclusion criteria,** is noteworthy for its variability: One person's reason to exclude another may be insignificant to someone else. For example, religion and politics do not matter to some people, but others would never befriend someone who is not, for instance, a fundamentalist Christian or a devout Muslim or a socialist. Behaviors may also be important. Some people might never befriend anyone who smoked cigarettes or drank heavily; others do not care.

exclusion criteria A person's reasons for omitting certain people from consideration as close friends or romantic partners. Exclusion criteria vary from one individual to another, but they are strong filters.

Exclusion criteria do not indicate intolerance. Most emerging adults appreciate diversity, value tolerance, and accept a wide variety of human choices (Pew, 2007). They believe that people who are, say, fundamentalist Christians or devout Muslims should live where they want and worship as they wish. However, when it comes to close confidants, people have two or three filters for screening potential friends. These filters are often connected to the identity they have developed for themselves: Friends tend to be similar in ethnicity, religious values, education, and so on (Fehr, 2000). Once people become close friends, they tend to assume more similarity between them than actually exists (Morry, 2005).

Especially for Emerging Adults Who Want More Close Friends Based on the four "gateways to attraction," what can a person do to make more friends?

Gender and Friendship

It is a mistake to imagine that men and women have opposite friendship needs. All humans seek intimacy, lifelong. Regarding sex differences, we need to avoid "adopting stereotypic thinking . . . a rather simple solution . . . inadequate because people do not reliably conform" to gender dichotomies (Canary et al., 1997, p. 3). Claiming that men are from Mars and women are from Venus ignores reality: People are from earth.

Nevertheless, for cultural and biological reasons, some sex differences can be found in typical friendships (Monsour, 2002; Radmacher & Azmitia, 2006; Wood, 2000). Men tend to share activities and interests. Male friends begin talking about external matters—sports, work, politics, cars—and are less likely to tell other men their weaknesses and problems. When they do bring up emotional and relationship difficulties, they expect practical advice rather than sympathy.

Women's friendships are more intimate and emotional. They tend to share secrets more than men do. Female friends are quicker to engage in self-disclosing talk, including difficulties with their health, romances, and relatives. Women expect to reveal their weaknesses and problems to friends and to receive an attentive and sympathetic ear and, if necessary, a shoulder to cry on or a reassuring hug.

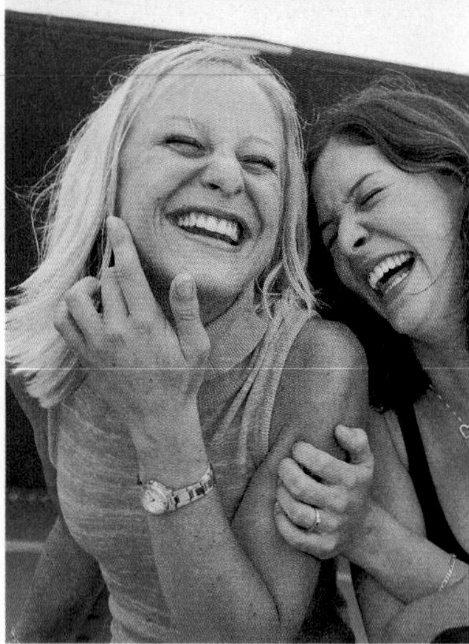

Such Good Friends Friendship patterns from person to person, and gender sterec types regarding these patterns are often wide of the mark. Nonetheless, friendshir between men tend to take a different dire tion from that taken by friendships betwe women. Men typically do things together- with outdoor activities frequently preferre especially if they lend themselves to shov off and friendly bragging. Women, in con- trast, tend to spend more time in intimate conversation, perhaps commiserating abc their problems rather than calling attentioı their accomplishments.

Observation Quiz (see answer, page 5C What have the young men at right just accomplished?

Especially for Young Men Why would want at least one close friend who is a woman?

➤Answer to Observation Quiz (from page 506): A day-long bike trek up and down a mountain. Among the clues are backpacks, bike shorts, sunglasses, smiles, and setting sun. The setting—Aspen Mountain, Colorado—
is harder to guess.

➤Response for Young Men (from page 506): Not for sex! Women friends are particularly responsive to deep conversations about family relationships, personal weaknesses, emotional confusion. But women friends might be offended by sexual advances, bragging, or advice-giving. Save these for a potential romance.

Since more than half of those aged 18 to 25 in North America and Europe have never married, we now discuss love, cohabitation, and lasting commitment—all issues of primary importance for emerging adults. (Divorce and parenthood are discussed in Chapter 22.)

The Dimensions of Love

Would you marry someone you didn't love if he or she had all the other qualities you seek? Most men and women in developed nations respond with a resounding NO!, but some young adults (especially women) in developing nations say yes (Hatfield & Rapson, 2006b).

Passion, Intimacy, and Commitment It seems as if "love" is not a simple emotion, not something universally recognized as the glue that holds a relationship together. In a classic analysis, Robert Sternberg (1988) described three distinct aspects of love—passion, intimacy, and commitment. Sternberg believes that the relative presence or absence of these three components gives rise to seven different forms of love (see Table 19.3).

Early in a relationship, *passion* is evident in "falling in love," an intense physical, cognitive, and emotional onslaught characterized by excitement, ecstasy, and euphoria. The entire body and mind, hormones and neurons, are activated (Aron et al., 2005). Such moonstruck joy can become bittersweet once the two people involved get to know each other. As one observer explains, "Falling in love is absolutely no way of getting to know someone" (Sullivan, 1999, p. 225).

There is some evidence that passion fades with familiarity. Siblings typically are not attracted to each other sexually. In India, future brides who have lived in the groom's household since they were children have fewer offspring than do those who first met their future spouse after puberty (Lieberman, 2006). Of course, the diminished fertility might not signify less passion. For example, if high-SES families are more likely to have child brides, then these wealthier families may also have better family planning. It is plausible, but not proven, that passion is less pronounced among children who grow up together.

Intimacy Shared laughter and overlapping legs, at midday in a public place, are universal indications of a couple who know each other well and enjoy their relationship. This couple is in San Sebastian, Spain, but they could be in any European or North American country.

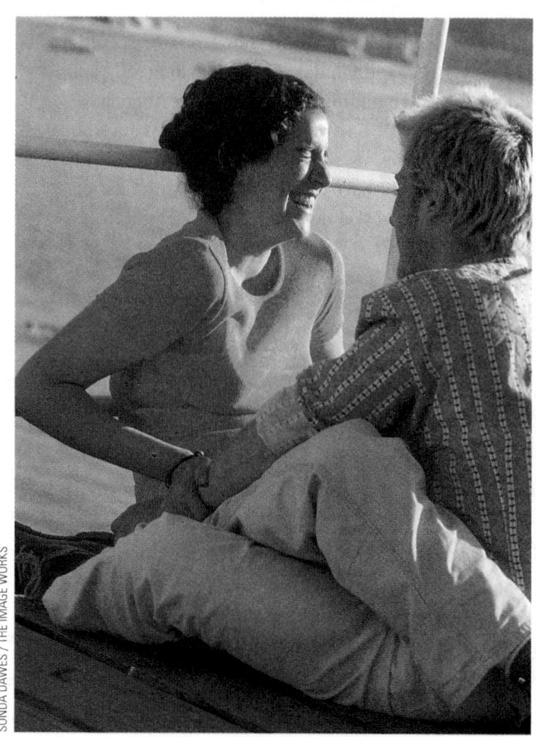

SONDA DAWES / THE IMAGE WORKS

Intimacy is knowing someone well, sharing secrets as well as sex. This phase of a relationship is reciprocal, with each partner gradually revealing more of himself or herself as well as accepting more of the other's revelations.

According to some research, lust and affection arise from different parts of the brain (L. M. Diamond, 2004). Establishing an intimate, nonsexual relationship, and later moving toward a sexual one, may be wiser than the opposite—sex first and friendship later (Furman & Hand, 2006). The research is not clear about the best sequence of passion and intimacy.

Commitment takes time. It grows gradually through decisions to be together, mutual caregiving, shared possessions, and forgiveness (Fincham et al., 2007). Maintaining a close romantic relationship over the years takes dedication and work (Dindia & Emmers-Sommers, 2006).

For both men and women, children add stress to a relationship but also make separation less likely, which is one reason most sexually active young adults are careful to avoid pregnancy. Social forces also strengthen commitment, which is why in-laws have become so important in jokes and relationships: They have the power to strengthen or weaken a couple's long-term relationship.

Ideal and Reality The Western ideal of consummate love is characterized by the presence of all three components: passion, intimacy, and commitment. This ideal combines "the view of love promulgated in the movies . . .

TABLE 19.3

Sternberg's Seven Forms of Love

Form of Love	Passion	Intimacy	Commitment
	Present in the Relationship?		
Liking	No	Yes	No
Infatuation	Yes	No	No
Empty love	No	No	Yes
Romantic love	Yes	Yes	No
Fatuous love	Yes	No	Yes
Companionate love	No	Yes	Yes
Consummate love	Yes	Yes	Yes

Source: Sternberg, 1988.

[and the] more prosaic conceptions of love rooted in daily and long-lived experience" (Gerstel, 2002, p. 555). For developmental reasons, this ideal is difficult to achieve. Passion seems to be sparked by unfamiliarity, uncertainty, and risk, all of which are diminished by the growing familiarity and security that contribute to intimacy as well as by the time needed to demonstrate commitment.

In short, with time, passion may fade, intimacy may grow and stabilize, and commitment may develop. This pattern occurs for all types of couples—married, unmarried, and remarried; heterosexual and homosexual; young and old (Ganong & Coleman, 1994; Kurdek, 1992). Romantic relationships move from passion to intimacy to commitment. Sexual attraction is part of the process, but it is not enough to keep a couple together. As one author explains, "Sex and love drift in and out of each other's territories and their foggy frontiers cannot be rigidly staked out. . . . Although lust does not contain love, love contains lust" (Sullivan, 1999, pp. 95–96).

As already explained, this sequence is not followed in every culture. Arranged marriages tend to begin with commitment; intimacy and passion sometimes follow. Families "make great efforts . . . to keep the couple together" (Georgas et al., 2006, p. 19) by providing practical support (such as child care) and emotional encouragement.

Given the diversity nationally and internationally, there is no one pattern that is guaranteed to lead to a happy relationship. It is apparent that some things are changing. One is that those who marry young are more likely to become depressed and then divorced; consequently, "finding a love partner in your teens and continuing in that relationship with that person through your early twenties, culminating in marriage, is now viewed as unhealthy, a mistake, a path likely to lead to disaster" (Arnett, 2004, p. 73).

Another change is the role of technology. Many emerging adults have profiles on matchmaking Web sites. Doing so indicates availability, increases exposure, and presets the exclusion criteria. Unfortunately, the first gateway, attractiveness, is hard to judge from a computer image. As one journalist puts it, many people face "profound disappointment when the process ends in a face-to-face meeting with an actual, flawed human being who doesn't look like a JPEG or talk like an email message" (D. Jones, 2006, p. 13). The most obvious change, however, is the likelihood of cohabitation.

Mail-Order Bride He was looking for a woman with green eyes and reddish hair but without strong religious convictions—his particular exclusion criteria, which he posted on the Web. That led to an e-mail courtship and eventually marriage to "the girl of my dreams."

Living Together, Not Married

cohabitation An arrangement in which a man and a woman live together in a committed sexual relationship but are not formally married.

Cohabitation, the term for living together in a romantic partnership without being married, has been called a stage of modern courtship. More than half of all emerging adults in the United States, Canada, northern Europe, England, and Australia cohabit during emerging adulthood. In other nations, including Japan, Ireland, and Italy, less than 10 percent of all adults have *ever* cohabited. (These international variations are evident in every survey, but specific percentages change by cohort and methodology.)

Variation is also apparent in the purpose of cohabitation (Casper & Bianchi, 2002). About half of all cohabiting couples in the United States consider living together as a prelude to marriage, which they expect to occur when they are financially and emotionally ready. Longitudinal research on this group finds that, in five to seven years, many marry, one-sixth are still cohabiting, and only one-third break up.

Some other couples live together but do not plan to marry each other; neither considers the relationship permanent. For them, longitudinal research finds that separation is likely (Casper & Bianchi, 2002).

Finally, cohabitation can be a substitute for marriage. Most adults in Sweden, France, Jamaica, and Puerto Rico live together but expect neither to wed nor to separate. In the United States (but not in Canada), committed homosexual couples are forced into this category. Many heterosexual couples—especially those who have been divorced—also expect to stay together but not to marry. These cohabitants tend to be older and to have more compatible relationships (King & Scott, 2005).

Especially for Social Scientists Suppose your 25-year-old Canadian friend, never married, says, "Look at the statistics. If I marry now, there is a 50/50 chance I will get divorced." What three statistical facts, found in the next few pages, allow you to insist, "Your odds of divorce are much lower"?

Although many people think of cohabitation as a good prelude to, or substitute for, marriage, research suggests they are mistaken. Cohabitants tend to be younger, poorer, and more likely to end their relationship than married couples—even when the relationship is actually quite satisfying (Bouchard, 2006; Brown et al., 2006). A Latin American study found that domestic violence is more common among cohabiting couples than among married couples (Flake & Forste, 2006). A study in the United States and Australia reported that, although the crime is rare, cohabitants are nine times more likely to kill their partner than married couples are (Shackelford & Mouzos, 2005).

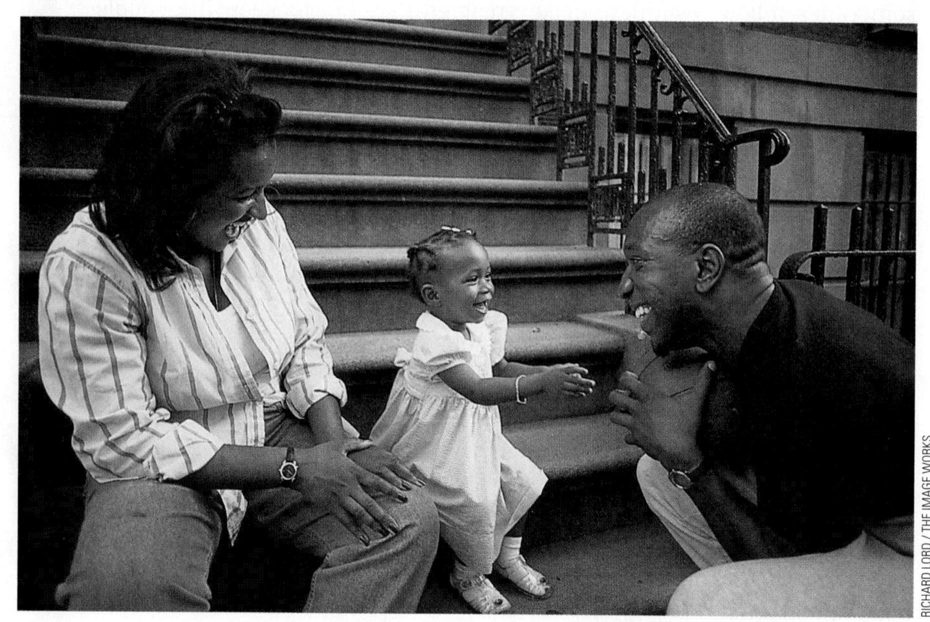

RICHARD LORD / THE IMAGE WORKS

What's Wrong with This Picture? The beaming man is a proud and responsive father, old enough to take his responsibilities seriously. A close look at his 22-month-old daughter suggests that he is doing a good job: She is delighted at the game he is playing with the ball, and he has moved his tall body way down, to be exactly at face level with her. Another fact also makes bonding easier: She is the biological child of these two young adults. So in terms of child and adult development, everything is right with this family picture—but some people might be troubled by one detail: Neither parent has a wedding ring. They have never married.

Contrary to widespread belief, living together before marriage does not preclude problems that might arise after a wedding. The opposite is more likely (Cohan & Kleinbaum, 2002; Kamp Dush & Amato, 2005). What, then, predicts a satisfying relationship? Several answers have been suggested; there is no answer that all researchers agree on.

What Makes Relationships Work

It is obvious that marriage is not what it once was—a legal and religious arrangement that couples sought as the exclusive avenue for sexual expression, the only legitimate prelude for childbearing, and a lifelong source of intimacy and support. As a sign of this change, the tie between marriage and childbearing is loosening in every nation. As many babies are born to unmarried as to married couples in some nations (including Denmark, France, and Sweden).

Further evidence is found in U.S. statistics (U.S. Bureau of the Census, 2006):

- Most adults aged 20 to 30 are not yet married.
- Compared to any year in the past, fewer adults are married (58 percent) and more are divorced.
- The divorce rate is half the marriage rate (3.4 compared to 7.8 per 1,000)—not primarily because more people are divorcing but because fewer people are marrying.

From a developmental perspective, it is noteworthy that marriages evolve over time, sometimes getting better and sometimes worse (Waite & Luo, 2002). Among the factors that lead to improvement are good communication, children growing up (newborns and adolescents seem to increase marital distress), financial shifts (income improvements or new employment), and the end of addiction or illness. Another developmental factor is maturity. In general, the younger the partners, the more likely they are to separate (Amato et al., 2003). This may be because, as Erikson pointed out, intimacy is hard to establish until identity is secure.

Compatibility

Commitment benefits from similarity, probably because similar people are likely to understand each other. Anthropologists distinguish between **homogamy,** or marriage within the same tribe or ethnic group, and **heterogamy,** marriage outside the group. Traditionally, homogamy meant marriage between people of the same cohort, religion, socioeconomic status, and ethnicity. For contemporary partners, homogamy and heterogamy also refer to similarity in interests, attitudes, and goals (Cramer, 1998; Hohmann-Marriott, 2006). Educational similarity is becoming increasingly important (Schoen & Cheng, 2006).

One study of 168 young couples found that **social homogamy,** defined as similarity in preferred activities and roles, increased long-term commitment (Houts et al., 1996). When both partners enjoyed (or hated) picnicking, dancing, swimming, going to the movies, listening to music, eating out, or any of 44 other activities, they tended to be more "in love" and more committed. Similarly, if they agreed on roles such as who should cook, pay bills, and shop for groceries, ambivalence and conflict were reduced.

The authors of this study do not believe that "finding a mate compatible on many dimensions is an achievable goal." In reality, "individuals who are seeking a compatible mate must make many compromises if they are to marry at all" (Houts et al., 1996, p. 18). They found that, for any young adult, fewer than 1 in 100 potential mates shares even three favorite leisure activities and three role preferences.

homogamy Defined by developmentalists as marriage between individuals who tend to be similar with respect to such variables as attitudes, interests, goals, socioeconomic status, religion, ethnic background, and local origin.

heterogamy Defined by developmentalists as marriage between individuals who tend to be dissimilar with repect to such variables as attitudes, interests, goals, socioeconomic status, religion, ethnic background, and local origin.

social homogamy The similarity of a couple's leisure interests and role preferences.

One thorny issue that arises among contemporary cohabiting couples as well as married ones is how housework is allocated. Many of today's couples include a woman who wants the man to do much more housework than he would prefer. If a couple cannot agree on division of household labor, cohabitants are more likely to go their separate ways and married people are less satisfied (Brown et al., 2006; Hohmann-Marriott, 2006).

A related factor is *equity,* the extent to which the two partners perceive a rough equality in the partnership (Hatfield & Rapson, 2006a). According to **social exchange theory,** marriage is an arrangement in which each person contributes something useful to the other (Astone et al., 1999; Edwards, 1969). In earlier decades, if the husband had a good job and the wife kept the household running smoothly, each partner was content. Both realized that they would have difficulty living alone. Today, partners expect each other to be friends, lovers, and confidants as well as wage earners and caregivers, and men and women both get paychecks, cook, and care for children.

social exchange theory The view that social behavior is a process of exchange aimed at maximizing the benefits one receives and minimizing the costs one pays.

Because both partners expect sensitivity to their many needs, happier relationships tend to be those in which both partners are adept at emotional perception and expression (Fitness, 2001). As women earn more money and men do more housework, overall marital satisfaction has improved. Indeed, many aspects of romantic relationships have changed over the decades, some increasing happiness, some not, but couples overall are as happy with their relationship as they ever were (Amato et al., 2003).

Conflict

Emotional sensitivity is crucial when couples disagree. According to John Gottman, who has videotaped thousands of couples, conflict is less predictive of later separation than disgust, because disgust closes down intimacy. If a couple "fights fair," using humor and attending to each other's emotions as they disagree, conflict can contribute to commitment and intimacy (Gottman et al., 2002).

The benefits of conflict are not found by other researchers. Other studies of young couples (dating, cohabiting, and married) report that conflict may undermine a relationship (Kim et al., 2007). Much depends on how the conflict ends—with better understanding or with resentment.

One particularly destructive pattern of interaction is called *demand/withdraw,* when one partner insists and the other retreats ("We need to talk about this" is met with "No. I'm too busy"). This is "consistently characteristic of ailing marriages," according to Gottman (Gottman et al., 2002, p. 22), and is probably evident among dating couples as well.

An international study of young adults in romantic relationships (some dating, some cohabiting, some married) in Brazil, Italy, Taiwan, and the United States found that constructive communication was crucial for satisfaction (Christensen et al., 2006; see Research Design). Women were more likely to be demanding and men withdrawing. As the authors explain:

> If couples cannot resolve their differences, then demand/withdraw interaction is likely not only to persist but also to become extreme. We believe that demand and withdraw may potentiate each other so that demanding leads to greater withdrawal and withdrawal leads to greater demanding. This repeated but frustrating and painful interaction can then damage relationship satisfaction.
>
> *[Christensen et al., 2006, p. 1040]*

Much worse, sometimes an unmet demand leads to domestic abuse. In such relationships, constructive communication is crucial but may be impossible, as the following explains.

Research Design

Scientists: Andrew Christensen, Kathleen Eldridge, Adriana Bokel Catta-Preta, Veronica R. Lim, and Rossella Santagata.

Publication: *Journal of Marriage and Family* (2006).

Participants: College students, aged 18 to 30, from Brazil, Italy, Taiwan, and the United States. Participants were self-selected, were required to be in a relationship less than 10 years (the average was 2½ years), and had to speak the native language.

Design: Participants answered many written questions, focusing on communication patterns. Particular attention was given to the demand/withdraw pattern and to relationship satisfaction.

Major conclusion: The importance of communication between members of a couple and the harm from the demand/withdraw pattern (which have been confirmed many times in the United States) are true for emerging adults in many nations, including many non-Western ones.

Comment: Such international research is needed and welcome. The authors note several drawbacks: The participants were volunteers and the data are based on self-report. Needed are longi-

issues and applications

Domestic Violence

Surveys in the United States and Canada find that each year, about 12 percent of all men say they have pushed, grabbed, shoved, or slapped their partner at least once. Between 1 and 3 percent have hit, kicked, beaten up, or threatened with a knife or a gun (MacMillan & Gartner, 1999; Straus & Gelles, 1995).

Surveys outside North America find higher rates. In China, 14 percent of the women experienced "severe physical abuse" (hitting, kicking, beating, strangling, choking, burning, threatening to use or using a weapon) in their lifetime, with 6 percent reporting such abuse in the past year (almost always at the hands of their husbands) (Xu et al., 2005). When verbal abuse (hostile or insulting comments such as "You're too fat" and "You're a lousy lover") was included, a New Zealand cohort of 25-year-olds reported that 70 percent of those who were in relationships (married or not) experienced domestic abuse (Fergusson et al., 2005).

These surveys were taken of women, because it was assumed that women were victims and men were abusers. It is true that more women are seriously injured or killed by their male lovers than vice versa, as evident in every hospital emergency room or homicide summary. However, it is now apparent that abuse includes threats, insults, and slaps as well as physical battering. With this expanded definition, more women than men are abusive to their partners (K. L. Anderson, 2002; Archer, 2000, Fergusson et al., 2005; Moffitt et al., 2001). Gay and lesbian couples can be abusive to their partners as well.

The original, mistaken male-abuser/female-victim assumption occurred because abusive men are physically stronger and thus cause more injury, and because socialization makes men reluctant to admit that they are victims. Likewise, homosexual couples hesitate to publicly proclaim that they have problems, although in domestic violence and most other aspects of relationships, they are very similar to heterosexual couples (Gelles, 1997; Kurdek, 2006).

Social scientists have identified numerous causes of domestic violence, including youth, poverty, personality (such as poor impulse control), mental illness (such as antisocial disorders), and drug and alcohol addiction. Developmentalists note that many children who are harshly punished, who are sexually abused, or who witness domestic assault grow up to become abusers and victims themselves (R. E. Heyman & Slep, 2002).

Knowing these causes points toward prevention. Halting child maltreatment, for instance, averts some later abuse. It is also useful to learn more about each abusive relationship. Researchers differentiate two forms of spouse abuse: common couple violence and intimate terrorism, each of which has distinct causes, patterns, and prevention (M. P. Johnson, 2005; M. P. Johnson & Ferraro, 2000).

Common couple violence (also called *situational couple violence*) is characterized by mutual outbursts of yelling, insults, and attack (Caetano et al., 2005). Often, both partners are depressed, both abuse alcohol or drugs, and both physically punish their children. They need help, but not necessarily separation or divorce, because the relationship may improve and the abuse may be halted by counseling, financial security, and addiction treatment.

Intimate terrorism occurs when one partner systematically isolates, degrades, and punishes the other. Intimate terrorism leads to the *battered-wife syndrome,* with the woman not only beaten but also psychologically and socially broken and vulnerable to permanent injury and death. This cycle of violence and submission feeds on itself, because each act that renders one partner helpless adds to the other's feeling of control.

Intimate terrorism is much less prevalent but far more dangerous than common couple violence. The perpetrator is usually antisocial and violent in many ways, with children and relatives in danger (M. P. Johnson, 2005; M. P. Johnson & Ferraro, 2000). The abuser is often irrationally jealous, reluctant for the partner to talk with friends, relatives, or anyone else or even to leave the house. Victims of intimate terrorism need immediate shelter, police protection, and help with self-confidence and independence.

Family members and friends should intervene in both types of conflict, since abuse hurts every adult and child. However, since domestic abuse often includes loss of social connections as both a cause and a consequence, no one may realize that help is needed. A survey of married Asian immigrants found that domestic violence was three times as common, and more severe, when the wife had no family members nearby (Raj & Silverman, 2003). Similar effects of isolation are found in couples from every ethnic group.

Family Connections

It is hard to overestimate the importance of the family at any time of the life span. Families are "our most important individual support system" (Schaie, 2002, p. 318), a "problem-solving system" (Wilson et al., 1995, p. 85) that "persists over time . . . as households wax and wane" (Troll, 1996, p. 246). Although made up of

common couple violence A form of abuse in which one or both partners of a couple engage in outbursts of verbal and physical attack. (Also called *situational couple violence.*)

intimate terrorism Spouse abuse in which, most often, the husband uses violent methods of accelerating intensity to isolate, degrade, and punish the wife.

individuals, a family is much more than the persons who belong to it. In dynamic synergy, children grow, adults find support, and everyone is part of an ethos that gives meaning to, and provides models for, personal aspirations and decisions.

➤Response for Social Scientists (from page 510): First, no other nation has a divorce rate as high as the United States. Second, even the 50 percent divorce rate in the United States comes from dividing the number of divorces by the number of marriages. Because some people get married and divorced many times, that minority provides data that drive up the ratio and skew the average. (Actually, even in the United States, only one first marriage in three—not one in two—ends in divorce.) Finally, because you have read that teenage marriages are especially likely to end, you can deduce that older brides and grooms are less likely to divorce. The odds of your friend getting divorced are about one in five, as long as the couple has established a fair degree of social homogamy.

Linked Lives

Emerging adults are said to set out on their own, leaving their childhood home and parents behind. They strive for independence (Arnett, 2004). It might seem as if they no longer need parental support and guidance, but the data show that parents continue to be crucial—perhaps even more so than for previous generations. Fewer emerging adults have established their own families, secured high-paying jobs, or found a definitive understanding of their identity and their goals.

All members of each family have **linked lives,** meaning that the experiences and needs of family members at one stage of life are affected by those at other stages (Macmillan & Copher, 2005).We have seen this in earlier chapters: Children are affected by their parents' relationship, even if they are not directly involved in domestic disputes, financial stresses, parental alliances, and so on.

linked lives Lives in which the success, health, and well-being of one generation in a family are connected to those of another generation, as in the relationship between parents and children.

Consider parents and emerging adults in the current context. Fewer parents have young children; both parents are usually employed, often with seniority and substantial income. In the United States in 2005, the highest incomes were in households headed by someone aged 45 to 54 (U.S. Bureau of the Census, 2007). Parents have always wanted to help their adult children, but now more of them are able to give both money and time.

Not surprisingly, then, one obvious connection between parents and adult children is financial. For example, very few young college students pay all their tuition and living expenses on their own. Parents provide support; loans, part-time employment, and partial scholarships also contribute.

Many emerging adults still live at home, partly because few entry-level jobs pay enough for true independence. This varies from nation to nation. Almost all unmarried young adults in Italy and Japan live with their parents, as do half those in England (Manzi et al., 2006). Fewer do so in the United States, but many parents underwrite their young adult children's independent living (Pew, 2007).

About half of all emerging adults receive cash from their parents (averaging $1,000 a year) in addition to tuition, medical care, food, and other material support.

The Same Event, A Thousand Miles Apart: Happy Young Women The British woman *(left)* and the Kenyan woman *(right)* are both developing just as their families and cultures had hoped they would. The major difference is that 23-year-old Kim is not yet married to Dave, while her contemporary already has a husband, son, and daughter.

CHRIS ROUTE / ALAMY

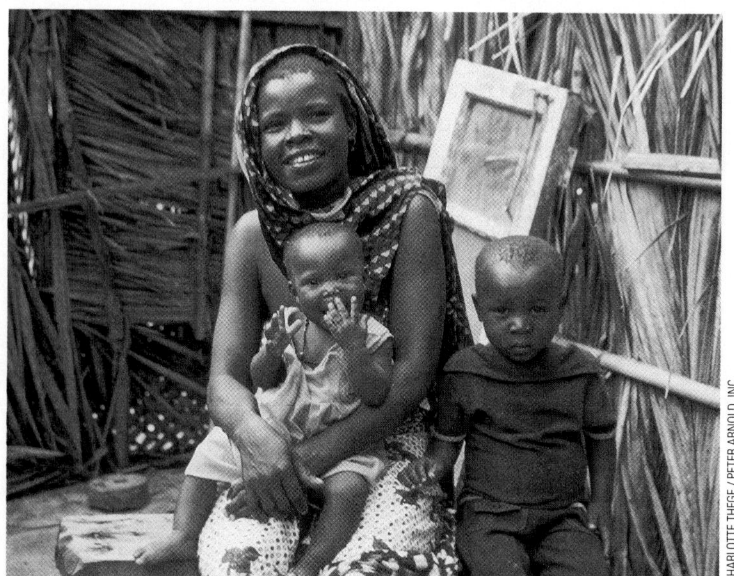

CHARLOTTE THEGE / PETER ARNOLD, INC.

Most are also given substantial gifts of time, such as help with laundry, moving, household repairs, and, if the young adult becomes a parent, free child care. This assistance makes achievement possible (Schoeni & Ross, 2005).

Emerging adults without family support (e.g., foster children who "age out" at age 18, or those whose families are too poor and overwhelmed to be helpful) find it difficult to meet the challenges of emerging adulthood (Foster & Gifford, 2005). Getting a college degree is especially hard without family help.

International Variations

Families can be destructive as well as helpful to emerging adults. For example, a study of enmeshment (e.g., parents always knowing what their emerging adult children are doing and thinking) found that British emerging adults were harmed if their parents were too intrusive. However, emerging adults in Italy seem able to remain closely connected with their parents without impairing their own development (Manzi et al., 2006).

Some Westerners believe that family dependence is more evident in developing nations. There is some truth in this. For example, many African young adults marry someone approved by their parents and work to support their many relatives—siblings, parents, cousins, uncles, and so on. Individuals sacrifice personal goals for family concerns, and "collectivism often takes precedence and overrides individual needs and interests," which makes "the family a source of both collective identity and tension" (Wilson & Ngige, 2006, p. 248).

There are advantages to this collectivism. Friendships are more practical, probably because relatives meet intimacy needs (Adams & Plout, 2003). Furthermore, each new baby is cared for by many people, so young adults are less burdened by children. This is in contrast to the United States, where parenthood is a major impediment to higher education and career success (Osgood et al., 2005). This may be one reason parenthood begins much earlier in poor nations.

However, in every nation young adults are encouraged to do well in school and get good jobs, partly to make their families proud, partly so that they will be able to care for their families when necessary, and partly for their own future. Immigrant young adults tend to be highly motivated to learn and work, and they reciprocate their parents' support. These values help them to become more successful than many native-born young adults (Mollenkopf et al., 2005).

When we look at actual lives, not the cultural image of independence or interdependence, emerging adults worldwide have much in common, including close family connections and a new freedom from parental limits (Georgas et al., 2006). Although specifics differ, it is a mistake to assume that emerging adults in Western nations abandon their parents when they leave home. Indeed, some studies find that family relationships improve when young adults leave (Graber & Brooks-Gunn, 1996; Smetana et al., 2004). One longitudinal study of four generations found that "most mothers and daughters had stormy relationships during the daughters' adolescence but close and friendly ones once the daughters left home, whether or not the daughters married" (Troll, 1996, p. 253).

Parents support their adult children indirectly as well, by what they did years earlier. In many nations, researchers find a connection between early attachment and adult relationships with friends, lovers, and children (Grossmann et al., 2005; Mikulincer & Goodman, 2006; Sroufe et al., 2005). Securely attached infants are more likely to become happily married adults; avoidant infants may hesitate to marry.

From a developmental perspective, it makes sense that emotional development and social skills learned in childhood would be relevant to adult relationships

(Mikulincer, 2006). Ponder this as we now look specifically at the emotions of emerging adults: Are they the outgrowth of early development, or do contextual factors in early adulthood determine them?

SUMMING UP

Intimacy needs are universal for all young adults, but the ways in which they are met vary by culture and cohort. In developed nations in the twenty-first century, most emerging adults have many friends, including some of the opposite sex, and a series of romantic relationships before marriage. Cohabitation is common, although it does not necessarily further the passion, intimacy, or commitment that emerging adults seek. In many other nations, arranged marriages are common. Parental support and linked lives are typical everywhere. In some nations, this support includes substantial financial assistance. ■

Emotional Development

As you know, people are at their peak—in strength, sexual impulses, health, cognitive growth, and much else—during emerging adulthood. Emotions, too, seem to run high during these years. When adults of various ages are asked to recall their happiest or most important memories, a cluster usually appears during the young-adult years (Berntsen & Rubin, 2002) (see Figure 19.1). Both positive and negative emotions seem to be especially strong at this time.

Well-Being

Emerging adults in most developed nations have the freedom to learn, explore, make friends, find lovers, and take whatever jobs, journeys, and risks they want. If a person is ever going to travel to another nation, or learn a new sport, or achieve some athletic, academic, or creative breakthrough, the most likely time is from age 18 to 25. One indication is found in the young-adult lives of highly successful or very creative adults. Often, the initial breakthrough came in early adulthood.

For example, among the winners of the Nobel Prize in 2005 were Harold Pinter (British) in literature, Barry Marshall (Australian) in medicine, and Mohamed

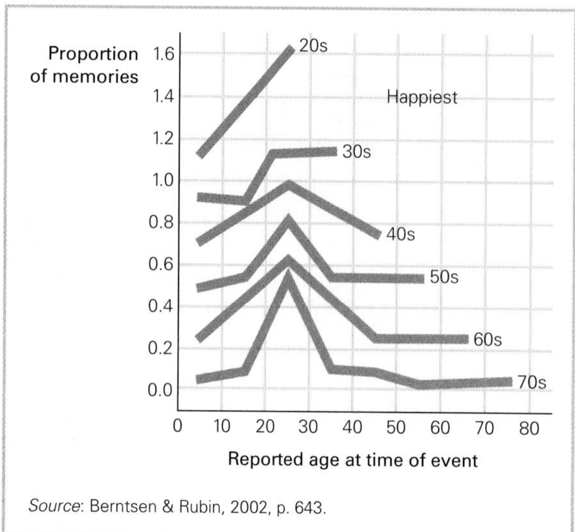

FIGURE 19.1

The Memory Bump A sizable proportion of adults of all ages report having had a "happiness bump" in their mid-20s. Participants in this study ranged in age from their 20s to their 70s, and the curves in this graph are labeled accordingly. To make the graph easier to read, the curve for each age group is offset by 0.2 from the curve for the next-oldest group. As a result, for the group in their 40s, for example, 0.6 is the equivalent of 0. Thus, about 15 percent of participants in their 40s said that they had experienced their happiest memories at age 10 or younger; 15 percent at ages 10–20; 35 percent at ages 20–29; 20 percent at ages 30–39; and about 15 percent at age 40 or older.

El-Baradei (Egyptian), in efforts to promote world peace. Pinter's first book of poems was published when he was just 20, and his first play was produced when he was 27; El-Baradei began to represent Egypt at the United Nations when he was 22; Marshall first decided that standard medicine was inadequate when he was a medical intern at age 22.

Marshall's example is particularly instructive. His rebellion against standard medicine included, by the mid-1980s, his conviction that a bacterium, *Helicobacter pylori,* caused peptic ulcers. The medical establishment continued to insist that the cause was excessive production of stomach acid in response to psychological stress.

In frustration, at age 32, as "a little known trainee doctor in a little known hospital . . . [Marshall] swallowed a broth of microbe-laced water" (Hamilton, 2001, p. 30). Soon afterward, he became violently ill with the symptoms of stomach ulcers. He cured himself by taking antibiotics, which killed off the *H. pylori*—proof that peptic ulcers are caused not by stress but by bacterial infection.

Marshall was technically past emerging adulthood when he swallowed the toxin, but his creative rebellion started much sooner. Further, some people take much longer to reach maturity than others. Marshall may have developed slowly; his wife said he was more like a boy than a man.

Boldness and creativity, evident in many young adults who become leaders, is not universal. However, the tendency to question authority and to feel pleased with oneself is common. In one U.S. study, 3,912 people were surveyed every two years from ages 18 to 24. They were quite happy with themselves at 18, and their self-esteem kept rising (Schulenberg et al., 2005) (see Figure 19.2). Similarly, 404 young adults in western Canada were repeatedly questioned from ages 18 to 25. They, too, evidenced rising self-esteem (Galambos et al., 2006).

Positive emotions increase when emerging adults have close relationships with friends, lovers, and parents, as well as when they undergo successful transitions such as leaving home, graduating from college, and securing a good job (Schulenberg et al., 2005). Some of the severe depressions and anxieties of adolescence lift when young people leave their high schools and distance themselves from their dysfunctional families.

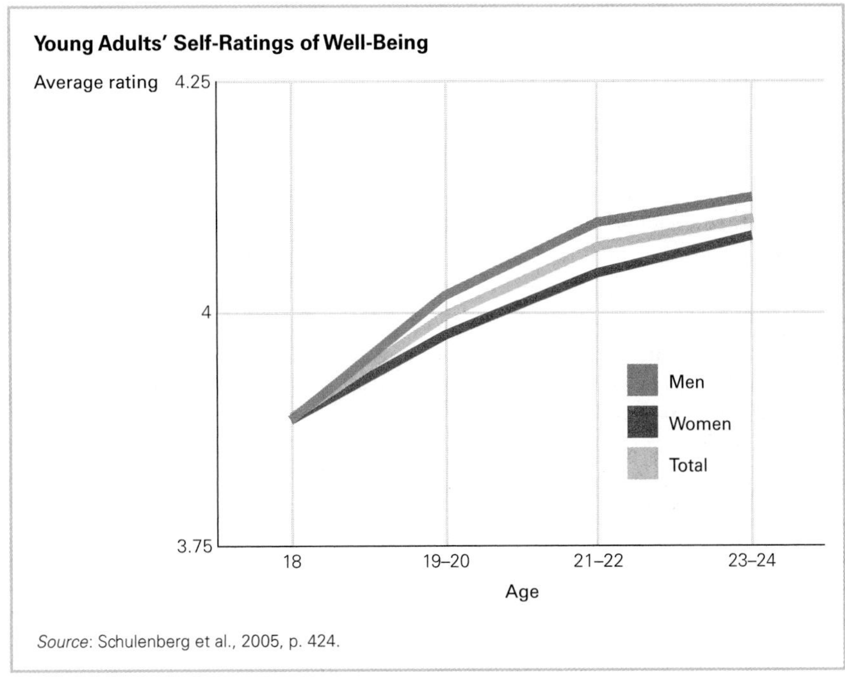

FIGURE 19.2

Worthy People This graph shows a steady increase in young adults' sense of well-being from age 18 to age 24, as measured by respondents' ratings of statements such as "I feel I am a person of worth." The ratings ranged from 1, indicating complete disagreement, to 5, indicating complete agreement. The average rating was already quite high at age 18, and it increased steadily over the years of emerging adulthood.

Psychopathology

It is a mistake to assume that every young adult benefits from independence. Although new experiences tend to improve self-esteem, some emerging adults, because of either their personality or their circumstances, have too many choices and too little guidance (Schwartz, 2004).

This was one conclusion from a study that began with seniors at 11 colleges who had requested help finding jobs. Some were "maximizers": They sought the best job possible, consulting experts and applying for 20 or so positions. The others were "satisficers": They consulted fewer people and submitted half as many applications as the maximizers. In follow-up research, after the graduating students had accepted jobs, the maximizers secured higher pay (averaging $7,430 more per year), but they were less pleased with their jobs than the satisficers were (Iyengar et al., 2006).

The dissatisfaction of the maximizers is one example of the problems that may detour young-adult growth. Some are overwhelmed by their many choices and challenges. From ages 18 to 25, "young people are coming to grips with their lives" (Galambos et al., 2006, p. 360). Some lose their grip. Average well-being increases in emerging adulthood, as just described, but so does the incidence of psychopathology (Mowbray et al., 2006; Schulenberg & Zarrett, 2006).

Worldwide, adults are more likely to have a mental illness during emerging adulthood than during any later time. Often, psychopathology continues throughout adult life. As the World Health Organization reports: "Although mental disorders cause fewer deaths than infectious diseases, they cause as much or more disability because they strike early and can last a long time" (G. Miller, 2006, p. 459).

Why this increase? Substantial research finds that vocational, financial, and interpersonal stresses are greater in early adulthood than later on (Kessler et al., 2005). Most developmentalists believe in the **diathesis-stress model,** which "views psychopathology as the consequence of stress interacting with an underlying predisposition (biological, psychosocial, or sociocultural) to produce a specific disorder" (Hooley, 2004, p. 204). Thus, the stresses of emerging adulthood are likely to cause problems when added to preexisting vulnerability. Now some specifics.

diathesis-stress model The view that mental disorders, such as schizophrenia, are produced by the interaction of a genetic vulnerability (the diathesis) with stressful environmental factors and life events.

Substance Abuse Disorders

As explained in Chapter 17, emerging adulthood is by far the most common time for substance abuse. One person in every eight is addicted (including alcohol addiction) before age 27 (Kessler et al., 2005).

At first, the social setting of many emerging adults may make drug abuse seem normal, even helpful (Schulenberg et al., 2005). As we have just seen, friends and romantic partners are chosen in part for similarities and common interests. One such common interest is drug and alcohol use, which can allow the heavy user to befriend other young adults who are more addicted than they are. Social norms within the friendship circle may prevent these young adults from recognizing their own addictions.

Many sufferers do manage to put an end to their abuse without professional counseling or residential rehabilitation. As explained in Chapter 17, when social norms make an emerging adult realize he or she has a problem, the social network can be helpful. Unfortunately, if professional help is needed, it often is not sought or even available until years or even decades after the problem has become evident.

Mood Disorders

Before age 30, 8 percent of U.S. residents suffer from a mood disorder, most commonly major depression, signaled by a "loss of interest or pleasure in nearly all activities" for two weeks or more. Other difficulties—in sleeping, concentrating, eating, carrying on friendships, and experiencing hope and meaning in life—are also present (American Psychiatric Association, 2000, p. 249). About a quarter of mood disorders in the United States begin in adolescence and another quarter begin in young adulthood. (Depression is also common among young adults in other nations, but reliable incidence statistics are unavailable.)

The origins of major depression may be biochemical, involving imbalances in neurotransmitters and hormones, but the stresses common in adolescence and emerging adulthood (e.g., a romantic breakup, an arrest) can be triggers. Young adults with psychological problems are less likely to have supportive friendships, and that itself can be depressing (King & Terrance, 2006).

Failure to get treatment for depression is a major problem for emerging adults. They tend to distance themselves from anyone who knows them well enough to realize that therapy is needed. Furthermore, depressed people of all ages characteristically believe that nothing will help. This makes them unlikely to seek treatment on their own. As a result, although effective treatment has been found for almost all types of depression, this disorder is a leading cause of impairment and premature death worldwide (World Health Organization, 2001).

Anxiety Disorders

Another major problem, evident in one-fourth of all U.S. residents below the age of 25, is anxiety disorders, which include post-traumatic stress disorder (PTSD), obsessive-compulsive disorder (OCD), and panic attacks. Note that anxiety disorders are even more prevalent than depression. Such incidence statistics vary from study to study, depending partly on definitions and cutoff scores, but all research finds that many emerging adults are anxious about themselves, their relationships, and their future.

Age and genetic vulnerability shape the symptoms of anxiety disorders. For instance, everyone with PTSD has had a frightening experience—near-death in battle, rape at knifepoint, watching the World Trade Center collapse on September 11, 2001. However, only about 15 percent of the people who experience such trauma develop PTSD (Ozer & Weiss, 2004). Young adults, especially if they have no support from close friends or relatives, are more likely to develop the disorder than people of other ages.

Anxiety disorders are also affected by cultural context. In the United States, social phobia—fear of talking to other people—is a common anxiety disorder, one that keeps young adults away from college, unable to make new friends, hesitant to apply for jobs. Eating disorders, as explained in Chapter 17, are more common among contemporary young women in college, probably for cultural reasons.

In Japan, a new anxiety disorder has appeared within the last 20 years that is said to affect more than 100,000 young adults. It is called ***hikikomori,*** or "pull away." The sufferer stays in his (or, less often, her) room almost all the time for six months or more. Typically, a person suffering with hikikomori is anxious about the social and academic pressures of high school and college. Parents bring food to their self-imprisoned children and "fear that their children won't survive without them" (M. Jones, 2005, p. 51).

hikikomori A Japanese word literally meaning "pull away," the name of an anxiety disorder common among young adults in Japan, in which sufferers isolate themselves from the outside world by staying inside their homes for months or even years at a time.

It is easier to see how another culture or family enables a particular anxiety disorder than it is to recognize aspects of the immediate social context that make

Recovering A young Japanese man sits alone in his room, which until recently was his self-imposed prison. He is one of thousands of Japanese young people (80 percent of whom are male) who have the anxiety disorder known as *hikikomori*.

Especially for Immigrants What can you do in your adopted country to avoid or relieve the psychic stresses of immigration?

emerging adults anxious. Japanese emerging adults are thought to experience more pressure, and parents are thought to be more indulgent. Yet everywhere, anxiety seems to be part of emerging adulthood. Manifestations vary, but the trait is universal. A U.S. survey found that neuroticism (one of the five basic traits of temperament, characterized by high anxiety) was highest in emerging adulthood (Chapman & Hayslip, 2006).

Schizophrenia

About 1 percent of all adults experience at least one episode of schizophrenia. They are overwhelmed by disorganized and bizarre thoughts, delusions, hallucinations, and emotions (American Psychiatric Association, 2000). This disorder is present in every nation, but some cultures and contexts have much higher rates than others (Cantor-Graae & Selten, 2005; Kirkbride et al., 2006).

No doubt the cause of schizophrenia is partly genetic, although most people with this disorder have no immediate family members suffering from it. Beyond genetics, some other vulnerabilities are known. One is malnutrition when the brain is developing: Women who are severely malnourished in the early months of pregnancy are twice as likely to have a child with schizophrenia than other women (St. Clair et al., 2005). Another is extensive social pressure. Among immigrants, the rate of schizophrenia triples when young adults have no familiar supports (Cantor-Graae & Selten, 2005; Morgan et al., 2007).

Symptoms typically begin in adolescence. Diagnosis is most common from ages 18 to 24, and males are particularly vulnerable (Kirkbride et al., 2006). If no symptoms appear by age 35, schizophrenia almost never develops. This raises the question: Does something in the bodies, minds, or social surroundings of emerging adults trigger schizophrenia? The diathesis-stress model of mental illness, which (as you saw earlier) proposes that a combination of genetic vulnerability and environmental stresses produces mental disorders, suggests that the answer is yes for all three.

Continuity and Discontinuity

Fortunately, most emerging adults, like humans at all ages, have strengths as well as liabilities. Many overcome their anxieties, their substance abuse, and other problems through "self-righting," social support, and ongoing maturation. A longitudinal study of children who had externalizing or internalizing problems found that their impact in early adulthood depended partly on what the problem was (Masten et al., 2005).

To be specific, childhood externalizing problems often become impediments in early adulthood because they diminish school achievement. This makes college less likely and thus increases the risk of other problems. By contrast, childhood internalizing problems are less likely to affect the emerging adult because academic achievement is typically unaffected and dangerous risks (such as with drugs) are avoided (Masten et al., 2005).

Every longitudinal study of the emotional development of emerging adults finds that the links are complex. No doubt, earlier problems have their impact, but some young adults escape unscathed. A happy marriage, a stellar college career, good human relationships, a satisfying job—all these are more likely if young adults have had a supportive childhood. But if a young adult with serious emotional problems manages to have even one of these, he or she stands a better chance of becoming successful (Hauser et al., 2006).

For example, Barry Marshall, the man who discovered the ulcer-causing bacteria, grew up in poverty and was considered a crank, showoff, and malcontent by many of his peers. Most people with that kind of background struggle through adulthood. Fortunately for Marshall, he had a good marriage, which gave him the support and stability necessary to make great strides in his research. Marshall is now a wealthy, proud, and widely admired researcher (Sweet, 1997).

SUMMING UP

Regarding emotional development during emerging adulthood, most people are quite pleased with themselves, and for good reason: Accomplishments begin to accumulate during these years. However, a sizable minority are emotionally disturbed. Substance abuse, depression, and anxiety disorders are particularly common. Although genetic vulnerability and early child rearing are crucial, the transitions and challenges of these years can either help or harm emotional development.

SUMMARY

Identity Achieved

1. Although Erikson thought that most people achieved identity by the end of adolescence, for today's youth the identity crisis continues into adulthood.

2. For emerging adults in multiethnic nations, ethnic identity needs to be established. This is difficult because combining local traditions and global concerns, or accommodating both parental wishes and peer pressures, is complex.

3. Vocational identity requires knowing what career one hopes to have. Few young adults are certain about their career goals. College is not only a moratorium on identity achievement but also a preparation for employment.

4. In today's job market, many adults of all ages switch jobs, with turnover particularly quick in emerging adulthood. Most short-term jobs are not connected to the young person's skills or ambitions. Vocational identity, as Erikson conceived it, is elusive, given the current job market and economic fluidity.

Intimacy

5. Close friendships are common during emerging adulthood, typically including some opposite-sex as well as same-sex friendships. Although male–female differences in friendships are diminishing, women still exchange more confidences and physical affection than men do. Male friendships often center on shared activities.

6. Romantic love is complex, involving passion, intimacy, and commitment. In some nations, commitment is crucial and parents arrange marriages with that in mind. Among emerging adults in developed nations, passion is more important but it does not necessarily lead to marriage.

7. More and more emerging adults are living together and postponing marriage. This arrangement does not necessarily improve marital happiness.

8. Marriages work best if couples are able to communicate well and share responsibilities. The pattern called demand/withdraw is particularly destructive.

9. Family support is needed lifelong. In emerging adulthood this often means that parents pay college costs and contribute in other ways to their young-adult children's independence.

10. In some nations, emerging adults and their parents are more closely connected than in others, but complete separation of the two generations is unusual and impairs young-adult achievement. Everywhere, members of families have linked lives.

Emotional Development

11. Many emerging adults come into their own. They find an appropriate combination of education, friendship, and achievement that improves their self-esteem. Some innovative leaders begin their extraordinary accomplishments during these years.

12. The incidence of many forms of psychopathology, including substance abuse, anxiety disorders, depression, and schizophrenia, rises during emerging adulthood. The origin is probably a combination of genes and early child rearing, but young adulthood is stressful for many.

KEY TERMS

intimacy versus isolation (p. 503)
gateways to attraction (p. 504)
exclusion criteria (p. 505)
cohabitation (p. 510)
homogamy (p. 511)
heterogamy (p. 511)
social homogamy (p. 511)
social exchange theory (p. 512)
common couple violence (p. 513)
intimate terrorism (p. 513)
linked lives (p. 514)
diathesis-stress model (p. 518)
hikikomori (p. 519)

KEY QUESTIONS

1. Why is vocational identity more complex for today's young adults than it was when Erikson developed his theory?

2. When, how, and why do people develop an ethnic identity?

3. What are the three main ways young adults meet their need for intimacy?

4. What are the differences between men's friendships and women's friendships?

5. What are the advantages and disadvantages of cross-sex friendships?

6. What are the main reasons for cohabitation?

7. How does cohabitation affect marriage?

8. What factors make romantic relationships endure?

9. What are the differences and similarities between developing and developed nations in family relationships?

10. Why is emerging adulthood an emotional peak for many people?

11. What factors increase the risk that a young adult will have an emotional disorder?

APPLICATIONS

1. Talk to three people you would expect to have contrasting views on love and marriage (differences in age, gender, upbringing, experience, and religion might affect attitudes). Ask each the same questions and then compare their answers.

2. Analyze 50 marriage announcements (with photographs of the couples) in your local paper. How much homogamy and heterogamy are evident?

3. Vocational identity is fluid in early adulthood. Talk with several people over age 30 about their work history. Are they doing what they expected when they were younger? Are they settled in their vocation and job? Pay attention to their age when they decided on their jobs. Was age 25 a turning point?

4. Observe couples walking together on your campus. Do your observation systematically, such as describing every third couple who walk past a particular spot. Can you tell the difference in body position or facial expression between men and women, and between lovers, friends, and acquaintances? Once you have an answer, test your hypothesis by asking several couples what their relationship is.

➤**Response for Immigrants** (from page 520): Maintain your social supports. Ideally, emigrate with members of your close family, and join a religious or cultural community where you will find emotional understanding.

PART VI The Developing Person So Far: Emerging Adulthood

BIOSOCIAL

Growth, Strength, and Health Bodies are strong, healthy, and active. Homeostasis and organ reserve are two biological processes that work to prevent adult illness and maintain all the organ systems. The sexual drive is strong, but most emerging adults do not want to marry or reproduce yet. One result is a high rate of sexually transmitted infections among this age group.

Health Habits Most young adults meet the ideal of daily exercise and healthy nutrition. A few, especially women, worry excessively about their weight, becoming vulnerable to two of the severe eating disorders of our era, anorexia and bulimia nervosa.

Taking Risks Early adulthood is the time of life when edgework is most attractive, especially for young men. In many ways, individuals find pleasure in, and societies benefit from, the risk taking of the young. But drug abuse and addiction, as well as serious injuries, may be destructive consequences.

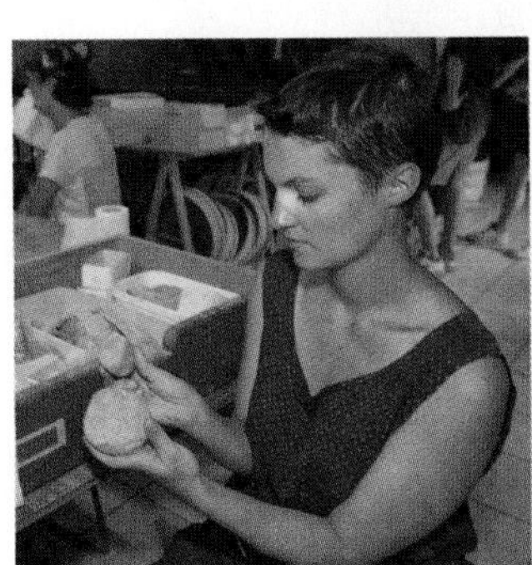

COGNITIVE

Postformal Thought Emerging adults may reach a fifth stage of cognitive development, in which they combine rational thought with emotional intuition. This manner of thinking requires experience and intellectual flexibility. The most advanced thinking may be dialectical, a dynamic process that synthesizes earlier ideas.

Morals and Religion Changes in moral thinking and religious faith occur in adulthood, when contact with other beliefs and unexpected experiences tends to make people think more deeply about their convictions. Since culture is a strong influence in such matters, it is difficult to conclude that ethical or spiritual thinking advances over the years of adulthood, although some research suggests that it does.

Education The institution of college is designed to advance thinking, via exposure to new people and ideas, intellectual challenges, and the mastery of communication and thinking skills. Current college students are far more numerous and diverse than those of half a century ago, but tertiary education probably still advances thought.

PSYCHOSOCIAL

Identity Achieved Emerging adults continue to seek identity. Ethnic and vocational identities are particularly difficult to achieve. Most emerging adults find employment, but few consider the jobs they have at this point in their lives to be their lifelong careers.

Intimacy Friendships are very important in meeting intimacy needs during emerging adulthood, as friends provide information as well as relief from stress. Many young people fall in love and live with a romantic partner, but some hesitate to marry, in part because divorce is common, as is conflict between partners. Generally, marriages are most likely to withstand the stresses of a long-term relationship if the two partners have similar attitudes and preferences. The family of origin continues to influence young adults, even if adult children live independently, as most do in the United States.

Emotional Development Most emerging adults think well of themselves. Some develop innovative ideas that will lead to later success. Others, however, experience psychopathology, including depression, anxiety, and even schizophrenia. Such disorders are caused in part by genes and childhood experiences, but the added stresses of growing up push some people over the edge.

Adulthood

PART VII

We now begin the seventh part of this text, another trio of chapters on another period of the life span. These three chapters cover 40 years (ages 25 to 65), a dramatic shift from the previous parts, each of which covered between two and seven years.

Developmentalists believe that much happens during these years of adulthood. Bodies grow more mature, minds master new material and consolidate what is already known; people work productively, nurture marriages, raise children, care for aging parents. Adults experience disaster, windfalls, divorce, illness, recovery, birth, death, travel, job loss, promotion, poverty, wealth.

All these are described in the next three chapters. A 40-year age span is covered because no particular age connects to any episode: Adults marry, or lose jobs, or whatever, at many ages. Thus adulthood is a long sweep, punctuated by events. Although not programmed by developmental age, those events are not random: Adults build on experiences, creating their own ecological niche, with chosen people, activities, communities, and habits. For the most part, these are good years, when each person's goals come closer and joys are manifest.

20

CHAPTER OUTLINE

Adulthood: Biosocial Development

How old are you? More important, do you feel your age? Will you feel young, or middle-aged, or old, when you are in your 60s? People in developed countries do not usually feel "old" until they are 70 or older (Lachman & Bertrand, 2001). For the most part, their bodies remain strong and capable.

Contemporary Western European and North American societies have been described as "age irrelevant," although that is not quite accurate (Perrig-Chiello & Perren, 2005, p. 143). True, adults of the same chronological age can be at very different points in their careers and family lives, and, true, bodies age at various rates such that one 60-year-old is dying while another has the vitality of a 30-year-old.

But age still matters. When a stranger says "Hello, young lady" to me, I bristle, resenting his attempt to please me. Yet I *am* pleased, which troubles me because it means I am caught up in my culture's view of aging. Particularly as a developmentalist, I know that aging is to be welcomed, not denied.

This chapter describes adult aging. Everybody grows older. As you will learn, it is not only health habits (smoking, exercising, and so on) but also gender, income, ethnicity, and nationality that affect how rapidly a body ages. No wonder I am caught by "young lady." I am proud that I appear young, but I guard against self-deception.

In fact, deception is unnecessary. Most of what you will learn here about adult biosocial development is encouraging. Although 25- to 65-year-olds show their age in many ways, essential organs work quite well, and adults of all ages (even those over age 65) are usually active, able, and vital, with specifics more dependent on habits and attitude than on age. One major advance is that priorities become clearer. As one woman wrote:

> These days I'm into the truth and the truth is I'm not crazy about my looks but I can live with them. . . . After the third funeral [of a friend], . . . I vowed to set my priorities straight before some fatal illness did it for me. Since then I have been trying to focus on the things that really matter. And I can assure you that being able to wear a bikini isn't one of them.
>
> *[Pogrebin, 1996]*

The Aging Process

We begin with the facts of aging, which may seem depressing if you are 20 years old or so. But physical aging is not discouraging to most people who experience it. Even in the one organ system that shows significant effects of aging, the sexual-reproductive system, some of the changes are welcome.

Senescence

senescence A gradual physical decline related to aging. Senescence occurs to everyone in every body part, but the rate of decline is highly variable.

Everyone ages, each at his or her own rate. When growth stops, **senescence** (a gradual physical decline that occurs with age, at a rate that is affected by many factors other than the passage of time) begins (Masoro, 2006).

Senescence affects every part of the body. For example, two invisible aspects of aging are increased blood pressure and higher levels of low-density lipoprotein (LDL), or "bad," cholesterol. Both of these occur to everyone over time (although not necessarily reaching dangerous levels) and both are harbingers of heart disease. In this example, coronary heart disease correlates with senescence, but it is not directly caused by any one aspect of aging.

Indeed, every known natural substance in the blood, every organ of the body, every bone and cell, is affected by aging—some more than others but all to some degree. Variations in the rate of senescence are apparent not only between one person and another but also between one organ and another within the same person.

Physical Appearance

Although most adults are strong and healthy, outward signs of senescence are present long before old age arrives. The first visible age-related changes are seen in the skin. Collagen, the connective tissue of the body, decreases by about 1 percent per year (M. Timiras, 2003). As a result, the skin becomes thinner and less flexible, and wrinkles become visible, particularly around the eyes.

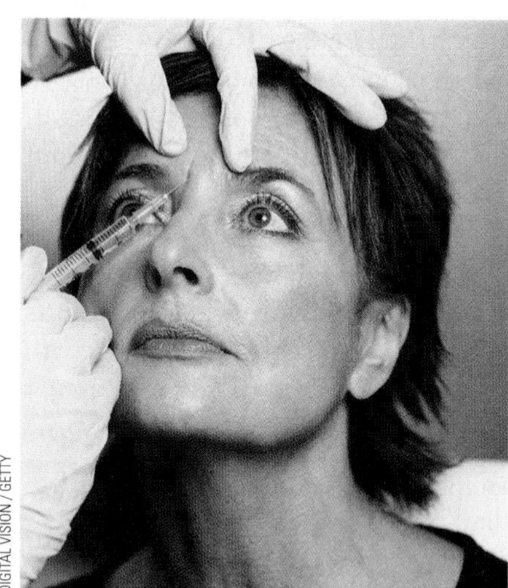

DIGITAL VISION / GETTY

No Wrinkles An injection of botox to plump the skin beneath her eyebrows is what this woman decided she needs, although she is quite beautiful and shows no signs of aging.

Especially on the face (most exposed to sun, rain, heat, cold, and pollution), skin shows "creases, discoloration, furrows, sagging, and loss of resiliency" (Whitbourne et al., 2002). This is barely noticeable in young adulthood, but if you know a typical pair of sisters, one 18 and the other 28, you can tell which one is older because of her skin. By age 60, all faces are wrinkled, some much more than others.

Aging is visible in dozens of other ways. Hair usually turns gray and gets thinner; skin becomes drier; "middle-age spread" appears as stomach muscles weaken; pockets of fat settle on parts of the body—most noticeably around the abdomen, but also on the upper arms, buttocks, eyelids, and the "infamous 'double chin'" (Whitbourne et al., 2002, p. 81).

People even get shorter. Back muscles, connective tissue, and bones lose strength, making the vertebrae in the spine collapse somewhat. This causes notable height loss (about an inch, or 2 to 3 centimeters) by age 65 (Merrill & Verbrugge, 1999).

Indeed, all the muscles weaken, not only because of disuse but also because the number of muscle fibers diminishes with age. The effect on appearance is in posture and movement, when an older person walks, stands, or sits. Walking "with a spring in their step" is more common in young adults than old ones.

Not all muscle fibers disappear at the same rate. The fibers for Type II muscles (the fast ones needed for forceful actions in many sports) are said to be reduced by 26 percent per decade beginning at age 30 (McCarter, 2006). Decline is much less significant in Type I fibers—those in slower, more routine muscle—and does not become evident until very old age.

Another visible effect is in breathing, which gets quicker and shallower with age. The reason is that lung efficiency is reduced beginning in the 20s, with vital capacity (the amount of air that can be expired after a deep breath) dropping by about 5 percent per decade (faster for smokers) (De Martinis & Timiras, 2003).

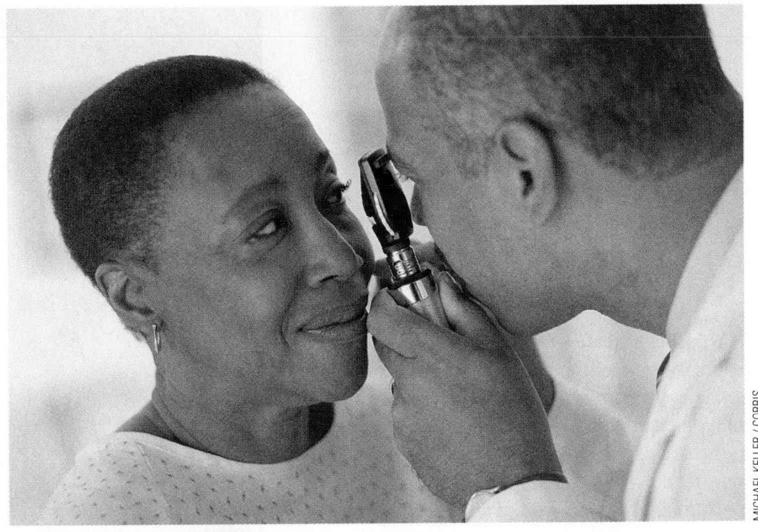

Healthy Eyes Annual examinations of the lens and retina are crucial for all middle-aged adults, especially those who are of African heritage.

Sense Organs

Not only does the rate of senescence vary from person to person and organ to organ, but the particular parts of each organ may also be on different timetables. This is particularly apparent in the organs associated with the five senses, all of which become less sharp over time. Each of the sense organs loses some functions faster than others.

The change in eyesight is perhaps the most obvious example of the varied rates within one organ. Difficulty seeing objects at a distance, or *nearsightedness*, increases gradually beginning in the 20s (see Figure 20.1). Within another 20 years or so, it also becomes harder to see objects that are close (called *farsightedness*), because the lens of the eye becomes less elastic and the cornea flattens (Schieber, 2006).

This explains why 40-year-olds tend to hold reading matter twice as far away from their eyes as 20-year-olds do and why many older adults use bifocals (Meisami et al., 2003). Younger adults with vision problems are usually either nearsighted *or* farsighted; most older adults are both.

Losses also occur in hearing. People have more acute hearing at age 10 than at any later age. Although some middle-aged people hear much better than others, none hear perfectly. Actually, "perfect" hearing is impossible; hearing is always a matter of degree. No one can hear a conversation on the other side of town. Deafness is rarely absolute, which is one reason the gradual hearing losses of age are not noticed until late middle age, when they begin to cause problems in daily life.

Not until about age 60 is **presbycusis** (literally, "aging hearing") often diagnosed. One practical measure of presbycusis is the "whisper test." A person is asked to repeat a whisper uttered by someone unseen, 3 feet away (Pirozzo et al.,

presbycusis The loss of hearing associated with senescence. Presbycusis often does not become apparent until after age 60.

FIGURE 20.1

Age-Related Declines in Vision Every aspect of bodily functioning follows its own rate of senescence. Vision is a prime example. *(a)* Sharpness of distance vision, as measured by the ability to see an object at 20 feet, reaches a peak at about age 20 and declines gradually until old age. *(b)* By contrast, ability to focus on a small point about 12 inches in front of the eyes declines from childhood on; at about age 60 the typical person becomes officially farsighted.

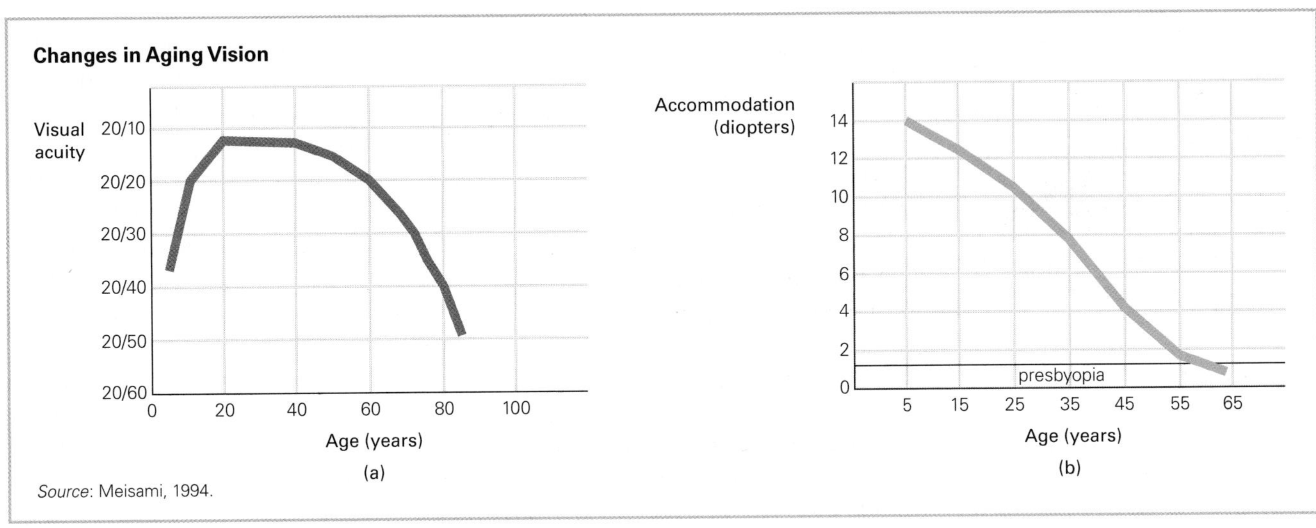

VAUGHN YOUTZ / LIAISON

Hard Rocking, Hard of Hearing Les Claypool is an example of the dangers posed by prolonged exposure to loud noise. Night after night of high-decibel rocking with his band, Primus, has damaged his hearing. When this photo was taken in 1999, Claypool was not only performing but also protecting his remaining hearing. He is active with HEAR—Hearing Education and Awareness for Rockers.

TABLE 20.1

Hearing Loss at Age 50

	Men	Women
Can understand even a whisper	65%	75%
Can understand soft conversation but cannot understand a whisper	28%	22%
Can understand loud conversation but cannot understand soft conversation	5%	2%
Cannot understand even loud conversation	2%	1%

2003). Almost all emerging adults pass this test, as do two-thirds of those age 50 and half of those over 65.

Again, specifics of hearing are affected differently by aging. The ability to distinguish pure tones declines faster than the ability to hear conversation (see Table 20.1), which means that the first sign of loss may be the inability to hear a doorbell or a telephone ringing in the next room. Deficits in hearing conversation begin with high-frequency tones, as when a young child talks. A 60-year-old may attend more to a teenage grandson than a preschool granddaughter because of selective hearing loss, not sexism.

The Aging Brain

Like every other part of the body, the brain slows down with aging. Neurons fire more slowly, and messages sent from the axon of one neuron are not picked up as quickly by the dendrite of another neuron. Further, the total size of the brain is reduced. Gray matter in particular declines; already by middle adulthood, there are fewer neurons and synapses (Buckner et al., 2006).

Overall, because of brain changes, reaction time is slower and complex memory tasks (e.g., repeating a series of eight numbers, then adding the first four, deleting the fifth one, subtracting the next two, and multiplying the new total by the last one—all in your head) become impossible. Multitasking is more difficult with every passing decade (Reuter-Lorenz & Sylvester, 2005). For example, driving while talking on a cell phone is dangerous at any age because the brain seems to ignore what the driver sees (Strayer & Drews, 2007); but trying to do two things at once is particularly hazardous with age because distractions are harder to ignore (Park & Gutchess, 2005). Stress further slows down reactions, especially with age.

Especially for Drivers A number of states have passed laws requiring that hands-free headphones be worn by people who use cell phones while driving. Do those measures cut down on accidents?

Regular sleep becomes increasingly essential. Skipping a night's sleep slows down thinking and problem solving. This was proven with medical interns, who once were required to be "on call" at hospitals for up to 48 hours at a time, snatching only bits of sleep (Lockley et al., 2004). Errors caused by lack of sleep led to regulations that doctors-in-training be on duty no more than 24 hours at a time, with at least 10 hours of rest between assignments.

Some adults risk sleep-walking, sleep-eating, and even sleep-driving. Normally, circadian rhythms (see Chapter 14) govern the sleep–wake cycle, and brain-produced chemicals prevent a sleeper from moving. These day–night, awake–asleep rhythms are disrupted by aging. Even in young adults, sleep deprivation and drugs can make a person seem awake when brain scans indicate sleep, often resulting in confused thoughts and dangerous actions (Gunn & Gunn, 2007). Aging makes the situation worse; disrupted sleep is characteristic of aging (as well as of diseases of all kinds) (Foley et al., 2004).

Even when they are not overtired, sick, stressed, or drugged, beginning in their 30s adults experience a "shallow decline" in abilities dependent on the brain. A steeper decline begins at about age 60 (Dangour et al., 2007, p. 54). Adults compensate by using more parts of their brain when called on to perform challenging tasks. As a result, brain declines are rarely evident throughout adulthood, although some changes are detected in fMRI or PET brain scans (Buckner et al., 2006; Reuter-Lorenz & Sylvester, 2005).

A few individuals, however, experience much greater losses. They "encounter a catastrophic rate of cognitive decline, passing through a threshold of cognitive functioning . . . sometimes termed the dementia threshold" (Dangour et al., 2007, p. 54). Less than 1 percent of adults under age 65 cross that frightening threshold.

When dementia does occur before old age, it rarely is a complete surprise: A person may have inherited a dominant gene for Alzheimer's, or been born with Down syndrome or another serious genetic condition, or have suffered major brain damage through trauma (such as being hit repeatedly on the head), or had a massive stroke (halting blood flow to the brain long enough that part of the brain dies).

It is reassuring to most adults that dementia is far more prevalent in late adulthood than from ages 25 to 65 and that adult brains usually perform as well at 60 as at 20. However, this does not mean that most adults are impervious to brain impairment. Senescence occurs in the brain as well as elsewhere in the body; the older a person is, the more likely it becomes that problems with the brain will reach the point at which illness is apparent.

Among the neurological problems that appear in middle age are Parkinson's disease and frontotemporal dementia (Hodges, 2007). A shaky signature may be the first sign of Parkinson's; a surprising loss of modesty may signify frontotemporal dementia. (Our main discussion of these and other types of dementia occurs in Chapter 24.)

Several other problems that occur in adulthood correlate with loss of brain cells:

- *Drug abuse.* People who consume large quantities of alcohol over decades risk a disease called Korsakoff's syndrome ("wetbrain"), signified by irreversible brain damage. Although research is not definitive, other psychoactive drugs are also suspected of permanently damaging the brain. The underlying problem may be severe vitamin deficiency (Stacey & Sullivan, 2004).
- *Excessive stress.* Stress hormones disrupt thought processes (as you may remember at a time when you were extremely stressed). This is temporary for most adults, but excessive stress in childhood disrupts the body's normal stress reactions. If adult bodies are flooded with stress hormones, that leads to depression and an overactive immune system, harming the brain (Pace et al., 2006).
- *Poor circulation.* Everything that protects the circulatory system—such as exercise, healthy diet, and low blood pressure—also protects brain functioning. Hypertension (high blood pressure) is particularly destructive of cognition, beginning in middle age (Elias et al., 2004).

➤Response for Drivers (from page 530): No. Car accidents occur when the mind is distracted, not the hands.

- *Viruses.* Although the "blood–brain barrier" serves to keep viruses out of the brain, some diseases and infections cross this barrier, with devastating results. The most dramatic recent example is HIV, which may attack the brain, causing personality changes and dementia.

What can be done to protect the brain from all these problems? Beyond such obvious measures as exercise and a healthy diet, two strategies have been suggested:

- *Intellectual challenges.* There is a correlation between brain activity (solving crossword puzzles and the like) and optimal brain functioning. The correlation between intellectual exercises and brain functioning may not be causal, however: Cognitive strength may lead to activity, not vice versa (Salthouse, 2006). Children and adolescents who are highly intelligent and reflective (writing in detail about their emotions, for instance) are less likely to become demented in late adulthood; but again, this may be merely a correlate, not a cause.
- *Replacing dead neurons.* It has recently been discovered that adult brains can grow new cells when old ones die, especially when a major trauma (such as a stroke) occurs (Yamashita et al., 2006). It is also known that *stem cells* (created very early in development) can become many kinds of body cells, perhaps replacing malfunctioning or absent neurons. However, the research is very preliminary, and cells of the cortex seem particularly difficult to replace (Shen et al., 2006). Aging of the brain may be irreversible.

Thus, it is known that adult brains can grow new cells, especially when a major brain injury has occurred. It is also known that certain cells of the body that arise early in development can become crucial body cells—although research has not yet determined whether this process can compensate for neurological cell death, as occurs in Parkinson's disease, multiple sclerosis, and many other illnesses. However, it may be that stem cells cannot create new neurons in the cortex and thus cannot slow senescence in the brain (Bhardwaj et al., 2006). Overall, this suggests that the best way to keep a well-functioning brain is to maintain one's general health.

FIGURE 20.2

Sexually Satisfied with Monogamy In a cross section of more than 2,000 adults in the United States, most were "comfortable monogamists," a category for those who were happy with their one partner, with whom they usually had sex once or twice a week. Note that the percentages in this category were quite similar for men and women. The other categories differed by gender. For example, women could be "enthusiastic cohabiters," a category that included 25 percent of the women aged 25 to 39 and 10 percent of those aged 40 to 59. Men could be "enthusiastic polygamists," a category that included 10 percent of the 25- to 39-year-old men and 4 percent of those aged 40 to 59. Almost no women were polygamists, but about one-third of the men were called "venturesome cohabiters."

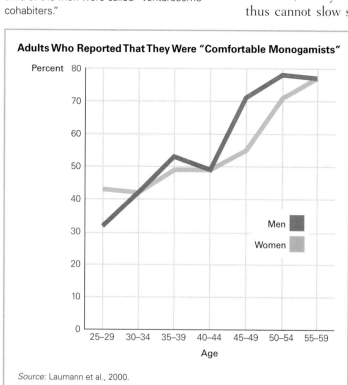

The Sexual-Reproductive System

Remember from Chapter 17 that the sexual-reproductive system peaks during early adulthood. But in this chapter we have seen that most physiological slowdowns are gradual, with little or no effect on daily life. To some extent, this is true for the sexual-reproductive system as well. Sexual responsiveness is slower and fertility is reduced with age, but adults of all ages enjoy "very high levels of emotional satisfaction and physical pleasure from sex within their relationships" (Laumann & Michael, 2000, p. 250).

In one study, men and women were most likely to report that they were "extremely satisfied" with sex if they were in a committed, monogamous relationship, a circumstance that was more likely to be true as they grew older (see Figure 20.2) (Laumann & Michael, 2000). Indeed, for people in long-term, committed relationships, sex may actually improve with age. Distress at slower responsiveness seems to be more affected by anxiety, the nature of a couple's relationship, and each person's own expectations than by age itself (Duplassie & Daniluk, 2006; Siegel & Siegel, 2006). There are also physiological reasons for sexual dysfunction, including the use of many prescription drugs that are more commonly prescribed as people age—but here again, age itself is not the problem.

Infertility

Historically, fertility was not just expected but also lauded. Women were admired for having a dozen children, and men were proud of fatherhood at any age. Currently, such fertility is no longer praised, but *infertility,* defined as the failure to conceive a child after a year or more of intercourse without contraception, is still distressing to many.

As few as 2 percent of healthy couples in their early 20s in medically advanced nations are infertile, as are almost one-third of 30-year-olds in poor nations. Ironically, the highest rates of infertility occur in countries with the highest birth rates, due in part to the lack of contraception as well as to the high incidence of untreated sexually transmitted infections (Bentley & Mascie-Taylor, 2000).

Overall in the United States, about 15 percent of all couples are infertile, primarily because many postpone childbearing until they are well past their peak reproductive years (Inhorn & van Balen, 2002). If a couple in their 40s wants a child, about half fail to conceive and the other half have higher rates of miscarriage, stillbirth, and seriously impaired births. Most physicians recommend that would-be mothers try to conceive before age 30 and would-be fathers before age 40. Both sexes are about equally likely to be the source of infertility when it occurs, but modern medicine can often solve the problem if the couple is under age 30. After age 40, medical solutions are less likely to succeed (Bhasin, 2007).

Some men are infertile because of specific problems with their reproductive organs, such as varicoceles, or varicose veins, in the testes or partially blocked genital ducts. A low sperm count is another reason for male infertility. Conception is most likely if a man ejaculates more than 20 million sperm per milliliter of semen, two-thirds of them mobile and viable, because each sperm's journey through the cervix and uterus is aided by millions of fellow travelers. The need for so many sperm to fertilize a single egg explains the effectiveness of a reversible type of male contraception that reduces sperm count to less than 3 million (Liu et al., 2006).

About 100 million sperm are developed every day as part of an ongoing cycle that lasts about 75 days. At any given moment, a man is developing billions of sperm. Over that two- to three-month period, anything that impairs body functioning (e.g., fever, radiation, prescription drugs, time in a sauna, excessive stress, environmental toxins, drug abuse, alcoholism, or cigarette smoking) reduces sperm number, shape, and motility (activity).

Age also reduces sperm count, and the reasons for this are many. One is that slower homeostasis (see Chapter 17) impedes recovery from, say, a weekend of drinking or a bout of radiation. Another reason is that male hormone levels are diminished, resulting in decreased sperm production. Low sperm count is the probable reason that men take five times as many months to impregnate a woman when they are over 45 as when they are under 25 (Hassan & Killick, 2003). (This study controlled for frequency of sex and age of the woman.)

Especially for Young Men A young man who impregnates a woman is often proud of his manhood. Is this reaction valid?

Female infertility also is affected by anything that impairs a woman's normal body functioning (including smoking, anorexia, and obesity). In addition, the fallopian tubes of some women can become blocked as a result of pelvic inflammatory disease (PID) if a sexually transmitted infection is not treated. The incidence of past, untreated STIs increases with age. Senescence also affects the entire process, from ovulation to implantation to fetal growth to birth, although many women have quite normal pregnancies in their 30s.

Assisted Reproduction

Good medical care can prevent many fertility problems. If prevention fails, various techniques can overcome several of the causes of infertility. Minor physical abnormalities are often correctable through surgery; lifestyle changes (no hot tubs!) and drugs can stimulate ovulation and sperm production. Many of the more elaborate methods used to restore fertility are collectively called **assisted reproductive technology (ART).**

assisted reproductive technology (ART) The collective name for the various methods of medical intervention that can help infertile couples have children.

in vitro fertilization (IVF) A technique in which ova (egg cells) are surgically removed from a woman and fertilized with sperm in a laboratory. After the original fertilized cells (the zygotes) have divided several times, they are inserted into the woman's uterus.

The most common ART method is **in vitro fertilization (IVF),** in which ova are surgically removed and fertilized in a laboratory (*in vitro* as contrasted with *in vivo*). Zygotes thus created divide until the eight- or sixteen-cell stage and then are implanted in the woman's uterus. IVF sidesteps problems with ovulation, with blocked fallopian tubes, and with low sperm count.

Currently, a typical IVF cycle also uses *intra-cytoplasmic sperm injection (ICSI)*, whereby one sperm is inserted into one ovum. This avoids the possibility that a viable ovum will not be fertilized and solves the problem of low sperm count. It also can be used when a man is HIV-positive and his wife is HIV-negative. Such couples use condoms for sexual intercourse, but sperm are collected and washed in the laboratory to rid them of the virus before one is inserted into an ovum (Kato et al., 2006).

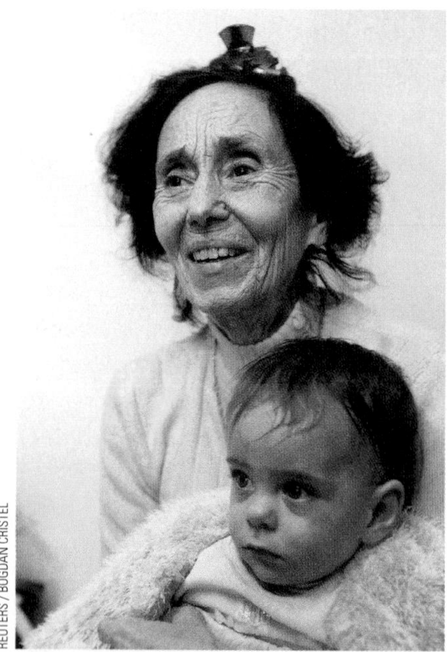

REUTERS / BOGDAN CRISTEL

A Happy 67-Year-Old Mother This Romanian woman gave birth after in vitro fertilization. Other nations would not allow IVF at her age, but every nation has new fathers who are that age or older.

Only about one-third of all IVF cycles produce a pregnancy, since implantation does not always occur. Nonetheless, since 1978, when the world's first "test-tube baby" was born in England, IVF has produced more than a million babies from almost all nations, currently including 1 percent of all U.S. newborns (MMWR, June 8, 2007).

Complications and birth defects increase with IVF, especially when several zygotes are implanted at once (MacKay et al., 2006; Shevell et al., 2005). Low-birthweight twins or triplets are born in almost half of all IVF pregnancies in the United States (MMWR, June 8, 2007).

No nation allows cloning, or laboratory-induced twinning (when a two-celled organism is split into monozygotic twins). Regulations vary on other aspects of ART, such as how many pre-embryos can be implanted at once and whether single or older women can undergo IVF. The United States has only voluntary guidelines.

The lack of uniform regulations has given rise to international controversies. Jeanne Salomone, a 62-year-old French woman, was refused ART in Europe because of her age. She flew to Los Angeles to obtain a donor egg that was fertilized with sperm she said was from her husband and then implanted in her uterus. She gave birth to a boy—and then revealed that the sperm came from her only sibling, her 52-year-old brother. His sperm was also used to impregnate a surrogate mother, who had a girl. The cost for those two babies was about $200,000 (Ananova, 2001). An international outcry erupted. Since neither sibling had other children, they were accused of having these babies in order to inherit their aged mother's fortune. Jeanne's response: "I have nothing on my conscience. I treasure these little ones and I get up three times a night like all mothers. I sing and rock them to sleep" (quoted in Ananova, 2001).

Menopause

At some point during adulthood, the level of sex hormones in the bloodstream is reduced, quite suddenly in women, gradually in men. As a result, sexual desire often decreases, as does the frequency of intercourse. Conception may become impossible. The specifics for women and men differ, so we discuss each in turn.

menopause The time in middle age, usually around age 50, when a woman's menstrual periods cease completely and the production of estrogen, progesterone, and testosterone drops considerably. Strictly speaking, menopause is dated one year after a woman's last menstrual period.

For women, sometime between ages 42 and 58 (the average age is 51), ovulation and menstruation stop because of a marked decrease in the production of several hormones (Wise, 2006). This is **menopause.** If a hysterectomy (surgical removal of the uterus, experienced by one in nine 35- to 45-year-old U.S. women) includes removal of the ovaries, then sudden, premature menopause occurs (MMWR, July 12, 2002).

Barring surgery, which always produces symptoms, most women (60 percent for women of Asian heritage, 75 percent for European and Hispanic women, 85 percent for women of African descent) experience some symptoms of natural menopause—most commonly, disturbances of body temperature, including hot flashes (feeling hot), hot flushes (looking hot), and cold sweats (feeling chilled) (Gold et al., 2006). Natural lubrication during sexual arousal is reduced, and, once ovulation stops, conception cannot naturally occur. Some women find that they become irritable, either because of the changing hormones or because of tiredness (if hot flashes interrupt sleep).

>**Response for Young Men** (from page 533): The answer depends on a person's definition of what a man is. No developmentalist would define a man as someone who has a high sperm count.

The psychic consequences of menopause are extremely variable. Although most women are not especially moody, the rate of depression increases (Cohen et al., 2006). Although some women become sad, others are relieved that contraception is no longer needed (Wise, 2003). In contrast to the historical Western notion that menopausal women "temporarily lose their minds" (Neugarten & Neugarten, 1986), the traditional view among Hindi women in India is that menopause represents liberation (Menon, 2001).

Over the past 20 or 30 years, millions of post-menopausal women used **hormone replacement therapy (HRT),** taking hormone supplements to replace those no longer produced by their ovaries. Some did so to alleviate hot and cold symptoms; others, to prevent osteoporosis (fragile bones), heart disease, or senility. All three of these conditions, in correlational studies, occur at lower rates in women using HRT.

hormone replacement therapy (HRT) Treatment to compensate for hormone reduction at menopause or following surgical removal of the ovaries. Such treatment, which usually involves estrogen and progesterone, minimizes menopausal symptoms and diminishes the risk of osteoporosis in later adulthood.

andropause A term coined to signify a drop in testosterone levels in older men, which normally results in reduced sexual desire, erections, and muscle mass. Also known as *male menopause*.

Researchers now believe that those studies were invalid, because most women who used HRT were also high in socioeconomic status. Their long-term good health resulted from their income, education, and better health habits rather than from HRT. In fact, in controlled longitudinal studies in the United States, the Women's Health Initiative found that long-term use of HRT (for 10 years or more) *increased* the risk of heart disease, stroke, and breast cancer, and had no proven effect on dementia (U.S. Preventive Task Force, 2002). It did, however, reduce hot flashes and decrease osteoporosis, which led the North American Menopause Society (2007) to urge that physicians and women consider individual needs.

Most women in the United States stopped taking HRT when they read about this research, but women and doctors in Europe were less alarmed. One reason is that the particular form of HRT used in Europe differs from that studied in the Women's Health Initiative, and another is that heart disease and dementia are affected by so many factors that it is difficult to connect HRT with them (Rosano et al., 2003). For example, many European women eat lower-fat diets and walk more, and therefore are at lower risk of heart disease.

Do men undergo anything like menopause? Some say yes, suggesting that the word **andropause** should be used to signify the lower testosterone levels of older men, which reduce sexual desire, erections, and muscle mass. Even with erection-inducing drugs such as Viagra and Levitra, sexual desire and speed of orgasm decline with age, as do many other physiological and cognitive functions (but not all, as the next chapter details).

But most experts think that the term *andropause* (or *male menopause*) is misleading, because it implies a sudden drop

Could This Be a Grandmother? Yes. Most middle-aged women are strong and competent, like this grandmother cutting wood in rural Italy.

JENS LUCKING / STONE / GETTY IMAGES

CLEO PHOTOGRAPHY / PHOTOEDIT, INC.

So Happy Together This long-married couple still demonstrate great affection for each other after years of familiarity.

in male reproductive ability or hormone levels, as with menopause. That does not occur (Siegel & Siegel, 2006). Most men continue to produce sperm indefinitely.

It is not just age but also sexual inactivity and anxiety that can reduce testosterone in men. As one review explains, "Retirement, financial problems, unresolved anger, and dwindling social relationships can wreak havoc on some men's sense of masculinity and virility" (Siegel & Siegel, 2006, p. 239). If aging leads to anxiety, that might further reduce testosterone, a phenomenon similar to menopause but with a psychological, not physiological, cause.

To combat this loss of testosterone, some men have turned to hormone replacement. Some women also take testosterone supplements to increase their sexual desire. But a two-year longitudinal study with testosterone or placebo supplements for both men and women found no benefits (sexual or otherwise) from taking testosterone (Nair et al., 2006). Researchers are understandably cautious; supplemental doses of hormones may be harmful (Bhasin, 2006; Moffat, 2005).

SUMMING UP

Growth stops and senescence progresses almost imperceptibly during adulthood (ages 25 to 65). While most adults remain strong and healthy, outward signs of senescence, such as wrinkles in the skin and weaker muscles, are apparent. All the sensory organs become less sharp every decade; reductions in visual acuity and auditory perception are often noticeable by middle age.

The sexual-reproductive system peaks during early adulthood, but most adults enjoy satisfying sexual relationships as they grow older. Nonetheless, hormone levels, sexual responsiveness, and fertility decline with age. Medical science can overcome many fertility problems with procedures such as in vitro fertilization (IVF) and a range of other techniques of assisted reproductive technology (ART). For women, ovulation ceases at menopause. Hormone replacement therapy (HRT) alleviates menopausal symptoms (e.g., hot flashes), but researchers report that long-term HRT may increase the risk of heart disease, stroke, and breast cancer. Men do not undergo a physiological equivalent of menopause, although some experience significant reductions in testosterone levels that can result in sexual problems. ■

The Impact of Poor Health Habits

Many age-related declines can be exacerbated and hastened by years of self-destructive behavior or long-time residence in an unhealthy community. Almost all diseases and chronic conditions that are normally associated with aging—from arthritis to strokes—are powerfully affected by the routines of daily life (Abeles, 2007; Crews, 2003). Whether the effects are positive or negative depends largely on people's habits.

This is evident even in the senescence just explained. For example, although the senses inevitably become less acute with age, every loud noise—traffic, music, construction—damages the eardrums to some extent. Some noise can be avoided, but many young adults (especially men) work with jackhammers without protection or listen to music at ear-splitting levels, developing hearing deficits that will appear later.

Decreasing sexual interest and reduced fertility depend a great deal on a person's relationship with a partner and medical care, as just described. Many experts in sexology insist that sexual changes with age can be improvements, as men's eroticism becomes less focused on intercourse and women become more aware of their sexual wishes. Now we focus on three habits that affect every aspect of aging: drug use, exercise, and eating.

Tobacco and Alcohol Use

Rates of addiction and drug abuse decrease markedly by age 30 in every nation, thanks partly to maturity and marriage. This is particularly true for illegal drugs, discussed in Chapter 17. Here we focus on two legal addictions for many adults: nicotine and alcohol.

Tobacco

Tobacco in all its forms—pipes, cigars, cigarettes, and chews—contains several harmful drugs. Nicotine is the most addictive. Which particular form of tobacco is used depends partly on culture and cohort; cigarettes are by far the most common in North America.

There is some good news about North American cigarette smokers: Fewer people are starting to smoke, and almost everyone quits by late adulthood. In 1970 in the United States, one-half of all adult men and one-third of all adult women smoked. Current rates are much lower (see Figure 20.3) (U.S. Bureau of the Census, 2007). Canadian and Mexican data also indicate a quitting trend over the last few decades (Franco-Marina et al., 2006; Shields, 2006).

Death rates for lung cancer (by far the leading cause of cancer deaths in North America) reflect smoking patterns of earlier decades, which differed for men and women. Because North American men have been quitting since 1970, lung cancer deaths for 35- to 65-year-old men are down 20 percent from the 1980 peak (see Appendix A, p. A-17). Currently in the United States, almost as many women smoke as men, and female lung cancer deaths increased 20 percent from 1980 to 1995.

Medical advances have been reducing deaths from all cancers, so women's lung cancer death rates are no longer rising. However, it is ironic that 50 years ago

FIGURE 20.3

Quitters Win This figure shows the well-known historical declines in the number of people who start smoking and also shows that many adults quit. Half of all men aged 25 to 64 in 1970 smoked; 35 years later almost all were over age 65 and almost all had quit. (Of course some had died, but most of that cohort were still alive and smoke-free.)

Observation Quiz (see answer, page 538): Are the two sexes growing closer together or farther apart in rates of smoking in the United States?

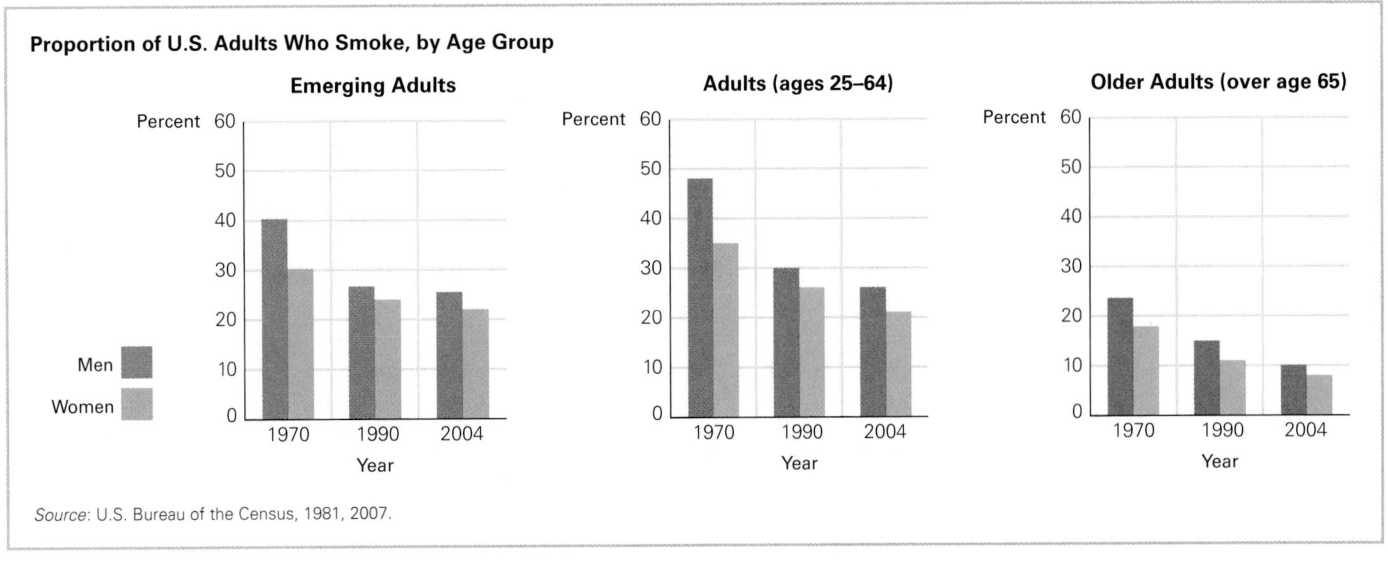

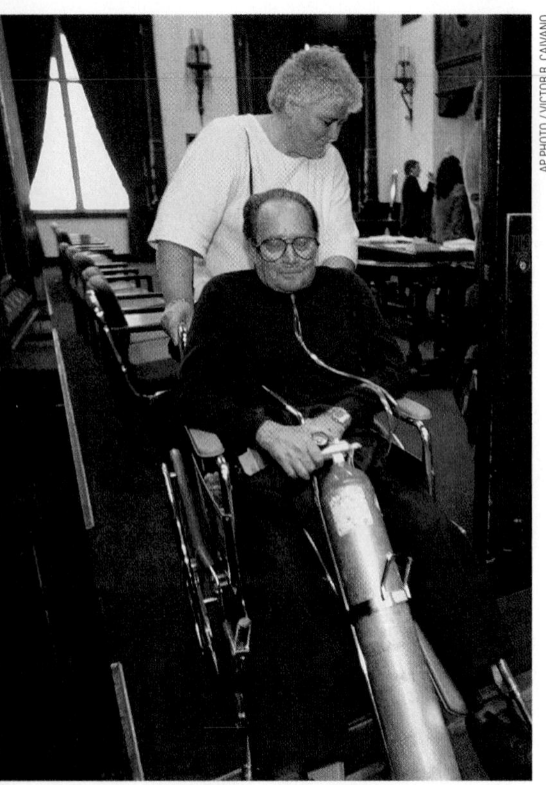
AP PHOTO / VICTOR R. CAIVANO

Working to Save Lives Ronald Bowell smoked for 30 years, and now his emphysema requires constant oxygen, a wheelchair, and his wife Lyliod's assistance. He tries to save lives through activism. He is shown here leaving a Florida courtroom, where he had testified in a class-action suit that eventually led to hard-hitting antismoking advertisements (showing teenagers hauling body bags). In the wake of this ad campaign, teen smoking was significantly reduced in Florida.

about twice as many women died from cancers of the breast, uterus, or ovary as of the lung; in 2005 about twice as many women died from lung cancer as from those other three forms of cancer combined (U.S. Bureau of the Census, 2006).

Worldwide trends are opposite those in North America, in that smoking is increasing. Almost half the adults in Germany, Denmark, Poland, Holland, Switzerland, and Spain are smokers. In developing nations, more than half of the men smoke, but only one-tenth of the women do—though women's rates are rising rapidly. The incidence of smoking and smoking-related cancers (lung, stomach, kidney, and so on) is increasing worldwide, especially in developing nations (Mackay & Eriksen, 2002; Mascie-Taylor & Karim, 2003). A news release by the World Health Organization (WHO) (2007) concluded:

> Tobacco use is the leading preventable cause of death globally, causing more than five million deaths a year. Tobacco use continues to expand most rapidly in the developing world, where currently half of tobacco-related deaths occur. By 2030, if current trends continue, 8 out of every 10 tobacco-related deaths will be in the developing world.

The wide variations from one nation, cohort, or gender to another are evidence that smoking is affected by social norms, laws, and advertisements. It now seems hard to believe that 50 years ago the U.S. government provided free cigarettes to everyone in the armed forces and some doctors agreed to endorse cigarettes in advertisements. In terms of developmental health over the years of adulthood, the history of smoking in North America is heartening—yet it shows that an enormous challenge still lies ahead.

Alcohol

The harm from cigarettes is directly dose-related—each additional puff, each additional day of smoking, each breath of secondhand smoke makes cancer, heart disease, emphysema, and strokes more likely. No such linear harm results from alcohol use. Adults who drink wine, beer, spirits, or other alcohol *in moderation*—no more than two moderate-sized drinks a day—live longer than those who never drink (Smith & Hart, 2002). But because it is widely abused, alcohol is nonetheless a major killer.

The major benefit of moderate drinking is a reduction in coronary heart disease. Alcohol increases HDL (high-density lipoprotein), the "good" cholesterol, and reduces LDL (low-density lipoprotein), the "bad" cholesterol that causes clogged arteries and blood clots. It also lowers blood pressure. High blood pressure (hypertension) correlates with heart attacks and strokes (Panagiotakos et al., 2007; Wannamethee & Shaper, 1999).

However, moderation is impossible for some drinkers. It is easier for an alcoholic to drink nothing than to have one, and only one, drink a day. Heavy drinking increases the risk of death from 60 diseases, including cancer of the breast, stomach, and throat (Hampton, 2005). Most of the 27,000 deaths from liver disease in the United States each year are caused by alcohol (U.S. Bureau of the Census, 2006). Worldwide, alcohol causes as many premature deaths as tobacco does (Room et al., 2005).

Further, alcohol destroys brain cells, contributes to osteoporosis, decreases fertility, and accompanies many suicides, homicides, and accidents. It has also wrecked many families, harming children in the process. Even moderate alcohol consumption is unhealthy if it leads to smoking or overeating. In the United States, people who are HIV-positive who never drink live, on average, three years longer than moderate drinkers and six years longer than heavy drinkers (Braithwaite et al., 2007).

➤Answer to Observation Quiz (from page 537): They are growing closer together. In fact, some data indicate that teenage girls are more likely to smoke than boys are.

Especially for Doctors and Nurses If you had to choose between recommending various screening tests and recommending various lifestyle changes to a 35-year-old, which would you do?

During the years between emerging and late adulthood, people are particularly subject to the deadly effects of alcohol. About half the deaths in Russia of men under age 60 are alcohol-related (Leon et al., 2007). Increased vodka consumption is one reason homicides skyrocketed and death from other causes rose there in the 1990s (Pridemore, 2002). All in all, the benefits of moderate drinking for the heart should not delude anyone. For millions of people, alcohol is deadly.

Staying on the Ball Professional athletes like New York Yankees pitcher Andy Pettitte know the value of regular exercise, especially as they get older—a lesson that many inactive adults need to learn.

Lack of Exercise

Chapter 17 described the many health benefits of regular exercise and recommended that adults bike to work, walk to school, play sports, or take classes in dance, aerobics, or karate. Three factors make it easier to exercise regularly: personal commitment, supportive friends, and community environment. Even though the health benefits of exercise, and the need for these three factors, are as apparent after age 25 as before it, adults in every nation tend to exercise less as they age. Figure 20.4 shows rates in the United States; other nations, even developing countries, show similar trends.

Low exercise rates can be blamed on any of the three factors. There may be a lack of individual commitment (why doesn't that person walk to work?), or a lack of support in the immediate social context (why doesn't that family go swimming together?), or the community's failure to provide appropriate facilities (why doesn't that city have bike paths?).

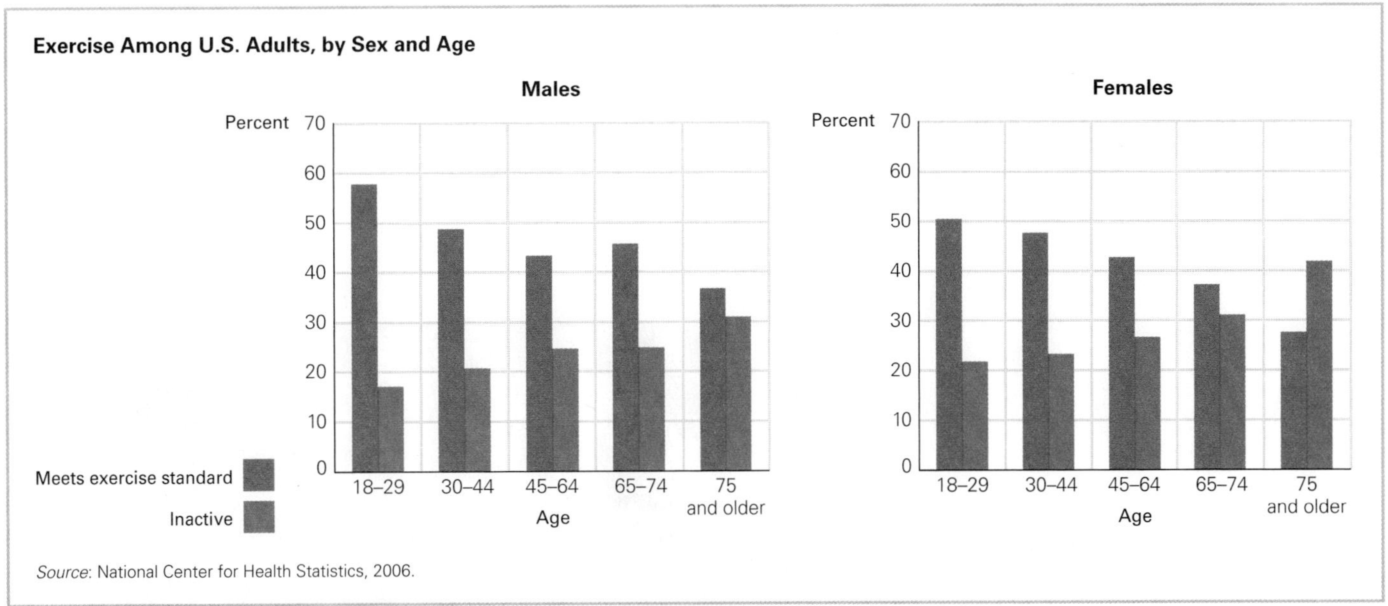

FIGURE 20.4

Even Worse Than It Seems If you are troubled to see that less than one-half of all adults meet the U.S. government's recommended standard for exercise and almost one-fourth are completely inactive, then you will be even more distressed to learn that these graphs portray adult exercise in the best light. These data are based on self-reports (which are generally rosier than reality) and combine three categories: transportation, work, and leisure. Further, the "standard" is only a weekly total of 2½ hours of moderate activity (including walking) or 1 hour of vigorous activity (such as running). Ideally, every adult should get more exercise than that.

Observation Quiz (see answer, page 541): Who is less likely to exercise: the typical 70-year-old man or the typical 50-year-old woman?

➤**Response for Doctors and Nurses** (from page 538): Obviously, much depends on the specific patient. Overall, however, far more people develop disease or die because of years of poor health habits than because of various illnesses not spotted early. With some exceptions, age 35 is too early to detect incipient cancers or circulatory problems, but it's prime time for stopping cigarette smoking, curbing alcohol abuse, and improving exercise and diet.

Overeating

Nutrition and exercise are closely connected. Too much eating combined with too little activity can worsen virtually every adult health problem.

Resistance to Good Nutrition

The basics of good nutrition are well known (He et al., 2006). Fresh fruits and vegetables, whole grains, fish with omega-3 fatty acids but no toxins, clean water, low-fat milk and cheese—all these reduce the risk of almost every adult disease. But resistance to good nutrition is common; people tend to look for excuses to avoid a healthy diet. One way they do so is by misinterpreting scientific research.

One recent example is from an eight-year study (part of the Women's Health Initiative) that compared 24,000 women who ate a low-fat diet (the goal was to obtain no more than 20 percent of daily calories from fat) with 24,000 who ate a regular diet (Howard et al., 2006; Prentice et al., 2006). Women on the low-fat diet were found to be marginally less likely to develop breast cancer (significant only at the 0.09 level) but had rates of heart disease similar to those of women on the regular diet. Skeptics concluded that a low-fat diet makes no difference to general health. For instance, Fox News proclaimed, "Low fat diet myth busted" (Milloy, 2006) and the *Washington Post* headlined, "Low-Fat Diet's Benefits Rejected" (Stein, 2006).

However, although the harm done to health by eating a high-fat diet (as from heavy drinking and smoking) takes decades to kill a person, this study lasted only eight years. Further, the experimental group never reached the goal of 20 percent calories from fat, and the control group did not consume the 40 percent level of fat that was the average for U.S. adults. The actual contrast in fat consumption was between 24 percent for the experimental group and 35 percent for the control group. Given the 11 percent rather than 20 percent difference in fat content, and given that cancer and heart disease are multifactorial, scientists were impressed that any benefits at all were found. No scientist would say that a myth was "busted" or that benefits were "rejected."

The same rush to dismissal occurs whenever specific foods (recently, apricots, spinach, nuts, garlic) are celebrated as fostering health and then later discovered to be less protective than the first research found. As scientists, developmentalists

ARIEL SKELLEY / CORBIS

Lettuce Eat Healthy If this couple regularly eats a well-balanced diet, with lots of vegetables, statistics predict that they are likely to continue enjoying each other's company into their 80s.

analyze the data from many studies and are convinced that a varied diet high in fruits, vegetables, and grains is better than one high in fat. Ignoring the evidence has resulted in a health crisis, as you will now see.

➤Answer to Observation Quiz (from page 539): The typical 50-year-old woman, but not by much. About one-fourth of both groups report that they never exercise.

Obesity

The World Health Organization recognizes obesity as a leading cause of premature adult death. As an editorial in the *Journal of the American Medical Association* warned, "Obesity is a worldwide epidemic and will be followed by a worldwide epidemic of diabetes" (Bray, 2003, p. 1853). Virtually every chronic disease becomes more common and more lethal with excess weight.

The United States is the world leader of the obesity and diabetes epidemics. Weight is increasing significantly for both sexes of every age group, cohort, and ethnicity, although members of some ethnicities (e.g., Latinos) tend to be heavier than others (e.g., Asians), as do some age groups (the highest rates of obesity are among adults aged 45 to 65). Of all adults in the United States, 66 percent are overweight (defined as having a body mass index, or BMI, above 25), 33 percent are obese (a BMI of 30 or more), and 5 percent are morbidly obese (a BMI of 40 or more) (NHANES, 2003–2004). (BMI is explained in Chapter 17; see Table 17.2 on page 450.)

To make these BMI guidelines seem less abstract, picture a person who is 5 feet, 8 inches tall. If that person weighs 150 pounds, the BMI is about 24 and that person is of normal weight. If he or she weighs 200 pounds or more, the BMI is 30 or higher and that person is obese. If he or she weighs more than 300 pounds, the BMI is over 40 and that person is morbidly obese.

The United States is the global leader, but every nation has seen an increase in obesity. In the United Kingdom, the rate of obesity has tripled since 1980 (Mascie-Taylor & Karim, 2003). Obesity was previously not a problem in Asia, but that is changing. As income is rising, so are the rates of obesity and heart disease in China, India, and other Asian nations (Lee, 2007).

Just to maintain the same weight, adults need to eat less each year. Even if a person eats and exercises as much as ever, metabolism slows down by a third between emerging adulthood and late adulthood. But few adults cut down on calories as they should. In the United States, adults now gain 1 to 2 pounds a year before age 65, much more than their grandparents did during those years (U.S. Bureau of the Census, 2006).

In late adulthood, fewer people are obese. It is not known whether the reason is that (1) the thinner ones are more likely to survive, (2) older people eat less, (3) the current cohort have always been thinner, or (4) older people are more protective of their health.

Similarly, there are several possible reasons for the high incidence of overweight among children and adults:

- Genes (regulating hunger, metabolism, and fat accumulation)
- Parental attitudes and practices (children are taught to overeat)
- Environment (modern cultures encourage overeating)

In all likelihood, all three of these factors contribute to overweight. The genetic theory has been bolstered by studies searching for genetic factors in diabetes. Researchers have found several such genes (diabetes is multifactorial) but have also stumbled upon two alleles that correlate with weight. One of those alternate gene forms is carried by about 10 percent of the population (Herbert et al., 2006); the other is carried by about 16 percent (Frayling et al., 2007). This and other research confirms that some people's genetic makeup makes it very difficult for them to lose weight.

Research Design

Scientists: T. Kue Young, Peter Bjerregaard, Eric Dewailly, Patricia Risica, Marit E. Jorgensen, & Sven E. O. Ebbesson.

Publication: *American Journal of Public Health* (2007).

Participants: In four separate surveys conducted between 1990 and 2001, participants included 2,545 adults from Inuit groups in Alaska, Canada, and Greenland. Data were compared with findings from 2,200 people of European heritage living in Manitoba, northern Canada.

Design: Many biophysiological measures were taken for each individual, including weight, height, blood pressure, cholesterol level, and glucose level.

Major conclusions: Although increased weight correlated with various measures of risk for heart disease and diabetes, weight-related risk was lower for the Inuit than for the European Canadians. The authors point out that the Inuit have relatively high sitting height compared with leg length and that centuries of adaptation to the Arctic climate may have resulted in increased body fat without the same mortality risk as for other peoples.

Comment: This research reminds us that no one indicator—such as BMI—has the same effect on health for everyone. Although obesity is a health hazard no matter what a person's genetic background, inherited body types differ, as do health risks with weight.

But remember that genes don't change much over the decades. That points to the influence of culture on the rate of obesity. Cultures do vary in this regard. For instance, Italians are less obese than the British, perhaps because of their lower-fat "Mediterranean diet"; rural Chinese weigh much less than urban Chinese, probably because they are more active; France has far fewer obese adults than the United States, perhaps because the French talk more during meals, eat more slowly, and consume smaller portions (Rozin et al., 2003).

Mentioning genes and culture raises another question: Are the international standards for overweight (a BMI between 25 and 30) and obesity (a BMI above 30) equally valid for every ethnic group? The answer is no. Obesity is always an indicator of medical risk for heart disease and diabetes, but the danger is not equivalent for every group. A high BMI is less risky for the Inuit in Canada, Alaska, and Greenland and more risky for East Asians than for Europeans (Asia Pacific Cohort Studies Collaboration, 2004; Young et al., 2007; see Research Design).

For everyone, however, obesity is unhealthy but sustained weight loss is difficult. Given the trends, people who weigh at age 60 what they did at 25 are to be congratulated; they weigh much less than the average (Hill, 2002). However, loss, not maintenance, of body weight is what millions want. Researchers have analyzed various weight-loss strategies in thousands of studies that compare results over time (see Table 20.2).

TABLE 20.2

Some Weight-Loss Methods Assessed

Diets

Name	Description	Results
Mediterranean	Lots of vegetables, legumes, fruits, grains, fish, olive oil; low in meat, dairy, saturated fat	Weight maintenance, longer life, less body fat
Atkins	Low in carbohydrates	Quick loss, then stable; better cholesterol, lower blood pressure
Weight Watchers	Low in calories; group support	Weight loss over time; good on maintenance
Ornish	Low in fat	Quick loss; hard to sustain

Sources: Dansinger et al., 2005; Estruch et al., 2006; Gardner et al., 2007; Trichopoulou et al., 2005; Truby et al., 2006.

Weight-Loss Drugs

Experience with weight-loss drugs urges caution (Li et al., 2005). Phen-fen was found to increase the risk of heart disease; commercial diet drugs are addictive and ineffective over time; other drugs upset the stomach. Thousands of researchers seek a low-risk weight-loss drug because profits would be in the billions of dollars. Two current candidates for such a miracle drug are rimonabant and sibutramine, but their long-term consequences are not yet known (Després et al., 2005; Wadden et al., 2005).

Surgery

Gastric bypass surgery, which permanently alters the anatomy of the digestive system, is increasingly common in every developed nation. In the United States, the number of such surgeries increased from 14,000 in 1998 to almost 100,000 in 2003 and continues to climb (Mitka, 2003; Smoot et al., 2006). The operations almost always produce substantial weight loss, but complications are common. Almost half the patients require another hospital visit, often for additional surgery. Deaths occur, but rates are lower for the morbidly obese than if they had never lost weight (Adams et al., 2007; Flum et al., 2005; Maggard et al., 2005; Torquati et al., 2007; Weber et al., 2004; Zingmond et al., 2005).

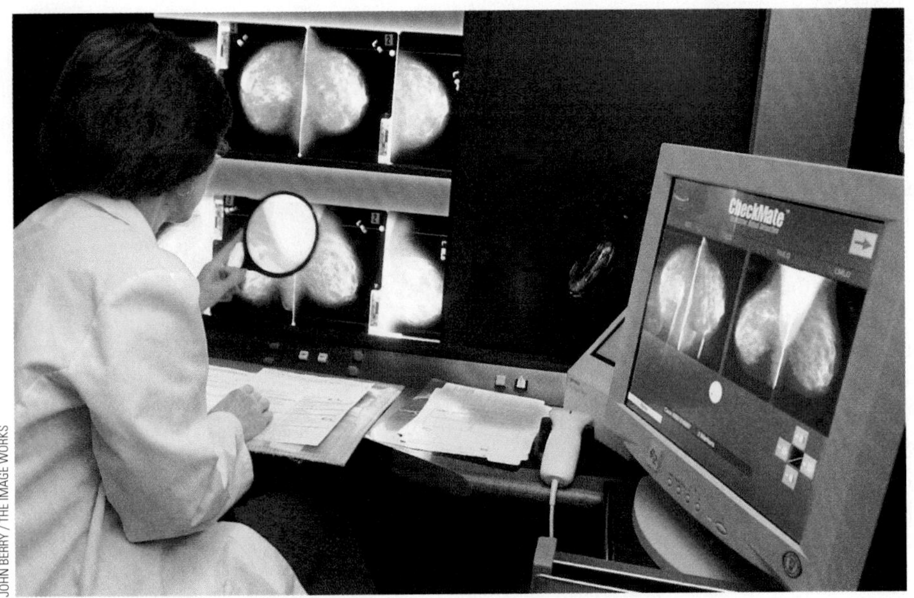

JOHN BERRY / THE IMAGE WORKS

Looking for Trouble A technician examines mammograms for breast abnormalities, such as tiny lumps that cannot be felt but may be malignant. The National Cancer Institute recommends a screening mammogram every one to two years for women who are 40 or older or who have certain risk factors for breast cancer.

Preventive Medicine

The damage and death caused by tobacco, alcohol, and obesity make it obvious that prevention is less risky than treatment. It is also more effective at increasing health, reducing disability, and prolonging life. As one review of midlife health concludes: "For most conditions and diseases, it's the way we live our lives that has the greatest influence on delaying and preventing physiological decline" (Merrill & Verbrugge, 1999, p. 86).

Although much of prevention involves choices people make on their own each day, some is medical, involving early detection and prompt treatment. As dramatic evidence, the rate of death from heart attacks in developed nations is only half that of 50 years ago. Less smoking and better diets are partly responsible, but so are drugs that reduce hypertension and cholesterol, surgery to repair heart damage, and quick treatment when an attack occurs (Unal et al., 2005).

No doubt some preventive screening and medical measures are helpful: Routine mammograms, for instance, have saved many lives (Otto et al., 2003). However, too much reliance on medical screening can be harmful. For prostate cancer, for example, *false positives* (test results indicating a problem where none really exists) cause needless surgery and anxiety (Kaplan, 2000; Welch et al., 2005).

Each patient has his or her own particular risks and needs; ideally, each has a personal doctor who knows the patient well. National incentives for preventive care may explain a surprising finding: Adults in England are healthier on almost every medical measure than adults in the United States, despite the fact that twice as much money is spent per capita on health care in the United States (Banks et al., 2006). Self-reported good health also tends to be higher in England than in the United States (Sacker et al., 2007).

Prevention depends not only on individuals and their doctors but also on social measures that protect against harm (such as seatbelts and earthquake-proof construction) and help for those who suffer from trauma. This was evident in the aftereffects of Hurricane Katrina on the people of Louisiana and Mississippi. Many say that the worst effects could have been prevented by better policies and public health measures, with some individuals resilient and others crushed. Primary, secondary, and tertiary prevention were all inadequate.

issues and applications

Responding to Stress

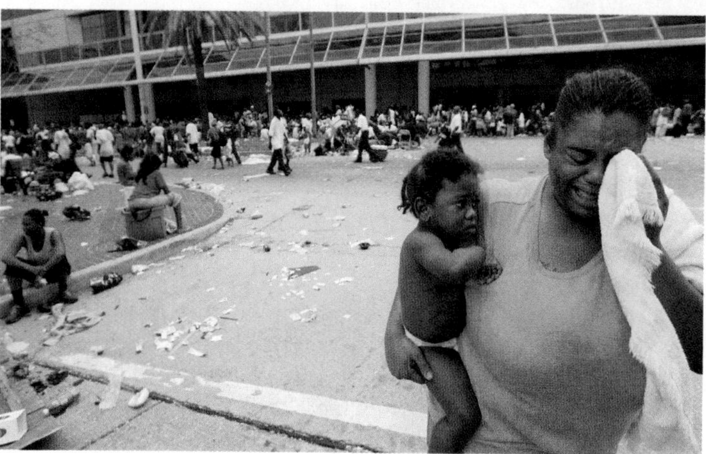

Adults learn to ignore some stresses and perceive others as challenges, even if outsiders would consider them threats. When challenges are successfully met, not only do people feel more effective and powerful, but also the body's damaging response to stress—increased heart and breathing rates, hormonal changes, and so on—is averted (Bandura, 1997). Effective coping may produce physiological changes, especially in the immune system, that promote health, not sickness. Among adults, potential stressors can become positive turning points (Aldwin & Levenson, 2001).

There are limits to this stress/challenge/victory process. For instance, psychologists are following the psychological reactions of the hundreds of thousands of people in Louisiana and Mississippi who were uprooted by Hurricane Katrina in 2005. Many of them lost their homes and jobs, went without food and water, knew people who died. Not surprisingly, their stress increased. For instance, one study of survivors from New Orleans six months after the flood (Kessler et al., 2006) found that most had stress reactions: Almost all reported feeling irritable and having upsetting thoughts, and half had nightmares (see Figure 20.5).

The accumulation of stressors led to psychological problems in many survivors. One in nine suffered serious mental health problems, twice as many as before Katrina. Another 20 percent had mild to moderate mental illness, again double the earlier rate (Kessler et al., 2006). Given the trauma of the storm and the frustratingly slow and inept official response, this is sad but not surprising.

However, there is one surprise. The same stresses led to increased resilience, with 3 out of 4 (including many who had psychological problems) reporting that they found a deeper sense of purpose after Katrina. Only 1 in 250 reported that they had made plans to commit suicide—only one-tenth of the rate reported before the storm. Adults aged 40–65 were particularly likely to cope well with the trauma (Kessler et al., 2006). Children were more likely to suffer (Abramson & Garfield, 2006).

Studies of the reactions of other groups to unexpected trauma find similar results: more stress-related symptoms but also more resilience and social support (Galea et al., 2002; Weissman et al., 1999). A college student who traveled to Mississippi to help Katrina survivors cope provides a firsthand account of this phenomenon. In her words:

> During spring break last March, I, along with more than 300 students from the University of Akron and Kent State University, came to Pass Christian, Miss., wanting to help alleviate the suffering that tugged at my conscience when I watched the news.
>
> What I didn't expect was how profoundly affected our group would be by the reality. More than six months after Katrina brought a vicious wall of sea water crashing down upon Pass Christian, it remained as if the hurricane had hit yesterday. Skeletons of homes littered the beachfront. Abandoned cars sat rusting in the street, clothing was strewn across tree branches and a crumbling doorstep signaled the spot where a home once

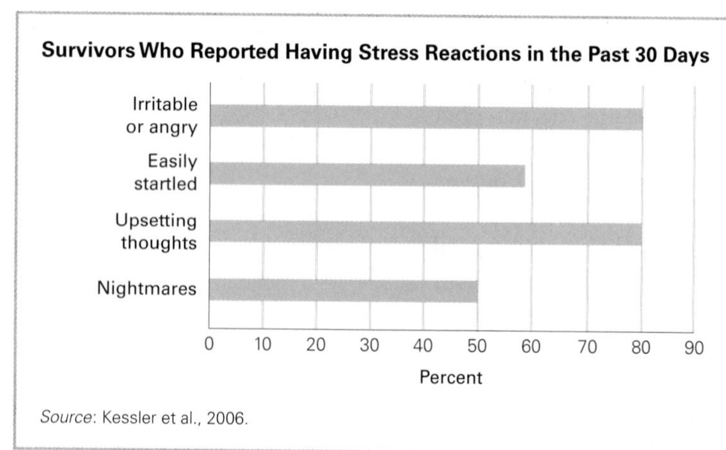

FIGURE 20.5

Lingering Effects of Hurricane Katrina Showing strong reactions to their stressful situation, the mother and child in the photograph above were among thousands of New Orleans residents who sought refuge in the city's convention center after the levees broke in September 2005. Typically, most people involved in a natural disaster recover within weeks, but, as the chart shows, most Katrina victims were still feeling the psychological effects 6 months later. Two years after the hurricane, death rates from all causes in New Orleans were double what they had been.

stood. As I adjusted to the devastation, the last thing I expected to see was resilient optimism rising above the rubble.

"You don't have time to sit down and cry. You've just got to get to work," said Ruby Blackwell, principal of the First Baptist Preschool. I met Blackwell as part of a group that assisted the school's teachers and helped sort through a mountain of donated books.

I was awed when Blackwell told me that a month after the hurricane, teachers were already asking how soon the school could reopen, even as many were reeling from their own disasters. . . .

From Blackwell and countless others, I learned a humbling truth. A local volunteer summarized the lesson in a simple, unforgettable phrase, "You make a living with what you earn; you make a life with what you give."

[Feerasta, 2006]

Of course, this does not mean that trauma and stress are benevolent. Many observers worry that ongoing stress may undermine even the most resilient survivors of Katrina, and some other research questions the conclusions of the Kessler study (Weissler et al., 2006).

However, humans seem to have a recovery reserve (similar to the organ reserve explained in Chapter 17) that is activated under stress. A related set of studies seemed to show that a reserve of effort and alertness is summoned when an emergency arises, even if the people involved are overtired and in a noisy environment. This reserve works well for the moments of the emergency, especially if people are expert at the task, although it takes a toll later on, when the emergency is over and the person must recover, unwind, sleep, relax, and so on (Hockey, 2005).

SUMMING UP

Health habits are crucial to physical well-being. If no adult smoked, drank heavily, underexercised, or overate, most would be active and vital throughout adulthood, living to at least 80. Cigarette smoking is decreasing in North America but increasing in most of the world. Overweight and obesity are rising to epidemic levels, especially in the United States. Regular exercise—even at moderate levels—averts many diseases and increases vitality. Preventive medicine, involving daily habits and good medical care, can maintain health and lessen the ill effects of senescence. ■

MARK RICHARDS / PHOTOEDIT, INC.

Working Out at Work Regular exercise enhances health as measured all four ways. Companies that provide exercise facilities at the workplace usually see declines in employee absenteeism and health-related expenses.

Measuring Health

Being healthy means much more than merely being alive. There are at least four distinct measures of health: mortality, morbidity, disability, and vitality.

Mortality and Morbidity

At the farthest extreme, death is the ultimate sign that efforts to protect health have failed. This basic indicator, **mortality,** is usually expressed as the number of deaths each year per 1,000 individuals in a particular population. For example, the mortality rate among people in the United States in 2004 was 8.1. The figure for various age, gender, and racial groups in the United States ranged from about 0.1 (1 in 10,000) for Asian American girls aged 5 to 14 to 153 (about 1 in 6 per year) for European American men over age 85 (U.S. Bureau of the Census, 2007).

Mortality statistics are compiled from death certificates, which indicate age, sex, and immediate cause of death. This allows valid international and historical comparisons, because deaths have been counted and recorded for decades, even (in some nations) for centuries. Mortality rates are often age-adjusted to take into account the higher death rate among the very old. By that measure, Japan has the lowest annual mortality (about 5 per 1,000) and Sierra Leone the highest (about 35 per 1,000).

A more comprehensive measure of health is **morbidity** (from the Latin word for "disease"), which refers to illnesses of all kinds—chronic as well as fatal. People are asked in surveys to identify any diseases they have, or doctors are asked to report on illnesses among a sample of their patients. Morbidity can be high even

mortality Death. As a measure of health, mortality usually refers to the number of deaths each year per 1,000 members of a given population.

morbidity Disease. As a measure of health, morbidity refers to the rate of diseases of all kinds in a given population—physical and emotional, acute (sudden) and chronic (ongoing).

when mortality is low (Michaud et al., 2001). For example, in many African nations, a parasite causes "river blindness," destroying energy and eyesight in millions but not directly causing death (Basáñez, 2006); in the United States, arthritis affects almost half of all women after age 50 but never kills them.

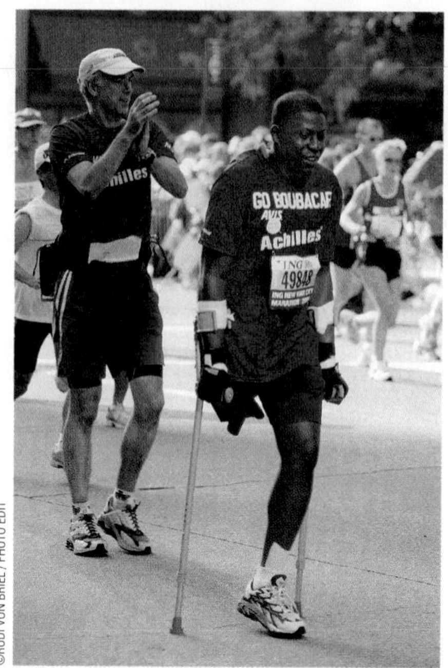

©RUDI VON BRIEL / PHOTO EDIT

Disabled but Vital Therapists find that the most serious consequence of losing a limb is losing the will to live. This young man not only learned to cope with crutches after losing a leg but also regained his spirit: He completed the 26.2-mile New York City marathon.

disability Long-term difficulty in performing normal activities of daily life because of some physical, mental, or emotional condition.

vitality A measure of health that refers to how healthy and energetic—physically, intellectually, and socially—an individual actually feels.

QALYs (quality-adjusted life years) A way of comparing mere survival without vitality to survival with good health. QALYs indicate how many years of full vitality are lost to a particular physical disease or disability. They are expressed in terms of life expectancy as adjusted for quality of life.

Disability and Vitality

Health is not only the absence of death and disease (mortality and morbidity) but also the ability to enjoy life. Two more indicators, disability and vitality, measure this aspect of health.

Disability refers to difficulty in performing normal activities of daily life because of a "physical, mental, or emotional condition" (U.S. Bureau of the Census, 2006). Limitation in functioning (not severity of disease) is the hallmark of disability.

Limitations, and hence disability, depend partly on the social context. For example, if heart disease prevents one from walking 200 feet without resting, that is a disability if a person's job requires a great deal of walking (a mail carrier, for instance) but not if the job is mostly sedentary (a post office clerk). Similarly, mental illness may be disabling for someone who lives alone in a city but not for someone who lives in a stable rural family, where there is less social isolation and more opportunity for meaningful routine work. (Specifics depend on the severity of the illness.)

Disability has a higher social cost than mortality or morbidity, because a disabled person needs special care and is less able to contribute to society. Social measures to reduce disability (e.g., public areas redesigned to include handrails and wheelchair ramps) therefore may also benefit society in the long run by making it possible for people with disabilities to participate more fully. Thanks to such measures, fewer adults aged 50 to 70 in the United States were disabled in 2005 than in 1960.

The fourth measure of health, **vitality,** refers to how healthy and energetic—physically, intellectually, and socially—an individual feels. Vitality is *joie de vivre,* the zest for living, the love of life (Gigante, 2007). A person can feel terrific despite having a chronic or fatal disease and disability. For example, in a Japanese study, most cancer survivors who were still in pain were also low in vitality, but others, even though they had cancer and were in pain, still scored high in vitality (Fujimori et al., 2006).

Personality correlates with vitality (van Straten et al., 2007), as does national culture. However, vitality does not always reflect more objective measures of health. For instance, the Danes seem to be the happiest people in the world (as measured by subjective reports of well-being), but they are not the longest living (Kahneman et al., 2003).

issues and applications

QALYs and DALYs

Every nation, every hospital, and every person makes hundreds of decisions regarding health. Public health advocates are troubled when decisions are made that seem to ignore measures that would protect the health of the population. Developmentalists note that sometimes actions that seem harmless at the moment will cause disabilities later on. Yet how can the impact of a particular decision be evaluated?

To answer this question, health economists have developed units of measure known as **QALYs (quality-adjusted life years).** If people are completely well, physically and psychologically, they have a top-notch quality of life. If that state of full well-being lasts a year, one quality-adjusted life year is counted. If a person lives to be 70 and is vital and active throughout, that is expressed as 70 QALYs.

When people die prematurely, before reaching the end of their life expectancy, then the years between actual and expected death are completely lost. For example, if a man's life expectancy is 70 but he is shot dead at age 30, then 40 QALYs are lost.

The calculation becomes more complicated when a person does not die but has a life of less than full quality. That necessitates measuring how much of a reduction in life's fullness is caused by a particular condition. If a 30-year-old is shot and permanently disabled—perhaps severely brain-injured—then each remaining year might be only of half quality, and thus 20 QALYs (40 divided by 2) would accrue by age 70.

In another scenario, if a 30-year-old is shot, undergoes 4 years of recovery that are so painful and disabling that he is thought to experience only one-fourth of full vitality, and then recovers completely to live fully until age 70, he would lose only 3 years ($4 \times \frac{1}{4} = 1$, subtracted from 4) which would give him 37 QALYs between ages 30 and 70.

To further complicate matters, it is even possible to have a negative QALY, if a person is alive but in extreme pain and unable to do anything. That state might well be considered even worse than death. Obviously, any estimate of the quality of someone's life is highly subjective.

Nonetheless, the concept is very useful. Doctors want to know how various medical treatments affect quality of life. For example, one group assessed patients who had spinal surgery (Mannion et al., 2007) and another group studied the effects of radiation on cancer patients (Strauss et al., 2007). Other indicators (pain, fatigue, disability) are also measured, but future quality of life is crucial in deciding on treatment.

DALYs (disability-adjusted life years) approaches the same concept from the other direction. A person with no disability incurs no DALYs. Each year lost due to premature death (earlier than would ordinarily be expected) adds one DALY, just as it would subtract one QALY. Similarly, a fraction of a DALY is added if the person is disabled.

Again, the problem is figuring out what that fraction should be. An outsider might think that someone is severely disabled, but that person may feel quite capable and be angry that others emphasize disability more than ability.

Professionals disagree about how to calculate DALYs and QALYs, especially when a person's vitality or well-being is part of the equation (Fayers & Machin, 2007; Ryan & Deci, 2001). One strategy is to assume that "people know the quality of their life and, if asked directly, will honestly and accurately report it" (Fleesen, 2004, p. 253). But some people, by nature, are more optimistic about their own lives than others are about theirs (Lawton et al., 1999).

One developmental disagreement concerns chronological age. The World Health Organization considers each year of life lost by a suddenly dead 30-year-old as a full DALY (40 years lost before age 70), but less than that (not 70 years) if a newborn dies. Many other professional organizations assign a lower value to disability after age 70 than before, assuming that the 70-year-old is already past the fullness of life (Kaiser, 2003).

Both of these assessments may seem callous, but no society spends enough on public health to enable everyone to live life to the fullest. Calculating DALYs provides a cost-benefit analysis to guide decisions about, for example, whether to subsidize a new well that will provide clean water for a village or intensive care for an extremely-low-birthweight newborn. Obviously, *if* care of 500-gram babies costs \$10 million per life saved (with survivors being severely brain-damaged and disabled) and *if* clean water costs \$10,000 per life saved (with survivors being vital adults), then clean water would be the priority.

This example is hypothetical; real choices are rarely so simple. Nations spend money on the health of their own citizens, and people want to save those they love—who would put a price on the life of their own tiny newborn? Calculating QALYs and DALYs helps doctors and public officials; it may not help individuals.

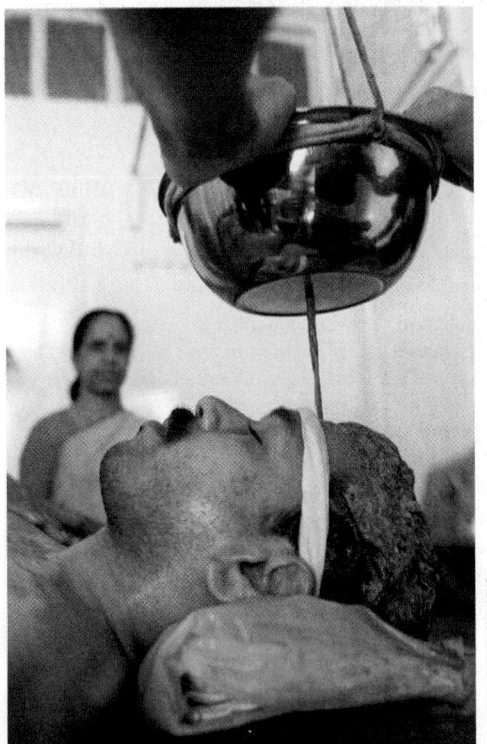
JOHN MOORE / THE IMAGE WORKS

Feeling Better The principles of quality-of-life self-assessment and attitude change were known thousands of years ago in India. At this ayurvedic-medicine clinic in New Delhi, a patient is treated with oils and massage prescribed for his particular needs. The desired results are lower blood pressure and increased vitality.

DALYs (disability-adjusted life years) A measure of the impact that disability has on quality of life. DALYs are the reciprocal of quality-adjusted life years: A reduction in QALYs means an increase in DALYs.

SUMMING UP

There are four main measures of health used by developmentalists: mortality, morbidity, disability, and vitality. Mortality in itself is not exclusively a measure of health, as it does not distinguish whether death comes as a result of disease, violence, or an overall weakening and aging of the body. The other three measures, however, indicate widespread health problems among adults. These can be quantified in terms of quality-adjusted life years (QALYs) and disability-adjusted life years (DALYs); such calculations are useful in setting public health priorities. ■

Variations in Aging

Rates of aging vary, but they are not random. Gender, genes, ethnicity, income, education, location, lifestyle, and culture speed up some aspects of senescence and slow down others. Indeed, a study of more than 7,000 adults in the United States found differences in physical and psychological health on dozens of dimensions, including income, gender, ethnicity, religion, personality, and residence (Brim et al., 2004; see Research Design).

Research Design

Scientists: Orville G. Brim, Carol D. Ryff, Ronald C. Kessler, and many others.

Publication: Hundreds of publications use these data, including the 2004 book *How Healthy Are We?*, edited by Brim, Ryff, and Kessler. This book is the outcome of a study called MIDUS (midlife, United States), sponsored by the John D. and Catherine T. MacArthur Foundation.

Participants: A nationwide sample of 7,189 U.S. residents, aged 25 to 74, completed a telephone interview; 3,032 of them also filled out a lengthy questionnaire.

Design: Answers were analyzed and compared by age (with ages 40 to 60 considered midlife), sex, and other ways.

Major conclusion: A person's health is affected by numerous aspects of his or her background and context, with those in midlife healthier in some respects (especially mental health) than those who are younger.

Comment: The extensive data from this study have led to many insights about midlife, a time given "surprisingly little attention" by developmentalists.

Gender Differences

In some ways, senescence affects women more than men, because small, superficial signs of aging—changes in skin, hair, weight—are of more concern (to both sexes) in women. In most ways, however, women age more slowly. Females live longer, by 5 years on average, with a wide range from one nation to another. For example, there are few gender differences in longevity in Africa, but men die 14 years earlier, on average, in Russia (see Table 20.3) (*World Factbook*, 2007).

Worldwide, there are more old women than old men (twice as many in the United States by age 85), not primarily because old men die at higher rates but because at every age (especially in infancy and adolescence) more males die. The effect is cumulative.

HERB SCHMITZ / STONE / GETTY IMAGES

Blue Skies Ahead Turkey is one of the nations where children still die at high rates, but some adults live long, happy, and active lives. The social context, illustrated by this man riding a donkey, is the reason.

Paradoxically, women are more likely to have every chronic disease—with one notable exception: heart disease under age 50 (Cleary et al., 2004). Some gender differences may be biological—the second X chromosome or extra estrogen could provide protection from some illnesses (Crews, 2003). Or the reason may be cultural. One public health expert wrote that, in the United States,

> Men are socialized to project strength, individuality, autonomy, dominance, stoicism, and physical aggression, and to avoid demonstrations of emotion or vulnerability that could be construed as weakness. These . . . combine to increase health risks.
>
> *[Williams, 2003, p. 726]*

For their part, women spend more time and effort on their health, and they are more likely to marry, have close friends, and seek help—all of which protect health. Most specific health habits also favor women, who drink and smoke less, eat less meat, and wear seat belts more often. Are such habits biological or cultural?

Socioeconomic Status

High SES is protective of health in every nation. Well-educated, financially secure people live longer, avoid chronic illness and disability, and feel healthier than the average person of their age, sex, and ethnicity. This explains a difference within nations: People who live near major cities generally are healthier than are people who live in the countryside.

Internationally, people in rich nations have lower rates of almost every disease, injury, and cause of death than people in poor nations. Thus, for example, babies born in the Asian Pacific region are expected to live to 73; in Southeast Asia to 63; and in sub-Saharan Africa to 48 (WHO, 2006).

Within nations and ethnic groups, economic disparities are evident (Marmot & Fuhrer, 2004). In the United States, among Hispanics, Cuban Americans live several years longer, on average, than Puerto Ricans and, among Asians, Japanese Americans live several years longer than Filipino Americans. The "10 million Americans with the best health" outlive—by about 30 years—the tens of millions who are low-SES and reside in neglected neighborhoods (Murray et al., 2006).

Certain "diseases of affluence" seemed to be exceptions to the generality that poverty is linked with poor health (Krieger, 2002, 2003). For example, at one time both lung and breast cancer were more common among the rich than among the poor, among the more educated than among the less educated, and, in the United States, among European Americans than among others. No longer. When smoking became cheaper and diagnosis of cancer improved and became more accessible, the diseases of affluence became more common in the poor.

This switch was detailed in a study of rates of cigarette smoking among three cohorts of Italians—those born in the 1940s, the 1950s, and the 1960s. A total of 58,727 people were surveyed as to whether they started smoking or not (Federico et al., 2007). An SES switch was apparent for both sexes, especially for the women. Among low-SES (and less educated) women, smoking increased: 28 percent of those born in the 1940s and 35 percent of those born in the 1960s started smoking.

TABLE 20.3

Life Expectancy by Gender, in Years, Selected Countries, 2007

Nation	Men	Women	Years More for Women
Argentina	76	79	3
Australia	78	84	6
Brazil	71	74	3
Canada	77	84	7
China	71	75	4
Cuba	75	80	5
Dominican Republic	71	75	4
Ethiopia	48	50	2
Germany	76	82	6
Ghana	58	60	2
Haiti	55	59	4
India	66	71	5
Indonesia	68	73	5
Israel	78	82	4
Japan	74	86	12
Mexico	73	79	6
Niger	44	44	0
Nigeria	47	49	2
Peru	68	72	4
Russia	59	73	14
Sierra Leone	38	43	5
South Africa	43	42	-1
Spain	77	83	5
United Kingdom	76	81	5
United States	75	81	6

Source: World Factbook, 2007.

Women Live Longer The actual life spans of individuals will vary and the totals change from decade to decade. Nonetheless, the trend for women to live longer than men is evident almost everywhere. The opposite was true in the nineteenth century, when many women died in childbirth, and the opposite is now true in only one nation, South Africa, where many women die of AIDS.

Observation Quiz (see answer, page 551): The 25 nations listed here are only about 10 percent of all the nations of the world. Can you think of criteria that may have been used to decide which countries to include?

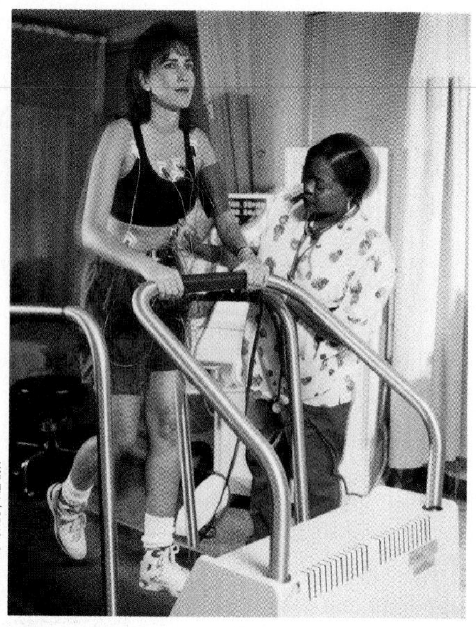

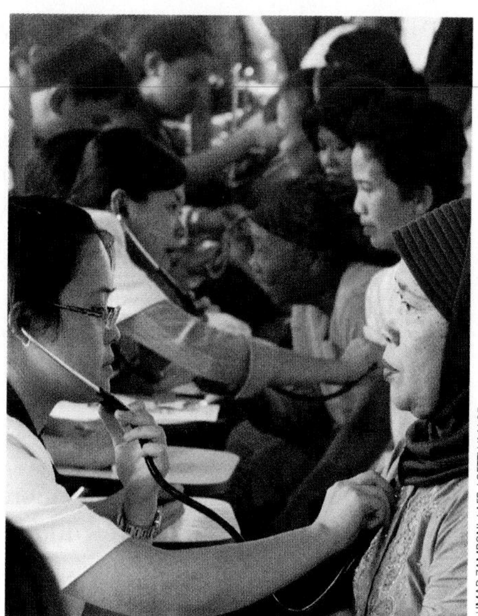

The Same Event, A Thousand Miles Apart: Female Heartbeats Nurses worldwide know that heart disease now kills more women than does any other disease, including cancer. Early diagnosis is protective, and that is why the woman in the United States *(left)* is taking a stress test of heart function and why the Indonesian women *(right)* are participating in a public health day.

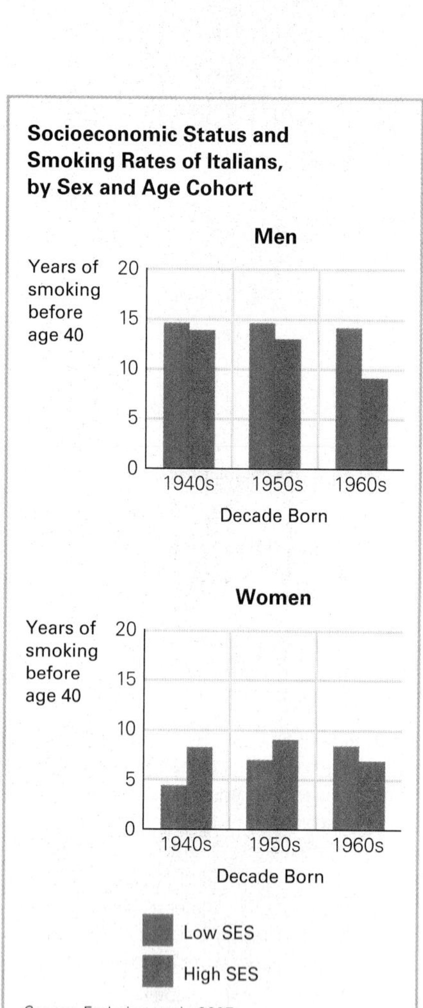

FIGURE 20.6

The Rich Get Sick? It used to be that high-SES educated Italians, especially women, were more likely to get lung cancer, breast cancer, and all the other diseases that correlate with cigarette smoking. That trend has been reversed because low-SES Italians are more likely to start smoking.

Among high-SES (and well-educated) women, smoking decreased: 35 percent of those born in the 1940s started smoking, as did 31 percent of those born in the 1960s. Educated Italians were also more likely to quit, so that, by the year 2000, high-SES Italians smoked (and had cancer) at lower rates than their low-SES contemporaries (see Figure 20.6).

Social context always affects health. For example, a study comparing adults in England and France found that, as expected, wealthier people were healthier. Reasons differed by social context, however. In England, but not in France, the rich ate more fruits and vegetables and smoked less than the poor; in France, but not in England, the wealthy drank less alcohol. According to these researchers, employment and neighborhood stresses for low-SES people in both nations led to poorer health habits, with the particulars (smoking in England and alcohol in France) dependent on the culture (Fuhrer et al., 2002).

Conclusion

All in all, when it comes to health-related variations in aging:

> There is a complex causal web involving socioeconomic determinants such as income, education, employment, . . . environmental factors such as tobacco use, physical activity, diet, . . . [and] physiological factors such as cholesterol levels, blood pressure, and genes that influence mortality and disability.
>
> [*Michaud et al., 2001, p. 537*]

This complex web cannot be disentangled, but it is obvious that health messages and practices should not be the same for everyone. The basics—avoiding drugs, eating healthy, exercising—are always useful, but specifics vary. Soon treatment will be tailored to each individual's genetic profile rather than to their ethnicity or gender. But in the meantime, practitioners are increasingly aware that many medical measures were validated mostly on European American men, who sometimes differ from members of other groups (Kee & Chiriboga, 2004).

For instance, heart failure is a leading cause of death for people of both sexes and all ethnicities, but the symptoms are different for women than for men. BiDil, a drug treatment for African Americans with congestive heart failure, is the first

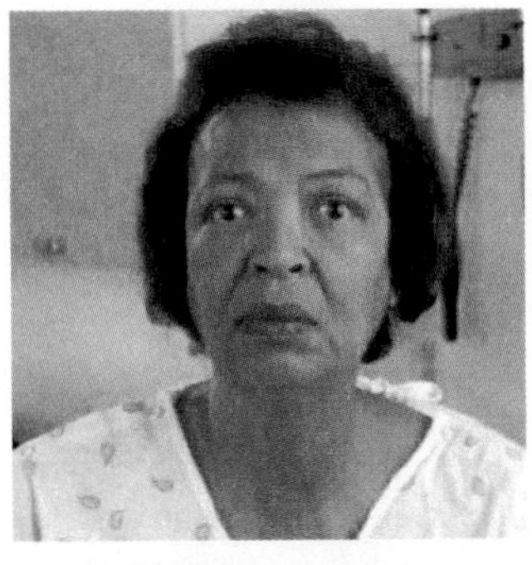
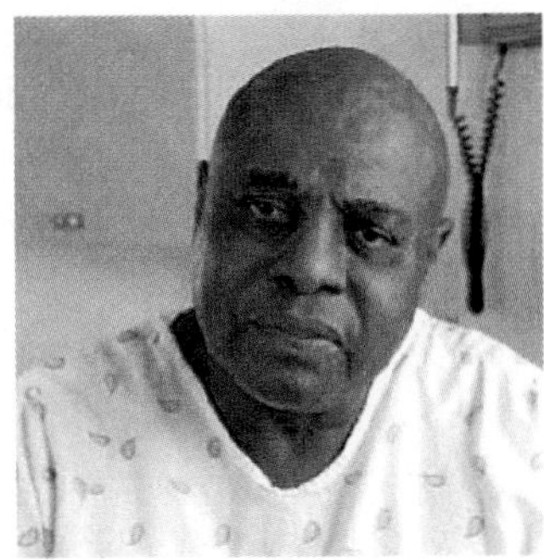

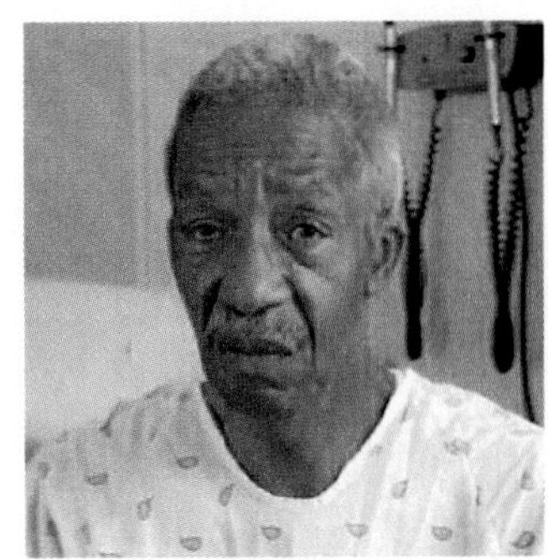
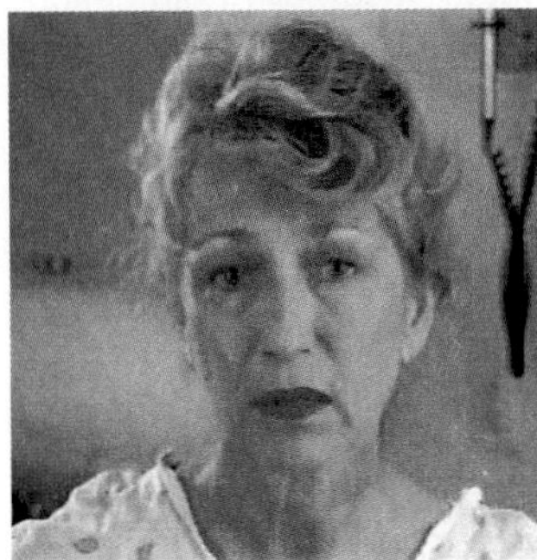

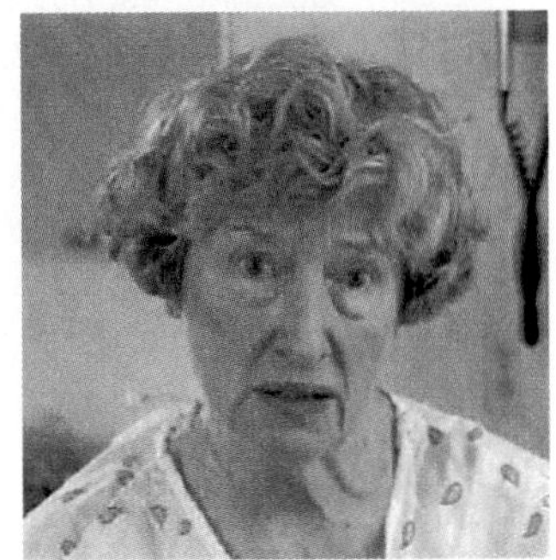

All Equally Sick? These photographs were used in a study that assessed physicians' biases in recommending treatment (Schulman et al., 1999). These supposed "heart patients" were described as identical in occupation, symptoms, and every other respect except age, race, and sex. However, the participating physicians who looked at the photos and the fictitious medical charts that accompanied them did not make identical recommendations. The appropriate treatment for the supposed symptoms would be catheterization; but for the younger, White, or male patients, catheterization was recommended 90, 91, and 91 percent of the time, respectively; for the older, female, or Black patients, 86, 85, and 85 percent of the time, respectively. Are you surprised that the bias differences were less than 10 percent? Or are you surprised that physician bias existed at all?

race-based prescription medication in the United States (Taylor et al., 2004).* In another example, Vietnamese American women have lower rates of breast cancer but a rate of cervical cancer four times higher than that of other women in the United States; accordingly, for them, Pap tests may be more essential than breast self-examination (Ro, 2002).

This leads to a final point. As you remember from Chapter 1, each of us is powerfully affected by all the contexts and cultures that surround us, but none of us is just like everyone else in our group. Social norms influence men to avoid doctors, women to worry about their appearance, low-income people to eat high-fat diets, and so on. Each of us is affected by our family and friends. However, no individual is permanently bound to the health customs of his or her group. Habits can change for individuals as well as for groups—as evidenced by the reduced smoking rates among North Americans of all ethnicities. Medical care can improve for groups as well.

For 20-year-old African American men, notable improvement in health has occurred in the past 35 years. In 1970 projections for such a man's life were death at age 60; today death is projected at age 71 (U.S. Bureau of the Census, 2006).

➤Answer to Observation Quiz (from page 549): With apologies to all the nations that were excluded, in general the countries included are large, geographically close, or similar (developed, democratic, English-speaking) to the United States.

* Since race is a social construction more than a biological category, many people object to this race-based approval for BiDil (Kahn, 2007). Nonetheless, the idea that diseases, drugs, and treatments are not the same for every person is endorsed by many developmentalists.

Those are averages: Some African Americans live to 100 or more, as 3,000 African American men were doing in 2005, beating all odds (U.S. Bureau of the Census, 2006).

This point is relevant to us all. The averages and generalities noted in this chapter do not apply equally to everyone. Each of us makes choices that change the outcome of the predictions; some of us will live vital lives to age 100 or beyond.

SUMMING UP

Marked variations are apparent in the risk of poor health between one person and another and in the quality of each day of each person's life. Men have higher mortality (death) rates, but women have higher morbidity (illness) rates. Income, within nations and among nations, has a dramatic impact on health no matter how it is measured. Low-income people are much more likely to experience poor health, get sick, and die. Health disparities are also evident between ethnic groups for many reasons, including variable genetic risks, cultural norms, stress, care provider prejudices, attitudes about preventive care, and social bias. ■

SUMMARY

The Aging Process

1. With each year of life, signs of senescence (a gradual physical decline associated with aging) become more apparent. All the body systems gradually become less efficient, though at varying rates, not only between different people but also between different organs within the same person.

2. A person's appearance undergoes gradual but noticeable changes as middle age progresses, including more wrinkles, less hair, and more fat, particularly around the abdomen. With the exception of excessive weight gain, changes in appearance have little impact on health.

3. The rate of senescence is most apparent in the sense organs. Vision becomes less sharp with age, with both nearsightedness and farsightedness increasing gradually beginning in the 20s. Hearing also becomes less acute, with noticeable losses being more likely for pure tones (such as doorbells) and high-frequency sounds (such as a child's excited speech).

4. The brain slows down and begins a slow, usually imperceptible decline. Beyond measures to protect overall health, the brain is affected by psychoactive drugs, lack of sleep, and lack of exercise.

5. Fertility problems become more common with increased age, for many reasons. The most common one for men is a reduced number of sperm, and for women, ovulation failure or blocked fallopian tubes. For both sexes, not only youth but also overall good health—especially sexual health—correlates with fertility.

6. A number of assisted reproductive technology (ART) procedures, including IVF (in vitro fertilization), offer potential answers to infertility. In the laboratory, a technician can fertilize an ovum by inserting a single sperm, thus avoiding the problem of low sperm count.

7. At menopause, as a woman's menstrual cycle stops, ovulation ceases, and levels of estrogen are markedly reduced. This hormonal change produces various symptoms, although most women find menopause much less troubling than they had expected.

8. Hormone production declines in men also, though not as suddenly as in women. For both sexes, hormone replacement therapy (HRT) should be used cautiously, if at all.

The Impact of Poor Health Habits

9. Adults in North America are smoking cigarettes much less than they once did, and rates of lung cancer and other diseases are falling, largely for that reason. Alcohol abuse remains a major health problem, however.

10. Good health habits include exercising regularly and not gaining weight. On both these counts, today's adults worldwide are faring worse than did previous generations. There is a worldwide "epidemic of obesity," as more people have access to abundant food and overeat as a result.

11. When used in conjunction with good health habits, preventive medicine (such as mammograms and other cancer screening, for example) and better treatment have been effective in extending life. The rate of fatal heart attacks in middle-aged men has been cut in half.

Measuring Health

12. Variations in health can be measured in terms of mortality, morbidity, disability, and vitality. Although death and disease are easier to quantify, in terms of the health of a population, disability and vitality may be more significant. Quality-adjusted life years (QALYs) and disability-adjusted life years (DALYs) help doctors and public health advocates figure out how to allocate limited resources.

Variations in Aging

13. Aging and health status vary by gender. Women tend to age more slowly and live longer than men, though they also have more chronic diseases. These differences may be biological, though culture is also thought to be influential. In general, women are more likely than men to engage in practices that are protective of health.

14. Both genes and culture affect the overall health of various ethnic groups. Social, economic, and psychological factors may be even more influential. Members of certain ethnic groups in certain settings are much more prone to health risks and to ongoing stress. Quality of care is powerfully affected by socioeconomic factors.

KEY TERMS

senescence (p. 528)
presbycusis (p. 529)
assisted reproductive technology (ART) (p. 534)
in vitro fertilization (IVF) (p. 534)
menopause (p. 534)
hormone replacement therapy (HRT) (p. 535)
andropause (p. 535)
mortality (p. 545)
morbidity (p. 545)
disability (p. 546)
vitality (p. 546)
QALYs (quality-adjusted life years) (p. 546)
DALYs (disability-adjusted life years) (p. 547)

KEY QUESTIONS

1. What age-related changes in appearance typically occur during adulthood?

2. How do vision and hearing change during adulthood?

3. As a person ages, how is the brain affected?

4. How do age and other factors affect a typical couple's sex life?

5. What are some of the factors that diminish fertility?

6. Why might a woman welcome menopause?

7. What changes in rates of tobacco use have occurred over the past few decades, and what are the consequences of those changes?

8. What is the effect of alcohol on a person's risk of mortality?

9. How does obesity affect physical and psychological health?

10. In what way(s) can preventive medicine have a positive effect on health?

11. What are the four measures of health, and what does each signify?

12. Why does health vary between and within ethnic groups?

APPLICATIONS

1. Guess the age of five people you know, and then ask them how old they are. Analyze the clues you used for your guesses and the people's reactions to your question.

2. Find a speaker who is willing to come to your class and who is an expert on weight loss, adult health, smoking, or drinking. Write a one-page proposal explaining why you think this speaker would be good and what topics he or she should address. Give this proposal to your instructor, with contact information for your speaker. The instructor will call the potential speakers, thank them for their willingness, and decide whether or not to actually invite them to speak.

3. Attend a gathering for people who want to stop a bad habit or start a good one, such as an open meeting of Alcoholics Anonymous or another 12-step program, an introductory session of Weight Watchers or Smoke Enders, or a meeting of prospective gym members. Report on who attended, what you learned, and what your reactions were.

4. Use behaviorist strategies (see Chapter 2 and/or read other sources) to change something you do. Take baseline data on one specific behavior (e.g., regarding talking in class, eating, exercising, watching TV, sleeping). The behavior must be operationally defined (see Appendix B). Use reinforcement or other measures to change the frequency or intensity of your behavior. Remove the reinforcement and continue to collect data to see if your pattern changed.

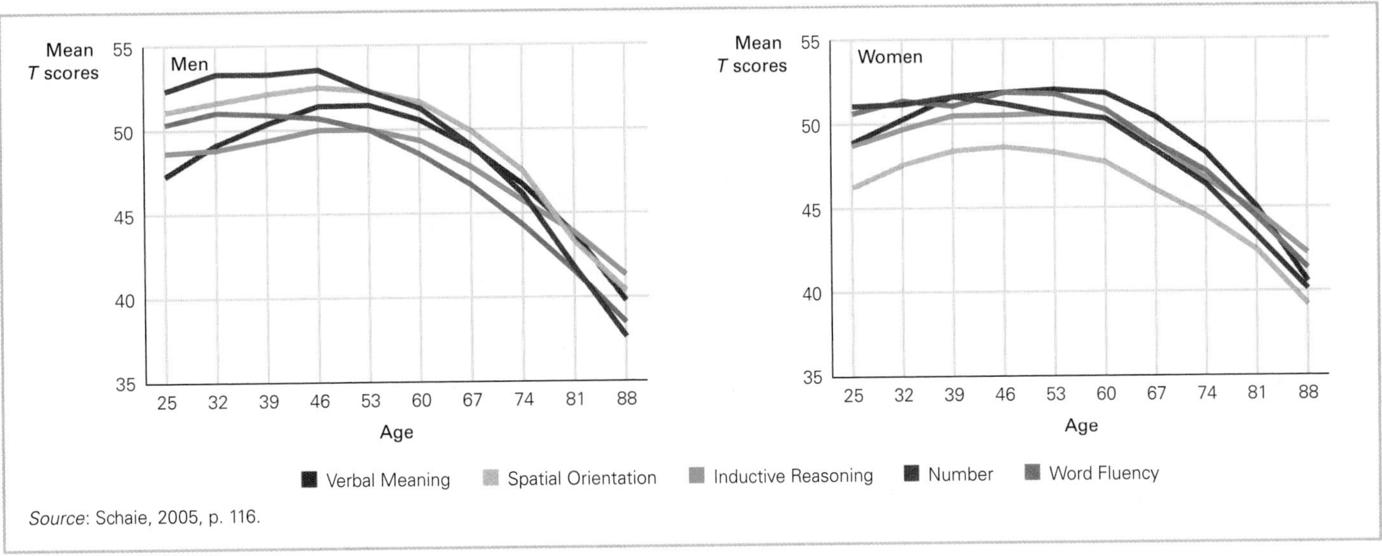

Source: Schaie, 2005, p. 116.

FIGURE 21.1

Age Differences in Intellectual Abilities
Cross-sectional data on intellectual abilities at various ages would show much steeper declines. Longitudinal research, in contrast, would show more notable rises. Because Schaie's research is cross-sequential, the trajectories it depicts are more revealing: None of the average scores for the five abilities at any age is above 55 or below 35. Because the methodology takes into account the cohort and historical effects, the age-related differences from age 25 to 60 are very small.

Note the gradual rise and the eventual decline of all abilities, with men initially better at spatial orientation and numbers and women later excelling at verbal skills —but the two genders are quite similar overall and eventually come together.

Other researchers from many nations agree. For example, Paul Baltes (2003) tested hundreds of older Germans in Berlin and found that only at age 80 did every cognitive ability show age-related average declines. Aduthood is usually a time of increasing, or at least maintaining, IQ (Martin & Zimprich, 2005).

Schaie has noted substantial cohort effects. Each successive cohort (born at seven-year intervals from 1889 to 1973) tends to score higher in adulthood than the previous cohorts in verbal memory and inductive reasoning, and lower in number ability. The most recent cohorts postpone the overall drop in scores (Schaie, 2005). These cohort effects may be attributed to the fact that younger cohorts complete more years of education, especially education that emphasizes logic and self-expression more than memorization of number facts.

One correlate of higher intelligence scores in the Seattle Longitudinal Study is intellectual complexity at work and in personal life, which is highest from age 39 to 53, and which favors more recent cohorts. Another correlate is social status, which peaks at age 46. Although these factors are among the reasons that IQ usually increases throughout adulthood, Schaie adds that "individual decline prior to 60 years of age is almost inevitably a symptom or precursor of pathological age changes" (Schaie, 2005, p. 418). In other words, most adults at some time between age 40 and 60 reach their peak of intellectual ability; those who show substantial decline are probably ill in some way.

Another crucial finding is that "virtually every possible permutation of individual profiles has been observed in our study" (Schaie, 1996, p. 351). One replication of the Seattle Longitudinal Study occurred in Sweden, among monozygotic and dizygotic twins aged 41 to 84 (Finkel et al., 1998). The results, markedly similar to Schaie's, reveal "vast individual differences in the aging process," even for monozygotic twins. Intellectual abilities sometimes rise, fall, stay the same, or fall and then rise higher than before. This can happen in one person even when it does not happen to a genetically identical twin. IQ is multidirectional and epigenetic (Fischer et al., 2003; Neisser, 1998). The following provides an example.

a case to study

"At Very Different Levels"

Adult intelligence may seem abstract when it is based on group averages, but individual cases also reveal remarkable growth, decline, and stability. Using data from his Seattle Longitudinal Study, K. Warner Schaie (1989) traced individual changes in one of the five primary mental abilities, verbal meaning. Examine the four patterns in Figure 21.2 and then read Schaie's explanations.

> The first two profiles represent two . . . women who throughout life functioned at very different levels. Subject 155510 is a high school graduate who has been a homemaker all of her adult life and whose husband is still alive and well-functioning. She started our testing program at a rather low level, but her performance has had a clear upward trend. The comparison participant subject (154503) had been professionally active as a teacher. Her performance remained fairly level and above the population average until her early sixties. Since that time she has been divorced and retired from her teaching job; her performance in 1984 dropped to an extremely low level, which may reflect her experiential losses but could also be a function of increasing health problems.
>
> The second pair of profiles shows the 28-year performance of two . . . men. . . . Subject 153003, who started out somewhat below the population average, completed only grade school and worked as a purchasing agent prior to his retirement. He showed virtually stable performance until the late sixties; his performance actually increased after he retired, but he is beginning to experience health problems and has recently become a widower, and his latest assessment was below the earlier stable level. By contrast, subject 153013, a high school graduate who held mostly clerical types of jobs, showed gain until the early sixties and stability over the next assessment interval. By age 76, however, he showed substantial decrement that continued through the last assessment, which occurred less than a year prior to his death.

Predictions about adult cognition are imprecise. No one could anticipate the late-life intellectual performance of these participants based on their early scores. In order to fully explore his data, Schaie added many other measures to his original five over the years, including QALYs (quality-adjusted life years; see Chapter 20); genetic analysis; and tests of latent abilities, personality, cognitive flexibility, and practical intelligence (Schaie, 2005). All these aid prediction of IQ, but even so, prediction is imperfect.

Education, occupation, and health—all of which vary from person to person—contribute to unique profiles. The lesson: Intellectual changes are woven into life circumstances. Eventually old age and poor health slow thinking; but this decline may not occur until late in life; moreover, the decline may be so gradual that those who were once high scorers slow down so little that they still score at the average for young adults (Salthouse, 2006).

Other researchers might downplay the importance of education, marriage, vocation, and health, all of which Schaie stresses. Instead they might focus on the economic background and ethnicity of each of these four individuals. Which do you think are the important factors in maintaining intelligence? If all the influential factors were in place, might someone's scores keep rising, even after age 80?

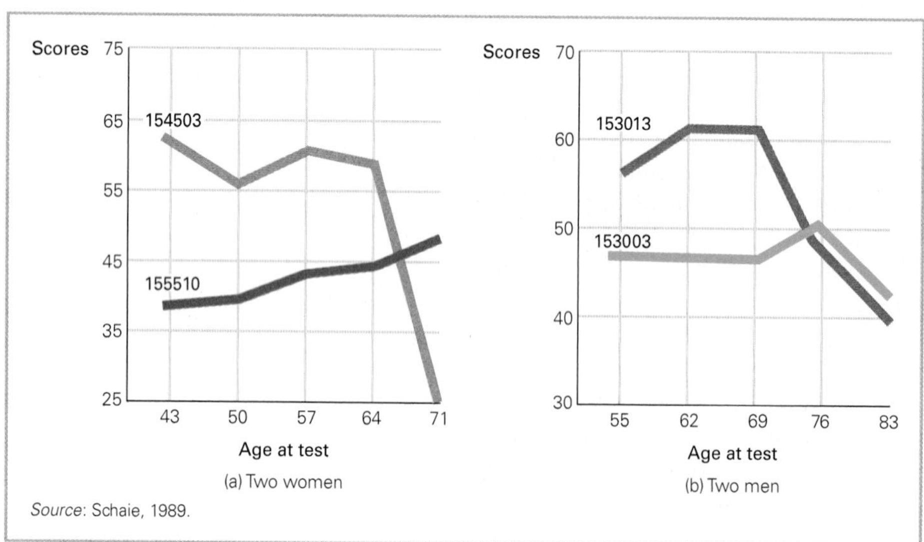

FIGURE 21.2

Profiles of Verbal Memory These figures index changes in word-recognition scores (which are used as a measure of crystallized intelligence) for two pairs of comparable adults over time. Notice how distinctly different the profiles are of individual change for each person—even though each is the same age, the same sex, and part of the same birth cohort. These differences underscore how much intellectual change in adulthood is affected by occupational, marital, health, and other experiences that vary from one person to another.

Components of Intelligence: Many and Varied

Responding to all these data, developmentalists are now looking closely at patterns of cognitive gains and losses over the adult years. Because virtually every pattern is possible, it is misleading to ask whether intelligence either increases or decreases; it does not move in lockstep, often zigzagging from one ability to another or within the same person over time. The questions to be asked are how many distinct abilities should be tested and whether it matters that a particular ability increases or decreases.

Although some psychologists believe that there may be a *g*, with perhaps speed or working memory underlying all the manifestations of intelligence, the data make it difficult to find such an ability. One reason for this difficulty is that there are no "pure" measures of intelligence. Every aspect of brain functioning is affected by health, emotions, and history, so proving that one particular ability underlies all IQ changes is impossible—especially from age 25 to 65, when a cognitive reserve compensates for any physiological loss (Kramer et al., 2006).

The search for a "single global factor . . . may make empirical findings uninterpretable" (Rabbitt et al., 2003). Many psychologists instead envision several intellectual abilities, each of which independently rises and falls. The debate concerns how many such abilities there are and how each might be affected by age. We now consider proposals that there are two, three, or eight such abilities.

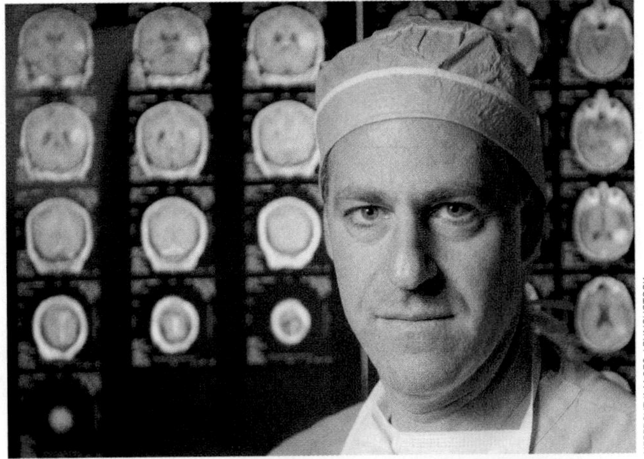

UPPERCUT IMAGES / PUNCHSTOCK

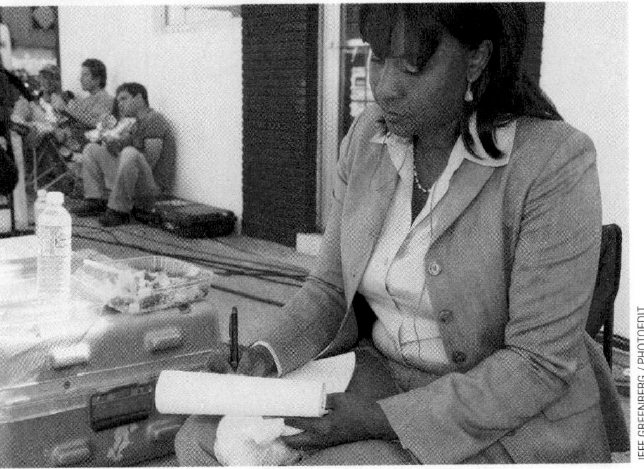

JEFF GREENBERG / PHOTOEDIT

Not Brain Surgery? Yes, it is! Both these adults need to combine fluid and crystallized intelligence, insight and intuition, logic and experience. One *(top)* is in fact a neurosurgeon, studying brain scans before picking up his scalpel. The other *(bottom)* is a court reporter for a TV station, jotting notes during a lunch recess before delivering her on-camera report on a trial.

Two Clusters: Fluid and Crystallized

In the 1960s a leading personality researcher, Raymond Cattell, teamed up with a promising PhD student, John Horn, to study the results of intelligence tests. They concluded that adult intelligence is best understood if it is clustered into two categories, called fluid and crystallized intelligence.

As its name implies, **fluid intelligence** is like water, flowing until it reaches its own level, no matter where that happens to be. Fluid intelligence is quick and flexible, enabling a person to learn anything, even things that are unfamiliar and unconnected to what is already known. Fluid intelligence allows people to draw inferences, to understand relations between concepts, to readily process new ideas and facts. Underlying fluid intelligence are basic mental abilities, such as inductive reasoning, abstract analysis, and working memory. Someone high in fluid intelligence is quick and creative with words and numbers and enjoys intellectual puzzles. The kind of question that tests fluid intelligence among Western adults might be:

fluid intelligence Those types of basic intelligence that make learning of all sorts quick and thorough. Abilities such as short-term memory, abstract thought, and speed of thinking are all usually considered part of fluid intelligence.

> What comes next in each of these two series?*
> 4 9 1 6 2 5 3
> V X Z B D

Puzzles are often used to measure fluid intelligence, with speedy solutions given bonus points (as on many IQ tests). Immediate recall—of nonsense words, of numbers, of a sentence just read—is one indicator of fluid intelligence, because working memory is considered crucial.

* The correct answers are 6 and F. These are fairly easy; some series are much more difficult to complete.

crystallized intelligence Those types of intellectual ability that reflect accumulated learning. Vocabulary and general information are examples. Some developmental psychologists think crystallized intelligence increases with age, while fluid intelligence declines.

Crystallized intelligence is the accumulation of facts, information, and knowledge as a result of education and experience. The size of vocabulary, the knowledge of chemical formulas, and long-term memory for dates in history all indicate crystallized intelligence. Tests designed to measure this intelligence might include questions like these:

> What is the meaning of the word *misanthrope*?
> Who would hold a harpoon?
> Explain the formula for the area of a circle.
> What was Sri Lanka called in 1950?

Although such questions seem to measure achievement more than aptitude, intelligent people do take in more information and remember what they learn. Vocabulary, for example, is a mainstay of most IQ tests, including the Wechsler and Stanford-Binet. The more people know, the more they can learn, which explains why high crystallized intelligence at one point in life predicts a high IQ later on.

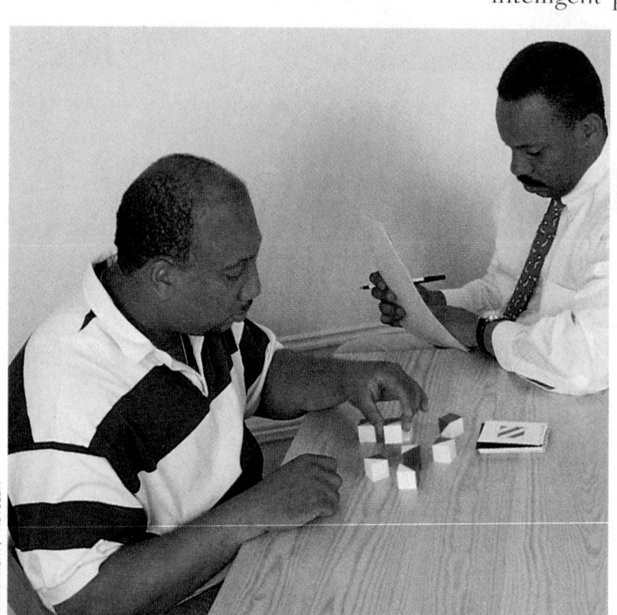

LAURA DWIGHT / PHOTOEDIT

The Wechsler Adult Intelligence Test This is a timed, one-on-one exam that involves 10 separate subtests, including the spatial-design item shown here.

Observation Quiz (see answer, page 564): Can you see three reasons why this test-taker might be made anxious by the testing context and thus score lower than he otherwise might?

To reflect the total picture of a person's intellectual potential, both fluid and crystallized intelligence must be measured. Age complicates the IQ calculation, because scores on items measuring fluid intelligence decrease with age whereas scores on items measuring crystallized intelligence increase. (Scores on subtests also follow one or the other of these patterns [Horn & Masunaga, 2000].) These two clusters, changing in opposite directions, make IQ scores fairly steady from ages 30 to 70, even though many particular abilities change.

The reason that age impairs fluid intelligence is that everything slows down with age, not only catching a speeding baseball but also processing a puzzle. Fluid intelligence is called aging-sensitive. Although brain slowdown (resulting from slower cerebral blood circulation and fewer new neurons and dendrites, among other things) begins at age 20 or so, it is rarely apparent until massive declines in fluid intelligence begin to affect crystallized intelligence and IQ scores overall start to fall (Lindenberger, 2001).

Horn and Cattell (1967) wrote that they had

> shown intelligence to both increase and decrease with age—depending upon the definition of intelligence adopted, fluid or crystallized! Our results illustrate an essential fallacy implicit in the construction of omnibus measures of intelligence.
>
> [p. 124]

In other words, it is foolish to try to measure *g* as a single omnibus intelligence, because both components need to be measured separately. Otherwise the real changes over time will be masked, because changes in fluid and crystallized abilities cancel each other out.

Three Forms of Intelligence: Sternberg

Robert Sternberg (1988, 2003) agrees that a single intelligence score is misleading. He has proposed three fundamental forms of intelligence: analytic, creative, and practical, each of which can be tested.

analytic intelligence A form of intelligence that involves such mental processes as abstract planning, strategy selection, focused attention, and information processing, as well as verbal and logical skills.

Analytic intelligence includes all the mental processes that foster academic proficiency by making efficient learning, remembering, and thinking possible. Thus, it draws on abstract planning, strategy selection, focused attention, and information processing, as well as on verbal and logical skills. Strengths in those areas are valuable in emerging adulthood, particularly in college, in graduate school, and in job training. Multiple-choice tests, with one and only one right answer, and brief essays that call forth remembered information assess analytic intelligence.

Creative intelligence involves the capacity to be intellectually flexible and innovative. Creative thinking is divergent rather than convergent, producing unexpected, imaginative, and unusual responses rather than standard and conventional answers.

creative intelligence A form of intelligence that involves the capacity to be intellectually flexible and innovative.

Tests of creative intelligence that Sternberg developed include writing a short story titled "The Octopus's Sneakers" and planning an advertising campaign for a new doorknob. High scores are earned by those who come up with many unusual ideas.

Practical intelligence involves the capacity to adapt one's behavior to the demands of a given situation. This capacity includes an accurate grasp of the expectations and needs of the people involved and an awareness of the particular skills that are called for, along with the ability to use these insights effectively. Practical intelligence is sometimes described as the product of "the school of hard knocks" or as "street smarts," not "book smarts."

practical intelligence The intellectual skills used in everyday problem solving.

Practical intelligence is useful for managing the conflicting personalities in a family or for convincing members of an organization (e.g., business, social group, school) to take some sort of action. Without practical intelligence, a solution found by analytic intelligence, or a stunningly creative idea, is doomed to fail. The reason is that many people resist academic brilliance when it is not coupled with practical intelligence, because they think it is unrealistic; likewise, they fear creative thinking because they think it is weird. For example, imagine a business manager, or a school principal, or a political leader without practical intelligence trying to change procedures. Unless the new policies are compatible with the organization and understood by at least some of the people, the workers or voters will misinterpret them, predict that they will fail, and balk at implementing them (Beach et al., 1997).

To assess practical intelligence, no abstract IQ test will do, because of the "centrality of context for understanding practical problem-solving" (Sternberg et al., 2001, p. 226). Adults must be observed dealing with their lives, not taking tests, to assess their practical intelligence. In a study of bank employees aged 24 to 58, the most successful workers (measured by authority, salary, and ratings) were not necessarily the ones who scored highest on standard measures of intelligence. Instead, they scored well on a measure of practical intelligence about bank management (Colonia-Willner, 1998).

Sternberg believes that each of these three forms of intelligence—analytic, creative, and practical—is useful and that adults should deploy the strengths and guard against the limitations of each:

TONY FREEMAN / PHOTOEDIT

Listening Quietly This elementary school teacher appears to be explaining academic work to one of her students, a boy who seems attentive and quiet.

Observation Quiz (see answer, page 565): If this situation is typical in this classroom, what kind of intelligence is valued?

> People attain success, in part, by finding out how to exploit their own patterns of strengths and weaknesses. . . . Analytic ability involves critical thinking; it is the ability to analyze and evaluate ideas, solve problems, and make decisions. Creative ability involves going beyond what is given to generate novel and interesting ideas. Practical ability involves implementing ideas; it is the ability involved when intelligence is applied to real world contexts.
>
> *[Sternberg et al., 2000, p. 31]*

Eight Intelligences: Gardner

As noted in Chapter 11, Howard Gardner (1983, 1998) believes that there are eight distinct intelligences: linguistic, logical-mathematical, musical, spatial, bodily-kinesthetic, naturalistic, social-understanding, and self-understanding. Gardner believes that each intelligence has a discrete neurological network in a particular section of the brain.

The fact that these intelligences are brain-based, according to Gardner, explains why brain-damaged people can be amazingly skilled in some intelligences (able to draw, play music, or calculate) despite enormous deficits in others (such as social interaction or language). Their patterns are part of the proof, Gardner argues, that there are eight intelligences.

Gardner believes that most people can achieve at least minimal proficiency in all eight. Each of us is more gifted in some areas than in others because of the particular patterns of our brains. However, our innate gifts may atrophy. Gardner explains that families and communities value, and life circumstances reward, some of these eight intelligences more than the others. Parents recognize and encourage prized abilities, and schools emphasize them. As a result, children develop and adults maintain certain talents, while allowing other skills to wither.

➤Answer to Observation Quiz (from page 562): The pressure is on him, as is made clear by the test-giver's timekeeping (he is looking at his watch), clothing (his white shirt and tie are signs of formal high status), and sex (men often feel more pressure when performing in front of other men). In addition, the test item, block design, is an abstract, out-of-context measure of performance IQ, which usually declines with age.

Consider school. Most American high schools value athletics: The popular students are star athletes (not captains of the chess team), and sports contests are occasions for rallies, cheers, dances, awards, and parental involvement. In effect, bodily-kinesthetic intelligence is celebrated, so students practice their athletic skills more than their academic or musical skills. An urban North American child who is naturally gifted in naturalistic intelligence might, for instance, be able to detect at a glance the difference in various types of trees but would never be acclaimed for this talent. This example illustrates that each social context evokes some intelligences more than others.

Diversity and Intelligence

Which kind of intelligence is most valued depends partly on age and partly on culture. Think about Sternberg's three over the life span. Analytic intelligence is usually valued in high school and college, as students are expected to remember and analyze various ideas.

Creative intelligence is prized if life circumstances change and new challenges arise; it is much more valued in some cultures and eras than in others (Kaufman & Sternberg, 2006). In times of social upheaval, creativity is a better predictor of accomplishment than are traditional measures, which tend to be too narrow. Creativity allows people to find "a better match to one's skills, values, or desires" (Sternberg, 2002, p. 456). However, creativity can be so innovative and out of touch with the mainstream that creative people are scorned, ignored, or even killed.

Practical intelligence may be particularly useful after the college days are over, when the demands of daily life are omnipresent (Berg & Klaczynski, 2002). Interestingly, scores on tests of practical intelligence do not always correlate with scores on traditional IQ tests (Sternberg et al., 2000), which are designed to correlate with school achievement.

The benefits of practical intelligence in adult life are obvious once we remember that few adults need to define obscure words or deduce the next element in a number sequence (analytic intelligence); nor do they need to imagine better ways to play music, to structure local government, or to write a poem (creative intelligence). Instead, adults need to solve real-world challenges: maintaining a home; advancing a career; managing family finances; analyzing information from media, mail, and the Internet; addressing the emotional needs of family members, neighbors, and colleagues. Schaie found that, even more than the five primary abilities, scores on tests of practical intelligence were steady, with no notable decrement, until people were in their 70s (Schaie, 2005).

Think about these three intelligences cross-culturally. Analytic intelligence has been looked at with suspicion if the "intellectuals" disagree with popular culture. Creative individuals would be critical of traditional authority, and hence would be tolerated only in some political situations (Sternberg, 2006). Practical intelligence, although valued less within school settings, might generally be most important, especially if food was scarce.

Especially for Prospective Parents In terms of the intellectual challenge, what type of intelligence is most needed for effective parenthood?

An Example of Practical Intelligence

Sternberg gives an example from rural Kenya, where a smart child is one who knows which herbal medicines cure which diseases, not one who excels in school. As Sternberg reported:

> Knowledge of these natural herbal medicines was negatively correlated both with school achievement in English and with scores on conventional tests of crystallized abilities. . . . [In rural Kenya,] children who spend a great deal of time on school-based learning may be viewed as rather foolish because they are taking away from the time they might be using to learn a trade and become economically self-sufficient. These results suggest that scores on ability or achievement tests always have to be understood in the cultural context in which they are obtained.
>
> *[Sternberg et al., 2000, p. 19]*

➤Answer to Observation Quiz (from page 563): Solely academic learning. Neither practical nor creative intelligence is fostered by a student working quietly at her desk (the girl at right) or the boy coming up to the teacher for private instruction. Fortunately, there are signs that this moment is not typical; notice the teacher's sweater, earrings, lipstick, and, especially, the apple on her desk.

This example highlights a problem: At every stage of life, people's intellectual abilities should be encouraged by their context as well as be useful in their communities. If a child is schooled in analytic intelligence but practical intelligence is more valued in the immediate environment, then that is a problem. If an adult is encouraged to develop creative intelligence but his or her only outlet for creativity is the decoration of birthday cakes, then that is a problem as well.

For that reason, if a school curriculum is only analytic, and if analytic intelligence is useless for adults in a certain culture, then children with high practical intelligence will not seek academic achievement because they realize that, practically speaking, school success is irrelevant. In Western cultures, children with high IQs will learn well in school and will therefore secure high-paying jobs. However, this may not be true in Kenya or other developing countries.

Which Intelligence Is Valued?

Broad cultural and historical contexts often emphasize one form of intelligence over the others. For example, as you read in Chapter 18, Chinese culture may be more dialectical and inclusive than others, placing a high priority on social compromises. As a result, Chinese people may emphasize interpersonal intelligence.

Likewise, the effect of the historical context is illustrated by the Puritans in colonial America in the seventeenth century. They considered dance and the visual arts the work of the devil. In that community, children's musical and spatial intelligences were never developed; whatever artistic talent (or any other manifestation of Sternberg's creative intelligence) they might have had would have faded by adulthood (Laplante, 2005).*

* This may overstate the case, in that some seventeenth-century creative adults designed practical objects (a pitcher, a chair) and others wrote sermons that were works of art. Nonetheless, every culture values some kinds of intelligence more than others, and children try hard to shine in whatever ways their community appreciates.

➤Response for Prospective Parents (from page 565): Because parenthood demands flexibility and patience, Sternberg's practical intelligence or Gardner's social-understanding is probably most needed. Anything that involves finding a single correct answer, such as analytic intelligence or number ability, would not be much help.

Every intelligence test and school curriculum reflects assumptions about the construct being measured. Psychometricians are increasingly aware that most tests of intelligence originated in western Europe (France and England) and have been refined and standardized by the academic elite in the United States. They are valid measures of the verbal and logical skills of North American, native-born, English-speaking children (who have always been the basis for setting the norms), but they may not be valid for other people or other skills.

Education, both deliberate (as in school) and inadvertent (as in a marriage) is a powerful expression of social values. Older adults can learn the skills valued by psychometricians if their particular cultural setting encourages it. In the Seattle Longitudinal Study, a group of 60-year-olds who had declined markedly in spatial or reasoning skills were given five one-hour sessions of personalized training. Forty percent of them improved so much that they reached the level they had been at 14 years earlier, and their gains were still evident 7 years later (Schaie, 2005). For them, time didn't just stop—it moved backward.

One overall conclusion from the array of intellectual tests and abilities is that cultural assumptions affect concepts of intelligence and the construction of IQ tests. How does this connect to developmental changes over adulthood? If a culture values youth and devalues age, this might explain why the very abilities that favor the young (quick reaction time, capacious short-term memory) are central to psychometric intelligence tests, whereas the strengths of older adults are not. Fluid intelligence is valued more in a youth-oriented culture than crystallized intelligence is. Curiously, a highly intelligent person is often described as *quick* whereas a stupid person is said to be *slow*—and slow is exactly what older adults are.

Often a person who values one kind of intelligence does not recognize the merits of another set of values. I became keenly aware of this when I counseled Jenny, one of my best students. I thought she would use her analytic intelligence to reach the same conclusions I did—but not so, as the following explains.

a case to study

Jenny: "Men Come and Go"

My students, especially the older ones who already have families of their own, seem surrounded by crushing stresses. Experience has taught me to listen when they talk about their problems. I ask questions, but I try not to recommend solutions.

Jenny was an A student in my child development class. She told us all that she was divorced, raising her own two children and two nephews of her former husband. The boys' parents had died—one from AIDS and the other from a bullet. She told her fellow students about free activities she had found for her children—parks, museums, the zoo, Fresh Air camps, and so on. I was awed by her ability to cope.

After that course ended, I didn't see Jenny again for two years. Then I chanced to meet her in the hall.

"God must have put you in my path," she said. "I need to talk with you."

I told her my office hours, and she came the next day.

Jenny told me she was four weeks pregnant—and the father was a married man named Billy. She thought she would abort, but she remembered a promise she'd made when her second child was born precipitously on her living room couch. He was blue from lack of oxygen; she prayed that he would live and promised God right then and there that she would never have an abortion. She wanted my theological opinion: Did she need to keep that promise, which had been made in desperation?

I asked more questions. Billy would not leave his wife and son, would not promise to stay with Jenny if she had the baby, but would pay for an abortion. Jenny was on public assistance, a single mother with two biological children and two unsubsidized foster children, living in the South Bronx. She was about to graduate with honors, and she had planned to get a job and leave her dangerous neighborhood before it destroyed her children. This embryo might develop sickle-cell anemia, since she was a carrier and Billy had not been tested. And, she added, she worried she was too old (31!) to have another baby.

As she spoke, the answer became obvious to me, as it did (or seemed to do) to her.

"Thank you; I know what I am going to do," she said.

Then the surprise. "I'll have the baby. Men come and go, but children are always with you."

Instead of attacking the problem, by having the abortion and getting rid of the man, Jenny, by thinking intuitively, reinterpreted this unexpected stress as an opportunity, another child to love.

It turned out to be a smart choice. Billy's wife hired a detective, who found out about Jenny. The wife told Billy he must never see Jenny again or she would sue for divorce. Two years later, the divorce became final, and Billy and Jenny were married. They moved to Florida, found good jobs, bought a house with a pool, and together raised their unplanned child well—a daughter who has now graduated from college. The son born on the couch now has his PhD in psychology.

None of this means that everyone, or even anyone, should follow Jenny's path. It does mean, however, that "we know more than we can tell" (Polanyi, quoted in Myers, 2002, p. 57); that is, experience sometimes leads to expert intuition that cannot be easily expressed. Jenny knew more about her baby's father than she conveyed to me, and talking helped her clarify her values and priorities. Her choice was wise, even expert, although quite different from the choice other experts might have made if they had only the facts, not the intuition.

SUMMING UP

Although psychometricians once believed that intelligence decreased beginning at about age 20, more sophisticated longitudinal testing demonstrates that many abilities increase throughout adulthood. Crystallized abilities such as vocabulary and general knowledge improve throughout adulthood, although some aspects of fluid intelligence, particularly speed, decrease. Intelligence may be not a single entity (*g*) but rather a combination of various abilities, which have been categorized as fluid and crystallized; analytic, creative, and practical; or linguistic, logical-mathematical, musical, spatial, bodily-kinesthetic, naturalistic, social-understanding, and self-understanding. These abilities rise and fall partly because of events in each person's life, partly because of culture and cohort, and partly because of age. The overall picture of adult intelligence, as measured by various tests, is complex. ■

Selective Gains and Losses

Thus far we have discussed intellectual changes over adulthood as if factors beyond individual control affected the patterns of change. In many ways, this assumption is valid. Aging neurons, cultural pressures, past education, and current life events all affect intelligence. None of these are under direct individual control, although, as Chapter 20 emphasized, some health habits (exercise, nutrition, drug use) are a personal choice.

Beyond that, many researchers believe that adults make deliberate choices about their intellectual development. For example, number skills have declined more for recent cohorts than for earlier ones, which may be the result not of past math curricula (as was suggested) but of modern adults' tendency to use calculators instead of doing paper-and-pencil (or mental) calculations. Any adult could choose to do otherwise.

Optimization with Compensation

Paul and Margaret Baltes (1990) developed a theory, called **selective optimization with compensation,** which holds that people seek to optimize their development, looking for the best ways to compensate for physical and cognitive losses and to become more proficient at activities they can already do well.

selective optimization with compensation The theory, developed by Paul and Margaret Baltes, that people try to maintain a balance in their lives by looking for the best way to compensate for physical and cognitive losses and to become more proficient in activities they can already do well.

One example might be an expert on China who notices that, with age, she is beginning to have difficulty reading the newspaper. She might buy reading glasses (compensation) and read only those articles (selection) whose headlines suggest they are about China, thus building on her existing expertise (optimization). Similarly, a 55-year-old aircraft mechanic might talk and walk more slowly than younger workers but might maintain his spatial and sequential abilities—and thus remain a valuable employee.

One father tried to explain this concept to his son as follows:

> I told my son: triage
> Is the main art of aging.
> At midlife, everything
> Sings of it. In law
> Or healing, learning or play,
> Buying or selling—above all
> In remembering—the rule is
> Cut losses, let profits ring.
> Specifics rise and fall
> By selection.
>
> *[Hamill, 1991]*

Selective optimization with compensation applies to every aspect of life, from choosing friends to playing baseball. To be specific, as people grow older their friendship circles become smaller but more intense, as they find ways to ensure intimacy without needing to socialize as widely (Schaie & Carstensen, 2006). Each adult seeks to maximize gains and minimize losses, therefore choosing to practice some abilities and ignore others (Wellman, 2003).

DAVIS BARBER / PHOTOEDIT

Handicapped Learner? This woman is using a computer in her ESL (English as a Second Language) class.

Observation Quiz (see answer, page 570): Do you see any evidence that this is a good way for her to learn a new language?

selective expert Someone who is notably more skilled and knowledgeable than the average person about whichever activities are personally meaningful.

Such choices are critical, because every ability can be enhanced or diminished, depending on how, when, and why a person uses it. It is possible to "teach an old dog new tricks," but learning requires that the adult choose and practice those "new tricks." As Baltes and Baltes (1990) explain, selective optimization means that each person selects aspects of intelligence to optimize and neglects the rest. If those aspects that are ignored happen to be the ones measured by IQ tests, then intelligence scores will fall, even if a person's selection results in improvement (optimization) in other areas.

Another way to express this idea is that everyone develops expertise. Each person becomes a **selective expert,** specializing in activities that are personally meaningful, whether they involve car repair, gourmet cooking, illness diagnosis, or fly-fishing. As people develop expertise in some areas, they pay less attention to others. For example, each adult tunes out most channels on the TV, ignores some realms of human experience, and has no interest in attending particular events that other people would wait in line for. This selectivity becomes increasingly evident with age, as is apparent when we note which age group is likely to try the latest food, fashion, or electronic gadgets.

Culture and context guide all of us in selecting our areas of expertise. Many adults born 60 years ago are much better than more recent cohorts at writing letters with distinctive but legible handwriting. Because of their childhood culture, they selected and practiced penmanship, becoming expert in it and maintaining that expertise. Today's schools and children make other choices: Reading, for instance, is now crucial for every child—unlike a century ago, when adult illiteracy was common.

Expert Cognition

Experts are not necessarily those with rare and outstanding proficiency. Although sometimes *expert* signifies an extraordinary genius, to researchers the term means more—and less—than that (Ericsson, 1996; Ericsson & Charness, 1994). As two scholars conclude, "There is more to human intelligence, namely expertise abilities, than has been measured in traditional IQ tests" (Masunaga & Horn, 2001, p. 308).

Developmentalists use a broader, more inclusive definition: An expert is notably more skilled, proficient, and knowledgeable at a particular task than the average person. Expertise is not innate; it does not necessarily correlate with basic abilities (such as those measured by IQ tests).

Although experts do not necessarily have extraordinary intellectual ability, what distinguishes them is not simply more knowledge about a subject (Wellman, 2003). At a certain point, the accumulation of knowledge, practice, and experience becomes transformative, putting the expert in a different league from the less adept person. The quality, as well as quantity, of cognition is advanced. Expert thought is intuitive, automatic, strategic, and flexible, as we now describe.

Intuitive

Novices follow formal procedures and rules. Experts rely more on their past experiences and on immediate contexts. Their actions are therefore more intuitive and less stereotypic. For example, when they look at X-rays, expert physicians interpret them more accurately than do young doctors, though they cannot always verbalize how they reached their diagnosis. As one team explains:

> The expert physician, with many years of experience, has so "compiled" his knowledge that a long chain of inference is likely to be reduced to a single association. This feature can make it difficult for an expert to verbalize information that he actually uses in solving a problem. Faced with a difficult problem, the apprentice fails to solve it at all, the journeyman solves it after long effort, and the master sees the answer immediately.
>
> *[Rybash et al., 1986]*

The role of experience and intuition is also evident during surgery. Another study begins by noting that outsiders might think medicine is straightforward, but that experts realize the hazards:

> Hospitals are filled with varieties of knives and poisons. Every time a medication is prescribed, there is potential for an unintended side effect. In surgery, collateral damage is inherent. External tisssue must be cut to allow internal access so that a diseased organ may be removed, or some other manipulation may be performed to return the patient to better health.
>
> *[Dominguez, 2001, p. 287]*

In this study, surgeons all saw the same videotape of a gallbladder operation and were asked to talk about it. The experienced surgeons anticipated and noted problems twice as often as the surgical residents (who also had removed gallbladders) (Dominguez, 2001).

Another example of expert intuition is *chicken-sexing*, the ability to tell if a newborn chicken is male or female. As David Myers (2002) tells it:

> Poultry owners once had to wait five to six weeks before the appearance of adult feathers enabled them to separate cockerels (males) from pullets (hens). Egg producers wanted to buy and feed only pullets, so they were intrigued to hear that some Japanese had developed an uncanny ability to sex day-old chicks. . . . Hatcheries elsewhere then gave some of their workers apprenticeships under the Japanese. . . . After months of training and experience, the best Americans and

> Australians could almost match the Japanese, by sexing 800 to 1,000 chicks per hour with 99 percent accuracy. But don't ask them how they do it. The sex difference, as any chicken sexer can tell you, is too subtle to explain.
>
> *[p. 55]*

Automatic

Many elements of expert performance are automatic; that is, the complex action and thought they involve have become routine, making it appear that most aspects of the task are performed instinctively. Experts process incoming information more quickly and analyze it more efficiently than nonexperts, and then they act in well-rehearsed ways that make their efforts appear nonconscious. In fact, some automatic actions are no longer accessible to the conscious mind. For example, adults are much better at tying their shoelaces than children are (adults can do it efficiently in the dark) but much worse at describing how they do it (McLeod et al., 2005).

This is no doubt apparent if you are an experienced driver and have attempted to teach someone else to drive. Excellent drivers who are inexperienced instructors find it hard to recognize or verbalize aspects of driving that have become automatic for them, such as noticing pedestrians and cyclists on the far side of the road, or feeling the car shift gears as it heads up an incline, or hearing the tires lose traction on a bit of sand. Yet such factors differentiate the expert from the novice.

Answer to Observation Quiz (from page 568): Individual learning styles differ, but there are three signs that this may be an effective method of language instruction: The equipment is new; both oral and auditory exercises are part of the curriculum; and she and each of her fellow students can learn at their own pace.

This explains why, despite powerful motivation, quicker reactions, and better vision, teenagers have far more car accidents than middle-aged drivers. Sometimes teenage drivers deliberately take risks, of course, but more often they simply misjudge and misperceive conditions that a more experienced driver would automatically notice.

Automatic processing is thought to be a crucial reason that expert chess and Go players are much better than novices. They see a configuration of game pieces and automatically encode it as a whole, rather than analyzing it bit by bit. Interestingly, one study of expert Go players (aged 23–76) found that recognition memory of Go pieces did not show age-related effects among experts, although recall memory diminishes with age. Apparently, automatic cognition is not abstract; it depends on a visual cue to trigger the process (Masunaga & Horn, 2001).

Another study of expert chess players (aged 17–81) found some age-related declines, but expertise was much more important than age. This was particularly apparent for speedy recognition that a player's king was threatened, even though standard tests of memory and speed showed a decline among older chess experts. They were still quick to defend the king (Jastrzembski et al., 2006).

Strategic

Experts have more and better strategies, especially when problems are unexpected (Ormerod, 2005). Indeed, strategy may be the most crucial difference between a skilled person and an unskilled one. For example, expert team leaders use ongoing communication, especially during slow times, so that when stress builds, no team member misinterprets plans, commands, and requirements. This strategy is used by effective military commanders as well as by civilian leaders in business and government (Sternberg et al., 2000).

Of course, strategies themselves need to be updated as situations change and people gain knowledge. The monthly fire drill required by some schools, the standard lecture given by some professors, and the pat safety instructions read by airline attendants before each flight may be less effective than they once were. I recently heard a flight attendant precede his standard talk with, "For those of you who have not ridden in an automobile since 1960, this is how you buckle a seat belt." That was one of the few times I actually listened to the words.

The superior strategies of the expert permit selective optimization with compensation. Many developmentalists regard the capacity to accommodate to changes over time (compensation) as essential to successful aging (M. M. Baltes & Carstensen, 2003; Rowe & Kahn, 1998). People need to compensate for any slippage in their fluid abilities.

Such compensation was evident in a study of airplane pilots, who were allowed to take notes on directions given by air traffic controllers in a flight simulation (Morrow et al., 2003). Experienced pilots took notes that were more accurate and complete. They used better graphic symbols (such as arrows) than did pilots who were trained to understand air traffic instructions but who did not have much flight experience. In other words, even though nonexperts were trained and had the proper tools (paper, pencil, and a suggestion that they might take notes), they did not use them as well as the experts did.

In actual flights, too, older pilots take more notes than younger ones do, because they have mastered this strategy, perhaps to compensate for their slower working memory. Probably as a result, these researchers found no differences in the ability to repeat complex instructions and conditions among experienced pilots of three age groups: 22–40, 50–59, and 60–76 (Morrow et al., 2003). People who are not experts show age-related deficits in many studies (including this one, on other abilities), but experts of all ages often maintain their proficiency at their occupation.

Flexible

Finally, perhaps because they are intuitive, automatic, and strategic, experts are also more flexible. The expert artist, musician, or scientist is creative and curious, deliberately experimenting and enjoying the challenge when things do not go according to plan (Csikszentmihalyi, 1996).

Consider the expert surgeon, who takes the most complex cases and prefers unusual patients over typical ones because operating on them might bring sudden, unexpected complications. Compared with the novice, the expert surgeon not only is more likely to notice telltale signs (an unexpected lesion, an oddly shaped organ, a rise or drop in a vital sign) that may signal a problem but also is more flexible, more willing to deviate from standard textbook procedures if they prove ineffective (Patel et al., 1999).

In the same way, experts in all walks of life adapt to individual cases and exceptions—somewhat like an expert chef who adjusts ingredients, temperature, technique, and timing as a dish develops and seldom follows a recipe exactly. Expert chess players, auto mechanics, and violinists do the same (Myers, 2002). Interestingly, a study of forensic scientists, who must find very individualized clues from a mishmash of relevant and irrelevant things, found that the most expert were more methodical as well as more flexible, using more strategies to study the most relevant objects (Schraagen & Leijenhorst, 2001).

Expertise and Age

The relationship between expertise and age is not straightforward. One of the essential requirements for expertise is time. Not everyone becomes an expert as he or she grows older, but everyone needs months or years (depending on the task) of practice to develop expertise. The study of chess and Go players found that "if there is intense, well-focused practice to attain expertise . . ., there may be no aging decline of abilities in the domain of that expertise" (Masunaga & Horn, 2001, p. 309).

Some researchers think practice must be extensive, involving at least 10 years and several hours a day (Charness et al., 1996; Ericsson, 1996). They were studying highly skilled experts, such as musicians. Motivation is crucial as well. As the

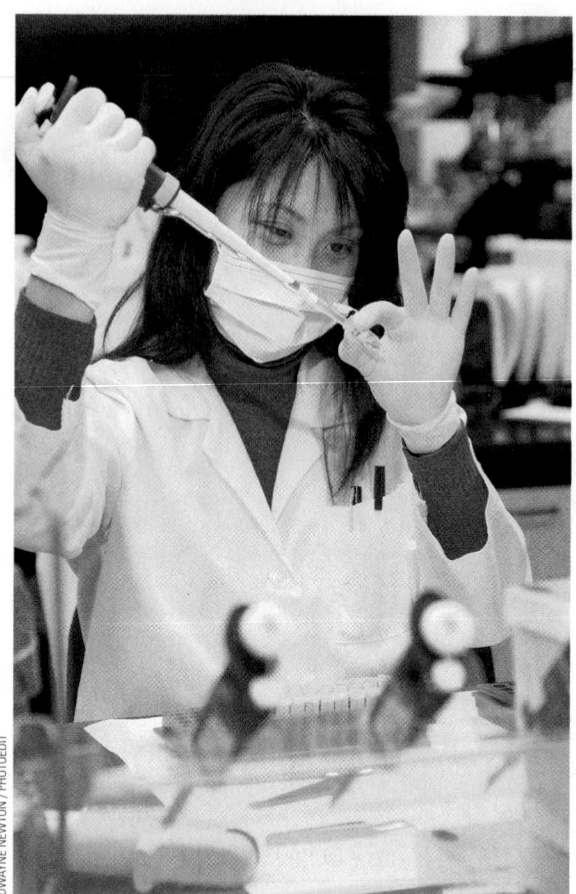

DWAYNE NEWTON / PHOTOEDIT

Make No Mistake Humans are not always expert at judging other humans. Juries have convicted some defendants who were later proved to be innocent and acquitted others who were actually guilty. If this lab technician is an expert at her work, and if the genetic evidence she is testing was carefully collected, DNA test results can provide objective proof of guilt or innocence.

authors of a study of figure skaters explain, "Everyone has the will to win, but there are only a few who have the will to prepare to win" (Starkes et al., 1996). Circumstances, training, talent, ability, practice, and age all affect expertise.

Expertise sometimes—but not always—overcomes the effects of age. For example, in one study, participants aged 17 to 79 were asked to identify nine common tunes (such as "Happy Birthday" and "Old MacDonald Had a Farm") when notes from midsong were first played very slowly and then gradually faster until the listener identified the tune. The listeners were grouped according to their musical experience, from virtually none to 10 or more years of training and performing.

In this slow-to-fast phase of the experiment, responses correlated with expertise but not with age. Those individuals who had played more music themselves were quicker to recognize songs played very slowly (Andrews et al., 1998). In other words, no matter what their age, novices were similar to one another and were slower than the experts, who were equally proficient at all ages.

In another phase of this study, the songs were played very fast at first and then gradually slowed down. In this condition, the older adults took longer to recognize the tunes. Although all the experts of every age did better than the novices, the older expert adults were slower than the younger expert adults (Andrews et al., 1998). Note that pace made the difference here; speed is one part of fluid intelligence. This harkens back to the question raised a few pages ago: What abilities should be tested on IQ tests? Perhaps "all measures of intelligence measure a form of developing expertise" (Sternberg, 2002, p. 452) and the specific measures used should depend on which kind of expertise is valued.

Older Workers: Experts or Has-Beens?

Research on cognitive plasticity confirms that experienced adults often use selective optimization with compensation. This is particularly apparent in the everyday workplace (Sterns & Huyck, 2001). The best employees may be the older ones—if they are motivated to do their best.

Complicated work requires more cognitive practice and expertise than routine work and may, as a result, have intellectual benefits for the workers themselves. In the Seattle Longitudinal Study, the cognitive complexity of the occupations of more than 500 workers was measured, including the complexities involved in the workers' interactions with other people, with things, and with data. All three kinds of occupational challenges maintained the workers' intellectual prowess (Schaie, 2005).

In another longitudinal study of adults, the authors found that

> the level of complexity of their paid work continued to affect the level of their intellectual functioning as it had when they were 20 and 30 years younger. Doing paid work that is substantially complex appears to raise the level of participants' intellectual functioning; doing paid work that is not intellectually challenging appears to decrease their level of intellectual functioning. Furthermore, the positive effect . . . appears even greater for older than for somewhat younger workers.
>
> *[Schooler et al., 1999, p. 491]*

An intriguing study of age and job effectiveness comes from an occupation everyone knows, waitressing. Waiting on tables in a restaurant demands many skills, including communication of menu items, memory for orders, knowledge of delivery procedures, time management of several groups at various stages, and the ability to smooth social interactions with customers and coworkers—as well as physical stamina! Adolescent and young adult waitresses have an advantage over older adults in their strength as well as in their speed and memory. Are older employees necessarily less efficient, or can they compensate?

Marion Perlmutter and her colleagues sought to answer this question. They identified the skills required for successful waitressing and then assessed those skills in 64 waitresses who varied in age (from 19 to 60) and work experience (from 2 months to 31 years) (Perlmutter et al., 1990).

The women were assessed on memory, strength, dexterity, knowledge of the technical and organizational requirements of the job, and social skills. They were also observed during different times of the workday, including rush and slack periods, to determine their effectiveness. Perlmutter and her colleagues wanted to know if younger and older employees differed in their overall job performance—and if so, whether the cause was physical and cognitive skills, work experience, or both.

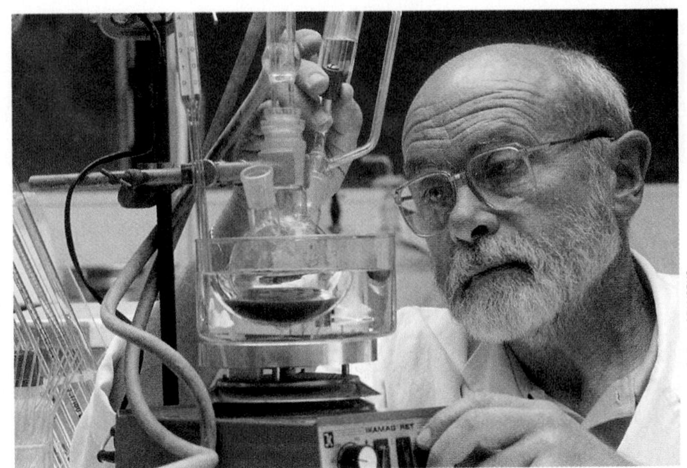
PHILIPPE GONTIER / THE IMAGE WORKS

Voilà! This chemist is thinking intensely and watching carefully for a result that will merit an excited *"Voilà!"* ("There it is!") He is in France, so we can guess his linguistic expertise; but unless we are also experienced chemists, we would not recognize an important result if it happened. Expertise is astonishingly selective.

They were surprised to discover that experience had little impact on work performance or on work-related physical or cognitive skills. Apparently, expertise at waiting on tables takes far less than 10 years to attain. As others have also found, after one has learned the basic requirements of some jobs, additional experience does not necessarily yield better performance (Ceci & Cornelius, 1990).

However, in the waitress study, the employees' age (independent of their experience) made a significant difference (Perlmutter et al., 1990). Younger women, as expected, had better physical skills and memory abilities, and they were quicker in calculating customers' checks. Nevertheless, older women outperformed their younger counterparts in the number of customers served, even during rush periods. One owner learned this the hard way. He said:

> A pretty girl is an asset to any business, but we tried them and they fell apart on us. . . . They could not keep up the pace of our fast and furious lunch hours. . . . Our clients want good service; if they want sex appeal they go elsewhere.
>
> *[quoted in Perlmutter et al., 1990, p. 189]*

The researchers noted that many restaurant managers

> consistently reported that older workers chunk tasks to save steps by combining orders for several customers at several tables and/or by employing time management strategies such as preparing checks while waiting for food delivery. . . . Although younger experienced food servers may have the knowledge and skills necessary for such organization and chunking, they do not seem to use the skills as often, perhaps because they do not believe they need to.
>
> *[Perlmutter et al., 1990, pp. 189–190]*

Thus, older waitresses developed strategies to compensate for their declining job-related abilities. The researchers concluded that "adaptive competence in adulthood represents functional improvements that probably are common, particularly in the workplace" (Perlmutter et al., 1990, p. 196).

Human Relations Expertise

Probably the most important skill for people of every age to learn is how to get along with other people, understanding their emotional needs and helping them function well. Think of an expert coach, therapist, or judge, and it becomes apparent that something is gained from life experience. The most common test of expert human relations occurs with parenting. Ideally, a parent is patient, good-humored, and consistent—all traits that become more common with age, as the following illustrates.

in person

An Experienced Parent

A mother I know joked, "I wish children were like pancakes, and I could throw out the first batch if they didn't turn out right." Her comment reflected the widespread belief that first-born children are more difficult to raise than later-borns. Children raise their parents while their parents raise them, which explains why first-time parents often seem bewildered and experienced parents seem more relaxed. I was much more worried about fevers, rashes, and laundry soap for my first-born than for my last-born, because I became more expert about babies.

When they were teenagers, Bethany, my eldest, told Rachel: "You have it easy, because I broke them in." I see the truth in that, although Rachel did not appreciate that Bethany had laid the groundwork. In fact, she complained, "It's not fair, Mommy. You like Bethany best because you've known her longer." As an experienced parent, I smiled; I had learned to take comments from teenagers "not too seriously, not too personally." With each, adolescence had become easier for me.

Bethany had a point. Research on parents of adolescents has found that parenting skills improve with experience. Specifically, mothers and fathers know more about the daily lives of their second teenager than their first, and such parental awareness, or monitoring, is thought to be pivotal in raising children well (Whiteman et al., 2003). Similarly, grandparents are believed to be more patient and playful (both qualities that benefit children) than they were when they were parents.

I do not doubt that. I have learned about parenthood from my years of practice, and I am more confident and skilled because of it. For example, I readily hold other people's children who reach out to me, something I was afraid to do before I had experience with my own. Many of my students ask me questions about their children, instead of asking my colleagues who know the research as well as I do but who have less personal experience. My students believe that parenting skills are learned on the job.

Like other parents, I am astonished at aspects of human experience that my children know about but I do not (current music being the most blatant example). They are amazed at things I do not know (Elissa once asked me how I dared teach American history when I didn't know how George Washington died), and I am troubled that there are things they have not learned (Bible stories, Shakespearean quotes, and, of course, psychology). They are experts and so am I, but our expertise does not necessarily overlap. The impact of culture, cohort, and context becomes obvious to every parent.

An enormous challenge of family life is to know when to advise, guide, or outright insist on certain actions from people you love—and when to bite your tongue, letting children make their own choices and learn their own lessons. This becomes easier with experience. I know more, but I say less.

The hardest challenge at any age is knowing when to take advice. I sometimes heed my daughters' suggestions about my clothes and hair; I know their expertise outshines mine. I resist their suggestions about other areas of my life, just as they resist mine. When I am old, I may recognize more of their expertise. Not yet.

SUMMING UP

People choose to become adept at some aspects of cognition, charting their course by using selective optimization with compensation. Choices and practice produce expertise, which is intuitive, automatic, strategic, and flexible. Expertise allows people to continue performing well throughout adulthood. This is evident in many occupations: Experienced workers can continue to hold their own even when some intellectual abilities start to slip. ■

SUMMARY

What Is Intelligence?

1. It was traditionally assumed that there is one general entity called intelligence that individuals have in greater or lesser quantity and that it decreases over the years of adulthood. However, current evidence does not support this idea.

2. Longitudinal research has found that each person tends to increase in IQ, particularly in vocabulary and general knowledge, until age 60 or so. In addition, James Flynn found that average IQ scores increased over the twentieth century, perhaps because later cohorts had more education.

3. K. Warner Schaie found that some primary abilities decline with age while others (such as vocabulary) increase. Education, vocation, and family, as well as age, seem to affect these abilities.

4. Cattell and Horn concluded that while crystallized intelligence, which is based on accumulated knowledge, increases with time, one's fluid, flexible reasoning skills inevitably decline with age.

5. Sternberg proposed three fundamental forms of intelligence: analytic, creative, and practical. Most adults believe that while analytic and creative abilities decline with age, their practical intelligence improves as they grow older; research supports this belief.

6. Gardner identified eight intelligences: linguistic, logical-mathematical, musical, spatial, bodily-kinesthetic, naturalistic, social-understanding, and self-understanding. The individual's genetic heritage and culture influence which of these intelligences are valued and thus more highly developed.

7. Overall, cultural values and changing demands with age reward some cognitive abilities more than others. Each person and each culture responds to these demands, which may not be reflected in psychometric tests.

Selective Gains and Losses

8. As people grow older, they select certain aspects of their lives to focus on, optimizing development in those areas and compensating for declines in others, if need be. Applied to cognition, this means that people become selective experts in whatever intellectual skills they choose to develop. Meanwhile, abilities that are not exercised may fade.

9. In addition to being more experienced, experts are better thinkers than novices are because they are more intuitive; their cognitive processes are automatic, often seeming to require little conscious thought; they use more and better strategies to perform whatever task is required; and they are more flexible.

10. Expertise in adulthood is particularly apparent at the workplace. Experienced workers often surpass younger workers because of their ability to specialize and harness their efforts, compensating for any deficits that may appear.

KEY TERMS

general intelligence (*g*) (p. 556)
Flynn effect (p. 557)
Seattle Longitudinal Study (p. 558)
fluid intelligence (p. 561)
crystallized intelligence (p. 562)
analytic intelligence (p. 562)
creative intelligence (p. 563)
practical intelligence (p. 563)
selective optimization with compensation (p. 567)
selective expert (p. 568)

KEY QUESTIONS

1. Why do cross-sectional and longitudinal studies of intelligence reach different conclusions?

2. How is fluid intelligence different from crystallized intelligence? How does each change in adulthood?

3. How do Sternberg's three fundamental forms of intelligence—analytic, creative, and practical—tend to vary with age?

4. Which of Gardner's eight intelligences tend to increase during adulthood in North America, and why?

5. How and why do context and cohort affect patterns of cognitive growth?

6. How is the plasticity of cognitive development related to education?

7. What are the differences between a selective expert and a novice?

8. What does research say about becoming an expert?

9. How do people compensate for the losses that come with age?

APPLICATIONS

1. The importance of context and culture is illustrated by the things that people think are basic knowledge. Write four questions that you think are hard but fair as measures of general intelligence. Then give your test to someone else, and answer the four questions that person has prepared for you. What did you learn from the results?

2. Skill at video games is sometimes thought to reflect intelligence. Go to a public place where people play such games, and interview three or four people who play them. What abilities do they think video games require? What do you think these games reflect in terms of experience, age, and motivation?

3. People choose to develop their expertise. Which of Gardner's eight intelligences are you least proficient in? Why is that? (Consider genes, family influences, culture, and personal choice.)

22

CHAPTER OUTLINE

Adulthood: Psychosocial Development

Throughout the past five chapters, you have read many times that chronological age does not determine adult development. Age boundaries are fluid, sometimes crossed in unexpected ways. Emotional reactions to events in adulthood are fluid, too, as I learned when I invited two married couples to our home for a dinner party.

"George and I will be arriving separately," one of the wives told me.

"No problem," I assured her. "I guess one or both of you will be coming directly from work."

"Actually, we will both be coming from our homes. We are divorced."

I was taken aback. I had no idea their marriage was in trouble.

"I'm so sorry. Should I have invited only one of you?"

"Don't be sorry. It's good for both of us. We are happier now, and good friends."

I was stunned. I thought divorce meant a "failed" marriage, a "broken" home, and at least one bitter spouse. Obviously, I was wrong. (The dinner party was a success, with lots of laughter.)

To avoid repetition, some topics (e.g., choosing friends, cohabitation) that affect people throughout life are discussed primarily in the emerging adulthood psychosocial chapter (19) and some events (grandparenthood, retirement) that often occur before age 65 are nonetheless assigned to the last psychosocial chapter (25). Marriage, parenthood, divorce, and the empty nest—each sometimes joyous and sometimes not—are in this chapter. That placement does not signify that these four necessarily occur between ages 25 and 65; fluid boundaries mean that these can occur at other ages, or never.

To tie all this together, we begin with a discussion of ages and stages of adulthood, which, like the divorce of my friends, may not be what you expect.

Ages and Stages

Often when developmentalists describe the psychosocial stages of adults, they begin with Erik Erikson, who was the first to realize that significant development occurs in adulthood. He emphasized the importance of the social context, using the term *psychosocial* instead of *psychosexual* (Freud's word).

> [Erikson] stands alone as the one thinker who changed our minds about what it means to live as a person who has arrived at a chronologically mature position and yet continues to grow, to change, and to develop.
>
> *[Hoare, 2002, p. 3]*

Especially for People Under 20 Will future "decade" birthdays—30, 40, 50, and so on—be major turning points in your life?

Erikson originally envisioned all eight stages in sequence, but it is apparent that adult age boundaries are not rigid. In Chapters 16 and 19, we stressed that, although the identity crisis begins in adolescence, finding identity is ongoing. Neither of Erikson's adult stages, *intimacy versus isolation* and *generativity versus stagnation*, is age invariant (Hoare, 2002; McAdams, 2006).

Erikson himself reassessed his eighth and final stage, *integrity versus despair*, when he reached retirement, writing that "the demand to develop integrity and wisdom in old age seems to be somewhat unfair, especially when made by middle-aged theorists—as, indeed, we then were" (Erikson, 1984, p. 160). He decided that the psychosocial virtues and concerns of late adulthood could and should be found much earlier (Hoare, 2002). A more detailed description of these four stages is shown in Table 22.1.

Erikson may have been the first to describe the psychosocial tensions and goals of adulthood, but he was not the only one. Social scientists who study adulthood typically recognize two complementary needs, similar to Erikson's *intimacy and*

TABLE 22.1

Erikson's Stages of Adulthood

Unlike Freud or other early theorists who thought adults simply worked through the legacy of their childhood, half of Erikson's eight stages described psychosocial needs after puberty. His most famous book, *Childhood and Society* (1963), devoted only two pages to each adult stage, but published and unpublished elaborations in later works led to a much richer depiction (Hoare, 2002).

Identity versus Role Diffusion
Although the identity crisis was originally set for adolescence, Erikson realized that identity concerns could be lifelong. Identity combines values and traditions from childhood with the current social context. Since contexts keep evolving, many adults reassess all four types of identity (sexual/gender, vocational/work, religious/spiritual, and political/ethnic).

Intimacy versus Isolation
Adults seek intimacy—a close, reciprocal connection with another human being. Intimacy is mutual, not self-absorbed, which means that adults need to devote time and energy to one other. This process begins in emerging adulthood and continues lifelong. Isolation is especially likely when divorce or death disrupts established intimate relationships.

Generativity versus Stagnation
Adults need to care for the next generation, either by raising their own children or by mentoring, teaching, and helping younger people. Erikson's first description of this stage focused on parenthood, but later he included other ways to achieve generativity. Adults extend the legacy of their culture and their generation with ongoing care, creativity, and sacrifice.

Integrity versus Despair
When Erikson himself was in his 70s, he decided that integrity, with the goal of combating prejudice and helping all humanity, was too important to be left to the elderly. He also thought that each person's entire life could be directed toward connecting a personal journey with the historical and cultural purpose of human society, the ultimate achievement of integrity.

generativity. Some write about *affiliation and achievement,* others *affection and instrumentality,* or *interdependence and independence,* or *communion and agency,* or *love/belonging and success/esteem.*

Each of these pairs has a somewhat different meaning, but all developmentalists realize that, as Freud (1935) succinctly put it, a healthy adult is one who can "love and work," as illustrated by the following feature.

a case to study

She "Began to Make a New Life on Her Own"

Linda was a client of therapist James Marcia, famous for interpreting the identity crisis. She had never established her own identity, and thus intimacy was difficult and generative work and parenthood were beyond her. Marcia (2002) wrote:

> Linda was the middle of three siblings in a blended family. . . . Although she had grown up Roman Catholic, she had not been at all religious and had never felt this to be an important issue to her. She said that she had been somewhat sexually promiscuous in high school—as a way of gaining attention and affection.
>
> She made several attempts at postsecondary education. The first was a brief stay in nursing school. This had been her mother's plan for her, but Linda found herself uninterested in school as well as unwelcome there. She then made several brief forays into courses in fashion design at two other institutions. . . .
>
> After she defaulted on her higher education, Linda went back to her small hometown and found a job waiting tables. She met and fell in love with Jacqueline, a French Canadian woman. . . . [Then] Linda met Greg, who took it on himself to "rescue" her. . . .
>
> Although she could have moved in with Greg after leaving Jacqueline, Linda decided to leave the whole area and move 3,000 miles away to the Pacific Northwest, to a strange city, and began to make a new life on her own . . . independent from her mother's designs, Jacqueline's demands, and Greg's directions.
>
> Her major issues were relationships and career, both of which had at their base questions of self-esteem. . . . Linda was still emotionally attached to Jacqueline and Greg, neither of whom provided her with any support. Jacqueline had cut off communication, and Greg was unreliable in contacting her and was emotionally unavailable when he did.
>
> *[pp. 23–24]*

As you see, Linda's failure to establish her own sexual, religious, or vocational identity made it difficult for her to move forward with her life. Her problems may be more dramatic than those of most adults, but her "major issues" bedevil adults of all ages—relationships and career, or intimacy and generativity. Linda's progress is described at the end of this chapter.

The Social Clock

Half a century ago, researchers already realized that the biological clock that measures physical aging in children does not apply to adulthood. Many nonbiological factors make one adult's body and brain age more quickly, or more slowly, than those of other people the same age, as emphasized in the previous chapters.

However, although the ticking of the biological clock is muted, adults still seem to check their developmental timing using a **social clock,** a timetable based on social norms (Neugarten & Neugarten, 1986). These norms set "best" ages for men or women to finish school, marry, establish a career, and have children (Greene, 2003; Keith, 1990; Settersten & Hagestad, 1996).

social clock Refers to the idea that the stages of life, and the behaviors "appropriate" to them, are set by social standards rather than by biological maturation. For instance, "middle age" begins when the culture believes it does, rather than at a particular age in all cultures.

The social clock guides adult social expectations for behavior. When people say that a woman is "too young to marry" or a man is "too old to become a father," they are referring to the social clock, not the biological one. Some markers on the social clock have been enacted into law, with minimum ages for driving, drinking, voting, getting married, or signing a mortgage. Cultures expect certain timing of adult transitions. As two psychologists who criticize standards for the expected age of marriage explain:

> Although life cycles are becoming more fluid, people are still at risk for being judged harshly if they do not reach developmental milestones on the timetable set by the social clock (defined by prevailing cultural norms).
>
> *[DePaulo & Morris, 2005]*

➤**Response for People Under 20** (from page 578): Probably not. While many younger people associate certain ages with particular attitudes or accomplishments, few people find those ages significant when they actually live through them.

Culture, Cohort, and SES

The specific ages of the social clock vary from nation to nation. In some South American countries, marriage is legal at age 12 for women and 14 for men. More than half of all new brides in Ecuador, Paraguay, Venezuela, and the Dominican Republic are under age 22 (Fussell & Palloni, 2004). By contrast, Germans cannot legally marry until they are at least 18. Most wait considerably longer; the median age in all of Germany for first marriage is 28 for women and 31 for men (EuroStat, 2006).

Historical conditions affect the social clock as well. In most nations a century ago, women were expected to have a baby before age 20. By contrast, in developed nations today, first births after age 30 are common (Bornstein & Putnick, 2007). For example, in Australia the median age of first birth is 31 (Lee & Gramotnev, 2007).

Beyond national and historical norms, the social clock is powerfully affected by socioeconomic status (SES): The lower the SES, the faster the social clock and the sooner life's major turning points occur, evident between nations as well as within them. Worldwide, many low-SES women still *finish* childbearing by age 30. Indeed, a recent cohort of women in India averaged marriage at age 16 and surgical sterilization (typically after two or three births) at age 26 (Padmadas et al., 2004).

In the United States, low-SES employed men expect to retire five years sooner than those of higher income (Pew Research Center, 2006). Of course, the social clock reflects economic reality as well as culture, since employment is harder to find for poor older men than wealthier ones. Health is also relevant: Disability and illness increase as income falls. Some men may anticipate inability to work or may want a few years of leisure. Cultures set social clocks to reflect reality as well as ideals.

Although many factors influence expectations, everywhere the social clock now moves more slowly and variably. That explains the appearance of "emerging adulthood" and the variation in age of marriage, parenthood, completion of education, and so on. The clock is quieter than it was a few decades ago.

The "Midlife Crisis"

midlife crisis A period of unusual anxiety, radical reexamination, and sudden transformation that is widely associated with middle age but which actually has more to do with developmental history than with chronological age.

If the social timetable is variable, why do people expect an age 40 **midlife crisis,** a time of anxiety and radical change? Midlife crisis is often referenced in popular movies and books. It was described in the *Wall Street Journal* as a time of unhappiness and anxiety for many successful men (Clements, 2005). A 2007 Google search found more than a million sites for "midlife crisis."

The idea of a midlife crisis was popularized 30 years ago, by Gail Sheehy (1976), who referred to the "age 40 crucible," and by Daniel Levinson (1978), who studied midlife men who experienced

> tumultuous struggles within the self and with the external world. . . . Every aspect of their lives comes into question, and they are horrified by much that is revealed. They are full of recriminations against themselves and others.
>
> [p. 199]

Contrary to Levinson and Sheehy, no large study in the United States or elsewhere has found anything like a midlife crisis. Adults quit jobs and abandon spouses, but they are no more likely to do so at age 40 than at any other age. Some adults quit work and leave marriages several times, and other adults never do. Developmentalists are convinced that a midlife crisis is *not* typical for either men or women.

How could earlier developmentalists have been misled? Men who were age 40 in 1970, who provided the data for Levinson and Sheehy, were affected by historical upheavals in their own families, with radically rebellious teenagers (the 60s generation) and suddenly assertive wives (the first wave of feminism). For some, being middle-aged during that era elicited questions and recriminations, creating an existential crisis. But their midlife crises were a result of history, not age.

In the twenty-first century, matching birthdays with stages or crises appears narrow, insensitive, and perhaps racist, classist, and sexist. Why do some people still imagine that a midlife crisis occurs? One theory is that the concept makes people feel better: They expect the worst and are "pleasantly surprised" (Heckhausen, 2001, p. 378). In other words, a midlife myth enables adults to cope with the specific frustrations of growing older and nonetheless feel fortunate.

Personality Throughout Adulthood

Personality is a major source of continuity, providing coherence and identity, allowing people to know themselves and be known (Caspi & Roberts, 1999; Cloninger, 2003). Genes, parental practices, culture, and adult experiences all contribute to personality. Of these four, genes are usually found to be the most influential, according to longitudinal studies of monozygotic and dizygotic twins and other research, but variations are evident (Pedersen et al., 2006).

The Big Five

As already mentioned in Chapter 7, extensive longitudinal, cross-sectional, and multicultural research has discovered basic clusters of personality traits—now referred to as the **Big Five**—that remain quite stable throughout adulthood (Digman, 1990; McCrae & Costa, 2003; Roberts et al., 2006). Although various experts use somewhat different terms to describe these clusters, five dimensions are often described:

Big Five The five basic clusters of personality traits that remain quite stable throughout adulthood: openness, conscientiousness, extroversion, agreeableness, and neuroticism.

- Openness—imaginative, curious, artistic, creative, open to new experiences
- Conscientiousness—organized, deliberate, conforming, self-disciplined
- Extroversion—outgoing, assertive, active
- Agreeableness—kind, helpful, easygoing, generous
- Neuroticism—anxious, moody, self-punishing, critical

Personality tests assess whether a person is high or low on each of these five dimensions (arranged here to spell the word *ocean,* to facilitate memory). Personality traits correlate with almost every aspect of adulthood, not only expected career choices and health habits but even college (conscientious people are more likely to graduate), marriage (extroverts do it more), and divorce (correlates with neuroticism) (Duckworth et al., 2007; Pedersen et al., 2006). Paradoxically, when discontinuity occurs, the continuity of personality becomes especially apparent. Under stress, people react in ways that reflect their distinctive traits.

Beginning in early adulthood, people choose a setting, called their **ecological niche,** that tends to stabilize their personality. Adults select vocations, neighborhoods, mates, and routines that led two researchers to quip, "Ask not how life's experiences change personality; ask instead how personality shapes lives" (McCrae & Costa, 2003, p. 235). This may be why personality is particularly stable from age 30 to 50 (Roberts et al., 2006).

ecological niche The particular lifestyle and social context that adults settle into because that setting is compatible with their individual personality needs and interests.

A hypothetical example helps clarify the ecological niche. A person high in extroversion is likely to find an outgoing mate. The couple's social life would include many friends and acquaintances, who would enjoy going to parties and

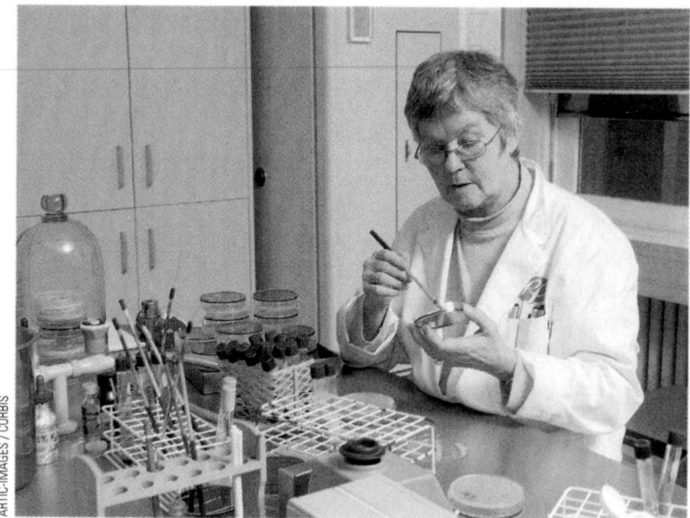

ARTIC-IMAGES / CORBIS

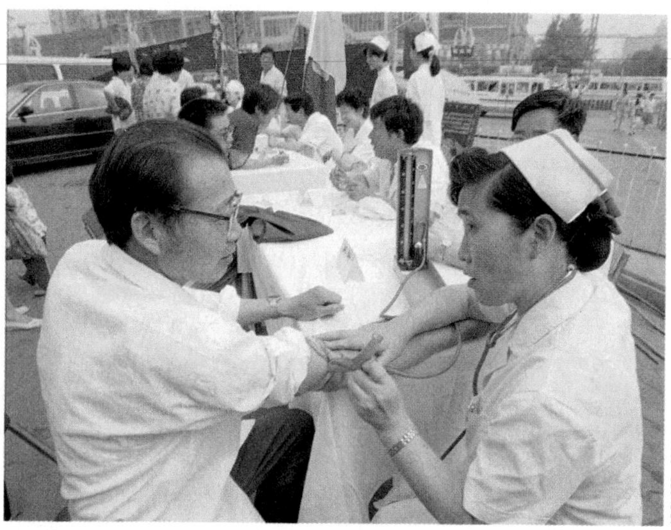

AP PHOTO / GREG BAKER

The Same Event, A Thousand Miles Apart: Culture or Personality? Personality is more evident here than is culture, according to research on the ecological niche. The women in both of these photographs studied biology, but the more introverted one in Iceland *(left)* prefers to analyze samples of fish tissue on her own, while the more extroverted one in China *(right)* takes blood pressure readings in a city square.

other gatherings. An extrovert's chosen career would require extensive social interaction (perhaps in sales, politics, or public relations). Niche-building would situate this couple in a busy neighborhood close to their sports league, political club, and religious group.

After 20 years together, this couple would have more friends and several children (extroverts tend to have large families), who would also have many friends (inheriting temperament from their parents). The couple would lead Parent–Teacher Associations, Scouts, Little League, and so on. Thus, their extroversion would be increasingly expressed as well as rewarded with social acclaim.

Although personality certainly begins with genes and is manifest in the decisions that form the ecological niche, adult personality can shift if the context shifts. For example, choosing a warm, supportive spouse affects the personality of the person who made that choice. Although those high in neuroticism are less likely to find an affectionate, loyal mate, if they do so, they become less neurotic (Rönkä et al., 2002). Hostile workplaces, ill health, and poverty—if experienced—affect personalities.

If life circumstances are dramatically altered (perhaps by divorce or widowhood, recovery from addiction, emigration, a treated depression, a disabling disease), people may behave in new ways (Mroczek et al., 2006). More often, new events bring out old personality patterns (McCrae & Costa, 2003; Roberts & Caspi, 2003). As two researchers note:

> People undoubtedly do change across the life span. Marriages end in divorce, professional careers are started in mid-life, fashions and attitudes change with the times. Yet often the same traits can be seen in new guises: Intellectual curiosity merely shifts from one field to another, avid gardening replaces avid tennis, one abusive relationship is followed by another. Many of these changes are best regarded as variations on the "uniform tune" played by individuals' enduring dispositions.
>
> *[McCrae & Costa, 1994, p. 174]*

People are often quite unaware of their distinctive characteristics, unless a particular trait (such as a violent temper) is one they seek to change. In describing their past personality and predicting their future one, college students imagine marked improvements (Haslam et al., 2007). When asked whether their personalities had changed since young adulthood, middle-aged adults usually say yes, believing they have improved more than the data suggest (Lachman & Bertrand, 2001).

Only small improvement occurs, on average. The MIDUS study of midlife (see Chapter 20, page 548) found that, of the Big Five, agreeableness and conscientiousness increased slightly in adulthood and that openness and neuroticism decreased (Lachman & Bertrand, 2001). Other research confirms this finding (Pulkkinen et al., 2005; Schaie, 2005). Although the average North American becomes a little less neurotic with maturity, those high in this trait at age 30 are still high at age 60 compared with other 60-year-olds.

Culture and Personality

The Big Five are also found in many other nations, again with relatively slight age-related trends (McCrae et al., 1999; McCrae & Allik, 2002; Schmitt et al., 2007). National and political upheavals have almost no impact. For example, East and West Germany experienced radically different political systems from 1945 to 1995, but that did not seem to affect basic personality patterns (Bode, 2003). Overall, personality variations are more evident between one person and another in the same nation than between one nation and another.

However, there do seem to be some national differences in the proportions of people within each nation who are high or low in each of the Big Five. A sixth personality dimension, known as dependence on others, is significant in Asia (Hofstede, 2007). Worldwide, adults strive to express those traits that are valued within their culture. For instance, a survey of 52 nations found that conscientiousness may be particularly valued in China, extroversion in Australia, openness in the United States, and agreeableness in the Philippines (McCrae & Allik, 2002; Schmitt et al., 2007).

We need to be careful with national stereotypes, however. Similarities are more apparent than differences. A case in point is that, although people tend to believe that Canadians are agreeable and U.S. citizens are anxious, assessments of personality in both nations show very similar distributions of these traits (McCrae & Terracciano, 2006).

If people are similar worldwide, why do stereotypes emerge? Perhaps people equate national policies with personality. For instance, "Canadians are proud of their benevolent universal health care system; Americans defiantly cherish their right to bear arms" (McCrae & Terracciano, 2006, p. 160). But policies are more a result of national history than of national personality. Canadian agreeableness and U.S. neuroticism are more myth than reality.

Gender Convergence

Reality may clash with stereotypes in gender as well. Men tend to express aggression and women nurturance; men take more risks and women are more cautious. Expression may differ, but that does not mean that underlying traits differ. On the Big Five, young men are only slightly more extroverted and young women slightly more conscientious, and the two sexes probably become even more similar as they mature, a phenomenon known as **gender convergence** (Gutmann, 1994).

gender convergence A tendency for men and women to become more similar as they move through middle age.

Gender convergence seemed evident, for example, in one longitudinal study that began with a representative sample of all the third-grade children in Finland and then followed them for 30 years (Pulkkinen et al., 2005). The Big Five scales had not been developed when this study began, but other personality measures found that, by age 42, the men had become less aggressive and more conforming while the opposite was true for the women. Scores on these two personality traits differed for the two sexes in adolescence but were almost identical by middle age.

Gender convergence in middle age has been described by Erikson and many others (Hoare, 2002). The psychoanalyst Carl Jung theorized that everyone has both a masculine and a feminine side but that young adults express only those traits

PETER HORREE / ALAMY

JOSE LUIS PELAEZ, INC. / CORBIS

The Same Event, A Thousand Miles Apart: Caregiving Dads Fathers are often caregivers for their young children, as shown here in the United States *(left)* and Indonesia *(right)*. Most developmentalists think that men have always nurtured their children, although in modern times employed mothers, plastic bottles, and sturdy baby carriers are among the specifics that have changed.

Observation Quiz (see answer, page 586): Is the man on the left really sleeping?

that "belong" to their own gender. Thus, young women strive to be more tender and deferential than they might naturally be, while young men try to be brave and assertive even when they feel afraid. Eventually, adults realize that

> the achievements which society rewards are won at the cost of a diminution of personality. Many—far too many—aspects of life which should have been experienced lie in the lumber-room among dusty memories.
>
> *[Jung, 1933, p. 104]*

Jung believed that adults eventually come to explore the *shadow side* of their personality—women, their repressed masculine traits and men, their repressed feminine traits.

Evidence for convergence can be found internationally. In every nation, warriors tend to be young men while caregivers tend to be young women. By late adulthood, older men are supposed to be judges and peacemakers and older women can be more assertive. Particularly in Asia, young women are expected to

AP PHOTO / DAVID GUTTENFELDER

From Warrior to Peacemaker Ariel Sharon joined the Haganah (a Jewish underground military organization that some called a terrorist group) when he was 14, earning a reputation as a brave commando. He served in the Israeli army until he was 45. Elected prime minister in 2001 at age 62, he became known as a champion of peace. He is shown here praying at the Western Wall in Jerusalem.

be submissive to their husbands and mothers-in-law, but older women are free to be dominant. Similarly, young Asian men are expected to be active, but older men are expected to be more meditative (Menon, 2001). A similar developmental shift may be evident in the West—if the stereotype of the bossy mother-in-law and the fun-loving grandfather reflect reality, not just prejudice.

SUMMING UP

Adulthood is the time for two universally acknowledged psychosocial needs. Developmentalists have many names for these: Erikson called them intimacy and generativity. Although originally Erikson thought generativity followed intimacy, both are sought throughout adulthood. In current times, the social clock is not as rigid as it was, and no midlife crisis seems to occur.

Personality characteristics have been clustered into the Big Five: openness, conscientiousness, extroversion, agreeableness, and neuroticism. Each individual in every culture is relatively high or low on each of these traits. Enduring traits become especially evident in the individual's reaction to unexpected or disruptive life events. Cultural, gender, and developmental differences may be found in the levels of the Big Five (over the years, neuroticism and openness may decrease slightly while agreeableness and conscientiousness may increase), but similarities are far more evident than differences. The two genders may move toward convergence in personality as adulthood progresses. ■

Intimacy

Intimacy needs are lifelong. As you remember from Chapter 19, adults meet their need for social connection with relatives, friends, coworkers, and romantic partners. Each adult gathers a specific set of personal relationships: Some adults are distant from their parents and close to partners and friends; others are close to their family members but not to any nonrelatives. Such variation is affected by culture, age, and circumstances. For example, as parents become elderly, family roles change. With time, friendships and marriages begin, continue, or end.

Each person has a **social convoy,** a group of people who "provide a protective layer of social relations to guide, encourage, and socialize individuals as they go through life" (Antonucci et al., 2001, p. 572). Convoys originally referred to protective groups, such as the pioneers in ox-drawn wagons headed for California or soldiers marching across unfamiliar terrain. In those examples, each individual was strengthened by being part of the convoy as well as buoyed by sharing the same conditions (hunger, cold, fear) with others. The social convoy works in the same way as people move through life (Crosnoe & Elder, 2002). Isolation is harmful, companionship is beneficial, and intimacy appears in many ways.

social convoy Collectively, the family members, friends, acquaintances, and even strangers who move through life with an individual.

Friends

Friends are typically the most supportive members of the social convoy, partly because they are chosen for the very traits that make them reliable fellow travelers through life. They are usually about the same age, with similar experiences and values, and thus they are a source of help and advice when serious problems—death of a family member, personal illness, loss of a job—arise.

Perhaps equally important, in daily life friends provide companionship, information, and laughter, helping each adult figure out how to get a child to eat his carrots, whether to remodel or replace the kitchen cabinets, what to do when a boss asks for coffee, or, as time goes on, how to deal with college children, menopause, or retirement.

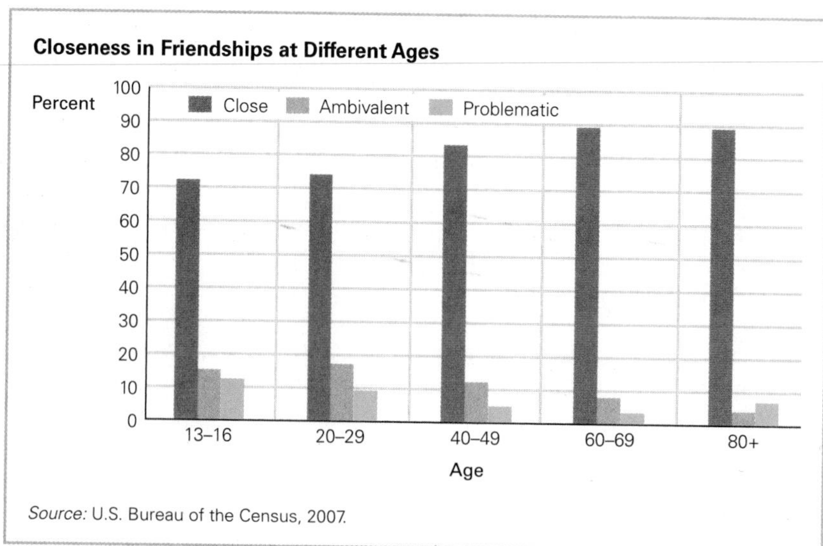

FIGURE 22.1

Good Friends In a survey in which people of various ages rated their relationships as close, ambivalent, or problematic, friends overall scored highest on closeness, with fewer ambivalent or problematic relationships. One reason that friendships seem to improve with age, of course, is that friends are chosen. If a particular friendship is problematic over time, that friendship may end.

Observation Quiz (see answer, page 588): At what age are virtually no friendships problematic?

A comprehensive research study (Fingerman et al., 2004) found that friendships tend to improve with age. As you see from Figure 22.1, friendships were usually rated as "close" by adolescents and emerging adults, but a significant minority of young people considered their friendships "ambivalent" or "problematic." By adulthood, almost all friendships are close, few are ambivalent, almost none are problematic. (Ironically, the same research found that more than half of the adults felt their relationship to their spouse was ambivalent or problematic.)

Protection Against Stress

Many psychologists have studied the effects of stress on adult development (Aldwin, 2007). Life is stress-filled, including both major stressors, such as a parent's serious illness, disability, or death and one's own employment crisis, and ongoing hassles, such as commuting to work, helping children with homework, paying bills, and hearing criticism. The total burden of stress and disease carried by each person is called **allostatic load.** A large allostatic load increases the risk of major disease, premature aging, and death (Geronimus et al., 2006). Friends can play an important role in alleviating some of the stress adults face.

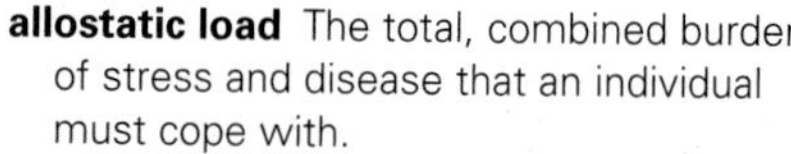
allostatic load The total, combined burden of stress and disease that an individual must cope with.

Both age and gender affect how a person responds to stress and thus affect allostatic load (Aldwin, 2007). Younger adults tend to be more *problem-focused,* attacking the issue directly. For example, if their work situation is difficult, they quit their job, complain to their boss, transfer to another location, or find some other way to solve the problem. Older adults tend to be more *emotion-focused.* For example, in a stressful work context, they might cope by reminding themselves that the boss's opinions are uninformed or singing as they perform an unpleasant task or joking with a coworker. They change their thinking and their feelings, not their jobs.

Men often respond to stress in problem-focused "fight-or-flight" manner. Their sympathetic nervous systems (faster heart rate, increased adrenaline) prepare them for attack or escape. Women may be more emotion-focused, likely to "tend and befriend," as their bodies produce oxytocin, a hormone that leads them to seek confidential and caring interactions (Taylor, 2006; Taylor et al., 2000).

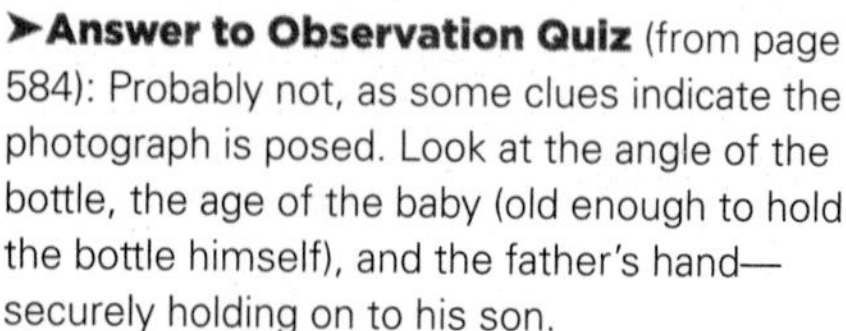
➤**Answer to Observation Quiz** (from page 584): Probably not, as some clues indicate the photograph is posed. Look at the angle of the bottle, the age of the baby (old enough to hold the bottle himself), and the father's hand—securely holding on to his son.

Problem- and emotion-focused coping are each effective in some situations; all adults need to fight sometimes and to befriend at others. Friends help adults cope in two crucial ways. First, they help analyze the situation, giving advice about the most effective responses. Second, companionship reduces cortisol, the stress hormone, which is one reason people call each other and gather together whenever tragedy occurs. Thus, having close friends helps with both physical and psychological health, reducing allostatic load (Krause, 2006).

Gender Differences

Many gender differences in friendship were already discussed in Chapter 19, and these differences continue in adulthood. Same-sex as well as opposite-sex friendships are valuable lifelong, although many married partners are suspicious of friendships, especially when a wife has a close friendship with another man. Partly for this reason, married adults tend to have fewer personal friends than unmarried adults, although many couples develop "couple friends," who are other married couples with whom they socialize.

This scarcity of personal friends may be unwise. Two psychologists explain:

> Adults in couples look to each other for companionship, sexual intimacy, soulmatery, coparenting, economic partnership, advice, sharing of household tasks, and just about everything else. . . . No mere mortal should be expected graciously and lovingly to fulfill every important role to another human.
>
> *[DePaulo & Morris, 2005, pp. 76, 77]*

Men often rely on their wives for companionship. That may explain some of the data on health that were reviewed in Chapter 20. Adult men who have recently been divorced or widowed are more likely to die than are women in the same circumstances. Men without wives tend to die of stress-related causes—heart attacks, drug abuse, and suicide. Friendless men and women are vulnerable to stress, illness, and depression.

linked lives The notion that family members tend to share all aspects of each other's lives, from triumph to tragedy.

household A group of people who live together in one dwelling and share its common spaces, such as kitchen and living room.

Family Bonds

No other group system has replaced the family in any nation or century, although the form taken by "family" varies among different cultures (Georgas et al., 2006). Family members are an important part of the social convoy. They tend to have **linked lives,** which means that each person's triumphs and tragedies are shared by everyone (Elder et al., 2003).

As already noted in Chapter 13, *family* should not be confused with **household**—who are people who live in the same dwelling. Increasingly, adults live apart from their parents. This is reflected in the decrease in the size of U.S. households. As Figure 22.2 shows, more than half of the U.S. population today live alone or with one other person, usually a spouse.

Living in separate households does not necessarily weaken family ties. A seven-nation study found that, whether they share a household or not, adults provide substantial help to other family members, ranging from advice and emotional support to gifts, loans, babysitting, home repair, and health care (Connidis, 2001; Farkas & Hogan, 1995). A large U.S. study found that, if anything, relationships between parents and adult children worsen when they live *together,* especially since the reason is usually that the children are unable to live on their own (Ward & Spitze, 2007).

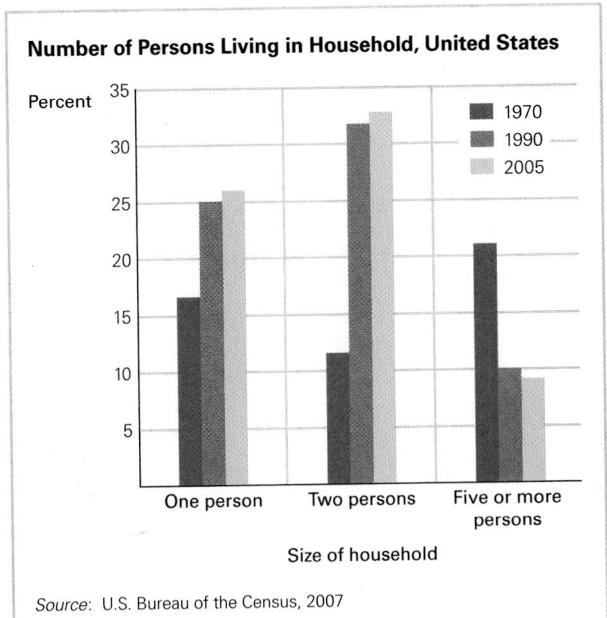

FIGURE 22.2

The Shrinking U.S. Household As the U.S. population has become less rural, less married, and longer living, the average household has gotten smaller.

A Developmental View

Parents and adult children typically increase in closeness, forgiveness, and pride as both generations gain maturity (Connidis, 2001). Current cohorts of younger

TRUJILLO-PAUMIER / STONE / GETTY IMAGES

DIGITAL VISION / GETTY IMAGES

Like Parent, Like Child Even when a child becomes bigger than a parent, as is evident with this Mexican son and California daughter, parents and adult children continue to admire each other.

adults often have friendly relationships with their parents, partly because the parents are usually healthy, active, and independent. Some of this is cultural: In North America, western Europe, and Australia, adults cherish their independence and dread burdening other generations; in most Asian and African nations that is not the case (Harvey & Yoshino, 2006).

The specifics depend on many factors, including childhood attachments, cultural norms, and the financial and practical resources of each generation. A particularly influential variable is **familism,** the belief that family members should care for each other, sacrificing personal freedom and success to do so. Members of some families believe they should always help each other, even if a relative is drug-addicted, abusive, or wanted by the law. Other families believe that adults should be independent and that those who have violated social standards do not deserve to be protected from their own mistakes.

familism The idea that family members should support one another because family unity is more important than individual freedom and success.

Health, single parenthood, and poverty also affect the likelihood of family members supporting each other. In many nations, immigrants and members of minority groups are more likely to live in three-generation households for practical as well as cultural reasons (Burr & Mutchler, 1999).

When adult children have serious problems—financial, legal, marital, and so on—their parents' overall well-being is also likely to suffer, as does the parent–child relationship. This is particularly true for middle-aged parents with no marriage partner to buffer their disappointment with their offspring (Greenfield & Marks, 2006).

Adult Siblings

Although only about one-third of adolescents consider themselves close to their siblings, two-thirds of adults do, as do almost all of the oldest adults (Fingerman et al., 2004) (see Figure 22.3). Adult siblings help each other with their teenage children, stressful marriages, and elderly relatives.

➤**Answer to Observation Quiz** (from page 586): Age 60 to 69.

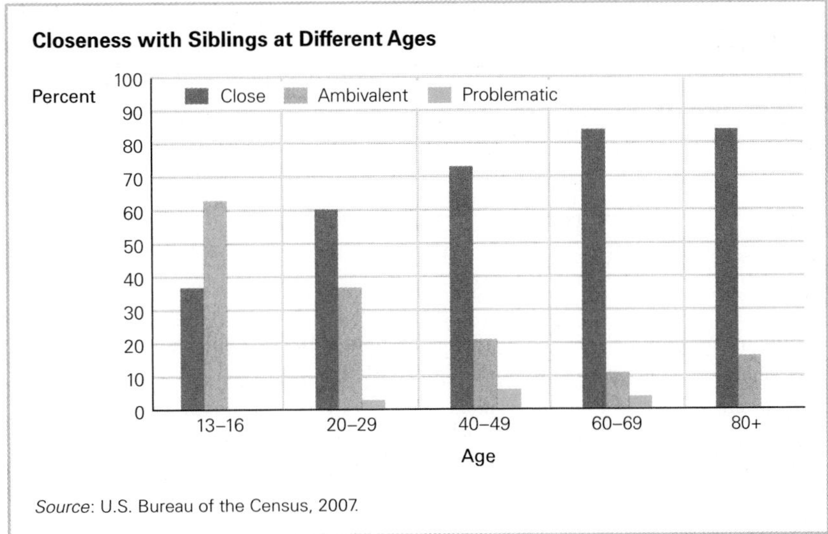

FIGURE 22.3

From Rival to Friend Adolescents are not usually close to their siblings, but that often changes with time. By late adulthood, brothers and sisters usually consider each other among their best friends.

Particularly in large families subject to stresses (for example, poverty, divorce, prejudice), siblings are connected throughout life. In adolescence, they may criticize each other, and in emerging adulthood many strive for independence. Then they become closer. One researcher described the usual sibling relationship as an hourglass: close during childhood, increasingly distant during adolescence and early adulthood, then closer together again, especially if a sibling's marriage ends (Bedford, 1995).

The possibility of adult sibling closeness is demonstrated by one woman who lived thousands of miles from her two brothers and two sisters but said:

> I have a good relationship with my brothers. . . . Every time I come they are very warm and loving, and I stayed with my brother for a week. . . . Sisters is another story. Sisters are best friends. Sisters is like forever. When I have a problem, I phone my sisters. When I'm feeling down, I phone my sisters. And they always pick me up.
>
> *[quoted in Connidis, 2007, p. 488]*

Some adults keep their distance from their blood relatives, perhaps becoming **fictive kin** in another family; that is, becoming accepted and treated like a family member. Fictive kin are usually brought into a family by a peer who considers them like a brother or sister, and then they are gradually accepted by the rest of the family. Especially for people rejected by their family of origin (perhaps because of their sexual orientation) or far from home (perhaps an immigrant), being "adopted" by a new family is beneficial (Ebaugh & Curry, 2000; Muraco, 2006).

fictive kin A term used to describe someone who becomes accepted as part of a family to which he or she has no blood relation.

Siblings' relationships can be strained if a parent becomes frail and needs care. One (and only one) sibling usually becomes the chief caregiver. The inequity of one sibling becoming the primary caregiver may be resented by other siblings. For example, in one family, the caregiving sister described one of her two siblings as "real immature . . . a little slow" and the other as "very irresponsible," adding, "When it came right down to having to bathe and having to take care of physical [tasks], neither of them would be able to handle it" (quoted in Ingersoll-Dayton et al., 2003, p. 209). A brother in another family resented his caregiving sister. "My sister reminds me all the time that she's taking care of them. They're actually pretty self-sufficient" (quoted in Ingersoll-Dayton et al., 2003, pp. 208–209).

The reality is that linked lives mean that everyone in the family, caregiver or not, is strained when a family member becomes ill or disabled (Amirkhanyan & Wolf, 2006). Old jealousies and resentments can reemerge as readily as old patterns of support, as I saw with my mother's siblings.

in person

Childhood Echoes

My mother and father were raised by their immigrant parents with a strong sense of familism. When I was 6 years old, my family moved to Pennsylvania, far from our Minnesota home. We kept in contact with the relatives back in the Midwest; we often visited aunts, uncles, and cousins. Later, when my parents retired, they decided not to go to sunny Arizona or Florida (where some of their friends had gone), but back to snowy Minnesota, near their 15 siblings. They returned to their linked lives.

Once they were surrounded by their siblings, I heard more about sibling support and rivalry. One of my aunts, a widow, apparently had developed a serious drinking problem. My mother and I were worried at first, but then I learned that two of my uncles, her brothers, had intervened. I had never known that they had been early members of Alcoholics Anonymous, but I quickly understood that they could help their sister when she needed it. They did, and she quit drinking.

My mother became distressed when her sisters Harriet and Laura became so angry at each other that they stopped speaking. Dumbfounded that aging siblings could hold a grudge, I asked my mother what the fight was about.

"It began long ago," Mom explained. "Papa favored Laura. She's the pretty one."

My mother's father died long before I was born, and the only difference I could see between my aunts was that Aunt Laura's eyes were blue and Aunt Harriet's were brown. Neither was "the pretty one" any longer; each had warmth and sparkle, but both were overweight and wore thick glasses.

Outside intervention can help resolve family conflict at any age, especially if it comes from someone who is part of the social convoy. My father told each of my aunts, individually, that the other really missed her and wished they were talking again. Harriet and Laura were both pleased to hear that the other was sorry, and each said she missed her sister. They resumed daily phone conversations several months before Laura died. As I watched the family dynamics, I understood why my parents had retired to their childhood home.

Marriage

As detailed earlier, people in every nation take longer than previous generations did to make a public commitment to one long-term sexual partner. Nonetheless, although specifics differ (in some cultures, age 18 is "late" to marry), adults still seek committed sexual partnerships to help meet their needs for intimacy as well as to raise children, share resources, and provide care.

U.S. statistics show that less than 3 percent marry before age 20, but by age 40, 85 percent have married (U.S. Bureau of the Census, 2007). Of those 15 percent not yet married, about a third have been cohabiting for years with a romantic partner. Probably only about 10 percent of adults now living in the United States will never make a marriage-like commitment.

That minority is even smaller in other nations and in prior centuries. Only 4 percent of U.S. residents now over age 65 have never been married (U.S. Bureau of the Census, 2007). They are not necessarily lonely or unhappy; they meet their intimacy needs in other ways (DePaulo, 2006).

Marriage and Happiness

From a developmental perspective, marriage is useful. Adults thrive if another person is committed to caring for them, children benefit when they have two parents legally and emotionally dedicated to them, societies benefit if individuals sort themselves into families. Generally, married people are a little happier, healthier, and richer than unmarried ones of the same age and background.

But not that much happier. When married adults are compared with those who have never married, their advantage is slight. Indeed, a survey of adults in 16 nations found one nation (Portugal) where single people were happier than married ones, another (France) where both groups were equal, and several where married adults were only slightly more often "very happy" than ones who never married. The largest differences were in the United States, where more married people than single people were "very happy" (37 versus 26 percent) (Inglehart, 1990).

One major factor affecting marital happiness is how old the newlyweds were. If a couple wed as teenagers, they are likely to be more depressed, more violent, and less educated than those who marry later (Glick et al., 2006; Teti et al., 1987).

Generally speaking, longitudinal research on individuals before and during long-term marriages finds that people tend to become happier during the honeymoon period (a year or so), with husbands tending throughout to be more pleased with marriage than are wives (Kiecolt-Glaser & Newton, 2001; Lucas et al., 2001). Adults between ages 25 and 40 are more likely to be pleased with their marriages than are adults at other ages (Lucas & Dyrenforth, 2005).

Another major factor is the quality of the relationship (Kiecolt-Glaser & Newton, 2001). In a large longitudinal study, those who stayed married tended to be slightly happier than those who did not. But there is a caveat:

> There were as many people who ended up less happy than they started as there were people who ended up happier than they started (a fact that is particularly striking given that we restricted the sample to people who stayed married).
>
> *[Lucas et al., 2003, p. 536]*

Thus, most adults will marry and will expect ongoing happiness because of it, but some will be disappointed (Coontz, 2005). This leads to the next two topics—how a marriage can get better over time and what happens after divorce.

Long-Term Marriage

Some of the long-term quality of a marriage relationship is affected by family relationships in childhood (Overbeek et al., 2007), some by factors explained in Chapter 19 (homogamy, cohabitation before marriage), and some by the Big Five traits described earlier in this chapter. In addition, there are reasons why adults find that marriages improve with time.

Older couples have less child-rearing stress (young children tend to increase marital dissatisfaction), fewer arguments, higher incomes, and more time together. In fact, in a survey of long-married people, most of them said they stayed married because of the love, trust, and joy in their partner, not primarily because it was difficult to break up (Previti & Amato, 2003). The **empty nest**—so named because it is the time when the children have gone, launched into their own lives—is often a happy time for a married couple, who now can spend time together again.

empty nest A time in the lives of parents when their grown children leave the family home to pursue their own lives.

There are also reasons for dissatisfaction during the course of a marriage. Marriages take work; wedded bliss is not guaranteed. Children cause financial pressure and provoke arguments about child-rearing assumptions that parents may not have known they held. If the couple married only because of sexual passion, then the other two parts of love (intimacy and commitment) may not appear.

Especially for Young Couples Suppose you are one-half of a turbulent relationship in which moments of intimacy alternate with episodes of abuse. Should you break up?

Fortunately, the advantages and disadvantages of marriage seem to balance each other out. Comparing marriages in recent decades with marriages of previous decades (Amato et al., 2007) reveals that husbands are now doing more housework, which makes them somewhat less happy but their wives happier, and more wives are employed, which eases financial stress but reduces time together. Although husbands and wives are each more independent today than they were in the past, marital satisfaction is as high as earlier.

ROLF BRUDERER / BLEND / JUPITER IMAGES

GARETH BROWN / CORBIS

The Same Event, A Thousand Miles Apart: More Than Yesterday Some older couples worldwide experience greater joy in being together than when they were younger. Culture influences the form of expression, not the level of affection.

Some marriages bring notable improvement to a person's life. One example comes from a longitudinal study of all the newborns of five distinct ethnicities born in 1955 in Kauai, Hawaii. As children, they had many health and family problems. By age 40, most were happier and more successful than was predicted. A marriage before age 30 that endured over the years was one of the best sources of resilience and satisfaction (Werner & Smith, 2001). Similar findings have been reported by researchers in many other nations (Rönkä et al., 2002; Rutter, 2004).

Of course, generalities obscure specifics. Some long-term marriages are blissful; others are horrific. Economic stress creates marital friction, no matter how many years a couple has been together (Conger et al., 1999), and contextual factors can undermine a couple's willingness to communicate and compromise (Karney & Bradbury, 2005). A long-standing relationship might crumble, especially with major financial and relationship stresses (such as demanding in-laws or angry children).

The opposite is also true: A relationship might improve with time. Several leading researchers (Fincham et al., 2007) cite evidence that many marriages are stressful and then rebound, with unhappy spouses becoming happy again as they learn to understand and forgive each other.

Homosexual Partners

Almost everything just described applies to homosexual partners as well as to heterosexual ones (Herek, 2006). Some same-sex couples are very supportive of each other, and their emotional well-being benefits from their interaction. Others are conflicted, with problems of finances, communication, and so on that resemble those of traditional marriages.

Partly because political and cultural contexts for homosexual couples are changing markedly, research on homosexual couples done 20 years ago may not be accurate today. Current research with a large, randomly selected sample of gay

➤**Response for Young Couples** (from page 591): There is no simple answer, but you should bear in mind that, while abuse usually decreases with age, breakups become more difficult with every year, especially if children are involved.

TABLE 22.2

Number of Unmarried Partner Households in the United States*

	Male/Female	Male/Male	Female/ Female	Total homosexual couples
2000	4,881,377	301,026	293,365	594,391
2004	5,133,637	374,397	332,799	707,196
Increase from 2000 to 2004: Number and Percent				
	252,260 (5%)	73,371 (24%)	39,434 (14%)	112,805 (19%)

*Officially declared.
Source: U.S. Bureau of the Census, 2002, 2007.

How Many Homosexual Couples? The 19 percent increase is probably the result of more gay and lesbian couples being willing to declare themselves in official U.S. statistics. It is not known how many more such couples are still undeclared. The 5 percent jump among heterosexuals may indicate increased willingness to publicly acknowledge their status, or it may reflect a genuine shift in the committed couples who do not want to marry. However, since the homosexual increase is four times as high as the heterosexual one, there were probably many undeclared gay and lesbian cohabitants in 2000 who were braver in 2004.

and lesbian couples is not yet available. It is not even known how many such couples there are. According to the U.S. Bureau of the Census (2007), only 0.6 percent (about 1 in 150) of households are headed by a homosexual couple. All gay and lesbian groups, and most social scientists, consider this an underestimate.

One reason this may be an underestimate is that homosexual couples were uncounted until recently, and many such couples are still reluctant to proclaim their status. Evidence for an undercount comes from data published by the Bureau of the Census. No official count of homosexual couples was available until 2000 because before that year an "unmarried couple" was defined as a cohabiting man and woman. Now "unmarried partners" are allowed to specify male/female, male/male, or female/female.

U.S. data (see Table 22.2) over four years show a 19 percent increase in homosexual couples (U.S. Bureau of the Census, 2002, 2007), a jump suggesting that more homosexual couples are willing to declare themselves. The next data wave will reveal whether the number continues to increase.

One recently published study of 5,000 adults (more than 1,000 each of the four kinds of couples—gay, lesbian, heterosexual unmarried, heterosexual married) found that, in most ways, the four kinds of couples were very similar (Kurdek, 2006; see Research Design). For instance, there were no significant differences in overall satisfaction with the relationship or in distribution of household chores. (Married heterosexuals with children were less equitable in household labor, but similar in satisfaction.)

The greatest difference among the types of child-free couples was in acceptance by their parents. Fathers were less likely to treat the mates of their homosexual children "like family" than the mates of their married heterosexual children. (Parental acceptance of cohabiting heterosexual partners was halfway between the two.) Homosexual couples scored higher on contact with friends. Apparently, these couples met their intimacy needs in somewhat different ways. Other research on homosexual couples also finds more similarities than differences between them and heterosexuals (Herek, 2006).

Research Design

Scientist: Lawrence Kurdek.

Publication: *Journal of Marriage and Family* (2006).

Participants: More than 5,000 couples (10,000 individuals) from Seattle, San Francisco, and New York filled out questionnaires for a study (Blumstein & Schwartz, 1983). Two-thirds of the couples provided follow-up data, via interviews or questionnaires. All the couples were volunteers.

Design: The Kurdek (2006) research analyzed data from that 1983 study to compare four types of couples without children (gay, lesbian, heterosexual unmarried, heterosexual married) and one type with children (married heterosexual). Data were collected on measures thought to predict couple satisfaction and stability (predispositions, social support, attitudes, interactions).

Major conclusions: The differences between the types of couples were quite small, especially when the homosexual couples were compared with the heterosexual cohabiting couples. Of the five, the most different group was the married heterosexuals with children, who were least likely to separate. Parents accepted the married partners significantly more than the cohabiting ones of any sexual orientation.

Comments: This study is noteworthy for comparing many homosexual and heterosexual couples. However, as the author recognizes, there were two serious drawbacks: (1) The couples were questioned 25 years ago, and (2) they selected themselves. Results may differ for recent couples, randomly selected.

Divorce

Throughout this text, developmental events that seem isolated, personal, and transitory are shown to be interconnected and socially mediated, with enduring consequences. Divorce is a prime example. Marriages never improve or end in a vacuum; they are influenced by the social and political context (Fine & Harvey, 2006).

Divorced adults are often affected (for better or for worse) in ways they never anticipated. The negative impacts tend to be greater as more years of marriage precede the divorce. Decades after divorce, the couple's income, family welfare, and self-esteem tend to be lower, on average, than those of nondivorced adults (married or single) of the same age. When the divorced couple have children, the separation is harder on the adults (Amato & Cheadle, 2005).

Although divorce is always stressful for adults and children, it is also sometimes beneficial. According to results in 39 nations, adults whose parents fought constantly but stayed married report less happiness than those with equally conflicted parents who divorced (Gohm et al., 1998). Much depends on the community and other relatives, who can punish (inadvertently) or support the children of divorce. This helps explain a curious phenomenon: African American marriages are more likely to end in divorce or separation, but the children are less troubled by it than are European American children whose parents split up (Fomby & Cherlin, 2007).

Divorce Rates

The power of the social context is evident in variations in divorce rates. In the United States, almost one out of every two marriages ends in divorce, a rate matched by several other nations. Compared to a decade ago, marriage rates have decreased and divorce rates have increased in almost every developed nation. Even in Ireland and Italy, where the divorce rate used to be close to zero, about one in every seven marriages now ends in divorce (see Figure 22.4).

Historical variations are more marked than national ones. In many countries (including the United States), divorces increased markedly in the 1970s. New laws allowed many long-troubled marriages to end. Rates have been stable, or even declining, since then. About half of the teenage marriages before 1970 that ended in divorce were precipitated by pregnancy. This is no longer the case (Wolfinger, 2005).

Social scientists have many explanations for divorce, as listed in Table 22.3. In addition, economists suggest that the marriage rate is falling because of lower income for young men and more employment for women. Since the divorce rate is calculated by dividing the number of divorces by the number of marriages, fewer marriages mean an increase in the rate of divorce even with no change in the number of divorces. Stress of all kinds, particularly chronic financial pressure, reduces a couple's ability to discuss their problems and forgive each other's faults (Karney & Bradbury, 2005).

Over the Years, Divorce and Remarriage

Divorce is most likely to occur within the first five years after a wedding. Divorced individuals usually try to re-establish friendships and romances. Often they marry again, especially if they are men who were relatively young (under age 30) when the divorce occurred. Women with children are less likely to remarry, but those who do often marry a man who also has children from a previous marriage (Goldscheider & Sassler, 2006). About half of all U.S. marriages are remarriages for at least one of the partners.

For long-term marriages, divorce is less likely but more devastating when it happens (Lucas et al., 2003). For both husbands and wives, divorce can reduce income, sever friendships (many couples had only other couples as friends), and weaken family ties, not only with children but also with all the relatives (Amato, 1999; Anderson, 2003; King, 2003). The severity of the impact depends partly on whether or not the adult has close relationships with family members, friends, or a new partner.

Initially, remarriage typically brings happiness, intimacy, and other benefits, including better health for men and financial security for women (Hetherington & Kelly, 2002). For remarried fathers, bonds with a new wife's custodial children or

Bearing and rearing children are labor-intensive expressions of generativity. Erikson says, "The fashionable insistence on dramatizing the dependence of children on adults often blinds us to the dependence of the older generation on the younger one" (1963, p. 266).

This dependence apparently is satisfied as much by having one child as by having several (Kohler, 2005). Adults want to be generative, but they also want the benefits of employment, so currently they limit childbearing. As a result, although there are fewer marriages without children, the birth rate is lower than the replacement rate in 31 nations.

Although the intimacy and satisfaction of marriage often decrease with parenthood, the level of commitment increases (Bradbury et al., 2000). Ideally, a *parental alliance* forms as the parents cooperate in child rearing. This is a challenge. Every parent is tested and transformed by the dynamic experiences of raising children. Just when adults think they have mastered the art of parenting, their child's advancement to the next stage requires major adjustment. Generativity is required.

➤Answer to Observation Quiz (from page 595): The populations of both Ireland and Italy are predominantly Roman Catholic, but that is also true of France and Spain. The probable reason for the low divorce rates in Ireland and Italy is that the laws of both those nations make divorce very difficult to obtain.

Over the decades in any family, new babies arrive and older children grow up, job opportunities emerge or disappear, financial burdens increase or decrease, income is almost never adequate, and seldom is every child thriving in every way. Extra caregiving may be suddenly needed if illness strikes a child or an elderly parent. Throughout, many families cope, evidence of generativity.

Many Paths to Parenthood

A parental alliance assumes two cooperating parents. However, as described in Chapter 13, children can develop well in any family structure—nuclear or extended; heterosexual or homosexual; single-parent, two-parent, or grandparent. Can adults also thrive in any kind of parenting relationship? The challenges for nonbiological parents are great, but opportunities for generativity for such adults are great as well.

Roughly one-third of all North American adults become stepparents, adoptive parents, or foster parents at some point in their lives. In such relationships, developing secure attachment is more difficult for both generations. The social construction about "real" parents (meaning biological parents) is misleading, but it

WAYNE SCARBERRY / AP / WIDE WORLD PHOTOS

Not Lonely When they were 2, 4, and 6 years old, these boys went to live with their grandparents in Virginia. The family is attending a picnic for grandparents who have become surrogate parents for their grandchildren. Events like this fill a need: Many such grandparents feel isolated from their peers.

Observation Quiz (see answer, page 599): This family is typical of grandparent–grandchild families in age and sex. Can you guess how?

may affect both parent and child. Further, some foster children are strongly attached to their birth parents, an attachment that can be especially troublesome because of the conditions that led to their separation. Other children have never been attached to anyone; they are suspicious of their new parents. Secure attachment between foster parents and children is further hampered because the connection can be severed regardless of the quality of caregiving.

Strong bonds are particularly hard to create if a child already has strong attachments to other available caregivers. This is usually the case with stepchildren, since the average new stepchild is about 9 years old. Stepmothers may enter a marriage hoping to heal a broken family through love and understanding, while stepfathers may believe that their new children will welcome a benevolent disciplinarian. Not necessarily so. Stepparent families sometimes become well-functioning ones (especially if the new parent is authoritative) and sometimes not, depending largely on the personality and relationship of the adults (Ganong & Coleman, 2004).

Often a stepparent becomes an "intimate outsider," more distant from the child's personal life than the stepparent hoped but much closer than any stranger (Hetherington & Kelly, 2002). Some stepchildren are fiercely loyal to the absent parent, sabotaging any effort by a new adult to fill the traditional parental role, perhaps directly challenging authority ("You're not my father, you can't tell me what to do") or perhaps interfering as much as possible with the new marriage.

Stepchildren and foster children also evoke guilt by getting hurt, sick, lost, or (if the child is a teenager) pregnant, drunk, or arrested. Such childish reactions, often unconscious, may cause adult overreaction or anger, further alienating the two generations (Coleman et al., 2000).

Adoptive families have an advantage here: Parents are legally connected to their adopted children for life and biological parents are usually absent. Nevertheless, during adolescence, emotional bonds may stretch and loosen. Some adoptive children become intensely rebellious, rejecting family control, even as they seek reunification with their birth parents (Kohler et al., 2002). The children's reasons—whether to test their parents' devotion or to discover their roots or to establish an identity—are understandable, but the adoptive parents need every ounce of selfless generativity they can muster.

Can You Make Rice Cakes? If you can, it's probably because you, like these Japanese American girls, were fortunate enough to have a grandmother nearby to teach you. Note how intently and carefully all three are working to prepare the food for a large family gathering.

Despite such complications, most adoptive and foster parents cherish their parenting experiences, typically seeking a second child within a few years of the arrival of the first. Similarly, stepparents usually find satisfaction in their role (Ganong & Coleman, 2004). For their part, children usually reciprocate—if not immediately, then later on.

Nonparents (grandparents, teachers, neighbors, aunts, and uncles) may also develop close relationships with children, cherishing their generative role. As one uncle explained about his nephew:

> I find I just like talking with him. He needs to express his ideas . . . and I think anything that develops companionship . . . really I don't mind.
>
> *[quoted in Milardo, 2005, p. 1230]*

Grandparents are often crucial during divorce, providing continuity and often a home.

Perhaps even more than biological parenthood, alternative routes to child rearing may make adults more humble, less self-absorbed, and more aware of the problems facing children everywhere. When this occurs, adults become true exemplars of generativity, as Erikson and others (1986) described it, characterized by the virtue that is perhaps the most important of all—caring for others.

➤Answer to Observation Quiz (from page 597): The grandparents are relatively young, and the grandchildren are boys, as is the case for most such surrogate parents and children.

Caregiving for Aging Parents

In the twenty-first century, the following demographic trends are evident:

- More than half of all mothers of young children, and more than two-thirds of middle-aged women, are employed. (In the United States, 74 percent of married women and 80 percent of single women aged 35 to 44 are in the labor force.)
- People are living longer: Many adults have two living parents and four living grandparents.
- Fewer children per family (down from five to two, on average, over the past century) mean fewer adult caregivers.

Each of these trends changes the patterns of care for the frail elderly family members. Because of their position in the generational hierarchy, many adults are expected to help both older and younger generations. They have been called the **sandwich generation,** a term that evokes an image of two slices of bread with a substantial filling in the middle. The analogy to a sandwich, making it seem as if the middle generation is squeezed by obligations to those younger and older, is vivid—but it is not very accurate (Grundy & Henretta, 2006).

sandwich generation A term for the generation of middle-aged people who are supposedly "squeezed" by the needs of the younger and older generations. Some adults do feel pressured by these obligations, but most are not burdened by them, either because they enjoy fulfilling them or because they choose to take on only some of them or none.

It is true that many adults in their late 20s and early 30s, including those who have partners and children, are active participants in the lives of their family of origin. As already explained, siblings remain connected to each other, and sometimes they are stressed by caregiving for parents. It is *not* true, however, that most adults are burdened by such obligations. Some hire professional caregivers, but most find that even that is not needed.

Here are some specifics that show that most adults do *not* provide major financial or caregiving help to any of the older generation. One study of married people aged 51 to 61 with living parents found that less than 20 percent committed significant income or time to aid their parents (Shuey & Hardy, 2003).

Similarly, a study in England found that most adults did not provide care for anyone, but when employed professionals began caring for someone sick, disabled, or elderly, they were unlikely to leave their jobs. Those who became full-time caregivers were already less engaged in their work (e.g., they worked

TABLE 22.4

Contacts and Help Provided by Middle-Aged Couples to Parents and In-Laws

	Phone Calls per Month	Visits per Month	Minutes of Help per Week
Wife to own parents	11	6	120
Husband to wife's parents	8	5	70
Total to wife's parents	19	11	190
Husband to own parents	7	4	100
Wife to husband's parents	5	4	58
Total to husband's parents	12	8	158

Source: Lee et al., 2003.

part-time at routine jobs) and had neither dependent children nor a needy spouse (Henz, 2006). In a study of Chinese American adults in California, all felt a filial duty to their aging parents, but when extensive care was needed, many hired an unemployed Chinese American to provide it (Lan, 2002).

Interestingly, care for elderly parents does not flow equally to all parents of a married couple. A detailed breakdown found that in the United States, both husbands and wives tend to tilt toward the wife's parents (Lee et al., 2003) (see Table 22.4). In some other nations, such as China, it is the husband's parents who are more likely to receive support (Lin et al., 2003; Zhan et al., 2006).

PHOTODISC

Four Generations of Caregiving These four women, from the great-grandmother to her 17-year-old great-granddaughter, all care for one another. Help flows to whoever needs it, not necessarily to the oldest or youngest.

Personality and familism are as influential as need in determining caregiving (Grundy & Henretta, 2006). The U.S. study which found that only 20 percent of married adults contributed care to any of their four parents also found that those same 20 percent were likely to provide support for their adult children. The researchers suggest that a personality trait (generosity), more than need, may be the reason (Shuey & Hardy, 2003).

This is a positive personality trait since caregiving may be vital for all the generations. Specifics of caregiving for the elderly are discussed in more detail in Chapter 25, since people over age 65 are often both caregivers and care receivers. Here we need to emphasize that although "sandwich generation" is a misleading term, the crucial role of mutual caregiving for the benefit of all family members should be recognized.

Employment

For most of the history of social science research, employment has been studied as part of the macrosystem (e.g., the correlation between unemployment and domestic abuse) or as a small part of individual development (e.g., matching an adolescent's talents and interests with a specific career). Both these approaches have merit, but missing has been the study of how work affects personal and family development, integrating "thinking about working into the broader fabric of psychological theory and practice" (Blustein, 2006, p. xiv).

Exactly how work affects development is not clear, however, especially considering the current employment scene, where much is changing. It is apparent, however, that work during adulthood has a major effect on each person's developmental well-being (Bianchi et al., 2005).

Many Benefits

A paycheck is only one of many benefits of employment. Work provides a structure for daily life, a setting for human interaction, a source of status and fulfillment (Wethington, 2002). Work meets generativity needs by allowing people to do the following:

- Develop and use their personal skills
- Express their creative energy
- Aid and advise coworkers, as a mentor or friend
- Support the education and health of their families
- Contribute to the community by providing goods or services

The pleasure of "a job well done" is universal, as is the joy in supportive supervisors and friendly coworkers. Job satisfaction correlates more strongly with challenge, creativity, productivity, and relationships among employees than with high pay or easy work. Abusive supervisors and hostile coworkers tend to reduce employee motivation (Le Blanc & Barling, 2004).

One important developmental distinction is between the **extrinsic rewards of work,** such as salary, health benefits, pension, and other aspects not connected with the actual job, and the **intrinsic rewards of work,** such as job satisfaction, friendship, pride, and self-esteem. Young adults tend to look for work that has high extrinsic rewards, choosing a job for the paycheck and benefits, for instance. However, the "intrinsic rewards of work, satisfaction, relationships with coworkers, and a sense of participation in meaningful work become more important as an individual ages" (Sterns & Huyck, 2001, p. 452). This is the probable explanation for lower rates of absenteeism and less job change among older workers. Many enjoy the work, not just the money.

extrinsic rewards of work The tangible rewards, usually in the form of compensation, that one receives for a job (e.g., salary, benefits, pension).

intrinsic rewards of work The intangible benefits one receives from a job (e.g., job satisfaction, self-esteem, pride) that come from within oneself.

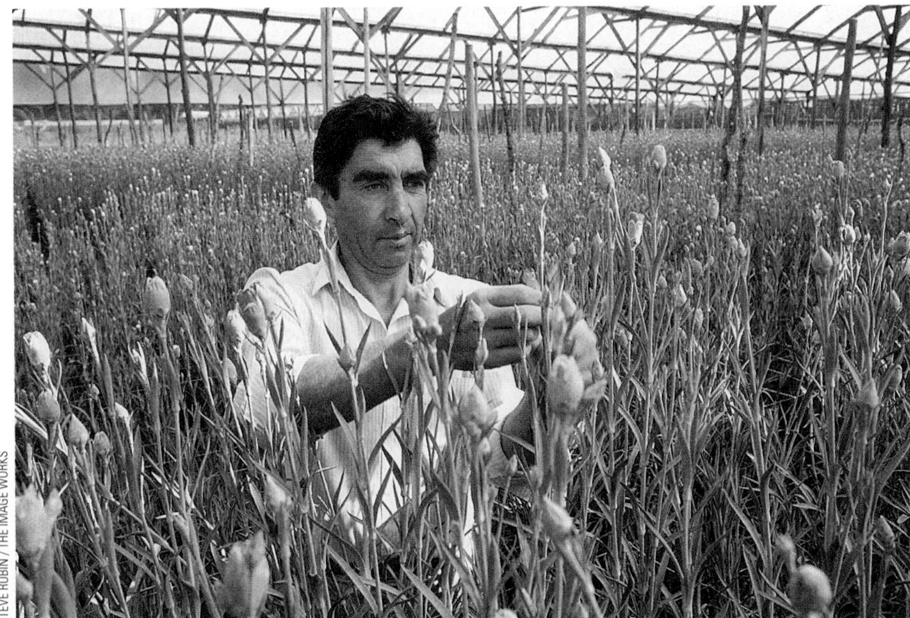

STEVE RUBIN / THE IMAGE WORKS

Tomorrow's Fresh-Cut Bouquet For guests to take imported fresh flowers to their hostess was impossible until relatively recently. This gardener in Chile takes satisfaction from growing and carefully tending flowers to be cut and flown overnight to the United States.

Human Needs

The work environment is changing in many ways. For instance, globalization has resulted in each nation exporting what it does best (and cheapest) and importing what it needs. Developed nations are shifting from industry-based economies to information and service economies; developing nations are shifting from subsistence agriculture to larger businesses. Multinational corporations are replacing small, local endeavors.

Financial and managerial companies seek to coordinate all this growth and change, with the goal of efficiency and profit. This is only the first step. It is crucial to learn how new work conditions support development, especially the generative functions of family caregiving, personal creativity, satisfaction and esteem from a job well done, and mentoring other workers (Bianchi et al., 2005). Research on this has not yet reached firm conclusions. Here we present some initial findings to encourage more study of the developmental implications of employment.

Companies downsize, level, outsource, merge, and hire temporary employees to produce goods "just in time." Workers increasingly change jobs several times during adulthood. As you can see from Figure 22.5, job change is particularly common in emerging adulthood but continues throughout adulthood. Even at age 40, about one-fourth of all workers have been at their current job for less than two

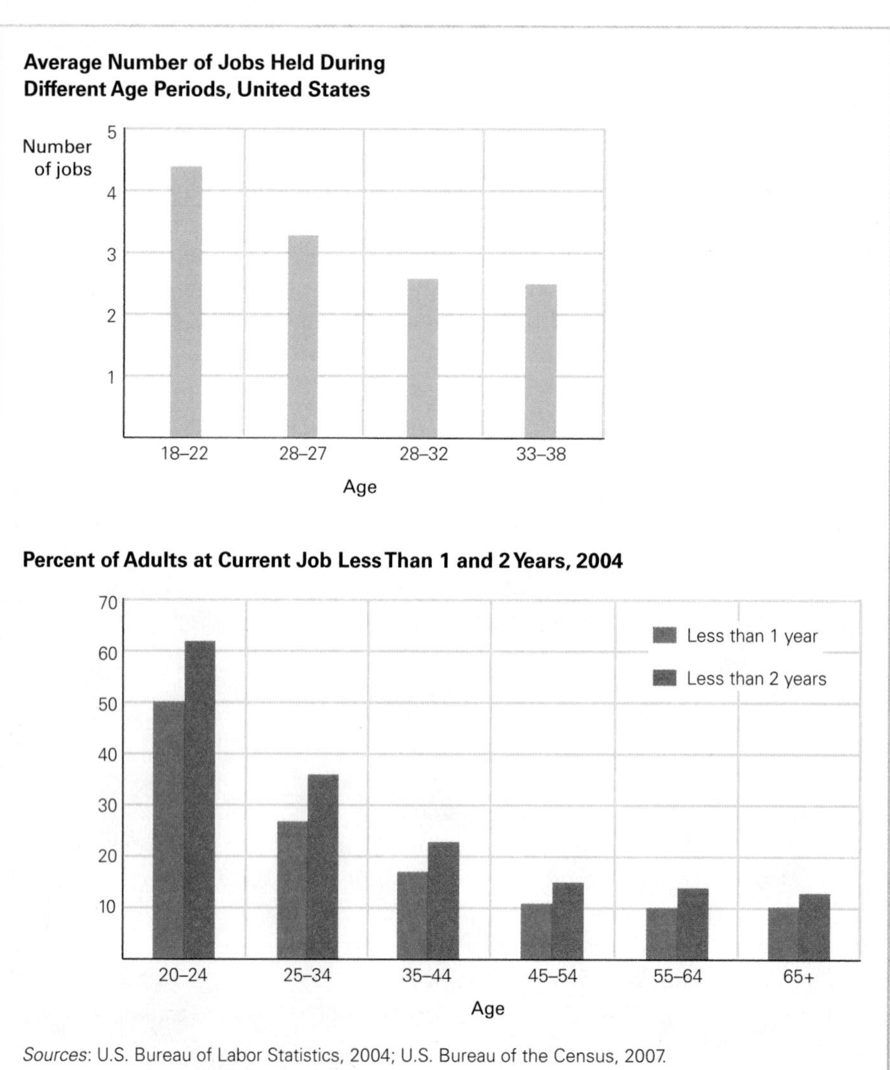

FIGURE 22.5

No Longer Married to the Job Most of our grandparents had one job in one place for their entire working lives. Today's workers frequently change jobs and locations. This kind of mobility affects their friendships, identity, and pension status in various ways.

The Global Market These women sorting cashews *(left)* and the men working on an offshore oil rig *(right)* are participants in globalization—a phenomenon that has changed the economies of every nation and every family in the world. Radical changes coexist with traditional inequities. For instance, the women here are said to have easy, unskilled work, which is the reason they are paid less than 10 percent of the men's wages.

years. From a developmental perspective, this is problematic. As with divorce and other family change, losing a job and finding another is more devastating the older the worker is, for three reasons.

1. Many of the skills and much of the knowledge required for a new job were never learned by older workers. The most obvious example is computer literacy. Almost every job now requires computer knowledge, often with software developed within the past few years. Yet adults who began work 20 or more years ago (now older than 40) were not exposed to computers in school or college.
2. Seniority means that older workers are paid more, are often mentors, and have become experts. This is an advantage when they stay put but a disadvantage when they seek work, because each area of expertise is specialized.
3. Older workers have established roots. Relocation is more difficult with age because friends and family must be left behind or move. The unemployment rate in Mississippi is more than three times the rate in Hawaii (U.S. Bureau of Labor Statistics, 2007). If you were a middle-aged adult in Mississippi, would you leave your family, church, and community for work? What if you were in Mexico?

Another major change in the current economy is an increase in shift work. Once, most employees worked from 9 A.M. to 5 P.M. and only on weekdays, but companies now seek to meet customers' demands for goods and services 24/7. In the United States in 2005, less than half of all full-time workers had traditional work schedules (U.S. Bureau of Labor Statistics, 2005). Some (27 percent) had flexible schedules, some (15 percent) worked odd shifts, some (4 percent) were temporary employees, some (7 percent) were independent contractors, and some (4 percent) were looking for work. In addition, 20 percent were working part time, usually by choice. All of these schedules disrupt family life.

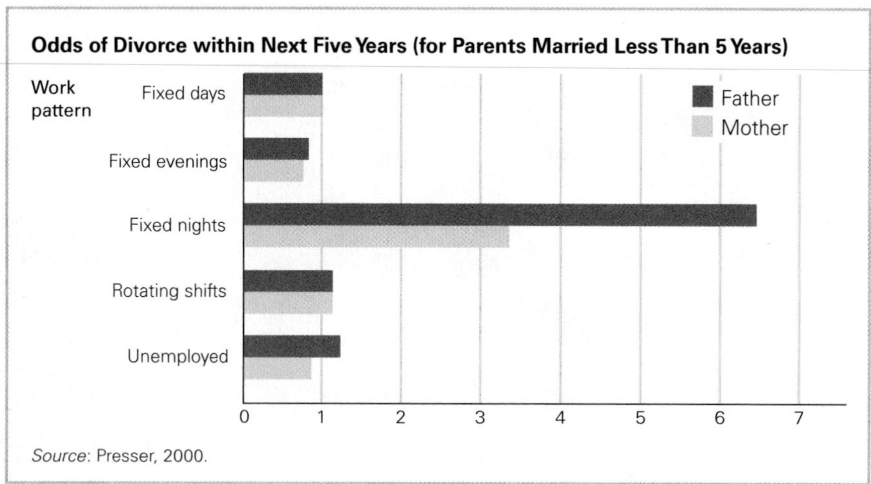

FIGURE 22.6

Parents' Work Schedules and the Risk of Divorce Both the wife's and the husband's work schedules affect their chances of getting divorced. To interpret this graph, you need to know that the odds of divorce are set at a baseline of 1.0 for those who are working "fixed days" (i.e., most work hours occur between 8 A.M. and 4 P.M.). The odds of divorce for other couples are higher or lower than 1, depending on whether the risk is greater or less than that of the fixed-days group.

This study was longitudinal, measuring work schedules of 3,476 married couples over five years. Of those who initially had been married less than five years, 21 percent had divorced; of those who had been married more than five years, 8 percent had divorced.

About one-third of all working couples with young children schedule their hours so that one parent provides child care while the other works (Presser, 2000). This is a logical solution that allows both parents to earn money and care for the children. But the emotional costs to the family may outweigh the benefits, especially when either parent works a night shift. Couples without young children do not seem to suffer when one of them has a night schedule, but those with small children and nighttime jobs are at high risk of divorce (see Figure 22.6). Remember that relationships require time together to sustain. As one woman explained:

> Right now I feel torn between a rock and a hard place—my husband and I work opposite shifts, so we do not have to put our children in day care. . . . Opposite shifts [are] putting a strain on our marriage. . . . It is very stressful.
>
> *[quoted in Glass, 1998]*

Shift work creates a practical problem as well: Adult body rhythms do not allow deep sleep at any time of the day or night, and a sleep-deprived parent is often cranky and impatient. While employees may like the flexibility of variable work schedules, from the perspective of optimal biosocial development of individuals and families, a regular schedule (even if it always includes odd hours) is better than an irregular one, and a steady job is better than one with intense overtime alternating with periods of no work.

When there is not enough time for everything, human relationships and family life tend to suffer. Developmentalists find that family bonds take time to develop, and child care is not always recognized as a family priority. This may be a negative side effect of economic pressure, at least according to one middle-class U.S. worker, who says that people are

> so pressed for time that they're always looking for a shortcut. . . . You look for a quick way to be able to juggle, you know, because you've got a lot of things you need to do. You need to go home and clean your house, you need to get groceries. . . . People are always trying to kind of shortcut the system. And society has encouraged that. I mean, you no longer have to wait in line for a bank teller. So we're getting to the point where we're always looking for a shortcut. Everybody, everybody is.
>
> *[quoted in Wolfe, 1998, pp. 244–245]*

Ironically, much of the stress begins with the misperception that mothers used to spend long hours caring for their children, reading and playing with them as well as providing direct care, while fathers earned all the money to support the family.

This makes many modern parents worry that their dual-income paychecks are hurting their children. However, time studies show that parents are actually spending more time with each child than they once did (partly because housework is easier and families are not as large), yet "the emergence of *intensive mothering* and *involved fathering* norms over recent decades has intensified feelings among parents that time with children is never sufficient" (Mattingly & Sayer, 2006, p. 207).

One solution to potential conflict between work and family roles, made possible by modern technology, is telecommuting, in which employees use their home computers, phones, and faxes to do many tasks that once had to be done at the office. This saves office rent and commuting time, but developmentalists are not sure this is good for human growth.

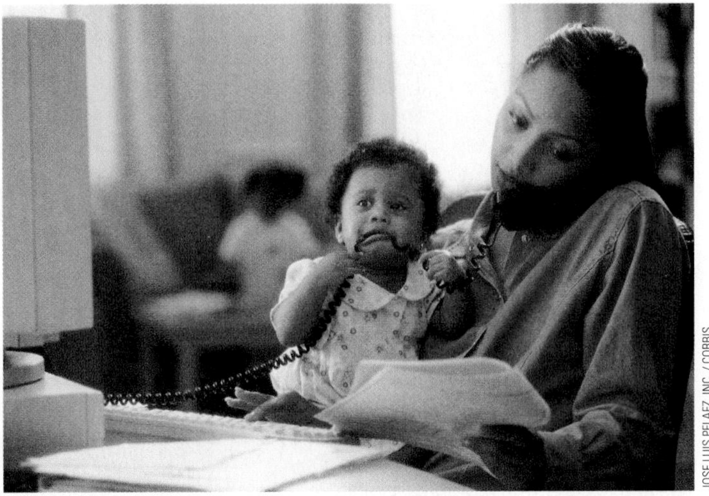

JOSE LUIS PELAEZ, INC. / CORBIS

Not Happy with Mommy Working at home sounds like an ideal way to combine motherhood and a career—until one tries it. Letting a child chew on a cord is risky, but so is asking your client to call you back at naptime.

A recent study found that families probably benefit, especially when telecommuters have flexibility as to what they do and when they do it (Golden et al., 2006). A worker can take a relative to the doctor, help a child with homework, or do a load of laundry in the middle of the workday. Fewer distractions and interruptions from the office but more from home benefits family life but may reduce work efficiency.

This study looked at how many family members each telecommuter had and found that the larger the family, the more likely family life interfered with work. However, "they may also experience the benefits of greater family enrichment," which makes the authors caution that the advantages of telecommuting may outweigh the problems for some workers (Golden et al., 2006, p. 1348). A noteworthy finding is that those who benefit least may be those who live alone, who miss the friendships and social interactions that work brings. Telecommuting has "an upside and a downside" (Golden et al., 2006, p. 1348), as do most changes in the workplace. Much depends on the individual situation of the worker and on his or her ability to balance intimacy and generativity needs.

Diversity

One of the benefits of the modern economy is increased diversity, with more employed women and members of minority groups (see Table 22.5). Since it is apparent that having a job adds to self-esteem as well as income, higher employment rates have helped those who were shut out before.

In many developed nations, almost half the civilian labor force is female. In the United States, two-thirds of the mothers of dependent children are employed. Some occupations continue to be segregated by sex or ethnicity, but less so than

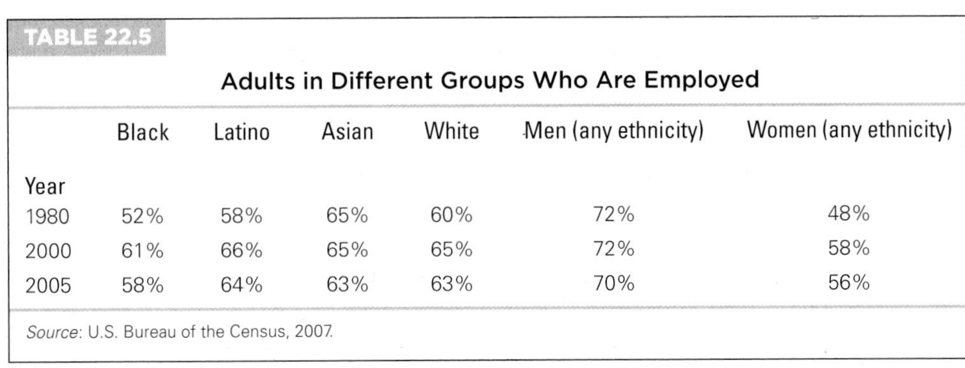

TABLE 22.5

Adults in Different Groups Who Are Employed

Year	Black	Latino	Asian	White	Men (any ethnicity)	Women (any ethnicity)
1980	52%	58%	65%	60%	72%	48%
2000	61%	66%	65%	65%	72%	58%
2005	58%	64%	63%	63%	70%	56%

Source: U.S. Bureau of the Census, 2007.

More Work to Be Done For every group, some of the adults who are not in the labor force may choose their status, often because they are retired or doing unpaid child care. Nonetheless, this table indicates improvements that have occurred and more that are needed. One bright spot in bad news: The recession at the beginning of the twenty-first century affected all groups equally.

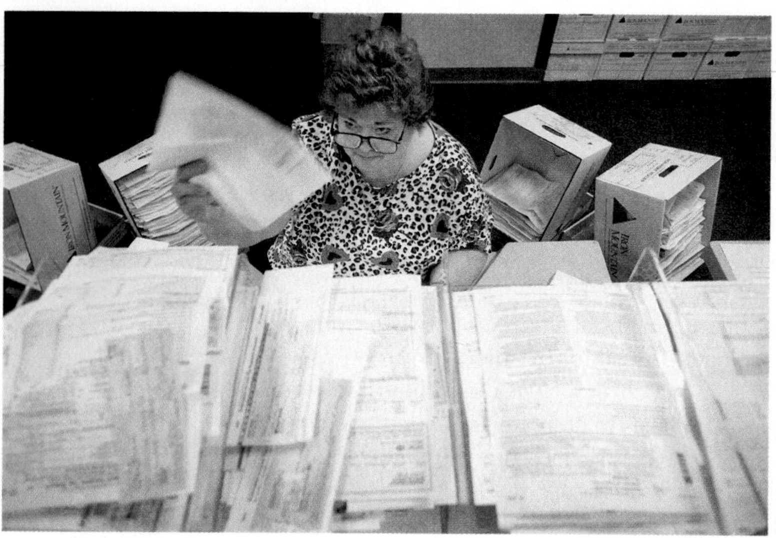

KATHLEEN MCLAUGHLIN / THE IMAGE WORKS

Stress or Stressor Facing a desk overflowing with income tax forms and checks is stressful, and this woman is new to the job—she began it less than a year ago. Will she quit? Probably not. She is mature enough to establish priorities and to cope with any unreasonable demands from her supervisor.

Especially for Entrepreneurs Suppose you are starting a business. In what ways would middle-aged adults be helpful to you?

before: For example, 8 percent of nurses are men and 5 percent of firefighters are women, more than double the proportions in 1980 (U.S. Bureau of the Census, 2006). Rates of minority employment have increased as well. For example, from 1980 to 2005, the proportion of African Americans in the labor force has increased from 52 to 58 percent and that of Hispanic Americans has increased from 58 to 64 percent (as illustrated in Table 22.5).

Functioning effectively and happily in a diverse workplace requires a mature perspective. Being a generative worker in a generative workplace is a goal recently articulated by psychologists but not often achieved (Blustein, 2006). Human resources counselors are developing selection procedures that assess personal skills and traits that predict whether a prospective employee will work effectively with others (Chan, 2005).

Diversity means that employees differ in what they expect and need from their jobs, which increases the need for mentors who show new employees what is required as well as the need for work conditions that take into account the specific needs of each person. This was already evident in the previous discussion of relocation and telecommuting.

It is also evident in the policies for reducing job stress. A study of employees in the United States and China found that the former were more stressed by lack of control and direct conflict with supervisors and the latter were more stressed by the possibility of negative job evaluations and indirect conflicts (Liu et al., 2007). The implications of different coping patterns (problem-focused versus emotion-focused) are that, in a diverse workplace, managers must be sensitive to various signals that all is not well.

Obviously, work can further the well-being of every adult, but the modern economy includes hazards to adult development. Much remains to be discovered, but adults of both sexes are physically and psychologically healthier if they have multiple roles—as workers, friends, partners, and parents. Job and home stresses are buffered by intimacy and caregiving in all their variations (Grzywacz & Bass, 2003; Rogers & May, 2003; Voydanoff, 2004).

ROBIN DAVIES / TAXI / GETTY IMAGES

Off to Work We Go Even from the back, this European mother and daughter seem to be thriving. Note that the mother is carrying a laptop computer, the daughter is well dressed, and the two are in step, literally as well as figuratively.

SUMMING UP

Generativity needs are met by caregiving, creative work, and employment. Each of these areas can be problematic. For example, parents experience pride and joy as they watch their children grow, but raising children requires substantial time, patience, and flexibility. This is sometimes difficult for parents raising their biological children and even harder (but perhaps more rewarding) for step-, foster, and adoptive parents. Caregiving in general is satisfying, eased by other family members and by the mutual relationships that sustain families, but stress can overwhelm some caregivers and kinkeepers. Similarly, work can provide many psychic rewards, but the current economic scene makes work satisfaction elusive for many people. ■

a case to study

Linda: "A Much Sturdier Self"

Remember Linda, whose story began this chapter? Her therapist reports on her progress:

> Linda decided that she wanted to apply to university to try again in an arena where she felt she had failed so badly. This move was not easy, particularly for someone haunted by shame. It would be difficult to describe the fear, ambivalence, and procrastination with which she approached this challenge. However, after much equivocation, Linda did send off her application and she was accepted for university admission. . . .
>
> She lost her job as an office receptionist because of the company's downsizing. Previously this would have been such a blow to her self-esteem that she would have given up on her plans to go to university. However, Linda picked herself up, got a job with another firm, finally let go emotionally of Jacqueline, gave Greg his ultimatum (on which he defaulted), began a relationship with an eligible partner in the new company, and made plans to move back east to begin university. . . .
>
> Linda's story is not over by any means. I do not know whether she will be the criminology major and psychological counselor she aims to be. I do not know what will become of her current relationship. However, I do know that she takes a much sturdier self and a much stronger identity into her new world.
>
> *[Marcia, 2002, pp. 24–25]*

Linda discovered her identity, found better ways to achieve intimacy, and is seeking more education in part to become more generative. She is on her way to a happier life, despite complications (with her earlier relationships, with downsizing) and, like other adults, has the potential to develop "a much sturdier self."

Given the complexity of intimacy and generativity in the current context, psychosocial growth for Linda and other adults is not guaranteed. Many are "on their way," however, taking a "much sturdier self and a much stronger identity into a new world."

SUMMARY

Ages and Stages

1. Adult development is remarkably diverse, yet it appears to be characterized by two basic needs. Throughout adulthood, people seek intimacy, which is achieved through friendships, family attachments, and romantic partnerships. The second need is for generativity, which is achieved through caregiving, parenthood, and work.

2. Traditional patterns of development following specific tasks at specific ages have been replaced by more varied and flexible patterns. The social clock still influences behavior, but less profoundly than it once did. The midlife crisis does not usually occur.

3. Personality traits are a source of continuity. The Big Five traits—openness, conscientiousness, extroversion, agreeableness, and neuroticism—are evident throughout the life span and are particularly stable in adulthood.

4. Each person selects an ecological niche of career and partner, which reinforces personality patterns. Although such choices typically strengthen traits, unexpected events (for instance, a major illness or financial windfall) can temporarily disrupt personality.

5. Culture and gender have some influence on personality, but this is more evident in expression than in underlying temperament. Asians may be more likely than other ethnic groups to depend on others, and the two sexes may become more similar to each other as people age.

Intimacy

6. Each person has a social convoy of other people with whom they travel through life. Friends are crucial for buffering stress and sharing secrets.

7. Family members have linked lives, continuing to affect one another as they all grow older. Siblings typically become closer over the years of adulthood, and adult children and their parents continue to help one another in practical and emotional ways.

8. Almost all adults find a partner to share life with, usually raising children together.

9. Although some research finds that marriage and parenthood increase happiness in adulthood, this is not always true and the relationship may be more correlational than causal. Some marriages improve with time; others do not.

10. Homosexual partnerships are similar in most ways to heterosexual ones. Single people fare well if they have close friends. Given the changing social contexts, research has not yet discovered all the similarities and differences in various types of partnerships.

11. Divorce is difficult for both partners and their family members. Remarriage solves some of the problems (particularly financial and intimacy troubles) that are common among divorced adults, but remarriage is complicated and may end in a second divorce.

Generativity

12. Adults need to feel generative, achieving, successful, instrumental—all words used to describe a major psychosocial need. This need is met through creative work, employment, and caregiving, especially those activities aimed toward supporting and assisting the next generation.

13. Caring for partners, parents, children, and others is a major expression of generativity. Often one family member becomes the chief kinkeeper and caregiver, usually by choice. The "sandwich generation" metaphor is misleading.

14. Parenthood typically begins with biological childbearing and then continues as a parental alliance forms between mother and father. Adults are changed by their children as they grow.

15. Many adults care for children who are not their biological offspring. Step-, foster, and adoptive parenting can be both challenging and satisfying. Aunts and uncles also can be generative for the next generation.

16. Employment brings many rewards to adults, particularly intrinsic benefits such as pride and friendship. Changes in employment pattern—including job switches, shift work, and diversity of fellow workers—can affect other aspects of adult development.

17. Combining work schedules, caregiving requirements, and intimacy needs is not automatic; adults find varied ways to fill numerous roles, some more successful than others.

KEY TERMS

social clock (p. 579)
midlife crisis (p. 580)
Big Five (p. 581)
ecological niche (p. 581)
gender convergence (p. 583)
social convoy (p. 585)
allostatic load (p. 586)
linked lives (p. 587)
household (p. 587)
familism (p. 588)
fictive kin (p. 589)
empty nest (p. 591)
kinkeeper (p. 596)
sandwich generation (p. 599)
extrinsic rewards of work (p. 601)
intrinsic rewards of work (p. 601)

KEY QUESTIONS

1. Describe the two basic needs of adulthood, using the words of several theorists as well as your own descriptions.

2. How does the social clock affect life choices for both high-income and low-income adults?

3. Explain how the midlife crisis, the empty nest, and gender convergence might reflect cohort rather than maturational changes.

4. Compare the three main sources of intimacy.

5. What are the psychological and social factors that make divorce better or worse for an adult?

6. How are family relationships affected by the passage of time?

7. Compare the advantages and disadvantages of biological and nonbiological parenthood.

8. Women are more often kinkeepers and caregivers than are men. How is this role both a blessing and a burden?

9. Pick one of the changes in work over the past decades and explain how it has affected family life and adults' development.

10. Who benefits and who suffers from the increased diversity of the workplace?

APPLICATIONS

1. Describe a relationship that you know of in which a middle-aged person and a younger adult learned from each other.

2. Did your parents' marital and employment status affect you? How would you have fared if they had chosen other marriage or work patterns?

3. Think about becoming a foster or adoptive parent yourself. What would you see as the personal benefits and costs?

4. Ask several people how their personalities have changed in the past decade. The research suggests that changes are usually minor. Is that what you found?

➤**Response for Entrepreneurs** (from page 606): As employees and as customers. Middle-aged workers are steady, with few absences and good "people skills," and they like to work. In addition, household income is likely to be higher at about age 50 than at any other time, so middle-aged adults will probably be able to afford your products or services.

PART VII The Developing Person So Far: Adulthood

BIOSOCIAL

The Aging Process Senescence begins as soon as growth stops. The signs of aging in the skin, hair, muscles, and body shape are benign but can be disconcerting. Losses of acuity in hearing and vision are usually gradual and are not debilitating for most people. Senescence of the sexual-reproductive system includes reduced levels of hormones and less urgent sexual desire as people age from 25 to 65. Some men become concerned about less reliable erections; some women are troubled by menopause, when estrogen levels fall dramatically, making reproduction impossible. For some younger adults, concerns about infertility have led to alternate means of reproduction.

Health Habits Avoiding tobacco and obesity, maintaining daily exercise and good nutrition, and moderate use of alcohol keep most adults healthy. In addition, medical treatment for some conditions that may begin in middle age (high blood pressure and diabetes among them) prevents mortality, morbidity, and disability. Income, culture, gender, and genes all affect health throughout life, notably during the adult years.

COGNITIVE

What Is Intelligence? Researchers describe adult intelligence in many ways, noting that some intellectual abilities improve with age, while others decline. Some believe that there is a general intelligence that underlies all cognitive abilities, but most find several distinct kinds of intelligence that vary with culture and age. For example, fluid intelligence decreases and crystallized intelligence increases; academic intelligence becomes less important after college, but practical intelligence is increasingly necessary. Overall, cohort differences and individual variations are more notable than age differences.

Selective Gains and Losses To cope with the effects that aging has on cognition, adults become selective, compensating for losses and specializing in tasks they do well (optimization). Choice and motivation lead to practice and thus expertise, which is characterized by cognition that is intuitive, automatic, strategic, and flexible.

PSYCHOSOCIAL

Ages and Stages Chronological age and the social clock are no longer as influential as they were, as adults develop in ways that reflect their Big Five personality traits and their ecological niches more than their age. The midlife crisis is more myth than reality. Nonetheless, gender, age, and culture affect personality to some degree, especially in the expression of various characteristics.

Intimacy Throughout adulthood, including before and after the ages (25–65) that are the focus of this period, people depend on friends, family members, and life partners to meet their needs for respect and affection. Adults usually have rewarding relationships with friends, with partners (heterosexual or homosexual), with adult children, and with aging siblings and parents. All these intimate connections can be problematic, especially the relationship with a spouse, which ends in divorce almost half the time.

Generativity Adults often become caregivers, typically as parents (whether biological or otherwise) or as children of elderly parents. Employment is another source of generativity as well as of income, status, and stress. Globalization and diversity have changed the careers of many adults, who today are more likely to change jobs and to work with people of many backgrounds. Many adults of both sexes successfully coordinate the demands of partner, children, and employers.

Late Adulthood

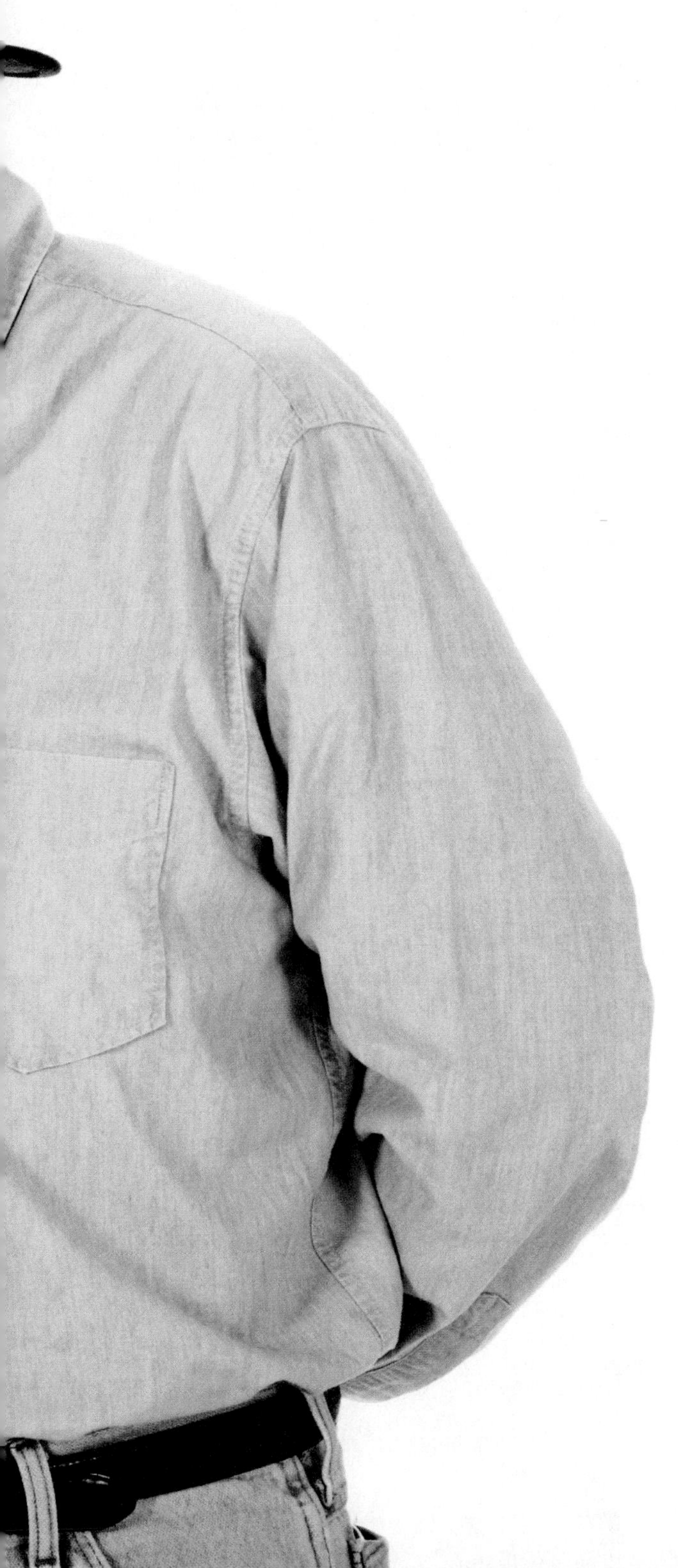

CHAPTER 23

CHAPTER 24

CHAPTER 25

PART VIII

What emotions do you anticipate as you read about development in late adulthood? Given the myths that abound, you might expect to feel discomfort, depression, resignation, and sorrow. At moments in the next three chapters, such emotions may be appropriate. However, your most frequent emotion might be surprise. For example, you will learn in Chapter 23 that thousands of centenarians are active, alert, and happy; in Chapter 24 that marked intellectual decline ("senility") is unusual; in Chapter 25 that relationships between older and younger generations are neither as close as some imagine nor as distant as others claim. Overall, late adulthood continues earlier patterns rather than breaks from them. Instead of resigning themselves to lonely isolation, most older adults remain social and independent.

This period of life, more than any other, is a magnet for misinformation and prejudice. Why? Think about the answer when the facts and research presented in the next three chapters surprise you.

23

CHAPTER OUTLINE

Late Adulthood: Biosocial Development

Now we begin our study of the last phase of life, from age 65 or so until death. This chapter describes biosocial changes—in the senses, the vital organs, morbidity, and mortality—and then raises the crucial question: Why does aging occur? The answer might allow you to live to age 100 or beyond.

If the thought of living more than a century evokes feelings of dread, remember that personal knowledge usually softens prejudice (both negative and positive). One way to combat prejudice is simply to ask someone old, as I did on my mother's 90th birthday.

"How does it feel to be 90?"

"Okay, but 89 felt better."

She looked old, but her wit was intact.

Another way is to take the following quiz to see how much you know about the realities of life after age 65.

1. In 2007, the proportion of the U.S. population over age 65 was about
   (a) 3 percent.
   (b) 13 percent.
   (c) 25 percent.
   (d) 33 percent.
   (e) 50 percent.
2. In 2005, the proportion of the world's population over age 65 was about
   (a) 2 percent.
   (b) 8 percent.
   (c) 12 percent.
   (d) 20 percent.
   (e) 35 percent.
3. Happiness in older people is
   (a) rare.
   (b) much less common than in younger adults.
   (c) at least as common as in younger adults.
   (d) apparent only in those who are grandparents.
   (e) apparent only among those who have dementia.

Especially for People Who Guess on Quizzes On a multiple-choice quiz, it is better to guess than to leave an answer blank. People tend to choose *b* as a guess when they are not certain of the answer. Is this true for you?

4. Which senses become less acute in old age?
   (a) Sight and hearing
   (b) Taste and smell
   (c) Varied, as each sense improves in some people and declines in others
   (d) None if the person is healthy
   (e) All
5. The automobile accident rate for licensed drivers over age 65 is
   (a) higher than for those under 65.
   (b) about the same as for those under age 65.
   (c) lower than for those under age 65.
   (d) unknown, because such statistics are not reported.
   (e) close to zero, because almost no one over age 65 drives.
6. About what percent of U.S. residents over age 65 are in nursing homes or hospitals?
   (a) 4 percent
   (b) 10 percent
   (c) 25 percent
   (d) 35 percent
   (e) 50 percent
7. Compared with that of younger adults, the reaction time of older adults is
   (a) slower.
   (b) about the same.
   (c) faster.
   (d) slower for men, faster for women.
   (e) faster for men, slower for women.
8. Lung capacity (measured by how much air a person expels in one breath)
   (a) is reduced with age.
   (b) stays the same among nonsmokers.
   (c) increases among healthy old people.
   (d) is unrelated to age.
   (e) is unaffected by smoking.
9. The most common living arrangement for a person over age 65 in the United States is
   (a) with a husband or wife.
   (b) with a grown child.
   (c) alone.
   (d) with an unrelated elderly person.
   (e) in a nursing home.
10. Compared with people under age 65, an older adult's chance of being a victim of a violent crime is
    (a) lower.
    (b) about the same.
    (c) higher.
    (d) lower for men, higher for women.
    (e) higher for men, lower for women.

This quiz is adapted from a much larger one called *Facts on Aging* (Palmore, 1998). Current data come primarily from the U.S. Bureau of the Census (2006), which includes some international statistics.

As you read this chapter, you will find the answers to these questions (on the following pages: 1, p. 617; 2, p. 617; 3, p. 616; 4, p. 620; 5, p. 624; 6, p. 619; 7, p. 620; 8, p. 622; 9, p. 619; 10, p. 627). Most people get at least half wrong, sometimes because they simply lack knowledge but usually because prejudice—more negative than positive—clouds their judgment (Palmore et al., 2005).

Prejudice and Predictions

Prejudice about late adulthood is common among people of all ages, including children and older adults themselves. As an example of the latter, most people over age 70 think that they themselves are doing well compared with other people their age, who, they believe, have worse problems and are too self-absorbed (Cruikshank, 2003; Townsend et al., 2006).

Ageism

Two leading scientists who study old age noted:

> Common beliefs about the aging process result in negative stereotypes—oversimplified and biased views of what old people are like. The "typical" old person is often viewed as uninterested in (and incapable of) sex, on the road to (if not arrived at) senility, conservative and rigid. The stereotype would have us believe that old people are tired and cranky, passive, without energy, weak, and dependent on others.
>
> *[Schaie & Willis, 1996, p. 17]*

All these stereotypes are false. They arise from a widespread prejudice called **ageism,** the tendency to categorize and judge people solely on the basis of chronological age. "Ageism is a social disease, much like racism and sexism" in that it relies on stereotypes, creating "needless fear, waste, illness, and misery" (Palmore, 2005, p. 90).

ageism A prejudice in which people are categorized and judged solely on the basis of their chronological age.

Ageism Against Young and Old

You read in Chapter 20 that calculation of QALYs (quality-adjusted life years) often discounts the years of late adulthood. That is ageist. Some curfew laws require all teenagers to be off the streets by 10 P.M. That, too, is ageist. (Imagine the public outcry if curfews applied only to all males or all non-Whites) Ageism is "pigeon-holing people and not allowing them to be individuals with unique ways of living their lives" (Butler et al., 1998, p. 208).

Teenagers rebel against ageism. Fortunately for them, they soon become adults, and anti-teen ageism no longer affects them. Unfortunately for the elderly, as they grow older, ageism gets worse. Restaurant staff patronize them, neighbors do not invite them to parties, employers refuse to hire them—all because they are old. Ageism is particularly damaging during late adulthood, because the targets succumb to policies and attitudes that reduce their pride, activity, health, and social involvement (Hess, 2006).

Elderspeak

One common expression of ageism is the demeaning kind of speech called **elderspeak.** Like baby talk, elderspeak uses simple and short sentences, exaggerated emphasis, slower talk, higher and louder pitch, and frequent repetition (See et al., 1999). Elderspeak often involves the use of demeaning clichés ("second childhood," "dirty old man," "senior moment," "doddering") or patronizing compliments ("spry," "having all her marbles"). Elderspeak is especially patronizing when people enunciate artificially, or call an older person "honey" or "dear," or use a nickname instead of a surname ("Johnny" instead of "Mr. White"). Some features of elderspeak reduce comprehension (Kemper & Harden, 1999): Lower pitch is more audible than higher pitch; stretching out words makes it harder to understand them. Elderspeak is often used by service providers (such as social workers and nurses) who know only the age, not the person (O'Conner & St. Pierre, 2004). Older adults react with anger or, worse, self-doubt.

elderspeak A condescending way of speaking to older adults that resembles baby talk, with simple and short sentences, exaggerated emphasis, repetition, and a slower rate and a higher pitch than normal speech.

Especially for Young Adults Should you always speak louder and slower when talking to a senior citizen?

At least with racism, the targets of the prejudice are taught to disbelieve the negative assumptions that others have. Many become proud of being members of their race. However, when children believe an ageist idea, no one teaches them otherwise. When those children become old, their lifetime prejudice is "extremely resistant to change," becoming a "self-fulfilling prophecy" that undercuts their health and intellect (Golub & Langer, 2007, pp. 12–13). They may tolerate elder-speak without realizing its effect on them.

Gerontology

gerontology The multidisciplinary study of old age.

Ageism is increasingly recognized as a prejudice, partly because of **gerontology,** the multidisciplinary study of old age. Many developmentalists who study the life span find late adulthood to be a continuation of earlier life, influenced by the same genetic, contextual, and familial factors that affect children and younger adults. Thus, gerontologists see late adulthood as similar to younger ages, with gains and losses, contextual influences, and plasticity as described in Chapter 1 (see page 15).

The people studied by gerontologists are typically community-dwelling adults (as opposed to older people who are living in nursing homes or other institutions). This population repeatedly provides evidence that they are usually healthy, active, and as happy and satisfied with their lives as younger adults (Myers, 2000) (*question* 3).

➤Response for People Who Guess on Quizzes (from page 614): If you chose *b* as the answer to more than two of these quiz questions, you have made at least one wrong guess.

Gerontologists, benefiting from the life-span perspective as well as the data they collect, conclude that aging is not necessarily problematic unless it is "socially constructed as a problem" (Cruikshank, 2003, p. 7). For example, with the inevitable declines that accompany aging, older people walk more slowly than younger ones; this is not a problem unless someone else is in a hurry or a red light is timed for faster-moving pedestrians.

geriatrics The medical specialty devoted to aging.

Gerontology reaches conclusions quite different from **geriatrics,** the traditional medical specialty devoted to aging. Since geriatric physicians and nurses see hundreds of patients who are ill and infirm, they equate aging and illness; that is their experience. One geriatrician described "the patient seen in most geriatric practices—old, somewhat frail, with multiple medical conditions and taking multiple medications, possibly with some cognitive, functional, or mood impairment" (Leipzig, 2003, p. 4).

More specialists are needed in both disciplines. Geriatricians must help their patients cope with chronic, disabling diseases (such as arthritis and emphysema), which are undertreated, underresearched, and underfinanced (Cassel et al., 2003; Kane & Kane, 2005). The challenge for gerontologists is different—not preventing morbidity as much as increasing older people's joy in life: "From a gerontologist's perspective, the twenty-first century will be a time of unprecedented promise and excitement . . . [for a] life of great quality, great longevity" (Hazzard, 2001, pp. 452, 455).

The Demographic Shift

Ageism is decreasing somewhat because millions of people worldwide are reaching old age, and it is harder to be ageist when many of one's neighbors and relatives are old. The increase in the number of elderly people is being studied in **demography** (population study), the science that describes the characteristics of people of a particular age, gender, or region. We are witnessing what demographers call a *demographic shift* in the proportions of the population of various ages. Once there were 20 times more children than older people; a shift is occurring as more people survive to later adulthood.

demography The study of the characteristics of human populations, including size, birth and death rates, density, and distribution.

The World's Aging Population

The United Nations estimates that nearly 8 percent of the world's population today is over age 65, compared with only 2 percent a century ago (*question* 2). In developed nations, the proportion is larger: 13 percent of the population in Canada, Australia, and the United States (*question 1*), 16 percent in Great Britain, 19 percent in Italy, and 20 percent in Japan are 65 years old or older. Some nations, notably Japan, have more people over 65 than under 15. This is a worldwide shift: People over age 65 are projected to make up 9 percent of the world's population by 2015 and 16 percent by 2050 (United Nations, 2007).

Most nations still have more children than older adults (worldwide in 2005 there were four times more people under age 15 as over 65), but every country's population is aging. The fastest-growing age group is the **centenarians,** people over age 100. Their numbers are still small, far fewer than 1 percent in any nation (0.02 percent in the United States in 2005, or 71,000 individuals). Given current survival rates, however, the United States will have more than 241,000 people over age 100 in 2020, according to the U.S. Bureau of the Census (2006). The world will have 3.2 million centenarians by the year 2050 (United Nations, 2007).

>Response for Young Adults (from page 615): No. Some seniors hear well, and they would resent it.

centenarian A person who has lived 100 years or more.

Graphing the Change

Demographers often depict a given population as a series of stacked bars, one bar for each age cohort, with the bar representing the youngest cohort at the bottom and the bar for the oldest cohort at the top (see Figure 1.8, p. 24). Historically, the result is a shape called a *demographic pyramid*. Like a wedding cake, this diagram is widest at the base, and each higher level is narrower than the one beneath it.

There were three reasons for this traditional pyramidal shape. First, far more children were born than the replacement rate of one per adult, so each new cohort was bigger than the last. Second, before modern sanitation and nutrition, about half of all children died before age 5. Finally, those who lived to be middle-aged rarely survived adult diseases like cancer or heart attacks. As a result, after age 50 or so, each five-year cohort was about 20 percent smaller than the next-younger group.

Sometimes unusual world events have caused a deviation from this wedding-cake pattern. For example, the Great Depression and World War II reduced the birth rate in every nation. Then postwar prosperity increased rates of marriage, home-buying, and births; a "baby boom" occurred between 1946 and 1964, notably in the United States but in most other nations as well. The survival rate of children also increased. Indeed, in the 1960s many demographers feared a worldwide population explosion, a disaster that would result in mass starvation and only a few feet of living space per person (Ehrlich, 1968).

That fear has subsided. Birth rates have fallen throughout the developed world and in some developing nations. Some experts now warn of a new and very different population problem: not enough babies (Booth & Crouter, 2005). Each new cohort may be no larger than the previous one, as death before late adulthood becomes less common. The demographic stacks for Germany, Italy, and Japan are already almost square.

The populations of some nations still reflect the pyramid pattern. For example, less than 3 percent of the populations of Afghanistan, Iraq, Nigeria, Ethiopia, and Sudan are over age 65, because medical care is scarce and war has killed many adults. However, even in the poorest nations, family size is shrinking, with a reduction from an average of eight to four children per woman. In those places almost no one lived past 65 twenty years ago; now about 1 person in 40 does.

Demographic data are often reported in ways designed to alarm. If you got *question 1,* about the proportion of elderly people, wrong, you can blame the media.

For instance, some reports state that people over age 85 are the fastest-growing age group and that their numbers will double by 2050. That is true, and it sounds frightening. But "fastest-growing" could mean that the number of elderly people will double from two to four! Those over 85 are now 2 percent of the U.S. population. Even with an unprecedented increase in longevity that would allow many baby boomers to live until their 90s, which would double the proportion over age 85 by 2050, only 1 in 25 of U.S. residents would be that old. The other 24 would not be overwhelmed.

If the new shape of the demographic stack is interpreted in ageist terms, it becomes a burden for younger adults. Or it can be welcomed as providing more volunteers, voters, and grandparents, benefiting everyone (Lloyd-Sherlock, 2004; Longino, 2005). Which of these opposite possibilities turns out to be more accurate depends partly on how healthy and socially active those over age 65 will be.

Dependents and Independence

Every society has independent, self-sufficient adults and "dependents" who need care. Traditionally, it was assumed that those aged 15 to 64 were independent and productive (either in the labor force or at home) while those under age 15 and over 65 were dependent. This assumption was invalid for some individuals, but it was used as a generality to calculate the **dependency ratio,** the number of self-supporting people (aged 15 to 65) in a given population divided by the number of dependents, young and old.

dependency ratio The ratio of self-sufficient, productive adults to dependents (children and the elderly) in a given population.

In most industrialized countries, the current dependency ratio—about 2:1, or two independent adults for every one dependent—is lower than it has been for a century. That's because the birth rate has been declining since 1970 and low birth rates during the Depression mean that relatively few people are now over age 65. By contrast, the poorest developing nations have so many children that their dependency ratio is 1:1.

What will happen worldwide as more people live longer? Especially as young people need more education to become self-sufficient (which typically does not happen until they are in their 20s) and as more baby boomers retire before age 65, the tax and caregiving burden may fall on a shrinking middle cohort. If people live to 90 or 100, and only the middle third of the population—young and middle-aged adults—are working, the dependency ratio will flip from 2:1 to 1:2.

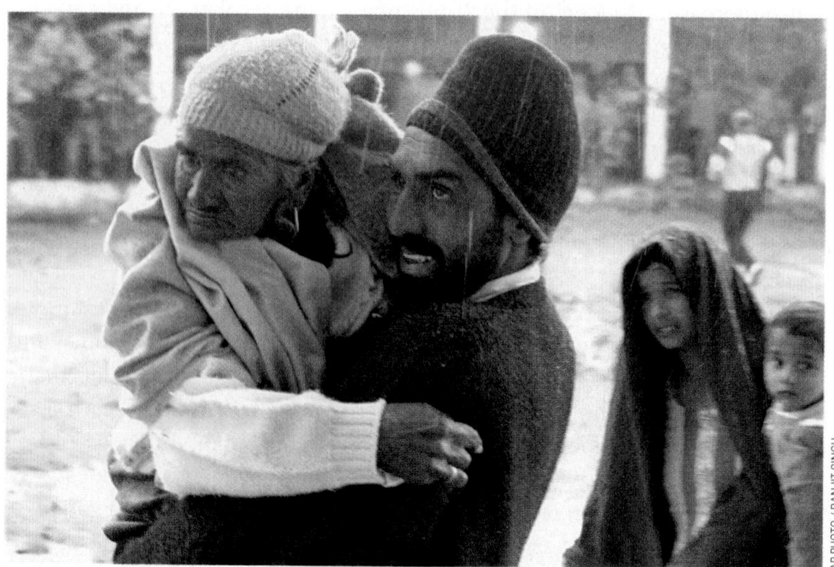

Determined to Vote Older voters tend to have stronger political opinions, more party loyalty, and higher voting rates than younger adults. This Punjabi woman takes an active interest in politics, even though she must depend on her son to carry her to the polling place.

One geriatrician has warned:

> America [is] facing financial and sociological destruction, burning in the flashpoint of a 76 million megaton age bomb . . . as 76 million aging baby boomers cause an unprecedented crisis in geriatric medicine and in our social and economic support system. . . . The coming juggernaut of the aged and infirm will crush our most beloved and important social support systems—Medicare, Social Security, and quality private health insurance—and, if not deflected, will bankrupt America.
>
> *[Klatz, 1997]*

Although this alarmist was from the United States, the demographic shift worries social scientists and demographers in every nation (Lloyd-Sherlock, 2004; Walker, 2005). For example, China has by far the largest population (more than a billion), an excellent dependency ratio (about 2.5:1), and twice as many citizens under 15 as over 65. Nonetheless, Chinese demographers ask, "Who will care for the elderly in China?" and fear the same "megaton age bomb" (Zhang & Goza, 2006).

Not So Bleak a Future

Fortunately, this time bomb is unlikely to explode, for three reasons.

First, modern technology means that fewer and fewer workers are needed to provide the food, shelter, and other goods that society needs. A century ago, 90 percent of the world's workers were farmers, who harvested just barely enough to feed themselves, their large families, and the other 10 percent. Now a few farmers feed everyone. For example, less than 2 percent of the current U.S. labor force are in agriculture (U.S. Bureau of the Census, 2006; see Research Design). No nation has more farmers than workers in any other category. Worldwide, a third of the people can produce adequate food and other necessities for everyone.

Second, there is an inverse relationship between birth rates and longevity (Kirkwood, 2003). Studies of human birth and death rates from many nations, as well as studies of animals from many species, find fewer births among long-lived social groups. This means that the birth rate will continue to fall as the aged population increases, reducing the caregiving demands on younger adults.

Finally and most important, the assumption that people over age 65 are "dependent" is ageist. Elders are "caregivers, guardians, leaders, stabilizing centers, teachers . . . culture bearers" (Carey, 2003, p. 231). Most of them are fiercely independent, providing for themselves and contributing to society. Older adults are more likely to care for others than to be cared for: They have high rates of voting, participating in community and religious groups, and donating to charity.

Contrary to the idea that most older people are infirm, only 10 percent of those over age 65 need extensive daily care, and in the United States less than half of those (about 4 percent of the total) are in nursing homes or hospitals (*question* 6). (Rates are even lower worldwide.)

In the United States, most people over 65 (about 55 percent) live with a spouse, about 30 percent (usually widows) live alone, and almost 10 percent live with grown children—half within the child's household and the other half as householders who allow their grown children to live with them (*question* 9) (U.S. Bureau of the Census, 2006). These percentages vary from nation to nation (in some cultures widows almost never live alone), but everywhere most older adults care for themselves.

People tend to overestimate the dependency of the elders (this question is most often missed on the quiz), because the frail and confused attract notice. However, think about your relatives over age 65. Most of them are probably self-sufficient, and if anyone is in a nursing home, he or she was probably self-sufficient for years.

Research Design

Scientists: Lars B. Johanson and hundreds of others.

Publication: *Statistical Abstract of the United States* (2007 and previous years).

Participants: The entire resident United States population is surveyed by the U.S. Bureau of the Census every 10 years, and samples are surveyed every year. The findings are analyzed, collated, and printed in the *Statistical Abstract*, published every year. Efforts are made to include the homeless, the hospitalized, the undocumented, although such groups are still undercounted.

Design: Questions are carefully crafted, asked by people with the same culture and language as the respondents. By law, answers are confidential and are safeguarded from inquiries by the immigration authorities. Other national and international agencies also provide data, which are checked for accuracy.

Major conclusion: Most results are what researchers would expect, but recent surprises include rising rates of low-birthweight infants, falling rates of teen pregnancy, more centenarians, and fewer serious crimes.

Comment: Social scientists rely on these data. Although not 100 percent accurate, the *Statistical Abstract* is more comprehensive than other sources. The main problems are omissions: questions not asked, data not collected, statistics not included. Ethnic backgrounds are not well distinguished: Mexicans and Puerto Ricans are placed in the same category, as are Jamaicans and African Americans, Germans and Greeks, Navajos and Hawaiians, Pakistanis and Japanese. Until 2000, mixed-race respondents had to identify themselves as belonging to only one racial group.

young-old Healthy, vigorous, financially secure older adults (generally, those aged 60 to 75) who are well integrated into the lives of their families and communities.

old-old Older adults (generally, those over age 75) who suffer from physical, mental, or social deficits.

oldest-old Elderly adults (generally, those over age 85) who are dependent on others for almost everything, requiring supportive services such as nursing homes and hospital stays.

Young, Old, and Oldest

It is ageist to lump all the older adults together, as often occurs the *Statistical Abstract of the United States.* Gerontologists distinguish among the **young-old,** the **old-old,** and the **oldest-old,** a distinction based not exclusively on age but also on health and well-being. The *young-old* make up the largest group of older adults. They are healthy, active, financially secure, and independent.

Many leaders in politics, entertainment, and business are young-old, although not usually perceived that way. One example is Dolly Parton, country singer, songwriter ("Jolene"), and actress (*9 to 5*), who is now in her 60s and still selling out concert halls.

The *old-old* suffer from some losses in body, mind, or social support, although they still have some strengths as well. The *oldest-old* (about 10 percent of the aged) are dependent, at risk for illness and injury. In general, the young-old are age 60 to 75 and the oldest-old are over age 85. However, age does not equate with dependency; some of the old-old are 100 years old, but others are only 60.

Many gerontologists prefer to label groups of people over 60 using terms that do not refer to age—*optimal aging, usual aging,* and *impaired aging* (Aldwin & Gilmer, 2003; Powell, 1994). The term *successful aging* is also used (Rowe & Kahn, 1998), signifying levels of social interaction and activity that are beyond the capacity of some people in their 60s and almost everyone over 100 (Motta et al., 2005).

AP PHOTO / KEVORK DJANSEZIAN

At Age 60 As one of 12 children, Dolly Parton grew up "dirt poor" in Tennessee; as a young-old woman, she is still a very popular singer, songwriter, and actress. Her Imagination Library program distributes more than 2.5 million free books to children every year. She maintains her image as a full-figured blonde bombshell via extensive cosmetic surgery, quipping, "It takes a lot of money to look this cheap."

SUMMING UP

Ageism is a common but destructive prejudice. Ageism is evident in the patronizing tones of elderspeak as well as the more common prejudice behind fearful predictions concerning the growing numbers of older people. The numbers of the population who are over age 65 are indeed increasing (from the current 13 percent in the United States and 7 percent worldwide), but most elders are quite self-sufficient and independent. They are far more likely to live with a spouse or alone than to be dependent on a grown child or to be in a long-term-care facility. Most elderly people may be considered the young-old, aging successfully, far more likely to support younger generations than to be dependent on them. Only the oldest-old (at most, 10 percent of the total number of people over age 65) need full-time care, whether at home with their family members or in residential care facilities. ■

Senescence

Senescence, you remember, is the aging process, which is evident from adolescence on. As discussed in Chapters 17 and 20, with each decade reaction time slows (*question* 7), all the senses become less acute (*question* 4), organ reserves are diminished, and homeostasis takes longer. In late adulthood, the visible signs of senescence become more obvious; as an unfortunate result, they may "serve as physical markers" for ageism (Calasanti, 2005, p. 9). Underlying those superficial signs are the invisible changes that take place in the internal organs.

primary aging The universal and irreversible physical changes that occur to all living creatures as they grow older.

secondary aging The specific physical illnesses or conditions that become more common with aging but are caused by health habits, genes, and other influences that vary from person to person.

Aging and Disease

Gerontologists distinguish between **primary aging,** the universal changes that occur with senescence, and **secondary aging,** the consequences of particular diseases. A leading gerontologist explains:

> Primary aging is defined as the universal changes occurring with age that are not caused by diseases or environmental influences. Secondary aging is defined as changes involving interactions of primary aging processes with environmental influences and disease processes.
>
> *[Masoro, 2006, p. 46]*

High Blood Pressure and Cardiovascular Disease

As you might imagine, the distinction between primary and secondary aging is not clear-cut. For example, the leading cause of death for both men and women is **cardiovascular disease,** which is disease that involves the heart (*cardio*) and circulatory system (*vascular*).

cardiovascular disease Disease that involves the heart and the circulatory system.

Cardiovascular disease is secondary aging, because, although common, it is far from universal and is more risk-related than age-related (Supiano, 2006). For example, the Cardiovascular Health Study began with more than 5,000 people over age 65 in the United States who did not have heart disease. After six years, some participants had developed heart disease that was not related to aging as much as to diabetes, smoking, abdominal fat, high blood pressure, lack of exercise, and high cholesterol (Fried et al., 1998).

However, the distinction between primary and secondary aging here is not as simple as it may seem. For example, high blood pressure (also called *hypertension*) is a risk factor for heart disease, stroke, cognitive impairment, and many other ailments of late adulthood. Hypertension is powerfully affected not only by some aspects of life style (salt consumption, weight) but also by genes and age. For example, a large sample of 65-year-old women with normal blood pressure were followed for 20 years. Most of them maintained their health habits, exercising and eating at age 85 as they had at age 65. Nonetheless, nearly 90 percent of them developed high blood pressure (Vasan et al., 2002).

Apparently hypertension is age-related, and cardiovascular disease is hypertension-related, so it is an oversimplification to conclude that hypertension is a risk factor for cardiovascular disease but age is not (Supiano, 2006). This kind of interaction between factors applies to almost every disease (Masoro, 2006). The mere passage of time does not cause secondary aging, but many biological changes of primary aging increase vulnerability to disease. For example, in addition to hypertension, other risks for heart disease that increase with age are cholesterol level, lipids (fats) in the blood, and stiffened arteries.

Diseases of the Elderly

The distinction between primary and secondary aging highlights an important fact: Most elderly people, even the oldest-old, do not have any particular disease. Less than half have cardiovascular disease, or diabetes, or dementia. But we cannot ignore another fact: Almost everyone has at least one disease, and many have several.

The precise meaning of "almost everyone" varies, depending on: (1) the medical cutoff point (for example, high blood pressure was traditionally diagnosed at a systolic reading of 160 or higher but is now diagnosed at 140 or higher), (2) detection methods (diabetes is more often detected than it used to be), (3) the population studied (some groups are healthier), and (4) definitions. One study defined disease as any condition that requires ongoing medical attention and/or interferes with daily life for at least a year. By that definition, 84 percent of U.S. residents over age 65 had at least one disease and 62 percent had two or more (Anderson & Horvath, 2004).

All the vital bodily systems—cardiovascular, respiratory, digestive, and renal/urinary—sustain life. Organ reserve and homeostasis enable each system to function well, even under stress, during most of adulthood, unless some particular problem (such as smoking, a virus, or drug abuse) results in illness.

Although primary aging is not the cause, it makes every bodily system slower and less efficient and thus makes disease more likely (Masoro, 2006). The heart pumps more slowly and the vascular network is less flexible, so blood pressure rises and increases the risk of stroke and heart attacks. The lungs take in and expel less air with each breath (*question* 8), so that the level of oxygen in the blood is reduced. The digestive system slows, becoming less able to absorb nutrients and expel toxins. The kidneys are less efficient at regulating levels of water, potassium, and other substances, a situation that is particularly problematic if the older adult drinks less to reduce incontinence—which itself can be caused by an imperfect renal/urinary system.

As a result of this slowdown and loss of efficiency, serious diseases—heart attacks, strokes, lower-respiratory diseases (e.g., emphysema), and most forms of cancer—are much more common in late adulthood. These examples of secondary aging are only indirectly caused by primary aging. Compared with 25- to 34-year-olds, those over age 85 in the United States today are:

- 1,000 times more likely to die of heart disease
- 1,000 times more likely to die of a stroke
- 800 times more likely to die of respiratory disease
- 200 times more likely to die of cancer
- 18 times more likely to die overall

The overall death rate (the last item on the list) is lower than the rate for any of the individual major diseases on the list because some causes of death are more common in the young than the old. Notably, the rate of homicide is eight times higher among those in their early 20s than among those 85 and older (National Center for Health Statistics, 2005).

Recuperation is slower in the very old, and weakened organs make the elderly more vulnerable if illness or an accident occurs (see Figure 23.1) (Arking, 2006). Young adults who contract pneumonia recover in a few weeks, but pneumonia can cause death if a person has no organ reserve. One in every five older people hospitalized for pneumonia dies of it (O'Meara et al., 2005).

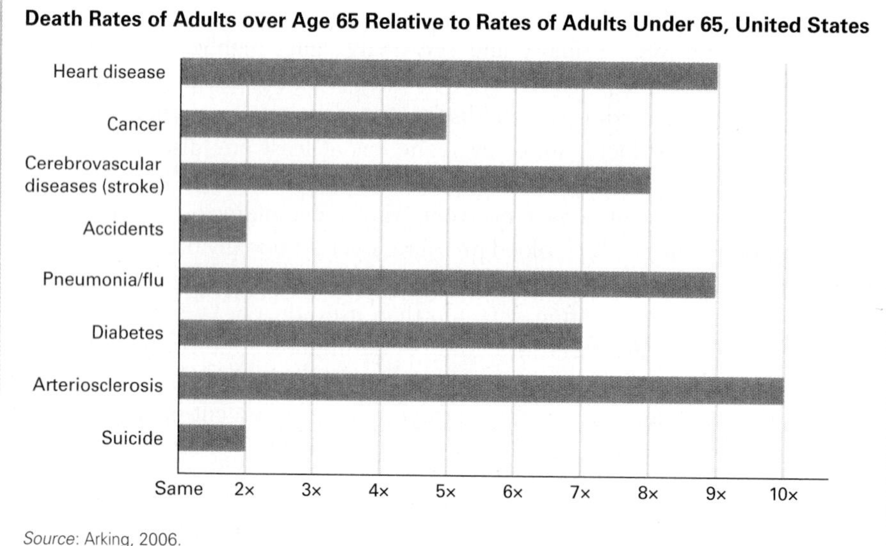

FIGURE 23.1

Leading Causes of Death Among the Elderly This chart shows approximate ratios between the death rates for Americans over and under 65. (The text compares adults aged 85 and over with those aged 25–34.) The death rate among people over age 65 is higher even for conditions that are not age-related. In fact, older adults do not have more accidents or flu than do younger adults, but if an elderly person's organs have lost their reserve capacity, an accident may cause heart failure, and the flu may lead to pneumonia.

Selective Optimization with Compensation

Secondary aging undermines quality of life. Primary aging is increasingly stressful as aging continues. A crucial factor is how well people respond with *selective optimization with compensation* (which was first discussed in Chapter 21, on page 567). Some people choose projects and activities (*selecting*) that they can do well (*optimizing*) as their adjustment (*compensation*) to aging.

Individual Compensation: Sleep

The need for selective optimization with compensation is illustrated by sleep patterns. Older adults spend more time in bed, take longer to fall asleep, wake up often (about 10 times per night), take naps, feel drowsy in the daytime, and, because of all this, are more distressed by their sleep patterns than younger adults are. Some experts find that "sleep deficit problems are widespread in the elderly, adversely affect[ing] memory, performance capabilities, and general quality of life" (Dunlap et al., 2004, p. 363). Insufficient deep sleep is particularly likely for smokers and for older men (Redline et al., 2004; Zhang et al., 2006).

One medical response is to prescribe narcotics, which may be harmful in late adulthood (Glass et al., 2005). The usual dose can overwhelm an older person's capacity for homeostasis, causing heavy sleep and rebound wakefulness, with confusion, nausea, depression, impaired cognition, and unsteadiness resulting in falls. A self-administered drug chosen by some elderly insomniacs is alcohol—which can create rebound symptoms (Aldwin & Gilmer, 2003). Many doctors advise people with insomnia to avoid all drugs, including caffeine.

The best solution may be cognitive and psychological, not medical (McCurry et al. 2007; Silversten et al., 2006). Not everyone should "sleep like a baby." As Figure 23.2 shows, sleep patterns change with age. Most of the elderly awaken several times a night to urinate, to move the legs, to adjust the blankets. With advancing years, the brain's electrical activity is reduced, which means less deep sleep, more half-awake time, and shorter dreams (Wise, 2006). Body rhythms change with age.

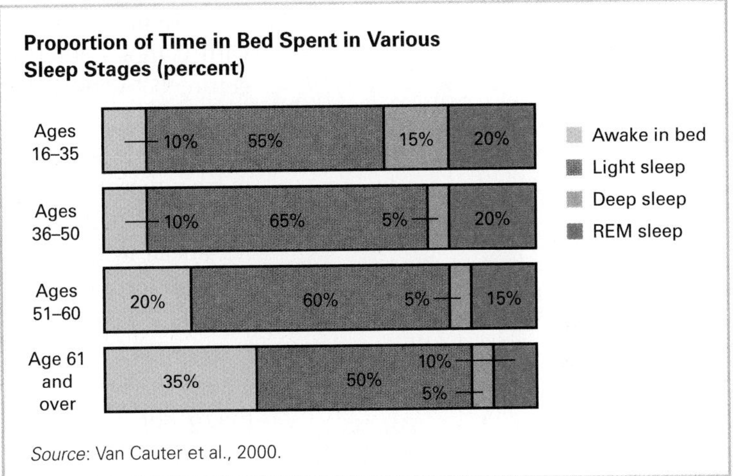

FIGURE 23.2

Don't Just Lie There One of the most common complaints of the elderly is that they spend too much time in bed but not sleeping. The solution is to get up and do something, not wait for sleep to come.

Optimization means making good use of sleep time. Evidence suggests that people with insomnia should restrict time in bed, avoid naps, and compress the time of their nightly sleep. Eventually, these measures will induce their bodies and brains to compensate by making good use of the limited sleep time (McCurry et al., 2007).

Social Compensation: Driving

Selective optimization with compensation is needed for the sake of families and societies, too. One example is in driving. Many family members question the driving ability of their oldest relatives but hesitate to do anything about it. Very few physicians advise their elderly patients about driving (Hakamies-Blomqvist & Wahlstrom, 1998). Most U.S. jurisdictions and many other nations renew driver's licenses automatically, without retesting (McKnight, 2003). Many of the elderly depend on their cars to preserve their health and independence (Scialfa & Fernie, 2006) and therefore continue to drive even when they should not.

If an older driver crashes, people blame the driver but not the family or laws that allowed driving. The ageist assumption is either that all older adults can drive or that none can. All older drivers are suspect, and some who can drive safely are

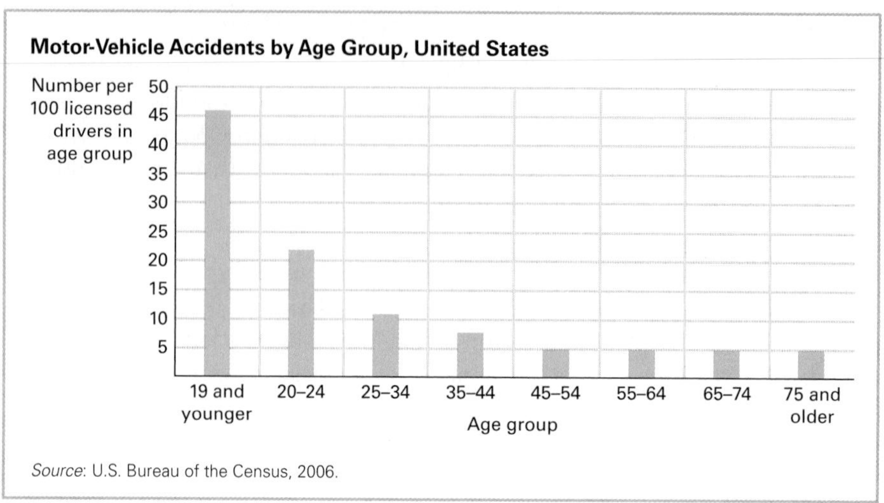

FIGURE 23.3

Nine Times as Many Accidents Among Teenagers This graph is based on data from licensed drivers only. Omitted are elderly drivers who have given up their licenses and unlicensed drivers of all ages.

afraid to do so. Ideally, everyone would periodically be required to take a road and vision test that mimicked actual driving conditions.

The fact is that elderly drivers have fewer auto accidents than younger adults (see Figure 23.3) (*question* 5), even though sign-reading takes longer, head-turning is reduced, and night vision is worse. Most older drivers use selective optimization with compensation on their own—taking their time, traversing familiar routes, getting home by dark, driving less.

Although many individuals compensate, few laws, highways, and automobile designers do so (Satariano, 2006). Bigger signs alerting drivers long before a turn, mirrors that make head-turning less crucial, direction and location devices, dashboard lighting, less glare from headlights or hazard flashes, and warnings of ice or fog ahead would reduce accidents for everyone, but especially for the aged. Cell phones, for instance, are dangerous for drivers of any age, especially the elderly (Scialfa & Fernie, 2006).

If protection were provided by well-designed cars, roads, and laws, then good elderly drivers would still be mobile, while dangerous drivers would be taken off the road. Families, societies, and the elderly themselves would benefit.

Health Habits

As emphasized in previous chapters, establishing and maintaining good health habits depend on a combination of individual choice and social context. Although all the habits we now discuss have been stressed many times in previous chapters, here we apply them specifically to the aging body.

Nutrition

With age, bodies become less efficient at digesting food and using its nutrients. Merely to stay at a steady weight, people need fewer daily calories as they grow older. Because more nutrients need to be packed into fewer calories, a varied and healthful diet, emphasizing fresh fruits and vegetables and complex carbohydrates (cereals and grains), is even more essential in late adulthood than earlier in life. Indeed, deficits of B vitamins, particularly B_{12} and folic acid, correlate with memory deficiencies (Rosenberg, 2001).

An added problem arises from drugs that affect nutrition. Aspirin (taken daily by many who have arthritis or who are trying to reduce their risk of stroke or heart attack) increases the need for vitamin C; antibiotics reduce the absorption of iron,

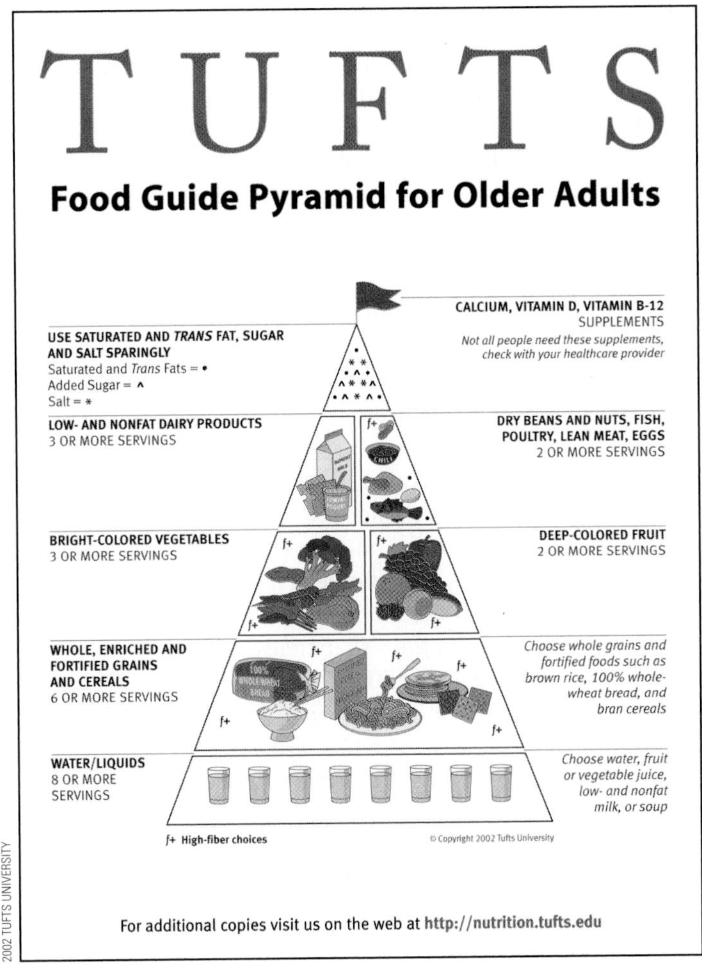

2002 TUFTS UNIVERSITY

FIGURE 23.4

Modified for Seniors Nutritionists at Tufts University in Massachusetts prepared this food pyramid, which is a modification of the U.S. Department of Agriculture's food pyramid for younger adults. One notable difference appears in the bottom row. Homeostasis for hydration (thirst) is diminished in late adulthood, so many older people need to consciously drink eight glasses of fluid each day.

calcium, and vitamin K; antacids reduce absorption of protein; oil-based laxatives deplete vitamins A and D (Lamy, 1994); caffeine reduces the water in the body. Even multivitamins can do more harm than good—if they include too much iron, for instance.

Thus, the elderly have additional demands for a balanced diet. As you can see in Figure 23.4, the basics are the same at every age but the quantities are adjusted to help the elderly avoid overeating. Another problem is undereating, which often occurs if an older person has low income, has dental problems, has digestive difficulties, or is newly widowed.

Exercise

Like nutrition, exercise may be even more important in later life than earlier, but it is increasingly difficult for an older person to walk as much as he or she did when younger. Wet leaves or ice on a sidewalk can keep a person inside; team sports are rarely organized for the elderly; traditional dancing is more difficult at an age when the sex ratio has changed so that there are more women than men; many yoga, aerobic, and other classes are paced for younger adults.

Moreover, muscles stiffen and atrophy, causing less range of motion in, for example, kicking from the knee, swinging the arms, and turning the torso (Masoro, 1999). With less flexibility, a sudden twist might lead to an aching back. For both sexes, reductions in balance and strength are especially apparent in the legs, necessitating a slower, stiffer gait and perhaps the use of a walker or cane (Newell et al., 2006).

AGE FOTOSTOCK / SUPERSTOCK

Moving Along Her stiffening joints have made a walker necessary, but this elderly woman in Gujarat, India, is maintaining her mobility by walking every day.

Self-perception is crucial. One 92-year-old man who used a cane explained:

> I look like a cripple. I'm not a cripple mentally. I don't feel that way. But I am physically. I hate it. . . . You know, when I hear people, particularly gals and ladies, their heels hitting the pavement . . . I feel so lacking in assurance—why can't I walk that way? . . . I have the same attitude now, toward life and living, as I did 30 years ago. That's why this idea of not being able to walk along with other people—it hurts my ego. Because inside, that's not really me.
>
> *[quoted in Kaufman, 1986, pp. 10–11]*

Older adults walk less if they start to think that they "look like a cripple." This change becomes debilitating if it leads to a fear of falling, which is "a common and modifiable cause of excess disability" (Lach, 2002–2003, p. 37). Note the phrase "excess disability," which means more disability than can be attributed to actual loss.

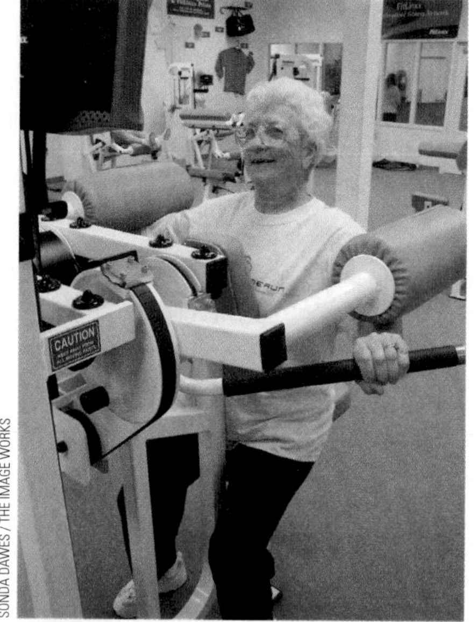
SONDA DAWES / THE IMAGE WORKS

Guess Her Age According to the stereotype, muscle-building equipment is for young men, but this 78-year-old grandmother works out at a gym four days a week.

Falls can be serious, partly because osteoporosis (fragile bones) can cause a broken hip from a tumble that would have merely bruised a younger person. (Osteoporosis is both primary and secondary aging, because it is caused by both the normal aging process and by specific behaviors—including a diet low in calcium, cigarette smoking, and lack of exercise.) Falls are the leading cause of injury leading to death after age 60, and the risk increases: Mortality rates from falls are 10 times higher at age 90 than at age 70 (Stevens, 2002–2003).

However, falls less often result in death than in functional decline (Satariano, 2006). Lack of movement increases the risk of every illness. A prospective, longitudinal study of Dutch elders (Stel et al., 2004) found that a third of those who fell became fearful and reduced their activity. Especially if they were female and already somewhat depressed and the accident occurred outside the home, all their organs often became less efficient. Ironically, only 6 percent of the falls resulted in serious injury, and those 6 percent were no more likely to lead to functional decline than the other, less serious 94 percent.

Exercise is another example of the need for compensation, because those who become unsteady need to strengthen their muscles, benefiting their cardiovascular, respiratory, and digestive bodily systems as well as their balance. Elders benefit more from weight-lifting than younger adults do, because "strength training has the greatest impact on the most debilitated subjects" (Rice & Cunningham, 2002, p. 138). Walking may need to replace running and care needs to be taken to make sure falling will not occur (walkers can be found that are very stable), but it is important for health at any age that a person exercise at least half an hour per day. Indeed, weight-bearing exercise slows down osteoporosis and thus protects should a fall occur.

issues and applications

Getting from Place to Place

One crucial indicator of elderly persons' physical and psychological health is mobility. Those who move around are healthier and more likely to maintain their well-being for years to come. This beneficial activity includes walking inside the house, but the correlation is especially strong between health (physical and psychological) and trips outside the house. By contrast, those who are homebound are likely to become sick, frail, depressed, and, especially if they spend most of their time in bed, mortally ill.

Yet ageism, younger adults, and society seem to discourage the elderly from leaving home. For example, whenever an older person is robbed, conned, raped, or assaulted, sensational news headlines make the elderly afraid and the young sympathetic toward their reluctance to venture outside. In fact, however, the

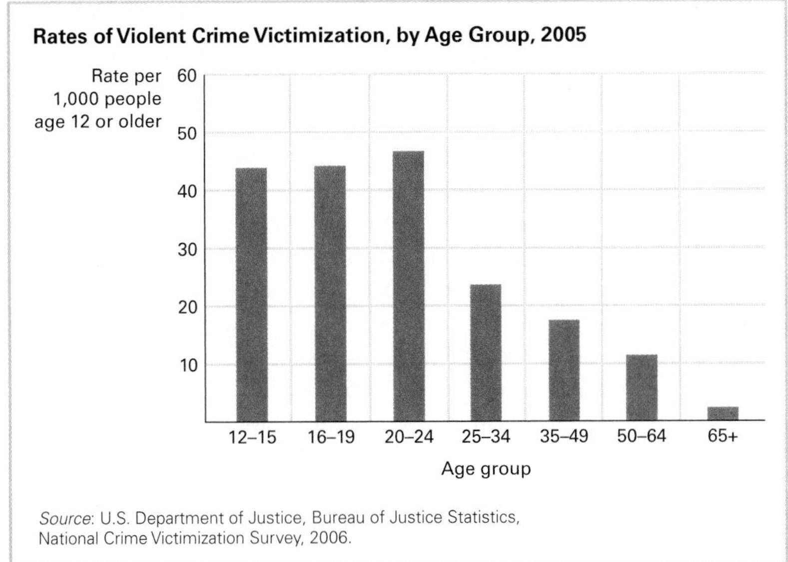

FIGURE 23.5

Victims of Crime As people grow older, they are less likely to be crime victims. These figures come from personal interviews in which respondents were asked whether they had been the victim of a violent crime—assault, sexual assault, rape, or robbery—in the past several months. This approach yields more accurate results than official crime statistics, because many crimes are never reported to the police.

aged are far less likely to be victims of street crime than are younger adults (see Figure 23.5) (*question 10*). News reports and advertisements work on the emotions of younger adults to induce them to buy locks and medical-alert devices for their older relatives, when it would be much better to go walking with them.

When it becomes necessary for an older person to stop driving, that could mean simply switching to public transportation. Yet, as the elderly complain, some areas have no public transport. Even when they are available, buses and trains run infrequently, waiting areas have no protection from weather or places to sit, and fellow passengers are rude—refusing to give up a seat, to move aside at the door, and to wait when a slower walker enters. Interestingly, such social complaints about public transportation are far more common than complaints about safety or crime (Mollenkopf et al., 2005).

Another possible form of transportation is the bicycle. Lest you think that bikes are only for children, an extensive study of five European nations (Germany, Italy, Finland, Hungary, the Netherlands) found that 15 percent of Europeans over age 75 ride their bicycles every day (Tacken & van Lamoen, 2005). In the United States, however, far fewer of the elderly ride bikes, perhaps because few bike paths are available and most bikes are designed for speed, not stability. Laws requiring bike helmets usually apply only to children—an example of ageism.

Finally, walking improves health and mobility. However, in many cities and suburbs, sidewalks are narrow or even nonexistent, traffic lights change quickly, few crosswalks have stop signs, young cyclists and skateboarders speed by, pedestrian bridges are scarce and require climbing. Those elderly who persist in walking despite such impediments are very determined, as is this legally blind man:

> I move about New York as much as ever, but with a healthy caution crossing streets. I slavishly wait for the light to change (I can usually see that) . . . and I have taken to crossing alongside other pedestrians—especially women with baby carriages, next to whom I feel safe.
>
> [*quoted in Grunwald, 2003, p. 103*]

Despite any precautions, the pedestrian death rate rises in late adulthood, because the social context—speeding drivers, streets without sidewalks, and so on—is hostile to older walkers. In the United States, the proportion of pedestrian deaths among the elderly is twice as high as their proportion of the population (U.S. Department of Transportation, 2003). In Europe also, especially among older women, the pedestrian accident rate is higher than for other forms of mobility (Mollenkopf et al., 2005).

DAVID W. HAMILTON / THE IMAGE BANK / GETTY IMAGES

His Daily Bread An older man rides his bicycle home in Fecamp, France, after buying a loaf of fresh bread.

Drug Use

As mentioned in Chapter 20, cigarette smoking is a leading killer at every age. In late adulthood, cigarettes contribute to virtually every health problem (not just with the lungs but also with the cardiovascular system and the brain). Cessation of smoking brings health benefits even if it does not occur until age 70.

Alcohol use is complicated, partly because many of the elderly are well aware of the moral prohibitions against alcohol, and thus they drink either not at all or, in rebellion against abstinence, too much. In fact, moderation is key: Elders are likely to be much healthier if they drink one or two glasses of wine or beer a day, but not more (Mukamal et al., 2006). The benefits of moderate drinking are well known for the heart, but they also apply to dementia.

The elderly tend to use legal drugs and are not usually at great risk of becoming addicted to the illegal drugs that ensnare young adults. However, prescription drugs do pose some risk, since many of them can be addictive. Here the social context is crucial, as family and physicians sometimes are unaware of or indifferent to overuse of drugs by elderly people. This topic is discussed further in Chapter 24, as overmedication is one cause of dementia.

The Brain

The fluid boundaries among the three major domains are particularly apparent in discussing the brain, which can be described in biological terms, as an organ subject to the same senescence and health habits that affect all the other organs, or in cognitive terms, emphasizing how the brain functions. This point is discussed extensively in the next chapter, on cognition in late adulthood. As with other aspects of secondary aging, the diseases of the brain (such as Alzheimer's, Pick's, and Parkinson's diseases) are not the usual outcome of senescence.

Primary aging, however, causes one cognitive change in everyone: The elderly think more slowly than younger adults do. This should come as no surprise: You have already read about the slowdown in reaction time, which affects walking, adjusting to sensory losses, and talking. The brain slowdown is part of the overall slower transmission of impulses from one cell to another, but it can also be traced to reduced production of neurotransmitters—glutamate, acetylcholine, serotonin, and especially dopamine—that allow nerve impulses to jump across the synapses between neurons (Bäckman & Farde, 2005). Furthermore, less neural fluid, a smaller prefrontal cortex, and slower cerebral blood flow all affect speed within the brain.

Especially for People Who Are Proud of Their Intellect What can you do to keep your mind sharp all your life?

Beyond the overall slowdown, there is a second crucial aspect of the physical aging of the brain: It gets smaller. Not only does the brain shrink in overall size, but some areas shrink more than others. For example, the hypothalamus—a key area for memory—and the prefrontal cortex—the area for planning ahead, inhibiting unwanted responses, and coordinating thoughts—markedly decrease (Kramer et al., 2006). As a result, both motor reaction time and brain processing are impaired.

A curious finding from brain scans (PET and fMRI) performed while a person is thinking is that, when presented with a problem, older adults use more parts of their brains, including both hemispheres, when younger adults may use more targeted areas of their brains, perhaps only in one hemisphere. This is thought to be compensation: Since older adults find that one small part of the brain is inadequate for complex thinking, they automatically use more of their brains. In this way, the ability to think may be unimpaired, even though the process of thinking is different (Daselaar & Cabeza, 2005).

As a part of the body, the brain is affected not only by the same senescence that affects the rest of the body but also, particularly, by inadequate nutrition and impaired circulation. High blood pressure, which, as you have read, is common in late adulthood, slows down cognition markedly, which means that controlling hypertension through diet or medication is as important for the brain as for the heart (Raz, 2005).

It is also important to keep the brain exercised throughout life, building up cognitive reserves so that thinking continues even as a person reaches age 90 or 100. This was shown in a study of the relationship between past education (used as an indicator of cognitive reserve) and infarcts, which are strokes that stop brain circulation for a few moments. Such strokes cause speech and motor problems as well as cognitive impairment. Education does not protect the elderly from infarcts. Those with and without college degrees have a similar incidence of strokes, in the same parts of their brains. However, education does help with recovery: Those stroke victims with greater cognitive reserve are more likely to recover their intellectual abilities (Elkins et al., 2006).

The implications of all this are discussed in Chapter 24. Much still needs to be understood about normal age-related changes in the brain, but it is safe to say here that selective optimization with compensation works for the brain as well as the body; people need to keep their brains working by keeping their overall health and circulation good.

Physical Appearance

Changes in appearance with senescence have been discussed in earlier chapters. These changes continue among the elderly, often with emotionally destructive results. In an ageist society, people who look old are treated as old, in a stereotyped way (Butler et al., 1998). When older people notice how they are treated or, for that matter, when they catch an unguarded glimpse of themselves in the mirror, they may be surprised by their own internalized ageism, even in late-late adulthood. As one 92-year-old woman related:

> There's this feeling of being out of one's skin. The feeling that you are not in your own body. . . . Whenever I'm walking downtown, and I see my reflection in a store window, I'm shocked at how old it is. I never think of myself that way.
>
> *[quoted in Kaufman, 1986, p. 9]*

What does the mirror typically show?

Skin and Hair

The skin reveals the first signs of aging: It becomes drier, thinner, and less elastic; wrinkles, visible blood vessels, and pockets of fat under the skin appear as "irrefutable evidence of the passage of time" (M. Timiras, 2003, p. 397). By late adulthood, dark patches known as "age spots" appear, and the overall reduction of the cells under the skin's surface makes people more vulnerable to cold, heat, and scratches (Whitbourne, 2002).

The hair becomes grayer and, in many people, turns white. Hair all over the body thins with age. Many men experience *male pattern baldness* because they have inherited a gene that becomes activated in adulthood. Ironically, although lower testosterone levels do not cause baldness, many men feel that hair loss signals loss of virility. Similarly, many women feel that sexual attractiveness depends on the color and thickness of their hair. Accordingly, both sexes seek to compensate, with dyes, transplants, and other means.

Body Shape and Muscles

Other visible physical changes include altered body shape (Spirduso et al., 2005). Older people are shorter than they were in early adulthood, losing a centimeter or so every decade, because the vertebrae of the spine begin settling closer together in middle age. Shape is also affected by redistribution of fat, which disappears from the arms, legs, and upper face and collects in the torso (especially the abdomen) and the lower face (especially the jowls and chin).

The change in shape obviously affects appearance, but it may also pose a health risk. If two people have the same BMI, the "apple-shaped" person, with a very wide waist, is more likely to develop heart disease than the pear-shaped person, with heavier hips and legs.

➤Response for People Who Are Proud of Their Intellect (from page 628): If you answered, "Use it or lose it" or "Do crossword puzzles," you need to read more carefully. No specific mental activity has been proved to prevent brain slowdown. Overall health is good for the brain as well as for the body, so exercise, a balanced diet, and well-controlled blood pressure are some smart answers.

Older adults often weigh less than they did in middle age, partly because they have less muscle tissue, which is relatively dense and heavy. This difference is particularly notable in men. Earlier in life, losing weight meant less fat and better health, but in old age it may indicate weakness, thinner bones, fracture risk, and disease onset (Aldwin & Gilmer, 2003).

Dulling of the Senses

For many of the elderly, the most troubling part of senescence is the loss of sensory ability. Much of social interaction depends on quick and accurate sensory responses, yet the senses become slower and less sharp with each decade (Meisami et al., 2003) (*question 4*). This is true for touch (particularly in the extremities), taste (particularly for sour and bitter), and smell as well as for the more critical senses of sight and hearing. Only 10 percent of people over age 65 see well without glasses; by age 90, the average man is almost deaf, hearing only 20 percent of what he once did (Aldwin & Gilmer, 2003).

As already described in earlier chapters, sensory decline begins as soon as puberty is over, but it is not usually devastating until old age. These losses may render the aged lonely and vulnerable.

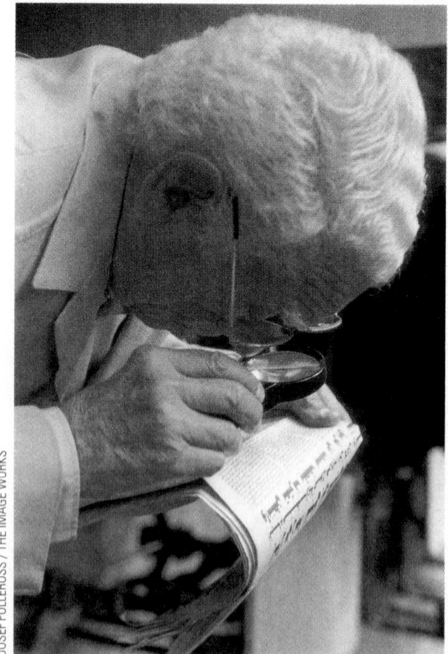

JOSEF POLLEROSS / THE IMAGE WORKS

Current Events If you had to choose between staying informed about current events and being able to see well without glasses, which one would you pick? Most elderly people can no longer see well without glasses, but, like this man reading a newspaper in Cairo, Egypt, older adults tend to be more knowledgeable than people half their age.

The crucial factor to emphasize in this chapter is not the ongoing loss but the many ways technology can modify that loss (Scialfa & Fernie, 2006). For instance, preservatives protect against food poisoning, making taste less crucial; smoke alarms and carbon monoxide alarms compensate for a diminished ability to smell; and visual and auditory losses can be moderated with aids of various kinds. To be specific, although only about 10 percent of the elderly see well, most visual losses of primary aging can be remedied. Simple corrections include brighter lights and more vivid colors, because the ability to see contrast diminishes with age. Another aid is glasses, typically two pairs (reading and distance) or bifocals, because the eyes are much less able to adjust than they used to be (Madden & Whiting, 2004).

About 17 percent of people aged 65 and over and 26 percent of those over age 75 have more serious vision impairment (not correctable with eyeglasses), usually cataracts, glaucoma, or macular degeneration (Houde, 2007):

- *Cataracts* involve a thickening of the lens, causing vision to become cloudy, opaque, and distorted. As early as age 50, about 10 percent of adults have such clouding, with 3 percent experiencing a partial loss of vision. By age 70, 30 percent have some visual loss because of cataracts. These losses are initially treatable with eyeglasses and then with outpatient surgery, in which the cloudy lens is removed and replaced with an artificial lens.
- *Glaucoma* is less common but more devastating if not detected. About 1 percent of those in their 70s and 10 percent in their 90s have glaucoma, a buildup of fluid within the eye. The pressure that results from this excess fluid damages the optic nerve, causing the visual field to narrow and eventually causing

sudden blindness. Until then, the person has no symptoms, but an ophthalmologist or optometrist can detect early signs and relieve the problem with eye drops or laser surgery. Glaucoma is partly genetic; it occurs at younger ages among African Americans and people with diabetes (Whitbourne, 2002).

- *Macular degeneration* is deterioration of the retina and is the most common cause of blindness. It affects one in twenty-five people in their 60s and one in six over age 80 (O'Neill et al., 2001). It can be diagnosed early by having regular eye exams or by noticing spotty vision (such as reading with some letters missing). Macular degeneration is progressive, becoming severe five years after it starts (Mukesh et al., 2004). Medication (ranibizumab) can restore some vision if treatment begins early enough (Rosenfeld et al., 2006).

For all sensory problems, including these three, early detection and treatment are needed. Ophthalomologists have many measures to prevent impairment but almost none to reverse damage once it has occurred. At that point, technology (from lighting to sound waves) can be useful. With accommodation, even those who are blind can be productive employees and self-sufficient family members (Houde, 2007).

As you remember from Chapter 20, age-related hearing loss, called *presbycusis*, affects every adult. People typically wait five years or more between getting the first hint that their hearing is fading and visiting an audiologist. By age 65, 40 percent have difficulty hearing normal conversation. If a hearing aid is recommended, ageism interferes. Many people refuse even tiny, digital, personalized hearing aids because they associate any such device with looking old (Meisami et al., 2003).

Through Different Eyes These photographs depict the same scene as it would be perceived by a person with (a) normal vision, (b) cataracts, (c) glaucoma, or (d) macular degeneration. Thinking about how difficult it would be to find your own car if you had one of these disorders may help you remember to have your vision checked regularly.

(a)

(b)

(c)

(d)

ALL: PHOTODISC / GETTY IMAGES

Ironically, individuals who mishear and misunderstand conversation may strike others not only as old but also as mentally deficient, and they may therefore be excluded from social give-and-take. Then the hard-of-hearing person may withdraw. Even compared to the visually impaired, "hard-of-hearing individuals are often mistakenly thought to be retarded or mentally ill . . . [and] are more subject to depression, demoralization, and even at times psychotic symptomatology" (Butler et al., 1998, p. 181).

When people first notice the loss of some sensory abilities—when a newspaper page blurs or a dinner conversation is misunderstood—their usual reaction is disbelief. Then the problem seems to disappear—eyes refocus, the brain completes the half-heard comments—so the person can blame the situation, not his or her own aging sensory system. This reaction may be life-threatening if, for example, diminished taste and smell cause an older person to eat spoiled food or fail to detect smoke or gas, or if hearing or vision impairment leads to crossing the street when a truck is coming.

More generally, many people become depressed when they realize that their senses are not functioning as well as they once did; they avoid social situations or even avoid leaving their home, sadly concluding that things will only get worse. Unless something is done, depression continues—and things do get worse, since primary aging is ongoing.

Recognition and compensation, not denial or passive acceptance, are crucial (Horowitz & Stuen, 2003). Fortunately, compensation is available for every sensory loss. Specific technological advances include not only smaller hearing aids and lighter glasses but also attachments to televisions, radios, and telephones, headsets for particular occasions, canes that sense when an object is near, infrared lenses that illuminate the darkness, closed-captioned TV programs, service animals (not just dogs, but birds and monkeys, too), computers that scan printed text and "speak" the words, or, for the hearing-impaired, computers that turn speech into print.

Millions of people are disabled by sensory losses, not only because advanced technology may be too expensive but also because "the technology is not yet so advanced as to prescribe itself for the person who needs it, nor does it teach people how to integrate it into their lives" (Goodrich, 2003, p. 69). Technology is not necessarily user-friendly, and those who care for the elderly are sometimes inclined to do things for them rather than help them learn to help themselves.

Remedies must be subsidized and individualized in order for people to be taught how to use them properly, so that frustration, denial, and resignation are prevented (Charness & Schaie, 2003). People with new hearing aids, for instance, need help to master the best settings, positioning, and maintenance procedures. Typically, six sessions over two months are required, because the equipment requires fine adjustment and new social patterns must be allowed to develop (Weinstein, 2000).

Thus far we have focused primarily on individuals adjusting to their losses. We should also take note of the adjustments that society makes—or, more often, fails to make—for children, the disabled, or the elderly.

Just about everything, from airplane seats to fashionable shoes, is designed for young, able-bodied adults. Many disabilities would disappear if the social setting were better designed (Satariano, 2006). Look around at the built environment (the layout and lighting of stores, streets, colleges, and homes) and notice the print on medicine bottles, the garbled public address systems in train stations, even the stairs on buses.

Like society as a whole, many individuals fail to take the needs of others into account. Relatives and friends need to remember that sensory loss does not mean

AP PHOTO / THE BRAINERD DISPATCH, STEVE KOHLS

Taking Her Ears for a Walk This profoundly deaf woman is greatly helped by Murphy, who is trained to get her attention whenever the telephone or doorbell rings or the smoke alarm goes off. Murphy's assistance enables her to remain in her home in Brainerd, Minnesota.

brain loss. Instead of yelling at an older person who does not hear well or oversimplifying what is communicated, younger people can pronounce their words clearly and speak slowly in settings where lip reading is easy (a well-lit living room, not a crowded, dimly lit restaurant).

Compression of Morbidity

Unlike childhood diseases that can be prevented by vaccination, most adult diseases are impossible to prevent, since they are caused by a combination of genes (present since conception), early childhood influences (too late to change), and senescence (increasing every year). As one editorial explains, "Aging . . . predisposes our bodies to fall apart. Organs, tissues, and even individual cells start misbehaving, rendering us susceptible to the familiar conditions that, for example, weaken our bones, scramble our neural messages, and condemn us to pain" (Chong et al., 2004). Often, however, the onset of illness can be postponed and its impact can be limited, reducing the amount of time that a person is seriously ill, disabled, or in pain. This is **compression of morbidity,** a shortening of the time spent in illness before death.

compression of morbidity A shortening of the time a person spends ill or infirm, accomplished by postponing illness.

Morbidity has, in fact, been compressed among the aged. Compared to 30 years ago, a smaller proportion of older adults report that their activity is limited, and fewer people are in hospitals. Many people have serious diseases but nonetheless continue to be independent and without pain (Hamerman, 2007; Manton et al., 2006).

Compression of morbidity is the result of lifestyle and attitude as well as medicine, as can be illustrated with a hypothetical example (see Figure 23.6). Say that pair of identical twins have the same genes and are exposed to the same

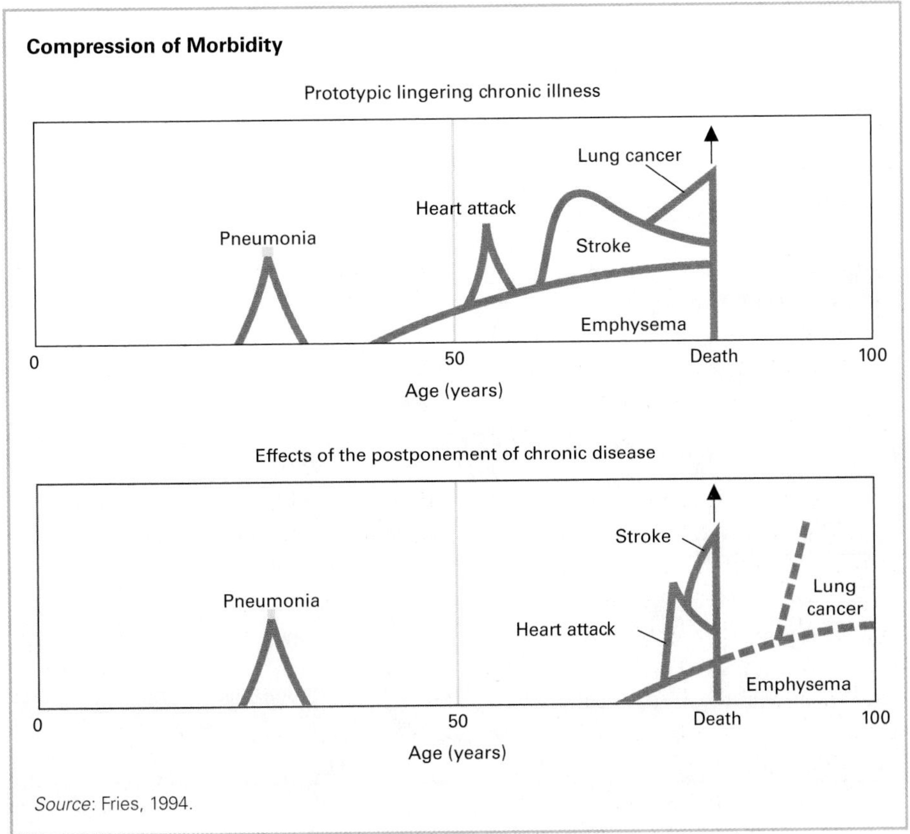

FIGURE 23.6

Primary and Secondary Aging The interplay of primary and secondary aging is shown in this diagram of the illness and death of a hypothetical pair of monozygotic twins. Both are equally subject to certain illnesses—so both experience a bout of pneumonia at about age 25. Both also carry the same genetic clock, so they both die at age 80. However, genetic vulnerabilities to circulatory, heart, and lung problems affect each quite differently. The nonexercising smoker (*top*) suffers from an extended period of morbidity, as his various illnesses become manifest when his organ reserve is depleted, beginning at about age 45. By contrast, the healthy lifestyle of his twin (*bottom*) keeps disability and disease at bay until primary aging is well advanced. Indeed, he dies years before the emergence of lung cancer—which had been developing throughout late adulthood but was slowed by the strength of his organ reserve and immune system.

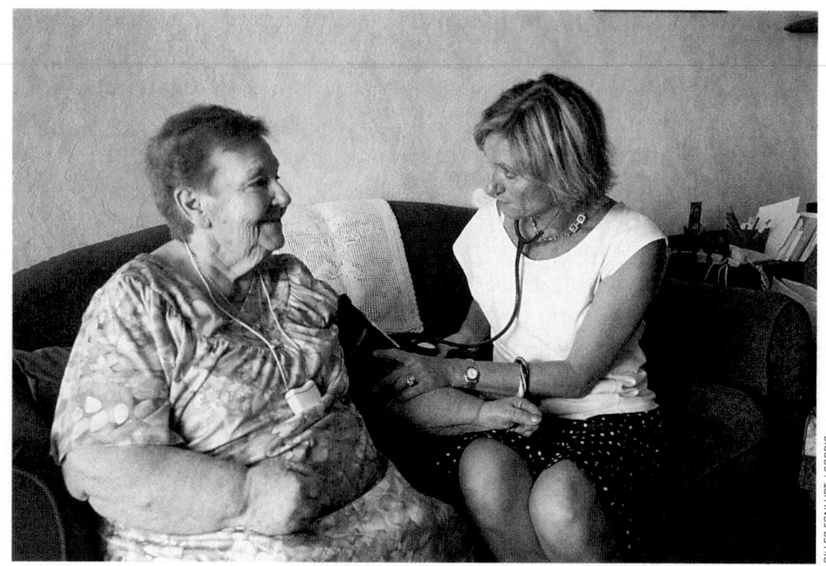

GILLES FONLUPT / CORBIS

Reducing Risk The woman at left has some lifestyle factors, especially her excessive weight, that increase her risk of illness. On the plus side, however, she evidently has a cheerful attitude and sees her doctor regularly.

Observation Quiz (see answer, page 636): Can you spot another sign that this patient is making an effort to protect her health?

pathogens, but one "smokes like a chimney, is fat, doesn't exercise, and has a poor diet," while the other has "fairly good health habits" (Fries, 1994, p. 314). Both get pneumonia at about age 25 (environmental exposure), and both recover quickly, because their organ reserves and immune systems have barely begun to age. Both are genetically predisposed to the same illnesses—emphysema, heart attack, stroke, and lung cancer.

Beginning in middle age, one twin is sick with several serious illnesses, but his brother is protected. Even if they die at the same age (not typical), the morbidity of the healthy twin is so delayed that his genetic vulnerability to cancer is not yet evident. He has only a few compressed weeks of illness after a long, healthy life. This example is hypothetical, but it echoes reality: Monozygotic twins experience dozens of nongenetic differences in QALYs (Finch & Kirkwood, 2000).

BARRY LEWIS / CORBIS

Happy Days Ahead This proud and happy couple in Romania are homeowners and gardeners and are likely to remain quite healthy until a series of illnesses occur in the last year of their lives. This is compression of morbidity at its best.

Compression of morbidity is a social and psychological blessing as well as a biological one. A healthier person is likely to remain more intellectually alert and socially active—in other words, to experience the optimal aging of the young-old person, not the impaired life of the oldest-old. Medical science has made compression of morbidity possible: Improved prevention, detection, and, most important, treatment allow today's older persons to live with less pain, more mobility, better vision, stronger teeth, sharper hearing, clearer thinking, and enhanced vitality.

SUMMING UP

Primary aging is inevitable and universal, its effects becoming apparent in many ways as people age. Secondary aging involves diseases that occur as a result of poor health habits and environmental toxins combined with primary aging. Successful coping with senescence requires selective optimization with compensation on the part of societies as well as individuals. The most obvious signs of senescence are superficial—in skin, hair, and body shape. Some of the most troubling developments relate to the senses, particularly vision and hearing, because sensory impairment often results in depression and social isolation. External compensation is available but requires a combination of technology, specialist help, and personal determination. The goal is compression of morbidity, so that aging is not accompanied by serious disease or severe disability except for a short time, right before death. ■

Theories of Aging

Can aging and even death itself be postponed, allowing the average person to live 100 healthy years or more instead of 75 or 85? There are many intriguing possibilities but not many definitive answers. Almost two decades ago, one expert categorized 300 theories of aging (Medvedev, 1990). Here we describe three that are still widely debated: wear and tear, genetic adaptation, and cellular aging.

Wear and Tear

The oldest, most general theory of aging is known as **wear and tear** (Masoro, 1999). Just as the parts of an automobile begin giving out as time and distance add up, so the body wears out, part by part, after years of exposure to pollution, radiation, unhealthy foods, drugs, diseases, and other stresses. This theory holds that just by living our lives, we wear out our bodies. In more technical terms, human bodies are built with a certain redundancy, with organ reserve and repair processes to overcome the inevitable assaults from time, pollution, illness, and injury (Gavrilov & Gavrilova, 2006).

wear-and-tear theory A view of aging as a process by which the human body wears out because of the passage of time and exposure to environmental stressors.

Can this be true? For some body parts, yes. Athletes who put repeated stress on their shoulders or knees have chronically painful joints by middle adulthood; people who regularly work outdoors in strong sunlight damage their skin; industrial workers who inhale asbestos and smoke cigarettes destroy their lungs.

These examples of unusual wear and tear are not typical, but by late adulthood, everyone's body has accumulated signs of wear. Scars leave their mark, bones reveal past fractures, eye lenses get cloudy, the inner ear has fewer hairs, fingernails become ridged, and so on.

At least three findings support the wear-and-tear theory. First, according to the "disposable soma" theory of aging, each body (soma) has a certain amount of physical energy and strength, which gradually is spent (disposed of) over a lifetime (Finch & Kirkwood, 2000). For this reason, women who have never been pregnant

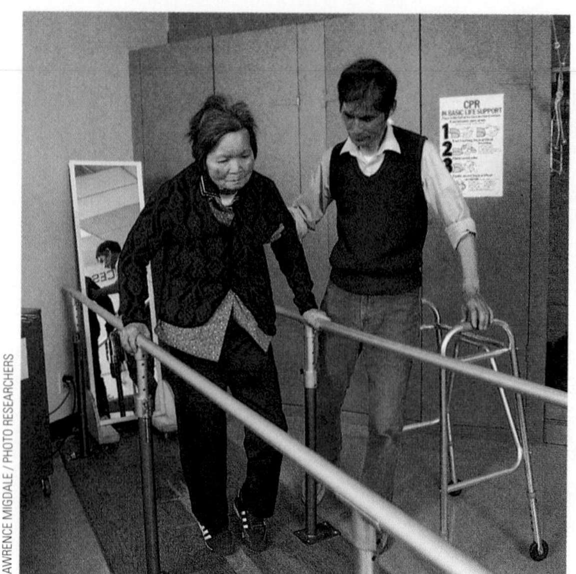

LAWRENCE MIGDALE / PHOTO RESEARCHERS

Use It So You Don't Lose It Although wear-and-tear theory might predict otherwise, the single most critical failure of body functions that accelerates aging is loss of mobility. We now know that after a stroke or other mobility-restricting event, the best therapy is to start walking again.

live longer than others with the same health habits; perhaps pregnancy helps to wear out a person's body.

Second, people who are overweight tend to sicken and die at younger ages, perhaps because it takes more energy to maintain their bodies and thus less life force is available to them as they approach old age. Gastric surgery on morbidly obese people increases the risk of death during recuperation, but seems to add years over the long term, because their bodies have a smaller day-to-day burden (Torquati et al., 2007).

Third, one breakthrough of modern medical technology is the ability to replace worn-out body parts. Transplanted hearts and livers, artificial knees and hips, implanted dentures add years to life.

The analogy to a machine does not explain all of human aging, because "unlike inanimate objects, living systems utilize external matter and energy to repair wear and tear" (Masoro, 1999, p. 50). In other words, we eat, we breathe, we move—and we get better! Unlike a machine, the human body benefits from use. Aerobic exercise improves heart and lung functioning; tai chi improves balance; weight training increases strength; sexual activity stimulates the sexual-reproductive system; digestion is improved by eating fruits and vegetables that require vigorous intestinal activity.

The converse is also true: Inactivity breeds illness. It seems as if people are more likely to "rust out" from disuse or suffer effects of misuse and abuse than to wear out. Thus, although the wear-and-tear theory applies to some aspects of aging and seems relevant for some people, it probably does not describe human aging overall (Austad, 2001).

Genetic Adaptation

genetic clock A purported mechanism in the DNA of cells that regulates the aging process by triggering hormonal changes and controlling cellular reproduction and repair.

Humans may have a kind of **genetic clock,** a mechanism in the DNA of cells that regulates the aging process by triggering hormonal changes and controlling cellular reproduction and repair. Just as a genetic clock "switches off" genes that promote growth (at about age 15), it might "switch on" genes that promote aging.

Evidence for genetic aging comes from several genetic conditions that produce premature aging and early death. People with Down syndrome (trisomy-21) develop heart disease, cancer, and Alzheimer's disease in middle age. Children born with a genetic disease called *progeria* stop growing at about age 5 and begin to look old, with wrinkled skin and balding heads. These children develop many other signs of premature aging and die in their teens of heart diseases typically found in the elderly (Clark, 1999; Spirduso et al., 2005).

➤Answer to Observation Quiz (from page 634): She is wearing a medical alert pendant, which enables her to summon help if she should fall or become ill. Not visible in the photograph is the fact that this doctor has practiced in Marseille, France, for 14 years; continuity in health care is life-prolonging.

How Long Is a Normal Life?

maximum life span The oldest possible age that members of a species can live, under ideal circumstances. For humans, that age is approximately 122 years.

Genes seem to bestow on every living species an inherent **maximum life span,** defined as the oldest possible age that members of that species can live. Under ideal circumstances, the maximum that rats live seems to be 4 years; rabbits, 13; tigers, 26; house cats, 30; brown bears, 37; chimpanzees, 55; Indian elephants, 70; finback whales, 80; humans, 122; lake sturgeon, 150; giant tortoises, 180 (Clark, 1999; Finch, 1999).

Such variations between species, and limits of life for each species, suggest that the maximum is set by the genes of each animal. Of course, everyone has different genes. Centenarians probably inherit genes for a long life (their siblings also tend to live about 15 years longer than average) (Perls, 2005), but every human has some genes that signal the end of life.

average life expectancy The number of years the average newborn in a particular population group is likely to live.

Maximum life span is quite different from **average life expectancy,** which is the average life span of individuals in a particular group. In human groups, average life expectancy varies a great deal, depending on historical, cultural, and socioeconomic factors.

In ancient times, the average life expectancy was about 20 years (because many infants died). In 1900, in developed nations, it was about 50. The main reasons for the increase were public health measures, including better sanitation and nutrition, that meant survival of young children. Since the middle of the twentieth century, immunization and antibiotics have further extended the life span (Crews, 2003).

More recent increases in life expectancy are attributed to reduction in deaths from adult diseases (heart attack, pneumonia, cancer, childbed fever). Many middle-aged men once died of heart attacks; now they usually survive. Childbirth was a leading killer for young women a century ago, was still hazardous 50 years ago, but now is virtually never fatal in the developed world. Cancer was once a death sentence; today more than half the people with cancer survive for at least five years.

In the United States in 2007, average life expectancy at birth was about 75 years for men and 81 years for women (U.S. Bureau of the Census, 2007). Those who are already 65 years old (no longer at risk of early death) are expected to live to 84; those who are already 80 die at age 89, on average. At about 90, the death rate seems to level off, which means that someone who is 95 is as likely to die within that year as is someone who is 105.

The marked historic variations in average life expectancy are mirrored by geographical variations. If your aunt lives in Boston and is now 60, she will probably live 35 more years, but if she lives in Botswana, it is astonishing that she is still alive (life expectancy at birth in Botswana is 34) and chances are she has only a few more years to live.

LIONEL CIRONNEAU / AP / WIDE WORLD PHOTOS

DIEGO GIUDICE / AP / WIDE WORLD PHOTOS

Celebrating a Dozen Decades Only a few people in the world have lived much beyond 100 years. Two of those oldest of the old are shown here. *(left)* Jeanne Calment of France celebrates her 121st birthday; she died at 122 in 1997. *(right)* Maria do Carmo Jeronimo of Brazil celebrates her 125th. Jeronimo was born in slavery and had no reliable birth records; she died in 2000, supposedly aged 129. Several other people are known to have lived to 120, and that age seems to be the upper limit for the human species. Even with the best medical care, most people die before age 80.

DAVID BARRIT / GAMMA LIAISON

Progeria This 16-year-old South African boy, embraced by his 81-year-old grandmother, has progeria, a genetic disorder that produces accelerated aging, including baldness, wrinkled skin, arthritis, heart and lung difficulties, and early death.

Despite such variations, the genetic theory of aging contends that the *maximum* life span is fixed at a few years past age 100, which was the maximum human life span a millennium or two ago. (The biblical patriarch Methuselah's age, 969, was probably measured in "years" that had fewer days than the modern year.) Thus, in ancient times those few who avoided accidents and illnesses died of the same aging-related causes that are evident in the twenty-first century. Just as we humans are genetically programmed to reach sexual maturity during the teen years, we may be genetically programmed to die during late adulthood.

Selective Adaptation

Epigenetic theory (discussed in Chapter 2) provides an explanation for the genetic diseases of late life. Since reproduction and child care are essential for the survival of the species, when genes appeared that were fatal to young adults, they were not transmitted; their existence ended when the person died or when their parentless children died.

However, "after the vagaries of reproductive adulthood, genetics begin to exert their effects" (Crews, 2003, p. 158). Thus, genes for diseases of late adulthood were already passed on to the next generation. This would explain why the disease rate does not merely increase year by year but accelerates sharply at the age when childbirth and child rearing are usually over (see Figure 23.7)

Consequently, death in early adulthood is almost always caused by nongenetic events (accidents, suicide, war, infections), but diseases that kill people after age 50 frequently result from genes that have been maintained (Finch & Kirkwood, 2000). Parkinson's disease, Huntington's disease, Alzheimer's disease, type 2 diabetes, coronary heart disease, and osteoporosis are among the many examples of genetic conditions that evolutionary processes allow (Satariano, 2006). These conditions begin in midlife but do not kill until later, perhaps because of the "grandmother hypothesis"—the idea that middle-aged people need to devote their energy to the well-being of future generations (Alvarez, 2000).

An alternative version of the genetic theory of aging is that each species has particular genes that directly cause aging and death, in order for a new generation to be born. This theory is bolstered by the discovery of alleles—SIR2, ApoE4, def-2, and several others—that cause aging (Hekimi & Guarente, 2003; R. Miller, 2001). For instance, the ApoE2 gene is protective. Of U.S. men in their 70s,

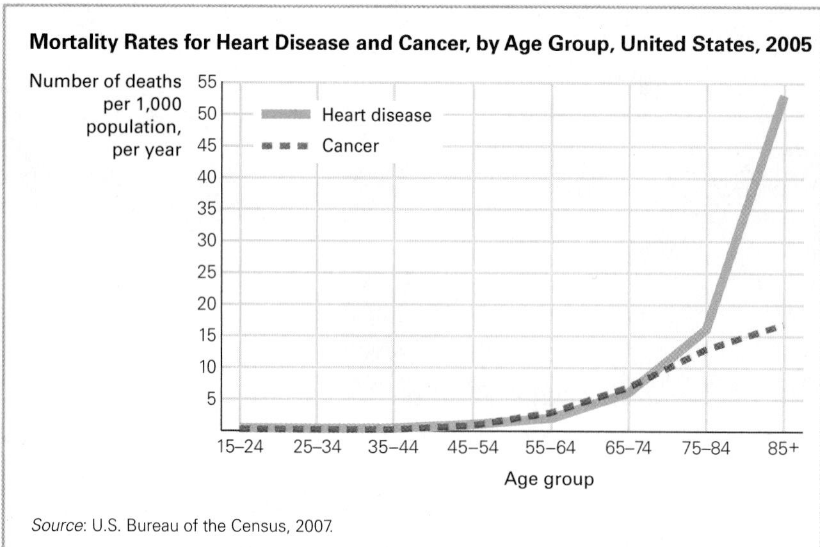

FIGURE 23.7

Not a Straight Line The two leading causes of human death, cancer and heart disease, are fatal to less than 1 person in 1,000 under age 55, but after that the death toll from these two conditions increases markedly, especially after age 65. The reason may be that younger adults are genetically protected from death but, after their child-rearing days are over, their genetic weaknesses are allowed expression.

12 percent have that gene, as do 17 percent of those over age 85; these statistics mean that a higher proportion of those without it die before age 85 (Crews, 2003). But another common allele of the same gene, ApoE4, causes senescence in the cardiovascular system and the brain. According to this theory, everyone has at least some genes, like ApoE4, that cause aging.

Cellular Aging

A related cluster of theories about aging begin with the idea that aging occurs at the cellular level: Perhaps people grow old because the cells of their bodies become old, damaged, or exhausted. Humans are composed of trillions of cells, many of which reproduce throughout life (although cell reproduction slows down with age). An obvious example is the outer cells of the skin, which normally are completely replaced every few years. When the skin gets cut or scraped, cell replacement occurs within a few days. Blood and tissue cells also duplicate rapidly. Cells of the ear, eye, and brain duplicate more slowly or not at all. New cells are continually created, each designed as the exact copy of an old cell.

Errors in Duplication

This ongoing cell duplication may produce aging, because each cell is so complex that minor errors inevitably accumulate (Fossel, 2004). Mutations occur because of toxins and stresses and also because DNA instructions for creating new cells become imperfect over thousands of duplications.

Since new cells are not quite exact copies of the old, some of them contain damaged elements. This transmission of cellular errors begins at conception. If the imperfection is severe (e.g., a missing chromosome anywhere except the 23rd pair), the organism is spontaneously aborted. If just one cell is imperfect, that does not cause the death of the entire organism, since bodies have many ways to repair cellular errors or destroy an abnormal cell. Over time, an "error catastrophe" may occur as imperfections multiply to the point that the organism can no longer repair or overcome all the damage. With the rapidly reproducing skin cells, for example, inexact replication results in slower replacement, benign growths, color changes, or skin cancer (P. Timiras, 2003). Invisibly, throughout the rest of the body, cellular imperfections accumulate (Vijg et al., 2005).

SARAH LEEN / NATIONAL GEOGRAPHIC / GETTY IMAGES

A Sun Worshipper When this Australian man was a young lifeguard, he says, "We rubbed our bodies with coconut oil"—which did nothing to protect his skin from the sun's damaging rays. Deep tanning damaged his skin cells. Every dot of light represents a lesion that was removed to halt the spread of skin cancer.

One specific theory that explains why cellular accidents increase over time begins with the fact that electrons of some atoms in our bodies are unattached to their nuclei. Such atoms are called *free radicals.* Free radicals are highly unstable, because unpaired electrons can react violently with other molecules, splitting them or tearing them apart.

Such damage is especially likely when free radicals of oxygen scramble DNA molecules or the mitochondria that provide energy for DNA duplication. These **oxygen free radicals** (also called ROS, reactive oxygen species) produce errors in cell maintenance that can eventually cause cancer, diabetes, and arteriosclerosis as a result of "oxidative stress" (Halliwell & Gutteridge, 2007).

oxygen free radicals Atoms of oxygen that, as a result of metabolic processes, have an unpaired electron. These atoms scramble DNA molecules or mitochondria, producing errors in cell maintenance and repair that, over time, may cause cancer, diabetes, and arteriosclerosis.

Indeed, although oxygen is essential for life and some oxygen free radicals are normal, every part of the body suffers if too many oxygen free radicals bombard the cells. As many as 10,000 hits per cell can occur per day (Sinclair & Howitz, 2006). Some believe that an abundance of oxygen free radicals, over time, is what causes aging. Slowing down the hit rate would thus slow down aging.

One way to do this would be to increase the body's supply of **antioxidants,** which are chemical compounds that bind with the unattached electrons of oxygen free radicals, preventing them from causing damage. Many people take supplements of antioxidants (vitamins A, C, and E and the mineral selenium) in hopes of

antioxidants Chemical compounds that nullify the effects of oxygen free radicals by forming a bond with their unattached oxygen electron.

living longer. However, research does not confirm that ingested antioxidants slow the aging process even in birds and mice, much less in humans (Barga, 2003; Halliwell & Gutteridge, 2007).

The Immune System

A variant of the cellular theory of aging focuses on the immune system, whose cells become less numerous as the person ages. In a young person, many cells in the body recognize foreign or abnormal substances in the circulatory system, isolate them, and destroy them. Among these immune cells, one type is called **B cells,** because they are manufactured in the *bone* marrow. B cells produce antibodies to destroy specific invading bacteria and viruses. These antibodies remain in the body lifelong, protecting it against a second bout of infectious diseases such as measles, mumps, and specific strains of influenza.

B cells Immune cells manufactured in the bone marrow that create antibodies for isolating and destroying bacteria and viruses that invade the body.

T cells Immune cells manufactured in the thymus gland that produce substances that attack infected cells in the body.

Another type of attack cells, called **T cells** (manufactured by the *thymus* gland), produce substances that destroy infected cells. They help the B cells produce more efficient antibodies and strengthen other aspects of the immune system. The immune system also includes NK ("natural killer") cells, K ("killer") cells, and white blood cells. Altogether, since humans are very complex and long-living creatures, they have developed an elaborate array of immune cells, which is necessary because humans are exposed to thousands of pathogens and parasites (Promislow et al., 2006).

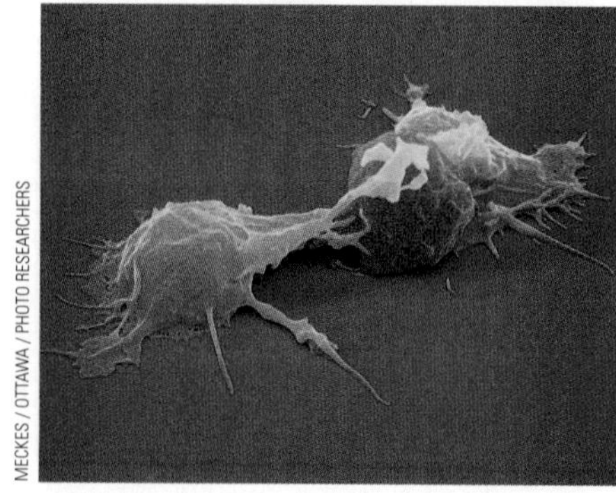

MECKES / OTTAWA / PHOTO RESEARCHERS

Normal Killers The immune system is always at war, attacking invading bacteria, viruses, and other destructive agents. Here two "natural killer" cells are overwhelming a leukemia cell. How healthy we are and how long we live are directly related to the strength and efficiency of our immune system.

In all age groups, individuals with weaker immune systems (measured by analysis of T and B cells in the blood) die sooner than others (Effros, 2001), and those with a high count of NK cells are likely still to be quite healthy at age 85. As the immune system declines, cancers may grow and shingles (caused by a latent herpes virus, which younger immune systems are able to keep in check) may appear.

Measures to stop cancer often involve killing all rapidly producing cells, which means temporarily shutting down the immune system. Measures to prevent shingles include a new inoculation to add immunity, which is not completely effective because the immune system of the aging body is more difficult to activate (Oxman et al., 2005).

Throughout life, immune systems are stronger in women than in men. The female thymus gland is larger. That is why females tend to live longer and, in many families, why fathers are more often incapacitated by a cold than are mothers. This advantage has a downside, because women have more autoimmune diseases (e.g., rheumatoid arthritis and lupus), which occur when a person's immune system turns against the body.

Replication No More

The idea that cellular aging limits the life span is also supported by laboratory research, beginning with the work of Leonard Hayflick (1994; Hayflick & Moorhead, 1961). At first Hayflick thought that cells, given the right conditions, would continue duplicating forever. Like thousands of other scientists worldwide, he worked with cultures of cells that duplicated time and time again. When the cells stopped duplicating, Hayflick and others believed, something in the environment was at fault (no laboratory could be completely free of contaminants in the air).

In a famous series of experiments, Hayflick allowed cells taken from human embryos to age "under glass" by providing them with all the nutrients necessary for cell growth and protecting them from external stress or contamination that would produce errors. In such ideal conditions, he expected the cells to double again and again, indefinitely.

Instead, cells stopped multiplying after about 50 divisions. This time Hayflick hypothesized that something other than laboratory contaminants was at work. In further research, he found that cells from adults divided fewer times than did cells from children and that children's cells doubled fewer times than did cells from embryos. Something was counting and keeping track of age.

Over the past several decades, this research has been replicated many times by hundreds of scientists, using various techniques and cells from people and animals. Healthy cells always stop replicating at a certain point, which is referred to as the **Hayflick limit;** it is roughly proportional to the maximum life span of the particular species.

When the Hayflick limit is reached, the aged cells differ from young cells in many ways. One major discovery is that the very ends of the chromosomes—called the **telomeres**—are much shorter in older cells. The length of telomeres signals longevity. Each cell duplication results in a shorter telomere, fewer remaining duplications, and therefore shorter life (Hornsby, 2007). Eventually, the telomere is completely gone, the cell stops duplicating, and the creature dies.

Some experts believe that "relengthening telomeres is the most efficient way to reset gene expression" (Fossel, 2004, p. 284), slowing the aging process. An enzyme called *telomerase* increases the length of telomeres; adding telomerase to an organism may slow down aging. There is one serious drawback: Cancer cells multiply more rapidly when telomerase is abundant (Feldser & Greider, 2007).

Another possibility is to implant stem cells with long telomeres and natural telomerase from embryos into an aging person, in the hope that the cells will duplicate and thus slow the aging process. This approach is highly speculative, and much more research is needed (Hiyama & Hiyama, 2007).

Hayflick himself believes that the Hayflick limit, and therefore aging, is caused by a natural loss of molecular fidelity—that is, by inevitable errors in transcription as each cell reproduces itself (Hayflick, 2001–2002). He does not dispute the telomere research, but believes that telomere shortening is a symptom of a basic process rather than the direct cause of aging.

Hayflick limit The number of times a human cell is capable of dividing into two new cells. The limit for most human cells is approximately 50 divisions, an indication that the life span is limited by our genetic program.

telomeres The ends of chromosomes in the cells, whose length decreases with each cell duplication and seems to correlate with longevity.

Especially for Biologists What are some immediate practical uses for research on the causes of aging?

thinking like a scientist

Can the Aging Process Be Stopped?

Leonard Hayflick (2004) calls *anti-aging* an oxymoron, a term that contradicts itself. He believes that aging is a natural process built into the very cells of our species. Humans can stave off morbidities and premature mortality, but they cannot (and should not) halt senescence. We can "add life to years" but we cannot "add years to life." Another scientist agrees, vehemently criticizing anyone who hopes to extend life as

> an utterly irresponsible citizen if you would dump this radical life extension on the rest of us, as if you expect your friends and neighbors to pay for your Social Security at age 125 and your Medicare at 145.
>
> *[Stock & Callahan, 2005, p. 218]*

Few scientists are that impassioned, but most agree that the research has not proven the effectiveness of any of the anti-aging methods now in use. Many people are already eating special foods or taking pills, with no proof that doing so will have any effect (Huang et al., 2006). One Australian scientist notes that "sixty-one percent of Australians and probably a larger percentage of Americans are already" taking dietary supplements, hoping for longer life and better health. "We're talking while the horse has already bolted, the stable is empty" (Dransfield, 1998, p. 471).

Some scientists are looking for effective ways to extend human life, pursuing leads from research on lower animals. One group has found a gene (UCP-2) in the mouse brain that regulates temperature. By changing the expression of that gene, they lowered core body temperature and extended mouse life (Conti et al., 2006). Might humans also be able to lower their body temperature and live longer?

As one skeptical scientist notes, however, no one knows "why this temperature [98.6° F, or 37° C] has been selected by evolution [as normal for humans]. . . . One would certainly want to know the consequences of hypothermia before pursuing it as a way to increase life span" (Saper, 2006, p. 774). As stressed throughout this book, scientists have good reason to be wary. Some measures that once seemed very promising (thalidomide to prevent miscarriage, abstinence education to prevent teen pregnancy, the D.A.R.E. program to stop adolescent drug use, hormone replacement therapy to stave off heart disease) have proven to be more harmful than helpful.

There is, however, one promising possibility that few humans—scientists or not—seem ready to pursue: **calorie restriction,** drastically reducing the intake of dietary energy (that is, food calories) while maintaining an adequate intake of vitamins, minerals, and other important nutrients. In dozens of experiments, first with fruit flies and mice and recently with dogs, monkeys, and chimpanzees, the animals that were given healthy foods, but only half their usual calories, lived much longer. For humans, this would mean eating about 1,000 calories a day, none of which would be fried, buttered, or sugared.

Groups of genetically similar animals have been compared after one group has been fed restricted meals since infancy while the other group has been allowed free access to food. The life span of the calorie-restricted animals doubles, and that group experiences fewer diseases of aging, such as cardiovascular disease, diabetes, and dementia (Sinclair & Howitz, 2006).

The main explanation for this extension of the life span in lower mammals is at the cellular level: Restricted nutrition slows down cell growth and duplication, resulting in fewer free radicals and slower metabolism. This allows much more time before the Hayflick limit is reached. The crucial question remains: Would restricted eating work for people?

About 1,000 North Americans belong to the Calorie Restriction Society, eating only about 1,000 nutritious calories a day. One is Michael Rae, from Calgary, Canada, who explained to a reporter:

> Aging is a horror and it's got to stop right now. People are popping antioxidants, getting face lifts, and injecting Botox, but none of that is working. At the moment, C.R. [calorie restriction] is the only tool we have to stay younger longer.
>
> *[quoted in Hochman, 2003, p. 5]*

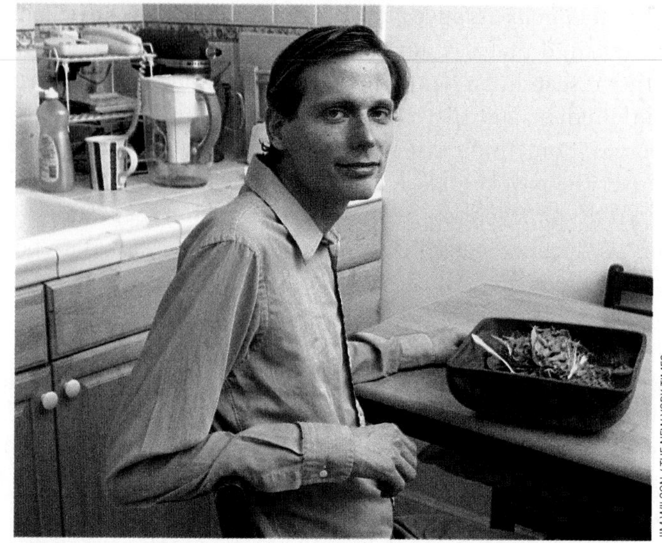

JIM WILSON / THE NEW YORK TIMES

112/63, 6 Feet, 135 Pounds These numbers are this man's blood pressure, height, and weight after six years on a calorie-restricted diet. So far, so good—he is now 36 years old.

The reporter notes, "Mr. Rae is 6 feet tall, weighs just 115 pounds, and is often very hungry." Are he and his fellow members merely deluding themselves? One scientist comments:

> We won't know whether calorie restriction really would extend life span in humans for a long time. . . . Actual studies are going to be brutally difficult, and it would be a very cruel irony if after years of trials, life span were not extended.
>
> *[Cutler et al., 2005, p. 59]*

Another says:

> The only proven method of life extension for mammals is caloric restriction in infancy, which is impractical for human purposes. Search for a Fountain of Youth has always been a delusion.
>
> *[Moody, 2001–2002, p. 34]*

Perhaps. Or perhaps most people (including most scientists) are deluding themselves by continuing to eat as much as they do.

calorie restriction The practice of limiting dietary energy intake (while consuming sufficient quantities of vitamins, minerals, and other important nutrients) for the purpose of improving health and slowing down the aging process.

SUMMING UP

There are hundreds of theories of aging. The wear-and-tear theory proposes that bodies wear out with age, but this theory does not explain the entire aging process. Genetic theories explain the evolutionary limits on the maximum life span for various species. One such theory holds that selective adaptation for humans may have required, or at least allowed, humans to inherit genes for aging and death that did not become active until after they had raised their replacement generation. Cellular theories reflect the fact that living organisms are collections of cells, which usually replicate themselves and repair damage—processes that become less effective with age. Some cellular theories focus on damage from oxygen free radicals; others on accumulated errors in cell duplication; others on telomere shortening, when cells no longer reproduce. Although not yet proven with humans, calorie restriction extends the life of many other species of mammals and raises the question: What are humans willing to do to live longer? ■

➤Response for Biologists (from page 641): Although ageism and ambivalence limit the funding of research on the causes of aging, the applications include prevention of AIDS, cancer, senility, and physical damage from pollution—all urgent social priorities.

The Centenarians

According to some scientists, most babies born today in developed countries will live to become centenarians (Kinsella, 2005). How might your life be at age 100?

Other Places, Other Stories

In the 1970s, three remote places—one in the Republic of Georgia, one in Pakistan, and one in Ecuador—were in the news because many vigorous old people were found to live there. As one researcher wrote:

> Most of the aged [about age 90] work regularly. . . . Some even continue to chop wood and haul water. Close to 40 percent of the aged men and 30 percent of the aged women report good vision; that is, that they do not need glasses for any sort of work, including reading or threading a needle. Between 40 and 50 percent have reasonably good hearing. Most have their own teeth. Their posture is unusually erect, even into advanced age. Many take walks of more than two miles a day and swim in mountain streams.
>
> *[Benet, 1974]*

Among the people described in this report are a woman said to be over 130 who drank a little vodka before breakfast and smoked a pack of cigarettes a day, a man who claimed to be 100 when he fathered a child, and a village storyteller who had an excellent memory at a reported age of 148.

A more comprehensive study (Pitskhelauri, 1982) found that the lifestyles in all three of these regions are similar in four ways:

- Diet is moderate, consisting mostly of fresh vegetables and herbs, with little consumption of meat and fat. A prevailing belief is that it is better to leave the dining table a little bit hungry than too full.
- Work continues throughout life. In these rural areas, even very elderly adults help with farm work and household tasks, including child care.
- Family and community are important. All the long-lived people are well integrated into families of several generations and interact frequently with friends and neighbors.
- Exercise and relaxation are part of the daily routine. Most of the long-lived take a stroll in the morning and another in the evening (often up and down mountains); most take a midday nap and socialize in the evening, telling stories and discussing the day's events.

Perhaps these factors—diet, activity, social respect, and exercise—lengthen life.

That the social context promotes longevity is buttressed by evidence from bumblebees. Genetically, worker bees and queen bees are the same, but worker bees die at about age 3 months while queen bees, which are fed special food and given respect, do not die until about age 5 years, living 20 times longer than their genetic relatives. Only when a queen dies is another worker bee chosen to become a queen. Could diet and respect extend the human life as well?

Surely your suspicions were raised by the preceding paragraphs. Humans have almost nothing in common with bumblebees, or mice or fruit flies for that matter,

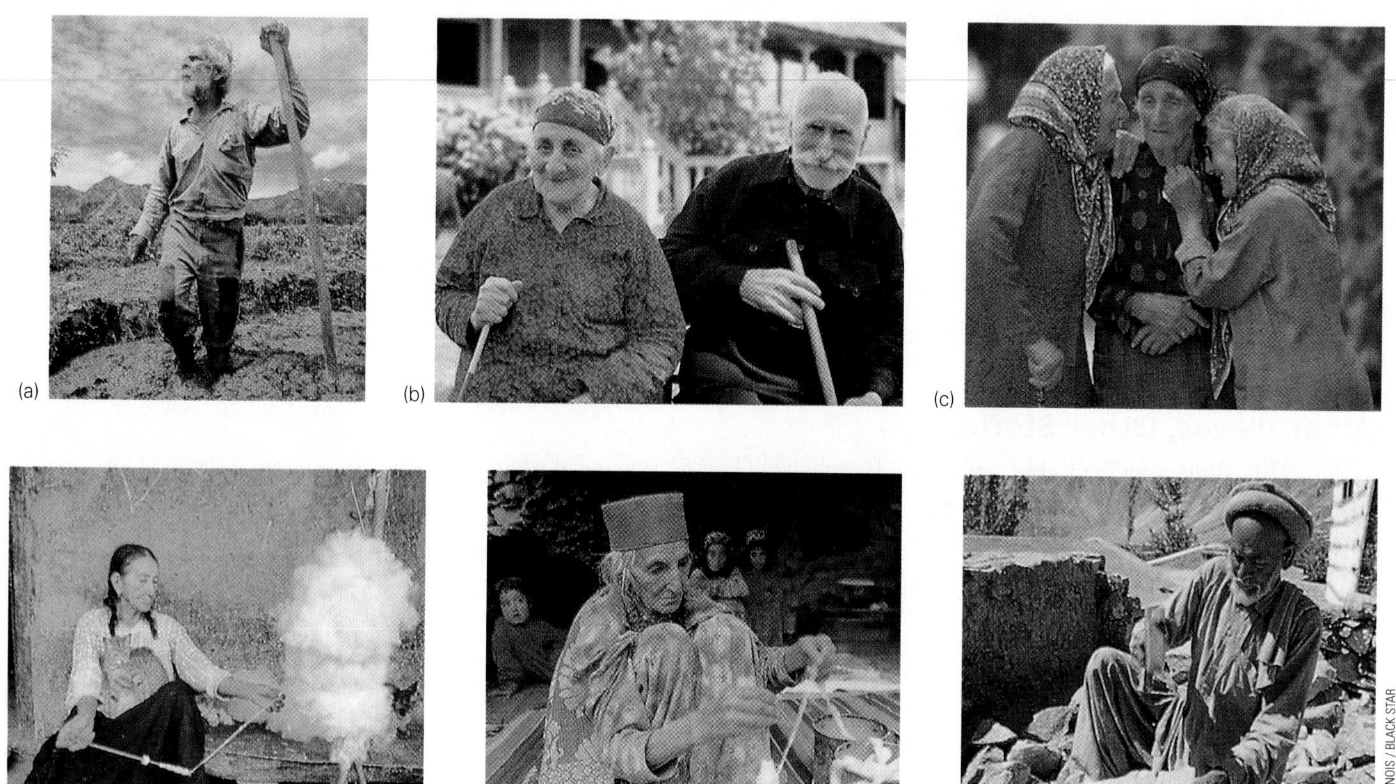

Longevity Three remote regions of the world are renowned for the longevity of their people (although verified birth certificates are unavailable). In Vilcabamba, Ecuador, (*a*) 87-year-old Jose Maria Roa stands on the mud from which he will make adobe for a new house, and (*d*) 102-year-old Micaela Quezada spins wool. In Abkhazia in the Republic of Georgia, companionship is an important part of late life, as shown by (*b*) Selekh Butka, 113, posing with his wife, Marusya, 101, and (*c*) Ougula Lodara talking with two "younger" friends. Finally, Shah Bibi (*e*), at 98, and Galum Mohammad Shad (*f*), at 100, from the Hunza area of Pakistan, spin wool and build houses.

and the information about those long-lived people came out more than 30 years ago. The phrases "reported age," "said to be," and "claimed" were used.

Indeed, the three regions famous for long-lived humans have no verifiable birth or marriage records from 100 years ago. Beginning at about age 70, many people in these areas systematically exaggerate their age (Thorson, 1995). Everyone who claimed to be a centenarian was probably exaggerating, and every researcher who believed them was too eager to accept the idea that life would be long and wonderful if only the ills of modern civilization could be avoided. The oldest well-documented person lived to be 122.

The Truth About Life After 100

Do not give up on centenarians too quickly. Several modern nations with good records report communities where many people live long, productive lives, including an island of Japan (Okinawa), an area of the United States (rural North Dakota), and a religious group (Seventh Day Adventists). Those who study the aged, wherever they live, are surprised to find many quite happy (Jopp & Rott, 2006). As one woman explained:

AP PHOTO / DANIEL OCHOA DEL OLZA

Francisco Ayala at 100 Ayala wrote his first novel at age 18. Eighty-one years later, he noted that he had always maintained his "curiosity and fundamental skepticism." Ayala left his native Spain after the civil war that brought a fascist regime to power in the 1930s. He taught in Argentina and the United States for 25 years. Since age 60 he has been writing and lecturing in his homeland, winning every Spanish literary prize.

> At 100, I have a sense of achievement and a sense of leisure as well. I'm not pushed as much as I was. Old age can be more relaxing and more contemplative. I'm enjoying it more than middle age.
>
> *[quoted in Adler, 1995]*

Researchers in western Europe, East Asia, and North America find similarities between the centenarians in their research and the aged individuals (many of whom, while not reaching 100, were at least in their 80s) in Georgia, Pakistan, and Ecuador: moderate diet, hard work, an optimistic attitude, intellectual curiosity, and social involvement. Fewer calories, more respect, lots of vegetables, and strong religious faith seem to be part of their lives.

Disease, disability, and dementia may eventually set in; studies disagree about how common these problems are at age 100. However, there is no doubt that many people celebrate a 100th birthday with energy, awareness, and optimism (Ellis, 2002; Hitt et al., 1999; Jopp & Rotte, 2006).

Virtually no centenarian is completely disease-free, but many seem to have escaped or delayed the serious infirmities of late adulthood, and some are intellectually intact (Perls, 2005). People who live past 100 tend to have achieved a compression of morbidity. They tend to minimize whatever problems they have and are quite upbeat about their health (Aldwin & Gilmer, 2003). That attitude may be one reason they have lived so long.

If this surprises you, you are not alone; many older people themselves would be surprised. Ironically, the older a person is, the less likely he or she is "to imagine large numbers of their peers as favored as they are" (Cruikshank, 2003, p. 11), instead believing that they are "exceptions to the usual pattern of aging, and that their health is superior to that of most of their age peers" (Hirslaho & Ruopplia, 2005, p. 79). Ageism affects all of us, at every age.

SUMMING UP

Research on centenarians finds no proof that anyone has lived longer than 122 years, but more and more people throughout the world are reaching 100. Many of them are quite happy and active. If people reach late adulthood in good health, their attitudes and activities may be crucial in determining the length and quality of their remaining years. It may be ageist to assume that a human will be less happy, less alert, and less interested in life at age 100 than at age 30 or 60. ■

SUMMARY

Prejudice and Predictions

1. Contrary to ageist stereotypes, most older adults are happy, quite healthy, and active. Although elderspeak persists, ageism is weakening because gerontologists provide a more optimistic picture of late adulthood than geriatricians do and an increasing percentage of the population is over age 65.

2. The dependency ratio expresses the relationship between the number of self-sufficient, productive adults and the number of children and elderly dependents in a population. Most elderly people are not dependent on younger generations.

3. Gerontologists sometimes distinguish among the young-old, the old-old, and the oldest-old, according to each age group's relative degree of dependency. Only 10 percent of the elderly are dependent, and only 4 percent are in nursing homes or hospitals.

Senescence

4. The many apparent changes in skin, hair, and body shape that began earlier in adulthood continue in old age. The senses all become less acute, including vision (90 percent of older people need glasses, and many have cataracts, glaucoma, or macular degeneration) and hearing (most older men are significantly hard-of-hearing, as are a smaller number of elderly women).

5. Selective optimization with compensation for sensory losses requires a combination of technology, specialist advice, and personal determination. These three have been underutilized in the past (exemplified by the underuse of hearing aids). The next cohort may compensate more than today's elderly do.

6. Primary aging happens to everyone, reducing organ reserve in body and brain. Although the particulars differ depending on the individual's past health habits and genes, eventually morbidity, disability, and risk of mortality increase. Compensation is possible and brings many benefits, including compression of morbidity, which means that the person suffers only a short period of infirmity right before death.

Theories of Aging

7. Hundreds of theories address the causes of aging. Wear-and-tear theory suggests that living wears out the body; it applies to some parts of the body, but not to overall aging.

8. Another theory is that genes allow humans to survive through the reproductive years but then to become seriously ill and inevitably die. Each species seems to have a genetic timetable for decline and death, expressed in the length of telomeres. Cell reproduction slows down and eventually stops.

9. Cellular theories of aging include the idea that the processes of DNA duplication and repair are affected by genetic factors that cause errors to accumulate as new cells are made. Oxidative stress, caused by oxygen free radicals, hinders cell maintenance and repair.

10. Age-related decline in the immune system may cause aging, as it contributes to elderly people's increasing vulnerability to disease.

11. One approach to extending life is calorie restriction, an approach that has been successful with many species of mammals.

The Centenarians

12. It was once believed that many people in certain parts of the world lived long past 100 as a result of moderate diet, high altitude, hard work, and respect for the aged. Such reports turned out to be exaggerated.

13. The number of centenarians is increasing, and many of these oldest-old are quite healthy and happy. The personality and attitudes of the very old suggest that long-term survival may be welcomed more than feared.

KEY TERMS

ageism (p. 615)
elderspeak (p. 615)
gerontology (p. 616)
geriatrics (p. 616)
demography (p. 616)
centenarian (p. 617)
dependency ratio (p. 618)
young-old (p. 620)
old-old (p. 620)
oldest-old (p. 620)
primary aging (p. 620)
secondary aging (p. 620)
cardiovascular disease (p. 621)
compression of morbidity (p. 633)
wear-and-tear theory (p. 635)
genetic clock (p. 636)
maximum life span (p. 636)
average life expectancy (p. 636)
oxygen free radicals (p. 639)
antioxidants (p. 639)
B cells (p. 640)
T cells (p. 640)
Hayflick limit (p. 641)
telomeres (p. 641)
calorie restriction (p. 642)

KEY QUESTIONS

1. How is ageism comparable to racism or sexism?

2. Why is the increasing number of people living past the age of 65 less of a problem than some people imagine it to be?

3. What is the difference between primary aging and secondary aging?

4. What changes occur in the sense organs in old age, and how can their effects be minimized?

5. Explain several factors that affect how long a person is sick before he or she dies.

6. Evaluate the validity of the wear-and-tear theory for senescence.

7. In what ways do the cellular theories of aging seem plausible?

8. What is the relationship between the immune system and aging?

9. How do genes contribute to the length of life?

10. Describe an epigenetic explanation for the the aging process.

11. What conclusions can be drawn from Hayflick's research?

12. What are some of the characteristics of people who live to a very old age?

APPLICATIONS

1. Analyze Web sites that have information about aging for evidence of ageism, anti-aging measures, and exaggeration of longevity.

2. Compensating for sensory losses is difficult, because it involves learning new habits. To better understand the experience, reduce your hearing or vision for a day by wearing earplugs or dark glasses that let in only bright lights. (Use caution and common sense: Don't drive a car while wearing earplugs or cross streets while wearing dark glasses.) Report on your emotions, the responses of others, and your conclusions.

3. Ask five people of various ages if they want to live to age 100, and record their responses. Would they be willing to eat half as much, exercise much more, experience weekly dialysis, or undergo other procedures in order to extend life? Analyze the responses.

24

CHAPTER OUTLINE

- The Usual: Information Processing After Age 65
  - Sensing and Perceiving
  - A CASE TO STUDY: "That Aide Was Very Rude"
  - Memory
  - THINKING LIKE A SCIENTIST: John, Paul, Ringo, and . . .
  - Control Processes
  - THINKING LIKE A SCIENTIST: Neuroscience and Brain Activity
  - Staying Healthy and Alert
  - Ageism
- The Impaired: Dementia
  - Alzheimer's Disease
  - Many Strokes
  - Subcortical Dementias
  - Reversible Dementia
  - A CASE TO STUDY: Is It Dementia or Drug Addiction?
  - Prevention and Treatment
- The Optimal: New Cognitive Development
  - Aesthetic Sense and Creativity
  - The Life Review
  - Wisdom

Late Adulthood: Cognitive Development

As you saw in the two earlier chapters on adult cognition (Chapters 18 and 21), during adulthood some abilities increase, others wane, and some remain stable. By the end of adulthood, physical impairment, reduced perception, decreased energy, and slower reactions take an increasing toll. Yet, even among the oldest-old, decline is not the entire story. The information-processing perspective, a focus of this chapter, highlights the complexity and variability of cognition in late adulthood.

Whenever I flew to Minnesota to visit my parents, who were in their 90s, friends would ask me, "How are their minds?"

"Good," I would answer.

"Isn't that wonderful!" they sometimes replied.

I wanted to shout "No! Not wonderful!" and then lecture about cognition in late adulthood. Instead I was quiet, thinking and remembering.

My parents were forgetful and repetitive; they could be stuck in the past, telling stories I had already heard. But my friends were asking if my parents were senile, and they were relieved to learn that this was not the case.

Like most of their peers, my parents were neither senile nor wonderful. Late-adulthood cognition is too complex to be captured in a brief social conversation.

The previous chapter explained that biosocial development in later adulthood may be "impaired," "usual," or "optimal." As you will see in this chapter, cognitive development can be separated into the same trio. Severe cognitive impairment (dementia) is discussed, as is optimal cognition (wisdom). Before describing the worst and the best, we begin with the usual, neither sad nor wonderful.

The Usual: Information Processing After Age 65

One helpful way to understand intellectual ability in late adulthood is to use an information-processing approach, breaking down cognition into the steps of input (sensing), storage (memory), program (control processes), and output. As you will see, some parts of the process decline and others do not.

Most intellectual abilities change little throughout early and middle adulthood (as documented in Chapter 21). At some point, however, everyone slows down in every domain. In the Seattle Longitudinal Study, the averages in all five primary mental abilities (verbal meaning, spatial orientation,

AP PHOTO / THE NEWS-STAR, ARELY CASTILLO

From Ten-Hut to Plant-Tending This man needed all his senses when he was on active duty as a colonel in the U.S. Marine Corps. Now, nearing age 90, he is partially deaf and has problems with balance. These sensory impairments don't keep him from enjoying the sights, smells, and textures of the plants he tends at a senior center's greenhouse in Louisiana.

inductive reasoning, number ability, and word fluency) began to fall at about age 60, a decline particularly notable in the subtests that measure spatial perception and processing speed (Schaie, 2005).

Other longitudinal research finds that, for some abilities, cognitive decline does not begin until age 80 or so (Singer et al., 2003). Still other researchers report losses earlier, by age 50 (Rabbitt & Anderson, 2006). Although scientists differ on timing, they agree that people do not think as quickly or remember as well at age 80 as they did at age 40.

Two impediments are often cited as typically contributing to this general decline and slowdown: too much interference and not enough inhibition. The information-processing perspective helps clarify at what point interference and lack of selectivity have an impact as well as what that impact is.

Sensing and Perceiving

Information processing starts with input—that is, with stimuli taken in by the senses. In order for stimuli to become information that is perceived by the mind, they must cross the *sensory threshold;* that is, the person must be able to sense them. Here significant decline begins with age. Remember that none of the senses are as sharp at age 65 as at age 16. Some information—the details of a road sign 300 feet away or the words of a conversation in a noisy place—never reaches sensory memory because the senses never detect the relevant stimuli.

Attention Deficits

Sensory-input problems are insidious because people miss information without realizing it. Cognition depends on perception, and perception depends on sensations, so elderly people whose senses are less sharp might be oblivious to their cognitive handicap.

Research confirms that reduced sensory input (missed sounds, sights, and even smells) impairs cognition (Anstey et al., 2003; Dulay & Murphy, 2002; Wingfield et al., 2005). One study of people of all ages found that 11 percent of the variance in cognitive scores for young adults, and 31 percent of the variance for older adults, was related to sensory impairment (Lindenberger & Baltes, 1997). That is, 31 percent of the difference in test scores between two older people could probably be attributed to the sharper senses (better sight or hearing, for example) of the "smarter" person.

Results like this imply that one simple way to predict an older person's intellect may be to measure vision, hearing, or smell. This raises another issue: How important is intellectual sharpness near the end of life? Consider the following.

a case to study

"That Aide Was Very Rude"

I knew an elderly couple, married 65 years, who shared a room in a nursing home because neither could walk far without help. They were loving, protective, and proud of each other. This led to trouble.

Once an aide lifted the woman from her bed.

"Stop, you're hurting me!" she yelled. The aide kept lifting until the husband hit him with his cane. One outcome was an "incident report," casting doubt on the husband's intellect since he did not understand that the aide was helping his wife. The other outcome, from the wife, was "I love you more than ever."

Another aide, in changing the man's bed, said, "This stinks." The man was almost deaf, so he didn't hear the comment, but his wife did and complained for weeks, saying things like,"That aide was very rude. How do you think my husband would feel if he heard that?"

In fact, the bed did stink, because the husband was incontinent. Neither he nor his wife could smell the stale urine on his bedsheets. She would have been ashamed; almost all her life she had cleaned and tidied for both of them, ensuring that he was always well-dressed and sweet-smelling.

In late adulthood, their reduced sensitivity, plus habituation, meant that neither noticed the odor and thus neither was ashamed—he of his incontinence and she of her failure to make sure the bed was clean.

Were their sensory limitations and their love a better combination than the aides' normal senses and insensitive behavior? If you had to choose between reduced sense of smell and reduced emotional awareness, which would you pick?

A similar situation was explored in a psychological study of decision making between older mothers (aged 65–94) and their caregiving children (aged 34–66). Researchers found that, in most cases, rather than exploring the six or more rational options for resolving a dilemma, the mother and child did "no evaluation of alternatives because the first one proposed was quickly selected" (Cicirelli, 2006, p. 215). Usually the adult child's solution was accepted by the mother. This can be interpreted either as evidence for "age-related declines" (p. 219) in decision making or as evidence that these dyads valued mutual respect and affection more than following a strictly logical process.

Interference

Reduced sensory input affects cognition in a second way, by increasing the power of interference. Interference is thought to be a major impediment to effective and efficient cognition in the elderly (Park & Payer, 2006). Not only is less information perceived by the mind because of reduced sensory input, but some vital information is obscured because other, less important information interferes by capturing attention.

For example, if reduced auditory input means that the word *interference* is faintly heard as *ear ants,* then cognitive resources are required to ignore background noises in order to analyze the sounds and the context to figure out what was probably said. This process might tire the mind, depleting the mental energy needed to take the next step in information processing—that is, to judge whether the words should be remembered or not. Thus, interference impedes thought because it slows down thinking (Kramer et al., 2006).

Memory

In the information-processing model of cognition (see Chapter 12), storage refers to memory. Some aspects of memory remain virtually unimpaired with age, but others become weaker. For example, memory for words (semantic memory) is usually quite good, but memory for events (episodic memory) usually declines. Here we will begin by discussing the two basic types of storage: working memory (previously called short-term memory) and long-term memory (see also Chapter 6).

Working Memory

You learned in Chapter 12 that *working memory* is the capacity to keep information in mind for a few seconds while processing it—evaluating, calculating, inferring, and so on. That is, working memory functions as both a repository and a processor (Baddeley, 1986, 2003).

Older individuals tend to have difficulty with working memory. Problems with reduced sensory input and interference are among the reasons. A **dual-task deficit** is often evident: The greater the number of tasks, the worse performance becomes (Kemper et al., 2003; Voelcker-Rehage & Alberts, 2007). The dual-task deficit has been demonstrated in experiments in which a person must simultaneously walk

dual-task deficit A situation in which a person's performance of one task is impeded by interference from the simultaneous performance of another task.

PAUL THOMAS / THE IMAGE BANK / GETTY IMAGES

Learning New Tricks Most older adults readily learn how to use anything that expands their memory capacity, from handwritten to-do lists to computer programs.

and read or tap a finger and add. Particularly difficult is performing a motor task and cognitive task simultaneously (Albinet et al., 2006).

The dual-task deficit is evident in daily life as well. Suppose a grandfather, reading the newspaper, is interrupted by a grandchild's questions, or a grandmother is getting dressed while figuring out what bus to take. Most likely the grandfather will put the newspaper down (or tell the child to be quiet) and the grandmother will first dress and then figure out transportation (avoiding mismatched shoes).

In fact, some scholars believe that the inability to multitask, which requires screening out distractions and inhibiting irrelevant thoughts, is the main reason that working memory suffers in late adulthood: The brain cannot handle too much at once. Others suggest that a decline in total mental energy—making it too hard to filter and think at the same time—may be at the root of weakening working memory.

Usually, if people can slow down and focus, performance is as good as in younger years (Verhaeghen et al., 2003). However, such focus may preclude other mental tasks that a younger person could be doing simultaneously, and make substantial storage and processing impossible, as in answering comprehension questions about a passage just read *and* repeating the last word of each sentence (a common challenge to working memory).

Long-Term Memory

Intellectual processing depends not only on input and working memory but also on the knowledge base—that is, the information already stored in *long-term memory*. Do you remember that definition of *knowledge base* from Chapter 12? If so, your long-term memory is good.

An important aspect of the knowledge base is vocabulary. Evidence suggests that long-term memory for words remains unimpaired over the decades. In fact, vocabulary typically increases at least until age 80 (Uttl & Van Alstine, 2003; Verhaeghen, 2003).

However, other aspects of long-term memory are vulnerable to alteration. Some memories are distorted by interference from other memories or from hopes and fears.

Especially for Students If you want to remember something you learn in class for the rest of your life, what should you do?

Some errors in long-term memory are to be expected, since at every age, "it is the rule rather than the exception for people to change, add, and delete things from a remembered event" (Engel, 1999, p. 6). However, especially with regard to recent long-term memory (covering the past five years), the particular details that an older person stores may not be what a younger person thinks should be stored. In this case, selection becomes a generational problem.

Selective Memory

Both working memory and long-term memory remain quite strong if the items to be remembered relate to the person's expertise (Krampe & Charness, 2006). As you learned in Chapter 21, when people become experts in particular areas, their knowledge base holds steady in those areas; in addition, their working memory remains adequate because some cognitive tasks in those areas have become habitual and require little thought. Certainly, expertise among the young-old continues at full strength, as seen in the performance of judges, businesspeople, artists, clergy, and many others who can make and execute decisions as well as ever.

However, in areas not related to expertise, selective deficits in long-term memory appear. Older adults often are less able to recall details of events in the recent past (Piolino et al., 2006).

This selectivity results in interesting patterns in long-term memory. Happy events that occurred between ages 10 and 30 are remembered better than events of any kind that happened earlier or later (Berntsen & Rubin, 2002). Emotions are also remembered better than are factual details. For example, people remember how they felt ("I was thrilled to hold my baby") more than exactly where, how, and when the events occurred. A mother with grown children may remember her thrill at holding a newborn and forget which child was born in the morning and which at night.

Source amnesia, forgetting who or what was the source of a specific fact, idea, or snippet of conversation, is another common problem among the elderly (Craik & Salthouse, 2000). An older person may sometimes feel sure that something was true that, in reality, was only a rumor from an unreliable source (Jacoby & Rhodes, 2006).

Bias toward happy events, especially from adolescence and young adulthood, emphasis on subjective emotions, and source amnesia are common at every age, but they are increasingly so in late adulthood. Such selective memories can be adaptive. For example, Tina was married for 56 years to Tim, who developed Parkinson's disease. She says:

> I think of him as a young man. I see him the same. He doesn't look any older to me. . . . I feel sorry that he can't walk. I can't believe it, because he would always be walking ahead of me as if we were from another culture . . . men in front, you know.
>
> *[quoted in Koch, 2000, p. 72]*

Tina's adult children complained that she put Tim's needs above her own; caring for him interfered with her sleep, exercise, and social life. Tina insisted that the children did not understand. This was true, since their impressions of their parents' relationship had been solidified during their emerging adulthood and thus were based on perceptions (such as the sexism of women walking behind men) that were quite different from Tina's.

thinking like a scientist

John, Paul, Ringo, and . . .

How can we measure the impact of age on long-term memory? One way might be to test people's memory for past public events. Older adults do well on this measure (Baier & Ackerman, 2001), but the test may not be objective.

For example, asking people to remember the names of the heads of state at Yalta is an easier question for those who were politically aware in 1945; asking for the names of the four Beatles gives an advantage to women who were teenagers in the 1960s; asking for the names of the current stars of the NBA gives an edge to North American young men who are interested in sports. (If this is not you, you may not know that NBA stands for National Basketball Association. If this *is* you, are you surprised that others do not know?)

Every question favors particular interests—here politics, music, and sports. Each cohort has its particular concerns, which are magnified by the media. For example, detailed accounts of battles and treaties filled the newspapers during World War II. Today celebrity gossip has largely replaced serious journalism. For all these reasons, scientists can find no kinds of questions that objectively measure long-term memory among all types of people at all ages, from 15 to 45 to 75.

COURTESY OF KATHLEEN BERGER

Recognition At every age, recognition memory is much better than recall. Chances are that few of my high school classmates could describe how I looked back then, but all of them could point out my picture among the hundreds of photos in our yearbook.

Another approach to assessing long-term memory is to measure knowledge that was learned in high school. One researcher found that those who had studied Spanish within the past three years remembered it best (Bahrick, 1984). Thereafter, forgetting was gradual: Those who had studied Spanish 50 years earlier remembered about 80 percent of what the young adults who had studied it five years earlier remembered.

The most significant variable was not how long ago the person had studied Spanish in high school but how well the person had learned the language at that time: Those who had gotten an A 50 years earlier outscored those who had gotten a C just 1 year before (Bahrick, 1984). Thus, as you might expect, many people who became fluent in a language in childhood but have rarely used it since are often able to converse in that language decades later. Memories are stored for decades, and neither age nor time erases them.

In long-term memory, much depends on the specifics. One researcher cites the example of a "lady of 100 years old who could still play (and win) Scrabble in three languages, even though she had marked difficulty remembering what she just had for lunch" (Parkin, 1993). Her Scrabble playing required that she remember words and their spelling in three languages and many Scrabble skills. Similarly, given 15 minutes to work on a crossword puzzle, participants filled in more words correctly the older they were (see Figure 24.1) (Salthouse, 2004).

Overall, then, although interference and sensory decline impair working memory, the picture is more complicated for long-term memory: "There are replicable findings of age-related decline, stability and even in some cases increase" (Zacks & Hasher, 2006, p. 162). Scientists hesitate to predict whether and when any of these things will occur.

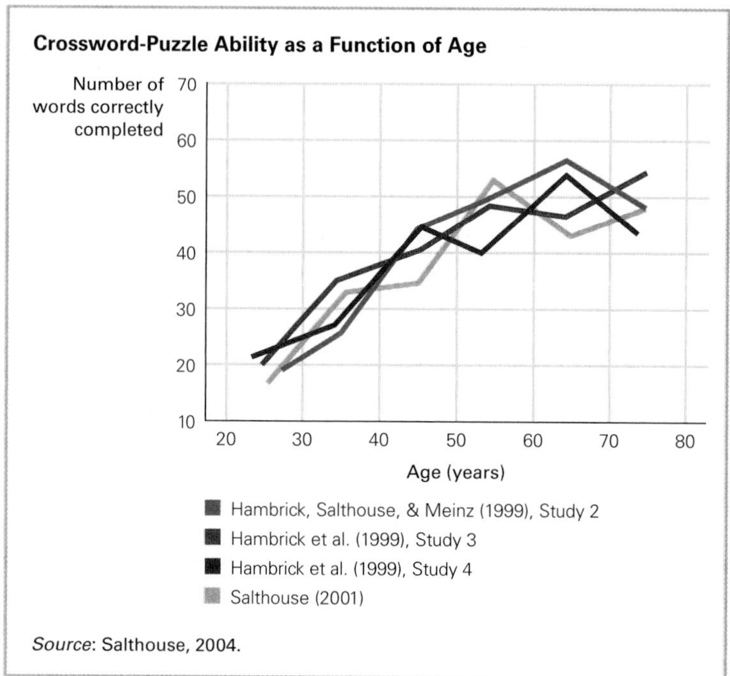

FIGURE 24.1

Quick Retrieval Experienced solvers were given 15 minutes to work on a *New York Times* crossword puzzle. Almost no one filled in all the blanks, but some of the oldest solvers came close.

Control Processes

Cognitive problems in later life seem greater than the input and memory impairments just described might suggest. If these problems involved merely senses and memory, then eyeglasses, hearing aids, and PDAs or written lists would correct them. But older adults also seem "impaired in controlled cognitive processes" (Jacoby et al., 2001, p. 250), and this difficulty is hard to remedy.

control processes That part of the information-processing system that regulates the analysis and flow of information. Memory and retrieval strategies, selective attention, and rules or strategies for problem solving are all useful control processes.

Control processes include strategies, selective attention, and storage mechanisms, already discussed, and logical analysis and retrieval—all the methods that help people think clearly and well. Such processes usually depend on activity in the prefrontal cortex (as first explained in Chapter 12), which shrinks with age more than most other parts of the brain do (Raz, 2005). Perhaps as a result, older adults do not seem to gather and consider all the relevant information as well as younger people do (Cicirelli, 2006; Zwahr et al., 1999).

Analysis

One aspect of impaired analysis is that the elderly are more likely to stick to preconceived ideas rather than consider new evidence and change their minds (Pierce et al., 2004). For example, political opinions are influenced by impressions formed in early adulthood. United States citizens who were young when a Republican was president are more likely to vote Republican, and the corresponding pattern holds

➤**Response for Students** (from page 652): Learn it very well now, and you will probably remember it in 50 years, with a little review.

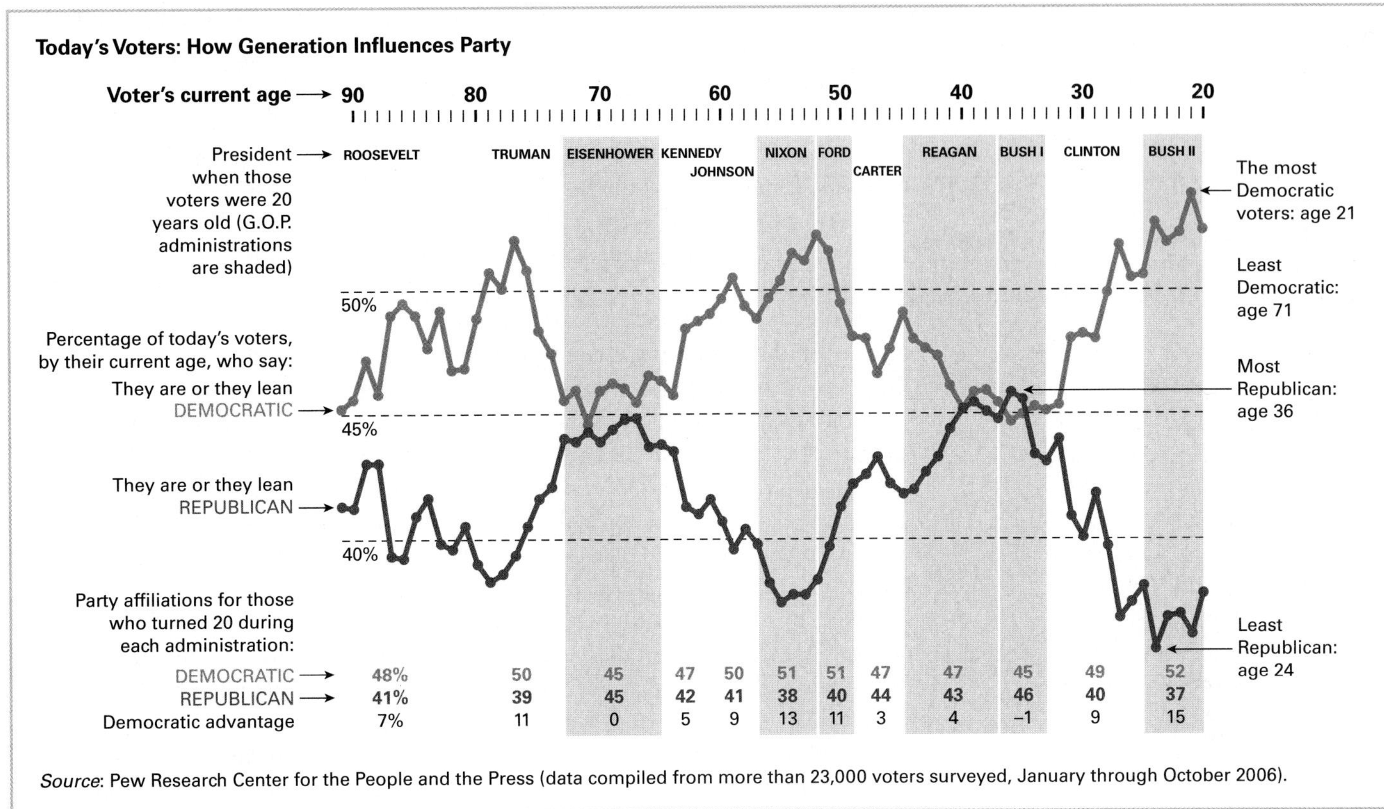

FIGURE 24.2

They Still Like Ike In the 2006 congressional elections, U.S. voters generally preferred Democratic candidates. The blue and red curves in this graph show their party preferences by age. Almost half the voters in two age cohorts leaned toward the Republican party: the 71-year-olds, who may have had good memories of Eisenhower, who was president when they were young, and the 36-year-olds, who may have felt loyal to Reagan for the same reason.

for those who were young adults during Democratic administrations (see Figure 24.2). Some older people (about age 60) chose the Republican George W. Bush in 2004 because they had liked the Republican Dwight Eisenhower in the 1950s; others (about age 75) chose the Democrat John Kerry because they had liked the Democrat Franklin D. Roosevelt in the 1930s. Of course, every voter of every age believes he or she makes a rational choice on current issues, but voters are much more influenced by past emotions and memories than they realize (Westen, 2007).

In general, the elderly rely on prior knowledge, general principles, familiarity, and rules of thumb in their decision making instead of learning new and novel approaches (Jacoby & Rhodes, 2006). This is called a top-down strategy, using deductive rather than inductive reasoning.

Attitudes about homosexuality, civil liberties, racial profiling, and many other issues shift among all generations, depending on current events and opinions; however, they also differ according to the age of the person, partly because each older generation maintains its "old-fashioned" attitudes (T. Smith, 2005). This resistance to change is not necessarily a disadvantage, but it does indicate less active analysis.

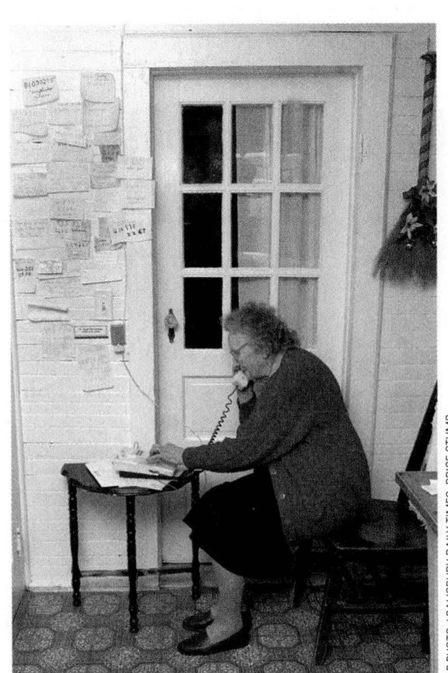
AP PHOTO / SALISBURY DAILY TIMES, BRICE STUMP

Don't Forget As a retrieval strategy, this Maryland shop owner posts dozens of reminders for herself on the wall.

Retrieval

Another control process involves using retrieval strategies. The ability to use this approach also worsens with age. Trying to recall the name of a childhood acquaintance, for example, a young adult might run through an alphabetical mental checklist or try to associate the person with a specific context—both effective strategies. In contrast, older adults might just give up, saying "I forget" or, more ominously, "My memory is failing."

The hypothesis that declines in control processes, more than declines in memory, are the reason for impaired cognition (i.e., that the problem is less in storage than in recall) is supported by the fact that older adults' impressive and extensive vocabulary is not matched by their verbal fluency. Compared with younger adults, they show more tip-of-the-tongue forgetfulness, less accurate memory for names, and poorer spelling (Burke & Shafto, 2004). All these deficits suggest that something is amiss with retrieval rather than with storage.

One part of a multifaceted study illustrates this (Thomas & Bulevich, 2005). Adults were given props with which they could perform 30 simple but bizarre (and therefore memorable) actions, such as kissing an artificial frog or stepping into a large plastic bag. Fifteen of these actions they were told to imagine (closing their eyes for 15 seconds) and fifteen they actually did.

Two weeks later, they were shown (one by one) a list of 45 bizarre actions and were asked whether they had imagined, performed, or never experienced each of them in the previous session. Half the participants were just presented with the list, with no special instructions; in that half, youth outscored age. For instance, on average, the young adults misjudged 22 percent of the actions on the list as imagined, performed, or never seen, while the older people mistakenly identified 48 percent.

The other half (both young and old) were given strategies for distinguishing imagined from experienced actions, such as trying to remember "how an object felt in your hand, how something looked or smelled . . . how you felt performing the action." These instructions helped the older adults: Their error rate was 34 percent. The younger participants were not helped by the strategy suggestion: They tied their counterparts in the other group, with 22 percent. Since the instructions were given two weeks after the first part of the experiment, the researchers concluded that the elderly had less of a problem with initially putting information into memory than with using strategies to retrieve that information later (Thomas & Bulevich, 2005).

thinking like a scientist

Neuroscience and Brain Activity

Neurological research has found that, over the life span, the brain is more multifaceted, and thought processes more diverse, than was once believed. Brains do become smaller with age, but the shrinkage varies substantially from part to part (Raz, 2005). Older adults tend to use more areas of the brain, from both hemispheres, than younger adults do.

Until recently, most aspects of the brain's complexity over the life span were obscure to scientists. They had only crude measures, such as overall volume and analysis at autopsy. Research on the effects of massive strokes or surgery also provided information, but it was not known whether conclusions from such research applied to healthy people. Today, however, noninvasive neuroimaging in vivo (that is, in living brains) allows researchers to observe the dynamic workings of the brain (Cabeza et al., 2005).

Although neuroscientists still have much work to do, they have already found that many parts of the brain can be used for almost every task. They no longer believe that the human brain has just one or two language areas; a dozen areas might be activated when people listen and talk. Neuroscience has also shown that neurons and dendrites can grow in adulthood (Yang et al., 2006), that intellectual ability does not correlate with brain size, that the prefrontal cortex is crucial for control processes, and that brain use changes with age (Kramer et al., 2006).

It has been widely assumed that brain activity decreases with age because older people themselves are less active. This assumption is often false. As one expert explains:

> When the neuroimaging techniques are applied to . . . young and old adults, there are three possible outcomes in terms of task-

> related activity in a given brain region: the two groups could have equivalent activity, the young group could have greater activity, or the older group could have greater activity. All three of these outcomes have been found, depending on the task and the particular brain region.
>
> *[Grady, 2002, p. 4]*

The third outcome, that sometimes older brains show more activity, was unexpected, yet it now has been replicated in many studies. Younger adults usually think within one hemisphere or the other, while older adults use both hemispheres. This "age-related decrease in lateralization" occurs in many cognitive tasks (Cabeza, 2002, p. 97).

One explanation involves compensation: Older adults may naturally compensate for cognitive slowdown by recruiting extra brain areas when they think. As one team explains: "The brain has the apparent ability to reorganize in the face of neural insults of aging in what is an apparently compensatory manner" (Park & Payer, 2006, p. 138).

A second, less optimistic explanation for greater brain activity among older adults is that, since control processes become weaker, the brain "dedifferentiates," no longer using a different region for each function. Inhibition fails, attention wanders, and thinking becomes diffuse (Nielson et al., 2002).

Interpretation of this evidence may be influenced by benign or hostile ageism, the prejudice against the elderly that we first discussed in Chapter 23. Is diffusion an admirable adaptation, combining intellectual and emotional skills, and a sign of "strategic diversity" that helps optimized cognition (Lindenberger & von Oertzen, 2006, p. 310), or does it represent a pathetic loss of focus?

Thinking like a scientist means suspending judgment until sufficient information is collected and avoiding ageist prejudices—favorable as well as unfavorable. Such objectivity is difficult to achieve, but that is the scientist's task (Salthouse, 2006; see Research Design).

Research Design

Scientist: Timothy A. Salthouse.

Publication: *Perspectives on Psychological Science* (2006).

Participants: Unlike most Research Designs reported in this book, this one consists primarily of reviews of other research on a topic of interest to the scientist. Included, however, are 1,200 adults, ages 18 to 97, who participated in a study in Salthouse's laboratory.

Design: Salthouse analyzed evidence for the "use it or lose it" hypothesis, that mental exercise reduces mental aging. In Salthouse's study, participants' time spent in various cognitive activities (of varied complexity) was compared with their age and intellect.

Major conclusion: "Although my professional opinion is that . . . the mental-exercise hypothesis is more of an optimistic hope than an empirical reality, my personal recommendation is that people should behave as if it is true" (p. 84).

Comment: Some good science, such as in this article, combines analysis of other studies with further exploration. Salthouse highlights inconsistencies and biases in the research.

Reminding People of What They Know

Everyone's memory benefits from **priming,** as when a person is given a clue before being asked to remember something or when some technique is used to jog the person's memory. For example, hearing a word in some context before being asked to remember it primes the brain to recall the word later. And when your professor begins class with a review of previously learned material, that teaching technique helps you connect what you already know to what you are about to learn, which is also a form of priming.

priming Preparation that makes it easier to perform some action. For example, it is easier to retrieve an item from memory if we are given a clue about it beforehand.

Some people use priming on their own as a retrieval strategy, such as recalling a person's name by remembering the first letter. Priming may benefit older people more than younger ones, although older people are less likely to use it on their own.

One way to understand why priming helps is to compare implicit and explicit memory. **Explicit memory** involves facts, definitions, data, concepts, and the like. Most of what is in explicit memory was consciously learned, usually through links made with verbal information already in memory and through deliberate repetition and review designed to facilitate later recall.

explicit memory Memory that is easy to retrieve on demand (as in a specific test), usually with words. Most explicit memory involves consciously learned words, data, and concepts.

Implicit memory is less conscious, more automatic. It involves habits, emotional responses, and routine procedures. For the most part, the contents of implicit memory were never deliberately memorized for later recall. Items in implicit memory are, accordingly, difficult to retrieve verbally on demand. However, they are easy to retrieve when priming provides a context.

implicit memory Unconscious or automatic memory that is usually stored via habits, emotional responses, routine procedures, and various sensations.

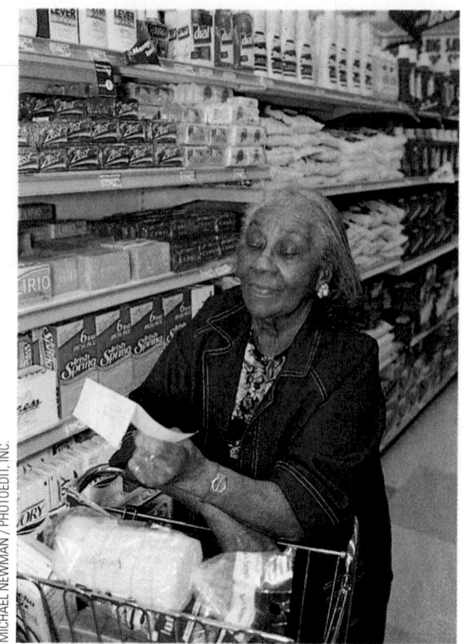
MICHAEL NEWMAN / PHOTOEDIT, INC.

Does She Need Her Shopping List? A shopping list may help when explicit memory fails. If this shopper wrote a list and then misplaced it, however, she could scan the store shelves and imagine her kitchen cupboards. Implicit memory would probably enable her to choose almost every item she needed.

Observation Quiz (see answer, page 660): What are two signs that this woman is over 60?

Explicit memory is especially shaky in elderly people who lack adequate control processes. For example, if older adults were asked to describe the face of their best friend in third grade, they might find that impossible, but if they were primed by being shown a class photo, they could pick out that friend immediately. When Jean Piaget (1970) asked people to explain how to crawl, most of them got it wrong. (What moves when—hands, feet, elbows, knees, right, left?) However, almost everyone, if primed by getting on the floor, can demonstrate crawling. That's implicit memory.

Children, brain-damaged people, and older adults are better at implicit than explicit memory (Rowe et al., 2006; Schneider & Björklund, 2003). With priming, healthy and intellectually sharp older adults access implicit memory as well as much younger adults do (Zacks & Hasher, 2006). Consider high school Spanish again. Implicit memory (comprehending an overheard Spanish phrase) is easier for the elderly than is performing an explicit task (translating a list of English words into Spanish).

Brain Slowdown

Even with good priming and adequate stimulation, the unavoidable process called senescence (see Chapters 17, 20, and 23) causes one cognitive change in everyone: The elderly react more slowly than younger adults do. This brain slowdown can be traced partly to reduced production of neurotransmitters—glutamate, acetylcholine, serotonin, and especially dopamine—that allow a nerve impulse to jump across the synapse from one neuron to another (Bäckman & Farde, 2005). Speed of cognition is also affected by a decrease in neural fluid, a smaller prefrontal cortex, and slower cerebral blood flow.

Speed is crucial for many aspects of cognition, especially working memory, since information stays in working memory for only a short time. If people cannot quickly process that information, some of it will be lost in order for other relevant information to be put into working memory.

As a result of this slowdown, people cannot hold all the relevant information in their minds, cannot sequentially analyze information that is lost before they get to it, and cannot respond to new information on the basis of prior information (now lost). Slower thinking also tends to be simpler and shallower because of these losses (Salthouse, 2000, 2006). Not surprisingly, fluid intelligence (requiring quick analysis) is powerfully affected by speed of processing (Zimprich & Martin, 2002).

Cognition that is unaffected by speed is usually unaffected by primary aging. For this reason, "aging impairs cognition on some tasks but spares it in others. . . . Individuals adapt, sometimes with great success" (Stern & Carstensen, 2000, p. 3).

Fortunately, although slower processing is detrimental in traditional tests of intelligence, speed is less relevant for everyday cognition, when

> decision time is controlled more by "appropriate programming" that uses our brains efficiently than by raw speed of information processing. . . . In most cases involving everyday activity, the young–old contrast should not be thought of as a contrast between a fast and a slow computer, but as a contrast between a fast computer with a limited library of programs and a slow computer with a large library.
>
> *[Hunt, 1993]*

An analysis of many measurements of cognition found that older adults were slower at almost everything, but were not always less accurate, than younger people (Verhaeghen et al., 2003). Many compensate for loss of speed by allowing additional time to solve problems, repeating instructions that might be confusing, asking others to slow down, focusing on meaningful cognitive tasks and ignoring irrelevant ones. All these strategies help older adults adjust to their slower rate of information processing. Further, expertise continues to buffer the effects of overall slowdown. For example, expert older chess players were almost as fast at assessing risks to the king as were expert younger players, and they were far faster than less experienced players who were accurate in their judgments but slower to decide (Jastrzembski et al., 2006; see Research Design).

Thus far, our discussion of compensation, control, and intellectual strengths has ignored the cognitive breakdown suffered by some of the elderly. Many people demonstrate a marked loss of intellectual power when death is near, even before a physician notices anything amiss. Changes in cognition and increased depression often precede a final worsening of health (Rabbitt et al., 2002). This **terminal decline** (also called *terminal drop*) is an overall slowdown of cognitive abilities in the weeks and months before death.

With terminal decline, a *compression of morbidity* (see Chapter 23) is evident, with the sudden drop in cognition followed by declines in many other functions (Bäckman et al., 2002; Small et al., 2003). Terminal decline is not directly caused by age; it is the result of being close to death (Maier et al., 2003).

terminal decline An overall slowdown of cognitive abilities in the weeks and months before death. (Also called *terminal drop*.)

Research Design

Scientists: Tiffany S. Jastrzembski, Neil Charness, and Catherine Vasyukova.

Publication: *Psychology and Aging* (2006).

Participants: A total of 59 chess players from Russia and the United States, at three levels of expertise: unranked, intermediate, and expert, according to international criteria. They were considered young (ages 17 to 44, average age 33) or old (45 to 81, average age 61).

Design: The participants were tested on general response speed and on working memory and then presented with a segment of a chess board, with a king and one other piece. They judged whether the king was in check, or one move from check, or not threatened. Judgments were very accurate, but some took longer than others to decide.

Major conclusion: Expertise overcomes most age effects. At the same skill level, the older participants were slower—in chess by about 20 percent (200 milliseconds) and in general speed by about 50 percent. However, the older experts were quicker than the intermediate young players and far quicker than the young unranked players. Thus, "experts maintain an earlier perceptual advantage over less skilled players in chess" (p. 405).

Comment: This is one of many studies that compare age and expertise. Conclusions vary depending on the specific skill. Age-related declines affect some skills, but experts in many areas (including chess) experience only minor age deficits.

Staying Healthy and Alert

We have focused thus far on *primary aging,* the inevitable and universal process of growing older and eventually dying. However, *secondary aging,* the particular illnesses and conditions that affect one person but not another, probably has more influence on the cognition of any particular individual. Secondary aging is a major reason for the remarkable variation in intellectual ability between one older person and another. Detailed studies support the conclusion that "variability pervades cognitive aging" (Lindenberger & von Oertzen, 2006, p. 297).

A study of 900 people in their 70s, 80s, and 90s living in the community (not in institutions) found "both greater-than-expected deterioration as well as less-than-expected deterioration (including improvement)" over a four-year period (Christensen et al., 1999). Another group of researchers agreed that "in some people cognition declines precipitously, but in many others cognition declines only slightly or not at all, or improves slightly" (Wilson et al., 2002, p. 179). Studies of the brain find that "older adults may activate less, more, or even different neural structures to perform a memory task than young adults do" (Park & Gutchess, 2005, p. 219).

The reasons for the variation include gender, education, biological aging, and the person's own assessment of whether everyday activities are restricted by the state of his or her health (Wahlin et al., 2006). Many diseases that are common among the elderly impair cognition (Raz, 2005). In addition to those that directly attack the brain (discussed later in this chapter), hypertension (high blood pressure), diabetes, arteriosclerosis, emphysema, and many other chronic conditions slow down cognition; their effects are most evident in middle age. Physical and mental health are crucial for intellectual health throughout adulthood (Caplan & Schooler, 2003; Elias et al., 2004). One review found that "aerobic fitness emerged as a potential modifier of brain aging" (Raz, 2005, p. 44).

Unfortunately, perhaps because of the poor eating and exercise habits described in previous chapters, few older adults are free from all the conditions that lead to secondary aging and cognitive decline. Of all 50- to 64-year-olds, 75 percent have at least one risk factor; for half of them, it is hypertension (MMWR, January 16, 2004). Thus, when older adults are cognitively impaired, secondary aging may be to blame. Exercise, moderate eating, and avoiding cigarettes may be as important for the mind as for the body.

➤Answer to Observation Quiz (from page 658): Her gray hair and poor vision. She is holding the paper about 24 inches away from her face, a sign of aging eyes. Younger people see best if an object is about 10 inches away.

Ageism

Some cognitive decline is rooted not in the older person's body and brain but in the surrounding social context. Cultural attitudes can lead directly to age differences in cognition (Hess, 2005).

Stereotype Threat Again

Stereotypes do most harm when individuals—regardless of age, sex, or ethnicity—internalize other people's prejudices and react with helplessness, self-doubt, or misplaced anger (as we saw in the discussion of *stereotype threat* in Chapter 18). If the elderly fear losing their minds because they have internalized the idea that old age brings dementia, that fear may become a stereotype threat, undermining normal thinking (Hess, 2005).

Influenced by expectations of decline, people aged 50 to 70 tend to overestimate the memory skills they had in young adulthood. They selectively forget their earlier forgetfulness! Lack of confidence impairs memory, as every student who has panicked about an exam knows. Confidence is further eroded when others interpret slow responses as failing memory. If they use elderspeak (explained in Chapter 23), not only is the older person made to feel stupid, but also to become less intelligent because of consistently oversimplified conversations (Levy, 2003). In many ways, expectations and responses affect cognition (Hess, 2005).

In one experiment, words that expressed either positive or negative ageism were flashed on a screen so quickly that the participants didn't even know they had seen them. Nonetheless, older adults performed better on cognitive tests after they saw words that reflected positive stereotypes (such as *guidance, wise, alert, sage, accomplished, learned, improving, creative, enlightened, insightful,* and *astute*) than they did after seeing words that reflected negative stereotypes (*Alzheimer's, decline, dependent, senile, misplaces, dementia, dying, forgets, confused, decrepit, incompetent,* and *diseased*) (Levy, 1996).

When the same experiment was repeated with younger adults, no significant differences in test scores were found. Apparently, negative stereotypes do damage only if a person identifies with them. The researcher concludes:

> Two messages emerge from this research. The pessimistic one is that older individuals' memory capabilities can be damaged by self-stereotypes that are derived from a prevalent and insidious stereotype about aging. Specifically, the stereotype that memory decline is inevitable can become a self-fulfilling prophecy. This research also offers an optimistic message. The findings indicate that memory decline is not inevitable. In fact, the studies show that memory performance can be enhanced in old age.
>
> *[Levy, 1996, p. 1105]*

Similar results were found when adults aged 24 to 86 were tested after reading an article confirming the stereotype that memory declines in old age. The performance of the youngest participants was unaffected, the middle-aged ones actually improved, and the oldest-old, like the young, were unfazed. However, the young-old, in their late 60s, were negatively affected, especially if they believed what they read (Hess & Hinson, 2006).

Especially for Busy People When does "speed reading" make sense?

The influence of stereotyping was also apparent in a study that began with a novel idea: Find people who are not influenced by ageism. The researchers found two groups: residents of China, where the old are traditionally venerated, and deaf people in North America, whose lack of hearing limits their exposure to ageist stereotypes (Levy & Langer, 1994). Memory tests were given to the two groups and to a third group, hearing North Americans. For that hearing group, the gap between scores of the younger and older test-takers was twice as great as the old/young gap among the deaf North Americans and five times as great as that for the Chinese. Similar trends were found in a study that compared recent Chinese immigrants to Canada with Chinese Canadians who had emigrated decades ago and presumably had been more influenced by North American ageism (Yoon et al., 2001).

Ageism Among Scientists

Traditionally, scientists measured age differences in memory in the same way they had always studied memory: in laboratories on university campuses, in the afternoon, using nonsense syllables. The researchers counted how many syllables participants could remember within a specific time. (Nonsense syllables were used so that the material to be remembered would be culturally neutral.)

However, each of these factors works against older adults, who tend to perform best in familiar settings, in the morning, with familiar words (Baltes et al., 1998). In addition, the young participants are usually college students, who have lots of practice with taking tests under pressure. Older adults, by contrast, have less practice and tend to be more fearful of performing poorly on memory tests. If stereotype threat is evoked, they may become anxious or ignore the instructions of the research assistant (who is often a young graduate student).

For example, in one experiment, adults were taught a memory technique called the *method of loci,* in which the person creates a mental picture of unusual locations in which the items to be remembered are "placed." Many older adults quietly resisted using the new method, even though the experiment required it. Instead, they used their own memory strategies. The older participants scored lower, but half of that difference could be traced to this resistance rather than to age-related decline (Verhaeghen & Marcoen, 1996).

The same problem may occur in daily life. Many older people, of their own accord, use compensatory strategies such as carrying a grocery list, keeping a calendar, or programming a phone to dial numbers automatically. However, if someone else tells them to do these things, they may refuse, either directly or indirectly (as by writing a grocery list but not bringing it to the store). Of course, resistance to suggestions from other generations is common among everyone—not every college student follows Mother's advice.

Older adults are more cautious, less inclined to take risks, so they would rather not guess if they think their answer might be wrong. But when they think they know something, they are more certain that they are right than young adults are (Jacoby & Rhodes, 2006). Because they use "more conservative decision criteria," the elderly may appear less accurate or slower on psychological tests, and less able to learn from mistakes, than they actually are (Ratcliffe et al., 2006, p. 353).

Beyond Ageism

Although laboratory experiments indicate memory loss in late adulthood, few older adults consider memory problems a significant handicap in their daily lives. They worry at the beginning of late adulthood or if they think they are experiencing symptoms of Alzheimer's disease, but otherwise, they take memory problems in stride. They think that they are better than the young at remembering to pay bills, take medicine, and keep appointments. They may be right (Park & Hedden, 2001).

One classic study was designed to mimic the memory demands of daily life (Moscovitch, 1982). Older and younger adults (all living busy lives) were asked to call an answering service every day for two weeks at a specific time of their own

➤Response for Busy People (from page 660): Faster is not always better, and people who believe a stereotype and develop research to prove it often find what they expect. Therefore, take a skeptical view of any claim that is made about speed reading.

choice. Only 20 percent of the younger adults made every call, but 90 percent of the older adults did. Why did the younger adults do so poorly? One reason is that many put excessive trust in their memories ("I have an internal alarm that always goes off at the right time") and therefore did not use memory aids. Older adults were more likely to use reminders, such as a note on the telephone or a shoe near the door.

The experimenters then attempted to increase forgetting. They required only one call per week at a time selected by the researchers, and they told the participants not to use visible reminders. About half of both groups, old and young, failed to call at the appointed time. More old people would probably have forgotten, but some of them bent the rules, using a memory-priming measure (such as carrying the phone number in plain sight in their wallets).

One of the researchers concluded:

> With more effort, we are sure we can bring old people's memory to its knees . . . but that hardly seems to be the point of this research. The main lesson of this venture into the dangerous real world is that old people have learned from experience what we have so consistently shown in the laboratory—that their memory is getting somewhat poorer—and they have structured their environment to compensate.
>
> *[Moscovitch, 1982]*

Many other researchers have assessed memory in older adults, not only in traditional experiments but also in more novel studies designed to accommodate the special abilities and needs of the elderly. Almost invariably, the more realistic the circumstances, the better an older person remembers. As one series of studies concludes, "Older adults, in their everyday life, are capable of accurate and reliable performance of important tasks" (Rendell & Thompson, 1999).

Fortunately, most older adults develop supportive environments for themselves. They use routines, memory strategies, and cues to "help ameliorate, and sometimes eliminate, age-related memory impairment" (Moscovitch et al., 2001). Ordinarily, compared with college students, older adults are less likely to forget birthdays, vitamins, or even brushing their teeth.

SUMMING UP

Cognitive processing among the elderly is hindered by diminished sensation and perception, more interference, and less inhibition. Working memory is affected, especially as reactions slow down. Control processes are particularly impaired. Exercise can prevent some of the secondary aging known to affect cognition, such as hypertension, diabetes, and lung diseases. Ageism and stereotype threat may make the elderly appear less intelligent than they actually are, especially in performing the activities of daily life. ■

The Impaired: Dementia

Loss of intellectual ability in elderly people has traditionally been called *senility*. That term is ageist, however, because *senile,* which simply means "old," is being used to signify cognitive impairment. The implication is that old age itself causes severe intellectual failure.

dementia Irreversible loss of intellectual functioning caused by organic brain damage or disease. Dementia becomes more common with age, but it is abnormal and pathological even in the very old.

A more precise term for pathological loss of brain functioning is **dementia**—literally, "out of mind," referring to severely impaired judgment, memory, or problem-solving ability. Traditionally, when dementia occurred before age 60, it was called *presenile dementia,* when it occurred after age 60, it was called *senile dementia* or *senile psychosis.* However, age 60 is a meaningless marker: A person may develop dementia at age 40 or age 80; the symptoms are the same at every age.

More than 70 diseases can cause dementia, each different in sequence, severity, and particulars, although all are characterized by mental confusion and forgetfulness (Fromholt & Bruhn, 1998). Dementia is chronic, which means it is long-lasting, unlike **delirium,** which refers to acute, severe memory loss and confusion that disappears in hours or days (Inouye, 2006).

delirium A temporary loss of memory, often accompanied by feelings of fear or grandiosity and irrational actions.

The precise cause of dementia is difficult to determine in the early stages. When adults become confused and memory fails, many assume that the problem is Alzheimer's disease. However, even when Alzheimer's disease is diagnosed by a physician, autopsies reveal that about 15 percent of the diagnoses were wrong.

Doctors are stuck in a dilemma: How much evidence should they collect before they diagnose the cause of dementia? A correct early diagnosis can lead to treatment that slows down or even halts dementia, but a wrong early diagnosis often leads to ineffective treatment and false hope or needless despair.

Alzheimer's Disease

The most feared yet most common cause of dementia (about half of cases worldwide, a total of 20 million people) is **Alzheimer's disease (AD),** also called *senile dementia of the Alzheimer type (SDAT)* (Goedert & Spillantini, 2006). Alzheimer's disease is characterized by the proliferation of plaques and tangles in the brain. These are abnormalities in the cerebral cortex that destroy the ability of neurons to communicate with each other and thus stop brain functioning.

Alzheimer's disease (AD) The most common cause of dementia, characterized by gradual deterioration of memory and personality and marked by the formation of plaques of beta-amyloid protein and tangles in the brain.

Plaques are clumps of a protein called *beta-amyloid,* which is found in the tissues surrounding the neurons; tangles are twisted masses of threads made of a protein called *tau* within the neurons. A normal brain contains some beta-amyloid and tau, but in AD the amounts are excessive, and the resulting plaques and tangles disrupt brain communication. This disturbance usually begins in the hippocampus, a brain structure that plays a vital role in memory, and memory loss is usually the first, and the dominant, symptom of AD.

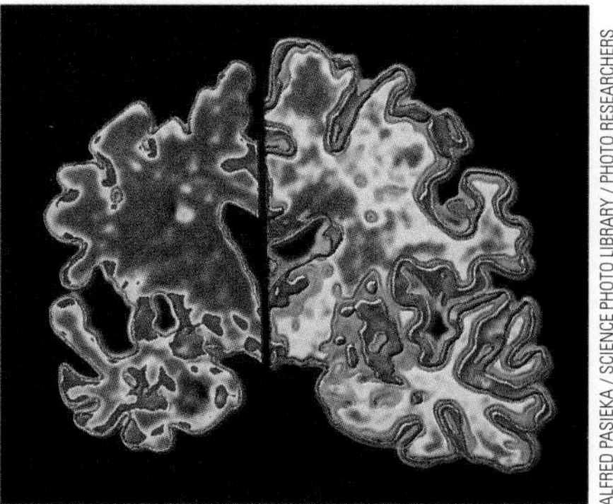

ALFRED PASIEKA / SCIENCE PHOTO LIBRARY / PHOTO RESEARCHERS

The Alzheimer's Brain This computer graphic shows a vertical slice through a brain ravaged by Alzheimer's disease *(left)* compared with a similar slice of a normal brain *(right).* The diseased brain is shrunken as the result of the degeneration of neurons. Not viewable in this cross section are tangles of protein filaments within the nerve cells as well as plaques that contain decaying dendrites and axons.

New techniques for analyzing brain tissue after death (the only sure way to diagnose AD) show that the amount of plaques and tangles correlates with the degree of intellectual impairment before death but not with the victim's age. In a living person, a diagnosis is typically based on reports of symptoms, a medical history, and some cognitive tests. This method is about 85 percent accurate, although autopsies find plaques and tangles in the brains of some very old people who had never been diagnosed as having dementia.

Risk Factors for Alzheimer's Disease

Gender, ethnicity, and especially age affect a person's odds of developing Alzheimer's disease. Women are at greater risk than men, and fewer East Asians than Europeans (no matter where they live) develop the disorder (Jellinger, 2002). Alzheimer's disease may also be less common among people of African descent, but life expectancy is far lower in Africa than on any other continent and diagnosis of illness in late adulthood is less certain. This means that the lower rates of AD in Africa may reflect earlier death or less frequent diagnosis rather than any genetic or cultural protection. Some experts believe childhood, adult context, and specific toxins in the environment affect Alzheimer's; others disagree.

In every nation, age is the chief risk factor for AD. According to a compilation of 13 studies from several nations (Ritchie et al., 1992), the incidence rises from about 1 percent of people age 65 to about 20 percent of people over age 85. Other research finds a doubling of incidence every 5 years after age 65, with about half of those over age 100 having the disease (Czech et al., 2000; Samuelsson et al., 2001). These data are approximate and are not found by every study, partly because diagnostic variations affect incidence rates.

As you learned in Chapter 3, Alzheimer's disease is partly genetic. When AD appears in middle age, the person either has trisomy-21 (Down syndrome) or has inherited at least one of three genes: APP (amyloid precursor protein), presenilin 1, or presenilin 2. Those genes are powerful: The disease in middle age progresses quickly, reaching the last phase within three to five years. However, most cases begin at age 75 or so, with much less genetic influence.

Many other genes probably have some impact, including genes called SORL1 and ApoE4 (allele 4 of the ApoE gene) (Marx, 2007). A person who inherits ApoE4 from only one parent, as one-fifth of all people in the United States do, has about a 50/50 chance of developing Alzheimer's by age 80; those who inherit the gene from both parents almost always develop Alzheimer's by their 90s. ApoE4 also increases the risk of heart disease and stroke, so many carriers die before dementia begins (Crews, 2003). Genetic tests are not used diagnostically before symptoms appear, because predictions and prevention are so uncertain.

Especially for Genetic Counselors Would you perform a test for ApoE4 if someone asked for it?

Genes can also reduce the risk of developing AD. For example, ApoE2 (allele 2 of ApoE) dissipates the amyloid that causes plaques. There is another allele that probably reduces the risks associated with exposure to Arctic weather as well as the risk of developing Alzheimer's disease, although it increases the risk of some other diseases (Ruiz-Pesini et al., 2004). For unknown reasons, the incidence of ApoE4 is higher in African Americans, but it is less predictive of Alzheimer's. People with no known genetic or environmental risk can nonetheless develop AD.

Stages: From Confusion to Death

Alzheimer's disease usually runs through a progressive course of five identifiable stages, beginning with forgetfulness and ending in death.

The *first stage* is characterized by absentmindedness about recent events or newly acquired information, particularly the names of people and places. A person in the first stage of the disease might be unable to remember where he or she just put something or might forget people's names after being introduced to them. In this early stage, most people recognize that they have a memory problem and try to cope with it, writing down names, addresses, appointments, shopping lists, and other items much more often than they once did.

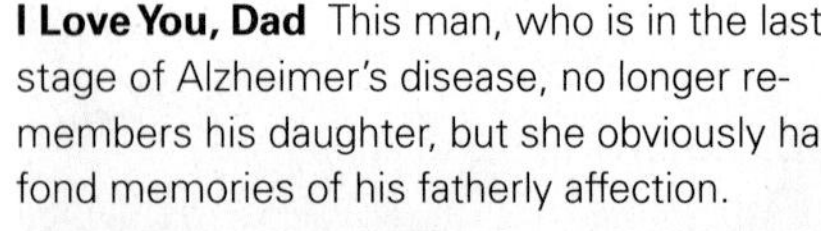

I Love You, Dad This man, who is in the last stage of Alzheimer's disease, no longer remembers his daughter, but she obviously has fond memories of his fatherly affection.

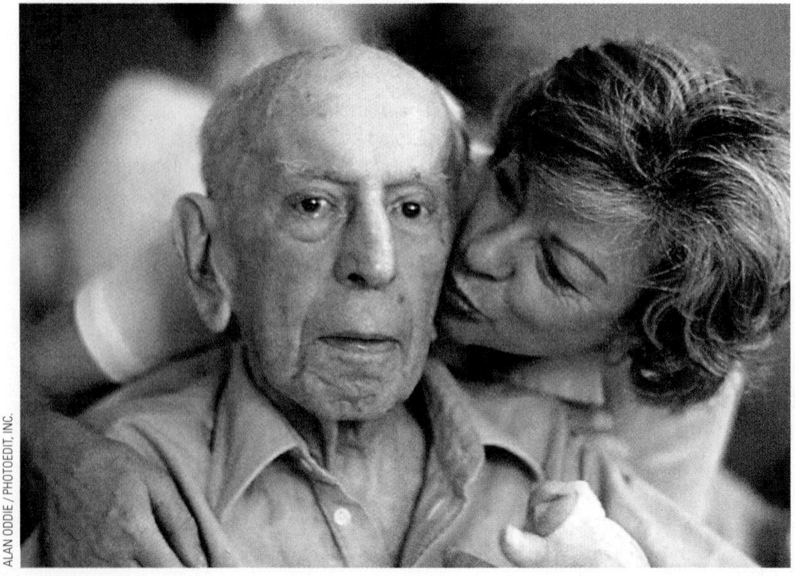

ALAN ODDIE / PHOTOEDIT, INC.

This first stage is sometimes confused with normal aging. For example, in a study of 1,883 people over age 65 (average age 75), 5 percent complained about memory problems. Three years later, 15 percent of those who complained, and 6 percent of those who had not, had developed dementia (Wang et al., 2004). Even experts cannot always distinguish early Alzheimer's disease from other conditions. For example, in retrospect, it seems clear that President Ronald Reagan had early AD symptoms while in office, but no doctor diagnosed it. Many tests, both cognitive and physiological, provide clues, but none are definitive (Peterson, 2003).

In the *second stage,* generalized confusion develops, with deficits in concentration and short-term memory. Speech becomes aimless and repetitious, vocabulary becomes much more limited, and words get mixed up. People at stage two are likely to read a newspaper article and forget it completely the next moment; they may put down their keys or eyeglasses and within seconds have no idea where they could be.

People with Alzheimer's disease who have always been suspicious by nature may decide that others have stolen the things that they themselves have mislaid. Then, "in the firm conviction of having been robbed, the patient starts hiding everything, but promptly forgets the hiding place. This reinforces the belief that thieves are at work" (Wirth, 1993).

Personality changes are common. The person begins to express long-repressed impulses as rational thought disappears. A previously tidy person may become compulsively neat; a person with a quick temper may begin to display explosive rages; a person who is asocial may become even more withdrawn. One writer, who worked obsessively to chronicle his losses, used spell-check to figure out how to write but quit in frustration after spending five minutes struggling to spell *hour* (DeBaggio, 2002).

In the *third stage,* memory loss becomes dangerous. Individuals with Alzheimer's disease may take to eating only one food, or they may forget to eat entirely. Often they fail to dress properly, leaving home barefoot in winter or walking naked about the neighborhood, crossing streets against the light. They might leave a lit stove or a hot iron, causing a fire. They might go out on some errand and then lose track not only of the errand but also of the way back home. And they cannot ask neighbors for help because they do not recognize them. Getting lost is a valid fear for people in this stage (Sabat, 2001).

The part of the brain that visualizes an object and realizes that it is a *K,* a hat, or a person may become tangled. In such cases, a person appears more helpless and incompetent than his or her overall cognitive losses would indicate.

By the *fourth stage,* people with AD need full-time care. They cannot care for themselves or respond normally to others, and they sometimes become irrationally angry or paranoid. They can no longer communicate or even recognize their closest loved ones, not because they have forgotten them completely but because the part of the brain that recognizes people has further deteriorated. A man might want to see his wife but refuse to believe that the person before him is, indeed, his wife.

Finally, in the *fifth stage,* people with AD become almost completely unresponsive, no longer even talking. Death usually comes 10 to 15 years after the beginning of stage one.

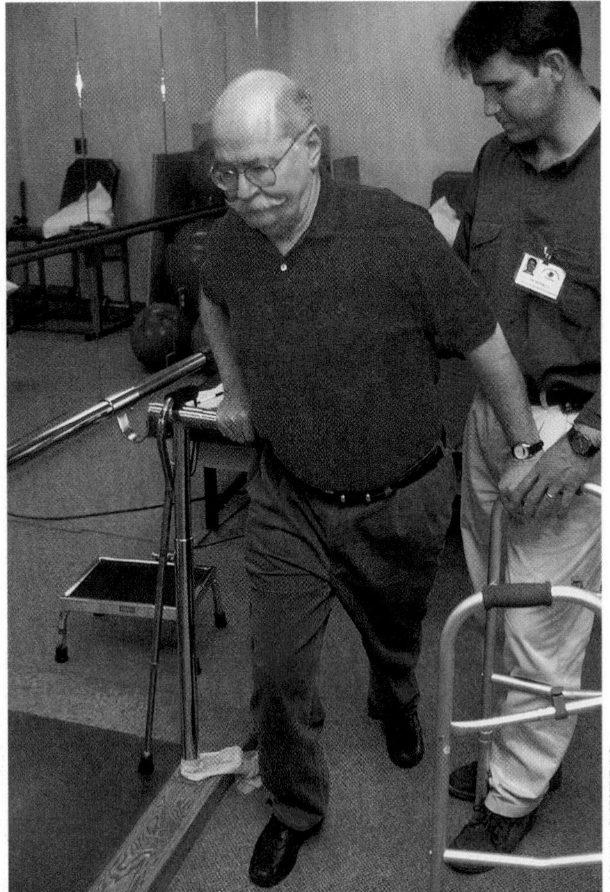

PAUL CONKLIN / PHOTOEDIT, INC.

Vascular Dementia Rehabilitation after a stroke is easier for the body than the mind because progress in physical therapy is more apparent to the patient and the therapist.

Many Strokes

The second most common cause of dementia is a stroke (a temporary obstruction of a blood vessel in the brain) or, more often, a series of many strokes, called TIAs (*transient ischemic attacks,* or ministrokes). Insufficient oxygen to the affected area of the brain, caused by the interruption in blood supply, results in the destruction of brain tissue, which produces immediate symptoms (blurred vision, weak or paralyzed limbs, slurred speech, and mental confusion).

vascular dementia (VaD)/multi-infarct dementia (MID) A form of dementia characterized by sporadic, and progressive, loss of intellectual functioning caused by repeated infarcts, or temporary obstructions of blood vessels, which prevent sufficient blood from reaching the brain.

In a TIA, symptoms typically disappear quickly—in hours or even minutes—and may be so slight that no one (including the victim) notices. Nevertheless, brain damage has occurred, and after a series of TIAs, the repeated brain damage leads to **vascular dementia (VaD),** also called **multi-infarct dementia,** or **MID** (Fromholt & Bruhn, 1998).

In North America and Europe, VaD causes 10 to 15 percent of all cases of dementia. The incidence is much higher in Japan and China, where VaD is more common than Alzheimer's disease (De la Torre et al., 2002). Worldwide, both VaD and Alzheimer's disease often occur in the same person. Some clinicians believe that most older people are affected by both VaD and AD, and that one or the other is diagnosed only when the combination of symptoms is too noticeable to be ignored.

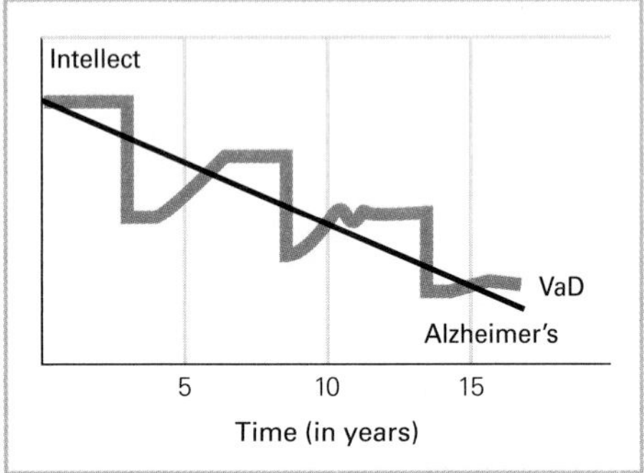

FIGURE 24.3

The Progression of Vascular Dementia and Alzheimer's Disease Cognitive decline is apparent in both Alzheimer's disease and multi-infarct dementia. However, the pattern of decline for each disease is different. Victims of AD show steady, gradual decline, while those who suffer from VaD get suddenly much worse, improve somewhat, and then experience another serious loss.

The progression of "pure" VaD differs from that of Alzheimer's disease (see Figure 24.3). Typically, the person suddenly loses some intellectual functioning following a ministroke. Other neurons take over, dendrites grow, and the person becomes better. People may think that the problem is solved, but that first ministroke is a warning that other strokes are likely (Van Wijk et al., 2005).

With each successive infarct, it becomes harder and harder for the remaining parts of the brain to compensate. If heart disease, major stroke, diabetes, or another illness does not kill the VaD victim, ministrokes continue to occur. The person's behavior eventually becomes indistinguishable from that of someone suffering from Alzheimer's disease. In pure VaD, autopsy reveals that parts of the brain have been completely destroyed while other parts seem normal; the proliferation of plaques and tangles characteristic of Alzheimer's disease is not apparent.

Subcortical Dementias

subcortical dementias Forms of dementia that begin with impairments in motor ability (which is governed by the subcortex) and produce cognitive impairment in later stages. Parkinson's disease, Huntington's disease, and multiple sclerosis are subcortical dementias.

Many other dementias are associated with conditions that originate not in the cortex, as with Alzheimer's disease and vascular dementia, but in the subcortex, the parts of the brain under the cortex. Because the brain damage resulting from these conditions is below, not inside, the cortex, thinking and memory are not initially affected. Instead, **subcortical dementias** cause a progressive loss of motor control.

Causes of subcortical dementias include Parkinson's disease, Huntington's disease, and multiple sclerosis. All begin with the person's realization that a serious, chronic illness has taken hold in the body and that his or her control of the movements of hands, legs, and other body parts is not what it once was. In later stages, when and if dementia appears, one sign that it is subcortical is that short-term memory is better than long-term memory, exactly the opposite of people with cortical degeneration.

Parkinson's disease A chronic, progressive disease that is characterized by muscle tremor and rigidity, and sometimes dementia, caused by a reduction of dopamine production in the brain.

The most common type of subcortical dementia results from **Parkinson's disease,** which begins with rigidity or tremor of the muscles. Neurons degenerate in a brain region that produces dopamine, a neurotransmitter essential to normal brain functioning. If destruction of neurons and slowed transmission reach a certain threshold, dementia may begin. Because cognitive reserve declines with age, older people with Parkinson's disease are more likely to develop dementia than are younger ones (Starkstein & Merello, 2002). An estimated 8 percent of newly diagnosed individuals are under age 40, but most are much older.

A related form of dementia is called *Lewy body dementia,* because of the round deposits of protein (Lewy bodies) seen in neurons (Whitbourne, 2002). These bodies are always found in Parkinson's disease, but in Lewy body dementia they are dispersed throughout the brain. Motor movements and cognition are both affected, but these effects are not as severe as the motor effects of Parkinson's or the memory loss of Alzheimer's. The main symptom is loss of inhibition.

Various infectious agents and toxins can also affect the brain. For instance, people with AIDS often develop a brain infection that produces dementia, as do those in the last stages of syphilis. Eating beef infected with bovine spongiform encephalitis (BSE, or "mad cow disease") eventually leads to dementia and death.

Any psychoactive drug can produce delirium, and chronic use can lead to dementia. When alcohol abuse is chronic, disruptions in the functioning of the central nervous system impair learning, reasoning, perception, and other mental processes. Over the long term, severe alcohol abuse can lead to *Korsakoff's syndrome,* with loss of short-term memory and increased confusion caused by brain lesions.

➤Response for Genetic Counselors (from page 664): A general guideline for genetic counselors is to provide clients with whatever information they seek; but because of both the uncertainty and the devastation of Alzheimer's disease, the ApoE4 test is not available at present. This may change (as was the case with the test for HIV) if early methods of prevention and treatment become more effective.

Reversible Dementia

The cortical and subcortical dementias already described damage the brain, and once brain damage has occurred, it cannot be reversed. However, proper treatment can slow the progression of dementia, and that is one reason early diagnosis is important.

Symptoms are sometimes caused by something whose effects *can* be reversed, such as medication, inadequate nutrition, alcohol abuse (short of Korsakoff's syndrome), depression, or other mental illness. Reversible dementia can also be caused by a brain injury or tumor; normal cognition may be restored by surgery and rehabilitation therapy.

Overmedication and Undernourishment

In hospitals, many forms of anesthesia can trigger delirium in the aged, and pain medication plus sleep deprivation in an unfamiliar setting can lead to ongoing dementia. At discharge, dementia may continue if the person is given medications that interact harmfully (Hajjar et al., 2005).

At home or in a nursing home, many elderly people take numerous different drugs each day—not only prescription medicines but also over-the-counter drugs, alcohol, and herbal remedies. The interaction of all these drugs often produces confusion and psychotic behavior. Also, doses given to the elderly may not be correct, since doses are usually determined by clinical trials using younger adults, whose metabolism and digestive systems differ from those of older adults and who are unlikely to be taking the same array of other medications.

Even without considering interactions, many drugs commonly taken by the elderly (such as most of those used to reduce high blood pressure, to combat Parkinson's disease, or to relieve pain) slow down mental processes (Davies & Thorn, 2002). The solution seems simple—moderation or elimination of problem drugs—but this solution requires that the cause be recognized and that the problem drugs not be necessary at their current dosages.

No drug is proven to protect against dementia, although many such drugs have been suggested. For example, as explained in Chapter 20, women who took estrogen after menopause were found to be less likely to develop Alzheimer's disease (Marriott & Wink, 2004). However, those who took the hormones were also more likely to exercise regularly, to be well-educated, and to eat healthy foods—all of which also correlate with a reduced incidence of dementia. As you remember from Chapter 1, correlation does not prove causation; so in this case, no conclusions can be drawn about the extent to which any or all of these factors reduce the risk of Alzheimer's.

Hormones are probably not protective. The same debate now focuses on statins, a group of drugs used to reduce cholesterol levels: Some believe that statins are protective against dementia, but they probably are not (Zandi et al., 2005).

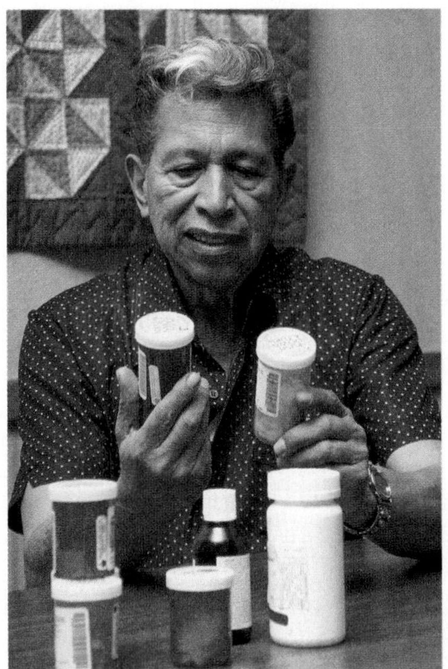

And the Print Is Too Small Patients, physicians, and pharmacists have reason to be confused about the eight or more drugs that the average elderly person takes. Very few patients take their medicines exactly as prescribed. Moreover, in addition to prescription drugs, most elderly people also take over-the-counter medications, vitamins, herbal remedies, and caffeinated or alcoholic drinks. It is no wonder that drug interactions cause drowsiness, unsteadiness, and confusion in about half of all elderly persons.

Anti-inflammatory drugs, such as aspirin and ibuprofen, may be protective but they, too, probably are not.

Inadequate nutrition is connected to overmedication, not only because some of the poorest elderly skimp on food in order to be able to afford their medications but also because many medications reduce absorption of vitamins. Undernutrition can also stem from reduced income, loss of appetite, loneliness, and impaired digestive processes. Extreme vitamin deficiencies and dehydration can lead to depression, confusion, and cognitive decline (Rosenberg, 2001), but vitamin pills are not a good substitute for a healthy diet.

Adequate healthy eating and drinking (water, not wine or coffee) correlate with reduced incidence of dementia. As was noted in Chapter 23, however, many elderly people, at home or in nursing homes, overmedicate and do not eat well or drink enough water (Wendland et al., 2003).

a case to study

Is It Dementia or Drug Addiction?

Many gerontologists are becoming aware of the problem of overmedication and drug abuse among the elderly, although ageism often prevents family members from realizing that an elderly relative's mood swings, rage, and confusion are not normal. As at every age, addicts hide their addiction and become angry at those who confront them. Fortunately, treatment and recovery are possible at any age. Consider Audrey.

> A 70-year-old widow named Audrey . . . was covered with large black bruises and burns from her kitchen stove. Audrey no longer had an appetite, so she ate little and was emaciated. One night she passed out in her driveway and scraped her face. The next morning, her neighbor found her face down on the pavement in her nightgown.
>
> Audrey couldn't be trusted with the grandchildren anymore, so family visits were fewer and farther between. She rarely showered and spent most days sitting in a chair alternating between drinking, sleeping, and watching television. She stopped calling friends, and social invitations had long since ceased.
>
> Audrey obtained prescriptions for Valium, a tranquilizer, and Placydil, a sleep inducer. Both medications, which are addictive and have more adverse effects in patients over age 60, should only be used for short periods of time. Audrey had taken both medications for years at three to four times the prescribed dosage. She mixed them with large quantities of alcohol. She was a full-fledged addict . . . close to death.
>
> Her children knew she had a problem, but they . . . couldn't agree among themselves on the best way to help her. Over time, they became desensitized to the seriousness of her problem—until it progressed to a dangerously advanced stage. Luckily for Audrey, she was referred to a new doctor who recognized her addiction. . . . Once Audrey was in treatment and weaned off the alcohol and drugs, she bloomed. Audrey's memory improved; her appetite returned; she regained her energy; and she started walking, swimming and exercising every day. Now, a decade later, Audrey plays an important role in her grandchildren's lives, gardens, and she lives creatively and with meaning.
>
> *[Colleran & Jay, 2003, p. 11]*

Audrey is a stunning example of the danger of ageist assumptions about senility. Her children did not realize that she could once again have an intellectually and socially productive life.

Psychological Illness

Elderly people have a lower incidence of psychological disorders than younger adults do. The rates of anxiety, antisocial personality disorder, bipolar disorder, schizophrenia, and depression are lower after age 65. One reason is that these problems can lead to poor health and thus higher mortality at younger ages. Another is that many disorders become less severe with age. Nonetheless, about 10 percent of the elderly who seem demented are experiencing psychological, more than physiological, illness.

Anxiety is particularly likely to be mistaken for dementia (Scogin, 1998) because anxiety can make even a healthy person forgetful. When an older person arrives at a hospital or nursing home, crippling anxiety may cause disorientation and memory loss. If the patient is assessed immediately, misdiagnosis is a real possibility.

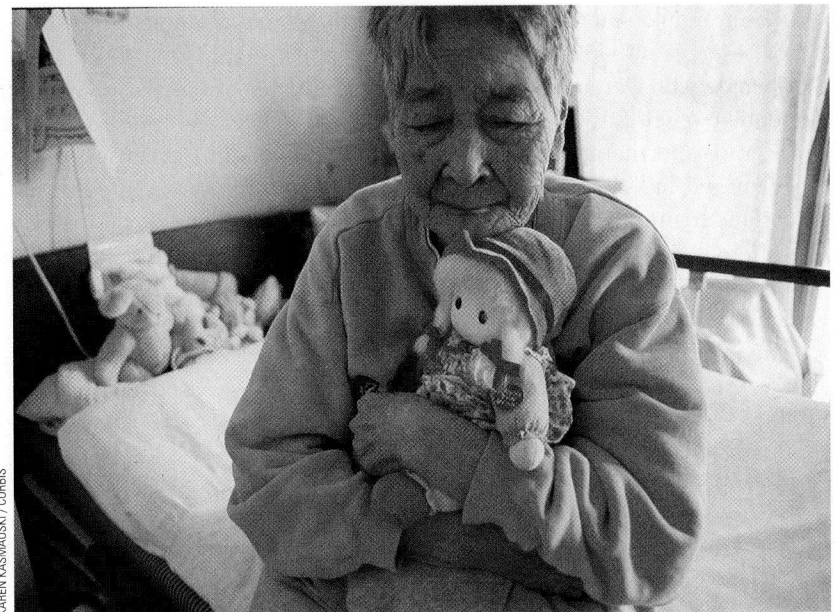

KAREN KASMAUSKI / CORBIS

Waiting for a Bath This woman is in a Tokyo facility that provides baths for physically or cognitively impaired elderly people—not just as a hygienic necessity, but also as a soothing, sensual experience.

Observation Quiz (see answer, page 670): Should someone take that doll away?

It might lead to prescriptions for psychotropic medicine, resulting in ongoing, though reversible, dementia.

Careful diagnosis is essential. If an older person is depressed, lonely, and inactive but is *not* treated, symptoms of dementia may occur (Davies & Thorn, 2002). Clues to the person's true condition are evident in his or her behavior. For example, many depressed older adults exaggerate minor memory losses or refuse to answer questions. Quite the opposite reaction comes from people with Alzheimer's, who try to answer and are embarrassed by their inability to do so (Sabat, 2001). People who suffer from mental illness are often impaired in episodic memory (memory of what happened) but not in short-term memory, unlike people with Alzheimer's disease (Vidailhet et al., 2001).

The most common problem in this regard is that many older adults who are depressed are not treated, even though therapy and careful use of medication usually bring improvement in a few weeks, and pseudodementia disappears (Davies & Thorn, 2002). However, as when they miss signs of addiction, some younger people expect the elderly to be sad and confused, so the depression goes untreated. The result may be suicide, which occurs almost twice as often in the United States among those over age 85 than among teenagers (U.S. Bureau of the Census, 2007). Rates are particularly high among men of European background (see Appendix A, p. A-27).

Prevention and Treatment

Irreversible dementia is not easy to prevent. The idea that people who keep their minds active will never develop dementia is simplistic. Doing the daily crossword puzzle will not prevent dementia. In short, there is no cure—or even effective prevention as yet.

However, many lifestyle factors that slow down senescence also delay the onset of dementia. For example, the underlying cause of the blood-vessel obstructions that lead to strokes and vascular dementia is arteriosclerosis (hardening of the arteries). Measures to improve circulation (such as regular exercise) or to prevent and control hypertension and diabetes (such as proper diet and drugs) slow arteriosclerosis and may delay the onset of dementia.

➤Answer to Observation Quiz (from page 669): No. Note that the woman is holding the doll close, with both hands and her chin. The photograph makes a valid point about the universal need for comfort.

In fact, regular exercise can reduce the incidence of dementia by half (Marx, 2005), especially if exercise also prevents overweight. One large study found that people who were obese in middle age were almost twice as likely to develop dementia by their 70s as were people of normal weight (Whitmer et al., 2005).

Exercise and therapy to retrain the brain's automatic responses and to repair the damaged links between neurons can sometimes restore intellectual health, and "some brain-cellular changes seen in normal aging can be slowed or reversed with exercise" (Woodlee & Schallert, 2006, p. 203). Antidepressants can also help if the person feels like giving up and doing nothing, as is often the case (Okamoto et al., 2002).

Once dementia begins, early diagnosis can signal the need for various drugs (Jellinger et al., 2002; Peterson, 2003). Several of these, especially cholinesterase inhibitors (e.g., donepezil) slow the progression of Alzheimer's disease (Kaduszkiewicz et al., 2005).

Many scientists are seeking to halt the production of beta-amyloid or tau (Marx, 2007; Roberson & Mucke, 2006). Some drugs succeed with mice that have been genetically engineered to develop Alzheimer's. Clinical trials with human participants are now underway to learn which drugs have unexpected toxic effects and to discover whether they slow the human disease. Hope is replacing despair because

> researchers have made tremendous progress toward understanding the molecular events that appear to trigger the illness, and they are now exploring a variety of strategies for slowing or halting these destructive processes. Perhaps one of these treatments, or a combination of them, could impede the degeneration of neurons enough to stop Alzheimer's disease in its tracks.
>
> *[Wolfe, 2006, p. 73]*

Similarly, while Parkinson's disease is incurable, many drugs are now used to relieve its symptoms. Surgery to repair the specific area of the brain affected by Parkinson's has had some success (Deuschl et al., 2006).

From a developmental perspective, the possibility of cure is thrilling, but even in the most optimistic scenario, millions now suffering from dementia will die before such therapy is available. Although research seeking a medical cure is necessary and thrilling, there is currently a much more pressing need to provide services and treatment for the millions of people with dementia and their caregivers.

SUMMING UP

Dementia, characterized by memory loss and confusion, is not rare among the elderly, but it is not the usual pattern. The three main causes of dementia are Alzheimer's disease, small strokes (TIAs) resulting in vascular dementia, and Parkinson's disease. Each of these conditions follows a somewhat different pattern. There are many other reasons for dementia, including drug addiction and mental disorders, which can be reversed. Researchers are discovering the causes of dementia and testing drugs that might stop its insidious progression. ■

The Optimal: New Cognitive Development

You have learned that, in adapting to later life, most adults maintain sufficient intellectual power. Their focus may shift from details to principles, from negative to positive, from criticism to acceptance, from speed to accuracy. It may be ageist to fault thinking at age 80 for not being as detailed, critical, or quick as at younger years. Wouldn't it be just as illogical to blame the young for undervaluing faith, tradition, and community?

Erik Erikson finds that older people are more interested than the young in the arts, in children, and in human experience as a whole. The elderly are "social witnesses" to life, more aware of the interdependence of the generations (Erikson et al., 1986). Abraham Maslow maintained that older adults are much more likely than younger people to reach what he considered the highest stage of development—self-actualization—which includes heightened aesthetic, creative, philosophical, and spiritual understanding (Maslow, 1970).

Erikson and Maslow have been criticized for selective perception (they chose their interviewees) (Hoare, 2002). But even Paul Baltes, with his data-based study of a representative cohort of the elderly in West Berlin, finds gains as well as losses at every stage of life (Baltes, 2003). What are some of the gains?

Aesthetic Sense and Creativity

Many elderly people seem to gain a greater appreciation of nature and aesthetic experiences. As one team of gerontologists explains:

> The elemental things of life—children, friendship, nature, human touching (physical and emotional), color, shape—assume greater significance as people sort out the more important from the less important. Old age can be a time of emotional sensory awareness and enjoyment.
>
> *[Butler et al., 1998, p. 65]*

For many older people, this heightened appreciation finds active expression. They may begin gardening, bird-watching, making ceramics, painting, or playing a musical instrument—and not simply because they have nothing better to do. The importance that creativity can have for some in old age is wonderfully expressed by a 79-year-old man, who was not famous, little educated, yet joyful at his workbench:

> This is the happiest time of my life. . . . I wish there was twenty-four hours in a day. Wuk hours, wake hours. Yew can keep y' sleep; plenty of time for that later on. . . . That's what I want all this here time for now—to make things. I draw and I paint too. . . . I don't copy anything. I make what I remember. I tarn wood. I paint the fields. As I say, I've niver bin so happy in my whole life and I only hope I last out.
>
> *[quoted in Blythe, 1979]*

For this man, the creative impulse did not suddenly arise in late adulthood; it was present, although infrequently expressed, in earlier years. Many older adults decide to stop deferring their creative expression.

One of the most famous examples of late creative development is Anna Moses, who was a farm wife and mother in upstate New York. For most of her life, she expressed her artistic impulses by stitching quilts and doing embroidery during the long winters on the farm. At age 75, arthritis made needlework impossible, so she took to "dabbling in oil" instead. Four years later, three of her oil paintings, displayed in a local drugstore, caught the eye of a New York City art dealer who was passing by. He bought them, drove to Anna Moses's house, bought 15 more, and began to exhibit them. One year later, at age 80, "Grandma Moses" had her first one-woman show in New York, receiving international recognition for her unique "primitive" style. She continued to paint, "incredibly gaining in assurance and artistic discretion," into her 90s (Yglesias, 1980).

It Pleases Me In young adulthood and middle age, many people feel that they must meet social expectations and conform to community values. With a strong hand, a vivid imagination, and bold colors, the elderly are finally free to express themselves as they never did before.

RHODA SIDNEY / PHOTOEDIT, INC.

For those who have been creative all their lives, old age is often a time of continuing productivity and even of renewed inspiration. There is something called the "old-age style" in the arts, when established artists change their usual pattern, developing a new style that may be more creative then the previous style (Lindauer, 2003). Famous examples abound: Michelangelo painted the amazing frescoes in the Sistine Chapel at age 75; Giuseppe Verdi composed the opera *Falstaff* when he was 80; Frank Lloyd Wright completed the design of the Guggenheim Museum in New York City, an innovative architectural masterpiece, when he was 91.

In a study of extraordinarily creative people (Csikszentmihalyi, 1996), almost none of the respondents felt that their ability, their goals, or the quality of their work had been much impaired with age. What had changed was their sense of urgency, sharpened by their realization that fewer years lay ahead and that their energy and physical strength were diminishing. The researcher observed, "In their seventies, eighties, and nineties, they may lack the fiery ambition of earlier years, but they are just as focused, efficient, and committed as before . . . perhaps more so" (p. 503).

Another reviewer of artistic expression in late adulthood drew similar conclusions, which the author feels apply to all the aged. He writes:

> The study of art in older age increases our awareness of the growth possibilities of aging. . . . A realization that old age can be a time of gains as indicated by the work of aging artists, or a time of cognitive stability, as shown by older non-artists' response to art and arts-related activities, gives a positive perspective on late life potential.
>
> *[Lindauer, 1998, p. 248]*

The Life Review

Many older people become more reflective and philosophical. Sometimes they think about their own history, putting their lives in perspective, assessing accomplishments and failures in narrative form (Birren & Schroots, 2006).

life review An examination of one's own part in life, engaged in by many elderly people.

One form of this attempt to assess one's own life is called the **life review,** as people recall and recount their lives, comparing the past with the present. In general, the life review helps elders connect their past with the future, as they tell their stories to younger generations. At the same time, it renews links with former generations as people remember parents, grandparents, and even great-grandparents. A person's relationship to humanity, to nature, to God, and to the whole of life becomes a topic of reflection, as various memories are revived, reinterpreted, and finally reintegrated (Kotre, 1995).

The life review is more social than solitary. Elderly people want to tell their stories to others, and often their tales are not solely about themselves but also about their family, cohort, or ethnic group. Such stories tend to be richer in interesting details than those told by younger adults (Pratt & Robins, 1991). Of course, not everyone, old or young, is a gifted storyteller. The authors of one study explain:

> Most of us can recall older family members or acquaintances from our youth who were legendary (sometimes, perhaps, notorious) as champion storytellers. These individuals shared important cultural and personal knowledge and information on a variety of topics with younger generations through the recounting of their own past experiences. Yet other adults may come to mind who were terrible storytellers. Clearly, adults vary dramatically in their capacities and motivation to engage in such adult storytelling with young persons.
>
> *[Pratt et al., 1999, p. 414]*

To someone who knows how to listen, the stories are often worth hearing (Kastenbaum, 2003). Even if the life review is merely nostalgia or reminiscence, that may still be helpful to older people, although not always easy for others to hear. It may be crucial to the elder's feelings of self-worth that others appreciate the significance of these reminiscences. As Robert Butler and his colleagues explain:

> We have been taught that this nostalgia represents living in the past and a preoccupation with self and that it is generally boring, meaningless, and time-consuming. Yet as a natural healing process it represents one of the underlying human capacities on which all psychotherapy depends. The life review should be recognized as a necessary and healthy process in daily life as well as a useful tool in the mental health care of older people.
>
> *[Butler et al., 1998, p. 91]*

The reflectiveness of old age may intensify attempts to put broader historical and cultural contexts into perspective (Cohen, 1999). A comparison of autobiographical memories found that younger people recalled more specific details but that older ones gave more integrative accounts, stressing social roles and broader implications (Levine et al., 2002). In other words, young adults used autobiography to say what occurred, older adults to gain insight. No wonder their own life review is meaningful to them.

Wisdom

Wisdom is the most positive attribute associated with older people. The idea that wisdom may be common in old age has become a "hoped-for antidote to views that have cast the process of aging in terms of intellectual deficit and regression" (Labouvie-Vief, 1990). Although many people believe that wisdom increases with age, this belief, like the belief that aging inevitably means intellectual decline, may not be generally true (Brugman, 2006).

Certainly, younger adults do not always believe that their own parents are wiser than they are. This is notable among immigrants to the United States from places where respect for the wisdom of the elderly is integral to the culture. Sometimes adult immigrants bring their aged parents to live with them. This situation often leads to disappointment: The elderly feel that their wisdom is devalued, and younger family members feel that the elderly do not understand the current context.

One spouse complained of his Italian in-laws, "Parents won't let go. They want to bury their child" (quoted in Olson, 2001, p. 201). A Haitian elder said, "The children are not well educated. Yet they make fun of me" (p. 109). Many elders feel that their children and grandchildren are "too American," a phrase that signifies rudeness and disrespect. Wisdom is not evident in either generation.

What is wisdom, after all? Any definition is subjective. Whether any given individual is perceived as wise depends on the immediate social context in which that person's thoughts or actions are being judged. Wisdom is a social virtue, one that involves recognizing and responding to both the enduring cultural values and the current human needs of one's social group (Staudinger & Werner, 2003).

Given these obstacles to precision, consider one of the more comprehensive, all-purpose definitions of **wisdom,** offered by Paul Baltes: "Expertise in the fundamental pragmatics of life, permitting exceptional insight and judgment involving complex and uncertain matters of the human condition" (Baltes et al., 1998, p. 1070). Wisdom includes dialectical thinking that emerges in early adulthood (Chapter 18) and expertise in human relations gained from experience (Chapter 21).

wisdom A cognitive perspective characterized by a broad, practical, comprehensive approach to life's problems, reflecting timeless truths rather than immediate expediency; said to be more common in the elderly than in the young.

Is wisdom characteristic of late adulthood? Maybe not. In one study, adults of all ages were asked to advise four fictitious persons who faced difficult decisions regarding their future (Smith & Baltes, 1990). Here is an example:

> Elizabeth, 33 years old and a successful professional for 8 years, was recently offered a major promotion. Her new responsibilities would require an increased time commitment. She and her husband would also like to have children before it is too late. Elizabeth is considering the following options: She could plan to accept the promotion, or she could plan to start a family.
>
> *[p. 497]*

The other three stories concerned parental responsibilities at home, accepting early retirement, and intergenerational commitments, respectively. Participants were asked to think out loud to decide what each person should do, indicating when they thought additional information was needed. Responses were transcribed. Professionals who did not know the ages of the respondents assessed their wisdom. They found that wisdom was in short supply. Of 240 respondents, only 5 percent were judged as truly wise, and those were about equally likely to be of any age (Smith & Baltes, 1990). The professionals were chosen because they were considered good judges, but again, the definition of who is wise is complex.

More recent research likewise finds wisdom at many ages—although it is rare at any age and the very wise are more likely to be old. Experience and practice in dealing with the problems of life tend to increase wisdom, but intelligence and chronological age do not (Baltes et al., 1998).

If wisdom includes warm social interactions, humor, and altruistic concern, another study also found little correlation between intelligence and wisdom (Vaillant & Davis, 2000). This study found that when boys who had low IQ scores (between 60 and 86) grew up, some led wise and good lives. For example, one man, called "slovenly, tardy, and lazy" by his boyhood teacher, became a pastor, first of a small parish, then of progressively larger ones. He loved "helping and teaching" people, and he excelled at it. Wisely, he appreciated that his wife did the paperwork and math, and he was thrilled that all his children attended college.

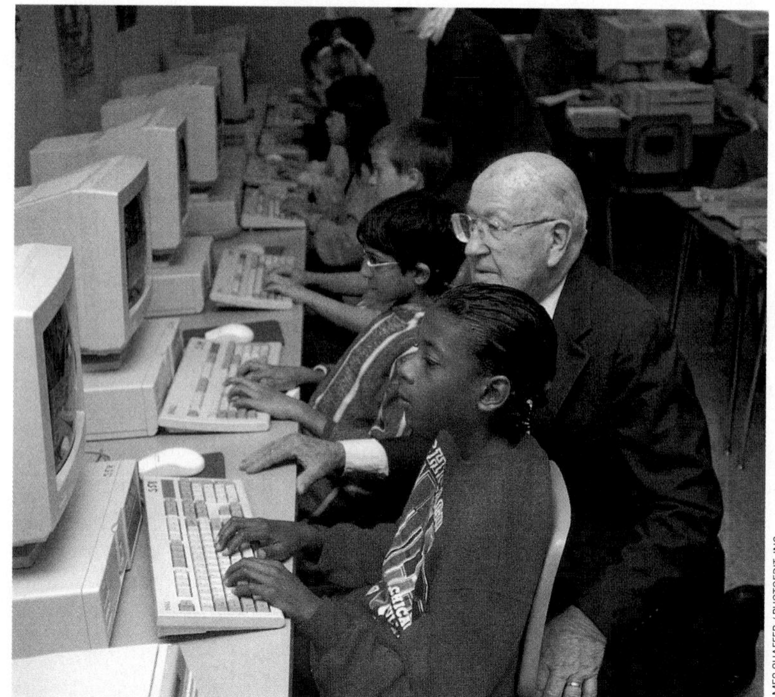

JAMES SHAFFER / PHOTOEDIT, INC.

So Much to Learn When it comes to computer savvy, these children will probably soon surpass their elderly volunteer teacher. But wisdom includes patience, appreciation of diversity, and willingness to learn, and on these qualities some older adults surpass the typical schoolchild.

Observation Quiz (see answer, page 676): What is it about the man's posture that suggests he is a dedicated teacher?

Not everyone achieved such success, but about half of the low-IQ participants in this study attained joy, connection, devotion, and caring that matched those attained by peers who had much higher IQs. One author of a longitudinal study of 814 people (including these low IQ boys) concludes that wisdom is not reserved for the old, although humor, perspective, and altruism often increase over the decades. He then writes:

> To be wise about wisdom we need to accept that wisdom does—and wisdom does not—increase with age. Age facilitates a widening social radius and more balanced ways of coping with adversity, but thus far no one can prove that wisdom is great in old age. Perhaps we are wisest when we keep our discussion of wisdom simple and when we confine ourselves to words of one and two syllables. Winston Churchill, that master of wise simplicity and simple wisdom, reminds us, "We are all happier in many ways when we are old than when we are young. The young sow wild oats. The old grow sage."
>
> *[Vaillant, 2002, p. 256]*

SUMMING UP

On balance, it seems fair to conclude that the mental processes in late adulthood can be adaptive and creative—not necessarily as efficient as thinking at younger ages, but more appropriate to the final period of life. These qualities are particularly apparent in the work of artists, who seem as creative and passionate about their work in later adulthood as they were earlier. Many others, who are not artistic, also have a strong aesthetic sense and seek to tell their life story to other people. Wisdom is not the sole domain of the old, nor are all older people wise. Nonetheless, many are insightful, creative, and reflective, using their life experience to gain wisdom. ■

Let us conclude with an exemplary case, the poet Henry Wadsworth Longfellow, who wrote these lines at age 68:

> . . . But why, you ask me, should this tale be told?
> Of men grown old, or who are growing old?
> Ah, nothing is too late
> Till the tired heart shall cease to palpitate;
> Cato learned Greek at eighty; Sophocles
> Wrote his grand Oedipus, and Simonides
> Bore off the prize of verse from his compeers,
> When each had numbered more than four score years,
> And Theophrastus, at four score and ten,
> Had just begun his Characters of Men.
> Chaucer, at Woodstock with the nightingales,
> At sixty wrote the Canterbury Tales;
> Goethe at Weimar, toiling to the last,
> Completed Faust when eighty years were past.
> These are indeed exceptions, but they show
> How far the gulf-stream of our youth may flow
> Into the arctic regions of our lives
> When little else than life itself survives. . . .
> Shall we then sit us idly down and say
> The night hath come; it is no longer day?
> The night hath not yet come; we are not quite
> Cut off from labor by the failing light;
> Some work remains for us to do and dare;
> Even the oldest tree some fruit may bear; . . .
> And as the evening twilight fades away
> The sky is filled with stars, invisible by day.

SUMMARY

The Usual: Information Processing After Age 65

1. Although thinking processes become slower and less sharp once a person reaches late adulthood, there is much individual variation in this decline, and each particular cognitive ability shows a different rate of age-related loss.

2. As the senses themselves become dulled, some material never reaches the sensory memory. Working memory shows notable declines, especially when the older person must simultaneously store and process information in complex ways. Processing takes longer with age.

3. Control processes are less effective with age, as retrieval strategies become less efficient. More parts of the brain are activated.

4. With increasing age, adults experience greater difficulty accessing information from working memory and long-term memory. Knowledge stored in implicit memory is more easily retrieved than are the facts and concepts stored in explicit memory.

5. One reason older adults perform less well than younger adults on tests of cognitive functioning is that more of the older group experience stereotype threat, forming negative self-perceptions. Some laboratory research creates contexts that impede the efficient use of adult cognition.

6. In daily life, most of the elderly are not seriously handicapped by cognitive difficulties. Usually, once they recognize problems in their memory or other intellectual abilities, they develop strategies to compensate.

The Impaired: Dementia

7. Dementia, whether it occurs in late adulthood or earlier, is characterized by memory loss—at first minor lapses, then more serious forgetfulness, and finally such extreme losses that recognition of even the closest family members fades.

8. The most common cause of dementia in the United States is Alzheimer's disease, an incurable ailment that becomes more prevalent with age. Genetic factors (especially the ApoE4 gene) play a role in Alzheimer's disease. Drug therapy offers some promise for the prevention and treatment of Alzheimer's disease.

9. Vascular dementia (also called multi-infarct dementia) results from a series of ministrokes (transient ischemic attacks, or TIAs, that occur when impairment of blood circulation destroys portions of brain tissue. Measures to improve circulation and to control hypertension can prevent or slow the course of vascular dementia.

10. Subcortical abnormalities, such as Lewy body dementia and Parkinson's disease, are also leading causes of dementia. Severe alcoholism and AIDS can cause dementia as well.

11. Dementia is sometimes mistakenly diagnosed when the individual is actually suffering from a reversible problem. Overuse or misuse of medication, anxiety, depression, and poor nutrition can cause dementia symptoms.

The Optimal: New Cognitive Development

12. Many people become more responsive to nature, more interested in creative endeavors, and more philosophical as they grow older. The life review is a personal reflection that many older people undertake, remembering earlier experiences and putting their entire lives into perspective.

13. Wisdom does not necessarily increase as a result of age, but some elderly people are unusually wise or insightful.

KEY TERMS

dual-task deficit (p. 651)
control processes (p. 654)
priming (p. 657)
explicit memory (p. 657)
implicit memory (p. 657)
terminal decline (p. 659)
dementia (p. 662)
delirium (p. 663)
Alzheimer's disease (AD) (p. 663)
vascular dementia (VaD)/multi-infarct dementia (MID) (p. 666)
subcortical dementias (p. 666)
Parkinson's disease (p. 666)
life review (p. 672)
wisdom (p. 673)

➤**Answer to Observation Quiz** (from page 674): He is kneeling in order to be at the right level and distance. Kneeling is harder for the old than for the young; the fact that he has made the effort is a sign of his dedication to instructing the children.

KEY QUESTIONS

1. How is each part of the information-processing system—sensory register, working memory, knowledge base, and control processes—affected by age?

2. How could a slowdown within the brain lead to cognitive decline?

3. Compare age differences in explicit and implicit memory.

4. What are the problems with, and the conclusions derived from, research on long-term memory?

5. How do stereotypes about aging held by researchers, by cultures, and by individuals affect research on memory?

6. Does everyone develop dementia if they live long enough?

7. What are the similarities between Alzheimer's disease and vascular dementia? What are the differences?

8. How reversible is dementia?

9. What are the purpose and the result of the life review?

10. What is a definition of wisdom, and how does this relate to aging?

APPLICATIONS

1. At all ages, memory is selective. People forget much more than they remember. Choose someone—a sibling, a former classmate, or a current friend—who went through some public event with you. Sit down together, write separate lists of all the details each of you remembers about the event, and then compare your accounts. What insight does this exercise give you into the kinds of things older adults remember and forget?

2. Many factors affect intellectual sharpness. Think of an occasion when you felt stupid and an occasion when you felt smart. How did the contexts of the two experiences differ? How might those differences affect the performance of elderly and young adults who go to a university laboratory for testing?

3. Visit someone in a hospital. Note all the elements in the environment—such as noise, lights, schedules, and personnel—that might cause an elderly patient to seem demented.

25

CHAPTER OUTLINE

Late Adulthood: Psychosocial Development

The range of possibilities for life after age 65 is vast, greater than at any earlier age. You already learned that some elderly people run marathons, while others hardly move; some write timeless poetry, while others cannot speak. This chapter describes some of the psychosocial possibilities, particularly regarding family relationships and other social interactions. Some problems, such as poverty, frailty, and elder abuse, are also discussed.

As a preview, consider a couple married for 80 years, retired for 40, both over age 100. They live together, without outside help. Gilbert is proud of his wife, Sadie:

> "She gets out of bed—I timed her this morning, just for fun. I got up first, but while I was in the bathroom, she gets up, she comes out here first and puts the coffee on. Got back and washed up and got dressed and just twelve minutes after she got out of bed—just twelve minutes this morning—I had her right on the watch."
>
> Sadie chuckles. "I don't have any secrets anymore."
>
> "So then you have breakfast together?" I ask.
>
> "Oh, yes!"
>
> "And then read the paper?"
>
> "After we get the dishes washed, we sit down and read the paper for a couple of hours."
>
> *[quoted in Ellis, 2002, pp. 107–108]*

Few centenarians live as well as Gilbert and Sadie: Many are widowed, most are no longer independent. Gilbert and Sadie are unusual in being still together and independent, but they are not unusual in taking comfort in their families, pleasure in their daily routines, and interest in current events.

Remember them as we describe the variability and complexity of development in later life. We begin with theories of psychosocial development in late adulthood and then focus on a range of possible activities in retirement, social relationships, and frailty.

Theories of Late Adulthood

Dozens of theories have been formulated to help us understand psychosocial development in late adulthood. To simplify, we consider these theories in three clusters: self theories, stratification theories, and dynamic theories.

Self Theories

self theories Theories of late adulthood that emphasize the core self, or the search to maintain one's integrity and identity.

Self theories begin with the premise that adults seek to be themselves. They make choices, confront problems, and interpret reality in such a way as to define, become, and express themselves as fully as possible. As Maslow (1968) described it, people attempt to self-actualize, or achieve their full potential.

Self theories emphasize "the ways people negotiate challenges to the self" (Sneed & Whitbourne, 2005, p. 380), an ability that is particularly crucial when older adults are confronted with multiple challenges: illnesses, retirement, death of loved ones. The central idea of self theory is that each person ultimately depends on him- or herself. As one woman explained:

> I actually think I value my sense of self more importantly than my family or relationships or health or wealth or wisdom. I do see myself as on my own, ultimately. . . . Statistics certainly show that older women are likely to end up being alone, so I really do value my own self when it comes right down to things in the end.
>
> *[quoted in Kroger, 2007, p. 203]*

Integrity Versus Despair

integrity versus despair The final stage of Erik Erikson's developmental sequence, in which older adults seek to integrate their unique experiences with their vision of community.

The most comprehensive self theory came from Erik Erikson, who was still writing in his 90s (Erikson et al., 1986). The developmental crisis of Erikson's final stage is **integrity versus despair,** when older adults seek to integrate their unique experiences with their vision of community. Many develop pride and contentment with their personal story, as well as with their community. Others despair, "feeling that the time is now short, too short for the attempt to start another life and to try out alternate roads to recovery" (Erikson, 1963, p. 269).

As at every other stage, tension between the two opposing aspects of the developmental crisis helps advance the person toward a fuller understanding. In this eighth stage,

> life brings many, quite realistic reasons for experiencing despair: aspects of the present that cause unremitting pain; aspects of a future that are uncertain and frightening. And, of course, there remains inescapable death, that one aspect of the future which is both wholly certain and wholly unknowable. Thus, some despair must be acknowledged and integrated as a component of old age.
>
> *[Erikson et al., 1986, p. 72]*

Ideally, the reality of death brings a "life-affirming involvement" in the present—for oneself, one's children, one's grandchildren, and all of humanity (Erikson et al., 1986).

To maintain integrity, older people are proud to be alert, independent, and respected. As you remember, each of Erikson's stages builds on the previous ones. Elders who have many close friends and family members, including a partner (intimacy), and who can look back on a productive life (generativity) are most able to feel integrity, approaching the end of life without despair. Integrity itself begins to build long before old age (Hoare, 2002).

An older person who is no longer independent can be buffered from despair by love and by the reassurance of his or her remaining abilities (Rothermund &

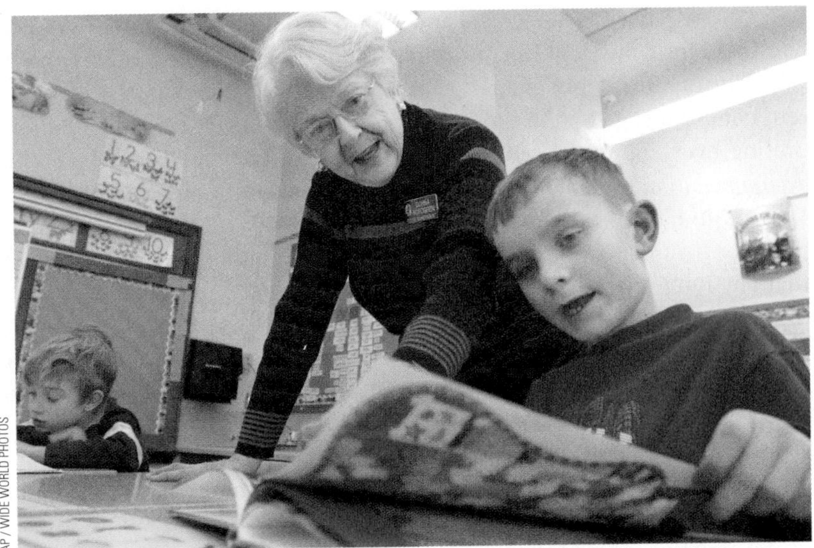
AP / WIDE WORLD PHOTOS

On the Same Page This school volunteer, working with "high-risk" children, pays close attention to the picture that has captured the boy's interest. The ability to care for others is one sign of integrity, as older adults realize all the "high risks" they have personally overcome.

Brandstädter, 2003; Steverink & Lindenberg, 2006). Thus, Gilbert and Sadie were delighted with each other and with the "just twelve minutes" it took her to get dressed (intimacy and generativity again).

Identity Theory

A second self theory originates in Erikson's fifth stage, *identity versus role confusion*. Throughout life, each new experience, each gain or loss, requires a reassessment of identity (Cross & Markus, 1991; Kroger, 2007; van der Meulen, 2001; Zucker et al., 2002).

Identity is challenged in old age. The usual pillars of the self-concept crumble, specifically appearance, health, and employment. One 70-year-old said, "I know who I've been, but who am I now?" (quoted in Kroger, 2007, p. 201).

Knowing oneself often means accepting one's key personality traits—generosity, shyness, good nature, and so on. Most older people consider their personalities and attitudes to have remained quite stable over their life span. One 103-year-old woman observed, "My core has stayed the same. Everything else has changed" (Troll & Skaff, 1997, p. 166). One nursing home resident,

> when asked whether she had changed much over the years, extracted a photo from a stack in her dresser drawer, one taken when she was in her early twenties, and said, "That's me, but I changed a little." She had indeed changed. She was now neither curvaceous nor animated, but was physically distorted from crippling arthritis and sullen from pain. To herself, however, she was still the same person she had always been.
>
> *[Tobin, 1996]*

When older adults are asked to select a "cherished object," most pick ordinary and inexpensive things that had great personal meaning (Sherman & Dacher, 2005). Objects and places become more precious in late adulthood than earlier, a way to hold on to identity (Kroger, 2007; Whitmore, 2001).

This trait may be problematic if it leads to compulsive hoarding, an urge that causes some elderly people to save so many old papers, pieces of furniture, and mementoes that little space is left in their homes for themselves (Thobaden, 2006). Hoarding becomes increasingly common with age. Many older people resist moving from a drafty and dangerous dwelling into a smaller, safer place, not because they do not recognize the social and health benefits of the move but because they fear that parting with objects may mean that they will lose themselves.

Unfortunately, some elderly people, instead of balancing past identity and current conditions, go to one extreme or the other. Some choose *assimilation* (reinterpreting every new experience as part of the same old pattern); others choose *accommodation* (abandoning old identity in the face of new contexts).

In assimilation, identity remains unchanged and new experiences are incorporated, or assimilated, into earlier structures. The individual distorts reality to deny that anything is new. To protect self-esteem, a person might refuse to eat an unfamiliar food or to learn to use e-mail, or might insist that the only way to worship God is with words from childhood. Older adults, by far, are the age group least likely to use technology of any kind, from cell phones to faxes, from microwaves to Internet shopping (Czaja et al., 2006). If an older person is nostalgic about "the good old days," believing that life was once uniformly better (ignoring the facts that racism, sexism, childhood diseases, and death in middle age were more prevalent), that may be assimilation.

Assimilation is useful in protecting the self-concept from ageism (Sneed & Whitbourne, 2005). However, assimilation may result in a refusal to take medication or ask for help. An assimilating person might ignore "shaky balance" to "venture out on an icy day wearing shoes that do not have nonskid soles" (Whitbourne, 2002, p. 11). Assimilation leads to rigidity.

The opposite strategy, accommodation, is worse for self-esteem (Whitbourne, 2002). In accommodation, people adapt to changes by abandoning their identity, adjusting too much. Accommodating individuals might accept ageist stereotypes, deciding that nothing can "stave off the onset of old age" (Whitbourne, 2002, p. 11). Incorporating the negative stereotypes of ageism leads to depression and poorer health. This outlook leads to deterioration and hastens mortality. Life is over, integrity is impossible, and all that is left is despair and death.

Ideally, then, a person combines long-standing identity with changing circumstances, avoiding both mindless resistance (assimilation) and total defeat (accommodation). Constructive identity "consists of both more or less enduring, stable beliefs as well as more short-term, variable ones" (van der Meulen, 2001, p. 29), as "individuals select pathways, act and appraise the consequences of their actions in terms of their self-identity" (Heinz, 2002, p. 58).

CHRISTIAN HIM / RETNA

Selective Optimization with Compensation Max Roach has was leading jazz drummer for over 50 years. His approach to his work at age 73 clearly reflects the idea of selective optimization with compensation: "I joined a health club. . . . I thought I'd tune up, you know, tone up. Playing my instrument is a lot of exercise. All four limbs going. . . . I don't play the way I did back in the 52nd Street days. We were playing long, hard hours in all that smoke. It would kill me now if I played like I did then. Now I play concerts, and the show goes on for just an hour." Roach died in 2007 at the age of 83.

Selective Optimization

As you remember from Chapter 23, people can choose to cope successfully with the changes of late adulthood through *selective optimization with compensation*. This concept is central to self theories. Individuals can set goals, assess their own abilities, and figure out how to accomplish what they want to achieve despite the limitations and declines of later life. Although at every age people seek new achievements, in later years the goal of simply maintaining abilities correlates with well-being (Ebner et al., 2006). In this way, optimization combines with compensation, assimilation with accommodation.

As an example of selective optimization, consider Artur Rubinstein, a world-famous concert pianist who "continued to perform with great success" in his 80s (Baltes et al., 2006, p. 592). He did this by limiting his repertoire to pieces he knew he could perform well (selection) and by practicing them more than he had when he was younger (optimization). Since he was slower at playing fast passages, he slowed the tempo of other parts, making the fast passages seem quicker by contrast (compensation) (Baltes et al., 2006).

More common examples are provided by elders who restructure their daily lives. One woman shopped for food at a distant store at the end of the bus line, so

Stratification by Age

Industrialized nations segregate older people. Increasingly as they grow older, people may be consigned to their own places and activities. This is especially true in modern societies (Achenbaum, 2005), where ageism harms everyone because "age segregation creates socialization deficits for members of all age groups" (Hagestad & Dannefer, 2001, p. 13).

The deficit arises from the fact that younger and older people are less often in places where they are equals, especially if the older people live in communities that exclude residents under age 55 and if they are forced to retire, leaving work to the younger adults. These structural aspects of age segregation are echoed in personal lives. When was the last time you went to a party of friends and people of all ages came?

The most controversial version of age stratification theory is **disengagement theory** (Cummings & Henry, 1961). According to this theory, traditional roles become unavailable or unimportant, the social circle shrinks, coworkers stop asking for help, and adult children focus on their own children. Once people reach their 60s, infirmity and slowness lead them to voluntarily avoid life's hustle and bustle. Thus, not only do younger people disengage from the old but the elderly also disengage, relinquishing past roles, withdrawing, and becoming passive.

disengagement theory The view that aging makes a person's social sphere increasingly narrow, resulting in role relinquishment, withdrawal, and passivity.

A study found that older adults were less upset at past mistakes than younger adults were, not because they had fewer regrets but because they cared less about wanting to undo the past. This could be seen as the positivity effect, or it could be seen as disengagement from their own past lives. The older people were happier than the younger adults, who were less able to disengage and thus felt their regrets more intensely. According to this researcher, disengagement was the best choice (Wrosch et al., 2005).

Disengagement theory provoked a storm of protest because people thought it encouraged age segregation and thus ageism. Many gerontologists insisted that older people need new involvements. Some developed an opposite theory, called **activity theory,** which holds that the elderly seek to remain active with relatives, friends, and community groups. If the elderly do disengage and withdraw, activity theorists contend, they do so unwillingly (Kelly, 1993; Rosow, 1985).

activity theory The view that elderly people want and need to remain active in a variety of social spheres—with relatives, friends, and community groups—and become withdrawn only unwillingly, as a result of ageism.

STEPHANIE MAZE / CORBIS

Silver on Display In the foreground is Layla Eneboldsen, enjoying the company of three other elderly people who live with her. Since more than 90 percent of the elderly in the United States are White (and mostly female), like this group of friends, and since the furniture, lights, and artwork date from 60 years ago, this might seem to be a scene from the 1940s in the United States. In fact, this is twenty-first-century Denmark.

Especially for Social Scientists The various social-science disciplines tend to favor different theories of aging. Can you tell which theories would be more acceptable to psychologists and which to sociologists?

Research has shown that, in general, the more active the elderly are and the more roles (worker, wife, mother, neighbor) they have, the greater their satisfaction and the longer their lives (Rowe & Kahn, 1998). Indeed, literally being active —bustling around the house, climbing stairs, walking to work—can lengthen a person's life as well as increase satisfaction (Manini et al., 2006). Other research also finds support for activity theory. A longitudinal study of 77- to 98-year-olds in Sweden found that quality of life was directly related to having many leisure activities. Over a 10-year period, one-third of those studied added activities rather than cutting back, with some of them substituting new activities if old ones were no longer available (Silverstein & Parker, 2002).

Another leading gerontologist suggests that both disengagement theory and activity theory may be too extreme:

> Care providers have reported that their feelings are very mixed when trying to "activate" certain old people. The workers say that while they believe activity is good, they nevertheless have the feeling that they are doing something wrong when they try to drag some older people to various forms of social activity or activity therapy.
>
> *[Tornstam, 1999–2000].*

This comment applies to every aspect of age segregation. If people of a certain age prefer to be with each other rather than with younger or older people, is that to be allowed, encouraged, or resisted? The same question can be asked about the other two forms of segregation apparent among the elderly: segregation by gender and by ethnicity.

Stratification by Gender

Feminist theory draws attention to gender separation. From the newborn's pink or blue blanket, continuing through childhood education, adult career choices, family caregiving, and older-adult living arrangements, males and females are guided and pressured into following divergent paths.

Feminists are particularly concerned about late adulthood, partly because "the study of aging, by sheer force of demography, is necessarily a woman's issue" (Ray, 1996, p. 674). A disproportionate number of the elderly are female. The ratio in the United States is almost two women to one man by age 70; that ratio is reached worldwide by age 80. Everywhere older women are segregated and, perhaps as a result, poorer than old men.

Past sexual discrimination is one reason for high rates of female poverty. Pension plans are often pegged to continuous employment, which is less common among wives and mothers than among men; Social Security pays more to a former worker than to his spouse; medical insurance covers men's illnesses (which are more likely to be acute problems, such as heart attacks) at a higher rate than women's (which are more often chronic problems, such as arthritis).

The ongoing implications of gender differences were revealed by a study of retirement and caregiving among older married couples. Both men and women provided care if their spouse needed it, but they did it in opposite ways: Women quit their jobs, but men worked longer. To be specific, employed women whose husbands needed care were five times more likely to retire than other older women who were not caregivers. By contrast, when employed husbands had a sick wife, they retired only half as often as other men (Dentinger & Clarkberg, 2002). Both responses make sense (the men could afford household help), but the female strategy is more likely to lead to poverty than the male one.

Irrational fear also limits women's independence. For example, adult children persuade their elderly mothers more than their fathers to stop traveling or living alone (even though only 2 percent of violent crime victims are women over age 65). The rate of violent-crime victimization among older women is only 1/50 that of young adults of both sexes; among older men it is 1/20 (Klaus, 2005).

Ethnic Discrimination

Another view of stratification comes from *critical race theory*, which sees ethnicity and race as "social construct[s] whose practical utility is determined by a particular society or social system" (King & Williams, 1995). According to this theory, long-standing ethnic discrimination and racism result in stratification, shaping experiences and attitudes throughout the life span.

How powerful such stratification is for young adults today is disputed. Certainly it has not disappeared. But there is no doubt that today's elderly were raised when most non-White populations worldwide were ruled by Europeans. In the United States, schools, hospitals, and even cemeteries were segregated until the 1960s. Children of color were often poor, dependent, and undereducated, and, since stratification effects are cumulative, the results are felt by today's elders. This effect is apparent physically, in allostatic load (see Chapter 23), and also financially and cognitively.

According to this theory, people who have experienced discrimination all their lives are, by old age, more likely to be poor and frail. Not only are they more often sick, but discrimination continues: They are less welcome at senior-citizen centers, clinics, and nursing homes. As a result, their health, vitality, and survival are at risk (Gelfand, 2003; Williams & Wilson, 2001).

Elderly immigrants experience similar exclusions—partly because of the majority culture and partly because of their own cultural values (Olson, 2000). In the United States, Hispanics over age 65 (the majority of them born in Mexico, receiving little education there) are twice as likely to be poor as are European Americans (21 percent compared to 9 percent) (U.S. Bureau of the Census, 2007).

Following the common cultural pattern of most of the world, many immigrant elders expect their adult children to care for them. However, that is not the custom in many modern developed nations; therefore, housing designs and locations, employment patterns, and cultural values make elder care difficult for grown children as well as for the elders. As an example, an elderly man born in Russia was placed by his U.S.-born son in an assisted-living center for senior citizens. The man hated the place and left. Instead he rented a room from an 85-year-old Russian widow, to whom he became very attached. But his son moved him out when the landlady became frail and the elderly man began taking care of her. Once again, the father was on his own and unhappy. He said:

> Would I like to live with my kids? Of course. But I know that's impossible. They don't want me. . . . It's not that they don't love me. I understand that. In the old days, a hundred years ago, old people stayed at home.
>
> *[quoted in Koch, 2000, p. 53]*

As a result of this cultural divide, the man's life was described as one of "lonely independence . . . a quintessentially American tragedy" (Koch, 2000, p. 55).

SONDA DAWES / THE IMAGE WORKS

Dig Deeper A glance at this woman at her outdoor pump might evoke sympathy. Her home's lack of plumbing suggests that she is experiencing late adulthood in poverty, in a rural community that probably offers few social services. Her race and gender put her at additional risk of problems as she ages. However, a deeper understanding might reveal many strengths: religious faith, strong family ties, and gritty survival skills.

Better to Be Female, Non-European, and Old?

The stratification theories just discussed may distort reality to some extent. Elderly African and Hispanic Americans are often nurtured and respected within their families and churches. It is true that African Americans are more likely to be in poor health and to die at younger ages, but Asian and Hispanic elders often outlive their European American contemporaries (Angel & Angel, 2006).

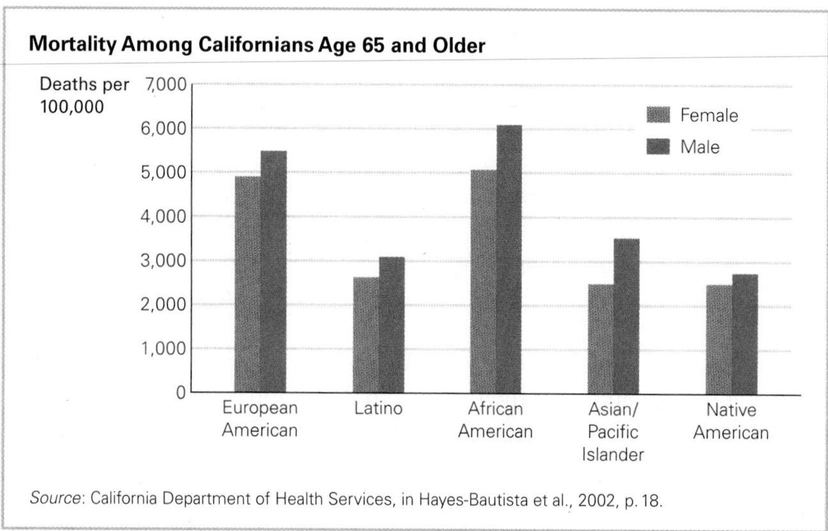

FIGURE 25.2

Longevity in California Greater family support may be one reason that Latino, Asian American, and Native American Californians over age 65 die at lower rates than do their White peers.

One study focused on mortality among Californians over age 65 in various ethnic groups (see Figure 25.2). In all groups, women outlived men, and Latinos, Asian Americans, and Native Americans outlived European Americans (Hayes-Bautista et al., 2002). European American men may seem to be advantaged, in that they have more education and money, but—in California at least—they die sooner.

Because women tend to be the caregivers and kinkeepers in their families, they are less likely than men to be lonely and depressed. One review finds that, because men are socialized to be self-sufficient, "gender is more problematic for men than women" (Huyck, 1995). Grown children are more nurturing toward their aging mothers than toward their aging fathers. This preference may reduce an older woman's independence but also may bring her joy. When elderly parents are divorced or never married, children maintain contact with mothers more than with fathers. It is the old men who suffer from loneliness more than the old women; men over age 65 have a suicide rate eight times as high as that for women that age (U.S. Bureau of the Census, 2007).

What seems to be the disadvantage of race or gender may actually be the disadvantage of low income, since those three factors overlap (Achenbaum, 2006). A detailed study of the income of various U.S. groups over the life span found that, as expected, non-White elders had less income and that poverty correlated with poor health. But then the researchers compared people of various groups living in similar neighborhoods (presumably with similar income). When housing quality was equal, elders of non-European ethnicity had a health advantage (Robert & Lee, 2002).

In other words, poverty and poor medical care are always problematic, but something else may benefit non-European elders. Two possibilities are familism and large family size. Interesting correlations appear between religious faith and aged women of all groups as well as between religious faith and African Americans and Hispanics of both sexes. Those groups are particularly likely to have a strong religious faith, to attend church regularly, and to feel that the church has helped them (Idler, 2006).

Other research, focusing particularly on gender, finds that gender stratification has eased, especially since more women are employed (Blau et al., 2006; Moen & Spencer, 2006). Further, some leading gerontologists contend that age stratification is lessening (Bengston & Putney, 2006).

Let us look closely at one case to study, Mrs. Edwards.

➤**Response for Social Scientists** (from page 686): In general, psychologists favor self theories, and sociologists favor stratification theories. Of course, each discipline respects the other, but each believes that its perspective is more honest and accurate.

a case to study

Doing Just Fine?

Mrs. Edwards is a 76-year-old African American widow, a retired practical nurse living in her small Victorian house (not in good repair) in San Francisco. She has eight children by her first husband and two by her second as well as several stepchildren and 52 grandchildren. One son and three grandchildren live with her.

When she was 72, Mrs. Edwards had surgery for breast cancer, which recently reappeared and is being treated with radiation. She takes taxis to visit her children and attend church, with the fare paid by city-issued vouchers that require her to contribute 10 percent. She feels busy and blessed, explaining:

> After this interview I will go to my daughter's for dinner. I can get up and go any time I want. I'm not nervous about my health now. I have cancer, so I can't say my health is excellent, but it is not poor. I guess it's fair. I don't worry about it. I'm more concerned about starting my fruitcakes for Thanksgiving dinner than I am about the cancer. The whole family will be here.
>
> I am fortunate that I have enough money. My children help me when I'm sick. I get social security and a pension and my children give me money. The only help I had after surgery was a visiting nurse who stopped by to show my son and daughter-in-law how to change the bandages. The social worker wanted to give me a nurse and someone to clean my house, but why should I pay for that when I have so many children and grandchildren to help me? My daughter gave me four nightshirts. She said she'd kill me if I was sitting in bed in an old sweater. . . .
>
> My eight children by Mr. Houston include my eldest son, who lives in Kentucky. He has a son who is a pediatrician. Next I have a daughter who works for the phone company. My third son has lost two children. A daughter died of crib death and a son died of an automobile accident.
>
> My fourth, a son, works for the state. His son got killed. Someone shot him over a drug deal. My fifth is Raymond, who has three children. He is a parole officer. His daughter, Angela, is asleep upstairs. Lots of my grandchildren stop by to spend the night. My sixth is David. He has a son who is paraplegic who lives here. His other son is in prison. I don't know when he will get out.
>
> My seventh is Kenneth who is also in prison at Vacaville. When I took sick, my doctor wrote a letter requesting he be transferred to a closer prison, but that didn't work out. As it is, I don't get to see him much. He has a wife and two children.
>
> My eighth son by Mr. Houston, oh I can't think who it is. Let's see. . . Oh, it's Richard. Richard came in the other day with a bottle of brandy and passed out on the couch. I took his brandy and hid it. It's what I need for my fruitcake. I talk to his wife every day. My daughter and my son from Mr. Moore are also around here a lot.
>
> *[quoted in Johnson & Barer, 2003, pp. 116–117]*

On a second visit, the researchers found Mrs. Edwards "much the same. She was still actively involved with her very large family and in the community. Some of her children and grandchildren moved out only to be replaced by other children and grandchildren" (Johnson & Barer, 2003, p. 117). She seemed quite happy, with her church, her family, and her large color television. Here is her idea of a good day:

> Nothing hurting and I can lie down and watch TV. I've lost a lot of weight, so I am a little bit depressed. And I am distressed about my son in prison. At least he didn't kill anyone. I read that the punishment is strict for that. But freedom and your health are the best things in life. If your freedom is taken from you, you have nothing.
>
> *[quoted in Johnson & Barer, 2003, p. 117]*

The authors of this case study believe that Mrs. Edwards is strong, has high spirits, and has living conditions and a social context that work well for her. Do you agree, or do you think she suffers from "triple jeopardy," being harmed by age, race, and gender stratification?

Predictions are difficult, but several ongoing changes might affect future stratification. In many nations, almost as many women are employed as men, and in the future more of the U.S. elderly will be of non-European ancestry (Jackson et al., 2004). Younger adults are less often married, have fewer children, and are less often church members than their counterparts were 50 years ago. Each of these changes will make a difference for future cohorts of the elderly.

Dynamic Theories

In contrast to self theories and stratification theories, dynamic theories focus on the transformations of late adulthood and on how individuals react to such events. **Dynamic theories** view each person's life as an active, ever-changing, largely self-propelled process, occurring within specific social contexts that are also

dynamic theories Theories of psychosocial development that emphasize change and readjustment rather than either the ongoing self or the impact of stratification. Each person's life is seen as an active, ever-changing, largely self-propelled process, occurring within specific social contexts that are also constantly changing.

constantly changing. These theories are the most recent way to look at late adulthood; they have been inspired in part by the dynamic-systems approach described in Chapter 1.

The best-known dynamic theory is called (somewhat ironically) **continuity theory;** it focuses on how selfhood shifts with social and biological changes. Continuity theory "assumes that a primary goal of adult development is adaptive change, not homeostatic equilibrium" (Atchley, 1999). Continuity is possible as people respond to their context. Thus, an intellectually curious person who had dropped out of high school in adolescence might earn a college degree in old age; this would be an example of continuity as well as dynamic change.

continuity theory The theory that each person experiences the changes of late adulthood and behaves toward others in much the same way he or she did in earlier periods of life.

One source of continuity is temperament. Reinforced by the ecological niches that individuals have carved out for themselves, the Big Five personality traits (see Chapter 22) are maintained throughout old age as in younger years, shifting somewhat but always oriented toward the same life goals (Cook et al., 2005). Therefore, a person's reactions to potentially disruptive problems reflect continuity, as do attitudes toward all other topics—drugs, sex, money, neatness, privacy, health, government.

Especially for People Who Are Unhappy If the circumstances of your life changed, would you be much happier?

How is this a dynamic theory and not an identity theory? The distinction is not clear-cut. Self theories have aspects of continuity, but the emphasis differs: Continuity theory stresses how people adjust to aging and circumstances, not how they protect their core. For example, elderly wives whose husbands are terminally ill will adjust their social lives, first becoming less socially active as they tend their husbands and then becoming more sociable after their husbands die. This is dynamic adjustment (Utz et al., 2002).

As another, more specific example of continuity in the midst of change, a young woman became a teacher because she liked to help others. When she retired, she did volunteer work and then, when she could no longer walk, she welcomed high school students who interviewed her at home. She finally entered a nursing home, where her presence made the entire staff and residents more outgoing. She still affected her former students, who visited her often, although the home was several miles away from the town where she had taught (Atchley, 1999).

Dynamic theories consider early experiences as psychic events that are incorporated throughout life, sometimes in unanticipated ways. A child of a very neat housekeeper might turn out to be either tidy or messy, but either way would probably not be indifferent to neatness. A specific example of the psychic continuity of long-ago events comes from a study of older adults who had suffered Nazi occupation and imprisonment as adolescents. In old age, they were more pessimistic about life than were other people their age, although many of them had had satisfying lives as adults (Berntsen & Rubin, 2006).

SUMMING UP

Self theories emphasize the idea that people define and express themselves, especially in late adulthood, when external pressures are reduced. Erikson's stages, including his final stage, integrity versus despair, and his fifth stage, identity versus role confusion, can be seen as self theories.

Arising from a sociocultural perspective, stratification theories emphasize the power of social groupings (often giving some groups an advantage over others) in shaping development from childhood on. Disengagement theory and activity theory reach opposite conclusions, but both focus on age stratification. Past and present stratification by gender and ethnicity also affects older people, although some argue that the gender and ethnic categories are no longer as potent.

Dynamic theories, such as continuity theory, stress fluctuations caused by interactions of the self, social context, and personal and historical events. The difference among the three groups of theories is viewpoint and practicality. The crucial question to answer is when it is best to focus on the self, or on the society, or on the dynamic relationship between the individual and the circumstances. ■

Coping with Retirement

All people fill their days with activities that they find useful in one way or another. Work is one such activity, recognized by "a growing body of research [that] points to the positive physical and psychological impacts, for women as well as men, of employment" (Moen & Spencer, 2006, p. 135). Both paid and unpaid work are a source of social support and status, bringing self-esteem. For many people, work allows generativity, the main task of middle age, and is symbolic of "productivity, effectiveness, and independence," which are cherished values in Western cultures (Tornstam, 2005, p. 23).

Many adults believe that employment is beneficial not only for society (employment rates are often used to indicate economic health) but also for individuals. Indeed, for younger adults, depression, drug abuse, and family stress all correlate with unemployment. For that reason, many social scientists have warned about "the presumed traumatic aspects of retirement" (Tornstam, 2005, p. 19).

Deciding When to Retire

Social scientists and political leaders have therefore assumed that older adults wanted employment; activity theory led to the conclusion that employed adults would be healthier and happier than unemployed ones. To curb the ageism that led to forced retirement, U.S. laws were passed in the 1980s to make mandatory retirement policies illegal (including for professors), except in certain occupations (e.g., police work).

However, more recent sociological and psychological research has found that most older adults want to stop working as soon as they are eligible to do so, even when employers want to keep them (Hardy, 2006). Some occupations, nursing and teaching among them, are losing too many experienced workers to early retirement. When pensions are adequate, as they are in more than a dozen European nations, half the people retire before age 60, and only 23 percent of those aged 60–64 are still working (Walker, 2005).

The age at which people choose to retire is strongly influenced by national policies (many nations are reversing inducements to early retirement) and specifics of the job. Work may "subject workers to physical strain, emotional stress, and hazardous conditions," making early retirement a desirable choice (Hardy, 2006, p. 215). Developmentalists now believe that each person's health status, job conditions, social networks, and financial reserves should determine retirement age. By these criteria, some people may be wise to retire at age 50 and some, never. Among people over age 65 in the United States, 20 percent of the men and 15 percent of the women are still in the labor force (U.S. Bureau of the Census, 2007), almost always by choice as well as from economic necessity.

Retirement and Marriage

Because many couples now have two earners, researchers have begun to look at the relationship between retirement and marriage. If both spouses are employed, it is best for them to retire together (Smith & Moen, 2004). In a study of 790 retirees, aged 57 to 67, most were quite happy with retirement (Szinovacz & Davey, 2005). However, if a husband retired but his wife was still working *and* made most family

➤Response for People Who Are Unhappy (from page 690): Continuity theorists would say no, reasoning that your core temperament will be expressed no matter what your circumstances are. You can assess the validity of this conclusion by recalling whether your mood changed markedly in the past when your situation changed.

decisions, the husband was rarely (only 25 percent) "very satisfied" with retirement, unlike 80 percent of the retired men whose wives were not working *or* who felt that they made most family decisions.

Retired wives followed the same pattern (Szinovacz & Davey, 2005). They were very satisfied *unless* their husbands were employed and dominant. Apparently older adults have two main sources of satisfaction: work and home. They are dissatisfied if they have control over neither sphere, which means that those who had more control at their workplace than they did at home need to carefully balance their retirement.

For both sexes (married or not), a major problem with retirement is inadequate planning (Moen et al., 2005). A common mistake is to plan how to manage the finances but not how to spend the time. There are many nonwork activities that are satisfying. However, it takes thought and planning to find the right mix. Older people often need to reorder their lives, "expanding, reducing, concentrating and diffusing" their former goals and activities (Nimrod, 2007, p. 91).

Although some new retirees flounder and have difficulty adjusting to retirement, most of them eventually find satisfying patterns of activity and leisure. In the previous chapter, you learned that many elders create works of art, write books, and make crafts. There is much else that retirees do, as we now describe.

Aging in Place

One of the favorite activities of many of the elderly is caring for their own homes and gardens. Many older people have become so firmly attached to their surroundings that they prefer to **age in place,** staying in the same house in the same neighborhood, adjusting but not leaving when health fades.

age in place Refers to a preference of elderly people to remain in the same home and community, adjusting but not leaving when health fades.

The age distribution of residents in each of the 50 U.S. states reveals the strength of the desire to age in place. Not everyone wants to retire to the sunny Southwest. A higher proportion of people over age 64 (15 percent) live in Maine, West Virginia, and North Dakota than in California (11 percent), New Mexico (12 percent), or Arizona (13 percent) (U.S. Bureau of the Census, 2007). Rather than moving to a place where falling on the ice is impossible, people remain in the chilly places they settled down in to raise their children. Sometimes a suburban development, large city apartment building, or rural town becomes a *NORC*, a *naturally occurring retirement community.* This is a neighborhood that has gradually become home to many older people, who stay there partly because their social convoy is there.

FIGURE 25.3

Dirty Fingernails Almost three times as many 60-year-olds as 20-year-olds are gardeners. What is it about dirt, growth, and time that makes gardening an increasingly popular hobby as people age?

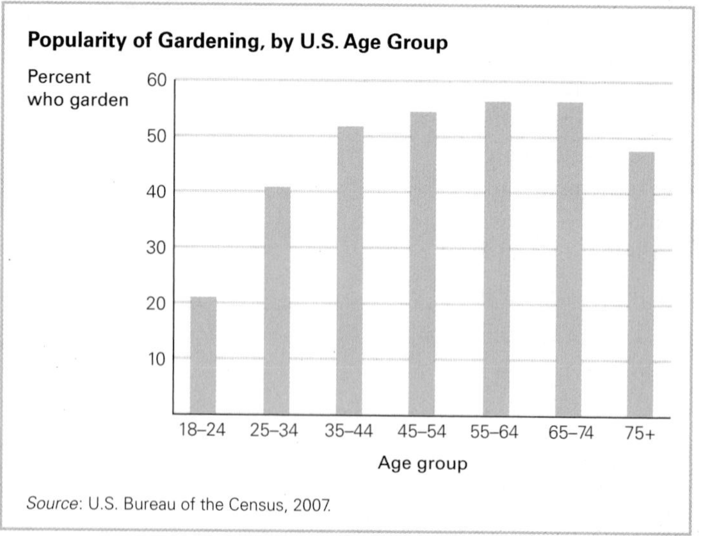

Source: U.S. Bureau of the Census, 2007.

One result of aging in place is that many of the elderly live alone, staying behind after family members move away and spouses die. Most prefer it that way (Cook et al., 2007). They appreciate neighbors, friends, relatives, nurses, and other people in their community who help them maintain their independence. Sometimes they allow children and grandchildren to move in with them (as Mrs. Edwards did). But the home is theirs.

Typically both men and woman do more housework after retirement (Kleiber, 1999; Szinovacz, 2000). They also take on longer-term projects in addition to their daily household chores: yard work, redecorating, building. Gardening is one leisure activity that becomes more common with age; more than half the elders in the United States cultivate a garden each year (see Figure 25.3).

Continuing Education

Retirement offers the time and opportunity to take classes, which appeal particularly to those who have already been to college. Even more of the elderly will probably seek education in the future because the baby boomers, approaching retirement, are much better educated than the current generation of elderly people.

About one out of four U.S. adults age 66 and older was enrolled in continuing education in 2005, most studying the practical arts (such as carpentry and quilting) and a few seeking advanced academic degrees (U.S. Bureau of the Census, 2007). Most elderly students (76 percent) are motivated primarily by a desire for personal or social development through such skills as mastering hobbies, managing income, learning about their roots, or understanding their grandchildren (Jeanneret, 1995).

Many elderly people hesitate to take college courses with younger students. When they do so, however, they usually earn excellent grades, because motivation, conscientiousness, and crystallized intelligence compensate for declines in reaction time and fluid intelligence. They also enjoy the experience. One man, who surprised himself by taking drawing, painting, and Spanish classes at a community college, explains:

> When I first retired, I couldn't wait to pack up and go to a warm climate and just goof off. But now, retirement is an enormous challenge. Once you start learning about yourself, you get the feeling that anything is possible.
>
> *[quoted in Goldman, 1991]*

Programs designed for the elderly circumvent that hesitation. One example is Elderhostel, a nonprofit program of continuing education for people aged 55 and over that started in New England in 1975 with 220 students. About 160,000 students enrolled in Elderhostel courses in 2005, usually taking short courses on college campuses while the regular students are on vacation. Some elders prefer more active learning. For example, a 2007 Elderhostel course in Belize involved snorkeling and sand analysis as well as classroom lectures on coral ecology.

Thousands of other learning programs worldwide are filled with retirees. At least a dozen European nations have Universities of the Third Age, which are college programs dedicated to older learners (Achenbaum, 2005). Many nations encourage and sponsor education for older people. For example, the Chinese government offers free courses in calligraphy, traditional arts, exercise, and health under "Five Guarantees"—a policy promising that "older people should be supported, have medical care, contribute to society, be engaged in lifelong learning, and have a happy life" (Peng & Phillips, 2004, p. 114).

Volunteer Work

Volunteer work offers the social advantages of working without the financial compensation of paid employment. Accordingly, volunteer work is especially suitable for elderly people who have adequate pensions or other sources of income.

Many feel a strong commitment to their community and believe that older people should be of service to others. Volunteering allows them to gain status and to find "new meaning . . . to perform useful services . . . [to] function as mentors, guides, and repositories of experience" (Settersten, 2002, p. 65).

In the United States, the rate of volunteering seems to decrease with age, although older volunteers put in more hours (see Figure 25.4 on page 694). The tendency for older adults to volunteer less often than younger adults, but to spend

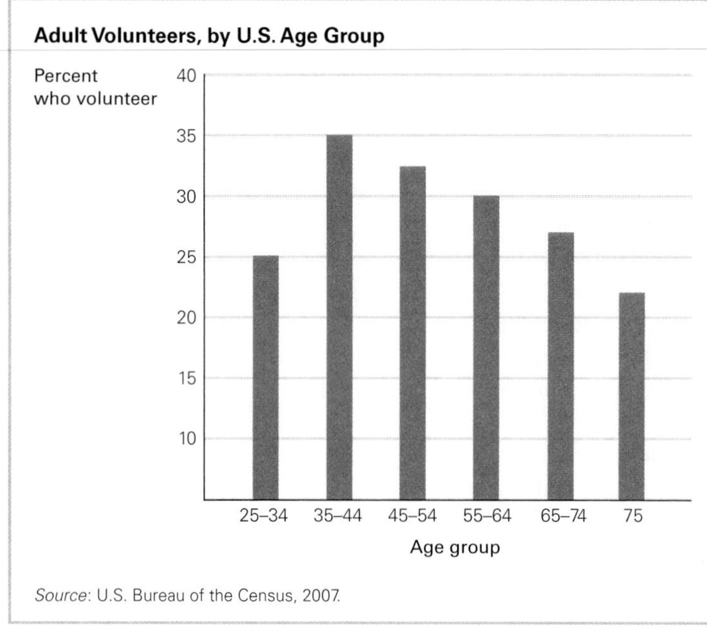

FIGURE 25.4

Giving Their Time These statistics count only hours spent in formal volunteer work, usually for a church or hospital. In addition, many older adults informally provide free services to friends and family members. Almost every grandparent babysits; many elders care for older relatives (spouses, siblings, parents). If these services are counted, the percentage who volunteer is much higher (Choi et al., 2007).

more hours when they do, is found in many nations (Walker, 2005). The overall rate of elderly volunteering varies by culture; Nordic nations (e.g., Sweden and Norway) have far more older volunteers than do Mediterranean nations (e.g., Italy and Greece). These differences persist when health is taken into account (Erlinghagen & Hank, 2006). This suggests that culture and opportunities affect whether an older person will do volunteer work.

A vital but undercounted service is the assistance that the elderly provide to their frail neighbors. Many people over age 65 run errands, make meals, repair broken appliances, and perform other services that help the disabled elderly to stay in their homes. Such neighborhood help is particularly notable within a NORC.

Volunteering has many benefits for retirees. A study that measured how excited, enthusiastic, alert, and inspired older adults felt found that such positive emotions did not correlate with feeling loved but did correlate with feeling recognized for accomplishments (which few of the elderly felt) (Steverink & Lindenberg, 2006). Other studies find that, particularly for the aged, the desire for social interaction and appreciation is a motivating force for becoming a volunteer (Tang, 2006).

There are many reasons volunteering should be encouraged among the elderly, not only to benefit those they serve but also to benefit the elderly themselves. Volunteers tend to live longer than people who do not volunteer, especially if they volunteer for only one organization (Musick et al., 1999). Volunteers also tend to be more involved with friends and religious organizations. Social involvement correlates with volunteering, probably as both a cause and a consequence (Okun et al., 2007). Feelings of well-being seem to come from volunteering, particularly among older adults (George, 2006).

Especially for Social Workers Your agency needs more personnel but does not have money to hire anyone. Should you go to your local senior-citizen center and recruit volunteers?

KAREN KASMAUSKI / CORBIS

Mutual Help Senior citizens are steady volunteers at this Tokyo day-care center. Small children benefit from personal attention as they learn new skills. The elders benefit from social interaction with the children.

Religious Involvement

Some form of religious involvement is another area of activity available to retired older adults. Perhaps surprisingly, the oldest-old are less likely to attend religious services than are the middle-aged. However, attendance is a poor indicator of spirituality. Many places of worship are not particularly welcoming to the old: They may be located far from senior housing; stairs may restrict access; the lighting and acoustics may be bad.

Belief is a better measure of religious involvement than is attendance at religious services. Faith increases with age, as do prayer and other religious practices (Ingersoll-Dayton et al., 2002). Many studies show that religious involvement of all kinds correlates with physical and emotional health as well as long life (Idler, 2006). Interestingly, religious faith does not necessarily speed recovery in the seriously ill as much as it reduces the risk of illness (Powell et al., 2003).

Many social scientists have wondered why this is true. The data come from longitudinal as well as cross-sectional research, which points toward cause and effect, not just a spurious correlation. Among the hypotheses offered to explain this connection are that faith encourages people to have a healthier life style (with less drug and alcohol use, for instance), to connect with other people, and to experience less stress.

As already mentioned, religious identity and religious institutions are a foundation for many older members of American minority groups, who may feel a stronger commitment to their religious heritage than to their national or cultural background. For example, although Westerners may note national background for Iranians or Iraqis or Turks, the immigrant elderly of those groups may focus on their Muslim, or Christian, or Jewish faith. They identify with a particular branch of their religion more than with national origin (Gelfand, 2003).

Religious institutions play many essential roles for the elderly, offering reasons to age in place. For example, "Little Tokyo" in Los Angeles is home to many Japanese elders who could move to better housing but who want to be able to walk to Japanese Christian churches and Buddhist temples (Shibusawa et al., 2001). Many African American elderly find cherished spiritual and practical activities, and close friends, in church (Billingsley, 1999).

For all elderly, no matter what their particular faith, confronting death and ensuring historical continuity are crucial for psychological health, as already explained with Erikson's integrity stage. At least one gerontologist believes that there is "increasing cosmic communion" with age, that older people are better able to see beyond their own immediate needs and care about other people, ask enduring questions, and emphasize spiritual concerns (Tornstam, 2005, p. 58). Every religion helps elders deal with these concerns (Idler, 2006).

Political Activism

On some measures, the elderly are more politically active than any other age group. Compared with younger people, they tend to be better informed, to write to their elected representatives, to vote in off-year elections, to identify with a political party, and to join groups that lobby on behalf of certain interests (Torres-Gil, 1992). Like Sadie and Gilbert in the anecdote that opens this chapter, many read newspapers and watch TV news.

However, they tend to be less active when it comes to attending rallies and door-to-door campaigning. Analyses in Europe as well as in the United States find that the elderly as a group are not particularly involved in such political activities (Walker, 2006).

DAVID YOUNG-WOLFF / PHOTOEDIT, INC.

Still Politically Active The man with the microphone is Floyd Red Crow Westerman, a Lakota Sioux who is an actor (in *Dances with Wolves,* among many other films) and director. Many members of his cohort fought in Vietnam. Disapproval of the war in Iraq was greater among his generation than among both older and younger cohorts.

The elderly have the potential, however, to be very powerful politically. Hundreds of organizations, in the United States and elsewhere, advocate for the elderly, who are often leaders as well as followers. In the United States, some are organized around a particular ethnicity or some other category of older people. Many organizations are multinational: The AARP cites 59 international or regional organizations focused on aging.

The **AARP** (originally the American Association of Retired Persons) is the major U.S. organization representing the elderly. It is also the largest organized interest group in the world. In 2006, the AARP had a membership of 37 million (many of them baby boomers in their 50s—members must be over 50 but need not be retired). The political influence of this organization is one reason that Social Security has been called "the third rail" of domestic politics, fatal to any politician who touches it to try to cut benefits—even though most economists and social scientists believe that reform of Social Security policies is needed (Delea, 2005; *The Economist,* 2007).

AARP A U.S. organization of people aged 50 and older, which advocates for the elderly. It was originally called the American Association of Retired Persons, but now only the initials AARP are used, to reflect the fact that the organization's members do not have to be retired.

Worldwide, many government policies affect the elderly, especially those related to poverty, housing, pensions, prescription drugs, and medical costs. As you learned in Chapter 23, the population of the elderly is growing in every nation, and choices about allocation of public resources need to be made. However, the elderly do not necessarily vote to protect their economic interests. One reason is that, like younger adults, they care about the environment, world affairs, crime, and many other issues of general concern. Their opinions tend to reflect national trends and their own history more than their age (Walker, 2006). Most have enough money to get by; today the median income of men over age 65 (including income from pensions) is 68 percent of the median income of all men of working age—far better than the 42 percent figure of 1960 (U.S. Bureau of the Census, 2007).

The suggestion that the political or economic concerns of the elderly clash with those of the young is not confirmed by the data: Most older people are concerned about the well-being of future generations. Often older and younger voters are divided along ideological or regional lines, not according to age. In fact, one analyst believes that "the idea of grey power" is a myth, designed to reduce support among younger people for programs to support health care for the elderly (Walker, 2006, p. 349).

➤**Response for Social Workers** (from page 694): Yes, but be careful. If people want to volunteer and are just waiting for an opportunity, you will probably benefit from their help and they will also benefit. But if you convince reluctant seniors to help you, the experience may benefit no one.

SUMMING UP

Retirement, whether by choice or necessity, requires careful planning by both the retiree and his or her spouse. Many retired people have a strong preference for aging in place. Besides working around the home, retired people may keep active by taking courses, doing volunteer work, participating in religious activities, or getting involved in politics. ■

Friends and Relatives

Remember from Chapter 22 that people travel the life course in the company of others, a reality captured by the term **social convoy** (Antonucci et al., 2001). At various points, other people join or leave the convoy. But, just as covered wagons grouped together to head west or ships formed convoys to cross the high seas, life's journey has a better chance of success if it is taken with fellow travelers.

social convoy Collectively, the family members, friends, acquaintances, and even strangers who move through life with an individual.

JEAN MICHEL FOUJOLS / ZEFA / CORBIS

SEAN SPRAGUE / THE IMAGE WORKS

The Same Event, A Thousand Miles Apart: Partners Whether in the living room of their home in the United States *(left)* or at a senior center in the Philippines *(right)*, elderly people are more likely to smile when they are with one another than when they are alone.

Observation Quiz (see answer, page 698): What does the clothing of the people in these photographs indicate about their economic status?

Bonds formed over a lifetime allow people to share triumphs with and to gather sympathy from those who understand their victories and defeats. Siblings, old friends, and spouses are ideal convoy members, but anyone (famous people, neighbors, acquaintances) from the same cohort can be part of a person's social convoy, especially in late adulthood.

We now discuss the typical components of the social convoy, beginning with life partners.

Long-Term Marriages

A spouse buffers against the problems of old age and extends life, as was shown by a meta-analysis of numerous studies with a combined total of 250,000 participants (Manzoli et al., 2007). More than in younger years, married adults are healthier, wealthier, and happier than other people their age who are unmarried. Separate studies of unmarried couples in long-term partnerships (usually homosexual relationships) have not been done, but research on younger homosexual couples suggests that gay people also benefit from having an intimate partner committed to their well-being.

Generally, personal happiness increases with the quality of the marriage or intimate relationship; this association shows up more clearly in longitudinal than in cross-sectional research (Proulx et al., 2007). Among the usual reasons for the advantages of long-lasting marriages are these: Children have left the house (young children are a major source of disputes); income is more predictable; both partners feel comforted by their familiarity (remember Sadie chuckling that she didn't have any more secrets); and equitable division of tasks has been achieved. A lifetime of shared experiences—living together, raising children, and dealing with financial and emotional crises—brings partners closer in memories and values as "spouses . . . increasingly internalize each other's ideas about appropriate behavior" (Huston, 2000, p. 314).

In general, older couples have learned how to disagree. A study that compared happy and unhappy couples reported that older couples discussed disputes with

ZAVE SMITH / CORBIS

Shared Laughter One characteristic of long-married couples is that they often mirror each other's moods. Thanks to the positivity effect, the mood is often one of joy.

more warmth, humor, and respect than younger couples did (Carstensen et al., 1995). I know a couple in their 60s who seem happily married and are both politically active, yet they vote for opposing candidates. That puzzled me until I heard the wife explain: "We sit together on the fence, seeing both perspectives, and then, when it is time to get off the fence and vote, Bob and I fall on opposite sides." Was she fooling herself, since I always knew which of them would fall where? No matter. Her explanation kept disagreements from becoming fights. Other long-married couples do the same.

Another aspect of long marriages also suggests mutual respect. Generally, older spouses accept each other's frailties, assisting with physical and psychological needs. When elders are disabled (have difficulty walking, bathing, and performing other activities of daily life), they are less depressed and anxious when they are in a close marital relationship (Mancini & Bonanno, 2006).

What about the nondisabled spouse in such a marriage? One study found that wives caring for disabled husbands usually felt more affection and less burden in the later stages of caregiving (when demands were greater) than at the start (Seltzer & Li, 1996). Other caregivers tend to be less tolerant. In the same study, caregiving daughters of frail parents felt less affection and more burden as time went on.

In part, a caregiver's response depends on intimate understanding. When men whose wives had severe arthritis were asked to estimate how much pain their wives felt (after watching them do a standard task), some husbands were much more accurate than others. Those who had the more accurate understanding were more helpful and less irritated. Husbands who overestimated pain were far more stressed (Martire et al., 2006).

Besides caregiving, sexual intimacy is another major aspect of long-lasting marriages. For many couples, their sexual relationship has changed but remains important (Johnson, 2007). This was evident when one elderly couple was asked about their sex life.

Husband: We have sex less frequently now, but it's satisfying to me. Now that we are both home, we could spend all our time in bed. But it's still more amorous when we go away. When we travel, it's like a second honeymoon.

Wife: Sex has been important in our marriage, but not the most important. The most important thing has been our personal relationship, our fondness, respect, and friendship.

[quoted in Wallerstein & Blakeslee, 1995, p. 318]

➤Answer to Observation Quiz (from page 697): The U.S. couple is relatively rich (their nightclothes look new, and pajamas are mostly the preference of well-to-do men); the Filipina women are relatively poor (they are wearing identical dresses, a gift from the agency that runs this senior center).

Losing a Spouse

Some older adults have always been single, and some have been divorced for decades. Together these two groups account for about 12 percent of those over age 65 in the United States (U.S. Bureau of the Census, 2007) (see Figure 25.5). Research usually finds that health and happiness are slightly lower in elderly single people than in those who are married, but income and personality, not the unmarried status, may be the reason for the discrepancy (Manzoli et al., 2007). Usually these unpartnered older adults have arranged their lives so that the absent spouse is not missed.

Widowhood among the elderly is common. It may also be problematic, particularly in the first two years after the death (Hagedoorn et al., 2006). The experience

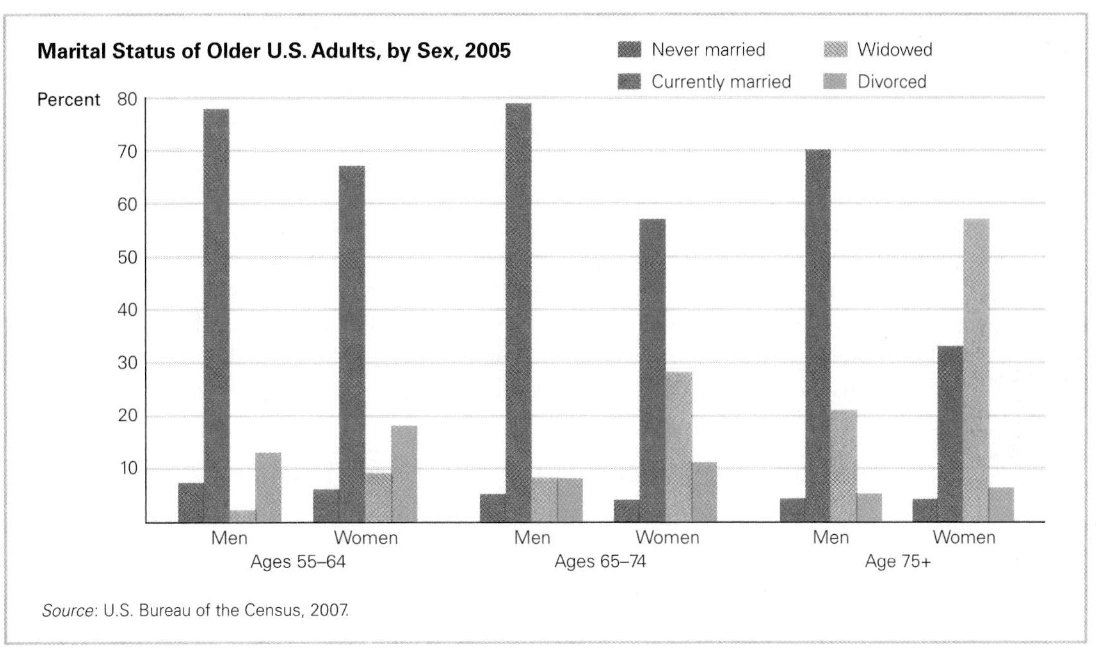

FIGURE 25.5

Gender Differences in Marital Status In old age, the differences in marital status between men and women become dramatic. There are more than four times as many widows as widowers after age 74. In the current cohort of the old-old, less than 10 percent are divorced or never married, but 20 percent of the baby boomers will fall into those categories.

of losing a spouse differs for men and women. Because women tend to marry older men (by three years, on average) and live longer than men (about three years, on average), the average married woman experiences six years or so of widowhood and the average man, none. Among the current cohort of older women, many centered their lives on their activities as spouse, caregiver, and homemaker, and thus the death of a husband is more than loss of a companion—it also reduces status, activities, identity, and income.

With time, many widows learn to enjoy their independence, typically not seeking to remarry. A prospective study found that 18 months after the death of their husbands, only 19 percent of widows were interested in remarrying and only 9 percent were currently dating (Carr, 2004). Widows rely on women friends (who are often widows as well) and grown children, typically increasing their social connections after a husband's death (Utz et al., 2002). Widows feel much more supported and comforted by their relatives than widowers do (Ha et al., 2006).

Widowers not only feel less supported by their families; they also have fewer men friends who have lost a partner, and they have more trouble seeking help. If they married when traditional gender divisions were still the custom, they depended on their mothers and wives for emotional and practical support (listening and encouraging, cooking

MARKO HAGERTY / THE IMAGE BANK / GETTY IMAGES

Alone, but Not Lonely Ten million women in the United States are widows. Most, like this woman, are over age 60 and live alone. Many, though not all, are financially secure and well adjusted to their newly independent way of life.

and cleaning) (Gurung et al., 2003). That pattern of dependency makes it particularly hard for them to keep house, to share their emotions, or even to ask someone over for dinner.

In the months following the death of their spouse, widowers are more likely than widows to be physically ill and socially isolated. Their risk of suicide increases, not only in the United States but also in Taiwan (Liu et al., 2006), Denmark (Erlangsen et al., 2004), and every other nation that reports data by age and marital status. Although most widowers do not seek to remarry, their likelihood of remarriage is far higher than that of widows, for two reasons: They tend to be lonelier than the women, and the sex ratio is in their favor. For widowers, but not widows, interest in remarriage or dating is particularly likely if the man has few friends (Carr, 2004; see Research Design).

Research Design

Scientist: Deborah Carr.

Publication: *Journal of Marriage and Family* (2004).

Participants: This study began with 1,531 married people age 65 and older from the Detroit area. After the initial interview, careful checking of death notices revealed that 319 of them had become widows or widowers. As many as possible (some refused, some died, some were seriously sick) were reinterviewed 6, 18, or 48 months after the death. This study is based on 210 participants who were interviewed 6 months after the death, 155 of whom were reinterviewed at 18 months.

Design: Data on social support, depression, quality of past marriage, interest in dating and remarriage, and other factors were collected. Since this was a longitudinal study, developmental change was assessed.

Major conclusions: Most widows and widowers were not eager to begin a new relationship. In fact, none of the 155 were interested in dating and remarriage at both 6 and 18 months after the death. Although sex differences were evident (at 6 months, 15 percent of the men and only 1 percent of the women were dating), most men were not eager to find a new wife, especially if their marriage had been satisfying and they had supportive friends.

Comment: By beginning with married elders, and then interviewing those who lost a partner, this study overcame many selection and memory biases. However, as the author points out, those who consented to be reinterviewed tended to be physically healthier than those who refused. Although efforts were made to account for this difference, an even smaller proportion of widows and widowers may be interested in remarriage than this study revealed.

Relationships with Younger Generations

In past centuries, most adults died before their grandchildren were born (Uhlenberg, 1996). Now most older adults live to see two or more generations of younger family members; often a member of their parents' generation is still alive as well. Some families today span five generations, often in a pattern called the *beanpole family,* with multiple generations but only a few members at each age (see Figure 25.6).

As more adults are having only one child, many children will have no aunts, uncles, cousins, brothers, or sisters—a pattern hard for many of today's elderly to imagine. It is predicted that intergenerational relationships will become even more important when each grandparent has fewer grandchildren (Bengtson, 2001; Silverstein, 2006). Fortunately, family ties across generations are as strong as or stronger than ever, even in nations such as Spain, where the beanpole family type is new (Meil, 2006).

Although relationships with younger generations are positive for the most part, they may also include tension and conflict, as explained in Chapter 22. Few older adults stop parenting simply because their children are fully grown and independent. As one 82-year-old woman put it: "No matter how old a mother is, she watches her middle-aged children for signs of improvement" (quoted in Scott-Maxwell, 1968). Obviously, the correlation between well-being in old age and marriage, parenthood, or grandparenthood depends on the specifics. A good relationship with one's successful children enhances well-being, but a poor relationship makes life worse (Greenfeld & Marks, 2006; Koropeckyj-Cox, 2002).

Adult Children

Generally, engagement and interaction are common between older adults and their grown children, with conflict more likely in emotionally close relationships than in distant ones (Van Gaalen & Dykstra, 2006). The mother–daughter relationship is particularly likely to be both close and conflicted. For example, in one study of 48 mother–daughter pairs (ages averaging 76 and 44, respectively) 75 percent of mothers and almost 60 percent of daughters included the other as one of the three most important persons in their lives. Yet 83 percent of the mothers and 100 percent of the daughters acknowledged recently being "irritated, hurt, or annoyed" by the other. The mothers usually blamed someone else for the tension ("Her husband kept on turning up the radio every time I turned it down"), while the daughters were more likely to blame their mother directly ("She tells me how to discipline my kids") (quoted in Fingerman, 1996).

Intergenerational relationships are affected by many factors (Hareven, 2001; van Geelan & Dykstra, 2006). In general:

- Assistance arises both from need and from the ability to provide it.
- Personal contact depends mostly on geographical proximity.
- Affection is influenced by the pair's history of mutual love and respect.
- Sons feel stronger obligation; daughters feel stronger affection.

Contrary to popular perceptions, financial and emotional assistance typically flows from the older generation to their children instead of vice versa, although much depends on the specific needs of each family member (Silverstein, 2006). As one expert describes it, the older generation is like a family National Guard: "Although remaining silent and unobserved for the most part, grandparents (and great-grandparents) muster up and march out when an emergency arises regarding younger generation members' well-being" (Bengtson, 2001, p. 7).

If the older generation becomes dependent on the younger generation, conflict may arise. The problem is that the specifics of assistance—how much, where, provided by whom—can be a source of hurt feelings and disagreement, although the idea of assistance is endorsed by almost everyone (Silverstein, 2006). The least satisfactory situations occur when parents want assistance but complain about the children or when children provide help but are critical of their parents. Mutual respect is crucial. As parents grow old, every family needs to adjust to "changing conditions and circumstances [by] renegotiating relationships" (Connidis, 2002, p. 565).

Such adjustments are often influenced by **filial responsibility,** the idea (often part of familism) that adult children are obligated to care for their aging parents. This idea is found in every culture and does not seem to depend on particulars of

filial responsibility The idea that adult children are obligated to care for their aging parents.

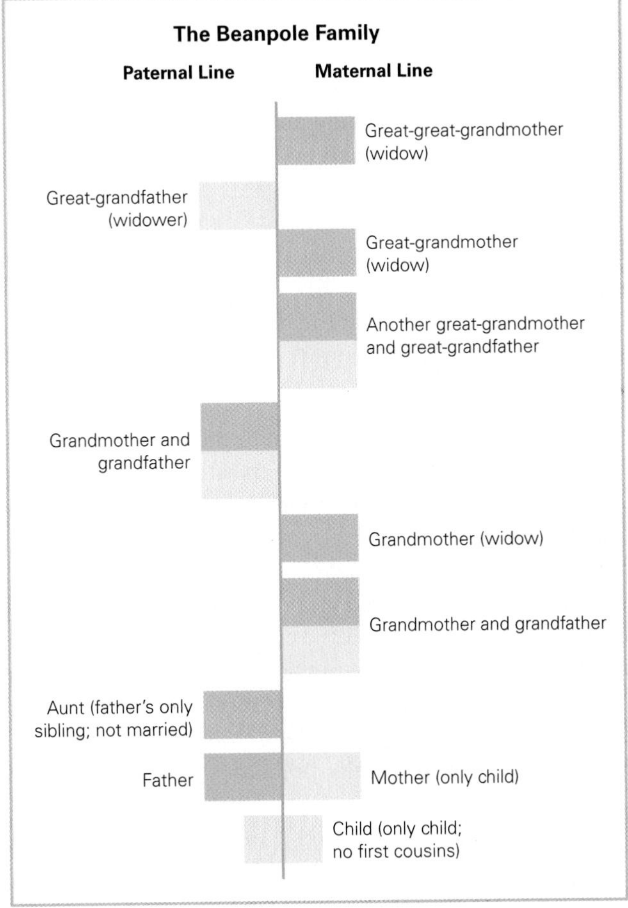

FIGURE 25.6

Many Households, Few Members The traditional nuclear family consists of two parents and their children living together. Today, as couples have fewer children, the beanpole family is becoming more common. This kind of family has many generations, each typically living in its own household, with only a few members in each generation.

economic self-interest. Although financial support is sometimes considered part of filial responsibility, emotional support seems more crucial and sometimes increases when financial support is not needed (Silverstein, 2006).

A longitudinal study of attitudes about filial responsibility in the United States found no evidence that changes in family structures (including increases in divorce) reduce the sense of filial responsibility (Gans & Silverstein, 2006). In fact, trends were in the opposite direction: Younger cohorts (born in the 1950s and 1960s) endorsed *more* responsibility from younger generations to older ones "regardless of the sacrifices involved" than did earlier cohorts (born in the 1930s and 1940s).

Amazingly, support for filial responsibility was weaker among those who were most likely to need care from their children. After midlife and especially after the death of their own parents, members of the older generation were *less* likely to express the belief that children should provide substantial care for their parents. The authors conclude that, as adults realize that they are more likely to become receivers than givers of intergenerational care, "reappraisals are likely the result of altruism (growing relevance as a potential receiver) or role loss (growing irrelevance as a provider)" (Gans & Silverstein, 2006, p. 974).

Grandchildren

Grandparenthood often begins in middle age. By age 70, 85 percent of all people in the current cohort are grandparents, which makes this a significant role for many older people, in the United States and elsewhere. The experience is highly variable, ranging from fulfilling to frustrating, from pivotal to peripheral. Not surprisingly, personality, ethnicity, national background, and past parent–child relationships all influence the nature of the grandparent–grandchild relationship, as do the age and the personality of the child (Mueller & Elder, 2003).

Ongoing grandparent–grandchild relationships usually reveal one of three approaches to grandparenting:

- *Remote grandparents* are emotionally distant. They are esteemed elders who are honored, respected, and obeyed by children, grandchildren, and great-grandchildren.
- *Companionate grandparents* entertain and "spoil" their grandchildren—especially in ways, or for reasons, that the parents would not—and do not discipline them.
- *Involved grandparents* are active in the day-to-day life of the grandchildren. They live in or near the grandchildren's household, see them daily, and provide substantial care.

Although remote grandparents were common in the past and are evident currently in rural areas of some nations, they are rare in most modern nations. Instead, grandparents "strive for love and friendship rather than demand respect and obedience" (Gratton & Haber, 1996), choosing to be companions rather than authority figures (Hayslip & Patrick, 2003).

Some elders who become involved grandparents do not do so by choice. One reason is cultural. If their values and traditions differ from those that surround their grandchildren, they attempt to transmit "the values, beliefs, language, and customs" of their cultural heritage (Silverstein & Chen, 1999; Taylor et al., 2005). Particularly if an elder lives with the grandchildren and is responsible for daily child care, this physical proximity precludes either the remote or companionate roles.

Although all three generations can benefit from involved grandparenting, closeness can cause conflicts. If an elder hoped to be a remote grandparent, respected and obeyed, but instead is thrust into the role of involved grandparent, frustration arises in all three generations. As one 60-year-old Cambodian immigrant explained:

> I'm afraid they might not be what I want them to be because in this country the children are very unpredictable. . . . I don't like to talk too much, because the more you talk the less respect they have toward you.
>
> *[quoted in Detzner, 1996, p. 47]*

Sometimes involved grandparents become *surrogate parents* (see Chapter 22), raising their grandchildren because the parents cannot. In 2005, an estimated 3 percent of all U.S. children were living with grandparents, without either parent (U.S. Bureau of the Census, 2007). Most grandparents have several grandchildren; this statistic refers to only one year. Therefore, when a grandparent's entire life span is considered, a far higher proportion of grandparents (about 20 percent) provide exclusive care of at least one grandchild for a month or more—and often for years.

Young parents with special problems (poverty, drug addiction, severe illness) are more likely to send their children to live with their parents, especially their most difficult children. Drug-affected infants and rebellious school-age boys, for example, are more likely to live with grandparents than preschool girls are. If the parents are judged to be neglectful or abusive, grandparents may provide *kinship care* for the children (see Chapter 8), with government subsidy and authority. However, most surrogate parents are not formally designated caretakers and may very well wonder whether they are up to the job. One grandmother explains:

> I don't know if God thought I did a poor job and wanted to give me a second chance, or thought I did well enough to be given the task one more time. My daughter tells me she cannot handle the children anymore, but maybe I won't be able to manage them either.
>
> *[quoted in Strom & Strom, 2000, p. 291]*

Sometimes surrogate parenting impairs the grandparent's own health and well-being, increasing the risk of physical illness, depression, and marital problems (Kelley & Whitley, 2003; Solomon & Marx, 2000). Having another child to raise "off-time" is part of the problem. As one surrogate parent says:

> We are participating in a life that in no way resembles that which was anticipated. . . . I grieve for my future, my hopes and aspirations for myself as well as those for my son, my loss of freedom, and my relationship with my husband and daughters. . . . And to make it worse, I cannot give voice to my grief for fear my granddaughter will feel it is her fault.
>
> *[quoted in Baird, 2003, pp. 62, 65]*

The special problems of surrogate parenting, while serious, are not the usual pattern. Most grandparents enjoy their role and are usually appreciated by younger family members. Given the longevity and health of today's grandparents, it is not unusual for an elder to have close friendships with adult grandchildren (Kemp, 2005). Indeed, international college students, despite being thousands of miles away from their grandparents, often express warmth, respect, and affection for at least one grandparent (usually their maternal grandmother) (Taylor et al., 2005).

Friendship

Of those currently over age 65 in the United States, only 4 percent (1.4 million) have never married, making this the most married cohort in history (U.S. Bureau of the Census, 2007). Most of these people also have children and grandchildren. As you have seen, in late life spouses and offspring provide social support for

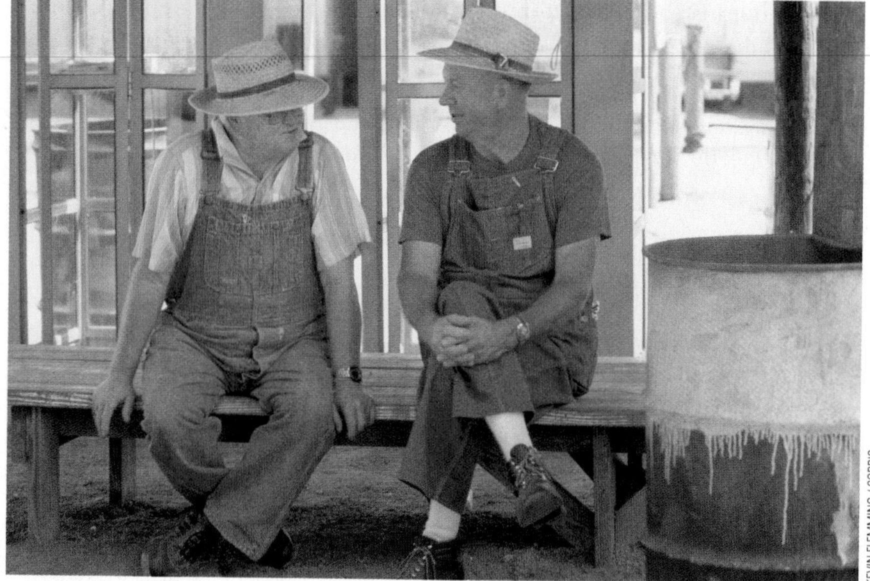

Good to See You Again Older men, like younger ones, appreciate each other's friendship but seldom get together just to talk. These Delaware farmers met again at a melon auction and took the opportunity to get caught up on their families, their aches and pains, and the price of watermelon.

KEVIN FLEMMING / CORBIS

many of the elderly—but not for all. The next cohort to reach old age will include far more unmarried people. Further, many older adults, both married and unmarried, will have no children or grandchildren. Will they be lonely and unsupported?

Probably not. All indications are that members of the current elder generation who never married are quite content. In future generations, as the numbers of unmarried older adults increase, their social networks are likely to increase as well. Since they have spent a lifetime without a spouse, they have usually developed friendships, activities, and social connections that keep them busy and happy (DePaulo, 2006). For instance, a Dutch study of 85 single elders found that their well-being was similar to that of people in long-term equitable marriages and better than that of people who were less satisfied with their social networks because they were recently widowed or were in an unequal marriage (Hagedoorn et al., 2006).

One problem with the research on single older adults is that some are not really single; they are partnered homosexuals, with longtime companions who are confidants and caregivers. In terms of health and well-being (although not always health benefits or hospital policies), they benefit from the partnerships just as longtime married couples do. More research is needed on single elders who are truly alone.

The research that has been published suggests that having a partner and children is not necessary for happiness in old age. In a study that asked older women to rank their regrets, older child-free women put the highest priority on such areas as education, occupation, and artistic expression. Those who were voluntarily child-free did not regret their decision. Those who were involuntarily childless regretted not having a child, but they regretted other things more. Ironically, older women who were mothers had more regrets related to their children than the nonmothers had about the absence of children (Jeffries & Konnert, 2002).

Life satisfaction in old age correlates more closely with friendships than with contact with younger relatives (Lawton et al., 1999; Newsom & Schultz, 1996). The reason is probably that friendships are voluntary and mutual, providing benefits beyond those provided by obligatory family relationships (Krause, 2006).

Quality (not quantity) of friendship is crucial. Having at least one close confidant acts as a buffer against many forms of lost status, poor health, and reduced companionship, especially among the oldest-old (Krause, 2006). Every old person experiences unwelcome changes in his or her social convoy, as dynamic theory would predict (Fung & Carstensen, 2004). Ideally, new intimates are added to the inner circle when death or distance cuts off old friends.

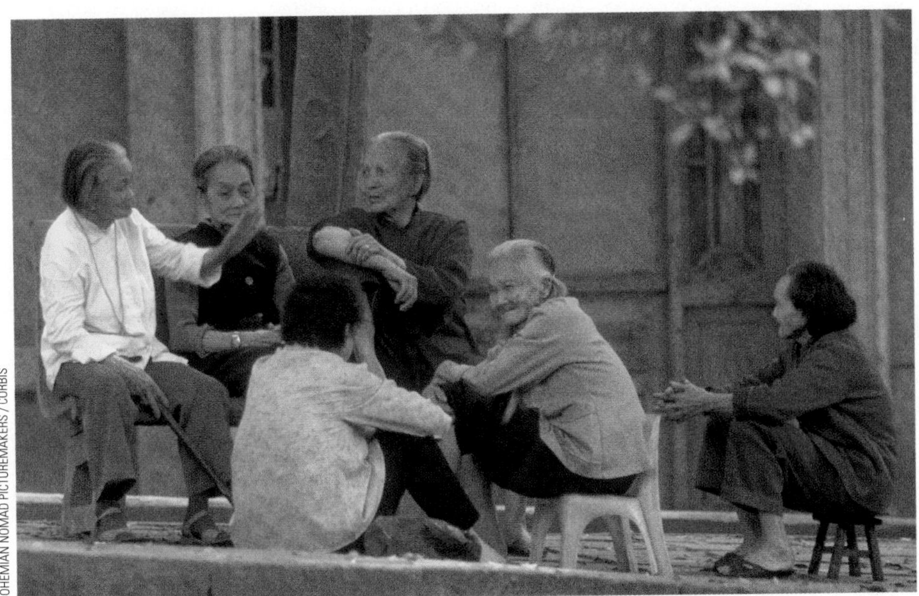
BOHEMIAN NOMAD PICTUREMAKERS / CORBIS

Together by Choice Elderly women outnumber elderly men in China by a very wide margin. Chinese cultural traditions include respect for the aged, group spirit, and self-efficacy. These six women in a public park in Guangzhou seek one another out for daily conversation.

These adjustments to changes in the social convoy demonstrate selection, compensation, and optimization (Baltes & Carstensen, 2003). Successful aging requires that people keep themselves from becoming socially isolated, a task that most of the elderly manage to accomplish. With fewer friends and relatives still alive, elders become more supportive (phoning more often, providing practical help) of those remaining (Gurung et al., 2003). Having a reliable, although small, social network buffers against almost any problem that can arise (Atchley, 1999).

Remember the elderly widower whose son insisted he move out of the home of the Russian widow who had become his friend? The man did not want to leave, but he said that his son

> probably couldn't understand because he told me all the time, "She's not your mother. Come on, you're free. You're young enough to live somewhere else." But I had a very hard time making up my mind what was the right thing to do because my landlady wanted me to stay.
>
> *[quoted in Koch, 2000, p. 51]*

In retrospect, this man should have maintained his friendship with the elderly woman, but instead he listened to his son. He moved to Florida, regretfully leaving his landlady friend. He died alone, with one child in Berlin, another in Hong Kong, and the third estranged and angry.

SUMMING UP

As at younger ages, each person's social convoy provides emotional and psychological support as well as practical help. People in long-term partnerships (heterosexual or homosexual) typically live longer, healthier, and happier because of their mutual dependence. Widows often have close friends to ease the loss; widowers have greater problems initially but are more likely to remarry. Grandparenting is usually companionate, bringing joy to elders, although stress as well as joy comes to grandparents who are remote, involved, or surrogate parents. Younger generations typically want to be supportive, but many older adults prefer to be independent. Friends are needed and wanted in late adulthood, by everyone. This is particularly true for those elderly people who are without close social support from relatives; for them, friends help maintain their health and happiness.

The Frail Elderly

frail elderly People over age 65 who are physically infirm, very ill, or cognitively impaired.

Remember that aging can be categorized as usual, impaired, or optimal. Thus far we have focused on the usual and optimal, those who are active and supported by friendship and family. Now we look at the **frail elderly,** those who are infirm, very ill, or cognitively impaired. Usually the frail are the oldest-old, past age 85.

Most older adults become frail if they live long enough, although, as you remember from the discussions of compression of morbidity in Chapter 23 and terminal decline in Chapter 24, ideally a person is frail only for a short period. Some elderly people, however, are frail for years, even decades.

Activities of Daily Life

activities of daily life (ADLs) Actions that are important to independent living, typically consisting of five tasks of self-care: eating, bathing, toileting, dressing, and transferring from a bed to a chair. The inability to perform any of these tasks is a sign of frailty.

Beyond age and illness, the crucial marker of frailty is the inability to perform, safely and adequately, the physical and cognitive tasks of self-care needed to maintain independence. Gerontologists refer to five physical **activities of daily life,** abbreviated **ADLs**—namely, eating, bathing, toileting, dressing, and transferring from a bed to a chair. If a person needs help with even one of these five tasks, he or she may be considered frail, although for some purposes (such as insurance) frailty does not begin until a person is unable to perform three or more ADLs.

In the aftermath of many illnesses and operations, doctors and nurses consider the ability to perform ADLs the crucial sign of recovery. ADL ability is affected by age as well as health status and pain (e.g., Osnes et al., 2004). Medical personnel strive to help all elderly persons perform their ADLs, providing occupational therapy or special equipment (such as a higher toilet seat) to help a person remain self-sufficient.

instrumental activities of daily life (IADLs) Actions that are important to independent living and that require some intellectual competence and forethought. The ability to perform these tasks may be even more critical to self-sufficiency than ADL ability.

Equally important may be the **instrumental activities of daily life,** or **IADLs,** which require intellectual competence and forethought (Stone, 2006). It is more difficult to measure competence at IADLs because they vary from culture to culture. In developed nations, IADLs include shopping for groceries, paying bills, driving a car, taking medications, and keeping appointments (see Table 25.1). In rural areas of other nations, feeding the chickens, cultivating the garden,

TABLE 25.1

Instrumental Activities of Daily Life

Domain	Exemplar Task
Managing medications	Determining how many doses of cough medicine can be taken in a 24-hour period Completing a patient medical history form
Shopping for necessities	Ordering merchandise from an online catalogue Comparison of brands of a product
Managing one's finances	Comparison of Medigap Insurance Plans Completing income tax returns
Using transportation	Computing taxi rates versus bus rates Interpreting driver's right-of-way laws
Using the telephone	Determining amount to pay from a phone bill Determining emergency phone information
Maintaining one's household	Following instructions for operating a household appliance Comprehending appliance warranty
Meal preparation and nutrition	Evaluating nutritional information on food label Following recipe directions

Source: Adapted from Willis, 1996.

Another Test The items in the right-hand column are adapted from a questionnaire to assess IADL competence. As you can see, managing daily life is not easy, but most of the elderly do it.

mending clothes, getting water from the well, and baking might be IADLs. Everywhere the inability to perform IADLs makes people frail, even if they can perform all five ADLs (Stone, 2006).

Worldwide, relatively few of the elderly are frail (Ahearn, 2001); less than 2 percent of the world's total population are unable to perform their ADLs or IADLs. However, this proportion is rising, for three reasons:

- People are living longer.
- Medical care emphasizes preventing death more than enhancing life.
- Adequate nutrition, safe housing, and health aids are able to prevent or postpone frailty, but some mobility, planning, and/or money is needed to access such measures, and that tends to exclude many who are already somewhat frail.

A. RAMEY / PHOTOEDIT, INC

Mobility Is Crucial The best help is the kind that permits self-sufficiency. This man's legs can no longer carry him everywhere, but his motorized wheelchair (with room for his furry companion) lets him get around on his own, without having to depend on other people for transportation. Thus, although he is not strong, he is also not frail.

These factors mean that frailty may soon be a serious problem in many nations. Ideally, compression of morbidity and good medical care will reduce the amount of time during which the average elderly person needs help with ADLs or IADLs. Some nations already depend on family members to care for the frail. Many Asian and African cultures emphasize family responsibility and respect for the aged. However, gerontologists criticize over-reliance on family obligation, noting that many families are unfairly burdened and some elderly people are inadequately supported (Aboderin, 2004; Ogawa, 2004; Phillipson, 2006).

Governments, families, and aging individuals sometimes blame one another for frailty. The responsibility actually rests with all three. To take a simple example, a person whose leg muscles are weakening might choose to start strength training, purchase a walker, avoid stairs, or become bed-bound. Family members can make each of those possibilities more or less attractive, and public policies can help as well. In this example, family members could walk with the elderly person on pathways that their city has constructed to be safe and unobstructed. Family members could purchase a steady walker, designed to further mobility, and public funds could pay for it. The older person could use those pathways and the walker safely.

As dynamic theories remind us, some people enter late adulthood well supported by family members and friends, prepared by past education and creative problem solving, possessed of an adequate pension and work opportunities, protected by a lifetime of good health habits. Others lack these buffers. Consider the differences between two hypothetical 80-year-olds.

issues and applications

Buffers Between Fragile and Frail

Imagine two 80-year-old childless widows, each living in a U.S. city on a small pension, with failing eyesight, adequate hearing, and advanced osteoporosis. These basics are identical, but their current state of mind and projected health are very different.

One widow lives alone in her old, rundown house with uneven hardwood floors covered with braided scatter rugs, a flight of steep stairs separating the bedroom and the kitchen, dimly lit hallways, and rumors of a recent robbery two blocks away. Temperamental fearfulness combines with her good hearing to make her cringe at every frightening creak of the old house.

Since falling and fracturing her wrist on the way to the toilet one night, she has been apprehensive about walking. She refuses to go downstairs to prepare meals. She never ventures outside or answers the doorbell or the phone. Further, she no longer tries to wash or dress herself, or even to eat as much as she should, citing some lingering pain in her fingers and her belief that "no one cares."

Obviously, this widow is very frail, requiring ongoing care. She has trouble with four of the five ADLs. At present, she has a home health aide, who comes daily to bathe her, bring in the mail, and prepare the day's food. This aide fears that one day she will arrive to find her patient dead, but health aides have almost no authority, so this aide is neither trained nor expected to intervene. A professional might set up an exercise program; arrange transportation to a senior center; send a housing consultant who would change the rugs, lights, and stairs; and find a program providing nutritious meals.

In the United States, assistance (e.g., Meals on Wheels) is available, but this widow is unlikely to find it. Family members usually locate public programs and augment them with private support; this woman has no one to do that. Her income is spent on utility bills, medicine, and subscriptions to magazines she no longer reads. A reverse mortgage, canceled subscriptions, public subsidies, and better insulation would make her financially secure, but each of those takes more planning than she is able to do.

The other widow is equally bereft of family, but she sold her old house and, with two lifelong friends, bought a large co-op apartment (with no stairs) near a small shopping center. As all three women are aging, they consulted an expert (recommended by the city's senior service agency) who suggested that they equip their apartment with bright lighting, sturdy furniture, grab rails, wall-to-wall carpeting, a telephone programmed to dial important numbers, a stove that automatically shuts off, and a front door that buzzes until locked.

The three housemates compensate for one another's impairments: The one who sees best reads the fine print on medicine bottles, legal papers, and cooking directions; the sturdiest one sweeps, mops, and vacuums; and our widow hears the phone, doorbell, and alarm clock. They regularly eat, converse, and laugh together—good for the digestion as well as the spirits. Their arrangement works partly because they chose each other; forced communal housing (when elders are placed together by outsiders in a home) is less successful (Folts & Muir, 2002).

Unlike the first widow, who will be institutionalized if she does not die soon, the second widow, with the same physical problems, cares for herself, socializes, and shops. Her buffers prevent frailty. If her health worsens, her friends will make sure she obtains good care, including cataract surgery, home delivery of audiobooks, a hip replacement, a motorized wheelchair—whatever is needed.

Just as a fine crystal goblet—admired, lovingly handled, and carefully stored—is unlikely to break despite its fragility, so an older person, surrounded by crucial buffering, may not become frail.

Caring for the Frail Elderly

Often the caregivers of the elderly are themselves elderly, typically a husband or wife. If the frail person has no living partner, often a sibling or an aging daughter takes over the care.

The Demands of Family Care

Family caregivers often experience substantial stress. Their health suffers and depression increases, especially if the care receiver has dementia (Pinquart & Sörensen, 2003). One daughter described the strain that she and her father experienced as her mother succumbed to Alzheimer's disease:

> I worked the entire time through four pregnancies . . . returning to work within six weeks of delivery. It was a piece of cake compared to trying to cope with a combative, frustrated adult who cannot dress, bathe, feed herself; who wanders constantly. A person faced with this situation . . . having to work a full day, raise a family, and take care of an "impaired" relative would be susceptible to suicide, "parent-abuse" . . . possibly murder.
>
> My father tried very hard to take care of her, but a man 84 years old cannot go without sleep, and cannot force her to take care of her personal cleanliness. Up until two years ago, she was taking care of the finances and household. Her signature was beautiful. . . . Now it's just a wavy line. An 84-year-old man does not learn to cook and balance the budget very easily, and he becomes bitter. He did not want to put her in the nursing homes he visited, and so he reluctantly sold his house and moved to a city he didn't like so that his children could help with her care. It has been a nightmare. . . . She obviously belonged in a secondary-care facility because no one can give her 24-hr. care and still maintain their sanity and families.
>
> *[quoted in Lund, 1988]*

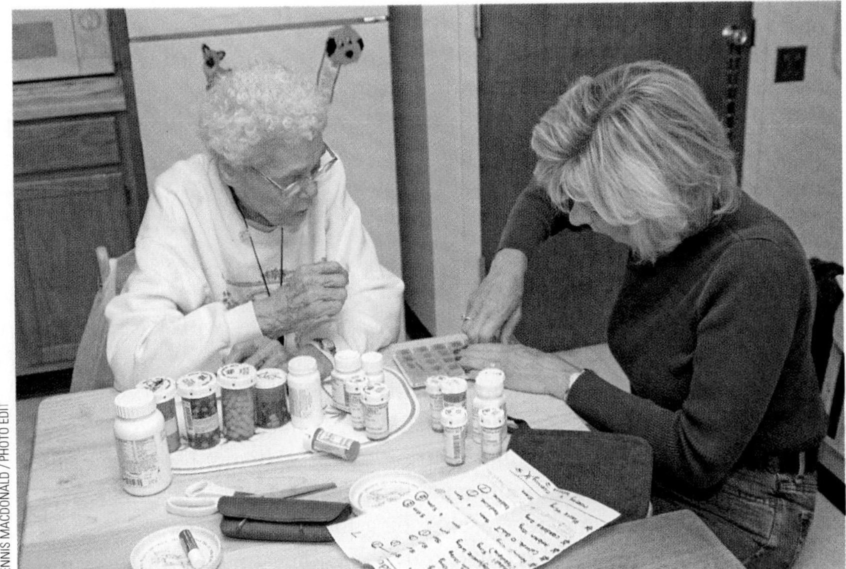
DENNIS MACDONALD / PHOTO EDIT

Morning, Afternoon, Evening, Bedtime Less than half of all adults follow doctors' orders about medication. For seniors, this negligence can lead to dementia or even death. Family caregiving usually begins with IADLs, as with this daughter, who is sorting her mother's 16 medications into a tray that is marked to help the older woman remember when to take them.

Observation Quiz (see answer, page 710): Do this mother and daughter live together?

Sometimes caregivers feel fulfilled by their experience because everyone, including the care receiver, appreciates their efforts. In fact, when a caregiver feels supported by family, even if the caregiving demands increase, the caregiver becomes less stressed (Roth et al., 2005).

Nonetheless, after listing the problems and frustrations of caring for someone who is mentally incapacitated but physically strong, one overview notes:

> The effects of these stresses on family caregivers can be catastrophic. Family caregiving has been associated with increased levels of depression and anxiety as well as higher use of psychotropic medicine, poorer self-reported health, compromised immune function, and increased mortality.
>
> *[Gitlin et al., 2003, p. 362]*

The designated caregiver is chosen less for practical reasons (such as who has the most time and skill) than because of cultural expectations. In the United States, a spouse is the usual caregiver, but in Asian nations the son and his wife feel responsible. In Korea, for instance, 80 percent of elderly people with dementia are cared for by daughters-in-law and only 7 percent by a spouse. That shifts for Korean Americans who have dementia: 19 percent are cared for by daughters-in-law and 40 percent by the spouse (Youn et al., 1999).

Even in ideal circumstances, caregivers may feel resentful, for three reasons:

- If one adult child is the primary caregiver, other siblings tend to feel relief or jealousy. The primary caregiver wants them to do more; they resist being told what to do.
- Care receivers and caregivers often disagree about schedules, menus, doctor visits, and so on. Resentments on both sides disrupt affection and appreciation.
- Public agencies rarely provide services unless an emergency arises. For example, **respite care,** when a professional caregiver takes over for a few hours, is not paid for by public funds in the United States (although it is in England), but hospital care is (Butler et al., 1998).

respite care An arrangement in which a professional caregiver relieves a frail elderly person's usual family caregiver for a few hours each day or for an occasional weekend.

The result of public policy and cultural values may be "a system that places inappropriate burdens of elder care upon the family" (Seki, 2001, p. 101). Developmentalists, concerned about the well-being of people of all ages, advocate more help for families of the frail elderly (see Fortinsky et al., 2007; Stone, 2006).

➤**Answer to Observation Quiz** (from page 709): Probably not. Clues include the small (not family-size) refrigerator, the mother's medical alert pendant, and the fact that the daughter is organizing medications for an entire week (as indicated by the large number of compartments in the tray), not just a single day.

Elder Abuse

When caregiving results in resentment and in social isolation, the risk of depression, poor health, and abuse (of the frail person or the caregiver) escalates. Most family members provide adequate care despite the stress, but abuse is likely if the caregiver suffers from emotional problems or substance abuse (Brandi et al., 2006). Maltreatment ranges from direct physical attack to ongoing emotional neglect.

Analysis of elder abuse is complicated because three distinct elements contribute to the problem: the victim, the abuser, and the setting (Gordon & Brill, 2001). Thus, an old person who is cranky and feeble, with severe memory loss (the care receiver), cared for by an alcoholic grandchild (the caregiver), in a place where visitors are few (the community), is a recipe for abuse. If only one of those three factors were different, abuse would be less likely.

The typical case of elder maltreatment begins benignly, as an outgrowth of caregiving. For example, an elder may provide money to a younger relative, who gradually spends all the elder's assets; or a family member may be pressured to care for an increasingly frail relative, only to become so overwhelmed and isolated that neglect occurs; or a husband may feel resentment when he unexpectedly must care for his wife, who no longer recognizes him. Benign beginnings make elder abuse difficult to recognize. Other family members are reluctant to notify authorities, and, as with other forms of abuse, the dependency of the victim makes prosecution difficult (Mellor & Brownell, 2006).

AP PHOTO / SERGE J-F. LEVY

Even in the Best Families The question of elder abuse became front-page news in the last months of Brooke Astor's life. The wealthy philanthropist and socialite is shown here at age 95; she died in 2007 at age 105. Her grandson accused his father, her only child, of plundering her fortune and neglecting her care. The truth of the accusation has not been established.

Researchers are not sure whether family abusers are more often husbands or wives or adult children, but it is clear that, while most caregivers do a good job, some do not. Sadly "perpetrators tend to be dependent on the individual they were mistreating," with that dependence usually including housing and financial assistance (Bonnie & Wallace, 2003, p. 96).

Overall, in "worldwide studies based on community surveys," elder abuse occurs in 5 to 6 percent of all caregiver–care receiver pairs (Wolf, 1998, p. 161). Because those who are mistreated by family members are ashamed to admit it, the actual rate is probably higher. Adding to the problem of accurate measurement are disagreements among elders, caregivers, and professionals regarding standards of care.

Families are less prepared to cope with difficult patients than professionals are, yet they typically provide round-the-clock care, with little outside help or supervision. Some caregivers believe that overdrugging, locked doors, and physical restraints (all abusive) are their only options. Extensive public and personal safety nets for the frail are needed to prevent maltreatment (Mellor & Brownell, 2006).

Long-Term Care

Many elders and their relatives feel that nursing homes should be avoided no matter what, although the reality of elder abuse—more easily detected in nursing homes, where physical restraints are now illegal except temporarily in exceptional circumstance—makes it apparent that many of the elderly would receive better care outside their homes. In North America and particularly in western Europe, good care is available for those who can afford it and know what to look for. The key elements are independence and privacy for the residents and a sufficient number of well-trained and well-paid staff.

Elderly people who are not self-sufficient have many options. Most prefer to age in place, remaining in their own home with help from family members and home health aides. At the other extreme are skilled nursing facilities, with medical personnel available and help with all ADLs available around the clock. Advanced age and mental impairment are the strongest correlates for admission to a nursing home (Adler, 1995). In the United States, the trend over the past 20 years has been toward fewer nursing home residents (still about 1.5 million people), more of whom are impaired than previously, typically needing assistance with both ADLs and IADLs (Stone, 2006).

Especially for Those Uncertain About Future Careers Would you like to work in a nursing home?

An intermediate form of elder care between one's own residence and a nursing home is **assisted living,** which provides some of the privacy and independence of living at home, along with some medical supervision (Imamoglu, 2007). For example, an assisted-living home might include a private room for each person, one communal meal per day, and a nurse who counts out pills and makes sure they are taken on time. There are many variations in assisted living, from a small group of three or four elderly people who live together to a large facility for hundreds of people (Stone, 2006).

assisted living A living arrangement for elderly people that combines privacy and independence with medical supervision.

Each state in the United States has its own standards for assisted-living arrangements, but many such places are unlicensed. International variation is also wide: Some nations have many more residential options for older residents than do others. The traditional choice—a person is either well enough to stay at home or so frail that he or she must be in an institution—is no longer accepted by political leaders, medical personnel, developmentalists, families, or the elderly themselves.

In the United States and most other nations, nursing homes are licensed and must conform to certain standards, but quality varies. If a nursing home is profit-making and has many patients subsidized entirely by Medicare and Medicaid, then costs will be tightly controlled. The easiest way to save money is to overwork and underpay the staff who provide direct services. Family members who visit their elderly relatives in places that offer substandard care are likely to feel depressed and guilty (Aneshensel et al., 1995).

Overall, the abuses that occurred 50 years ago with unregulated expansion of nursing homes are rare today. Many professionals consider it their mission to help

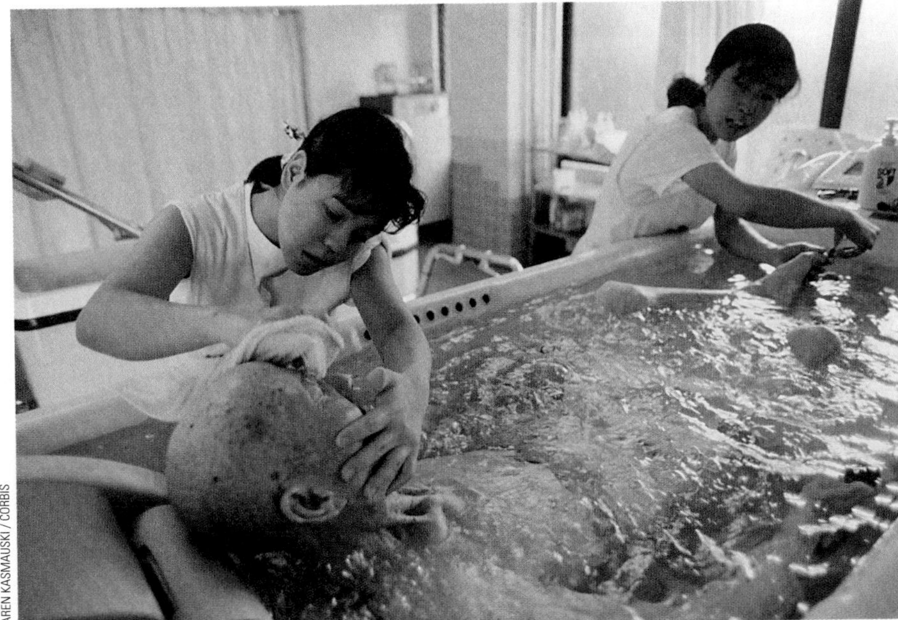

KAREN KASMAUSKI / CORBIS

Help with an ADL A frail elderly man who can no longer bathe himself (one of the basic activities of daily living) is assisted by trained attendants in a model home for the aged in Tokyo.

each resident retain independence, control, and self-respect (Hill et al., 2002). Not only is this good health practice (self-management and independence correlate with physical and mental well-being), it also is the law (Allen, 2007).

The best long-term-care facilities encourage individual choice. Such minor things as when, where, and what a person eats can be controlled by either the resident or the facility. Individualized care is expensive; the national average for nursing-home care in the United States is $75,000 a year. Some facilities cost three times that amount. An AARP survey of people over age 40 in the United States found that only 8 percent could accurately (within 20 percent) estimate the cost of a year of such care in their community. Most people underestimate the amount and mistakenly think that Medicare or Medicaid will pay for it (Barrett, 2006).

➤Response for Those Uncertain About Future Careers (from page 711): Why not? The demand for good workers will obviously increase as the population ages, and the working conditions will improve. An important problem is that the quality of nursing homes varies, so you need to make sure you work in one whose policies incorporate the view that the elderly can be quite capable, social, and independent.

Actually, in the United States, only a fraction of long-term care is paid by public insurance (precise numbers vary, depending on the specifics of illness and care). Sometimes care is more readily funded if it occurs in a hospital than at home, but that situation is changing. Almost every American family spends substantial private funds if an elderly person becomes frail.

This is a topic that should concern everyone. About one in two North Americans will probably need nursing-home care at some point, and one in eight will need such care for more than a year (Stone, 2006). Since admission usually begins with a medical emergency, it is wise to plan ahead, before such a crisis occurs.

SUMMING UP

Some elderly people become frail, unable to perform the activities of daily life (such as bathing and dressing) or the instrumental activities of daily life (such as taking medication and paying bills). Frailty is not inevitable with age or illness; it can be prevented or postponed with the help of family, friends, and community. If an elderly person needs full-time care, usually the spouse or another family member provides it, usually with major self-sacrifice. Stress on the caregiver and care receiver can be reduced if the entire family and many public agencies are supportive, but that is seldom the case. Sometimes caregiving stress leads to abuse, and sometimes the elderly person is best cared for in an assisted-living setting or a nursing home, where good care may be available. ■

We close with an example of family and nursing-home care at their best. A young adult named Rob related that his 98-year-old great-grandmother "began to fail. We had no idea why and thought, well, maybe she is growing old" (quoted in Adler, 1995, p. 242). All three younger generations of the family conferred and reluctantly decided that it was time to move her from her suburban home, where she had lived for decades, into a nursing home.

Fortunately, this nursing home encouraged independence and did not assume that decline is always a sign of "final failing." The doctors there discovered that the woman's pacemaker was not working properly. As Rob explains:

> We were very concerned to have her undergo surgery at her age, but we finally agreed. . . . Soon she was back to being herself, a strong, spirited, energetic, independent woman. It was the pacemaker that was wearing out, not Great-grandmother.
>
> *[quoted in Adler, 1995, p. 242]*

This story contains a lesson repeated throughout this book. When an older person seems to be failing, or a preschooler is selfish, or a teenager uses alcohol, or an emerging adult takes dangerous risks, one might conclude that such problems are normal for that particular age. It is true that each of these behaviors is more common at those stages. But just because people act their age, we cannot assume that they do not need protection and guidance. The life-span perspective holds that, at every age, people can be "strong, spirited, and energetic" if the rest of us do our part. At every age, life can be lived to the fullest.

SUMMARY

Theories of Late Adulthood

1. Several self theories hold that adults make personal choices in ways that allow them to become fully themselves. Erikson believed that individuals seek integrity that connects them to the human community. Identity theory suggests that people try to maintain a sense of themselves.

2. A dominant interpretation of the goal of later life is that selective optimization with compensation can help in adjusting to physical and cognitive decline. This is a way of preserving the self. Most older adults compensate for their decline partly by taking a more positive view of life.

3. Stratification theories maintain that social forces limit personal choices, especially the disengagement that may come with age. Activity theory predicts the opposite, that older people who are active are also healthier and happier.

4. Lifelong stratification by gender or race may also limit an elder's ability to live a full life. However, many older members of minority groups function very well, primarily because of strong family and religious connections.

5. Dynamic theories see human development as an ever-changing process, influenced by social contexts, which themselves are constantly changing, as well as by genetic and historical factors that are unique to each person. For instance, continuity theory emphasizes that the changes that occur with age may be much less disruptive than they appear to be.

Coping with Retirement

6. Retirement is often welcomed by the elderly, especially when their jobs are no longer satisfying and their finances are adequate. Some older people prefer to keep working, deriving satisfaction from continued productivity.

7. Many retired people continue their education or perform volunteer work in their communities. Both of these activities enhance the health and well-being of the elderly and benefit the larger society. Even more common is involvement in home and garden enhancement. Most elderly people prefer to age in place, staying in their own homes.

Friends and Relatives

8. A spouse is the most important member of a person's social convoy. Older adults in long-standing marriages tend to be quite satisfied with their relationships and to safeguard each other's health. As a result, married elders tend to live longer, happier, and healthier lives than unmarried elders.

9. The death of a spouse is always difficult, but wives are more likely to experience this loss and, partly for that reason, are more likely to adjust and continue with their lives.

10. Relationships with adult children and grandchildren are usually mutually supportive. Most of the elderly prefer to maintain their independence, living alone, but some become surrogate parents, raising their grandchildren. This situation has many benefits for the families and society as a whole, but it adds to the stress of the older generation.

The Frail Elderly

11. Most elderly people are self-sufficient, but some eventually become frail. They need help with their activities of daily life, either with physical tasks (such as eating and bathing) or with instrumental ones (such as paying bills and arranging transportation).

12. Care of the frail elderly is usually undertaken by family members, either spouses or children (who are often elderly themselves). Many families have a strong sense of filial responsibility, although elder abuse may occur when the stress of care is great and social support is lacking.

13. Nursing homes, assisted living, and professional home care are of varying quality and availability. Each of these arrangements can provide necessary and beneficial care, but good care for the frail elderly cannot be taken for granted.

KEY TERMS

self theories (p. 680)
integrity versus despair (p. 680)
positivity effect (p. 683)
stratification theories (p. 684)
disengagement theory (p. 685)
activity theory (p. 685)
dynamic theories (p. 689)
continuity theory (p. 690)
age in place (p. 692)
AARP (p. 696)
social convoy (p. 696)
filial responsibility (p. 701)
frail elderly (p. 706)
activities of daily life (ADLs) (p. 706)
instrumental activities of daily life (IADLs) (p. 706)
respite care (p. 709)
assisted living (p. 711)

KEY QUESTIONS

1. What are the similarities and differences between self theories and identity theories?

2. Compare the three types of stratification in late adulthood.

3. How can continuity theory be considered a dynamic theory?

4. What kinds of activities do older people undertake after they retire?

5. What changes typically occur in long-term marriages in late adulthood?

6. Compare the roles of friends and family in late adulthood.

7. How does reaction to the death of a spouse differ for men and women?

8. What factors affect the ability to perform ADLs and IADLs?

9. What accounts for the increasing prevalence of the frail elderly?

10. What problems might arise in caring for a frail elderly person?

11. What are the advantages and disadvantages of nursing home care?

APPLICATIONS

1. Attitudes about disabilities are influential. Visit the disability office on your campus, asking both staff and students what they see as effects of attitude on the performance of students. How do you think attitudes toward disability affect the elderly?

2. People of different ages, cultures, and experiences vary in their values regarding family caregiving, including the need for safety, privacy, independence, and professional help. Find four people whose views on this issue will probably differ. Ask their opinions, and analyze the results.

3. Visit a nursing home or assisted-living residence in your community. Notice details of the physical setting, the social interaction of the residents, and the staff. Would you like to work or live in this place? Why or why not?

PART VIII

Late Adulthood

BIOSOCIAL

Prejudice and Predictions As a result of ageism, the functioning of the elderly is restricted and younger people overestimate how many of the aged are impaired. Although people are living longer in every nation, most of the elderly are "young-old"—quite healthy and independent.

Senescence Primary aging is inevitable. Appearance changes, and the brain slows down. Deficits in vision and hearing are widespread, although much can be done to prevent or remedy sensory losses. Because of declines in organ reserve, both primary and secondary aging put older adults at risk of chronic and acute diseases. Compression of morbidity can improve the quality of life for the elderly.

Theories of Aging Research on the causes of aging indicates that genes and cell senescence are both crucial. Specific theories of aging focus on the immune system, a genetic clock, damage from oxygen free radicals, or innate maximum life span. Calorie restriction has not yet been shown to prolong life in humans.

COGNITIVE

The Usual: Information Processing After Age 65 As the senses become less acute and as senescence slows down brain functioning, some aspects of cognition become less effective in late adulthood. Working (or short-term) memory is the first to slow down; long-term memory is more durable. Deficits may result from a decrease of neurotransmitters and blood flow in the brain, from reliance on less effective strategies, and from ageist social expectations. Keeping healthy aids cognition. Most older adults develop ways to compensate for memory loss and slower thinking.

The Impaired: Dementia Symptoms of dementia (memory loss, confusion) may be caused by Alzheimer's disease, strokes, Parkinson's disease, other diseases, depression, or drugs. There is no cure for dementia, but several methods slow down decline. Sometimes a temporary problem or mental illness is misdiagnosed as dementia.

Optimal: New Cognitive Development Many older individuals develop or intensify their aesthetic and philosophical interests and values in later life. An opportunity to remember and to recount the past, called life review, can be very useful. Wisdom is rare at any age, but the elderly who benefit from their experiences may become wise.

PSYCHOSOCIAL

Coping with Retirement Variability is evident throughout late adulthood, with some choosing to retire in their 50s and others wanting to keep working in their 70s. Couples need to plan and coordinate their retirements. Most retired people prefer to age in place, fixing up their homes and gardens. Many find ways to expand their horizons after retirement, through education, volunteer work, and political involvement.

Friends and Relatives Older adults' satisfaction with life depends in large part on continuing contact with friends and family. Generally, marital satisfaction continues to improve. The greatest source of social support is likely to be other elders, either relatives or friends. Family members continue to be connected to one another; adult children generally embrace filial responsibility.

The Frail Elderly The number of elderly people needing help with the activities of daily life is growing, although most are proud of their ability to manage their own lives. Social support can reduce caregiver stress and guard against elder abuse.

Epilogue

CHAPTER OUTLINE

Death and Dying

Death mirrors the complexity of life, as each death highlights cultural differences and ethical dilemmas. Neither complexity nor morbidity should deter us, however, because understanding death and dying helps people live their lives to the fullest. That is the goal of **thanatology,** the study of death and dying, especially social and emotional aspects.

We begin this epilogue as we did Chapter 1, with a multicultural and developmental perspective. Humans have always had beliefs, practices, and rituals that bring *hope* in death, *acceptance* of dying, and *reaffirmation* of life through bereavement.

The diversity of death rituals is often striking. In India, mourners sit on the floor and neither eat nor wash until the funeral pyre is extinguished; in the southern United States and elsewhere, funerals may include food, music, and dancing. In many Muslim cultures, the dead person is bathed by the next of kin; among the Navajo, no one touches the dead person, for fear that his or her restless spirit will return.

But in all cultures, death has been regarded as a passage, not an endpoint, and as a reason for people to come together, not a time when differences are magnified. Hope, acceptance, and reaffirmation of the family, faith, and community have been the result.

That may be changing. Modern medicine and the structures of daily life undercut many customs and beliefs related to death and bereavement. People often argue over when death should occur, what should happen to the corpse, and who deserves the inheritance. Death separates as often as it unites. This is tragic, because our entire study makes it apparent that humans need each other for dying and mourning as well as for living and rejoicing. Perhaps this chapter will help.

Death and Hope

What is death? This simple question has no simple answer. Death could be an end or a beginning, a private and personal event or a part of the larger culture, something to deny or avoid or something to welcome.

A life-span perspective (which, as you learned in Chapter 1, is multidirectional, multicontextual, multicultural, multidisciplinary, and plastic) considers age, culture, training, and experience. Those complexities are further complicated by historical changes (see Table EP.1). A new understanding of death is required.

thanatology The study of death and dying, especially in their social and emotional aspects.

DENIS FARRELL / AP / WIDE WORLD PHOTOS

Not Forgotten Archeologists have determined that remembrance of the dead is one of the oldest rituals of humankind. Each generation and circumstance evoke different rituals. Here, in one of the most recent and tragic circumstances, a worker at the Cotlands Baby Sanctuary of South Africa places the ashes of a young child who died of AIDS into a wall of remembrance in a cemetery. The baby had been found abandoned after both of its parents died of AIDS.

TABLE EP.1

How Death Has Changed in the Past 100 Years

Death occurs later. A century ago, the average life span worldwide was less than 40 years (though it was 47 in the rapidly industrializing United States). Half of the world's babies died before age 5. Now newborns are expected to live to age 78; in many nations, elderly people age 85 and over are the fastest-growing age group.

Dying takes longer. In the early 1900s, death was usually fast and unstoppable; once the brain, the heart, or other vital organs failed, the rest of the body quickly followed. Now death can often be postponed through medical intervention: Hearts can beat for years after the brain stops functioning, respirators can replace lungs, and dialysis can do the work of failing kidneys. As a result, dying is often a lengthy process.

Death often occurs in hospitals. A hundred years ago, death almost always occurred at home, with the dying person surrounded by familiar faces. Now many deaths occur in hospitals, surrounded by medical personnel and technology.

The main causes of death have changed. People of all ages once died of infectious diseases (tuberculosis, typhoid, smallpox), and many women and infants died in childbirth. Now disease deaths before age 50 are rare, and almost all newborns (99 percent) and their mothers (99.99 percent) live, unless the infant is very frail or medical care of the mother is grossly inadequate.

And after death . . . People once knew about life after death. Some believed in heaven and hell; others, in reincarnation; others, in the spirit world. Many prayers were repeated—some on behalf of the souls of the deceased, some for remembrance, some to the dead asking for protection. Believers were certain that their prayers were heard. Today's young adults are aware of cultural and religious diversity, which makes them question what earlier generations believed, raising doubts that never occurred to their ancestors.

Source: Adapted from Kastenbaum, 2006; data from U.S. Bureau of the Census, 2007 and earlier editions.

Death Throughout the Life Span

In order to understand what death means to people, we begin with developmental differences. The meaning assigned to death—either the person's own death or the death of another person—depends partly on cognitive maturation and personal experience.

Death in Childhood

Some adults mistakenly think that children do not understand death; others believe that children should participate in the rituals accompanying the death of a loved one exactly as adults do. You know from your study of childhood cognition that neither approach is correct.

Children as young as 2 have some understanding of death, but their perspective differs from that of older family members. Adults should listen carefully to children who have lost a loved one or who themselves are dying, neither ignoring nor dismissing their concerns (Kenyon, 2001).

Dying children often fear that death means being abandoned by the people they love. Consequently, parents must stay with very sick children day and night, holding their hands, reading to them, telling them they are loved. For a child who loses a friend, a relative, or a pet, sadness, loneliness, and other signs of mourning are typical and should not be ignored.

Current, frequent contact is more important to a child than logic. Thus, one 7-year-old boy who lost three grandparents and an uncle within two years was especially upset when his dog, Twick, died. His parents, each grieving for a dead mother, were taken aback by the depth of the boy's emotions, and regretted that they had not taken their son to the veterinarian's office to see the dog before it

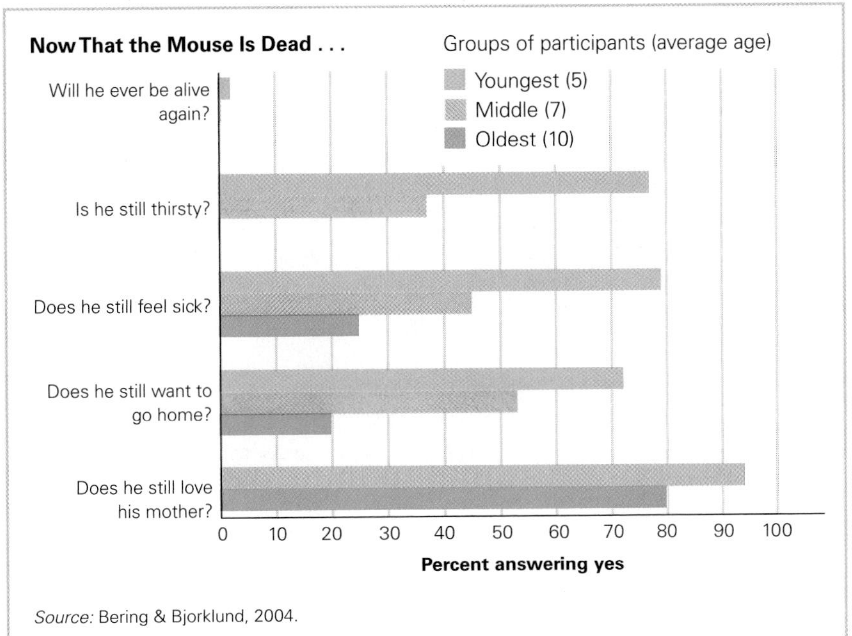

FIGURE EP.1

Love Endures Even the youngest children knew that the mouse was dead, but most of them believed that it still had feelings, needs, and wishes. For children, death does not stop life. These researchers also surveyed 20 college students, 13 of whom (65 percent) thought that love for one's mother continues after death. (In this series of studies, not every age group was asked every question; that explains why only two sets of responses are shown for two of the questions here.)

died. The boy refused to go back to school, saying, "I wanted to see him one more time. . . . You don't understand. . . . I play with Twick every day" (Kaufman & Kaufman, 2006. pp. 65–66).

Because loss of companionship is a crucial concern, telling children that Grandma is sleeping or that God wanted their sister in heaven or that Grandpa went on a long trip is not helpful; children may take such statements literally. In the child's preoperational or concrete operational mind, someone should wake up Grandma, complain to God, or get angry at Grandpa.

Although children have some comprehension of death, adults cannot assume that children share their perceptions. This was shown by a Florida study (Bering & Bjorklund, 2004; see Research Design) in which children saw a puppet skit about a sick mouse that was eaten by an alligator. When questioned afterward, nearly all the children asserted that the mouse was dead and would never be alive again, but most of the younger children thought the dead mouse still felt sick, and most children of all ages thought the mouse still loved his mother (see Figure EP.1).

This study was replicated in Spain (Bering et al., 2005). Children from Spanish public and religious schools followed the same pattern as the Florida children, although children in Catholic schools were more likely to believe that biological functions, such as hearing and tasting, continued.

Research Design

Scientist: James Bering and David Bjorklund.

Publication: *Developmental Psychology* (2004).

Participants: A total of 199 children, age 3 years 2 months to 12 years 10 months, all enrolled in schools affiliated with Florida Atlantic University.

Design: Three experiments, each with different children who answered questions about a skit they saw about a mouse that was eaten by an alligator. Specifics varied (the mouse was lost, sick, jealous of brother, loved mother).

Major conclusion: Children usually expect biological functions (hearing, tasting) to cease at death, but not psychological ones (desires, emotions, ideas).

Comment: Although replication has begun in Spain, replication by other researchers, using participants at other locales and of other ages (including adults), is needed.

Death in Adolescence and Emerging Adulthood

"Live fast and leave a good-looking corpse. . . . Never have a normal day or a boring night" (Kastenbaum, 2004, p. 356). At what age would a person be most likely to agree? Ages 15 to 25, of course, when death is less feared, risk taking increases, appearance is valued, and thrills are sought. Worldwide, fear of death diminishes and life is considered less precious once puberty occurs (Chikako, 2004; Gullone & King, 1997).

Especially when people age 15 to 24 have guns and cars, this developmental trend can be deadly (see Figure EP.2). Adolescents and emerging adults die in suicides, accidents (e.g., car accidents resulting from drunk driving), and homicides

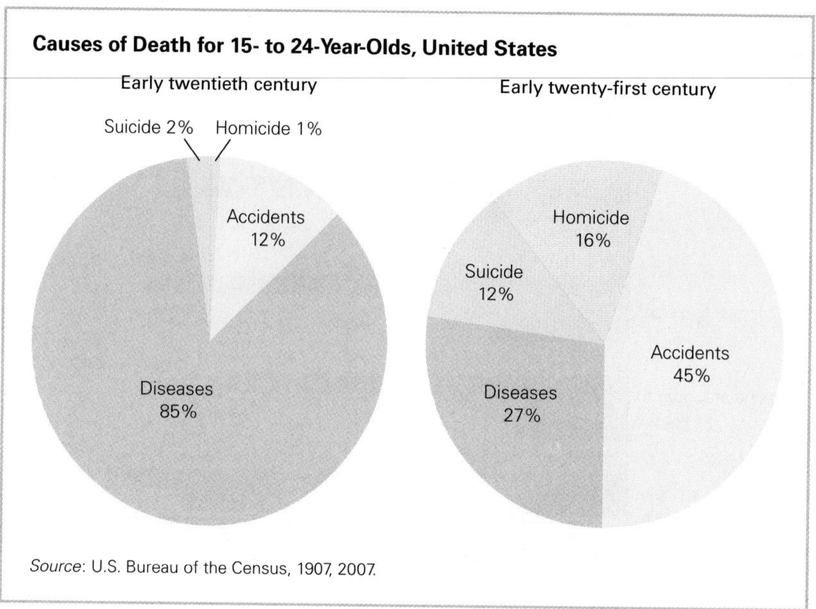

FIGURE EP.2

Typhoid versus Driving into a Tree In 1905, most young adults in the United States who died were victims of diseases, usually infectious ones like tuberculosis and typhoid. In 2005, 25 times more died in the most common type of accident (motor vehicle) than died of the most common lethal disease (leukemia).

Observation Quiz (see answer, page Ep-6): Do these two pie charts show that 16 times more 15- to 24-year-olds were victims of homicide in 2005 than in 1907?

partly because they romanticize death. This outlook makes young people vulnerable to cluster suicides (see Chapter 16), fatal gang wars, and foolish dares (see Chapter 17).

Death in Adulthood

A major shift in attitudes about death occurs when adults become responsible for work and family. Death is not romanticized, but is dreaded as something to be avoided, or at least postponed. These are the years when many people stop taking addictive drugs and start wearing seat belts. They do not want to think about their own death, nor do they accept the death of others. Thus, when Dylan Thomas was about 30, he addressed his most famous poem to his dying father: "Do not go gentle into that good night. / Rage, rage against the dying of the light" (Thomas, 1957).

From age 25 to 60, terminally ill adults do not fear their own death as much as they worry about leaving something undone: One dying 30-year-old mother of a 3-year-old and a 9-month-old strained

> to stay alert for as long as possible so that she could take care of all her unfinished business . . . [including writing] letters to her children for . . . graduation, marriage, and the birth of their first children. She wanted them to know that she would love them always.
>
> *[Deremo & Meert, 2004, p. 66]*

Many scholars have noted that adults' attitudes about death are quite different for a public tragedy and for a private one (Lattanzi-Licht & Doka, 2003). Reasons are many, including the circumstances of death and the fame of the person, but age is one factor, as is evident in news reports that highlight the ages of the dead and the bereaved.

Consider the contrast between public sadness at the death of two U.S. presidents: John F. Kennedy and Ronald Reagan. Even though the latter was president for longer, survived an assassination attempt, and had far more supporters (Kennedy was elected with 34,220,984 popular votes, Reagan with 43,903,230), Kennedy's death, at age 46, evoked more public sorrow.

As another example, fewer than 3,000 people died in the terror attack on the World Trade Center; in the United States, more people than that die *each day* of heart disease. The former was a public tragedy, one that still affects government policy and people's emotions, while heart disease is a private and insidious problem.

Death in Late Adulthood

Finally, in late adulthood, anxiety about death decreases. Many developmentalists believe that a sign of mental health in older adults is acceptance of their mortality (e.g., Baltes & Carstensen, 2003; Erikson et al., 1986). Older people write their wills, designate health proxies, read scriptures, reconcile with family members, and, in general, tie up all the loose ends that young adults avoid dealing with (Kastenbaum, 2006).

Performing these actions does not mean that the elderly have given up on life. Even after age 85 people still work to maintain their health and independence. But developing an understanding of death is one of the normal tasks of late adulthood (Schindler et al., 2006). Many older people make quite specific death plans, such as deciding who will get which heirloom, choosing funeral music, buying a burial plot, and ending each family visit with loving goodbyes.

Belief in life after death is directly related to people's estimate of how likely it is that they themselves might die. This is one reason that the aged in the United States tend to be more religious than the young. It is also why nations in which many people die young tend to be more devout (Idler, 2006).

Research has described the difference in priorities between those who think about their death and those who do not. In an intriguing series of studies, people were presented with the following scenario:

> Imagine that in carrying out the activities of everyday life, you find that you have half an hour of free time, with no pressing commitments. You have decided that you'd like to spend this time with another person. Assuming that the following three persons are available to you, which of them would you choose to spend that time with?
>
> A member of your immediate family
> The author of a book you have just read
> An acquaintance with whom you seem to have much in common

Older adults, more than younger ones, choose the family member, presumably because such conversations become more important when death may occur soon. This explanation is supported by a comparison of three groups of middle-aged homosexual men—one group that had AIDS, one that was HIV-positive without symptoms, and one that was HIV-negative. Those with AIDS more often chose to spend their half-hour with a family member (Carstensen & Fredrickson, 1998).

Another study of these three choices began with 329 people recently diagnosed with cancer and another group of 170 people (matched for age and education) who had no life-threatening illness (Pinquart & Silbereisen, 2006). The most marked difference in choices was between those who had cancer and those who did not, regardless of age (see Figure EP.3). Adults who were cancer-free were more likely to choose an author or a potential friend over a family member.

FIGURE EP.3

Turning to Family as Death Approaches Both young and old people diagnosed with cancer (a fourth of whom died within five years) were found to be more likely to prefer to spend a free half-hour having a conversation with a family member rather than with an interesting person whom they did not know well. A larger difference was found between older and younger adults who did not have a serious disease: The healthy younger people were less likely to say that they would prefer to spend the time with a family member rather than with an interesting acquaintance.

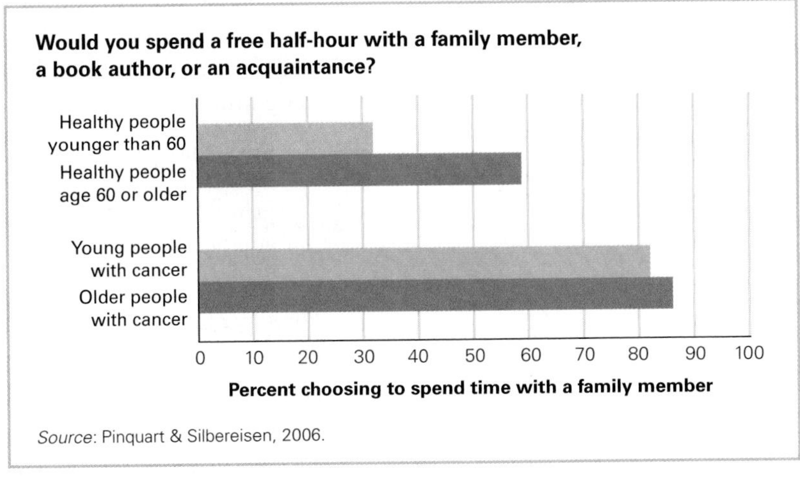

Source: Pinquart & Silbereisen, 2006.

STEVEN M. STONE / PICTURE CUBE

Last Rites This colorful Balinese funeral procession on its way to a Buddhist cremation is a marked contrast to the somber memorial service that is more common in the West. No matter what form it takes, community involvement in death and dying seems to benefit the living.

Many Religions, Many Cultures

A second major contextual factor involved in people's understanding of death is religion. First, a disclaimer: As one review notes, "Rituals in the world's religions, especially those for the major tragic and significant events of bereavement and death, have a bewildering diversity" (Idler, 2006, p. 285). The summaries offered in this brief overview are greatly simplified; readers are encouraged to read more deeply about each faith.

Views of Death in Major Religions

Buddhism Among Buddhists, disease and death are regarded as inevitable sufferings, which may eventually bring enlightenment (Nakasone, 2000). Birth, life, and death are merely phases of the great circle of existence: "Life melds gradually into death. And death itself is part of the recurring cycle of being and becoming" (Kastenbaum, 2004, p. 337).

In Buddhism, death occurs in eight stages: Eyesight dims, hearing diminishes, smell disappears, breathing ceases, white moonlight is perceived, red sunlight appears, darkness descends, the clear light of death arrives. Note that the last four stages occur after a physician would certify death (Kastenbaum, 2006).

The task of the individual is to gain insight from dying. Relatives and friends help by ensuring that the person does not receive mind-altering medication or death-delaying intervention. Death is not an end of the individual, who will be reborn and, if all goes well, will eventually reach *nirvana*—a state of perfect enlightenment, in which all desires end and reincarnation stops. If a dying person feels hope or fear, the reason is not death itself but rebirth.

Hinduism Among Hindus, helping the dying person to surrender his or her ties to this world and prepare for the next is a particularly important obligation for the immediate family. A holy death is one that is welcomed by the dying person, who should be resting on the ground, chanting prayers, lips moistened with water from the sacred Ganges River, surrounded by family members who are reciting sacred texts. Such a holy death is believed to ease entry into the next life.

Achieving a holy Hindu death is elusive in Western hospitals, where, in addition to other problems, the dying person cannot be placed on the floor. It is crucial for a Hindu family to know when someone is about to die so that preparations can be made and the entire family can be present when the soul leaves the body.

A dying Hindu woman, Shanti, had lived in the United States for 32 years. She did not want to know the cause of her fatal illness because, she said, "It is in the hands of the gods." She refused medication because she believed that pain would purify her spirit; she insisted on dying at home. A nurse who understood her culture reported:

> Shanti died in relatively unrelieved pain, but the beauty of her story is that she died with strong karma, at home, with her family around her . . . with her head facing North, with the water of the river Ganges sprinkled in her mouth . . . at peace.
>
> *[Doorenbos, 2005, pp. 178–179]*

➤Answer to Observation Quiz (from page Ep-4): No. The charts show the proportion of deaths, not the absolute number.

For some people, including many Hindus, death is a way toward spiritual enlightenment, a part of karma; achieving enlightenment is more important than avoiding pain.

Native American Traditions Although the more than 400 tribes of Native Americans (called Indians, Aboriginals, or members of First Nations in Canada) vary significantly in their customs, all consider death an affirmation of nature and community. This contrasts with the Western emphasis on individualism and science (Van Winkle, 2000). Unless this is appreciated by medical personnel, Native Americans may shun dying in hospitals.

In one example, the adult sons of a Lakota Sioux man began chanting in his hospital room as soon as he died, a ritual affirmation of their dedication to their father and his legacy:

> A nurse entered the room, heard the chants and called hospital security to remove "those drunken Indians." . . . A doctor arrived to announce that an autopsy should be performed . . . [although the] tribe was firmly opposed to autopsies.
>
> *[Brokenleg & Middleton, 1993]*

A contrasting example comes from the death of a 76-year-old Ojibwa woman in Canada. Perhaps because Mary (the dying woman's daughter) was a nurse, the hospital allowed the family to have a private room, which they cleansed with sweet grass and sage. At first, some younger family members wanted life-prolonging measures (such as a stomach tube when the woman stopped eating), but Mary insisted that her mother should die "the Indian way . . . taking cues from the universe, the earth" (quoted in Chapleski, 2005, p. 52).

Perhaps respect for Indian customs was the reason that the hospital allowed death without medication or other measures. According to Mary, however, the reason was indifference: "It didn't matter to them. In Canada it was just another Indian dying, . . . but that was okay, it made my work [of caring for Mother] easier" (quoted in Chapleski, 2005, p. 52).

Judaism Jews believe that life should be celebrated and hope sustained. Death is not emphasized, nor final judgment stressed. The person is never left alone during and after the process of dying, because each person is regarded as part of the community, deserving attention and respect. On the day after death, the body is buried, unembalmed and in a plain wooden coffin to symbolize that physical preservation is not possible.

The family mourns at home for a week (a ritual called *sitting shiva*), joined by many visitors, who bring food and comfort, tears and laughter. "The Jew is forbidden to mourn alone. . . . The door of the house of mourning is never locked: the assumption is that the community will come in and out, and the mourner should not have to open or close the door" (Gillman, 2005, p. 148).

The immediate family recites a prayer called the Kaddish (which does not mention death) every evening and curtails social activities for a year. Family members also attend services and say the Kaddish on each anniversary of the death. The person lives on in the memory and respect of mourners, not in heaven or hell.

Christianity Many Christians believe that death is not an end but rather the beginning of eternity in heaven or hell. Therefore, death may be either welcomed or feared, depending on the person's belief (and sometimes on his or her behavior and piety as well).

Particular customs vary widely from denomination to denomination and from place to place. Funerals may involve gathering relatives and neighbors (a "wake") to view the body, to express sorrow, to eat and drink; or funerals may be quiet events only for those who were close to the deceased, with emotional restraint and a closed coffin.

The variability is such that in Mexico, for example, Christianity blends with Aztec customs in the Day of the Dead on November 1 and 2, the holiday on which people visit the cemetery to bring flowers and food. They tell stories about the

Differences and Similarities An open coffin, pictures of saints, and burning candles are traditional features of many Christian funerals, like this Ukrainian Orthodox ceremony.

ED KASHI / IPN / AURORA PHOTOS

dead person, leave sweets on the grave, and eat a festive meal at the graveside, celebrating life and death (Talamantes et al., 1999; Younoszai, 1993).

In the United States, the equivalent holiday is Halloween (from All Hallows Eve, the night before All Saints Day, November 1). Among African American Christians, death is a community event, with family sorrow blending with community hopes in a crowded church, which echoes with joyful as well as mournful gospel music (Collins & Doolittle, 2006; Rosenblatt & Wallace, 2005).

Islam The prophet Muhammad said, "Live as though one is going to live forever and, at the same time, live as though one is going to die tomorrow." Allah, or God, is part of every aspect of life, from the mundane to the sublime, thus death is not seen as separate from living or believing (Lord et al., 2003).

For Muslims, death affirms faith. Islam teaches that the achievements, problems, and pleasures of this life are fleeting; everyone should be mindful of, and ready for, death at any time. Therefore, caring for the dying is a holy reminder of mortality and of the potential for a happy life in the afterworld.

Rituals before and after death (including reciting prayers, washing the body, carrying the coffin, and attending the funeral) are performed by devout strangers as well as by relatives and friends; death is meaningful for every Muslim.

Public and noisy lamenting over death may be expressed by everyone (Nobles & Sciarra, 2000), especially in the first three days after death. Mourners need also accept Allah's will, remembering that the end of mortal life is the transition to a better world (Hai & Husain, 2000). In Islam, there is a judgment before that passage into a better world, although, as in Christianity, various branches of Islam differ in the specifics.

Respect for Ancestors

In many African and Asian religions, adults gain new status through death, joining other ancestors who watch over their descendants. The entire community (most members of which are related to one another) participates in each adult's funeral, preparing the body and providing food and money for the journey to the ancestral realm. Mourning helps everyone to celebrate their connection with each other and with their history (Opoku, 1989).

In many Asian homes, a special altar is set up for the dead person, with photographs, flowers, and other memorial objects. In Japan, the person's spirit is believed to stay with the family for seven weeks and to return on each anniversary of death (Morgan & Laungani, 2005). In Borneo, the head of the dead person was once preserved and hung above the family's living area, to be fed and respected. The idea of all these practices is that the spirits of the dead are still around, protecting (or, in some cases, disturbing) the living (Kastenbaum, 2004).

Spiritual and Cultural Affirmation

Some people who survive a very serious injury or illness report having had a **near-death experience** in which they left their body and moved toward a bright, white light while feeling peacefulness and joy. The following report is typical:

near-death experience An episode in which a person comes close to dying but survives and reports having left his or her body and having moved toward a bright, white light while feeling peacefulness and joy.

> I was in a coma for approximately a week. . . . I felt as though I were lifted right up, just as though I didn't have a physical body at all. A brilliant white light appeared. . . . The most wonderful feelings came over me—feelings of peace, tranquility, a vanishing of all worries.
>
> [*quoted in Moody, 1975, p. 56*]

Near-death experiences often include religious elements (angels have been seen, celestial music heard), and survivors often adopt a more spiritual, less materialistic view of life. Note that Buddhists also describe a white light after breathing ceases. To some, near-death experiences prove that there is "life after life" (Moody, 1975). However,

> there is no evidence that what happens when a person really dies and "stays dead" has any relationship to the experience reported by those who have recovered from a life-threatening episode. In fact, it is difficult to imagine how there could ever be such evidence.
>
> [*Kastenbaum, 2006, p. 448*]

Nonetheless, the role of religion in providing hope at death is evident in every tradition (Kemp & Bhungalia, 2002). In addition to those just described, for example, detailed descriptions of life after death have been provided by the ancient Greeks and the ancient Egyptians (whose focus on the afterlife is evidenced by their *Book of the Dead*, magnificent pyramid tombs, and preservation of mummies for eternal life).

For all people throughout history, religious and spiritual concerns often become particularly important at death (Idler, 2006). Many elderly people seek to return to their religious roots through devotion to traditional rituals, deeper spirituality, or an actual journey. Many dying adults ask that their bodies or ashes be returned to their birthplace.

In one study, seriously ill Hindus who had emigrated to Canada spoke nostalgically about their origins (Fry, 1999). Contrary to assumptions about acculturation, the more time an immigrant had spent in Canada, the more he or she wanted a Hindu funeral (see Figure EP.4). In the words of one woman who had spent 22 years abroad:

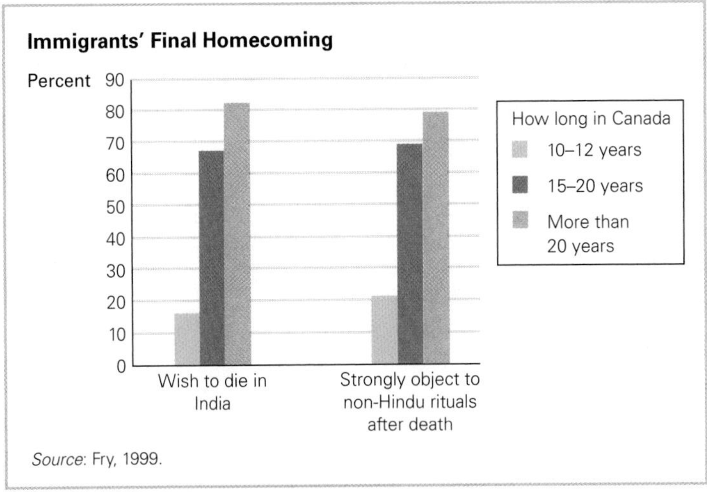

FIGURE EP.4

Strong Homeland and Religious Impulses Open-ended interviews with seriously ill Indians who had emigrated to Canada found that the longer they had been away, the more important India and Hinduism became as they thought about their deaths.

> I long to die among my relatives in the old country. . . . I miss the music, the chantings, the smells and sounds and the ringing of the temple bells in my hometown. I worry whether my own Hindu God will take me back or reject me because I am not a pure Hindu any more and have not been in communion with the elders of the Hindu faith for the years and years I have spent in Canada.
>
> [*quoted in Fry, 1999*]

Spiritual beliefs and a connection to religious community give hope that is desperately needed at death, a sense "that individual lives cannot be reduced to insignificance, that they can and do make a difference worth making, that the world is better for their existing" (Attig, 2003, pp. 62–63).

SUMMING UP

A major concern regarding death is the hope that the dying person and his or her family have for the future. This concern is affected by modern medical measures (which prolong life and make death more lonely), by age (both mourners and the dying are affected by their stage of life), and by religion. All the world's religions have rituals and beliefs regarding death and the afterlife. These are very important to both the dying and the mourners, but they differ among and within the various traditions. ■

Dying and Acceptance

good death A death that is peaceful, quick, and painless and that occurs at the end of a long life, in the company of family and friends, and in familiar surroundings.

People in all religious and cultural contexts hope for a **good death:** one that is peaceful and quick and occurs at the end of a long life; in familiar surroundings; with family and friends present; and without pain, confusion, or discomfort (Abramovitch, 2005). By contrast, a bad death is dreaded, particularly by the elderly, who do not want to die over months or years, semiconscious and alone, surrounded only by medical technology.

Attending to the Needs of the Dying

In some ways, modern medicine has made a good death more likely. Because of clean drinking water, improved sanitation, and widespread immunization, billions of lives are saved, mostly of the young. Doctors, not priests, are sought when someone is ill. Surgery, drugs, radiation, and rehabilitation mean that, in developed countries, people of all ages get sick, go to the hospital, and . . . return home, well again.

However, modern medicine can also make a bad death more likely. When a cure is impossible, physical and emotional care can deteriorate. A study by a leading thanatologist, Robert Kastenbaum, found that when a patient was known to be dying, doctors spent fewer minutes with the patient, inadequate medication was given, visitors were kept away, and nurses responded more slowly to the call button:

> Nurses took a significantly longer time before going to the bedside of a dying patient. . . . The nurses were surprised and upset when told of this differential response pattern . . . [and] resolved to . . . respond promptly to terminally ill patients. After a few weeks, however, the original pattern reinstated itself. As much as they wanted to treat all patients equally, the nurses found it difficult to avoid being influenced by their society's fear of contact with dying people.
>
> *[Kastenbaum, 2006, p. 113]*

Has modern medicine made dying better or worse? It depends, but Kastenbaum and many others report that three recent trends make a good death more likely: truthful talk, the hospice, and palliative care.

Honest Conversation

In about 1960, Elisabeth Kübler-Ross (1969, 1975) asked the administrator of a large Chicago hospital for permission to speak with dying patients. He informed her that none of the patients were dying! Eventually she found a few terminally ill patients, who, to everyone's surprise, were grateful for the opportunity to talk. From ongoing interviews, Kübler-Ross described many emotions of the dying, which she divided into a sequence of five stages:

1. Denial ("I am not really dying.")
2. Anger ("I blame doctors, or family, or God for my death.")
3. Bargaining ("I will be good from now on if I can live.")
4. Depression ("I don't care about anything; nothing matters anymore.")
5. Acceptance ("I accept my death as part of life.")

Another set of stages of dying is based on Abraham Maslow's hierarchy of human needs:

1. Physiological needs (freedom from pain)
2. Safety (no abandonment)
3. Love and acceptance (from close family and friends)
4. Respect (from caregivers)
5. Self-actualization (spiritual transcendence) (Zalenski & Raspa, 2006)

Other researchers have *not* found sequential stages in dying people's approach to death. Denial, anger, and depression disappear and reappear; bargaining is brief because it's fruitless; and acceptance may never occur. Comfort, safety, love, and respect are important throughout the dying process, and achieving transcendence does not depend on completion of Maslow's first four stages.

However, as Kübler-Ross and others have proven, dying people want to spend time with loved ones and to talk honestly with medical and religious professionals. As a result of this knowledge, the patient's right to know about his or her impending death is now widely accepted in Western hospitals. Many medical personnel are taken aback when Asian or Latino family members assert that giving their dying loved one too much information would destroy hope. Consider, for example, the experience of Mrs. Y, in the following.

a case to study

"Ask My Son and My Husband"

Mrs. Y's case was referred to the ethics committee by a hospital staff person who was concerned about a violation of her autonomy. . . . Mrs. Y was an alert 83-year-old Japanese woman who was admitted to the hospital for shortness of breath. During the evaluation of this symptom, she was found to have an advanced case of lung cancer.

Her physician informed her older son and her husband, both of whom told the physician that they did not want Mrs. Y to be informed about the diagnosis. They told the physician that, in Japanese culture, cancer is felt to be a diagnosis that robs the patient of hope. The physician asked Mrs. Y whether she would like to be told of her diagnosis when it was discovered and whether she would like to make decisions about her treatment. . . . Mrs. Y clearly answered, "No, you ask my son and my husband."

[quoted in Kogan et al., 2000, p. 320]

This case was brought to the hospital ethics committee because the wishes of Mrs Y. and her family were contrary to the belief that patients need to be informed. This belief is expressed in respect for individuals, as reflected in medical ethics, incorporated in lists of patients' rights, and upheld by Western law. In Mrs. Y's case, this value conflicted with Japanese beliefs in hope, death, and family. The discrepancy may also reflect the status of women in Japanese culture, which led Mrs. Y to defer to her husband and son.

Is truthful communication and individual autonomy more important than family wishes and cultural taboos? The hospital ethics committee allowed Mrs. Y to die without knowing her diagnosis or prognosis. Is that what you would have done?

The Hospice

hospice An institution in which terminally ill patients receive palliative care.

In London in the 1950s, Cecily Saunders opened the first modern **hospice,** where terminally ill people could spend their last days in comfort (Saunders, 1978). Thousands of other such places have since opened throughout the world. Instead of moving into a hospice facility, many patients remain in their homes, receiving services from visiting hospice workers.

Hospice caregivers provide skilled treatment but avoid desperate measures to try to delay death; their focus is on making dying easier. There are two principles for hospice care: (1) Each patient's autonomy and decisions are respected (for example, pain medication is given when requested, not on a schedule); (2) family members and friends are counseled and helped before the death, as well as being shown how to provide care. When the patient's home is the hospice, family members provide most of the care; when a person is in a hospice facility, relatives and close friends are encouraged (sometimes required) to be with the patient day and night. After death, the hospice staff attends to the needs of the bereaved.

Originally hospices were designed for adults dying of cancer. Few people with other illnesses (such as heart disease or kidney failure, both of which cause many deaths among the elderly) entered hospices. There were also few children and few patients of non-European ancestry. This is changing, as demonstrated by two statistics: The United Kingdom has 40 hospices for children, and in South Carolina African Americans are as likely to be in hospice as European Americans (Han et al., 2006; Mash & Lloyd-Williams, 2006).

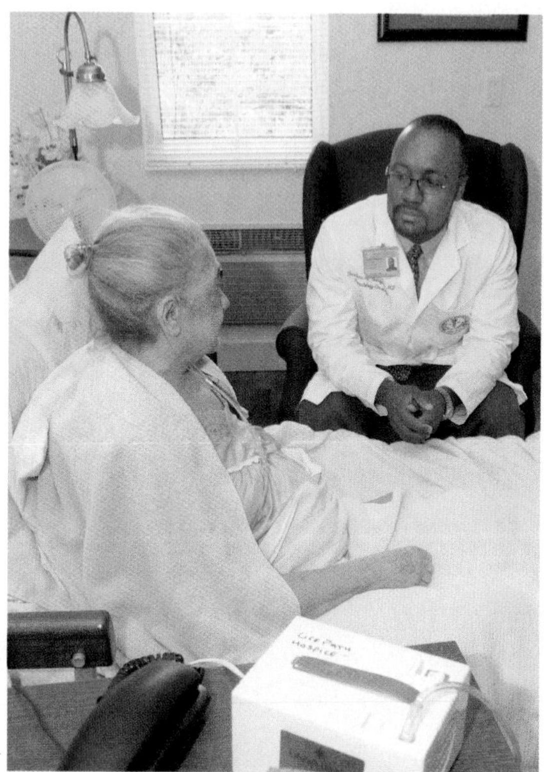

AP / WIDE WORLD PHOTOS

To Meet a Need The idea of hospice care has traveled far from its birthplace in London. Dr. Theodore Turnquest, shown here speaking with a patient in Lifepath Hospice House in Florida, plans to open the first hospice in his native country, the Bahamas.

Nonetheless, there are several reasons why many of the dying never begin hospice care or begin only in the last days before death. These reasons are detailed in Table EP.2. One report says that half of all hospice patients have less than three weeks of specialized care before they die; that is too short a time for all the individualized medical and emotional needs of a dying person to be assessed and satisfied (Brody, 2007). In the United States, the number of patients in hospice care doubled from 2000 to 2005 (to 1.2 million)

TABLE EP.2

Barriers to Entering Hospice Care

- Hospice patients must be terminally ill, with death anticipated within six months, but such predictions are difficult to make. For example, in one study of noncancer patients, physician predictions were 90 percent accurate for those who died within a week but only 13 percent accurate when death was predicted in three to six weeks (usually the patients died sooner) (Brandt et al., 2006).
- Patients and caregivers must accept death. Traditionally, entering a hospice meant the end of curative treatment (chemotherapy, dialysis, and so on). This is no longer true (Abelson, 2007; Sulmasy, 2006). About 12 percent of patients live longer than expected, and about 2 to 3 percent are discharged (Finn, 2005). Nonetheless, many people avoid hospice because they want to keep hope alive.
- Hospice care is expensive, especially if curative therapy continues. Many skilled workers—doctors, nurses, psychologists, social workers, clergy, music therapists, and so on—provide individualized care day and night.
- Availability varies. Hospice care is more common in England than in mainland Europe and is a luxury in poor nations. In the United States, western states have more hospices than southern states do. Even in one region (northern California) and among clients of one insurance company (Kaiser), the likelihood that people with terminal cancer will enter hospice depends on exactly where they live (Keating et al., 2006)

and now includes almost half of all dying people. In other nations, from 1 to 50 percent of deaths occur in hospice (Abelson, 2007; Loewy, 2004).

Especially for Relatives of a Person Who Is Dying Why would a healthy person want the attention of hospice caregivers?

Comfort Care

The same "bad death" conditions that inspired the hospice movement have led to the creation of a new field of medicine called **palliative care,** designed not to treat illness but to relieve suffering (Hallenbeck, 2003). Many people fear pain more than any other symptom of fatal illness, and most doctors now recognize the importance of controlling pain.

palliative care Care designed not to treat an illness but to relieve the pain and suffering of the patient and his or her family.

Good palliative care can control most pain through the use of morphine and many other drugs. Medications are also available to control symptoms such as nausea, constipation, itchy skin, bedsores, and muscle aches (Hallenbeck, 2003; Preston et al., 2003).

Pain medication was once sparingly prescribed to prevent addiction—until medical policy makers realized that drug dependence is not a problem in dying people. There is another possible problem with morphine and other opiates: They improve the dying person's quality of life but also hasten death by slowing respiration. This is called **double effect,** and it is considered acceptable in law, ethics, and practice. In England, for instance, almost no physician does anything intended primarily to cause death, but about a third of all deaths are hastened because of double effect (Seale, 2006).

double effect An ethical situation in which a person performs an action that is good or morally neutral but has ill effects that are foreseen, though not desired.

Choices and Controversies

Because talking with the dying and providing hospice and palliative care are now widely accepted by doctors and nurses, a good death is more likely today than it was 50 years ago. But new controversies have emerged as a result of medical advances: A dying person's breathing can be continued with respirators, a heart that has stopped can be restarted, and nutrition can be provided via a PEG (percutaneous endoscopic gastronomy—i.e., a stomach tube).

Choices are made in almost every hospital death: Treatments are avoided, started, or stopped, with life-prolonging or death-hastening effects (Rosenfeld, 2004). People disagree vehemently about appropriate care, not only between nations but also within them, not only between families and experts but also within families (Engelhardt, 2005).

When Is a Person Dead?

With life-support measures so widely available, when does death occur? In the late 1970s, a group of Harvard physicians decided that the crucial organ was the brain. When brain waves ceased, the brain was dead, and therefore the person was dead. This definition was accepted by a U.S. presidential commission in 1981 and is now used worldwide. But what if some primitive brain activity continues, but the person is in a vegetative state? In such a situation, the definition of death is not so clear-cut (see Table EP.3).

Words can fuel conflicts. People who want to "let nature take its course" or "halt suffering" would not want to "cause death," even though all these phrases can be used to describe the same action. Thanatologists use terms carefully; we will try to do the same here, as we discuss the various aspects of the controversy over how people should respond to dying.

In **passive euthanasia,** a person is allowed to die. No respirators facilitate breathing, no shocks restart the heart, no PEG provides nutrition, no antibiotics halt infections. The chart of a patient who is dying may be coded **DNR (do not resuscitate),** which directs the medical staff not to try to restore breathing if it

passive euthanasia A situation in which a seriously ill person is allowed to die naturally, through the cessation of medical interventions.

DNR (do not resuscitate) A written order from a physician (sometimes initiated by a patient's advance directive or by a health care proxy's request) that no attempt should be made to revive a patient if he or she suffers cardiac or respiratory arrest.

TABLE EP.3

Dead or Not? Yes, No, and Maybe

Brain death: Prolonged cessation of all brain activity with complete absence of voluntary movements; no spontaneous breathing; no response to pain, noise, and other stimuli. Brain waves have ceased; the EEG is flat; *the person is dead.*
Locked-in syndrome: The person cannot move, except for the eyes, but brain waves are still apparent; *the person is not dead.*
Coma: A state of deep unconsciousness from which the person cannot be aroused. Some people awaken spontaneously from a coma; others enter a vegetative state; *the person is not dead.*
Vegetative state: A state of deep unconsciousness in which all cognitive functions are absent, although eyes may open, sounds may be emitted, and breathing may continue; *the person is not dead.* This state can be *transient,* with recovery possible, *persistent,* or *permanent.* No one has ever recovered after two years; most who do recover (about 15 percent) improve within three weeks (Preston & Kelly, 2006). After time has elapsed, the person may, effectively, be dead.

active euthanasia A situation in which someone takes action to bring about another person's death, with the intention of ending that person's suffering.

physician-assisted suicide A form of active euthanasia in which a doctor provides the means for someone to end his or her own life.

stops. Passive euthanasia is legal everywhere, although a distinction can be made between removing life-support equipment and not starting it in the first place. Both have the same result.

Active euthanasia involves doing something to bring about death, such as giving a person a drug. Some physicians perform active euthanasia when they are confronted with suffering that they cannot relieve and they believe that the person would want death to be hastened. It is definitely legal in the Netherlands, probably legal in Belgium and Switzerland, and considered unethical and illegal (but rarely prosecuted) everywhere else (Laurie, 2005; Magnusson, 2004; Rosenfeld, 2004).

In **physician-assisted suicide,** a person takes his or her own life, using medication provided by a doctor. In the state of Oregon, a law permits physician-assisted suicide under certain conditions but explicitly states that such a death should be considered not suicide, but "death with dignity."

The morality of suicide is controversial. In Eastern nations, suicides can be noble, as when Buddhist monks burned themselves publicly to protest the war in Vietnam or when people choose to die for their nation or their honor. In Western nations, suicide is illegal for any reason. Even prisoners on death row are rescued from suicide attempts.

Nonetheless, physician-assisted deaths occur everywhere. Some patients hoard sedatives or other drugs and then swallow an overdose to die, with or without their doctors' awareness. In the United Kingdom, a disabled, dying woman named Diane Pretty sued the government because her disability meant she could not hoard and overdose, which prevented her from exercising her "right to die." She lost and had to wait for death to occur naturally.

Many healthy people and medical professionals think that the primary reason for passive and active euthanasia as well as for physician-assisted suicide is to avoid intense pain. One physician complained, "It is criminal the way my colleagues fail to treat pain. . . . Physician-assisted suicide . . . is a problem of physical ignorance and abandonment" (quoted in Curry et al., 2002). In fact, however, pain is not the primary motivation for patients who wish to die in either the Netherlands or Oregon. Loss of dignity, of cognition, of choice is much more crucial.

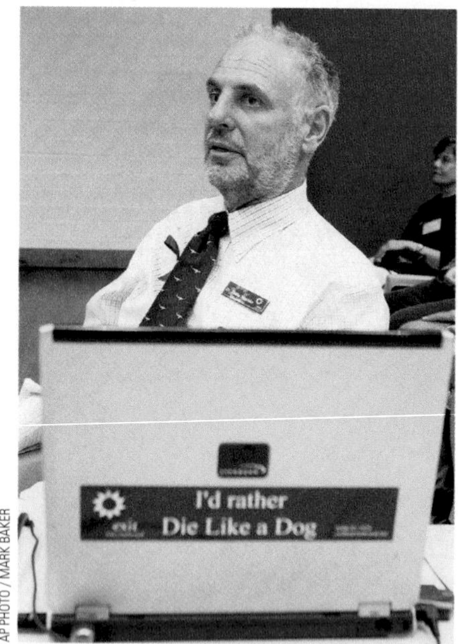

AP PHOTO / MARK BAKER

Speaking Out in Australia Philip Nitschke speaks in favor of voluntary euthanasia on the tenth anniversary of the first such death legally allowed in the Northern Territory of Australia. Since that time, the national government has ruled that states cannot make such laws. The controversy continues, in Australia and elsewhere.

Observation Quiz (see answer, page Ep-16): Does something in this photograph indicate how passionate Mr. Nitschke is about making death easier for the terminally ill?

The Netherlands

The law in the Netherlands (Holland) has permitted voluntary euthanasia and physician-assisted suicide since 1980. A doctor must approve and report each such death, and only half the patients who ask for help in dying receive it (a fourth die before approval and a fourth are denied or dissuaded) (Jansen-van der Weide, 2005). One doctor explains:

> The process and procedure take so much emotional energy that physicians hope that nature will take its course before matters reach the point where euthanasia is appropriate. I am grateful when patients die peacefully on their own.
>
> *[quoted in Thomasma et al., 1998]*

Most (but not all) Dutch physicians believe that hospice and palliative care have improved in their country since euthanasia became legal and regulated (Georges et al., 2006). Nonetheless, the number of people dying with medical help in the Netherlands has been increasing slightly, to 2 or 3 percent of all deaths.

➤Response for Relatives of a Person Who Is Dying (from page Ep-13): Death affects the entire family, including children and grandchildren. I learned this myself when my mother was dying. A hospice nurse not only gave her pain medication (which made it easier for me to be with her) but also counseled me. At the nurse's suggestion, I asked for forgiveness. My mother indicated that there was nothing to forgive. We both felt a peace that would have eluded us without hospice care.

Oregon

Oregon voters approved physician-assisted suicide (but not active euthanasia) in 1994 and again in 1997. Under the new law, only 28 percent of requests are approved, according to one account (Orentlicher & Callahan, 2005). The law states that:

- The person must be an adult and an Oregon resident.
- The dying person must request the lethal drugs twice orally and once in writing.
- Fifteen days must elapse between the first request and the prescription.
- Two physicians must confirm that the person is terminally ill, with less than six months to live, and is competent to make a decision (i.e., is not mentally impaired or depressed).

Between 1998 and 2005, of the 75,000 people in Oregon who died of a terminal illness, only 246 were assisted suicides. As Table EP.4 shows, the reasons for requesting physician-assisted suicide were more psychological than biological (Oregon Department of Human Services, 2006).

In 2005, 64 Oregonians obtained a lethal prescription. Half of them did not use it; 15 died naturally, and 17 were still alive at year's end. Doctors explain alternatives to patients who request the drugs, often recommending a hospice (where physician-assisted death may occur). Oregon hospices are said to be excellent (Kastenbaum, 2006).

Many are concerned that legalizing euthanasia or physician-assisted suicide will create a **slippery slope** (Foley & Hendin, 2002; Rosenfeld, 2004). That is, if societies begin hastening death, they may slide into killing people—especially the old and the poor—who are not ready to die.

Data from the Netherlands and Oregon do not support this fear. People whose doctors legally help them to die tend to be advantaged, not disadvantaged (unless being unmarried is considered a disadvantage) (see Table EP.5). It could be less

TABLE EP.4

Reasons Oregon Residents Gave for Requesting Physician Assistance in Dying, 1998–2005

Reason	Patients Giving Reason (%)
Loss of autonomy	86
Less able to enjoy life	85
Loss of dignity	83
Loss of control over body	57
Burden on others	37
Pain	22

Source: Oregon Department of Human Services, 2006.

slippery slope The argument that a given action will start a chain of events that will culminate in an undesirable outcome.

TABLE EP.5

Characteristics of People Who Request and Consume Lethal Drugs in Oregon

Compared with those who die of the same diseases, those dying with a doctor's help are:

- Younger: The average age was 69, compared to 76. The range of ages was 25 to 94.
- Better educated: 41 percent were college graduates.
- More often divorced or never married: 33 percent, compared to 19 percent.
- Richer: 62 percent had private health insurance.
- Less often of minority ethnicity: 97 percent were European Americans.

Source: Oregon Department of Human Services, 2006.

➤Answer to Observation Quiz (from page Ep-14): On his computer is a sticker reading "I'd rather die like a dog"—a sardonic but emphatic way of expressing a preference for being painlessly euthanized if suffering from a terminal illness.

slippery for these practices to be regulated than for them to exist illegally, as may occur in every community (Magnusson, 2004).

Voters are not convinced that Oregon and the Netherlands are moving in the right direction. In five states of the United States, and in the legislative bodies of many nations (e.g., the British House of Lords in 2006), proposals to legalize physician-assisted suicide have been defeated.

Advance Directives

A massive effort in Hawaii to inform people about end-of-life issues resulted in *less* support for physician-assisted suicide but *more* support for *advance directives*—an individual's instructions regarding end-of-life medical care (Braun et al., 2005). At least in Hawaii, once people understood the processes and complications of dying, they realized that they already had substantial control over their own deaths. That control is exerted via two documents, a living will and a health care proxy.

living will A document that indicates what medical intervention an individual wants if he or she becomes incapable of expressing those wishes.

health care proxy A person chosen by another person to make medical decisions if the second person becomes unable to do so.

A **living will** indicates what medical intervention is wanted or not wanted if a person is unable to express any preferences. Living wills use phrases such as "incurable," "reasonable chance of recovery," and "extraordinary measures," but each of these phrases is a generality that may not be interpreted the same way by everyone else when the time comes. Accordingly, people also designate a **health care proxy,** a person who will make more specific medical decisions if need be. Only about 25 percent of all North Americans (mostly older adults) have both these documents, although they are recommended for everyone (Preston & Kelly, 2006).

Even with a living will and a proxy, care may not always be what a person wants. For one thing, it is difficult for a proxy to choose death for a loved one. Further, hospital staff members do not necessarily agree with a patient's advance directives, yet they are the ones who must take the final action. For example, many medical people think the PEG is overused, as it prolongs life but does not cure. Most laypeople, however, regard eating as a basic function, and thus they are unlikely to consider a PEG an "extraordinary measure" (Orentlicher & Callahan, 2004).

Especially for People Without Advance Directives Why do very few young adults have living wills?

The discrepancy between care providers and care receivers was evident in a survey conducted in six European nations. Doctors were more likely than family members to choose quality of life over length of life (see Figure EP.5) (Sprung et al., 2007).

Many patients choose their doctors for their values as well as their training, and most doctors who provide ongoing care discuss treatment issues with them. The data show that doctors in the Netherlands and in Oregon who assisted with death

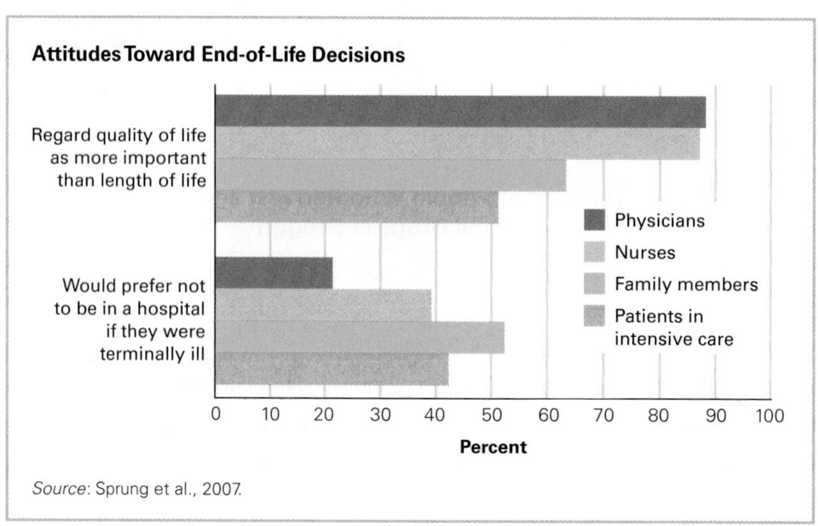

FIGURE EP.5

Interesting Discrepancies Responding to a survey based in intensive-care units in six European nations, higher percentages of ICU doctors and nurses than of ICU patients and their families said that they considered quality of life more important than a long life; they would rather be at home (or in a hospice) than in a hospital if they were terminally ill and had only a short time left to live.

usually knew the dying person well, typically hastening death for fewer than one person per year.

Demographic characteristics may influence decisions about dying. In the past 30 years, passive euthanasia has been publicly debated for three young U.S. women who had no advance directives: Karen Ann Quinlan, Nancy Cruzan, and Teresa Schiavo. The following feature presents six reasons why Terri Schiavo captured national attention, unlike thousands of other U.S. patients who are in persistent vegetative states. Should her youth, female gender, and European ethnicity be counted as additional reasons?

issues and applications

Let Terri Schiavo Live/Die/Live/Die

On February 25, 1990, 26-year-old Theresa Marie Schiavo collapsed in her Florida home. She had had an eating disorder and had recently been treated for infertility. The combination may have triggered her heart failure. Her heart was restarted, but she never recovered.

At first, Terri's parents and her husband of six years, Michael, cooperated to care for her at home. Later they paid for her care in a good nursing home. They refused to believe that her vegetative state was permanent, visiting her every day, talking with her, making sure that her PEG was working properly and that her body was turned regularly to avoid bedsores. They even flew her to California to try an experimental treatment to reawaken her brain. It failed. Because Terri had no advance directive, the court designated Michael as her health care proxy.

Four years after Terri's collapse, Michael finally accepted the medical diagnosis of persistent vegetative state and had a DNR order put on her chart. Seven years later, Michael petitioned to have the feeding tube removed. Amid growing public controversy, the court agreed, partly because witnesses said that before her illness, Terri had told them that she never wanted to be on life support. The judges did not order the PEG removed immediately, because Terri's parents appealed the decision. They lost, and the PEG was taken out (a quick and painless procedure).

Immediately, Florida governor Jeb Bush and the state legislature passed "Terri's Law," requiring that the tube be reinserted. It was.

Florida courts ruled that Terri's Law was unconstitutional. Three more years of court cases ensued. Finally, the U.S. Supreme Court ruled that the lower courts were correct. By that point, every newspaper and TV station in the nation was following the case. Terri's parents insisted that she had some degree of consciousness and accused her husband of having abused her. Thousands of people joined vigils, some supporting Terri's "right to life" and others supporting her "right to die."

The U.S. Congress passed, and President George W. Bush signed, a law requiring that artificial feeding be continued, but that law, too, was overturned by the Supreme Court. A week after the tube was removed, Terri died, on March 31, 2005. Or had she really died 15 years earlier? An autopsy found that her brain was half the normal size.

"The battle over the death of Theresa Marie Schiavo left the entire country drained and frustrated" (Cerminara, 2006, p. 101). There were at least six reasons why this case unfolded as it did and caused such powerful reactions:

1. Terri had no advance directive (few 26-year-olds do), so people were free to think that she would want what they themselves would want.
2. Family disputes capture the attention of all of us. Terri's parents wanted her kept alive, but her husband wanted to let her die. Both thought they were advocating for Terri.
3. Conflicts between branches of government (in this case, between the judiciary on one side and the executive and the legislative on the other) can be virulent. The courts at all levels consistently upheld the legality of removing Terri's feeding tube, and the executive and legislative branches consistently disputed the courts' rulings.
4. There is no universally accepted definition of death. Doctors consider a persistent vegetative state a kind of death, allowing withdrawal of life support. Some laypeople believe that the heart, not the brain, is critical.
5. People disagree about medical judgment. All the doctors who examined Terri diagnosed a persistent vegetative state, while others, including U.S. Senator Bill Frist, a physician, insisted that Terri was conscious after watching a home video that showed her seeming to smile at her mother and respond to her surroundings.
6. Social values made people on both sides predict dire consequences. The courts imagined being overwhelmed with similar family disputes, hospitals feared providing extensive free care for people who had no hope of cure, and many others feared that slippery slope toward widespread euthanasia.

Given these historic conflicts and deep convictions, "in the end there were no winners" in the Terri Schiavo case (Cerminara, 2006, p. 101)—and it is hard to see how there could have been any.

➤Response for People Without Advance Directives (from page Ep-16): Young adults tend to avoid thinking realistically about their own deaths. This attitude is emotional, not rational. The actual task of preparing the documents is easy (the forms can be downloaded; no lawyer is needed). Young adults have no trouble doing other future-oriented things, such as getting a tetanus shot or enrolling in a pension plan.

SUMMING UP

Hospice and palliative care help people achieve a "good death" by relieving pain, discomfort, and deception. Passive euthanasia (allowing a seriously ill person to die) is generally accepted and legal, but active euthanasia and physician-assisted suicide are usually opposed. Both the Netherlands and Oregon have made it legal for doctors to help with dying, but few terminally ill people in those places request that service. In preparing for death, about one North American in four signs a living will and designates a health care proxy. Thanatologists wish far more people would do so, because without those advance directives, patients' families and doctors may become embroiled in painful conflicts over whether and how a dying person should be treated. ■

Bereavement

Humans sometimes act and think in ways that make no sense. This is apparent at every stage of development and continues to be evident when a loved one dies. In her book *The Year of Magical Thinking,* Joan Didion, a highly respected author known for logical thinking, explains that for a long time after her husband died, she did not give away his shoes because she believed that he was coming back and would need them (Didion, 2005). With similar illogic, many people wonder, when a loved one dies, how the world seems to continue as it did before.

Normal Grief

When someone dies, those who loved the person typically feel powerful emotions, including anger and shock, sadness and depression. Denial, as in Didion's refusal to accept that the person is never coming back, is combined with deep waves of sadness. Humans may be overwhelmed by one death and yet indifferent to millions of others who die each day. As one woman said:

> Although I'm 62 I still miss my mother. . . . Since 9/11 it has been even harder. People make me feel ashamed. After all, they're right when they say to me, "Look at all the youngsters who were killed; their lives were just beginning. Your mother lived a full life, what more do you want?"
>
> *[quoted in Schachter, 2003, p. 20]*

Grief and Mourning

bereavement The sense of loss following a death.

grief An individual's emotional response to the death of another.

Bereavement is the sense of loss following a death. Grief and mourning are both aspects of bereavement, but they are quite different from each other. (Small, 2001). **Grief** is a powerful and personal emotion, a sadness that overtakes daily life. It is manifested in uncontrollable crying, sleeplessness, and irrational and delusional thoughts—the "magical thinking" of Didion's title:

> Grief has no distance. Grief comes in waves, paroxysms, sudden apprehensions that weaken the knees and blind the eyes and obliterate the dailiness of life. . . . I see now that my insistence on spending that first night alone was more complicated than it seemed, a primitive instinct. . . . There was a level on which I believed that what had happened remained reversible. That is why I needed to be alone. . . . I needed to be alone so that he could come back. This was the beginning of my year of magical thinking.
>
> *[Didion, 2005, pp. 27, 32, 33]*

mourning The ceremonies and behaviors that a religion or culture prescribes for bereaved people.

Mourning is a more public and ritualistic expression of bereavement. It is manifested in ceremonies and behaviors that a religion or culture prescribes to honor all who die. These may include special clothing, food, prayers, or informal shrines at the place where someone died, as well as the gestures of friends, who may send cards, bring food, and stay near the bereaved person.

A. RAMEY / PHOTOEDIT, INC.

The Flowers of Youth In many cultural traditions, mourners bring a token of their presence to funeral rites. Such items as pebbles, stuffed animals, notes, candles, and flowers are left at gravesites throughout the world. These young women are placing flowers on the coffin of a friend who was killed in a drive-by shooting.

Mourning customs are designed to move grief toward reaffirmation (Harlow, 2005). For this reason, eulogies emphasize the dead person's good qualities; people who did not know the deceased attend wakes, funerals, or memorial services. Mourning is needed because the grief-stricken are vulnerable not only to irrational thoughts but also to self-destructive acts.

Health, physical as well as mental, dips in the recently bereaved, and the rate of suicide increases (Stroebe & Stroebe, 1993). After natural or human-caused disasters, including war, many people who die are those who fall victim to their own diminished self-care and the indifference of others. More people died of human violence and negligence after Hurricane Katrina than died in the catastrophe itself. Grief splinters a person into jumbled pieces; mourning reassembles him or her, making the person whole again, once more a part of the larger community.

Mourning is often time-limited—the week of sitting shiva at home in Judaism, three days of active sorrow for Muslims and Catholics, and so on. Since memories spontaneously return on the anniversary of a death, many religions prescribe anniversary rituals such as visiting a grave or lighting a candle. Having a specific time, prayer, and place for remembering the dead (such as a home altar in China or a gravesite in most places) helps the bereaved express grief without being overwhelmed by it.

Seeking Blame and Meaning

A common impulse after death is for the survivors to assess blame, such as for medical measures not taken, laws not enforced, habits not changed. The bereaved sometimes blame the dead person, sometimes themselves, and sometimes distant others. For public tragedies, nations blame each other. Blame is not necessarily rational, as when the assassination of Archduke Francis Ferdinand in Sarajevo in 1914 led to the four years of World War I. On a much smaller scale, I have experienced this blaming impulse myself.

in person

Blaming Martin, Hitler, and Me

On September 11, 2001, I left lower Manhattan at 7:00 in the morning to teach in the Bronx. Two hours later, students told me about the terrorist attack on the World Trade Center. I thought first about my family (not about the thousands of other people who might be affected). Three of my daughters were far away. I phoned Elissa, who was on a Brooklyn street corner. My husband, Martin, worked near the towers, but when I left home that morning, he had been dressing for an 8:00 A.M. appointment uptown. I felt relief. When classes were canceled, I felt gratitude for a chance to mark papers.

When I finally got home (having had to walk for miles, with subway and bus service suspended), I learned that Martin had been less than logical. After his appointment, he had taken a taxi to his office. When all traffic stopped, he got out to walk—while thousands of people fled in the other direction. Finally the police made him turn around. He also said that he had tried to give blood but was rejected because two years before he had had surgery for lung cancer.

Martin died 16 months later. The immediate cause was an infection, which quickly became virulent because he was taking massive doses of steroids. His lung cancer had returned, and the drugs helped him breathe. Perhaps the cancer came back partly because of the toxins he had breathed as he walked downtown on 9/11 and for weeks afterward, when the smell of smoke was constantly in our home.

The reason he walked downtown is the same reason I marked papers; we could not comprehend what had occurred; we were experiencing denial. The origin of the lung cancer was 50 years of cigarette smoking. Martin was to blame for that. So was I, since I never got him to quit.

The U.S. military was also at fault, because when Martin was a 17-year-old recruit, the army provided free cigarettes. He accepted that free gift because of a cultural belief: Smoking helped boys think they were men. Even Adolf Hitler might be to blame, because Martin grew up wanting to kill him. Hitler had died before Martin was old enough to join the army, but his boyhood hatred of the German dictator may be one reason he volunteered.

I would like to pinpoint a single target to blame for my husband's death, but a life-span perspective recognizes too many causes: steroids, 9/11, cancer, pollution, his habits, my failure, military policy, machismo, tobacco advertising, Hitler, and more. I am a scientist, but I am not always rational. I am even more anti-tobacco than most other scientists are. Now you know why.

As you remember, denial and blame are early on the list of reactions to death; ideally, people move on to accept the deeper meaning of life and death. It seems that the need to find meaning is crucial to the reaffirmation that follows grief. In some cases, this search starts with preserving memories: Photographs, personal effects, and anecdotes are central to many memorial services.

AP PHOTO / ROBERT F. BUKATY

Shared Grief When Seung-Hui Cho, a disturbed student, killed 32 people and wounded 17 on the campus of Virginia Tech in April 2007, many outsiders looked for something or someone to blame—the university's security arrangements and mental health policies, the state's gun laws, even Korean Americans as a group. Students, preferring to seek meaning rather than blame, gathered to pray, sing, and embrace one another.

Mourners may also be helped by strangers who have experienced a similar loss, especially when friends are unlikely to understand. This explains why there are gatherings of parents of murdered children, of mothers whose adolescents were killed by drunk drivers, of widows of firefighters who died at the World Trade Center, of relatives of passengers who died in the same plane crash, and so on.

Sometimes "meaning becomes grounded in action" to honor the dead (Armour, 2003, p. 538). Organizations devoted to causes such as fighting cancer and banning handguns are supported by people who have lost a loved one to that particular enemy. Often when someone dies, the close family designates a charity and others send contributions in the name of the deceased. One mother carries a bag with the personal effects of her murdered son and shows them, item by item, to groups of young gang members, telling them

> "This is all I had left of my son. A pair of tennis shoes and a pair of underwear that had no blood on them. He loved this little chain he had on. And you see it's broken up, with a shot?" . . . These groups of young kids are sitting there . . . and I tell them exactly about my son. . . . Driving home from that group, I just get warm, like affirmation.
>
> *[quoted in Armour, 2003, p. 532]*

The normal grief reaction is intense and irrational at first but gradually eases, as time, social support, and traditions help with both the initial outpouring of emotion and then with the search for meaning and reaffirmation. The individual may engage in *grief work,* experiencing and expressing strong emotions and then moving toward wholeness, which includes recognizing the larger story of human life and death.

Complicated Grief

In recent times, mourning has become more private, less emotional, and less religious. As a result, new complications in the grieving process have emerged. Emblematic of this change are funeral trends in the United States: Whereas older generations prefer burial after a traditional funeral, younger generations are likely to prefer small memorial services after cremation (Hayslip et al., 1999).

As mourning rituals diminish, many bereavement counselors have noted specific problems that may become pathological. One is **absent grief,** in which a person who is bereaved is not expected, or even allowed, to go through a mourning period. If an aged parent or a close friend dies, a person might not have any rituals or time to grieve. In such a situation, grief is "absent."

absent grief A situation in which overly private people cut themselves off from the community and customs of expected grief; can lead to social isolation.

Since many people now live and work where no one knows about their personal lives, they are cut off from the community and the customs that allow and expect grief. This leads to social isolation, exactly the opposite of what bereaved people need. Absent grief may erupt later in unexpected ways.

For workers or students at large corporations or universities, grief becomes "an unwelcome intrusion (or violent intercession) into the normal efficient running of everyday life" (Anderson, 2001, p. 141). Many counselors fear that, without grief work, absent grief will interfere with the person's life (Rando, 1993).

Modern life also increases the incidence of **disenfranchised grief,** a situation in which certain people, although they are bereaved, are not allowed to mourn publicly (Doka, 2002). Unmarried lovers (of the same or opposite sex) of the deceased, an ex-spouse, the dead person's young children, grandparents, or siblings, and his or her best friends at work may be excluded from seeing the dying person or participating in the aftermath of death. Sometimes only adults of the immediate family (a spouse or parents) are allowed to make decisions about the funeral, disposing of the body, and so on.

disenfranchised grief A situation in which certain people, although they are bereaved, are not allowed to mourn publicly.

Another problem is **incomplete grief.** Murders and suicides often trigger police investigations and press reports, which interfere with the grief process. An autopsy complicates grieving for those who believe that the body will rise again or that the soul does not leave the body immediately. Death without a body impedes mourning and hence halts reaffirmation, as for relatives of soldiers who are reported to be missing in action.

incomplete grief A situation in which circumstances, such as a police investigation or an autopsy, interfere with the process of grieving.

Sometimes events interrupt the responses of the community. The bereaved need attention to their particular loss, and the grief process may be incomplete if mourning is cut short. When death occurs on a major holiday, after another death or disaster, or during wartime, it is harder for the survivors to grieve.

AP PHOTO / JOHN MOORE

Empty Boots The body of a young army corporal killed near Baghdad has been shipped home to his family in Mississippi for a funeral and burial, but his fellow soldiers in Iraq also need to express their grief. The custom is to hold an informal memorial service, placing the dead solder's boots, helmet, and rifle in the middle of a circle of mourners, who weep, pray, and reminisce.

One widow whose husband died of cancer on September 10, 2001, complained, "People who attended the funeral talked only about the [terrorist] attack [of September 11], and my husband wasn't given the respect he deserved" (quoted in Schachter, 2003, p. 20). Although she was expressing concern for her husband's memory, it is apparent that this woman was also upset because she herself did not get the sympathy she needed.

Diversity of Reactions

Bereaved people depend on the customs and attitudes of their culture to guide them through their irrational thoughts (remember Joan Didion's "magical thinking") and personal grief. The particulars depend on the specific culture. For example, mourners who, four months after a loved one's death, still kept the dead person's possessions, talked to the deceased, and frequently reviewed memories are, at 18 months after the death, notably *less* well adjusted if they are in the United States but notably *better* adjusted if they are in China (Lalande & Bonanno, 2006).

Childhood experiences also affect bereavement. A person whose parents died when he or she was younger than 18 is more vulnerable to adult losses. Attachment history may be important (Hansson & Stroebe, 2007). Older adults who were securely attached may be more likely to experience normal grief; those who were resistant may have absent grief; and those who were anxious may become stuck, unable to find meaning in the living and dying of someone they love, and thus may be unable to reaffirm their own lives.

Research on Grief

Reaffirmation of life does not necessarily mean forgetting the person, because many *continuing bonds* are evident years after death. There is a

> lack of empirical support for the presumed necessity of working through loss [which] has prompted a reversal of the historical trend in bereavement theory; moving away from the traditional focus on severing the attachment bond.
>
> *[Field & Friedrichs, 2006]*

As this quotation implies, bereavement theory once held that everyone should do grief work and then move on, realizing that the person was gone forever. If this did not happen, pathological grief could result, with the person either not grieving enough (absent grief) or grieving too long (incomplete grief). Current research finds a much wider variety of reactions.

It is easy to see why some earlier studies overestimated the frequency of pathological grief. For obvious reasons, scientists often began their research on mourning with mourners—that is, with people who had recently experienced the death of a loved one. Further, they often studied people who needed to express their absent grief; who felt disenfranchised; who were overcome by unremitting sadness many months after the loss; or who could not find meaning in a violent, sudden, unexpected death.

Such mourners are *not* typical. Almost everyone experiences several deaths over their lifetime, of parents and grandparents, of a spouse or close friend. Most feel sadness at first but then resume their customary activities, functioning as well a few months later as they had before.

This was evident in a longitudinal study that began by interviewing and assessing married older adults who lived in greater Detroit. Over several years, 319 became widows or widowers. Most (205) were reinterviewed at 6 and 18 months after the death (Bonanno et al., 2004; see Research Design). Some (92) were seen again three years later, or 4½ years after the death (Boerner et al., 2005).

General trends were evident: Almost all the widows and widowers idealized their marriages, remembering them as better than when they had assessed them while their spouse was still living. With time, most thought less about their dead spouse.

Reactions to the spouse's death varied but can be clustered into five categories:

- 11 percent experienced normal grief, with increased depression for 6 months after the death but recovery at 18 months.
- 11 percent were slow to recover, not approaching pre-loss levels until four years after the death.
- 50 percent were resilient. They may have been grief-stricken at first, but by 6 months they were about as happy and productive as when their spouse was alive.
- 18 percent were *less* depressed after the death than before, perhaps because they had been caregivers for their seriously ill partners.
- 10 percent were depressed at every assessment after the loss, but they also had been depressed while they were married. If this study had begun only after the death, one might conclude that the loss caused the depression. However, because of the pre-loss assessment, it can more legitimately be claimed that these individuals were chronically depressed, not stuck in grief.

Research Design

Scientists: George Bonanno and colleagues.

Publication: Reported in many journals, including *Psychology and Aging* (2004).

Participants: Out of a group of 1,522 married participants (English-speaking, from Detroit, with the husband age 65 or older), this study included the 205 individuals whose spouse later died and who were reinterviewed at 6 and 18 months after the death, and 92 of whom were interviewed again 3 years after that.

Design: Interviews and questionnaires, including a standard measure of depression and responses to questions such as "During the past month, how often have you had thoughts or memories of your husband/wife?"

Major conclusion: Many people cope quite well with the death of a spouse. A majority "appeared to make an excellent adjustment" (p. 269).

Comment: These encouraging results of a large, prospective, longitudinal study add to several smaller studies that find that pathological and delayed grief are not typical, nor is grief work necessary. However, the specifics may be limited. The participants were English-speaking, living in Michigan, and many did not complete three follow-up interviews. Some dropouts had died, but others may have been too depressed or stuck in grief.

Practical Applications

Could this research help someone who is grieving or suggest what friends can do to help? The first step is simply to be aware that powerful, complicated, and unexpected emotions are likely: A friend should listen and sympathize, never implying that the person is too grief-stricken or not grief-stricken enough.

The bereaved person *might or might not* want to visit the grave, light a candle, cherish a memento, pray, or sob. Those who have been taught to bear grief stoically may be doubly distressed if they are advised to cry and cannot. Those whose cultures expect loud wailing may become confused and resentful if they are told to hush.

Even so-called absent grief—in which the bereaved refuses to do any of these things—might be appropriate. In contrast, some people may want to talk about their loss, especially to assess blame and find meaning. If such emotions can find expression in action—joining a bereavement group, protesting some government policy, walking, running, or biking to raise money for some cause—that may help.

Remember the 7-year-old whose grandparents, uncle, and dog died? The boy wrote a memorial poem only for the dog, and his parents framed the poem and hung it in the living room. A wide variety of reactions to death are normal. No specific emotion or timetable is required (Kaufman & Kaufman, 2006).

No matter what rituals are followed or what pattern is evident in human reactions to death, the result may give the living a deeper appreciation of themselves as well as of the value of human relationships. In fact, a theme frequently sounded by those who work with the dying and the bereaved is that the lessons of death may lead to a greater appreciation of life, especially of the value of intimate, caring relationships.

Especially for Educators How might a teacher help a young child cope with death?

It is fitting to end this chapter, and this book, with a reminder of the creative work of loving. As first described in Chapter 1, the study of human development is a science, with topics to be researched, understood, and explained. But the process of living is an art as well as a science, with strands of love and sorrow and resilience woven into each person's unique tapestry. Dying, when accepted; death,

➤Response for Educators (from page Ep-23): Death has varied meanings, so a teacher needs to take care not to contradict the child's cultural background. In general, however, specific expressions of mourning are useful, and acting as if the death did not happen is destructive.

when it leads to hope; grief, when it is allowed expression; and mourning, when it fosters reaffirmation—all give added meaning to birth, growth, development, and human relationships.

SUMMING UP

Rituals help the bereaved come to terms with both mourning (the public process) and grief (the private emotion). Grief is not necessarily rational or predictable. Each person's childhood, recent experiences, and personality affect the experience of grief. Modern lifestyles have added to the complications of grief, as close relationships are not always family ones, yet family members usually make decisions regarding dying and mourning. Unlike traditional communities, in which everyone knew who died and who was grieving, modern societies do not recognize mourners. Further, reactions to death are varied; outsiders must be especially responsive to whatever needs a grieving person may have. ■

SUMMARY

Death and Hope

1. Death has various meanings, depending partly on the age of the person involved, whether that person is dying or mourning. For example, children are more concerned about being separated from those they see every day; older adults are hopeful that their values and contributions will live on.

2. Each of the many religions of the world has rituals and beliefs regarding death. Although there are many variations, all religions affirm that individual lives and deaths have an enduring significance.

Dying and Acceptance

3. People who are dying need to be treated with honestly and respect. Their emotions may change over time; for example, they may move from denial to acceptance of impending death.

4. A hospice is a place where the needs of fatally ill people and their families are met. Some people prefer to die at home, and in those cases a hospice professional can help the patient's family and friends care for him or her and can allow everyone to cope emotionally with the impending death.

5. Palliative care, particularly care that relieves pain, has become part of modern hospitals as well as hospices. Such care makes a good death much more possible.

6. The range of medical measures is vast, and doctors as well as patients have varied opinions about their use. A living will and a health care proxy can help to clarify what steps should be taken when the need arises.

7. Whether or not passive or active euthanasia or physician-assisted suicide is legal is controversial. At the moment, such deaths occur everywhere but are legal in only two jurisdictions, the Netherlands and the U.S. state of Oregon.

8. One of the problems in dying is deciding when a person is dead. The definition used to be that death occurred when the brain waves stopped. A person in a "persistent vegetative state" is dead in every function, but people disagree over whether life support should continue in that case.

Bereavement

9. Grief may be irrational and complicated. Many bereavement counselors believe that absent or disenfranchised grief will eventually take a psychic toll on those who have lost a loved one.

10. Mourning rituals are cultural or religious expressions which aid survivors and the entire community. Variations in grief and mourning are so great that it now seems that there is no single best way to cope with death.

KEY TERMS

thanatology (p. Ep-1)
near-death experience (p. Ep-9)
good death (p. Ep-10)
hospice (p. Ep-12)
palliative care (p. Ep-13)
double effect (p. Ep-13)
passive euthanasia (p. Ep-13)
DNR (do not resuscitate) (p. Ep-13)
active euthanasia (p. Ep-14)
physician-assisted suicide (p. Ep-14)
slippery slope (p. Ep-15)
living will (p. Ep-16)
health care proxy (p. Ep-16)
bereavement (p. Ep-18)
grief (p. Ep-18)
mourning (p. Ep-18)
absent grief (p. Ep-21)
disenfranchised grief (p. Ep-21)
incomplete grief (p. Ep-21)

KEY QUESTIONS

1. How is a contemporary death different from a death a century ago?

2. How do dying people tend to feel about family members?

3. What is the goal of a holy death in Buddhism, Hinduism, and Islam?

4. What are the similarities and differences in death rituals of Jews and Christians?

5. How does a near-death experience relate to developmental science?

6. Why did Kübler-Ross initially have trouble interviewing dying people?

7. Why do many people *not* die in hospice care?

8. What is the difference between passive and active euthanasia?

9. Why do relatively few people in Oregon die via physician-assisted suicide?

10. What are the differences among bereavement, grief, and mourning? Give examples of each.

APPLICATIONS

1. Death is sometimes said to be hidden, even taboo. Ask 10 people if they have ever been with someone who was dying. Note not only the yes and no answers, but also the details and reactions. For instance, how many of the deaths occurred in the hospital, how many at home?

2. Find quotes about death in *Bartlett's Familiar Quotations* or a similar collection. Do you see any historical or cultural patterns of acceptance, denial, or fear?

3. Every aspect of dying is controversial in modern society. Do an Internet search for a key term such as *euthanasia* or *grief*. Analyze the information and the underlying assumptions. What is your opinion, and why?

4. People of varying ages have different attitudes toward death. Ask at least three people (ideally one teenager, one adult under 60, and one older person) what thoughts they have about their own death. What differences do you find?

Appendix A

Supplemental Charts, Graphs, and Tables

Often, examining specific data is useful, even fascinating, to developmental researchers. The particular numbers reveal trends and nuances not apparent from a more general view. For instance, many people mistakenly believe that the incidence of Down syndrome babies rises sharply for mothers over 35, or that even the tiniest newborns usually survive. Each chart, graph, or table in this appendix contains information not generally known.

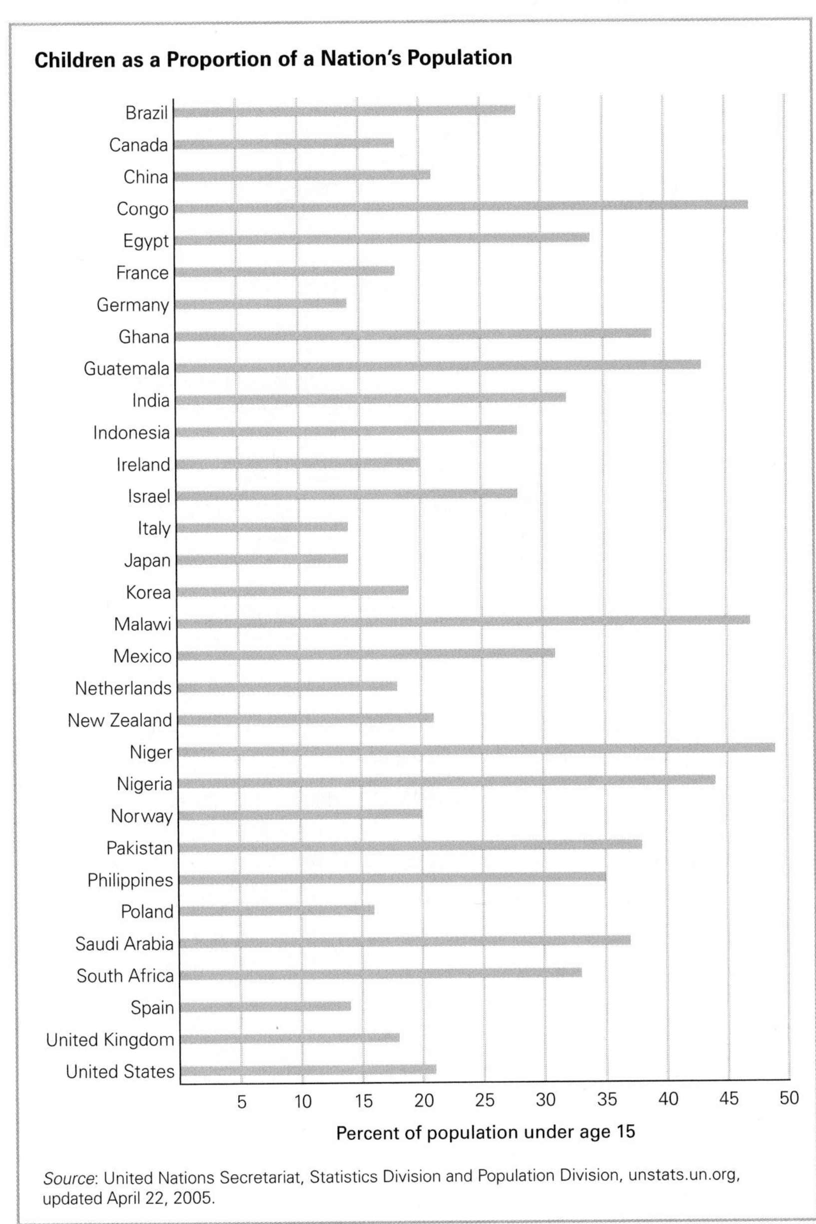

Source: United Nations Secretariat, Statistics Division and Population Division, unstats.un.org, updated April 22, 2005.

More Children, Worse Schools? (Chapter 1)

Nations that have high birth rates also have high death rates, short life spans, and more illiteracy. A systems approach suggests that these variables are connected: For example, the Montessori and Reggio Emilia early-childhood education programs, said to be the best in the world, originated in Italy, and Italy has the lowest proportion of children under 15.

Ethnic Composition of the U.S. Population (Chapter 2)

Thinking about the ethnic makeup of the U.S. population can be an interesting exercise in social comparison. If you look only at the table, you will conclude that not much has changed over the past 30 years: Whites are still the majority, Native Americans are still a tiny minority, and African Americans are still about 12 percent of the population. However, if you look at the chart, you can see why every group feels that much has changed. Because the proportions of Hispanic Americans and Asian Americans have increased dramatically, European Americans see the current non-white population at almost one-third of the total, and African Americans see that Hispanics now outnumber them. There are also interesting regional differences within the United States; for example, Los Angeles County has the largest number of Native Americans (156,000) and the largest number of Asians (1.3 million).

Observation Quiz (see answer, page A-4): Which ethnic group is growing most rapidly?

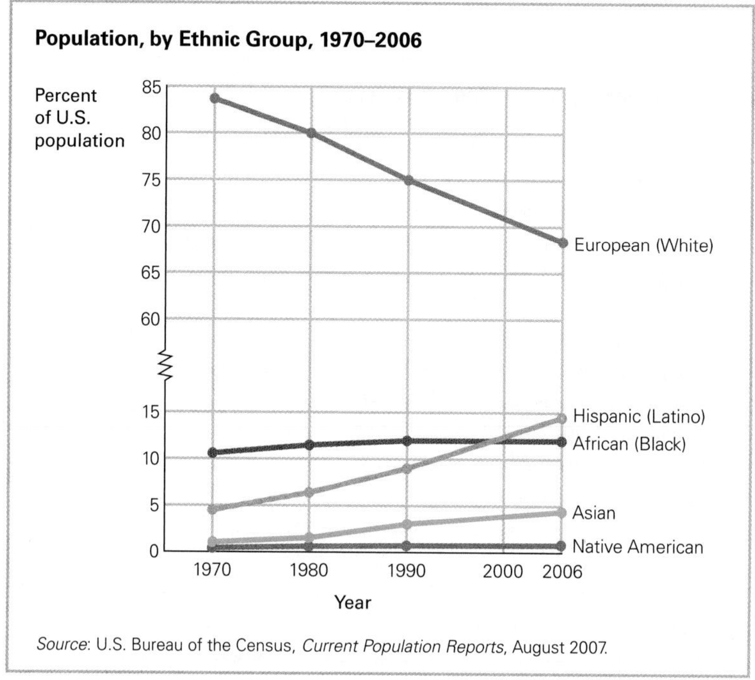

Source: U.S. Bureau of the Census, *Current Population Reports*, August 2007.

	Percent of U.S. population			
Ethnic origin	1970	1980	1990	2006
European (White)	83.7	80	75	68.4
African (Black)	10.6	11.5	12	12
Hispanic (Latino)	4.5	6.4	9	14.5
Asian	1.0	1.5	3	4.3
Native American	.4	.6	.7	0.82

The Genetics of Blood Types (Chapter 3)

Blood types A and B are dominant traits, and type O is recessive. The percentages given in the first column of this chart represent the odds that a child born to the parents with the various combinations of genotypes will have the genotype given in the second column.

Genotypes of Parents*	Genotype of Offspring	Phenotype	Can Donate Blood to (Phenotype)	Can Receive Blood from (Phenotype)
AA + AA (100%) AA + AB (50%) AA + AO (50%) AB + AB (25%) AB + AO (25%) AO + AO (25%)	AA (inherits one A from each parent)	A	A or AB	A or O
AA + OO (100%) AB + OO (50%) AO + AO (50%) AO + OO (50%) AB + AO (25%) AB + BO (25%)	AO	A	A or AB	A or O
BB + BB (100%) AB + BB (50%) BB + BO (50%) AB + AB (25%) AB + BO (25%) BO + BO (25%)	BB	B	B or AB	B or O
BB + OO (100%) AB + OO (50%) BO + BO (50%) BO + OO (50%) AB + AO (25%) AB + BO (25%)	BO	B	B or AB	B or O
AA + BB (100%) AA + AB (50%) AA + BO (50%) AB + AB (50%) AB + BB (50%) AO + BB (50%) AB + BO (25%) AO + BO (25%)	AB	AB	AB only	A, B, AB, O ("universal recipient")
OO + OO (100%) AO + OO (50%) BO + OO (50%) AO + AO (25%) AO + BO (25%) BO + BO (25%)	OO	O	A, B, AB, O ("universal donor")	O only

*Blood type is not a sex-linked trait, so any of these pairs can be either mother-plus-father or father-plus-mother.
Source: Adapted from Hartl & Jones, 1999.

Odds of Down Syndrome by Maternal Age and Gestational Age (Chapter 4)

The odds of any given fetus, at the end of the first trimester, having three chromosomes at the 21st site (trisomy 21) and thus having Down syndrome is shown in the 10-weeks column. Every year of maternal age increases the incidence of trisomy 21. The number of Down syndrome infants born alive is only half the number who survived the first trimester. Although obviously the least risk is at age 20 (younger is even better), there is no year when the odds suddenly increase (age 35 is an arbitrary cut-off). Even at age 44, less than 4 percent of all newborns have Down syndrome. Other chromosomal abnormalities in fetuses also increase with mother's age, but the rate of spontaneous abortion is much higher, so births of babies with chromosomal defects is not the norm, even for women over age 45.

Age (yrs)	Gestation (weeks) 10	35	Live Births
20	1/804	1/1,464	1/1,527
21	1/793	1/1,445	1/1,507
22	1/780	1/1,421	1/1,482
23	1/762	1/1,389	1/1,448
24	1/740	1/1,348	1/1,406
25	1/712	1/1,297	1/1,352
26	1/677	1/1,233	1/1,286
27	1/635	1/1,157	1/1,206
28	1/586	1/1,068	1/1,113
29	1/531	1/967	1/1,008
30	1/471	1/858	1/895
31	1/409	1/745	1/776
32	1/347	1/632	1/659
33	1/288	1/525	1/547
34	1/235	1/427	1/446
35	1/187	1/342	1/356
36	1/148	1/269	1/280
37	1/115	1/209	1/218
38	1/88	1/160	1/167
39	1/67	1/122	1/128
40	1/51	1/93	1/97
41	1/38	1/70	1/73
42	1/29	1/52	1/55
43	1/21	1/39	1/41
44	1/16	1/29	1/30

Source: Snijders & Nicolaides, 1996.

Saving Young Lives: Childhood and Adolescent Immunizations (Chapter 5)

Recommended Childhood and Adolescent Immunization Schedule, United States, 2005

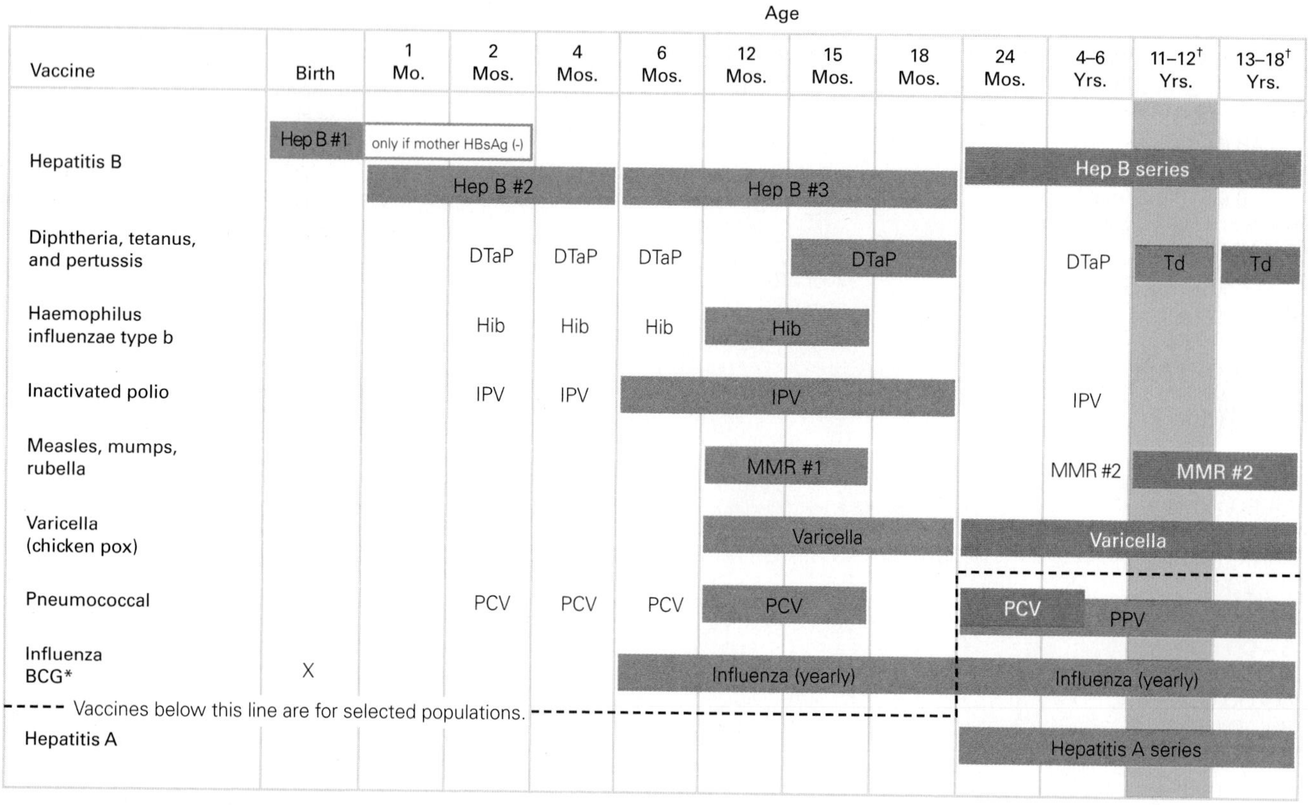

Vaccine	Age: Birth	1 Mo.	2 Mos.	4 Mos.	6 Mos.	12 Mos.	15 Mos.	18 Mos.	24 Mos.	4–6 Yrs.	11–12† Yrs.	13–18† Yrs.
Hepatitis B	Hep B #1	only if mother HBsAg (-)							Hep B series			
		Hep B #2			Hep B #3							
Diphtheria, tetanus, and pertussis			DTaP	DTaP	DTaP		DTaP			DTaP	Td	Td
Haemophilus influenzae type b			Hib	Hib	Hib	Hib						
Inactivated polio			IPV	IPV	IPV					IPV		
Measles, mumps, rubella						MMR #1				MMR #2	MMR #2	
Varicella (chicken pox)						Varicella			Varicella			
Pneumococcal			PCV	PCV	PCV	PCV			PCV	PPV		
Influenza					Influenza (yearly)				Influenza (yearly)			
BCG*	X											
- - - - Vaccines below this line are for selected populations. - - - -												
Hepatitis A									Hepatitis A series			

■ Range of recommended ages for vaccination
■ Catch-up immunization—age groups that warrant special effort to administer those vaccines not given previously
■ Preadolescent assessment

Note: For many diseases, repeated doses are recommended, as shown.
†See HPV, in Adult Immunizations table that follows.
*BCG vaccine is highly recommended in most nations, but is not required in the United States because the prevalence of tuberculosis is low.

Source: CDC Web site (http://cdc.gov/nip/recs/child-schedule), accessed July 24, 2007.

Adult Immunizations (Chapter 5)

Vaccine	Recommended Immunization Schedule
Tetanus, diphtheria, pertussis	Dtap: Before age 65—Dtap every 10 years. Adults older than 65—1 dose Td booster every 10 years.
Human papillomavirus (HPV)	Females age 9–26 (before any sexual activity)
Influenza	Before age 50—recommended if some other risk factor is present. Adults older than 50—every year.
Pneumococcal	Before age 65—recommended if some other risk factor is present. Adults older than 65—every year.
Meningococcal	Recommended if other risk factor is present.

➤Answer to Observation Quiz (from page A-2): Asian Americans, whose share of the U.S. population has quadrupled in the past 30 years. Latinos are increasing most rapidly in numbers, but not in proportion.

First Sounds and First Words: Similarities Among Many Languages (Chapter 6)

Language	Baby's word for: Mother	Father
English	mama, mommy	dada, daddy
Spanish	mama	papa
French	maman, mama	papa
Italian	mamma	babbo, papa
Latvian	mama	te-te
Syrian Arabic	mama	baba
Bantu	ba-mama	taata
Swahili	mama	baba
Sanskrit	nana	tata
Hebrew	ema	abba
Korean	oma	apa

Which Mothers Breast-feed? (Chapter 7)

Differentiating excellent from destructive mothering is not easy, once the child's basic needs for food and protection are met. However, as the Jacob example in Chapter 7 makes clear, psychosocial development depends on responsive parent–infant relationships. Breast-feeding is one sign of intimacy between mother and infant.

Regions of the world differ dramatically in rates of breast-feeding, with the highest worldwide in Southeast Asia, where half of all 2-year-olds are still breast-fed. In the United States, factors that affect the likelihood of breast-feeding are ethnicity, maternal age, and education.

Breast-feeding Rates by Socio-demographic Factors, 2005

Socio-demographic factors	Ever breast-feeding	Breast-feeding at 6 months	Breast-feeding at 12 months	Exclusive breast-feeding* at 3 months	Exclusive breast-feeding* at 6 months
U.S. National	72.9%	39.1%	20.1%	38.7%	13.9%
Sex of baby					
Male	72.7	38.7	19.6	38.2	13.6
Female	73.2	39.5	20.5	39.3	14.2
Birth order					
First born	74.0	36.6	17.7	36.4	12.3
Not first born	72.1	41.2	22.1	40.7	15.2
Ethnicity					
Native American	67.3	33.7	16.7	30.7	11.3
Asian or Pacific islander	81.4	47.5	24.5	43.1	18.1
Hispanic or Latino	79.0	42.0	22.0	43.9	14.1
African American (non-Hispanic)	55.4	24.8	11.9	26.8	9.2
European (non-Hispanic)	74.1	41.1	21.0	39.3	14.7
Mother's age					
Less than 20	50.0	14.8	5.4	17.5	6.7
20–30	68.4	31.7	15.8	32.8	10.1
More than 30	77.7	46.2	24.2	44.6	17.3
Mother's education					
Less than high school	63.6	32.2	17.9	33.6	12.3
High school	64.8	29.3	14.9	30.6	10.2
Some college	76.8	39.3	19.5	39.5	13.3
College graduate	84.5	52.5	26.6	49.3	18.6
Mother's marital status					
Married	78.4	45.2	23.7	43.7	16.1
Unmarried†	60.3	25.0	11.6	27.2	8.8
Residence					
Central city	74.2	41.0	21.9	40.2	15.1
Urban	74.8	40.7	20.2	40.3	13.9
Suburban and rural	64.9	30.0	14.8	30.6	10.8

*Exclusive breast-feeding is defined in this 2005 study as only breast milk—no solids, no water, and no other liquids.
†Unmarried includes never married, widowed, separated, and divorced.
Source: Adapted from CDC's National Immunization Survey, Table 1: http://www.cdc.gov/breastfeeding/data/NIX_data/socio-demographic.htm, accessed July 24, 2007.

Height Gains from Birth to Age 18 (Chapter 8)

The range of height (on this page) and weight (see page A-7) of children in the United States. The columns labeled "50th" (the fiftieth percentile) show the average; the columns labeled "90th" (the ninetieth percentile) show the size of children taller and heavier than 90 percent of their contemporaries; and the columns labeled "10th" (the tenth percentile) show the size of children who are taller than only 10 percent of their peers. Note that girls are slightly shorter, on average, than boys.

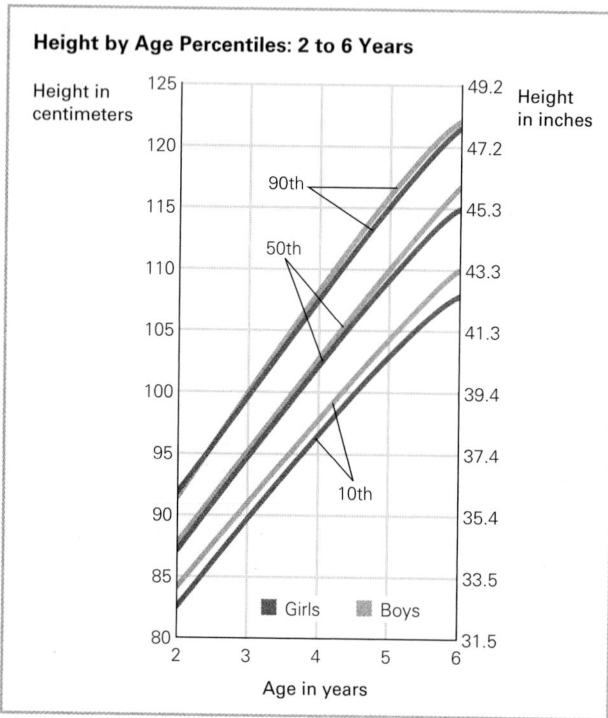

Same Data, Different Form

The columns of numbers in the table at the right provide detailed and precise information about height ranges for every year of childhood. The illustration above shows the same information in graphic form for ages 2–6. The same is done for weight ranges on page A-7. Ages 2–6 are singled out because that is the period during which a child's eating habits are set. Which form of data presentation do you think is easier to understand?

Length in Centimeters (and Inches)

	Boys: percentiles			Girls: percentiles		
AGE	10th	50th	90th	10th	50th	90th
Birth	47.5 (18¾)	50.5 (20)	53.5 (21)	46.5 (18¼)	49.9 (19¾)	52.0 (20½)
1 month	51.3 (20¼)	54.6 (21½)	57.7 (22¾)	50.2 (19¾)	53.5 (21)	56.1 (22)
3 months	57.7 (22¾)	61.1 (24)	64.5 (25½)	56.2 (22¼)	59.5 (23½)	62.7 (24¾)
6 months	64.4 (25¼)	67.8 (26¾)	71.3 (28)	62.6 (24¾)	65.9 (26)	69.4 (27¼)
9 months	69.1 (27¼)	72.3 (28½)	75.9 (30)	67.0 (26½)	70.4 (27¾)	74.0 (29¼)
12 months	72.8 (28¾)	76.1 (30)	79.8 (31½)	70.8 (27¾)	74.3 (29¼)	78.0 (30¾)
18 months	78.7 (31)	82.4 (32½)	86.6 (34)	77.2 (30½)	80.9 (31¾)	85.0 (33½)
24 months	83.5 (32¾)	87.6 (34½)	92.2 (36¼)	82.5 (32½)	86.5 (34)	90.8 (35¾)
3 years	90.3 (35½)	94.9 (37¼)	100.1 (39½)	89.3 (35¼)	94.1 (37)	99.0 (39)
4 years	97.3 (38¼)	102.9 (40½)	108.2 (42½)	96.4 (38)	101.6 (40)	106.6 (42)
5 years	103.7 (40¾)	109.9 (43¼)	115.4 (45½)	102.7 (40½)	108.4 (42¾)	113.8 (44¾)
6 years	109.6 (43¼)	116.1 (45¾)	121.9 (48)	108.4 (42¾)	114.6 (45)	120.8 (47½)
7 years	115.0 (45¼)	121.7 (48)	127.9 (50¼)	113.6 (44¾)	120.6 (47½)	127.6 (50¼)
8 years	120.2 (47¼)	127.0 (50)	133.6 (52½)	118.7 (46¾)	126.4 (49¾)	134.2 (52¾)
9 years	125.2 (49¼)	132.2 (52)	139.4 (55)	123.9 (48¾)	132.2 (52)	140.7 (55½)
10 years	130.1 (51¼)	137.5 (54¼)	145.5 (57¼)	129.5 (51)	138.3 (54½)	147.2 (58)
11 years	135.1 (53¼)	143.33 (56½)	152.1 (60)	135.6 (53½)	144.8 (57)	153.7 (60½)
12 years	140.3 (55¼)	149.7 (59)	159.4 (62¾)	142.3 (56)	151.5 (59¾)	160.0 (63)
13 years	145.8 (57½)	156.5 (61½)	167.0 (65¾)	148.0 (58¼)	157.1 (61¾)	165.3 (65)
14 years	151.8 (59¾)	63.1 (64¼)	173.8 (68½)	151.5 (59¾)	160.4 (63¼)	168.7 (66½)
15 years	158.2 (62¼)	169.0 (66½)	178.9 (70½)	153.2 (60¼)	161.8 (63¾)	170.5 (67¼)
16 years	163.9 (64½)	173.5 (68¼)	182.4 (71¾)	154.1 (60¾)	162.4 (64)	171.1 (67¼)
17 years	167.7 (66)	176.2 (69¼)	184.4 (72½)	155.1 (61)	163.1 (64¼)	171.2 (67½)
18 years	168.7 (66½)	176.8 (69½)	185.3 (73)	156.0 (61½)	163.7 (64½)	171.0 (67¼)

Source: These data are those of the National Center for Health Statistics (NCHS), Health Resources Administration, DHHS. They were based on studies of The Fels Research Institute, Yellow Springs, Ohio. These data were first made available with the help of William M. Moore, M.D., of Ross Laboratories, who supplied the conversion from metric measurements to approximate inches and pounds. This help is gratefully acknowledged.

Weight Gains from Birth to Age 18 (Chapter 8)

These height and weight charts present rough guidelines; a child might differ from these norms and be quite healthy and normal. However, if a particular child shows a discrepancy between height and weight (for instance, at the 90th percentile in height but only the 20th percentile in weight) or is much larger or smaller than most children the same age, a pediatrician should see if disease, malnutrition, or genetic abnormality is part of the reason.

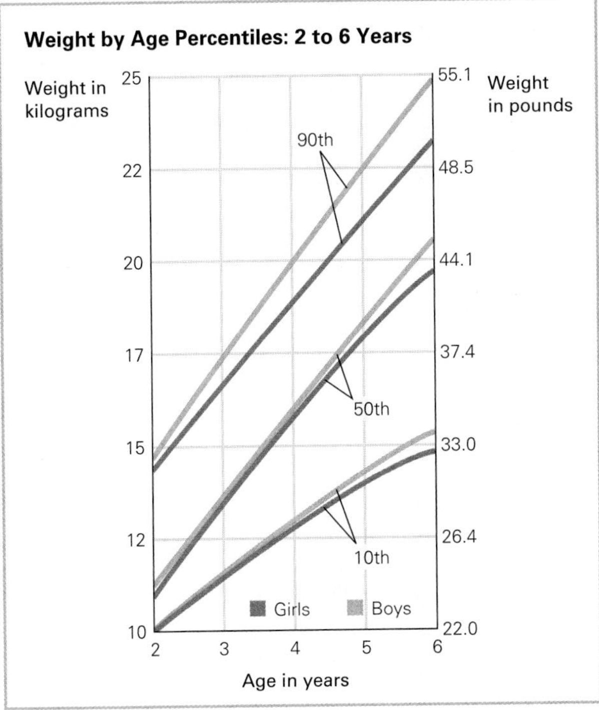

Weight in Kilograms (and Pounds)						
	Boys: percentiles			Girls: percentiles		
AGE	10th	50th	90th	10th	50th	90th
Birth	2.78 (6¼)	3.27 (7¼)	3.82 (8½)	2.58 (5¾)	3.23 (7)	3.64 (8)
1 month	3.43 (7½)	4.29 (9½)	5.14 (11¼)	3.22 (7)	3.98 (8¾)	4.65 (10¼)
3 months	4.78 (10½)	5.98 (13¼)	7.14 (15¾)	4.47 (9¾)	5.40 (12)	6.39 (14)
6 months	6.61 (14½)	7.85 (17¼)	9.10 (20)	6.12 (13½)	7.21 (16)	8.38 (18½)
9 months	7.95 (17½)	9.18 (20¼)	10.49 (23¼)	7.34 (16¼)	8.56 (18¾)	9.83 (21¾)
12 months	8.84 (19½)	10.15 (22½)	11.54 (25½)	8.19 (18)	9.53 (21)	10.87 (24)
18 months	9.92 (21¾)	11.47 (25¼)	13.05 (28¾)	9.30 (20½)	10.82 (23¾)	12.30 (27)
24 months	10.85 (24)	12.59 (27¾)	14.29 (31½)	10.26 (22½)	11.90 (26¼)	13.57 (30)
3 years	12.58 (27¾)	14.62 (32¼)	16.95 (37¼)	12.26 (27)	14.10 (31)	16.54 (36½)
4 years	14.24 (31½)	16.69 (36¾)	19.32 (42½)	13.84 (30½)	15.96 (35¼)	18.93 (41¾)
5 years	15.96 (35¼)	18.67 (41¼)	21.70 (47¾)	15.26 (33¾)	17.66 (39)	21.23 (46¾)
6 years	17.72 (39)	20.69 (45½)	24.31 (53½)	16.72 (36¾)	19.52 (43)	23.89 (52¾)
7 years	19.53 (43)	22.85 (50¼)	27.36 (60¼)	18.39 (40½)	21.84 (48¼)	27.39 (60½)
8 years	21.39 (47¼)	25.30 (55¾)	31.06 (68½)	20.45 (45)	24.84 (54¾)	32.04 (70¾)
9 years	23.33 (51½)	28.13 (62)	35.57 (78½)	22.92 (50½)	28.46 (62¾)	37.60 (83)
10 years	25.52 (56¼)	31.44 (69¼)	40.80 (90)	25.76 (56¾)	32.55 (71¾)	43.70 (96¼)
11 years	28.17 (62)	35.30 (77¾)	46.57 (102¾)	28.97 (63¾)	36.95 (81½)	49.96 (110¼)
12 years	31.46 (69¼)	39.78 (87¾)	52.73 (116¼)	32.53 (71¼)	41.53 (91½)	55.99 (123½)
13 years	35.60 (78½)	44.95 (99)	59.12 (130¼)	36.35 (80¼)	46.10 (101¾)	61.45 (135½)
14 years	40.64 (89½)	50.77 (112)	65.57 (144½)	40.11 (88½)	50.28 (110¾)	66.04 (145½)
15 years	46.06 (101½)	56.71 (125)	71.91 (158½)	43.38 (95¾)	53.68 (118¼)	69.64 (153¼)
16 years	51.16 (112¾)	62.10 (137)	77.97 (172)	45.78 (101)	55.89 (123¼)	71.68 (158)
17 years	55.28 (121¾)	66.31 (146¼)	83.58 (184¼)	47.04 (103¾)	56.69 (125)	72.38 (159½)
18 years	57.89 (127½)	68.88 (151¾)	88.41 (195)	47.47 (104¾)	56.62 (124¾)	72.25 (159¼)

Source: Data are those of the National Center for Health Statistics, Health Resources Administration, DHHS, collected in its Health Examination Surveys.

Comparisons

Notice that the height trajectories for boys and girls on page A-6 are much closer together than the weight trajectories shown above. By age 18, the height range amounts to only about 6 inches, but there is a difference of about 65 pounds between the 10th and the 90th percentiles.

Critical Thinking Question (see answer, page A-8): How can this discrepancy between height and weight ranges be explained?

Day Care and Family Income (Chapter 9)

Note that, in both years, the wealthier families were less likely to have children exclusively in parental care and more likely to have children in center-based care.

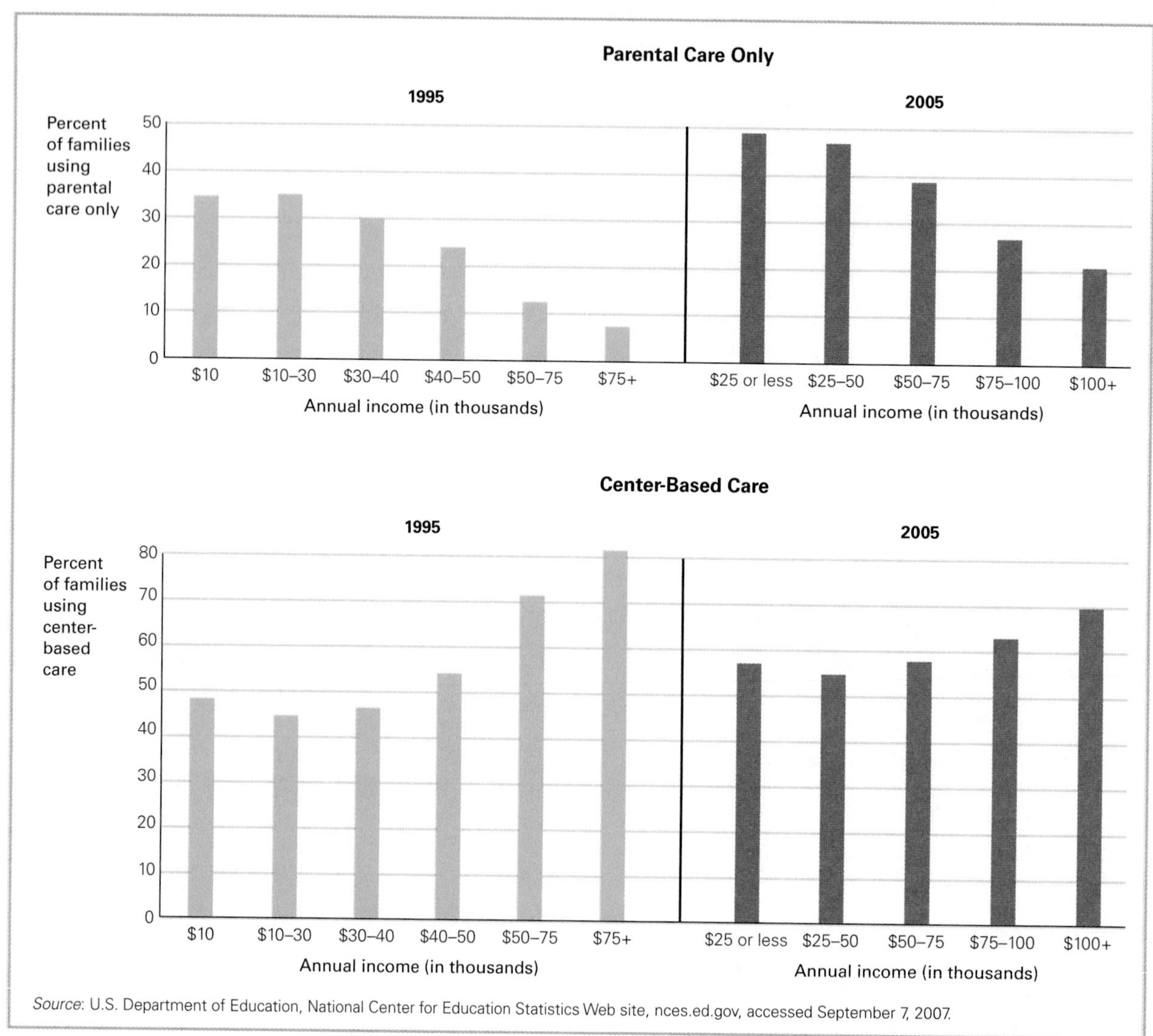

Source: U.S. Department of Education, National Center for Education Statistics Web site, nces.ed.gov, accessed September 7, 2007.

➤Answer to Critical Thinking Question (from page A-7): Nutrition is generally adequate in the United States, and that is why height differences are small. But as a result of the strong influence that family and culture have on eating habits, almost half of all North Americans are overweight or obese.

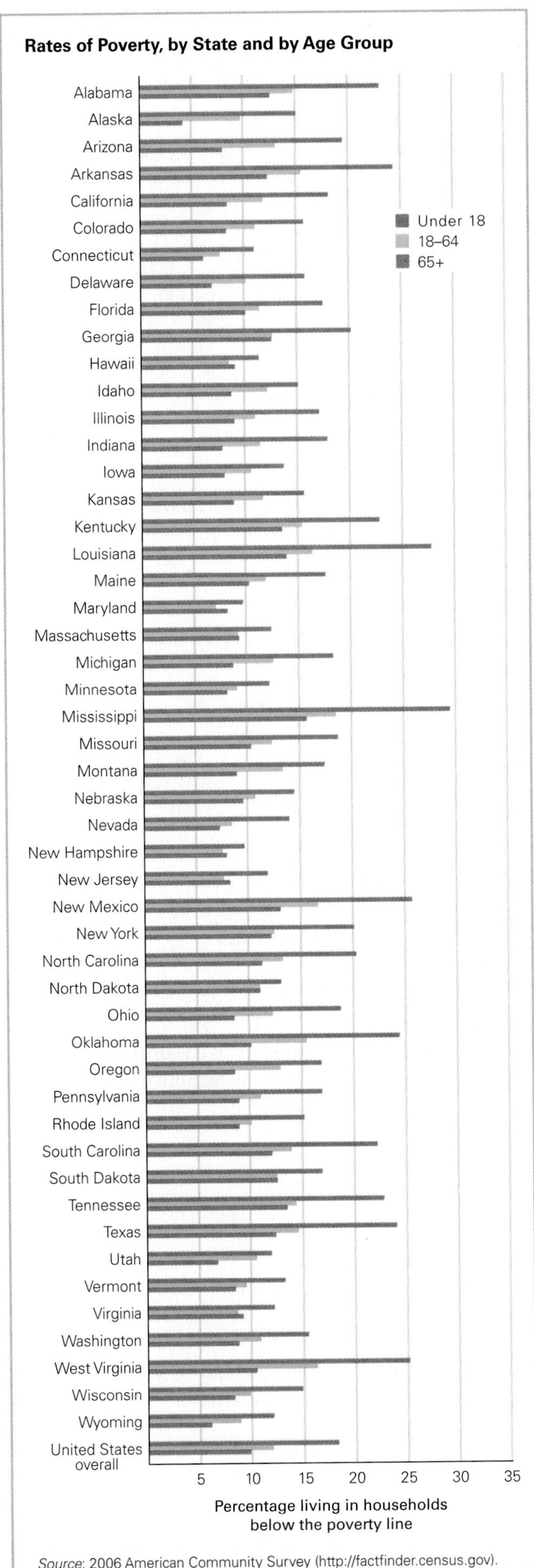

Source: 2006 American Community Survey (http://factfinder.census.gov).

Children Are the Poorest Americans (Chapter 10)

It probably comes as no surprise that the rate of poverty is twice as high in some states as in others. What is surprising is how much the rates vary between age groups within the same state.

Observation Quiz (see answer, page A-10): In which nine states is the proportion of poor children more than twice as high as the proportion of poor people over age 65?

➤Answer to Observation Quiz (from page A-9): Alaska, Arizona, California, Delaware, Indiana, Michigan, Oklahoma, West Virginia, and Wisconsin.

DSM-IV-TR Criteria for Attention-Deficit/Hyperactivity Disorder (ADHD), Conduct Disorder (CD), Oppositional Defiant Disorder (ODD), Autistic Disorder, and Asperger's Disorder (Chapter 11)

The specific symptoms for these various disorders overlap. Many other childhood disorders also have some of the same symptoms. Differentiating one problem from another is the main purpose of DSM-IV-TR. That is no easy task, which is one reason the book is now in its fourth major revision and is more than 900 pages long. Those pages include not only the type of diagnostic criteria shown here but also discussions of prevalence, age and gender statistics, cultural aspects, and prognosis for about 400 disorders or subtypes, 40 of which appear primarily in childhood. Thus, the diagnostic criteria reprinted here for three disorders represent less than 1 percent of the contents of DSM-IV-TR.

Diagnostic Criteria for Attention-Deficit/Hyperactivity Disorder

A. Either (1) or (2):

(1) Six (or more) of the following symptoms of **inattention** have persisted for at least 6 months to a degree that is maladaptive and inconsistent with developmental level:

Inattention

(a) often fails to give close attention to details or makes careless mistakes in schoolwork, work, or other activities
(b) often has difficulty sustaining attention in tasks or play activities
(c) often does not seem to listen when spoken to directly
(d) often does not follow through on instructions and fails to finish schoolwork, chores, or duties in the workplace (not due to oppositional behavior or failure to understand instructions)
(e) often has difficulty organizing tasks and activities
(f) often avoids, dislikes, or is reluctant to engage in tasks that require sustained mental effort (such as schoolwork or homework)
(g) often loses things necessary for tasks or activities (e.g., toys, school assignments, pencils, books, or tools)
(h) is often easily distracted by extraneous stimuli
(i) is often forgetful in daily activities

(2) Six (or more) of the following symptoms of **hyperactivity-impulsivity** have persisted for at least 6 months to a degree that is maladaptive and inconsistent with developmental level:

Hyperactivity

(a) often fidgets with hands or feet or squirms in seat
(b) often leaves seat in classroom or in other situations in which remaining seated is expected
(c) often runs about or climbs excessively in situations in which it is inappropriate (in adolescents or adults, may be limited to subjective feelings of restlessness)
(d) often has difficulty playing or engaging in leisure activities quietly
(e) is often "on the go" or often acts as if "driven by a motor"
(f) often talks excessively

Impulsivity

(g) often blurts out answers before questions have been completed
(h) often has difficulty awaiting turn
(i) often interrupts or intrudes on others (e.g., butts into conversations or games)

B. Some hyperactive-impulsive or inattentive symptoms that caused impairment were present before age 7 years.
C. Some impairment from the symptoms is present in two or more settings (e.g., at school [or work] and at home).
D. There must be clear evidence of clinically significant impairment in social, academic, or occupational functioning.

Diagnostic Criteria for Conduct Disorder

A. A repetitive and persistent pattern of behavior in which the basic rights of others or major age-appropriate societal norms or rules are violated, as manifested by the presence of three (or more) of the following criteria in the past 12 months, with at least one criterion present in the past 6 months:

Aggression to people and animals

(1) often bullies, threatens, or intimidates others
(2) often initiates physical fights
(3) has used a weapon that can cause serious physical harm to others (e.g., a bat, brick, broken bottle, knife, gun)
(4) has been physically cruel to people
(5) has been physically cruel to animals
(6) has stolen while confronting a victim (e.g., mugging, purse snatching, extortion, armed robbery)
(7) has forced someone into sexual activity

Destruction of property

(8) has deliberately engaged in fire setting with the intention of causing serious damage
(9) has deliberately destroyed others' property (other than by fire setting)

Deceitfulness or theft

(10) has broken into someone else's house, building, or car
(11) often lies to obtain goods or favors or to avoid obligations (i.e., "cons" others)
(12) has stolen items of nontrivial value without confronting a victim (e.g., shoplifting, but without breaking and entering; forgery)

Serious violations of rules

(13) often stays out at night despite parental prohibitions, beginning before age 13 years
(14) has run away from home overnight at least twice while living in parental or parental surrogate home (or once without returning for a lengthy period)
(15) is often truant from school, beginning before age 13 years

B. The disturbance in behavior causes clinically significant impairment in social, academic, or occupational functioning.

Diagnostic Criteria for Oppositional Defiant Disorder

A. A pattern of negativistic, hostile, and defiant behavior lasting at least 6 months, during which four (or more) of the following are present:

(1) often loses temper
(2) often argues with adults
(3) often actively defies or refuses to comply with adults' requests or rules
(4) often deliberately annoys people
(5) often blames others for his or her mistakes or misbehavior
(6) is often touchy or easily annoyed by others
(7) is often angry and resentful
(8) is often spiteful or vindictive

Note: Consider a criterion met only if the behavior occurs more frequently than is typically observed in individuals of comparable age and developmental level.

B. The disturbance in behavior causes clinically significant impairment in social, academic, or occupational functioning.

Source: American Psychiatric Association, 2004.

Diagnostic Criteria for Autistic Disorder

A. A total of six (or more) items from (1), (2), and (3), with at least two from (1) and one each from (2) and (3):

(1) qualitative impairment in social interaction, as manifested by at least two of the following:
  (a) marked impairment in the use of multiple nonverbal behaviors such as eye-to-eye gaze, facial expression, body postures, and gestures to regulate social interaction
  (b) failure to develop peer relationships appropriate to developmental level
  (c) a lack of spontaneous seeking to share enjoyment, interests, or achievements with other people (e.g., by a lack of showing, bringing, or pointing out objects of interest)
  (d) lack of social or emotional reciprocity

(2) qualitative impairments in communication as manifested by at least one of the following:
  (a) delay in, or total lack of, the development of spoken language (not accompanied by an attempt to compensate through alternative modes of communication such as gesture or mime)
  (b) in individuals with adequate speech, marked impairment in the ability to initiate or sustain a conversation with others
  (c) stereotyped and repetitive use of language or idiosyncratic language
  (d) lack of varied, spontaneous make-believe play or social imitative play appropriate to developmental level

(3) restricted repetitive and stereotyped patterns of behavior, interests, and activities, as manifested by at least one of the following:
   (a) encompassing preoccupation with one or more stereotyped and restricted patterns of interest that is abnormal either in intensity or focus
   (b) apparently inflexible adherence to specific, nonfunctional routines or rituals
   (c) stereotyped and repetitive motor mannerisms (e.g., hand or finger flapping or twisting, or complex whole-body movements)
   (d) persistent preoccupation with parts of objects

B. Delays or abnormal functioning in at least one of the following areas, with onset prior to age 3 years: (1) social interaction, (2) language as used in social communication, or (3) symbolic or imaginative play

C. The disturbance is not better accounted for by Rett's Disorder or Childhood Disintegrative Disorder.

Diagnostic Criteria for Asperger's Disorder

A. Qualitative impairment in social interaction, as manifested by at least two of the following:
   (1) marked impairment in the use of multiple nonverbal behaviors such as eye-to-eye gaze, facial expression, body postures, and gestures to regulate social interaction
   (2) failure to develop peer relationships appropriate to developmental level
   (3) a lack of spontaneous seeking to share enjoyment, interests, or achievements with other people (e.g., by a lack of showing, bringing, or pointing out objects of interest to other people)
   (4) lack of social or emotional reciprocity

B. Restricted repetitive and stereotyped patterns of behavior, interests, and activities, as manifested by at least one of the following:
   (1) encompassing preoccupation with one or more stereotyped and restricted patterns of interest that is abnormal either in intensity or focus
   (2) apparently inflexible adherence to specific, nonfunctional routines or rituals
   (3) stereotyped and repetitive motor mannerisms (e.g., hand or finger flapping or twisting, or complex whole-body movements)
   (4) persistent preoccupation with parts of objects

C. The disturbance causes clinically significant impairment in social, occupational, or other important areas of functioning.

D. There is no clinically significant general delay in language (e.g., single words used by age 2 years, communicative phrases used by age 3 years).

E. There is no clinically significant delay in cognitive development or in the development of age-appropriate self-help skills, adaptive behavior (other than in social interaction), and curiosity about the environment in childhood.

F. Criteria are not met for another specific Pervasive Developmental Disorder or Schizophrenia.

Changes in Ranking of 16 Nations on Science and Math Knowledge Between Fourth and Eighth Grades (Chapter 12)

Only the 16 highest-scoring nations are included in these rankings. Many other countries, such as Chile and Morocco, rank much lower. Still others, including all the nations of Latin America and Africa, do not administer the tests on which these rankings are based. Identical rankings indicate ties between nations on overall scores. International comparisons are always difficult and often unfair, but two general conclusions have been confirmed: Children in East Asian countries tend to be high achievers in math and science, and children in the United States lose ground in science and just hold their own in math between the fourth and eighth grades.

Science Knowledge				Math Knowledge			
Nation	Rank in Fourth Grade	Rank in Eighth Grade	Change in Rank	Nation	Rank in Fourth Grade	Rank in Eighth Grade	Change in Rank
Singapore	1	1	0	Singapore	1	1	0
Chinese Taipei	2	2	0	Hong Kong	2	3	−1
Japan	3	6	−3	Japan	3	5	−2
Hong Kong	4	4	0	Chinese Taipei	4	4	0
England	5	*	—	Belgium	5	6	−1
United States	6	9	−3	Netherlands	6	7	−1
Latvia	7	18	−11	Latvia	7	11†	−4
Hungary	8	7	+1	Lithuania	8	13	−5
Russian Federation	9	17	−8	Russian Federation	9	11†	−2
Netherlands	10	8	+2	England	10	*	—
Australia	11	10	+1	Hungary	11	9	−2
New Zealand	12	13	−1	United States	12	12	0
Belgium	13	16	−3	Cyprus	13	26	−13
Italy	14	22	−8	Moldova	14	25	−11
Lithuania	15	14	+1	Italy	15	19	−4
Scotland	16	19	−3	Australia	16	11	+5

*Did not participate.
†Average scale scores were tied.
Source: Third International Mathematics and Science Study (TIMSS), 2003.

Changes in the Average Weekly Amount of Time Spent by 6- to 11-Year-Olds in Various Activities (Chapter 12)

Data can be presented graphically in many ways. The data given here were collected in the same way in 1981, 1997, and 2004, so the changes are real (although the age cutoff in 1997 was 12, not 11). What do you think would be the best way to show this information? What is encouraging and what is problematic in the changes that you see? What were children doing in 2004 that is not accounted for in this list of activities and wasn't even available in 1981?

	Average Amount of Time Spent in Activity, per Week, United States			
Activity	In 1981	In 1997	In 2004	Change in Time Spent Since 1981
School	25 hrs, 17 min.	33 hrs, 52 min.	33 hrs, 33 min.	+8 hrs, 16 min.
Organized sports	3 hrs, 5 min.	4 hrs, 56 min.	2 hrs, 28 min.	–32 min.
Studying	1 hr, 46 min.	2 hrs, 50 min.	3 hrs, 25 min.	+1 hr, 21 min.
Reading	57 min.	1 hr, 15 min.	1 hr, 28 min.	+31 min.
Being outdoors	1 hr, 17 min.	39 min.	56 min.	–21 min.
Playing	12 hrs, 52 min.	10 hrs, 5 min.	10 hrs, 25 min.	–2 hrs, 27 min.
Watching TV	15 hrs, 34 min.	13 hrs, 7 min.	14 hrs, 19 min.	–1 hr, 15 min.

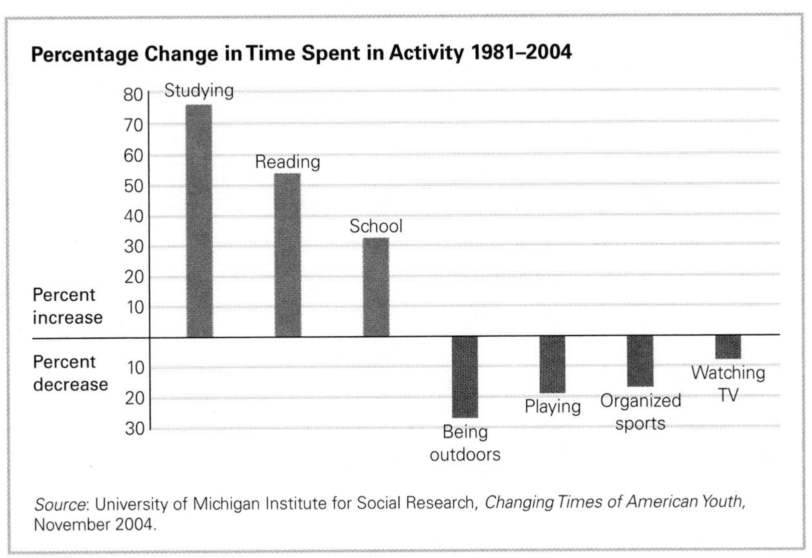

Source: University of Michigan Institute for Social Research, *Changing Times of American Youth*, November 2004.

Who Is Raising the Children? (Chapter 13)

Most children still live in households with a male/female couple, who may be the children's married or unmarried biological parents, grandparents, stepparents, foster parents, or adoptive parents. However, the proportion of households headed by single parents has risen—by 500 percent for single fathers and by almost 200 percent for single mothers. (In 2005, 52 percent of U.S. households had *no* children under age 18.)

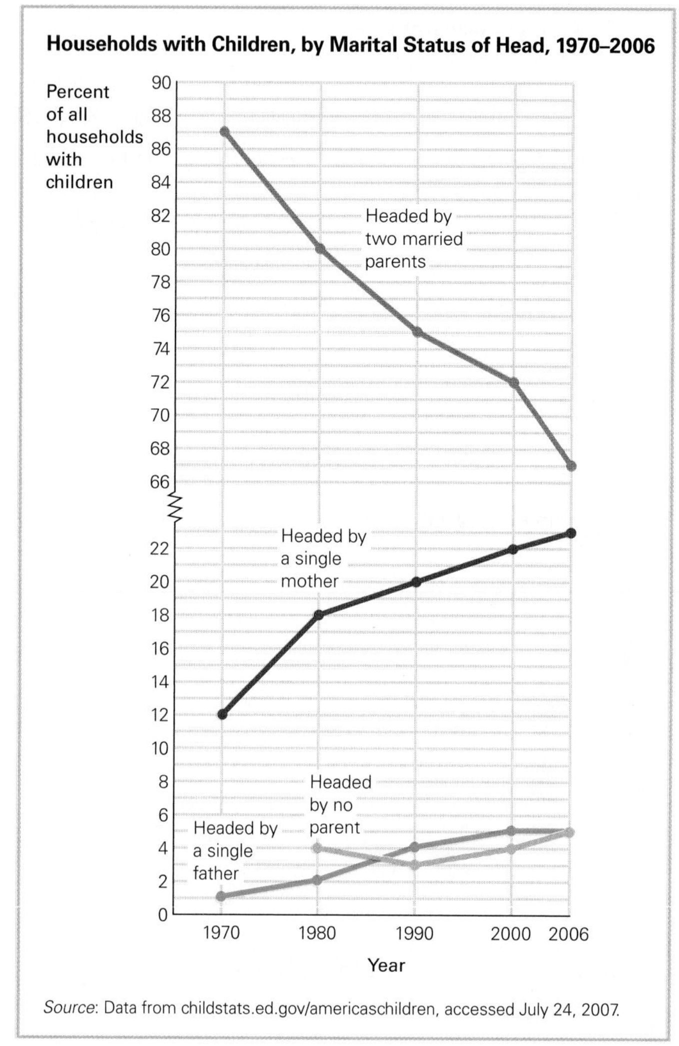

Source: Data from childstats.ed.gov/americaschildren, accessed July 24, 2007.

Smoking Behavior Among U.S. High School Students, 1991–2005 (Chapter 14)

The data in these two tables reveal many trends. For example, do you see that African American adolescents are much less likely to smoke than Hispanics or European Americans, but that this racial advantage is decreasing? Are you surprised to see that White females smoke more than White males?

Percentage of High School Students Who Reported Smoking Cigarettes

Smoking Behavior	1991	1995	1999	2003	2005
Lifetime (ever smoked)	70.1	71.3	70.4	58.4	54.3
Current (smoked at least once in past 30 days)	27.5	34.8	34.8	21.9	23.0
Current frequent (smoked 20 or more times in past 30 days)	12.7	16.1	16.8	9.7	9.4

Percentage of High School Students Who Reported Current Smoking, by Sex, Ethnicity, and Grade

Characteristic	1991	1995	1999	2003	2005
Sex					
Female	27.3	34.3	34.9	21.9	23.0
Male	27.6	35.4	34.7	21.8	22.9
Ethnicity					
White, non-Hispanic	30.9	38.3	38.6	24.9	25.9
Female	*31.7*	*39.8*	*39.1*	*26.6*	*27*
Male	*30.2*	*37.0*	*38.2*	*23.3*	*24.9*
Black, non-Hispanic	12.6	19.2	19.7	15.1	12.9
Female	*11.3*	*12.2*	*17.7*	*10.8*	*11.9*
Male	*14.1*	*27.8*	*21.8*	*19.3*	*14.0*
Hispanic	25.3	34.0	32.7	18.4	22.0
Female	*22.9*	*32.9*	*31.5*	*17.7*	*19.2*
Male	*27.9*	*34.9*	*34.0*	*19.1*	*24.8*
Grade					
9th	23.2	31.2	27.6	17.4	19.7
10th	25.2	33.1	34.7	21.8	21.4
11th	31.6	35.9	36.0	23.6	24.3
12th	30.1	38.2	42.8	26.2	27.6

Source: MMWR (2006, July 7)

Sexual Behaviors of U.S. High School Students, 2005 (Chapter 15)

These percentages, as high as they may seem, are actually lower than they were in the early 1990s. (States not listed did not participate fully in the survey.) The data in this table reflect responses from students in the 9th to 12th grades. When only high school seniors are surveyed, the percentages are higher. In every state, more than half of all high school seniors say they have had sexual intercourse, and about 20 percent have had four or more sex partners.

	Ever had sexual intercourse (%)			Had first sexual intercourse before age 13 (%)			Has had four or more sex partners during lifetime (%)			Is currently sexually active (%)		
State	Female	Male	Total	Female	Male	Total	Female	Male	Total	Female	Male	Total
Alabama	46.8	54.6	**50.6**	4.9	12.8	**8.8**	9.5	21.1	**15.1**	37.7	38.0	**38.0**
Arizona	42.8	42.9	**42.8**	3.6	7.9	**5.7**	10.5	16.5	**13.5**	32.9	27.4	**30.2**
Arkansas	53.6	54.3	**54.0**	5.5	12.7	**9.2**	15.8	21.0	**18.3**	42.3	38.8	**40.6**
Colorado	37.2	41.3	**39.3**	2.3	7.0	**4.7**	8.7	13.9	**11.3**	29.3	29.4	**29.5**
Delaware	51.3	58.6	**55.1**	4.5	16.9	**10.8**	15.7	22.1	**19.1**	39.8	38.6	**39.2**
Florida	47.1	53.5	**50.5**	4.0	13.6	**8.8**	11.5	21.1	**16.3**	35.3	36.7	**36.2**
Hawaii	37.6	33.7	**35.7**	4.4	5.8	**5.1**	7.9	10.0	**9.0**	29.4	18.7	**24.1**
Idaho	39.5	37.4	**38.5**	4.2	9.0	**6.7**	—	—	**—**	—	—	**—**
Iowa	44.0	43.0	**43.5**	3.0	5.4	**4.2**	11.8	13.7	**12.7**	34.5	31.2	**32.8**
Kansas	44.3	45.3	**44.8**	2.8	7.9	**5.5**	11.7	14.7	**13.3**	36.3	30.0	**33.3**
Kentucky	44.6	48.0	**46.3**	4.1	11.5	**7.9**	10.6	16.6	**13.6**	34.5	32.5	**33.5**
Maine	46.4	43.0	**44.8**	3.0	6.1	**4.5**	10.6	13.4	**11.9**	36.9	30.1	**33.5**
Massachusetts	42.9	47.9	**45.4**	2.2	8.1	**5.2**	10.5	14.5	**12.6**	35.4	32.7	**34.1**
Michigan	41.2	43.2	**42.2**	3.9	8.5	**6.2**	9.6	14.1	**11.8**	31.1	27.7	**29.4**
Missouri	47.1	46.3	**46.7**	3.5	8.4	**5.9**	11.3	16.7	**14.0**	34.7	31.5	**33.2**
Montana	42.6	44.4	**43.6**	2.8	7.0	**5.1**	12.5	13.3	**13.1**	32.4	30.0	**31.2**
Nebraska	40.9	40.6	**40.8**	3.3	5.5	**4.4**	12.2	11.7	**11.9**	29.6	30.2	**29.9**
Nevada	39.6	48.5	**44.1**	3.8	11.5	**7.7**	11.5	18.7	**15.2**	30.6	30.8	**30.8**
New York	39.3	44.6	**42.0**	3.0	8.6	**5.8**	8.6	16.3	**12.5**	29.2	29.0	**29.2**
North Carolina	47.6	54.3	**50.8**	5.0	11.2	**8.1**	13.9	20.6	**17.2**	35.3	39.1	**37.1**
North Dakota	40.7	41.6	**41.2**	1.7	4.7	**3.3**	10.7	12.0	**11.3**	33.3	31.4	**32.4**
Ohio	46.5	49.0	**47.8**	3.5	7.2	**5.3**	15.1	18.5	**16.9**	35.5	37.2	**36.4**
Oklahoma	48.2	50.2	**49.3**	4.0	8.9	**6.5**	14.3	21.2	**17.8**	37.0	35.4	**36.3**
Rhode Island	44.9	48.3	**46.7**	2.3	9.4	**5.9**	9.3	16.8	**13.0**	36.4	36.6	**36.5**
South Carolina	49.7	55.1	**52.3**	4.8	13.9	**4.7**	14.5	23.5	**18.8**	38.2	36.7	**37.5**
South Dakota	47.1	41.4	**44.3**	3.6	8.0	**5.8**	16.9	11.5	**14.2**	33.7	28.7	**31.2**
Tennessee	55.6	53.7	**54.7**	5.8	11.2	**8.5**	14.7	19.1	**17.0**	41.1	35.3	**38.2**
Texas	49.6	55.2	**52.5**	4.0	10.7	**7.4**	13.1	19.5	**16.3**	37.5	37.6	**37.6**
West Virginia	51.1	53.8	**52.5**	3.7	11.0	**7.3**	11.0	18.5	**14.8**	41.1	37.3	**39.3**
Wisconsin	40.3	40.2	**40.3**	2.6	5.0	**3.9**	9.9	10.9	**10.4**	31.8	27.3	**29.5**
Wyoming	47.4	46.9	**47.1**	3.7	6.6	**5.2**	15.2	15.9	**15.5**	37.6	32.0	**34.7**
U.S. median	**44.9**	**46.3**	**44.8**	**3.6**	**8.4**	**5.8**	**11.3**	**16.3**	**13.6**	**35.3**	**31.4**	**33.3**

Source: National Center for Chronic Disease Prevention and Health Promotion, Youth Risk Behavior Surveillance System, *MMWR,* June 9, 2006.

United States Homicide Victim and Offender Rates, by Race and Gender, Ages 14–17 (Chapter 16)

Teenage boys are more often violent offenders than victims. The ratio of victimization to offense has varied for teenage girls over the years. The good news is that rates have decreased dramatically over the past ten years for every category of adolescents—male and female, Black and White. (Similar declines are apparent for Asian and Hispanic Americans.) The bad news is that rates are still higher in the United States than in any other developed nation.

Homicide Victimization Rates per 100,000 Population for 14- to 17-Year-Olds

	Male		Female	
Year	White	Black	White	Black
1976	3.7	24.6	2.2	6.4
1981	4.4	23.6	2.4	6.2
1986	4.2	27.4	2.3	6.6
1991	8.7	73.6	2.6	9.6
1996	8.4	53.3	2.1	8.9
2002	3.6	22.6	1.5	6.1
2006	4.4	26.4	1.1	4.0

Source: U. S. Bureau of Justice Statistics, 2006.
Tabulations based on FBI Supplementary Homicide Reports and U.S. Census Bureau, Current Population Reports.

Homicide Offending Rates per 100,000 Population for 14- to 17-Year-Olds

	Male		Female	
Year	White	Black	White	Black
1976	10.4	72.4	1.3	10.3
1981	10.9	73.1	1.3	8.6
1986	12.3	72.2	1.1	5.6
1991	21.9	199.1	1.3	12.1
1996	17.4	134.8	1.7	7.8
2002	9.2	54.5	.9	3.7
2006	7.9	64.1	.7	4.0

Source: U. S. Bureau of Justice Statistics, 2006.
Tabulations based on FBI Supplementary Homicide Reports and U.S. Census Bureau, Current Population Reports. Rates include both known perpetrators and estimated share of unidentified perpetrators.

All the charts, graphs, and tables in this Appendix offer readers the opportunity to analyze raw data and draw their own conclusions. The same information may be presented in a variety of ways. On this page, you can create your own bar graph or line graph, depicting some noteworthy aspect of the data presented in the three tables. First, consider all the possibilities the tables offer by answering these six questions:

1. Are white male or female teenagers more likely to be victims of homicide?
2. These are annual rates. How many African Americans in 1,000 were likely to commit homicide in 2006?
3. Which age group is *most* likely to commit homicide?
4. Which age group is *least* likely to be victims of homicide?
5. Which age group is *almost equally* likely to be either perpetrators or victims of homicide?
6. Of the four groups of adolescents, which has shown the greatest decline in rates of both victimization and perpetration of homicide over the past decade? Which has shown the least decline?

Answers: 1. Boys—at least twice as often. 2. Less than one. 3. 18–24. 4. 0–13. 5. 35–49. 6. Black males had the greatest decline, and White females had the least (but these two groups have always been highest and lowest, respectively, in every year). *Now*—use the grid provided at right to make your own graph.

Overall Rate of Homicide by Age, 2005, United States (Chapter 16)

Late adolescence and early adulthood are the peak times for murders—both as victims and offenders. The question for developmentalists is whether something changes before age 18 to decrease the rates in young adulthood.

Age group	Victims (per 100,000 in age group)	Killers (per 100,000 in age group)
0–13	1.4	.1
14–17	4.8	9.3
18–24	14.9	26.5
25–34	11.6	13.5
35–49	5.7	5.1
50–64	2.6	1.4

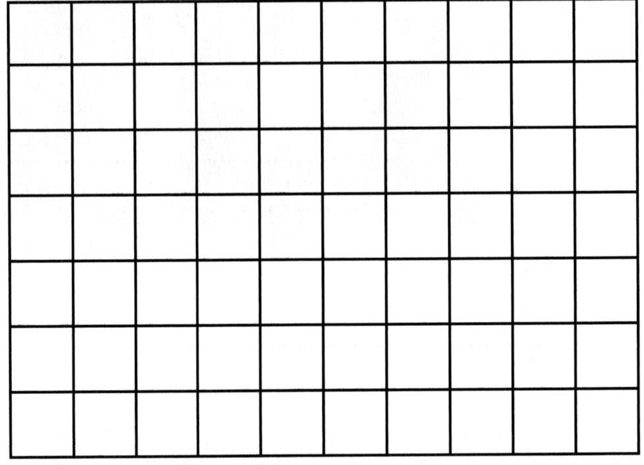

Too Young for Motherhood (Chapter 17)

These numbers show dramatic shifts in family planning, with teenage births continuing to fall and births after age 30 rising again. These data come from the United States, but the same trends are apparent in almost every nation (see top of page A-21). Can you tell when contraception became widely available?

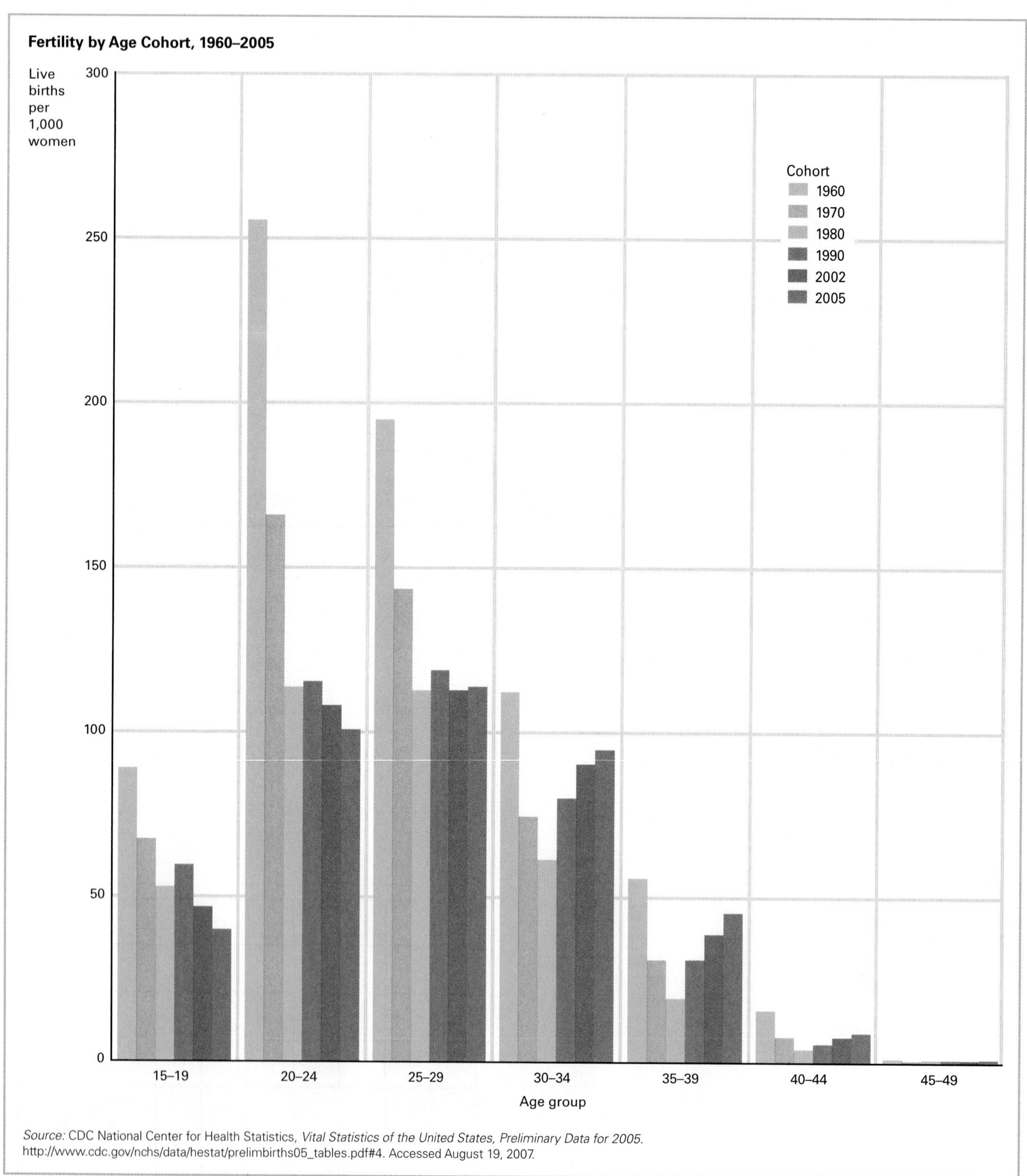

Source: CDC National Center for Health Statistics, *Vital Statistics of the United States, Preliminary Data for 2005.* http://www.cdc.gov/nchs/data/hestat/prelimbirths05_tables.pdf#4. Accessed August 19, 2007.

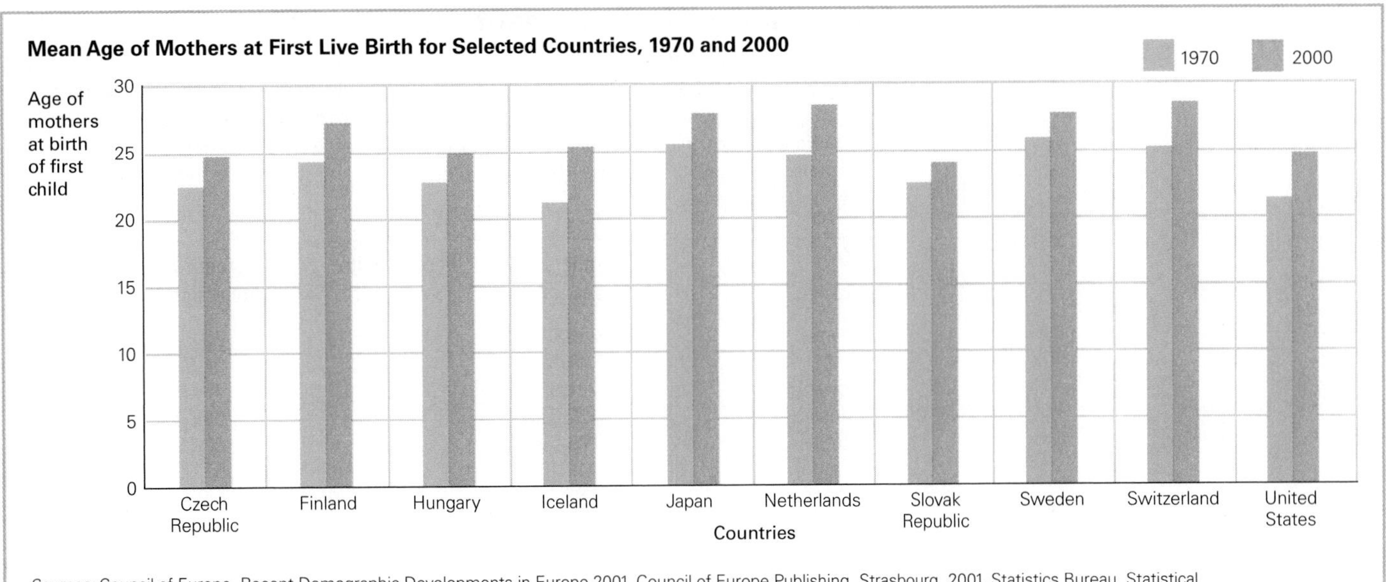

Sources: Council of Europe. Recent Demographic Developments in Europe 2001. Council of Europe Publishing, Strasbourg, 2001. Statistics Bureau. Statistical Handbook of Japan 2001. Ministry of Public Management, Home Affairs, Ports, and Telecommunications, 2001. Japan Information Network. Women's Life Cycle (1983–2000). Released August 29, 2001. http://www.cdc.gov/nchs/data/nvsr/nvsr51/nvsr51_01.pdf.

Education Affects Income (Chapter 18)

Although there is some debate about the cognitive benefits of college education, there is no doubt about the financial benefits. No matter what a person's ethnicity or gender is, an associate's degree more than doubles his or her income compared to that of someone who has not completed high school. These data are for the United States; similar trends, often with steeper increases, are found in other nations.

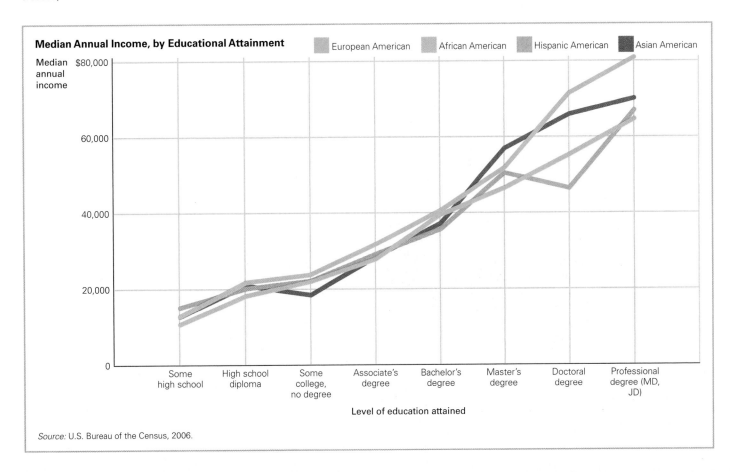

Median Annual Income, by Educational Attainment

European American | African American | Hispanic American | Asian American

Median annual income: $80,000 · 60,000 · 40,000 · 20,000 · 0

Some high school · High school diploma · Some college, no degree · Associate's degree · Bachelor's degree · Master's degree · Doctoral degree · Professional degree (MD, JD)

Level of education attained

Source: U.S. Bureau of the Census, 2006.

Child Support Enforcement, by State, 2006 (Chapter 19)

Everyone loses when fathers do not support their children. Mothers become poor and angry, fathers feel burdened (the less income a man has, the less likely he is to pay what the courts require), and children suffer the most, in that fathers who do not support their children financially often withdraw emotionally. The ranks here are the percent of fathers who have court-ordered payment and who pay it. Note that even in the best state (South Dakota), a third of the fathers did not pay what was needed.

State	Number of cases	Percent with court order	Percent with collection	Rank
Alabama	226,838	50.91	52.87	50
Alaska	44,989	92.24	54.9	23
Arizona	211,039	76.48	46.55	42
Arkansas	122,667	83.61	59.02	25
California	1,705,561	80.57	50.39	33
Colorado	142,154	86.29	59.09	21
Connecticut	202,174	70.99	54.99	38
Delaware	56,971	75.11	60.48	29
District of Columbia	77,651	45.43	52.53	51
Florida	742,584	73.79	54.38	34
Georgia	482,495	75.67	51.93	37
Hawaii	102,023	58.53	56.93	47
Idaho	110,112	79.49	55.86	31
Illinois	602,533	66.86	51.76	44
Indiana	355,757	68.44	53.82	40
Iowa	184,197	85.87	65.66	9
Kansas	130,845	74.72	55.29	32
Kentucky	320,412	79.73	56.64	30
Louisiana	284,244	73.1	54.05	36
Maine	67,045	87.67	61.05	14
Maryland	265,146	77.66	64.19	24
Massachusetts	273,213	74.85	65.44	26
Michigan	958,128	79.79	61.38	27
Minnesota	249,944	82.54	68.83	8
Mississippi	301,355	54.13	54.32	49
Missouri	367,918	82.81	55.68	28
Montana	40,048	87.96	61.49	12
Nebraska	104,974	78.42	67.44	18
Nevada	111,258	66.8	45.92	48
New Hampshire	36,747	82.54	64.38	16
New Jersey	359,530	82.03	65.57	13
New Mexico	68,210	63.24	52.97	46
New York	893,768	81.6	64.91	17
North Carolina	410,399	81.05	65.64	15
North Dakota	41,029	87.5	73.42	2
Ohio	956,541	73.33	69.14	22
Oklahoma	174,065	69.63	52.68	41
Oregon	251,412	66.36	60.42	35
Pennsylvania	550,150	84.5	74.65	3
Rhode Island	58,171	58.57	58.57	45
South Carolina	212,085	75.65	49.31	39
South Dakota	45,746	92.98	69.47	1
Tennessee	386,180	63.87	55.68	43
Texas	980,497	82.74	62.33	20
Utah	78,083	87.83	63.57	10
Vermont	22,711	85.87	67.46	6
Virginia	351,930	85.19	61.61	19
Washington	344,972	89.86	64.33	7
West Virginia	113,473	85.42	64.48	11
Wisconsin	359,126	83.81	70.64	4
Wyoming	35,099	89.09	65.85	5
United States	**15,574,199**	**76.92**	**59.8**	

Source: Office of Child Support Enforcement, Fiscal Year 2006 Preliminary Report, March 2007. Department of Health and Human Services, Administration for Children and Families, Office of Child Support Enforcement. www.acf.hhs.gov/programs/cse/pubs/2007/preliminary_report/ accessed August 19, 2007.

Obesity in the United States, 1976 to 2004 (Chapter 20)

About a third of all adults in the United States have a BMI of 30 or higher, which is not just overweight but seriously too heavy. Other data show that another third are overweight, again with increases over the past decades.

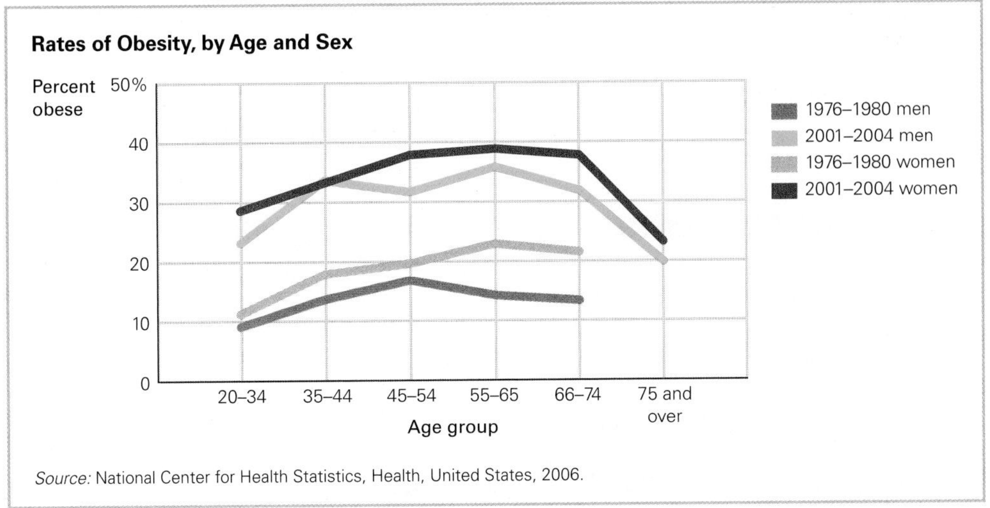

Source: National Center for Health Statistics, Health, United States, 2006.

Dying of Lung Cancer: It's Not Just Genes and Gender (Chapter 20)

For lung cancer as well as most other diseases, the male death rate is markedly higher than the female death rate in the United States. Moreover, the death rate for African Americans is almost twice the average, and for Asian Americans it is almost half the average. Genes and gender do not explain these discrepancies, however. As you can see, White women are at greater risk than Hispanic or Native American men, and the rate for Black men went down as the rate for some other groups rose. (These are "age-adjusted" rates, which means that they reflect the fact that more Asians reach old age and fewer Native Americans do. In other words, the sex and ethnic differences shown here are real—not artifacts of the age distribution.)

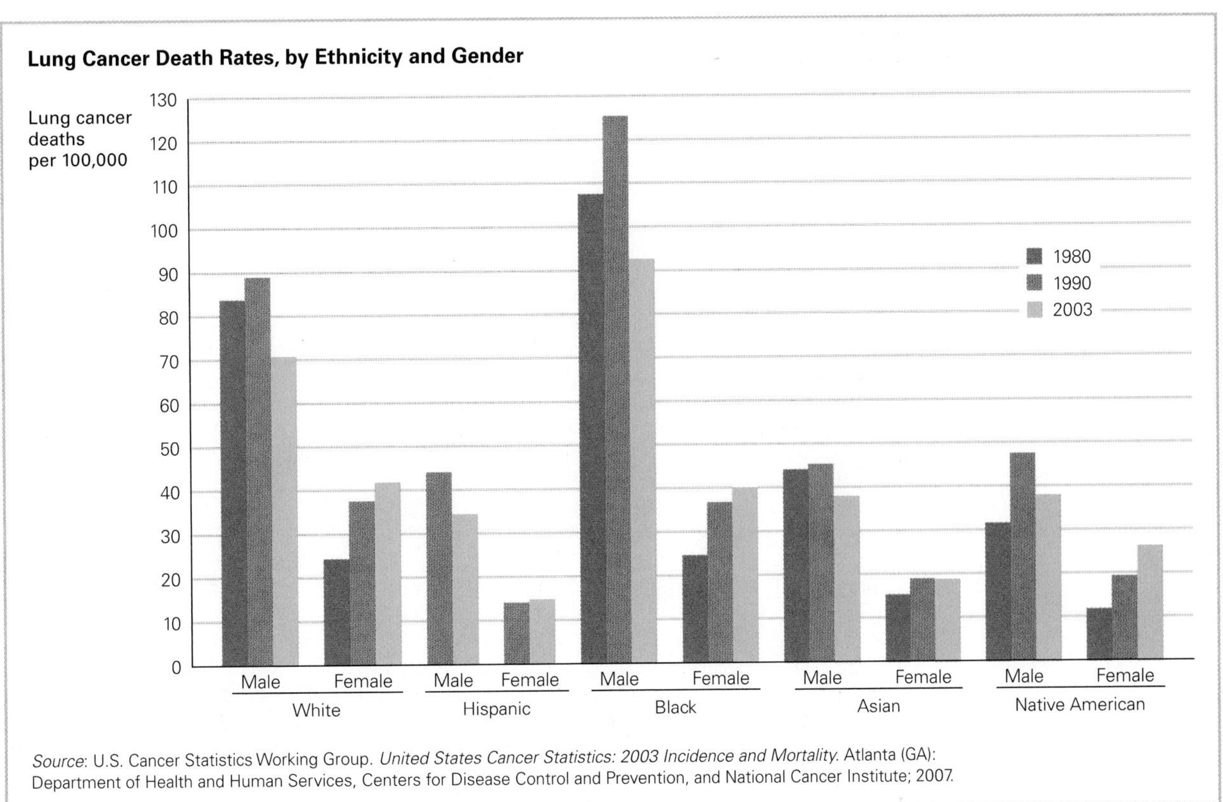

Source: U.S. Cancer Statistics Working Group. *United States Cancer Statistics: 2003 Incidence and Mortality.* Atlanta (GA): Department of Health and Human Services, Centers for Disease Control and Prevention, and National Cancer Institute; 2007.

Continuing Education (Chapter 21)

This chart shows the percentage of adults (aged 24–64) involved in job-related training.

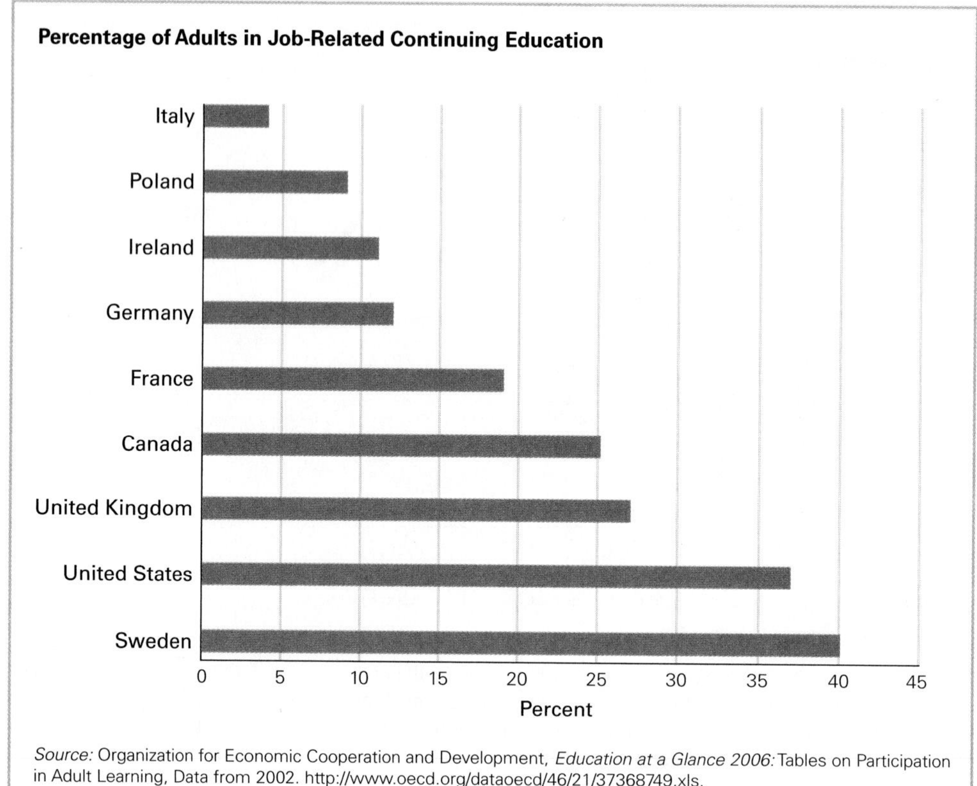

Source: Organization for Economic Cooperation and Development, *Education at a Glance 2006:* Tables on Participation in Adult Learning, Data from 2002. http://www.oecd.org/dataoecd/46/21/37368749.xls.

Grandparents Parenting Grandchildren (Chapter 22)

In 2005, 3.6% of U.S. households included grandparents living with grandchildren. In 40 percent of those households, 2.45 million grandparents were directly responsible for the care of their grandchildren.

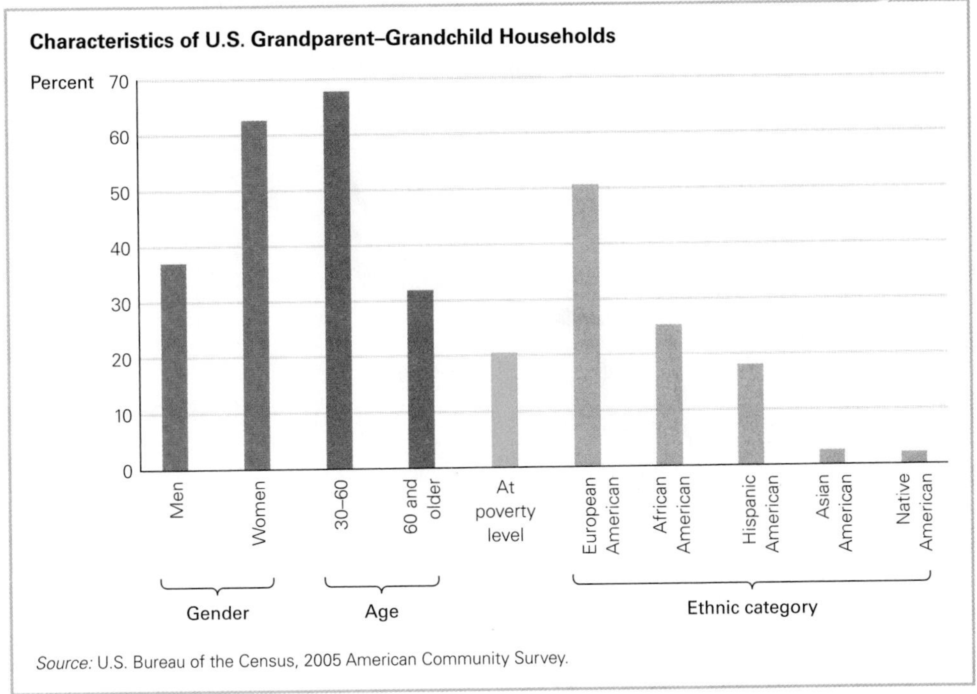

Source: U.S. Bureau of the Census, 2005 American Community Survey.

Trouble with Personal Care (Chapter 23)

As you see, with age people are more likely to need help with daily activities, such as taking a shower, getting dressed, and even getting out of bed. What is not shown is who provides that help. Usually it is a husband or wife, sometimes a grown child (who often is elderly), and, only for the oldest and least capable, the aides in a nursing home.

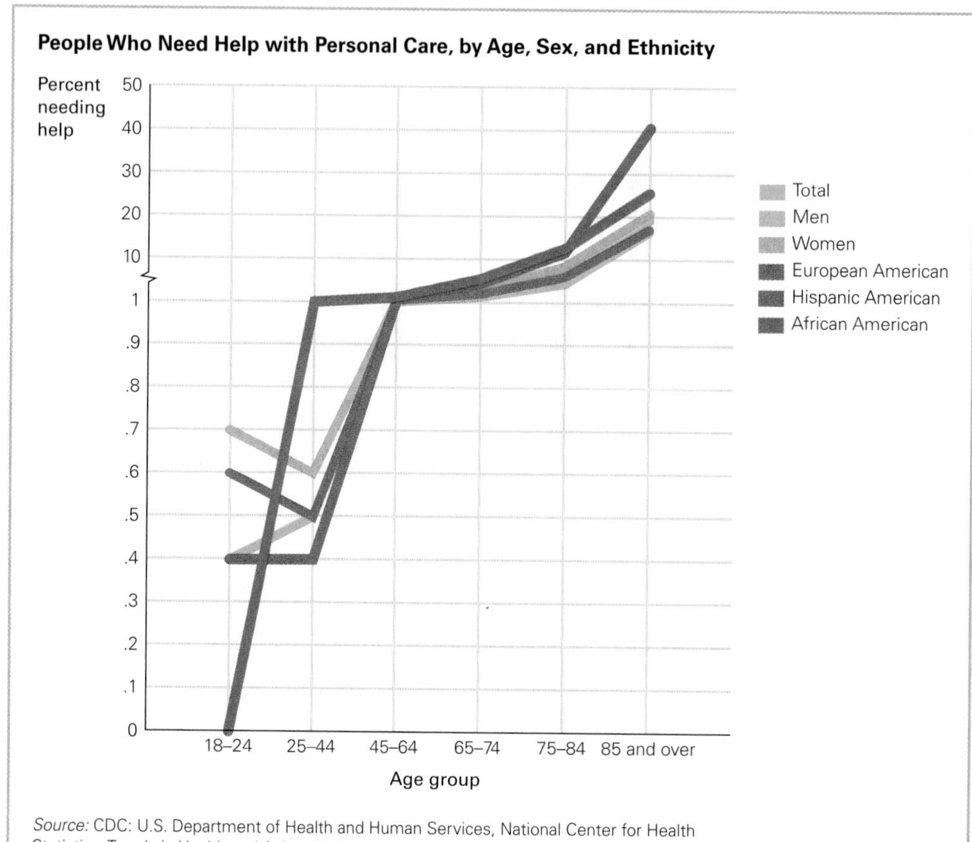

People Who Need Help with Personal Care, by Age, Sex, and Ethnicity

Source: CDC: U.S. Department of Health and Human Services, National Center for Health Statistics, Trends in Health and Aging, 2005 (http://209.217.72.34/aging/ ReportFolders/reportFolders.aspx, accessed August 1, 2007).

Dementia Around the World (Chapter 24)

More than 24 million of the 6 billion people worldwide have been diagnosed with Alzheimer's disease. This number is expected to double by 2020, since one of the major risk factors is advanced age. That also is the main reason rates are lower in nations with poor medical care—most people with health problems die and fewer are diagnosed. At the moment, 60 percent of people with Alzheimer's disease live in developing countries, making it a "disease of affluence."

Region	Percentage of population over 60 with dementia, 2001
Africa	1.6
India and South Asia	1.9
Indonesia, Sri Lanka, and Thailand	2.7
Middle East and North Africa	3.6
Developing western Pacific countries (including China, Korea, Vietnam)	4.0
Developed countries in the western Pacific (including Japan, Australia, New Zealand)	4.3
Europe	4.36
Latin America	4.6
North America	6.4

Source: C. P. Ferri et al. (2005). Global prevalence of dementia: A Delphi consensus study. *The Lancet, 366:* 2112–2117. Adapted from Table 2.

Suicide Rates in the United States (Chapter 25)

These are the rates per 100,000. When there is no bar for a given age group, that means there are too few suicides in that age group to calculate an accurate rate. Overall, the highest rates are among older European American men.

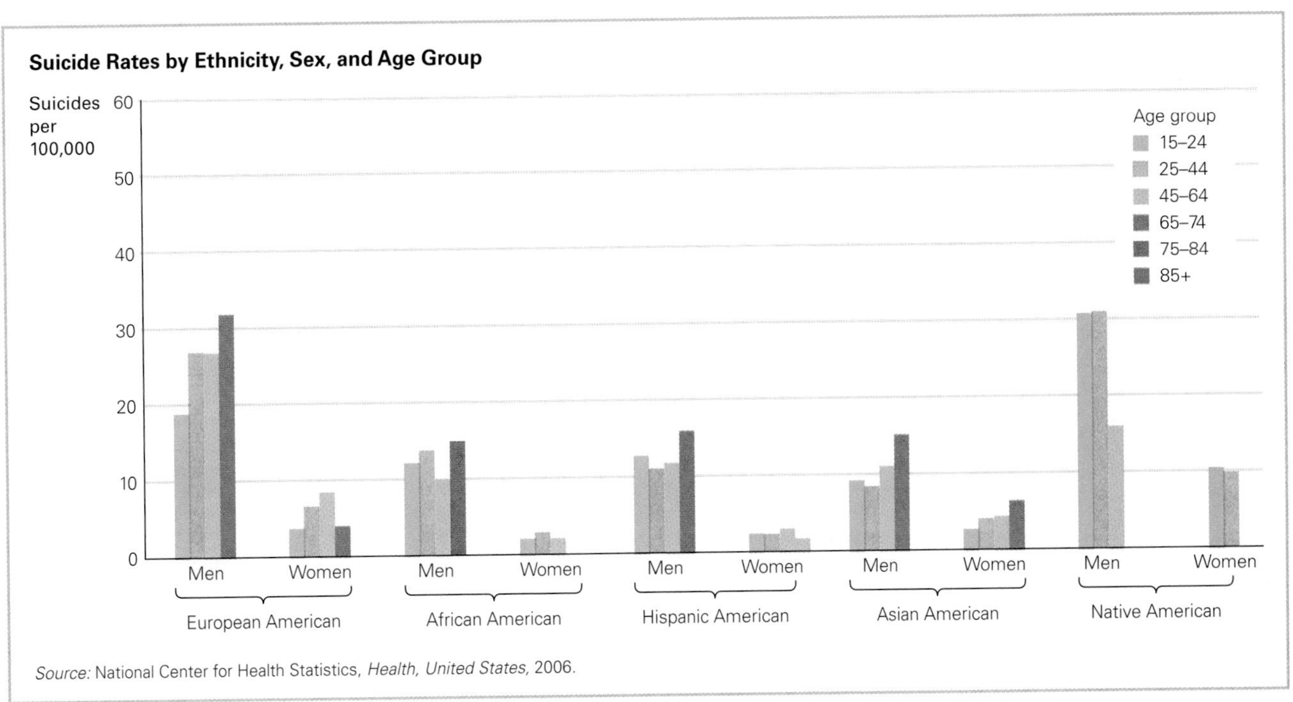

Source: National Center for Health Statistics, *Health, United States,* 2006.

Suicide Rates Around the World (Chapter 25)

In almost every nation, unmarried older men are most likely to kill themselves. The major exception is China. China's sexism is one explanation, but the difference may be simply accessible poison. Usually people kill themselves with guns, and men have more guns than women. In China, swallowing pesticides is the most common means, and lethal pesticides are readily available to every rural woman.

Suicide Rates for Selected Countries, by Gender

Argentina
Canada
China
France
Greece
India
Japan
Mauritius
Mexico
Poland
Russia
United States

Women
Men

0 10 20 30 40 50 60 70

Suicides per 100,000 population

Sources: World Health Organization, May 2007; *Japanese data*: J. Sean Curtin (2004). Suicide in Japan: Part Eleven—Comparing International Rates of Suicide. *Social Trends #79*, August 8, 2004. U.S. data: from Health, United States, 2006. Chinese data: M. R. Phillips (2002). Suicide rates in China, 1995–99. *Lancet, 359*: 835–840.

Aging Around the World (Chapter 25)

Almost always, the nations with the fewest older people have the most children, and generally, the more older people a nation has the wealthier the nation is.

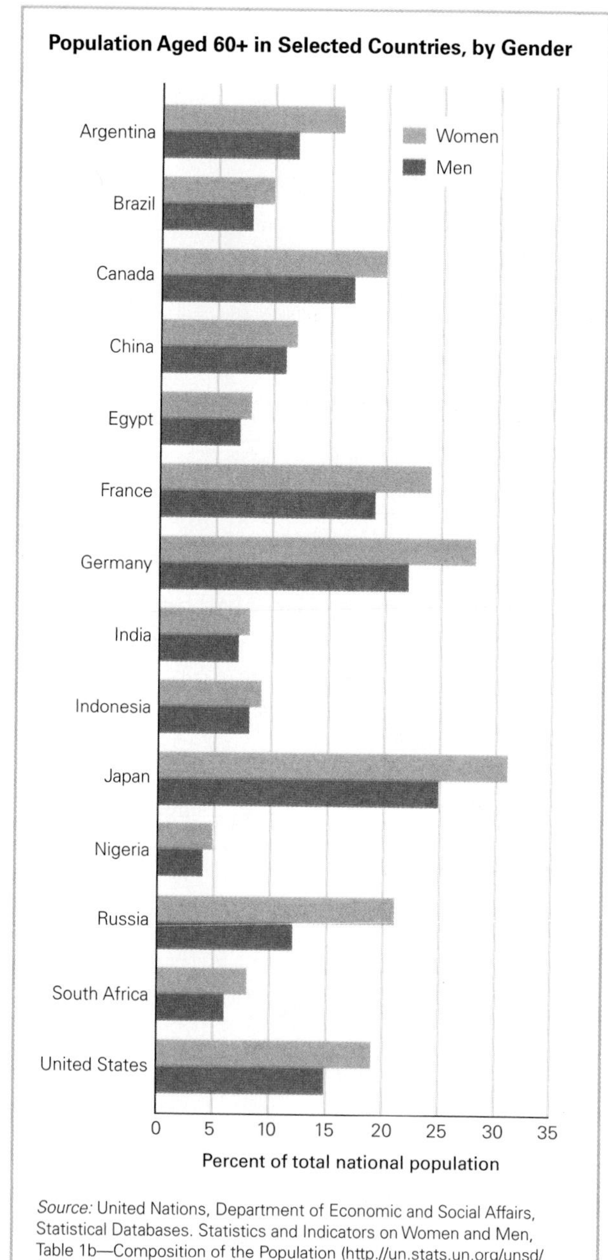

Source: United Nations, Department of Economic and Social Affairs, Statistical Databases. Statistics and Indicators on Women and Men, Table 1b—Composition of the Population (http.//un.stats.un.org/unsd/demographic/products/indwm/tab1b.htm, accessed September 11, 2007).

Hospice Care Patients (Epilogue)

Hospice helps people die without pain and other discomforts, and with family and friends nearby. As you see, most of the people in hospice care are over age 75 and diagnosed with cancer. Is this ageism, or are they the ones most likely to die soon?

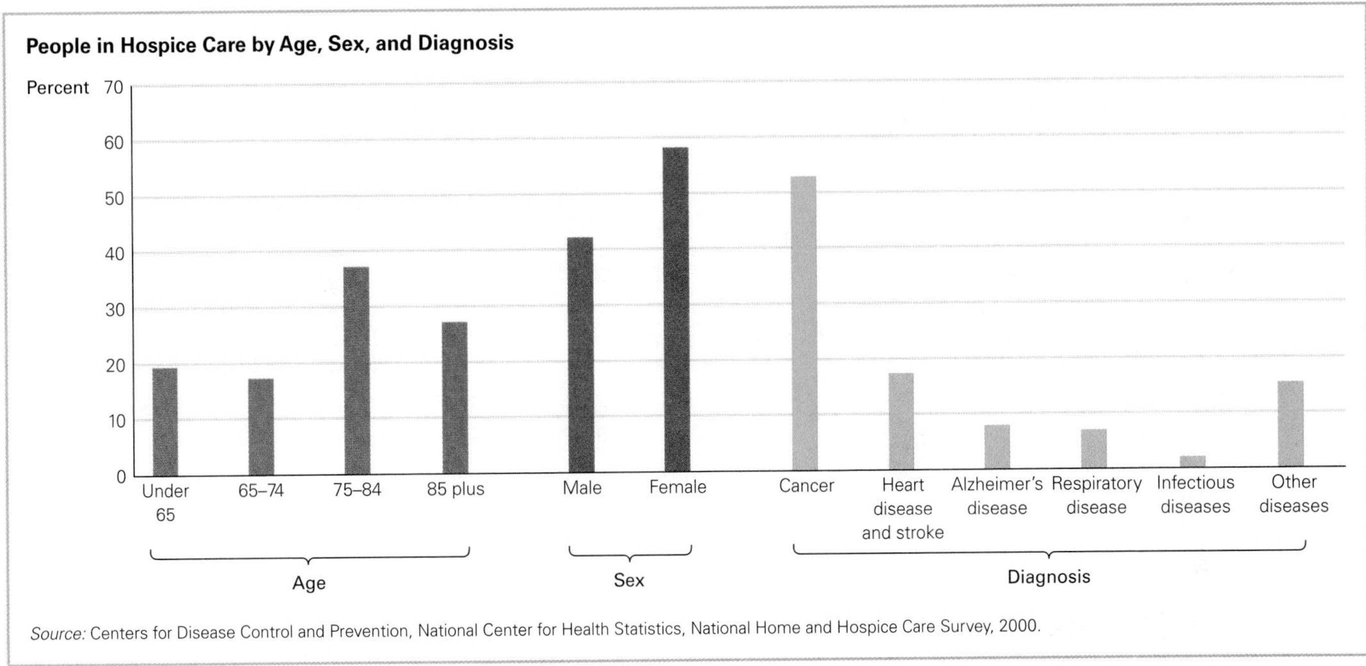

The Human Brain

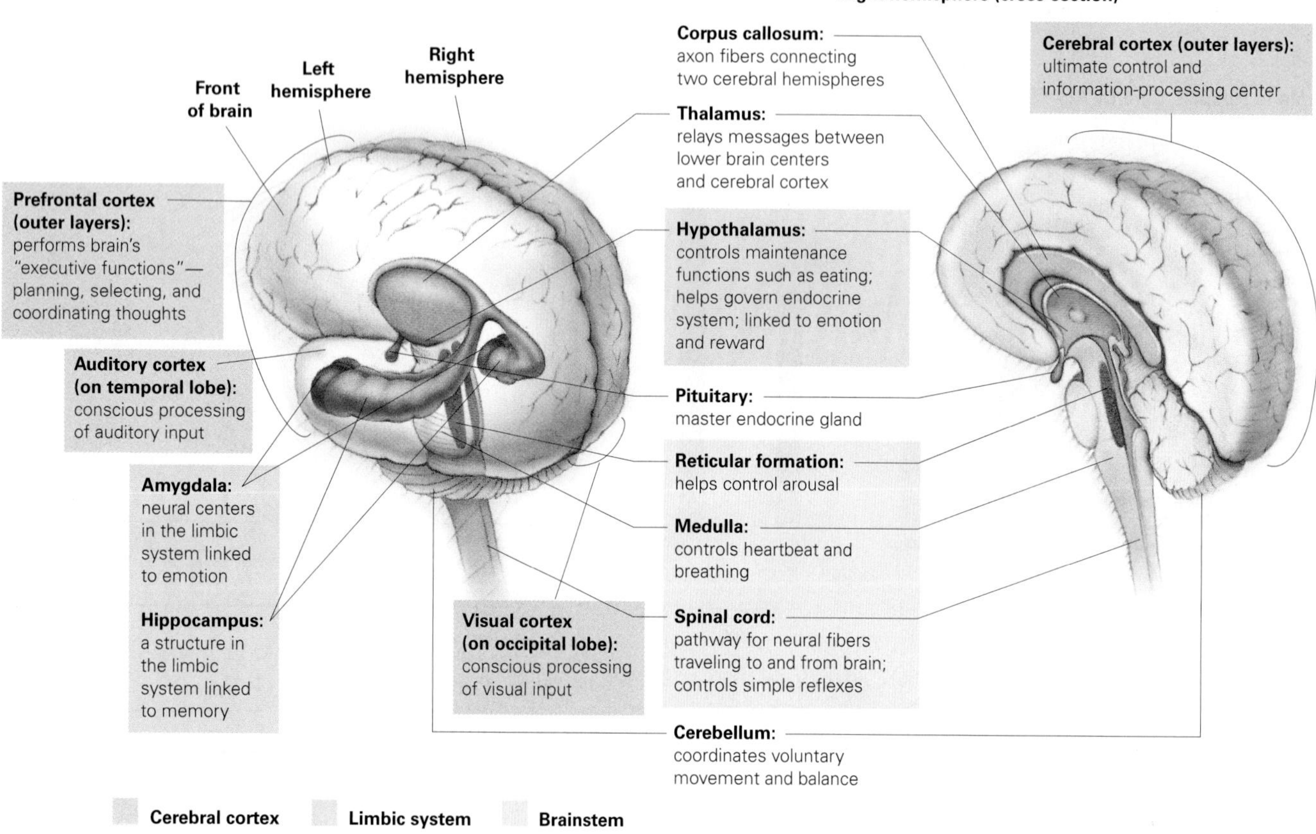
Front of brain
Left hemisphere
Right hemisphere
Right hemisphere (cross-section)
Prefrontal cortex (outer layers): performs brain's "executive functions"—planning, selecting, and coordinating thoughts
Auditory cortex (on temporal lobe): conscious processing of auditory input
Amygdala: neural centers in the limbic system linked to emotion
Hippocampus: a structure in the limbic system linked to memory
Visual cortex (on occipital lobe): conscious processing of visual input
Corpus callosum: axon fibers connecting two cerebral hemispheres
Thalamus: relays messages between lower brain centers and cerebral cortex
Hypothalamus: controls maintenance functions such as eating; helps govern endocrine system; linked to emotion and reward
Pituitary: master endocrine gland
Reticular formation: helps control arousal
Medulla: controls heartbeat and breathing
Spinal cord: pathway for neural fibers traveling to and from brain; controls simple reflexes
Cerebellum: coordinates voluntary movement and balance
Cerebral cortex (outer layers): ultimate control and information-processing center
Cerebral cortex
Limbic system
Brainstem

Appendix B More About Research Methods

Appendix A provides charts and numbers that lead to questions, hypotheses, surprises, and conclusions. The Research Design boxes in every chapter illustrate some ways to study any topic and show why additional research is needed. Appendix C guides students who want to conduct an observational or experimental study.

Here Appendix B explains how to learn about any topic. It is crucial that you distinguish valid conclusions from wishful thinking. This begins with your personal experience.

Make It Personal

Think about your life, observe your behavior, and watch the people around you. Pay careful attention to details of expression, emotion, and behavior. The more you see, the more fascinated, curious, and reflective you will become. Then, as is often suggested in the Applications that appear at the end of each chapter, listen carefully and respectfully to what other people say regarding development.

Whenever you ask specific questions as part of an assignment, **remember that observing ethical standards (see Chapter 1) comes first.** *Before* you interview anyone, inform the person of your purpose and assure him or her of confidentiality. Promise not to identify the person in your report (use a pseudonym) and do not repeat any personal details that emerge in the interview to anyone (friends or strangers).Your instructor will provide further ethical guidance. If you might publish what you've learned, inform your college's Institutional Research Board (IRB).

Read the Research

No matter how deeply you think about your own experiences, and no matter how intently you listen to others whose background is unlike yours, you also need to read scholarly published work in order to fully understand whatever topic interests you. Don't believe magazine or newspaper reports; some are bound to be simplified, exaggerated, or biased.

Professional Journals and Books

Part of the process of science is that conclusions are not considered solid until they are corroborated in many studies, which means that you should consult several sources on any topic. Four **professional journals in human development** that cover all three domains (biosocial, cognitive, and psychosocial) are:

- *Developmental Psychology* (published by the American Psychological Association)
- *Child Development* (Society for Research in Child Development)
- *Developmental Review* (Elsevier)
- *Human Development* (Karger)

These journals differ in the types of articles and studies they publish, but all are well respected. Every article includes references to other recent work.

Beyond these four are literally thousands of other professional journals, each with a particular perspective or topic. To judge them, look for journals that are *peer-reviewed,* which means that scientists (other than the authors of each article) read the submissions and decided whether each should be accepted, rejected, or revised. Also consider the following details: the background of the author (research funded by corporations tends to favor their products); the nature of the publisher (professional organizations, as in the first two journals above, protect their reputations); how long the journal has been published (the volume number tells you that). Some interesting work does not meet these criteria, but these are guides to quality.

Many **books** cover some aspect of development. Single-author books are likely to present only one viewpoint. That view may be insightful, but it is limited. You might consult a *handbook,* which is a book that includes many authors and many topics. Two good handbooks in development, both now in their sixth editions (a sign that past scholars have found them useful) are:

- *Handbook of Child Psychology* (2006), four volumes, published by Wiley
- *Handbook of Aging* (2006), three volumes (Biology, Psychology, and Social Sciences), published by Academic Press

The Internet

The **Internet** is a mixed blessing, useful to every novice and experienced researcher but dangerous as well. Every library has computers that provide access to journals and other information. Ask for help from the librarians; many are highly skilled. In addition, other students, friends, and even strangers can be helpful.

Virtually everything is on the Internet, not only massive national and international statistics but also very personal accounts. Photos, charts, quizzes, ongoing experiments, newspapers from around the world, videos, and much more are available at the click of a mouse. Every journal has a Web site, with tables of contents, abstracts, and sometimes full texts (an abstract gives the key findings; for the full text, you may need to consult the library's copy of the print version).

Unfortunately, you can spend many frustrating hours sifting through information that is useless, trash, or tangential. *Directories* (which list general topics or areas and then move you step by step in the direction you choose) and *search engines* (which give you all the sites that use a particular word or words) can help you select appropriate information. Each directory or search engine provides somewhat different lists; none provides only the most comprehensive and accurate sites. With experience and help, you will find the best sites for you, but you will also encounter some junk no matter how experienced you are.

Another problem is that anybody can put anything on the Web, regardless of its truth or fairness, so evaluate with a very critical eye everything you find. Make sure you have several divergent sources for every "fact" you find; consider who provided the information and why. Every controversial issue has sites that forcefully advocate opposite viewpoints, sometimes with biased statistics and narrow perspectives.

Here are nine Internet sites that are quite reliable:

- *www.worthpublishers.com/berger* Includes links to Web sites, quizzes, PowerPoint slides, and activities keyed to every chapter of the textbook.
- *embryo.soad.umich.edu* The Multidimensional Human Embryo. Presents MRI images of a human embryo at various stages of development, accompanied by brief explanations.

- *www.cdipage.com* A useful site, with links and articles on child development and information on common childhood psychological disorders.
- *ericeece.org/* ERIC Clearinghouse. Provides links to many education-related sites and includes brief descriptions of each.
- *site.educ.indiana.edu/cafs* Adolescence Directory online (ADOL) is an electronic guide to information on adolescent issues. It is a service of the Center for Adolescent and Family Studies at Indiana University.
- *www.nih.gov.nia/* National Institutes on Aging. Includes information about current research on aging.
- *www.cdc.gov/nchs/hus.htm* The National Center for Health Statistics issues an annual report on health trends, called "Health, United States."
- *www.aarp.org/life/grandparents* The AARP's Web site provides a wealth of information on grandparenting.
- *www.psy.pdx.edu/PsiCafe/Areas/Developmental/CogDev-Adult/* A good site for information on learning, memory, creativity, and other aspects of adult cognition.

Every source—you, your interviewees, journals, books, and the Internet— is helpful. Do not depend on any particular one. Especially if you use the Web, also check print resources. Avoid plagiarism and prejudice by citing every source and noting objectivity, validity, and credibility. Your own analysis, opinions, words, and conclusions are crucial.

Additional Terms and Concepts

As emphasized throughout this text, the study of development is a science. Social scientists study methods and statistics for years. Chapter 1 touches on some of these matters (observation and experiments; correlation and statistical significance; independent and dependent variables; experimental and control groups; cross-sectional, longitudinal, and cross-sequential research), but there is much more. A few additional aspects of research are presented here, to help you evaluate research wherever you find it.

Who Participates?

The entire group of people about whom a scientist wants to learn is called the **population.** Generally, a research population is quite large—not usually the world's entire population of almost 7 billion, but perhaps all the 4 million babies born in the United States last year, or all the 25 million Japanese currently over age 65.

The particular individuals who are studied in a specific research project are called the **participants.** They are used as a **sample** of the larger group. Ideally, a large number of people are used as a **representative sample,** that is, a sample who reflect the entire population. Every published study reports details on the sample.

Selection of the sample is crucial. Volunteers, or people with telephones, or people treated with some particular condition, are not a *random sample,* in which everyone in that population is equally likely to be selected. To avoid *selection bias,* some studies are *prospective,* beginning with an entire cluster (for instance, every baby born on a particular day) and then tracing the development of some particular characteristic.

For example, prospective studies find the antecedents of heart disease, or child abuse, or high school dropout rates—all of which are much harder to find if the study is *retrospective,* beginning with those who had heart attacks, experienced

population The entire group of individuals who are of particular concern in a scientific study, such as all the children of the world or all newborns who weigh less than 3 pounds.

participants The people who are studied in a research project.

sample A group of individuals drawn from a specified population. A sample might be the low-birthweight babies born in four particular hospitals that are representative of all hospitals.

representative sample A group of research participants who reflect the relevant characteristics of the larger population whose attributes are under study.

abuse, or left school. Thus, although retrospective research finds that most high school dropouts say they disliked school, prospective research finds that some who like school still decide to drop out and then later say they hated school, while others dislike school but stay to graduate. Prospective research discovers how many students are in these last two categories; retrospective research on people who have already dropped out does not.

Research Design

Every researcher begins not only by formulating a hypothesis but also by learning what other scientists have discovered about the topic in question and what methods might be useful and ethical in designing research. Often they include methods to guard against inadvertently finding the results they expect. Often the people who actually gather the data do not know the purpose of the research. Scientists say that these data gatherers are **blind** to the hypothesized outcome. Adult participants are sometimes blind as well, because otherwise they might, for instance, answer a survey question the way they think they should.

blind The condition of data gatherers (and sometimes participants as well) who are deliberately kept ignorant of the purpose of the research so that they cannot unintentionally bias the results.

operational definition A description of the specific, observable behavior that will constitute the variable that is to be studied, so that any reader will know whether that behavior occurred or not. Operational definitions may be arbitrary (e.g., an IQ score at or above 130 is operationally defined as "gifted"), but they must be precise.

Another crucial aspect of research design is to define exactly what is to be studied. Researchers establish an **operational definition** of whatever phenomenon they will be examining, defining each variable by describing specific, observable behavior. This is essential in quantitative research (see Chapter 1), but it is also useful in qualitative research. For example, if a researcher wants to know when babies begin to walk, does *walking* include steps taken while holding on, and is one unsteady step enough? Some parents say yes, but the usual operational definition of walking is "takes at least three steps without holding on." This operational definition allows comparisons worldwide, making it possible to discover, for example, that well-fed African babies tend to walk earlier than well-fed European babies.

Operational definitions are difficult but essential when personality traits are studied. How should *aggression* or *sharing* or *shyness* be defined? Lack of an operational definition leads to contradictory results. For instance, some say that infant day care makes children more aggressive, but others say it makes them less passive. For any scientists, or any parent, operational definitions are crucial.

Reporting Results

You already know that results should be reported in sufficient detail so that another scientist can analyze the conclusions and replicate the research. Various methods, population, and research designs may produce divergent conclusions. For that reason, handbooks, some journals, and some articles are called *reviews:* They summarize past research. Often, when studies are similar in operational definitions and methods, the review is a **meta-analysis,** combining the findings of many studies to present an overall conclusion.

meta-analysis A technique of combining results of many studies to come to an overall conclusion. Meta-analysis is powerful, in that small samples can be added together to lead to significant conclusions, although variations from study to study sometimes make combining them impossible.

effect size A way to indicate, statistically, how much of an impact the independent variable had on the dependent variable.

You also remember *statistical significance,* which indicates whether or not a particular result could have occurred by chance. Many studies report other statistics and statistical measures—all helpful to scientists as they evaluate the conclusions.

One other statistic that is often crucial is **effect size,** a way of measuring how much impact one variable has on another. Effect size ranges from 0 (no effect) to 1 (total transformation, never found in actual studies). Effect size may be particularly important when the sample size is large, because a large sample often leads to highly "significant" results (unlikely to have occurred by chance) that have only a tiny effect on the variable of interest.

This is the case for many gender differences, which are statistically significant but minuscule (Hyde, 2001). For example, if, after testing thousands of high school students, researchers found that the average boy scored a point higher on a test of math ability than the average girl (see Chapter 15), that would be highly significant but only a very small effect of gender.

A specific example involved methods to improve student's writing ability between grades 4 and 12. A meta-analysis found that many methods of writing instruction have a significant impact, but effect size is much larger for some methods (teaching strategies and summarizing) than for others (prewriting exercises and studying models). For teachers, this statistic is crucial, for they want to know what has a big effect, not merely what is better than chance (significant).

To read examples of meta-analysis and effect size, you might look at the following:

- Dixon, Kim E., Keefe, Francis J., & Scipio, Cindy D. (2007). Psychological interventions for arthritis pain management in adults: A meta-analysis. *Health Psychology, 26,* 241–250. [The overall effect size was 0.17, considered small, but some pain-management methods were found to be better than others.]
- Graham, Steve, & Perin, Dolores. (2007). A meta-analysis of writing instruction for adolescent students. *Journal of Educational Psychology, 99,* 445–476. [This article, mentioned above, contains many interesting details, including operational definitions and specific effect sizes.]
- Grissom, R. J., & Kim, J. J. (2005). Effect sizes for research: A broad practical approach. Mahwah, NJ: Erlbaum. [This article provides many specifics about this statistical measure; it makes for heavy reading but is useful for researchers.]
- Hyde, Janet Shibley. (2001). Reporting effect sizes: The roles of editors, textbook authors, and publication manuals. *Educational and Psychological Measurement, 61,* 225–228. [Explains why effect size is important, using gender differences as an example.]
- Olatunji, Bunmi O., Cisler, Josh M., & Tolin, David F. (2007). Quality of life in the anxiety disorders: A meta-analytic review. *Clinical Psychology Review,* 2, 572–581. [This review concludes that anxiety disorders reduce the quality of life, but some of them, such as post-traumatic stress disorder, have a greater negative effect than others.].
- Oosterman, Mirjam, Schuengel, Carlo, & Slot, N. Wim. (2007). Disruptions in foster care: A review and meta-analysis. *Children and Youth Services Review, 29,* 53–76. [This review finds that a child with behavior problems is likely to experience more changes in placement, but kinship care is unexpectedly stable.]

Appendix C
Suggestions for Research Assignments

The best way to study human development is to do some investigation yourself, not only by reading the textbook and expressing your ideas in speech and writing but also by undertaking some research of your own. Writing a term paper is the usual mode in most college courses: You and your instructor already know the importance of setting a deadline for each stage (topic selection, outline, first draft, final draft), of asking several readers to evaluate your paper (perhaps including other students or a professor), and of having the final version typed with references correctly cited and listed. Some suggestions for effective use of journals and the Internet are given in Appendix B.

The subject of human development is also ideal for more personal study, so suggestions for conducting observations, case studies, surveys, and experiments are offered here.

Learning Through Observation

Much can be learned by becoming more systematic in your observations of the adults and children around you. One way to begin is to collect observations of ten different children, in differing contexts, during the semester. Each profile should be approximately one page and should cover the following four items:

1. *Describe the physical and social context.* You will want to describe where you are, what day and time it is, and how many people you are observing. The weather and age and gender of those who are being observed might also be relevant. For example:

    Neighborhood playground on (street), at about 4 P.M. on (day, date), 30 children and 10 adults present.
    OR
    Supermarket at (location) on Saturday morning (day, date), about 20 shoppers present.

2. *Describe the specific child who is the focus of your attention.* Estimate age, gender, and so on of the target child and anyone else who interacts with the child. Do not ask the age of the child until after the observation, if at all. Your goal is to conduct a naturalistic observation that is unobtrusive. For example:

    Boy, about 7 years old, playing with four other boys, who seem a year or two older. All are dressed warmly (it is a cold day) in similar clothes.
    OR
    Girl, about 18 months old, in supermarket cart pushed by woman, about 30 years old. The cart is half full of groceries.

3. *Write down everything that the child does or says in three minutes.* (Use a watch with a second hand.) Record gestures, facial expressions, movements, and words. Accurate reporting is the goal, and three minutes becomes a surprisingly long time if you write down everything. For example:

    Child runs away about 20 feet, returns, and says, "Try to catch me." Two boys look at him, but they do not move. Boy frowns. He runs away and comes back in 10 seconds, stands about four feet away from the boys, and says, "Anyone want to play tag?" [And so on.]

OR
Child points to a package of Frosted Flakes cereal and makes a noise. (I could not hear if it was a word.) Mother says nothing and pushes the cart past the cereal. Child makes a whining noise, looks at the cereal, and kicks her left foot. Mother puts pacifier in child's mouth. [And so on.]

4. *Interpret what you just observed.* Is the child's behavior typical of children that age? Is the reaction of others helpful or not helpful? What values are being encouraged, and what skills are being mastered? What could have happened differently? This section is your opinion, but it must be based on the particulars you have just observed and on your knowledge of child development, ideally with specific reference to concepts (e.g., the first may be a rejected child; the second child's language development may not be encouraged).

Structuring a Case Study

A case study is more elaborate and detailed than an observation report. Select one child (ask your instructor if family members can be used), and secure written permission from the caregiver and, if the child is old enough, the child him- or herself. Explain that you are not going to report the name of the child, that the material is for your class, that the child or caregiver can stop the project at any time, and that they would be doing you a big favor in helping you learn about child development. Most people are quite happy to help in your education, if you explain this properly.

Gather Your Data

First, collect the information for your paper by using all the research methods you have learned. These methods include:

1. *Naturalistic observation.* Ask the caregiver when the child is likely to be awake and active, and observe the child for an hour during this time. Try to be as unobtrusive as possible; you are not there to play with, or care for, the child. If the child wants to play, explain that you must sit and write for now and that you will play later.

    Write down, minute by minute, everything the child does and that others do with the child. Try to be objective, focusing on behavior rather than interpretation. Thus, instead of writing "Jennifer was delighted when her father came home, and he dotes on her," you should write "5:33: Her father opened the door, Jennifer looked up, smiled, said 'dada,' and ran to him. He bent down, stretched out his arms, picked her up, and said, 'How's my little angel?' 5:34: He put her on his shoulders, and she said, 'Giddy up, horsey.'"

    After your observation, summarize the data in two ways: (a) Note the percentage of time spent in various activities. For instance, "Playing alone, 15 percent; playing with brother, 20 percent; crying, 3 percent." (b) Note the frequency of various behaviors: "Asked adult for something five times; adult granted request four times. Aggressive acts (punch, kick, etc.) directed at brother, 2; aggressive acts initiated by brother, 6." Making notations like these will help you evaluate and quantify your observations. Also, note any circumstances that might have made your observation atypical (e.g., "Jenny's mother said she hasn't been herself since she had the flu a week ago," or "Jenny kept trying to take my pen, so it was hard to write").

    Note: Remember that a percentage can be found by dividing the total number of minutes spent on a specific activity by the total number of minutes you spent observing. For example, if, during your 45-minute observation, the child played by herself for periods of 2 minutes, 4 minutes, and 5 minutes, "playing alone" would total 11 minutes. Dividing 11 by 45 yields 0.244; thus the child spent 24 percent of the time playing alone.

2. *Informal interaction.* Interact with the child for at least half an hour. Your goal is to observe the child's personality and abilities in a relaxed setting. The particular activities you engage in will depend on the child's age and temperament. Most children enjoy playing games, reading books, drawing, and talking. Asking a younger child to show you his or her room and favorite toys is a good way to break the ice; asking an older child to show you the neighborhood can provide insights.
3. *Interview adults responsible for the child's care.* Keep these interviews loose and open-ended. Your goals are to learn (a) the child's history, especially any illnesses, stresses, or problems that might affect development; (b) the child's daily routine, including play patterns; (c) current problems that might affect the child; (d) a description of the child's temperament and personality, including special strengths and weaknesses.

   You are just as interested in adult values and attitudes as in the facts; therefore, you might concentrate on conversing during the interview, perhaps writing down a few words. Then write down all you remember as soon as the interview has been completed.
4. *Testing the child.* Assess the child's perceptual, motor, language, and intellectual abilities by using specific test items you have prepared in advance. The actual items you use will depend on the age of the child. For instance, you might test object permanence in a child between 6 and 24 months old; you would test conservation in a child between 3 and 9 years old. Likewise, testing language abilities might involve babbling with an infant, counting words per sentence with a preschooler, and asking a school-age child to make up a story.

Write Up Your Findings

Second, write the report, using the following steps:

1. Begin by reporting relevant background information, including the child's birth date and sex, age and sex of siblings, economic and ethnic background of the family, and the educational and marital status of the parents.
2. Describe the child's biosocial, cognitive, and psychosocial development, citing supporting data from your research to substantiate any conclusions you have reached. Do not simply transcribe your interview, test, or observation data, although you can attach your notes as an appendix, if you wish.
3. Predict the child's development in the next year, the next five years, and the next ten years. List the strengths in the child, the family, and the community that you think will foster optimal development. Also note whatever potential problems you see (either in the child's current behavior or in the family and community support system) that may lead to future difficulties for the child. Include discussion of the reasons, either methodological or theoretical, that your predictions may not be completely accurate.

Finally, show your report to a classmate (your instructor may assign you to a peer mentor) and ask if you have been clear in your description and predictions. Discuss the child with your classmate to see if you should add more details to your report. Your revised case study should be typed and given to your professor, who will evaluate it. If you wish, send me a copy (Professor Kathleen Berger, c/o Worth Publishers, 41 Madison Avenue, New York, NY 10010).

Experiments and Surveys

As you learned in Chapter 1, experiments and surveys are wonderful ways to learn more about development, but each study needs to be very carefully designed and undertaken to avoid bias and to ensure that all the ethical considerations are taken into account. Accordingly, I recommend that an experiment or survey be undertaken by a group of students, not by an individual. Listening carefully to other opinions, using more than one person to collect data, and checking with your professor before beginning the actual study are ways to make sure that your results have some validity.

If you do this, structure your work in such a way that everyone contributes and that contrary opinions are encouraged. (The normal human response is for everyone to agree with everyone else, but, as you learned in Chapter 15, seeking alternate, logical explanations can move an entire group forward to deeper, more analytic thought.) You might designate one person to be the critic, or your group might spend one day designing your study and another day finding problems with the design. (Some problems simply need to be recognized and acknowledged, but some of them can be fixed by changing the design.)

Specific topics for experiments or surveys depend on your group's interests and on your professor's requirements for the course. For ideas, check this book's Subject Index or Study Guide. Since development is multidisciplinary and multicontextual, almost any topic can be related to it. Just remember to consider theory and practice, change and continuity, social interaction and cultural impact . . . and then try to limit your initial experiment or survey to one small part of this fascinating, ever-changing subject!

Glossary

A

AARP A U.S. organization of people aged 50 and older, which advocates for the elderly. It was originally called the American Association of Retired Persons, but now only the initials AARP are used, to reflect the fact that the organization's members do not have to be retired.

absent grief A situation in which overly private people cut themselves off from the community and customs of expected grief; can lead to social isolation.

achievement tests Measures of mastery or proficiency in reading, math, writing, science, or any other subject.

active euthanasia A situation in which someone takes action to bring about another person's death, with the intention of ending that person's suffering.

activities of daily life (ADLs) Actions that are important to independent living, typically consisting of five tasks of self-care: eating, bathing, toileting, dressing, and transferring from a bed to a chair. The inability to perform any of these tasks is a sign of frailty.

activity theory The view that elderly people want and need to remain active in a variety of social spheres—with relatives, friends, and community groups—and become withdrawn only unwillingly, as a result of ageism.

additive gene A gene that has several alleles, each of which contributes to the final phenotype (such as skin color or height).

adolescence-limited offender A person whose criminal activity stops by age 21.

adolescent egocentrism A characteristic of adolescent thinking that leads young people (ages 10 to 13) to focus on themselves to the exclusion of others. A young person might believe, for example, that his or her thoughts, feelings, and experiences are unique, more wonderful or awful than anyone else's.

adrenal glands Two glands, located above the kidneys, that produce hormones (including the "stress hormones" epinephrine [adrenaline] and norepinephrine).

affordance An opportunity for perception and interaction that is offered by a person, place, or object in the environment.

age in place Refers to a preference of elderly people to remain in the same home and community, adjusting but not leaving when health fades.

age of viability The age (about 22 weeks after conception) at which a fetus can survive outside the mother's uterus if specialized medical care is available.

ageism A prejudice in which people are categorized and judged solely on the basis of their chronological age.

aggressive-rejected Rejected by peers because of antagonistic, confrontational behavior.

allele A slight, normal variation of a particular gene.

allostatic load The total, combined burden of stress and disease that an individual must cope with.

Alzheimer's disease (AD) The most common cause of dementia, characterized by gradual deterioration of memory and personality and marked by the formation of plaques of beta-amyloid protein and tangles in the brain.

amygdala A tiny brain structure that registers emotions, particularly fear and anxiety.

analytic intelligence A form of intelligence that involves such mental processes as abstract planning, strategy selection, focused attention, and information processing, as well as verbal and logical skills.

analytic thought Thought that results from analysis, such as a systematic ranking of pros and cons, risks and consequences, possibilities and facts. Analytic thought depends on logic and rationality.

androgyny A balance, within a person, of traditionally male and female psychological characteristics.

andropause A term coined to signify a drop in testosterone levels in older men, which normally results in reduced sexual desire, erections, and muscle mass. Also known as *male menopause*.

anorexia nervosa A serious eating disorder in which a person restricts eating to the point of emaciation and possible starvation. Most victims are high-achieving females in early puberty or early adulthood.

anoxia A lack of oxygen that, if prolonged during birth, can cause brain damage or death to the baby.

antioxidants Chemical compounds that nullify the effects of oxygen free radicals by forming a bond with their unattached oxygen electron.

antipathy Feelings of anger, distrust, dislike, or even hatred toward another person.

antisocial behavior Feeling and acting in ways that are deliberately hurtful or destructive to another person.

antithesis A proposition or statement of belief that opposes the thesis; the second stage of the process of dialectical thinking.

Apgar scale A quick assessment of a newborn's body functioning. The baby's color, heart rate, reflexes, muscle tone, and respiratory effort are given a score of 0, 1, or 2 twice—at one minute and five minutes after birth—and the total of all the scores is compared with the ideal score of 10.

apprentice in thinking Vygotsky's term for a person whose cognition is stimulated and directed by older and more skilled members of society.

aptitude The potential to master a particular skill or to learn a particular body of knowledge.

Asperger syndrome A specific type of autistic spectrum disorder characterized by extreme attention to details and deficient social understanding.

assisted living A living arrangement for elderly people that combines privacy and independence with medical supervision.

assisted reproductive technology (ART) A general term for the techniques designed to help infertile couples conceive and then sustain a pregnancy.

asthma A chronic disease of the respiratory system in which inflammation narrows the airways from the lungs to the nose and mouth, causing difficulty in breathing. Signs and symptoms include wheezing, shortness of breath, chest tightness, and coughing.

attachment According to Ainsworth, "an affectional tie" that an infant forms with the caregiver—a tie that binds them together in space and endures over time.

attention-deficit/hyperactivity disorder (ADHD) A condition in which a person not only has great difficulty concentrating for more than a few moments but also is inattentive, impulsive, and overactive.

authoritarian parenting Child rearing with high behavioral standards, punishment of misconduct, and low communication.

authoritative parenting Child rearing in which the parents set limits but listen to the child and are flexible.

autism A developmental disorder marked by an inability to relate to other people normally, extreme self-absorption, and an inability to acquire normal speech.

autistic spectrum disorder Any of several disorders characterized by inadequate social skills, unusual communication, and abnormal play.

automatization A process in which repetition of a sequence of thoughts and actions makes the sequence routine, so that it no longer requires conscious thought.

autonomy versus shame and doubt Erikson's second crisis of psychosocial development. Toddlers either succeed or fail in gaining a sense of self-rule over their own actions and bodies.

average life expectancy The number of years the average newborn in a particular population group is likely to live.

axon A nerve fiber that extends from a neuron and transmits electrical impulses from that neuron to the dendrites of other neurons.

B

B cells Immune cells manufactured in the bone marrow that create antibodies for isolating and destroying bacteria and viruses that are invading the body.

babbling The extended repetition of certain syllables, such as *ba-ba-ba,* that begins between 6 and 9 months of age.

balanced bilingual A person who is fluent in two languages, not favoring one or the other.

behavioral teratogens Agents and conditions that can harm the prenatal brain, impairing the future child's intellectual and emotional functioning.

behaviorism A grand theory of human development that studies observable behavior. Behaviorism is also called *learning theory* because it describes the laws and processes by which behavior is learned.

bereavement The sense of loss following a death.

bickering Petty, peevish arguing, usually repeated and ongoing.

Big Five The five basic clusters of personality traits that remain quite stable throughout adulthood: openness, conscientiousness, extroversion, agreeableness, and neuroticism.

bilingual education A strategy in which school subjects are taught in both the learner's original language and the second (majority) language.

binocular vision The ability to focus the two eyes in a coordinated manner in order to see one image.

blastocyst A cell mass that develops from the zygote in the first few days after conception, during the germinal period, and forms a hollow sphere in preparation for implantation.

blended family A family that consists of two adults and the children of the prior relationships of one or both parents and/or the new partnership.

body image A person's idea of how his or her body looks.

body mass index (BMI) The ratio of a person's weight in kilograms divided by his or her height in meters squared.

bulimia nervosa An eating disorder in which the person, usually female, engages repeatedly in episodes of binge eating followed by purging through induced vomiting or use of laxatives.

bully-victim Someone who attacks others, and who is attacked as well. (Also called *provocative victims* because they do things that elicit bullying, such as taking a bully's pencil.)

bullying aggression Unprovoked, repeated physical or verbal attack, especially on victims who are unlikely to defend themselves.

bullying Repeated, systematic efforts to inflict harm through physical, verbal, or social attack on a weaker person.

butterfly effect The idea that a small effect or thing can have a large impact if it happens to tip the balance, causing other changes that create a major event.

C

calorie restriction The practice of limiting dietary energy intake (while consuming sufficient quantities of vitamins, minerals, and other important nutrients) for the purpose of improving health and slowing down the aging process.

cardiovascular disease Disease that involves the heart and the circulatory system.

carrier A person whose genotype includes a gene that is not expressed in the phenotype. Such an unexpressed gene occurs in half of the carrier's gametes and thus is passed on to half of the carrier's children, who will most likely be carriers, too. Generally, only when the gene is inherited from both parents does the characteristic appear in the phenotype.

case study A research method in which one individual is studied intensively.

centenarian A person who has lived 100 years or more.

center day care Child care in a place especially designed for the purpose, where several paid providers care for many children. Usually the children are grouped by age, the day-care center is licensed, and providers are trained and certified in child development.

centration A characteristic of preoperational thought in which a young child focuses (centers) on one idea, excluding all others.

cerebral palsy A disorder that results from damage to the brain's motor centers. People with cerebral palsy have difficulty with muscle control, so their speech and body movements are impaired.

cesarean section A surgical birth, in which incisions through the mother's abdomen and uterus allow the fetus to be removed quickly, instead of being delivered through the vagina. (Also called *c-section* or simply *section*.)

child abuse Deliberate action that is harmful to a child's physical, emotional, or sexual well-being.

child maltreatment Intentional harm to or avoidable endangerment of anyone under 18 years of age.

child neglect Failure to meet a child's basic physical, educational, or emotional needs.

child sexual abuse Any erotic activity that arouses an adult and excites, shames, or confuses a child, whether or not the victim protests and whether or not genital contact is involved.

child-directed speech The high-pitched, simplified, and repetitive way adults speak to infants. (Also called *baby talk* or *motherese*.)

children with special needs Children who, because of a physical or mental disability, require extra help in order to learn.

chromosome One of the 46 molecules of DNA (in 23 pairs) that each cell of the human body contains and that, together, contain all the genes. Other species have more or fewer chromosomes.

classical conditioning The learning process that connects a meaningful stimulus (such as the smell of food to a hungry animal) with a neutral stimulus (such as the sound of a bell) that had no special meaning before conditioning. Also called *respondent conditioning*.

classification The logical principle that things can be organized into groups (or categories or classes) according to some characteristic they have in common.

clinical depression Feelings of hopelessness, lethargy, and worthlessness that last two weeks or more.

clique A group of adolescents made up of close friends who are loyal to one another while excluding outsiders.

clone An organism that is produced from another organism through artificial replication of cells and is genetically identical to that organism.

cluster suicides Several suicides committed by members of a group within a brief period of time.

co-sleeping A custom in which parents and their children (usually infants) sleep together. (Also called *bed-sharing*.)

code of ethics A set of moral principles that members of a profession or group are expected to follow.

cognitive equilibrium In cognitive theory, a state of mental balance in which people are not confused because they can use their existing thought processes to understand current experiences and ideas.

cognitive theory A grand theory of human development that focuses on changes in how people think over time. According to this theory, our thoughts shape our attitudes, beliefs, and behaviors.

cohabitation An arrangement in which a man and a woman live together in a committed sexual relationship but are not formally married.

cohort A group of people who were born at about the same time and thus move through life together, experiencing the same historical events and cultural shifts.

common couple violence A form of abuse in which one or both partners of a couple engage in outbursts of verbal and physical attack. (Also called *situational couple violence*.)

comorbidity The presence of two or more unrelated disease conditions at the same time in the same person.

comparison group/control group A group of participants in a research study who are similar to the experimental group in all relevant ways but who do not experience the experimental condition (the independent variable).

compression of morbidity A lessening of the time a person spends ill or infirm, accomplished by postponing illness.

concrete operational thought Piaget's term for the ability to reason logically about direct experiences and perceptions.

conditioning According to behaviorism, the processes by which reponses become linked to particular stimuli and learning takes place. The word *conditioning* is used to emphasize the importance of repeated practice, as when an athlete gets into physical condition by training for a long time.

conservation The idea that the amount of a substance remains the same (i.e., is conserved) when its appearance changes.

continuity theory The theory that each person experiences the changes of late adulthood and behaves toward others in much the same way he or she did in earlier periods of life.

control processes Mechanisms (including selective attention, metacognition, and emotional regulation) that combine memory, processing speed, and knowledge to regulate the analysis and flow of information within the information-processing system.

conventional moral reasoning Kohlberg's second level of moral reasoning, emphasizing social rules.

corpus callosum A long band of nerve fibers that connect the left and right hemispheres of the brain.

correlation A number indicating the degree of relationship between two variables, expressed in terms of the likelihood that one variable will (or will not) occur when the other variable does (or does not). A correlation is not an indication that one variable causes the other, only that the two variables are related to the indicated degree.

cortex The outer layers of the brain in humans and other mammals. Most thinking, feeling, and sensing involve the cortex. (Sometimes called the *neocortex*.)

creative intelligence A form of intelligence that involves the capacity to be intellectually flexible and innovative.

critical period In prenatal development, the time when a particular organ or other body part of the embryo or fetus is most susceptible to damage by teratogens. Also, a time when a certain development *must* happen if it is ever to happen. For example, the embryonic period is critical for the development of arms and legs.

cross-sectional research A research design that compares groups of people who differ in age but are similar in other important characteristics.

cross-sequential research A hybrid research method in which researchers first study several groups of people of different ages (a cross-sectional approach) and then follow those groups over the years (a longitudinal approach). (Also called *cohort-sequential research* or *time-sequential research*.)

crowd A larger group of adolescents who have something in common but who are not necessarily friends.

crystallized intelligence Those types of intellectual ability that reflect accumulated learning. Vocabulary and general information are examples. Some developmental psychologists think crystallized intelligence increases with age, while fluid intelligence declines.

culture of children The particular habits, styles, and values that reflect the set of rules and rituals that characterize children as distinct from adult society.

D

DALYs (disability-adjusted life years) A measure of the impact that disability has on quality of life. DALYs are the reciprocal of quality-adjusted life years: A reduction in QALYs means an increase in DALYs.

deductive reasoning Reasoning from a general statement, premise, or principle, through logical steps, to figure out (deduce) specifics. (Sometimes called *top-down thinking*.)

deferred imitation A sequence in which an infant first perceives something that someone else does and then performs the same action a few hours or even days later.

Defining Issues Test (DIT) A series of questions developed by James Rest and designed to assess respondents' level of moral development by having them rank possible solutions to moral dilemmas.

delay discounting The tendency to undervalue, or downright ignore, future consequences and rewards in favor of more immediate gratification.

delirium A temporary loss of memory, often accompanied by emotions of fear or grandiosity and irrational actions.

dementia Irreversible loss of intellectual functioning caused by organic brain damage or disease. Dementia becomes more common with age, but it is abnormal and pathological even in the very old.

demography The study of the characteristics of human populations, including size, birth and death rates, density, and distribution.

dendrite A nerve fiber that extends from a neuron and receives electrical impulses transmitted from other neurons via their axons.

dependency ratio The ratio of self-sufficient, productive adults to dependents (children and the elderly) in a given population.

dependent variable In an experiment, the variable that may change as a result of whatever new condition or situation the experimenter adds. In other words, the dependent variable *depends* on the independent variable.

developmental psychopathology The field that uses insights into typical development to study and treat developmental disorders, and vice versa.

developmental theory A group of ideas, assumptions, and generalizations that interpret and illuminate the thousands of observations that have been made about human growth. In this way, developmental theories provide a framework for explaining the patterns and problems of development.

deviancy training The process whereby children are taught by their peers how to rebel against authority or social norms.

Diagnostic and Statistical Manual of Mental Disorders (DSM-IV-TR) The American Psychiatric Association's official guide to the diagnosis (not treatment) of mental disorders. (*IV-TR* means "fourth edition, Test Revision.")

dialectical thought The most advanced cognitive process, characterized by the ability to consider a thesis and its antithesis simultaneously and thus to arrive at a synthesis. Dialectical thought makes possible an ongoing awareness of pros and cons, advantages and disadvantages, possibilities and limitations.

diathesis-stress model The view that mental disorders, such as schizophrenia, are produced by the interaction of a genetic vulnerability (the diathesis) with stressful environmental factors and life events.

disability Long-term difficulty in performing normal activities of daily life because of some physical, mental, or emotional condition.

disenfranchised grief A situation in which certain people, although they are bereaved, are not allowed to mourn publicly.

disengagement theory The view that aging makes a person's social sphere increasingly narrow, resulting in role relinquishment, withdrawal, and passivity.

disorganized attachment A type of attachment that is marked by an infant's inconsistent reactions to the caregiver's departure and return.

distal parenting Parenting practices that focus on the intellect more than the body, such as talking with the baby and playing with an object.

diversity For developmentalists, diversity involves differences among groups of people based on such characteristics as race, gender, culture, age, family income, and sexuality.

dizygotic (DZ) twins Twins who are formed when two separate ova are fertilized by two separate sperm at roughly the same time. (Also called *fraternal twins*.)

DNA (deoxyribonucleic acid) The molecule that contains the chemical instructions for cells to manufacture various proteins.

DNR (do not resuscitate) A written order from a physician (sometimes initiated by a patient's advance directive or by a health care proxy's request) that no attempt should be made to revive a patient if he or she suffers cardiac or respiratory arrest.

dominant–recessive pattern The interaction of a pair of alleles in such a way that the phenotype reveals the influence of one allele (the dominant gene) more than that of the other (the recessive gene).

double effect An ethical situation in which a person performs an action that is good or morally neutral but has ill effects that are foreseen, though not desired.

doula A woman who helps with the birth process. Traditionally in Latin America, a doula was like a midwife, the only professional who attended childbirths. Now doulas are likely to work alongside a hospital's medical staff to help mothers through labor and delivery.

Down syndrome A condition in which a person has 47 chromosomes instead of the usual 46, with three rather than two chromosomes at the 21st position. People with Down syndrome typically have distinctive characteristics, including unusual facial features, heart abnormalities, and language difficulties. (Also called *trisomy-21*.)

drug abuse The ingestion of a drug to the extent that it impairs the user's biological or psychological well-being.

drug addiction A condition of drug dependence in which the absence of the given drug in the individual's system produces a drive—physiological, psychological, or both—to ingest more of the drug.

dual-process model The notion that two networks exist within the human brain, one for emotional and one for analytical processing of stimuli.

dual-task deficit A situation in which a person's performance of one task is impeded by interference from the simultaneous performance of another task.

dynamic perception Perception that is primed to focus on movement and change.

dynamic theories Theories of psychosocial development that emphasize change and readjustment rather than either the ongoing self or the impact of stratification. Each person's life is seen as an active, ever-changing, largely self-propelled process, occurring within specific social contexts that are also constantly changing.

dynamic-systems theory A view of human development as always changing. Life is the product of ongoing interaction between the physical and emotional being and between the person and every aspect of his or her environment, including the family and society. Flux is constant, and each change affects all the others.

dyslexia Unusual difficulty with reading; thought to be the result of some neurological underdevelopment.

E

eclectic perspective The approach taken by most developmentalists, in which they apply aspects of each of the various theories of development rather than adhering exclusively to one theory.

ecological niche The particular lifestyle and social context adults settle into that are compatible with their individual personality needs and interests.

ecological-systems approach A vision of how human development should be studied, with the person considered in all the contexts and interactions that constitute a life.

edgework Occupations or recreational activities that require a degree of risk or danger; it is this prospect of "living on the edge" that makes edgework compelling to some individuals.

effortful control The ability to regulate one's emotions and actions through effort, not simply through natural inclination.

egocentrism Piaget's term for children's tendency to think about the world entirely from their own personal perspective.

elderspeak A condescending way of speaking to older adults that resembles baby talk, with simple and short sentence, exaggerated emphasis, repetition, and a slower rate and a higher pitch than normal speech.

Electra complex The unconscious desire of girls to replace their mother and win their father's exclusive love.

embryo The name for a developing organism from about the third through the eighth week after conception.

embryonic period The stage of prenatal development from approximately the third through the eighth week after conception, during which the basic forms of all body structures, including internal organs, develop.

emergent theories Theories that bring together information from many disciplines in addition to psychology and that are becoming comprehensive and systematic in their interpretations of development but are not yet established and detailed enough to be considered grand theories.

emotional regulation The ability to control when and how emotions are expressed. This is the most important psychosocial development to occur between the ages of 2 and 6, though it continues throughout life.

empathy The ability to understand the emotions of another person, especially when those emotions differ from one's own.

empirical Based on observation, experience, or experiment; not theoretical.

empty nest A time in the lives of parents when their grown children leave the family home to pursue their own lives.

English-language learner (ELL) A child who is learning English as a second language.

epigenetic theory An emergent theory of development that considers both the genetic origins of behavior (within each person and within each species) and the direct, systematic influence that environmental forces have, over time, on genes.

ESL (English as a second language) An approach to teaching English in which all children who do not speak English are placed together and given an intensive course in basic English so that they can be educated in the same classroom as native English speakers.

estradiol A sex hormone, considered the chief estrogen. Females produce more estradiol than males do.

ethnic group People whose ancestors were born in the same region and who often share a language, culture, and religion.

ethnotheory A theory that underlies the values and practices of a culture and that becomes apparent through analysis and comparison of those practices, although it is not usually apparent to the people within the culture.

exclusion criteria A person's reasons for omitting certain people from consideration as close friends or romantic partners. Exclusion criteria vary from one individual to another, but they are strong filters.

experience-dependent Refers to brain functions that depend on particular, variable experiences and that therefore may or may not develop in a particular infant.

experience-expectant Refers to brain functions that require certain basic common experiences (which an infant can be expected to have) in order to develop normally.

experiment A research method in which the researcher tries to determine the cause-and-effect relationship between two variables by manipulating one variable (called the *independent variable*) and then observing and recording the resulting changes in the other variable (called the *dependent variable*).

experimental group A group of participants in a research study who experience some special treatment or condition (the independent variable).

explicit memory Memory that is easy to retrieve on demand (as in a specific test), usually with words. Most explicit memory involves consciously learned words, data, and concepts.

extended family A family of three or more generations living in one household.

externalizing problems Difficulty with emotional regulation that involves outwardly expressing emotions in uncontrolled ways, such as by lashing out in impulsive anger or attacking other people or things.

extreme sports Forms of recreation that include apparent risk of injury or death and that are attractive and thrilling as a result. Motocross is one example.

extremely low birthweight (ELBW) A body weight at birth of less than 3 pounds (1,360 grams).

extrinsic motivation The need for rewards from outside, such as material possessions or someone else's esteem.

extrinsic rewards of work The tangible rewards, usually in the form of compensation, that one receives for a job (e.g., salary, benefits, pension).

F

familism The idea that family members should support one another because family unity is more important than individual freedom and success or failure.

family day care Child care that occurs in another caregiver's home. Usually the caregiver is paid at a lower rate than in center care, and usually one person cares for several children of various ages.

family function The way a family works to meet the needs of its members. Children need families to provide basic material necessities, encourage learning, develop self-respect, nurture friendships, and foster harmony and stability.

family structure The legal and genetic relationships (e.g., nuclear, extended, step) among relatives in the same home.

fast-mapping The speedy and sometimes imprecise way in which children learn new words by mentally charting them into categories according to their meaning.

fetal alcohol syndrome (FAS) A cluster of birth defects, including abnormal facial characteristics, slow physical growth, and retarded mental development, caused by the mother's drinking alcohol while pregnant.

fetal period The stage of prenatal development from the ninth week after after conception until birth, during which the organs grow in size and mature in functioning.

fetus The name for a developing organism from the ninth week after conception until birth.

fictive kin A term used to describe someone who becomes accepted as part of a family to whom he or she has no blood relation.

filial responsibility The idea that adult children are obligated to care for their aging parents.

fine motor skills Physical abilities involving small body movements, especially of the hands and fingers, such as drawing and picking up a coin. (The word *fine* here means "small.")

fluid intelligence Those types of basic intelligence that make learning of all sorts quick and thorough. Abilities such as short-term memory, abstract thought, and speed of thinking are all usually considered part of fluid intelligence.

Flynn Effect The rise in average IQ scores that has occurred over the decades in developed nations.

fMRI Functional magnetic resonance imaging, a measuring technique in which the brain's electrical excitement indicates activation anywhere in the brain; fMRI helps researchers locate neurological responses to stimuli.

focus on appearance A characteristic of preoperational thought in which a young child ignores all attributes that are not apparent.

foreclosure Erikson's term for premature identity formation, which occurs when an adolescent adopts parents' or society's roles and values wholesale, without questioning and analysis.

formal operational thought In Piaget's theory, the fourth and final stage of cognitive development, characterized by more systematic logic and the ability to think about abstract ideas.

foster care A legal, publicly supported plan in which a maltreated child is removed from the parents' custody and entrusted to another adult, who is paid to be the child's caregiver.

fragile X syndrome A genetic disorder in which part of the X chromosome seems to be attached to the rest of it by a very thin string of molecules. The actual cause is too many repetitions of a particular part of a gene's code.

frail elderly People over age 65 who are physically infirm, very ill, or cognitively impaired.

G

gamete A reproductive cell; that is, a sperm or ovum that can produce a new individual if it combines with a gamete from the other sex to make a zygote.

gateways to attraction The various qualities, such as appearance and proximity, that are prerequisites for the formation of close friendships and intimate relationships.

gender convergence A tendency for men and women to become more similar as they move through middle age.

gender differences Differences in the roles and behavior of males and females that originate in the culture.

gender identity A person's acceptance of the roles and behaviors that society associates with the biological categories of male and female.

gene A section of a chromosome and the basic unit for the transmission of heredity, consisting of a string of chemicals that code for the manufacture of certain proteins.

general intelligence (*g*) The idea that intelligence is one basic trait, underlying all cognitive abilities. According to this concept, people have varying levels of this general ability.

generational forgetting The idea that each new generation forgets what the previous generation learned about harmful drugs.

genetic clock A purported mechanism in the DNA of cells that regulates the aging process by triggering hormonal changes and controlling cellular reproduction and repair.

genetic counseling Consultation and testing by trained experts that enable individuals to learn about their genetic heritage, including harmful conditions that they might pass along to any children they may conceive.

genome The full set of genes that are the instructions to make an individual member of a certain species.

genotype An organism's entire genetic inheritance, or genetic potential.

geriatrics The medical specialty devoted to aging.

germinal period The first two weeks of prenatal development after conception, characterized by rapid cell division and the beginning of cell differentiation.

gerontology The multidisciplinary study of old age.

gonads The paired sex glands (ovaries in females, testicles in males). The gonads produce hormones and gametes.

good death A death that is peaceful, quick, and painless and that occurs at the end of a long life, in the company of family and friends, and in familiar surroundings.

goodness of fit A similarity of temperament and values that produces a smooth interaction between an individual and his or her social context, including family, school, and community.

grammar All the methods—word order, verb forms, and so on—that languages use to communicate meaning, apart from the words themselves.

grand theories Comprehensive theories of psychology, which have traditionally inspired and directed psychologists' thinking about child development. Psychoanalytic theory, behaviorism, and cognitive theory are all grand theories.

grief An individual's emotional response to the death of another.

gross motor skills Physical abilities involving large body movements, such as walking and jumping. (The word *gross* here means "big.")

growth spurt The relatively sudden and rapid physical growth that occurs during puberty. Each body part increases in size on a schedule. Weight usually precedes height, and the limbs precede the torso.

guided participation In sociocultural theory, a technique in which skilled mentors help novices learn not only by providing instruction but also by allowing direct, shared involvement in the activity. Also called *apprenticeship in thinking*.

H

habituation The process of getting used to an object or event through repeated exposure to it.

Hayflick limit The number of times a human cell is capable of dividing into two new cells. The limit for most human cells is approximately 50 divisions, an indication that the life span is limited by our genetic program.

head-sparing The biological protection of the brain when malnutrition affects body growth. The brain is the last part of the body to be damaged by malnutrition.

health care proxy A person chosen by another person to make medical decisions if the second person becomes unable to do so.

heterogamy Defined by developmentalists as marriage between individuals who tend to be dissimilar with repect to such variables as attitudes, interests, goals, socioeconomic status, religion, ethnic background, and local origin.

hidden curriculum The unofficial, unstated, or implicit rules and priorities that influence the academic curriculum and every other aspect of learning in school.

high-stakes test An evaluation that is critical in determining success or failure. If a single test determines whether a student will graduate or be promoted, that is a high-stakes test.

hikikomori A Japanese word meaning "pull away," a common anxiety disorder in Japan in which emerging adults refuse to leave their rooms.

hippocampus A brain structure that is a central processor of memory, especially the memory of locations.

holophrase A single word that is used to express a complete, meaningful thought.

homeostasis The adjustment of the body's systems to keep physiological functions in a state of equilibrium. As the body ages, it takes longer for these homeostatic adjustments to occur, so it becomes harder for older bodies to adapt to stress.

homogamy Defined by developmentalists as marriage between individuals who tend to be similar with respect to such variables as attitudes, interests, goals, socioeconomic status, religion, ethnic background, and local origin.

hormone An organic chemical substance that is produced by one body tissue and conveyed via the bloodstream to another to affect some physiological function. Various hormones influence thoughts, urges, emotions, and behavior.

hormone replacement therapy (HRT) Treatment to compensate for hormone reduction at menopause or following surgical removal of the ovaries. Such treatment, which usually involves estrogen and progesterone, minimizes menopausal symptoms and diminishes the risk of osteoporosis in later adulthood.

hospice An institution in which terminally ill patients receive palliative care.

household A group of people who live together in one dwelling and share its common spaces, such as kitchen and living room.

HPA axis The hypothalamus-pituitary-adrenal axis, a route followed by many kinds of hormones to trigger the changes of puberty and to regulate stress, growth, sleep, appetite, sexual excitement, and various other bodily changes.

Human Genome Project An international effort to map the complete human genetic code. This effort was essentially completed in 2001, though analysis is ongoing.

hypothalamus A brain area that responds to the amygdala and the hippocampus to produce hormones that activate other parts of the brain and body.

hypothesis A specific prediction that is stated in such a way that it can be tested and either confirmed or refuted.

hypothetical thought Reasoning that includes propositions and possibilities that may not reflect reality.

I

identification An attempt to defend one's self-concept by taking on the behaviors and attitudes of someone else.

identity The logical principle that certain characteristics of an object remain the same even if other characteristics change. Also, a consistent definition of one's self as a unique individual, in terms of roles, attitudes, beliefs, and aspirations.

identity achievement Erikson's term for the attainment of identity, or the point at which a person understands who he or she is as a unique individual, in accord with past experiences and future plans.

identity diffusion A situation in which an adolescent does not seem to know or care what his or her identity is.

identity versus diffusion Erikson's term for the fifth stage of development, in which the person tries to figure out "Who am I?" but is confused as to which of many possible roles to adopt.

imaginary audience The other people who, in an adolescent's egocentric belief, are watching, and taking note of, his or her appearance, ideas, and behavior. This belief makes many teenagers very self-conscious.

immunization A process that stimulates the body's immune system to defend against attack by a particular contagious disease. A person may acquire immunization either naturally (by having the disease) or through vaccination (by having an injection, wearing a patch, swallowing, or inhaling).

implantation The process, beginning about 10 days after conception, in which the developing organism burrows into the placenta that lines the uterus, where it can be nourished and protected as it continues to develop.

implicit memory Unconscious or automatic memory that is usually stored via habits, emotional responses, routine procedures, and various sensations.

in vitro fertilization (IVF) Fertilization that takes place outside a woman's body (as in a glass laboratory dish). Sperm are mixed with ova that have been surgically removed from the woman's ovary. If the combination produces a zygote, it is inserted into the woman's uterus, where it may implant and develop into a baby.

incidence How often a particular behavior or circumstance occurs.

inclusion An approach to educating children with special needs in which they are included in regular classrooms, with "appropriate aids and services," as required by law.

incomplete grief A situation in which circumstances, such as a police investigation or an autopsy, interfere with the process of grieving.

independent variable In an experiment, the variable that is introduced to see what effect it has on the dependent variable. (Also called *experimental variable.*)

individual education plan (IEP) A document that specifies educational goals and plans for a child with special needs.

induced abortion The intentional termination of a pregnancy.

inductive reasoning Reasoning from one or more specific experiences or facts to a general conclusion; may be less cognitively advanced than deduction. (Sometimes called *bottom-up reasoning.*)

industry versus inferiority The fourth of Erikson's eight psychosocial development crises, during which children attempt to master many skills, developing a sense of themselves as either industrious or inferior, competent or incompetent.

infertility The inability to produce a baby after at least a year of trying to conceive via sexual intercourse.

information-processing theory A perspective that compares human thinking processes, by analogy, to computer analysis of data, including sensory input, connections, stored memories, and output.

initiative versus guilt Erikson's third psychosocial crisis. Children begin new activities and feel guilty when they fail.

injury control/harm reduction Practices that are aimed at anticipating, controlling, and preventing dangerous activities; these practices reflect the beliefs that accidents are not random and that injuries can be made less harmful if proper controls are in place.

insecure-avoidant attachment A pattern of attachment in which an infant avoids connection with the caregiver, as when the infant seems not to care about the caregiver's presence, departure, or return.

insecure-resistant/ambivalent attachment A pattern of attachment in which anxiety and uncertainty are evident, as when an infant is very upset at separation from the caregiver and both resists and seeks contact on reunion.

instrumental activities of daily life (IADLs) Actions that are important to independent living and that require some intellectual competence and forethought. The ability to perform these tasks may be even more critical to self-sufficiency than ADL ability.

instrumental aggression Hurtful behavior that is intended to get or keep something that another person has.

integrity versus despair The final stage of Erik Erikson's developmental sequence, in which older adults seek to integrate their unique experiences with their vision of community.

interaction effect The result of a combination of teratogens. Sometimes risk is greatly magnified when an embryo or fetus is exposed to more than one teratogen at the same time.

internalizing problems Difficulty with emotional regulation that involves turning one's emotional distress inward, as by feeling excessively guilty, ashamed, or worthless.

intimacy versus isolation The sixth of Erikson's eight stages of development. Adults seek someone with whom to share their lives in an enduring and self-sacrificing commitment. Without such commitment, they risk profound aloneness and isolation.

intimate terrorism Spouse abuse in which, most often, the husband uses violent methods of accelerating intensity to isolate, degrade, and punish the wife.

intrinsic motivation Goals or drives that come from inside a person, such as the need to feel smart or competent. This contrasts with external motivation, the need for rewards from outside, such as material possessions or someone else's esteem.

intrinsic rewards of work The intangible benefits one receives from a job (e.g., job satisfaction, self-esteem, pride) that come from within oneself.

intuitive thought Thought that arises from an emotion or a hunch, beyond rational explanation. Past experiences, cultural assumptions, and sudden impulses are the precursors of intuitive thought. (Also called *contextualized* or *experiential thought.*)

invincibility fable An adolescent's egocentric conviction that he or she cannot be overcome or even harmed by anything that might defeat a normal mortal, such as unprotected sex, drug abuse, or high-speed driving.

IQ tests Tests designed to measure intellectual aptitude, or ability to learn in school. Originally, intelligence was defined as mental age divided by chronological age, times 100—hence the term *intelligence quotient,* or *IQ.*

irreversibility The idea that nothing can be undone; the inability to recognize that something can sometimes be restored to the way it was before a change occurred.

K

kangaroo care A form of child care in which the mother of a low-birthweight infant spends at least an hour a day holding the baby between her breasts, like a kangaroo that carries her immature newborn in a pouch on her abdomen. If the infant is capable, he or she can easily breast-feed in this position.

kinkeeper The person who takes primary responsibility for celebrating family achievements, gathering the family together, and keeping in touch with family members who do not live nearby.

kinship care A form of foster care in which a relative of a maltreated child becomes the approved caregiver.

knowledge base A body of knowledge in a particular area that makes it easier to master new information in that area.

kwashiorkor A disease of chronic malnutrition during childhood, in which a protein deficiency makes the child more vulnerable to other diseases, such as measles, diarrhea, and influenza.

L

language acquisition device (LAD) Chomsky's term for a hypothesized mental structure that enables humans to learn language, including the basic aspects of grammar, vocabulary, and intonation.

latency Freud's term for middle childhood, during which children's emotional drives and psychosocial needs are quiet (latent). Freud thought that sexual conflicts from earlier stages are only temporarily submerged, to burst forth again at puberty.

lateralization Literally, sidedness. The specialization in certain functions by each side of the brain, with one side dominant for each activity. The left side of the brain controls the right side of the body, and vice versa.

learning disability A marked delay in a particular area of learning that is not caused by an apparent physical disability, by mental retardation, or by an unusually stressful home environment.

least restrictive environment (LRE) A legal requirement that children with special needs be assigned to the most general educational context in which they can be expected to learn.

life review An examination of one's own part in life, engaged in by many elderly people.

life-course-persistent offender A person whose criminal activity typically begins in early adolescence and continues throughout life; a career criminal.

linked lives The notion that family members tend to share all aspects of each other's lives, from triumph to tragedy.

"little scientist" Piaget's term for the stage-five toddler (age 12 to 18months) who experiments without anticipating the results.

living will A document that indicates what medical intervention an individual wants if he or she becomes incapable of expressing those wishes.

long-term memory The component of the information-processing system in which virtually limitless amounts of information can be stored indefinitely.

longitudinal research A research design in which the same individuals are followed over time and their development is repeatedly assessed.

low birthweight (LBW) A body weight at birth of less than 5½ pounds (2,500 grams).

M

marasmus A disease of severe protein-calorie malnutrition during early infancy, in which growth stops, body tissues waste away, and the infant eventually dies.

maximum life span The oldest possible age that members of a species can live, under ideal circumstances. For humans, that age is approximately 122 years.

menarche A girl's first menstrual period, signaling that she has begun ovulation. Pregnancy is biologically possible, but ovulation and menstruation are often irregular for years after menarche.

menopause The time in middle age, usually around age 50, when a woman's menstrual periods cease completely and the production of estrogen, progesterone, and testosterone drops considerably. Strictly speaking, menopause is dated one year after a woman's last menstrual period.

mental retardation Literally, slow, or late, thinking. In practice, people are considered mentally retarded if they score below 70 on an IQ test and if they are markedly behind their peers in adaptation to daily life.

metacognition "Thinking about thinking," or the ability to evaluate a cognitive task to determine how best to accomplish it, and then to monitor and adjust one's performance on that task.

middle childhood The period between early childhood and early adolescence, approximately from age 7 to 11.

middle school A school for the grades between elementary and high school. Middle school can begin with grade 5 or 6 and usually ends with grade 8.

midlife crisis A period of unusual anxiety, radical reexamination, and sudden transformation that is widely associated with middle age but which actually has more to do with developmental history than with chronological age.

mirror neurons Brain cells that respond to actions performed by someone else, as if the observer had done that action. For example, the brains of dancers who witness another dancer moving onstage are activated in the same movement areas as would be activated if they themselves did that dance step, because their mirror neurons reflect the activity.

modeling The central process of social learning, by which a person observes the actions of others and then copies them.

monozygotic (MZ) twins Twins who originate from one zygote that splits apart very early in development. (Also called *identical twins*.) Other monozygotic multiple births (for example, quadruplets) can occur as well.

morality of care In Gilligan's view, the tendency of females to be reluctant to judge right and wrong in absolute terms because they are socialized to be more nurturant, compassionate, and nonjudgmental.

morality of justice In Gilligan's view, the tendency of males to emphasize justice over compassion, judging right and wrong in absolute terms.

moratorium A way for adolescents to postpone making identity achievement choices by finding an accepted way to avoid identity achievement. Going to college is the most common example.

morbidity Disease. As a measure of health, morbidity refers to the rate of diseases of all kinds in a given population—physical and emotional, acute (sudden) and chronic (ongoing).

mortality Death. As a measure of health, mortality usually refers to the number of deaths each year per 1,000 members of a given population.

mosaic Having a condition (*mosaicism*) that involves having a mixture of cells, some normal and some with an odd number of chromosomes or a series of missing genes.

motor skill The learned ability to move some part of the body, from a large leap to a flicker of the eyelid. (The word *motor* here refers to movement of muscles.)

mourning The ceremonies and behaviors that a religion or culture prescribes for bereaved people.

multifactorial Referring to a trait that is affected by many factors, both genetic and environmental.

myelination The process by which axons become coated with myelin, a fatty substance that speeds the transmission of nerve impulses from neuron to neuron.

N

naming explosion A sudden increase in an infant's vocabulary, especially in the number of nouns, that begins at about 18 months of age.

National Assessment of Educational Progress (NAEP) An ongoing and nationally representative measure of children's achievement in reading, mathematics, and other subjects over time; nicknamed "the Nation's Report Card."

nature A general term for the traits, capacities, and limitations that each individual inherits genetically from his or her parents at the moment of conception.

near-death experience An episode in which a person comes close to dying but survives and reports having left his or her body and having moved toward a bright, white light while feeling peacefulness and joy.

neuron One of the billions of nerve cells in the central nervous system, especially the brain.

No Child Left Behind Act A U.S. law passed by Congress in 2001 that was intended to increase accountability in education by requiring standardized tests to measure school achievement. Many critics, especially teachers, say the law undercuts learning and fails to take local needs into consideration.

norm An average, or standard, measurement, calculated from the measurements of many individuals within a specific group or population.

nuclear family A family that consists of a father, a mother, and their biological children under age 18.

nurture A general term for all the environmental influences that affect development after an individual is conceived.

O

obesity In an adult, having a BMI (body mass index) of 30 or more. In a child, being above the 95th percentile, based on the U.S. Centers for Disease Control's 1980 standards for his or her age and sex.

object permanence The realization that objects (including people) still exist when they cannot be seen, touched, or heard.

objective thought Thinking that is not influenced by personal qualities, such as facts and numbers that are considered true and valid by every observer.

Oedipus complex The unconscious desire of young boys to replace their father and win their mother's exclusive love.

old-old Older adults (generally, those over age 75) who suffer from physical, mental, or social deficits.

oldest-old Elderly adults (generally, those over age 85) who are dependent on others for almost everything, requiring supportive services such as nursing homes and hospital stays.

operant conditioning The learning process by which a particular action is followed by something desired (which makes the person or animal more likely to repeat the action) or by something unwanted (which makes the action less likely to be repeated). Also called *instrumental conditioning*.

organ reserve The capacity of young adults' organs to allow the body to cope with stress.

overregularization The application of rules of grammar even when exceptions occur, so that the language is made to seem more "regular" than it actually is.

overweight In an adult, having a BMI (body mass index) of 25 to 29. In a child, being above the 85th percentile, based on the U.S. Centers for Disease Control's 1980 standards for his or her age and sex.

oxygen free radicals Atoms of oxygen that, as a result of metabolic processes, have an unpaired electron. These atoms scramble DNA molecules or mitochondria, producing errors in cell maintenance and repair that, over time, may cause cancer, diabetes, and arteriosclerosis.

P

palliative care Care designed not to treat an illness but to relieve the pain and suffering of the patient and his or her family.

parasuicide Any potentially lethal action against the self that does not result in death.

parental alliance Cooperation between a mother and a father based on their mutual commitment to their children. In a parental alliance, the parents agree to support each other in their shared parental roles.

parental monitoring Parents' ongoing awareness of what their children are doing, where, and with whom.

parent–infant bond The strong, loving connection that forms as parents hold their newborn.

Parkinson's disease A chronic, progressive disease that is characterized by muscle tremor and rigidity, and sometimes dementia, caused by a reduction of dopamine production in the brain.

passive euthanasia A situation in which a seriously ill person is allowed to die naturally, through the cessation of medical interventions.

peer facilitation The encouragement adolescent peers give one another to partake in activities or behaviors they would not otherwise do alone, whether constructive or destructive.

peer pressure Encouragement to conform with one's friends or contemporaries in behavior, dress, and attitude; usually considered a negative force, as when adolescent peers encourage one another to defy adult authority.

peer selection An ongoing, active process whereby adolescents select friends based on shared interests and values.

people preference A universal principle of infant perception, consisting of an innate attraction to other humans, which is evident in visual, auditory, tactile, and other preferences.

percentile A point on a ranking scale of 1 to 99. The 50th percentile is the midpoint; half the people in the population rank higher and half rank lower.

perception The mental processing of sensory information, when the brain interprets a sensation.

permanency planning An effort by authorities to find a long-term living situation that will provide stability and support for a maltreated child. A goal is to avoid repeated changes of caregiver or school, which can be particularly harmful for the child.

permissive parenting Child rearing with high nurturance and communication but rare punishment, guidance, or control.

perseveration The tendency to persevere in, or stick to, one thought or action for a long time.

phallic stage Freud's third stage of development, when the penis becomes the focus of concern and pleasure.

phenotype The observable characteristics of a person, including appearance, personality, intelligence, and all other traits.

phenylketonuria (PKU) A genetic disorder in which a child's body is unable to metabolize an amino acid called phenylalanine. Unless phenylalanine is eliminated from the child's diet, the resulting buildup of that substance in body fluids causes brain damage, progressive mental retardation, and other symptoms.

phonics approach Teaching reading by first teaching the sounds of each letter and of various letter combinations.

physician-assisted suicide A form of active euthanasia in which a doctor provides the means for someone to end his or her own life.

pituitary gland A gland that, in response to a signal from the hypothalamus, produces many hormones, including those that regulate growth and control other glands, among them the adrenal and sex glands.

placenta The organ that surrounds the developing embryo and fetus, sustaining life via the umbilical cord. The placenta is attached to the wall of the uterus.

polygenic Referring to a trait that is influenced by many genes.

positivity effect The tendency for elderly people to perceive, prefer, and remember positive images and experiences more than negative ones.

post-traumatic stress disorder (PTSD) A delayed reaction to a trauma or shock, which may include hyperactivity and hypervigilance, displaced anger, sleeplessness, sudden terror or anxiety, and confusion between fantasy and reality.

postconventional moral reasoning Kohlberg's third level of moral reasoning, emphasizing moral principles.

postformal thought A proposed adult stage of cognitive development, following Piaget's four stages, that goes beyond adolescent thinking by being more practical, more flexible, and more dialectical (that is, more capable of combining contradictory elements into a comprehensive whole).

postpartum depression A new mother's feelings of inadequacy and sadness in the days and weeks after giving birth.

practical intelligence The intellectual skills used in everyday problem solving.

preconventional moral reasoning Kohlberg's first level of moral reasoning, emphasizing rewards and punishments.

prefrontal cortex The area of cortex at the front of the brain that specializes in anticipation, planning, and impulse control.

preoperational intelligence Piaget's term for cognitive development between the ages of about 2 and 6; it includes language and imagination (in addition to the senses and motor skills of infancy), but logical, operational thinking is not yet possible.

presbycusis The loss of hearing associated with senescence. Presbycusis often does not become apparent until after age 60.

preterm birth A birth that occurs three or more weeks before the full 38 weeks of the typical pregnancy has elapsed—that is, at 35 or fewer weeks after conception.

prevalence How widespread within a population a particular behavior or circumstance is.

primary aging The universal and irreversible physical changes that occur to all living creatures as they grow older.

primary circular reactions The first of three types of feedback loops in sensorimotor intelligence, this one involving the infant's own body. The infant senses motion, sucking, noise, and so on, and tries to understand them.

primary prevention Actions that change overall background conditions to prevent some unwanted event or circumstance, such as injury, disease, or abuse.

primary sex characteristics The parts of the body that are directly involved in reproduction, including the vagina, uterus, ovaries, testicles, and penis.

priming Preparation that makes it easier to perform some action. For example, it is easier to retrieve an item from memory if we are given a clue about it beforehand.

private speech The internal dialogue that occurs when people talk to themselves (either silently or out loud).

Progress in International Reading Literacy Study (PIRLS) Inaugurated in 2001, a planned five-year cycle of international trend studies in the reading ability of fourth-graders.

prosocial behavior Feeling and acting in ways that are helpful and kind, without obvious benefit to oneself.

protein-calorie malnutrition A condition in which a person does not consume sufficient food of any kind. This deprivation can result in several illnesses, severe weight loss, and sometimes death.

proximal parenting Parenting practices that involve close physical contact with the child's entire body, such as cradling and swinging.

psychoanalytic theory A grand theory of human development that holds that irrational, unconscious drives and motives, often originating in childhood, underlie human behavior.

psychological control A disciplinary technique that involves threatening to withdraw love and support and that relies on a child's feelings of guilt and gratitude to the parents.

puberty The time between the first onrush of hormones and full adult physical development. Puberty usually lasts three to five years. Many more years are required to achieve psychosocial maturity.

Q

QALYs (quality-adjusted life years) A way of comparing mere survival without vitality to survival with good health. QALYs indicate how many years of full vitality are lost to a particular physical disease or disability. They are expressed in terms of life expectancy as adjusted for quality of life.

qualitative research Research that considers qualities instead of quantities. Descriptions of particular conditions and participants' expressed ideas are often part of qualitative studies.

quantitative research Research that provides data that can be expressed with numbers, such as ranks or scales.

R

race A group of people who are regarded (by themselves or by others) as genetically distinct from other groups on the basis of physical appearance.

reaction time The time it takes to respond to a stimulus, either physically (with a reflexive movement such as an eye blink) or cognitively (with a thought).

reactive aggression An impulsive retaliation for another person's intentional or accidental actions, verbal or physical.

Reading First A federal program that was established by the No Child Left Behind Act and that provides states with funding for early reading instruction in public schools, aimed at ensuring that all children learn to read well by the end of the third grade.

reflex A responsive movement that seems automatic because it almost always occurs in reaction to a particular stimulus. Newborns have many reflexes, some of which disappear with maturation.

reinforcement A technique for conditioning behavior in which that behavior is followed by something desired, such as food for a hungry animal or a welcoming smile for a lonely person.

REM sleep Rapid eye movement sleep, a stage of sleep characterized by flickering eyes behind closed lids, dreaming, and rapid brain waves.

reminder session A perceptual experience that is intended to help a person recollect an idea, a thing, or an experience, without testing whether the person remembers it at the moment.

replication The repetition of a scientific study, using the same procedures on a similar (but not identical) group of participants, in order to verify, or refine, or dispute the original study's conclusions.

reported maltreatment Harm or endangerment about which someone has notified the authorities.

resilience The capacity to develop optimally by adapting positively to significant adversity.

resource room A room in which trained teachers help children with special needs, using specialized curricula and equipment.

respite care An arrangement in which a professional caregiver relieves a frail elderly person's usual family caregiver for a few hours each day or for an occasional weekend.

reversibility The logical principle that a thing that has been changed can sometimes be returned to its original state by reversing the process by which it was changed.

risk analysis The science of weighing the potential effects of a particular event, substance, or experience to determine the likelihood of harm. In teratology, risk analysis attempts to evaluate everything that affects the chances that a particular agent or condition will cause damage to an embryo or fetus.

rumination Repeatedly thinking and talking about past experiences that can contribute to depression.

S

sandwich generation A term for the generation of middle-aged people who are supposedly "squeezed" by the needs of the younger and older generations. Some adults do feel pressured by these obligations, but most are not burdened by them, either because they enjoy fulfilling them or because they choose to take on only some of them, or none.

scaffolding Temporary support that is tailored to a learner's needs and abilities and aimed at helping the learner master the next task in a given learning process.

science of human development The science that seeks to understand how and why people change or remain the same over time. Developmentalists study people of all ages and circumstances.

science of human development The science that seeks to understand how and why people change or remain the same over time. Developmentalists study people of all ages and circumstances.

scientific method A way to answer questions that requires empirical research and data-based conclusions.

scientific observation A method of testing hypotheses by unobtrusively watching and recording participants' behavior in a systematic and objective manner, either in a laboratory or in a natural setting.

Seattle Longitudinal Study The first cross-sequential study of adult intelligence. This study began in 1956; the most recent testing was conducted in 2005.

secondary aging The specific physical illnesses or conditions that become more common with aging but are caused by health habits, genes, and other influences that vary from person to person.

secondary circular reactions The second of three types of feedback loops in sensorimotor intelligence, this one involving people and objects. The infant is responsive to other people and to toys and other objects the infant can touch and move.

secondary education Literally the period after primary education and before tertiary education. It usually occurs from about age 12 to 18, although there is some variation by school and by nation.

secondary prevention Actions that avert harm in a high-risk situation, such as stopping a car before it hits a pedestrian.

secondary sex characteristics Physical traits that are not directly involved in reproduction but that indicate sexual maturity, such as a man's beard and a woman's breasts.

secular trend A term that refers to the earlier and greater growth of children due to improved nutrition and medical care over the last two centuries.

secure attachment A relationship in which an infant obtains both comfort and confidence from the presence of his or her caregiver.

selective adaptation The process by which humans and other organisms gradually adjust to their environment. Specifically, the frequency of a particular genetic trait in a population increases or decreases over generations, depending on whether or not the trait contributes to the survival and reproductive ability of members of that population.

selective attention The ability to concentrate on some stimuli while ignoring others.

selective expert Someone who is notably more skilled and knowledgeable than the average person about whichever activities are personally meaningful.

selective optimization with compensation The theory, developed by Paul and Margaret Baltes, that people try to maintain a balance in their lives by looking for the best way to compensate for physical and cognitive losses and to become more proficient in activities they can already do well.

self theories Theories of late adulthood that emphasize the core self, or the search to maintain one's integrity and identity.

self-awareness A person's realization that he or she is a distinct individual, with body, mind, and actions that are separate from those of other people.

self-concept A person's understanding of who he or she is. Self-concept includes appearance, personality, and various traits.

self-efficacy In social learning theory, the belief that some people have that they are able to change themselves and effectively alter the social context.

self-esteem How a person evaluates his or her own worth, either in specifics (e.g., intelligence, attractiveness) or overall.

self-righting The inborn drive to remedy a developmental deficit.

senescence The process of aging, whereby the body becomes less strong and efficient.

sensation The response of a sensory system (eyes, ears, skin, tongue, nose) when it detects a stimulus.

sensitive period A time when a certain type of development is most likely to happen and happens most easily. For example, early childhood is considered a sensitive period for language learning.

sensorimotor intelligence Piaget's term for the way infants think—by using their senses and motor skills during the first period of cognitive development.

sensory memory The component of the information-processing system in which incoming stimulus information is stored for a split second to allow it to be processed. (Also called the *sensory register*.)

separation anxiety An infant's distress when a familiar caregiver leaves; most obvious between 9 and 14 months.

set point A particular body weight that an individual's homeostatic processes strive to maintain.

sex differences Biological differences between males and females, in organs, hormones, and body type.

sexual orientation A person's impulses and internal direction regarding sexual interest. A person may be oriented to people of the same sex, of the other sex, or of both sexes. Sexual orientation may differ from sexual expression, appearance, identity, or lifestyle.

sexually transmitted infection (STI) A disease spread by sexual contact, including syphilis, gonorrhea, genital herpes, chlamydia, and HIV.

shaken baby syndrome A life-threatening condition that occurs when an infant is forcefully shaken back and forth, rupturing blood vessels in the brain and breaking neural connections.

single-parent family A family that consists of only one parent and his or her biological children under age 18.

slippery slope The argument that a given action will start a chain of events that will culminate in an undesirable outcome.

small for gestational age (SGA) A term for a baby whose birthweight is significantly lower than expected, given the time since conception. For example, a 5-pound (2,200-gram) newborn is considered SGA if born on time but not SGA if born two months early. (Also called *small for dates*.)

social clock Refers to the idea that the stages of life, and the behaviors "appropriate" to them, are set by social standards rather than by biological maturation. For instance, "middle age" begins when the culture believes it does, rather than at a particular age in all cultures.

social cognition The ability to understand social interactions, including the causes and consequences of human behavior.

social comparison The tendency to assess one's abilities, achievements, social status, and other attributes by measuring them against those of other people, especially one's peers.

social construction An idea that is built more on shared perceptions than on objective reality. Many age-related terms, such as childhood, adolescents, yuppies, and senior citizens are social constructions.

social homogamy The similarity of a couple's leisure interests and role preferences.

social learning Learning by observing others.

social learning theory An extension of behaviorism that emphasizes the influence that other people have over a person's behavior. Even without specific reinforcement, every individual learns many things via observation and imitation of other people.

social mediation A function of speech by which a person's cognitive skills are refined and extended through both formal instruction and casual conversation.

social norms The standards of behavior within a given society or culture.

social norms approach A method of reducing risky behavior that uses emerging adults' desire to follow social norms by making them aware, through the use of surveys, of the prevalence of various behaviors within their peer group.

social referencing Seeking information about how to react to an unfamiliar or ambiguous object or event by observing someone else's expressions and reactions. That other person becomes a social reference.

social smile A smile evoked by a human face, normally evident in infants about 6 weeks after birth.

sociocultural theory An emergent theory that holds that development results from the dynamic interaction between each person and the surrounding social and cultural forces.

socioeconomic status (SES) A person's position in society as determined by income, wealth, occupation, education, place of residence, and other factors.

spermarche A boy's first ejaculation of sperm. Erections can occur as early as infancy, but ejaculation signals sperm production. Spermache occurs during sleep (in a "wet dream") or via direct stimulation.

spontaneous abortion The naturally occurring termination of a pregnancy before the embryo or fetus is fully developed. (Also called *miscarriage*.)

static reasoning Thinking that nothing changes: Whatever is now has always been and always will be.

stereotype threat The possibility that one's appearance or behavior will be misread to confirm another person's oversimplified, prejudiced attitudes.

still-face technique An experimental practice in which an adult keeps his or her face unmoving and expressionless in face-to-face interaction with an infant.

Strange Situation A laboratory procedure for measuring attachment by evoking infants' reactions to stress.

stranger wariness An infant's expression of concern—a quiet stare, clinging to a familiar person, or sadness—when a stranger appears.

stratification theories Theories that emphasize that social forces, particularly those related to a person's social stratum or social category, limit individual choices and affect the ability to function in late adulthood as past stratification continues to limit life in various ways.

subcortical dementias Forms of dementia that begin with impairments in motor ability (which is governed by the subcortex) and produce cognitive impairment in later stages. Parkinson's disease, Huntington's disease, and multiple sclerosis are subcortical dementias.

subjective thought Thinking that is strongly influenced by personal qualities of the individual thinker, such as past experiences, cultural assumptions, and goals for the future.

substantiated maltreatment Harm or endangerment that has been reported, investigated, and verified.

sudden infant death syndrome (SIDS) A situation in which a seemingly healthy infant, at least 2 months of age, suddenly stops breathing and dies unexpectedly while asleep. The cause is unknown, but it is correlated with sleeping on the stomach and having parents who smoke.

suicidal ideation Thinking about suicide, usually with some serious emotional and intellectual or cognitive overtones.

sunk cost fallacy The belief that if time or money has already been invested in something, then more time or money should be invested. Because of this fallacy, people spend money trying to fix a "lemon" of a car or sending more troops to win a losing war. Ample amounts of these expenditure have already been made. It is an error made by people of all ages.

superego In psychoanalytic theory, the judgmental part of the personality that internalizes moral standards of the parents.

survey A research method in which information is collected from a large number of people by interviews, written questionnaires, or some other means.

synapse The intersection between the axon of one neuron and the dendrites of other neurons.

synchrony A coordinated, rapid, and smooth exchange of responses between a caregiver and an infant.

synthesis A new idea that integrates the thesis and its antithesis, thus representing a new and more comprehensive level of truth; the third stage of the process of dialectical thinking.

T

T cells Immune cells manufactured in the thymus gland that produce substances that attack infected cells in the body.

telomeres The ends of chromosomes in the cells, whose length decreases with each cell duplication and seems to correlate with longevity.

temperament Inborn differences between one person and another in emotions, activity, and self-control. Temperament is epigenetic, originating in genes but affected by child-rearing practices.

teratogens Agents and conditions, including viruses, drugs, and chemicals, that can impair prenatal development and result in birth defects or even death.

terminal decline An overall slowdown of cognitive abilities in the weeks and months before death. (Also called *terminal drop*.)

tertiary circular reactions The third of three types of feedback loops in sensorimotor intlligence, this one involving active exploration and experimentation. The infant explores a range of new activities, varying his or her responses as a way of learning about the world.

tertiary prevention Actions, such as immediate and effective medical treatment, that are taken after an adverse event such as illness or injury occurs, and are aimed at reducing the harm or preventing disability.

testosterone A sex hormone, the best known of the androgens (male hormones); secreted in far greater amounts by males than by females.

thanatology The study of death and dying, especially in their social and emotional aspects.

thanatology The study of death and dying, especially in their social and emotional aspects.

theory of mind A person's theory of what other people might be thinking. In order to have a theory of mind, children must realize that other people are not necessarily thinking the same thoughts that they themselves are. That realization is seldom possible before age 4.

theory-theory The idea that children attempt to explain everything they see and hear by constructing theories.

thesis A proposition or statement of belief; the first stage of the process of dialectical thinking.

threshold effect A situation in which a certain teratogen is relatively harmless in small doses but becomes harmful once exposure reaches a certain level (the threshold).

time-out A disciplinary technique in which a child is separated from other people for a specified time.

TIMSS (Trends in Math and Science Study) An international assessment of the math and science skills of fourth- and eighth-graders. Although the TIMSS is very useful, scores are not always comparable, because sample selection, test administration, and content validity are hard to keep uniform.

total immersion A strategy in which instruction in all school subjects occurs in the second (majority) language that a child is learning.

transient exuberance The great increase in the number of dendrites that occurs in an infant's brain during the first two years of life.

trust versus mistrust Erikson's first psychosocial crisis. Infants learn basic trust if the world is a secure place where their basic needs (for food, comfort, attention, etc.) are met.

23rd pair The chromosome pair that, in humans, determines the zygote's (and hence the person's) sex. The other 22 pairs are autosomes, the same whether the 23rd pair is for a male or a female.

type 2 diabetes A chronic disease in which the body does not produce enough insulin to adequately metabolize carbohydrates (glucose). It was once called *adult-onset diabetes* because it typically developed in people aged 50 to 60; today, however, it often appears in younger people.

V

vascular dementia (VaD)/multi-infarct dementia (MID) A form of dementia characterized by sporadic, and progressive, loss of intellectual functioning caused by repeated infarcts, or temporary obstructions of blood vessels, which prevent sufficient blood from reaching the brain.

very low birthweight (VLBW) A body weight at birth of less than 3 pounds, 5 ounces (1,500 grams).

visual cliff An experimental apparatus that gives an illusion of a sudden drop between one horizontal surface and another.

vitality A measure of health that refers to how healthy and energetic—physically, intellectually, and socially—an individual actually feels.

W

wear-and-tear theory A view of aging as a process by which the human body wears out because of the passage of time and exposure to environmental stressors.

Wechsler Intelligence Scale for Children (WISC) An IQ test designed for school-age children. The test assesses potential in many areas, including vocabulary, general knowledge, memory, and spatial comprehension.

whole-language approach Teaching reading by encouraging early use of all language skills—talking and listening, reading and writing.

wisdom A cognitive perspective characterized by a broad, practical, comprehensive approach to life's problems, reflecting timeless truths rather than immediate expediency; said to be more common in the elderly than in the young.

withdrawn-rejected Rejected by peers because of timid, withdrawn, and anxious behavior.

working memory The component of the information-processing system in which current conscious mental activity occurs. (Also called *short-term memory.*)

working model In cognitive theory, a set of assumptions that the individual uses to organize perceptions and experiences. For example, a person might assume that other people are trustworthy, and be surprised when this model of human behavior seems in error.

X

X-linked Referring to a gene carried on the X chromosome. If a boy inherits an X-linked recessive trait from his mother, he expresses that trait, since the Y from his father has no counteracting gene. Girls are more likely to be carriers of X-linked traits but are less likely to express them.

XX A 23rd chromosome pair consisting of two X-shaped chromosomes, one each from the mother and the father. XX zygotes become female embryos, female fetuses, and girls.

XY A 23rd chromosome pair consisting of an X-shaped chromosome from the mother and a Y-shaped chromosome from the father. XY zygotes become male embryos, male fetuses, and boys.

Y

young-old Healthy, vigorous, financially secure older adults (generally, those aged 60 to 75) who are well integrated into the lives of their families and communities.

Z

zone of proximal development (ZPD) In sociocultural theory, a metaphorical area, or "zone," surrounding a learner that includes all the skills, knowledge, and concepts that the person is close ("proximal") to acquiring but cannot yet master without help.

zygote The single cell formed from the fusing of two gametes, a sperm and an ovum.

References

Abbott, Lesley, & Nutbrown, Cathy (Eds.). (2001). *Experiencing Reggio Emilia: Implications for pre-school provision.* Buckingham, England: Open University Press.

Abeles, Ronald P. (2007). Foreword. In Carolyn M. Aldwin, Crystal L. Park, & Avron Spiro, III (Eds.), *Handbook of health psychology and aging* (pp. ix–xii). New York: Guilford Press.

Abelson, Reed. (2007, February 10). A chance to pick hospice, and still hope to live. *New York Times,* pp. A1, C4.

Abikoff, Howard B., & Hechtman, Lily. (1996). Multimodal therapy and stimulants in the treatment of children with ADHD. In Euthymia D. Hibbs & Peter S. Jensen (Eds.), *Psychosocial treatments for child and adolescent disorders: Empirically based strategies for clinical practice* (pp. 341–369). Washington, DC: American Psychological Association.

Aboderin, Isabella. (2004). Intergenerational family support and old age economic security in sub-Saharan Africa: The importance of understanding shifts, processes and expectations. An example from Ghana. In Peter Lloyd-Sherlock (Ed.), *Living longer: Ageing, development and social protection* (pp. 210–229). London: Zed Books.

Aboud, Frances E., & Amato, Maria. (2001). Developmental and socialization influences on intergroup bias. In Rupert Brown & Samuel L. Gaertner (Eds.), *Blackwell handbook of social psychology: Intergroup processes* (pp. 65–85). Malden, MA: Blackwell.

Aboud, Frances E., & Mendelson, Morton J. (1998). Determinants of friendship selection and quality: Developmental perspectives. In William M. Bukowski, Andrew F. Newcomb, & Willard W. Hartup (Eds.), *The company they keep: Friendship in childhood and adolescence* (pp. 87–112). New York: Cambridge University Press.

Abramovitch, Henry. (2005). Where are the dead? Bad death, the missing, and the inability to mourn. In Samuel Heilman (Ed.), *Death, bereavement, and mourning* (pp. 53–67). New Brunswick, NJ: Transaction.

Abramson, David, & Garfield, Richard. (2006). *On the edge: Children and families displaced by hurricanes Katrina and Rita face a looming medical and mental health crisis.* New York: Columbia University Mailman School of Public Health.

Achenbaum, W. Andrew. (2005). *Older Americans, vital communities: A bold vision for societal aging.* Baltimore: Johns Hopkins University Press.

Achenbaum, W. Andrew. (2006). Historical gerontology: It is a matter of time. In Debra J. Sheets, Dana Burr Bradley, & Jon Hendricks (Eds.), *Enduring questions in gerontology* (pp. 203–224). New York: Springer.

Adams, Glenn, & Plaut, Victoria C. (2003). The cultural grounding of personal relationship: Friendship in North American and West African worlds. *Personal Relationships, 10,* 333–347.

Adams, Ted D., Gress, Richard E., Smith, Sherman C., Halverson, R. Chad, Simper, Steven C., Rosamond, Wayne D., et al. (2007). Long-term mortality after gastric bypass surgery. *New England Journal of Medicine, 357,* 753–761.

Adams-Price, Carolyn E. (Ed.). (1998). *Creativity and successful aging: Theoretical and empirical approaches.* New York: Springer.

Adamson, Lauren B., & Bakeman, Roger. (2006). Development of displaced speech in early mother-child conversations. *Child Development, 77,* 186–200.

Adenzato, Mauro, & Garbarini, Francesca. (2006). The as if in cognitive science, neuroscience and anthropology: A journey among robots, blacksmiths and neurons. *Theory & Psychology, 16,* 747–759.

Adler, Lynn Peters. (1995). *Centenarians: The bonus years.* Santa Fe, NM: Health Press.

Adler, Nancy E., & Snibbe, Alana Conner. (2003). The role of psychosocial processes in explaining the gradient between socioeconomic status and health. *Current Directions in Psychological Science, 12,* 119–123.

Adolph, Karen E., & Berger, Sarah E. (2005). Physical and motor development. In Marc H. Bornstein & Michael E. Lamb (Eds.), *Developmental science: An advanced textbook* (5th ed., pp. 223–281). Mahwah, NJ: Erlbaum.

Adolph, Karen E., & Berger, Sarah E. (2006). Motor development. In William Damon & Richard M. Lerner (Series Eds.) & Deanna Kuhn & Robert S. Siegler (Vol. Eds.), *Handbook of child psychology: Vol. 2. Cognition, perception, and language* (6th ed., pp. 161–213). Hoboken, NJ: Wiley.

Adolph, Karen E., Vereijken, Beatrix, & Denny, Mark A. (1998). Learning to crawl. *Child Development, 69,* 1299–1312.

Adolph, Karen E., Vereijken, Beatrix, & Shrout, Patrick E. (2003). What changes in infant walking and why. *Child Development, 74,* 475–497.

Agarwal, Dharam P., & Seitz, Helmut K. (Eds.). (2001). *Alcohol in health and disease.* New York: Dekker.

Aguirre-Molina, Marilyn, Molina, Carlos W., & Zambrana, Ruth Enid (Eds.). (2001). *Health issues in the Latino community.* San Francisco: Jossey Bass.

Ahearn, Frederick L. (2001). *Issues in global aging.* New York: Haworth Press.

Ahmed, Saifuddin, Koenig, Michael A., & Stephenson, Rob. (2006). Effects of domestic violence on perinatal and early-childhood mortality: Evidence from North India. *American Journal of Public Health, 96,* 1423–1428.

Ainsworth, Mary D. Salter. (1973). The development of infant-mother attachment. In Bettye M. Caldwell & Henry N. Ricciuti (Eds.), *Review of child development research* (Vol. 3, pp. 1–94). Chicago: University of Chicago Press.

Akhtar, Nameera, Jipson, Jennifer, & Callanan, Maureen A. (2001). Learning words through overhearing. *Child Development, 72,* 416–430.

Akiba, Daisuke, & García Coll, Cynthia. (2004). Effective interventions with children of color and their families: A contextual developmental approach. In Timothy B. Smith (Ed.), *Practicing multiculturalism: Affirming diversity in counseling and psychology* (pp. 123–144). Boston: Pearson/Allyn and Bacon.

Akinbami, Lara J. (2006). *The state of childhood asthma, United States, 1980–2005.* National Center for Health Statistics. Retrieved 2007, July 17, from the World Wide Web: http://www.cdc.gov/nchs/data/ad/ad381.pdf

Albinet, Cédric, Tomporowski, Phillip, & Beasman, Kathryn. (2006). Aging and concurrent task performance: Cognitive demand and motor control. *Educational Gerontology, 32,* 689–706.

Alcohol Policy Information System. (n.d.). *Alcohol and pregnancy: Civil commitment.* National Institute on Alcohol Abuse and Addiction. Retrieved September 1, 2007, from the World Wide Web: http://alcoholpolicy.niaaa.nih.gov/index.asp?SEC={51364079–6EFF-4B09–9C9D-AB32E98F4A4F}&Type=BAS_APIS

Aldwin, Carolyn M. (2007). *Stress, coping, and development: An integrative perspective* (2nd ed.). New York: Guilford Press.

Aldwin, Carolyn M., & Gilmer, Diane F. (2003). *Health, illness, and optimal aging: Biological and psychosocial perspectives.* Thousand Oaks, CA: Sage.

Aldwin, Carolyn M., & Levenson, Michael R. (2001). Stress, coping, and health at midlife: A developmental perspective. In Margie E. Lachman (Ed.), *Handbook of midlife development* (pp. 188–214). New York: Wiley.

Alexander, Karl L., Entwisle, Doris R., & Olson, Linda Steffel. (2007). Lasting consequences of the summer learning gap. *American Sociological Review, 72,* 167–180.

Alexander, Robin. (2000). *Culture and pedagogy: International comparisons in primary education.* Malden, MA: Blackwell.

Allen, James E. (2007). *Nursing home administration* (5th ed.). New York: Springer.

Allen, Joseph P., Porter, Maryfrances R., McFarland, F. Christy, Marsh, Penny, & McElhaney, Kathleen Boykin. (2005). The two faces of adolescents' success with peers: Adolescent popularity, social adaptation, and deviant behavior. *Child Development, 76,* 747–760.

Alloy, Lauren B., & Abramson, Lyn Y. (2007). The adolescent surge in depression and emergence of gender differences: a biocognitive vulnerability-stress model in developmental context. In Daniel Romer & Elaine F. Walker (Eds.), *Adolescent psychopathology and the developing brain: integrating brain and prevention science* (pp. x, 514 p., [515] p. of plates). New York: Oxford University Press.

Alloy, Lauren B., Zhu, Lin, & Abramson, Lyn. (2003). Cognitive vulnerability to depression: Implications for adolescent risk behavior in general. In Daniel Romer (Ed.), *Reducing adolescent risk: Toward an integrated approach* (pp. 171–182). Thousand Oaks, CA: Sage.

Alsaker, Françoise D., & Flammer, August (2006). Pubertal development. In Sandy Jackson & Luc Goossens (Eds.), *Handbook of adolescent development* (pp. 30–50). Hove, East Sussex, UK: Psychology Press.

Alvarez, Helen Perich. (2000). Grandmother hypothesis and primate life histories. *American Journal of Physical Anthropology, 113,* 435–450.

Amato, Paul R. (1999). The postdivorce society: How divorce is shaping the family and other forms of social organization. In Ross A. Thompson & Paul R. Amato (Eds.), *The postdivorce family: Children, parenting, and society* (pp. 161–190). Thousand Oaks, CA: Sage.

Amato, Paul R. (2007). *Alone together: How marriage in America is changing.* Cambridge, MA: Harvard University Press.

Amato, Paul R., & Afifi, Tamara D. (2006). Feeling caught between parents: Adult children's relations with parents and subjective well-being. *Journal of Marriage and Family, 68,* 222–235.

Amato, Paul R., & Cheadle, Jacob. (2005). The long reach of divorce: Divorce and child well-being across three generations. *Journal of Marriage and Family, 67,* 191–206.

Amato, Paul R., & Fowler, Frieda. (2002). Parenting practices, child adjustment, and family diversity. *Journal of Marriage & the Family, 64,* 703–716.

Amato, Paul R., Johnson, David R., Booth, Alan, & Rogers, Stacy J. (2003). Continuity and change in marital quality between 1980 and 2000. *Journal of Marriage & Family, 65,* 1–22.

American Demographics. (2002). The Gen Y budget. *American Demographics, 24,* S4.

American Psychiatric Association. (2000). *Diagnostic and statistical manual of mental disorders: DSM-IV-TR* (4th ed.). Washington, DC: Author.

Amirkhanyan, Anna A., & Wolf, Douglas A. (2006). Parent care and the stress process: Findings from panel data. *Journals of Gerontology: Series B: Psychological Sciences and Social Sciences, 61,* S248–S255.

Ammerman, Robert T., Ott, Peggy J., & Tarter, Ralph E. (1999). *Prevention and societal impact of drug and alcohol abuse.* Mahwah, NJ: Erlbaum.

Ananova. (2001, June 21). *Brother and sister have baby to keep mother's fortune.* Retrieved July 21, 2001, from the World Wide Web: Ananova.co.uk/news/story/sm_333307.html

Ananth, Cande V., Demissie, Kitaw, Kramer, Michael S., & Vintzileos, Anthony M. (2003). Small-for-gestational-age births among black and white women: Temporal trends in the United States. *American Journal of Public Health, 93,* 577–579.

Anderson, Carol. (2003). The diversity, strength, and challenges of single-parent households. In Froma Walsh (Ed.), *Normal family processes: Growing diversity and complexity* (3rd ed., pp. 121–152). New York: Guilford Press.

Anderson, Craig A., Berkowitz, Leonard, Donnerstein, Edward, Huesmann, L. Rowell, Johnson, James D., Linz, Daniel, et al. (2003). The influence of media violence on youth. *Psychological Science in the Public Interest, 4,* 81–110.

Anderson, Craig A., & Bushman, Brad J. (2002). Human aggression. *Annual Review of Psychology, 53,* 27–51.

Anderson, Daniel R., Huston, Aletha C., Schmitt, Kelly L., Linebarger, Deborah L., & Wright, John C. (2001). Early childhood television viewing and adolescent behavior: The recontact study. *Monographs of the Society for Research in Child Development, 66*(1, Serial No. 264).

Anderson, Gerard, & Horvath, Jane. (2004). The growing burden of chronic disease in America. *Public Health Reports, 119,* 263–270.

Anderson, Kristin L. (2002). Perpetrator or victim? Relationships between intimate partner violence and well-being. *Journal of Marriage & Family, 64,* 851–863.

Anderson, Michael. (2001). 'You have to get inside the person' or making grief private: Image and metaphor in the therapeutic reconstruction of bereavement. In Jenny Hockey, Jeanne Katz, & Neil Small (Eds.), *Grief, mourning, and death ritual* (pp. 135–143). Buckingham, England: Open University Press.

Anderson, Mark, Johnson, Daniel, & Batal, Holly. (2005). *Sudden infant death syndrome and prenatal maternal smoking: Rising attributed risk in the Back to Sleep era.* Retrieved June 23, 2005, from the World Wide Web: http://www.biomedcentral.com/1741–7015/3/4

Anderson, Robert N., & Smith, Betty L. (2005, March 7). Table 2. Deaths, percentage of total deaths, and death rates for the 10 leading causes of death in selected age groups, by Hispanic origin, race for non-Hispanic population, and sex: United States, 2002. *National Vital Statistics Reports,* 53(17), 50–71.

Andrade, Miriam, & Menna-Barreto, Luiz. (2002). Sleep patterns of high school students living in Sao Paulo, Brazil. In Mary A. Carskadon (Ed.), *Adolescent sleep patterns: Biological, social, and psychological influences* (pp. 118–131). New York: Cambridge University Press.

Andrade, Susan E., Gurwitz, Jerry H., Davis, Robert L., Chan, K. Arnold, Finkelstein, Jonathan A., Fortman, Kris, et al. (2004). Prescription drug use in pregnancy. *American Journal of Obstetrics and Gynecology, 191,* 398–407.

Andrews, Melinda W., Dowling, W. Jay, Bartlett, James C., & Halpern, Andrea R. (1998). Identification of speeded and slowed familiar melodies by younger, middle-aged, and older musicians and nonmusicians. *Psychology & Aging, 13,* 462–471.

Aneshensel, Carol S., Pearlin, Leonard I., Mullan, Joseph T., Zarit, Steven H., & Whitlatch, Carol I. (1995). *Profiles in caregiving: The unexpected career.* San Diego, CA: Academic Press.

Angelou, Maya. (1970). *I know why the caged bird sings.* New York: Random House.

Angold, Adrian, Erkanli, Alaattin, Egger, Helen L., & Costello, E. Jane. (2000). Stimulant treatment for children: A community perspective. *Journal of the American Academy of Child & Adolescent Psychiatry, 39,* 975–984.

Anis, Tarek. (2007). Hormones involved in male sexual function. In Annette Fuglsang Owens & Mitchell S. Tepper (Eds.), *Sexual health: Vol. 2. Physical foundations* (pp. 79–113). Westport, CT: Praeger/Greenwood.

Anstey, Kaarin J., Hofer, Scott M., & Luszcz, Mary A. (2003). A latent growth curve analysis of late-life sensory and cognitive function over 8 years: Evidence for specific and common factors underlying change. *Psychology & Aging, 18,* 714–726.

Antonucci, Toni C., Akiyama, Hiroko, & Merline, Alicia. (2001). Dynamics of social relationships in midlife. In Margie E. Lachman (Ed.), *Handbook of midlife development* (pp. 571–598). New York: Wiley.

Apgar, Virginia. (1953). A proposal for a new method of evaluation of the newborn infant. *Current Researches in Anesthesia and Analgesia, 32,* 260–267.

Archer, John. (2000). Sex differences in aggression between heterosexual partners: A meta-analytic review. *Psychological Bulletin, 126,* 651–680.

Archer, John. (2004). Sex differences in aggression in real-world settings: A meta-analytic review. *Review of General Psychology, 8,* 291–322.

Argyle, Michael. (2001). *The psychology of happiness* (2nd ed.). New York: Routledge.

Arita, Isao, Nakane, Miyuki, & Fenner, Frank. (2006, May 12). Is polio eradication realistic? *Science, 312,* 852–854.

Arking, Robert. (2006). *The biology of aging: Observations and principles* (3rd ed.). New York: Oxford University Press.

Arlin, Patricia Kennedy. (1984). Adolescent and adult thought: A structural interpretation. In Michael L. Commons, Francis A. Richards, & Cheryl Armon (Eds.), *Beyond formal operations: Late adolescent and adult cognitive development* (pp. 258–271). New York: Praeger.

Arlin, Patricia Kennedy. (1989). Problem solving and problem finding in young artists and young scientists. In Michael L. Commons, Jan D. Sinnott, Francis A. Richards, & Cheryl Armon (Eds.), *Adult development: Vol. 1. Comparisons and applications of developmental models* (pp. 197–216). New York: Praeger.

Armour, Marilyn. (2003). Meaning making in the aftermath of homicide. *Death Studies, 27,* 519–540.

Armour-Thomas, Eleanor, & Gopaul-McNicol, Sharon-Ann. (1998). *Assessing intelligence: Applying a bio-cultural model.* Thousand Oaks, CA: Sage.

Armson, B. Anthony. (2007). Is planned cesarean childbirth a safe alternative? *Canadian Medical Association Journal 176,* 475–476.

Arnett, Jeffrey Jensen. (1999). Adolescent storm and stress, reconsidered. *American Psychologist, 54,* 317–326.

Arnett, Jeffrey Jensen. (2004). *Emerging adulthood: The winding road from the late teens through the twenties.* New York: Oxford University Press.

Arnett, Jeffrey Jensen, & Tanner, Jennifer Lynn. (2006). *Emerging adults in America: Coming of age in the 21st century.* Washington, DC: American Psychological Association.

Aron, Arthur, Fisher, Helen, Mashek, Debra J., Strong, Greg, Li, Haifang, & Brown, Lucy L. (2005). Reward, motivation, and emotion systems associated with early-stage intense romantic love. *Journal of Neurophysiology, 94,* 327–337.

Aron, Arthur, McLaughlin-Volpe, Tracy, Mashek, Debra, Lewandowski, Gary, Wright, Stephen C., & Aron, Elaine N. (2005). Including others in the self. *European Review of Social Psychology, 15,* 101–132.

Aronson, Joshua, Fried, Carrie B., & Good, Catherine. (2002). Reducing the effects of stereotype threat on African American college students by shaping theories of intelligence. *Journal of Experimental Social Psychology, 38,* 113–125.

Artistico, Daniele, Cervone, Daniel, & Pezzuti, Lina. (2003). Perceived self-efficacy and everyday problem solving among young and older adults. *Psychology & Aging, 18,* 68–79.

Aseltine, Robert H., Jr., & DeMartino, Robert. (2004). An outcome evaluation of the SOS suicide prevention program. *American Journal of Public Health, 94,* 446–451.

Ashman, Sharon B., & Dawson, Geraldine. (2002). Maternal depression, infant psychobiological development, and risk for depression. In Sherryl H. Goodman & Ian H. Gotlib (Eds.), *Children of depressed parents: Mechanisms of risk and implications for treatment* (pp. 37–58). Washington, DC: American Psychological Association.

Asia Pacific Cohort Studies Collaboration. (2004). Body mass index and cardiovascular disease in the Asia-Pacific Region: an overview of 33 cohorts involving 310,000 participants. *International Journal of Epidemiology, 33,* 751–758.

Aslin, Richard N., & Hunt, Ruskin H. (2001). Development, plasticity, and learning in the auditory system. In Charles A. Nelson & Monica Luciana (Eds.), *Handbook of developmental cognitive neuroscience* (pp. 149–158). Cambridge, MA: MIT Press.

Aspinall, Richard J. (2003). *Aging of organs and systems.* Boston: Kluwer Academic.

Astin, Alexander W., & Oseguera, Leticia. (2002). *Degree attainment rates at American colleges and universities.* Los Angeles: Higher Education Research Institute.

Astington, Janet Wilde, & Gopnik, Alison. (1988). Knowing you've changed your mind: Children's understanding of representational change. In Janet W. Astington, Paul L. Harris, & David R. Olson (Eds.), *Developing theories of mind* (pp. 193–206). New York: Cambridge University Press.

Astone, Nan Marie, Nathanson, Constance A., Schoen, Robert, & Kim, Young J. (1999). Family demography, social theory, and investment in social capital. *Population and Development Review, 25,* 1–31.

Astuti, Rita, Solomon, Gregg E. A., & Carey, Susan. (2004). Constraints on conceptual development. *Monographs of the Society for Research in Child Development, 69*(3, Serial No. 277), vii–135.

Atchley, Robert C. (1999). *Continuity and adaptation in aging: Creating positive experiences.* Baltimore: Johns Hopkins University Press.

Atkinson, Janette, & Braddick, Oliver. (2003). Neurobiological models of normal and abnormal visual development. In Michelle De Haan & Mark H. Johnson (Eds.), *The cognitive neuroscience of development* (pp. 43–71). New York: Psychology Press.

Attig, Thomas. (2003). Respecting the spirituality of the dying and bereaved. In Inge Corless, Barbara B. Germino, & Mary A. Pittman (Eds.), *Dying, death, and bereavement: A challenge for living* (2nd ed., pp. 61–75). New York: Springer.

Aunola, Kaisa, & Nurmi, Jari-Erik. (2004). Maternal affection moderates the impact of psychological control on a child's mathematical performance. *Developmental Psychology, 40,* 965–978.

Austad, Steven N. (2001). Concepts and theories of aging. In Edward J. Masoro & Steven N. Austad (Eds.), *Handbook of the biology of aging* (5th ed., pp. 3–22). San Diego, CA: Academic Press.

Bäckman, Lars, & Farde, Lars. (2005). The role of dopamine systems in cognitive aging. In Roberto Cabeza, Lars Nyberg, & Denise Park (Eds.), *Cognitive neuroscience of aging: Linking cognitive and cerebral aging* (pp. 58–84). New York: Oxford University Press.

Bäckman, Lars, Laukka, Erika Jonsson, Wahlin, Åke, Small, Brent J., & Fratiglioni, Laura. (2002). Influences of preclinical dementia and impending death on the magnitude of age-related cognitive deficits. *Psychology & Aging, 17,* 435–442.

Baddeley, Alan. (1986). *Working memory.* New York: Clarendon Press.

Baddeley, Alan. (2003). Working memory and language: An overview. *Journal of Communication Disorders, 36*(3), 189–208.

Bagwell, Catherine L., Schmidt, Michelle E., Newcomb, Andrew F., & Bukowski, William M. (2001). Friendship and peer rejection as predictors of adult adjustment. In William Damon (Series Ed.) & Douglas W. Nangle & Cynthia A. Erdley (Vol. Eds.), *New directions for child and adolescent development: No. 91. The role of friendship in psychological adjustment* (pp. 25–49). San Francisco: Jossey-Bass.

Bahrick, Harry P. (1984). Semantic memory content in permastore: Fifty years of memory for Spanish learned in school. *Journal of Experimental Psychology: General, 113,* 1–29.

Baildam, Eileen M., Hillier, V. F., Menon, S., Bannister, R. P., Bamford, F. N., Moore, W. M. O., et al. (2000). Attention to infants in the first year. *Child: Care, Health and Development, 26,* 199–216.

Baillargeon, Renée. (1994). How do infants learn about the physical world? *Current Directions in Psychological Science, 3,* 133–140.

Baillargeon, Renée, & DeVos, Julie. (1991). Object permanence in young infants: Further evidence. *Child Development, 62,* 1227–1246.

Baird, Annabel H. (2003). Through my eyes: Service needs of grandparents who raise their grandchildren, from the perspective of a custodial grandmother. In Bert Hayslip Jr. & Julie Hicks Patrick (Eds.), *Working with custodial grandparents* (pp. 59–65). New York: Springer.

Baker, Jeffrey P. (2000). Immunization and the American way: 4 childhood vaccines. *American Journal of Public Health, 90,* 199–207.

Baker, Susan P. (2000). Where have we been and where are we going with injury control? In Dinesh Mohan & Geetam Tiwari (Eds.), *Injury prevention and control* (pp. 19–26). London: Taylor & Francis.

Baker, Timothy B., Japuntich, Sandra J., Hogle, Joanne M., McCarthy, Danielle E., & Curtin, John J. (2006). Pharmacologic and behavioral withdrawal from addictive drugs. *Current Directions in Psychological Science, 15,* 232–236.

Baldwin, Dare A. (1993). Infants' ability to consult the speaker for clues to word reference. *Journal of Child Language, 20,* 395–418.

Baldwin, Dare A. (2000). Interpersonal understanding fuels knowledge acquisition. *Current Directions in Psychological Science, 9,* 40–45.

Balmford, Andrew, Clegg, Lizzie, Coulson, Tim, & Taylor, Jennie. (2002, March 29). Why conservationists should heed Pokémon [Letter to the editor]. *Science, 295,* 2367.

Baltes, Margret M., & Carstensen, Laura L. (2003). The process of successful aging: Selection, optimization and compensation. In Ursula M. Staudinger & Ulman Lindenberger (Eds.), *Understanding human development: Dialogues with lifespan psychology* (pp. 81–104). Dordrecht, The Netherlands: Kluwer.

Baltes, Paul B. (2003). On the incomplete architechture of human ontogeny: Selection, optimization and compensation as foundation of developmental theory. In Ursula M. Staudinger & Ulman Lindenberger (Eds.), *Understanding human development: Dialogues with lifespan psychology* (pp. 17–43). Dordrecht, The Netherlands: Kluwer.

Baltes, Paul B., & Baltes, Margret M. (1990). Psychological perspectives on successful aging: The model of selective optimization with compensation. In Paul B. Baltes & Margret M. Baltes (Eds.), *Successful aging: Perspectives from the behavioral sciences* (pp. 1–34). New York: Cambridge University Press.

Baltes, Paul B., Lindenberger, Ulman, & Staudinger, Ursula M. (1998). Life-span theory in developmental psychology. In William Damon (Series Ed.) & Richard M. Lerner (Vol. Ed.), *Handbook of child psychology: Vol. 1. Theoretical models of human development* (5th ed., pp. 1029–1144). New York: Wiley.

Baltes, Paul B., Lindenberger, Ulman, & Staudinger, Ursula M. (2006). Life span theory in developmental psychology. In William Damon & Richard M. Lerner (Series Eds.) & Richard M. Lerner (Vol. Ed.), *Handbook of child psychology: Vol. 1. Theoretical models of human development* (6th ed., pp. 569–664). Hoboken, NJ: Wiley

Bamford, Christi, & Lagattuta, Kristin H. (2007, April). *Children really do "talk to god": What children know about prayer and its emotional contexts.* Poster session presented at the Society for Research in Child Development, Boston, MA.

Bandura, Albert. (1977). *Social learning theory.* Englewood Cliffs, NJ: Prentice Hall.

Bandura, Albert. (1986). *Social foundations of thought and action: A social cognitive theory.* Englewood Cliffs, NJ: Prentice-Hall.

Bandura, Albert. (1997). The anatomy of stages of change. *American Journal of Health Promotion, 12,* 8–10.

Bandura, Albert. (2006). Toward a psychology of human agency. *Perspectives on Psychological Science, 1,* 164–180.

Bandura, Albert, & Bussey, Kay. (2004). On broadening the cognitive, motivational, and sociostructural scope of theorizing about gender development and functioning: Comment on Martin, Ruble, and Szkrybalo (2002). *Psychological Bulletin, 130,* 691–701.

Banerjee, Robin, & Lintern, Vicki. (2000). Boys will be boys: The effect of social evaluation concerns on gender-typing. *Social Development, 9,* 397–408.

Bank, Lew, Burraston, Bert, & Snyder, Jim. (2004). Sibling conflict and ineffective parenting as predictors of adolescent boys'

antisocial behavior and peer difficulties: Additive and interactional effects. *Journal of Research on Adolescence, 14,* 99–125.

Banks, James, Marmot, Michael, Oldfield, Zoe, & Smith, James P. (2006). Disease and disadvantage in the United States and in England. *Journal of the American Medical Association, 295,* 2037–2045.

Barbaree, Howard E., & Marshall, William L. (2006). *The juvenile sex offender* (2nd ed.). New York: Guilford Press.

Barber, Bonnie L. (2006). To have loved and lost . . . adolescent romantic relationships and rejection. In Ann C. Crouter & Alan Booth (Eds.), *Romance and sex in adolescence and emerging adulthood: Risks and opportunities* (pp. 29–40). Mahwah, NJ: Erlbaum.

Barber, Brian K. (Ed.). (2002). *Intrusive parenting: How psychological control affects children and adolescents.* Washington, DC: American Psychological Association.

Barinaga, Marcia. (2003, January 3). Newborn neurons search for meaning. *Science, 299,* 32–34.

Barja, Gustavo. (2004). Mammalian and bird aging, oxygen radicals, and restricted feeding In Thomas Nyström & Heinz D. Osiewacz (Eds.), *Model systems in aging* (pp. 173–190). New York: Springer.

Barkley, Russell A. (2006). *Attention-deficit hyperactivity disorder: A handbook for diagnosis and treatment* (3rd ed.). New York: Guilford Press.

Barnard, Kathryn E., & Martell, Louise K. (1995). Mothering. In Marc H. Bornstein (Ed.), *Handbook of parenting: Vol. 3. Status and social conditions of parenting* (pp. 3–26). Hillsdale, NJ: Erlbaum.

Barnes, Grace M., Hoffman, Joseph H., Welte, John W., Farrell, Michael P., & Dintcheff, Barbara A. (2006). Effects of parental monitoring and peer deviance on substance use and delinquency. *Journal of Marriage and Family, 68,* 1084–1104.

Barnett, Rosalind C., & Rivers, Caryl. (2004). *Same difference: How gender myths are hurting our relationships, our children, and our jobs.* New York: Basic Books.

Baron, Andrew Scott, & Banaji, Mahzarin R. (2006). The development of implicit attitudes: Evidence of race evaluations from ages 6 and 10 and adulthood. *Psychological Science, 17,* 53–58.

Baron-Cohen, Simon. (1995). *Mindblindness: An essay on autism and theory of mind.* Cambridge, MA: MIT Press.

Barrett, Linda L. (2006). *The costs of long-term care: Public perceptions versus reality in 2006.* Washington, DC AARP.

Barrett, Martyn. (1999). An introduction to the nature of language and to the central themes and issues in the study of language development. In Martyn Barrett (Ed.), *The development of language* (pp. 1–24). Hove, England: Psychology Press.

Barros, Fernando C., Victora, Cesar G., Barros, Aluisio J. D., Santos, Ina S., Albernaz, Elaine, Matijasevich, Alicia, et al. (2005). The challenge of reducing neonatal mortality in middle-income countries: Findings from three Brazilian birth cohorts in 1982, 1993, and 2004. *Lancet, 365,* 847–854.

Barry, John M. (2005). *The great influenza: The epic story of the deadliest plague in history.* New York: Penguin Books.

Basáñez, María-Gloria , Pion, Sébastien D. S., Churcher, Thomas S., Breitling, Lutz P., Little, Mark P., & Boussinesq, Michel. (2006). River blindness: A success story under threat? *PLoS Medicine, 3,* e371.

Basili, Marcello, & Franzini, Maurizio. (2006). Understanding the risk of an avian flu pandemic: Rational waiting or precautionary failure? *Risk Analysis, 26,* 617–630.

Basseches, Michael. (1984). *Dialectical thinking and adult development.* Norwood, NJ: Ablex.

Basseches, Michael. (1989). Dialectical thinking as an organized whole: Comments on Irwin and Kramer. In Michael L. Commons, Jan D. Sinnott, Francis A. Richards, & Cheryl Armon (Eds.), *Adult development: Vol. 1. Comparisons and applications of developmental models* (pp. 161–178). New York: Praeger.

Batalova, Jeanne A., & Cohen, Philip N. (2002). Premarital cohabitation and housework: Couples in cross-national perspective. *Journal of Marriage and Family, 64,* 743–755.

Bateman, Belinda, Warner, John O., Hutchinson, Emma, Dean, Tara, Rowlandson, Piers, Gant, Carole, et al. (2004). The effects of a double blind, placebo controlled, artificial food colourings and benzoate preservative challenge on hyperactivity in a general population sample of preschool children. *Archives of Disease in Childhood, 89,* 506–511.

Bates, Elizabeth, Devescovi, Antonella, & Wulfeck, Beverly. (2001). Psycholinguistics: A cross-language perspective. *Annual Review of Psychology, 52,* 369–396.

Bates, John E., Viken, Richard J., Alexander, Douglas B., Beyers, Jennifer, & Stockton, Lesley. (2002). Sleep and adjustment in preschool children: Sleep diary reports by mothers relate to behavior reports by teachers. *Child Development, 73,* 62–74.

Bateson, Patrick. (2005, February 4). Desirable scientific conduct. *Science, 307,* 645.

Bau, Claiton H. D., Almeida, Silvana, Costa, Fabiana T., Garcia, Carlos E. D., Elias, Elvenise P., Ponso, Alexandra C., et al. (2001). DRD4 and DAT1 as modifying genes in alcoholism: Interaction with novelty seeking on level of alcohol consumption. *Molecular Psychiatry, 6,* 7–9.

Bauer, Patricia J. (2006). Event memory. In William Damon & Richard M. Lerner (Series Eds.) & Deanna Kuhn & Robert S. Siegler (Vol. Eds.), *Handbook of child psychology: Vol. 2. Cognition, perception, and language* (6th ed., pp. 373–425). Hoboken, NJ: Wiley.

Bauer, Patricia J., & Dow, Gina Annunziato. (1994). Episodic memory in 16- and 20-month-old children: Specifics are generalized but not forgotten. *Developmental Psychology, 30,* 403–417.

Bauer, Patricia J., Liebl, Monica, & Stennes, Leif. (1998). PRETTY is to DRESS as BRAVE is to SUITCOAT: Gender-based property-to-property inferences by 4–1/2-year-old children. *Merrill-Palmer Quarterly, 44,* 355–377.

Baumeister, Roy F., & Blackhart, Ginnette C. (2007). Three perspectives on gender differences in adolescent sexual development. In Rutger C. M. E. Engels, Margaret Kerr, & Håkan Stattin (Eds.), *Friends, lovers, and groups: Key relationships in adolescence* (pp. 93–104). Hoboken, NJ: Wiley.

Baumeister, Roy F., Campbell, Jennifer D., Krueger, Joachim I., & Vohs, Kathleen D. (2003). Does high self-esteem cause better performance, interpersonal success, happiness, or healthier lifestyles? *Psychological Science in the Public Interest, 4,* 1–44.

Baumrind, Diana. (1967). Child care practices anteceding three patterns of preschool behavior. *Genetic Psychology Monographs, 75,* 43–88.

Baumrind, Diana. (1971). Current patterns of parental authority. *Developmental Psychology, 4*(1, Pt. 2), 1–103.

Baumrind, Diana. (1991). The influence of parenting style on adolescent competence and substance use. *Journal of Early Adolescence, 11,* 56–95.

Bayer, Carey Roth. (2007). Understanding family planning, birth control, and contraception. In Annette Fuglsang Owens & Mitchell S. Tepper (Eds.), *Sexual health: Vol. 4. State-of-the-art treatments and research* (pp. 211–233). Westport, CT: Praeger/Greenwood.

Bayley, Nancy. (1966). Learning in adulthood: The role of intelligence. In Herbert J. Klausmeier & Chester William Harris (Eds.), *Analyses of concept learning* (pp. 000–000). New York: Academic Press.

Bayley, Nancy, & Oden, Melita H. (1955). The maintenance of intellectual ability in gifted adults. *Journal of Gerontology Series B, 10,* 91–107.

Beach, Lee Roy, Chi, Michelene, Klein, Gary, Smith, Philip, & Vicente, Kim. (1997). Naturalistic decision making and related research lines. In Caroline E. Zsambok & Gary Klein (Eds.), *Naturalistic decision making* (pp. 29–35). Hillsdale, NJ: Erlbaum.

Beal, S., & Porter, C. (1991). Sudden infant death syndrome related to climate. *Acta Paediatrica Scandinavica, 80,* 278–287.

Bearison, David J., Minian, Nadia, & Granowetter, Linda. (2002). Medical management of asthma and folk medicine in a Hispanic community. *Journal of Pediatric Psychology, 27,* 385–392.

Bearman, Peter S., & Brückner, Hannah. (2001). Promising the future: Virginity pledges and first intercourse. *American Journal of Sociology, 106,* 859–912.

Beauvais, Fred. (2000). Indian adolescence: Opportunity and challenge. In Raymond Montemayor, Gerald R. Adams, & Thomas Gullotta (Eds.), *Advances in adolescent development: Vol. 10. Adolescent diversity in ethnic, economic, and cultural contexts* (pp. 110–140). Thousand Oaks, CA: Sage.

Beck, Martha Nibley. (1999). *Expecting Adam: A true story of birth, rebirth, and everyday magic.* New York: Times Books.

Bedford, Victoria Hilkevitch. (1995). Sibling relationships in middle and old age. In Rosemary Blieszner & Victoria Hilkevitch Bedford (Eds.), *Handbook of aging and the family* (pp. 201–222). Westport, CT: Greenwood Press.

Behne, Tanya, Carpenter, Malinda, Call, Josep, & Tomasello, Michael. (2005). Unwilling versus unable: Infants' understanding of intentional action. *Developmental Psychology, 41,* 328–337.

Behrend, Douglas A., Scofield, Jason, & Kleinknecht, Erica E. (2001). Beyond fast mapping: Young children's extensions of novel words and novel facts. *Developmental Psychology, 37,* 698–705.

Beier, Margaret E., & Ackerman, Phillip L. (2001). Current-events knowledge in adults: An investigation of age, intelligence, and nonability determinants. *Psychology & Aging, 16,* 615–628.

Belamarich, Peter, & Ayoob, Keith-Thomas. (2001). Keeping teenage vegetarians healthy and in the know. *Contemporary Pediatrics, 10,* 89–108.

Belizan, Jose M., Althabe, Fernando, Barros, Fernando C., & Alexander, Sophie. (1999). Rates and implications of caesarean sections in Latin America: Ecological study. *British Medical Journal, 319,* 1397–1402.

Belka, David. (2004). Substituting skill learning for traditional games in early childhood. *Teaching Elementary Physical Education, 15,* 25–27.

Bell, Joanna H., & Bromnick, Rachel D. (2003). The social reality of the imaginary audience: A ground theory approach. *Adolescence, 38,* 205–219.

Bell, Ruth. (1998). *Changing bodies, changing lives: A book for teens on sex and relationships* (Expanded 3rd ed.). New York: Times Books.

Bem, Sandra Lipsitz. (1993). *The lenses of gender: Transforming the debate on sexual inequality.* New Haven, CT: Yale University Press.

Benes, Francine M. (2001). The development of prefrontal cortex: The maturation of neurotransmitter systems and their interactions. In Charles A. Nelson & Monica Luciana (Eds.), *Handbook of developmental cognitive neuroscience* (pp. 79–92). Cambridge, MA: MIT Press.

Benet, Sula. (1974). *Abkhasians: The long-living people of the Caucasus.* New York: Holt, Rinehart & Winston.

Bengtson, Vern L. (2001). Beyond the nuclear family: The increasing importance of multigenerational bonds (The Burgess Award Lecture). *Journal of Marriage & the Family, 63,* 1–16.

Bengtson, Vern L., & Putney, Norella M. (2006). Future 'conflicts' across generations and cohorts? In John A. Vincent, Chris R. Phillipson, & Murna Downs (Eds.), *The futures of old age* (pp. 20–29). Thousand Oaks, CA: Sage.

Ben-Itzchak, Esther, & Zachor, Ditza A. (2007). The effects of intellectual functioning and autism severity on outcome of early behavioral intervention for children with autism. *Research in Developmental Disabilities, 28,* 287–303.

Benjamin, Georges C. (2004). The solution is injury prevention. *American Journal of Public Health, 94,* 521.

Benjamin, Roger. (2003). *The coming transformation of the American university.* New York: Council for Aid to Education/An Independent Subsidiary of RAND.

Benner, Aprile D., & Graham, Sandra. (2007). Navigating the transition to multiethnic urban high schools: Changing ethnic congruence and adolescents' school-related affect. *Journal of Research on Adolescence, 17,* 207–220.

Benson, Peter L. (2003). Developmental assets and asset-building community: Conceptual and empirical foundations. In Richard M. Lerner & Peter L. Benson (Eds.), *Developmental assets and asset-building communities: Implications for research, policy, and practice* (pp. 19–43). New York: Kluwer/Plenum.

Bentley, Gillian R., & Mascie-Taylor, C. G. Nicholas. (2000). Introduction. In Gillian R. Bentley & C. G. Nicholas Mascie-Taylor (Eds.), *Infertility in the modern world: Present and future prospects* (pp. 1–13). Cambridge, England: Cambridge University Press.

Bentley, Tanya G. K., Willett, Walter C., Weinstein, Milton C., & Kuntz, Karen M. (2006). Population-level changes in folate intake by age, gender, and race/ethnicity after folic acid fortification. *American Journal of Public Health, 96,* 2040–2047.

Benton, David. (2004). Role of parents in the determination of the food preferences of children and the development of obesity. *International Journal of Obesity & Related Metabolic Disorders, 28,* 858–869.

Beppu, Satoshi. (2005). Social cognitive development of autistic children: Attachment relationships and understanding the existence of minds of others. In David W. Shwalb, Jun Nakazawa, & Barbara J. Shwalb (Eds.), *Applied developmental psychology: Theory, practice, and research from Japan* (pp. 199–221). Greenwich, CT: Information Age.

Berg, Cynthia A., & Klaczynski, Paul A. (2002). Contextual variability in the expression and meaning of intelligence. In Robert J. Sternberg & Elena L. Grigorenko (Eds.), *The general factor of intelligence: How general is it?* (pp. 381–412). Mahwah, NJ: Erlbaum.

Berg, Sandra J., & Wynne-Edwards, Katherine E. (2002). Salivary hormone concentrations in mothers and fathers becoming parents are not correlated. *Hormones & Behavior, 42,* 424–436.

Berger, Kathleen Stassen. (2007). Update on bullying at school: Science forgotten? *Developmental Review, 27,* 90–126.

Bering, Jesse M., & Bjorklund, David F. (2004). The natural emergence of reasoning about the afterlife as a developmental regularity. *Developmental Psychology, 40,* 217–233.

Bering, Jesse M., Blasi, Carlos Hernández, & Bjorklund, David F. (2005). The development of 'afterlife' beliefs in religiously and secularly schooled children. *British Journal of Developmental Psychology, 23,* 587–607.

Berkey, Catherine S., Gardner, Jane D., Lindsay Frazier, A., & Colditz, Graham A. (2000). Relation of childhood diet and body size to menarche and adolescent growth in girls. *American Journal of Epidemiology, 152,* 446–452.

Berkowitz, Alan D. (2005). An overview of the social norms approach. In Linda Costigan Lederman & Lea Stewart (Eds.), *Changing the culture of college drinking: A socially situated health communication campaign* (pp. 193–214). Cresskill, NJ: Hampton Press.

Berman, Alan L., Jobes, David A., & Silverman, Morton M. (2006). *Adolescent suicide: Assessment and intervention* (2nd ed.). Washington, DC: American Psychological Association.

Berndt, Thomas J., & Murphy, Lonna M. (2002). Influences of friends and friendships: Myths, truths, and research recommendations. In Robert V. Kail (Ed.), *Advances in child development and behavior* (Vol. 30, pp. 275–310). San Diego, CA: Academic Press.

Berninger, Virginia Wise, & Richards, Todd L. (2002). *Brain literacy for educators and psychologists.* Amsterdam: Academic Press.

Berntsen, Dorthe, & Rubin, David C. (2002). Emotionally charged autobiographical memories across the life span: The recall of happy, sad, traumatic and involuntary memories. *Psychology & Aging, 17,* 636–652.

Berntsen, Dorthe, & Rubin, David C. (2006). The Centrality of Event Scale: A measure of integrating a trauma into one's identity and its relation to post-traumatic stress disorder symptoms. *Behaviour Research and Therapy, 44,* 219–231.

Berrick, Jill Duerr. (1998). When children cannot remain home: Foster family care and kinship care. *The Future of Children: Protecting Children from Abuse and Neglect, 8*(1), 72–87.

Berry, John W. (2006). *Immigrant youth in cultural transition: Acculturation, identity, and adaptation across national contexts.* Mahwah, NJ: Erlbaum.

Bertenthal, Bennett I., & Clifton, Rachel K. (1998). Perception and action. In William Damon (Series Ed.) & Deanna Kuhn & Robert S. Siegler (Vol. Eds.), *Handbook of child psychology: Vol. 2. Cognition, perception, and language* (5th ed., pp. 51–102). New York: Wiley.

Bhardwaj, Ratan D., Curtis, Maurice A., Spalding, Kirsty L., Buchholz, Bruce A., Fink, David, Björk-Eriksson, Thomas, et al. (2006). Neocortical neurogenesis in humans is restricted to development. *Proceedings of the National Academy of Sciences, 103,* 12564–12568.

Bhasin, Shalender. (2007). Approach to the infertile man. *Journal of Clinical Endocrinology & Metabolism, 92,* 1995–2004.

Bhasin, Shalender, Cunningham, Glenn R., Hayes, Frances J., Matsumoto, Alvin M., Snyder, Peter J., Swerdloff, Ronald S., et al. (2006). Testosterone therapy in adult men with androgen deficiency syndromes: An endocrine society clinical practice guideline. *Journal of Clinical Endocrinology & Metabolism, 91,* 1995–2010.

Bialystok, Ellen. (2001). *Bilingualism in development: Language, literacy, and cognition.* New York: Cambridge University Press.

Bianchi, Suzanne M., Casper, Lynne M., & King, Rosalind Berkowitz (Eds.). (2005). *Work, family, health, and well-being.* Mahwah, NJ: Erlbaum.

Biddle, Stuart, & Mutrie, Nanette. (2001). *Psychology of physical activity: Determinants, well-being, and interventions.* London: Routledge.

Bienvenu, Thierry. (2005). Rett syndrome. In Merlin Gene Butler & F. John Meaney (Eds.), *Genetics of developmental disabilities* (pp. 477–519). Boca Raton, FL: Taylor & Francis.

Billingsley, Andrew. (1999). *Mighty like a river: The black church and social reform.* New York: Oxford University Press.

Bingham, C. Raymond, Shope, Jean T., & Tang, Xianli. (2005). Drinking behavior from high school to young adulthood: differences by college education. *Alcoholism: Clinical & Experimental Research, 29*(12), 2170–2180.

Birch, Susan A. J., & Bloom, Paul. (2003). Children are cursed: An asymmetric bias in mental-state attribution. *Psychological Science, 14,* 283–286.

Birney, Damian P., Citron-Pousty, Jill H., Lutz, Donna J., & Sternberg, Robert J. (2005). The development of cognitive and intellectual abilities. In Marc H. Bornstein & Michael E. Lamb (Eds.), *Developmental science: An advanced textbook* (5th ed., pp. 327–358). Mahwah, NJ: Erlbaum.

Biro, Frank M., McMahon, Robert P., Striegel-Moore, Ruth, Crawford, Patricia B., Obarzanek, Eva, Morrison, John A., et al. (2001). Impact of timing of pubertal maturation on growth in black and white female adolescents: The National Heart, Lung, and Blood Institute Growth and Health Study. *Journal of Pediatrics, 138,* 636–643.

Birren, James E., & Schroots, Johannes J. F. (2006). Autobiographical memory and the narrative self over the life span. In James E. Birren & K. Warner Schaie (Eds.), *Handbook of the psychology of aging* (6th ed., pp. 477–498). Amsterdam: Elsevier.

Blackburn, Susan Tucker. (2003). *Maternal, fetal & neonatal physiology: A clinical perspective* (2nd ed.). St. Louis, MO: Saunders.

Blair, Peter S., & Ball, Helen L. (2004). The prevalence and characteristics associated with parent-infant bed-sharing in England. *Archives of Disease in Childhood, 89,* 1106–1110.

Blake, Susan M., Simkin, Linda, Ledsky, Rebecca, Perkins, Cheryl, & Calabrese, Joseph M. (2001). Effects of a parent-child communications intervention on young adolescents' risk for early onset of sexual intercourse. *Family Planning Perspectives, 33,* 52–61.

Blanchard-Fields, Fredda, Baldi, Renee, & Stein, Renee. (1999). Age relevance and context effects on attributions across the adult lifespan. *International Journal of Behavioral Development, 23,* 665–683.

Blatchford, Peter. (2003). *The class size debate: Is small better?* Maidenhead, Berkshire, England: Open University.

Blau, Francine D., Brinton, Mary C., & Grusky, David B. (2006). *The declining significance of gender?* New York: Russell Sage Foundation.

Bleske-Rechek, April L., & Buss, David M. (2001). Opposite-sex friendship: Sex differences and similarities in initiation, selection, and dissolution. *Personality and Social Psychology Bulletin, 27,* 1310–1323.

Block, Lauren G., Morwitz, Vicki G., Putsis, William P., Jr., & Sen, Subrata K. (2002). Assessing the impact of antidrug advertising on adolescent drug consumption: Results from a behavioral economic model. *American Journal of Public Health, 92,* 1346–1351.

Bloom, Floyd E., Nelson, Charles A., & Lazerson, Arlyne. (2001). *Brain, mind, and behavior* (3rd ed.). New York: Worth.

Bloom, Lois. (1993). *The transition from infancy to language: Acquiring the power of expression.* New York: Cambridge University Press.

Bloom, Lois. (1998). Language acquisition in its developmental context. In William Damon (Series Ed.) & Deanna Kuhn & Robert S. Siegler (Vol. Eds.), *Handbook of child psychology: Vol. 2. Cognition, perception, and language* (5th ed., pp. 309–370). New York: Wiley.

Bloom, Lois. (2000). Pushing the limits on theories of word learning. *Monographs of the Society for Research in Child Development, 65*(3, Serial No. 262), 124–135.

Blum, Deborah. (2002). *Love at Goon Park: Harry Harlow and the science of affection.* Cambridge, MA: Perseus.

Blum, Robert W., Beuhring, Trisha, Shew, Marcia L., Bearinger, Linda H., Sieving, Renee E., & Resnick, Michael D. (2000). The effects of race/ethnicity, income, and family structure on adolescent risk behaviors. *American Journal of Public Health, 90,* 1879–1884.

Blum, Robert W., & Nelson-Mmari, Kristin. (2004). Adolescent health from an international perspective. In Richard M. Lerner & Laurence D. Steinberg (Eds.), *Handbook of adolescent psychology* (2nd ed., pp. 553–586). Hoboken, NJ: Wiley.

Blustein, David Larry. (2006). *The psychology of working: A new perspective for career development, counseling, and public policy.* Mahwah, NJ: Lawrence Erlbaum Publishers.

Blythe, Ronald. (1979). *The view in winter: Reflections on old age.* New York: Harcourt Brace Jovanovich.

Boaler, Jo. (2002). *Experiencing school mathematics: Traditional and reform approaches to teaching and their impact on student learning* (Rev. ed.). Mahwah, NJ: Erlbaum.

Bode, Christina. (2003). *Individuality and relatedness in middle and late adulthood: A study of women and men in the Netherlands, East-, and West-Germany.* Enschede, The Netherlands: PrintPartners Ipskamp.

Boerner, Kathrin, Wortman, Camille B., & Bonanno, George A. (2005). Resilient or at risk? A 4–year study of older adults who initially showed high or low distress following conjugal loss. *Journals of Gerontology: Series B: Psychological Sciences and Social Sciences, 60,* P67–P73.

Bolger, Kerry E., & Patterson, Charlotte J. (2003). Sequelae of child maltreatment: Vulnerability and resilience. In Suniya S. Luthar (Ed.), *Resilience and vulnerability: Adaptation in the context of childhood adversities* (pp. 156–181). New York: Cambridge University Press.

Bonanno, George A., Wortman, Camille B., & Nesse, Randolph M. (2004). Prospective patterns of resilience and maladjustment during widowhood. *Psychology and Aging, 19,* 260–271.

Bonner, Barbara L., Crow, Sheila M., & Logue, Mary Beth. (1999). Fatal child neglect. In Howard Dubowitz (Ed.), *Neglected children: Research, practice, and policy* (pp. 156–173). Thousand Oaks, CA: Sage.

Bonnie, Richard J., & Wallace, Robert B. (2003). *Elder mistreatment: Abuse, neglect, and exploitation in an aging America.* Washington, DC: National Academies Press.

Booth, Alan, & Crouter, Ann C. (2005). *The new population problem: Why families in developed countries are shrinking and what it means.* Mahwah, NJ: Erlbaum.

Borgaonkar, Digamber S. (1997). *Chromosomal variation in man: A catalog of chromosomal variants and anomalies* (8th ed.). New York: Wiley-Liss.

Borkowski, John G., Farris, Jaelyn Renee, Whitman, Thomas L., Carothers, Shannon S., Weed, Keri, & Keogh, Deborah A. (2007). *Risk and resilience: Adolescent mothers and their children grow up.* Mahwah, NJ: Erlbaum.

Borkowski, John G., Smith, Leann E., & Akai, Carol E. (2007). Designing effective prevention programs: How good science makes good art. *Infants & Young Children, 20,* 229–241.

Borland, Moira. (1998). *Middle childhood: The perspectives of children and parents.* London: Jessica Kingsley.

Bornstein, Marc H. (2002). Parenting infants. In Marc H. Bornstein (Ed.), *Handbook of parenting: Vol. 1. Children and parenting* (2nd ed., pp. 3–43). Mahwah, NJ: Erlbaum.

Bornstein, Marc H. (2006). Parenting science and practice. In William Damon & Richard M. Lerner (Series Eds.) & K. Ann Renninger & Irving E. Sigel (Vol. Eds.), *Handbook of child psychology: Vol. 4. Child psychology in practice* (6th ed., pp. 893–949). Hoboken, NJ: Wiley.

Bornstein, Marc H., Arterberry, Martha E., & Mash, Clay. (2005). Perceptual development. In Marc H. Bornstein & Michael E. Lamb (Eds.), *Developmental science: An advanced textbook* (5th ed., pp. 283–325). Mahwah, NJ: Erlbaum.

Bornstein, Marc H., Cote, Linda R., Maital, Sharone, Painter, Kathleen, Park, Sung-Yun, Pascual, Liliana, et al. (2004). Cross-linguistic analysis of vocabulary in young children: Spanish, Dutch, French, Hebrew, Italian, Korean, and American English. *Child Development, 75,* 1115–1139.

Bornstein, Marc H., & Putnick, Diane L. (2007). Chronological age, cognitions, and practices in European American mothers: A multivariate study of parenting. *Developmental Psychology, 43,* 850–864.

Bornstein, Robert F. (1989). Exposure and affect: Overview and meta-analysis of research, 1968–1987. *Psychological Bulletin, 106,* 265–289.

Bortz, Walter M. (2005). Biological basis of determinants of health. *American Journal of Public Health, 95,* 389–392.

Borzekowski, Dina L. G., & Rickert, Vaughn I. (2001). Adolescents, the internet, and health: Issues of access and content. *Journal of Applied Developmental Psychology, 22,* 49–59.

Bossé, Yohan, & Hudson, Thomas J. (2007). Toward a comprehensive set of asthma susceptibility genes. *Annual Review of Medicine, 58,* 171–184.

Botto, Lorenzo D., Lisi, Alessandra, Robert-Gnansia, Elisabeth, Erickson, J. David, Vollset, Stein Emil, Mastroiacovo, Pierpaolo, et al. (2005, March 12, 2005). *International retrospective cohort study of neural tube defects in relation to folic acid recommendations: Are the recommendations working?* Retrieved, 330, from the World Wide Web: http://www.bmj.com/cgi/content/abstract/330/7491/571

Botto, Lorenzo D., Olney, Richard S., & Erickson, J. David. (2004). Vitamin supplements and the risk for congenital anomalies other than neural tube defects. *American Journal of Medical Genetics Part C: Seminars in Medical Genetics, 125C,* 12–21.

Bouchard, Geneviève. (2006). Cohabitation versus marriage: The role of dyadic adjustment in relationship dissolution. *Journal of Divorce & Remarriage, 46,* 107–117.

Bouchard, Thomas J., Segal, Nancy L., Tellegen, Auke, McGue, Matt, Keyes, Margaret, & Krueger, Robert. (2004). Genetic influence on social attitudes: Another challenge to psychology from behavior genetics. In Lisabeth F. DiLalla (Ed.), *Behavior genetics principles: Perspectives in development, personality, and psychopathology* (pp. 89–104). Washington, DC: American Psychological Association.

Bousquet, Jean, Dahl, Ronald, & Khaltaev, Nikolai. (2007). Global alliance against chronic respiratory diseases. *Allergy, 62,* 216–223.

Bower, Bruce. (2006, August 12). Outside looking in: Researchers open new windows on Asperger syndrome and related disorders. *Science News, 170,* 106.

Bowlby, John. (1969). *Attachment and loss: Vol. 1. Attachment.* New York: Basic Books.

Bowlby, John. (1973). *Attachment and loss: Vol. 2. Separation: Anxiety and anger.* New York: Basic Books.

Bowlby, John. (1988). *A secure base: Clinical applications of attachment theory.* London: Routledge.

Bowman, Shanthy A., & Vinyard, Bryan T. (2004). Fast food consumption of U.S. adults: Impact on energy and nutrient intakes and overweight status. *Journal of the American College of Nutrition, 23,* 163–168.

Boyd, William L. (2007). The politics of privatization in American education. *Educational Policy, 21,* 7–14.

Bozik, Mary. (2002). The college student as learner: Insight gained through metaphor analysis. *College Student Journal, 36,* 142–151.

Bradbury, Thomas N., Fincham, Frank D., & Beach, Steven R. H. (2000). Research on the nature and determinants of marital satisfaction: A decade in review. *Journal of Marriage & the Family, 62,* 964–980.

Bradley, Robert H., & Corwyn, Robert F. (2005). Productive activity and the prevention of behavior problems. *Developmental Psychology, 41,* 89–98.

Braithwaite, R. Scott, Conigliaro, Joseph, Roberts, Mark S., Shechter, Steven, Schaefer, Andrew, McGinnis, Kathleen, et al. (2007). Estimating the impact of alcohol consumption on survival for HIV+ individuals. *AIDS Care, 19,* 459–466.

Brandl, Bonnie. (2000). Power and control: Understanding domestic abuse in later life. *Generations, 24*(2), 39–45.

Brandt, Hella E., Ooms, Marcel E., Ribbe, Miel W., Wal, Gerrit van der, & Deliens, Luc. (2006). Predicted survival vs. actual survival in terminally ill noncancer patients in Dutch nursing homes. *Journal of Pain and Symptom Management, 32,* 560–566.

Branson, Ruth, Potoczna, Natascha, Kral, John G., Lentes, Klaus-Ulrich, Hoehe, Margret R., & Horber, Fritz F. (2003). Binge eating as a major phenotype of melanocortin 4 receptor gene mutations. *New England Journal of Medicine, 348,* 1096–1103.

Braun, Kathryn L., Zir, Ana, Crocker, Joanna, & Seely, Marilyn R. (2005). Kokua Mau: A statewide effort to improve end-of-life care. *Journal of Palliative Medicine, 8,* 313–323.

Bray, George A. (2003). Low-carbohydrate diets and realities of weight loss. *Journal of the American Medical Association, 289,* 1853–1855.

Breggin, Peter Roger. (2001). *Talking back to ritalin: What doctors aren't telling you about stimulants and ADHD* (Rev. ed.). Cambridge, MA: Perseus.

Breggin, Peter R., & Baughman, Fred A., Jr. (2001, January 26). Questioning the treatment for ADHD [Letter to the editor]. *Science, 291,* 595.

Brendgen, Mara, Vitaro, Frank, Bukowski, William M., Doyle, Anna Beth, & Markiewicz, Dorothy. (2001). Developmental profiles of peer social preference over the course of elementary school: Associations with trajectories of externalizing and internalizing behavior. *Developmental Psychology, 37,* 308–320.

Brennan, Patricia A., Grekin, Emily R., & Mednick, Sarnoff A. (2003). Prenatal and perinatal influences on conduct disorder and serious delinquency. In Benjamin B. Lahey, Terrie E. Moffitt, & Avshalom Caspi (Eds.), *Causes of conduct disorder and juvenile delinquency* (pp. 319–341). New York: Guilford Press.

Brenner, Ruth A., Trumble, Ann C., Smith, Gordon S., Kessler, Eileen P., & Overpeck, Mary D. (2001). Where children drown, United States, 1995. *Pediatrics, 108,* 85–89.

Bretherton, Inge, & Munholland, Kristine A. (1999). Internal working models in attachment relationships: A construct revisited. In Jude Cassidy & Phillip R. Shaver (Eds.), *Handbook of attachment: Theory, research, and clinical applications* (pp. 89–111). New York: Guilford Press.

Breunlin, Douglas C., Bryant-Edwards, Tara L., Hetherington, Joshua S., & Cimmarusti, Rocco A. (2002). Conflict resolution training as an alternative to suspension for violent behavior. *Journal of Educational Research, 95,* 349–357.

Bridge, Jeffrey A., Iyengar, Satish, Salary, Cheryl B., Barbe, Remy P., Birmaher, Boris, Pincus, Harold Alan, et al. (2007). Clinical response and risk for reported suicidal ideation and suicide attempts in pediatric antidepressant treatment: A meta-analysis of randomized controlled trials. *Journal of the American Medical Association, 297,* 1683–1696.

Briley, Mike, & Sulser, Fridolin (Eds.). (2001). *Molecular genetics of mental disorders: The place of molecular genetics in basic mechanisms and clinical applications in mental disorders.* London: Martin Dunitz.

Brim, Orville Gilbert, Ryff, Carol D., & Kessler, Ronald C. (2004). *How healthy are we? A national study of well-being at midlife.* Chicago: University of Chicago Press.

Brint, Steven. (2003). Few remaining dreams: Community colleges since 1985. In Kathleen M. Shaw & Jerry A. Jacobs (Eds.), *Community colleges: New environments, new directions* (Vol. 586, pp. 16–37). Thousand Oaks, CA: Sage.

Brody, Gene H. (2004). Siblings' direct and indirect contributions to child development. *Current Directions in Psychological Science, 13,* 124–126.

Brody, Jane E. (2007, January 23). A humorist illuminates the blessings of hospice. *New York Times,* p. F7.

Broidy, Lisa M., Nagin, Daniel S., Tremblay, Richard E., Bates, John E., Brame, Bobby, Dodge, Kenneth A., et al. (2003). Developmental trajectories of childhood disruptive behaviors and adolescent delinquency: A six-site, cross-national study. *Developmental Psychology, 39,* 222–245.

Brokenleg, Martin, & Middleton, David. (1993). Native Americans: Adapting, yet retaining. In Donald P. Irish, Kathleen F. Lundquist, & Vivian Jenkins Nelsen (Eds.), *Ethnic variations in dying, death, and grief: Diversity in universality* (pp. 101–112). Philadelphia: Taylor & Francis.

Bronfenbrenner, Urie. (1974). Developmental research, public policy, and the ecology of childhood. *Child Development, 45,* 1–5.

Bronfenbrenner, Urie, & Morris, Pamela A. (2006). The bioecological model of human development. In William Damon & Richard M. Lerner (Eds.), *Handbook of child psychology: Vol. 1. Theoretical models of human development* (6th ed., pp. 793–828). Hoboken, NJ: Wiley.

Brooks-Gunn, Jeanne, Han, Wen-Jui, & Waldfogel, Jane. (2002). Maternal employment and child cognitive outcomes in the first three years of life: The NICHD study of early child care. *Child Development, 73,* 1052–1072.

Brown, B. Bradford. (2004). Adolescents' relationships with peers. In Richard M. Lerner & Laurence D. Steinberg (Eds.), *Handbook of adolescent psychology* (2nd ed., pp. 363–394). Hoboken, NJ: Wiley.

Brown, B. Bradford. (2005). Moving forward with research on adolescence: Some reflections on the state of JRA and the state of the field. *Journal of Research on Adolescence, 15,* 657–673.

Brown, B. Bradford. (2006). A few "course corrections" to Collins & van Dulmen's "The course of true love". In Ann C. Crouter & Alan Booth (Eds.), *Romance and sex in adolescence and emerging adulthood: Risks and opportunities* (pp. 113–123). Mahwah, NJ: Erlbaum.

Brown, B. Bradford, & Klute, Christa. (2003). Friendships, cliques, and crowds. In Gerald R. Adams & Michael D. Berzonsky (Eds.), *Blackwell handbook of adolescence* (pp. 330–348). Malden, MA: Blackwell.

Brown, B. Bradford, & Larson, Reed W. (2002). The kaleidoscope of adolescence: Experiences of the world's youth at the beginning of the 21st century. In B. Bradford Brown, Reed W. Larson, & T. S. Saraswathi (Eds.), *The world's youth: Adolescence in eight regions of the globe* (pp. 1–20). New York: Cambridge University Press.

Brown, Christia Spears, & Bigler, Rebecca S. (2005). Children's perceptions of discrimination: A developmental model. *Child Development, 76,* 533–553.

Brown, Kathryn. (2003, March 14). The medication merry-go-round. *Science, 299,* 1646–1649.

Brown, Sandra A., Tapert, Susan F., Granholm, Eric, & Delis, Dean C. (2000). Neurocognitive functioning of adolescents: Effects of protracted alcohol use. *Alcoholism: Clinical and Experimental Research, 24,* 164–171.

Brown, Susan L. (2004). Family structure and child well-being: The significance of parental cohabitation. *Journal of Marriage and Family, 66,* 351–367.

Brown, Susan L., Sanchez, Laura Ann, Nock, Steven L., & Wright, James D. (2006). Links between premarital cohabitation and subsequent marital quality, stability, and divorce: A comparison of covenant versus standard marriages. *Social Science Research, 35,* 454–470.

Bruck, Maggie, Ceci, Stephen J., & Principe, Gabrielle F. (2006). The child and the law. In William Damon & Richard M. Lerner (Series Eds.) & K. Ann Renninger & Irving E. Sigel (Vol. Eds.), *Handbook of child psychology: Vol. 4. Child psychology in practice* (6th ed., pp. 776–816). Hoboken, NJ: Wiley.

Brugman, Gerard M. (2006). Wisdom and aging. In James E. Birren & K. Warner Schaie (Eds.), *Handbook of the psychology of aging* (6th ed., pp. 445–475). Amsterdam: Elsevier.

Buccino, Giovanni, Binkofski, Ferdinand, & Riggio, Lucia. (2004). The mirror neuron system and action recognition. *Brain and Language, 89,* 370–376.

Buckhalt, Joseph A., El-Sheikh, Mona, & Keller, Peggy. (2007). Children's sleep and cognitive functioning: Race and socioeconomic status as moderators of effects. *Child Development, 78,* 213–231.

Buckner, John C., Bassuk, Ellen L., Weinreb, Linda F., & Brooks, Margaret G. (1999). Homelessness and its relation to the mental health and behavior of low-income school-age children. *Developmental Psychology, 35,* 246–257.

Buckner, Randy, Head, Denise, & Lustig, Cindy. (2006). Brain changes in aging: A lifespan perspective. In Ellen Bialystok & Fergus I. M. Craik (Eds.), *Lifespan cognition: Mechanisms of change* (pp. 27–42). Oxford, UK: Oxford University Press.

Buehler, Cheryl. (2006). Parents and peers in relation to early adolescent problem behavior. *Journal of Marriage and Family, 68,* 109–124.

Buehler, Cheryl, & Gerard, Jean M. (2002). Marital conflict, ineffective parenting, and children's and adolescents' maladjustment. *Journal of Marriage & Family, 64,* 78–92.

Buelga, Sofia, Ravenna, Marcella, Musitu, Gonzalo, & Lila, Marisol. (2006). Epidemiology and psychosocial risk factors associated with adolescent drug consumption. In Sandy Jackson & Luc Goossens (Eds.), *Handbook of adolescent development* (pp. 337–364). Hove, East Sussex, UK: Psychology Press.

Bugental, Daphne Blunt, & Grusec, Joan E. (2006). Socialization theory. In William Damon & Richard M. Lerner (Series Eds.) & Nancy Eisenberg (Vol. Ed.), *Handbook of child psychology: Vol. 3. Social, emotional, and personality development* (6th ed., pp. 366–428). Hoboken, NJ: Wiley.

Bugental, Daphne Blunt, & Happaney, Keith. (2004). Predicting infant maltreatment in low-income families: The interactive effects of maternal attributions and child status at birth. *Developmental Psychology, 40,* 234–243.

Bukowski, William M., Newcomb, Andrew F., & Hartup, Willard W. (Eds.). (1996). *The company they keep: Friendship in childhood and adolescence.* New York: Cambridge University Press.

Bumpass, Larry, & Lu, Hsien-Hen. (2000). Trends in cohabitation and implications for children's family contexts in the United States. *Population Studies, 54,* 29–41.

Burke, Deborah M., & Shafto, Meredith A. (2004). Aging and language production. *Current Directions in Psychological Science, 13,* 21–24.

Burr, Jeffrey A., & Mutchler, Jan E. (1999). Race and ethnic variation in norms of filial responsibility among older persons. *Journal of Marriage & the Family, 61,* 674–687.

Burton, Sarah, & Mitchell, Peter. (2003). Judging who knows best about yourself: Developmental change in citing the self across middle childhood. *Child Development, 74,* 426–443.

Buschman, Nina A., Foster, G., & Vickers, Pauline. (2001). Adolescent girls and their babies: Achieving optimal birthweight. Gestational weight gain and pregnancy outcome in terms of gestation at delivery and infant birth weight: A comparison between adolescents under 16 and adult women. *Child: Care, Health & Development, 27,* 163–171.

Buss, David M., Haselton, Martie G., Shackelford, Todd K., Bleske, April L., & Wakefield, Jerome C. (1998). Adaptations, exaptations, and spandrels. *American Psychologist, 53,* 533–548.

Busse, William W., & Lemanske, Robert F. (Eds.). (2005). *Lung biology in health and disease: Vol. 195. Asthma prevention.* Boca Raton, FL: Taylor & Francis.

Bussey, Kay, & Bandura, Albert. (1999). Social cognitive theory of gender development and differentiation. *Psychological Review, 106,* 676–713.

Butler, Merlin Gene, & Meaney, F. John. (2005). *Genetics of developmental disabilities.* Boca Raton, FL: Taylor & Francis.

Butler, Robert N., Lewis, Myrna I., & Sunderland, Trey. (1998). *Aging and mental health: Positive psychosocial and biomedical approaches* (5th ed.). Boston: Allyn & Bacon.

Buzsáki, György. (2006). *Rhythms of the brain.* Oxford, UK: Oxford University Press.

Byard, Roger W. (2004). *Sudden death in infancy, childhood, and adolescence* (2nd ed.). Cambridge, England: Cambridge University Press.

Bybee, Jane (Ed.). (1998). *Guilt and children.* San Diego, CA: Academic Press.

Byram, Michael S., & Feng, Anwei. (2005). Teaching and researching intercultural competence. In Eli Hinkel (Ed.), *Handbook of research in second language teaching and learning* (pp. 911–930). Mahwah, NJ: Erlbaum.

Byrnes, James P. (2005). The development of self-regulated decision making. In Janis E. Jacobs & Paul A. Klaczynski (Eds.), *The development of judgment and decision making in children and adolescents* (pp. 5–38). Mahwah, NJ: Erlbaum.

Cabeza, Roberto. (2002). Hemispheric asymmetry reduction in older adults: The HAROLD model. *Psychology & Aging, 17,* 85–100.

Cabeza, Roberto, Nyberg, Lars, & Park, Denise C. (2005). *Cognitive neuroscience of aging: Linking cognitive and cerebral aging.* New York: Oxford University Press.

Cabrera, Natasha J., Shannon, Jacqueline D., West, Jerry, & Brooks-Gunn, Jeanne. (2006). Parental interactions with Latino infants: Variation by country of origin and English proficiency. *Child Development, 77,* 1190–1207.

Caetano, Raul, Ramisetty-Mikler, Suhasini, & Field, Craig A. (2005). Unidirectional and bidirectional intimate partner violence among White, Black, and Hispanic couples in the United States. *Violence and Victims, 20,* 393–406.

Cairns, Robert B., & Cairns, Beverley D. (2001). Aggression and attachment: The folly of separatism. In Arthur C. Bohart & Deborah J. Stipek (Eds.), *Constructive & destructive behavior: Implications for family, school, & society* (pp. 21–47). Washington, DC: American Psychological Association.

Cairns, Robert B., & Cairns, Beverley D. (2006). The making of developmental psychology. In William Damon & Richard M. Lerner (Series Eds.) & Richard M. Lerner (Vol. Ed.), *Handbook of child psychology: Vol. 1. Theoretical models of human development* (6th ed., pp. 89–165). Hoboken, NJ: Wiley.

Calasanti, Toni M. (2005). Ageism, gravity, and gender: Experiences of aging bodies. *Generations, 29*(3), 8–12.

Caldwell, Christopher. (2007, May 27). Where every generation is first-generation. *New York Times Magazine,* pp. 44–29.

Callaghan, Tara, Rochat, Philippe, Lillard, Angeline, Claux, Mary Louise, Odden, Hal, Itakura, Shoji, et al. (2005). Synchrony in the onset of mental-state reasoning: Evidence from five cultures. *Psychological Science, 16,* 378–384.

Callaghan, Tara C., Rochat, Philippe, MacGillivray, Tanya, & MacLellan, Crystal. (2004). Modeling referential actions in 6-to 18-month-old infants: A precursor to symbolic understanding. *Child Development, 75,* 1733–1744.

Calvert, Karin. (2003). Patterns of childrearing in America. In Willem Koops & Michael Zuckerman (Eds.), *Beyond the century of the child: Cultural history and developmental psychology* (pp. 62–81). Baltimore: University of Pennsylvania Press.

Calvo-Merino, B., Glaser, D. E., Grèzes, J., Passingham, R. E., & Haggard, P. (2005). Action observation and acquired motor skills: An fMRI study with expert dancers. *Cerebral Cortex, 15,* 1243–1249.

Cameron, James D., & Bulpitt, Christopher J. (2003). Aging of the cardiovascular system. In Richard J. Aspinall (Ed.), *Aging of organs and systems* (pp. 137–152). Boston: Kluwer Academic.

Cameron, Judy L. (2001). Effects of sex hormones on brain development. In Charles A. Nelson & Monica Luciana (Eds.), *Handbook of developmental cognitive neuroscience* (pp. 59–78). Cambridge, MA: MIT Press.

Cameron, Judy L. (2004). Interrelationships between hormones, behavior, and affect during adolescence: Understanding hormonal, physical, and brain changes occurring in association with pubertal activation of the reproductive axis. Introduction to Part III. In Ronald E. Dahl & Linda Patia Spear (Eds.), *Adolescent brain development: Vulnerabilities and opportunities* (Vol. 1021, pp. 110–123). New York: New York Academy of Sciences

Cameron, Judy, & Pierce, W. David. (2002). *Rewards and intrinsic motivation: Resolving the controversy.* Westport, CT: Bergin & Garvey.

Camilli, Gregory, Vargas, Sadako, & Yurecko, Michele. (2003). Teaching children to read: The fragile link between science and federal education policy. *Education Policy Analysis Archives, 11,* 1–52.

Campaign for Fiscal Equity v. State of New York, 719 N.Y.S.2d 475 (2001).

Campbell, Frances A., Pungello, Elizabeth P., Miller-Johnson, Shari, Burchinal, Margaret, & Ramey, Craig T. (2001). The development of cognitive and academic abilities: Growth curves from an early childhood educational experiment. *Developmental Psychology, 37,* 231–242.

Campos, Paul F. (2004). *The obesity myth: Why America's obsession with weight is hazardous to your health.* New York: Gotham Books.

Canadian Psychological Association. (2000). *Canadian code of ethics for psychologists* (3rd ed.). Ottawa, Ontario, Canada: Author.

Canary, Daniel J., Emmers-Sommer, Tara M., & Faulkner, Sandra. (1997). *Sex and gender differences in personal relationships.* New York: Guilford Press.

Canetto, Silvia Sara. (1997). Meaning of gender and suicidal behavior during adolescence. *Suicide and Life-Threatening Behavior, 27,* 339–351.

Canli, Turhan. (2006). *Biology of personality and individual differences.* New York: Guilford Press.

Cantor-Graae, Elizabeth, & Selten, Jean-Paul. (2005). Schizophrenia and migration: A meta-analysis and review. *American Journal of Psychiatry, 162,* 12–24.

Caplan, Leslie J., & Schooler, Carmi. (2003). The roles of fatalism, self-confidence, and intellectual resources in the disablement process in older adults. *Psychology & Aging, 18,* 551–561.

Caprara, Gian Vittorio, Barbaranelli, Claudio, & Pastorelli, Concetta. (2001). Prosocial behavior and aggression in childhood and pre-adolescence. In Arthur C. Bohart & Deborah J. Stipek (Eds.), *Constructive & destructive behavior: Implications for family, school, & society* (pp. 187–203). Washington, DC: American Psychological Association.

Caretta, Carla Mucignat, Caretta, Antonio, & Cavaggioni, Andrea. (1995). Pheromonally accelerated puberty is enhanced by previous experience of the same stimulus. *Physiology & Behavior, 57,* 901–903.

Carey, James R. (2003). *Longevity: The biology and demography of life span.* Princeton, NJ: Princeton University Press.

Carey, Susan. (1985). *Conceptual change in childhood.* Cambridge, MA: MIT Press.

Carlo, Mara S., August, Diane, McLaughlin, Barry, Snow, Catherine E., Dressler, Cheryl, Lippman, David N., et al. (2004). Closing the gap: Addressing the vocabulary needs of English-language learners in bilingual and mainstream classrooms. *Reading Research Quarterly, 39,* 188–215.

Carlson, Marcia J., & Corcoran, Mary E. (2001). Family structure and children's behavioral and cognitive outcomes. *Journal of Marriage & the Family, 63,* 779–792.

Carlson, Stephanie M. (2003). Executive function in context: Development, measurement, theory and experience. *Monographs of the Society for Research in Child Development, 68*(3, Serial No. 274), 138–151.

Carnethon, Mercedes R., Gidding, Samuel S., Nehgme, Rodrigo, Sidney, Stephen, Jacobs, David R., Jr., & Liu, Kiang. (2003). Cardiorespiratory fitness in young adulthood and the development of cardiovascular disease risk factors. *Journal of the American Medical Association, 290,* 3092–3100.

Carr, Deborah. (2004). The desire to date and remarry among older widows and widowers. *Journal of Marriage and Family, 66,* 1051–1068.

Carskadon, Mary A. (2002a). Factors influencing sleep patterns of adolescents. In Mary A. Carskadon (Ed.), *Adolescent sleep patterns: Biological, social, and psychological influences* (pp. 4–26). New York: Cambridge University Press.

Carskadon, Mary A. (2002b). Risks of driving while sleepy in adolescents and young adults. In Mary A. Carskadon (Ed.), *Adolescent sleep patterns: Biological, social, and psychological influences* (pp. 148–158). New York: Cambridge University Press.

Carstensen, Laura L., & Fredrickson, Barbara L. (1998). Influence of HIV status and age on cognitive representations of others. *Health Psychology, 17,* 494–503.

Carstensen, Laura L., Gottman, John M., & Levenson, Robert W. (1995). Emotional behavior in long-term marriage. *Psychology & Aging, 10,* 140–149.

Carstensen, Laura L., Mikels, Joseph A., & Mather, Mara. (2006). Aging and the intersection of cognition, motivation, and emotion. In James E. Birren & K. Warner Schaie (Eds.), *Handbook of the psychology of aging* (6th ed., pp. 343–362). Amsterdam: Elsevier.

Casey, Patrick H., Whiteside-Mansell, Leanne, Barrett, Kathleen, Bradley, Robert H., & Gargus, Regina. (2006). Impact of prenatal and/or postnatal growth problems in low birth weight preterm infants on school-age outcomes: An 8-year longitudinal evaluation. *Pediatrics, 118,* 1078–1086.

Casper, Lynne M., & Bianchi, Suzanne M. (2002). *Continuity & change in the American family.* Thousand Oaks, CA: Sage.

Caspi, Avshalom, Harrington, HonaLee, Milne, Barry, Amell, James W., Theodore, Reremoana F., & Moffitt, Terrie E. (2003). Children's behavioral styles at age 3 are linked to their adult personality traits at age 26. *Journal of Personality, 71,* 495–513.

Caspi, Avshalom, McClay, Joseph, Moffitt, Terrie, Mill, Jonathan, Martin, Judy, Craig, Ian W., et al. (2002, August 2). Role of genotype in the cycle of violence in maltreated children. *Science, 297,* 851–854.

Caspi, Avshalom, Moffitt, Terrie E., Morgan, Julia, Rutter, Michael, Taylor, Alan, Arseneault, Louise, et al. (2004). Maternal expressed emotion predicts children's antisocial behavior problems: Using monozygotic-twin differences to identify environmental effects on behavioral development. *Developmental Psychology, 40,* 149–161.

Caspi, Avshalom, & Roberts, Brent W. (1999). Personality continuity and change across the life course. In Lawrence A. Pervin & Oliver P. John (Eds.), *Handbook of personality: Theory and research* (2nd ed., pp. 300–326). New York: Guilford Press.

Caspi, Avshalom, & Shiner, Rebecca L. (2006). Personality development. In William Damon & Richard M. Lerner (Series Eds.) & Nancy Eisenberg (Vol. Ed.), *Handbook of child psychology: Vol. 3. Social, emotional, and personality development* (Vol. 6th, pp. 300–365). Hoboken, NJ: Wiley.

Caspi, Avshalom, Sugden, Karen, Moffitt, Terrie E., Taylor, Alan, Craig, Ian W., Harrington, HonaLee, et al. (2003, July 18). Influence of life stress on depression: Moderation by a polymorphism in the 5–HTT gene. *Science, 301,* 386–389.

Cassel, Christine K., Leipzig, Rosanne, Cohen, Harvey Jay, Larson, Eric B., & Meier, Diane E. (Eds.). (2003). *Geriatric medicine: An evidence-based approach* (4th ed.). New York: Springer.

Cassell, Justine, Huffaker, David, Tversky, Dona, & Ferriman, Kim. (2006). The language of online leadership: Gender and youth engagement on the internet. *Developmental Psychology, 42,* 436–449.

Cassidy, Jude, & Shaver, Phillip R. (Eds.). (1999). *Handbook of attachment: Theory, research, and clinical applications.* New York: Guilford Press.

Cavanaugh, Sean. (2005, January 5). Poor math scores on world stage trouble U.S. *Education Week, 25,* 1, 18.

CBS/The Associated Press. (2005, September 21). *Tiniest baby marks major milestone.* Retrieved April 23, 2007, from the World Wide Web: http://www.cbsnews.com/stories/2005/09/21/earlyshow/main870763.shtml?source=search_story

Ceci, Stephen J., & Cornelius, Steven W. (1990). "Development of adaptive competence in adulthood": Commentary. *Human Development, 33,* 198–201.

Cedergren, Marie I. (2004). Maternal morbid obesity and the risk of adverse pregnancy outcome. *Obstetrics & Gynecology, 103,* 219–224.

Centers for Disease Control and Prevention. (2006, August 26). *Overweight prevalence.* Centers for Disease Control and Prevention. Retrieved May 12, 2007, from the World Wide Web: http://www.cdc.gov/nccdphp/dnpa/obesity/childhood/prevalence.htm

Centers for Disease Control and Prevention (CDC) (Ed.). (2007). *Epidemiology and prevention of vaccine-preventable diseases* (10th ed.). Washington, DC: Public Health Foundation.

Central Intelligence Agency. *The world factbook 2007.* Washington, DC: Central Intelligence Agency.

Cerminara, Kathy L. (2006). Theresa Marie Schiavo's long road to peace. *Death Studies, 30,* 101–112.

Chamberlain, Patricia, Fisher, Philip A., & Moore, Kevin. (2002). Multidimensional treatment foster care: Applications of the OSLC intervention model to high-risk youth and their families. In John B. Reid, Gerald R. Patterson, & James Snyder (Eds.), *Antisocial*

behavior in children and adolescents: A developmental analysis and model for intervention (pp. 203–218). Washington, DC: American Psychological Association.

Chan, David. (2005). Current directions in personnel selection research. *Current Directions in Psychological Science, 14,* 220–223.

Chandler, Michael J., Lalonde, Christopher E., Sokol, Bryan W., & Hallett, Darcy. (2003). Personal persistence, identity development, and suicide: A study of Native and non-Native North American adolescents. *Monographs of the Society for Research in Child Development, 68*(2, Serial No. 273), vii–130.

Chao, Ruth K. (2001). Extending research on the consequences of parenting style for Chinese Americans and European Americans. *Child Development, 72,* 1832–1843.

Chapleski, Elizabeth E. (2005). Stories of Abby: An Ojibwa journal. In Donald E. Gelfand, Richard Raspa, Sherylyn H. Briller, & Stephanie Myers Schim (Eds.), *End-of-life stories: Crossing disciplinary boundaries* (pp. 51–63). New York: Springer.

Chapman, Benjamin P., & Hayslip, Bert. (2006). Emotional intelligence in young and middle adulthood: Cross-sectional analysis of latent structure and means. *Psychology and Aging, 21,* 411–418.

Charness, Neil, Krampe, Ralf, & Mayr, Ulrich. (1996). The role of practice and coaching in entrepreneurial skill domains: An international comparison of life-span chess skill acquisition. In Karl Anders Ericsson (Ed.), *The road to excellence: The acquisition of expert performance in the arts and sciences, sports, and games* (pp. 51–80). Hillsdale, NJ: Erlbaum.

Charness, Neil, & Schaie, K. Warner. (2003). *Impact of technology on successful aging.* New York: Springer.

Chassin, Laurie, Hussong, Andrea, Barrera, Manuel, Jr., Molina, Brooke S. G., Trim, Ryan, & Ritter, Jennifer. (2004). Adolescent substance use. In Richard M. Lerner & Laurence D. Steinberg (Eds.), *Handbook of adolescent psychology* (2nd ed., pp. 665–696). Hoboken, NJ: Wiley.

Chawarska, Katarzyna, Klin, Ami, Paul, Rhea, & Volkmar, Fred. (2007). Autism spectrum disorder in the second year: Stability and change in syndrome expression. *Journal of Child Psychology and Psychiatry, 48,* 128–138.

Chen, Kevin, & Kandel, Denise B. (1995). The natural history of drug use from adolescence to the mid-thirties in a general population sample. *American Journal of Public Health, 85,* 41–47.

Chen, Xinyin, Cen, Guozhen, Li, Dan, & He, Yunfeng. (2005). Social functioning and adjustment in Chinese children: The imprint of historical time. *Child Development, 76,* 182–195.

Chen, Xinyin, Rubin, Kenneth H., & Sun, Yuerong. (1992). Social reputation and peer relationships in Chinese and Canadian children: A cross-cultural study. *Child Development, 63,* 1336–1343.

Chen, Xin, Striano, Tricia, & Rakoczy, Hannes. (2004). Auditory-oral matching behavior in newborns. *Developmental Science, 7,* 42–47.

Cherbuin, Nicolas, & Brinkman, Cobie. (2006). Hemispheric interactions are different in left-handed individuals. *Neuropsychology, 20,* 700–707.

Cherlin, Andrew J. (1998). Marriage and marital dissolution among Black Americans. *Journal of Comparative Family Studies, 29,* 147–158.

Chess, Stella, Thomas, Alexander, & Birch, Herbert G. (1965). *Your child is a person: A psychological approach to parenthood without guilt.* Oxford, England: Viking Press.

Cheurprakobkit, Sutham, & Bartsch, Robert A. (2005). Security measures on school crime in Texas middle and high schools. *Educational Research, 47,* 235–250.

Chikako, Tange. (2004). [Changes in attitudes toward death in early and middle adolescence]. *Japanese Journal of Developmental Psychology, 15,* 65–76.

Chisholm, Kim. (1998). A three year follow-up of attachment and indiscriminate friendliness in children adopted from Romanian orphanages. *Child Development, 69,* 1092–1106.

Choi, Incheol, Dalal, Reeshad, Kim-Prieto, Chu, & Park, Hyekyung. (2003). Culture and judgment of causal relevance. *Journal of Personality & Social Psychology, 84,* 46–59.

Choi, Namkee G., Burr, Jeffrey A., Mutchler, Jan E., & Caro, Francis G. (2007). Formal and informal volunteer activity and spousal caregiving among older adults. *Research on Aging, 29,* 99–124.

Chomsky, Noam. (1968). *Language and mind.* New York: Harcourt Brace & World.

Chomsky, Noam. (1980). *Rules and representations.* New York: Columbia University Press.

Chong, Lisa, McDonald, Heather, & Strauss, Evelyn. (2004, September 3). Deconstructing aging. *Science, 305,* 1419.

Christensen, Andrew, Eldridge, Kathleen, Catta-Preta, Adriana Bokel, Lim, Veronica R., & Santagata, Rossella. (2006). Cross-cultural consistency of the demand/withdraw interaction pattern in couples. *Journal of Marriage and Family, 68,* 1029–1044.

Christensen, Helen, Mackinnon, Andrew J., Korten, Ailsa E., Jorm, Anthony F., Henderson, A. Scott, Jacomb, Patricia A., et al. (1999). An analysis of diversity in the cognitive performance of elderly community dwellers: Individual differences in change scores as a function of age. *Psychology & Aging, 14,* 365–379.

Christenson, Sandra L., & Thurlow, Martha L. (2004). School dropouts: Prevention considerations, interventions, and challenges. *Current Directions in Psychological Science, 13,* 36–39.

Christoffel, Tom, & Gallagher, Susan Scavo. (1999). *Injury prevention and public health: Practical knowledge, skills, and strategies.* Gaithersburg, MD: Aspen.

Chronicle of Higher Education. (2006). *The almanac of higher education 2006–7.* Washington, DC: Author.

Chumlea, William Cameron, Schubert, Christine M., Roche, Alex F., Kulin, Howard E., Lee, Peter A., Himes, John H., et al. (2003). Age at menarche and racial comparisons in US girls. *Pediatrics, 111,* 110–113.

Cianciolo, Anna T., & Sternberg, Robert J. (2004). *Intelligence: A brief history.* Malden, MA: Blackwell.

Cicchetti, Dante, & Toth, Sheree L. (1998). Perspectives on research and practice in developmental psychopathology. In William Damon (Series Ed.) & Irving E. Sigel & K. Ann Renninger (Vol. Eds.), *Handbook of child psychology: Vol. 4. Child psychology in practice* (5th ed., pp. 479–483). New York: Wiley.

Cicchetti, Dante, & Walker, Elaine F. (2001). Stress and development: Biological and psychological consequences. *Development and Psychopathology, 13,* 413–418.

Cicirelli, Victor G. (2006). Caregiving decision making by older mothers and adult children: Process and expected outcome. *Psychology and Aging, 21,* 209–221.

Cillessen, Antonius H. N., & Mayeux, Lara. (2004a). From censure to reinforcement: Developmental changes in the association between aggression and social status. *Child Development, 75,* 147–163.

Clark, Eve Vivienne. (1995). Later lexical development and word formation. In Paul Fletcher & Brian MacWhinney (Eds.), *The handbook of child language* (pp. 393–412). Cambridge, MA: Blackwell.

Clark, William R. (1999). *A means to an end: The biological basis of aging and death.* New York: Oxford University Press.

Clarke, Ann M., & Clarke, Alan D. B. (2003). *Human resilience: A fifty year quest.* London: Jessica Kingsley.

Clarke-Stewart, Alison, & Allhusen, Virginia D. (2005). *What we know about childcare.* Cambridge, MA: Harvard University Press.

Cleary, Paul D., Zaborski, Lawrence B., & Ayanian, John Z. (2004). Sex differences in health over the course of midlife. In Orville Gilbert Brim, Carol D. Ryff, & Ronald C. Kessler (Eds.), *How healthy are we? A national study of well-being at midlife* (pp. 37–63). Chicago: University of Chicago Press.

Clements, Jonathan. (2005, October 5). *Rich, successful—and miserable: New research probes mid-life angst.* Retrieved September 15, 2007, from the World Wide Web: http://online.wsj.com/public/article/SB112846380547659946.html

Cleveland, Michael J., Gibbons, Frederick X., Gerrard, Meg, Pomery, Elizabeth A., & Brody, Gene H. (2005). The impact of parenting on risk cognitions and risk behavior: A study of mediation and moderation in a panel of African American adolescents. *Child Development, 76,* 900–916.

Clinchy, Blythe McVicker. (1993). Ways of knowing and ways of being: Epistemological and moral development in undergraduate women. In Andrew Garrod (Ed.), *Approaches to moral development: New research and emerging themes* (pp. 180–200). New York: Teachers College Press.

Cloninger, C. Robert. (2003). Completing the psychobiological architecture of human personality development: Temperament, character and coherence. In Ursula M. Staudinger & Ulman Lindenberger (Eds.), *Understanding human development: Dialogues with lifespan psychology* (pp. 159–181). Dordrecht, The Netherlands: Kluwer.

Cockerham, William C. (2006). *Society of risk-takers: Living life on the edge.* New York: Worth.

Cohan, Catherine L., & Kleinbaum, Stacey. (2002). Toward a greater understanding of the cohabitation effect: Premarital cohabitation and marital communication. *Journal of Marriage & Family, 64,* 180–192.

Cohen, Gillian. (1998). The effects of aging on autobiographical memory. In Charles P. Thompson, Douglas J. Herrmann, Darryl Bruce, J. Don Read, David G. Payne, Mike Toglia, & Michael P. Toglia (Eds.), *Autobiographical memory: Theoretical and applied perspectives* (pp. 105–124). Mahwah, NJ: Erlbaum.

Cohen, Jon. (2004, June 4). HIV/AIDS in China: Poised for takeoff? *Science, 304,* 1430–1432.

Cohen, Larry, Chávez, Vivian, & Chehimi, Sana. (2007). *Prevention is primary: Strategies for community well-being.* San Francisco: Jossey-Bass.

Cohen, Lee S., Altshuler, Lori L., Harlow, Bernard L., Nonacs, Ruta, Newport, D. Jeffrey, Viguera, Adele C., et al. (2006). Relapse of major depression during pregnancy in women who maintain or discontinue antidepressant treatment. *Journal of the American Medical Association, 295,* 499–507.

Cohen, Lee S., Soares, Claudio N., Vitonis, Allison F., Otto, Michael W., & Harlow, Bernard L. (2006). Risk for new onset of depression during the menopausal transition. *Archives of General Psychiatry, 63,* 385–390.

Cohen, Leslie B., & Cashon, Cara H. (2006). Infant cognition. In William Damon & Richard M. Lerner (Series Eds.) & Deanna Kuhn & Robert S. Siegler (Vol. Eds.), *Handbook of child psychology: Vol. 2. Cognition, perception, and language* (6th ed., pp. 214–251). Hoboken, NJ: Wiley.

Cohen, Robert, Hsueh, Yeh, Zhou, Zongkui, Hancock, Miriam H., & Floyd, Randy. (2006). Respect, liking, and peer social competence in China and the United States. In David W. Shwalb & Barbara J. Shwalb (Eds.), *New Directions for Child and Adolescent Development: Vol. 114. Respect and disrespect: Cultural and developmental origins* (pp. 53–66). San Francisco: Jossey-Bass.

Cohen, William I. (2005). Medical care of the child with Down syndrome. In Merlin Gene Butler & F. John Meaney (Eds.), *Genetics of developmental disabilities* (pp. 223–245). Boca Raton, FL: Taylor & Francis.

Cokley, Kevin O. (2003). What do we know about the motivation of African American students? Challenging the "anti-intellectual" myth. *Harvard Educational Review, 73,* 524–558.

Colder, Craig R., Mott, Joshua A., & Berman, Arielle S. (2002). The interactive effects of infant activity level and fear on growth trajectories of early childhood behavior problems. *Development & Psychopathology, 14,* 1–23.

Cole, Michael. (2005). Culture in development. In Marc H. Bornstein & Michael E. Lamb (Eds.), *Developmental science: An advanced textbook* (5th ed., pp. 45–101). Mahwah, NJ: Erlbaum.

Coleman, Marilyn, Ganong, Lawrence, & Fine, Mark. (2000). Reinvestigating remarriage: Another decade of progress. *Journal of Marriage & the Family, 62,* 1288–1307.

Coles, Robert. (1997). *The moral intelligence of children: How to raise a moral child.* New York: Random House.

Colleran, Carol, & Jay, Debra. (2003). Surviving addiction: Audrey's story. *Aging Today, 24*(1).

Collins, Michael F. (with Kay, Tess). (2003). *Sport and social exclusion.* London: Routledge.

Collins, W. Andrew, & Laursen, Brett. (2004). Parent-adolescent relationships and influences. In Richard M. Lerner & Laurence D. Steinberg (Eds.), *Handbook of adolescent psychology* (2nd ed., pp. 331–361). Hoboken, NJ: Wiley.

Collins, W. Andrew, & Steinberg, Laurence. (2006). Adolescent development in interpersonal context. In William Damon & Richard M. Lerner (Series Eds.) & Nancy Eisenberg (Vol. Ed.), *Handbook of child psychology: Vol. 3. Social, emotional, and personality development* (6th ed., pp. 1003–1067). Hoboken, NJ: Wiley.

Collins, W. Andrew, & van Dulmen, Manfred. (2006). "The course of true love(s) . . . ": Origins and pathways in the development of romantic relationships. In Ann C. Crouter & Alan Booth (Eds.), *Romance and sex in adolescence and emerging adulthood: Risks and opportunities* (pp. 63–86). Mahwah, NJ: Erlbaum.

Collins, Wanda Lott, & Doolittle, Amy. (2006). Personal reflections of funeral rituals and spirituality in a Kentucky African American family. *Death Studies, 30,* 957–969.

Colonia-Willner, Regina. (1998). Practical intelligence at work: Relationship between aging and cognitive efficiency among managers in a bank environment. *Psychology & Aging, 13,* 45–57.

Coltrane, Scott. (2000). Research on household labor: Modeling and measuring the social embeddedness of routine family work. *Journal of Marriage & the Family, 62,* 1208–1233.

Compas, Bruce E. (2004). Processes of risk and resilience during adolescence: Linking contexts and individuals. In Richard M. Lerner & Laurence D. Steinberg (Eds.), *Handbook of adolescent psychology* (2nd ed., pp. 263–296). Hoboken, NJ: Wiley.

Compian, Laura, Gowen, L. Kris, & Hayward, Chris. (2004). Peripubertal girls' romantic and platonic involvement with boys: Associations with body image and depression symptoms. *Journal of Research on Adolescence, 14,* 23–47.

Comstock, George, & Scharrer, Erica. (2006). Media and popular culture. In William Damon & Richard M. Lerner (Series Eds.) & K. Ann Renninger & Irving E. Sigel (Vol. Eds.), *Handbook of child psychology: Vol. 4. Child psychology in practice* (6th ed., pp. 817–863). Hoboken, NJ: Wiley.

Conboy, Barbara T., & Thal, Donna J. (2006). Ties between the lexicon and grammar: Cross-sectional and longitudinal studies of bilingual toddlers. *Child Development, 77,* 712–735.

Conger, Rand D., & Donnellan, M. Brent. (2007). An interactionist perspective on the socioeconomic context of human development. *Annual Review of Psychology, 58,* 175–199.

Conger, Rand D., Rueter, Martha A., & Elder, Glen H. (1999). Couple resilience to economic pressure. *Journal of Personality & Social Psychology, 76,* 54–71.

Conger, Rand D., Wallace, Lora Ebert, Sun, Yumei, Simons, Ronald L., McLoyd, Vonnie C., & Brody, Gene H. (2002). Economic pressure in African American families: A replication and extension of the family stress model. *Developmental Psychology, 38,* 179–193.

Connidis, Ingrid Arnet. (2001). *Family ties & aging.* Thousand Oaks, CA: Sage.

Connidis, Ingrid Arnet. (2007). Negotiating inequality among adult siblings: Two case studies. *Journal of Marriage and Family, 69,* 482–499.

Connolly, Jennifer, Furman, Wyndol, & Konarski, Roman. (2000). The role of peers in the emergence of heterosexual romantic relationships in adolescence. *Child Development, 71,* 1395–1408.

Connor, David J., & Ferri, Beth A. (2007). The conflict within: Resistance to inclusion and other paradoxes in special education. *Disability & Society, 22,* 63–77.

Conti, Bruno, Sanchez-Alavez, Manuel, Winsky-Sommerer, Raphaelle, Morale, Maria Concetta, Lucero, Jacinta, Brownell, Sara, et al. (2006, November 3). Transgenic mice with a reduced core body temperature have an increased life span. *Science, 314,* 825–828.

Cook, Christine C., Martin, Peter, Yearns, Mary, & Damhorst, Mary Lynn. (2007). Attachment to "place" and coping with losses in changed communities: A paradox for aging adults. *Family & Consumer Sciences Research Journal, 35,* 201–214.

Cook, Diane B., Casillas, Alex, Robbins, Steven B., & Dougherty, Linda M. (2005). Goal continuity and the "Big Five" as predictors of older adult marital adjustment. *Personality and Individual Differences, 38,* 519–531.

Coontz, Stephanie. (2005). *Marriage, a history: From obedience to intimacy or how love conquered marriage.* New York: Viking.

Coontz, Stephanie. (2006). Romance and sex in adolescence and emerging adulthood. In Ann C. Crouter & Alan Booth (Eds.), *Romance and sex in adolescence and emerging adulthood: Risks and opportunities* (pp. 87–91). Mahwah, NJ: Erlbaum.

Coovadia, H. M., & Wittenberg, D.F. (Eds.). (2004). *Paediatrics and child health: A manual for health professionals in developing countries* (5th ed.). New York: Oxford University Press.

Correa-Chavez, Maricela, Rogoff, Barbara, & Arauz, Rebeca Mejia. (2005). Cultural patterns in attending to two events at once. *Child Development, 76,* 664–678.

Corsaro, William A., & Molinari, Luisa. (2000). Entering and observing in children's worlds: A reflection on a longitudinal ethnography of early education in Italy. In Pia Monrad Christensen & Allison James (Eds.), *Research with children: Perspectives and practices* (pp. 179–200). London: Falmer Press.

Costello, E. Jane, Compton, Scott N., Keeler, Gordon, & Angold, Adrian. (2003). Relationships between poverty and psychopathology: A natural experiment. *Journal of the American Medical Association, 290,* 2023–2029.

Côté, James E. (2006). Emerging adulthood as an institutionalized moratorium: Risks and benefits to identity formation. In Jeffrey Jensen Arnett & Jennifer Lynn Tanner (Eds.), *Emerging adults in America: Coming of age in the 21st century* (pp. 85–116). Washington, DC: American Psychological Association.

Courage, Mary L., Reynolds, Greg D., & Richards, John E. (2006). Infants' attention to patterned stimuli: Developmental change from 3 to 12 months of age. *Child Development, 77,* 680–695.

Coutinho, Sonia Bechara, Cabral de Lira, Pedro Israel, de Carvalho Lima, Marilia, & Ashworth, Ann. (2005). Comparison of the effect of two systems for the promotion of exclusive breastfeeding. *Lancet, 366,* 1094–1100.

Covington, Martin V., & Dray, Elizabeth. (2002). The developmental course of achievement motivation: A need-based approach. In Allan Wigfield & Jacquelynne S. Eccles (Eds.), *Development of achievement motivation* (pp. 33–56). San Diego, CA: Academic Press.

Covington, Sharon N., & Burns, Linda Hammer. (2006). *Infertility counseling: A comprehensive handbook for clinicians* (2nd ed.). New York: Cambridge University Press.

Cowan, Nelson (Ed.). (1997). *The development of memory in childhood.* Hove, East Sussex, UK: Psychology Press.

Cox, Maureen V. (1993). *Children's drawings of the human figure.* Hillsdale, NJ: Erlbaum.

Coyle, Karin, Basen-Engquist, Karen, Kirby, Douglas, Parcel, Guy, Banspach, Stephen, Collins, Janet, et al. (2001). Safer choices: Reducing teen pregnancy, HIV, and STDs. *Public Health Reports, 116*(Suppl. 1), 82–93.

Crabbe, John C. (2003). Finding genes for complex behaviors: Progress in mouse models of the addictions. In Robert Plomin, John C. DeFries, Ian W. Craig, & Peter McGuffin (Eds.), *Behavioral genetics in the postgenomic era* (pp. 291–308). Washington, DC: American Psychological Association.

Craik, Fergus I. M., & Salthouse, Timothy A. (2000). *The handbook of aging and cognition* (2nd ed.). Mahwah, NJ: Erlbaum.

Crain, William C. (2005). *Theories of development: Concepts and applications* (5th ed.). Upper Saddle River, NJ: Prentice Hall.

Cramer, Duncan. (1998). *Close relationships: The study of love and friendship.* London: Arnold.

Crews, Douglas E. (2003). *Human senescence: Evolutionary and biocultural perspectives.* New York: Cambridge University Press.

Crick, Nicki R., Nelson, David A., Morales, Julie R., Cullerton-Sen, Crystal, Casas, Juan F., & Hickman, Susan E. (2001). Relational victimization in childhood and adolescence: I hurt you through the grapevine. In Jaana Juvonen & Sandra Graham (Eds.), *Peer harassment in school: The plight of the vulnerable and victimized* (pp. 196–214). New York: Guilford Press.

Crinion, Jenny, Turner, R., Grogan, Alice, Hanakawa, Takashi, Noppeney, Uta, Devlin, Joseph T., et al. (2006, June 9). Language control in the bilingual brain. *Science, 312,* 1537–1540.

Criss, Michael M., Pettit, Gregory S., Bates, John E., Dodge, Kenneth A., & Lapp, Amie L. (2002). Family adversity, positive peer relationships, and children's externalizing behavior: A longitudinal perspective on risk and resilience. *Child Development, 73,* 1220–1237.

Crncec, Rudi, Wilson, Sarah J., & Prior, Margot. (2006). The cognitive and academic benefits of music to children: Facts and fiction. *Educational Psychology, 26,* 579–594.

Crockett, Lisa J., Moilanen, Kristin L., Raffaelli, Marcela, & Randall, Brandy A. (2006). Psychological profiles and adolescent adjustment: A person-centered approach. *Development and Psychopathology, 18,* 195–214.

Crombag, Hans S., & Robinson, Terry E. (2004). Drugs, environment, brain, and behavior. *Current Directions in Psychological Science, 13,* 107–111.

Crosnoe, Robert, & Elder, Glen H., Jr,. (2002). Successful adaptation in the later years: A life course approach to aging. *Social Psychology Quarterly, 65,* 309–328.

Crosnoe, Robert, Johnson, Monica Kirkpatrick, & Elder, Glen H., Jr. (2004). Intergenerational bonding in school: The behavioral and contextual correlates of student-teacher relationships. *Sociology of Education, 77,* 60–81.

Crosnoe, Robert, & Needham, Belinda. (2004). Holism, contextual variability, and the study of friendships in adolescent development. *Child Development, 75,* 264–279.

Cross, Susan, & Markus, Hazel. (1991). Possible selves across the life span. *Human Development, 34,* 230–255.

Croteau, Agathe, Marcoux, Sylvie, & Brisson, Chantal. (2006). Work activity in pregnancy, preventive measures, and the risk of delivering a small-for-gestational-age infant. *American Journal of Public Health, 96,* 846–855.

Crouter, Ann C., & Booth, Alan. (2006). *Romance and sex in adolescence and emerging adulthood: Risks and opportunities.* Mahwah, NJ: Erlbaum.

Crow, James F. (2003, August 1). There's something curious about paternal-age effects. *Science, 301,* 606–607.

Crowe, Michael, Andel, Ross, Pedersen, Nancy L., Fratiglioni, Laura, & Gatz, Margaret. (2006). Personality and risk of cognitive impairment 25 years later. *Psychology and Aging, 21,* 573–580.

Cruikshank, Margaret. (2003). *Learning to be old: Gender, culture, and aging.* Lanham, MD: Rowman & Littlefield.

Csikszentmihalyi, Mihaly. (1996). *Creativity: Flow and the psychology of discovery and invention.* New York: HarperCollins.

Csikszentmihalyi, Mihaly, & Schneider, Barbara. (2000). *Becoming adult: How teenagers prepare for the world of work.* New York: Basic Books.

Cullen, Karen Weber, & Zakeri, Issa. (2004). Fruits, vegetables, milk, and sweetened beverages consumption and access to a la carte/snack bar meals at school. *American Journal of Public Health, 94,* 463–467.

Cumming, Elaine, & Henry, William Earl. (1961). *Growing old: The process of disengagement.* New York: Basic Books.

Cummings, E. Mark, Goeke-Morey, Marcie C., & Papp, Lauren M. (2003). Children's responses to everyday marital conflict tactics in the home. *Child Development, 74,* 1918–1929.

Curry, Leslie, Schwartz, Harold I., Gruman, Cindy, & Blank, Karen. (2002). Could adequate palliative care obviate assisted suicide? *Death Studies, 26,* 757–774.

Curtis, W. John, & Cicchetti, Dante. (2003). Moving research on resilience into the 21st century: Theoretical and methodological considerations in examining the biological contributors to resilience. *Development & Psychopathology, 15,* 773–810.

Curtis, W. John, & Nelson, Charles A. (2003). Toward building a better brain: Neurobehavioral outcomes, mechanisms, and processes of environmental enrichment. In Suniya S. Luthar (Ed.), *Resilience and vulnerability: Adaptation in the context of childhood adversities* (pp. 463–488). New York: Cambridge University Press.

Cutler, Richard, Guarante, Leonard P., Kensler, Thomas W., Naftolin, Fred, Jones, Dean P., Cantor, Charles R., et al. (2005). Longevity determinant genes: What is the evidence? What's the importance? Panel discussion. In Richard G. Cutler, S. Mitchell Harman, Chris Heward, & Mike Gibbons (Eds.), *Longevity health sciences: The Phoenix Conference* (Vol. 1055, pp. 58–63). New York: New York Academy of Sciences.

Cycowicz, Yael M., Friedman, David, & Duff, Martin. (2003). Pictures and their colors: What do children remember? *Journal of Cognitive Neuroscience, 15,* 759–768.

Czaja, Sara J., Charness, Neil, Fisk, Arthur D., Hertzog, Christopher, Nair, Sankaran N., Rogers, Wendy A., et al. (2006). Factors predicting the use of technology: Findings from the Center for Research and Education on Aging and Technology Enhancement (CREATE). *Psychology and Aging, 21,* 333–352.

Czech, Christian, Tremp, Günter, & Pradier, Laurent. (2000). Presenilins and Alzheimer's disease: Biological functions and pathogenic mechanisms. *Progress in Neurobiology, 60,* 363–384.

Dahl, Ronald E. (2004). Adolescent brain development: A period of vulnerabilities and opportunities. Keynote address. In Ronald E. Dahl & Linda Patia Spear (Eds.), *Adolescent brain development: Vulnerabilities and opportunities* (Vol. 1021, pp. 1–22). New York: New York Academy of Sciences.

Dales, Loring, Hammer, Sandra Jo, & Smith, Natalie J. (2001). Time trends in autism and in MMR immunization coverage in California. *Journal of the American Medical Association, 285,* 1183–1185.

Damasio, Antonio R. (2003). *Looking for Spinoza: Joy, sorrow, and the feeling brain.* Orlando, FL: Harcourt.

Danel, Isabella, Berg, Cynthia, Johnson, Christopher H., & Atrash, Hani. (2003). Magnitude of maternal morbidity during labor and delivery: United States, 1993–1997. *American Journal of Public Health, 93,* 631–634.

Dangour, Alan D., Fletcher, Astrid E., & Grundy, Emily M. D. (2007). *Ageing well: Nutrition, health, and social interventions.* Boca Raton, FL: CRC Press/Taylor & Francis.

Danis, Agnes, Bernard, Jean-Marc, & Leproux, Christine. (2000). Shared picture-book reading: A sequential analysis of adult-child verbal interactions. *British Journal of Developmental Psychology, 18,* 369–388.

Dansinger, Michael L., Gleason, Joi Augustin, Griffith, John L., Selker, Harry P., & Schaefer, Ernst J. (2005). Comparison of the Atkins, Ornish, Weight Watchers, and Zone diets for weight loss and heart disease risk reduction: A randomized trial. *Journal of the American Medical Association, 293,* 43–53.

Daro, Deborah. (2002). Public perception of child sexual abuse: Who is to blame? *Child Abuse & Neglect, 26,* 1131–1133.

Daselaar, Sander, & Cabeza, Roberto. (2005). Age-related changes in hemispheric organization. In Roberto Cabeza, Lars Nyberg, & Denise Park (Eds.), *Cognitive neuroscience of aging: Linking cognitive and cerebral aging* (pp. 325–353). New York: Oxford University Press.

Dasen, Pierre R. (2003). Theoretical frameworks in cross-cultural developmental psychology: An attempt at integration. In T. S. Saraswati (Ed.), *Cross-cultural perspectives in human development: Theory, research, and applications* (pp. 128–165). New Delhi, India: Sage.

Datan, Nancy. (1986). Oedipal conflict, platonic love: Centrifugal forces in intergenerational relations. In Nancy Datan, Anita L. Greene, & Hayne W. Reese (Eds.), *Life-span developmental psychology: Intergenerational relations* (pp. 29–50). Hillsdale, NJ: Erlbaum.

Daulaire, Nils, Leidl, Pat, Mackin, Laurel, Murphy, Colleen, & Stark, Laura. (2002). *Promises to keep: The toll of unintended pregnancies on women's lives in the developing world.* Washington, DC: Global Health Council.

David, Barbara, Grace, Diane, & Ryan, Michelle K. (2004). The gender wars: A self-categorization perspective on the development of gender identity. In Mark Bennett & Fabio Sani (Eds.), *The development of the social self* (pp. 135–157). Hove, East Sussex, England: Psychology Press.

Davidson, Julia O'Connell. (2005). *Children in the global sex trade.* Malden, MA: Polity.

Davies, Chris G., & Thorn, Brian L. (2002). Psychopharmacology with older adults in residential care. In Robert D. Hill, Brian L. Thorn, John Bowling, & Anthony Morrison (Eds.), *Geriatric residential care* (pp. 161–181). Mahwah, NJ: Erlbaum.

Davies, Patrick T., & Cicchetti, Dante. (2004). Toward an integration of family systems and developmental psychopathology approaches. *Development & Psychopathology, 16,* 477–481.

Davies, P. T., Harold, G. T., Goeke-Morey, M. C., & Cummings, E. M. (2002). Child emotional security and interparental conflict. *Monographs of the Society for Research in Child Development, 67*(3, Serial No. 270).

Davis, Elysia Poggi, Parker, Susan Whitmore, Tottenham, Nim, & Gunnar, Megan R. (2003). Emotion, cognition, and the hypothalamic-pituitary-adrenocortical axis: A developmental perspective. In Michelle de Haan & Mark H. Johnson (Eds.), *The cognitive neuroscience of development* (pp. 181–206). New York: Psychology Press.

Day, James, & Naedts, Myriam H. L. (1999). Constructivist and post-constructivist perspectives on moral and religious judgement research. In Ralph L. Mosher, Deborah J. Youngman, & James M. Day (Eds.), *Human development across the lifespan: Educational and psychological applications* (pp. 239–264). Westport, CT: Praeger.

DeBaggio, Thomas. (2002). *Losing my mind: An intimate look at life with Alzheimer's.* New York: Free Press.

De Bellis, Michael D. (2001). Developmental traumatology: The psychobiological development of maltreated children and its implications for research, treatment, and policy. *Development and Psychopathology, 13,* 539–564.

De Bellis, Michael D., Narasimhan, Anandhi, Thatcher, Dawn L., Keshavan, Matcheri S., Soloff, Paul, & Clark, Duncan B. (2005). Prefrontal cortex, thalamus, and cerebellar volumes in adolescents and young adults with adolescent-onset alcohol use disorders and comorbid mental disorders. *Alcoholism: Clinical and Experimental Research, 29,* 1590–1600.

Deci, Edward L., Koestner, Richard, & Ryan, Richard M. (1999). A meta-analytic review of experiments examining the effects of extrinsic rewards on intrinsic motivation. *Psychological Bulletin, 125,* 627–668.

de Haan, Michelle, & Johnson, Mark H. (2003). Mechanisms and theories of brain development. In Michelle De Haan & Mark H. Johnson (Eds.), *The cognitive neuroscience of development* (pp. 1–18). Hove, East Sussex, England: Psychology Press.

Deil-Amen, Regina, & Rosenbaum, James E. (2003). The social prerequisites of success: Can college structure reduce the need for social know-how? In Kathleen M. Shaw & Jerry A. Jacobs (Eds.), *Community colleges: New environments, new directions* (Vol. 586, pp. 120–143). Thousand Oaks, CA: Sage.

DeKeyser, Robert, & Larson-Hall, Jenifer. (2005). What does the critical period really mean? In Judith F. Kroll & Annette M. B. de Groot (Eds.), *Handbook of bilingualism: Psycholinguistic approaches* (pp. 88–108). Oxford, UK: Oxford University Press.

Delaney, Carol. (2000). Making babies in a Turkish village. In Judy S. DeLoache & Alma Gottlieb (Eds.), *A world of babies: Imagined childcare guides for seven societies* (pp. 117–144). New York: Cambridge University Press.

De la Torre, Jack C., Kalaria, Raj, Nakajima, Kenji, & Nagata, Ken (Eds.). (2002). *Annals of the New York Academy of Sciences: Vol. 977. Alzheimer's disease: Vascular etiology and pathology.* New York: New York Academy of Sciences.

Delea, Peter. (2005). International Social Science Review. *Point: The case for Social Security reform, 80,* 53–55.

De Lee, Joseph Bolivar. (1938). *The principles and practice of obstetrics* (7th ed.). Philadelphia: Saunders.

Delva, Jorge, Wallace, John M., O'Malley, Patrick M., Bachman, Jerald G., Johnston, Lloyd D., & Schulenberg, John E. (2005). The epidemiology of alcohol, marijuana, and cocaine use among Mexican American, Puerto Rican, Cuban American, and other Latin American eighth-grade students in the United States: 1991–2002. *American Journal of Public Health, 95,* 696–702.

De Martinis, Massimo, & Timiras, Paola S. (2003). The pulmonary respiration, hematopoiesis and erythrocytes. In Paola S. Timiras (Ed.), *Physiological basis of aging and geriatrics* (3rd ed., pp. 319–336). Boca Raton, FL: CRC Press.

Demetriou, Andreas, Christou, Constantinos, Spanoudis, George, & Platsidou, Maria. (2002). The development of mental processing: Efficiency, working memory, and thinking. *Monographs of the Society for Research in Child Development, 67*(1, Serial No. 268).

De Neys, Wim. (2006). Dual processing in reasoning: Two systems but one reasoner. *Psychological Science, 17,* 428–433.

Denham, Susanne A., Blair, Kimberly A., DeMulder, Elizabeth, Levitas, Jennifer, Sawyer, Katherine, Auerbach-Major, Sharon, et al. (2003). Preschool emotional competence: Pathway to social competence. *Child Development, 74,* 238–256.

Denney, Nancy W., & Pearce, Kathy A. (1989). A developmental study of practical problem solving in adults. *Psychology & Aging, 4,* 438–442.

Dennis, Tracy A., Cole, Pamela M., Zahn-Waxler, Carolyn, & Mizuta, Ichiro. (2002). Self in context: Autonomy and relatedness in Japanese and U.S. mother-preschooler dyads. *Child Development, 73,* 1803–1817.

Denny, Dallas, & Pittman, Cathy. (2007). Gender identity: From dualism to diversity. In Mitchell S. Tepper & Annette Fuglsang Owens (Eds.), *Sexual health: Vol. 1. Psychological foundations* (pp. 205–229). Westport, CT: Praeger/Greenwood.

Dentinger, Emma, & Clarkberg, Marin. (2002). Informal caregiving and retirement timing among men and women: Gender and caregiving relationships in late midlife. *Journal of Family Issues, 23,* 857–879.

DePaulo, Bella M. (2006). *Singled out: How singles are stereotyped, stigmatized, and ignored and still live happily ever after.* New York: St. Martin's Press.

DePaulo, Bella M., & Morris, Wendy L. (2005). Singles in society and in science. *Psychological Inquiry, 16,* 57–83.

Deremo, Dorothy, & Meert, Kathleen L. (2005). Stories of Grace: Gifts and givers. In Donald E. Gelfand, Richard Raspa, Sherylyn H. Briller, & Stephanie Myers Schim (Eds.), *End-of-life stories: Crossing disciplinary boundaries.* New York: Springer.

Derryberry, Douglas, Reed, Marjorie A., & Pilkenton-Taylor, Carolyn. (2003). Temperament and coping: Advantages of an individual differences perspective. *Development & Psychopathology, 15,* 1049–1066.

Dershewitz, Robert A. (2002, December 28). *Another good year for immunizations.* Journal Watch Gastroenterology. Retrieved June 22, 2005, from the World Wide Web: http://gastroenterology.jwatch.org/cgi/content/full/2002/1228/11

de Schipper, Elles J., Riksen-Walraven, J. Marianne, & Geurts, Sabine A. E. (2006). Effects of child-caregiver ratio on the interactions between caregivers and children in child-care centers: An experimental study. *Child Development, 77,* 861–874.

Després, Jean-Pierre, Golay, Alain, & Sjöström, Lars. (2005). Effects of rimonabant on metabolic risk factors in overweight patients with dyslipidemia. *New England Journal of Medicine, 353,* 2121–2134.

Detzner, Daniel F. (1996). No place without a home: Southeast Asian grandparents in refugee families. *Generations, 20*(1), 45–48.

Deuschl, Günther, Schade-Brittinger, Carmen, Krack, Paul, Volkmann, Jens, Schäfer, Helmut, Bötzel, Kai, et al. (2006). A randomized trial of deep-brain stimulation for Parkinson's disease. *New England Journal of Medicine, 355,* 896–908.

Deveraux, Lara L., & Hammerman, Ann Jackoway. (1998). *Infertility and identity: New strategies for treatment.* San Francisco: Jossey-Bass.

Diamond, Adele, & Kirkham, Natasha. (2005). Not quite as grown-up as we like to think: Parallels between cognition in childhood and adulthood. *Psychological Science, 16,* 291–297.

Diamond, David M., Dunwiddie, Thomas V., & Rose, G. M. (1988). Characteristics of hippocampal primed burst potentiation in vitro and in the awake rat. *Journal of Neuroscience, 8,* 4079–4088.

Diamond, Lisa M. (2004). Emerging perspectives on distinctions between romantic love and sexual desire. *Current Directions in Psychological Science, 13,* 116–119.

Diamond, Lisa M., & Savin-Williams, Ritch C. (2003). The intimate relationships of sexual-minority youths. In Gerald R. Adams & Michael D. Berzonsky (Eds.), *Blackwell handbook of adolescence* (pp. 393–412). Malden, MA: Blackwell.

Didion, Joan. (2005). *The year of magical thinking.* New York: Knopf.

Diener, Marissa. (2000). Gift from the gods: A Balinese guide to early child rearing. In Judy S. DeLoache & Alma Gottlieb (Eds.), *A world of babies: Imagined childcare guides for seven societies* (pp. 96–116). New York: Cambridge University Press.

DiGirolamo, Ann, Thompson, Nancy, Martorell, Reynaldo, Fein, Sara, & Grummer-Strawn, Laurence. (2005). Intention or experience? Predictors of continued breastfeeding. *Health Education & Behavior, 32,* 208–226.

Digman, John M. (1990). Personality structure: Emergence of the five-factor model. *Annual Review of Psychology, 41,* 417–440.

Dijk, Jan A. G. M. van. (2005). *The deepening divide: Inequality in the information society.* Thousand Oaks, CA: Sage.

Dilworth-Bart, Janean E., & Moore, Colleen F. (2006). Mercy mercy me: Social injustice and the prevention of environmental pollutant exposures among ethnic minority and poor children. *Child Development, 77,* 247–265.

Dindia, Kathryn, & Emmers-Sommer, Tara M. (2006). What partners do to maintain their close relationships. In Patricia Noller & Judith A. Feeney (Eds.), *Close relationships: Functions, forms and processes* (pp. 305–324). Hove, England: Psychology Press/Taylor & Francis.

Dion, Karen Kisiel. (2006). On the development of identity: Perspectives from immigrant families. In Ramaswami Mahalingam (Ed.), *Cultural psychology of immigrants* (pp. 299–314). Mahwah, NJ: Erlbaum

Dionne, Ginette, Dale, Philip S., Boivin, Michel, & Plomin, Robert. (2003). Genetic evidence for bidirectional effects of early lexical and grammatical development. *Child Development, 74,* 394–412.

DiPietro, Janet A., Hilton, Sterling C., Hawkins, Melissa, Costigan, Kathleen A., & Pressman, Eva K. (2002). Maternal stress and affect influence fetal neurobehavioral development. *Developmental Psychology, 38,* 659–668.

Dishion, Thomas J., & Bullock, Bernadette Marie. (2002). Parenting and adolescent problem behavior: An ecological analysis of the nurturance hypothesis. In John G. Borkowski, Sharon Landesman Ramey, & Marie Bristol-Power (Eds.), *Parenting and the child's world: Influences on academic, intellectual, and social-emotional development* (pp. 231–249). Mahwah, NJ: Erlbaum.

Dishion, Thomas J., & Owen, Lee D. (2002). A longitudinal analysis of friendships and substance use: Bidirectional influence from adolescence to adulthood. *Developmental Psychology, 38,* 480–491.

Dishion, Thomas J., Poulin, François, & Burraston, Bert. (2001). Peer group dynamics associated with iatrogenic effects in group interventions with high-risk young adolescents. In William Damon (Series Ed.) & Douglas W. Nangle & Cynthia A. Erdley (Vol. Eds.), *New directions for child and adolescent development: No. 91. The role of friendship in* *psychological adjustment* (pp. 79–92). San Francisco: Jossey-Bass.

Diwadkar, Vaibhav A., & Keshavan, Matcheri S. (2006). White matter pathology, brain development, and psychiatric disorders: Lessons from corpus callosum studies. In Dante Cicchetti & Donald J. Cohen (Eds.), *Developmental psychopathology: Vol. 2. Developmental neuroscience* (2nd ed., pp. 742–761). Hoboken, NJ: Wiley.

Dixon, Roger A., & Lerner, Richard M. (1999). History and systems in developmental psychology. In Marc H. Bornstein & Michael E. Lamb (Eds.), *Developmental psychology: An advanced textbook* (4th ed., pp. 3–45). Mahwah, NJ: Erlbaum.

Dodge, Kenneth A., Coie, John D., & Lynam, Donald R. (2006). Aggression and antisocial behavior in youth. In William Damon & Richard M. Lerner (Series Eds.) & Nancy Eisenberg (Vol. Ed.), *Handbook of child psychology: Vol. 3. Social, emotional, and personality development* (6th ed., pp. 719–788). New York: Wiley.

Doka, Kenneth J. (2002). *Disenfranchised grief: New directions, challenges, and strategies for practice.* Champaign, IL: Research Press.

Dominguez, Cynthia O. (2001). Expertise in laparoscopic surgery: Anticipation and affordances. In Eduardo Salas & Gary Klein (Eds.), *Linking expertise and naturalistic decision making* (pp. 287–301). Mahwah, NJ: Erlbaum.

Dooley, Dolores, Dalla-Vorgia, Panagiota, Garanis-Papadatos, Tina, & McCarthy, Joan. (2003). *Ethics of new reproductive technologies: Cases and questions.* New York: Berghahn Books.

Doorenbos, Ardith Z. (2005). Stories of Shanti: Culture and karma. In Donald E. Gelfand, Richard Raspa, Sherylyn H. Briller, & Stephanie Myers Schim (Eds.), *End-of-life stories: Crossing disciplinary boundaries* (pp. 177–188). New York: Springer.

Douglas, Ann. (2002). *The mother of all pregnancy books.* New York: Hungry Minds.

Doumbo, Ogobara K. (2005, February 4). It takes a village: Medical research and ethics in Mali. *Science, 307,* 679–681.

Dounchis, Jennifer Zoler, Hayden, Helen A., & Wilfley, Denise E. (2001). Obesity, body image, and eating disorders in ethnically diverse children and adolescents. In J. Kevin Thompson & Linda Smolak (Eds.), *Body image, eating disorders, and obesity in youth: Assessment, prevention, and treatment* (pp. 67–98). Washington, DC: American Psychological Association.

Duckworth, Angela L., Peterson, Christopher, Matthews, Michael D., & Kelly, Dennis R. (2007). Grit: Perseverance and passion for long-term goals. *Journal of Personality and Social Psychology, 92,* 1087–1101.

Dugger, Celia W. (2001, April 22). Abortion in India is tipping scales sharply against girls. *New York Times,* pp. A1, A10.

Dugger, Celia W. (2006, April 30). Mothers of Nepal vanquish a killer of children. *New York Times,* pp. A1, A16.

Dulay, Mario F., & Murphy, Claire. (2002). Olfactory acuity and cognitive function converge in older adulthood: Support for the common cause hypothesis. *Psychology & Aging, 17,* 392–404.

Dunlap, Jay C., Loros, Jennifer J., & DeCoursey, Patricia J. (2004). *Chronobiology: Biological timekeeping.* Sunderland, MA: Sinauer Associates.

Dunphy, Dexter C. (1963). The social structure of urban adolescent peer groups. *Sociometry, 26,* 230–246.

Duplassie, Danielle, & Daniluk, Judith C. (2007). Sexuality: Young and middle adulthood. In Mitchell S. Tepper & Annette Fuglsang Owens (Eds.), *Sexual health: Vol. 1. Psychological foundations* (pp. 263–289). Westport, CT: Praeger/Greenwood.

Durvasula, Srinivas, Lysonski, Steven, & Watson, John. (2001). Does vanity describe other cultures? A cross-cultural examination of the vanity scale. *Journal of Consumer Affairs, 35,* 180–199.

Duster, Troy. (1999). The social consequences of genetic disclosure. In Ronald A. Carson & Mark A. Rothstein (Eds.), *Behavioral genetics: The clash of culture and biology* (pp. 172—188). Baltimore: Johns Hopkins University Press.

Dutton, Donald G. (2000). Witnessing parental violence as a traumatic experience shaping the abusive personality. In Robert A. Geffner, Peter G. Jaffe, & Marlies Sudermann (Eds.), *Children exposed to domestic violence: Current issues in research, intervention, prevention, and policy development* (pp. 59–67). Binghamton, NY: Haworth Press.

Dye, Jane Lawler. (2005). *Fertility of American women: June 2004* (Current Population Reports P20–555). Washington, DC: U.S. Census Bureau.

East, Patricia L., & Kiernan, Elizabeth A. (2001). Risks among youths who have multiple sisters who were adolescent parents. *Family Planning Perspectives, 33,* 75–80.

Ebaugh, Helen Rose, & Curry, Mary. (2000). Fictive kin as social capital in new immigrant communities. *Sociological Perspectives, 43,* 189–209.

Ebner, Natalie C., Freund, Alexandra M., & Baltes, Paul B. (2006). Developmental changes in personal goal orientation from young to late adulthood: From striving for gains to maintenance and prevention of losses. *Psychology and Aging, 21,* 664–678.

Eccles, Jacquelynne S. (2004). Schools, academic motivation, and stage-environment fit. In Richard M. Lerner & Laurence D. Steinberg (Eds.), *Handbook of adolescent psychology* (2nd ed., pp. 125–153). Hoboken, NJ: Wiley.

Eccles, Jacquelynne S., Barber, Bonnie L., Stone, Margaret, & Hunt, James. (2003). Extracurricular activities and adolescent development. *Journal of Social Issues, 59,* 865–889.

Eckert, Penelope. (1989). *Jocks and burnouts: Social categories and identity in the high school.* New York: Teachers College Press.

Eckstein, Daniel G., Rasmussen, Paul R., & Wittschen, Lori. (1999). Understanding and dealing with adolescents. *Journal of Individual Psychology, 55,* 31–50.

Eddleman, Keith A., Malone, Fergal D., Sullivan, Lisa, Dukes, Kim, Berkowitz, Richard L., Kharbutli, Yara, et al. (2006). Pregnancy loss rates after midtrimester amniocentesis. *Obstetrics & Gynecology, 108,* 1067–1072.

Editors. (2004). Preventing early reading failure. *American Educator, 28,* 5.

Edwards, Carolyn, Gandini, Lella, & Forman, George (Eds.). (1998). *The hundred languages of children: The Reggio Emilia approach—Advanced reflections* (2nd ed.). Greenwich, CT: Ablex.

Edwards, John N. (1969). Familial behavior as social exchange. *Journal of Marriage and the Family, 31,* 518—526.

Edwards, Oliver W. (2006). Special education disproportionality and the influence of intelligence test selection. *Journal of Intellectual & Developmental Disability, 31,* 246–248.

Effros, Rita B. (2001). Immune system activity. In Edward J. Masoro & Steven N. Austad (Eds.), *Handbook of the biology of aging* (5th ed., pp. 324–352). San Diego, CA: Academic Press.

Egan, Kieran, & Ling, Michael. (2002). We began as poets: Conceptual tools and the arts in early childhood. In Liora Bresler & Christine Marme Thompson (Eds.), *The arts in children's lives: Context, culture, and curriculum* (pp. 93–100). Dordrecht, The Netherlands: Kluwer.

Ehrenberg, Ronald G., Brewer, Dominic J., Gamoran, Adam, & Willms, J. Douglas. (2001). Class size and student achievement. *Psychological Science in the Public Interest, 2,* 1–30.

Ehrlich, Paul R. (1968). *The population bomb.* New York: Ballantine Books.

Eid, Michael, & Diener, Ed. (2001). Norms for experiencing emotions in different cultures: Inter- and intranational differences. *Journal of Personality & Social Psychology, 81,* 869–885.

Eisenberg, Marla E., Bearinger, Linda H., Sieving, Renee E., Swain, Carolyne, & Resnick, Michael D. (2004). Parents' beliefs about condoms and oral contraceptives: Are they medically accurate? *Perspectives on Sexual and Reproductive Health, 36,* 50–57.

Eisenberg, Nancy, Cumberland, Amanda, Guthrie, Ivanna K., Murphy, Bridget C., & Shepard, Stephanie A. (2005). Age changes in prosocial responding and moral reasoning in adolescence and early adulthood. *Journal of Research on Adolescence, 15,* 235–260.

Eisenberg, Nancy, & Fabes, Richard A. (1998). Prosocial development. In William Damon (Series Ed.) & Nancy Eisenberg (Vol. Ed.), *Handbook of child psychology: Vol. 3. Social, emotional, and personality development* (5th ed., pp. 701–778). New York: Wiley.

Eisenberg, Nancy, Fabes, Richard A., & Spinrad, Tracy L. (2006). Prosocial development. In William Damon & Richard M. Lerner (Series Eds.) & Nancy Eisenberg (Vol. Ed.), *Handbook of child psychology: Vol. 3. Social, emotional, and personality development* (6th ed., pp. 646–718). Hoboken, NJ: Wiley.

Eisenberg, Nancy, Spinrad, Tracy L., Fabes, Richard A., Reiser, Mark, Cumberland, Amanda, Shepard, Stephanie A., et al. (2004). The relations of effortful control and impulsivity to children's resiliency and adjustment. *Child Development, 75,* 25–46.

Eisner, Manuel. (2002). Crime, problem drinking, and drug use: Patterns of problem behavior in cross-national perspective. *Annals of the American Academy of Political & Social Science, 580,* 201–225.

Elder, Glen H., Jr., Johnson, Monica Kirkpatrick, & Crosnoe, Robert. (2003). The emergence and development of life course theory. In Jeylan T. Mortimer & Michael J. Shanahan (Eds.), *Handbook of the life course* (pp. 3–19). New York: Kluwer Academic/Plenum Publishers.

Elder, Glen H., Jr,, & Shanahan, Michael J. (2006). The life course and human development. In William Damon & Richard M. Lerner (Series Eds.) & Richard M. Lerner (Vol. Ed.), *Handbook of child psychology: Vol. 1. Theoretical models of human development* (6th ed., pp. 665–715). Hoboken, NJ: Wiley.

Elias, Merrill F., Robbins, Michael A., Budge, Marc M., Elias, Penelope K., Hermann, Barbara A., & Dore, Gregory A. (2004). Studies of aging, hypertension and cognitive functioning: With contributions from the Maine-Syracuse Study. In Paul T. Costa & Ilene C. Siegler (Eds.), *Recent advances in psychology and aging* (Vol. 15, pp. 89–132). Amsterdam: Elsevier.

Elkind, David. (1967). Egocentrism in adolescence. *Child Development, 38,* 1025–1034.

Elkins, Jacob S., Longstreth, Jr., W. T., Manolio, T. A., Newman, A. B., Bhadelia, Rafeeque A., & Johnston, S. Claiborne. (2006). Education and the cognitive decline associated with MRI-defined brain infarct. *Neurology, 67,* 435–440.

Elliott, Leslie, Jr., Samuel J. Arbes, Harvey, Eric S., Lee, Robert C., Salo, Päivi M., Cohn, Richard D., et al. (2007). Dust weight and asthma prevalence in the National Survey of Lead and Allergens in Housing (NSLAH). *Environmental Health Perspectives, 115,* 215–220.

Ellis, Bruce J. (2004). Timing of pubertal maturation in girls: An integrated life history approach. *Psychological Bulletin, 130,* 920–958.

Ellis, Bruce J., Bates, John E., Dodge, Kenneth A., Fergusson, David M., Horwood, L. John, Pettit, Gregory S., et al. (2003). Does father absence place daughters at special risk for early sexual activity and teenage pregnancy? *Child Development, 74,* 801–821.

Ellis, Bruce J., & Bjorklund, David F. (2005). *Origins of the social mind: Evolutionary psychology and child development.* New York: Guilford Press.

Ellis, Bruce J., & Garber, Judy. (2000). Psychosocial antecedents of variation in girls' pubertal timing: Maternal depression, stepfather presence, and marital and family stress. *Child Development, 71,* 485–501.

Ellis, Neenah. (2002). *If I live to be 100: Lessons from the centenarians.* New York: Crown.

Ellison, Peter Thorpe. (2002). Puberty. In Noël Cameron (Ed.), *Human growth and development* (pp. 65–84). San Diego, CA: Academic Press.

Elmore, Richard, Ablemann, Charles, Even, Johanna, Kenyon, Susan, & Marshall, Joanne. (2004). When accountability knocks, will anyone answer? In Richard F. Elmore (Ed.), *School reform from the inside out: Policy, practice, and performance* (pp. 133–200). Cambridge, MA: Harvard Education Press.

El-Sheikh, Mona, & Harger, JoAnn. (2001). Appraisals of marital conflict and children's adjustment, health, and physiological reactivity. *Developmental Psychology, 37,* 875–885.

Emanuel, Ezekiel J., & Wertheimer, Alan. (2006, May 12). Who should get influenza vaccine when not all can? *Science, 312,* 854–855.

Engel, Susan. (1999). *Context is everything: The nature of memory.* New York: Freeman.

Engelhardt, H. Tristram, Jr. (1998). Critical care: Why there is no global bioethics. *The Journal of Medicine and Philosophy, 23,* 643–651.

Engels, Rutger C. M. E., Scholte, Ron H. J., van Lieshout, Cornelis F. M., de Kemp, Raymond, & Overbeek, Geertjan. (2006). Peer group reputation and smoking and alcohol consumption in early adolescence. *Addictive Behaviors, 31,* 440–449.

Enserink, Martin. (2006, September 15). Ground the planes during a flu pandemic? Studies disagree. *Science, 313,* 1555a.

Enserink, Martin. (2007, May 25). Indonesia earns flu accord at world health assembly. *Science, 316,* 1108.

Epstein, Leonard H., Handley, Elizabeth A., Dearing, Kelly K., Cho, David D., Roemmich, James N., Paluch, Rocco A., et al. (2006). Purchases of food in youth: Influence of price and income. *Psychological Science, 17,* 82–89.

Erickson, Rebecca J. (2005). Why emotion work matters: Sex, gender, and the division of household labor. *Journal of Marriage and Family, 67,* 337–351.

Ericsson, K. Anders. (1996). The acquisition of expert performance: An introduction to some of the issues. In Karl Anders

Ericsson (Ed.), *The road to excellence: The acquisition of expert performance in the arts and sciences, sports, and games* (pp. 1–50). Hillsdale, NJ: Erlbaum.

Ericsson, K. Anders, & Charness, Neil. (1994). Expert performance: Its structure and acquisition. *American Psychologist, 49,* 725–747.

Eriks-Brophy, Alice, & Crago, Martha. (2003). Variation in instructional discourse features: Cultural or linguistic? Evidence from Inuit and Non-Inuit teachers of Nunavik. *Anthropology & Education Quarterly, 34,* 396–419.

Erikson, Erik H. (1963). *Childhood and society* (2nd ed.). New York: Norton.

Erikson, Erik H. (1968). *Identity: Youth and crisis.* New York: Norton.

Erikson, Erik H. (1969). *Gandhi's truth: On the origins of militant nonviolence.* New York: Norton.

Erikson, Erik H. (1982). *The life cycle completed: A review.* New York: Norton.

Erikson, Erik H. (1984). Reflections on the last stage—and the first. *The Psychoanalytic Study of the Child, 39,* 155–165.

Erikson, Erik H., Erikson, Joan M., & Kivnick, Helen Q. (1986). *Vital involvement in old age.* New York: Norton.

Eriksson, Birgitta Sandén, & Pehrsson, Gunnel. (2005). Emotional reactions of parents after the birth of an infant with extremely low birth weight. *Journal of Child Health Care, 9,* 122–136.

Erlangsen, Annette, Jeune, Bernard, Bille-Brahe, Unni, & Vaupel, James W. (2004). Loss of partner and suicide risks among oldest old: A population-based register study. *Age and Ageing, 33,* 378–383.

Erlinghagen, Marcel, & Hank, Karsten. (2006). The participation of older Europeans in volunteer work. *Ageing & Society, 26,* 567–584.

Erwin, Phil. (1998). *Friendship in childhood and adolescence.* London: Routledge.

Estruch, Ramon, Martinez-Gonzalez, Miguel Angel, Corella, Dolores, Salas-Salvado, Jordi, Ruiz-Gutierrez, Valentina, Covas, Maria Isabel, et al. (2006). Effects of a Mediterranean-style diet on cardiovascular risk factors: A randomized trial. *Annals of Internal Medicine, 145,* 1–11.

Eurostat—Statistical Office of the European Communities. (2006). *Eurostat Yearbook 2006/07.* Luxembourg: Author.

Evans, David W., Leckman, James F., Carter, Alice, Reznick, J. Steven, Henshaw, Desiree, King, Robert A., et al. (1997). Ritual, habit, and perfectionism: The prevalence and development of compulsive-like behavior in normal young children. *Child Development, 68,* 58–68.

Eyer, Diane E. (1992). *Mother-infant bonding: A scientific fiction.* New Haven, CT: Yale University Press.

Fackelmann, Kathy A. (1994, November 5). Beyond the genome: The ethics of DNA testing. *Science News, 146,* 298–299.

Fagot, Beverly I. (1995). Parenting boys and girls. In Marc H. Bornstein (Ed.), *Handbook of parenting: Vol. 1. Children and parenting* (pp. 163–183). Hillsdale, NJ: Erlbaum.

Fairburn, Christopher G., & Brownell, Kelly D. (2002). *Eating disorders and obesity: A comprehensive handbook* (2nd ed.). New York: Guilford Press.

Faraone, Stephen V., Perlis, Roy H., Doyle, Alysa E., Smoller, Jordan W., Goralnick, Jennifer J., Holmgren, Meredith A., et al. (2005). Molecular genetics of attention-deficit/hyperactivity disorder. *Biological Psychiatry, 57,* 1313–1323.

Faraone, Stephen V., & Wilens, Timothy. (2003). Does stimulant treatment lead to substance use disorders? *Journal of Clinical Psychiatry, 64,* 9–13.

Farbrother, Jane E., & Guggenheim, Jeremy A. (2001). Myopia genetics: The family study of myopia. *Optometry Today, 41,* 41–44.

Farkas, Janice I., & Hogan, Dennis P. (1995). The demography of changing intergenerational relationships. In Vern L. Bengtson, Klaus Warner Schaie, & Linda M. Burton (Eds.), *Adult intergenerational relations: Effects of societal change* (pp. 1–29). New York: Springer.

Farrington, David P. (2004). Conduct disorder, aggression, and delinquency. In Richard M. Lerner & Laurence D. Steinberg (Eds.), *Handbook of adolescent psychology* (2nd ed., pp. 627–664). Hoboken, NJ: Wiley.

Fayers, Peter M., & Machin, David. (2007). *Quality of life: The assessment, analysis, and interpretation of patient-reported outcomes* (2nd ed.). Hoboken, NJ: Wiley.

Federico, Bruno, Costa, Giuseppe, & Kunst, Anton E. (2007). Educational inequalities in initiation, cessation, and prevalence of smoking among 3 Italian birth cohorts. *American Journal of Public Health, 97,* 838–845.

Fedson, David S. (2005). Preparing for pandemic vaccination: An international policy agenda for vaccine development. *Journal of Public Health Policy, 26,* 4–29.

Feerasta, Aniqa. (2006, August 28). "Voices of Katrina: 'A humbling truth.'" *USA Today,* p. A12.

Fehr, Beverley. (1996). *Friendship processes.* Thousand Oaks, CA: Sage.

Fehr, Beverley. (2000). The life cycle of friendship. In Clyde Hendrick & Susan S. Hendrick (Eds.), *Close relationships: A sourcebook* (pp. 71–82). Thousand Oaks, CA: Sage.

Feiring, Candice. (1999). Other-sex friendship networks and the development of romantic relationships in adolescence. *Journal of Youth & Adolescence, 28,* 495–512.

Feldman, Ruth, & Eidelman, Arthur I. (2004). Parent-infant synchrony and the social-emotional development of triplets. *Developmental Psychology, 40,* 1133–1147.

Feldman, Ruth, & Eidelman, Arthur I. (2005). Does a triplet birth pose a special risk for infant development? Assessing cognitive development in relation to intrauterine growth and mother-infant interaction across the first 2 years. *Pediatrics, 115,* 443–452.

Feldman, Ruth, Eidelman, Arthur I., & Rotenberg, Noa. (2004). Parenting stress, infant emotion regulation, maternal sensitivity, and the cognitive development of triplets: A model for parent and child influences in a unique ecology. *Child Development, 75,* 1774–1791.

Feldman, Ruth, Weller, Aron, Sirota, Lea, & Eidelman, Arthur I. (2002). Skin-to-skin contact (kangaroo care) promotes self-regulation in premature infants: Sleep-wake cyclicity, arousal modulation, and sustained exploration. *Developmental Psychology, 38,* 194–207.

Feldser, David M., & Greider, Carol W. (2007). Short telomeres limit tumor progression in vivo by inducing senescence. *Cancer Cell, 11,* 461–469.

Fenson, Larry, Bates, Elizabeth, Dale, Philip, Goodman, Judith, Reznick, J. Steven, & Thal, Donna. (2000). Measuring variability in early child language: Don't shoot the messenger. *Child Development, 71,* 323–328.

Ferguson, Mark W. J, & Joanen, Ted. (1982, April 29). Temperature of egg incubation determines sex in *Alligator mississippiensis. Nature, 296,* 850–853.

Fergusson, David M., & Horwood, L. John. (2002). Male and female offending trajectories. *Development & Psychopathology, 14,* 159–177.

Fergusson, David M., & Horwood, L. John. (2003). Resilience to childhood adversity: Results of a 12–year study. In Suniya S. Luthar (Ed.), *Resilience and vulnerability: Adaptation in the context of childhood adversities* (pp. 130–155). New York: Cambridge University Press.

Fergusson, David M., Horwood, L. John, & Ridder, Elizabeth M. (2005). Partner violence and mental health outcomes in a New Zealand birth cohort. *Journal of Marriage and Family, 67,* 1103–1119.

Ferrari, Josheph R., Kapoor, Monica, & Cowman, Shaun. (2005). Exploring the relationship between students' values and the values of postsecondary institutions. *Social Psychology of Education, 8,* 207–221.

Field, Nigel P., & Friedrichs, Michael. (2004). Continuing bonds in coping with the death of a husband. *Death Studies, 28,* 597–620.

Field, Tiffany. (2001). Massage therapy facilitates weight gain in preterm infants. *Current Directions in Psychological Science, 10,* 51–54.

Finch, Caleb E. (1999). Longevity without senescence: Possible examples. In Jean-Marie Robine, Bernard Forette, Claudio Franceschi, & Michel Allard (Eds.), *The paradoxes of longevity* (pp. 1–9). New York: Springer.

Finch, Caleb E., & Kirkwood, Thomas B. L. (2000). *Chance, development, and aging.* New York: Oxford University Press.

Fincham, Frank D., Stanley, Scott M., & Beach, Steven R. H. (2007). Transformative processes in marriage: An analysis of emerging trends. *Journal of Marriage and Family, 69,* 275–292.

Fine, Mark A., & Harvey, John H. (2006). *Handbook of divorce and relationship dissolution.* Mahwah, NJ: Erlbaum.

Fingerman, Karen L. (1996). Sources of tension in the aging mother and adult daughter relationship. *Psychology & Aging, 11,* 591–606.

Fingerman, Karen L., Hay, Elizabeth L., & Birditt, Kira S. (2004). The best of ties, the worst of ties: Close, problematic, and ambivalent social relationships. *Journal of Marriage and Family, 66,* 792–808.

Finkel, Deborah, Pedersen, Nancy L., Plomin, Robert, & McClearn, Gerald E. (1998). Longitudinal and cross-sectional twin data on cognitive abilities in adulthood: The Swedish Adoption/Twin Study of Aging. *Developmental Psychology, 34,* 1400–1413.

Finkelhor, David, & Jones, Lisa M. (2004). *Explanations for the decline in child sexual abuse cases.* Office of Juvenile Justice and Delinquency Prevention. Retrieved August 11, 2007, from the World Wide Web: http://www.ncjrs.gov/html/ojjdp/199298/contents.html

Finn, Jeremy D., & Achilles, Charles M. (1999). Tennessee's class size study: Findings, implications, misconceptions. *Educational Evaluation and Policy Analysis, 21,* 97–109.

Finn, John W. (2005). Stories of Pearl: Surviving end-of-life care. In Donald E. Gelfand, Richard Raspa, Sherylyn H. Briller, & Stephanie Myers Schim (Eds.), *End-of-life stories: Crossing disciplinary boundaries* (pp. 134–147). New York: Springer.

Fischer, Kurt W., & Bidell, Thomas R. (1998). Dynamic development of psychological structures in action and thought. In William Damon (Series Ed.) & Richard M. Lerner (Vol. Ed.), *Handbook of child psychology: Vol. 1. Theoretical models of human development* (5th ed., pp. 467–561). New York: Wiley.

Fischer, Kurt, W., Yan, Zheng, & Stewart, Jeffrey. (2003). Adult cognitive development: Dynamics in the developmental web. In Jaan Valsiner & Kevin J. Connolly (Eds.), *Handbook of developmental psychology* (pp. 491–516). Thousand Oaks, CA: Sage.

Fish, Jefferson M. (2002). The myth of race. In Jefferson M. Fish (Ed.), *Race and intelligence: Separating science from myth* (pp. 113–141). Mahwah, NJ: Erlbaum.

Fishbein, Martin, Hall-Jamieson, Kathleen, Zimmer, Eric, von Haeften, Ina, & Nabi, Robin. (2002). Avoiding the boomerang: Testing the relative effectiveness of antidrug public service announcements before a national campaign. *American Journal of Public Health, 92,* 238–245.

Fisher, Helen E. (2006). Broken hearts: The nature and risks of romantic rejection. In Ann C. Crouter & Alan Booth (Eds.), *Romance and sex in adolescence and emerging adulthood: Risks and opportunities* (pp. 3–28). Mahwah, NJ: Erlbaum.

Fisher, Jennifer O., & Birch, Leann L. (2001). Early experience with food and eating: Implications for the development of eating disorders. In J. Kevin Thompson & Linda Smolak (Eds.), *Body image, eating disorders, and obesity in youth: Assessment, prevention, and treatment* (pp. 23–39). Washington, DC: American Psychological Association.

Fitness, Julie. (2001). Emotional intelligence and intimate relationships. In Joseph Ciarrochi, Joseph P. Forgas, & John D. Mayer (Eds.), *Emotional intelligence in everyday life: A scientific inquiry* (pp. 98–112). New York: Psychology Press.

Flake, Dallan F., & Forste, Renata. (2006). Fighting families: Family characteristics associated with domestic violence in five latin american countries. *Journal of Family Violence, 21,* 19–29.

Flavell, John H., Miller, Patricia H., & Miller, Scott A. (2002). *Cognitive development* (4th ed.). Upper Saddle River, NJ: Prentice Hall.

Fleeson, William. (2004). The quality of American life at the end of the century. In Orville Gilbert Brim, Carol D. Ryff, & Ronald C. Kessler (Eds.), *How healthy are we? A national study of well-being at midlife* (pp. 252–272). Chicago: University of Chicago Press.

Fletcher, Anne C., Steinberg, Laurence, & Williams-Wheeler, Meeshay. (2004). Parental influences on adolescent problem behavior: Revisiting Stattin and Kerr. *Child Development, 75,* 781–796.

Flook, Lisa, Repetti, Rena L., & Ullman, Jodie B. (2005). Classroom social experiences as predictors of academic performance. *Developmental Psychology, 41,* 319–327.

Flory, Richard W., & Miller, Donald E. (2000). *GenX religion.* New York: Routledge.

Flum, David R., Salem, Leon, Broeckel Elrod, Jo Ann, Dellinger, E. Patchen, Cheadle, Allen, & Chan, Leighton. (2005). Early mortality among Medicare beneficiaries undergoing bariatric surgical procedures. *Journal of the American Medical Association, 294,* 1903–1908.

Flynn, James R. (1984). The mean IQ of Americans: Massive gains 1932 to 1978. *Psychological Bulletin, 95,* 29–51.

Flynn, James R. (1987). Massive IQ gains in 14 nations: What IQ tests really measure. *Psychological Bulletin, 101,* 171–191.

Flynn, James R. (1999). Searching for justice: The discovery of IQ gains over time. *American Psychologist, 54,* 5–20.

Foley, Daniel, Ancoli-Israel, Sonia, Britz, Patricia, & Walsh, James. (2004). Sleep disturbances and chronic disease in older adults: Results of the 2003 National

Sleep Foundation Sleep in America Survey. *Journal of Psychosomatic Research, 56,* 497–502.

Foley, Kathleen M., & Hendin, Herbert (Eds.). (2002). *The case against assisted suicide: For the right to end-of-life care.* Baltimore: Johns Hopkins University Press.

Folts, W. Edward, & Muir, Kenneth B. (2002). Housing for older adults: New lessons from the past. *Research on Aging, 24,* 10–28.

Fomby, Paula, & Cherlin, Andrew J. (2007). Family instability and child well-being. *American Sociological Review, 72,* 181–204.

Fortinsky, Richard H., Tennen, Howard, Frank, Natalie, & Affleck, Glenn. (2007). Health and psychological consequences of caregiving. In Carolyn M. Aldwin, Crystal L. Park, & Avron Spiro III (Eds.), *Handbook of health psychology and aging* (pp. 227–249). New York: Guilford Press.

Fossel, Michael. (2004). *Cells, aging, and human disease.* New York: Oxford University Press.

Foster, E. Michael, & Gifford, Elizabeth J. (2005). The transition to adulthood for youth leaving public systems: Challenges to policies and research. In Richard A. Settersten, Jr., Frank F. Furstenberg, Jr., & Rubén G. Rumbaut (Eds.), *On the frontier of adulthood: Theory, research, and public policy* (pp. 501–533). Chicago: University of Chicago Press.

Fowler, James W. (1981). *Stages of faith: The psychology of human development and the quest for meaning.* San Francisco: Harper & Row.

Fowler, James W. (1986). Faith and the structuring of meaning. In Craig Dykstra & Sharon Parks (Eds.), *Faith development and Fowler* (pp. 15–42). Birmingham, AL: Religious Education Press.

Fox, Nathan A., Henderson, Heather A., Rubin, Kenneth H., Calkins, Susan D., & Schmidt, Louis A. (2001). Continuity and discontinuity of behavioral inhibition and exuberance: Psychophysiological and behavioral influences across the first four years of life. *Child Development, 72,* 1–21.

Foxman, Betsy, Newman, Mark, Percha, Bethany, Holmes, King K., & Aral, Sevgi O. (2006). Measures of sexual partnerships: Lengths, gaps, overlaps, and sexually transmitted infection. *Sexually Transmitted Diseases, 33,* 209–214.

Franco-Marina, Francisco, Caloca, Jaime Villalba, Corcho-Berdugo, Alexander, & Grupo interinstitucional de cáncer pulmonar. (2006). Role of active and passive smoking on lung cancer etiology in Mexico City. *Salud Pública de México, 48*(Suppl. 1), s75–s82.

Frankenburg, William K., Dodds, Josiah, Archer, Philip, Shapiro, Howard, & Bresnick, Beverly. (1992). The Denver II: A major revision and restandardization of the Denver Developmental Screening Test. *Pediatrics, 89,* 91–97.

Frayling, Timothy M., Timpson, Nicholas J., Weedon, Michael N., Zeggini, Eleftheria, Freathy, Rachel M., Lindgren, Cecilia M., et al. (2007, May 11). A common variant in the FTO gene is associated with body mass index and predisposes to childhood and adult obesity. *Science, 316,* 889–894.

Fredricks, Jennifer A., Blumenfeld, Phyllis C., & Paris, Alison H. (2004). School engagement: Potential of the concept, state of the evidence. *Review of Educational Research, 74,* 59–109.

Fredricks, Jennifer A., & Eccles, Jacquelynne S. (2002). Children's competence and value beliefs from childhood through adolescence: Growth trajectories in two male-sex-typed domains. *Developmental Psychology, 38,* 519–533.

Fredricks, Jennifer A., & Eccles, Jacquelynne S. (2006). Is extracurricular participation associated with beneficial outcomes? Concurrent and longitudinal relations. *Developmental Psychology, 42,* 698–713.

Fredriksen, Katia, Rhodes, Jean, Reddy, Ranjini, & Way, Niobe. (2004). Sleepless in Chicago: Tracking the effects of adolescent sleep loss during the middle school years. *Child Development, 75,* 84–95.

Freeman, Kassie, & Thomas, Gail E. (2002). Black colleges and college choice: Characteristics of students who choose HBCUs. *Review of Higher Education, 25,* 349–358.

French, Howard W. (2005, February 17). As girls 'vanish,' Chinese city battles tide of abortions. *New York Times,* p. A4.

French, Sabine Elizabeth, Seidman, Edward, Allen, LaRue, & Aber, J. Lawrence. (2006). The development of ethnic identity during adolescence. *Developmental Psychology, 42,* 1–10.

Frensch, Peter A., & Buchner, Axel. (1999). Domain-generality versus domain-specificity in cognition. In Robert J. Sternberg (Ed.), *The nature of cognition* (pp. 137–172). Cambridge, MA: MIT Press.

Freud, Anna. (2000). Adolescence. In James B. McCarthy (Ed.), *Adolescent development and psychopathology* (Vol. 13, pp. 29–52). Lanham, MD: University Press of America. (Reprinted from *Psychoanalytic Study of the Child,* pp. 255–278, 1958, New Haven, CT: Yale University Press)

Freud, Sigmund. (1935). *A general introduction to psychoanalysis* (A. A. Brill, Ed., Joan Riviere, Trans.). New York: Liveright.

Freud, Sigmund (Ed.). (1938). *The basic writings of Sigmund Freud.* New York: Modern Library.

Freud, Sigmund. (1964). An outline of psycho-analysis. In James Strachey (Ed. and Trans.), *The standard edition of the complete psychological works of Sigmund Freud* (Vol. 23, pp. 144–207). London: Hogarth Press. (Original work published 1940)

Frey, Karin S., Hirschstein, Miriam K., Snell, Jennie L., Van Schoiack-Edstrom, Leihua, MacKenzie, Elizabeth P., & Broderick, Carole J. (2005). Reducing playground bullying and supporting beliefs: An experimental trial of the Steps to Respect program. *Developmental Psychology, 41,* 479–491.

Fried, Linda P., Kronmal, Richard A., Newman, Anne B., Bild, Diane E., Mittelmark, Maurice B., Polak, Joseph F., et al. (1998). Risk factors for 5-year mortality in older adults: The Cardiovascular Health Study. *Journal of the American Medical Association, 279,* 585–592.

Friedlander, Samuel L., Larkin, Emma K., Rosen, Carol L., Palermo, Tonya M., & Redline, Susan. (2003). Decreased quality of life associated with obesity in school-aged children. *Archives of Pediatrics & Adolescent Medicine, 157,* 1206–1211.

Friedman, Michael S., Powell, Kenneth E., Hutwagner, Lori, Graham, LeRoy M., & Teague, W. Gerald. (2001). Impact of changes in transportation and commuting behaviors during the 1996 Summer Olympic Games in Atlanta on air quality and childhood asthma. *Journal of the American Medical Association, 285,* 897–905.

Fries, James F. (1994). *Living well: Taking care of your health in the middle and later years.* Reading, MA: Addison-Wesley.

Fromholt, Pia, & Bruhn, Peter. (1998). Cognitive dysfunction and dementia. In Inger Hilde Nordhus, Gary R. VandenBos, Stig Berg, & Pia Fromholt (Eds.), *Clinical geropsychology* (pp. 183–188). Washington, DC: American Psychological Association.

Fry, Prem S. (1999). The sociocultural meaning of dying with dignity: An exploratory study of the perceptions of a group of Asian Indian elderly persons. In Brian de Vries (Ed.), *End of life issues: Interdisciplinary and multidimensional perspectives* (pp. 297–318). New York: Springer.

Fry, Prem S. (2003). Perceived self-efficacy domains as predictors of fear of the unknown and fear of dying among older adults. *Psychology & Aging, 18,* 474–486.

Fuhrer, R., Shipley, M. J., Chastang, J. F., Schmaus, A., Niedhammer, I., Stansfeld, S. A., et al. (2002). Socioeconomic position, health, and possible explanations: A tale of two cohorts. *American Journal of Public Health, 92,* 1290–1294.

Fujimori, Maiko, Kobayakawa, Makoto, Nakaya, Naoki, Nagai, Kanji, Nishiwaki, Yutaka, Inagaki, Masatoshi, et al. (2006). Psychometric properties of the Japanese version of the quality of life-Cancer Survivors Instrument. *Quality of Life Research, 15,* 1633–1638.

Fujita, Hidenori. (2000). Education reform and education politics in Japan. *The American Sociologist, 31*(3), 42–57.

Fuligni, Andrew J. (1998). Authority, autonomy, and parent-adolescent conflict and cohesion: A study of adolescents from Mexican, Chinese, Filipino, and European backgrounds. *Developmental Psychology, 34,* 782–792.

Fuligni, Andrew J. (2001). A comparative longitudinal approach to acculturation among children from immigrant families. *Harvard Educational Review, 71,* 566–578.

Fuligni, Andrew J., & Hardway, Christina. (2006). Daily variation in adolescents' sleep, activities, and psychological well-being. *Journal of Research on Adolescence, 16,* 353–378.

Fuligni, Andrew J., Witkow, Melissa, & Garcia, Carla. (2005). Ethnic identity and the academic adjustment of adolescents From Mexican, Chinese, and European backgrounds. *Developmental Psychology, 41,* 799–811.

Fung, Helene H., & Carstensen, Laura L. (2004). Motivational changes in response to blocked goals and foreshortened time: Testing alternatives to socioemotional selectivity theory. *Psychology and Aging, 19,* 68–78.

Fung, Helene H., & Ng, Siu-Kei. (2006). Age differences in the sixth personality factor: Age differences in interpersonal relatedness Among Canadians and Hong Kong Chinese. *Psychology and Aging, 21,* 810–814.

Furman, Wyndol, & Hand, Laura Shaffer. (2006). The slippery nature of romantic relationships: Issues in definition and differentiation. In Ann C. Crouter & Alan Booth (Eds.), *Romance and sex in adolescence and emerging adulthood: Risks and opportunities* (pp. 171–178). Mahwah, NJ: Erlbaum.

Furman, Wyndol, Ho, Martin J., & Low, Sabina M. (2007). The rocky road of adolescent romantic experience: Dating and adjustment. In Rutger C. M. E. Engels, Margaret Kerr, & Håkan Stattin (Eds.), *Friends, lovers, and groups: Key relationships in adolescence* (pp. 61–80). Hoboken, NJ: Wiley.

Fussell, Elizabeth, & Palloni, Alberto. (2004). Persistent marriage regimes in changing times. *Journal of Marriage and Family, 66,* 1201–1213.

Gagnon, John H., Giami, Alain, Michaels, Stuart, & de Colomby, Patrick. (2001). A comparative study of the couple in the social organization of sexuality in France and the United States. *Journal of Sex Research, 38,* 24–34.

Galambos, Nancy L. (2004). Gender and gender role development in adolescence. In Richard M. Lerner & Laurence D. Steinberg (Eds.), *Handbook of adolescent psychology* (2nd ed., pp. 233–262). Hoboken, NJ: Wiley.

Galambos, Nancy L., Barker, Erin T., & Almeida, David M. (2003). Parents do matter: Trajectories of change in externalizing and internalizing problems in early adolescence. *Child Development, 74,* 578–594.

Galambos, Nancy L., Barker, Erin T., & Krahn, Harvey J. (2006). Depression, self-esteem, and anger in emerging adulthood: Seven-year trajectories. *Developmental Psychology, 42,* 350–365.

Galea, Sandro, Ahern, Jennifer, Resnick, Heidi, Kilpatrick, Dean, Bucuvalas, Michael, Gold, Joel, et al. (2002). Psychological sequelae of the September 11 terrorist attacks in New York City. *New England Journal of Medicine, 346,* 982–987.

Gall, Stanley (Ed.). (1996). *Multiple pregnancy and delivery.* St. Louis, MO: Mosby.

Gallup, Gordon G., Anderson, James R., & Shillito, Daniel J. (2002). The mirror test. In Marc Bekoff, Colin Allen, & Gordon M. Burghardt (Eds.), *The cognitive animal: Empirical and theoretical perspectives on animal cognition* (pp. 325–333). Cambridge, MA: MIT Press.

Galotti, Kathleen M. (2002). *Making decisions that matter: How people face important life choices.* Mahwah, NJ: Erlbaum.

Ganong, Lawrence H., & Coleman, Marilyn. (1994). *Remarried family relationships.* Thousand Oaks, CA: Sage.

Ganong, Lawrence H., & Coleman, Marilyn. (2004). *Stepfamily relationships: Development, dynamics, and interventions.* New York: Kluwer Academic/Plenum.

Gans, Daphna, & Silverstein, Merril. (2006). Norms of filial responsibility for aging parents across time and generations. *Journal of Marriage and Family, 68,* 961–976.

Gantley, M., Davies, D. P., & Murcott, A. (1993). Sudden infant death syndrome: Links with infant care practices. *British Medical Journal, 306,* 16–20.

Garbarini, Francesca, & Adenzato, Mauro. (2004). At the root of embodied cognition: Cognitive science meets neurophysiology. *Brain and Cognition, 56,* 100–106.

Garcia, Cristina. (2004). *Monkey hunting.* New York: Ballantine Books.

Gardner, Christopher D., Kiazand, Alexandre, Alhassan, Sofiya, Kim, Soowon, Stafford, Randall S., Balise, Raymond R., et al. (2007). Comparison of the Atkins, Zone, Ornish, and LEARN diets for change in weight and related risk factors among overweight premenopausal women: The A to Z Weight Loss Study: a randomized trial. *Journal of the American Medical Association, 297,* 969–977.

Gardner, Howard. (1983). *Frames of mind: The theory of multiple intelligences.* New York: Basic Books.

Gardner, Howard. (1999). Are there additional intelligences? The case for naturalist, spiritual, and existential intelligences. In Jeffrey Kane (Ed.), *Education, information, and transformation: Essays on learning and thinking* (pp. 111–131). Upper Saddle River, NJ: Merrill.

Gardner, Howard, & Moran, Seana. (2006). The science of multiple intelligences theory: A response to Lynn Waterhouse. *Educational Psychologist, 41,* 227–232.

Gardner, Howard E. (1998). Extraordinary cognitive achievements (ECA): A symbol systems approach. In William Damon (Series Ed.) & Richard M. Lerner (Vol. Ed.), *Handbook of child psychology: Volume 1: Theoretical models of human development* (5th ed., pp. 415–466). Hoboken, NJ: Wiley.

Gardner, Margo, & Steinberg, Laurence. (2005). Peer influence on risk taking, risk preference, and risky decision making in adolescence and adulthood: An experimental study. *Developmental Psychology, 41*, 625–635.

Garofalo, Robert, Wolf, R. Cameron, Wissow, Lawrence S., Woods, Elizabeth R., & Goodman, Elizabeth. (1999). Sexual orientation and risk of suicide attempts among a representative sample of youth. *Archives of Pediatrics & Adolescent Medicine, 153*, 487–493.

Garvin, James. (1994). *Learning how to kiss a frog: Advice for those who work with pre- and early adolescents*. Topsfield, MA: New England League of Middle Schools.

Gaspar de Alba, Alicia. (2003). Rights of passage: From cultural schizophrenia to border consciousness in Cheech Marin's *Born in East L.A.* In Alicia Gaspar de Alba (Ed.), *Velvet barrios: Popular culture & Chicana/o sexualities*. Basingstoke, England: Palgrave Macmillan.

Gathercole, Susan E., Pickering, Susan J., Ambridge, Benjamin, & Wearing, Hannah. (2004). The structure of working memory from 4 to 15 years of age. *Developmental Psychology, 40*, 177–190.

Gauvain, Mary. (1998). Cognitive development in social and cultural context. *Current Directions in Psychological Science, 7*, 188–192.

Gavrilov, Leonid A., & Gavrilova, Natalia S. (2006). Reliability theory of aging and longevity. In Edward J. Masoro & Steven N. Austad (Eds.), *Handbook of the biology of aging* (6th ed., pp. 3–42). Amsterdam: Elsevier Academic Press.

Gdalevich, Michael, Mimouni, Daniel, & Mimouni, Marc. (2001). Breast-feeding and the risk of bronchial asthma in childhood: A systematic review with meta-analysis of prospective studies. *Journal of Pediatrics, 139*, 261–266.

Ge, Xiaojia, Brody, Gene H., Conger, Rand D., Simons, Ronald L., & Murry, Velma McBride. (2002). Contextual amplification of pubertal transition effects on deviant peer affiliation and externalizing behavior among African American children. *Developmental Psychology, 38*, 42–54.

Ge, Xiaojia, Conger, Rand D., & Elder, Glen H., Jr. (2001). Pubertal transition, stressful life events, and the emergence of gender differences in adolescent depressive symptoms. *Developmental Psychology, 37*, 404–417.

Ge, Xiaojia, Kim, Irene J., Brody, Gene H., Conger, Rand D., Simons, Ronald L., Gibbons, Frederick X., et al. (2003). It's about timing and change: Pubertal transition effects on symptoms of major depression among African American youths. *Developmental Psychology, 39*, 430–439.

Gelfand, Donald E. (2003). *Aging and ethnicity: Knowledge and services* (2nd ed.). New York: Springer.

Gelles, Richard J. (1997). *Intimate violence in families* (3rd ed.). Thousand Oaks, CA: Sage.

Gennetian, Lisa A., & Miller, Cynthia. (2002). Children and welfare reform: A view from an experimental welfare program in Minnesota. *Child Development, 73*, 601–620.

Gentner, Dedre, & Boroditsky, Lera. (2001). Individuation, relativity, and early word learning. In Melissa Bowerman & Stephen C. Levinson (Eds.), *Language acquisition and conceptual development* (pp. 215–256). Cambridge, UK: Cambridge University Press.

Georgas, James, Berry, John W., van de Vijver, Fons J. R., Kagitçibasi, Çigdem, & Poortinga, Ype H. (2006). *Families across cultures: A 30–nation psychological study*. Cambridge, UK: Cambridge University Press.

George, Linda K. (2006). Perceived quality of life. In Robert H. Binstock & Linda K. George (Eds.), *Handbook of aging and the social sciences* (6th ed., pp. 320–336). Amsterdam: Elsevier.

Georges, Jean-Jacques, Onwuteaka-Philipsen, Bregje D., Van Der Heide, Agnes, Van Der Wal, Gerrit, & Van Der Maas, Paul J. (2006). Physicians' opinions on palliative care and euthanasia in The Netherlands. *Journal of Palliative Medicine, 9*, 1137–1144.

Georgieff, Michael K., & Rao, Raghavendra. (2001). The role of nutrition in cognitive development. In Charles A. Nelson & Monica Luciana (Eds.), *Handbook of developmental cognitive neuroscience* (pp. 149–158). Cambridge, MA: MIT Press.

Geronimus, Arline T., Hicken, Margaret, Keene, Danya, & Bound, John. (2006). "Weathering" and age patterns of allostatic load scores among Blacks and Whites in the United States. *American Journal of Public Health, 96*(5), 826–833.

Gerris, Jan, De Sutter, Paul, De Neubourg, Diane D., Van Royen, Eric, Vander Elst, Josiane, Mangelschots, Katelijne, et al. (2004). A real-life prospective health economic study of elective single embryo transfer versus two-embryo transfer in first IVF/ICSI cycles. *Human Reproduction, 19*, 917–923.

Gershoff, Elizabeth Thompson. (2002). Corporal punishment by parents and associated child behaviors and experiences: A meta-analytic and theoretical review. *Psychological Bulletin, 128*, 539–579.

Gershoff, Elizabeth T., Aber, J. Lawrence, Raver, C. Cybele, & Lennon, Mary Clare. (2007). Income is not enough: Incorporating material hardship into models of income associations with parenting and child development. *Child Development, 78*, 70–95.

Gerstel, Naomi Ruth. (2002). Book reviews [Review of the book *Talk of love: How culture matters*]. *Journal of Marriage and the Family, 64*, 549–556.

Gerstorf, Denis, Smith, Jacqui, & Baltes, Paul B. (2006). A systemic-wholistic approach to differential aging: Longitudinal findings from the Berlin Aging Study. *Psychology and Aging, 21*, 645–663.

Getahun, Darios, Oyelese, Yinka, Salihu, Hamisu M., & Ananth, Cande V. (2006). Previous cesarean delivery and risks of placenta previa and placental abruption. *Obstetrics & Gynecology, 107*, 771–778.

Ghuman, Paul A. Singh. (2003). *Double loyalties: South Asian adolescents in the West*. Cardiff, United Kingdom: University of Wales Press.

Gibbons, Ann. (2006, December 15). There's more than one way to have your milk and drink it, too. *Science, 314*, 1672a.

Gibson, Eleanor J. (1969). *Principles of perceptual learning and development*. New York: Appleton-Century-Crofts.

Gibson, Eleanor J. (1988). Levels of description and constraints on perceptual development. In Albert Yonas (Ed.), *Perceptual development in infancy* (pp. 283–296). Hillsdale, NJ: Erlbaum.

Gibson, Eleanor J. (1997). An ecological psychologist's prolegomena for perceptual development: A functional approach. In Cathy Dent-Read & Patricia Zukow-Goldring (Eds.), *Evolving explanations of development: Ecological approaches to organism-environment systems* (pp. 23–54). Washington, DC: American Psychological Association.

Gibson, Eleanor J., & Walk, Richard D. (1960). The "visual cliff." *Scientific American, 202*(4), 64–71.

Gibson, James Jerome. (1979). *The ecological approach to visual perception.* Boston: Houghton Mifflin.

Gibson-Davis, Christina M., & Brooks-Gunn, Jeanne. (2006). Couples' immigration status and ethnicity as determinants of breastfeeding. *American Journal of Public Health, 96,* 641–646.

Gibson-Davis, Christina M., Edin, Kathryn, & McLanahan, Sara. (2005). High hopes but even higher expectations: The retreat from marriage among low-income couples. *Journal of Marriage and Family, 67,* 1301–1312.

Giele, Janet Zollinger. (2002). Life careers and the theory of action. In Richard A. Settersten & Timothy J. Owens (Eds.), *Advances in life course research: Vol. 7. New frontiers in socialization* (pp. 65–88). Amsterdam: JAI.

Gifford-Smith, Mary E., & Rabiner, David L. (2004). Social information processing and children's social adjustment. In Janis B. Kupersmidt & Kenneth A. Dodge (Eds.), *Children's peer relations: From development to intervention* (pp. 61–79). Washington, DC: American Psychological Association.

Gigante, Denise. (2007). Zeitgeist. *European Romantic Review, 18,* 265–272.

Gigerenzer, Gerd, Todd, Peter M., & ABC Research Group. (1999). *Simple heuristics that make us smart.* New York: Oxford University Press.

Gilbert, Daniel. (2006). *Stumbling on happiness.* New York: Knopf.

Gilhooly, Mary. (2002). Ethical issues in researching later life. In Anne Jamieson & Christina R. Victor (Eds.), *Researching ageing and later life: The practice of social gerontology* (pp. 211–225). Philadelphia: Open University Press.

Gilligan, Carol. (1981). Moral development in the college years. In A. Chickering (Ed.), *The modern American college: Responding to the new realities of diverse students and a changing society* (pp. 139–156). San Francisco: Jossey-Bass.

Gilligan, Carol, Murphy, John Michael, & Tappan, Mark B. (1990). Moral development beyond adolescence. In Charles N. Alexander & Ellen J. Langer (Eds.), *Higher stages of human development: Perspectives on adult growth* (pp. 208–225). London: Oxford University Press.

Gilliom, Miles, Shaw, Daniel S., Beck, Joy E., Schonberg, Michael A., & Lukon, JoElla L. (2002). Anger regulation in disadvantaged preschool boys: Strategies, antecedents, and the development of self-control. *Developmental Psychology, 38,* 222–235.

Gillman, Neil. (2005). Coping with chaos: Jewish theological-and ritual resources. In Samuel Heilman (Ed.), *Death, bereavement, and mourning* (pp. 135–150). New Brunswick, NJ: Transaction.

Ginsburg, Herbert P., Klein, Alice, & Starkey, Prentice. (1998). The development of children's mathematical thinking: Connecting research with practice. In William Damon (Series Ed.) & Irving E. Sigel & K. Ann Renninger (Vol. Eds.), *Handbook of child psychology: Vol. 4. Child psychology in practice* (5th ed., pp. 401–476). New York: Wiley.

Gitlin, Laura N., Belle, Steven H., Burgio, Louis D., Czaja, Sara J., Mahoney, Diane, Gallagher-Thompson, Dolores, et al. (2003). Effect of multicomponent interventions on caregiver burden and depression: The REACH multisite initiative at 6-month follow-up. *Psychology & Aging, 18,* 361–374.

Glass, Jennifer. (1998). Gender liberation, economic squeeze, or fear of strangers: Why fathers provide infant care in dual-earner families. *Journal of Marriage & the Family, 60,* 821–834.

Glass, Jennifer, Lanctôt, Krista L., Herrmann, Nathan, Sproule, Beth A., & Busto, Usoa E. (2005). Sedative hypnotics in older people with insomnia: Meta-analysis of risks and benefits. *British Medical Journal, 331,* 1–7.

Glass, Roger I., & Parashar, Umesh D. (2006). The promise of new rotavirus vaccines. *New England Journal of Medicine, 354,* 75–77.

Glauber, James H., Farber, Harold J., & Homer, Charles J. (2001). Asthma clinical pathways: Toward what end? *Pediatrics, 107,* 590–592.

Gleason, Jean Berko, & Ely, Richard. (2002). Gender differences in language development. In Ann McGillicuddy-De Lisi & Richard De Lisi (Eds.), *Advances in applied developmental psychology: Vol. 21. Biology, society, and behavior: The development of sex differences in cognition* (pp. 127–154). Westport, CT: Ablex.

Glenn, Norval D. (1998). The course of marital success and failure in five American 10–year marriage cohorts. *Journal of Marriage & the Family, 60,* 569–576.

Glick, Jennifer E., Ruf, Stacey D., White, Michael J., & Goldscheider, Frances. (2006). Educational engagement and early family formation: Differences by ethnicity and generation. *Social Forces, 84,* 1391–1415.

Glover, Evam Kofi, Bannerman, Angela, Pence, Brian Wells, Jones, Heidi, Miller, Robert, Weiss, Eugene, et al. (2003). Sexual health experiences of adolescents in three Ghanaian towns. *International Family Planning Perspectives, 29,* 32–40.

Gluckman, Peter D., & Hanson, Mark A. (2006). *Developmental origins of health and disease.* Cambridge, England: Cambridge University Press.

Gluckman, Peter D., & Hanson, Mark A. (2006). *Mismatch: Why our world no longer fits our bodies.* Oxford, UK: Oxford University Press.

Goedert, Michel, & Spillantini, Maria Grazia. (2006, November 3). A century of Alzheimer's disease. *Science, 314,* 777–781.

Goel, Mita Sanghavi, McCarthy, Ellen P., Phillips, Russell S., & Wee, Christina C. (2004). Obesity among US immigrant subgroups by duration of residence. *Journal of the American Medical Association, 292,* 2860–2867.

Gogate, Lakshmi J., Bahrick, Lorraine E., & Watson, Jilayne D. (2000). A study of multimodal motherese: The role of temporal synchrony between verbal labels and gestures. *Child Development, 71,* 878–894.

Gohm, Carol L., Oishi, Shigehiro, Darlington, Janet, & Diener, Ed. (1998). Culture, parental conflict, parental marital status, and the subjective well-being of young adults. *Journal of Marriage & the Family, 60,* 319–334.

Gold, Ellen B., Colvin, Alicia, Avis, Nancy, Bromberger, Joyce, Greendale, Gail A., Powell, Lynda, et al. (2006). Longitudinal analysis of the association between vasomotor symptoms and race/ethnicity across the menopausal transition: Study of women's health across the nation. *American Journal of Public Health, 96,* 1226–1235.

Golden, Timothy D., Veiga, John F., & Simsek, Zeki. (2006). Telecommuting's differential impact on work-family conflict: Is there no place like home? *Journal of Applied Psychology, 91,* 1340–1350.

Goldin-Meadow, Susan. (2006). Nonverbal communication: The hand's role in talking and thinking. In William Damon & Richard M. Lerner (Series Eds.) & Deanna Kuhn & Robert S. Siegler (Vol. Eds.), *Handbook of child psychology: Vol. 2. Cognition,* *perception, and language* (6th ed., pp. 336–369). Hoboken, NJ: Wiley.

Goldman, Connie. (1991). Late bloomers: Growing older or still growing? *Generations, 15*(2), 41–48.

Goldman, Herbert I. (2001). Parental reports of 'MAMA' sounds in infants: An exploratory study. *Journal of Child Language, 28,* 497–506.

Goldscheider, Frances, & Sassler, Sharon. (2006). Creating stepfamilies: Integrating children into the study of union formation. *Journal of Marriage and Family, 68,* 275–291.

Goldsmith, Marshall, Bennis, Warren, O'Neil, John, Robertson, Alastair, Greenberg, Cathy, & Hu-Chan, Maya. (2003). *Global leadership: The next generation.* Upper Saddle River, NJ: FT/Prentice Hall.

Goldsmith, Sara K., Pellmar, Terry C., Kleinman, Arthur M., & Bunney, William E. (Eds.). (2002). *Reducing suicide: A national imperative.* Washington, DC: National Academies Press.

Goldstein, Sara E., Davis-Kean, Pamela E., & Eccles, Jacquelynne S. (2005). Parents, peers, and problem behavior: A longitudinal investigation of the impact of relationship perceptions and characteristics on the development of adolescent problem behavior. *Developmental Psychology, 41,* 401–413.

Goleman, Daniel. (1998, August). *Building emotional intelligence.* Keynote address presented at the 106th Annual Convention of the American Psychological Association, San Francisco, CA.

Golub, Sarit A., & Langer, Ellen J. (2007). Challenging assumptions about adult development: implications for the health of older adults. In Carolyn M. Aldwin, Crystal L. Park, & Avron Spiro, III (Eds.), *Handbook of health psychology and aging* (pp. 9–29). New York: Guilford Press.

Good, Catherine, Aronson, Joshua, & Inzlicht, Michael. (2003). Improving adolescents' standardized test performance: An intervention to reduce the effects of stereotype threat. *Journal of Applied Developmental Psychology, 24,* 645–662.

Goodrich, Gregory L. (2003). Available and emerging technologies for people with visual impairment. *Generations, 27*(1), 64–70.

Gopnik, Alison. (2001). Theories, language, and culture: Whorf without wincing. In Melissa Bowerman & Stephen C. Levinson (Eds.), *Language acquisition and conceptual development* (pp. 45–69). Cambridge, UK: Cambridge University Press.

Gordon, Peter. (2004, August 19). Numerical cognition without words: Evidence from Amazonia. *Science, 306,* 496–499.

Gordon, Richard Allan. (2000). *Eating disorders: Anatomy of a social epidemic* (2nd ed.). Malden, MA: Blackwell.

Gordon, Robert M., & Brill, Deborah. (2001). The abuse and neglect of the elderly. In David N. Weisstub, David C. Thomasma, Serge Gauthier, & George F. Tomossy (Eds.), *Aging: Caring for our elders* (pp. 203–218). Dordrecht, The Netherlands: Kluwer.

Gore, Jonathan S., Cross, Susan E., & Morris, Michael L. (2006). Let's be friends: Relational self-construal and the development of intimacy. *Personal Relationships, 13,* 83–102.

Gorenstein, Ethan E., & Comer, Ronald J. (2002). *Case studies in abnormal psychology.* New York: Worth.

Gorski, Peter A. (2002). Racing cain. *Journal of Developmental & Behavioral Pediatrics, 23,* 95.

Goss, David A. (2002). More evidence that near work contributes to myopia development. *Indiana Journal of Optometry, 5,* 11–13.

Gottlieb, Alma. (2000). Luring your child into this life: A Beng path for infant care. In Judy S. DeLoache & Alma Gottlieb (Eds.), *A world of babies: Imagined childcare guides for seven societies* (pp. 55–90). New York: Cambridge University Press.

Gottlieb, Gilbert. (1992). *Individual development and evolution: The genesis of novel behavior.* New York: Oxford University Press.

Gottlieb, Gilbert. (2002). *Individual development and evolution: The genesis of novel behavior.* Mahwah, NJ: Erlbaum. (Original work published 1992)

Gottlieb, Gilbert. (2003). Probabilistic epigenesis of development. In Jaan Valsiner & Kevin J. Connolly (Eds.), *Handbook of developmental psychology* (pp. 3–17). Thousand Oaks, CA: Sage.

Gottman, John Mordechai, Murray, James D., Swanson, Catherine, Tyson, Rebecca, & Swanson, Kristin R. (2002). *The mathematics of marriage: Dynamic nonlinear models.* Cambridge, MA: MIT Press.

Gould, Madelyn. (2003). Suicide risk among adolescents. In Daniel Romer (Ed.), *Reducing adolescent risk: Toward an integrated approach* (pp. 303–320). Thousand Oaks, CA: Sage.

Graber, Julia A. (2004). Internalizing problems during adolescence. In Richard M. Lerner & Laurence D. Steinberg (Eds.), *Handbook of adolescent psychology* (2nd ed., pp. 587–626). Hoboken, NJ: Wiley.

Graber, Julia A., & Brooks-Gunn, Jeanne. (1996). Expectations for and precursors to leaving home in young women. In Julia A. Graber & Judith Semon Dubas (Eds.), *Leaving home: Understanding the transition to adulthood* (pp. 21–38). San Francisco: Jossey-Bass.

Gradin, Maria, Eriksson, Mats, Holmqvist, Gunilla, Holstein, Åsa, & Schollin, Jens. (2002). Pain reduction at venipuncture in newborns: Oral glucose compared with local anesthetic cream. *Pediatrics, 110,* 1053–1057.

Grady, Cheryl L. (2002). Introduction to the special section on aging, cognition, and neuroimaging. *Psychology and Aging, 17,* 3–6.

Graham, John W., & Beller, Andrea H. (2002). Nonresident fathers and their children: Child support and visitation from an economic perspective. In Catherine S. Tamis-LeMonda & Natasha Cabrera (Eds.), *Handbook of father involvement: Multidisciplinary perspectives* (pp. 431–453). Mahwah, NJ: Erlbaum.

Graham, Susan A., Kilbreath, Cari S., & Welder, Andrea N. (2004). Thirteen-month-olds rely on shared labels and shape similarity for inductive inferences. *Child Development, 75,* 409–427.

Granic, Isabela, Dishion, Thomas J., & Hollenstein, Tom. (2003). The family ecology of adolescence: A dynamic systems perspective on normative development. In Gerald R. Adams & Michael D. Berzonsky (Eds.), *Blackwell handbook of adolescence* (pp. 60–91). Malden, MA: Blackwell.

Grantham-McGregor, Sally M., & Ani, Cornelius. (2001). Undernutrition and mental development. In John D. Fernstrom, Ricardo Uauy, & Pedro Arroyo (Eds.), *Nutrition and brain* (pp. 1–18). Basel, Switzerland: Karger.

Gratton, Brian, & Haber, Carole. (1996). Three phases in the history of American grandparents: Authority, burden, companion. *Generations, 20,* 7–12.

Gray, Nicola J., Klein, Jonathan D., Noyce, Peter R., Sesselberg, Tracy S., & Cantrill, Judith A. (2005). Health information-seeking behaviour in adolescence: The place of the internet. *Social Science & Medicine, 60,* 1467–1478.

Green, Christa L., & Hoover-Dempsey, Kathleen V. (2007). Why do parents homeschool? A systematic examination of parental involvement. *Education and Urban Society, 39,* 264–285.

Green, Nancy S., Dolan, Siobhan M., & Murray, Thomas H. (2006). Newborn screening: Complexities in universal genetic testing. *American Journal of Public Health, 96,* 1955–1959.

Greenberger, Ellen, & Steinberg, Laurence D. (1986). *When teenagers work: The psychological and social costs of adolescent employment.* New York: Basic Books.

Greene, Melissa L., & Way, Niobe. (2005). Self-esteem trajectories among ethnic minority adolescents: A growth curve analysis of the patterns and predictors of change. *Journal of Research on Adolescence, 15,* 151–178.

Greene, Melissa L., Way, Niobe, & Pahl, Kerstin. (2006). Trajectories of perceived adult and peer discrimination among Black, Latino, and Asian American adolescents: Patterns and psychological correlates. *Developmental Psychology, 42,* 218–238.

Greene, Sheila. (2003). *The psychological development of girls and women: Rethinking change in time.* New York: Routledge.

Greenfield, Emily A., & Marks, Nadine F. (2006). Linked lives: adult children's problems and their parents' psychological and relational well-being. *Journal of Marriage and Family, 68,* 442–454.

Greenfield, Patricia M., Keller, Heidi, Fuligni, Andrew, & Maynard, Ashley. (2003). Cultural pathways through universal development. *Annual Review of Psychology, 54,* 461–490.

Greenough, William T. (1993). Brain adaptation to experience: An update. In Mark H. Johnson (Ed.), *Brain development and cognition: A reader* (pp. 319–322). Oxford, UK: Blackwell.

Greenough, William T., Black, James E., & Wallace, Christopher S. (1987). Experience and brain development. *Child Development, 58,* 539–559.

Greenough, William T., & Volkmar, Fred R. (1973). Pattern of dendritic branching in occipital cortex of rats reared in complex environments. *Experimental Neurology, 40,* 491–504.

Greenspan, Stanley I., & Wieder, Serena. (2006). *Engaging autism: Using the floortime approach to help children relate, communicate, and think.* Cambridge, MA: Da Capo Lifelong Books.

Griebel, Wilfried, & Niesel, Renate. (2002). Co-constructing transition into kindergarten and school by children, parents, and teachers. In Hilary Fabian & Aline-Wendy Dunlop (Eds.), *Transitions in the early years: Debating continuity and progression for young children in early education* (pp. 64–75). New York: RoutledgeFalmer.

Grigorenko, Elena L. (2003). Epistasis and the genetics of complex traits. In Robert Plomin, John C. DeFries, Ian W. Craig, & Peter McGuffin (Eds.), *Behavioral genetics in the postgenomic era* (pp. 247–266). Washington, DC: American Psychological Association.

Grigorenko, Elena L., & O'Keefe, Paul A. (2004). What do children do when they cannot go to school? In Robert J. Sternberg & Elena L. Grigorenko (Eds.), *Culture and competence: Contexts of life success* (pp. 23–53). Washington, DC: American Psychological Association.

Grolnick, Wendy S., Deci, Edward L., & Ryan, Richard M. (1997). Internalization within the family: The self-determination theory perspective. In Joan E. Grusec & Leon Kuczynski (Eds.), *Parenting and children's internalization of values: A handbook of contemporary theory* (pp. 135–161). New York: Wiley.

Grolnick, Wendy S., McMenamy, Jannette M., & Kurowski, Carolyn O. (2006). Emotional self-regulation in infancy and toddlerhood. In Lawrence Balter & Catherine S. Tamis-LeMonda (Eds.), *Child psychology: A handbook of contemporary issues* (2nd ed., pp. 3–25). New York: Psychology Press.

Grossmann, Klaus E., Grossmann, Karin, & Waters, Everett (Eds.). (2005). *Attachment from infancy to adulthood: The major longitudinal studies.* New York: Guilford Press.

Grosvenor, Theodore. (2003). Why is there an epidemic of myopia? *Clinical and Experimental Optometry, 86,* 273–275.

Grundy, Emily, & Henretta, John C. (2006). Between elderly parents and adult children: A new look at the intergenerational care provided by the 'sandwich generation'. *Ageing & Society, 26,* 707–722.

Grunwald, Henry. (2003). Twilight: Losing sight, gaining insight. *Generations, 27*(1), 102–104.

Grzywacz, Joseph G., & Bass, Brenda L. (2003). Work, family, and mental health: Testing different models of work-family fit. *Journal of Marriage & Family, 65,* 248–262.

Gu, Dongfeng, Reynolds, Kristi, Wu, Xigui, Chen, Jing, Duan, Xiufang, Reynolds, Robert F., et al. (2005). Prevalence of the metabolic syndrome and overweight among adults in China. *Lancet, 365,* 1398–1405.

Guilamo-Ramos, Vincent, Jaccard, James, Dittus, Patricia, & Bouris, Alida M. (2006). Parental expertise, trustworthiness, and accessibility: Parent-adolescent communication and adolescent risk behavior. *Journal of Marriage and Family, 68,* 1229–1246.

Guillaume, Michele, & Lissau, Inge. (2002). Epidemiology. In Walter Burniat, Tim J. Cole, Inge Lissau, & Elizabeth M. E. Poskitt (Eds.), *Child and adolescent obesity: Causes and consequences, prevention and management* (pp. 28–49). New York: Cambridge University Press.

Gullone, Eleonora, & King, Neville J. (1997). Three-year-follow-up of normal fear in children and adolescents aged 7 to 18 years. *British Journal of Developmental Psychology, 15,* 97–111.

Gunn, Shelly R., & Gunn, W. Stewart. (2007). Are we in the dark about sleepwalking's dangers? In Cynthia A. Read (Ed.), *Cerebrum 2007: Emerging ideas in brain science* (pp. 71–84). Washington, DC: Dana Press.

Gunnar, Megan R., & Vazquez, Delia M. (2001). Low cortisol and a flattening of expected daytime rhythm: Potential indices of risk in human development. *Development & Psychopathology, 13,* 515–538.

Gurney, James G., Fritz, Melissa S., Ness, Kirsten K., Sievers, Phillip, Newschaffer, Craig J., & Shapiro, Elsa G. (2003). Analysis of prevalence trends of autism spectrum disorder in Minnesota. *Archives of Pediatrics & Adolescent Medicine, 157,* 622–627.

Gurung, Regan A. R., Taylor, Shelley E., & Seeman, Teresa E. (2003). Accounting for changes in social support among married older adults: Insights from the MacArthur Studies of Successful Aging. *Psychology & Aging, 18,* 487–496.

Gustafson, Kathryn E., Bonner, Melanie J., Hardy, Kristina K., & Thompson Jr, Robert J. (2006). Biopsychosocial and developmental issues in sickle cell disease. In Ronald T. Brown (Ed.), *Comprehensive handbook of childhood cancer and sickle cell disease: A biopsychosocial approach* (pp. 431–448). New York: Oxford University Press.

Gutmann, David. (1994). *Reclaimed powers: Men and women in later life* (2nd ed.). Evanston, IL: Northwestern University Press.

Guzell, Jacqueline R., & Vernon-Feagans, Lynne. (2004). Parental perceived control over caregiving and its relationship to parent-infant interaction. *Child Development, 75,* 134–146.

Ha, Jung-Hwa, Carr, Deborah, Utz, Rebecca L., & Nesse, Randolph. (2006). Older adults' perceptions of intergenerational support after widowhood: How do men and women differ? *Journal of Family Issues, 27,* 3–30.

Hack, Maureen, Flannery, Daniel J., Schluchter, Mark, Cartar, Lydia, Borawski, Elaine, & Klein, Nancy. (2002). Outcomes in young adulthood for very-low-birth-weight infants. *New England Journal of Medicine, 346,* 149–157.

Haden, Catherine A., Ornstein, Peter A., Eckerman, Carol O., & Didow, Sharon M. (2001). Mother-child conversational interactions as events unfold: Linkages to subsequent remembering. *Child Development, 72,* 1016–1031.

Hagedoorn, Mariët, Van Yperen, Nico W., Coyne, James C., van Jaarsveld, Cornelia H. M., Ranchor, Adelita V., van Sonderen, Eric, et al. (2006). Does marriage protect older people from distress? The role of equity and recency of bereavement. *Psychology and Aging, 21,* 611–620.

Hagerman, Randi Jenssen, & Hagerman, Paul J. (2002). *Fragile X syndrome: Diagnosis, treatment, and research* (3rd ed.). Baltimore: Johns Hopkins University Press.

Hagestad, Gunhild O., & Dannefer, Dale. (2001). Concepts and theories of aging: Beyond microfication in social science approaches. In Robert H. Binstock (Ed.), *Handbook of aging and the social sciences* (5th ed., pp. 3–21). San Diego, CA: Academic Press.

Hai, Hamid Abdul, & Husain, Asad. (2000). Muslim perspectives regarding death, dying, and end-of-life decision making. In Kathryn Braun, James H. Pietsch, & Patricia L. Blanchette (Eds.), *Cultural issues in end-of-life decision making* (pp. 199–212). Thousand Oaks, CA: Sage.

Haidt, Jonathan. (2007, May 18). The new synthesis in moral psychology. *Science, 316,* 998–1002.

Hajjar, Emily R., Hanlon, Joseph T., Sloane, Richard J., Lindblad, Catherine I., Pieper, Carl F., Ruby, Christine M., et al. (2005). Unnecessary drug use in frail older people at hospital discharge. *Journal of the American Geriatrics Society, 53,* 1518–1523.

Hakamies-Blomqvist, L., & Wahlstrom, B. (1998). Why do older drivers give up driving? *Accident Analysis and Prevention, 30,* 305–312.

Hakuta, Kenji, Bialystok, Ellen, & Wiley, Edward. (2003). Critical evidence: A test of the critical-period hypothesis for second-language acquisition. *Psychological Science, 14,* 31–38.

Haley, David W., & Stansbury, Kathy. (2003). Infant stress and parent responsiveness: Regulation of physiology and behavior during still-face and reunion. *Child Development, 74,* 1534–1546.

Halford, Graeme S., & Andrews, Glenda. (2006). Reasoning and problem solving. In William Damon & Richard M. Lerner (Series Eds.) & Deanna Kuhn & Robert S. Siegler (Vol. Eds.), *Handbook of child psychology: Vol. 2. Cognition, perception, and language* (6th ed., pp. 557–608). Hoboken, NJ: Wiley.

Hallenbeck, James. (2003). *Palliative care perspectives.* New York: Oxford University Press.

Halliwell, Barry, & Gutteridge, John M. C. (2007). *Free radicals in biology and medicine* (4th ed.). New York: Oxford University Press.

Halpern, Carolyn Tucker, King, Rosalind Berkowitz, Oslak, Selene G., & Udry, J. Richard. (2005). Body mass index, dieting, romance, and sexual activity in adolescent girls: Relationships over time. *Journal of Research on Adolescence, 15,* 535–559.

Hambrick, David Z., Salthouse, Timothy A., & Meinz, Elizabeth J. (1999). Predictors of crossword puzzle proficiency and moderators of age-cognition relations. *Journal of Experimental Psychology: General, 128,* 131–164.

Hamerman, David. (2007). *Geriatric bioscience: The link between aging and disease.* Baltimore: Johns Hopkins University Press.

Hamermesh, Daniel S., Meng, Xin, & Zhang, Junsen. (2002). Dress for success—Does primping pay? *Labour Economics, 9,* 361–373.

Hamerton, John L., & Evans, Jane A. (2005). Sex chromosome anomalies. In Merlin Gene Butler & F. John Meaney (Eds.), *Genetics of developmental disabilities* (pp. 585–650). Boca Raton, FL: Taylor & Francis.

Hamill, Paul J. (1991). Triage: An essay. *The Georgia Review, 45,* 463–469.

Hamilton, Brady E., Martin, Joyce A., & Sutton, Paul P. (2004, November 23). Births: Preliminary data for 2003. *National Vital Statistics Reports, 53*(9), 1–17.

Hamilton, Garry. (2001, August 11). Dead man walking. *New Scientist, 2303,* 30–33.

Hamm, Jill V., & Faircloth, Beverly S. (2005). The role of friendship in adolescents' sense of school belonging. *New Directions for Child and Adolescent Development, 107,* 61–78.

Hammen, Constance. (2003). Risk and protective factors for children of depressed parents. In Suniya S. Luthar (Ed.), *Resilience and vulnerability: Adaptation in the context of childhood adversities* (pp. 50–75). New York: Cambridge University Press.

Hammond, Christopher J., Andrew, Toby, Mak, Ying Tat, & Spector, Tim D. (2004). A susceptibility locus for myopia in the normal population is linked to the PAX6 gene region on chromosome 11: A genomewide scan of dizygotic twins. *American Journal of Human Genetics, 75,* 294–304.

Hampton, Tracy. (2005). Alcohol and cancer. *Journal of the American Medical Association, 294,* 1481.

Han, Beth, Remsburg, Robin E., & Iwashyna, Theodore J. (2006). Differences in hospice use between black and white patients during the period 1992 through 2000. *Medical Care, 44,* 731–737.

Hane, Amie Ashley, & Fox, Nathan A. (2006). Ordinary variations in maternal caregiving influence human infants' stress reactivity. *Psychological Science, 17,* 550–556.

Hankin, Benjamin L., & Abramson, Lyn Y. (2001). Development of gender differences in depression: An elaborated cognitive vulnerability-transactional stress theory. *Psychological Bulletin, 127,* 773–796.

Hansson, Robert O., & Stroebe, Margaret S. (2007). *Bereavement in late life: Coping, adaptation, and developmental influences.* Washington, DC: American Psychological Association.

Hanushek, Eric A. (1999). The evidence on class size. In Susan E. Mayer & Paul E. Peterson (Eds.), *Earning and learning: How schools matter* (pp. 131–168). Washington, DC: Brookings Institution Press/Russell Sage Foundation.

Hard, Stephen F., Conway, James M., & Moran, Antonia C. (2006). Faculty and college student beliefs about the frequency of student academic misconduct. *Journal of Higher Education, 77,* 1058–1080.

Hardy, Melissa. (2006). Older workers. In Robert H. Binstock & Linda K. George (Eds.), *Handbook of aging and the social sciences* (6th ed., pp. 201–218). Amsterdam: Elsevier.

Hareven, Tamara K. (2001). Historical perspectives on aging and family relations. In Robert H. Binstock (Ed.), *Handbook of aging and the social sciences* (5th ed., pp. 141–159). San Diego, CA: Academic Press.

Harlow, Harry F. (1958). The nature of love. *American Psychologist, 13,* 673–685.

Harlow, Harry Frederick. (1986). *From learning to love: The selected papers of H. F. Harlow* (Clara Mears Harlow, Ed.). New York: Praeger.

Harlow, Ilana. (2005). Shaping sorrow: Creative aspects of public and private mourning. In Samuel Heilman (Ed.), *Death, bereavement, and mourning* (pp. 33–52). New Brunswick, NJ: Transaction.

Harmon, Amy. (2004, June 20). In new tests for fetal defects, agonizing choices for parents. *New York Times,* pp. A1, A19.

Harris, James C. (2003). Social neuroscience, empathy, brain integration, and neurodevelopmental disorders. *Physiology & Behavior, 79,* 525–531.

Harris, Judith Rich. (1998). *The nurture assumption: Why children turn out the way they do.* New York: Free Press.

Harris, Judith Rich. (2002). Beyond the nurture assumption: Testing hypotheses about the child's environment. In John G. Borkowski, Sharon Landesman Ramey, & Marie Bristol-Power (Eds.), *Parenting and the child's world: Influences on academic, intellectual, and social-emotional development* (pp. 3–20). Mahwah, NJ: Erlbaum.

Hart, Betty, & Risley, Todd R. (1995). *Meaningful differences in the everyday experience of young American children.* Baltimore: Brookes.

Hart, Carole L., Smith, George Davey, Hole, David J., & Hawthorne, Victor M. (1999). Alcohol consumption and mortality from all causes, coronary heart disease, and stroke: Results from a prospective cohort study of Scottish men with 21 years of follow up. *British Medical Journal, 318,* 1725–1729.

Hart, Daniel, Atkins, Robert, & Fegley, Suzanne. (2003). Personality and development in childhood: A person-centered approach. *Monographs of the Society for Research in Child Development, 68*(Serial No. 272), vii-109.

Harter, Susan. (1998). The development of self-representations. In William Damon (Series Ed.) & Nancy Eisenberg (Vol. Ed.), *Handbook of child psychology: Vol. 3. Social, emotional and personality development* (5th ed., pp. 553–618). New York: Wiley.

Harter, Susan. (1999). *The construction of the self: A developmental perspective.* New York: Guilford Press.

Harter, Susan. (2006). The self. In William Damon & Richard M. Lerner (Series Eds.) & Nancy Eisenberg (Vol. Ed.), *Handbook of child psychology: Vol. 3. Social, emotional, and personality development* (6th ed., pp. 505–570). Hoboken, NJ: Wiley.

Hartl, Daniel L., & Jones, Elizabeth W. (1999). *Essential genetics* (2nd ed.). Sudbury, MA: Jones and Bartlett.

Hartmann, Donald P., & Pelzel, Kelly E. (2005). Design, measurement, and analysis in developmental research. In Marc H. Bornstein & Michael E. Lamb (Eds.), *Developmental science: An advanced textbook* (5th ed., pp. 103–184). Mahwah, NJ: Erlbaum.

Harvey, Carol D. H., & Yoshino, Satomi. (2006). Social policy for family caregivers of elderly: A Canadian, Japanese, and Australian Comparison. *Marriage & Family Review, 39,* 143–158.

Harwood, Robin L., Miller, Joan G., & Irizarry, Nydia Lucca. (1995). *Culture and attachment: Perceptions of the child in context.* New York: Guilford Press.

Hasebe, Yuki, Nucci, Larry, & Nucci, Maria S. (2004). Parental control of the personal domain and adolescent symptoms of psychopathology: A cross-national study in the United States and Japan. *Child Development, 75,* 815–828.

Haskins, Ron. (2005). Child development and child-care policy: Modest impacts. In David B. Pillemer & Sheldon Harold White (Eds.), *Developmental psychology and social change: Research, history, and policy* (pp. 140–170). New York: Cambridge University Press.

Haslam, Nick, Bastian, Brock, Fox, Christopher, & Whelan, Jennifer. (2007). Beliefs about personality change and continuity. *Personality and Individual Differences, 42,* 1621–1631.

Hassan, Mohamed A. M., & Killick, Stephen R. (2003). Effect of male age on fertility: Evidence for the decline in male fertility with increasing age. *Fertility and Sterility, 79*(Suppl. 3), 1520–1527.

Hassold, Terry J., & Patterson, David (Eds.). (1999). *Down syndrome: A promising future, together.* New York: Wiley-Liss.

Hastie, Peter A. (2004). Problem-solving in teaching sports. In Jan Wright, Lisette Burrows, & Doune MacDonald (Eds.), *Critical inquiry and problem-solving in physical education* (pp. 62–73). London: Routledge.

Hatfield, Elaine, & Rapson, Richard L. (2006). Passionate love, sexual desire, and mate selection: Cross-cultural and historical perspectives. In Patricia Noller & Judith A. Feeney (Eds.), *Close relationships: Functions, forms and processes* (pp. 227–243). Hove, England: Psychology Press/Taylor & Francis.

Hauser, Stuart T., Allen, Joseph P., & Golden, Eve. (2006). *Out of the woods: Tales of resilient teens.* Cambridge, MA: Harvard University Press.

Hawley, Patricia H. (1999). The ontogenesis of social dominance: A strategy-based evolutionary perspective. *Developmental Review, 19,* 97–132.

Hayes, Brett K., & Younger, Katherine. (2004). Category-use effects in children. *Child Development, 75,* 1719–1732.

Hayes, Richard, & Weiss, Helen. (2006, February 3). Understanding HIV epidemic trends in Africa. *Science, 311,* 620–621.

Hayes-Bautista, David E., Hsu, Paul, Perez, Aide, & Gamboa, Cristina. (2002). The "browning" of the graying of America: Diversity in the elderly population and policy implications. *Generations, 26*(3), 15–24.

Hayflick, Leonard. (1994). *How and why we age.* New York: Ballantine Books.

Hayflick, Leonard. (2001–2002). Anti-aging medicine: Hype, hope, and reality. *Generations, 25*(4), 20–26.

Hayflick, Leonard. (2004). "Anti-aging" is an oxymoron. *Journals of Gerontology: Series A: Biological Sciences and Medical Sciences, 59A,* 573–578.

Hayflick, Leonard, & Moorhead, Paul S. (1961). The serial cultivation of human diploid cell strains. *Experimental Cell Research, 25,* 585–621.

Hayslip, Bert, Jr., & Patrick, Julie Hicks. (2003). Custodial grandparenting viewed from within a life-span perpective. In Bert Hayslip, Jr., & Julie Hicks Patrick (Eds.), *Working with custodial grandparents* (pp. 3–11). New York: Springer.

Hayslip, Bert, Jr., Servaty, Heather L., & Guarnaccia, Charles A. (1999). Age cohort differences in perceptions of funerals. In Brian de Vries (Ed.), *End of life issues: Interdisciplinary and multidimensional perspectives* (pp. 23–36). New York: Springer.

Hazzard, William R. (2001). Aging, health, longevity, and the promise of biomedical research: The perspective of a gerontologist and geriatrician. In Edward J. Masoro & Steven N. Austad (Eds.), *Handbook of the biology of aging* (5th ed., pp. 445–456). San Diego, CA: Academic Press.

Heath, Andrew C., Madden, Pamela A. F., Bucholz, Kathleen K., Nelson, Elliot C., Todorov, Alexandre, Price, Rumi Kato, et al. (2003). Genetic and environmental risks of dependence on alcohol, tobacco, and other drugs. In Robert Plomin, John C. DeFries, Ian W. Craig, & Peter McGuffin (Eds.), *Behavioral genetics in the postgenomic era* (pp. 309–334). Washington, DC: American Psychological Association.

Hechtman, Lily, Abikoff, Howard B., & Jensen, Peter S. (2005). Multimodal therapy and stimulants in the treatment of children with attention-deficit/hyperactivity disorder. In Euthymia D. Hibbs & Peter S. Jensen (Eds.), *Psychosocial treatments for child and adolescent disorders: Empirically based strategies for clinical practice* (2nd ed., pp. 411–437). Washington, DC: American Psychological Association.

Heckhausen, Jutta. (2001). Adaptation and resilience in midlife. In Margie E. Lachman (Ed.), *Handbook of midlife development* (pp. 345–394). New York: Wiley.

Heinz, Walter R. (2002). Self-socialization and post-traditional society. In Richard A. Settersten Jr. & Timothy J. Owens (Eds.), *Advances in life course research: Vol. 7: New frontiers in socialization* (pp. 41–64). Amsterdam: JAI.

Hekimi, Siegfried, & Guarente, Leonard. (2003, February 28). Genetics and the specificity of the aging process. *Science, 299,* 1351–1354.

Henig, Robin Marantz. (2004, November 30). Sorry. Your eating disorder doesn't meet our criteria. *New York Times Magazine,* pp. 32–37.

Henson, Sian M., & Aspinall, Richard J. (2003). Ageing and the immune response. In Richard J. Aspinall (Ed.), *Aging of organs and systems* (pp. 225–242). Boston: Kluwer Academic.

Henz, Ursula. (2006). Informal caregiving at working age: Effects of job characteristics and family configuration. *Journal of Marriage and Family, 68,* 411–429.

Herbert, Alan, Gerry, Norman P., McQueen, Matthew B., Heid, Iris M., Pfeufer, Arne, Illig, Thomas, et al. (2006, April 14). A common genetic variant is associated with adult and childhood obesity. *Science, 312,* 279–283.

Herek, Gregory M. (2006). Legal recognition of same-sex relationships in the United States: A social science perspective. *American Psychologist, 61,* 607–621.

Herman, Melissa. (2004). Forced to choose: Some determinants of racial identification in multiracial adolescents. *Child Development, 75,* 730–748.

Herman-Giddens, Marcia E., Wang, Lily, & Koch, Gary. (2001). Secondary sexual characteristics in boys: Estimates from the National Health and Nutrition Examination Survey III, 1988–1994. *Archives of Pediatrics & Adolescent Medicine, 155,* 1022–1028.

Hern, Matt, & Chaulk, Stu. (1997). The internet, democracy and community: another.big.lie. *Journal of Family Life, 3*(4), 36–39.

Hertenstein, Matthew J., & Campos, Joseph J. (2001). Emotion regulation via maternal touch. *Infancy, 2,* 549–566.

Hess, Thomas M. (2005). Memory and aging in context. *Psychological Bulletin, 131,* 383–406.

Hess, Thomas M. (2006). Attitudes toward aging and their effects on behavior. In James E. Birren & K. Warner Schaie (Eds.), *Handbook of the psychology of aging* (6th ed., pp. 379–406). Amsterdam: Elsevier.

Hess, Thomas M., & Hinson, Joey T. (2006). Age-related variation in the influences of aging stereotypes on memory in adulthood. *Psychology and Aging, 21,* 621–625.

Hetherington, E. Mavis, & Kelly, John. (2002). *For better or for worse: Divorce reconsidered.* New York: Norton.

Heuveline, Patrick. (2002). An international comparison of adolescent and young adult mortality. *Annals of the American Academy of Political and Social Science, 580,* 172–200.

Heuveline, Patrick, & Timberlake, Jeffrey M. (2004). The role of cohabitation in family formation: The United States in comparative perspective. *Journal of Marriage & Family, 66,* 1214–1230.

Heyman, Richard E., & Slep, Amy M. Smith. (2002). Do child abuse and interparental violence lead to adulthood family violence? *Journal of Marriage & Family, 64,* 864–870.

Higgins, Matt. (2006a, August 5). Risk of injury is simply an element of motocross. *New York Times,* p. D5.

Higgins, Matt. (2006b, August 7). A series of flips creates some serious buzz. *New York Times,* p. D7.

Higuchi, Susumu, Matsushita, Sachio, Muramatsu, Taro, Murayama, Masanobu, & Hayashida, Motoi. (1996). Alcohol and aldehyde dehydrogenase genotypes and drinking behavior in Japanese. *Alcoholism: Clinical and Experimental Research, 20,* 493–497.

Hildyard, Kathryn L., & Wolfe, David A. (2002). Child neglect: Developmental issues and outcomes. *Child Abuse & Neglect,* 26(6–7), 679–695.

Hill, James O. (2002). The nature of the regulation of energy balance. In Christopher G. Fairburn & Kelly D. Brownell (Eds.), *Eating disorders and obesity: A comprehensive handbook* (2nd ed., pp. 67–72). New York: Guilford Press.

Hill, Robert D., Thorn, Brian L., Bowling, John, & Morrison, Anthony (Eds.). (2002). *Geriatric residential care.* Mahwah, NJ: Erlbaum.

Hill, Shirley A. (2007). Transformative processes: Some sociological questions. *Journal of Marriage and Family, 69,* 293–298.

Hillman, Richard. (2005). Expanded newborn screening and phenylketonuria (PKU). In Merlin Gene Butler & F. John Meaney (Eds.), *Genetics of developmental disabilities* (pp. 651–664). Boca Raton, FL: Taylor & Francis.

Hinds, David A., Stuve, Laura L., Nilsen, Geoffrey B., Halperin, Eran, Eskin, Eleazar, Ballinger, Dennis G., et al. (2005, February 18). Whole-genome patterns of common DNA variation in three human populations. *Science, 307,* 1072–1079.

Hines, Melissa. (2004). *Brain gender.* Oxford, England: Oxford University Press.

Hinkel, Eli. (2005). *Handbook of research in second language teaching and learning.* Mahwah, NJ: Erlbaum.

Hirsiaho, Nina, & Ruoppila, Isto. (2005). Physical health and mobility. In Heidrun Mollenkopf, Fiorella Marcellini, Isto Ruoppila, Zsuzsa Széman, & Mart Tacken (Eds.),

Enhancing mobility in later life: Personal coping, environmental resources and technical support. The out-of-home mobility of older adults in urban and rural regions of five European countries (pp. 77–104). Amsterdam: IOS Press.

Hitt, Rachel, Young-Xu, Yinong, Silver, Margery, & Perls, Thomas. (1999). Centenarians: the older you get, the healthier you have been. *Lancet, 354,* 652.

Hiyama, E., & Hiyama, K. (2007). Telomere and telomerase in stem cells. *British Journal of Cancer 96,* 1020–1024.

Hoare, Carol Hren. (2002). *Erikson on development in adulthood: New insights from the unpublished papers.* New York: Oxford University Press.

Hobbes, Thomas. (1997). *Leviathan: Authoritative text, backgrounds, interpretations* (Richard E. Flathman & David Johnston, Eds.). New York: Norton. (Original work published 1651)

Hobbs, Frank, & Stoops, Nicole. (2002). *Demographic trends in the 20th century* (CENSR-4). Washington, DC: U.S. Government Printing Office.

Hochman, David. (2003, November 23). Food for holiday thought: Eat less, live to 140? *The New York Times,* p. A9.

Hockey, Robert J. (2005). Operator functional state: The prediction of breakdown in human performance. In John Duncan, Peter McLeod, & Louise H. Phillips (Eds.), *Measuring the mind: Speed, control, and age* (pp. 373–394). New York: Oxford University Press.

Hodges, John R. (Ed.). (2007). *Frontotemporal dementia syndromes.* New York: Cambridge University Press.

Hofer, Myron A. (2006). Psychobiological roots of early attachment. *Current Directions in Psychological Science, 15,* 84–88.

Hoff, David J. (2005, July 27). Efforts seek better data on graduates. *Education Week, 43*(24), 1, 31.

Hoff, Erika. (2003). The specificity of environmental influence: Socioeconomic status affects early vocabulary development via maternal speech. *Child Development, 74,* 1368–1378.

Hoff, Erika, & Naigles, Letitia. (2002). How children use input to acquire a lexicon. *Child Development, 73,* 418–433.

Hofferth, Sandra L., & Anderson, Kermyt G. (2003). Are all dads equal? Biology versus marriage as a basis for paternal investment. *Journal of Marriage & Family, 65,* 213–232.

Hofmann, Adele Dellenbaugh. (1997). Adolescent growth and development. In Adele Dellenbaugh Hofmann & Donald Everett Greydanus (Eds.), *Adolescent medicine* (3rd ed., pp. 11–22). Norwalk, CT: Appleton & Lange.

Hofstede, Geert. (2007). A European in Asia. *Asian Journal of Social Psychology, 10,* 16–21.

Hohmann-Marriott, Bryndl E. (2006). Shared beliefs and the union stability of married and cohabiting couples. *Journal of Marriage and Family, 68,* 1015–1028.

Holden, Constance. (2000, July 28). The violence of the lambs. *Science, 289,* 580–581.

Holden, Constance. (2006, June 30). An evolutionary squeeze on brain size. *Science, 312,* 1867b.

Holder, Harold D. (2006). Racial and gender differences in substance use: What should communities do about them? In William R. Miller & Kathleen Carroll (Eds.), *Rethinking substance abuse: What the science shows, and what we should do about it* (pp. 153–165). New York: Guilford Press.

Hollich, George J., Hirsh-Pasek, Kathy, Golinkoff, Roberta Michnick, Brand, Rebecca J., Brown, Ellie, Chung, He Len, et al. (2000). Breaking the language barrier: An emergentist coalition model for the origins of word learning. *Monographs of the Society for Research in Child Development, 65*(3, Serial No. 262), v-123.

Holliday, Robin. (1995). *Understanding ageing.* Cambridge, England: Cambridge University Press.

Hong, Ying-yi, Morris, Michael W., Chiu, Chi-yue, & Benet-Martinez, Veronica. (2000). Multicultural minds: A dynamic constructivist approach to culture and cognition. *American Psychologist, 55,* 709–720.

Hooley, Jill M. (2004). Do psychiatric patients do better clinically if they live with certain kinds of families? *Current Directions in Psychological Science, 13,* 202–205.

Horn, John L., & Cattell, Raymond B. (1967). Age differences in fluid and crystallized intelligence. *Acta Psychologica, 26,* 107–129.

Horn, John L., & Masunaga, Hiromi. (2000). New directions for research into aging and intelligence: The development of expertise. In Timothy J. Perfect & Elizabeth A. Maylor (Eds.), *Models of cognitive aging* (pp. 125–159). London: Oxford University Press.

Hornsby, Peter J. (2007). Telomerase and the aging process. *Experimental Gerontology, 42,* 575–581.

Horowitz, Amy, & Stuen, Cynthia. (2003). Introduction: Aging and the senses. *Generations, 27*(1), 6–7.

Hosaka, Toru. (2005). School absenteeism, bullying, and loss of peer relationships in Japanese children. In David W. Shwalb, Jun Nakazawa, & Barbara J. Shwalb (Eds.), *Applied developmental psychology: Theory, practice, and research from Japan* (pp. 283–299). Greenwich, CT: Information Age.

Houde, Susan Crocker. (2007). *Vision loss in older adults: Nursing assessment and care management.* New York: Springer.

Houts, Renate M., Robins, Elliot, & Huston, Ted L. (1996). Compatibility and the development of premarital relationships. *Journal of Marriage & the Family, 58,* 7–20.

Howard, Barbara V., Van Horn, Linda, Hsia, Judith, Manson, JoAnn E., Stefanick, Marcia L., Wassertheil-Smoller, Sylvia, et al. (2006). Low-fat dietary pattern and risk of cardiovascular disease: The Women's Health Initiative Randomized Controlled Dietary Modification Trial. *Journal of the American Medical Association, 295,* 655–666.

Howard, Jeffrey A. (2005). Why should we care about student expectations? In Thomas E. Miller, Barbara E. Bender, John H. Schuh, & Associates (Eds.), *Promoting reasonable expectations: Aligning student and institutional views of the college experience* (pp. 10–33). San Francisco: Jossey-Bass.

Howe, Christine. (1998). *Conceptual structure in childhood and adolescence: The case of everyday physics.* London: Routledge.

Howe, Mark L. (2004). The role of conceptual recoding in reducing children's retroactive interference. *Developmental Psychology, 40,* 131–139.

Hrdy, Sarah Blaffer. (2000). *Mother nature: A history of mothers, infants, and natural selection* (Paperback ed.). New York: Ballantine Books.

Hsu, Hui-Chin, Fogel, Alan, & Cooper, Rebecca B. (2000). Infant vocal development during the first 6 months: Speech quality and melodic complexity. *Infant & Child Development, 9,* 1–16.

Hu, Frank B., Li, Tricia Y., Colditz, Graham A., Willett, Walter C., & Manson,

JoAnn E. (2003). Television watching and other sedentary behaviors in relation to risk of obesity and type 2 diabetes mellitus in women. *Journal of the American Medical Association, 289*, 1785–1791.

Huang, Han-Yao, Caballero, Benjamin, Chang, Stephanie, Alberg, Anthony J., Semba, Richard D., Schneyer, Christine R., et al. (2006). The efficacy and safety of multivitamin and mineral supplement use to prevent cancer and chronic disease in adults: A systematic review for a National Institutes of Health state-of-the-science conference. *Annals of Internal Medicine, 145*, 372–385.

Huang, Jannet. (2007). Hormones and female sexuality. In Annette Fuglsang Owens & Mitchell S. Tepper (Eds.), *Sexual health: Vol. 2. Physical foundations* (pp. 43–78). Westport, CT: Praeger/Greenwood.

Hubbs-Tait, Laura, Culp, Anne McDonald, Culp, Rex E., & Miller, Carrie E. (2002). Relation of maternal cognitive stimulation, emotional support, and intrusive behavior during Head Start to children's kindergarten cognitive abilities. *Child Development, 73*, 110–131.

Huesmann, L. Rowell, Moise-Titus, Jessica, Podolski, Cheryl-Lynn, & Eron, Leonard D. (2003). Longitudinal relations between children's exposure to TV violence and their aggressive and violent behavior in young adulthood: 1977–1992. *Developmental Psychology, 39*, 201–221.

Hugdahl, Kenneth, & Davidson, Richard J. (Eds.). (2002). *The asymmetrical brain*. Cambridge, MA: MIT Press.

Hulanicka, Barbara. (1999). Acceleration of menarcheal age of girls from dysfunctional families. *Journal of Reproductive & Infant Psychology, 17*, 119–132.

Hunt, Earl. (1993). What do we need to know about aging? In John Cerella, John Rybash, Michael Commons, & William Hoyer (Eds.), *Adult information processing: Limits on loss* (pp. 587–598). San Diego, CA: Academic Press.

Husain, Nusrat, Bevc, Irene, Husain, M., Chaudhry, Imram B., Atif, N., & Rahman, A. (2006). Prevalence and social correlates of postnatal depression in a low income country. *Archives of Women's Mental Health, 9*, 197–202.

Hussey, Jon M., Chang, Jen Jen, & Kotch, Jonathan B. (2006). Child maltreatment in the United States: Prevalence, risk factors, and adolescent health consequences. *Pediatrics, 118*, 933–942.

Huston, Aletha C., & Aronson, Stacey Rosenkrantz. (2005). Mothers' time with infant and time in employment as predictors of mother-child relationships and children's early development. *Child Development, 76*, 467–482.

Huston, Ted L. (2000). The social ecology of marriage and other intimate unions. *Journal of Marriage & the Family, 62*, 298–319.

Huttenlocher, Janellen, Levine, Susan, & Vevea, Jack. (1998). Environmental input and cognitive growth: A study using time-period comparisons. *Child Development, 69*, 1012–1029.

Huyck, Margaret Hellie. (1995). Marriage and close relationships of the marital kind. In Rosemary Blieszner & Victoria Hilkevitch Bedford (Eds.), *Handbook of aging and the family* (pp. 181–200). Westport, CT: Greenwood Press.

Hyde, Janet Shibley. (2001). Reporting effect sizes: The roles of editors, textbook authors, and publication manuals. *Educational and Psychological Measurement, 61*, 225–228.

Hyde, Janet Shibley, & Linn, Marcia C. (2006, October 27). Gender similarities in mathematics and science. *Science, 314*, 599–600.

Hyson, Marilou, Copple, Carol, & Jones, Jacqueline. (2006). Early childhood development and education. In William Damon & Richard M. Lerner (Series Eds.) & K. Ann Renninger & Irving E. Sigel (Vol. Eds.), *Handbook of child psychology: Vol. 4. Child psychology in practice* (6th ed., pp. 3–47). Hoboken, NJ: Wiley.

Ichikawa, Shin'ichi. (2005). Cognitive counseling to improve students' metacognition and cognitive skills. In David W. Shwalb, Jun Nakazawa, & Barbara J. Shwalb (Eds.), *Applied developmental psychology: Theory, practice, and research from Japan* (pp. 67–87). Greenwich, CT: Information Age.

Idler, Ellen. (2006). Religion and aging. In Robert H. Binstock & Linda K. George (Eds.), *Handbook of aging and the social sciences* (6th ed., pp. 277–300). Amsterdam: Elsevier.

Imamoglu, Çagri. (2007). Assisted living as a new place schema: A comparison with homes and nursing homes. *Environment and Behavior, 39*, 246–268.

Ingersoll-Dayton, Berit, Krause, Neal, & Morgan, David. (2002). Religious trajectories and transitions over the life course. *International Journal of Aging & Human Development, 55*, 51–70.

Ingersoll-Dayton, Berit, Neal, Margaret B., Ha, Jung-Hwa, & Hammer, Leslie B. (2003). Redressing inequity in parent care among siblings. *Journal of Marriage & Family, 65*, 201–212.

Inglehart, Ronald. (1990). *Culture shift in advanced industrial society*. Princeton, NJ: Princeton University Press.

Inhelder, Bärbel, & Piaget, Jean. (1958). *The growth of logical thinking from childhood to adolescence: An essay on the construction of formal operational structures*. New York: Basic Books.

Inhelder, Bärbel, & Piaget, Jean. (1964). *The early growth of logic in the child*. New York: Harper & Row.

Inhorn, Marcia Claire, & van Balen, Frank (Eds.). (2002). *Infertility around the globe: New thinking on childlessness, gender, and reproductive technologies*. Berkeley, CA: University of California Press.

Inouye, Sharon K. (2006). Delirium in older persons. *New England Journal of Medicine, 354*, 1157–1165.

Institute of Medicine (U.S.), Committee on Food Marketing and the Diets of Children and Youth. (2006). *Food marketing to children and youth: Threat or opportunity?* Washington, DC: National Academies Press.

International Association for the Evaluation of Educational Achievement. (2003). *TIMSS & PIRLS International Study Center*. Retrieved 2007, July 28, from the World Wide Web: http://timss.bc.edu/

Inzlicht, Michael, McKay, Linda, & Aronson, Joshua. (2006). Stigma as ego depletion: How being the target of prejudice affects self-control. *Psychological Science, 17*, 262–269.

Irwin, Scott, Galvez, Roberto, Weiler, Ivan Jeanne, Beckel-Mitchener, Andrea, & Greenough, William. (2002). Brain structure and the functions of FMR1 protein. In Randi Jenssen Hagerman & Paul J. Hagerman (Eds.), *Fragile X syndrome: Diagnosis, treatment, and research* (3rd ed., pp. 191–205). Baltimore: Johns Hopkins University Press.

Isolauri, Erika, Sutas, Yelda, Salo, Matti K., Isosomppi, Riitta, & Kaila, Minna. (1998). Elimination diet in cow's milk allergy: Risk for impaired growth in young children. *Journal of Pediatrics, 132*, 1004–1009.

Iverson, Jana M., & Fagan, Mary K. (2004). Infant vocal-motor coordination: Precursor to the gesture-speech system? *Child Development, 75*, 1053–1066.

Iyengar, Sheena S., Wells, Rachael E., & Schwartz, Barry. (2006). Doing better but feeling worse: Looking for the "best" job undermines satisfaction. *Psychological Science, 17*, 143–150.

Izard, Carroll E., Fine, Sarah, Mostow, Allison, Trentacosta, Christopher, & Campbell, Jan. (2002). Emotion processes in normal and abnormal development and preventive intervention. *Development & Psychopathology, 14*, 761–787.

Jaccard, James, Dittus, Patricia J., & Gordon, Vivian V. (1998). Parent-adolescent congruency in reports of adolescent sexual behavior and in communications about sexual behavior. *Child Development, 69*, 247–261.

Jaccard, James, Dittus, Patricia J., & Gordon, Vivian V. (2000). Parent-teen communication about premarital sex: Factors associated with the extent of communication. *Journal of Adolescent Research, 15*, 187–208.

Jaccard, James, Dodge, Tonya, & Dittus, Patricia. (2002). Parent-adolescent communication about sex and birth control: A conceptual framework. In S. Shirley Feldman & Doreen A. Rosenthal (Eds.), *Talking sexuality: Parent-adolescent communication* (pp. 9–41). San Francisco: Jossey-Bass.

Jackson, James S., Antonucci, Toni C., & Brown, Edna. (2004). A cultural lens on biopsychosocial models of aging. In Paul T. Costa & Ilene C. Siegler (Eds.), *Recent advances in psychology and aging* (Vol. 15, pp. 221–241). Amsterdam: Elsevier.

Jackson, Linda A., von Eye, Alexander, Biocca, Frank A., Barbatsis, Gretchen, Zhao, Yong, & Fitzgerald, Hiram E. (2006). Does home internet use influence the academic performance of low-income children? *Developmental Psychology, 42*, 429–435.

Jackson, Richard J. (2003). The impact of the built environment on health: An emerging field. *American Journal of Public Health, 93*, 1382–1384.

Jackson, Yo, & Warren, Jared S. (2000). Appraisal, social support, and life events: Predicting outcome behavior in school-age children. *Child Development, 71*, 1441–1457.

Jacob's father. (1997). Jacob's story: A miracle of the heart. *Zero to Three, 17*, 59–64.

Jacobs, Janis E., Lanza, Stephanie, Osgood, D. Wayne, Eccles, Jacquelynne S., & Wigfield, Allan. (2002). Changes in children's self-competence and values: Gender and domain differences across grades one though twelve. *Child Development, 73*, 509–527.

Jacobson, Linda. (2006, June 7). Latest decision keeps Calif. exit-exam law as graduations near. *Education Week, 25*(39), 25.

Jacoby, Larry L., Marsh, Elizabeth J., & Dolan, Patrick O. (2001). Forms of bias: Age-related differences in memory and cognition. In Moshe Naveh-Benjamin, Morris Moscovitch, & Henry L. Roediger (Eds.), *Perspectives on human memory and cognitive aging: Essays in honour of Fergus Craik* (pp. 240–252). New York: Psychology Press.

Jacoby, Larry L., & Rhodes, Matthew G. (2006). False remembering in the aged. *Current Directions in Psychological Science, 15*, 49–53.

Jaffee, Sara, Caspi, Avshalom, Moffitt, Terrie E., Belsky, Jay, & Silva, Phil. (2001). Why are children born to teen mothers at risk for adverse outcomes in young adulthood? Results from a 20-year longitudinal study. *Development & Psychopathology, 13*, 377–397.

Jaffee, Sara R., Caspi, Avshalom, Moffitt, Terrie E., Polo-Tomas, Monica, Price, Thomas S., & Taylor, Alan. (2004). The limits of child effects: Evidence for genetically mediated child effects on corporal punishment but not on physical maltreatment. *Developmental Psychology, 40*, 1047–1058.

Jahns, Lisa, Siega-Riz, Anna Maria, & Popkin, Barry M. (2001). The increasing prevalence of snacking among U.S. children from 1977 to 1996. *Journal of Pediatrics, 138*, 493–498.

James, Raven. (2007). Sexually transmitted infections. In Annette Fuglsang Owens & Mitchell S. Tepper (Eds.), *Sexual health: Vol. 4. State-of-the-art treatments and research* (pp. 235–267). Westport, CT: Praeger/Greenwood.

Jansen-van der Weide, Marijke C., Onwuteaka-Philipsen, Bregje D., & van der Wal, Gerrit. (2005). Granted, undecided, withdrawn, and refused requests for euthanasia and physician-assisted suicide. *Archives of Internal Medicine, 165*, 1698–1704.

Jastrzembski, Tiffany S., Charness, Neil, & Vasyukova, Catherine. (2006). Expertise and age effects on knowledge activation in chess. *Psychology and Aging, 21*, 401–405.

Jeanneret, Rene. (1995). The role of a preparation for retirement in the improvement of the quality of life for elderly people. In Eino Heikkinen, Jorma Kuusinen, & Isto Ruoppila (Eds.), *Preparation for aging* (pp. 55–62). New York: Plenum Press.

Jeffries, Sherryl, & Konnert, Candace. (2002). Regret and psychological well-being among voluntarily and involuntarily childless women and mothers. *International Journal of Aging & Human Development, 54*, 89–106.

Jellinger, Kurt A. (2002). Alzheimer disease and cerebrovascular pathology: An update. *Journal of Neural Transmission, 109*, 813–836.

Jellinger, Kurt A., Schmidt, Reinhold, & Windisch, Manfred. (2002). *Ageing and dementia: Current and future concepts*. Vienna: Springer.

Jenkins, Jennifer M., & Astington, Janet Wilde. (1996). Cognitive factors and family structure associated with theory of mind development in young children. *Developmental Psychology, 32*, 70–78.

Jensen, Arthur Robert. (1998). *The g factor: The science of mental ability*. Westport, CT: Praeger.

Jenson, Jeffrey M., & Fraser, Mark W. (2006). *Social policy for children & families: A risk and resilience perspective*. Thousand Oaks, CA: Sage.

Joe, Sean. (2003). Implications of focusing on black youth self-destructive behaviors instead of suicide when designing preventative interventions. In Daniel Romer (Ed.), *Reducing adolescent risk: Toward an integrated approach* (pp. 325–332). Thousand Oaks, CA: Sage.

John-Steiner, Vera, Panofsky, Carolyn P., & Smith, Larry W. (Eds.). (1994). *Sociocultural approaches to language and literacy: An interactionist perspective*. Cambridge, UK: Cambridge University Press.

Johnson, Beverly. (2006). Sexuality at midlife and beyond. In Mitchell S. Tepper & Annette Fuglsang Owens (Eds.), *Sexual health: Vol. 1. Psychological foundations* (pp. 291–300). Westport: Praeger/Greenwood.

Johnson, Colleen L., & Barer, Barbara M. (1993). Coping and a sense of control among the oldest old: An exploratory analysis. *Journal of Aging Studies, 7*, 67–80.

Johnson, Colleen L., & Barer, Barbara M. (2003). Family lives of aging black Americans. In Jaber F. Gubrium & James A. Holstein (Eds.), *Ways of aging* (pp. 111–131). Malden, MA: Blackwell.

Johnson, Dana E. (2000). Medical and developmental sequelae of early childhood institutionalization in Eastern European adoptees. In Charles A. Nelson (Ed.), *The Minnesota symposia on child psychology: Vol. 31. The effects of early adversity on neurobehavioral development* (pp. 113–162). Mahwah, NJ: Erlbaum.

Johnson, Jeffrey G., Cohen, Patricia, Smailes, Elizabeth M., Kasen, Stephanie, & Brook, Judith S. (2002, March 29). Television viewing and aggressive behavior during adolescence and adulthood. *Science, 295,* 2468–2471.

Johnson, Kirk A., & Rector, Robert. (2004). *Adolescents who take virginity pledges have lower rates of out-of-wedlock births.* The Heritage Foundation. Retrieved November 29, 2006, from the World Wide Web: http://www.heritage.org/Research/Family/upload/63285_1.pdf

Johnson, Kevin R. (1999). *How did you get to be Mexican? A white/brown man's search for identity.* Philadelphia: Temple University Press.

Johnson, Mark H. (2005). Developmental neuroscience, psychophysiology and genetics. In Marc H. Bornstein & Michael E. Lamb (Eds.), *Developmental science: An advanced textbook* (5th ed., pp. 187–222). Mahwah, NJ: Erlbaum.

Johnson, Mark H., & Morton, John. (1991). *Biology and cognitive development: The case of face recognition.* Oxford, UK: Blackwell.

Johnson, Michael P. (2005). Domestic violence: It's not about gender—Or is it? *Journal of Marriage and Family, 67,* 1126–1130.

Johnson, Michael P., & Ferraro, Kathleen J. (2000). Research on domestic violence in the 1990s: Making distinctions. *Journal of Marriage & the Family, 62,* 948–963.

Johnson, Norine G. (2003). Psychology and health: Research, practice, and policy. *American Psychologist, 58,* 670–677.

Johnson, Ruth S. (2002). *Using data to close the achievement gap: How to measure equity in our schools.* Thousand Oaks, CA: Corwin Press.

Johnson, Scott P., Bremner, J. Gavin, Slater, Alan, Mason, Uschi, Foster, Kirsty, & Cheshire, Andrea. (2003). Infants' perception of object trajectories. *Child Development, 74,* 94–108.

Johnston, Lloyd D., O'Malley, Patrick M., Bachman, Jerald G., & Schulenberg, John E. (2006). *Monitoring the Future: National survey results on drug use, 1975–2006: Vol. 2. College students and adults ages 19–45* (NIH Publication No. 06–5884). Bethesda, MD: National Institute on Drug Abuse.

Johnston, Lloyd D., O'Malley, Patrick M., Bachman, Jerald G., & Schulenberg, John E. (2007). *Monitoring the Future: National survey results on drug use, 1975–2006. Volume I: Secondary school students* (NIH Publication No. 07–6205). Bethesda, MD: National Institute on Drug Abuse.

Johnston, Timothy D., & Edwards, Laura. (2002). Genes, interactions, and the development of behavior. *Psychological Review, 109,* 26–34.

Joiner, Thomas E. (1999). The clustering and contagion of suicide. *Current Directions in Psychological Science, 8,* 89–92.

Jones, Daniel. (2006, February 12). You're not sick, you're just in love. *New York Times,* pp. 1, 13.

Jones, Diane, & Crawford, Joy. (2005). Adolescent boys and body image: Weight and muscularity concerns as dual pathways to body dissatisfaction. *Journal of Youth and Adolescence, 34,* 629–636.

Jones, Edward P. (2003). *The known world.* New York: Amistad.

Jones, Edward P. (2003). *Lost in the city: Stories.* New York: Amistad. (Original work published 1992)

Jones, Harold Ellis , & Conrad, Herbert S. (1933). The growth and decline of intelligence: A study of a homogeneous group between the ages of ten and sixty. *Genetic Psychology Monographs, 13,* 223–298.

Jones, Howard W., Jr., & Cohen, Jean. (2001). IFFS surveillance 01. *Fertility and Sterility, 76*(5, Suppl. 1), 5–36.

Jones, Ian. (2006). Why do women experience mood disorders following childbirth? *British Journal of Midwifery, 14,* 654–657.

Jones, Maggie. (2006, January 15). Shutting themselves in. *New York Times Magazine,* pp. 46–51.

Jones, Mary Cover. (1965). Psychological correlates of somatic development. *Child Development, 36,* 899–911.

Jones, Steve. (2006, December 22). Prosperous people, penurious genes. *Science, 314,* 1879.

Jongbloed, Ben W. A., Maassen, Peter A. M., & Neave, Guy R. (Eds.). (1999). *From the eye of the storm: Higher education's changing institution.* Dordrecht, The Netherlands: Kluwer Academic Publishers.

Jopp, Daniela, & Rott, Christoph. (2006). Adaptation in very old age: Exploring the role of resources, beliefs, and attitudes for centenarians' happiness. *Psychology and Aging, 21,* 266–280.

Joseph, Rhawn. (2000). Fetal brain behavior and cognitive development. *Developmental Review, 20,* 81–98.

Jung, C. G. (1933). *Modern man in search of a soul.* Oxford, England: Harcourt.

Juujärvi, Soile. (2005). Care and justice in real-life moral reasoning. *Journal of Adult Development, 12,* 199–210.

Juvonen, Jaana, Nishina, Adrienne, & Graham, Sandra. (2006). Ethnic diversity and perceptions of safety in urban middle schools. *Psychological Science, 17,* 393–400.

Kaduszkiewicz, Hanna, Zimmermann, Thomas, Beck-Bornholdt, Hans-Peter, & van den Bussche, Hendrik. (2005). Cholinesterase inhibitors for patients with Alzheimer's disease: Systematic review of randomised clinical trials. *British Medical Journal, 331,* 321–327.

Kaestle, Christine E., Halpern, Carolyn T., Miller, William C., & Ford, Carol A. (2005). Young age at first sexual intercourse and sexually transmitted infections in adolescents and young adults. *American Journal of Epidemiology, 161,* 774–780.

Kagan, Jerome. (1998). *Galen's prophecy: Temperament in human nature.* Boulder, CO: Westview Press.

Kagan, Jerome. (2002). *Surprise, uncertainty, and mental structures.* Cambridge, MA: Harvard University Press.

Kagan, Jerome, & Fox, Nathan A. (2006). Biology, culture, and temperamental biases. In William Damon & Richard M. Lerner (Series Eds.) & Nancy Eisenberg (Vol. Ed.), *Handbook of child psychology: Vol. 3. Social, emotional, and personality development* (6th ed., pp. 167–225). Hoboken, NJ: Wiley.

Kagan, Jerome, & Herschkowitz, Elinore Chapman. (2005). *Young mind in a growing brain.* Mahwah, NJ: Erlbaum.

Kagan, Jerome, & Snidman, Nancy C. (2004). *The long shadow of temperament.* Cambridge, MA: Belknap Press.

Kagitcibasi, Cigdem. (2003). Human development across cultures: A contextual-functional analysis and implications for interventions. In T. S. Saraswati (Ed.), *Cross-cultural perspectives in human development:*

Theory, research, and applications (pp. 166–191). New Delhi, India: Sage.

Kahana-Kalman, Ronit, & Walker-Andrews, Arlene S. (2001). The role of person familiarity in young infants' perception of emotional expressions. *Child Development, 72*, 352–369.

Kahn, Jonathan. (2007, August). Race in a bottle. *Scientific American, 297*, 40–45.

Kahneman, Daniel, Diener, Ed, & Schwarz, Norbert (Eds.). (2003). *Well-being: The foundations of hedonic psychology* (Paperback ed.). New York: Russell Sage Foundation.

Kaiser, Jocelyn. (2003, March 21). How much are human lives and health worth? *Science, 299*, 1836–1837.

Källén, Bengt. (2004). Neonate characteristics after maternal use of antidepressants in late pregnancy. *Archives of Pediatric and Adolescent Medicine, 158*, 312–316.

Kalmijn, Matthijs. (2003). Shared friendship networks and the life course: An analysis of survey data on married and cohabiting couples. *Social Networks, 25*, 231–249.

Kalmuss, Debra, Davidson, Andrew, Cohall, Alwyn, Laraque, Danielle, & Cassell, Carol. (2003). Preventing sexual risk behaviors and pregnancy among teenagers: Linking research and programs. *Perspectives on Sexual and Reproductive Health, 35*, 87–93.

Kamlin, C. Omar F., O'Donnell, Colm P. F., Davis, Peter G., & Morley, Colin J. (2006). Oxygen saturation in healthy infants immediately after birth. *Journal of Pediatrics, 148*, 585–589.

Kamp Dush, Claire M., Cohan, Catherine L., & Amato, Paul R. (2003). The relationship between cohabitation and marital quality and stability: change across cohorts? *Journal of Marriage & Family, 65*, 539–549.

Kanaya, Tomoe, Scullin, Matthew H., & Ceci, Stephen J. (2003). The Flynn effect and U.S. policies: The impact of rising IQ scores on American society via mental retardation diagnoses. *American Psychologist, 58*, 778–790.

Kane, Robert L., & Kane, Rosalie A. (2005). Ageism in healthcare and long-term care. *Generations, 29*, 49–54.

Kanner, Leo. (1943). Autistic disturbances of affective contact. *Nervous Child, 2*, 217–250.

Kaplan, Robert M. (2000). Two pathways to prevention. *American Psychologist, 55*, 382–396.

Karney, Benjamin R., & Bradbury, Thomas N. (2005). Contextual influences on marriage: Implications for policy and intervention. *Current Directions in Psychological Science, 14*, 171–174.

Karpov, Yuriy V., & Haywood, H. Carl. (1998). Two ways to elaborate Vygotsky's concept of mediation. *American Psychologist, 53*, 27–36.

Kastenbaum, Robert. (2003). Where is the self in elder self-narratives? *Generations, 27*(3), 000–000.

Kastenbaum, Robert. (2004). *On our way: The final passage through life and death*. Berkeley, CA: University of California Press.

Kastenbaum, Robert. (2006). *Death, society, and human experience* (9th ed.). Boston, MA: Allyn and Bacon.

Kato, Shingo, Hanabusa, Hideji, Kaneko, Satoru, Takakuwa, Koichi, Suzuki, Mina, Kuji, Naoaki, et al. (2006). Complete removal of HIV-1 RNA and proviral DNA from semen by the swim-up method: assisted reproduction technique using spermatozoa free from HIV-1. *Aids, 20*, 967–973.

Kaufman, James C., & Sternberg, Robert J. (2006). *The international handbook of creativity*. New York: Cambridge University Press.

Kaufman, Joan, & Charney, Dennis. (2001). Effects of early stress on brain structure and function: Implications for understanding the relationship between child maltreatment and depression. *Development & Psychopathology, 13*, 451–471.

Kaufman, Kenneth R., & Kaufman, Nathaniel D. (2006). And then the dog died. *Death Studies, 30*, 61–76.

Kaufman, Sharon R. (1986). *The ageless self: Sources of meaning in late life*. Madison, WI: University of Wisconsin Press.

Kazdin, Alan E. (2001). *Behavior modification in applied settings* (6th ed.). Belmont, CA: Wadsworth/Thomson Learning.

Keating, Daniel P. (2004). Cognitive and brain development. In Richard M. Lerner & Laurence D. Steinberg (Eds.), *Handbook of adolescent psychology* (2nd ed., pp. 45–84). Hoboken, NJ: Wiley.

Keating, Nancy L., Herrinton, Lisa J., Zaslavsky, Alan M., Liu, Liyan, & Ayanian, John Z. (2006). Variations in hospice use among cancer patients. *Journal of the National Cancer Institute, 98*, 1053–1059.

Kedar, Yarden, Casasola, Marianella, & Lust, Barbara. (2006). Getting there faster: 18- and 24-month-old infants' use of function words to determine reference. *Child Development, 77*, 325–338.

Keil, Frank C., & Lockhart, Kristi L. (1999). Explanatory understanding in conceptual development. In Ellin Kofsky Scholnick, Katherine Nelson, Susan A. Gelman, & Patricia H. Miller (Eds.), *Conceptual development: Piaget's legacy* (pp. 103–130). Mahwah, NJ: Erlbaum.

Keith, Jennie. (1990). Age in social and cultural context: Anthropological perspectives. In Robert H. Binstock & Linda K. George (Eds.), *Handbook of aging and the social sciences* (3rd ed., pp. 91–111). San Diego, CA: Academic Press.

Kelemen, Deborah, Callanan, Maureen A., Casler, Krista, & Perez-Granados, Deanne R. (2005). Why things happen: Teleological explanation in parent-child conversation. *Developmental Psychology, 41*, 251–264.

Keller, Heidi, Yovsi, Relindis, Borke, Joern, Kartner, Joscha, Jensen, Henning, & Papaligoura, Zaira. (2004). Developmental consequences of early parenting experiences: Self-recognition and self-regulation in three cultural communities. *Child Development, 75*, 1745–1760.

Keller, Meret A., & Goldberg, Wendy A. (2004). Co-sleeping: Help or hindrance for young children's independence? *Infant and Child Development, 13*, 369–388.

Kelley, Sue A., Brownell, Celia A., & Campbell, Susan B. (2000). Mastery motivation and self-evaluative affect in toddlers: Longitudinal relations with maternal behavior. *Child Development, 71*, 1061–1071.

Kelley, Susan J., & Whitley, Deborah M. (2003). Psychological distress and physical health problems in grandparents raising grandchildren: Development of an empirically-based intervention model. In Bert Hayslip Jr. & Julie Hicks Patrick (Eds.), *Working with custodial grandparents* (pp. 127–144). New York: Springer.

Kelly, John R. (1993). *Activity and aging: Staying involved in later life*. Newbury Park, CA: Sage.

Kelly, Michelle M. (2006). The medically complex premature infant in primary care. *Journal of Pediatric Health Care, 20*, 367–373.

Kemp, Candace L. (2007). Grandparent-grandchild ties: Reflections on continuity and change across three generations. *Journal of Family Issues, 28*, 855–881.

Kemp, Charles, & Bhungalia, Sonal. (2002). Culture and the end of life: A review of major world religions. *Journal of Hospice & Palliative Nursing, 4*, 235–242.

Kempe, Ruth S., & Kempe, C. Henry. (1978). *Child abuse*. Cambridge, MA: Harvard University Press.

Kemper, Susan, & Harden, Tamara. (1999). Experimentally disentangling what's beneficial about elderspeak from what's not. *Psychology & Aging, 14*, 656–670.

Kemper, Susan, Herman, Ruth E., & Lian, Cindy H. T. (2003). The costs of doing two things at once for young and older adults: Talking while walking, finger tapping, and ignoring speech or noise. *Psychology & Aging, 18*, 181–192.

Kendall-Tackett, Kathleen. (2002). The health effects of childhood abuse: Four pathways by which abuse can influence health. *Child Abuse & Neglect, 26*, 715–729.

Kendler, Howard H. (2002). Unified knowledge: Fantasy or reality? [Review of the book *Unity of knowledge: The convergence of natural and human science*]. *Contemporary Psychology: APA Review of Books, 47*, 501–503.

Kennedy, Colin R., McCann, Donna C., Campbell, Michael J., Law, Catherine M., Mullee, Mark, Petrou, Stavros, et al. (2006). Language ability after early detection of permanent childhood hearing impairment. *New England Journal of Medicine, 354*, 2131–2141.

Kenyon, Brenda L. (2001). Current research in children's conceptions of death: A critical review. *Omega: Journal of Death and Dying, 43*, 63–91.

Keogh, Barbara K. (2004). The importance of longitudinal research for early intervention practices. In Peggy D. McCardle & Vinita Chhabra (Eds.), *The voice of evidence in reading research* (pp. 81–102). Baltimore: Brookes.

Kessler, Ronald C., Berglund, Patricia, Demler, Olga, Jin, Robert, & Walters, Ellen E. (2005). Lifetime prevalence and age-of-onset distributions of DSM-IV disorders in the National Comorbidity Survey Replication. *Archives of General Psychiatry, 62*, 593–602.

Kessler, Ronald C., Galea, Sandro, Jones, Russell T., & Parker, Holly A. (2006). Mental illness and suicidality after Hurricane Katrina. *Bulletin of the World Health Organization, 84*, 930–939.

Khaleque, Abdul, & Rohner, Ronald P. (2002). Perceived parental acceptance-rejection and psychological adjustment: A meta-analysis of cross-cultural and intracultural studies. *Journal of Marriage & the Family, 64*, 54–64.

Khawaja, Marwan, Jurdi, Rozzet, & Kabakian-Khasholian, Tamar. (2004). Rising trends in cesarean section rates in Egypt. *Birth: Issues in Perinatal Care, 31*, 12–16.

Kiberstis, Paula A. (2005, January 21). A surfeit of suspects. *Science, 307*, 369.

Kidder, Jeffrey L. (2006). "It's the job that I love": Bike messengers and edgework. *Sociological Forum, 21*, 31–54.

Kiecolt-Glaser, Janice K., & Newton, Tamara L. (2001). Marriage and health: His and hers. *Psychological Bulletin, 127*, 472–503.

Kiefer, Heather Mason. (2004, May 11). *U.S. schools: Whole lotta cheatin' going on*. Retrieved January 4, 2007, from the World Wide Web: http://www.galluppoll.com/content/?ci=11644&pg=1

Killen, Melanie. (2007). Children's social and moral reasoning about exclusion. *Current Directions in Psychological Science, 16*, 32–36.

Killen, Melanie, Margie, Nancy Geyelin, & Sinno, Stefanie. (2006). Morality in the context of intergroup relationships. In Melanie Killen & Judith G. Smetana (Eds.), *Handbook of moral development* (pp. 155–183). Mahwah: Erlbaum.

Killgore, William D. S., Vo, Alexander H., Castro, Carl A., & Hoge, Charles W. (2006). Assessing risk propensity in American soldiers: Preliminary reliability and validity of the Evaluation of Risks (EVAR) scale-English version. *Military Medicine, 171*, 233–239.

Kim, Hyoun K., Capaldi, Deborah M., & Crosby, Lynn. (2007). Generalizability of Gottman and colleagues' affective process models Of couples' relationship outcomes. *Journal of Marriage and Family, 69*(1), 55–72.

Kim, Jungmeen, & Cicchetti, Dante. (2006). Longitudinal trajectories of self-system processes and depressive symptoms among maltreated and nonmaltreated children. *Child Development, 77*, 624–639.

Kim-Cohen, Julia, Moffitt, Terrie E., Caspi, Avshalom, & Taylor, Alan. (2004). Genetic and environmental processes in young children's resilience and vulnerability to socioeconomic deprivation. *Child Development, 75*, 651–668.

Kimmel, Michael S. (2004). *The gendered society* (2nd ed.). New York: Oxford University Press.

Kincheloe, Joe L. (2004). *Multiple intelligences reconsidered*. New York: Peter Lang.

Kinder, Donald R. (2006, June 30). Politics and the life cycle. *Science, 312*, 1905–1908.

King, Alan R., & Terrance, Cheryl. (2006). Relationships between personality disorder attributes and friendship qualities among college students. *Journal of Social and Personal Relationships, 23*, 5–20.

King, Gary, & Williams, David R. (1995). Race and health: A multi-dimensional approach to African American health. In Benjamin C. Amick III, Sol Levine, Alvin R. Tarlov, & Diana Chapman Walsh (Eds.), *Society and health* (pp. 80–92). New York: Oxford University Press.

King, Jacqueline E. (2004). *Missed opportunities: Students who do not apply for financial aid*. Washington, DC: American Council on Education.

King, Jacqueline E. (2005). Academic success and financial decisions: Helping students make crucial choices. In Robert S. Feldman (Ed.), *Improving the first year of college: Research and practice* (pp. 3–25). Mahwah, NJ: Erlbaum.

King, Pamela Ebstyne, & Furrow, James L. (2004). Religion as a resource for positive youth development: Religion, social capital, and moral outcomes. *Developmental Psychology, 40*, 703–713.

King, Patricia M., & Kitchener, Karen S. (1994). *Developing reflective judgment: Understanding and promoting intellectual growth and critical thinking in adolescents and adults*. San Francisco: Jossey-Bass.

King, Valarie. (2003). The legacy of a grandparent's divorce: Consequences for ties between grandparents and grandchildren. *Journal of Marriage and Family, 65*, 170–183.

King, Valarie, Harris, Kathleen Mullan, & Heard, Holly E. (2004). Racial and ethnic diversity in nonresident father involvement. *Journal of Marriage & Family, 66*, 1–21.

King, Valarie, & Scott, Mindy E. (2005). A comparison of cohabiting relationships among older and younger adults. *Journal of Marriage and Family, 67*(2), 271–285.

Kinsella, Kevin G. (2005). Future longevity-demographic concerns and consequences. *Journal of the American Geriatrics Society, 53*(Suppl. l9), S299–S303.

Kirby, Douglas. (2001). *Emerging answers: Research findings on programs to reduce teen pregnancy*. Washington, DC: The National Campaign To Prevent Teen Pregnancy.

Kirby, Douglas. (2002). Effective approaches to reducing adolescent unprotected sex, pregnancy, and childbearing. *Journal of Sex Research, 39*, 51–57.

Kirkbride, James B., Fearon, Paul, Morgan, Craig, Dazzan, Paola, Morgan, Kevin, Tarrant, Jane, et al. (2006). Heterogeneity in incidence rates of schizophrenia and other psychotic syndromes: Findings from the 3–center ÆSOP study. *Archives of General Psychiatry, 63*, 250–258.

Kirkwood, Thomas B. L. (2003). Age differences in evolutionary selection benefits. In Ursula M. Staudinger & Ulman Lindenberger (Eds.), *Understanding human development: Dialogues with lifespan psychology* (pp. 45–57). Dordrecht, The Netherlands: Kluwer.

Kitzinger, Sheila. (2001). *Rediscovering birth*. New York: Simon & Schuster.

Klaczynski, Paul A. (2001). Analytic and heuristic processing influences on adolescent reasoning and decision-making. *Child Development, 72*, 844–861.

Klaczynski, Paul A. (2005). Metacognition and cognitive variability: A dual-process model of decision making and its development. In Janis E. Jacobs & Paul A. Klaczynski (Eds.), *The development of judgment and decision making in children and adolescents* (pp. 39–76). Mahwah, NJ: Erlbaum.

Klaczynski, Paul A., & Cottrell, Jennifer M. (2004). A dual-process approach to cognitive development: The case of children's understanding of sunk cost decisions. *Thinking & Reasoning, 10*, 147–174.

Klaczynski, Paul A., & Robinson, Billi. (2000). Personal theories, intellectual ability, and epistemological beliefs: Adult age differences in everyday reasoning biases. *Psychology and Aging, 15*, 400–416.

Klatz, Ronald M. (1997). Introduction. In Ronald M. Klatz & Robert Goldman (Eds.), *Anti-aging medical therapeutics* (Vol. 00, pp. 000–000). Marina del Rey, CA: Health Quest.

Klaus, Marshall H., & Kennell, John H. (1976). *Maternal-infant bonding: The impact of early separation or loss on family development*. St. Louis, MO: Mosby.

Klaus, Patsy. (2005). *Crimes against persons age 65 or older, 1993–2002* (NCJ 206154). Washington, DC: Bureau of Justice Statistics.

Kleiber, Douglas A. (1999). *Leisure experience and human development: A dialectical interpretation*. New York: Basic Books.

Klug, William S., & Cummings, Michael R. (2000). *Concepts of genetics* (6th ed.). Upper Saddle River, NJ: Prentice Hall.

Knudsen, Eric I. (1999). Mechanisms of experience-dependent plasticity in the auditory localization pathway of the barn owl. *Journal of Comparative Physiology A: Sensory, Neural, and Behavioral Physiology, 185*, 305–321.

Koch, Tom. (2000). *Age speaks for itself: Silent voices of the elderly*. Westport, CT: Praeger.

Kochanska, Grazyna, Coy, Katherine C., & Murray, Kathleen T. (2001). The development of self-regulation in the first four years of life. *Child Development, 72*, 1091–1111.

Kogan, Shari L., Blanchette, Patricia L., & Masaki, Kamal. (2000). Talking to patients about death and dying: Improving communication across cultures. In Kathryn Braun, James H. Pietsch, & Patricia L. Blanchette (Eds.), *Cultural issues in end-of-life decision making* (pp. 305–325). Thousand Oaks, CA: Sage.

Kohlberg, Lawrence. (1963). The development of children's orientations toward a moral order: I. Sequence in the development of moral thought. *Vita Humana, 6*(1–2), 11–33.

Kohlberg, Lawrence, Levine, Charles, & Hewer, Alexandra. (1983). *Moral stages: A current formulation and a response to critics*. New York: Karger.

Kohler, Hans-Peter. (2005). Attitudes and low fertility: Reflections based on danish twin data. In Alane Booth & Ann C. Crouter (Eds.), *The new population problem: Why families in developed countries are shrinking and what it means* (pp. 99–113). Mahwah, NJ: Erlbaum.

Kohler, Julie K., Grotevant, Harold D., & McRoy, Ruth G. (2002). Adopted adolescents' preoccupation with adoption: The impact on adoptive family relationships. *Journal of Marriage & Family, 64*, 93–104.

Kohn, Alfie. (2006). *The homework myth*. Cambridge, MA: Da Capo Lifelong Books.

Koivisto, Maila. (2004). A follow-up survey of anti-bullying interventions in the comprehensive schools of Kempele in 1990–98. In Peter K. Smith, Debra Pepler, & Ken Rigby (Eds.), *Bullying in schools: How successful can interventions be?* (pp. 235–249). New York: Cambridge University Press.

Kolb, Bryan, & Whishaw, Ian Q. (2003). *Fundamentals of human neuropsychology* (5th ed.). New York: Worth.

Komives, Susan R., & Nuss, Elizabeth M. (2005). Life after college. In Thomas E. Miller, Barbara E. Bender, John H. Schuh, & Associates (Eds.), *Promoting reasonable expectations: Aligning student and institutional views of the college experience* (pp. 140–174). San Francisco: Jossey-Bass.

Koolhaas, Jaap M., de Boer, Sietse F., & Buwalda, Bauke. (2006). Stress and adaptation. *Current Directions in Psychological Science, 15*, 109–112.

Koops, Willem. (2003). Imaging childhood. In Willem Koops & Michael Zuckerman (Eds.), *Beyond the century of the child: Cultural history and developmental psychology* (pp. 1–18). Philadelphia: University of Pennsylvania Press.

Koropeckyj-Cox, Tanya. (2002). Beyond parental status: Psychological well-being in middle and old age. *Journal of Marriage & Family, 64*, 957–971.

Kotre, John N. (1995). *White gloves: How we create ourselves through memory*. New York: Free Press.

Kovas, Yulia, Hayiou-Thomas, Marianna E., Oliver, Bonamy, Dale, Philip S., Bishop, Dorothy V. M., & Plomin, Robert. (2005). Genetic influences in different aspects of language development: The etiology of language skills in 4.5-year-old twins. *Child Development, 76*, 632–651.

Kramer, Arthur F., Fabiani, Monica, & Colcombe, Stanley J. (2006). Contributions of cognitive neuroscience to the understanding of behavior and aging. In James E. Birren & K. Warner Schaie (Eds.), *Handbook of the psychology of aging* (6th ed., pp. 57–83). Amsterdam: Elsevier.

Krampe, Ralf Th., & Charness, Neil. (2006). Aging and expertise. In K. Anders Ericsson, Neil Charness, Paul J. Feltovich, & Robert R. Hoffman (Eds.), *The Cambridge handbook of expertise and expert performance* (pp. 723–742). New York: Cambridge University Press.

Krause, Neal. (2006). Social relationships in late life. In Robert H. Binstock & Linda K. George (Eds.), *Handbook of aging and the social sciences* (6th ed., pp. 181–200). Amsterdam: Elsevier.

Krieger, Nancy. (2002). Is breast cancer a disease of affluence, poverty, or both? The case of African American women. *American Journal of Public Health, 92*, 611–613.

Krieger, Nancy. (2003). Does racism harm health? Did child abuse exist before 1962? On explicit questions, critical science, and current controversies: An ecosocial perspective. *American Journal of Public Health, 93,* 194–199.

Krieger, Nancy, Chen, Jarvis T., Waterman, Pamela D., Rehkopf, David H., & Subramanian, S. V. (2005). Painting a truer picture of U.S. socioeconomic and racial/ethnic health inequalities: The Public Health Disparities Geocoding Project. *American Journal of Public Health, 95,* 312–323.

Kroger, Jane. (2007). *Identity development: Adolescence through adulthood* (2nd ed.). Thousand Oaks, CA: Sage.

Kroger, Rolf O. (2006). The development of a postmodern self: A computer-assisted comparative analysis of personal documents. *PsycCRITIQUES,* No Pagination Specified.

Krueger, Robert F., & Markon, Kristian E. (2006). Reinterpreting comorbidity: A model-based approach to understanding and classifying psychopathology. *Annual Review of Clinical Psychology, 2,* 111–133.

Kübler-Ross, Elisabeth. (1969). *On death and dying.* New York: Macmillan.

Kübler-Ross, Elisabeth. (1975). *Death: The final stage of growth.* Englewood Cliffs, NJ: Prentice-Hall.

Kuh, George D., Gonyea, Robert M., & Williams, Julie M. (2005). What students expect from college and what they get. In Thomas E. Miller, Barbara E. Bender, John H. Schuh, & Associates (Eds.), *Promoting reasonable expectations: Aligning student and institutional views of the college experience* (pp. 34–64). San Francisco: Jossey-Bass.

Kuhn, Deanna. (2006). Do cognitive changes accompany developments in the adolescent brain? *Perspectives on Psychological Science, 1,* 59–67.

Kuhn, Deanna, & Franklin, Sam. (2006). The second decade: What develops (and how). In William Damon & Richard M. Lerner (Series Eds.) & Nancy Eisenberg (Vol. Ed.), *Handbook of child psychology: Vol. 2. Cognition, perception, and language* (6th ed., pp. 953–993). Hoboken, NJ: Wiley.

Kuller, Jeffrey A., Strauss, Robert A., & Cefalo, Robert C. (2001). Preconceptional and prenatal care. In Frank W. Ling & W. Patrick Duff (Eds.), *Obstetrics and gynecology: Principles for practice* (pp. 25–54). New York: McGraw-Hill.

Kumar, Rajesh, Jha, Prabhat, Arora, Paul, Mony, Prem, Bhatia, Prakash, Millson, Peggy, et al. (2006). Trends in HIV-1 in young adults in South India from 2000 to 2004: A prevalence study. *Lancet, 367,* 1164–1172.

Kumpfer, Karol L., & Alvarado, Rose. (2003). Family-strengthening approaches for the prevention of youth problem behaviors. *American Psychologist, 58,* 457–465.

Kupersmidt, Janis B., Coie, John D., & Howell, James C. (2004). Resilience in children exposed to negative peer influences. In Kenneth I. Maton, Cynthia J. Schellenbach, Bonnie J. Leadbeater, & Andrea L. Solarz (Eds.), *Investing in children, youth, families, and communities: Strengths-based research and policy* (pp. 251–268). Washington, DC: American Psychological Association.

Kurdek, Lawrence A. (1992). Relationship stability and relationship satisfaction in cohabiting gay and lesbian couples: A prospective longitudinal test of the contextual and interdependence models. *Journal of Social & Personal Relationships, 9,* 125–142.

Kurdek, Lawrence A. (2006). Differences between partners from heterosexual, gay, and lesbian cohabiting couples. *Journal of Marriage and Family, 68,* 509–528.

Kwong See, Sheree T., & Ryan, Ellen Bouchard. (1999). Intergenerational communication: The survey interview as a social exchange. In Norbert Schwarz, Denise C. Park, Bärbel Knaüper, & Seymour Sudman (Eds.), *Cognition, aging, and self-reports* (pp. 245–262). Hove, England: Psychology Press.

Labouvie-Vief, Gisela. (1990). Wisdom as integrated thought: Historical and developmental perspectives. In Robert J. Sternberg (Ed.), *Wisdom: Its nature, origins, and development* (pp. 52–83). Cambridge, England: Cambridge University Press.

Labouvie-Vief, Gisela. (2006). Emerging structures of adult thought. In Jeffrey Jensen Arnett & Jennifer Lynn Tanner (Eds.), *Emerging adults in America: Coming of age in the 21st century* (pp. 59–84). Washington, DC: American Psychological Association.

Lach, Helen W. (2002–2003). Fear of falling: An emerging public health problem. *Generations, 26*(4), 33–37.

Lachman, Margie E., & Bertrand, Rosanna M. (2001). Personality and the self in midlife. In Margie E. Lachman (Ed.), *Handbook of midlife development* (pp. 279–309). New York: Wiley.

Lacourse, Eric, Nagin, Daniel, Tremblay, Richard E., Vitaro, Frank, & Claes, Michel. (2003). Developmental trajectories of boys' delinquent group membership and facilitation of violent behaviors during adolescence. *Development & Psychopathology, 15,* 183–197.

Ladd, Gary W. (1999). Peer relationships and social competence during early and middle childhood. *Annual Review of Psychology, 50,* 333–359.

Ladd, Gary W. (2005). *Children's peer relations and social competence: A century of progress.* New Haven, CT: Yale University Press.

Ladd, Gary W., & Pettit, Gregory S. (2002). Parenting and the development of children's peer relationships. In Marc H. Bornstein (Ed.), *Handbook of parenting: Vol. 5. Practical issues in parenting* (2nd ed., pp. 269–309). Mahwah, NJ: Erlbaum.

Lagattuta, Kristin Hansen. (2005). When you shouldn't do what you want to do: Young children's understanding of desires, rules, and emotions. *Child Development, 76,* 713–733.

Lahey, Benjamin B., Moffitt, Terrie E., & Caspi, Avshalom (Eds.). (2003). *Causes of conduct disorder and juvenile delinquency.* New York: Guilford Press.

Lalande, Kathleen M., & Bonanno, George A. (2006). Culture and continuing bonds: A prospective comparison of bereavement in the United States and the People's Republic of China. *Death Studies, 30,* 303–324.

Lamb, Michael E. (1982). Maternal employment and child development: A review. In Michael E. Lamb (Ed.), *Nontraditional families: Parenting and child development* (pp. 45–69). Hillsdale, NJ: Erlbaum.

Lamb, Michael E. (1998). Nonparental child care: Context, quality, correlates, and consequences. In William Damon (Series Ed.) & Irving E. Sigel & K. Ann Renninger (Vol. Eds.), *Handbook of child psychology: Vol. 4. Child psychology in practice* (5th ed., pp. 73–133). New York: Wiley.

Lamb, Michael E. (2000). The history of research on father involvement: An overview. In H. Elizabeth Peters, Gary W. Peterson, Suzanne K. Steinmetz, & Randal D. Day (Eds.), *Fatherhood: Research, interventions, and policies* (pp. 23–42). New York: Haworth Press.

Lamb, Michael E., & Lewis, Charlie (2005). The role of parent-child relationships in child development. In Marc H. Bornstein & Michael E. Lamb (Eds.), *Developmental science: An advanced textbook* (5th ed., pp. 429–468). Mahwah, NJ: Erlbaum.

Lamy, Peter P. (1994). Drug-nutrient interactions in the aged. In Ronald R. Watson (Ed.), *Handbook of nutrition in the aged* (2nd ed., pp. 165–200). Boca Raton, FL: CRC Press.

Lan, Pei-Chia. (2002). Subcontracting filial piety: Elder care in ethnic Chinese immigrant families in California. *Journal of Family Issues, 23,* 812–835.

Landry, David J., Darroch, Jacqueline E., Singh, Susheela, & Higgins, Jenny. (2003). Factors associated with the content of sex education in U.S. public secondary schools. *Perspectives on Sexual and Reproductive Health, 35,* 261–269.

Lane, Scott D., Cherek, Don R., Pietras, Cynthia J., & Steinberg, Joel L. (2005). Performance of heavy marijuana-smoking adolescents on a laboratory measure of motivation. *Addictive Behaviors, 30,* 815–828.

Lansford, Jennifer E., Ceballo, Rosario, Abbey, Antonia, & Stewart, Abigail J. (2001). Does family structure matter? A comparison of adoptive, two-parent biological, single-mother, stepfather, and stepmother households. *Journal of Marriage & the Family, 63,* 840–851.

LaPlante, Eve. (2004). *American Jezebel: The uncommon life of Anne Hutchinson, the woman who defied the Puritans.* San Francisco: HarperSanFrancisco.

Lapsley, Daniel K. (1993). Toward an integrated theory of adolescent ego development: The "new look" at adolescent egocentrism. *American Journal of Orthopsychiatry, 63,* 562–571.

Larcombe, Duncan. (2005). Content matters: Sometimes even more than we think. *American Educator, 29,* 42–43.

Larson, Nicole I., Neumark-Sztainer, Dianne, Hannan, Peter J., & Story, Mary. (2007). Trends in adolescent fruit and vegetable consumption, 1999–2004: Project EAT. *American Journal of Preventive Medicine, 32,* 147–150.

Larson, Reed W. (2000). Toward a psychology of positive youth development. *American Psychologist, 55,* 170–183.

Larson, Reed W., & Wilson, Suzanne. (2004). Adolescence across place and time: Globalization and the changing pathways to adulthood. In Richard M. Lerner & Laurence D. Steinberg (Eds.), *Handbook of adolescent psychology* (2nd ed., pp. 299–330). Hoboken, NJ: Wiley.

Lattanzi-Licht, Marcia E., & Doka, Kenneth J. (Eds.). (2003). *Living with grief: Coping with public tragedy.* New York: Brunner-Routledge.

Laumann, Edward O., Gagnon, John H., Michael, Robert T., & Michaels, Stuart. (1994). *The social organization of sexuality: Sexual practices in the United States.* Chicago: University of Chicago Press.

Laumann, Edward O., & Michael, Robert T. (2000). *Sex, love, and health in America: Private choices and public policies.* Chicago: University of Chicago Press.

Laumann, Edward O., & Michael, Robert T. (2001). Setting the scene. In Edward O. Laumann & Robert T. Michael (Eds.), *Sex, love, and health in America: Private choices and public policies* (pp. 1–38). Chicago: University of Chicago Press.

Laurendeau, Jason, & Van Brunschot, Erin E. Gibbs (2006). Policing the edge: Risk and social control in skydiving. *Deviant Behavior, 27,* 173–201.

Laurie, Graeme. (2005). Physician assisted suicide in Europe: Some lessons and trends. *European Journal of Health Law, 12,* 5–10.

Laursen, Brett, Coy, Katherine C., & Collins, W. Andrew. (1998). Reconsidering changes in parent-child conflict across adolescence: A meta-analysis. *Child Development, 69,* 817–832.

Laursen, Brett, & Mooney, Karen S. (2007). Individual differences in adolescent dating and adjustment. In Rutger C. M. E. Engels, Margaret Kerr, & Håkan Stattin (Eds.), *Friends, lovers, and groups: Key relationships in adolescence* (pp. 81–92). Hoboken, NJ: Wiley.

Lavelli, Manuela, & Fogel, Alan. (2005). Developmental changes in the relationship between the infant's attention and emotion during early face-to-face communication: The 2-month transition. *Developmental Psychology, 41,* 265–280.

Lawton, M. Powell, Winter, Laraine, Kleban, Morton H., & Ruckdeschel, Katy. (1999). Affect and quality of life: Objective and subjective. *Journal of Aging & Health, 11,* 169–198.

Layden, Tim. (2004, November 15). Get out and play! *Sports Illustrated, 101,* 80–93.

Lazar, Mitchell A. (2005, January 21). How obesity causes diabetes: Not a tall tale. *Science, 307,* 373–375.

Leach, Penelope. (1997). *Your baby & child: From birth to age five* (3rd ed.). New York: Knopf.

Leaper, Campbell. (2002). Parenting girls and boys. In Marc H. Bornstein (Ed.), *Handbook of parenting: Vol. 1. Children and parenting* (2nd ed., pp. 189–225). Mahwah, NJ: Erlbaum.

Leaper, Campbell, & Smith, Tara E. (2004). A meta-analytic review of gender variations in children's language use: Talkativeness, affiliative speech, and assertive speech. *Developmental Psychology, 40,* 993–1027.

LeBlanc, Manon Mireille, & Barling, Julian. (2004). Workplace aggression. *Current Directions in Psychological Science, 13,* 9–12.

Lee, Christina, & Gramotnev, Helen. (2007). Life transitions and mental health in a national cohort of young Australian women. *Developmental Psychology, 43,* 877–888.

Lee, Crystal Man Ying, Martiniuk, Alexandra Lynda Conboy, Woodward, Mark, Feigin, Valery, Gu, Dongfeng, Jamrozik, Konrad, et al. (2007). The burden of overweight and obesity in the Asia-Pacific region. *Obesity Reviews, 8,* 191–196.

Lee, Eunju, Spitze, Glenna, & Logan, John R. (2003). Social support to parents-in-law: The interplay of gender and kin hierarchies. *Journal of Marriage and Family, 65,* 396–403.

Lee, Keun. (2000). Crying patterns of Korean infants in institutions. *Child: Care, Health and Development, 26,* 217–228.

Lefkowitz, Eva S., & Gillen, Meghan M. (2006). "Sex is just a normal part of life": Sexuality in emerging adulthood. In Jeffrey Jensen Arnett & Jennifer Lynn Tanner (Eds.), *Emerging adults in America: Coming of age in the 21st century* (pp. 235–255). Washington, DC: American Psychological Association.

Lehn, Hanne, Derks, Eske M., Hudziak, James J., Heutink, Peter, van Beijsterveldt, Toos C. E. M., & Boomsma, Dorret I. (2007). Attention problems and attention-deficit/hyperactivity disorder in discordant and concordant monozygotic twins: Evidence of environmental mediators. *Journal of the American Academy of Child and Adolescent Psychiatry, 46,* 83–91.

Lei, Joy L. (2003). (Un)necessary toughness?: Those "loud black girls" and those "quiet Asian boys". *Anthropology & Education Quarterly, 34,* 158–181.

Leipzig, Rosanne M. (2003). Evidence-based medicine and geriatrics. In Christine K. Cassel, Rosanne Leipzig, Harvey Jay Cohen, Eric B. Larson, & Diane E. Meier (Eds.), *Geriatric medicine: An evidence-based approach* (4th ed., pp. 3–14). New York: Springer.

Lenneberg, Eric H. (1967). *Biological foundations of language*. New York: Wiley.

Lenton, Alison, & Webber, Laura. (2006). Cross-sex friendships: Who has more? *Sex Roles, 54*, 809–820.

Leon, David A., Saburova, Ludmila, Tomkins, Susannah, Andreev, Evgueni M., Kiryanov, Nikolay, McKee, Martin, et al. (2007, June 16). Hazardous alcohol drinking and premature mortality in Russia: A population based case-control study. *Lancet, 369*, 2001–2009.

Leonard, Christiana M. (2003). Neural substrate of speech and language development. In Michelle De Haan & Mark H. Johnson (Eds.), *The cognitive neuroscience of development* (pp. 127–156). New York: Psychology Press.

Leone, Tiziana, Matthews, Zoë, & Dalla Zuanna, Gianpiero. (2003). Impact and determinants of sex preference in Nepal. *International Family Planning Perspectives, 29*, 69–75.

Lepage, Jean-Fran ois, & Théoret, Hugo. (2006). EEG evidence for the presence of an action observation-execution matching system in children. *European Journal of Neuroscience, 23*, 2505–2510.

Lepper, Mark R., Greene, David, & Nisbett, Richard E. (1973). Undermining children's intrinsic interest with extrinsic reward: A test of the "overjustification" hypothesis. *Journal of Personality & Social Psychology, 28*, 129–137.

Lerner, Richard M., Theokas, Christina, & Bobek, Deborah L. (2005). Concepts and theories of human development: Historical and contemporary dimensions. In Marc H. Bornstein & Michael E. Lamb (Eds.), *Developmental science: An advanced textbook* (5th ed., pp. 3–43). Mahwah, NJ: Erlbaum.

Leslie, Alan M., Knobe, Joshua, & Cohen, Adam. (2006). Acting intentionally and the side-effect effect: Theory of mind and moral judgment. *Psychological Science, 17*, 421–427.

Levesque, Roger J. R. (2002). *Not by faith alone: Religion, law, and adolescence*. New York: New York University Press.

Levine, Brian, Svoboda, Eva, Hay, Janine F., Winocur, Gordon, & Moscovitch, Morris. (2002). Aging and autobiographical memory: Dissociating episodic from semantic retrieval. *Psychology & Aging, 17*, 677–689.

Levine, James A., Lanningham-Foster, Lorraine M., McCrady, Shelly K., Krizan, Alisa C., Olson, Leslie R., Kane, Paul H., et al. (2005, January 28). Interindividual variation in posture allocation: Possible role in human obesity. *Science, 307*, 584–586.

Levinson, Daniel J. (1978). *The seasons of a man's life*. New York: Knopf.

Levy, Becca. (1996). Improving memory in old age through implicit self-stereotyping. *Journal of Personality & Social Psychology, 71*, 1092–1107.

Levy, Becca R. (2003). Mind matters: Cognitive and physical effects of aging self-stereotypes. *Journals of Gerontology: Series B: Psychological Sciences and Social Sciences, 58*, P203–P211.

Levy, Becca, & Langer, Ellen. (1994). Aging free from negative stereotypes: Successful memory in China among the American deaf. *Journal of Personality & Social Psychology, 66*, 989–997.

Lewin, Kurt. (1943). Psychology and the process of group living. *Journal of Social Psychology, 17*, 113–131.

Lewis, Hunter. (2000). *A question of values: Six ways we make personal choices that shape our lives* (Rev. and updated ed.). Crozet, VA: Axios Press.

Lewis, Lawrence B., Antone, Carol, & Johnson, Jacqueline S. (1999). Effects of prosodic stress and serial position on syllable omission in first words. *Developmental Psychology, 35*, 45–59.

Lewis, Michael. (1997). *Altering fate: Why the past does not predict the future*. New York: Guilford Press.

Lewis, Michael, & Brooks, Jeanne. (1978). Self-knowledge and emotional development. In Michael Lewis & L. A. Rosenblum (Eds.), *Genesis of behavior: Vol. 1. The development of affect* (pp. 205–226). New York: Plenum Press.

Lewis, Michael, & Ramsay, Douglas. (2005). Infant emotional and cortisol responses to goal blockage. *Child Development, 76*, 518–530.

Lewis, Pamela, Abbeduto, Leonard, Murphy, Melissa, Richmond, Erica, Giles, Nancy, Bruno, Loredana, et al. (2006). Psychological well-being of mothers of youth with fragile X syndrome: Syndrome specificity and within-syndrome variability. *Journal of Intellectual Disability Research, 50*, 894–904.

Lewit, Eugene M., & Kerrebrock, Nancy. (1998). Child indicators: Dental health. *The Future of Children: Protecting Children from Abuse and Neglect, 8*(1), 133–142.

Li, De-Kun, Willinger, Marian, Petitti, Diana B., Odouli, Roxana, Liu, Liyan, & Hoffman, Howard J. (2006). Use of a dummy (pacifier) during sleep and risk of sudden infant death syndrome (SIDS): Population based case-control study. *British Medical Journal, 332*, 18–21.

Li, Qing. (2007). New bottle but old wine: A research of cyberbullying in schools. *Computers in Human Behavior, 23*, 1777–1791.

Li, Xiaoming, Stanton, Bonita, & Feigelman, Susan. (2000). Impact of perceived parental monitoring on adolescent risk behavior over 4 years. *Journal of Adolescent Health, 27*, 49–56.

Li, Zhaoping, Maglione, Margaret, Tu, Wenli, Mojica, Walter, Arterburn, David, Shugarman, Lisa R., et al. (2005). Meta-analysis: Pharmacologic treatment of obesity. *Annals of Internal Medicine, 142*, 532–546.

Lieberman, Debra. (2006). Mate selection: Adaptive problems and evolved cognitive programs. In Patricia Noller & Judith A. Feeney (Eds.), *Close relationships: Functions, forms and processes* (pp. 245–266). Hove, England: Psychology Press/Taylor & Francis.

Lieu, Tracy A., Ray, G. Thomas, Black, Steven B., Butler, Jay C., Klein, Jerome O., Breiman, Robert F., et al. (2000). Projected cost-effectiveness of pneumococcal conjugate vaccination of healthy infants and young children. *Journal of the American Medical Association, 283*, 1460–1468.

Lightfoot, Cynthia. (1997). *The culture of adolescent risk-taking*. New York: Guilford Press.

Lillard, Angeline, & Else-Quest, Nicole. (2006, September 29). Evaluating Montessori education. *Science, 313*, 1893–1894.

Lillard, Angeline Stoll. (2005). *Montessori: The science behind the genius*. New York: Oxford University Press.

Lin, I. Fen, Goldman, Noreen, Weinstein, Maxine, Lin, Yu-Hsuan, Gorrindo, Tristan, & Seeman, Teresa. (2003). Gender differences in adult children's support of their parents in Taiwan. *Journal of Marriage and Family, 65*, 184–200.

Lindauer, Martin S. (1998). Artists, art, and arts activities: What do they tell us about aging? In Carolyn E. Adams-Price (Ed.), *Creativity and successful aging: Theoretical and empirical approaches* (pp. 237–250). New York: Springer.

Lindauer, Martin S. (2003). *Aging, creativity, and art: A positive perspective on late-life development*. New York: Plenum.

Lindenberger, Ulman. (2001). Lifespan theories of cognitive development. In Neil J. Smelser & Paul B. Baltes (Eds.), *International encyclopedia of the social & behavioral sciences* (pp. 8848–8854). Oxford, England: Elsevier.

Lindenberger, Ulman, & Baltes, Paul B. (1997). Intellectual functioning in old and very old age: Cross-sectional results from the Berlin Aging Study. *Psychology & Aging, 12*, 410–432.

Lindenberger, Ulman, & von Oertzen, Timo. (2006). Variability in cognitive aging: From taxonomy to theory. In Ellen Bialystok & Fergus I. M. Craik (Eds.), *Lifespan cognition: Mechanisms of change* (pp. 297–314). New York: Oxford University Press.

Lindsay, Geoff. (2000). Researching children's perspectives: Ethical issues. In Ann Lewis & Geoff Lindsay (Eds.), *Researching children's perspectives* (pp. 3–20). Philadelphia: Open University Press.

Lippa, Richard A. (2002). *Gender, nature, and nurture*. Mahwah, NJ: Erlbaum.

Lissau, Inge, Overpeck, Mary D., Ruan, W. June, Due, Pernille, Holstein, Bjorn E., & Hediger, Mary L. (2004). Body mass index and overweight in adolescents in 13 European countries, Israel, and the United States. *Archives of Pediatrics & Adolescent Medicine, 158*, 27–33.

Little, Emma. (2005). Secondary school teachers' perceptions of students' problem behaviours. *Educational Psychology, 25*, 369–377.

Little, Peter (Ed.). (2002). *Genetic destinies*. Oxford, England: Oxford University Press.

Liu, Cong, Spector, Paul E., & Shi, Lin. (2007). Cross-national job stress: A quantitative and qualitative study. *Journal of Organizational Behavior, 28*, 209–239.

Liu, Hui-li, Wang, Hong-Chung, & Yang, Ming-Jen. (2006). Factors associated with an unusual increase in the elderly suicide rate in Taiwan. *International Journal of Geriatric Psychiatry, 21*, 1219–1221.

Liu, Ping. (2006). Community-based Chinese schools in Southern California: A survey of teachers. *Language, Culture and Curriculum, 19*, 237–246.

Liu, Peter Y., Swerdloff, Ronald S., Christenson, Peter D., Handelsman, David J., Wang, Christina, & Hormonal Male Contraception Summit Group. (2006). Rate, extent, and modifiers of spermatogenic recovery after hormonal male contraception: an integrated analysis. *Lancet, 367*, 1412–1420.

Lloyd-Sherlock, Peter (Ed.). (2004). *Living longer: Ageing, development and social protection*. London: Zed Books.

Lockhart, Kristi L., Chang, Bernard, & Story, Tyler. (2002). Young children's beliefs about the stability of traits: Protective optimism? *Child Development, 73*, 1408–1430.

Lockley, Steven W., Cronin, John W., Evans, Erin E., Cade, Brian E., Lee, Clark J., Landrigan, Christopher P., et al. (2004). Effect of reducing interns' weekly work hours on sleep and attentional failures. *New England Journal of Medicine, 351*, 1829–1837.

Loeb, Susanna, Fuller, Bruce, Kagan, Sharon Lynn, & Carrol, Bidemi. (2004). Child care in poor communities: Early learning effects of type, quality, and stability. *Child Development, 75*, 47–65.

Loeber, Rolf, Lacourse, Eric, & Homish, D. Lynn. (2005). Homicide, violence, and developmental trajectories. In Richard Ernest Tremblay, Willard W. Hartup, & John Archer (Eds.), *Developmental origins of aggression* (pp. 202–222). New York: Guilford Press.

Loewy, Erich H. (2004). Euthanasia, physician assisted suicide and other methods of helping along death. *Health Care Analysis, 12*, 181–193.

Loland, Sigmund. (2002). *Fair play in sport: A moral norm system*. London: Routledge.

Lombardi, Joan, & Cubbage, Amy Stephens. (2004). Head Start in the 1990s: Striving for quality through a decade of improvement. In Edward Zigler & Sally J. Styfco (Eds.), *The Head Start debates* (pp. 283–295). Baltimore: Brookes.

Long, Lynellyn, & Oxfeld, Ellen (Eds.). (2004). *Coming home? Refugees, migrants, and those who stayed behind*. Philadelphia: University of Pennsylvania Press.

Longino, Charles F., Jr. (2005). The future of ageism: Baby boomers at the doorstep. *Generations, 29*(3), 79–83.

López, Frank A. (2006). ADHD: New pharmacological treatments on the horizon. *Journal of Developmental & Behavioral Pediatrics, 27*, 410–416.

Lopez, Nestor L., Vazquez, Delia M., & Olson, Sheryl L. (2004). An integrative approach to the neurophysiological substrates of social withdrawal and aggression. *Development & Psychopathology, 16*, 69–93.

Lord, Janice, Hook, Melissa, & English, Sharon. (2003). Different faiths, different perceptions of public tragedy. In Marcia E. Lattanzi-Licht & Kenneth J. Doka (Eds.), *Living with grief: Coping with public tragedy* (pp. 91–107). New York: Brunner-Routledge.

Lorenz, Edward. (1972, December). *Predictability: Does the flap of a butterfly's wings in Brazil set off a tornado in Texas?* Paper presented at the American Association for the Advancement of Science, Washington, DC.

Lu, Luo. (2005). In pursuit of happiness: The cultural psychological study of SWB. *Chinese Journal of Psychology, 47*, 99–112.

Lubienski, Sarah Theule, & Lubienski, Christopher. (2005). *A new look at public and private schools: Student background and mathematics achievement*. Retrieved September 4, 2007, from the World Wide Web: http://www.pdkintl.org/kappan/k_v86/k0505lub.htm

Lucas, Richard E., & Dyrenforth, Portia S. (2005). The myth of marital bliss? *Psychological Inquiry, 16*, 111–115.

Luciana, Monica. (2003). Cognitive development in children born preterm: Implications for theories of brain plasticity following early injury. *Development and Psychopathology, 15*, 1017–1047.

Luciana, Monica. (2003). The neural and functional development of human prefrontal cortex. In Michelle de Haan & Mark H. Johnson (Eds.), *The cognitive neuroscience of development* (pp. 157–179). New York: Psychology Press.

Ludington-Hoe, Susan M., Johnson, Mark W., Morgan, Kathy, Lewis, Tina, Gutman, Judy, Wilson, P. David, et al. (2006). Neurophysiologic assessment of neonatal sleep organization: Preliminary results of a randomized, controlled trial of skin contact with preterm infants. *Pediatrics, 117*, e909–923.

Lundy, Jean E. B. (2002). Age and language skills of deaf children in relation to theory of mind development. *Journal of Deaf Studies & Deaf Education, 7*, 41–56.

Luthar, Suniya S. (2003). The culture of affluence: Psychological costs of material wealth. *Child Development, 74*, 1581–1593.

Luthar, Suniya S., Cicchetti, Dante, & Becker, Bronwyn. (2000). The construct of resilience: A critical evaluation and guidelines for future work. *Child Development, 71*, 543–562.

Luthar, Suniya S., D'Avanzo, Karen, & Hites, Sarah. (2003). Maternal drug abuse versus other psychological disturbances: Risks and resilience among children. In Suniya S. Luthar (Ed.), *Resilience and vulnerability: Adaptation in the context of childhood adversities* (pp. 104–129). New York: Cambridge University Press.

Luthar, Suniya S., & Zelazo, Laurel Bidwell. (2003). Research on resilience: An integrative review. In Suniya S. Luthar (Ed.), *Resilience and vulnerability: Adaptation in the context of childhood adversities* (pp. 510–549). New York: Cambridge University Press.

Lutz, Donna J., & Sternberg, Robert J. (1999). Cognitive development. In Marc H. Bornstein & Michael E. Lamb (Eds.), *Developmental psychology: An advanced textbook* (4th ed., pp. 275–311). Mahwah, NJ: Erlbaum.

Lykken, David T. (2006). The mechanism of emergenesis. *Genes, Brain & Behavior, 5*, 306–310.

Lynch, Robert G. (2004). *Exceptional returns: Economic, fiscal, and social benefits of investment in early childhood development.* Washington, DC: Economic Policy Institute.

Lyng, Stephen (Ed.). (2005). *Edgework: The sociology of risk taking*. New York: Routledge.

Lynn, Richard, & Mikk, Jaan. (2007). National differences in intelligence and educational attainment. *Intelligence, 35*, 115–121.

Lynn, Richard, & Vanhanen, Tatu. (2002). *IQ and the wealth of nations*. Westport, CT: Praeger.

Lyons, Linda. (2004, June 8). *Most teens associate school with boredom, fatigue*. Retrieved September 15, 2007, from the World Wide Web: http://www.galluppoll.com/content/?ci=11893&pg=1

Lyons-Ruth, Karlen, Bronfman, Elisa, & Parsons, Elizabeth. (1999). IV. Maternal frightened, frightening, or atypical behavior and disorganized infant attachment patterns. *Monographs of the Society for Research in Child Development, 64*(3, Serial No. 258), 67–96.

Maccoby, Eleanor E. (1998). *The two sexes: Growing up apart, coming together.* Cambridge, MA: Belknap Press of Harvard University Press.

Maccoby, Eleanor E. (2000). Parenting and its effects on children: On reading and misreading behavior genetics. *Annual Review of Psychology, 51*, 1–27.

MacKay, Andrea P., Berg, Cynthia J., King, Jeffrey C., Duran, Catherine, & Chang, Jeani. (2006). Pregnancy-related mortality among women with multifetal pregnancies. *Obstetrics & Gynecology, 107*, 563–568.

Mackay, Judith, & Eriksen, Michael P. (2002). *The tobacco atlas*. Geneva, Switzerland: World Health Organization.

Macmillan, Ross, & Copher, Ronda. (2005). Families in the life course: Interdependency of roles, role configurations, and pathways. *Journal of Marriage and Family, 67*, 858–879.

Macmillan, Ross, & Gartner, Rosemary. (1999). When she brings home the bacon: Labor-force participation and the risk of spousal violence against women. *Journal of Marriage & the Family, 61*, 947–958.

Madden, David J., & Whiting, Wythe L. (2004). Age-related changes in visual attention. In Paul T. Costa & Ilene C. Siegler (Eds.), *Recent advances in psychology and aging* (pp. 41–88). Boston: Elsevier.

Madsen, Kreesten Meldgaard, Hviid, Anders, Vestergaard, Mogens, Schendel, Diana, Wohlfahrt, Jan, Thorsen, Poul, et al. (2002). A population-based study of measles, mumps, and rubella vaccination and autism. *New England Journal of Medicine, 347*, 1477–1482.

Magara, Keiichi. (2005). Children's misconceptions: Research on improving understanding of mathematics and science. In David W. Shwalb, Jun Nakazawa, & Barbara J. Shwalb (Eds.), *Applied developmental psychology: Theory, practice, and research from Japan* (pp. 89–108). Greenwich, CT: Information Age Publishing.

Magen, Zipora. (1998). *Exploring adolescent happiness: Commitment, purpose, and fulfillment*. Thousand Oaks, CA: Sage.

Maggard, Melinda A., Shugarman, Lisa R., Suttorp, Marika, Maglione, Margaret, Sugerman, Harvey J., Livingston, Edward H., et al. (2005). Meta-analysis: Surgical treatment of obesity. *Annals of Internal Medicine, 142*, 547–559.

Magnusson, Roger S. (2004). Euthanasia: Above ground, below ground. *Journal of Medical Ethics, 30*, 441–446.

Maguen, Shira, Floyd, Frank J., Bakeman, Roger, & Armistead, Lisa. (2002). Developmental milestones and disclosure of sexual orientation among gay, lesbian, and bisexual youths. *Journal of Applied Developmental Psychology, 23*, 219–233.

Mahler, Margaret S., Pine, Fred, & Bergman, Anni. (1975). *The psychological birth of the human infant: Symbiosis and individuation*. New York: Basic Books.

Mahmoud, Adel. (2004, July 9). The global vaccination gap. *Science, 305*, 147.

Mahoney, Joseph L., Larson, Reed W., & Eccles, Jacquelynne S. (Eds.). (2005). *Organized activities as contexts of development: Extracurricular activities, after-school and community programs*. Mahwah, NJ: Erlbaum.

Maier, Heiner, McGue, Matt, Vaupel, James W., & Christensen, Kaare. (2003). Cognitive impairment and survival at older ages. In Caleb Ellicott Finch, Jean-Marie Robine, & Yves Christen (Eds.), *Brain and longevity* (pp. 131–144). Berlin, Germany: Springer.

Malatesta, Carol Z., Culver, Clayton, Tesman, Johanna Rich, & Shepard, Beth (with commentary by Alan Fogel & Mark Reimers, & Gail Zivin). (1989). The development of emotional expression during the first two years of life. *Monographs of the Society for Research in Child Development, 54*(1–2, Serial No. 219).

Malina, Robert M., Bouchard, Claude, & Bar-Or, Oded. (2004). *Growth, maturation, and physical activity* (2nd ed.). Champaign, IL: Human Kinetics.

Malone, Fergal D., Canick, Jacob A., Ball, Robert H., Nyberg, David A., Comstock, Christine H., Bukowski, Radek, et al. (2005). First-trimester or second-trimester screening, or both, for Down's syndrome. *New England Journal of Medicine, 353*, 2001–2011.

Mancini, Anthony D., & Bonanno, George A. (2006). Marital closeness, functional disability, and adjustment in late life. *Psychology and Aging, 21*, 600–610.

Mandler, Jean Matter. (2004). *The foundations of mind: Origins of conceptual thought*. Oxford, England: Oxford University Press.

Mange, Elaine Johansen, & Mange, Arthur P. (1999). *Basic human genetics* (2nd ed.). Sunderland, MA: Sinauer Associates.

Manini, Todd M., Everhart, James E., Patel, Kushang V., Schoeller, Dale A., Colbert, Lisa H., Visser, Marjolein, et al. (2006). Daily activity energy expenditure and mortality among older adults. *Journal of the American Medical Association, 296*, 171–179.

Manlove, Jennifer, Ryan, Suzanne, & Franzetta, Kerry. (2003). Patterns of contraceptive use within teenagers' first sexual relationships. *Perspectives on Sexual and Reproductive Health, 35*, 246–255.

Manly, Jody Todd, Kim, Jungmeen E., Rogosch, Fred A., & Cicchetti, Dante. (2001). Dimensions of child maltreatment and children's adjustment: Contributions of developmental timing and subtype. *Development & Psychopathology, 13*, 759–782.

Mann, Ronald D., & Andrews, Elizabeth B. (Eds.). (2007). *Pharmacovigilance* (2nd ed.). Hoboken, NJ: Wiley.

Mannion, Anne F., Elfering, A., Staerkle, R., Junge, A., Grob, D., Dvorak, J., et al. (2007). Predictors of multidimensional outcome after spinal surgery. *European Spine Journal, 16*, 777–786.

Manson, JoAnn E., Hu, Frank B., Rich-Edwards, Janet W., Colditz, Graham A., Stampfer, Meir J., Willett, Walter C., et al. (1999). A prospective study of walking as compared with vigorous exercise in the prevention of coronary heart disease in women. *New England Journal of Medicine, 341*, 650–658.

Manton, Kenneth G., Gu, XiLiang, & Lamb, Vicki L. (2006). Change in chronic disability from 1982 to 2004/2005 as measured by long-term changes in function and health in the U.S. elderly population. *Proceedings of the National Academy of Sciences, 103*, 18374–18379.

Manzi, Claudia, Vignoles, Vivian L., Regalia, Camillo, & Scabini, Eugenia. (2006). Cohesion and enmeshment revisited: Differentiation, identity, and well-being in two European cultures. *Journal of Marriage and Family, 68*, 673–689.

Manzo, Kathleen Kennedy. (2006, October 4). Scathing report casts cloud over 'Reading First'. *Education Week, 26*, 1.

Manzo, Kathleen Kennedy. (2007, March 14). Australia grapples with national content standards. *Education Week, 26*, 10.

Manzoli, Lamberto, Villari, Paolo, Pironec, Giovanni M., & Boccia, Antonio. (2007). Marital status and mortality in the elderly: A systematic review and meta-analysis. *Social Science & Medicine, 64*, 77–94.

Mao, Amy, Burnham, Melissa M., Goodlin-Jones, Beth L., Gaylor, Erika E., & Anders, Thomas F. (2004). A comparison of the sleep-wake patterns of cosleeping and solitary-sleeping infants. *Child Psychiatry and Human Development, 35*, 95–105.

March, John, Silva, Susan, Petrycki, Stephen, Curry, John, Wells, Karen, Fairbank, John, et al. (2004). Fluoxetine, cognitive-behavioral therapy, and their combination for adolescents with depression: Treatment For Adolescents With Depression Study (TADS) randomized controlled trial. *Journal of the American Medical Association, 292*, 807–820.

Marcia, James E. (1966). Development and validation of ego-identity status. *Journal of Personality & Social Psychology, 3*, 551–558.

Marcia, James E. (2002). Identity and psychosocial development in adulthood. *Identity, 2*, 7–28.

Marcia, James E., Waterman, Alan S., Matteson, David R., Archer, Sally L., & Orlofsky, Jacob L. (1993). *Ego identity: A handbook for psychosocial research*. New York: Springer-Verlag.

Marcus, Gary. (2004). *The birth of the mind: How a tiny number of genes creates the complexities of human thought*. New York: Basic Books.

Marian, Viorica, & Fausey, Caitlin M. (2006). Language-dependent memory in bilingual learning. *Applied Cognitive Psychology, 20*, 1025–1047.

Marlow, Neil, Wolke, Dieter, Bracewell, Melanie A., & Samara, Muthanna. (2005). Neurologic and developmental disability at six years of age after extremely preterm birth. *New England Journal of Medicine, 352*, 9–19.

Marlow-Ferguson, Rebecca (Ed.). (2002). *World education encyclopedia: A survey of educational systems worldwide* (2nd ed.). Detroit, MI: Gale Group.

Marmot, Michael G., & Fuhrer, Rebecca. (2004). Socioeconomic position and health across midlife. In Orville Gilbert Brim, Carol D. Ryff, & Ronald C. Kessler (Eds.), *How healthy are we? A national study of well-being at midlife* (pp. 64–89). Chicago: University of Chicago Press.

Marriott, L. K., & Wenk, Gary L. (2004). Neurobiological consequences of long-term estrogen therapy. *Current Directions in Psychological Science, 13*, 173–176.

Marsiske, Michael, & Willis, Sherry L. (1995). Dimensionality of everyday problem solving in older adults. *Psychology & Aging, 10*, 269–283.

Marsiske, Michael, & Willis, Sherry L. (1998). Practical creativity in older adults' everyday problem solving: Life span perspectives. In Carolyn E. Adams-Price (Ed.), *Creativity and successful aging: Theoretical and empirical approaches* (pp. 73–113). New York: Springer.

Martin, Andres, & Leslie, Douglas. (2003). Trends in psychotropic medication costs for children and adolescents, 1997–2000. *Archives of Pediatrics & Adolescent Medicine, 157*, 997–1004.

Martin, Carol Lynn, Ruble, Diane N., & Szkrybalo, Joel. (2002). Cognitive theories of early gender development. *Psychological Bulletin, 128*, 903–933.

Martin, Joyce A., Hamilton, Brady E., Ventura, Stephanie J., Menacker, Fay, & Park, Melissa M. (2002, February 12). Births: Final data for 2000. *National Vital Statistics Reports, 50*(5).

Martin, Mike, & Zimprich, Daniel. (2005). Cognitive development in midlife. In Sherry L. Willis & Mike Martin (Eds.), *Middle adulthood: A lifespan perspective* (pp. 179–206). Thousand Oaks, CA: Sage.

Martino, Steven C., Collins, Rebecca L., Elliott, Marc N., Strachman, Amy, Kanouse, David E., & Berry, Sandra H. (2006). Exposure to degrading versus nondegrading music lyrics and sexual behavior among youth. *Pediatrics, 118*, e430–441.

Martire, Lynn M., Keefe, Francis J., Schulz, Richard, Ready, Rebecca, Beach, Scott R., Rudy, Thomas E., et al. (2006). Older spouses' perceptions of partners' chronic arthritis pain: implications for spousal responses, support provision, and caregiving experiences. *Psychology and Aging, 21*, 222–230.

Marx, Jean. (2005, August 5). Preventing Alzheimer's: A lifelong commitment? *Science, 309*, 864–866.

Marx, Jean. (2007, January 19, 2007). Trafficking protein suspected in Alzheimer's disease. *Science, 315*, 314.

Mascie-Taylor, C. G. Nicholas, & Karim, Enamul. (2003, December 12). The burden of chronic disease. *Science, 302*, 1921–1922.

Mascolo, Michael F., Fischer, Kurt W., & Li, Jin. (2003). Dynamic development of component systems of emotions: Pride, shame, and guilt in China and the United States. In Richard J. Davidson, Klaus R. Scherer, & H. Hill Goldsmith (Eds.), *Handbook of affective sciences* (pp. 375–408). Oxford, England: Oxford University Press.

Mash, Elisabeth, & Lloyd-Williams, Mari. (2006). A survey of the services provided by children's hospices in the United Kingdom. *Supportive Care in Cancer, 14*, 1169–1172.

Maslow, Abraham H. (1968). *Toward a psychology of being* (2nd ed.). Princeton, NJ: Van Nostrand.

Maslow, Abraham H. (1970). *Motivation and personality* (2nd ed.). New York: Harper & Row.

Masoro, Edward J. (1999). *Challenges of biological aging*. New York: Springer.

Masoro, Edward J. (2006). Are age-associated diseases an integral part of aging? In Edward J. Masoro & Steven N. Austad (Eds.), *Handbook of the biology of aging* (6th ed., pp. 43–62). Amsterdam: Elsevier Academic Press.

Masten, Ann S. (2001). Ordinary magic: Resilience processes in development. *American Psychologist, 56*, 227–238.

Masten, Ann S. (2004). Regulatory processes, risk, and resilience in adolescent development. In Ronald E. Dahl & Linda Patia Spear (Eds.), *Adolescent brain development: Vulnerabilities and opportunities* (Vol. 1021, pp. 310–319). New York: New York Academy of Sciences.

Masten, Ann S., & Coatsworth, J. Douglas. (1998). The development of competence in favorable and unfavorable environments: Lessons from research on successful children. *American Psychologist, 53*, 205–220.

Masten, Ann S., Roisman, Glenn I., Long, Jeffrey D., Burt, Keith B., Obradovic, Jelena, Riley, Jennifer R., et al. (2005). Developmental cascades: Linking academic achievement and externalizing and internalizing symptoms over 20 years. *Developmental Psychology, 41*, 733–746.

Masterpasqua, Frank, & Perna, Phyllis A. (Eds.). (1997). *The psychological meaning of chaos: Translating theory into practice*. Washington, DC: American Psychological Association.

Masunaga, Hiromi, & Horn, John. (2001). Expertise and age-related changes in components of intelligence. *Psychology & Aging, 16*, 293–311.

Maton, Kenneth I., Schellenbach, Cynthia J., Leadbeater, Bonnie J., & Solarz, Andrea L. (Eds.). (2004). *Investing in children, youth, families, and communities: Strengths-based research and policy*. Washington, DC: American Psychological Association.

Matsumoto, David. (2004). Reflections on culture and competence. In Robert J. Sternberg & Elena L. Grigorenko (Eds.), *Culture and competence: Contexts of life success* (pp. 273–282). Washington, DC: American Psychological Association.

Matsumoto, David, & Yoo, Seung Hee. (2006). Toward a new generation of cross-cultural research. *Perspectives on Psychological Science, 1*, 234–250.

Mattingly, Marybeth J., & Sayer, Liana C. (2006). Under pressure: Gender differences in the relationship between free time and feeling rushed. *Journal of Marriage and Family, 68*, 205–221.

Maughan, Angeline, & Cicchetti, Dante. (2002). Impact of child maltreatment and interadult violence on children's emotion regulation abilities and socioemotional adjustment. *Child Development, 73*, 1525–1542.

May, Henry, & Supovitz, Jonathan A. (2006). Capturing the cumulative effects of school reform: An 11–year study of the impacts of America's choice on student achievement. *Educational Evaluation and Policy Analysis, 28*, 231–257.

May, Philip A., Gossage, J. Phillip, Brooke, Lesley E., Snell, Cudore L., Marais, Anna-Susan, Hendricks, Loretta S., et al. (2005). Maternal risk factors for fetal alcohol syndrome in the Western Cape Province of South Africa: A population-based study. *American Journal of Public Health, 95*, 1190–1199.

May, Stephen. (2005). Language policy and minority language rights. In Eli Hinkel (Ed.), *Handbook of research in second language teaching and learning* (pp. 1055–1073). Mahwah, NJ: Erlbaum.

Mayberry, Rachel I., & Nicoladis, Elena. (2000). Gesture reflects language development: Evidence from bilingual children. *Current Directions in Psychological Science, 9*, 192–196.

Mayeux, Lara, & Cillessen, Antonius H. N. (2007). Peer influence and the development of antisocial behavior. In Rutger C. M. E. Engels, Margaret Kerr, & Håkan Stattin (Eds.), *Friends, lovers, and groups: Key relationships in adolescence* (pp. 33–46). Hoboken, NJ: Wiley.

Maynard, Ashley E. (2002). Cultural teaching: The development of teaching skills in Maya sibling interactions. *Child Development, 73*, 969–982.

McAdams, Dan P. (2006). The redemptive self: Generativity and the stories Americans live by. *Research in Human Development, 3*, 81–100.

McAdams, Dan P., & Pals, Jennifer L. (2006). A new big five: Fundamental principles for an integrative science of personality. *American Psychologist, 61*, 204–217.

McCabe, Donald L, & Trevino, Linda Klebe. (1996). What we know about cheating in college. *Change, 28*, 28–33.

McCardle, Peggy, & Chhabra, Vinita. (2004). The accumulation of evidence: A continuing process. In Peggy D. McCardle & Vinita Chhabra (Eds.), *The voice of evidence in reading research* (pp. 463–478). Baltimore: Brookes.

McCarter, Roger J. M. (2006). Differential aging among skeletal muscles In Edward J. Masoro & Steven N. Austad (Eds.), *Handbook of the biology of aging* (6th ed., pp. 470–497). Amsterdam: Elsevier Academic Press.

McCarthy, Barry W., & McCarthy, Emily J. (2004). *Getting it right the first time: Creating a healthy marriage*. New York: Brunner-Routledge.

McCarty, Michael E., & Ashmead, Daniel H. (1999). Visual control of reaching and grasping in infants. *Developmental Psychology, 35*, 620–631.

McCloskey, Laura Ann, & Stuewig, Jeffrey. (2001). The quality of peer relationships among children exposed to family violence. *Development & Psychopathology, 13*, 83–96.

McCrae, Robert R., & Allik, Jüri (Eds.). (2002). *The five-factor model of personality across cultures*. New York: Kluwer.

McCrae, Robert R., & Costa, Paul T. (1994). The stability of personality: Observation and evaluations. *Current Directions in Psychological Science, 3*, 173–175.

McCrae, Robert R., & Costa, Paul T. (2003). *Personality in adulthood: A five-factor theory perspective* (2nd ed.). New York: Guilford Press.

McCrae, Robert R., Costa, Paul T., de Lima, Margarida Pedroso, Simões, António, Ostendorf, Fritz, Angleitner, Alois, et al. (1999). Age differences in personality across the adult life span: Parallels in five cultures. *Developmental Psychology, 35*, 466–477.

McCrae, Robert R., & Terracciano, Antonio. (2006). National character and personality. *Current Directions in Psychological Science, 15*, 156–161.

McCurry, Susan M., Logsdon, Rebecca G., Teri, Linda, & Vitiello, Michael V. (2007). Evidence-based psychological treatments for insomnia in older adults. *Psychology and Aging, 22*, 18–27.

McDonald, C., Lambert, J., Nayagam, D., Welz, T., Poulton, M., Aleksin, D., et al. (2007). Why are children still being infected with HIV? Experiences in the prevention of mother-to-child transmission of HIV in south London. *Sexually Transmitted Infections, 83*, 59–63.

McElroy, Mary. (2002). *Resistance to exercise: A social analysis of inactivity*. Champaign, IL: Human Kinetics.

McKelvie, Pippa, & Low, Jason. (2002). Listening to Mozart does not improve children's spatial ability: Final curtains for the Mozart effect. *British Journal of Developmental Psychology, 20*, 241–258.

McKinley, Jesse. (2006, May 10). Two setbacks for exit exams taken by high school seniors. *New York Times*, p. A21.

McKinstry, Leo. (2005). *Not ill—Just naughty*. The Spectator. Retrieved July 22, 2007, from the World Wide Web: http://www.spectator.co.uk/archive/features/13287/not-ill-just-naughty.thtml

McKnight, A. James. (2003). The freedom of the open road: Driving and older adults. *Generations, 27*(2), 25–31.

McLanahan, Sara, Donahue, Elisabeth, & Haskins, Ron (Eds.). (2005). *The future of children: Marriage and child wellbeing*. Washington, DC: Brookings Institution.

McLeod, Bryce D., Wood, Jeffrey J., & Weisz, John R. (2007). Examining the association between parenting and childhood anxiety: A meta-analysis. *Clinical Psychology Review, 27*, 155–172.

McLeod, Peter, Sommerville, Peter, & Reed, Nick. (2005). Are automated actions beyond conscious access? In John Duncan, Peter McLeod, & Louise H. Phillips (Eds.), *Measuring the mind: Speed, control, and age* (pp. 359–372). New York: Oxford University Press.

McLoyd, Vonnie C., Aikens, Nikki L., & Burton, Linda M. (2006). Childhood poverty, policy, and practice. In William Damon & Richard M. Lerner (Series Eds.) & K. Ann Renninger & Irving E. Sigel (Vol. Eds.), *Handbook of child psychology: Vol. 4. Child psychology in practice* (6th ed., pp. 700–775). Hoboken, NJ: Wiley.

McLoyd, Vonnie C., & Smith, Julia. (2002). Physical discipline and behavior problems in African American, European American, and Hispanic children: Emotional support as a moderator. *Journal of Marriage & the Family, 64*, 40–53.

McNeil, Michele. (2007, May). Rigorous courses, fresh enrollment. *Education Week, 26*, 28–31.

McQuaid, Elizabeth L., Kopel, Sheryl J., Klein, Robert B., & Fritz, Gregory K. (2003). Medication adherence in pediatric asthma: Reasoning, responsibility, and behavior. *Journal of Pediatric Psychology, 28*, 323–333.

Mealey, Linda. (2003). Anorexia: A "disease" of low, low fertility. In Joseph Lee Rodgers & Hans-Peter Kohler (Eds.), *The biodemography of human reproduction and fertility* (pp. 1–21). Boston: Kluwer.

Medscape Psychiatry & Mental Health. (2005). *Autism first-hand: An expert interview with Temple Grandin, PhD*. Retrieved September 3, 2007, from the World Wide Web: http://www.medscape.com/viewarticle/498153

Medvedev, Zhores A. (1990). An attempt at a rational classification of theories of ageing. *Biological Reviews, 65*, 375–398.

Meil, Gerardo. (2006). The consequences of the development of a beanpole kin structure on exchanges between generations: The case of Spain. *Journal of Family Issues, 27*, 1085–1099.

Meisami, Esmail. (1994). Aging of the sensory systems. In Paola S. Timiras (Ed.), *Physiological basis of aging and geriatrics* (2nd ed., pp. 115–132). Boca Raton, FL: CRC Press.

Meisami, Esmail, Brown, Chester M., & Emerle, Henry F. (2003). Sensory systems: Normal aging, disorders, and treatments of vision and hearing in humans. In Paola S. Timiras (Ed.), *Physiological basis of aging and geriatrics* (3rd ed., pp. 141–165). Boca Raton, FL: CRC Press.

Mell, Loren K., Ogren, David S., Davis, Robert L., Mullooly, John P., Black, Steven B., Shinefield, Henry R., et al. (2005). Compliance with national immunization guidelines for children younger than 2 years, 1996–1999. *Pediatrics, 115*, 461–467.

Mellor, M. Joanna, & Brownell, Patricia J. (Eds.). (2006). *Elder abuse and mistreatment: Policy, practice, and research*. New York: Haworth Press.

Meltzoff, Andrew N., & Moore, M. Keith. (1999). A new foundation for cognitive development in infancy: The birth of the representational infant. In Ellin Kofsky Scholnick, Katherine Nelson, Susan A. Gelman, & Patricia H. Miller (Eds.), *Conceptual development: Piaget's legacy* (pp. 53–78). Mahwah, NJ: Erlbaum.

Menacker, Fay, Martin, Joyce A., & MacDorman, Marian F. (2004, November 15). Births to 10–14 year-old mothers, 1990–2002: Trends and health outcomes. *National Vital Statistics Reports, 53*(7).

Mendle, Jane, Turkheimer, Eric, & Emery, Robert E. (2007). Detrimental psychological outcomes associated with early pubertal timing in adolescent girls. *Developmental Review, 27*, 151–171.

Menon, Usha. (2001). Middle adulthood in cultural perspectives: The imagined and the experienced in three cultures. In Margie E. Lachman (Ed.), *Handbook of midlife development* (pp. 40–74). New York: Wiley.

Merline, Alicia C., O'Malley, Patrick M., Schulenberg, John E., Bachman, Jerald G., & Johnston, Lloyd D. (2004). Substance use among adults 35 years of age: Prevalence, adulthood predictors, and impact of adolescent substance use. *American Journal of Public Health, 94*, 96–102.

Merrell, Kenneth W., & Gimpel, Gretchen A. (1998). *Social skills of children and adolescents: Conceptualization, assessment, treatment*. Mahwah, NJ: Erlbaum.

Merrill, Susan S., & Verbrugge, Lois M. (1999). Health and disease in midlife. In Sherry L. Willis & James D. Reid (Eds.), *Life in the middle: Psychological and social development in middle age* (pp. 77–103). San Diego, CA: Academic Press.

Merriman, William E. (1999). Competition, attention, and young children's lexical processing. In Brian MacWhinney (Ed.), *The emergence of language* (pp. 331–358). Mahwah, NJ: Erlbaum.

Mervis, Jeffrey. (2006, May 19). Well-balanced panel to tackle algebra reform. *Science, 312*, 982a.

Merzenich, Michael M. (2001). Cortical plasticity contributing to child development. In James L. McClelland & Robert S. Siegler (Eds.), *Mechanisms of cognitive development: Behavioral and neural perspectives* (pp. 67–95). Mahwah, NJ: Erlbaum.

Michaud, Catherine, Murray, Christopher J. L., & Bloom, Barry R. (2001). Burden of disease—Implications for future research. *Journal of the American Medical Association, 285*, 535–539.

Michaud, Pierre-Andre, Chossis, Isabelle, & Suris, Joan-Carles. (2006). Health-related behavior: Current situation, trends, and prevention. In Sandy Jackson & Luc Goossens (Eds.), *Handbook of adolescent development* (pp. 284–307). Hove, East Sussex, UK: Psychology Press.

Michels, Tricia M., Kropp, Rhonda Y., Eyre, Stephen L., & Halpern-Felsher, Bonnie L. (2005). Initiating sexual experiences: How do young adolescents make decisions regarding early sexual activity? *Journal of Research on Adolescence, 15*, 583–607.

Mikels, Joseph A., Larkin, Gregory R., Reuter-Lorenz, Patricia A., & Cartensen, Laura L. (2006). Divergent trajectories in the aging mind: Changes in working memory for affective versus visual information with age. *Psychology and Aging, 20,* 542–553.

Mikulincer, Mario, & Goodman, Gail S. (2006). *Dynamics of romantic love: Attachment, caregiving, and sex.* New York: Guilford Press.

Milardo, Robert M. (2005). Generative uncle and nephew relationships. *Journal of Marriage and Family, 67,* 1226–1236.

Miller, Brent C., Benson, Brad, & Galbraith, Kevin A. (2001). Family relationships and adolescent pregnancy risk: A research synthesis. *Developmental Review, 21,* 1–38.

Miller, Greg. (2005, May 13). Reflecting on another's mind. *Science, 308,* 945–947.

Miller, Greg. (2006, January 27). The unseen: Mental illness's global toll. *Science, 311,* 458–461.

Miller, Greg. (2006, March 31). The thick and thin of brainpower: Developmental timing linked to IQ. *Science, 311,* 1851.

Miller, Joan G. (2004). The cultural deep structure of psychological theories of social development. In Robert J. Sternberg & Elena L. Grigorenko (Eds.), *Culture and competence: Contexts of life success* (pp. 111–138). Washington, DC: American Psychological Association.

Miller, Orlando J., & Therman, Eeva. (2001). *Human chromosomes* (4th ed.). New York: Springer.

Miller, Patricia H. (2002). *Theories of developmental psychology* (4th ed.). New York: Worth Publishers.

Miller, Patricia Y., & Simon, William. (1980). The development of sexuality in adolescence. In Joseph Adelson (Ed.), *Handbook of adolescent psychology* (pp. 383–407). New York: Wiley.

Miller, Richard A. (2001). Genetics of increased longevity and retarded aging in mice. In Edward J. Masoro & Steven N. Austad (Eds.), *Handbook of the biology of aging* (5th ed., pp. 369–395). San Diego, CA: Academic Press.

Miller, Thomas E., Bender, Barbara E., Schuh, John H., & Associates. (2005). *Promoting reasonable expectations: Aligning student and institutional views of the college experience.* San Francisco: Jossey-Bass.

Miller, William R., & Carroll, Kathleen. (2006). *Rethinking substance abuse: What the science shows, and what we should do about it.* New York: Guilford Press.

Miller, William R., & Thoresen, Carl E. (2003). Spirituality, religion, and health: An emerging research field. *American Psychologist, 58,* 24–35.

Miller-Day, Michelle A. (2004). *Communication among grandmothers, mothers, and adult daughters: A qualitative study of maternal relationships.* Mahwah, NJ: Erlbaum.

Milloy, Steven. (2006, February 9). *Low-fat diet myth busted.* Retrieved September 15, 2007, from the World Wide Web: http://www.foxnews.com/story/0,2933,184409,00.html

Mills, James L., McPartlin, Joseph M., Kirke, Peadar N., Lee, Young J., Conley, Mary R., Weir, Donald G., et al. (1995). Homocysteine metabolism in pregnancies complicated by neural-tube defects. *Lancet, 345,* 149–151.

Min, Pyong Gap. (2000). Korean Americans' language use. In Sandra Lee McKay & Sau-ling Cynthia Wong (Eds.), *New immigrants in the United States: Readings for second language educators* (pp. 306–332). Cambridge, UK: Cambridge University Press.

Mintz, Laurie B., & Kashubeck, Susan. (1999). Body image and disordered eating among Asian American and Caucasian college students: An examination of race and gender differences. *Psychology of Women Quarterly, 23,* 781–796.

Mintz, Toben H. (2005). Linguistic and conceptual influences on adjective acquisition in 24- and 36-month-olds. *Developmental Psychology, 41,* 17–29.

Mitchell, Jean, & McCarthy, Helen. (2000). Eating disorders. In Lorna Champion & Mick Power (Eds.), *Adult psychological problems: An introduction* (2nd ed., pp. 103–130). Hove, England: Psychology Press.

Mitchell, Katharyne. (2001). Education for democratic citizenship: Transnationalism, multiculturalism, and the limits of liberalism. *Harvard Educational Review, 71,* 51–78.

Mitka, Mike. (2003). Surgery for obesity: Demand soars amid scientific, ethical questions. *Journal of the American Medical Association, 289,* 1761–1762.

Mix, Kelly S., Huttenlocher, Janellen, & Levine, Susan Cohen. (2002). *Quantitative development in infancy and early childhood.* New York: Oxford University Press.

MMWR. (1998, August 14). Youth risk behavior surveillance—United States, 1997. *MMWR Surveillance Summaries, 47*(SS-3).

MMWR. (2002, April 5). Alcohol use among women of childbearing age—United States, 1991–1999. *Morbidity and Mortality Weekly Report, 51*(13), 273–276.

MMWR. (2002, July 12). Hysterectomy surveillance—United States, 1994–1999. *Morbidity and Mortality Weekly Report Surveillance Summaries, 51*(SS05), 1–8.

MMWR. (2002, September 13). Folic acid and prevention of spina bifida and anencephaly: 10 years after the U.S. public health service recommendation. *MMWR Recommendations and Reports, 51*(RR13), 1–3.

MMWR. (2003, June 13). Varicella-related deaths—United States, 2002. *Morbidity and Mortality Weekly Report, 52,* 545–547.

MMWR. (2003, August 22). State-specific prevalence of selected chronic disease-related characteristics—Behavioral Risk Factor Surveillance System, 2001. *Surveillance Summaries, 52*(SS08), 1–80.

MMWR. (2004, January 16). Declining prevalence of no known major risk factors for heart disease and stroke among adults—United States, 1991–2001. *Morbidity and Mortality Weekly Report, 53*(1), 4–7.

MMWR. (2004, September 3). Surveillance for fatal and nonfatal injuries—United States, 2001. *MMWR Surveillance Summaries,* 53(SS07), 1–57.

MMWR. (2004, September 17). Use of vitamins containing folic acid among women of childbearing age—United States, 2004. *Morbidity and Mortality Weekly Report, 53,* 847–850.

MMWR. (2004, October 15). Newborn screening for cystic fibrosis: Evaluation of benefits and risks and recommendations for state newborn screening programs. *MMWR: Recommendations and Reports,* 53(RR13), 1–36.

MMWR. (2004, October 29). Chlamydia screening among sexually active young female enrollees of health plans—United States, 1999–2001. *Morbidity and Mortality Weekly Report,* 53, 983–985.

MMWR. (2004, December 24). Alcohol consumption among women who are pregnant or who might become pregnant—United States, 2002. *Morbidity and Mortality Weekly Report,* 53, 1178–1181.

MMWR. (2005, January 14). Reducing childhood asthma through community-based service delivery—New York City, 2001–2004. *Morbidity and Mortality Weekly Report, 54,* 11–14.

MMWR. (2005, February 4). Quickstats: Pregnancy, birth, and abortion rates for teenagers aged 15–17 years—United States, 1976–2003. *Morbidity and Mortality Weekly Report,* 54(4).

MMWR. (2005, May 27). Blood lead levels—United States, 1999–2002. *Morbidity and Mortality Weekly Report, 54,* 513–516.

MMWR. (2006, February 24). Mumps epidemic—United Kingdom, 2004–2005. *Morbidity and Mortality Weekly Report,* 55(7), 173–175.

MMWR. (2006, June 9). Youth risk behavior surveillance—United States, 2005. *MMWR Surveillance Summaries,* 55(SS05), 1–108.

MMWR. (2006, July 14). Cigarette use among high school students—United States, 1991–2005. *Morbidity and Mortality Weekly Report, 55,* 724–726.

MMWR. (2006, July 14). Surveillance for certain health behaviors among states and selected local areas—Behavioral Risk Factor Surveillance System, United States, 2004. *MMWR Surveillance Summaries,* 55(SS07), 1–124.

MMWR. (2006, August 4). Sexually transmitted diseases treatment guidelines, 2006. *MMWR Recommendations and Reports,* 55(RR11), 1–94.

MMWR. (2006, August 11). Trends in HIV-related risk behaviors among high school students—United States, 1991–2005. *Morbidity and Mortality Weekly Report,* 55(31), 851–854.

MMWR. (2006, November 24). Abortion surveillance—United States, 2003. *MMWR Surveillance Summaries,* 55(SS11), 1–32.

MMWR. (2006, October 20). ST-prevention counseling practices and human papillomavirus opinions among clinicians with adolescent patients—United States, 2004. *Morbidity and Mortality Weekly Report,* 55(41), 1117–1120.

MMWR. (2007, January 12). Table II: Provisional cases of selected notifiable diseases, United States, weeks ending January 6, 2007 and January 7, 2006 (1st Week) *Morbidity and Mortality Weekly Report,* 56(1), 12–20.

MMWR. (2007, February 9). Prevalence of autism spectrum disorders—Autism and Developmental Disabilities Monitoring Network, six sites, United States, 2000. *MMWR Surveillance Summaries,* 56(SS01), 1–11.

MMWR. (2007, February 16). Prevalence of heart disease—United States, 2005. *Morbidity and Mortality Weekly Report,* 56(06), 113–118.

MMWR. (2007, June 8). Assisted reproductive technology surveillance—United States, 2004. *Morbidity and Mortality Weekly Report Surveillance Summaries,* 56(SS06), 1–22.

Mocan, H. Naci, & Tekin, Erdal. (2006). *Ugly criminals.* Social Science Electronic Publishing. Retrieved December 12, 2006, from the World Wide Web: http://ssrn.com/abstract=894062

Moen, Phyllis, & Roehling, Patricia. (2005). *The career mystique: Cracks in the American dream.* Lanham, MD: Rowman & Littlefield.

Moen, Phyllis, & Spencer, Donna. (2006). Converging divergences in age, gender, health, and well-being: Strategic selection in the third age. In Robert H. Binstock & Linda K. George (Eds.), *Handbook of aging and the social sciences* (6th ed., pp. 127–144). Amsterdam: Elsevier.

Moen, Phyllis, Sweet, Stephen, & Swisher, Raymond. (2005). Embedded career clocks: The case of retirement planning. In Ross Macmillan (Ed.), *The structure of the life course: Standardized? Individualized? Differentiated?* (pp. 237–265). Greenwich, CT: Elsevier/JAI Press.

Moffat, Scott D. (2005). Effects of testosterone on cognitive and brain aging in elderly men. In Richard G. Cutler, S. Mitchell Harman, Chris Heward, & Mike Gibbons (Eds.), *Longevity health sciences: The Phoenix conference* (Vol. 1055, pp. 80–92). New York: New York Academy of Sciences.

Moffitt, Terrie E. (1997). Adolescence-limited and life-course-persistent offending: A complementary pair of developmental theories. In Terence P. Thornberry (Ed.), *Developmental theories of crime and delinquency* (pp. 11–54). New Brunswick, NJ: Transaction.

Moffitt, Terrie E. (2003). Life-course-persistent and adolescence-limited antisocial behavior: A 10–year research review and a research agenda. In Benjamin B. Lahey, Terrie E. Moffitt, & Avshalom Caspi (Eds.), *Causes of conduct disorder and juvenile delinquency* (pp. 49–75). New York: Guilford Press.

Moffitt, Terrie E., Caspi, Avshalom, Belsky, Jay, & Silva, Phil A. (1992). Childhood experience and the onset of menarche: A test of a sociobiological model. *Child Development, 63,* 47–58.

Moffitt, Terrie E., Caspi, Avshalom, & Rutter, Michael. (2006). Measured gene-environment interactions in psychopathology: Concepts, research strategies, and implications for research, intervention, and public understanding of genetics. *Perspectives on Psychological Science, 1,* 5–27.

Moffitt, Terrie E., Caspi, Avshalom, Rutter, Michael, & Silva, Phil A. (2001). *Sex differences in antisocial behaviour: Conduct disorder, delinquency, and violence in the Dunedin longitudinal study.* New York: Cambridge University Press.

Mollenkopf, Heidrun, Marcellini, Fiorella, Ruoppila, Isto, Széman, Zsuzsa, & Tacken, Mart (Eds.). (2005). *Enhancing mobility in later life: Personal coping, environmental resources and technical support. The out-of-home mobility of older adults in urban and rural regions of five European countries.* Amsterdam: IOS Press.

Mollenkopf, John, Waters, Mary C., Holdaway, Jennifer, & Kasinitz, Philip. (2005). The ever-winding path: ethnic and racial diversity in the transition to adulthood. In Richard A. Settersten, Jr., Frank F. Furstenberg, Jr., & Rubén G. Rumbaut (Eds.), *On the frontier of adulthood: Theory, research, and public policy* (pp. 454–497). Chicago: University of Chicago Press.

Monastersky, Richard. (2007, January 12). Who's minding the teenage brain? *Chronicle of Higher Education, 53,* A14.

Moneta, L., & Kuh, G. D. (2005). When expectations and realities collide: Environmental influences on student expectations and student experiences. In Thomas E. Miller, Barbara E. Bender, John H. Schuh, & Associates (Eds.), *Promoting reasonable expectations: Aligning student and institutional views of the college experience* (pp. 65–83). San Francisco: Jossey-Bass.

Monsour, Michael. (2002). *Women and men as friends: Relationships across the life span in the 21st century.* Mahwah, NJ: Erlbaum.

Monteiro, Carlos A., Conde, Wolney L., & Popkin, Barry M. (2004). The burden of disease from undernutrition and overnutrition in countries undergoing rapid nutrition transition: A view from Brazil. *American Journal of Public Health, 94,* 433–434.

Montessori, Maria. (1966). *The secret of childhood* (M. Joseph Costelloe, Trans.). Notre Dame, IN: Fides. (Original work published 1936)

Montgomery, Barbara M., & Baxter, Leslie A. (1998). *Dialectical approaches to*

studying personal relationships. Mahwah, NJ: Erlbaum.

Moody, Harry R. (2001–2002). Who's afraid of life extension? *Generations, 25*(4), 33–37.

Moody, Raymond A. (1975). *Life after life: The investigation of a phenomenon—Survival of bodily death*. Atlanta, GA: Mockingbird Books.

Moore, Celia L. (2002). On differences and development. In David J. Lewkowicz & Robert Lickliter (Eds.), *Conceptions of development: Lessons from the laboratory* (pp. 57–76). New York: Psychology Press.

Moore, Ginger A., & Calkins, Susan D. (2004). Infants' vagal regulation in the still-face paradigm is related to dyadic coordination of mother-infant interaction. *Developmental Psychology, 40*, 1068–1080.

Moore, Keith L., & Persaud, Trivedi V. N. (2003). *The developing human: Clinically oriented embryology* (7th ed.). Philadelphia: Saunders.

Moore, Susan, & Rosenthal, Doreen. (2006). *Sexuality in adolescence: Current trends* (2nd ed.). New York: Routledge.

Morgan, Craig, Kirkbride, James, Leff, Julian, Craig, Tom, Hutchinson, Gerard, McKenzie, Kwame, et al. (2007). Parental separation, loss and psychosis in different ethnic groups: A case-control study. *Psychological Medicine, 37*, 495–503.

Morgan, Ian G. (2003). The biological basis of myopic refractive error. *Clinical and Experimental Optometry, 86*, 276–288.

Morgan, John D., & Laungani, Pittu (Eds.). (2005). *Death and bereavement around the world: Vol. 4. Death and bereavement in Asia, Australia and New Zealand*. Amityville, NY: Baywood.

Morgenstern, Hal, Bingham, Trista, & Reza, Avid. (2000). Effects of pool-fencing ordinances and other factors on childhood drowning in Los Angeles County, 1990–1995. *American Journal of Public Health, 90*, 595–601.

Morris, Jenny. (1998). *Still missing? Vol 1: The experiences of disabled children living away from their families*. London: The Who Cares? Trust.

Morrison, India. (2002). Mirror neurons and cultural transmission. In Maxim I. Stamenov & Vittorio Gallese (Eds.), *Mirror neurons and the evolution of brain and language* (pp. 333–340). Amsterdam: John Benjamins Publishing Company.

Morrongiello, Barbara A., Fenwick, Kimberley D., & Chance, Graham. (1998). Crossmodal learning in newborn infants: Inferences about properties of auditory-visual events. *Infant Behavior & Development, 21*, 543–553.

Morrow, Daniel G., Ridolfo, Heather E., Menard, William E., Sanborn, Adam, Stine-Morrow, Elizabeth A. L., Magnor, Cliff, et al. (2003). Environmental support promotes expertise-based mitigation of age differences on pilot communication tasks. *Psychology & Aging, 18*, 268–284.

Morry, Marian M. (2005). Relationship satisfaction as a predictor of similarity ratings: A test of the attraction-similarity hypothesis. *Journal of Social and Personal Relationships, 22*, 561–584.

Morse, Stephen S., Garwin, Richard L., & Olsiewski, Paula J. (2006, November 10). Next flu pandemic: What to do until the vaccine arrives? *Science, 314*, 929.

Morton, J. Bruce, Trehub, Sandra E., & Zelazo, Philip David. (2003). Sources of inflexibility in 6-year-olds' understanding of emotion in speech. *Child Development, 74*, 1857–1868.

Moscovitch, Morris. (1982). A neuropsychological approach to perception and memory in normal and pathological aging. In Fergus I. M. Craik & Sandra Trehub (Eds.), *Aging and cognitive processes* (pp. 000–000). New York: Plenum Press.

Moscovitch, Morris, Fernandes, Myra, & Troyer, Angela. (2001). Working-with-memory and cognitive resources: A component-process account of divided attention and memory. In Moshe Naveh-Benjamin, Morris Moscovitch, & Henry L. Roediger (Eds.), *Perspectives on human memory and cognitive aging: Essays in honour of Fergus Craik* (pp. 171–192). New York: Psychology Press.

Moshman, David. (1999). *Adolescent psychological development: Rationality, morality, and identity*. Mahwah, NJ: Erlbaum.

Moshman, David. (2005). *Adolescent psychological development: Rationality, morality, and identity* (2nd ed.). Mahwah, NJ: Erlbaum.

Moshman, David, & Geil, Molly. (1998). Collaborative reasoning: Evidence for collective rationality. *Thinking & Reasoning, 4*, 231–248.

Moss, Ellen, Cyr, Chantal, & Dubois-Comtois, Karine. (2004). Attachment at early school age and developmental risk: Examining family contexts and behavior problems of controlling-caregiving, controlling-punitive, and behaviorally disorganized children. *Developmental Psychology, 40*, 519–532.

Moster, Dag, Lie, Rolv T., Irgens, Lorentz M., Bjerkedal, Tor, & Markestad, Trond. (2001). The association of Apgar score with subsequent death and cerebral palsy: A population-based study in term infants. *Journal of Pediatrics, 138*, 798–803.

Motta, M., Bennati, E., Ferlito, L., Malaguarnera, M., & Motta, L. (2005). Successful aging in centenarians: Myths and reality. *Archives of Gerontology and Geriatrics, 40*, 241–251.

Mowbray, Carol T., Megivern, Deborah, Mandiberg, James M., Strauss, Shari, Stein, Catherine H., Collins, Kim, et al. (2006). Campus mental health services: Recommendations for change. *American Journal of Orthopsychiatry, 76*, 226–237.

Mpofu, Elias, & van de Vijver, Fons J. R. (2000). Taxonomic structure in early to middle childhood: A longitudinal study with Zimbabwean schoolchildren. *International Journal of Behavioral Development, 24*, 204–212.

Mroczek, Daniel K., Spiro, Avion, III, & Griffin, Paul W. (2006). Personality and aging. In James E. Birren & K. Warner Schaie (Eds.), *Handbook of the psychology of aging* (6th ed., pp. 363–377). Amsterdam: Elsevier.

Mueller, Margaret M., & Elder, Glen H. (2003). Family contingencies across the generations: Grandparent-grandchild relationships in holistic perspective. *Journal of Marriage & Family, 65*, 404–417.

Mukamal, Kenneth J., Lumley, Thomas, Luepker, Russell V., Lapin, Pauline, Mittleman, Murray A., McBean, A. Marshall, et al. (2006). Alcohol consumption in older adults and Medicare costs. *Health Care Financing Review, 27*, 49–61.

Mukesh, Bickol N., Dimitrov, Peter N., Leikin, Sophia, Wang, Jie J., Mitchell, Paul, McCarty, Catherine A., et al. (2004). Five-year incidence of age-related maculopathy: The Visual Impairment Project. *Ophthalmology, 111*, 1176–1182.

Müller, Ulrich, Dick, Anthony Steven, Gela, Katherine, Overton, Willis F., & Zelazo, Philip David. (2006). The role of negative priming in preschoolers' flexible rule use on the dimensional change card sort task. *Child Development, 77*, 395–412.

Mullis, Ina V. S., Martin, Michael O., Gonzalez, Eugenio J., & Chrostowski, Steven J. (2004). *TIMSS 2003 international mathematics report: Findings from IEA's Trends in International Mathematics and Science Study at the eighth and fourth grades.* Chestnut Hill, MA: TIMSS & PIRLS International Study Center, Lynch School of Education, Boston College.

Mullis, Ina V. S., Martin, Michael O., Gonzalez, Eugenio J., & Kennedy, Ann M. (2003). *PIRLS 2001 international report: IEA's study of reading literacy achievement in primary school in 35 countries.* Chestnut Hill, MA: PIRLS International Study Center, Lynch School of Education, Boston College.

Mulvey, Edward P., & Cauffman, Elizabeth. (2001). The inherent limits of predicting school violence. *American Psychologist, 56,* 797–802.

Munakata, Yuko. (2006). Information processing approaches to development. In William Damon & Richard M. Lerner (Series Eds.) & Deanna Kuhn & Robert S. Siegler (Vol. Eds.), *Handbook of child psychology: Vol. 2. Cognition, perception, and language* (6th ed., pp. 426–463). Hoboken, NJ: Wiley.

Muraco, Anna. (2006). Intentional families: Fictive kin ties between cross-gender, different sexual orientation friends. *Journal of Marriage and Family, 68,* 1313–1325.

Murray, Christopher J. L., Kulkarni, Sandeep C., Michaud, Catherine, Tomijima, Niels, Bulzacchelli, Maria T., Iandiorio, Terrell J., et al. (2006). Eight Americas: Investigating mortality disparities across races, counties, and race-counties in the United States. *PLoS Medicine, 3*(9), e260.

Murray, Lynne, Halligan, Sarah L., Adams, Gillian, Patterson, Paul, & Goodyer, Ian M. (2006). Socioemotional development in adolescents at risk for depression: The role of maternal depression and attachment style. *Development and Psychopathology, 18,* 489–516.

Musick, Kelly. (2002). Planned and unplanned childbearing among unmarried women. *Journal of Marriage & Family, 64,* 915–929.

Musick, Marc A., Herzog, A. Regula, & House, James S. (1999). Volunteering and mortality among older adults: Findings from a national sample. *Journals of Gerontology: Series B: Psychological Sciences & Social Sciences, 54B,* S173–S180.

Mustillo, Sarah, Worthman, Carol, Erkanli, Alaattin, Keeler, Gordon, Angold, Adrian, & Costello, E. Jane. (2003). Obesity and psychiatric disorder: Developmental trajectories. *Pediatrics, 111,* 851–859.

Muter, Valerie, Hulme, Charles, Snowling, Margaret J., & Stevenson, Jim. (2004). Phonemes, rimes, vocabulary, and grammatical skills as foundations of early reading development: Evidence from a longitudinal study. *Developmental Psychology, 40,* 665–681.

Myers, David G. (2000). The funds, friends, and faith of happy people. *American Psychologist, 55,* 56–67.

Myers, David G. (2002). *Intuition: Its powers and perils.* New Haven, CT: Yale University Press.

Myers-Scotton, Carol, & Bolonyai, Agnes. (2001). Calculating speakers: Codeswitching in a rational choice model. *Language in Society, 30,* 1–28.

Nagda, Biren A., Gurin, Patricia, & Johnson, Shawnti M. (2005). Living, doing and thinking diversity: How does precollege diversity experience affect first-year students' engagement with college diversity? In Robert S. Feldman (Ed.), *Improving the first year of college: Research and practice* (pp. 73–108). Mahwah, NJ: Erlbaum.

Nair, K. Sreekumaran, Rizza, Robert A., O'Brien, Peter, Dhatariya, Ketan, Short, Kevin R., Nehra, Ajay, et al. (2006). DHEA in elderly women and DHEA or testosterone in elderly men. *New England Journal of Medicine, 355*(16), 1647–1659.

Nakahara, Kiyoshi, & Miyashita, Yasushi. (2005, April 29). Understanding intentions: Through the looking glass. *Science, 308,* 644–645.

Nakamura, Suad, Wind, Marilyn, & Danello, Mary Ann. (1999). Review of hazards associated with children placed in adult beds. *Archives of Pediatrics and Adolescent Medicine, 153,* 1019–1023.

Nakasone, Ronald Y. (2000). Buddhist issues in end-of-life decision making. In Kathryn Braun, James H. Pietsch, & Patricia L. Blanchette (Eds.), *Cultural issues in end-of-life decision making* (pp. 213–228). Thousand Oaks, CA: Sage.

Nathan, Rebekah. (2005). An anthropologist goes under cover. *The Chronicle of Higher Education: The Chronicle Review, 51*(47), B11

National Center for Health Statistics. (2000, September 21). Deaths: Final data for 1999. *National vital statistics reports, 49*(8).

National Center for Health Statistics. (2004, October 12). *Deaths: Final data for 2002, table* 3. Retrieved July 21, 2007, from the World Wide Web: http://www.cdc.gov/nchs/fastats/pdf/mortality/nvsr53_05t03.pdf

National Center for Health Statistics. (2005). *Health, United States, 2005, with chartbook on trends in the health of Americans* (PHS 2005–1232). Hyattsville, MD: Author.

National Center for Health Statistics. (2006). *Health, United States, 2006, with chartbook on trends in the health of Americans.* Retrieved April 28, 2007, from the World Wide Web: http://www.cdc.gov/nchs/data/hus/hus06.pdf#chartbookontrends

National Heart, Lung, and Blood Institute. (n.d.). *Body mass index table.* Retrieved August 21, 2007, from the World Wide Web: http://www.nhlbi.nih.gov/guidelines/obesity/bmi_tbl.htm

National Research Council and Institute of Medicine. (2000). *From neurons to neighborhoods: The science of early childhood development.* Washington, DC: National Academy Press.

Neal, David T., Wood, Wendy, & Quinn, Jeffrey M. (2006). Habits—A repeat performance. *Current Directions in Psychological Science, 15,* 198–202.

Neisser, Ulric (Ed.). (1998). *The rising curve: Long-term gains in IQ and related measures.* Washington, DC: American Psychological Association.

Nelson, Charles A., de Haan, Michelle, & Thomas, Kathleen M. (2006). *Neuroscience of cognitive development: The role of experience and the developing brain.* Hoboken, NJ: Wiley.

Nelson, Charles A., III, Thomas, Kathleen M., & de Haan, Michelle. (2006). Neural bases of cognitive development. In William Damon & Richard M. Lerner (Series Eds.) & Deanna Kuhn & Robert S. Siegler (Vol. Eds.), *Handbook of child psychology: Vol. 2. Cognition, perception, and language* (6th ed., pp. 3–57). Hoboken, NJ: Wiley.

Nelson, Charles A., & Webb, Sara J. (2003). A cognitive neuroscience perspective on early memory development. In Michelle de Haan & Mark H. Johnson (Eds.), *The cognitive neuroscience of development* (pp. 99–126). New York: Psychology Press.

Nelson, Jennifer A., Chiasson, Mary Ann, & Ford, Viola. (2004). Childhood overweight in a New York City WIC population. *American Journal of Public Health, 94,* 458–462.

Nemy, Enid (with Alexander, Ron). (1998, November 2). Metropolitan diary. *New York Times,* p. B2.

Nerlich, Brigitte, & Halliday, Christopher. (2007). Avian flu: The creation of expectations in the interplay between science and the media. *Sociology of Health & Illness, 29,* 46–65.

Nesdale, Drew. (2004). Social identity processes and children's ethnic prejudice. In Mark Bennett & Fabio Sani (Eds.), *The development of the social self* (pp. 219–245). Hove, East Sussex, England: Psychology Press.

Nesselroade, John R., & Molenaar, Peter C. M. (2003). Quantitative models for developmental processes. In Jaan Valsiner & Kevin J. Connolly (Eds.), *Handbook of developmental psychology* (pp. 622–639). Thousand Oaks, CA: Sage.

Netting, Nancy S., & Burnett, Matthew L. (2004). Twenty years of student sexual behavior: Subcultural adaptations to a changing health environment. *Adolescence, 39,* 19–38.

Neugarten, Bernice L., & Neugarten, Dail A. (1986). Changing meanings of age in the aging society. In Alan J. Pifer & Lydia Bronte (Eds.), *Our aging society: Paradox and promise* (pp. 33–52). New York: Norton.

Newell, Karl M., Vaillancourt, David E., & Sosnoff, Jacob J. (2006). Aging, complexity, and motor performance. In James E. Birren & K. Warner Schaie (Eds.), *Handbook of the psychology of aging* (6th ed., pp. 163–182). Amsterdam: Elsevier.

Newirth, Joseph. (2003). *Between emotion and cognition: The generative unconscious.* New York: Other Press.

Newman, Stuart A., & Müller, Gerd B. (2006). Genes and form: Inherency in the evolution of developmental mechanisms. In Eva M. Neumann-Held & Christoph Rehmann-Sutter (Eds.), *Genes in development: Re-reading the molecular paradigm* (pp. 38–73). Durham, NC: Duke University Press.

Newnham, John P., Doherty, Dorota A., Kendall, Garth E., Zubrick, Stephen R., Landau, Louis L., & Stanley, Fiona J. (2004). Effects of repeated prenatal ultrasound examinations on childhood outcome up to 8 years of age: Follow-up of a randomised controlled trial. *Lancet, 364,* 2038–2044.

Newschaffer, Craig J., Falb, Matthew D., & Gurney, James G. (2005). National autism prevalence trends from United States special education data. *Pediatrics, 115,* e277–282.

Newsom, Jason T., & Schulz, Richard. (1996). Social support as a mediator in the relation between functional status and quality of life in older adults. *Psychology & Aging, 11,* 34–44.

Newton, Christopher R., McBride, Joanna, Feyles, Valter, Tekpetey, Francis, & Power, Stephen. (2007). Factors affecting patients' attitudes toward single- and multiple-embryo transfer. *Fertility and Sterility, 87,* 269–278.

Nguyen, Huong Q., Jumaan, Aisha O., & Seward, Jane F. (2005). Decline in mortality due to varicella after implementation of varicella vaccination in the United States. *New England Journal of Medicine, 352,* 450–458.

Nguyen, Simone P., & Murphy, Gregory L. (2003). An apple is more than just a fruit: Cross-classification in children's concepts. *Child Development, 74,* 1783–1806.

NICHD Early Child Care Research Network. (2001). Child care and children's peer interaction at 24 and 36 months: The NICHD study of early child care. *Child Development, 72,* 1478–1500.

NICHD Early Child Care Research Network. (2003). Does amount of time spent in child care predict socioemotional adjustment during the transition to kindergarten? *Child Development, 74,* 976–1005.

NICHD Early Child Care Research Network. (2003). Do children's attention processes mediate the link between family predictors and school readiness? *Developmental Psychology, 39,* 581–593.

NICHD Early Child Care Research Network. (2004). Trajectories of physical aggression from toddlerhood to middle childhood. *Monographs of the Society for Research in Child Development, 69*(Serial No. 278), vii-129.

NICHD Early Child Care Research Network. (2004). Does class size in first grade relate to children's academic and social performance or observed classroom processes? *Developmental Psychology, 40,* 651–664.

NICHD Early Child Care Research Network. (2004). Are child developmental outcomes related to before- and after-school care arrangements? Results from the NICHD Study of Early Child Care. *Child Development, 75,* 280–295.

NICHD Early Child Care Research Network (Ed.). (2005). *Child care and child development: Results from the NICHD study of early child care and youth development.* New York: Guilford Press.

Nichols, Sharon L., & Berliner, David C. (2007). *Collateral damage: How high-stakes testing corrupts America's schools.* Cambridge, MA: Harvard Education Press.

Nichols, Tracy R., Graber, Julia A., Brooks-Gunn, Jeanne, & Botvin, Gilbert J. (2006). Sex differences in overt aggression and delinquency among urban minority middle school students. *Journal of Applied Developmental Psychology, 27,* 78–91.

Nielsen, David A., Virkkunen, Matti, Lappalainen, Jaakko, Eggert, Monica, Brown, Gerald L., Long, Jeffrey C., et al. (1998). A tryptophan hydroxylase gene marker for suicidality and alcoholism. *Archives of General Psychiatry, 55,* 593–602.

Nielsen, Mark, Suddendorf, Thomas, & Slaughter, Virginia. (2006). Mirror self-recognition beyond the face. *Child Development, 77,* 176–185.

Nielson, Kristy A., Langenecker, Scott A., & Garavan, Hugh. (2002). Differences in the functional neuroanatomy of inhibitory control across the adult life span. *Psychology & Aging, 17,* 56–71.

Nieto, Sonia. (2000). *Affirming diversity: The sociopolitical context of multicultural education* (3rd ed.). New York: Longman.

Nimrod, Galit. (2007). Expanding, reducing, concentrating and diffusing: Post retirement leisure behavior and life satisfaction. *Leisure Sciences, 29,* 91–111.

Nisbett, Richard E., Peng, Kaiping, Choi, Incheol, & Norenzayan, Ara. (2001). Culture and systems of thought: Holistic versus analytic cognition. *Psychological Review, 108,* 291–310.

Nishina, Adrienne, & Juvonen, Jaana. (2005). Daily reports of witnessing and experiencing peer harassment in middle school. *Child Development, 76,* 435–450.

Nobles, Anna Y., & Sciarra, Daniel T. (2000). Cultural determinants in the treatment of Arab Americans: A primer for mainstream therapists. *American Journal of Orthopsychiatry, 70,* 182–191.

Normile, Dennis. (2007, April 13). Japan picks up the 'innovation' mantra. *Science, 316,* 186.

Norris, Pippa. (2001). *Digital divide: Civic engagement, information poverty, and the internet worldwide.* New York: Cambridge University Press.

North American Menopause Society. (2007). Estrogen and progestogen use in peri- and postmenopausal women: March 2007 position statement of The North American Menopause Society. *Menopause: The Journal of The North American Menopause Society, 14*, 168–182.

Nurmi, Jari-Erik. (2004). Socialization and self-development: Channeling, selection, adjustment, and reflection. In Richard M. Lerner & Laurence D. Steinberg (Eds.), *Handbook of adolescent psychology* (2nd ed., pp. 85–124). Hoboken, NJ: Wiley.

O'Connor, Brian P., & St. Pierre, Edouard S. (2004). Older persons' perceptions of the frequency and meaning of elderspeak from family, friends, and service workers. *International Journal of Aging & Human Development, 58*, 197–221.

O'Connor, Thomas G. (2002). The 'effects' of parenting reconsidered: Findings, challenges, and applications. *Journal of Child Psychology & Psychiatry, 43*, 555–572.

O'Connor, Thomas G., Rutter, Michael, Beckett, Celia, Keaveney, Lisa, Kreppner, Jana M., & English & Romanian Adoptees Study Team. (2000). The effects of global severe privation on cognitive competence: Extension and longitudinal follow-up. *Child Development, 71*, 376–390.

O'Doherty, Kieran. (2006). Risk communication in genetic counselling: A discursive approach to probability. *Theory & Psychology, 16*, 225–256.

O'Meara, Ellen S., White, Mark, Siscovick, David S., Lyles, Mary F., & Kuller, Lewis H. (2005). Hospitalization for pneumonia in the cardiovascular health study: Incidence, mortality, and influence on longer-term survival. *Journal of the American Geriatrics Society, 53*, 1108–1116.

O'Neill, Ciaran, Jamison, James , McCulloch, Douglas, & Smith, David. (2001). Age-related macular degeneration: Cost-of-illness issues. *Drugs and Aging, 18*, 233–241.

O'Rahilly, Ronan R., & Müller, Fabiola. (2001). *Human embryology & teratology* (3rd ed.). New York: Wiley-Liss.

O'Rand, Angela M. (2006). Stratification and the life course: Life course capital, life course risks, and social inequality. In Robert H. Binstock & Linda K. George (Eds.), *Handbook of aging and the social sciences* (6th ed., pp. 145–162). Amsterdam: Elsevier.

Oberman, Lindsay M., & Ramachandran, Vilayanur S. (2007). The simulating social mind: The role of the mirror neuron system and simulation in the social and communicative deficits of autism spectrum disorders. *Psychological Bulletin, 133*, 310–327.

Oddy, Wendy H. (2004). A review of the effects of breastfeeding on respiratory infections, atopy, and childhood asthma. *Journal of Asthma, 41*, 605–621.

Ogawa, Tetsuo. (2004). Ageing in Japan: An issue of social contract in welfare transfer or generational conflict? In Peter Lloyd-Sherlock (Ed.), *Living longer: Ageing, development and social protection* (pp. 141–159). London: Zed Books.

Ogbu, John U. (2003). *Black American students in an affluent suburb: A study of academic disengagement*. Mahwah, NJ: Erlbaum.

Ogden, Cynthia L., Carroll, Margaret D., Curtin, Lester R., McDowell, Margaret A., Tabak, Carolyn J., & Flegal, Katherine M. (2006). Prevalence of overweight and obesity in the United States, 1999–2004. *Journal of the American Medical Association, 295*, 1549–1555.

Okamoto, Koichi, Tanaka, Makoto, & Kondo, Susumu. (2002). Treatment of vascular dementia. In Denham Harman, Robin Holliday, & Mohsen Meydani (Eds.), *Towards prolongation of the healthy life span: Practical approaches to intervention* (Vol. 977, pp. 507–512). New York: New York Academy of Sciences.

Okun, Morris A., Pugliese, John, & Rook, Karen S. (2007). Unpacking the relation between extraversion and volunteering in later life: The role of social capital. *Personality and Individual Differences, 42*, 1467–1477.

Olausson, Petra Otterblad, Haglund, Bengt, Weitoft, Gunilla Ringbäck, & Cnattingius, Sven. (2001). Teenage childbearing and long-term socioeconomic consequences: A case study in Sweden. *Family Planning Perspectives, 33*, 70–74.

Olson, Laura Katz (Ed.). (2001). *Age through ethnic lenses: Caring for the elderly in a multicultural society*. Lanham, MD: Rowman & Littlefield.

Olson, Lynn. (2005, June 22). States raise bar for high school diploma. *Education Week, 24*, 1, 28.

Olson, Lynn. (2007, June 12). What does 'ready' mean? *Education Week, 26*, 7–8, 10, 12.

Olson, Steve. (2004, September 3). Making sense of Tourette's. *Science, 305*, 1390–1392.

Olweus, Dan. (1992). Bullying among schoolchildren: Intervention and prevention. In Ray DeV. Peters, Robert Joseph McMahon, & Vernon L. Quinsey (Eds.), *Aggression and violence throughout the life span* (pp. 100–125). Thousand Oaks, CA: Sage.

Olweus, Dan. (1993). Victimization by peers: Antecedents and long-term outcomes. In Kenneth H. Rubin & Jens B. Asendorpf (Eds.), *Social withdrawal, inhibition, and shyness in childhood* (pp. 315–341). Hillsdale, NJ: Erlbaum.

Olweus, Dan, Limber, Sue, & Mahalic, Sharon F. (1999). *Bullying prevention program*. Boulder, CO: Center for the Study and Prevention of Violence, Institute of Behavioral Science, University of Colorado at Boulder.

Ombelet, Willem. (2007). Access to assisted reproduction services and infertility treatment in Belgium in the context of the European countries. *Pharmaceuticals Policy and Law, 9*, 189–201.

Omoto, Allen M., & Kurtzman, Howard S. (2006). *Sexual orientation and mental health: Examining identity and development in lesbian, gay, and bisexual people*. Washington, DC: American Psychological Association.

Opoku, Kofi Asare. (1989). African perspectives on death and dying. In Arthur Berger, Paul Badham, Austin Kutscher, Joyce Berger, Michael Perry, & John Beloff (Eds.), *Perspectives on death and dying: Cross-cultural and multi-disciplinary views* (pp. 14–23). Philadelphia: Charles Press.

Oregon Department of Human Services. (2006). *State of Oregon: Death with dignity act*. Retrieved September 8, 2007, from the World Wide Web: http://oregon.gov/DHS/ph/pas/index.shtml

Orentlicher, David, & Callahan, Christopher M. (2004). Feeding tubes, slippery slopes, and physician-assisted suicide. *Journal of Legal Medicine, 25*, 389–409.

Orfield, Gary (Ed.). (2004). *Dropouts in America: Confronting the graduation rate crisis*. Cambridge, MA: Harvard Education Press.

Organisation for Economic Co-operation and Development. (2004). *Problem solving for tomorrow's world: First measures of cross-curricular competencies from PISA 2003*. Paris: Author.

Ormerod, Thomas C. (2005). Planning and ill-defined problems. In Robin Morris & Geoff Ward (Eds.), *The cognitive psychology of planning* (pp. 53–70). New York: Psychology Press.

Osgood, D. Wayne, Ruth, Gretchen, Eccles, Jacquelynne S., Jacobs, Janis E., & Barber, Bonnie L. (2005). Six paths to adulthood: Fast starters, parents without careers, educated partners, educated singles, working singles, and slow starters. In Richard A. Settersten, Jr., Frank F. Furstenberg, Jr., & Rubén G. Rumbaut (Eds.), *On the frontier of adulthood: Theory, research, and public policy* (pp. 320–355). Chicago: University of Chicago Press.

Osnes, E., Lofthus, C., Meyer, H., Falch, J., Nordsletten, L., Cappelen, I., et al. (2004). Consequences of hip fracture on activities of daily life and residential needs. *Osteoporosis International, 15,* 567–574.

Oswald, Debra L., Clark, Eddie M., & Kelly, Cheryl M. (2004). Friendship maintenance: An analysis of individual and dyad behaviors. *Journal of Social & Clinical Psychology, 23,* 413–441.

Otto, Suzie J., Fracheboud, Jacques, Looman, Caspar W. N., Broeders, Mireille J. M., Boer, Rob, Hendriks, Jan H. C. L., et al. (2003). Initiation of population-based mammography screening in Dutch municipalities and effect on breast-cancer mortality: A systematic review. *Lancet, 361,* 1411–1417.

Overbeek, Geertjan, Stattin, Håkan, Vermulst, Ad, Ha, Thao, & Engels, Rutger C. M. E. (2007). Parent-child relationships, partner relationships, and emotional adjustment: A birth-to-maturity prospective study. *Developmental Psychology, 43,* 429–437.

Oxman, M. N., Levin, M. J., Johnson, G. R., Schmader, K. E., Straus, S. E., Gelb, L. D., et al. (2005). A vaccine to prevent herpes zoster and postherpetic neuralgia in older adults. *New England Journal of Medicine, 352,* 2271–2284.

Ozer, Emily J., & Weiss, Daniel S. (2004). Who develops posttraumatic stress disorder? *Current Directions in Psychological Science, 13,* 169–172.

Pace, Thaddeus W. W., Mletzko, Tanja C., Alagbe, Oyetunde, Musselman, Dominique L., Nemeroff, Charles B., Miller, Andrew H., et al. (2006). Increased stress-induced inflammatory responses in male patients with major depression and increased early life stress. *American Journal of Psychiatry, 163,* 1630–1633.

Padmadas, Sabu S., Hutter, Inge, & Willekens, Frans. (2004). Compression of women's reproductive spans in Andhra Pradesh, India. *International Family Planning Perspectives, 30,* 12–19.

Pahl, Kerstin, & Way, Niobe. (2006). Longitudinal trajectories of ethnic identity among urban Black and Latino adolescents. *Child Development, 77,* 1403–1415.

Palmer, Raymond F., Blanchard, Stephen, Jean, Carlos R., & Mandell, David S. (2005). School district resources and identification of children with autistic disorder. *American Journal of Public Health, 95,* 125–130.

Palmore, Erdman. (1998). *The facts on aging quiz* (2nd ed.). New York: Springer.

Palmore, Erdman. (2005). Three decades of research on ageism. *Generations, 29,* 87–90.

Palmore, Erdman, Branch, Laurence G., & Harris, Diana K. (2005). *Encyclopedia of ageism.* Binghamton, NY: Haworth.

Pan, Xiaochuan, Yue, Wei, He, Kebin, & Tong, Shilu. (2007). Health benefit evaluation of the energy use scenarios in Beijing, China. *Science of The Total Environment, 374,* 242–251.

Panagiotakos, D. B., Kourlaba, G., Zeimbekis, A., Toutouzas, P., & Polychronopoulos, E. (2007). The J-shape association of alcohol consumption on blood pressure levels, in elderly people from Mediterranean Islands (MEDIS epidemiological study). *Journal of Human Hypertension, 21,* 585–587.

Pang, Jenny W. Y., Heffelfinger, James D., Huang, Greg J., Benedetti, Thomas J., & Weiss, Noel S. (2002). Outcomes of planned home births in Washington State: 1989–1996. *Obstetrics & Gynecology, 100,* 253–259.

Park, Denise C., & Gutchess, Angela H. (2005). Long-term memory and aging: A cognitive neuroscience perspective. In Roberto Cabeza, Lars Nyberg, & Denise Park (Eds.), *Cognitive neuroscience of aging: Linking cognitive and cerebral aging* (pp. 218–245). New York: Oxford University Press.

Park, Denise C., & Hedden, Trey. (2001). Working memory and aging. In Moshe Naveh-Benjamin, Morris Moscovitch, & Henry L. Roediger (Eds.), *Perspectives on human memory and cognitive aging: Essays in honour of Fergus Craik* (pp. 148–160). New York: Psychology Press.

Park, Denise C., & Payer, Doris. (2006). Working memory across the adult lifespan. In Ellen Bialystok & Fergus I. M. Craik (Eds.), *Lifespan cognition: Mechanisms of change* (pp. 128–142). New York: Oxford University Press.

Park, D. J. J., & Congdon, Nathan G. (2004). Evidence for an "epidemic" of myopia. *Annals, Academy of Medicine, Singapore, 33,* 21–26.

Parke, Ross D. (1996). *Fatherhood.* Cambridge, MA: Harvard University Press.

Parke, Ross D., & Buriel, Raymond. (2006). Socialization in the family: Ethnic and ecological perspectives. In William Damon & Richard M. Lerner (Series Eds.) & Nancy Eisenberg (Vol. Ed.), *Handbook of child psychology: Vol. 3. Social, emotional, and personality development* (6th ed., pp. 429–504). Hoboken, NJ: Wiley.

Parke, Ross D., Coltrane, Scott, Duffy, Sharon, Buriel, Raymond, Dennis, Jessica, Powers, Justina, et al. (2004). Economic stress, parenting, and child adjustment in Mexican American and European American families. *Child Development, 75,* 1632–1656.

Parker, Susan W., & Nelson, Charles A. (2005). The impact of early institutional rearing on the ability to discriminate facial expressions of emotion: An event-related potential study. *Child Development, 76,* 54–72.

Parkin, Alan J. (1993). *Memory: Phenomena, experiment, and theory.* Oxford, England: Blackwell.

Parsell, Diana. (2004, November 13). Assault on autism. *Science News, 166,* 311–312.

Pascarella, Ernest T. (2005). Cognitive impacts of the first year of college. In Robert S. Feldman (Ed.), *Improving the first year of college: Research and practice* (pp. 111–140). Mahwah, NJ: Erlbaum.

Pascarella, Ernest T., & Terenzini, Patrick T. (1991). *How college affects students: Findings and insights from twenty years of research.* San Francisco: Jossey-Bass Publishers.

Pascual-Leone, Alvaro, & Torres, Fernando. (1993). Plasticity of the sensorimotor cortex representation of the reading finger in Braille readers. *Brain, 116,* 39–52.

Pastore, Ann L., & Maguire, Kathleen. (2005). *Sourcebook of criminal justice statistics, 2003* (NCJ 208756). Rockville, MD: Justice Statistics Clearinghouse/NCJRS.

Pastore, Ann L., & Maguire, Kathleen. (n.d.). *Sourcebook of criminal justice statistics online: Firearm suicide rate (per 100,000 per-*

sons in each age group), by age, United States, 1980–2004. Retrieved August 25, 2007, from the World Wide Web: http://www.albany.edu/sourcebook/pdf/t31392004.pdf

Patel, Vimla L., Arocha, José F., & Kaufman, David R. (1999). Expertise and tacit knowledge in medicine. In Robert J. Sternberg & Joseph A. Horvath (Eds.), *Tacit knowledge in professional practice: Researcher and practitioner perspectives* (pp. 75–99). Mahwah, NJ: Erlbaum.

Paterson, David S., Trachtenberg, Felicia L., Thompson, Eric G., Belliveau, Richard A., Beggs, Alan H., Darnall, Ryan, et al. (2006). Multiple serotonergic brainstem abnormalities in sudden infant death syndrome. *Journal of the American Medical Association, 296*, 2124–2132.

Patrick, Kevin, Norman, Gregory J., Calfas, Karen J., Sallis, James F., Zabinski, Marion F., Rupp, Joan, et al. (2004). Diet, physical activity, and sedentary behaviors as risk factors for overweight in adolescence. *Archives of Pediatrics & Adolescent Medicine, 158*, 385–390.

Patterson, Charlotte J. (2006). Children of lesbian and gay parents. *Current Directions in Psychological Science, 15*, 241–244.

Paul, David, Leef, Kathleen, Locke, Robert, Bartoshesky, Louis, Walrath, Judy, & Stefano, John. (2006). Increasing illness severity in very low birth weight infants over a 9-year period. *BMC Pediatrics, 6*, 2.

Pauli-Pott, Ursula, Mertesacker, Bettina, & Beckmann, Dieter. (2004). Predicting the development of infant emotionality from maternal characteristics. *Development & Psychopathology, 16*, 19–42.

Pedersen, Nancy L., Spotts, Erica, & Kato, Kenji. (2005). Genetic influences on midlife functioning. In Sherry L. Willis & Mike Martin (Eds.), *Middle adulthood: A lifespan perspective* (pp. 65–98). Thousand Oaks, CA: Sage.

Peng, Du, & Phillips, David R. (2004). Potential consequences of population ageing for social development in China. In Peter Lloyd-Sherlock (Ed.), *Living longer: Ageing, development and social protection* (pp. 97–116). London: Zed Books.

Peng, Kaiping, & Nisbett, Richard E. (1999). Culture, dialectics, and reasoning about contradiction. *American Psychologist, 54*, 741–754.

Pennington, Bruce Franklin. (2002). *The development of psychopathology: Nature and nurture*. New York: Guilford Press.

Pepler, Debra, Craig, Wendy, Yuile, Amy, & Connolly, Jennifer. (2004). Girls who bully: A developmental and relational perspective. In Martha Putallaz & Karen L. Bierman (Eds.), *Aggression, antisocial behavior, and violence among girls: A developmental perspective* (pp. 90–109). New York: Guilford.

Perfect, Timothy J., & Maylor, Elizabeth A. (Eds.). (2000). *Models of cognitive aging*. New York: Oxford University Press.

Perfetti, Jennifer, Clark, Roseanne, & Fillmore, Capri-Mara. (2004). Postpartum depression: Identification, screening, and treatment. *Wisconsin Medical Journal, 103*, 56–63.

Perie, Marianne, Grigg, Wendy S., & Dion, Gloria S. (2005). *The nation's report card: Mathematics 2005* (NCES 2006–453). Washington, DC: U.S. Department of Education, National Center for Education Statistics.

Perlmutter, Marion, Kaplan, Michael, & Nyquist, Linda. (1990). Development of adaptive competence in adulthood. *Human Development, 33*, 185–197.

Perls, Thomas. (2005). The different paths to age one hundred. In Richard G. Cutler, S. Mitchell Harman, Chris Heward, & Mike Gibbons (Eds.), *Longevity health sciences: The Phoenix conference* (pp. 13–25). New York: New York Academy of Sciences.

Perner, Josef. (2000). About + belief + counterfactual. In Peter Mitchell & Kevin John Riggs (Eds.), *Children's reasoning and the mind* (pp. 367–401). Hove, England: Psychology Press.

Perner, Josef, Lang, Birgit, & Kloo, Daniela. (2002). Theory of mind and self-control: More than a common problem of inhibition. *Child Development, 73*, 752–767.

Perrig-Chiello, Pasqualina, & Perren, Sonja. (2005). Impact of past transitions on well-being in middle age. In Sherry L. Willis & Mike Martin (Eds.), *Middle adulthood: A lifespan perspective* (pp. 143–178). Thousand Oaks, CA: Sage Publications.

Perry, William G., Jr. (1981). Cognitive and ethical growth: The making of meaning. In A. Chickering (Ed.), *The modern American college: Responding to the new realities of diverse students and a changing society* (pp. 76–116). San Francisco: Jossey-Bass.

Perry, William G. (1999). *Forms of intellectual and ethical development in the college years: A scheme*. San Francisco: Jossey-Bass.

Persaud, Trivedi V. N., Chudley, Albert E., & Skalko, Richard G. (1985). *Basic concepts in teratology*. New York: Liss.

Petersen, Ronald C. (Ed.). (2003). *Mild cognitive impairment: Aging to Alzheimer's disease*. Oxford, England: Oxford University Press.

Peterson, Jordan B., & Flanders, Joseph L. (2005). Play and the regulation of aggression. In Richard Ernest Tremblay, Willard W. Hartup, & John Archer (Eds.), *Developmental origins of aggression* (pp. 133–157). New York: Guilford Press.

Pett, Marjorie A., Caserta, Michael S., Hutton, Ann P., & Lund, Dale A. (1988). Intergenerational conflict: Middle-aged women caring for demented older relatives. *American Journal of Orthopsychiatry, 58*, 405–417.

Pettit, Gregory S. (2004). Violent children in developmental perspective: Risk and protective factors and the mechanisms through which they (may) operate. *Current Directions in Psychological Science, 13*, 194–197.

Pew Commission on Children in Foster Care. (2004). *Safety, permanence and well-being for children in foster care*. Retrieved June 23, 2007, from the World Wide Web: http://pewfostercare.org/research/docs/FinalReport.pdf

Pew Research Center. (2006). *Working after retirement: The gap between expectations and reality*. Pew Research Center. Retrieved February 14, 2007, from the World Wide Web: http://pewresearch.org/assets/social/pdf/Retirement.pdf

Pew Research Center. (2007). *How young people view their lives, futures and politics: A portrait of "Generation Next"*. Pew Research Center. Retrieved August 26, 2007, from the World Wide Web: http://people-press.org/reports/pdf/300.pdf

Philip, John, Silver, Richard K., Wilson, R. Douglas, Thom, Elizabeth A., Zachary, Julia M., Mohide, Patrick, et al. (2004). Late first-trimester invasive prenatal diagnosis: Results of an international randomized trial. *Obstetrics & Gynecology, 103*, 1164–1173.

Phillips, Deborah A., & White, Sheldon H. (2004). New possibilities for research on Head Start. In Edward Zigler & Sally J. Styfco (Eds.), *The Head Start debates* (pp. 263–278). Baltimore: Brookes.

Phillipson, Chris. (2006). Ageing and globalization. In John A. Vincent, Chris R. Phillipson, & Murna Downs (Eds.), *The futures of old age* (pp. 201–207). Thousand Oaks, CA: Sage.

Phinney, Jean S. (2006). Ethnic identity exploration in emerging adulthood. In Jeffrey Jensen Arnett & Jennifer Lynn Tanner (Eds.), *Emerging adults in America: Coming of age in the 21st century* (pp. 117–134). Washington, DC: American Psychological Association.

Piaget, Jean. (1952b). *The origins of intelligence in children.* (M. Cook, Trans.). Oxford, England: International Universities Press.

Piaget, Jean. (1962). *Play, dreams and imitation in childhood* (C. Gattegno & F. M. Hodgson, Trans.). New York: Norton. (Original work published 1945)

Piaget, Jean. (1970). *The child's conception of movement and speed* (G. E. T. Holloway and M. J. Mackenzie, Trans.). New York: Basic Books.

Piaget, Jean. (1997). *The moral judgment of the child* (Marjorie Gabain, Trans.). New York: Simon and Schuster. (Original work published 1932)

Piaget, Jean, Voelin-Liambey, Daphne, & Berthoud-Papandropoulou, Ioanna. (2001). *Problems of class inclusion and logical implication* (Robert L. Campbell, Ed. & Trans.). Hove, E. Sussex, England: Psychology Press. (Original work published 1977)

Pierce, Benton H., Simons, Jon S., & Schacter, Daniel L. (2004). Aging and the seven sins of memory. In Paul T. Costa & Ilene C. Siegler (Eds.), *Recent advances in psychology and aging* (Vol. 15, pp. 1–40). Amsterdam: Elsevier.

Pinborg, Anja, Loft, Anne, & Nyboe Andersen, Anders. (2004). Neonatal outcome in a Danish national cohort of 8602 children born after in vitro fertilization or intracytoplasmic sperm injection: The role of twin pregnancy. *Acta Obstetricia et Gynecologica Scandinavica, 83*, 1071–1078.

Pinheiro, Paulo Sèrgio (Ed.). (2006). *World report on violence against children.* Geneva, Switzerland: United Nations.

Pinker, Steven. (1994). *The language instinct.* New York: William Morrow.

Pinquart, Martin, & Silbereisen, Rainer K. (2006). Socioemotional selectivity in cancer patients. *Psychology and Aging, 21*, 419–423.

Pinquart, Martin, & Sörensen, Silvia. (2003). Associations of stressors and uplifts of caregiving with caregiver burden and depressive mood: A meta-analysis. *Journals of Gerontology: Series B: Psychological Sciences & Social Sciences, 58B*, P112–P128.

Piolino, Pascale, Desgranges, Béatrice, Clarys, David, Guillery-Girard, Bérengère, Taconnat, Laurence, Isingrini, Michel, et al. (2006). Autobiographical memory, autonoetic consciousness, and self-perspective in aging. *Psychology and Aging, 21*, 510–525.

Piontelli, Alessandra. (2002). *Twins: From fetus to child.* London: Routledge.

Pirozzo, Sandi, Papinczak, Tracey, & Glasziou, Paul. (2003). Whispered voice test for screening for hearing impairment in adults and children: Systematic review. *British Medical Journal, 327*, 967–960.

Pitskhelauri, G. Z. (1982). *The longliving of Soviet Georgia* (Gari Lesnoff-Caravaglia, Ed. & Trans.). New York: Human Sciences Press.

Plank, Stephen B., & MacIver, Douglas J. (2003). Educational achievement. In Marc H. Bornstein, Lucy Davidson, Corey L. M. Keyes, & Kristin Moore (Eds.), *Well-being: Positive development across the life course* (pp. 341–354). Mahwah, NJ: Erlbaum.

Plomin, Robert. (2002). Behavioural genetics in the 21st century. In Willard W. Hartup & Rainer K. Silbereisen (Eds.), *Growing points in developmental science: An introduction* (pp. 47–63). Philadelphia: Psychology Press.

Plomin, Robert, DeFries, John C., Craig, Ian W., & McGuffin, Peter. (2003). *Behavioral genetics in the postgenomic era.* Washington, DC: American Psychological Association.

Plomin, Robert, Happé, Francesca, & Caspi, Avshalom. (2002). Personality and cognitive abilities. In Peter McGuffin, Michael J. Owen, & Irving I. Gottesman (Eds.), *Psychiatric genetics and genomics* (pp. 77–112). New York: Oxford University Press.

Plomin, Robert, & McGuffin, Peter. (2003). Psychopathology in the postgenomic era. *Annual Review of Psychology, 54*, 205–228.

Plutchik, Robert. (2003). *Emotions and life: Perspectives from psychology, biology, and evolution.* Washington, DC: American Psychological Association.

Pogrebin, Letty Cottin. (1996). *Getting over getting older: An intimate journey.* Boston: Little Brown.

Poland, Gregory A. (2006). Vaccines against avian influenza—A race against time. *New England Journal of Medicine, 354*, 1411–1413.

Pollack, Harold, & Frohna, John. (2001). A competing risk model of sudden infant death syndrome incidence in two U.S. birth cohorts. *Journal of Pediatrics, 138*, 661–667.

Pollak, Seth D., Cicchetti, Dante, Hornung, Katherine, & Reed, Alex. (2000). Recognizing emotion in faces: Developmental effects of child abuse and neglect. *Developmental Psychology, 36*, 679–688.

Pomerantz, Eva M., & Rudolph, Karen D. (2003). What ensues from emotional distress? Implications for competence estimation. *Child Development, 74*, 329–345.

Pong, Suet-ling, Dronkers, Jaap, & Hampden-Thompson, Gillian. (2003). Family policies and children's school achievement in single- versus two-parent families. *Journal of Marriage and Family, 65*, 681–699.

Ponsonby, Anne-Louise, Dwyer, Terence, Gibbons, Laura E., Cochrane, Jennifer A., & Wang, You-Gan. (1993). Factors potentiating the risk of sudden infant death syndrome associated with the prone position. *New England Journal of Medicine, 329*, 377–382.

Porche, Michelle V., Ross, Stephanie J., & Snow, Catherine E. (2004). From preschool to middle school: The role of masculinity in low-income urban adolescent boys' literacy skills and academic achievement. In Niobe Way & Judy Y. Chu (Eds.), *Adolescent boys: Exploring diverse cultures of boyhood* (pp. 338–360). New York: New York University Press.

Portes, Alejandro, & Rumbaut, Rubén G. (2001). *Legacies: The story of the immigrant second generation.* Berkeley, CA and New York: University of California Press and the Russell Sage Foundation.

Posthuma, Daniëlle, de Geus, Eco J. C., & Boomsma, Dorret I. (2003). Genetic contributions to anatomical, behavioral, and neurophysiological indices of cognition. In Robert Plomin, John C. DeFries, Ian W. Craig, & Peter McGuffin (Eds.), *Behavioral genetics in the postgenomic era* (pp. 141–161). Washington, DC: American Psychological Association.

Powell, Douglas H. (with Whitla, Dean K.). (1994). *Profiles in cognitive aging.* Cambridge, MA: Harvard University Press.

Powell, Douglas R. (2006). Families and early childhood interventions. In William Damon & Richard M. Lerner (Series Eds.) & K. Ann Renninger & Irving E. Sigel (Vol. Eds.), *Handbook of child psychology: Vol. 4. Child psychology in practice* (6th ed., pp. 548–591). Hoboken: Wiley.

Powell, Lynda H., Shahabi, Leila, & Thoresen, Carl E. (2003). Religion and spirituality: Linkages to physical health. *American Psychologist, 58,* 36–52.

Powlishta, Kimberly. (2004). Gender as a social category: Intergroup processes and gender-role development. In Mark Bennett & Fabio Sani (Eds.), *The development of the social self* (pp. 103–133). Hove, East Sussex, England: Psychology Press.

Pratt, Michael W., & Norris, Joan E. (1999). Moral development in maturity: Lifespan perspectives on the processes of successful aging. In Thomas M. Hess & Fredda Blanchard-Fields (Eds.), *Social cognition and aging* (pp. 291–317). San Diego, CA: Academic Press.

Pratt, Michael W., Norris, Joan E., Arnold, Mary Louise, & Filyer, Rebecca. (1999). Generativity and moral development as predictors of value-socialization narratives for young persons across the adult life span: From lessons learned to stories shared. *Psychology & Aging, 14,* 414–426.

Pratt, Michael W., & Robins, Susan L. (1991). That's the way it was: Age differences in the structure and quality of adults' personal narratives. *Discourse Processes, 14,* 73–85.

Prentice, Ross L., Caan, Bette, Chlebowski, Rowan T., Patterson, Ruth, Kuller, Lewis H., Ockene, Judith K., et al. (2006). Low-fat dietary pattern and risk of invasive breast cancer: The Women's Health Initiative Randomized Controlled Dietary Modification Trial. *Journal of the American Medical Association, 295,* 629–642.

Presser, Harriet B. (2000). Nonstandard work schedules and marital instability. *Journal of Marriage & the Family, 62,* 93–110.

Pressley, Michael, & Hilden, Katherine. (2006). Cognitive strategies: Production deficiencies and successful strategy instruction everywhere. In William Damon & Richard M. Lerner (Series Eds.) & Deanna Kuhn & Robert S. Siegler (Vol. Eds.), *Handbook of child psychology: Vol. 2. Cognition, perception, and language* (6th ed., pp. 511–556). Hoboken, NJ: Wiley.

Preston, Fredrica, Tang, Siew Tzuh, & McCorkle, Ruth. (2003). Symptom management for the terminally ill. In Inge Corless, Barbara B. Germino, & Mary A. Pittman (Eds.), *Dying, death, and bereavement: A challenge for living* (2nd ed., pp. 145–180). New York: Springer.

Preston, Tom, & Kelly, Michael. (2006). A medical ethics assessment of the case of Terri Schiavo. *Death Studies, 30,* 121–133.

Previti, Denise, & Amato, Paul R. (2003). Why stay married? Rewards, barriers, and marital stability. *Journal of Marriage & Family, 65,* 561–573.

Pridemore, William Alex. (2002). Vodka and violence: Alcohol consumption and homicide rates in Russia. *American Journal of Public Health, 92,* 1921–1930.

Promislow, Daniel, Fedorka, Ken, & Burger, Joep. (2006). Evolutionary biology of aging: Future directions. In Edward J. Masoro & Steven N. Austad (Eds.), *Handbook of the biology of aging* (6th ed., pp. 217–242). Amsterdam: Elsevier Academic Press.

Proulx, Christine M., Helms, Heather M., & Buehler, Cheryl. (2007). Marital quality and personal well-being: A meta-analysis. *Journal of Marriage and Family, 69,* 576–593.

Pruden, Shannon M., Hirsh-Pasek, Kathy, Golinkoff, Roberta Michnick, & Hennon, Elizabeth A. (2006). The birth of words: Ten-month-olds learn words through perceptual salience. *Child Development, 77,* 266–280.

Pucher, John, & Dijkstra, Lewis. (2003). Promoting safe walking and cycling to improve public health: Lessons from the Netherlands and Germany. *American Journal of Public Health, 93,* 1509–1516.

Pulkkinen, Lea, Feldt, Taru, & Kokko, Katja. (2005). Personality in young adulthood and functioning in middle age. In Sherry L. Willis & Mike Martin (Eds.), *Middle adulthood: A lifespan perspective* (pp. 99–141). Thousand Oaks, CA: Sage.

Quas, Jodi A., Bauer, Amy, & Boyce, W. Thomas. (2004). Physiological reactivity, social support, and memory in early childhood. *Child Development, 75,* 797–814.

Quinn, Paul C. (2004). Development of subordinate-level categorization in 3- to 7-month-old infants. *Child Development, 75,* 886–899.

Quintana, Stephen M., Aboud, Frances E., Chao, Ruth K., Contreras-Grau, Josefina, Cross, William E., Hudley, Cynthia, et al. (2006). Race, ethnicity, and culture in child development: Contemporary research and future directions. *Child Development, 77,* 1129–1141.

Raaijmakers, Quinten A. W., Engels, Rutger C. M. E., & Van Hoof, Anne. (2005). Delinquency and moral reasoning in adolescence and young adulthood. *International Journal of Behavioral Development, 29,* 247–258.

Rabbitt, Patrick, & Anderson, Mike. (2006). The lacunae of loss? Aging and the differentiation of cognitive abilities. In Ellen Bialystok & Fergus I. M. Craik (Eds.), *Lifespan cognition: Mechanisms of change* (pp. 331–343). New York: Oxford University Press.

Rabbitt, Patrick, Anderson, Michael, Davis, Helen, & Shilling, Val. (2003). Cognitive processes in ageing. In Jaan Valsiner & Kevin J. Connolly (Eds.), *Handbook of developmental psychology* (pp. 560–583). Thousand Oaks, CA: Sage.

Rabbitt, Patrick, Watson, Peter, Donlan, Chris, Mc Innes, Lynn, Horan, Michael, Pendleton, Neil, et al. (2002). Effects of death within 11 years on cognitive performance in old age. *Psychology & Aging, 17,* 468–481.

Radmacher, Kimberley, & Azmitia, Margarita. (2006). Are there gendered pathways to intimacy in early adolescents' and emerging adults' friendships? *Journal of Adolescent Research, 21,* 415–448.

Raikes, Helen, Luze, Gayle, Brooks-Gunn, Jeanne, Raikes, H. Abigail, Pan, Barbara Alexander, Tamis-LeMonda, Catherine S., et al. (2006). Mother-child bookreading in low-income families: Correlates and outcomes during the first three years of life. *Child Development, 77,* 924–953.

Raj, Anita, & Silverman, Jay G. (2003). Immigrant South Asian women at greater risk for injury from intimate partner violence. *American Journal of Public Health, 93,* 435–437.

Raley, R. Kelly, & Wildsmith, Elizabeth. (2004). Cohabitation and children's family instability. *Journal of Marriage & Family, 66,* 210–219.

Ramchandani, Paul, Stein, Alan, Evans, Jonathan, & O'Connor, Thomas G. (2005). Paternal depression in the postnatal period and child development: A prospective population study. *Lancet, 365,* 2201–2205.

Ramey, Craig T., Ramey, Sharon Landesman, Lanzi, Robin Gaines, & Cotton, Janice N. (2002). Early educational interventions for high-risk children: How center-based treatment can augment and improve parenting effectiveness. In John G. Borkowski, Sharon Landesman Ramey, & Marie Bristol-Power (Eds.), *Parenting and the child's world: Influences on academic, intellectual, and social-emotional development* (pp. 125–140). Mahwah, NJ: Erlbaum.

Rando, Therese A. (1993). *Treatment of complicated mourning.* Champaign, IL: Research Press.

Rankin, Jane L., Lane, David J., Gibbons, Frederick X., & Gerrard, Meg. (2004). Adolescent self-consciousness: Longitudinal age changes and gender differences in two cohorts. *Journal of Research on Adolescence, 14*, 1–21.

Ratcliff, Roger, Thapar, Anjali, & McKoon, Gail. (2006). Aging, practice, and perceptual tasks: A diffusion model analysis. *Psychology and Aging, 21*, 353–371.

Rauscher, Frances H., & Shaw, Gordon L. (1998). Key components of the Mozart effect. *Perceptual & Motor Skills, 86*(3, Pt. 1), 835–841.

Rauscher, Frances H., Shaw, Gordon L., & Ky, Catherine N. (1993, 14 Oct). Music and spatial task performance. *Nature, 365*, 611.

Ray, Ruth E. (1996). A postmodern perspective on feminist gerontology. *Gerontologist, 36*, 674–680.

Rayco-Solon, Pura, Fulford, Anthony J., & Prentice, Andrew M. (2005). Differential effects of seasonality on preterm birth and intrauterine growth restriction in rural Africans. *American Journal of Clinical Nutrition, 81*, 134–139.

Rayner, Keith, Foorman, Barbara R., Perfetti, Charles A., Pesetsky, David, & Seidenberg, Mark S. (2001). How psychological science informs the teaching of reading. *Psychological Science in the Public Interest, 2*, 31–74.

Raz, Naftali. (2005). The aging brain observed in vivo: Differential changes and their modifiers. In Roberto Cabeza, Lars Nyberg, & Denise Park (Eds.), *Cognitive neuroscience of aging: Linking cognitive and cerebral aging* (pp. 19–57). New York: Oxford University Press.

Read, Jennifer S. (2004). Prevention of mother-to-child transmission of HIV In Steven L. Zeichner & Jennifer S. Read (Eds.), *Textbook of pediatric HIV care* (pp. 111–133). Cambridge, UK: Cambridge University Press.

Ream, Geoffrey L., & Savin-Williams, Ritch C. (2003). Religious development in adolescence. In Gerald R. Adams & Michael D. Berzonsky (Eds.), *Blackwell handbook of adolescence* (pp. 51–59). Malden, MA: Blackwell.

Redline, Susan, Schluchter, Mark D., Larkin, Emma K., & Tishler, Peter V. (2003). Predictors of longitudinal change in sleep-disordered breathing in a nonclinic population. *Sleep: Journal of Sleep and Sleep Disorders Research, 26*, 703–709.

Reece, E. Albert, & Hobbins, John C. (Eds.). (2007). *Handbook of clinical obstetrics: The fetus & mother handbook* (2nd ed.). Malden, MA: Blackwell.

Reeve, Christopher. (1999). *Still me*. New York: Ballantine Books.

Regnerus, Mark D. (2005). Talking about sex: Religion and patterns of parent-child communication about sex and contraception. *Sociological Quarterly, 46*, 79–105.

Reichert, Monika, & Weidekamp-Maicher, Manuela. (2004). Germany: Quality of life in old age II. In Alan Walker (Ed.), *Growing older in Europe* (pp. 159–178). Maidenhead, United Kingdom: Open University Press.

Reis, Harry T., & Collins, W. Andrew. (2004). Relationships, human behavior, and psychological science. *Current Directions in Psychological Science, 13*, 233–237.

Reiss, David, Neiderhiser, Jenae M., Hetherington, E. Mavis, & Plomin, Robert. (2000). *The relationship code: Deciphering genetic and social influences on adolescent development*. Cambridge, MA: Harvard University Press.

Reiter, Russel J. (1998). Roundtable discussion: How best to ensure daily intake of antioxidants (from the diet and supplements) that is optimal for life span, disease, and general health. In Denham Harman, Robin Holliday, & Mohsen Meydani (Eds.), *Towards prolongation of the healthy life span: Practical approaches to intervention* (Vol. 854, pp. 463–476). New York: New York Academy of Sciences.

Reith, Gerda. (2005). On the edge: Drugs and the consumption of risk in late modernity. In Stephen Lyng (Ed.), *Edgework: The sociology of risk taking* (pp. 227–246). New York: Routledge.

Remage-Healey, Luke, & Bass, Andrew H. (2004). Rapid, hierarchical modulation of vocal patterning by steroid hormones. *Journal of Neuroscience, 24*, 5892–5900.

Rendell, Peter G., & Thomson, Donald M. (1999). Aging and prospective memory: Differences between naturalistic and laboratory tasks. *Journals of Gerontology: Series B: Psychological Sciences & Social Sciences, 54B*, P256–P269.

Renninger, K. Ann, & Amsel, Eric. (1997). Change and development: An introduction. In Eric Amsel & K. Ann Renninger (Eds.), *Change and development: Issues of theory, method, and application* (pp. ix-xv). Mahwah, NJ: Erlbaum.

Rentner, Diane Stark, Scott, Caitlin, Kober, Nancy, Chudowsky, Naomi, Chudowsky, Victor, Joftus, Scott, et al. (2006). *From the capital to the classroom: Year 4 of the No Child Left Behind Act*. Washington, DC: Center on Education Policy.

Rest, James. (1993). Research on moral judgment in college students. In Andrew Garrod (Ed.), *Approaches to moral development: New research and emerging themes* (pp. 201–211). New York: Teachers College Press.

Rest, James, Narvaez, Darcia, Bebeau, Muriel J., & Thoma, Stephen J. (1999). *Postconventional moral thinking: A neo-Kohlbergian approach*. Mahwah, NJ: Erlbaum.

Rettig, Michael. (2005). Using the multiple intelligences to enhance instruction for young children and young children with disabilities. *Early Childhood Education Journal, 32*, 255–259.

Retting, Richard A., Ferguson, Susan A., & McCartt, Anne T. (2003). A review of evidence-based traffic engineering measures designed to reduce pedestrian-motor vehicle crashes. *American Journal of Public Health, 93*, 1456–1463.

Reuter-Lorenz, Patricia A., Sylvester, Ching-Yune C., Cabeza, Roberto, Nyberg, Lars, & Park, Denise. (2005). The cognitive neuroscience of working memory and aging, *Cognitive neuroscience of aging: Linking cognitive and cerebral aging* (pp. 186–217). New York: Oxford University Press.

Reyna, Valerie F. (2004). How people make decisions that involve risk: A dual-processes approach. *Current Directions in Psychological Science, 13*, 60–66.

Reyna, Valerie F., & Farley, Frank. (2006). Risk and rationality in adolescent decision making: Implications for theory, practice, and public policy. *Psychological Science in the Public Interest, 7*, 1–44.

Reynolds, Arthur J. (2000). *Success in early intervention: The Chicago child-parent centers*. Lincoln, NE: University of Nebraska Press.

Reynolds, Arthur J., Ou, Suh-Ruu, & Topitzes, James W. (2004). Paths of effects of early childhood intervention on educational attainment and delinquency: A confirmatory analysis of the Chicago Child-Parent Centers. *Child Development, 75*, 1299–1328.

Reynolds, Heidi W., Wong, Emelita L., & Tucker, Heidi. (2006). Adolescents' use of maternal and child health services in developing countries. *International Family Planning Perspectives, 32*(1), 6–16.

Rhodes, Frank Harold Trevor. (2001). *The creation of the future: The role of the American university*. Ithaca, NY: Cornell University Press.

Rhodes, Jean E., & Roffman, Jennifer G. (2003). Nonparental adults as asset builders in the lives of youth. In Richard M. Lerner & Peter L. Benson (Eds.), *Developmental assets and asset-building communities: Implications for research, policy, and practice* (pp. 195–209). New York: Kluwer/Plenum.

Rice, Charles L., & Cunningham, David A. (2002). Aging of the neuromuscular system: Influences of gender and physical activity. In Roy J. Shephard (Ed.), *Gender, physical activity, and aging* (pp. 121–150). Boca Raton, FL: CRC Press.

Rich, John A., & Grey, Courtney M. (2005). Pathways to recurrent trauma among young black men: Traumatic stress, substance use, and the "code of the street". *American Journal of Public Health, 95,* 816–824.

Richardson, Rhonda A. (2004). Early adolescence talking points: Questions that middle school students want to ask their parents. *Family Relations, 53,* 87–94.

Ridley, Matt. (1999). *Genome: The autobiography of a species in 23 chapters*. London: Fourth Estate.

Riegel, Klaus F. (1975). Toward a dialectical theory of development. *Human Development, 18,* 50–64.

Riordan, Jan (Ed.). (2005). *Breastfeeding and human lactation* (3rd ed.). Sudbury, MA: Jones and Bartlett.

Ritchie, Karen, Kildea, Daniel, & Robine, Jean-Marie. (1992). The relationship between age and the prevalence of senile dementia: a meta-analysis of recent data. *International Journal of Epidemiology, 21,* 763–769.

Rizzolatti, Giacomo, & Craighero, Laila. (2004). The mirror-neuron system. *Annual Review of Neuroscience, 27,* 169–192.

Ro, Marguerite. (2002). Moving forward: Addressing the health of Asian American and Pacific Islander women. *American Journal of Public Health, 92,* 516–519.

Robelen, Erik W. (2006, June 20). Exit exams found to depress H. S. graduation rates. *Education Week,* p. 30.

Roberson, Erik D., & Mucke, Lennart. (2006, November 3). 100 years and counting: Prospects for defeating Alzheimer's disease. *Science, 314,* 781–784.

Robert, Stephanie A., & Lee, Kum Yi. (2002). Explaining race differences in health among older adults: The contribution of community socioeconomic context. *Research on Aging, 24,* 654–683.

Roberts, Brent W., & Caspi, Avshalom. (2003). The cumulative continuity model of personality development: Striking a balance between continuity and change in personality traits accross the life course. In Ursula M. Staudinger & Ulman Lindenberger (Eds.), *Understanding human development: Dialogues with lifespan psychology* (pp. 183–214). Dordrecht, The Netherlands: Kluwer.

Roberts, Brent W., Walton, Kate E., & Viechtbauer, Wolfgang. (2006). Patterns of mean-level change in personality traits across the life course: A meta-analysis of longitudinal studies. *Psychological Bulletin, 132,* 1–25.

Roberts, Donald F., & Foehr, Ulla G. (2004). *Kids and media in America: Patterns of use at the millennium*. New York: Cambridge University Press.

Roberts, Eric M. (2003). Does your child have asthma? Parent reports and medication use for pediatric asthma. *Archives of Pediatrics and Adolescent Medicine, 157,* 449–455.

Robin, Daniel J., Berthier, Neil E., & Clifton, Rachel K. (1996). Infants' predictive reaching for moving objects in the dark. *Developmental Psychology, 32,* 824–835.

Robins, Lee N., Helzer, John E., & Davis, Darlene H. (1975). Narcotic use in Southeast Asia and afterward: An interview study of 898 Vietnam returnees. *Archives of General Psychiatry, 32,* 955–961.

Robinson-Zañartu, Carol, Peña, Elizabeth D., Cook-Morales, Valerie, Peña, Anna M., Afshani, Rosalyn, & Nguyen, Lynda. (2005). Academic crime and punishment: Faculty members' perceptions of and responses to plagiarism. *School Psychology Quarterly, 20,* 318–337.

Robitaille, David F., & Beaton, Albert E. (Eds.). (2002). *Secondary analysis of the TIMSS data*. Boston: Kluwer.

Rochat, Philippe. (2001). *The infant's world*. Cambridge, MA: Harvard University Press.

Roche, Alex F., & Sun, Shumei S. (2003). *Human growth: Assessment and interpretation*. Cambridge, UK: Cambridge University Press.

Rodgers, Joseph. (2003). EMOSA sexuality models, memes, and the tipping point: Policy & program implications. In Daniel Romer (Ed.), *Reducing adolescent risk: Toward an integrated approach* (pp. 185–192). Thousand Oaks, CA: Sage.

Rodgers, Joseph Lee, & Wänström, Linda. (2007). Identification of a Flynn Effect in the NLSY: Moving from the center to the boundaries. *Intelligence, 35,* 187–196.

Rogers, Chrissie. (2007). Experiencing an 'inclusive' education: Parents and their children with 'special educational needs'. *British Journal of Sociology of Education, 28,* 55–68.

Rogers, Stacy J., & May, Dee C. (2003). Spillover between marital quality and job satisfaction: Long-term patterns and gender differences. *Journal of Marriage & Family, 65,* 482–495.

Rogoff, Barbara. (1998). Cognition as a collaborative process. In William Damon (Series Ed.) & Deanna Kuhn & Robert S. Siegler (Vol. Eds.), *Handbook of child psychology: Vol. 2. Cognition, perception, and language* (5th ed., pp. 679–744). New York: Wiley.

Rogoff, Barbara. (2003). *The cultural nature of human development*. New York: Oxford University Press.

Rogoff, Barbara, Correa-Chávez, Maricela, & Cotuc, Marta Navichoc. (2005). A cultural/historical view of schooling in human development. In David B. Pillemer & Sheldon H. White (Eds.), *Developmental psychology and social change: Research, history and policy* (pp. 225–263). New York: Cambridge University Press.

Roid, Gale H. (2003). *Stanford-Binet intelligence scales* (5th ed.). Itasca, IL: Riverside.

Roisman, Glenn I., & Fraley, R. Chris. (2006). The limits of genetic influence: A behavior-genetic analysis of infant-caregiver relationship quality and temperament. *Child Development, 77,* 1656–1667.

Romans, Sarah E., Martin, M., Gendall, Kelly, & Herbison, G. P. (2003). Age of menarche: The role of some psychosocial factors. *Psychological Medicine, 33,* 933–939.

Roney, Kathleen, Brown, Kathleen M., & Anfara, Vincent A., Jr. (2004). Middle-level reform in high- and low-performing middle schools: A question of implementation? *Clearing House, 77,* 153–159.

Rönkä, Anna, Oravala, Sanna, & Pulkkinen, Lea. (2002). "I met this wife of mine and things got onto a better track": Turning points in risk development. *Journal of Adolescence, 25,* 47–63.

Room, Robin, Babor, Thomas, & Rehm, Jürgen. (2005). Alcohol and public health. *Lancet, 365*, 519–530.

Rosano, Giuseppe M. C., Vitale, Cristiana, Silvestri, Antonello, & Fini, Massimo. (2003). Hormone replacement therapy and cardioprotection: The end of the tale? In George Creatsas, George Mastorakos, & George P. Chrousos (Eds.), *Women's health and disease: Gynecologic and reproductive issues* (Vol. 997, pp. 351–357). New York: New York Academy of Sciences.

Roschelle, Jeremy M., Pea, Roy D., Hoadley, Christopher M., Gordin, Douglas N., & Means, Barbara M. (2000). Changing how and what children learn in school with computer-based technologies. *The Future of Children, 10*(2), 76–101.

Rose, Amanda J., & Asher, Steven R. (1999). Children's goals and strategies in response to conflicts within a friendship. *Developmental Psychology, 35*, 69–79.

Rose, Amanda J., Swenson, Lance P., & Waller, Erika M. (2004). Overt and relational aggression and perceived popularity: Developmental differences in concurrent and prospective relations. *Developmental Psychology, 40*, 378–387.

Rose, Richard J. (2007). Peers, parents, and processes of adolescent socialization: A twin-study perspective. In Rutger C. M. E. Engels, Margaret Kerr, & Håkan Stattin (Eds.), *Friends, lovers, and groups: Key relationships in adolescence* (pp. 105–124). Hoboken, NJ: Wiley.

Rosenberg, Irwin H. (2001). Aging, B vitamins and cognitive decline. In John D. Fernstrom, Ricardo Uauy, & Pedro Arroyo (Eds.), *Nutrition and brain* (pp. 201–218.). Basel, Switzerland: Karger.

Rosenblatt, Paul C., & Wallace, Beverly R. (2005). *African American grief*. New York: Routledge.

Rosenbluth, Barri, Whitaker, Daniel J., Sanchez, Ellen, & Valle, Linda Anne. (2004). The Expect Respect project: Preventing bullying and sexual harassment in US elementary schools. In Peter K. Smith, Debra Pepler, & Ken Rigby (Eds.), *Bullying in schools: How successful can interventions be?* (pp. 211–233). New York: Cambridge University Press

Rosenfeld, Barry. (2004). *Assisted suicide and the right to die: The interface of social science, public policy, and medical ethics*. Washington, DC: American Psychological Association.

Rosenfeld, Philip J., Brown, David M., Heier, Jeffrey S., Boyer, David S., Kaiser, Peter K., Chung, Carol Y., et al. (2006). Ranibizumab for neovascular age-related macular degeneration. *New England Journal of Medicine, 355*, 1419–1431.

Rosow, Irving. (1985). Status and role change through the life cycle. In Robert H. Binstock & Ethel Shanas (Eds.), *Handbook of aging and the social sciences* (2nd ed., pp. 62–93). New York: Van Nostrand Reinhold.

Roth, David L., Mittelman, Mary S., Clay, Olivio J., Madan, Alok, & Haley, William E. (2005). Changes in social support as mediators of the impact of a psychosocial intervention for spouse caregivers of persons with Alzheimer's disease. *Psychology and Aging, 20*, 634–644.

Rothbart, Mary K., Ahadi, Stephan A., & Evans, David E. (2000). Temperament and personality: Origins and outcomes. *Journal of Personality and Social Psychology, 78*, 122–135.

Rothbart, Mary K., & Bates, John E. (2006). Temperament. In William Damon & Richard M. Lerner (Series Eds.) & Nancy Eisenberg (Vol. Ed.), *Handbook of child psychology: Vol. 3. Social, emotional, and personality development* (6th ed., pp. 99–166). Hoboken, NJ: Wiley.

Rothbaum, Fred, Pott, Martha, Azuma, Hiroshi, Miyake, Kazuo, & Weisz, John. (2000). The development of close relationships in Japan and the United States: Paths of symbiotic harmony and generative tension. *Child Development, 71*, 1121–1142.

Rothermund, Klaus, & Brandstädter, Jochen. (2003). Coping with deficits and losses in later life: From compensatory action to accommodation. *Psychology & Aging, 18*, 896–905.

Rovee-Collier, Carolyn. (1987). Learning and memory in infancy. In Joy Doniger Osofsky (Ed.), *Handbook of infant development* (2nd ed., pp. 98–148). New York: Wiley.

Rovee-Collier, Carolyn. (1990). The "memory system" of prelinguistic infants. In Adele Diamond (Ed.), *The development and neural bases of higher cognitive functions* (Vol. 608, pp. 517–542). New York: New York Academy of Sciences.

Rovee-Collier, Carolyn. (2001). Information pick-up by infants: What is it, and how can we tell? *Journal of Experimental Child Psychology, 78*, 35–49.

Rovee-Collier, Carolyn, & Gerhardstein, Peter. (1997). The development of infant memory. In Nelson Cowan (Ed.), *The development of memory in childhood* (pp. 5–39). Hove, East Sussex, UK: Psychology Press.

Rovee-Collier, Carolyn, & Hayne, Harlene. (1987). Reactivation of infant memory: Implications for cognitive development. In Hayne W. Reese (Ed.), *Advances in child development and behavior* (Vol. 20, pp. 185–238). San Diego, CA: Academic Press.

Rovi, Sue, Chen, Ping-Hsin, & Johnson, Mark S. (2004). The economic burden of hospitalizations associated with child abuse and neglect. *American Journal of Public Health, 94*, 586–590.

Rowe, Gillian, Valderrama, Steven, Hasher, Lynn, & Lenartowicz, Agatha. (2006). Attentional disregulation: A benefit for implicit memory. *Psychology and Aging, 21*, 826–830.

Rowe, John W., & Kahn, Robert Louis. (1998). *Successful aging*. New York: Pantheon.

Rowland, Andrew S., Umbach, David M., Stallone, Lil, Naftel, A. Jack, Bohlig, E. Michael, & Sandler, Dale P. (2002). Prevalence of medication treatment for attention deficit-hyperactivity disorder among elementary school children in Johnston County, North Carolina. *American Journal of Public Health, 92*, 231–234.

Rozin, Paul, Kabnick, Kimberly, Pete, Erin, Fischler, Claude, & Shields, Christy. (2003). The ecology of eating: Smaller portion sizes in France than in the United States help explain the French paradox. *Psychological Science, 14*, 450–454.

Rubin, Kenneth H., Bukowski, William M., & Parker, Jeffrey G. (2006). Peer interactions, relationships, and groups. In William Damon & Richard M. Lerner (Series Eds.) & Nancy Eisenberg (Vol. Ed.), *Handbook of child psychology: Vol. 3. Social, emotional, and personality development* (6th ed., pp. 619–700). Hoboken, NJ: Wiley.

Ruble, Diane, Alvarez, Jeanette, Bachman, Meredith, Cameron, Jessica, Fuligni, Andrew, Coll, Cynthia Garcia, et al. (2004). The development of a sense of "we": The emergence and implications of children's collective identity. In Mark Bennett & Fabio Sani (Eds.), *The development of the social self* (pp. 29–76). Hove, East Sussex, England: Psychology Press.

Ruble, Diane N., Martin, Carol Lynn, & Berenbaum, Sheri. (2006). Gender development. In William Damon & Richard M. Lerner (Series Eds.) & Nancy Eisenberg (Vol. Ed.), *Handbook of child psychology:*

Vol. 3. Social, emotional, and personality development (6th ed., pp. 858–932). Hoboken, NJ: Wiley.

Rueda, M. Rosario, Rothbart, Mary K., Saccomanno, Lisa, & Posner, Michael I. (2007). Modifying brain networks underlying self regulation. In Daniel Romer & Elaine F. Walker (Eds.), *Adolescent psychopathology and the developing brain: Integrating brain and prevention science* (pp. 401–419). Oxford, UK: Oxford University Press.

Rueter, Martha A., & Kwon, Hee-Kyung. (2005). Developmental trends in adolescent suicidal ideation. *Journal of Research on Adolescence, 15*, 205–222.

Ruffman, Ted, Slade, Lance, & Crowe, Elena. (2002). The relation between children's and mothers' mental state language and theory-of-mind understanding. *Child Development, 73*, 734–751.

Ruffman, Ted, Slade, Lance, Sandino, Juan Carlos, & Fletcher, Amanda. (2005). Are A-not-B errors caused by a belief about object location? *Child Development, 76*, 122–136.

Ruiz-Pesini, Eduardo, Mishmar, Dan, Brandon, Martin, Procaccio, Vincent, & Wallace, Douglas C. (2004, January 9). Effects of purifying and adaptive selection on regional variation in human mtDNA. *Science, 303*, 223–226.

Rumbaut, Rubén G., & Portes, Alejandro (Eds.). (2001). *Ethnicities: Children of immigrants in America*. Berkeley, CA and New York: University of California Press and the Russell Sage Foundation.

Russell, Mark. (2002, January 25). South Korea: Institute helps spread use of vaccines in Asia. *Science, 295*, 611–612.

Rutstein, Shea O. (2000). Factors associated with trends in infant and child mortality in developing countries during the 1990s. *Bulletin of the World Health Organization, 78*, 1256–1270.

Rutter, Michael. (1998). Some research considerations on intergenerational continuities and discontinuities: Comment on the special section. *Developmental Psychology, 34*, 1269–1273.

Rutter, Michael. (2004). Intergenerational continuities and discontinuities in psychological problems. In P. Lindsay Chase-Lansdale, Kathleen Kiernan, & Ruth J. Friedman (Eds.), *Human development across lives and generations: The potential for change* (pp. 239–277). New York: Cambridge University Press.

Rutter, Michael. (2006). The psychological effects of early institutional rearing. In Peter J. Marshall & Nathan A. Fox (Eds.), *The development of social engagement: Neurobiological perspectives* (pp. 355–391). New York: Oxford University Press.

Rutter, Michael, & O'Connor, Thomas G. (2004). Are there biological programming effects for psychological development? Findings from a study of Romanian adoptees. *Developmental Psychology, 40*, 81–94.

Rutter, Michael, Thorpe, Karen, Greenwood, Rosemary, Northstone, Kate, & Golding, Jean. (2003). Twins as a natural experiment to study the causes of mild language delay: I: Design; twin-singleton differences in language, and obstetric risks. *Journal of Child Psychology and Psychiatry, 44*, 326–341.

Ryalls, Brigette Oliver. (2000). Dimensional adjectives: Factors affecting children's ability to compare objects using novel words. *Journal of Experimental Child Psychology, 76*, 26–49.

Ryan, Michael J. (2005, June 8). *Punching out in Little League. Boston Herald*. Retrieved September 11, 2005, from the World Wide Web: http://news.bostonherald.com/blogs/rapSheet/index.bg?mode=viewid&post_id=190

Ryan, Richard M., & Deci, Edward L. (2001). On happiness and human potentials: A review of research on hedonic and eudaimonic well-being. *Annual Review of Psychology, 52*(1), 141–166.

Rybash, John M., Hoyer, William J., & Roodin, Paul. (1986). *Adult cognition and aging: Developmental changes in processing, knowing and thinking*. New York: Pergamon Press.

Saarni, Carolyn, Campos, Joseph J., Camras, Linda A., & Witherington, David. (2006). Emotional development: Action, communication, and understanding. In William Damon & Richard M. Lerner (Series Eds.) & Nancy Eisenberg (Vol. Ed.), *Handbook of child psychology: Vol. 3. Social, emotional, and personality development* (6th ed., pp. 226–299). Hoboken, NJ: Wiley.

Sabat, Steven R. (2001). *The experience of Alzheimer's disease: Life through a tangled veil*. Oxford, UK: Blackwell.

Sacker, Amanda, Wiggins, Richard D., Bartley, Mel, & McDonough, Peggy. (2007). Self-rated health trajectories in the United States and the United Kingdom: A comparative study. *American Journal of Public Health, 97*, 812–818.

Sackett, Paul R., Hardison, Chaitra M., & Cullen, Michael J. (2004). On interpreting stereotype threat as accounting for African American-White differences on cognitive tests. *American Psychologist, 59*, 7–13.

Sacks, Oliver W. (1995). *An anthropologist on Mars: Seven paradoxical tales*. New York: Knopf.

Sadeh, Avi, Raviv, Amiram, & Gruber, Reut. (2000). Sleep patterns and sleep disruptions in school-age children. *Developmental Psychology, 36*, 291–301.

Saffran, Jenny R., Werker, Janet F., & Werner, Lynne A. (2006). The infant's auditory world: Hearing, speech, and the beginnings of language. In William Damon & Richard M. Lerner (Series Eds.) & Deanna Kuhn & Robert S. Siegler (Vol. Eds.), *Handbook of child psychology: Vol. 2. Cognition, perception, and language* (pp. 58–108). Hoboken, NJ: Wiley.

Sagi, Abraham, Koren-Karie, Nina, Gini, Motti, Ziv, Yair, & Joels, Tirtsa. (2002). Shedding further light on the effects of various types and quality of early child care on infant-mother attachment relationship: The Haifa study of early child care. *Child Development, 73*, 1166–1186.

Sahar, Gail, & Karasawa, Kaori. (2005). Is the personal always political? A cross-cultural analysis of abortion attitudes. *Basic and Applied Social Psychology, 27*, 285–296.

Sakata, Mariko, Utsu, Masaji, & Maeda, Kazuo. (2006). Fetal circulation and placental blood flow in monochorionic twins. *The Ultrasound Review of Obstetrics & Gynecology, 6*, 135 - 140.

Salkind, Neil J. (2004). *An introduction to theories of human development*. Thousand Oaks, CA: Sage.

Salmivalli, Christina, Ojanen, Tiina, Haanpaa, Jemina, & Peets, Katlin. (2005). "I'm OK but you're not" and other peer-relational schemas: Explaining individual differences in children's social goals. *Developmental Psychology, 41*, 363–375.

Salovey, Peter, & Grewal, Daisy. (2005). The science of emotional intelligence. *Current Directions in Psychological Science, 14*, 281–285.

Salthouse, Timothy A. (2000). Steps toward the explanation of adult age differences in cognition. In Timothy J. Perfect & Elizabeth A. Maylor (Eds.), *Models of cognitive aging* (pp. 19–49). London: Oxford University Press.

Salthouse, Timothy A. (2001). Attempted decomposition of age-related influences on

two tests of reasoning. *Psychology and Aging, 16,* 251–263.

Salthouse, Timothy A. (2004). What and when of cognitive aging. *Current Directions in Psychological Science, 13,* 140–144.

Salthouse, Timothy A. (2006). Mental exercise and mental aging: Evaluating the validity of the "use it or lose it" hypothesis. *Perspectives on Psychological Science, 1,* 68–87.

Salzarulo, Piero, & Fagioli, Igino. (1999). Changes of sleep states and physiological activities across the first year of life. In Alex Fedde Kalverboer, Maria Luisa Genta, & J. B. Hopkins (Eds.), *Current issues in developmental psychology: Biopsychological perspectives* (pp. 53–73). Dordrecht, The Netherlands: Kluwer.

Sameroff, Arnold J., & MacKenzie, Michael J. (2003). Research strategies for capturing transactional models of development: The limits of the possible. *Development & Psychopathology, 15,* 613–640.

Sampaio, Ricardo C., & Truwit, Charles L. (2001). Myelination in the developing human brain. In Charles A. Nelson & Monica Luciana (Eds.), *Handbook of developmental cognitive neuroscience* (pp. 35–44). Cambridge, MA: MIT Press.

Samuels, Christina A. (2007, May 8). Lack of research, data hurts dropout efforts, experts say. *Education Week,* p. 8.

Samuelsson, Gillis, Dehlin, Ove, Hagberg, Bo, & Sundström, Gerdt. (2003). Incidence of dementia in relation to medical, psychological and social risk factors: A longitudinal cohort study during a 25-year period. In Caleb Ellicott Finch, Jean-Marie Robine, & Yves Christen (Eds.), *Brain and longevity* (pp. 131–144). Berlin, Germany: Springer.

Sanchez, Maria del Mar, Ladd, Charlotte O., & Plotsky, Paul M. (2001). Early adverse experience as a developmental risk factor for later psychopathology: Evidence from rodent and primate models. *Development & Psychopathology, 13,* 419–449.

Sandstrom, Marlene J., & Zakriski, Audrey L. (2004). Understanding the experience of peer rejection. In Janis B. Kupersmidt & Kenneth A. Dodge (Eds.), *Children's peer relations: From development to intervention* (pp. 101–118). Washington, DC: American Psychological Association.

Sanger, David E. (2007, February 28). Afghan bombing sends a danger signal to U.S. *New York Times,* p. A1.

Sani, Fabio, & Bennett, Mark. (2004). Developmental aspects of social identity. In Mark Bennett & Fabio Sani (Eds.), *The development of the social self* (pp. 77–100). Hove, East Sussex, England: Psychology Press.

Saper, Clifford B. (2006, November 3). Life, the universe, and body temperature. *Science, 314,* 773–774.

Sapp, Felicity, Lee, Kang, & Muir, Darwin. (2000). Three-year-olds' difficulty with the appearance-reality distinction: Is it real or is it apparent? *Developmental Psychology, 36,* 547–560.

Saraswathi, T. S. (2005). Hindu worldview in the development of selfways: The "Atman" as the real self. In Lene Arnett Jensen & Reed W. Larson (Eds.), *New Horizons in Developmental Theory and Research* (pp. 43–50). San Francisco: Jossey-Bass.

Sarroub, Loukia K. (2001). The sojourner experience of Yemeni American high school students: An ethnographic portrait. *Harvard Educational Review, 71,* 390–415.

Satariano, William. (2006). *Epidemiology of aging: An ecological approach.* Sudbury, MA: Jones and Bartlett Publishers.

Saunders, Cicely M. (1978). *The management of terminal disease.* London: Arnold.

Savin-Williams, Ritch C. (2005). *The new gay teenager.* Cambridge, MA: Harvard University Press.

Savin-Williams, Ritch C. (2006). Who's gay? Does it matter? *Current Directions in Psychological Science, 15,* 40–44.

Savin-Williams, Ritch C., & Diamond, Lisa M. (1997). Sexual orientation as a developmental context for lesbians, gays, and bisexuals: Biological perspectives. In Nancy L. Segal, Glenn E. Weisfeld, & Carol C. Weisfeld (Eds.), *Uniting psychology and biology: Integrative perspectives on human development* (pp. 217–238). Washington, DC: American Psychological Association.

Savin-Williams, Ritch C., & Diamond, Lisa M. (2004). Sex. In Richard M. Lerner & Laurence D. Steinberg (Eds.), *Handbook of adolescent psychology* (2nd ed., pp. 189–231). Hoboken, NJ: Wiley.

Saw, Seang-Mei. (2003). A synopsis of the prevalence rates and environmental risk factors for myopia. *Clinical and Experimental Optometry, 86,* 289–294.

Saxe, Geoffrey B. (1991). *Culture and cognitive development: Studies in mathematical understanding.* Hillsdale, NJ: Erlbaum.

Saxe, Geoffrey B. (1999). Sources of concepts: A cultural-developmental perspective. In Ellin Kofsky Scholnick, Katherine Nelson, Susan A. Gelman, & Patricia H. Miller (Eds.), *Conceptual development: Piaget's legacy* (pp. 253–267). Mahwah, NJ: Erlbaum.

Saylor, Megan M., & Sabbagh, Mark A. (2004). Different kinds of information affect word learning in the preschool years: The case of part-term learning. *Child Development, 75,* 395–408.

Scambler, Douglas J., Hepburn, Susan L., Rutherford, Mel, Wehner, Elizabeth A., & Rogers, Sally J. (2007). Emotional responsivity in children with autism, children with other developmental disabilities, and children with typical development. *Journal of Autism and Developmental Disorders, 37,* 553–563.

Scannapieco, Maria, & Connell-Carrick, Kelli. (2005). *Understanding child maltreatment: An ecological and developmental perspective.* New York: Oxford University Press.

Schachter, Sherry R. (2003). 9/11: A grief therapist's journal. In Marcia Lattanzi-Licht & Kenneth J. Doka (Eds.), *Living with grief: Coping with public tragedy* (pp. 15–25). New York: Brunner-Routledge.

Schacter, Daniel L., & Badgaiyan, Rajendra D. (2001). Neuroimaging of priming: New perspectives on implicit and explicit memory. *Current Directions in Psychological Science, 10,* 1–4.

Schafer, Graham. (2005). Infants can learn decontextualized words before their first birthday. *Child Development, 76,* 87–96.

Schaffer, H. Rudolph. (2000). The early experience assumption: Past, present, and future. *International Journal of Behavioral Development, 24,* 5–14.

Schaie, K. Warner. (1989). Perceptual speed in adulthood: Cross-sectional and longitudinal studies. *Psychology & Aging, 4,* 443–453.

Schaie, K. Warner. (1996). *Intellectual development in adulthood: The Seattle Longitudinal Study.* New York: Cambridge University Press.

Schaie, K. Warner. (2002). The impact of longitudinal studies on understanding development from young adulthood to old age. In Willard W. Hartup & Rainer K. Silbereisen (Eds.), *Growing points in developmental science: An introduction* (pp. 307–328). New York: Psychology Press.

Schaie, K. Warner. (2005). What can we learn from longitudinal studies of adult

development? *Research in Human Development, 2,* 133–158.

Schaie, K. Warner. (2005). *Developmental influences on adult intelligence: The Seattle longitudinal study* (Rev. ed.). New York: Oxford University Press.

Schaie, K. Warner, & Carstensen, Laura L. (Eds.). (2006). *Social structures, aging, and self-regulation in the elderly.* New York: Springer.

Schaie, K. Warner, & Willis, Sherry L. (1996). *Adult development and aging* (4th ed.). New York: HarperCollins.

Schaie, K. Warner, & Willis, Sherry L. (2000). A stage theory model of adult cognitive development revisited. In Robert L. Rubinstein, Miriam Moss, & Morton H. Kleban (Eds.), *The many dimensions of aging* (pp. 175–193). New York: Springer.

Schardein, James L. (1976). *Drugs as teratogens.* Cleveland, OH: CRC Press.

Schellenberg, E. Glenn, Nakata, Takayuki, Hunter, Patrick G., & Tamoto, Sachiko. (2007). Exposure to music and cognitive performance: Tests of children and adults. *Psychology of Music, 35,* 5–19.

Schieber, Frank. (2006). Vision and aging. In James E. Birren & K. Warner Schaie (Eds.), *Handbook of the psychology of aging* (6th ed., pp. 129–161). Amsterdam: Elsevier.

Schiller, Ruth A. (1998). The relationship of developmental tasks to life satisfaction, moral reasoning, and occupational attainment at age 28. *Journal of Adult Development, 5,* 239–254.

Schindler, Ines, Staudinger, Ursula M., & Nesselroade, John R. (2006). Development and structural dynamics of personal life investment in old age. *Psychology and Aging, 21,* 737–753.

Schlegel, Alice. (2003). Modernization and changes in adolescent social life. In T. S. Saraswati (Ed.), *Cross-cultural perspectives in human development: Theory, research, and applications* (pp. 236–257). New Delhi, India: Sage.

Schmader, Toni. (2002). Gender identification moderates stereotype threat effects on women's math performance. *Journal of Experimental Social Psychology, 38,* 194–201.

Schmitt, David P., Allik, Jüri, McCrae, Robert R., & Benet-Martínez, Verónica. (2007). The geographic distribution of big five personality traits: Patterns and profiles of human self-description across 56 nations. *Journal of Cross-Cultural Psychology, 38,* 173–212.

Schneider, Wolfgang, & Bjorklund, David F. (2003). Memory and knowledge development. In Jaan Valsiner & Kevin J. Connolly (Eds.), *Handbook of developmental psychology* (pp. 370–403). Thousand Oaks, CA: Sage.

Schneider, Wolfgang, & Pressley, Michael. (1997). *Memory development between two and twenty* (2nd ed.). Mahwah, NJ: Erlbaum.

Schoen, Robert, & Cheng, Yen-Hsin Alice. (2006). Partner choice and the differential retreat from marriage. *Journal of Marriage and Family, 68,* 1–10.

Schoeni, Robert F., & Ross, Karen E. (2005). Material assistance from families during the transition to adulthood. In Richard A. Settersten, Jr., Frank F. Furstenberg, Jr., & Rubén G. Rumbaut (Eds.), *On the frontier of adulthood: Theory, research, and public policy* (pp. 396–416). Chicago: University of Chicago Press.

Schooler, Carmi, Mulatu, Mesfin Samuel, & Oates, Gary. (1999). The continuing effects of substantively complex work on the intellectual functioning of older workers. *Psychology & Aging, 14,* 483–506.

Schore, Allan N. (2001). Effects of a secure attachment relationship on right brain development, affect regulation, and infant mental health. *Infant Mental Health Journal, 22,* 7–66.

Schraagen, Jan Maarten, & Leijenhorst, Henk. (2001). Searching for evidence: Knowledge and search strategies used by forensic scientists. In Eduardo Salas & Gary A. Klein (Eds.), *Linking expertise and naturalistic decision making* (pp. 263–274). Mahwah, NJ: Erlbaum.

Schulenberg, John, O'Malley, Patrick M., Bachman, Jerald G., & Johnston, Lloyd D. (2005). Early adult transitions and their relation to well-being and substance use. In Richard A. Settersten, Jr., Frank F. Furstenberg, Jr., & Rubén G. Rumbaut (Eds.), *On the frontier of adulthood: Theory, research, and public policy* (pp. 417–453). Chicago: University of Chicago Press.

Schulenberg, John, & Zarrett, Nicole R. (2006). Mental health during emerging adulthood: Continuity and discontinuity in courses, causes, and functions. In Jeffrey Jensen Arnett & Jennifer Lynn Tanner (Eds.), *Emerging adults in America: Coming of age in the 21st century* (pp. 135–172). Washington, DC: American Psychological Association.

Schulman, Kevin A., Berlin, Jesse A., Harless, William, Kerner, Jon F., Sistrunk, Shyrl, Gersh, Bernard J., et al. (1999). The effect of race and sex on physicians' recommendations for cardiac catheterization. *New England Journal of Medicine, 340,* 618–626.

Schult, Carolyn A. (2002). Children's understanding of the distinction between intentions and desires. *Child Development, 73,* 1727–1747.

Schultz, P. Wesley, Nolan, Jessica M., Cialdini, Robert B., Goldstein, Noah J., & Griskevicius, Vladas. (2007). The constructive, destructive, and reconstructive power of social norms. *Psychological Science, 18,* 429–434.

Schumann, Cynthia Mills, Hamstra, Julia, Goodlin-Jones, Beth L., Lotspeich, Linda J., Kwon, Hower, Buonocore, Michael H., et al. (2004). The amygdala is enlarged in children but not adolescents with autism; the hippocampus is enlarged at all ages. *Journal of Neuroscience, 24,* 6392–6401.

Schwab, Jacqueline, Kulin, Howard E., Susman, Elizabeth J., Finkelstein, Jordan W., Chinchilli, Vernon M., Kunselman, Susan J., et al. (2001). The role of sex hormone replacement therapy on self-perceived competence in adolescents with delayed puberty. *Child Development, 72,* 1439–1450.

Schwartz, Barry. (2004). *The paradox of choice: Why more is less.* New York: Ecco.

Schwartz, Jeffrey, & Begley, Sharon. (2002). *The mind and the brain: Neuroplasticity and the power of mental force.* New York: Regan Books.

Schwartz, Michael W., & Porte, Daniel. (2005, January 21). Diabetes, obesity, and the brain. *Science, 307,* 375–379.

Schwartz, Pepper. (2006). What elicits romance, passion, and attachment, and how do they affect our lives throughout the life cycle? In Ann C. Crouter & Alan Booth (Eds.), *Romance and sex in adolescence and emerging adulthood: Risks and opportunities* (pp. 49–60). Mahwah, NJ: Erlbaum.

Schweinhart, Lawrence J., Montie, Jeanne, Xiang, Zongping, Barnett, W. Steven, Belfield, Clive R., & Nores, Milagros. (2005). *Lifetime effects: The High/Scope Perry Preschool study through age 40.* Ypsilanti, MI: High/Scope Press.

Schweinhart, Lawrence J., & Weikart, David P. (1997). *Lasting differences: The High/Scope preschool curriculum comparison study through age 23.* Ypsilanti, MI: High/Scope Educational Research Foundation.

Scialfa, Charles T., & Fernie, Geoff R. (2006). Adaptive technology. In James E. Birren & K. Warner Schaie (Eds.), *Handbook of the psychology of aging* (6th ed., pp. 425–441). Amsterdam: Elsevier.

Scogin, Forrest R. (1998). Anxiety in old age. In Inger Hilde Nordhus, Gary R. VandenBos, Stig Berg, & Pia Fromholt (Eds.), *Clinical geropsychology* (pp. 205–209). Washington, DC: American Psychological Association.

Scollon, Christie Napa, Diener, Ed, Oishi, Shigehiro, & Biswas-Diener, Robert. (2005). An experience sampling and cross-cultural investigation of the relation between pleasant and unpleasant affect. *Cognition & Emotion, 19*, 27–52.

Scott, Jacqueline. (2000). Children as respondents: The challenge for quantitative methods. In Pia Monrad Christensen & Allison James (Eds.), *Research with children: Perspectives and practices* (pp. 98–119). London: Falmer Press.

Scott-Maxwell, Florida. (1968). *The measure of my days*. New York: Knopf.

Seale, Clive. (2006). Characteristics of end-of-life decisions: Survey of UK medical practitioners. *Palliative Medicine, 20*, 653–659.

Sears, Malcolm R., Greene, Justina M., Willan, Andrew R., Wiecek, Elizabeth M., Taylor, D. Robin, Flannery, Erin M., et al. (2003). A longitudinal, population-based, cohort study of childhood asthma followed to adulthood. *New England Journal of Medicine, 349*, 1414–1422.

Segal, Nancy L. (1999). *Entwined lives: Twins and what they tell us about human behavior*. New York: Dutton.

Segalowitz, Sidney J., & Schmidt, Louis A. (2003). Developmental psychology and the neurosciences. In Jaan Valsiner & Kevin J. Connolly (Eds.), *Handbook of developmental psychology* (pp. 48–71). Thousand Oaks, CA: Sage.

Seifer, Ronald, LaGasse, Linda L., Lester, Barry, Bauer, Charles R., Shankaran, Seetha, Bada, Henrietta S., et al. (2004). Attachment status in children prenatally exposed to cocaine and other substances. *Child Development, 75*, 850–868.

Seki, Fusako. (2001). The role of the government and the family in taking care of the frail elderly: A comparison of the United States and Japan. In David N. Weisstub, David C. Thomasma, Serge Gauthier, & George F. Tomossy (Eds.), *Aging: Caring for our elders* (pp. 83–105). Dordrecht, The Netherlands: Kluwer.

Seltzer, Marsha Mailick, & Li, Lydia Wailing. (1996). The transitions of caregiving: Subjective and objective definitions. *Gerontologist, 36*, 614–626.

Serpell, Robert, & Haynes, Brenda Pitts. (2004). The cultural practice of intelligence testing: Problems of international export. In Robert J. Sternberg & Elena L. Grigorenko (Eds.), *Culture and competence: Contexts of life success* (pp. 163–185). Washington, DC: American Psychological Association.

Settersten, Richard A. (2002). Social sources of meaning in later life. In Robert S. Weiss & Scott A. Bass (Eds.), *Challenges of the third age: Meaning and purpose in later life* (pp. 55–79). London: Oxford University Press.

Settersten, Richard A., Furstenberg, Frank F., & Rumbaut, Rubén G. (2005). *On the frontier of adulthood: Theory, research, and public policy*. Chicago, IL: University of Chicago Press.

Settersten, Richard A., & Hagestad, Gunhild O. (1996). What's the latest? Cultural age deadlines for family transitions. *Gerontologist, 36*, 602–613.

Shackelford, Todd K., & Mouzos, Jenny. (2005). Partner killing by men in cohabiting and marital relationships: A comparative, cross-national analysis of data from Australia and the United States. *Journal of Interpersonal Violence, 20*, 1310–1324.

Shahin, Hashem, Walsh, Tom, Sobe, Tama, Lynch, Eric, King, Mary-Claire, Avraham, Karen, et al. (2002). Genetics of congenital deafness in the Palestinian population: Multiple connexin 26 alleles with shared origins in the Middle East. *Human Genetics, 110*, 284–289.

Shanahan, Lilly, McHale, Susan M., Osgood, Wayne, & Crouter, Ann C. (2007). Conflict frequency with mothers and fathers from middle childhood to late adolescence: Within- and between-families comparisons. *Developmental Psychology, 43*, 539–550.

Shannon, Joyce Brennfleck (Ed.). (2007). *Eating disorders sourcebook: Basic consumer health information about anorexia nervosa, bulimia nervosa, binge eating, compulsive exercise, female athlete triad, and other eating disorders* (2nd ed.). Detroit, MI: Omnigraphics.

Shattuck, Paul T. (2006). The contribution of diagnostic substitution to the growing administrative prevalence of autism in US special education. *Pediatrics, 117*, 1028–1037.

Sheehy, Gail. (1976). *Passages: Predictable crises of adult life*. New York: Dutton.

Sheldon, Kennon M., & Kasser, Tim. (2001). Getting older, getting better? Personal strivings and psychological maturity across the life span. *Developmental Psychology, 37*, 491–501.

Shen, Qin, Wang, Yue, Dimos, John T., Fasano, Christopher A., Phoenix, Timothy N., Lemischka, Ihor R., et al. (2006). The timing of cortical neurogenesis is encoded within lineages of individual progenitor cells. *Nature Neuroscience, 9*, 743–751.

Shepard, Thomas H., & Lemire, Ronald J. (2004). *Catalog of teratogenic agents* (11th ed.). Baltimore: Johns Hopkins University Press.

Sher, Kenneth J., & Gotham, Heather J. (1999). Pathological alcohol involvement: A developmental disorder of young adulthood. *Development and Psychopathology, 11*, 933–956.

Sherman, Edmund, & Dacher, Joan. (2005). Cherished objects and the home: Their meaning and roles in late life. In Graham D. Rowles & Habib Chaudhury (Eds.), *Home and identity in late life international perspectives* (pp. 63–79). New York: Springer.

Sherman, Stephanie. (2002). Epidemiology. In Randi Jenssen Hagerman & Paul J. Hagerman (Eds.), *Fragile X syndrome: Diagnosis, treatment, and research* (3rd ed., pp. 136–168). Baltimore: Johns Hopkins University Press.

Shevell, Tracy, Malone, Fergal D., Vidaver, John, Porter, T. Flint, Luthy, David A., Comstock, Christine H., et al. (2005). Assisted reproductive technology and pregnancy outcome. *Obstetrics & Gynecology, 106*, 1039–1045.

Shibusawa, Tazuko, Lubben, James, & Kitano, Harry H. L. (2001). Japanese American elderly. In Laura Katz Olson (Ed.), *Age through ethnic lenses: Caring for the elderly in a multicultural society* (pp. 33–44). Lanham, MD: Rowman & Littlefield.

Shields, Margot. (2005). An update on smoking from the 2005 Canadian Community Health Survey. *Your Community, Your Health: Findings from the Canadian Community Health Survey (CCHS), 2*, 8–47.

Shuey, Kim, & Hardy, Melissa A. (2003). Assistance to aging parents and parents-in-law: Does lineage affect family allocation decisions? *Journal of Marriage and Family, 65*, 418–431.

Siebenbruner, Jessica, Zimmer-Gembeck, Melanie J., & Egeland, By-

ron. (2007). Sexual partners and contraceptive use: A 16–year prospective study predicting abstinence and risk behavior. *Journal of Research on Adolescence, 17*, 179–206.

Siegal, Michael. (2004, September 17). Signposts to the essence of language. *Science, 305*, 1720–1721.

Siegel, Judith M., Yancey, Antronette K., Aneshensel, Carol S., & Schuler, Roberleigh. (1999). Body image, perceived pubertal timing, and adolescent mental health. *Journal of Adolescent Health, 25*, 155–165.

Siegel, Larry. (2006). *Post-publication peer reviews: Correlation is not causation*. Retrieved September 11, 2007, from the World Wide Web: http://pediatrics.aappublications.org/cgi/eletters/118/2/e430#2217

Siegel, Lawrence A., & Siegel, Richard M. (2007). Sexual changes in the aging male. In Annette Fuglsang Owens & Mitchell S. Tepper (Eds.), *Sexual health: Vol. 2. Physical foundations* (pp. 223–255). Westport, CT: Praeger/Greenwood.

Silver, Archie A., & Hagin, Rosa A. (2002). *Disorders of learning in childhood* (2nd ed.). New York: Wiley.

Silverman, Wendy K., & Dick-Niederhauser, Andreas. (2004). Separation anxiety disorder. In Tracy L. Morris & John S. March (Eds.), *Anxiety disorders in children and adolescents* (2nd ed., pp. 164–188). New York: Guilford Press.

Silverstein, Alvin, Silverstein, Virginia B., & Nunn, Laura Silverstein. (2006). *The flu and pneumonia update*. Berkeley Heights, NJ: Enslow Elementary.

Silverstein, Merril. (2006). Intergenerational family transfers in social context. In Robert H. Binstock & Linda K. George (Eds.), *Handbook of aging and the social sciences* (6th ed., pp. 165–180). Amsterdam: Elsevier.

Silverstein, Merril, & Chen, Xuan. (1999). The impact of acculturation in Mexican American families on the quality of adult grandchild-grandparent relationships. *Journal of Marriage & the Family, 61*, 188–198.

Silverstein, Merril, & Parker, Marti G. (2002). Leisure activities and quality of life among the oldest old in Sweden. *Research on Aging, 24*, 528–547.

Sinclair, David A., & Howitz, Konrad T. (2006). Dietary restriction, hormesis and small molecule mimetics In Edward J. Masoro & Steven N. Austad (Eds.), *Handbook of the biology of aging* (6th ed., pp. 63–104). Amsterdam: Elsevier Academic Press.

Singer, Dorothy G., & Singer, Jerome L. (2005). *Imagination and play in the electronic age*. Cambridge, MA: Harvard University Press.

Singer, Lynn T., Arendt, Robert, Minnes, Sonia, Farkas, Kathleen, Salvator, Ann, Kirchner, H. Lester, et al. (2002). Cognitive and motor outcomes of cocaine-exposed infants. *Journal of the American Medical Association, 287*, 1952–1960.

Singer, Tania, Verhaeghen, Paul, Ghisletta, Paolo, Lindenberger, Ulman, & Baltes, Paul B. (2003). The fate of cognition in very old age: Six-year longitudinal findings in the Berlin Aging Study (BASE). *Psychology and Aging, 18*, 318–331.

Singer, Wolf. (2003). The nature-nurture problem revisited. In Ursula M. Staudinger & Ulman Lindenberger (Eds.), *Understanding human development: Dialogues with lifespan psychology* (pp. 437–447). Dordrecht, The Netherlands: Kluwer.

Singh, Devendra. (2004). Mating strategies of young women: Role of physical attractiveness. *Journal of Sex Research, 41*, 43–54.

Sinnott, Jan D. (1998). *The development of logic in adulthood: Postformal thought and its applications*. New York: Plenum Press.

Siqueira, Lorena M., Rolnitzky, Linda M., & Rickert, Vaughn I. (2001). Smoking cessation in adolescents: The role of nicotine dependence, stress, and coping methods. *Archives of Pediatrics & Adolescent Medicine, 155*, 489–495.

Sirard, John R., Ainsworth, Barbara E., McIver, Kerri L., & Pate, Russell R. (2005). Prevalence of active commuting at urban and suburban elementary schools in Columbia, SC. *American Journal of Public Health, 95*, 236–237.

Sircar, Ratna, & Sircar, Debashish. (2005). Adolescent rats exposed to repeated ethanol treatment show lingering behavioral impairments. *Alcoholism: Clinical and Experimental Research, 29*, 1402–1410.

Sirin, Selcuk R. (2005). Socioeconomic status and academic achievement: A meta-analytic review of research. *Review of Educational Research, 75*, 417–453.

Sivertsen, Borge, Omvik, Siri, Pallesen, Ståle, Bjorvatn, Bjorn, Havik, Odd E., Kvale, Gerd, et al. (2006). Cognitive behavioral therapy vs zopiclone for treatment of chronic primary insomnia in older adults: A randomized controlled trial. *Journal of the American Medical Association, 295*, 2851–2858.

Skinner, B. F. (1957). *Verbal behavior*. New York: Appleton-Century-Crofts.

Skirton, Heather, & Patch, Christine. (2002). *Genetics for healthcare professionals: A lifestage approach*. Oxford, UK: Bios.

Sliwinski, Martin J., Hofer, Scott M., Hall, Charles, Buschke, Herman, & Lipton, Richard B. (2003). Modeling memory decline in older adults: The importance of preclinical dementia, attrition, and chronological age. *Psychology & Aging, 18*, 658–671.

Slobin, Dan I. (2001). Form-function relations: How do children find out what they are? In Melissa Bowerman & Stephen C. Levinson (Eds.), *Language acquisition and conceptual development* (pp. 406–449). Cambridge, UK: Cambridge University Press.

Slonim, Amy B., Roberto, Anthony J., Downing, Christi R., Adams, Inez F., Fasano, Nancy J., Davis-Satterla, Loretta, et al. (2005). Adolescents' knowledge, beliefs, and behaviors regarding hepatitis B: Insights and implications for programs targeting vaccine-preventable diseases. *Journal of Adolescent Health, 36*, 178–186.

Small, Brent J., Fratiglioni, Laura, von Strauss, Eva, & Bäckman, Lars. (2003). Terminal decline and cognitive performance in very old age: Does cause of death matter? *Psychology & Aging, 18*, 193–202.

Small, Neil. (2001). Theories of grief: A critical review. In Jenny Hockey, Jeanne Katz, & Neil Small (Eds.), *Grief, mourning, and death ritual* (pp. 19–48). Buckingham, England: Open University Press.

Smedley, Audrey, & Smedley, Brian D. (2005). Race as biology is fiction, racism as a social problem is real: Anthropological and historical perspectives on the social construction of race. *American Psychologist, 60*, 16–26.

Smetana, Judith G., Metzger, Aaron, & Campione-Barr, Nicole. (2004). African American late adolescents' relationships with parents: Developmental transitions and longitudinal patterns. *Child Development, 75*, 932–947.

Smith, Christian (with Denton, Melinda Lundquist). (2005). *Soul searching: The religious and spiritual lives of American teenagers*. Oxford, UK: Oxford University Press.

Smith, Deborah B., & Moen, Phyllis. (2004). Retirement satisfaction for retirees and their spouses: Do gender and the retirement decision-making process matter? *Journal of Family Issues, 25*, 262–285.

Scialfa, Charles T., & Fernie, Geoff R. (2006). Adaptive technology. In James E. Birren & K. Warner Schaie (Eds.), *Handbook of the psychology of aging* (6th ed., pp. 425–441). Amsterdam: Elsevier.

Scogin, Forrest R. (1998). Anxiety in old age. In Inger Hilde Nordhus, Gary R. VandenBos, Stig Berg, & Pia Fromholt (Eds.), *Clinical geropsychology* (pp. 205–209). Washington, DC: American Psychological Association.

Scollon, Christie Napa, Diener, Ed, Oishi, Shigehiro, & Biswas-Diener, Robert. (2005). An experience sampling and cross-cultural investigation of the relation between pleasant and unpleasant affect. *Cognition & Emotion, 19*, 27–52.

Scott, Jacqueline. (2000). Children as respondents: The challenge for quantitative methods. In Pia Monrad Christensen & Allison James (Eds.), *Research with children: Perspectives and practices* (pp. 98–119). London: Falmer Press.

Scott-Maxwell, Florida. (1968). *The measure of my days*. New York: Knopf.

Seale, Clive. (2006). Characteristics of end-of-life decisions: Survey of UK medical practitioners. *Palliative Medicine, 20*, 653–659.

Sears, Malcolm R., Greene, Justina M., Willan, Andrew R., Wiecek, Elizabeth M., Taylor, D. Robin, Flannery, Erin M., et al. (2003). A longitudinal, population-based, cohort study of childhood asthma followed to adulthood. *New England Journal of Medicine, 349*, 1414–1422.

Segal, Nancy L. (1999). *Entwined lives: Twins and what they tell us about human behavior*. New York: Dutton.

Segalowitz, Sidney J., & Schmidt, Louis A. (2003). Developmental psychology and the neurosciences. In Jaan Valsiner & Kevin J. Connolly (Eds.), *Handbook of developmental psychology* (pp. 48–71). Thousand Oaks, CA: Sage.

Seifer, Ronald, LaGasse, Linda L., Lester, Barry, Bauer, Charles R., Shankaran, Seetha, Bada, Henrietta S., et al. (2004). Attachment status in children prenatally exposed to cocaine and other substances. *Child Development, 75*, 850–868.

Seki, Fusako. (2001). The role of the government and the family in taking care of the frail elderly: A comparison of the United States and Japan. In David N. Weisstub, David C. Thomasma, Serge Gauthier, & George F. Tomossy (Eds.), *Aging: Caring for our elders* (pp. 83–105). Dordrecht, The Netherlands: Kluwer.

Seltzer, Marsha Mailick, & Li, Lydia Wailing. (1996). The transitions of caregiving: Subjective and objective definitions. *Gerontologist, 36*, 614–626.

Serpell, Robert, & Haynes, Brenda Pitts. (2004). The cultural practice of intelligence testing: Problems of international export. In Robert J. Sternberg & Elena L. Grigorenko (Eds.), *Culture and competence: Contexts of life success* (pp. 163–185). Washington, DC: American Psychological Association.

Settersten, Richard A. (2002). Social sources of meaning in later life. In Robert S. Weiss & Scott A. Bass (Eds.), *Challenges of the third age: Meaning and purpose in later life* (pp. 55–79). London: Oxford University Press.

Settersten, Richard A., Furstenberg, Frank F., & Rumbaut, Rubén G. (2005). *On the frontier of adulthood: Theory, research, and public policy*. Chicago, IL: University of Chicago Press.

Settersten, Richard A., & Hagestad, Gunhild O. (1996). What's the latest? Cultural age deadlines for family transitions. *Gerontologist, 36*, 602–613.

Shackelford, Todd K., & Mouzos, Jenny. (2005). Partner killing by men in cohabiting and marital relationships: A comparative, cross-national analysis of data from Australia and the United States. *Journal of Interpersonal Violence, 20*, 1310–1324.

Shahin, Hashem, Walsh, Tom, Sobe, Tama, Lynch, Eric, King, Mary-Claire, Avraham, Karen, et al. (2002). Genetics of congenital deafness in the Palestinian population: Multiple connexin 26 alleles with shared origins in the Middle East. *Human Genetics, 110*, 284–289.

Shanahan, Lilly, McHale, Susan M., Osgood, Wayne, & Crouter, Ann C. (2007). Conflict frequency with mothers and fathers from middle childhood to late adolescence: Within- and between-families comparisons. *Developmental Psychology, 43*, 539–550.

Shannon, Joyce Brennfleck (Ed.). (2007). *Eating disorders sourcebook: Basic consumer health information about anorexia nervosa, bulimia nervosa, binge eating, compulsive exercise, female athlete triad, and other eating disorders* (2nd ed.). Detroit, MI: Omnigraphics.

Shattuck, Paul T. (2006). The contribution of diagnostic substitution to the growing administrative prevalence of autism in US special education. *Pediatrics, 117*, 1028–1037.

Sheehy, Gail. (1976). *Passages: Predictable crises of adult life*. New York: Dutton.

Sheldon, Kennon M., & Kasser, Tim. (2001). Getting older, getting better? Personal strivings and psychological maturity across the life span. *Developmental Psychology, 37*, 491–501.

Shen, Qin, Wang, Yue, Dimos, John T., Fasano, Christopher A., Phoenix, Timothy N., Lemischka, Ihor R., et al. (2006). The timing of cortical neurogenesis is encoded within lineages of individual progenitor cells. *Nature Neuroscience, 9*, 743–751.

Shepard, Thomas H., & Lemire, Ronald J. (2004). *Catalog of teratogenic agents* (11th ed.). Baltimore: Johns Hopkins University Press.

Sher, Kenneth J., & Gotham, Heather J. (1999). Pathological alcohol involvement: A developmental disorder of young adulthood. *Development and Psychopathology, 11*, 933–956.

Sherman, Edmund, & Dacher, Joan. (2005). Cherished objects and the home: Their meaning and roles in late life. In Graham D. Rowles & Habib Chaudhury (Eds.), *Home and identity in late life international perspectives* (pp. 63–79). New York: Springer.

Sherman, Stephanie. (2002). Epidemiology. In Randi Jenssen Hagerman & Paul J. Hagerman (Eds.), *Fragile X syndrome: Diagnosis, treatment, and research* (3rd ed., pp. 136–168). Baltimore: Johns Hopkins University Press.

Shevell, Tracy, Malone, Fergal D., Vidaver, John, Porter, T. Flint, Luthy, David A., Comstock, Christine H., et al. (2005). Assisted reproductive technology and pregnancy outcome. *Obstetrics & Gynecology, 106*, 1039–1045.

Shibusawa, Tazuko, Lubben, James, & Kitano, Harry H. L. (2001). Japanese American elderly. In Laura Katz Olson (Ed.), *Age through ethnic lenses: Caring for the elderly in a multicultural society* (pp. 33–44). Lanham, MD: Rowman & Littlefield.

Shields, Margot. (2005). An update on smoking from the 2005 Canadian Community Health Survey. *Your Community, Your Health: Findings from the Canadian Community Health Survey (CCHS), 2*, 8–47.

Shuey, Kim, & Hardy, Melissa A. (2003). Assistance to aging parents and parents-in-law: Does lineage affect family allocation decisions? *Journal of Marriage and Family, 65*, 418–431.

Siebenbruner, Jessica, Zimmer-Gembeck, Melanie J., & Egeland, By-

Physical dimensions of aging (2nd ed.). Champaign, IL: Human Kinetics.

Spock, Benjamin. (1976). *Baby and child care* (Newly rev., updated, and enl. ed.). New York: Pocket Books.

Sprung, Charles L., Carmel, Sara, Sjokvist, Peter, Baras, Mario, Cohen, Simon L., Maia, Paulo, et al. (2007). Attitudes of European physicians, nurses, patients, and families regarding end-of-life decisions: The ETHICATT study. *Intensive Care Medicine, 33*, 104–110.

Sroufe, L. Alan, Egeland, Byron, Carlson, Elizabeth A., & Collins, W. Andrew. (2005). *The development of the person: The Minnesota study of risk and adaptation from birth to adulthood.* New York: Guilford.

Stacey, Phillip S., & Sullivan, Karen A. (2004). Preliminary investigation of thiamine and alcohol intake in clinical and healthy samples. *Psychological Reports, 94*(3, Pt. 1), 845–848.

Staff, Jeremy, Mortimer, Jeylan T., & Uggen, Christopher. (2004). Work and leisure in adolescence. In Richard M. Lerner & Laurence D. Steinberg (Eds.), *Handbook of adolescent psychology* (2nd ed., pp. 429–450). Hoboken, NJ: Wiley.

Staiger, Annegret Daniela. (2006). *Learning difference: Race and schooling in the multiracial metropolis.* Stanford, CA: Stanford University Press.

Stansfeld, Stephen A., Berglund, Birgitta, Clark, Charlotte, Lopez-Barrio, Isabel, Fischer, Paul, Öhrström, Evy, et al. (2005). Aircraft and road traffic noise and children's cognition and health: A cross-national study. *Lancet, 365*, 1942–1949.

Stanton, Bonita, & Burns, James. (2003). Sustaining and broadening intervention effect: Social norms, core values, and parents. In Daniel Romer (Ed.), *Reducing adolescent risk: Toward an integrated approach* (pp. 193–200). Thousand Oaks, CA: Sage.

Stanton, Cynthia K., & Holtz, Sara A. (2006). Levels and trends in cesarean birth in the developing world. *Studies in Family Planning, 37*, 41–48.

Starkes, Janet L., Deakin, Janice M., Allard, Fran, Hodges, Nicola J., & Hayes, A. (1996). Deliberate practice in sports: What is it anyway? In Karl Anders Ericsson (Ed.), *The road to excellence: The acquisition of expert performance in the arts and sciences, sports, and games* (pp. 81–106). Hillsdale, NJ: Erlbaum.

Starkstein, Sergio E., & Merello, Marcelo J. (2002). *Psychiatric and cognitive disorders in Parkinson's disease.* New York: Cambridge University Press.

Stattin, Hakan, & Kerr, Margaret. (2000). Parental monitoring: A reinterpretation. *Child Development, 71*, 1072–1085.

Staudinger, Ursula M., & Lindenberger, Ulman. (2003). Why read another book on human development? Understanding human development takes a metatheory and multiple disciplines. In Ursula M. Staudinger & Ulman E. R. Lindenberger (Eds.), *Understanding human development: Dialogues with lifespan psychology* (pp. 1–13). Boston: Kluwer.

Staudinger, Ursula M., & Werner, Ines. (2003). Wisdom: Its social nature and lifespan development. In Jaan Valsiner & Kevin J. Connolly (Eds.), *Handbook of developmental psychology* (pp. 584–602). Thousand Oaks, CA: Sage.

St. Clair, David, Xu, Mingqing, Wang, Peng, Yu, Yaqin, Fang, Yourong, Zhang, Feng, et al. (2005). Rates of adult schizophrenia following prenatal exposure to the Chinese famine of 1959–1961. *Journal of the American Medical Association, 294*, 557–562.

Steele, Claude M. (1997). A threat in the air: How stereotypes shape intellectual identity and performance. *American Psychologist, 52*, 613–629.

Stein, Rob. (2006, February 8). Low-fat diet's benefits rejected: Study finds no drop in risk for disease. *Washington Post*, p. A1.

Steinberg, Adria. (1993). *Adolescents and schools: Improving the fit.* Cambridge, MA: Harvard Education Letter.

Steinberg, Laurence. (2004). Risk taking in adolescence: What changes, and why? In Ronald E. Dahl & Linda Patia Spear (Eds.), *Adolescent brain development: Vulnerabilities and opportunities* (Vol. 1021, pp. 51–58). New York: New York Academy of Sciences

Steinberg, Laurence. (2007). Risk taking in adolescence: New perspectives from brain and behavioral science. *Current Directions in Psychological Science, 16*, 55–59.

Steinberg, Laurence, Lamborn, Susie D., Darling, Nancy, Mounts, Nina S., & Dornbusch, Sanford M. (1994). Over-time changes in adjustment and competence among adolescents from authoritative, authoritarian, indulgent, and neglectful families. *Child Development, 65*, 754–770.

Stel, Vianda S., Smit, Johannes H., Pluijm, Saskia M. F., & Lips, Paul. (2004). Consequences of falling in older men and women and risk factors for health service use and functional decline. *Age and Ageing, 33*, 58–65.

Stern, Daniel N. (1985). *The interpersonal world of the infant: A view from psychoanalysis and developmental psychology.* New York: Basic Books.

Stern, Paul C., & Carstensen, Laura L. (Eds.). (2000). *The aging mind: Opportunities in cognitive research.* Washington, DC: National Academy Press.

Sternberg, Robert J. (1988). Triangulating love. In Robert J. Sternberg & Michael L. Barnes (Eds.), *The psychology of love* (pp. 119–138). New Haven, CT: Yale University Press.

Sternberg, Robert J. (1988). *The triarchic mind: A new theory of human intelligence.* New York: Viking.

Sternberg, Robert J. (1996). *Successful intelligence: How practical and creative intelligence determine success in life.* New York: Simon & Schuster.

Sternberg, Robert J. (2002). Beyond g: The theory of successful intelligence. In Robert J. Sternberg & Elena L. Grigorenko (Eds.), *The general factor of intelligence: How general is it?* (pp. 447–479). Mahwah, NJ: Erlbaum.

Sternberg, Robert J. (2003). *Wisdom, intelligence, and creativity synthesized.* New York: Cambridge University Press.

Sternberg, Robert J. (2006). Introduction. In James C. Kaufman & Robert J. Sternberg (Eds.), *The international handbook of creativity* (pp. 1–9). New York: Cambridge University Press.

Sternberg, Robert J., Forsythe, George B., Hedlund, Jennifer, Horvath, Joseph A., Wagner, Richard K., Williams, Wendy M., et al. (2000). *Practical intelligence in everyday life.* New York: Cambridge University Press.

Sternberg, Robert J., & Grigorenko, Elena (Eds.). (2002). *The general factor of intelligence: How general is it?* Mahwah, NJ: Erlbaum.

Sternberg, Robert J., & Grigorenko, Elena (Eds.). (2004). *Culture and competence: Contexts of life success.* Washington, DC: American Psychological Association.

Sternberg, Robert J., Grigorenko, Elena L., & Bundy, Donald A. (2001). The predictive value of IQ. *Merrill-Palmer Quarterly, 47*, 1–41.

Sternberg, Robert J., Grigorenko, Elena L., & Kidd, Kenneth K. (2005).

Intelligence, race, and genetics. *American Psychologist, 60,* 46–59.

Sternberg, Robert J., Grigorenko, Elena L., & Oh, Stella. (2001). The development of intelligence at midlife. In Margie E. Lachman (Ed.), *Handbook of midlife development* (pp. 217–247). Hoboken, NJ: Wiley.

Sterns, Harvey L., & Huyck, Margaret Hellie. (2001). The role of work in midlife. In Margie E. Lachman (Ed.), *Handbook of midlife development* (pp. 447–486). New York: Wiley.

Stevens, Judy A. (2002–2003). Falls among older adults: Public health impact and prevention strategies. *Generations, 26*(4), 7–14.

Stevenson, Harold W., Chen, Chuansheng, & Lee, Shin-ying. (1993, January 1). Mathematics achievement of Chinese, Japanese, and American children: Ten years later. *Science, 259,* 53–58.

Stevenson, Harold W., Lee, Shin-ying, Chen, Chuansheng, Stigler, James W., Hsu, Chen-Chin, & Kitamura, Seiro. (1990). Contexts of achievement: A study of American, Chinese, and Japanese children. *Monographs of the Society for Research in Child Development, 55*(1–2, Serial No. 221), 1–123.

Steverink, Nardi, & Lindenberg, Siegwart. (2006). Which social needs are important for subjective well-being? What happens to them with aging? *Psychology and Aging, 21,* 281–290.

Stevick, Richard A. (2001). The Amish: Case study of a religious community. In Clive Erricker & Jane Erricker (Eds.), *Contemporary spiritualities: Social and religious contexts* (pp. 159–172). London: Continuum.

Stewart, Susan D., Manning, Wendy D., & Smock, Pamela J. (2003). Union formation among men in the U.S.: Does having prior children matter? *Journal of Marriage and Family, 65,* 90–104.

Stigler, James W., & Hiebert, James. (1999). *The teaching gap: Best ideas from the world's teachers for improving education in the classroom.* New York: Free Press.

Still the third rail. (2007, February 22). *The Economist, 382,* 38.

Stipek, Deborah, Feiler, Rachelle, Daniels, Denise, & Milburn, Sharon. (1995). Effects of different instructional approaches on young children's achievement and motivation. *Child Development, 66,* 209–223.

Stock, Gregory B., & Callahan, Daniel. (2005). Would doubling the human lifespan be a net positive or negative for us, either as individuals or as a society? Point-counterpoint. In Richard G. Cutler, S. Mitchell Harman, Chris Heward, & Mike Gibbons (Eds.), *Longevity health sciences: The Phoenix Conference* (Vol. 1055, pp. 207–218). New York: New York Academy of Sciences.

Stokstad, Erik. (2003, December 12). The vitamin D deficit. *Science, 302,* 1886–1888.

Stone, Robyn I. (2006). Emerging issues in long-term care. In Robert H. Binstock & Linda K. George (Eds.), *Handbook of aging and the social sciences* (6th ed., pp. 397–418). Amsterdam: Elsevier

Storch, Eric A., & Storch, Jason B. (2002). Fraternities, sororities, and academic dishonesty. *College Student Journal, 36,* 247–252.

Straus, Murray A. (with Donnelly, Denise A.). (1994). *Beating the devil out of them: Corporal punishment in American families.* New York: Lexington Books.

Straus, Murray A., & Gelles, Richard J. (with Smith, Christine) (Eds.). (1995). *Physical violence in American families: Risk factors and adaptations to violence in 8,145 families* (Paperback ed.). New Brunswick, NJ: Transaction.

Strauss, Bernhard, Brix, Christina, Fischer, Sebastian, Leppert, Karena, Füller, Jürgen, Roehrig, Bernd, et al. (2007). The influence of resilience on fatigue in cancer patients undergoing radiation therapy (RT). *Journal of Cancer Research and Clinical Oncology, 133,* 511–518.

Strayer, David L., & Drews, Frank A. (2007). Cell-phone-induced driver distraction. *Current Directions in Psychological Science, 16,* 128–131.

Streissguth, Ann P., & Connor, Paul D. (2001). Fetal alcohol syndrome and other effects of prenatal alcohol: Developmental cognitive neuroscience implications. In Charles A. Nelson & Monica Luciana (Eds.), *Handbook of developmental cognitive neuroscience* (pp. 505–518). Cambridge, MA: MIT Press.

Striano, Tricia. (2004). Direction of regard and the still-face effect in the first year: Does intention matter? *Child Development, 75,* 468–479.

Stroebe, Margaret S., & Stroebe, Wolfgang. (1993). The mortality of bereavement: A review. In Margaret S. Stroebe, Wolfgang Stroebe, & Robert O. Hansson (Eds.), *Handbook of bereavement: Theory, research, and intervention* (pp. 175–195). New York: Cambridge University Press.

Strom, Robert D., & Strom, Shirley K. (2000). Goals for grandparents and support groups. In Bert Hayslip Jr. & Robin Goldberg-Glen (Eds.), *Grandparents raising grandchildren: Theoretical, empirical, and clinical perspectives* (pp. 289–303). New York: Springer.

Strouse, Darcy L. (1999). Adolescent crowd orientations: A social and temporal analysis. In Jeffrey A. McLellan & Mary Jo V. Pugh (Eds.), *The role of peer groups in adolescent social identity: Exploring the importance of stability and change* (pp. 37–54). San Francisco, CA: Jossey-Bass.

Suarez-Orozco, Carola, & Suarez-Orozco, Marcelo M. (2001). *Children of immigration.* Cambridge, MA: Harvard University Press.

Subrahmanyam, Kaveri, Greenfield, Patricia M., Kraut, Robert, & Gross, Elisheva. (2002). The impact of computer use on children's and adolescent's development. In Sandra L. Calvert, Amy B. Jordan, & Rodney R. Cocking (Eds.), *Children in the digital age: Influences of electronic media on development* (pp. 3–33). Westport, CT: Praeger/Greenwood.

Suellentrop, Katherine, Morrow, Brian, Williams, Letitia, & D'Angelo, Denise. (2006, October 6). Monitoring progress toward achieving maternal and infant Healthy People 2010 objectives—19 states, Pregnancy Risk Assessment Monitoring System (PRAMS), 2000–2003. *MMWR Surveillance Summaries, 55*(SS09), 1–11.

Sugie, Shuji, Shwalb, David W., & Shwalb, Barbara J. (2006). Respect in Japanese childhood, adolescence, and society. *New Directions for Child and Adolescent Development, 114,* 39–52.

Sullivan, Sheila. (1999). *Falling in love: A history of torment and enchantment.* London: Macmillan.

Sulmasy, Daniel P. (2006). Spiritual issues in the care of dying patients: '...It's okay between me and god". *Journal of the American Medical Association, 296,* 1385–1392.

Suomi, Steven J. (2002). Parents, peers, and the process of socialization in primates. In John G. Borkowski, Sharon Landesman Ramey, & Marie Bristol-Power (Eds.), *Parenting and the child's world: Influences on academic, intellectual, and social-emotional development* (pp. 265–279). Mahwah, NJ: Erlbaum.

Supiano, Mark A. (2006). Hypertension in later life. *Generations, 30*(3), 11–16.

Susman, Elizabeth J., & Rogol, Alan. (2004). Puberty and psychological development. In Richard M. Lerner & Laurence D. Steinberg (Eds.), *Handbook of adolescent psychology* (2nd ed., pp. 15–44). Hoboken, NJ: Wiley.

Suzuki, Lalita K., & Calzo, Jerel P. (2004). The search for peer advice in cyberspace: An examination of online teen bulletin boards about health and sexuality. *Journal of Applied Developmental Psychology, 25*, 685–698.

Swanson, Richard A. (2007). *Analysis for improving performance: Tools for diagnosing organizations and documenting workplace expertise* (2nd ed.). San Francisco: Berrett-Koehler Publishers.

Sweet, Melissa. (1997, August 2). Smug as a bug. *Sydney Morning Herald.*

Szinovacz, Maximiliane E. (2000). Changes in housework after retirement: A panel analysis. *Journal of Marriage & the Family, 62*, 78–92.

Szinovacz, Maximiliane E., & Davey, Adam. (2005). Retirement and marital decision making: Effects on retirement satisfaction. *Journal of Marriage and Family, 67*, 387–398.

Szkrybalo, Joel, & Ruble, Diane N. (1999). "God made me a girl": Sex-category constancy judgments and explanations revisited. *Developmental Psychology, 35*, 392–402.

Tacken, Mart, & van Lamoen, Ellemieke (2005). Transport behaviour and realised journeys and trips. In Heidrun Mollenkopf, Fiorella Marcellini, Isto Ruoppila, Zsuzsa Széman, & Mart Tacken (Eds.), *Enhancing mobility in later life: Personal coping, environmental resources and technical support. The out-of-home mobility of older adults in urban and rural regions of five European countries* (pp. 105–139). Amsterdam: IOS Press.

Taga, Keiko A., Markey, Charlotte N., & Friedman, Howard S. (2006). A longitudinal investigation of associations between boys' pubertal timing and adult behavioral health and well-being. *Journal of Youth and Adolescence, 35*, 401–411.

Talamantes, Melissa A., Gomez, Celina, & Braun, Kathryn L. (1999). Advance directives and end-of-life care: The Hispanic perspective. In Kathryn Braun, James H. Pietsch, & Patricia L. Blanchette (Eds.), *Cultural issues in end-of-life decision making* (pp. 83–100). Thousand Oaks, CA: Sage.

Tallandini, Maria Anna, & Scalembra, Chiara. (2006). Kangaroo mother care and mother-premature infant dyadic interaction. *Infant Mental Health Journal, 27*, 251–275.

Tamay, Zeynep, Akcay, Ahmet, Ones, Ulker, Guler, Nermin, Kilic, Gurkan, & Zencir, Mehmet. (2007). Prevalence and risk factors for allergic rhinitis in primary school children. *International Journal of Pediatric Otorhinolaryngology, 71*, 463–471.

Tamis-LeMonda, Catherine S., Bornstein, Marc H., & Baumwell, Lisa. (2001). Maternal responsiveness and children's achievement of language milestones. *Child Development, 72*, 748–767.

Tanaka, Yuko, & Nakazawa, Jun. (2005). Job-related temporary father absence (Tanshinfunin) and child development. In David W. Shwalb, Jun Nakazawa, & Barbara J. Shwalb (Eds.), *Applied developmental psychology: Theory, practice, and research from Japan* (pp. 241–260). Greenwich, CT: Information Age.

Tang, Chao-Hsiun, Wang, Han-I., Hsu, Chun-Sen, Su, Hung-Wen, Chen, Mei-Ju, & Lin, Herng-Ching. (2006). *Risk-adjusted cesarean section rates for the assessment of physician performance in Taiwan: A population-based study*. Retrieved April 27, 2007, from the World Wide Web: http://www.biomedcentral.com/1471–2458/6/246

Tang, Fengyan. (2006). What resources are needed for volunteerism? A life course perspective. *Journal of Applied Gerontology, 25*, 375–390.

Tangney, June Price. (2001). Constructive and destructive aspects of shame and guilt. In Arthur C. Bohart & Deborah J. Stipek (Eds.), *Constructive & destructive behavior: Implications for family, school, & society* (pp. 127–145). Washington, DC: American Psychological Association.

Tanner, James Mourilyan. (1990). *Foetus into man: Physical growth from conception to maturity* (Rev. and enl. ed.). Cambridge, MA: Harvard University Press.

Tarter, Ralph E., Vanyukov, Michael, Giancola, Peter, Dawes, Michael, Blackson, Timothy, Mezzich, Ada, et al. (1999). Etiology of early age onset substance use disorder: A maturational perspective. *Development & Psychopathology, 11*, 657–683.

Tatz, Colin Martin. (2001). *Aboriginal suicide is different: A portrait of life and self-destruction*. Canberra, Australia: Aboriginal Studies Press.

Tay, Marc Tze-Hsin, Au Eong, Kah Guan, Ng, C. Y., & Lim, M. K. (1992). Myopia and educational attainment in 421,116 young Singaporean males. *Annals, Academy of Medicine, Singapore, 21*, 785–791.

Taylor, Alan C., Robila, Mihaela, & Lee, Hae Seung. (2005). Distance, contact, and intergenerational relationships: Grandparents and adult grandchildren from an international perspective. *Journal of Adult Development, 12*, 33–41.

Taylor, Anne L., Ziesche, Susan, Yancy, Clyde, Carson, Peter, D'Agostino, Ralph, Jr., Ferdinand, Keith, et al. (2004). Combination of isosorbide dinitrate and hydralazine in blacks with heart failure. *New England Journal of Medicine, 351*, 2049–2057.

Taylor, Shelley E. (2006). Tend and befriend: Biobehavioral bases of affiliation under stress. *Current Directions in Psychological Science, 15*, 273–277.

Taylor, Shelley E., Klein, Laura Cousino, Lewis, Brian P., Gruenewald, Tara L., Gurung, Regan A. R., & Updegraff, John A. (2000). Biobehavioral responses to stress in females: Tend-and-befriend, not fight-or-flight. *Psychological Review, 107*, 411–429.

Tedeschi, Alberto, & Airaghi, Lorena. (2006). Is affluence a risk factor for bronchial asthma and type 1 diabetes? *Pediatric Allergy and Immunology, 17*, 533–537.

Teicher, Martin H. (2002, March). Scars that won't heal: The neurobiology of child abuse. *Scientific American, 286*, 68–75.

Teitler, Julien O. (2002). Trends in youth sexual initiation and fertility in developed countries: 1960–1995. *Annals of the American Academy of Political & Social Science, 580*, 134–152.

Tenenbaum, Harriet R., & Leaper, Campbell. (2002). Are parents' gender schemas related to their children's gender-related cognitions? A meta-analysis. *Developmental Psychology, 38*, 615–630.

ter Bogt, Tom, Schmid, Holger, Gabhainn, Saoirse Nic, Fotiou, Anastasios, & Vollebergh, Wilma. (2006). Economic and cultural correlates of cannabis use among mid-adolescents in 31 countries. *Addiction, 101*, 241–251.

Tester, June M., Rutherford, George W., Wald, Zachary, & Rutherford, Mary W. (2004). A matched case-control study evaluating the effectiveness of speed humps in reducing child pedestrian injuries. *American Journal of Public Health, 94*, 646–650.

Teti, Douglas M., Lamb, Michael E., & Elster, Arthur B. (1987). Long-range

socioeconomic and marital consequences of adolescent marriage in three cohorts of adult males. *Journal of Marriage & the Family, 49,* 499–506.

Thelen, Esther, & Corbetta, Daniela. (2002). Microdevelopment and dynamic systems: Applications to infant motor development. In Nira Granott & Jim Parziale (Eds.), *Microdevelopment: Transition processes in development and learning* (pp. 59–79). New York: Cambridge University Press.

Thelen, Esther, & Smith, Linda B. (2006). Dynamic systems theories. In William Damon & Richard M. Lerner (Series Eds.) & Richard M. Lerner (Vol. Ed.), *Handbook of child psychology: Vol. 1. Theoretical models of human development* (6th ed., pp. 258–312). Hoboken, NJ: Wiley.

Thelen, Esther, & Ulrich, Beverly D. (1991). Hidden skills: A dynamic systems analysis of treadmill stepping during the first year. *Monographs of the Society for Research in Child Development, 56,* 104.

Thobaben, Marshelle. (2006). Understanding compulsive hoarding. *Home Health Care Management Practice, 18,* 152–154.

Thomas, Ayanna K., & Bulevich, John B. (2006). Effective cue utilization reduces memory errors in older adults. *Psychology and Aging, 21,* 379–389.

Thomas, Dylan. (1957). *The collected poems of Dylan Thomas* (6th ed.). New York: New Directions.

Thomasma, David C., Kimbrough Kushner, Thomasine, Kimsma, Gerrit K., & Ciesielski-Carlucci, Chris (1998). *Asking to die: Inside the Dutch debate about euthanasia.* Dordrecht, The Netherlands: Kluwer.

Thompson, Christine. (2002). Drawing together: Peer influence in preschool-kindergarten art classes. In Liora Bresler & Christine Marme Thompson (Eds.), *The arts in children's lives: Context, culture, and curriculum* (pp. 129–138). Dordrecht, The Netherlands: Kluwer.

Thompson, Ross A. (2006). The development of the person: Social understanding, relationships, conscience, self. In William Damon & Richard M. Lerner (Series Eds.) & Nancy Eisenberg (Vol. Ed.), *Handbook of child psychology: Vol. 3. Social, emotional, and personality development* (6th ed., pp. 24–98). Hoboken, NJ: Wiley.

Thompson, Ross A., & Nelson, Charles A. (2001). Developmental science and the media: Early brain development. *American Psychologist, 56,* 5–15.

Thompson, Ross A., & Raikes, H. Abigail. (2003). Toward the next quarter-century: Conceptual and methodological challenges for attachment theory. *Development & Psychopathology, 15,* 691–718.

Thompson, Ross A., & Wyatt, Jennifer M. (1999). Values, policy, and research on divorce: Seeking fairness for children. In Ross A. Thompson & Paul R. Amato (Eds.), *The post-divorce family: Children, parenting, and society* (pp. 191–232). Thousand Oaks, CA: Sage.

Thornton, Wendy J. L., & Dumke, Heike A. (2005). Age differences in everyday problem-solving and decision-making effectiveness: A meta-analytic review. *Psychology and Aging, 20,* 85–99.

Thorson, James A. (1995). *Aging in a changing society*. Belmont, CA: Wadsworth.

Tiggemann, Marika, & Lynch, Jessica E. (2001). Body image across the life span in adult women: The role of self-objectification. *Developmental Psychology, 37,* 243–253.

Timiras, Mary Letitia. (2003). The skin. In Paola S. Timiras (Ed.), *Physiological basis of aging and geriatrics* (3rd ed., pp. 397–404). Boca Raton, FL: CRC Press.

Timiras, Paola S. (2003). Cardiovascular alterations with aging: Atherosclerosis and coronary heart disease. In Paola S. Timiras (Ed.), *Physiological basis of aging and geriatrics* (3rd ed., pp. 375–395). Boca Raton, FL: CRC Press.

TIMSS. (2004). *Highlights from the Trends in International Mathematics and Science Study: TIMSS 2003* (NCES 2005005). Washington, DC: National Center for Education Statistics.

Tishkoff, Sarah A., & Kidd, Kenneth K. (2004). Implications of biogeography of human populations for 'race' and medicine. *Nature Genetics, 36,* S21–S27.

Tobin, Sheldon S. (1996). Cherished possessions: The meaning of things. *Generations, 20*(3), 46–48.

Tomasello, Michael. (2001). Perceiving intentions and learning words in the second year of life. In Melissa Bowerman & Stephen C. Levinson (Eds.), *Language acquisition and conceptual development* (pp. 132–158). Cambridge, UK: Cambridge University Press.

Tomasello, Michael. (2006). Acquiring linguistic constructions. In William Damon & Richard M. Lerner (Series Eds.) & Deanna Kuhn & Robert S. Siegler (Vol. Eds.), *Handbook of child psychology: Vol. 2. Cognition, perception, and language* (6th ed., pp. 255–298). Hoboken, NJ: Wiley.

Tonn, Jessica L. (2006, March 22). Later high school start times: A reaction to research. *Education Week, 25,* 5, 17.

Torgesen, Joseph K. (2004). Preventing early reading failure—And its devastating downward spiral. *American Educator, 28,* 6–9, 12–13, 17–19, 45–47.

Torney-Purta, Judith, Lehmann, Rainer, Oswald, Hans, & Schulz, Wolfram. (2001). *Citizenship and education in twenty-eight countries: Civic knowledge and engagement at age fourteen.* Amsterdam: International Association for the Evaluation of Educational Achievement.

Tornstam, Lars. (1999–2000). Transcendence in later life. *Generations, 23*(4), 10–14.

Tornstam, Lars. (2005). *Gerotranscendence: A developmental theory of positive aging*. New York: Springer.

Torquati, Alfonso, Wright, Kelly, Melvin, Willie, & Richards, William. (2007). Effect of gastric bypass operation on Framingham and actual risk of cardiovascular events in class II to III obesity. *Journal of the American College of Surgeons 204,* 776–782.

Torres-Gil, Fernando M. (1992). *The new aging: Politics and change in America*. New York: Auburn House.

Townsend, Jean, Godfrey, Mary, & Denby, Tracy. (2006). Heroines, villains and victims: Older people's perceptions of others. *Ageing & Society, 26,* 883–900.

Toyama, Miki. (2001). Developmental changes in social comparison in preschool and elementary school children: Perceptions, feelings, and behavior. *Japanese Journal of Educational Psychology, 49,* 500–507.

Tremblay, Richard E., & Nagin, Daniel S. (2005). Developmental origins of physical aggression in humans. In Richard Ernest Tremblay, Willard W. Hartup, & John Archer (Eds.), *Developmental origins of aggression* (pp. 83–106). New York: Guilford Press.

Trenholm, Christopher, Devaney, Barbara, Fortson, Ken, Quay, Lisa, Wheeler, Justin, & Clark, Melissa. (2007). *Impacts of four Title V, Section 510 abstinence education programs final report*. U.S. Department of Health and Human Services. Retrieved August 22, 2007, from the World Wide Web: http://www.mathematica-mpr.com/abstinencereport.asp

Trichopoulou, Antonia, Naska, Androniki, & Oikonomou, Eleni. (2005). The DAFNE databank: The past and future of monitoring the dietary habits of Europeans. *Journal of Public Health, 13,* 69–73.

Trillo, Alex. (2004). Somewhere between Wall Street and El Barrio: Community college as a second chance for second-generation Latino students. In Philip Kasinitz, John H. Mollenkopf, & Mary C. Waters (Eds.), *Becoming New Yorkers: Ethnographies of the new second generation* (pp. 57–78). New York: Russell Sage.

Trimble, Joseph, Root, Maria P. P., & Helms, Janet E. (2003). Psychological perspectives on ethnic and racial psychology. In Guillermo Bernal, Joseph E. Trimble, Ann Kathleen Burlew, & Frederick T. Leong (Eds.), *Racial and ethnic minority psychology series: Vol. 4. Handbook of racial & ethnic minority psychology* (pp. 239–275). Thousand Oaks, CA: Sage.

Troll, Lillian E. (1996). Modified-extended families over time: Discontinuity in parts, continuity in wholes. In Vern L. Bengtson (Ed.), *Adulthood and aging: Research on continuities and discontinuities* (pp. 246–268). New York: Springer.

Troll, Lillian E., & Skaff, Marilyn McKean. (1997). Perceived continuity of self in very old age. *Psychology & Aging, 12*, 162–169.

Tronick, Edward, Als, Heidelise, Adamson, Lauren, Wise, Susan, & Brazelton, T. Berry. (1978). The infant's response to entrapment between contradictory messages in face-to-face interaction. *Journal of the American Academy of Child Psychiatry, 17*, 1–13.

Tronick, Edward Z. (1989). Emotions and emotional communication in infants. *American Psychologist, 44*, 112–119.

Tronick, Edward Z., & Weinberg, M. Katherine. (1997). Depressed mothers and infants: Failure to form dyadic states of consciousness. In Lynne Murray & Peter J. Cooper (Eds.), *Postpartum depression and child development* (pp. 54–81). New York: Guilford Press.

Truby, Helen, Baic, Sue, deLooy, Anne, Fox, Kenneth R., Livingstone, M. Barbara E., Logan, Catherine M., et al. (2006). Randomised controlled trial of four commercial weight loss programmes in the UK: Initial findings from the BBC "diet trials". *British Medical Journal, 332*, 1309–1314.

Trzesniewski, Kali H., Robins, Richard W., Roberts, Brent W., & Caspi, Avshalom. (2004). Personality and self-esteem development across the life span. In Paul T. Costa & Ilene C. Siegler (Eds.), *Recent advances in psychology and aging* (Vol. 15, pp. 163–185). Amsterdam: Elsevier.

Tsao, Feng-Ming, Liu, Huei-Mei, & Kuhl, Patricia K. (2004). Speech perception in infancy predicts language development in the second year of life: A longitudinal study. *Child Development, 75*, 1067–1084.

Tse, Lucy. (2001). *"Why don't they learn English?" Separating fact from fallacy in the U.S. language debate*. New York: Teachers College Press.

Tseng, Vivian. (2004). Family interdependence and academic adjustment in college: Youth from immigrant and U.S.-born families. *Child Development, 75*, 966–983.

Tucker, Joan S., Friedman, Howard S., Wingard, Deborah L., & Schwartz, Joseph E. (1996). Marital history at midlife as a predictor of longevity: Alternative explanations to the protective effect of marriage. *Health Psychology, 15*, 94–101.

Tudge, Jonathan R. H., Doucet, Fabienne, Odero, Dolphine, Sperb, Tania M., Piccinini, Cesar A., & Lopes, Rita S. (2006). A window into different cultural worlds: Young children's everyday activities in the United States, Brazil, and Kenya. *Child Development, 77*, 1446–1469.

Turiel, Elliot. (2006). The development of morality. In William Damon & Richard M. Lerner (Series Eds.) & Nancy Eisenberg (Vol. Ed.), *Handbook of child psychology: Vol. 3. Social, emotional, and personality development* (6th ed., pp. 789–857). Hoboken, NJ: Wiley.

Twomey, John G. (2006). Issues in genetic testing of children. *MCN: The American Journal of Maternal/Child Nursing, 31*, 156–163.

U.S. Bureau of the Census. (1907). *Statistical abstract of the United States: 1907* (30th ed.). Washington, DC: U.S. Government Printing Office.

U.S. Bureau of the Census. (1952). *Statistical abstract of the United States: 1952* (73rd ed.). Washington, DC: U.S. Government Printing Office.

U.S. Bureau of the Census. (1972). *Statistical abstract of the United States: 1972* (93rd ed.). Washington, DC: U.S. Government Printing Office.

U.S. Bureau of the Census. (1975). *Statistical abstract of the United States: 1975* (96th ed.). Washington, DC: U.S. Government Printing Office.

U.S. Bureau of the Census. (2002). *Statistical abstract of the United States, 2001: The national data book* (121st ed.). Washington, DC: U.S. Department of Commerce.

U.S. Bureau of the Census. (2004). *Statistical abstract of the United States: 2004–2005* (124th ed.). Washington, DC: U.S. Government Printing Office.

U.S. Bureau of the Census. (2006). *Statistical abstract of the United States: 2007* (126th ed.). Washington, DC: U.S. Government Printing Office.

U.S. Census Bureau. (2006, August 24). *International Data Base (IDB)*. Retrieved May 1, 2007, from the World Wide Web: http://www.census.gov/ipc/www/idbsum.html

U.S. Department of Health and Human Services. (2004). *Trends in the well-being of America's children and youth, 2003* (No. 017–022–01571–4). Washington, DC: U.S. Government Printing Office.

U.S. Department of Health and Human Services, Administration on Children Youth and Families. (2006). *Child maltreatment 2004*. Washington, DC: U.S. Government Printing Office.

U.S. Department of Justice. (2006). *National crime victimization survey*. Hyattsville, MD: Bureau of Justice Statistics.

U.S. Department of Labor. (2007). *Bureau of Labor Statistics*. Retrieved September 15, 2007, from the World Wide Web: http://www.bls.gov/

U.S. Department of Labor. (2007, August 17). *Regional and state employment and unemployment summary: Table 3. Civilian labor force and unemployment by state and selected area, seasonally adjusted*. Retrieved September 23, 2007, from the World Wide Web: http://www.bls.gov/news.release/laus.nr0.htm

U.S. Department of Labor, Bureau of Labor Statistics. (2004, August 25). *Number of jobs held, labor market activity, and earnings growth among younger baby boomers: Recent results from a longitudinal survey* (Press Release USDL 04–1678). Washington, DC: U.S. Department of Labor.

U.S. Department of Labor, Bureau of Labor Statistics. (2005, July 1). *Workers on flexible and shift schedules in 2004 summary* (Press Release USDL 05–1198). Washington, DC: U.S. Department of Labor.

U.S. Department of Transportation, National Highway Traffic Safety Administration. (2003, April). *Pedestrian roadway fatalities* (DOT HS 809 456). Springfield, VA: National Center for Statistics and Analysis.

U.S. Preventive Services Task Force. (2002). Postmenopausal hormone replacement therapy for primary prevention of chronic conditions: Recommendations and

rationale. *Annals of Internal Medicine, 137,* 834–839.

Udry, J. Richard, & Chantala, Kim. (2005). Risk factors differ according to same-sex and opposite-sex interest. *Journal of Biosocial Science, 37,* 481–497.

Uhlenberg, Peter. (1996). The burden of aging: A theoretical framework for understanding the shifting balance of caregiving and care receiving as cohorts age. *Gerontologist, 36,* 761–767.

UNAIDS. (2006). *Report on the global AIDS epidemic 2006.* Geneva, Switzerland: World Health Organization.

Unal, Belgin, Critchley, Julia Alison, & Capewell, Simon. (2005). Modelling the decline in coronary heart disease deaths in England and Wales, 1981–2000: Comparing contributions from primary prevention and secondary prevention. *British Medical Journal, 331,* 614–617.

Underwood, Marion K. (2003). *Social aggression among girls.* New York: Guilford Press.

Underwood, Marion K. (2004). Gender and peer relations: Are the two gender cultures really all that different? In Janis B. Kupersmidt & Kenneth A. Dodge (Eds.), *Children's peer relations: From development to intervention* (pp. 21–36). Washington, DC: American Psychological Association.

UNESCO. (2006). *Global education digest 2006: Comparing education statistics across the world* (UIS/SD/06–01). Montreal, Canada: UNESCO Institute for Statistics.

Ungar, Michael T. (2000). The myth of peer pressure. *Adolescence, 35,* 167–180.

UNICEF (United Nations Children's Fund). (2003). *The state of the world's children 2004: Infants with low birthweight.* Retrieved September 3, 2005, from the World Wide Web: http://hdr.undp.org/statistics/data/indic/indic_68_1_1.html

UNICEF (United Nations Children's Fund). (2005). *The state of the world's children 2006—Excluded and invisible.* New York: UNICEF.

UNICEF (United Nations Children's Fund). (2006). *The state of the world's children 2007: Women and children: The double dividend of gender equality.* New York: UNICEF.

United Nations Department of Economic and Social Affairs, Population Division. (2007). *World population ageing, 2007.* New York: United Nations.

United Nations Development Programme. (2006). *Human development report 2006: Beyond scarcity: Power, poverty and the global water crisis.* Retrieved April 27, 2007, from the World Wide Web: http://hdr.undp.org/hdr2006/pdfs/report/HDR06–complete.pdf

Unnever, James D. (2005). Bullies, aggressive victims, and victims: Are they distinct groups? *Aggressive Behavior, 31,* 153–171.

Uttl, Bob, & Van Alstine, Cory L. (2003). Rising verbal intelligence scores: Implications for research and clinical practice. *Psychology & Aging, 18,* 616–621.

Utz, Rebecca L., Carr, Deborah, Nesse, Randolph, & Wortman, Camille B. (2002). The effect of widowhood on older adults' social participation: An evaluation of activity, disengagement, and continuity theories. *The Gerontologist, 42,* 522–533.

Vaillant, George E. (2002). *Aging well: Surprising guideposts to a happier life from the landmark Harvard study of adult development.* Boston: Little Brown.

Vaillant, George E., & Davis, J. Timothy. (2000). Social/emotional intelligence and midlife resilience in schoolboys with low tested intelligence. *American Journal of Orthopsychiatry, 70,* 215–222.

Valentino, Kristin, Cicchetti, Dante, Toth, Sheree L., & Rogosch, Fred A. (2006). Mother-child play and emerging social behaviors among infants from maltreating families. *Developmental Psychology, 42,* 474–485.

Valkenburg, Patti M., & Peter, Jochen. (2007). Preadolescents' and adolescents' online communication and their closeness to friends. *Developmental Psychology, 43,* 267–277.

Valsiner, Jaan. (2006). Developmental epistemology and implications for methodology. In William Damon & Richard M. Lerner (Series Eds.) & Richard M. Lerner (Vol. Ed.), *Handbook of child psychology: Vol. 1. Theoretical models of human development* (6th ed., pp. 166–209). Hoboken, NJ: Wiley.

Van Cauter, Eve, Leproult, Rachel, & Plat, Laurence. (2000). Age-related changes in slow wave sleep and REM sleep and relationship with growth hormone and cortisol levels in healthy men. *Journal of the American Medical Association, 284,* 861–868.

van Dam, Rob M., Willett, Walter C., Manson, JoAnn E., & Hu, Frank B. (2006). The relationship between overweight in adolescence and premature death in women. *Annals of Internal Medicine, 145,* 91–97.

van der Meulen, Matty. (2001). Developments in self-concept theory and research: Affect, context, and variability. In Harke A. Bosma & E. Saskia Kunnen (Eds.), *Identity and emotion: Development through self-organization* (pp. 10–38). New York: Cambridge University Press.

Van Gaalen, Ruben I., & Dykstra, Pearl A. (2006). Solidarity and conflict between adult children and parents: A latent class analysis. *Journal of Marriage and Family, 68,* 947–960.

Van Goozen, Stephanie H. M. (2005). Hormones and the developmental origins of aggression. In Richard E. Tremblay, Willard W. Hartup, & John Archer (Eds.), *Developmental origins of aggression* (pp. 281–306). New York: Guilford Press.

Van Hoorn, Judith Lieberman, Komlosi, Akos, Suchar, Elzbieta, & Samelson, Doreen A. (2000). *Adolescent development and rapid social change: Perspectives from Eastern Europe.* Albany, NY: State University of New York Press.

Van Leeuwen, Karla G., Mervielde, Ivan, Braet, Caroline, & Bosmans, Guy. (2004). Child personality and parental behavior as moderators of problem behavior: Variable- and person-centered approaches. *Developmental Psychology, 40,* 1028–1046.

van Straten, Annemieke, Cuijpers, Pim, Zuuren, Florence, Smits, Niels, & Donker, Marianne. (2007). Personality traits and health-related quality of life in patients with mood and anxiety disorders. *Quality of Life Research, 16,* 1–8.

van Wijk, I., Kappelle, L. J., van Gijn, J., Koudstaal, P. J., Franke, C. L., Vermeulen, M., et al. (2005, June 18–24). Long-term survival and vascular event risk after transient ischaemic attack or minor ischaemic stroke: A cohort study. *Lancet, 365,* 2098–2104.

Van Winkle, Nancy Westlake. (2000). End-of-life decision making in American Indian and Alaska native cultures. In Kathryn Braun, James H. Pietsch, & Patricia L. Blanchette (Eds.), *Cultural issues in end-of-life decision making* (pp. 127–146). Thousand Oaks, CA: Sage.

Vartanian, Lesa Rae. (2001). Adolescents' reactions to hypothetical peer group conversations: Evidence for an imaginary audience? *Adolescence, 36,* 347–380.

Vasa, Roma A., & Pine, Daniel S. (2004). Neurobiology. In Tracy L. Morris & John S. March (Eds.), *Anxiety disorders in children*

and adolescents (2nd ed., pp. 3–26). New York: Guilford Press.

Vasan, Ramachandran S., Beiser, Alexa, Seshadri, Sudha, Larson, Martin G., Kannel, William B., D'Agostino, Ralph B., et al. (2002). Residual lifetime risk for developing hypertension in middle-aged women and men: The Framingham Heart Study. *Journal of the American Medical Association, 287*, 1003–1010.

Vaupel, James W., & Loichinger, Elke. (2006, June 30, 2006). Redistributing work in aging Europe. *Science, 312*, 1911–1913.

Venn, John J. (Ed.). (2004). *Assessing children with special needs* (3rd ed.). Upper Saddle River, NJ: Pearson.

Verhaeghen, Paul. (2003). Aging and vocabulary score: A meta-analysis. *Psychology and Aging, 18*, 332–339.

Verhaeghen, Paul, & Marcoen, Alfons. (1996). On the mechanisms of plasticity in young and older adults after instruction in the method of loci: Evidence for an amplification model. *Psychology & Aging, 11*, 164–178.

Verhaeghen, Paul, Steitz, David W., Sliwinski, Martin J., & Cerella, John. (2003). Aging and dual-task performance: A meta-analysis. *Psychology & Aging, 18*, 443–460.

Verkuyten, Maykel. (2004). Ethnic minority identity and social context. In Mark Bennett & Fabio Sani (Eds.), *The development of the social self* (pp. 189–216). Hove, East Sussex, England: Psychology Press.

Verona, Sergiu. (2003). Romanian policy regarding adoptions. In Victor Littel (Ed.), *Adoption update* (pp. 5–10). New York: Nova Science.

Verté, Sylvie, Geurts, Hilde M., Roeyers, Herbert, Oosterlaan, Jaap, & Sergeant, Joseph A. (2005). Executive functioning in children with autism and Tourette syndrome. *Development & Psychopathology, 17*, 415–445.

Viadero, Debra. (2006, February 15). Scholars warn of overstating gains from AP classes alone. *Education Week* 25(23), 14.

Viadero, Debra. (2007, April 5). Long after Katrina, children show symptoms of psychological distress. *Education Week, 26*, 7.

Vianna, Eduardo, & Stetsenko, Anna. (2006). Embracing history through transforming it: Contrasting Piagetian versus Vygotskian (activity) theories of learning and development to expand constructivism within a dialectical view of history. *Theory & Psychology, 16*, 81–108.

Vidailhet, Pierre, Christensen, Bruce K., Danion, Jean-Marie, & Kapur, Shitij. (2001). Episodic memory impairment in schizophrenia: A view from cognitive psychopathology. In Moshe Naveh-Benjamin, Morris Moscovitch, & Henry L. Roediger (Eds.), *Perspectives on human memory and cognitive aging: Essays in honour of Fergus Craik* (pp. 348–361). New York: Psychology Press.

Viinanen, Arja, Munhbayarlah, S., Zevgee, T., Narantsetseg, L., Naidansuren, Ts, Koskenvuo, M., et al. (2007). The protective effect of rural living against atopy in Mongolia. *Allergy, 62*, 272–280.

Vijg, J. A. N., Busuttil, Rita A., Bahar, Rumana, & Dolle, Martijn E. T. (2005). Aging and genome maintenance. In Richard G. Cutler, S. Mitchell Harman, Chris Heward, & Mike Gibbons (Eds.), *Longevity health sciences: The Phoenix Conference* (Vol. 1055, pp. 35–47). New York: New York Academy of Sciences.

Vikan, Arne, Camino, Cleonice, & Biaggio, Angela. (2005). Note on a cross-cultural test of Gilligan's ethic of care. *Journal of Moral Education, 34*, 107–111.

Viner, Russell M., & Cole, Tim J. (2005). Adult socioeconomic, educational, social, and psychological outcomes of childhood obesity: A national birth cohort study. *British Medical Journal, 330*, 1354–1357.

Visser, Beth A., Ashton, Michael C., & Vernon, Philip A. (2006). Beyond g: Putting multiple intelligences theory to the test. *Intelligence, 34*, 487–502.

Voelcker-Rehage, Claudia, & Alberts, Jay L. (2007). Effect of motor practice on dual-task performance in older adult. *Journals of Gerontology: Series B: Psychological Sciences and Social Sciences, 62*, P141–P148.

Vogler, George P. (2006). Behavior genetics and aging. In James E. Birren & K. Warner Schaie (Eds.), *Handbook of the psychology of aging* (6th ed., pp. 41–55). Amsterdam: Elsevier.

Votruba-Drzal, Elizabeth, Coley, Rebekah Levine, & Chase-Lansdale, P. Lindsay. (2004). Child care and low-income children's development: Direct and moderated effects. *Child Development, 75*, 296–312.

Voydanoff, Patricia. (2004). The effects of work demands and resources on work-to-family conflict and facilitation. *Journal of Marriage and Family, 66*, 398–412.

Vu, Pauline. (2007). *Lake Wobegon, U.S.A.* Retrieved July 27, 2007, from the World Wide Web: http://pewresearch.org/pubs/403/lake-wobegon-usa

Vukman, Karin Bakracevic. (2005). Developmental differences in metacognition and their connections with cognitive development in adulthood. *Journal of Adult Development, 12*, 211–221.

Vygotsky, Lev S. (1978). *Mind in society: The development of higher psychological processes* (Michael Cole, Vera John-Steiner, Sylvia Scribner, & Ellen Souberman, Eds.). Cambridge, MA: Harvard University Press. (Original work published 1935)

Vygotsky, Lev S. (1986). *Thought and language* (Eugenia Hanfmann & Gertrude Vakar, Trans., Revised ed.). Cambridge, MA: MIT Press. (Original work published 1934)

Vygotsky, Lev S. (1987). *Thinking and speech* (R. W. Rieber, & Aaron S. Carton, Eds., Norris Minick, Trans., Vol. 1). New York: Plenum Press. (Original work published 1934)

Vygotsky, Lev S. (1994). Principles of social education for deaf and dumb children in Russia (Theresa Prout, Trans.). In Rene van der Veer & Jaan Valsiner (Eds.), *The Vygotsky reader* (pp. 19–26). Cambridge, MA: Blackwell. (Original work published 1925)

Vygotsky, Lev S. (1994). The development of academic concepts in school aged children (Theresa Prout, Trans.). In Rene van der Veer & Jaan Valsiner (Eds.), *The Vygotsky reader* (pp. 355–370). Cambridge, MA: Blackwell. (Original work published 1934)

Wachs, Theodore D. (1999). Celebrating complexity: Conceptualization and assessment of the environment. In Sarah L. Friedman & Theodore D. Wachs (Eds.), *Measuring environment across the life span: Emerging methods and concepts* (pp. 357–392). Washington, DC: American Psychological Association.

Waddell, Charlotte, Macmillan, Harriet, & Pietrantonio, Anna Marie. (2004). How important is permanency planning for children? Considerations for pediatricians involved in child protection. *Journal of Developmental & Behavioral Pediatrics, 25*, 285–292.

Wadden, Thomas A., Berkowitz, Robert I., Womble, Leslie G., Sarwer, David B., Phelan, Suzanne, Cato, Robert K., et al.

(2005). Randomized trial of lifestyle modification and pharmacotherapy for obesity. *New England Journal of Medicine, 353*, 2111–2120.

Wahlin, Åke, MacDonald, Stuart W. S., de Frias, Cindy M., Nilsson, Lars-Göran, & Dixon, Roger A. (2006). How do health and biological age influence chronological age and sex differences in cognitive aging: Moderating, mediating, or both? *Psychology and Aging, 21*, 318–332.

Wahlstrom, Kyla L. (2002). Accommodating the sleep patterns of adolescents within current educational structures: An uncharted path. In Mary A. Carskadon (Ed.), *Adolescent sleep patterns: Biological, social, and psychological influences* (pp. 172–197). New York: Cambridge University Press.

Wailoo, Michael, Ball, Helen L., Fleming, Peter, & Ward Platt, Martin. (2004). Infants bed-sharing with mothers. *Archives of Disease in Childhood, 89*, 1082–1083.

Wainright, Jennifer L., Russell, Stephen T., & Patterson, Charlotte J. (2004). Psychosocial adjustment, school outcomes, and romantic relationships of adolescents with same-sex parents. *Child Development, 75*, 1886–1898.

Wainryb, Cecilia, Shaw, Leigh A., Langley, Marcie, Cottam, Kim, & Lewis, Renee. (2004). Children's thinking about diversity of belief in the early school years: Judgments of relativism, tolerance, and disagreeing persons. *Child Development, 75*, 687–703.

Waite, Linda J., & Luo, Ye. (2002, August). *Marital quality and marital stability: Consequences for psychological well-being.* Paper presented at the Annual Meetings of the American Sociological Association, Chicago.

Walcott, Delores D., Pratt, Helen D., & Patel, Dilip R. (2003). Adolescents and eating disorders: Gender, racial, ethnic, sociocultural and socioeconomic issues. *Journal of Adolescent Research, 18*, 223–243.

Waldfogel, J. (2006). What do children need? *Public Policy Research, 13*, 26–34.

Walker, Alan. (2004). *Growing older in Europe.* Maidenhead, United Kingdom: Open University Press.

Walker, Alan. (2006). Aging and politics: An international perspective. In Robert H. Binstock & Linda K. George (Eds.), *Handbook of aging and the social sciences* (6th ed., pp. 339–359). Amsterdam: Elsevier.

Walker, Elaine F. (2002). Adolescent neurodevelopment and psychopathology. *Current Directions in Psychological Science, 11*, 24–28.

Walker, Lawrence J. (1984). Sex differences in the development of moral reasoning: A critical review. *Child Development, 55*, 677–691.

Wallerstein, Judith S., & Blakeslee, Sandra. (1995). *The good marriage: How and why love lasts.* Boston: Houghton Mifflin.

Walsh, Froma. (2002). A family resilience framework: Innovative practice applications. *Family Relations, 51*, 130–137.

Wang, Li, van Belle, Gerald, Crane, Paul K., Kukull, Walter A., Bowen, James D., McCormick, Wayne C., et al. (2004). Subjective memory deterioration and future dementia in people aged 65 and older. *Journal of the American Geriatrics Society, 52*, 2045–2051.

Wannamethee, S. Goya, & Shaper, A. Gerald. (1999). Type of alcoholic drink and risk of major coronary heart disease events and all-cause mortality. *American Journal of Public Health, 89*, 685–690.

Ward, Russell A., & Spitze, Glenna D. (2007). Nestleaving and coresidence by young adult children: The role of family relations. *Research on Aging, 29*, 257–277.

Warren, Charles W., Jones, Nathan R., Eriksen, Michael P., & Asma, Samira. (2006). Patterns of global tobacco use in young people and implications for future chronic disease burden in adults. *Lancet, 367*, 749–753.

Warshofsky, Fred. (1999). *Stealing time: The new science of aging.* New York: TV Books.

Washington, Harriet A. (2006). *Medical apartheid: The dark history of medical experimentation on Black Americans from colonial times to the present.* New York: Doubleday.

Wassenberg, Renske, Feron, Frans J. M., Kessels, Alfons G. H., Hendriksen, Jos G. M., Kalff, Ariane C., Kroes, Marielle, et al. (2005). Relation between cognitive and motor performance in 5- to 6-year-old children: Results from a large-scale cross-sectional study. *Child Development, 76*, 1092–1103.

Waterhouse, Lynn. (2006). Multiple intelligences, the Mozart effect, and emotional intelligence: A critical review. *Educational Psychologist, 41*, 207–225.

Watson, John B. (1928). *Psychological care of infant and child.* New York: Norton.

Watson, John B. (1998). *Behaviorism.* New Brunswick, NJ: Transaction. (Original work published 1924)

Waxman, Sandra R., & Lidz, Jeffrey L. (2006). Early word learning. In William Damon & Richard M. Lerner (Series Eds.) & Deanna Kuhn & Robert S. Siegler (Vol. Eds.), *Handbook of child psychology: Vol. 2. Cognition, perception, and language* (6th ed., pp. 299–335). Hoboken, NJ: Wiley.

Way, Niobe, Gingold, Rachel, Rotenberg, Mariana, & Kuriakose, Geena. (2005). Close friendships among urban, ethnic-minority adolescents. In Niobe Way & Jill V. Hamm (Eds.), *The experience of close friendships in adolescence* (Vol. 107, pp. 41–59). San Francisco: Jossey-Bass.

Way, Niobe, & Hamm, Jill V. (Eds.). (2005). *The experience of close friendships in adolescence.* San Francisco: Jossey-Bass.

Wayne, Andrew J., & Youngs, Peter. (2003). Teacher characteristics and student achievement gains: A review. *Review of Educational Research, 73*, 89–122.

Weaver, Chelsea M., Blodgett, Elizabeth H., & Carothers, Shannon S. (2006). Preventing risky sexual behavior. In John G. Borkowski & Chelsea M. Weaver (Eds.), *Prevention: The science and art of promoting healthy child and adolescent development* (pp. 185–214). Baltimore: Brookes.

Weber, Markus, Müller, Markus K., Bucher, Tanja, Wildi, Stefan, Dindo, Daniel, Horber, Fritz, et al. (2004). Laparoscopic gastric bypass is superior to laparoscopic gastric banding for treatment of morbid obesity. *Annals of Surgery, 240*, 975–982.

Wechsler, David. (2003). *Wechsler intelligence scale for children—Fourth edition (WISC-IV).* San Antonio, TX: The Psychological Corporation.

Wechsler, Henry, Nelson, Toben F., Lee, Jae Eun, Seibring, Mark, Lewis, Catherine, & Keeling, Richard P. (2003). Perception and reality: A national evaluation of social norms marketing interventions to reduce college students' heavy alcohol use. *Quarterly Journal of Studies on Alcohol, 64*, 484–494.

Weichold, Karina, Silbereisen, Rainer K., Schmitt-Rodermund, Eva, & Hayward, Chris. (2003). Short-term and long-term consequences of early versus late physical maturation in adolescents, *Gender differences at puberty* (pp. 241–276). New York: Cambridge University Press.

Weikart, David P. (Ed.). (1999). *What should young children learn? Teacher and parent views in 15 countries.* Ypsilanti, MI: High/Scope Press.

Weil, Elizabeth. (2007, June 3). When should a kid start kindergarten? *New York Times Magazine,* pp. 46–51.

Weinstein, Barbara E. (2000). *Geriatric audiology*. New York: Thieme.

Weisfeld, Glenn E. (1999). *Evolutionary principles of human adolescence*. New York: Basic Books.

Weisler, Richard H., Barbee, James G. I. V., & Townsend, Mark H. (2006). Mental health and recovery in the Gulf Coast after hurricanes Katrina and Rita. *Journal of the American Medical Association, 296,* 585–588.

Weissman, Myrna M., Bland, Roger C., Canino, Glorisa J., Greenwald, Steven, Hwu, Hai-Gwo, Joyce, Peter R., et al. (2000). Prevalence of suicide ideation and suicide attempts in nine countries. *Psychological Medicine, 29,* 9–17.

Weizman, Zehava Oz, & Snow, Catherine E. (2001). Lexical output as related to children's vocabulary acquisition: Effects of sophisticated exposure and support for meaning. *Developmental Psychology, 37,* 265–279.

Welch, H. Gilbert, Schwartz, Lisa M., & Woloshin, Steven. (2005). Prostate-specific antigen levels in the United States: Implications of various definitions for abnormal. *Journal of the National Cancer Institute, 97,* 1132–1137.

Wellman, Henry M. (2003). Enablement and constraint. In Ursula M. Staudinger & Ulman Lindenberger (Eds.), *Understanding human development: Dialogues with lifespan psychology* (pp. 245–263). Dordrecht, The Netherlands: Kluwer.

Wellman, Henry M., Cross, David, & Watson, Julanne. (2001). Meta-analysis of theory-of-mind development: The truth about false belief. *Child Development, 72,* 655–684.

Welsh, Marilyn, & Pennington, Bruce. (2000). Phenylketonuria. In Keith Owen Yeates, M. Douglas Ris, & H. Gerry Taylor (Eds.), *Pediatric neuropsychology: Research, theory, and practice* (pp. 275–299). New York: Guilford Press.

Wendland, Barbara E., Greenwood, Carol E., Weinberg, Iris, & Young, Karen W. H. (2003). Malnutrition in institutionalized seniors: The iatrogenic component. *Journal of the American Geriatrics Society, 51,* 85–90.

Werner, Emmy E., & Smith, Ruth S. (1992). *Overcoming the odds: High risk children from birth to adulthood*. Ithaca, NY: Cornell University Press.

Werner, Emmy E., & Smith, Ruth S. (2001). *Journeys from childhood to midlife: Risk, resilience, and recovery*. Ithaca, NY: Cornell University Press.

Wertsch, James V. (1998). *Mind as action*. New York: Oxford University Press.

Wertsch, James V., & Tulviste, Peeter. (2005). L. S. Vygotsky and contemporary developmental psychology (pp. xii, 322). New York: Routledge.

West, Sheila, & Sommer, Alfred. (2001). Prevention of blindness and priorities for the future. *Bulletin of the World Health Organization, 79,* 244–248.

West, Steven L., & O'Neal, Keri K. (2004). Project D.A.R.E. outcome effectiveness revisited. *American Journal of Public Health, 94,* 1027–1029.

Westen, Drew. (2007). *The political brain: The role of emotion in deciding the fate of the nation*. New York: PublicAffairs.

Wethington, Elaine. (2000). Expecting stress: Americans and the "midlife crisis." *Motivation & Emotion, 24,* 85–103.

Wethington, Elaine. (2002). The relationship of turning points at work to perceptions of psychological growth and change. In Richard A. Settersten & Timothy J. Owens (Eds.), *Advances in life course research: Vol. 7. New frontiers in socialization* (pp. 93–110). Amsterdam: JAI.

Whitbourne, Susan Krauss. (2002). *The aging individual: Physical and psychological perspectives* (2nd ed.). New York: Springer.

Whitbourne, Susan Krauss, Sneed, Joel R., & Skultety, Karyn M. (2002). Identity processes in adulthood: Theoretical and methodological challenges. *Identity, 2,* 29–45.

White, Aaron M., & Swartzwelder, H. Scott. (2004). Hippocampal function during adolescence: A unique target of ethanol effects. In Ronald E. Dahl & Linda Patia Spear (Eds.), *Adolescent brain development: Vulnerabilities and opportunities* (Vol. 1021, pp. 206–220). New York: New York Academy of Sciences.

Whitehurst, Grover J., & Massetti, Greta M. (2004). How well does Head Start prepare children to learn to read? In Edward Zigler & Sally J. Styfco (Eds.), *The Head Start debates* (pp. 251–262). Baltimore: Brookes.

Whiteman, Shawn D., McHale, Susan M., & Crouter, Ann C. (2003). What parents learn from experience: The first child as a first draft? *Journal of Marriage & Family, 65,* 608–621.

Whitfield, Keith E., & McClearn, Gerald. (2005). Genes, environment, and race: Quantitative genetic approaches. *American Psychologist, 60,* 104–114.

Whitley, Bernard E., & Keith-Spiegel, Patricia. (2002). *Academic dishonesty: An educator's guide*. Mahwah, NJ: Erlbaum.

Whitlock, Janis L., Powers, Jane L., & Eckenrode, John. (2006). The virtual cutting edge: The internet and adolescent self-injury. *Developmental Psychology, 42,* 407–417.

Whitmer, Rachel A., Gunderson, Erica P., Barrett-Connor, Elizabeth, Quesenberry, Charles P., & Yaffe, Kristine. (2005). Obesity in middle age and future risk of dementia: A 27 year longitudinal population based study. *British Medical Journal, 330,* 1360.

Whitmore, Heather. (2001). Value that marketing cannot manufacture: Cherished possessions as links to identity and wisdom. *Generations, 25*(3), 57–63.

Wiener, Judith, & Schneider, Barry H. (2002). A multisource exploration of the friendship patterns of children with and without learning disabilities. *Journal of Abnormal Child Psychology, 30,* 127–141.

Wiesner, Margit, Kim, Hyoun K., & Capaldi, Deborah M. (2005). Developmental trajectories of offending: Validation and prediction to young adult alcohol use, drug use, and depressive symptoms. *Development and Psychopathology, 17,* 251–270.

Wigfield, Allan, Eccles, Jacquelynne S., Yoon, Kwang Suk, Harold, Rena D., Arbreton, Amy J. A., Freedman-Doan, Carol, et al. (1997). Change in children's competence beliefs and subjective task values across the elementary school years: A 3-year study. *Journal of Educational Psychology, 89,* 451–469.

Wilhelm, Mark O., Rooney, Patrick M., & Tempel, Eugene R. (2007). Changes in religious giving reflect changes in involvement: Age and cohort effects in religious giving, secular giving, and attendance. *Journal for the Scientific Study of Religion, 46,* 217–232.

Willatts, Peter. (1999). Development of means-end behavior in young infants: Pulling a support to retrieve a distant object. *Developmental Psychology, 35,* 651–667.

Williams, David R. (2003). The health of men: Structured inequalities and opportunities. *American Journal of Public Health, 93,* 724–731.

Williams, David R., & Wilson, Colwick M. (2001). Race, ethnicity, and aging. In Robert H. Binstock (Ed.), *Handbook of aging and the social sciences* (5th ed., pp. 160–178). San Diego, CA: Academic Press.

Williams, Julie. (2003). Dementia and genetics. In Robert Plomin, John C. DeFries, Ian W. Craig, & Peter McGuffin (Eds.), *Behavioral genetics in the postgenomic era* (pp. 503–527). Washington, DC: American Psychological Association.

Williams, Justin H. G., Waiter, Gordon D., Gilchrist, Anne, Perrett, David I., Murray, Alison D., & Whiten, Andrew. (2006). Neural mechanisms of imitation and 'mirror neuron' functioning in autistic spectrum disorder. *Neuropsychologia, 44*, 610–621.

Williams, Shirlan A. (2005). Jealousy in the cross-sex friendship. *Journal of Loss and Trauma, 10*(5), 471 - 485.

Willis, Sherry L. (1996). Everyday cognitive competence in elderly persons: Conceptual issues and empirical findings. *Gerontologist, 36*, 595–601.

Wilmut, Ian, & Highfield, Roger. (2006). *After Dolly: The uses and misuses of human cloning*. New York: W.W. Norton.

Wilson, Margaret, & Knoblich, Günther. (2005). The case for motor involvement in perceiving conspecifics. *Psychological Bulletin, 131*, 460–473.

Wilson, Melvin N., Lewis, Joyce B., Hinton, Ivora D., Kohn, Laura P., Underwood, Alex, Phuong Hogue, Lan Kho, et al. (1995). Promotion of African American family life: Families, poverty, and social programs. In Melvin N. Wilson (Ed.), *African American family life: Its structural and ecological aspects* (pp. 85–99). San Francisco: Jossey-Bass.

Wilson, Robert S., Beckett, Laurel A., Barnes, Lisa L., Schneider, Julie A., Bach, Julie, Evans, Denis A., et al. (2002). Individual differences in rates of change in cognitive abilities of older persons. *Psychology & Aging, 17*, 179–193.

Wilson, Stephan M., & Ngige, Lucy W. (2006). Families in sub-Saharan Africa. In Bron B. Ingoldsby & Suzanna D. Smith (Eds.), *Families in global and multicultural perspective* (2nd ed., pp. 247–273). Thousand Oaks, CA: Sage.

Wilson-Costello, Deanne, Friedman, Harriet, Minich, Nori, Siner, Bonnie, Taylor, Gerry, Schluchter, Mark, et al. (2007). Improved neurodevelopmental outcomes for extremely low birth weight infants in 2000–2002. *Pediatrics, 119*, 37–45.

Wingert, Pat. (2007, March 5). The baby who's not supposed to be alive. *Newsweek*, 59.

Wingfield, Arthur, Tun, Patricia A., & McCoy, Sandra L. (2005). Hearing loss in older adulthood: What it is and how it interacts with cognitive performance. *Current Directions in Psychological Science, 14*, 144–148.

Winsler, Adam, Carlton, Martha P., & Barry, Maryann J. (2000). Age-related changes in preschool children's systematic use of private speech in a natural setting. *Journal of Child Language, 27*, 665–687.

Winsler, Adam, Díaz, Rafael M., Espinosa, Linda, & Rodríguez, James L. (1999). When learning a second language does not mean losing the first: Bilingual language development in low-income, Spanish-speaking children attending bilingual preschool. *Child Development, 70*, 349–362.

Wirth, H.-P. (1993). Caring for a chronically demented patient within the family. In W. Meier-Ruge (Ed.), *Dementing brain disease in old age* (pp. 171–206). Basel, Switzerland: Karger.

Wise, Phyllis M. (2003). The female reproductive system. In Paola S. Timiras (Ed.), *Physiological basis of aging and geriatrics* (3rd ed., pp. 189–212). Boca Raton, FL: CRC Press.

Wise, Phyllis M. (2006). Aging of the female reproductive system. In Edward J. Masoro & Steven N. Austad (Eds.), *Handbook of the biology of aging* (6th ed., pp. 570–590). Amsterdam: Elsevier Academic Press.

Wishart, Jennifer G. (1999). Learning and development in children with Down's syndrome. In Alan Slater & Darwin Muir (Eds.), *The Blackwell reader in development psychology* (pp. 493–508). Malden, MA: Blackwell Publishers.

Witt, Whitney P., Riley, Anne W., & Coiro, Mary Jo. (2003). Childhood functional status, family stressors, and psychosocial adjustment among school-aged children with disabilities in the United States. *Archives of Pediatrics & Adolescent Medicine, 157*, 687–695.

Woessner, Matthew C. (2004). Beating the house: How inadequate penalties for cheating make plagiarism an excellent gamble. *PS: Political Science & Politics, 37*, 313–320.

Wolery, Mark, Barton, Erin E., & Hine, Jeffrey F. (2005). Evolution of applied behavior analysis in the treatment of individuals with autism. *Exceptionality, 13*, 11–23.

Wolf, Rosalie S. (1998). Domestic elder abuse and neglect. In Inger Hilde Nordhus, Gary R. VandenBos, Stig Berg, & Pia Fromholt (Eds.), *Clinical geropsychology* (pp. 161–165). Washington, DC: American Psychological Association.

Wolfe, Alan. (1998). *One nation, after all: What middle-class Americans really think about: God, country, family, racism, welfare, immigration, homosexuality, work, the right, the left, and each other*. New York: Viking.

Wolfe, Michael S. (2006, May). Shutting down Alzheimer's. *Scientific American, 294*, 72–79.

Wolfinger, Nicholas H. (2005). *Understanding the divorce cycle: The children of divorce in their own marriages*. New York: Cambridge University Press.

Wolraich, Mark L., & Doffing, Melissa A. (2005). Attention deficit hyperactivity disorder. In Merlin Gene Butler & F. John Meaney (Eds.), *Genetics of developmental disabilities* (pp. 783–807). Boca Raton, FL: Taylor & Francis.

Wong, Sau-ling Cynthia, & Lopez, Miguel G. (2000). English language learners of Chinese background: A portrait of diversity. In Sandra Lee McKay & Sau-ling Cynthia Wong (Eds.), *New immigrants in the United States: Readings for second language educators* (pp. 263–305). Cambridge, UK: Cambridge University Press.

Wong, Sheila, Chan, Kingsley, Wong, Virginia, & Wong, Wilfred. (2002). Use of chopsticks in Chinese children. *Child: Care, Health & Development, 28*, 157–161.

Wong, Wan-chi. (2006). Understanding dialectical thinking from a cultural-historical perspective. *Philosophical Psychology, 19*, 239–260.

Wood, Alex, & Joseph, Stephen. (2007). Grand theories of personality cannot be integrated. *American Psychologist, 62*, 57–58.

Wood, Julia T. (2000). Gender and personal relationships. In Clyde Hendrick & Susan S. Hendrick (Eds.), *Close relationships: A sourcebook* (pp. 301–313). Thousand Oaks, CA: Sage.

Woodlee, Martin T., & Schallert, Timothy. (2006). The impact of motor activity and inactivity on the brain: Implications for the prevention and treatment of nervous-system disorders. *Current Directions in Psychological Science, 15*, 203–206.

Woodward, Amanda L., & Markman, Ellen M. (1998). Early word learning. In William Damon (Series Ed.) & Deanna Kuhn & Robert S. Siegler (Vol. Eds.), *Handbook of child psychology: Vol. 2. Cognition, perception and language* (5th ed., pp. 371–420). New York: Wiley.

Woolley, Jacqueline D., & Boerger, Elizabeth A. (2002). Development of beliefs about the origins and controllability of dreams. *Developmental Psychology, 38,* 24–41.

World Bank. (2005). *Expanding opportunities and building competencies for young people: A new agenda for secondary education.* Washington, DC: World Bank.

World Health Organization. (2000). *New data on the prevention of mother-to-child transmission of HIV and their policy implications—Conclusions and recommendations.* Retrieved September 3, 2005, from the World Wide Web: http://www.who.int/child-adolescent-health/New_Publications/CHILD_HEALTH/MTCT_Consultation.htm

World Health Organization. (2001). *The World Health Report 2001: Mental health: New understanding, new hope.* Geneva, Switzerland: World Health Organization.

World Health Organization. (2003). *World atlas of birth defects* (2nd ed.). Geneva, Switzerland: Author.

World Health Organization. (2005). *Sexually transmitted infections among adolescents: Issues in adolescent health and development.* Geneva, Switzerland: Author.

World Health Organization. (2006). *World health statistics 2006*. Geneva, Switzerland: Author.

World Health Organization. (2007, May 29). *Only 100% smoke-free environments adequately protect from dangers of second-hand smoke [News release].* Retrieved September 15, 2007, from the World Wide Web: http://www.who.int/mediacentre/news/releases/2007/pr26/en/index.html

Wright, Dave, Bradbury, Ian, Cuckle, Howard, Gardosi, Jason, Tonks, Ann, Standing, Sue, et al. (2006). Three-stage contingent screening for Down syndrome. *Prenatal Diagnosis, 26,* 528–534.

Wright, Lawrence. (1999). *Twins: And what they tell us about who we are.* New York: Wiley.

Wrosch, Carsten, Bauer, Isabelle, & Scheier, Michael F. (2005). Regret and quality of life across the adult life span: The influence of disengagement and available future goals. *Psychology and Aging, 20,* 657–670.

Wyman, Peter A., Cowen, Emory L., Work, William C., Hoyt-Meyers, Lynn, Magnus, Keith B., & Fagen, Douglas B. (1999). Caregiving and developmental factors differentiating young at-risk urban children showing resilient versus stress-affected outcomes: A replication and extension. *Child Development, 70,* 645–659.

Xu, Xiao, Zhu, Fengchuan, O'Campo, Patricia, Koenig, Michael A., Mock, Victoria, & Campbell, Jacquelyn. (2005). Prevalence of and risk factors for intimate partner violence in China. *American Journal of Public Health, 95,* 78–85.

Yamashita, Toru, Ninomiya, Mikiko, Hernandez Acosta, Pilar, Garcia-Verdugo, Jose Manuel, Sunabori, Takehiko, Sakaguchi, Masanori, et al. (2006). Subventricular zone-derived neuroblasts migrate and differentiate into mature neurons in the post-stroke adult striatum. *Journal of Neuroscience, 26,* 6627–6636.

Yang, Lixia, Krampe, Ralf T., & Baltes, Paul B. (2006). Basic forms of cognitive plasticity extended into the oldest-old: Retest learning, age, and cognitive functioning. *Psychology and Aging, 21,* 372–378.

Yarber, William L., Milhausen, Robin R., Crosby, Richard A., & Torabi, Mohammad R. (2005). Public opinion about condoms for HIV and STD prevention: A midwestern state telephone survey. *Perspectives on Sexual and Reproductive Health, 37,* 148–154.

Yates, Tuppett M. (2004). The developmental psychopathology of self-injurious behavior: Compensatory regulation in posttraumatic adaptation. *Clinical Psychology Review, 24,* 35–74.

Yates, Tuppett M., Egeland, Byron, & Sroufe, L. Alan. (2003). Rethinking resilience: A developmental process perspective. In Suniya S. Luthar (Ed.), *Resilience and vulnerability: Adaptation in the context of childhood adversities* (pp. 243–266). New York: Cambridge University Press.

Yee, Barbara W. K., & Chiriboga, David A. (2007). Issues of diversity in health psychology and aging. In Carolyn M. Aldwin, Crystal L. Park, & Avron Spiro, III (Eds.), *Handbook of health psychology and aging* (pp. 286–312). New York: Guilford Press.

Yehuda, Rachel (Ed.). (2006). *Annals of the New York Academy of Sciences: Vol. 1071. Psychobiology of posttraumatic stress disorder: A decade of progress.* Boston: Blackwell.

Yerkes, Robert Mearns. (1923). Testing the human mind. *Atlantic Monthly, 131,* 358–370.

Yerys, Benjamin E., & Munakata, Yuko. (2006). When labels hurt but novelty helps: Children's perseveration and flexibility in a card-sorting task. *Child Development, 77,* 1589–1607.

Yeung, W. Jean, Linver, Miriam R., & Brooks-Gunn, Jeanne. (2002). How money matters for young children's development: Parental investment and family processes. *Child Development, 73,* 1861–1879.

Yglesias, Helen. (1980). Moses, Anna Mary Robertson (Grandma). In Barbara Sicherman & Carol Hurd Green (Eds.), *Notable American women: The modern period.* Cambridge, MA: Belknap Press.

Yoon, Carolyn, Hasher, Lynn, Feinberg, Fred, Rahhal, Tamara A., & Winocur, Gordon. (2000). Cross-cultural differences in memory: The role of culture-based stereotypes about aging. *Psychology & Aging, 15,* 694–704.

Youn, Gahyun, Knight, Bob G., Jeong, Hyun-Suk, & Benton, Donna. (1999). Differences in familism values and caregiving outcomes among Korean, Korean American, and White American dementia caregivers. *Psychology & Aging, 14,* 355–364.

Young, T. Kue, Bjerregaard, Peter, Dewailly, Eric, Risica, Patricia M., Jorgensen, Marit E., & Ebbesson, Sven E. O. (2007). Prevalence of obesity and its metabolic correlates among the circumpolar Inuit in 3 countries. *American Journal of Public Health, 97,* 691–695.

Young-Hyman, Deborah, Schlundt, David G., Herman-Wenderoth, Leanna, & Bozylinski, Khristine. (2003). Obesity, appearance, and psychosocial adaptation in young African American children. *Journal of Pediatric Psychology, 28,* 463–472.

Younoszai, Barbara. (1993). Mexican American perspectives related to death. In Donald P. Irish, Kathleen F. Lundquist, & Vivian Jenkins Nelsen (Eds.), *Ethnic variations in dying, death, and grief: Diversity in universality* (pp. 67–78). Philadelphia: Taylor & Francis.

Zacks, Rose T., & Hasher, Lynn. (2006). Aging and long-term memory: Deficits are not inevitable. In Ellen Bialystok & Fergus I. M. Craik (Eds.), *Lifespan cognition: Mechanisms of change* (pp. 162–177). New York: Oxford University Press.

Zahn-Waxler, Carolyn. (2000). The development of empathy, guilt, and internalization of distress: Implications for gender differentiation in internalizing and externalizing problems. In Richard J. Davidson (Ed.), *Anxiety, depression, and emotion* (pp. 222–265). New York: Oxford University Press.

Zalenski, Robert J., & Raspa, Richard. (2006). Maslow's hierarchy of needs: A framework for achieving human potential in hospice. *Journal of Palliative Medicine, 9,* 1120–1127.

Zandi, Peter P., Sparks, D. Larry, Khachaturian, Ara S., Tschanz, JoAnn, Norton, Maria, Steinberg, Martin, et al. (2005). Do statins reduce risk of incident dementia and Alzheimer disease? The Cache County Study. *Archives of General Psychiatry, 62,* 217–224.

Zani, Bruna, & Cicognani, Elvira. (2006). Sexuality and intimate relationships in adolescence. In Sandy Jackson & Luc Goossens (Eds.), *Handbook of adolescent development* (pp. 200–222). Hove, East Sussex, UK: Psychology Press.

Zeedyk, M. Suzanne, Wallace, Linda, & Spry, Linsay. (2002). Stop, look, listen, and think? What young children really do when crossing the road. *Accident Analysis & Prevention, 34,* 43–50.

Zehler, Annette M., Fleischman, Howard L., Hopstock, Paul J., Stephenson, Todd G., Pendzick, Michelle L., & Sapru, Saloni. (2003). *Descriptive study of services to LEP students and LEP students with disabilities: Vol. 1. Research report*. Arlington, VA: Development Associates.

Zeifman, Debra, Delaney, Sarah, & Blass, Elliott M. (1996). Sweet taste, looking, and calm in 2- and 4-week-old infants: The eyes have it. *Developmental Psychology, 32,* 1090–1099.

Zelazo, Philip David, Müller, Ulrich, Frye, Douglas, & Marcovitch, Stuart. (2003). The development of executive function in early childhood. *Monographs of the Society for Research in Child Development, 68*(3, Serial No. 274), 11–27.

Zhan, Heying Jenny, Liu, Guangya, & Guan, Xinping. (2006). Willingness and availability: Explaining new attitudes toward institutional elder care among Chinese elderly parents and their adult. *Journal of Aging Studies, 20,* 279–290.

Zhang, Lin, Samet, Jonathan, Caffo, Brian, & Punjabi, Naresh M. (2006). Cigarette smoking and nocturnal sleep architecture. *American Journal of Epidemiology, 164,* 529–537.

Zhang, Yuanting, & Goza, Franklin W. (2006). Who will care for the elderly in China? A review of the problems caused by China's one-child policy and their potential solutions. *Journal of Aging Studies, 20,* 151–164.

Zigler, Edward F., Kagan, Sharon Lynn, & Hall, Nancy Wilson (Eds.). (1996). *Children, families, and government: Preparing for the twenty-first century*. New York: Cambridge University Press.

Zigler, Edward, & Styfco, Sally J. (2001). Can early childhood intervention prevent delinquency? A real possibility. In Arthur C. Bohart & Deborah J. Stipek (Eds.), *Constructive & destructive behavior: Implications for family, school, & society* (pp. 231–248). Washington, DC: American Psychological Association.

Zigler, Edward, & Styfco, Sally J. (Eds.). (2004). *The Head Start debates*. Baltimore: Brookes.

Zimmer-Gembeck, Melanie J., & Collins, W. Andrew. (2003). Autonomy development during adolescence. In Gerald R. Adams & Michael D. Berzonsky (Eds.), *Blackwell handbook of adolescence* (pp. 175–204). Malden, MA: Blackwell.

Zimprich, Daniel, & Martin, Mike. (2002). Can longitudinal changes in processing speed explain longitudinal age changes in fluid intelligence? *Psychology & Aging, 17,* 690–695.

Zingmond, David S., McGory, Marcia L., & Ko, Clifford Y. (2005). Hospitalization before and after gastric bypass surgery. *Journal of the American Medical Association, 294,* 1918–1924.

Zito, Julie Magno, Safer, Daniel J., dosReis, Susan, Gardner, James F., Magder, Laurence, Soeken, Karen, et al. (2003). Psychotropic practice patterns for youth: A 10-year perspective. *Archives of Pediatrics & Adolescent Medicine, 157,* 17–25.

Zucker, Alyssa N., Ostrove, Joan M., & Stewart, Abigail J. (2002). College-educated women's personality development in adulthood: Perceptions and age differences. *Psychology & Aging, 17,* 236–244.

Zuvekas, Samuel H., Vitiello, Benedetto, & Norquist, Grayson S. (2006). Recent trends in stimulant medication use among U.S. children. *American Journal of Psychiatry, 163,* 579–585.

Zwahr, Melissa D., Park, Denise C., & Shifren, Kim. (1999). Judgments about estrogen replacement therapy: The role of age, cognitive abilities, and beliefs. *Psychology & Aging, 14,* 179–191.

Name Index

Subject Index

Note: Page numbers followed by f indicate figures; those followed by t indicate tables; and those preceded by Ep indicate the Epilogue.